The Definitive Source Book For The Three Stooges

THE COMPLETE THREE STOOGES

The Official Filmography and Three Stooges Companion

JON SOLOMON

Comedy III Productions, Inc.

ISBN 0971186804

LIBRARY OF CONGRESS CATALOG CARD NUMBER 2001095020

Published by Comedy III Productions, Inc.
1725 Victory Boulevard
Glendale, CA 91201
www.threestooges.com

Cover and Interior Design by Nathan Boldman

10 9 8 7 6 5 4 3 2 1

Printed in the United States of America

THE COMPLETE THREE STOOGES

The Official Filmography and Three Stooges Companion

TABLE OF CONTENTS

FORWARD

Although much has been written about The Three Stooges over the years, until now there has never been a complete study of the entire rich body of work of The Three Stooges. After all, The Three Stooges work spanned almost forty years and includes more than 200 films. Over seventy five years since they first began their comedy antics, The Three Stooges still regularly appear on television every day of the week all over the world. The faces of Larry, Moe and Curly are more recognizable than many of our most popular film stars of today. Many performers of today repeatedly borrow from and mimic the great comedy routines of The Three Stooges. No other entertainer can boast such claims. Which is why we can easily state that The Three Stooges are the greatest comedy team of all time.

It is only fitting that The Three Stooges have a definitive collection for their entire great body of work that pays tribute to the comedy genius of The Three Stooges. When I became the President and CEO of Comedy III Productions, one of our most important tasks was to gather together all existing materials on the men who make millions of people laugh. In order to properly manage all of the interests of The Three Stooges, we needed to know everything there was to know about these comedy legends. We decided to commission a complete filmography to include all of the films of The Three Stooges. The works of The Three Stooges are so vast and complex, we soon concluded that we needed more than a summary of their films.

Indeed, The Three Stooges deserved a detailed study and analysis of all their films from beginning to end. We were fortunate to find Professor Jon Solomon to take on this daunting task. Not only is Professor Solomon a scholar, and a talented researcher and writer, equally important he is a huge Three Stooges fan. Born in Philadelphia, he grew up in the same town that gave us three members of The Three Stooges. Like many of us, he was raised on The Three Stooges shorts, which aired on television everyday during his youth.

When I first spoke to Professor Solomon about this book, it was obvious that he was perfect for this project. It was never about money. With Jon, it was only about The Three Stooges. His love of The Three Stooges and their work was apparent from the beginning. That was over five years ago. Since then he has worked tirelessly and faithfully on this book. Not only did he spend thousands of hours reviewing every Three Stooges film; he also reviewed just about everything that has ever been written about The Three Stooges. Meticulous in detail, and precise with respect to every fact, Professor Solomon produced a complete work fit for the kings of comedy – *The Complete Three Stooges: The Official Filmography and Three Stooges Companion.* It was well worth the wait. Everybody at Comedy III is so pleased and proud of this book that we decided to publish it ourselves. It is, and will be, the definitive source book for everything about the great film work of The Three Stooges. We hope all of The Three Stooges Fans all over the world enjoy it.

Earl M. Benjamin

INTRODUCTION

The Three Stooges have been popular for four generations. They achieved such stardom in vaudeville in the late 1920s, that in the early 1930s they were offered film contracts by five major film studios. The Three Stooges finally settled in at Columbia Pictures where they made 190 short-films and a variety of features for twenty-four years. Throughout the 1930s and 1940s they continued performing live on stages around the country and even in Europe. In the 1950s they began starring in a series of feature films, and by the time they made a TV pilot in 1970, most of their 220 films had already been showing nationwide on television for a decade. Thirty years later, as we begin a new millennium, their films are still being shown daily on national television, and every one of their short films has been released for home viewing.

No other comedians have had such a run, not the Marx Brothers, not Laurel & Hardy, not Abbott & Costello, not Martin & Lewis, nor any other comedy team, or comedian for that matter. In fact, the Stooges get more regular exposure on television than any other film stars. Who else has had their films shown on their own daily *and* weekly shows nationwide for four decades? Simply put, The Three Stooges are one of the most widely recognized and easily identifiable icons of American popular culture.

Just mention the Stooges in a crowded room: immediately people begin gouging, slapping, finger-waving, and woo-wooing as if society had just abolished all its norms and rules. A few people will groan, of course, because there are those who dislike the Stooges for bringing out in many an adult, particularly male adults, the embarrassing imbecility of a ten year-old. But the participants will remind each other about great Stooge films like "the plumbing one" with such memorable lines as "this house is sho' goin' crazy," and they will all have a favorite Stooge - usually Curly. It is as if there is a hidden universe of Stoogedom out there which periodically compels people to interact by summoning up fond memories of anti-social physical mayhem. There is no other anti-cultural cultural phenomenon quite like it.

Yet even their millions of admirers assume that the Stooges were just, well, stooges, whose function in life was to louse things up and be slapped and gouged and bossed around by Moe. And it is true, whether the Stooges worked as census takers or doctors, or whether they mouthed the words to an operatic recording or designed evening dresses to look like furniture, what mattered really was that the ineptly versatile Stooges carried on their *shtick* in film after film year after year. But the Stooges were not 'just stooges.' They were artists, professional comedians who constantly developed their craft and varied their seemingly endless repertoire of gags as their career progressed. Ted Healy gave their first stage slap in the 1920s, Shemp accidentally delivered the first eye-gouge in the early 1930s, they threw their first cream puff in 1936, Moe first ripped out a clump of Larry's hair in 1938, Curly's iron-like skull first ruined a saw in 1939, and when Curly's health forced his retirement in 1946, Shemp gave the Stooges an entirely new look. Their membership kept changing, too: over the years the 'third Stooge' role was played by Shemp, Curly, Shemp again, Joe Besser, and Curly-Joe DeRita. In between there were on-stage auditions for other vaudeville veterans, and months before his death in 1975 Moe was planning still another triadic configuration with Emil Sitka. But at any given time the Stooges were actually more than a trio. They were very ably assisted by inventive gag writers, directors well schooled in silent-film visual/physical comedy, a keen technical crew capable of working within shoe-string budgets, and a host of talented actors who took pies to the face, saw their priceless vases smashed, and were soaked by water gushing out of their TV set, all with gaping-mouthed surprise and appropriate outrage.

Ironically and unfortunately, the Stooges were such successful imbeciles on film that few have ever taken them seriously as artists or their films as works of art. Libraries are filled with scholarly studies and biographies of the Marx Brothers, Buster Keaton, Charlie Chaplin, and almost every other classic comedian who is considered a 'comedian' and not just a knucklehead. But this is changing. Since Joan Howard Maurer set the record straight in 1982's *The Three Stooges Scrapbook*, Stooge scholars - oxymoronic as that phrase may seem - have researched scripts, interviewed surviving cast and crew members, and resurrected 'lost' films. In 1995 the UCLA Film & Television Archive finished its restoration of *Soup to Nuts*, the Stooges' first feature film, and still another resurgence in Stooge popularity has made their early MGM and Paramount films resurface. Work continues even now on understanding the Stooge films within the cultural contexts of the Depression, World War II, the Cold War, and the pre-psychedelic Sixties.

The writing of this book would have been impossible without the pioneering efforts of many other Three Stooges authors and scholars, whose publications gave me a solid foundation of reliable information. Russel Forsythe and John Shetler helped me early on in the project by providing me with valuable perspective and much needed input. Special thanks to Leo Banks; I would never have had the opportunity to work on this project had he not interviewed me, put me in the *L.A. Times*, and made Comedy III aware of my research. Professor Don Morlan of the University of Dayton also deserves special recognition for his work on *You Nazty Spy!*, which made me aware of just how much twentieth-century history was contained in these films. I also wish to thank Pat and Ray Brown of the Popular Culture Association for allowing me to make 'Stooge Studies' an intellectual pursuit recognized by an academic organization, Carla Van West for her Yiddish help, and David Sider of the American Philological Association for giving me 'erysipelas.' My Humanities Seminar class in the fall of 1995 assisted me greatly in pointing out some of the historical and cultural references that were before my time, as did my mother, Vita P.

I would be remiss if I did not recall my earliest memories and interest in the Stooges back in Philadelphia in the late 1950s, so many thanks to Sally Starr, my two older brothers Andy and Bob (with whom I could identify myself as a third Stooge), and my father, who struggled to allow my almost nightly performances of a chicken-with-its-head-cut-off not five feet from the dinner table. My college days at the University of Chicago would not have kept the flame lit had not my friends David Paley and Liz Norment found frequent use for the appellation "knucklehead," and may my graduate school friend and fellow classicist Jim May finally get to that town named 'Goslow.' My children - Jem, Jesi, Dani - have demonstrated to me the universal timelessness of the humor in Stooge films and kept on the lookout for Stooge references.

I am most grateful to my wife Lois for supporting and encouraging my efforts for well over three years; without complaint she allowed me to remain locked in my office until all hours of the night with little more than Stooge videos, an odd array books, and the half-dozen drafts of this project. Lastly I have to thank The Three Stooges themselves and their writers, directors, and crews at Columbia and elsewhere. If their films were not so interesting, I would not have been so inspired to apply twenty years of training as a classical scholar to these years of research on the Stooges, comedy, film, and twentieth-century American popular culture.

The Three Stooges made both feature films and short films. The feature films are divided into four chapters, *Soup to Nuts* (1930), and then early (1933-1934), middle (1934-1951), and late features (1959-1970). The early short films at Paramount and MGM (1934) are combined in a single chapter. The 190 Columbia shorts are numbered and then divided according to the years in which they were released.

Each film is treated individually, first listed by title, release date, and running time. The running times listed here have been checked against Columbia's master copies.

There follow lists of credited cast members, credited crew members, and uncredited cast members. Of several problem areas in the Stooge film corpus, cast lists are the most vexing. The films themselves rarely credit more than one or two cast members other than the Stooges, Columbia's records are not always available or reliable, the films themselves sometimes offer us only a momentary, non-frontal glimpse of a cast member, and many minor roles are played by actors who do not appear again in a Stooge film. Accuracy here cannot be guaranteed.

Each film then has a 'Perspective,' an essay describing the film's unique quality. Most explain the film's historical/cultural perspective, examine its narrative structure or comic pedigree, or discuss its place in the Stooge corpus. In the later Shemp films, many of which were refurbished versions of earlier films, the method of refurbishing is detailed.

The section labeled 'Visual Humor' analyzes slapstick developments, sight gags, prop gags, accompanying sound effects, and camera or editing techniques. 'Stooge firsts' are noted. The section usually closes with a listing of where well known visual gags appear first, or, if appropriate, most recently in the Stooge corpus, or, in the case of the pre-Columbia films, where they will appear first in the Columbia films. For a complete listing of where gags appear, see the separate indices. These listings do not include such basic Stooge moves as the slap, gouge, nosebonk, belly pound, bonk, or hand-wave, but significant developments and variations are referenced.

The section labeled 'Verbal Humor' analyzes the verbal gags, particularly puns, pattern gags, internal rhymes, malapropisms (misspoken words), neologisms (made-up words), and ethnic humor. 'Stooge firsts' are noted. This section also contains an explanation of verbal references, translations of foreign words and phrases, and a listing of the epithets Moe uses (e.g. "grape-head"). The section usually closes with a listing of where well known verbal gags appear first, or, where appropriate, most recently in the Stooge corpus. These listings do not include such basic Stooge sounds as Curly's "nyuk, nyuk, nyuk" or "woob-woob-woob" or Shemp's "ee-bee-bee," but significant developments and variations are discussed.

The final section, 'Other Notes,' contains information about production, including working titles and shooting dates (when known). Brief biographical information is given when important cast and crew members appear for the first or last time. Continuity problems are noted, as are relevant quotes or anecdotes.

Citations are given by name of author and page number; select references are given in the bibliography.

So here, nearly three quarters of a century after The Three Stooges made their first film, and after almost two decades of research, is a study of their 220 films, a classical commentary on the complete oeuvre of the most beloved, longest-enduring comedy act in history.

Jon Solomon

THE BEGINNING
1930 SOUP TO NUTS

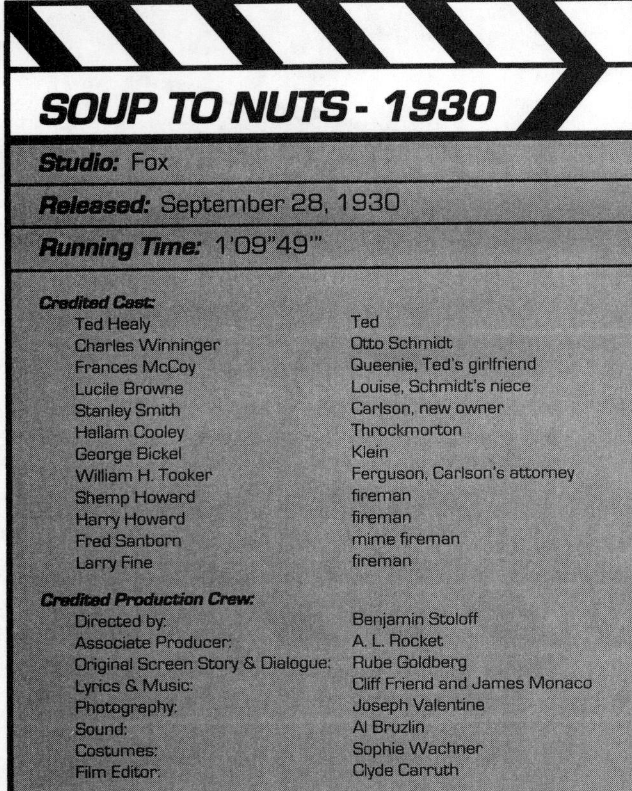

SOUP TO NUTS - 1930

Studio: Fox

Released: September 28, 1930

Running Time: 1'09"49'"

Credited Cast:

Ted Healy	Ted
Charles Winninger	Otto Schmidt
Frances McCoy	Queenie, Ted's girlfriend
Lucile Browne	Louise, Schmidt's niece
Stanley Smith	Carlson, new owner
Hallam Cooley	Throckmorton
George Bickel	Klein
William H. Tooker	Ferguson, Carlson's attorney
Shemp Howard	fireman
Harry Howard	fireman
Fred Sanborn	mime fireman
Larry Fine	fireman

Credited Production Crew:

Directed by:	Benjamin Stoloff
Associate Producer:	A. L. Rocket
Original Screen Story & Dialogue:	Rube Goldberg
Lyrics & Music:	Cliff Friend and James Monaco
Photography:	Joseph Valentine
Sound:	Al Bruzlin
Costumes:	Sophie Wachner
Film Editor:	Clyde Carruth

PERSPECTIVE: In 1929 Moe, Larry, and Shemp were not yet 'The Three Stooges.' Working in vaudeville for Ted Healy as his 'Racketeers' or 'Three Southern Gentlemen,' they neither had star-billing nor earned much money. But the foursome did gain popularity. From May 21, 1929 until just after the October Wall Street crash, they performed in J. J. Shubert's Broadway revue *A Night in Venice*, and, with Fred Sanborn added to the act, a few months thereafter at the Palace Theatre. These high-profile shows impressed Fox representatives who were eager to cast stage stars in their new 'talkie' films. The resulting *Soup to Nuts* credited Healy, Sanborn and each Stooge individually, but film publicity advertised all five of them as 'Ted Healy and His Racketeers.' Nonetheless, like all of their feature films of the 1930s, *Soup to Nuts* is not primarily a Stooge film. Its plot concerns Healy and several dramatic actors. But Moe, Larry and Shemp do get thirty minutes of screen time that captured the earliest performance by the pre-'Three Stooges' for us and impressed Fox executives enough to offer the trio a seven-year film contract. Healy was unwilling to break up the act, though, and unilaterally terminated the contract. This was the last straw: Moe, Larry, and Shemp quit Healy and began working on their own.

Healy's screen dominance creates an inter-Stooge equality and submissiveness very different from the relationships to be developed after the Healy years. Appearing both fatherly and cross - qualities Moe would eventually tailor to his own Stooge role - the charismatic, multi-faceted Healy could be variously mean-spirited, clownlike or debonair, and *Soup to Nuts* shows us how the Stooges supplied the frequent interruptions and submissive clowns his act required. Yet even while playing sidekicks, the Stooges make it clear here in their earliest footage how well they naturally fill a screen with human-like poses, gestures and actions unlike those of any other three humanoids. Whether hanging off the fire truck or shoved across the stage into a pile, the Stooges move in a uniquely busy blur of arms, legs and heads. All of this, mind you, is without the benefit of careful film editing, added sound effects or a writer and director well aware of the Stooges' physical capacities. The audience at the fireman's ball loves their stage act, suggesting why the Stooges became so popular on stage in the late Twenties and showing us why the Stooges were destined to flourish on film for the next four decades.

The significance of the title we learn from writer Rube Goldberg's introductory statement: "There can never be harmony in the home while people loudly gurgle their soup. There can never be peace in matrimony while wives throw broken nutshells on the floor for their husbands to step on with their bare feet. Somewhere between the soup and the nuts,perhaps in the fish or

Ted Healy and His Racketeers shortly before and after they traveled to Hollywood for the first time. Healy, the star of the act, paid each Stooge only $100 weekly though he bought them occasional gifts.

the applesauce, there must be joy and contentment." The expression 'soup to nuts' applies to the plot of the film in that Ted and Queenie and Louise and Carlson will recognize their love for each other only after there has been plenty of chaos along the way. Chaos? That is where the Stooges come in and begin their film career.

VISUAL HUMOR: The Stooges' first filmed visual gag is Ted and Sanborn's failed attempt at dropping sandbags on them. Ironically, this gag features the Stooges *escaping* physical abuse; almost all of their future gags will feature their taking and giving physical abuse. The slapping, which is real, was the mainstay of their early routines; according to contemporaries, Ted Healy invented this kind of authentic stage slap. Moe's grabbing Larry by the head and delivering a relatively mean-spirited uppercut slap to Larry's face demonstrates how violent their stage routines tended to be. In future years, the slapstick will soften and not appear so mean-spirited. Sound effects will help tone down the violence inherent in Stooge slapstick and make it more intensely comical rather than painfully realistic. There are no added sound effects aside from the cuckoo sound when Otto gets punched. A number of slapstick movements have not been developed yet, most notably the head bonk, the eye gouge, the fist game, and getting hit with a tool. Filmed Stooge firsts: a Stooge huddle as well as Moe and Shemp exchanging slaps before finally turning and slapping Larry. We will see something similar to the latter in *Hoi Polloi.* Contemporaries say Healy also invented the stage huddle, but *Scripts* 101 adds a variant: the huddle was invented on stage after Moe missed Curly with a slap and hit Larry so hard he needed time to recover. Shemp will again be rescued by a woman (Daphne Pollard) in his 1935 Vitaphone film *His First Flame.* Shemp's coin flipping losses will be reprised in *Restless Knights* and *Men in Black.* The three bearded creditors crowd into a narrow doorway much as the Stooges will in *Saved By the Belle* and *Oily to Bed, Oily to Rise.*

Writer (inventor/cartoonist) Rube Goldberg's infamous gadgets may have influenced such Stooge gadgetry as we will see in *Termites of 1938, Three Pests in a Mess, Cactus Makes Perfect* and many other films. The large mallet in the burglar alarm is recalled in the pinball mallet in *Three Little Pirates.* Lou Breslow, who will direct *Punch Drunks,* assisted in writing this script, and claimed [*Scripts* 46] to have invented most of the gadgetry. Carlson walking through the door that had fallen off the building onto the sidewalk will reappear in the classic door-installation scene in *Pardon My Scotch.* During the gag in which Larry passes out, the doctor says "I'm afraid he's done for" and then Larry gets up, as we will see in *Even as IOU.* Moe's "You wanna make a fool out of the doctor?!" will be reused in *Fright Night,* Shemp's first film after rejoining the team in 1946. Early in his career, Moe was a dramatic actor, as we can see when he calls for a doctor to help Larry. The Stooges take their girls to Coney Island - the first example of Stooge womanizing in their films. The audience at the fireman's ball enjoys the Stooges' live performance, a technique used later in *Ants In the Pantry, Gents Without Cents,* and *4 For Texas.*

VERBAL HUMOR: The Stooges' first filmed verbal utterance is, appropriately, a three-pattern (Shemp: "Say 'Hello' for us." Moe: "Give her my regards, will ya?" Larry: "Me too!"). Already Stooge verbal humor results from ignorance (Moe: "Say, this is the hottest June we've had since last July!"; and Shemp: "He don't know the lyrics [lie-rics]" Moe: "He means the larynx.") and slovenliness (Shemp: "Yeah, it was so hot night last night I had to get up and take off my socks!"). The barber-shop quartet song 'You'll Never Know [What Tears Are, Till You Cry Like You Made Me Cry]' was a Stooge favorite in the early years; it will be sung in seven films. Epithets: Larry calls Moe "lunk-head," and Healy calls Queenie "apple-head," both to be used later. Schmidt's punchline to the suit of armor ("My gallant knight, I raised you from a tin can!") resembles Curly-Joe's gag in *The Outlaws Is Coming* ("I got a horse pistol. I raised it from a colt!"). The Depression is reflected in Ted's song 'One Pair of Pants at a Time' and a set-gag (Ted: "What's your name?" Moe: "George Washington."

Rube Goldberg gadgets and contraptions from a 1929 cartoon in *Collier's.* This is an invention ("that fell off the professor's head along with the rest of the dandruff") for carving a turkey. It is set into motion by the rooster weeping for his wife in the chicken salad on the window sill.

Ted: "Are you the fella that chopped down the cherry tree?" Moe: "No, I ain't worked in a year and a half!"]. Moe will crave "bologna and whipped cream" in *Idiots Deluxe*. The 'George Washington' and 'Pick a number' gags from their stage act will be filmed in stage form in *Plane Nuts*. Moe's "The arrow points halfway. I don't know if it's half empty or half full!" was used in *A Night in Venice*, and will reappear in *False Alarms* [like *Flat Foot Stooges*, another film in which the Stooges portray firemen] and even *Kook's Tour*. A gag in the form - Healy: "Did he have on a gray hat? With a black band? And tan shoes? I don't know him!" - will be used in *Termites of 1938*. Ted says "soup to nuts" to describe his array of costumes, Shemp ["soup *with* some nuts"] to describe his lunch. Laurel & Hardy first received top billing in *From Soup to Nuts* [1928].

OTHER NOTES: The restoration of *Soup to Nuts* by the UCLA Film and Television Archive is a milestone in film preservation. For details, see Jim Shemansky, "The Search for Soup to Nuts," *The Three Stooges Journal* 56 [1990] 10-11. The film had its television debut on Oct. 8, 1995 on American Movie Classics. *A Night in Venice* played for 175 performances; cf. *Plane Nuts*. The Wall Street crash killed vaudeville; it forced the closing of its mecca, the Palace Theatre, which later reopened as RKO's Orpheum movie theater.

Although this is his first film appearance as a Stooge, Moe, credited here as 'Harry Howard,' had appeared as a juvenile extra in many Vitagraph silents from 1909. Also, in 1923, he appeared in a dozen films with Pittsburgh Pirates Baseball Hall of Famer Honus Wagner, although some sources attribute these films to Shemp. Shemp will not make another Stooge feature film until *Gold Raiders* [1951].

Benjamin Stoloff began directing in 1926; his best known work is *Destry Rides Again* [1932]. Charles Winninger [Otto] was best known as Captain Andy in *Showboat*, a role he created on Broadway in 1927, played in the Universal musical of the same name in 1936, and played again – though vaguely disguised – as Captain Henry on Maxwell House's *Show Boat* on NBC radio. Lucile Browne [Louise] played the heroine in Gene Autry's first Republic film, *Tumbling Tumbleweeds* [1935]. Richard Finegan hears Moe, Larry, and Shemp call their dates "Helen," "Mabel," and "Babe," the names of their real-life wives. Before the restoration made the film available for public viewing, an erroneous rumor circulated that the Stooges doubled as three of the 'San Stevedorean' Revolutionaries. According to *Moe* [45], Healy met privately with Fox's Winnie Sheehan to terminate the Stooges' film contract. Moe, whom Healy told simply that Fox had changed its mind, did not find out about Healy's interference until later.

This publicity photo from the Stooges' first film, *Soup to Nuts* [1930], shows four Stooges. Ted Healy was always the star and boss, as illustrated in the photos on the previous pages. Shemp Howard, Moe Howard, and Larry Fine were his regular stooges, called variously "Three Southern Gentleman" or "Racketeers," and here Fred Sanborn joins the troupe. Healy's act was reconfigured for each contract. According to Larry's autobiography [68], producer J. J. Shubert signed Sanborn as Healy's third Stooge for his 1929 Broadway show *A Night in Venice*, but Healy, preferring Larry Fine, hired Larry on his own.

Fred Sanborn is technically a fifth 'third' Stooge besides Shemp and successors Curly Howard, Joe Besser, and Joe DeRita. After Shemp left the group in 1932, Moe and Larry toured with Healy on the Balaban & Katz Circuit for six weeks; Sanborn filled in for Shemp. Soon after Curly would replace Shemp for fourteen years.

1933 - 1934
EARLY SHORT FILMS

Hollywood on Parade • *Nertsery Rhymes* • *Beer and Pretzels*

Hello Pop! • *Plane Nuts* • *The Big Idea*

HOLLYWOOD ON PARADE

Studio: Paramount; released by Criterion Pictures Corp.

Released: March 30, 1934

Running Time: 11"00"'

Uncredited Production Crew:
Producer: Louis Lewyn
Director: unknown

Uncredited Cast:
Jimmy Durante
Mack Gordon & Harry Revel
Florence Desmond
Ted Healy
Bonnie Bonnell
Curly Howard
Larry Fine
Moe Howard
Ben Turpin
Rudy Vallee
Benny Rubin

PERSPECTIVE: Like many film studios in the early days of sound pictures, Paramount was signing talented stars from East coast stage revues but did not always know at first how to write film scripts for them. In this low budget and plotless but historically interesting revue, we see Jimmy Durante singing "I Gotta See a Man About a Dog" and songwriters Mack Gordon and Harry Revel crooning "Did You Ever See a Dream Walking?". In addition to a variety of first lines with Rudy Vallee, we see Florence Desmond doing several of her famous impersonations; Ben Turpin looking cross-eyed and doing a spectacular pratfall; and Ted Healy, Bonnie Bonnell and the Stooges [uncredited] performing a slapping gag by the bar tended by Turpin. There are no choral production numbers, as there would be in the next year's MGM two-reelers. And unlike the two-reeler MGM and Columbia shorts to follow in ensuing years, this film is merely a one-reeler. So it is relatively brief.

There is considerable confusion about the date of this film. Neither Moe nor Larry in their autobiographies, nor the Stooge authorities in the *The Three Stooges Scrapbook*, discuss the circumstances surrounding its production. But Larry, in his *Stroke of Luck* [84-85], recollects that in 1933 – around the time they were performing at Club New Yorker in Hollywood – film producer Bryan Foy [a Catholic school friend of Ted Healy's] invited Healy and company to perform at a party attended by Jack Warner, Harry Cohn and Louis B. Mayer, the heads of Warner's, Columbia, and MGM, respectively. Their act was so well received that each studio offered them a contract. Healy, who handled all business matters for the group, signed with MGM and they worked at that studio during the second half of 1933. A little later they were offered contracts by Universal and Columbia, the latter turning out to be a 24-year relationship. Apparently, Paramount was in the mix, too, for *Hollywood On Parade* was released by Paramount in 1934. But there are several reasons for believing that it was the Stooges' first short film, perhaps dating back to late 1932. Most of the arguments for this early dating are internal.

Above all, Curly sports a short crop of hair on his head; we would not see this hair again until Curly's retirement more than a decade hence when he made his hirsute cameo appearance in 1947's *Hold That Lion*. Moe makes a sound and motion which will be later developed and identified almost exclusively with Curly: clenching his fists and squealing "Hhmm!" In addition, Larry slaps Moe with impunity, although Moe does get even by slapping Curly twice. If indeed *Hollywood on Parade* preserves Curly's first Stooge appearance on film, it includes Curly's first face rub, an early staple of his repertoire. Besides their great age and previous rarity, each of these early Stooge films has something

In Paramount's *Hollywood on Parade*, songwriters Mack Gordon [right] and Harry Revel sing their new song, "Did You Ever See a Dream Walking?", to be heard in Fox's 1933 film, *Sitting Pretty* that introduced Clifton Webb as 'Mr. Belvedere.' The song was used more recently in *The Green Mile* [1999]. Gordon and Revel went on to write the tunes for such 1934 Paramount films as *College Rhythm* starring Dick Powell; for *We're Not Dressing* [1934] with Bing Crosby, Carole Lombard, Burns and Allen, and Ethel Merman [*It's a Mad, Mad, Mad, Mad World*]; and for the Fox/Shirley Temple vehicle *Stowaway* [1936].

Ben Turpin fakes a California snow scene - with cotton icicles in the foreground - in a postcard issued about the same year *Hollywood on Parade* was made. The photo was shot on the grounds of the Mack Sennett studios in Edendale, where the Stooges would play golf and chase beer barrels [*Three Little Beers*] in a few years.

unique about it and either introduces some person, movement, gag, or line the Stooges will develop and reprise in future films – or one which they will never use again. This early production is to be treasured above all for preserving the first triple-slap, a slapstick maneuver used effectively some three dozen times in future films. Those would include the Stooges' father [*Restless Knights*] or mother [*Cactus Makes Perfect*] or a sophisticated woman [*Crash Goes the Hash*] or even Dean Martin [*4 for Texas*] delivering the blow(s).

VISUAL HUMOR: Besides Larry's unrevenged slap of Moe, we also see Bonnie slapping Healy with impunity. Curly will not use the clenched fist "Hhmm!" to full effect until *Hoi Polloi* and *Three Little Beers*. Moe would use the 'Hhmm!' again in 1948's *Shivering Sherlocks*, as would Shemp in 1947's *Sing a Song of Six Pants*. Monty Collins, as the Stooges' mother in *Cactus Makes Perfect*, also, appropriately, goes, "Hhmm!". After the Stooges' slapfest, Ben Turpin slaps himself and renders quite a sideways reaction.

VERBAL HUMOR: Effeminacy was a common topic for humor in the early 1930s. Fred Sanborn's walk (imitated by Curly in *Plane Nuts*) is one example. In this film, we hear the exchange (Healy: "Your fairy godmother always watches over you." Bonnie: "I've got an uncle I'm not sure of."). Bonnie's "Are you Ted Heal?" will be used again by Moe in *Plane Nuts*.

OTHER NOTES: Paramount in 1932-1934 released twenty-six 'Hollywood on Parade' one-reelers, of which this [B-9] was the twenty-second. Some years later, Criterion Pictures re-released all twenty-six films and added a generic title screen with 'COPYRIGHT - 1932.' Richard Finegan [in 'Ted Healy Update,' *The 3 Stooges Journal* 60 (1991) 6] confirms this film's March 30, 1934 release date, pointing out that MGM's *The Big Idea* and *Hollywood Party* were the only films containing the foursome of Ted Healy, Moe, Larry, and Curly which had a later release. But because none of our sources make any mention of the Stooges working for any film studio other than MGM or Columbia during 1934, and since Curly's hairstyle is unique, one might assume a production date earlier than the Stooges' MGM period in 1933.

As in all of the ensuing MGM two-reelers with Ted Healy and the Stooges, Bonnie Bonnell, Ted Healy's paramour in real life, is part of their act. The Stooges will appear with Jimmy Durante a number of times in the next two years, most notably in MGM's *Meet the Baron*, and they will mimic him in some of their Columbia films. In *Fifi Blows Her Top* Larry will say "She went to see a dog about a man". For Rudy Vallee, see *Time Out For Rhythm*. Ben Turpin's trademark gags were exactly what he does here: looking cross-eyed and taking pratfalls. The British dancer Florence Desmond, known for her impersonations, did not appear in many films. Here she impersonates Greta Garbo and Helen Broderick; on a 1932 Victor record she 'did' Janet Gaynor, Zasu Pitts, Jimmy Durante, Tallulah Bankhead, Marlene Dietrich, Gracie Fields and Marie Dressler. Bryan Foy, the eldest of the 'Seven Little Foys,' knew Ted Healy from their Catholic school days and wound up defraying the indebted star's funeral costs in 1937. Years later, Foy produced such memorable films as *Guadalcanal Diary* (1942) and *House of Wax* (1953).

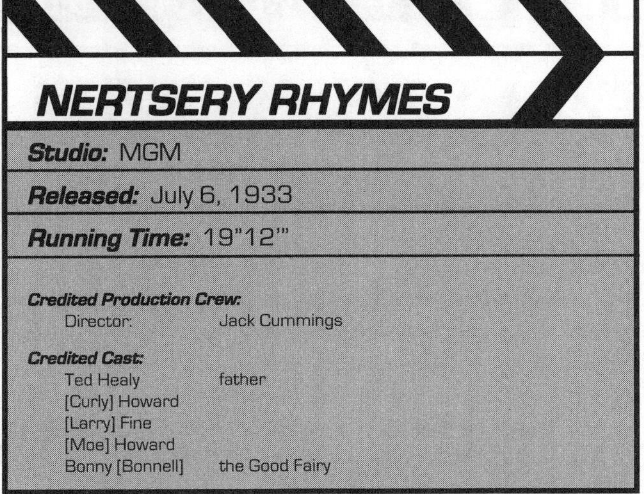

NERTSERY RHYMES

Studio: MGM

Released: July 6, 1933

Running Time: 19"12'"

Credited Production Crew:

Director: Jack Cummings

Credited Cast:

Ted Healy — father
[Curly] Howard
[Larry] Fine
[Moe] Howard
Bonny [Bonnell] — the Good Fairy

PERSPECTIVE: When Ted Healy destroyed the seven-year film contract Fox offered Moe, Larry, and Shemp after their debut in *Soup to Nuts*, they left him and played coast-to-coast as the "Three Lost Souls." In 1931, they added straight man Jack Walsh and played the RKO-Keith Theatre Circuit so successfully that Healy threatened, cajoled and made promises to them. He even tried forming his own rival 'Stooges' with three other actors – anything to get the Stooges back. It worked. But just four weeks after they were booked into J. J. Shubert's *The Passing Show of 1932*, Healy broke the contract. Tired of Healy's volatility and underhanded methods, Shemp quit the act to begin his own film career at Vitaphone. Meanwhile, Healy, Moe and Larry signed with the Balaban & Katz Circuit and temporarily hired Fred Sanborn [*Soup to Nuts*] as the third Stooge. But following that booking, Moe's younger brother Jerome – forever after to be known as Curly – took Sanborn's place. It was shortly after this new foursome performed at Hollywood's Club New Yorker in 1933 that Harry Rapf signed them to an MGM studio contract for both feature films and two-reelers in a variety of personnel configurations.

A linen postcard of the Balaban & Katz Chicago Theater, 1930

Nertsery Rhymes earns its unique niche in Stoogedom as the initial Stooges short-film release, the first of five at MGM, (although *The Big Idea*, *Plane Nuts* and *Turn Back the Clock* may have been produced earlier). MGM was the only major studio to turn a healthy profit in these early years of the Depression, and the studio used the profits to sign big name stars, develop a short-film unit and, inspired by the success of Warner's *42nd Street,* create musicals. Some of the production numbers edited out of their feature-length musicals were inserted into short films, so *Nertsery Rhymes* contains two musical numbers from the unreleased feature *The March of Time*. Despite making up to 80 short films each year, MGM made some of them relatively elaborate. *Nertsery Rhymes* and *Hello Pop!* were even photographed by Technicolor Process, the two-strip dye transfer process in use before 1935.

The production numbers consume seven minutes of *Nertsery Rhymes*, but the Stooges appear in the other twelve. They play Healy's three sons, whom he tries to soothe with bedtime stories so he can go out on a date with the Good Fairy. The father-sons relationship works very well for Healy and the Stooges since it accounts for how loving Healy can be toward the Stooges one minute yet dominant or abusive the next. It also explains the Stooges' child-like behavior: demanding bedtime stories, slapping one another, listening intently to 'father' and ultimately imitating him by taking three dates to an outing at the beer hall. Already in this first short film release, we can see that the Stooges thrive on inter-Stooge slapstick. That includes pushing and shoving each other; telling set-jokes and puns; listening to but blatantly challenging a dominant person; and striking memorable group poses. There remain noticeable differences between these early MGM Stooge films and the better known Columbia shorts to follow, but it was clear that the slapping, gouging, singing and joking Stooges had arrived in Hollywood for good.

VISUAL HUMOR: The eye gouge – filmed here for the first time – had been created after filming *Soup to Nuts* while the Stooges were preparing for their West coast debut as "Three Lost Souls" in 1930. During a bridge game, Shemp – accusing Larry of cheating – jammed his fingers into Larry's eyes. Moe (who laughed so hard he fell off his chair, broke a glass door pane and cut his arm) used the move the very next morning at the Paramount Theatre in Los Angeles by simultaneously gouging Shemp and Larry [*Moe* 46]. In this film, Moe uses it as soon as Curly falls backwards and wakes him and Larry, gouging them both. Interestingly, a contemporary gouge is used on Gus Shy in Vitaphone's *I Scream* (also featuring Shemp), released May 19, 1934. The gouge gives both Healy and the Stooges their first opportunity to use threatening language along with their slapstick (Healy to Curly: "I'll gouge your eyes out!"; later: "I'll gouge your tonsils out!"). Another first here finds Ted hitting the Stooges with a mallet to put them to sleep. This is the first use of a tool in a Stooge film and will appear later (e.g. *Men in Black*) as a means of delivering an anesthetic. We see the first Stooge sleeping scene, but at this point it is without the trademark rhythmic snoring. Other Stooge film firsts here include Curly fanning his ear (*Horses' Collars*); the three of them forming a train (*Three Sappy People*); an Indian dance; pretending to watch a horse race (*Back to the Woods*); and the collapsing bed (*Movie Maniacs*). Their huddle (near the finale) is something we already saw in *Soup to Nuts*. In their pair of intense slapstick scenes, Moe takes the dominant role among the three Stooges. He stands in the middle dishing out gouges and slaps and receiving only a few slaps in return, never suffering a gouge. Typically, the spatial arrangement finds Moe striking Larry or Curly while Healy hits the other. Because he stands in the middle, Moe often gives backhanded slaps to Larry or Curly, a technique that he will use for only a year or two after this film. The slapstick is devoid of accompanying sound effects aside from an occasional wood block. Minus other sound effects, we hear the real slapping. Early on, however, Healy hits a certain spot on Curly's forehead and creates a musical tone that he twice uses as his starting pitch. In the future, slapstick sound effects will not be so musically useful. Having Moe mark an 'X' on Curly's forehead is unique. It will be several years before the metal-like hardness of Curly's skull becomes established (*A Pain in the Pullman*, et al.).

VERBAL HUMOR: There is an important three pattern (Curly: "They followed in their father's footsteps." Moe: "And then they went to the beer joint for a drink." Larry: "And they lived happily ever after." All: "Woo-woo-woo!"). This unison "Woo-woo-woo!" and the "Woo-woo" Indian cries earlier in the film are the predecessors to Curly's characteristic "Woob-woob". We hear their first triadic harmonizing ("You said it!") at the end of "The Woman in the Shoe". The script by Healy, Moe and Matty Brooks -- who co-wrote the other MGM shorts gives us our first version of the "You don't know my father" joke (Fairy: "My little man, if I gave you a dollar and your father gave you a dollar, how many dollars would you have?" Larry: "One dollar." Fairy: "I can see you don't know your arithmetic." Larry: "I can see you don't know my father!") It would be used again in *Half-Wits Holiday*. In this case, the father (Healy) is actually present. Other verbal gags to be reused in the Columbia short films include: Father: "What happened in 1776?" Curly: "What street?"; "Chief Belch in the Face"; the reference to the reform school (*Ants in the Pantry*); "What do you think they are – baboons?" (*Dizzy Detectives*); "Remember: It's every man for himself!" (*Restless Knights*); "Are you getting personal?" (*Back to the Woods*); the reference to Sitting Bull (*Rockin' Thru the Rockies*); and Moe: "Little fly upon the wall / Ain't you got no clothes at all?" (*All the World's a Stooge*). Healy's "That's for nothin', son" will have echoes from Moe in later films (e.g. *Hoi Polloi*) as will Healy's "I'll gouge your eyes out!" (*Punch Drunks*). Healy's "I'll gouge your tonsils out!" is unique. In the second production number, the fairy sings about other nursery rhymes – in particular Little Miss Muffet, Jack and Jill and the one about "Four and Twenty Blackbirds' Baked in a Pie." The first two of these will be revisited (with Simple Simon and the Pie Man) during a Stooge-like production number of their own in *Fiddlers Three*. References: The "shimmy shirt" in Moe's fly poem is a type of chemise. "Nerts" was 1930s slang for "nuts" (as in "Ahh, nerts!"), hence the title.

OTHER NOTES: The working title was *Nursery Rhymes*. The Stooges are billed as 'TED HEALY - Howard, Fine and Howard.' They would not become 'The Three Stooges' until after they signed with Columbia. An RKO theater bill illustrated in *Scripts* (20) labels the sans-Healy Stooges as the 'Three Lost Soles'. According to Larry's autobiography (75-84), the Stooges were paid $30,000 as compensation for the broken Fox contract. He recalls being unable to cash his check in Febrary because a local earthquake closed the banks. Actually, the quake hit on March 11, and banks were closed for President Franklin D. Roosevelt's infusion of several hundred million dollars into the depressed banking system. After quitting Healy and the Stooges in 1932, Shemp stayed on the Shubert circuit and worked with Joe Besser, who decades later became the third Stooge when, in 1956, he replaced Shemp – who had replaced Curly in 1946, who had replaced Shemp in 1933. Shemp formed his own Stooges for RKO's two-reeler *Knife of the Party* (1934). In his autobiography, *Besser* (81) relates that Curly, eager to enter show business, used to hang around the theater during rehearsals for J. J. Shubert's *The Passing Show of 1932*. He would fetch sandwiches and sodas for Healy, Moe, Larry, and Shemp. According to Moe's account [59-60], it was Healy who inspired Curly to shave his head of wavy brown hair and his waxed mustache. But the authors of the *Scrapbook* [63] cite photographs of Curly without his hair (but with a mustache) dating from those few months before they signed their MGM contract. Forrester (*Lost Episodes* (23-24) heard that Shemp got Curly to shave his head. All seem to agree that the ironic nickname of Curly was Jerome's own idea. Marion [Bonny/Bonnie] Bonnell, Ted's girlfriend, appeared in all five MGM short films. For a biography, see Bill Cappello, "The Search for...Bonnie Bonnell" *The 3 Stooges Journal* 57 (1991) 6-7. Director Jack Cummings worked with the Stooges throughout their MGM tenure and, like the Stooges, he made films well into the 1960s. Those movies include *Seven Brides for Seven Brothers* and *Viva Las Vegas*. He also directed the Marx Brothers' *Go West* (1940). Harry Rapf was the head of MGM's short films, the same position Jules White would have at Columbia.

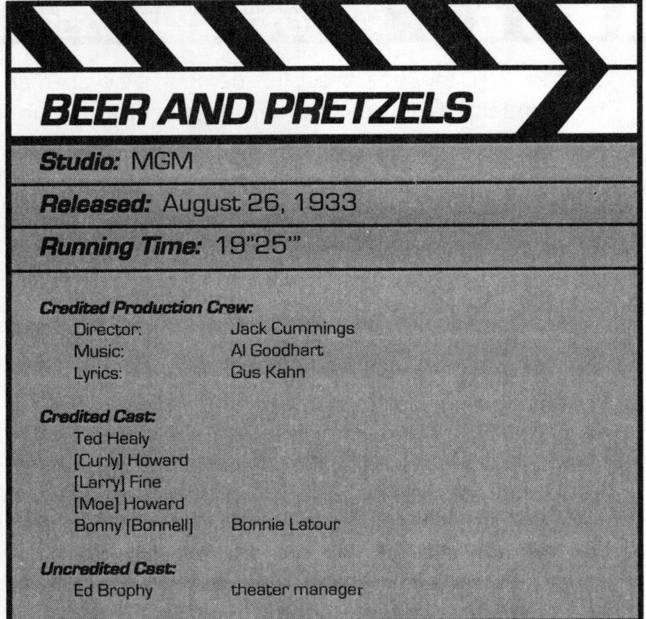

BEER AND PRETZELS

Studio: MGM

Released: August 26, 1933

Running Time: 19"25'"

Credited Production Crew:

Director:	Jack Cummings
Music:	Al Goodhart
Lyrics:	Gus Kahn

Credited Cast:

Ted Healy	
[Curly] Howard	
[Larry] Fine	
[Moe] Howard	
Bonny [Bonnell]	Bonnie Latour

Uncredited Cast:

Ed Brophy	theater manager

PERSPECTIVE: Billed as 'Heely, Heely, Heely, & Heely,' Ted Healy and his Stooges venture beyond the interior setting of *Nertsery Rhymes*. The opening and closing scenes take them outdoors for the first time in a two-reeler. It launches them into a backstage plot surpassing the limited narrative parameters of the previous month's *Nertsery Rhymes* and their functional cameo in the feature *Turn Back the Clock*, which was released just the day before *Beer and Pretzels*. This musical short does not include a large production number, as did their previous MGM short. Instead, it incorporates a few setup scenes featuring Ted Healy and "Howard, Fine and Howard," a revue- a song and dance by Bonny, a trio of singing bartenders, a threesome of barrel-top tap dancers seen from some interesting camera angles - and a denouement. That's not to mention periodic doses of slapstick, antics and even a brief riot.

Because the backstage plot by nature and design focuses on the presentation of the club's musical entertainment program, Healy and the Stooges are reduced to book-ending that program and interrupting it at comically poignant intervals. This narrative design works well for them, since often their stage act flourished when one of the four interrupted the others. (We see this most clearly in *Plane Nuts*.) It also enhances another of their act's comic staples: their self-defacement. At the outset, the four of them are tossed onto the ground and leave a dazed Bonny on the sidewalk as they scramble to enter the club, get tossed back onto the sidewalk again and ultimately faint back onto it at the end of the film. They thrive on being characterized as lousy performers. This clever device allows the film audience to laugh when a manager, scout or lead dislikes their act or makes fun of it. Yet it also sets up the audience to enjoy the act when they happen to give a good performance beyond expectations. In this sense, the plot gives Healy and the Stooges a no-lose situation. We laugh at them for being bad because the film tells us they are bad; we laugh at them for being good despite what the film has told us. This "lousy act" characterization and backstage narrative scheme will be adopted several times in their Columbia films, most notably in *A Pain in the Pullman*, *What's the Matador?* and *Gents Without Cents* as well as in one of their last films, *Sweet and Hot*.

Once they get off the sidewalk and inside the club, the Stooges do not stand up any better than they did outside. They land on the floor diving after a quarter, wrestle a customer and the manager and pelt everyone with furniture. We found them on the stage floor in *Soup to Nuts* and will do so again in *Woman Haters*. But while these scenes are riotous and do not have the organized chaos we will see in future multi-door corridor chases (e.g. *Restless Knights*), they do feature the Stooges' ability to cause chaos in an otherwise controlled situation. Once Del Lord directs them in Columbia's *Pop Goes the Easel*, *Hoi Polloi* and *Ants in the Pantry*, this will become second nature. Similarly, the interior scenes give us our first – albeit brief – glimpse of what kind of damage the Stooges can do to a kitchen.

VISUAL HUMOR: In their MGM configuration with Ted Healy, Stooge dynamics depend largely on Healy's dialogue with another person (the two women and the two managers), his joke telling and his physicality. But it is mostly Curly who receives the slaps, and in this film he endures them from Healy, Moe and Larry as well. This evokes the first filmed "victim of circumstance." It is also Curly who burps and is featured playing spoons. He does all of this without any of the high-pitched sounds or extraordinary hand motions and facial gestures he will develop in the next year or two, save for forming his mouth into a tight 'O' shape and interlocking his thumbs and forefingers (which he also does in his solo effort *Roast-Beef and Movies*). Curly receives a head bonk; the sound effect is not the resonant BONG-G-G of *Nertsery Rhymes*, but a wood block sound that approaches the sound effect to be used at Columbia.

When they rush through the club door, there is no body scrunching or coattail grabbing as we will see in the classic entry/movement routines in *Rockin' Thru the Rockies*, *Saved By the Belle* and *Oily to Bed, Oily to Rise* many years hence. Ignorance will always be a part of Stoogedom, so here they jump in the lake when "ordered" to do so. Larry slaps Curly, something he will do only occasionally in the Columbia films. Curly's pants are too short, as will be the case in many early Columbia films. Other firsts: the Stooges diving for the coin (diving for the cigar in *Uncivil Warriors*); slipping on the soapy floor (*Loco Boy Makes Good*); and Healy threatening the theater manager himself but then sending Curly to fight him [*The Sitter Downers; Dizzy Detectives*].

VERBAL HUMOR: The opening billing includes "Venetian Street Singers," the first ethnic joke in a Stooge short, since these Italians have the Irish names "O'Toole, Flannigan, & Murphy"; cf. the Yiddish/Irish booking agency in *A Pain in the Pullman*. The Stooges will themselves play Venetians in *Hello Pop!* and *Meet the Baron*, as they did in *A Night in Venice* on the New York stage in 1929. Larry will reprise the "Pate de foie gras" / "We'll I'll see if the band can play that" joke in *Loco Boy Makes Good*, another film which has the Stooges portray actors/waiters in a club. Other Stooge firsts: Healy: "If I'm lyin', I hope you drop dead" [Larry in *Pop Goes the Easel*]; and Healy: "Junior, would you watch your Ps and Qs, please?" [*Three Missing Links*]. Moe will use this line frequently. Ted again uses "I'll gouge your eyes out," as in *Nertsery Rhymes*. The Stooges will sing more of the barbershop quartet song "You'll Never Know" [*Soup to Nuts*] in three part harmony during *Horses' Collars*, *A Ducking They Did Go*, and elsewhere. Observe that when Curly laughs after jumping into the lake, he has not yet developed the 'nyuk' laugh. References: when Healy asks Bonny, "Did you ever hear of Garbo or Harlow?" he mentions two fellow MGM contract stars, Greta Garbo and Jean Harlow.

OTHER NOTES: The working title was *Beer Gardens*. Ed Brophy [theater manager], who would also play in *Hello Pop!*, would many years later provide one of the voices in *Dumbo* [1941]. Richard Finegan [in 'Ted Healy Update,' *The 3 Stooges Journal* 60 [1991] 14] identifies the trio of singing bartenders as 'The Three Ambassadores'. The riot at the end is reminiscent of the incident "Ted Healy and His Gang" experienced in 1927 at the Black and White Society, described in *Moe* 37. *Moe* 59 confirms that Curly was an expert at playing spoons, as we see here first and later in *Disorder in the Court* and *Horses' Collars*. There is some irony in the plot, for in real life Ted was a womanizer and got the Stooges in trouble on occasion with his big mouth; he once got them fired from the Loew's circuit for using the word "crap."

When Moe, Larry, and Curly signed with MGM, they became part of the largest film factory in the world, with "more stars than there are in heaven." The studio made all personnel decisions, so they produced two short films separating the trio. At the time Moe, Larry, and Curly were simply actors who used to be Ted's Stooges, not the 'Three Stooges.' On the title page of this chapter is a photo from the non-extant *Jailbirds of Paradise* [1934] with Moe and Curly. Here, Curly alone joins George Grivot and Bobby Callahan in *Roast Beef and Movies* [1933].

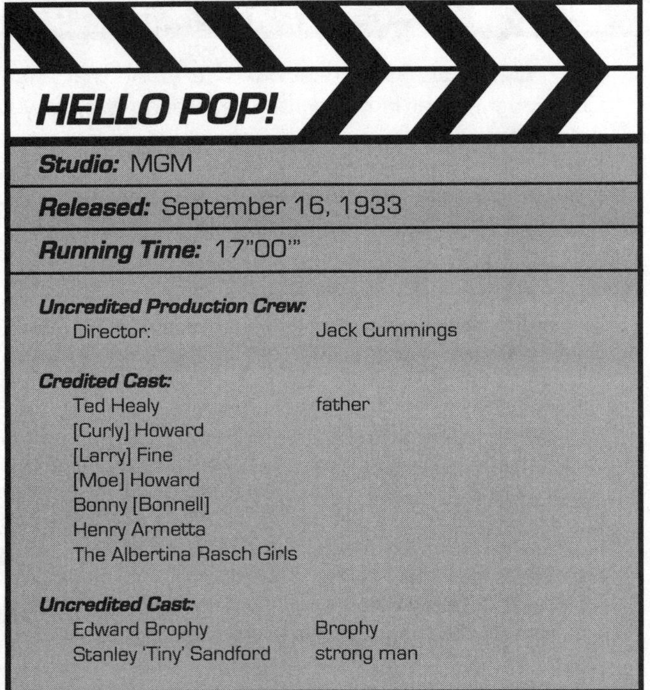

HELLO POP!

Studio: MGM

Released: September 16, 1933

Running Time: 17"00'"

Uncredited Production Crew:

Director:	Jack Cummings

Credited Cast:

Ted Healy	father
[Curly] Howard	
[Larry] Fine	
[Moe] Howard	
Bonny [Bonnell]	
Henry Armetta	
The Albertina Rasch Girls	

Uncredited Cast:

Edward Brophy	Brophy
Stanley 'Tiny' Sandford	strong man

PERSPECTIVE: This seems to have been the final musical short the Stooges and Healy made at MGM. Unfortunately, no prints or negatives of *Hello Pop!* are known to exist, which makes it unique in the Stooge corpus. Each of the other 219 MGM and Columbia Stooge shorts and features are extant. The loss of *Hello Pop!* is particularly regrettable since it seems to have been a high quality production filmed entirely in Technicolor and enhanced by several inserted production numbers. We mourn the absence of a print of this film, but *Soup to Nuts* was also for decades unavailable for viewing. Perhaps there is hope that someday a print will surface.

We do have a good idea of what happened in the film, for Stooge aficionado Richard Finegan spent years tracking down the script, still photographs and related materials. He published his findings in *The Three Stooges Journal* [64 (1992) 10-12]], in which he offers a plot summary, a discussion of the musical numbers and their origins and several lines of dialogue.

The backstage setting for the film is a first for Healy and the Stooges, but the pace of the film is typically Healy-esque in that it starts and stops each time Ted is interrupted. After Ted complains to Edward Brophy that his name does not appear enough on the script, Bonny Bonnell (like Fred Sanborn in *Soup to Nuts*) keeps trying to tell him something, but is pushed away before she can say it. Actors complain about costumes. And blustery Italian musician Henry Armetta cannot find his flute or music. The Stooges dressed as Ted's children (*Nertsery Rhymes*) give him more to worry about. Moe says their mother has gone out to play bridge but Larry and Curly suspect she is with another man. But Ted has to get his show started, so he tells Brophy to lock them in a dressing room. The Stooges want out (Moe: "Our Papa owns this show, and we're going to see the show!"), so they sneak out dressed in Venetian costumes. Ted discovers them slapping and fighting [Larry slaps Ted!],

so he grabs Larry and Moe by the hair and drags them back to the dressing room. While the chorus girls do the "Moon Ballet," a kaleidoscopic production number, the Stooges stick their heads around the scenery to watch. After that number Moe jumps into the arms of a chorus girl who asks him his age (Moe: "35." Curly: "41!" Larry: "50!"). But she ends up with Ted, so Brophy bribes the Stooges: "Now little pals, be nice, good little children and Uncle Eddie will give you a nice clean dollar." When Ted and the chorus girl wearing a large hoop skirt sing his number "Wedding Bells," he is accompanied by Armetta, who has finally found his flute. But the Stooges run under her skirt and ruin the song, ushering in the kaleidoscopic production number, "I'm Sailing on a Sunbeam", with a schematic series of golden sunbeam slides in the sky down which the chorus girls slide. For the finale, Ted slaps Moe ("I'm warning you, when I get you home"). But Bonny interrupts, "Mr. Billingham!" Ted: "My name happens to be Ted Healy." Bonny: "Oh, I'm in the wrong theater!"

VISUAL HUMOR: Two possible Stooge firsts: Finegan reports that Ted grabs Larry and Moe by the hair, possibly the first Stooge hair pull; and he reports that the Stooges stick their heads around the corner of the scenery. Did they place their heads one on top of the other as they will often after *Whoops, I'm an Indian*?

VERBAL HUMOR: We already met a blustery Italian as the club manager in *Beer and Pretzels*. The best known irate Italians in the Columbia shorts will be the gardener in *Three Little Beers* and the bespectacled violinist in *Micro-Phonies*. Finegan reports that Moe says, as Ted

Although there are no extant prints of *Hello Pop!* (1933), several photographic stills help us visualize the Stooges' roles. They play Ted Healy's children, and in this scene they dress as Venetians - just as they had in *A Night in Venice*, the 1929 Shubert New York production. They will ride and sing on a Venetian gondola in MGM's *Meet the Baron* (1933).

is about to hit Curly: "Papa! Don't hit him on the head, you know he's not normal." This line will be used again in *Loco Boy Makes Good* and *Dizzy Pilots*. Each Stooge shouting out a different number (Moe: "35." Curly: "41!" Larry: "50!") will be varied in *Three Little Pigskins*.

OTHER NOTES: The working titles were *Back Stage*, *New Musical Short by Suber* and a generic '*Ted Healy Short*'. The reason this film seems to have been the final musical short the Stooges and Healy made at MGM is its high production number (#696); the others are: *The Big Idea* (#628/740), *Plane Nuts* (#680), *Nertsery Rhymes* (#685) and *Beer and Pretzels* (#690). Higher production numbers do not always mean later shooting dates, however. The Stooges will sing their own version of a wedding song in *Three Smart Saps* and elsewhere.

Finegan offers the following pedigree for the three numbers in *Hello Pop!* 1): "I'm Sailing on a Sunbeam," used both for the opening credits and as the finale, was taken from the MGM musical feature *It's a Great Life* (1929) starring the Duncan Sisters (Vivian and Rosetta). There, too, the number was used as the finale. The music was written by Dave Dreyer to lyrics by Ballard MacDonald (not by Irving Berlin as has been reported elsewhere). Only a brief segment in the middle of the number, where the Duncan Sisters sing part of this song and a few lines from "There's a Rainbow 'Round My Shoulder" and "I'm Following You," is omitted from *Hello Pop!*. 2) Ted Healy's song "Wedding Bells" (including the tune "Air Louis XIII" by Ghys) was written by Al Goodhart. 3) The "Garden Ballet" ("Moon Ballet") segment was composed and arranged by Dmitri Tiomkin, so (following Finegan's argument) it must derive from a pre-1933 MGM Technicolor feature including a ballet sequence composed by Dmitri Tiomkin and featuring the Albertina Rasch Girls. *Devil-May-Care* (1930) and *The Rogue Song* (1930) meet these parameters, but the ballet sequences do not match the one in *Hello Pop!*. Finegan suggests that the *Hello Pop!* number might derive from an unreleased portion of one of these films or from the 1930 MGM musical feature *The March of Time*, which was never completed or released but from which segments were used in other films (including *Nertsery Rhymes*).

In the following issue of the *Journal* [65 (1993) 8-10, 14], Finegan reconstructs MGM's short *Jailbirds of Paradise* (1934) that featured Moe and Curly without Larry. Albertina Rasch, famous for ensemble ballet patterns, worked at MGM in the mid-1930s.

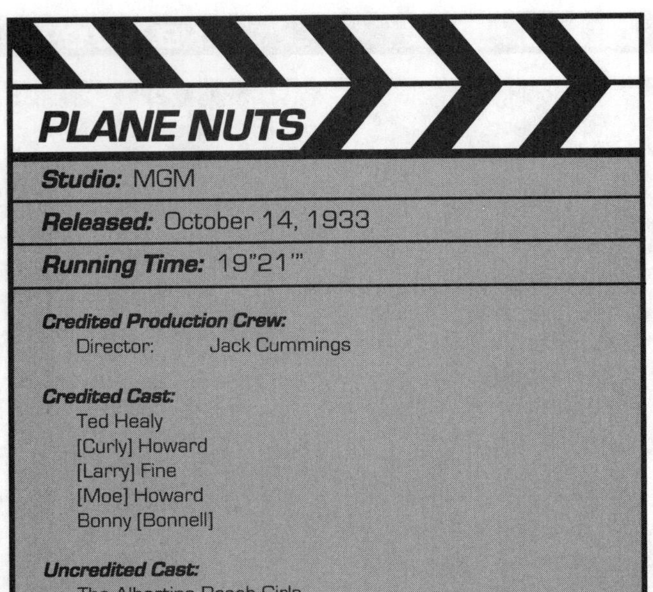

PERSPECTIVE: *Plane Nuts*, one of the earliest MGM films featuring Ted Healy and "Howard, Fine, Howard," is a most precious Stooge film. It preserves twelve minutes of the type of stage act they performed in 1929 for J. J. Shubert's Broadway revue, *A Night in Venice*, before they came to Hollywood. Modern viewers have become so accustomed to seeing the Stooges' Columbia short films – which did not begin production until 1934, when Moe was turning 37, Larry 32, and Curly 30 – that they forget the Stooges had earlier careers on stage. In 1909, when Moe (age 12) was already appearing as a Vitagraph film extra in his native Brooklyn, he met Ted Healy (age 13), and in the summer of 1912, the two men dove as "Annette Kellerman Diving Girls." By 1914, Moe was working on the Mississippi showboat Sunflower in dramatic roles. He and brother Shemp, having changed their last name from Horvitz to Howard, performed blackface and whiteface roles on both the RKO and Loew's vaudeville circuits until 1922, when they teamed up with Healy again. In 1925, Larry joined their act now known as "Ted Healy and His Three Southern Gentlemen." By 1929, they made it to Broadway, and we see the last vestiges of this act when we look at *Plane Nuts*.

Part of their highly praised stage act is preserved in MGM's *Plane Nuts* (1933). This original handbill was crudely printed.

Moe recalls some of their routines in his autobiography *Moe Howard and the Three Stooges* (41), e.g. Healy: "Did you boys ever hear of Abraham Lincoln?" Curly (extending his hand): "Glad to meet you, stranger!", and Moe: "Did you take a bath this morning?" Curly: "Nah, somebody was in the bathroom." Moe: "What time was that?" Curly: "About nine o'clock." Moe: "That was my wife!" Curly: "Ain't she skinny!" A few of their other stage gags were already filmed in *Soup to Nuts* (Healy: "What's your name?" Moe: "George Washington." Healy: "Are you the fella that chopped down the cherry tree?" Moe: "No, I ain't worked in a year and a half!"; and the "Take a number between 1 and 10" gag). We even see Larry speaking a little Yiddish, dancing on feet moving a mile a minute and shouting 'Hallelujah!' – three bits he used in his solo act before joining the others.

Plane Nuts differs from the other MGM shorts written by Healy, Moe and Matty Brooks in preserving some greatest hits of the Healy/Stooge theatrical act. It offers a comparison between the techniques used for staged comedy-musical revues, filmed comedy-musical revues, and the subsequent Columbia non-musical films.

On stage, each gag would finish with laughter and applause from the live audience and requires nothing more from the actors. But in the filmed *Plane Nuts,* the players have to end each gag with a hubbub between the four or five actors on stage and then blend with the next gag without a natural pause. Someone has to walk on from offstage or speak additional dialogue to tie the two gags together. In the Columbia films, there will be more options; gags will usually end in a slapstick flurry, a physical escape, a film dissolve or wipe, or a throwaway line either ad-libbed or written.

VISUAL HUMOR: Curly sways and swings his arms for the first time, and we see a hint of his footwork in his stocking-foot entrance. However, with both arms up, the right elbow held immobile and cocked at a right angle, Curly's movement and pose are clearly adapted from Fred Sanborn's running poses that we see in *Soup to Nuts*. Also like Sanborn is Curly's non-verbal initial approach to Healy. Curly had not had as many years of stage experience as the others; he was seven years younger than Moe and spent his youth more as a dancer than an actor. According to Gertrude Frank "Babe" Howard [Shemp's wife], Curly also tended to imitate Hugh Herbert, who was known for saying "Hoo-hoo!" -- developing into Curly's "Woob-woob!"; later, Herbert, too, made short films at Columbia. The Stooges huddled in *Soup to Nuts*, but here they do it with a fourth person [Bonny]. The two upbeat production numbers are kaleidoscopically choreographed and photographed as they were for *Hello Pop!*. Busby Berkeley, the master of this technique, had staged the musical numbers for 1929's *A Night in Venice*. The next time we will see Larry shirtless will be for his Marlon Brando imitation in *Cuckoo on a Choo Choo*. Boxer shorts will return in 1941 [*Dutiful But Dumb*; *All the World's a Stooge*]. Future Stooge motifs: Moe and Curly linking arms and dancing from here to there in big sweeps behind Healy [*Woman Haters*]; the pianist not giving Healy a chance to sing [*Loco Boy Makes Good*]; and directing Ted to stand a certain way [*Pop Goes the Easel; Slippery Silks*].

VERBAL HUMOR: The "Take a Number From 1 to 10" gag from their stage act is varied here with the addition of both Bonnie and the slapstick conclusion. The Stooges will vary their gags for decades, rarely performing anything the same way twice. Joking about Stooge verbal ignorance [Ted: "Get this guy with big words - 'resume'"; Moe: "What are you walkin' out here interrumpin' Ted Heal?"; Curly: "You don't care if we wear a 'truxedo'?"] and the failed attempt at spelling [Healy: "A bat-h? How do you spell it?" Moe: "I never heard of it!"] will be revisited in *Pop Goes the Easel, Hoi Polloi, Cactus Makes Perfect* and other films. Stooge ignorance is quintessential to their characterization. When Curly laughs in Ted's face, it is almost the first filmed "nyuk, nyuk, nyuk"; it is a haughty sound here. When Curly says "Ain't she skinny!" his voice is almost fully in the falsetto he will use in the years ahead. The first part of the bath exchange [Curly: "'Did you take a bat-h?'" Healy: "Did you take a what?" Curly: "A bat-h."] will be varied in *A Plumbing We Will Go*. Larry's "Woo-hoo!!" resembles his Tarzan yell in *Disorder in the Court*. His "Hallelujah!" will be reprised in such classic films as *Uncivil Warriors, Pardon My Scotch, Back to the Woods* and *You Nazty Spy!*. Healy will refer to Moe again as "hatchet-head" in MGM's feature *Meet the Baron*.

Other future Stooge motifs: Curly's "Not me!"; Moe's "Spread out!"; Larry's "I'll take it when I'm ready!. Yeah, I'm ready"; Moe speaking in a foreign accent; Larry speaking Yiddish; Moe's "comedy, singing, dancin' and talkin'" [*A Pain in the Pullman*]; Moe's "spittoon haircut" [*Three Little Beers*]; Curly saluting: "Vive la France!" [*Half Shot Shooters*]; and rats references like "Back to the rat trap" and Moe: "That's the wrong answer, you rat!" Larry: "What'd you say?!" Moe: "He's a rat!" Bonny: "Did you call me?" ["trapped like rats" in *Back to the Woods*].

Larry gives a unique verbal response to a gouge: "Give me my eyes back!". Ted's joking about "Curly/Girly" may be historically ironic if it's true that Ted originally inspired Curly to shave his head. Many of the verbal gags are typical of Healy's style, ranging from indirect insults ("I know you're here. Now the pool rooms are empty!"); flat, confusing, exchange patterns (Healy: "What's my name?" Moe: "Ted Heal?"); and extended exchanges (Healy: "Where'd you get that whistle, son?" Larry: "My father gave me the whistle" Healy: "What is he, a cop?" Larry: "Nah, he's a street cleaner, but he couldn't work yesterday. The wind was against him!"). Only the insults will regularly be used in the later Stooge films. Confusing patterns and extended exchanges take too long to decipher or deliver in their rapidly paced Columbia films.

References: 'Noel Coward stuff' refers to the darling of the international theater in the 1920s/1930s; he made several films in 1933. The chorus' aeronautic references are to Richard E. Byrd, who flew over the North and South poles in 1926 and 1929; Charles Lindbergh, who crossed the Atlantic solo in 1927; and Frank Monroe, who set a number of speed and distance records in 1932-1933. Ted's mentioning the "market crash" on the phone dates this routine to post-1929, although the stock market continued to move lower in 1932. Ted's comments about "Park Avenue" refer to the high class residential area in Manhattan, paralleling his dinner comments in *Beer and Pretzels*. When Moe says, "Oh, mutiny, huh?", it is uncertain if he is referring to the MGM film *Mutiny on the Bounty*, which would already have been in production at MGM, but would not be released until 1935. They certainly refer to it later in *Movie Maniacs*. Larry's "O.K. America!' was a popular exclamation, heard also in *The Big Idea* and *Meet the Baron*.

OTHER NOTES: The two production numbers, "Dance Until the Dawn" and 'Happy Landing", choreographed by Busby Berkeley, were originally made for the 1931 MGM musical/comedy feature *Flying High* starring Pat O'Brien, Bert Lahr and Charlotte Greenwood and directed by Charles Riesner. It was released in England under the title *Happy Landing*. Although *Flying High* ran almost 90 minutes, it contained only these two production numbers. The song "Dance Until the Dawn" was also used as background music in MGM's *Red-Headed Woman* (1932) starring Jean Harlow. The Australian Annette Kellerman, with whom Moe and Healy performed in the summer of 1912, was portrayed by Esther Williams in MGM's *Million Dollar Mermaid* (1952).

The working titles for *Plane Nuts - Aviation Short* and *Around the World Backwards* - as well as several photographic stills like the one, confirm that the film was originally conceived as a three-reel short or a theatrical feature, the deleted footage of which showed Healy and the Stooges flying around the world backwards. Their stage act in *A Night in Venice* featured a scene in a mock airplane; in fact, that scene was the first in which they used the gas-gauge "half-empty or half-full" gag reprised in their first film *Soup to Nuts* (1930) and their last film *Kook's Tour* (1970).

THE BIG IDEA

Studio: MGM

Released: May 12, 1934

Running Time: 18"40"'

Credited Production Crew:

Director:	William Crowley
Dance Director:	Sammy Lee

Credited Cast:

Ted Healy	
[Curly] Howard	
[Larry] Fine	
[Moe] Howard	
Bonny Bonnell	cleaning woman
Muriel Evans	Healy's fiancee
Three Radio Rogues	
Tut Mace	
The M-G-M Dancing Girls	

PERSPECTIVE: *The Big Idea* has a very simple narrative design. Ted Healy is trying to write a scenario but finds himself continually interrupted by his fiancée, the cleaning lady, workmen (ironically *not* the Stooges), a gangster, and the Stooges – not to mention two production sequences. Such a sketch is vintage Ted Healy, whose stage and screen appearances tend toward narrative incompleteness and rely heavily on minor characters rescuing him from the need to complete a song, story or sketch. In *Soup to Nuts*, it was primarily Fred Sanborn who interrupted Ted. In *Plane Nuts*, it was the Stooges and co-star/girlfriend Bonny Bonnell. In *The Big Idea,* it is the Stooges along with a number of others. Reduced simply to the role of interrupters, the Stooges are given only a few brief screen moments in three separate entrances.

This scarce use of the Stooges suggests that this last MGM Stooge short film release was made early in their brief tenure at MGM. It is MGM production number is #628 – the lowest of any Stooge short or feature – and internal evidence suggests it was the earliest of the five MGM Stooge shorts. It has the least complex narrative and the least elaborate production of any of the Stooge MGM shorts; focuses largely on Ted Healy and Bonny Bonnell; and uses the woodblock sound effect for a head bonk as did *Nertsery Rhymes*, their first MGM short film release. On the other hand, at least one of the publicity stills from the production is numbered #740, which would suggest that it was indeed the last of the MGM shorts. In either case, MGM did not release the film until May 12, 1934, at which point the Stooges were no longer under an MGM contract. No doubt MGM was competing with Columbia, which had issued its first "Three Stooges" short, *Woman Haters*, a week earlier on May 5. Because the trio was to become known as "The Three Stooges" shortly after (June 1, 1934), MGM included their new name on a reissued credit screen that reads, "Ted Healy with His Three Stooges (Howard, Fine and Howard)."

The Stooges appear here in three odd musical interludes with no dialogue. In fact, the sequences are designed for the Stooges to remain stone-faced throughout. Such sequences are interesting in that they demonstrate how subservient a role the Stooges could play early on in their film careers, as we see in the MGM feature film, *Turn Back the Clock,* as well as toward the end of their career (we see in 1963's *It's a Mad, Mad, Mad, Mad World).* By that time, however, the audience knew very well what destruction the Stooges could inflict. And yet, the slapstick sequence in *The Big Idea* preserves for us the only MGM example of a triple-slap, a pound/bonk, Curly revving up his legs and Moe and Larry alternating gouges and defensive countermeasures. Judging by this film alone, whether it is to be understood as the first MGM Stooge film production or the last one released, viewers today can see that the Stooges had developed artistically as much as they were allowed at MGM. They needed greener pastures of the sort awaiting them at Columbia.

These six Paramount and MGM short films from 1933/1934 are historically fascinating and conceptually instructive. Many decades after these films were produced and distributed, they demonstrate that the act so well known today as "The Three Stooges" was not born out of whole cloth. It took many years of development on stage, several reconfigurations of the actors – Ted Healy, Moe Howard, Shemp Howard, Curly Howard, Larry Fine, Fred Sanborn, and Jack Walsh – and a number contracts offered, signed, fulfilled or nullified. They demonstrate as well that although the Stooges' slapstick is indeed their artistic trademark, it would take something much more significant to turn the Stooges' presence on film into a wide-reaching and long-lasting phenomenon. This would be compelling comic narratives (i.e. stories), and the author of the first great Stooge story would be none other than Moe Howard.

VISUAL HUMOR: Ted delivers his first triple-slap on the Stooges' hats, not on their faces. The pound/bonk Moe gives Curly is accompanied by the drum/woodblock sound effect similar to that used at Columbia (beginning with *Punch Drunks*) for head bonks. Larry covers his eyes with both hands to keep from being gouged. He will not use Curly's trademark one-hand gouge block until *Vagabond Loafers* (1949). The Stooges try to bow and foul each other up. In subsequent films they will bonk heads when they do this (*Uncivil Warriors*). Squirting water into Healy's face from their trumpets is the first of many squirtings; the next will be in *Woman Haters* and *Three Little Pigskins*, the most in *Calling All Curs*. The Stooges' left hands should be the top hands when playing their saxophones. This is intentional, and Curly will reprise it in *Rhythm and Weep*.

VERBAL HUMOR: *Amos 'n' Andy*, whom the Three Radio Rogues imitate, received national attention in 1928 and were regularly attracting as many as 40 million listeners weekly at the time this film was made. There was no more popular radio program, and historians credit *Amos 'n' Andy* with making radio popular just as Milton Berle would make television popular two decades later. Creators Freeman Gosden and Charles Correll did all of their own voices; here, all of those voices are done by one person. The Stooges will do their own *Amos 'n' Andy* imitation in *Some More of Samoa*. Bing Crosby had become very popular by this time as well. He joined the Paul Whiteman Band as one of the Rhythm Boys in 1927 and began crooning as a soloist in the early 1930s. The pun on his name is "double-cross-by". One of the Three Radio Rogues finishes his bit with "O.K. America!", which Larry says in response to 'Vive la France" in *Plane Nuts*. The phrase belonged to an old Art Kassel song.

OTHER NOTES: The beginning of the first fanfare the Stooges play sounds a little like their future "Three Blind Mice" theme. The disk props used in the final production number resemble those used in *Dancing Lady*. The film ends with the N(ational) R(ecovery) A(dministration) logo seen also in *Woman Haters*, which was released the same week. The NRA was created in June 1933 as part of Roosevelt's New Deal legislation. MGM was at this time making about 80 shorts per year, including the comedies produced at the Hal Roach studios. Many of these featured Laurel & Hardy as well as Charley Chase, all of whom would eventually appear with or work with the Stooges. In his autobiography, Larry [85-86] explains that when freed from their MGM contract, the Stooges had an opportunity to appear in Fox' *One in a Million*, ice-skating star Sonja Henie's debut film. Ted Healy left them out of the deal, though, and the Ritz Brothers comedy team was featured instead. Ironically, some thirty years later, the Stooges would appear in ice-skating star Carol Heiss' debut film, *Snow White and the Three Stooges* (1961).

The Big Idea (1934) preseves the quintessence of Ted Healy's comic style. He preferred a static, understated narrative decorated with verbal misdirections and puns, and punctuated with abrupt physical slapstick from his 'stooges.' Though he played in more than a dozen features at MGM after the Stooges left him, he rarely had the opportunity to perform in his own style. He does get some brief solo moments in MGM's *San Francisco* (1936) and *Hollywood Hotel* (1938).

This poster for *The Big Idea* (1934), the final release of the Stooges' MGM short film series, confirms what a well-known celebrity Ted Healy was and how relatively insignificant the Stooges were. In fact, when the film was first released in early May of 1934, the credits and MGM publicity listed the trio as merely "Howard, Fine and Howard." But after Columbia recast the trio as the 'Three Stooges' in early June, subsequent MGM publicity billed them as "Ted Healy and His Three Stooges (Howard, Fine and Howard)." This poster is from that secondary release. Intriguingly, this particular poster is a modern reproduction; at the time of its original release, the film was a minor production from a studio as vast as MGM. Sixty-seven years later, few of the other MGM 1934 releases – including features – are recalled at all, and the Ted Healy/Three Stooges poster is being reproduced and sold.

Turn Back the Clock • *Meet the Baron* • *Dancing Lady*

Fugitive Lovers • *Hollywood Party* • *Myrt and Marge*

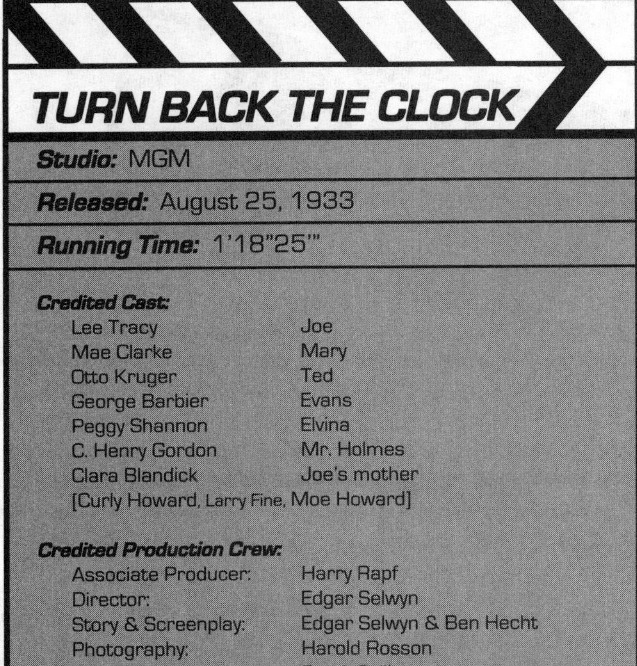

TURN BACK THE CLOCK

Studio: MGM

Released: August 25, 1933

Running Time: 1'18"25'"

Credited Cast:

Lee Tracy	Joe
Mae Clarke	Mary
Otto Kruger	Ted
George Barbier	Evans
Peggy Shannon	Elvina
C. Henry Gordon	Mr. Holmes
Clara Blandick	Joe's mother

[Curly Howard, Larry Fine, Moe Howard]

Credited Production Crew:

Associate Producer:	Harry Rapf
Director:	Edgar Selwyn
Story & Screenplay:	Edgar Selwyn & Ben Hecht
Photography:	Harold Rosson
Editor:	Frank Sullivan

PERSPECTIVE: Their MGM contract called for the Stooges and Ted Healy to appear in a variety of studio projects. Those included two-reelers, three-reelers and feature films – whether together as a foursome, as a trio of Stooges, in duos (Moe & Curly's *Jailbirds of Paradise*) or individually (Curly's *Roast-Beef and Movies*). The Stooges ultimately appeared in five feature films at MGM. None were in a starring role, but some gave them considerable exposure. *Turn Back the Clock* was their first MGM feature and one of the first projects (#689) MGM assigned to them. Shooting took place at about the same time the Stooges and Healy made the short films *Plane Nuts* (#680), *Nertsery Rhymes* (#685), and *Beer and Pretzels* (#690), and the film was released in late August, just one day before *Beer and Pretzels*.

Hollywood studios at the time were signing stars from the theatrical circuits and the world of radio. No studio signed more than MGM, which had sixty-one players under contract by year's end and boasted that it had "more stars than there are in Heaven." But having signed them, the studios then had the equally difficult task of matching the stars with the proper cinematic vehicle to translate their talent to the big screen. The vaudevillian slapstick/musical style of Ted Healy and his three "Racketeers"/"Southern Gentlemen" required a film that featured their comic shtick rather than an involved narrative, so the MGM brass decided to put them in musical two-reelers. Their appearance here precedes that decision. *Turn Back the Clock* is not a musical, but a lighthearted dramatic fantasy; the only live music in the film is the Stooges singing "By the Light of the Silvery Moon." The Stooges were probably chosen to appear as a trio singing by the piano since their very first scene in Fox's *Soup to Nuts* featured them singing 'You'll Never Know' in fine three-part harmony (while Ted Healy and Fred Sanborn try to drop sandbags on their heads). This kind of singing was a staple of their stage act and an ancient relic of vaudeville. Because the flashback in *Turn Back the Clock* goes back several decades from its target date of March 6, 1933 and requires someone to sing turn-of-the-century music, the Stooges were a perfect chronological fit. Incidental as this appearance is, it turned out to be a significant first in the career of the trio America would come to know as "The Three Stooges," as it was their first film without Ted Healy. Healy was featured in *Soup to Nuts*, but now the Stooges appear as a trio (if only for a minute or so) in a feature film all by themselves, without verbal humor or slapstick and uncredited on the screen.

VERBAL HUMOR: What little dialogue is given to the Stooges does not include gag lines (Joe: "Why sing us somethin', why don't ya'?" Larry: "What'll we sing?" Joe: "Anything to pep the thing up." Moe: "All right, Joe."). The closest is perhaps, Joe: "Somethin' that's got some life in it: 'Tony's Wife.'" Moe: "Tony's wife - who is she?" But this is meant to emphasize the confusion between the contemporary Stooges and the time-traveling protagonist. Joe knows the song "Tony's Wife" because it was written by the time he died, but it was not written yet in the period into which he time-travels; hence, Moe's confusion. "Tony's Wife" was written this same year (1933) by Burton Lane (*Dancing Lady*) and Harold Adamson. The old songs the Stooges sing are "By the Light of the Silvery Moon," composed by Gus Edwards and Edward Madden in 1909 for *The Ziegfeld Follies of 1909*; and Stephen Foster's "My Old Kentucky Home" (1853).

OTHER NOTES: Director/writer Edgar Selwyn was a stage star who came to Hollywood in 1915. In 1917, he joined into a partnership with the legendary Samuel Goldfish to form 'Goldwyn Pictures'; Goldfish kept the hybrid name even after their partnership dissolved. Selwyn's wife, Ruth, a comedienne who had worked with Buster Keaton and who plays 'Babe Callahan' in *Fugitive Lovers*, was the sister-in-law of Nicholas Schenck. Schenk headed Loew's, the parent company of MGM and the man largely responsible for negotiating Loew's absorption of Goldwyn Pictures and Louis B. Meyer Productions to form Metro-Goldwyn-Mayer. Lee Tracy and Mae Clarke were popular MGM stars. Tracy alone starred in seven features in 1933, including *Dinner At Eight*. He was an Oscar nominee for 1964's *The Best Man*. Clarke took the infamous grapefruit in the face from James Cagney in *Public Enemy* (1931). Associate producer Harry Rapf was the MGM executive who signed the Stooges to their studio contract. Though his hand is not evident, future Columbia Stooge producer/director Jules White worked on several scenes in this film.

Elvina [Peggy Shannon] and Joe [Lee Tracy] are the toast of their wedding in MGM's *Turn Back the Clock* (1933). The Stooges are scattered - Larry to the right of the groom, Moe to the far left, and Curly in the far back left beneath the painting. Their hair is uncharacteristically slicked down for the pre-World War I period of the film. In terms of their physical arrangement, this kind of separation would soon give way to a dynamic triadic unity which would make the Stooges thrive for years.

In the early period of their career, The Three Stooges were influenced and assisted by several multi-talented, comedic stars. Ted Healy [right] laid the foundations for the concepts of a Stooge trio, slapstick punctuation, and Moe's bossy characterization. Jack Pearl [center] was a radio star in 1933, and it was in his premier film vehicle, MGM's *Meet the Baron*, that the Stooges first had an opportunity to shine on screen. Jimmy Durante [left] appeared in several films with the Stooges, and they would imitate him in several films in future years.

MEET THE BARON

Studio: MGM

Released: October 20, 1933

Running Time: 1'06"23'"

Credited Cast:

Jack Pearl	Julius, impersonating Baron Munchausen
Jimmy Durante	Joseph McGoo
ZaSu Pitts	upstairs maid
Ted Healy & His Stooges [Moe Howard, Jerry Howard, Larry Fine]	
Edna May Oliver	Dean Primrose
Ben Bard	Charley
Henry Kolker	Baron Munchausen
William B. Davidson	radio interviewer
The Metro-Goldwyn-Mayer Girls	

Credited Production Crew:

Produced by:	David O. Selznick
Directed by:	Walter Lang
Story by:	Herman Mankiewicz & Norman Krasna
Screen Play by :	Allen Rivkin & P. J. Wolfson
Dialogue by:	Arthur Kober & William K. Wells
Lyrics by:	Dorothy Fields
Music by :	Jimmy McHigh
Photographed by:	Allen Siegler
Art Directors:	Frank H. Webster & Howard Fisher
Wardrobe by:	Dolly Tree
Film Editor:	James E. Newcom

PERSPECTIVE: Gathering "more stars than there are in Heaven" in the 1930s, MGM signed not only dramatic actors and Broadway musical stars but popular radio personalities as well. Harry Rapf, the producer who had signed Healy and the Stooges, created the film aptly titled *The Chief* for Texaco's radio "Fire Chief" Ed Wynn, and David O. Selznick, who would produce *Gone With the Wind* six years later, He created *Meet the Baron* as a vehicle for Jack Pearl, "the famous Baron Munchausen of the Air." Pearl's radio characterization of the legendary Eighteenth century spinner of fantastical adventure stories delighted audiences, with an interview format punctuated by his trademark tag: "Vass you dere, Sharlie?" So Pearl does what he does best: he uses the question and answer format to deliver puns (Charley: "What was your Aunt Sophie doing in the middle of the ocean?" Baron Munchausen: "Light house keeping!") and speak in dyspropisms ("a bathroom with a bath, a pantry with pants!").

Seeking a Marx Brothers-like zaniness, Selznick assigned six writers and six additional comedians to supplement Pearl's radio-style humor. Jimmy Durante fills the voids with head-shaking raspiness ("Humiliatin'! Under a bed and no husband in sight!") and interacts with the lower levels of comic support: the dean [Edna May Oliver] and "Ted Healy and His Stooges." The latter add the quadruple-bodied physicality Selznick sought, and though subservient to the dean and Durante ("I smell treachery! [to Curly] Or is that you?"), they get more screen time than in most of their MGM features.

According to the *Times-Mirror* reviewer, "Ted Healy and His Stooges nearly steal the picture," and one of the structural reasons for this is their very subservience. The Stooges thrive on being ordered around, yelled at and hit while they move unswervingly along their comic vector. Another reason is that for the first time the Stooges portray tradesmen, a situation they will use countless times in the future. Acting as tradesmen allows their energies and timing to flourish, mostly because it gives them a chance to use hand tools. No, we do not yet see them dropping tool bags on Moe's foot to start a Cossack dance or ruining a saw on Curly's iron skull. Such routines will take several years to develop. The plumbing scene downplays physical humor in favor of verbal gags (Curly: "He's great at chiseling!"; Dean: "Will you get to those pipes?" Stooges & Healy: "Will we?!"). But we do at least see Ted miss the chisel Curly holds and hit Curly on the head, with Curly merely brushing his ear in response -- a precursor of much to come. Comparing the plumbing sequences in *Meet the Baron* and *A Plumbing We Will Go* makes it clear that it took the Stooges a number of years to find their true personae and discover what they could do with/to each other. Being a Stooge is not as easy as it looks. It takes talent, trial and experiment, developed routines, and writers and directors who understand the essence of Stoogeness. Nonetheless, this tool scene is a giant leap for Stoogekind.

VISUAL HUMOR: The use of tools inspires a verbal/physical three-pattern (Healy to Curly: "Are you gonna work?" Curly: "No!" [SLAP] Healy to Moe: "Are you gonna work?" Moe: "No!" [SLAP] Healy to Larry: "Are you gonna work?"). Such down-the-line patterns will be used often after *Uncivil Warriors.* Another physical three-pattern occurs when the Stooges each strike a peaking pose when told: "Cover your eyes!". We see several slapstick setups. For instance, Curly and Larry do their trick and Healy says, "You like sugar in your coffee? Here's a lump!" Moe will do this often in the near future. The Stooges pretend to be busy while they are supposed to be working. This will be reprised in the opening of *Ants in the Pantry*, again with the Stooges playing cards.

Stooge firsts: Riding a tandem bicycle, and disappearing around the corner of the hallway and then returning into view (*Men in Black*); wearing tuxedoes; Healy aiming at a chisel but hitting Curly in the head; Moe tweaking Curly's nose; Moe slapping Curly with a back-and-forth motion of the hand; the use of fast motion

The most significant development in 1933's *Meet the Baron* is the use of tools. The Stooges are cast as Ted Healy's assistants, and as college tradesmen they embark on a decades-long journey that will see them explore the comic possibilities of saws, pipes, wiring, glue, hammers and much more. Still, it will take a few years to perfect this sort of comedy, develop their timing and defenses and acquire the verbal gags and sound effects that will accompany the movements.

(after the cannon blast); and Curly telling the dean to mind her own business after Ted hits him on the head (the sweater sequence of *How High is Up?*). Curly's leg revving is not yet full steam, thigh high, or coordinated with his arm movements. Also, he bumps his head on the steam pipe, but there is no sound effect and little is made of it. Lastly, Curly delivers several of his lines while cross-eyed. Perhaps he was influenced by his brief encounter with Ben Turpin in *Hollywood on Parade.* The dean grabbing Larry by the hair as he runs by is the first extant example of a hair pull. Ted reportedly did the first filmed hair pull in *Hello Pop!.* The Stooges singing on the boat brings to mind their Venetian costumes in that same film and on stage in *A Night in Venice.* The Stooges dive for money, as they did in *Beer and Pretzels* and will (for a cigar) in *Uncivil Warriors.* Other variations: Curly wiping his hand by his ear (*Nertsery Rhymes*) and the phone hopping up and down (the smoking phone in *Soup to Nuts*).

VERBAL HUMOR: Several of the Stooge scenes offer memorable pattern jokes. Besides the standard three pattern (Curly: "Local 464." Larry: "Telephone Main 1-234." Moe: "And if a man answers, hang up.") there is a double three pattern (Larry: "I gotta fish!" Curly: "I gotta fish!" Moe: "All us children got fish!" Healy: "That's the first fish of the season. Make a wish!" Larry: "'I wish I was in Dixie!'" Moe: "He would!" Curly: "He should!") derived from their "Southern Gentlemen" routine. A number of pattern gags are filmed Stooge firsts. One is the pattern bridge betting (Healy: "I bid four spades." Curly: "I double." Larry: "I redouble." Moe: "I triple.") to be heard next in *Restless Knights*. Another is the "Will we?" routine (Dean: "Will you get to those pipes?" Stooges & Healy: "Will we?!") to be heard in *An Ache in Every Stake*; and the classic 'Get the tools!' routine (Healy: "Boys, get the tools." Moe: "What tools?" Healy: "The tools we've been usin' for the last ten years." Stooges: "Oh! Those tools!") to be heard next in *Pardon My Scotch*; and, an early version of the "When I'm Ready" routine (Larry: "I'll work if I feel like it!" Healy: "Do you feel like it?!" Larry: "Yeah, I feel like it.") to be heard next in *Men in Black*.

Other Stooge firsts: "Give him the bird" (*Pop Goes the Easel*); Healy: "For two pins I'd knock your head off!" (*Cactus Makes Perfect*); Larry: "Nah, we're union men!" (*Half-Wits Holiday*); Healy: "Are we men or are we rats?" (*Three Troubledoers*); and Healy: "Concentrate!" (the seance in *You Nazty Spy!*). When Curly is ordered to put on a blindfold, he says, "Like the time we held up the bank." They will often pretend to be convicts, e.g. "Reminds me of the reform school!". Curly's "Certainly" is low voiced and not his fully pronounced "*soitenly!*". One of Healy's most effective responses (Dean: "One slip of those blindfolds and you'll feel my wrath!" Healy: "Don't try to bribe the boys.") resembles a gag that will become standard in future years – when someone tries to threaten the Stooges and they ignorantly mistake it for a compliment, e.g. *Hula-la-la* (Witch Doctor: "Why you impertinent swine!" Moe: "Flattery will get you nowhere!");

Healy here is not being ignorant, just tough. Because this film is not a Ted Healy vehicle either, he has time for only one of his extended pun/insults ["How do you want 'em fixed, lady – rare, medium, or well done? [to the Stooges] I'm gonna take you to the land of beyond. You're going to see a beautiful woman, a gorgeous lookin' creature." Dean: "What's the meaning of this?" Healy: "I'm givin' it to you 'medium'"]. Healy used the "We'll quit first!" gag in *Beer and Pretzels*, and there was reference to a Healy/Stooge "mutiny" in *Plane Nuts*.

References: Moe's "That ain't the Culbertson System" refers to Ely Culbertson's system for contract bridge developed recently in 1930. The "dean, dean, dean, Gunga Dean" reference is to Rudyard Kipling's poem "Gunga Din" [to be made into an RKO film in 1939]. The two old songs the Stooges play/sing are Giuseppe Verdi's "Anvil Chorus" from the opera *Il Trovatore* and "Tramp, Tramp, Tramp the Boys are Marching," originally a Civil War lyric by George Root. Epithets: In the first scene, the Baron calls Julius a pair of future Stooge favorites: "imbecile" and "moron." Elsewhere, Healy calls Larry "mousehead," and the dean calls Curly "sluggard". Two of the Baron's better silly malapropisms: "When I sees your eyes, my heart goes pitty." Nurse: "You mean pitty patty." Baron: "I got a weak heart"; and Maid: "I'll bet you're awfully fickle." Baron: "When the sun shines I get 'fickled' all over."

OTHER NOTES: Although *Meet the Baron* had a later production number [#710] than both *Dancing Lady* [#694] and *Hollywood Party* [#695], it had an earlier release. Jack Pearl began creating a number of characters for "The Lucky Strike Program" in late 1932. By 1933, he had his own hit show about which *Variety* [1/9/34] remarked: "Pearl is the premier radio exponent of the question-and-answer school of comedy". Director Walter Lang would three decades later direct *Snow White and the Three Stooges* [1961], while photographer Allen Siegler would work on the Columbia Stooge shorts from 1937-1951. Co-writer Herman Mankiewicz assisted in writing *Citizen Kane*. The Stooges would make another film set on a college campus, *Start Cheering*; the Marx Brothers had already made one, *Horse Feathers* [1932]. Associated with the womanizing Healy [in real life and *Beer and Pretzels*] – and with all the coeds around, particularly in the shower scene -- it is no wonder the Stooges are characterized as womanizers here as well. Womanizing will become a constant in their first few years of Columbia films and then beyond. Absent sound: Healy tells the Stooges to cover their eyes with handkerchiefs; the dean [Edna May Oliver] says something inaudible and winces at the response.

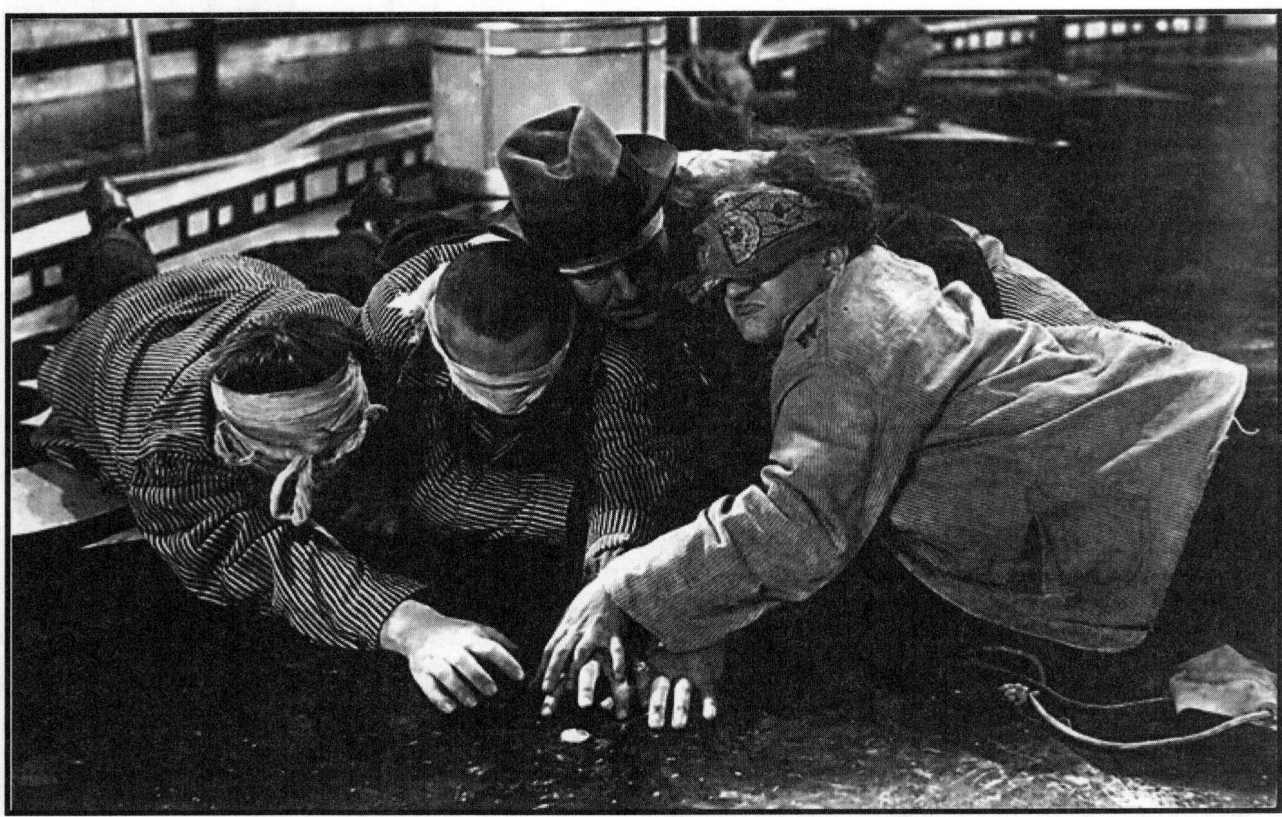

DANCING LADY

Studio: MGM

Released: November 24, 1933

Running Time: 1'31"26'"

Credited Cast:

Joan Crawford	Janie Barlow
Clark Gable	Patch Gallagher
Franchot Tone	Tod Newton
May Robson	Grandma Newton
Winnie Lightner	Rosette La Rue
Fred Astaire	himself
Robert Benchley	Ward King
Ted Healy and His Stooges	Steve and stage hands
Art Jarrett	Art Jarrett
Grant Mitchell	Jasper Bradley
Nelson Eddy	singer
Maynard Holmes	Bradley, Jr.
Sterling Holloway	author Mickey
Gloria Foy	Vivian Warner
Moe Howard	
Jerry Howard	
Larry Fine	

Credited Production Crew:

Directed by:	Robert Z. Leonard
Executive Producer:	David O. Selznick
Assoc. Producer:	John W. Considine, Jr.
Screen Play by:	Allen Rivkin and P. J. Wolfson
From the book by:	James Warner Bellah
Lyrics by:	Harold Adamson, Lorenz Hart ('That's the Rhythm of the Day'), & Dorothy Fields ('My Dancing Lady')
Music by:	Burton Lane, Richard Rodgers ('That's the Rhythm of the Day'), & Jimmy McHigh ('My Dancing Lady')
Musical Ensembles Directed by:	Sammy Lee and Eddie Prinz
Photographed by:	Oliver T. Marsh
Special Effects by:	Slavko Vorkapich
Recording Director:	Douglas Shearer
Art Director:	Merril Pye
Interior Decoration by:	Edwin B. Willis
Gowns by:	Adrian
Film Editor:	Margaret Booth

PERSPECTIVE: MGM's *Dancing Lady* is the highest profile film the Stooges ever made. Breaking MGM box office records, it co-starred the emerging Clark Gable (who had his first major role in *Red Dust* the previous year and would win an Oscar for *It Happened One Night* the year after) and Joan Crawford in one of her spunkiest roles. It was also produced by David O. Selznick (*Gone With the Wind*). The short featured a song by Richard Rodgers (*The Sound of Music*) and was directed by the recently Oscar-nominated Robert Z. Leonard. The short was also based on a James Warner Bellah (*Fort Apache, Rio Bravo*) story, and included Fred Astaire's screen debut and the first major singing role for Nelson Eddy. Like Warner's archetypal *42nd Street* released the same year, *Dancing Lady* is a formulaic Depression-era backstage musical. This is a formula in which a broke but determined young woman comes out of the chorus to star in a Broadway show directed by a hypertensive, hard-boiled director assisted by a wise guy manager, pianist or stagehand. Cast Joan Crawford as the woman, Clark Gable as the director, and Ted Healy and His Stooges as the wise guys and you have a historic, unique screen chemistry.

Although they appear for only a few minutes in several scenes, the Stooges provide comic relief to the tension between the high-strung director and the love-torn show girl. Sixty-some years later, it is particularly fascinating to see these soon-to-be titans of American film working in the same scene. Crawford dances, flings her hair about and manipulates her magnificent, dark-trimmed eyes. Gable glares back with an external disdain that masks his warm admiration and internal confidence. In the same scene, Moe is bashing Curly with a set of cymbals! This is a Stooge moment to savor. There is also a bit of film irony: one of the themes of the film has Clark Gable chastising Joan Crawford for "trading Broadway for Park Avenue," i.e. marrying for money instead of being true to the show business profession. This same year, Gable starred in *Men in White*, in which he plays a doctor who marries into money instead of being true to his medical profession. The following year (1934), the Stooges would parody Gable's *Men in White* with their first and only Academy Award nominated short film, *Men in Black*.

Dancing Lady shows us an arrangement of Stooges that is only rarely seen; Larry is separated from the other two Stooges. Larry will be separated like this in *Three Loan Wolves, Cuckoo on a Choo Choo* and in a few other films, but is important to observe here that whenever one Stooge is isolated from the others, the triadic comic arrangement necessarily changes. In the Healy films, e.g. *Meet the Baron*, there are usually four people involved in slapstick routines, but here Larry plays the piano while Healy is elsewhere and Moe is bombarding Curly with cymbals in the background. This was an MGM experiment in how to place and arrange Healy's three Stooges in a film, and it lessens their impact. It would not be the final solution.

VISUAL HUMOR: We see several gags the Stooges will re-use. Healy walks through the unattached stage door (*Pardon My Scotch*; previously in *Soup to Nuts*) and the Stooges hit each other with celery stalks (*Woman Haters*). Moe alternately gouges and slaps Curly while Curly alternately covers his eyes and his head to protect himself with his hands (*Three Little Beers*). Moe finishes with a POUND-BONK-SLAP combination. Ted closes the piano lid on Larry as will Moe in *Loco Boy Makes Good*. Larry will be a piano player again in *Wee Wee Monsieur*, *Hula-la-la* and *Brideless Groom* [although he has different uses for a piano in *Ants in the Pantry* and *Crash Goes the Hash*]. In later rehearsal scenes in the film, the pianist is 'Harry'. We see Curly womanizing, as in *Meet the Baron*. Moe slaps him, but then Curly sees a chorus girl and chases her.

VERBAL HUMOR: Stooge firsts include Healy saying "Spread Out!" [also in *Plane Nuts*] and the Stooges each saying "Right!" "Right!" "Right!". The latter will reappear in *Dizzy Doctors*, *Violent is the Word for Curly* and *Mutts to You*. The Stooges use the "Hallelujah!" from their vaudevillean "Southern Gentlemen" routine [*Plane Nuts*], and they sing "You'll Never Know" as they did in *Soup to Nuts* and *Beer and Pretzels*. Curly's ignorance shines through (Steve: "We're gonna have an audition." Curly: "A 'raw-dition?'").

OTHER NOTES: In order of production, *Dancing Lady* [#694] preceded *Hollywood Party* [#695] and *Meet the Baron* [#710], but came after the cameo appearance in *Turn Back the Clock* [#689]. Credited first as "Ted Healy and His Stooges," the Stooges are credited a second time as "Moe Howard, Jerry Howard, and Larry Fine" under "Supporting Players" after Art Jarrett, Grant Mitchell, Nelson Eddy, Maynard Holmes, Sterling Holloway and Gloria Foy. Director Robert Z. Leonard won a second Oscar nomination the following year for *The Great Ziegfeld*; in 1938 he would direct Nelson Eddy again in *Maytime*. Rodgers & Hart, who wrote the finale here, later wrote *The Boys from Syracuse*, a musical the Stooges will refer to in *You Nazty Spy!*; cf. *A Merry Mix-Up*. Jimmy McHigh, who wrote "My Dancing Lady," also wrote such standards as "The Sunny Side of the Street" and "I Can't Give You Anything But Love, Baby". After the Cuba montage, the chorus members hold silver disks similar to those used in the Busby Berkeley production number in *Plane Nuts*, originally created for the feature *Flying High*.

1933/1934 was an exciting period for the Stooge act. Along with Ted Healy, Moe, Larry and Curly [then 'Curley'] made short films and features at Paramount, MGM, Universal, and Columbia, and they worked alongside such luminaries as Clark Gable [chapter title page] and Joan Crawford in *Dancing Lady* (1933), the most significant feature the Stooges ever made at MGM. Larry actually could play piano, and Curly was fond of playing spoons at nightclubs.

FUGITIVE LOVERS

Studio: MGM

Released: January 5, 1934

Running Time: 1'21"10'"

Credited Cast:

Robert Montgomery	Paul Porter
Madge Evans	Letty Morris
Ted Healy	Hector Withington, Jr.
Nat Pendleton	Legs Caffee
C. Henry Gordon	Detective Daly
Ruth Selwyn	Babe Callahan
Larry Fine	
Moe Howard	Three Julians [Bill,Jabez, PeeWee]
Jerry Howard	

Credited Production Crew:

Assoc. Producer:	Lucien Hubbard
Director:	Richard Boleslavsky
Screenplay:	Albert Hackett, Frances Goodrich, & George B. Seitz
Story:	Ferdinand Reyher & Frank Wead
Art Director:	Arnold Gillespie
Interior Decoration:	Edwin B. Willis
Photography:	Ted Tetzlaff
Editor:	William S. Gray

PERSPECTIVE: Several high-profile feature films produced in 1932-1934 used long distance bus trips as settings for criminal chases and personal odysseys. This was no coincidence. Hollywood studios and producers have always imitated themes and borrowed concepts from each other. And with transcontinental bus travel beginning to burgeon in those years, movie studios found both drama and comedy inside these large, dark, confining vehicles. *Fugitive Lovers* is one of these films, but what distinguishes it from the multi-award-winning *It Happened One Night* (1934) is that its passenger list includes Healy, Howard, Fine and Howard. Having just appeared in the *42nd Street*-style musical *Dancing Lady* and with radio star Jack Pearl in *Meet the Baron*, the Stooges are now part of another Hollywood trend. This will remain a constant throughout the trio's career. They will make Depression films in the 1930s; patriotic and noir gangster movies in the 1940s; 3-D flicks (*Spooks!*) and films about (*Goof on the Roof*) and satirizing (*Blunder Boys*) television in the 1950s; and even sci-fi films (*The Three Stooges in Orbit*) in the 1960s.

Once again playing show business people, the Stooges have only a limited role in *Fugitive Lovers*. Letty, Legs and Porter, the principals of the love triangle, carry the plot along while an ensemble of actors joins them on the bus. Along the way, we learn that the Stooges are a vaudevillian team of brothers led by Moe, who repeatedly fears that his throat is closing up on him. At the bus depot, he sings a line of a song and in the middle of the night he belts out a high note to ensure that his throat stays open. Moe also gets to speak briefly to the protagonist Letty, though Larry barely speaks a line and Curly merely gets to threaten Moe twice. Their only slapstick event occurs when Legs pulls Moe's ear and hair and shoves him back onto Curly and Larry. Once Letty, Legs and Porter leave that bus, the Stooges are out of the picture. Healy's role continues on into the next scene.

Healy's continuing on his own in this, their last MGM feature, symbolizes the most significant development in the Stooges' cinematic maturation: their separation from Ted Healy. Healy, who plays here the wisecracking, hard-drinking Hector Withington, Jr., does indeed board the bus at the same time as the Stooges, but he does not interact with them. He does not insult or hit any of them, nor does he joke. The Stooges had appeared independent of Healy previously in *Turn Back the Clock*, but this film mirrors their actual break with Healy and subsequent signing of an independent contract with Columbia. Something else here is a prelude to the Columbia films. In *Fugitive Lovers*, we never hear Moe's name, but we do hear he and Larry worry about "Bill" [Curly] getting back on the bus after the first stop. Giving the Stooges stage names – rather than using 'Moe,' 'Larry,' and 'Curly' – will continue in several of the early Columbia shorts, the first of which (*Woman Haters*) was shot less than three months after *Fugitive Lovers* was released.

A contemporary cigarette ad featuring Robert Montgomery, star of *Fugitive Lovers* (1934), the Stooges' last MGM feature-film.

VISUAL HUMOR: This is one of the few films in which the Stooges do not slap each other even once, although Legs pulls Moe's ear and hair and shoves him. When the Stooges learn that the man roughing up Moe is Legs Caffey, all three Stooges faint. Fainting had been their exit technique in *Beer and Pretzels* and will be used again in such future films as *Men in Black* and *Horses' Collars*.

VERBAL HUMOR: Curly's threats ("Pipe down! Save it for Harrisburg!"; "Wake me again and I'll close it for good!") are his most forceful to date. He will reprise this tough-guy role a bit in the Stooges' lone Universal film, *Myrt and Marge*. Curly is also given the punchline when Larry and he interrupt Moe's pick-up lines ("Legs Caffey, he and I are like that." Curly: "Who's on top?" Larry: "Skip it!"). The Stooges twice sing the opening line of "You'll Never Know," which they also performed in *Soup to Nuts*, *Beer and Pretzels* and *Dancing Lady*. The kid who gives Moe "the bird" recalls the scene in *Meet the Baron* where the Stooges give the Baron "the bird". Moe's fear that his throat is closing up ironically prestages the problem Curly will pretend to experience as Senorita Cucaracha in *Micro-Phonies*. Asthma, as in Moe's "That's the worst case of asthma I ever heard!", will turn up again in *Oily to Bed, Oily to Rise* and *You Nazty Spy!*. Larry's "Ahh, that's professional jealousy!" will show up again in *Three Little Pigskins*.

Reference: Moe's "Who's afraid of the big bad wolf?" parodies the 1933 animated Disney short *The Three Little Pigs*, from which derives the Stooges' film title *Three Little Pigskins* later the same year. The song he begins to sing, "I ought to be good but I guess I'll be bad instead," is of a typical gag type, e.g. 1916's "I Want To Be Good But My Eyes Won't Let Me" by Sigmund Romberg.

OTHER NOTES: The working titles were *Overland Bus* and *Transcontinental Bus*. Robert Montgomery had a long career that earned him two Academy Award nominations, the second for 1941's *Here Comes Mr. Jordon*, which inspired the Stooges' *Heavenly Daze*. Madge Evans had been a child star in silent films, including *The Sign of the Cross* (1914). Nat Pendleton [Legs] was an ex-Olympic and professional wrestler and acted with other well-known comedians, including the Marx Brothers (*Horse Feathers, At the Circus*) and Abbott & Costello (*Buck Privates*). For Ruth Selwyn ('Babe Callahan'), see *Turn Back the Clock*. The next project for director Richard Boleslawski was MGM's *Men in White* with Clark Gable, which the Stooges parody in their Oscar-nominated *Men in Black*. After Moe hears another man singing and describes it as "the worst case of asthma I ever heard," Curly says, "Why don't you do somethin' for your throat?" Moe responds, "What do you suggest?" but Curly's response apparently no longer exists in extant prints of the film.

The Stooges and Ted Healy are literally left out in the dark in *Hollywood Party* (1934), a star-revue film from MGM. As with most of their featurefilm appearances before1959, they have very minor roles.

HOLLYWOOD PARTY

Studio: MGM

Released: June 1, 1934

Running Time: 1'08"21'"

Credited Cast:

Stan Laurel & Oliver Hardy	themselves
Jimmy Durante	'Schnarzan' (himself)
Jack Pearl	Baron Munchausen
Polly Moran	Henrietta
Charles Butterworth	Harvey Clemp
Eddie Quillan	Bob
June Clyde	Linda
Mickey Mouse	
Lupe Velez	Durante's co-star and girl friend
George Givot	Liondora
Richard Carle	Knapp

Uncredited Cast:

Robert Young	
Arthur Treacher	butler
Joe E. Brown	butler [?]
Frances Williams	
Ben Bard	Charley
Tom Kennedy	butler
Ted Healy and His Stooges	

Credited Production Crew:

Director:	uncredited
Screenplay:	Howard Dietz and Arthur Kober
Art Director:	Fredric Hope
Interior Decoration:	Edwin B. Willis
Costumes:	Adrian
Photography:	James Wong Howe
Songs:	Richard Rodgers & Lorenz Hart, Walter Donaldson & Gus Kahn, Nacio Herb Brown & Arthur Freed
Editor:	George Boemler
Animated Sequence:	Walt Disney Productions, Ltd.

PERSPECTIVE: *Hollywood Party* belongs to the star revue film genre that became popular in the early 1930s as a byproduct of Hollywood's studio system. At MGM and the other major studios, dozens of stars signed studio contracts of the type Harry Rapf (who produced this film, *Turn Back the Clock*, and *Meet the Baron*) offered to Healy and the Stooges. These contracts obligated actors to appear in specific, tailor-made features as well as studio promotional films that gloried in a revue of stars, multiple production sequences directed by different directors and and even color sequences, all loosely connected by something resembling a plot. Some of the best examples include MGM's *The Hollywood Revue of 1929*, Paramount's *Paramount on Parade* (1930) and MGM's *Dinner at Eight* (1933), but by far the most successful of the all-star cast films was MGM's non-musical *Grand Hotel* (1932). MGM's *Hollywood Party* is a Hollywood dream and has very little plot except to throw together Jimmy Durante, Jack Pearl [Baron Munchausen], Laurel & Hardy and a number of lesser stars. Despite their minor roles, Laurel & Hardy actually received top billing, no doubt because of the cast assembled for the film they were the best known nationally and the most loyal locally, having produced over five-dozen MGM releases for producer Hal Roach since 1927.

The Stooges were so undervalued at MGM at this time that they did not even warrant an actual invitation to the Hollywood party in *Hollywood Party*. They play autograph hounds who look for movie stars but encounter only Ted Healy – playing a photographer with whom they exchange some BONKS and a triple slap – and a quartet of scientists who identify the Stooges as primitive humanoid specimens. As it turned out, future Stooge films would portray the Stooges as cavemen (*I'm a Monkey's Uncle*). Others would portray Curly in particular as a special sort of humanoid whose head could keep doctors and scientists (not to mention hard objects) busy for years (*From Nurse to Worse*; *A Bird in the Head*). In still others, the Stooges would have occasion to interact with professors (*Hoi Polloi*; *Violent is the Word for Curly*). But the goal here was merely to cameo some Stooge slapstick and ignorance. In other words, MGM considered the Stooges' personae to be, well, stooge-like. As in *Fugitive Lovers*, the Stooges interact separately from Ted Healy when they encounter the scientists. They both hit and are hit by Healy and the professors for the bulk of their two-minute, eighteen-second cameo.

This would not be the end of Hollywood cameos for the Stooges. They will have several more, including an animated cameo in the Warner Brothers' cartoon *Hollywood Steps Out* (1941) in which they dance a slapstick rumba – an animated Mickey Mouse has a cameo in *Hollywood Party* – and appearances in 1963's *It's a Mad, Mad, Mad, Mad World* and *4 for Texas*.

VISUAL HUMOR: Stooge firsts: One professor sees Larry and says, "Ahh!". So Larry turns away to see who the professor is looking at. In *Horses' Collars*, the Stooges will begin turning like that when anyone addresses them as "gentlemen." Also, Moe yanks one professor's beard, as in *Hold That Lion*. The Stooges only rarely get hit one after the other in sequence by a non-Stooge, but the professor has a scientific point to prove. Healy hit one after the other in *Meet the Baron*, although Larry gets out of it. Scientific tests will reappear in *Three Sappy People*, *From Nurse to Worse*, and elsewhere. The cane raps from the scientists elicit sound effects similar to those we will soon hear regularly in the Columbia films, particularly the wood block for the head bonk. In the

These were the last few films the Stooges made with Ted Healy. Charles Earnest Lee Nash was a boyhood friend of Moe and Shemp Howard, and, after a failed venture in his family's business, Nash took on the stage name 'Ted Healy' and worked his way up to vaudeville stardom. He sang and devised skits featuring silly, subtle and absurd gags while slapping his "stooges." Earning thousands of dollars a week, he paid these stooges only $100 each. But he also brought 'Howard, Fine and Howard' to Hollywood and new opportunities. The underpaid Stooges were essential to Healy's act. Although Healy went on without them to play in a dozen or so more films, most notably *San Francisco* (1936) and *Hollywood Hotel* (1938), his career in film was not nearly as successful as it had been with his stooges on stage. His alcoholism got the best of him during several periods in his life, and he died a violent death in 1937.

MGM shorts, *Beer and Pretzels* and *The Big Idea,* we hear the wood block used for head bonks. Healy triple slaps the Stooges here as he did in *Meet the Baron*, *The Big Idea* (hats only) and Paramount's *Hollywood on Parade*. The first full-fledged triple slap from an outsider will be from Walter Brennan in *Restless Knights*. Unique is the setup to the triple slap: each Stooge in succession hits Healy with his own cane. Also unique is Larry's showing Healy his book full of autographs by rapidly flipping through the pages while saying, "Look-a-that, look-a-that, look-a-that, look-a-that!"

VERBAL HUMOR: The woman scientist is indeed brilliant in recognizing the Stooges as "morons" at first glance ("Out of the way, morons!"). Years hence, they will be the dictatorial troika of "Moronika" in *You Nazty Spy!* and badge-holding members of the Amalgamated Association of Morons in *Half-Wits Holiday* and *Pies and Guys*. Moe's suspecting the bearded scientists of being Clark Gable in disguise is ironic, since the Stooges just worked with Gable in MGM's *Dancing Lady*. As for the humanoid types, the "Neanderthal," the immediate predecessor to our own species (Homo Sapiens) is the only authentic one. "Androgynous" refers to having both male and female genital characteristics; "Anthropidon" and "Anthropidia" refer generally to the class Anthropidae, the human group of mammals. "Androphobia," meanwhile, refers to fear of the male sex, while Curly's "Androgenes" sounds like a nonsense Greek name, but is no doubt Curly's unintentional mispronunciation of "Androgynous." (Moe tells us that Curly had trouble remembering his lines on occasion). Speaking of Greek names, the scientist uses the term "Thespis," the founder of Greek tragedy: "We are of the scientific world, not of Thespis." We will not hear the term again until Shemp uses it in *Three Hams on Rye* in 1950.

OTHER NOTES: The working title was *Broadway to Hollywood*. According to its MGM Production Number (#695), this film was scheduled just after *Dancing Lady* (#694) and just before *Hello Pop!* (#696), but before *Meet the Baron* (#710) and *Fugitive Lovers* (#716). The release date turned out to be the month after *The Big Idea* and *Woman Haters*. The film was thought at the time to be so dismal that no one wanted credit as director. The directors who worked on the film, as reported in the *Scrapbook* and compiled by Randy Skretvedt, include Russel Mach, Richard Boleslavsky [*Fugitive Lovers*] (musical sequences), George Stevens (comedy sequences), Sam Wood, Allan Dwan, Edmund Goulding [*Grand Hotel*] and Charles Reisner [*The Big Store*]. Co-writer Howard Dietz was also MGM's publicity chief. Tom Kennedy [the butler who chases Laurel & Hardy] will work with the Stooges again in tough guy roles in *Loose Loot* [man with the swollen hand] and *Spooks!* [Mr. Hyde]. He had his own short-lived comedy series at Columbia from 1935 to 1938, teamed up with Shemp in some of his solo efforts, and appearing along with the Stooges one final time in *It's a Mad, Mad, Mad, Mad World*.

MYRT AND MARGE

Studio: Universal

Released: December 4, 1934

Running Time: 1'05"08'"

Credited Cast:

Myrtle Vail	Myrt Winter
Donna Maereal	Marge Spear
Clarence	Ray Hedges
Eddie Foy, Jr.	Eddie Hanley
Grace Hayes	Grace
Trixie Friganza	Mrs. Minter
J. Farrell MacDonald	Grady
Thomas Jackson	Jackson
Ted Healy	Mullins
Howard, Fine and Howard	Mullin's helpers
The Colenette Ballet	

Uncredited Cast:

Bonnie Bonnell	Bonnie

Credited Production Crew:

Screenplay:	Beatrice Banyard
Music:	M. K. Jerome
Lyrics:	Joan Jasmyn
Musical Director:	Paul Van Loan
Dance Director:	Jack Haskell
Art Director:	W. L. Vogel
Photographer:	Joseph Valentine
Film Editor:	Arthur Hilton
Directed by:	Al Boasberg

PERSPECTIVE: In 1933, when 'Ted Healy and His Stooges' made *Meet the Baron* with radio star Jack Pearl, the title alone suggested MGM's purpose was to transfer radio's 'famous Baron Munchausen' to the silver screen. *Myrt and Marge* was Universal's attempt at creating a film version of the radio tandem of Myrtle Vail and Donna Damerell, 'Myrt and Marge, Radio's Sweethearts.' Debuting in 1931 on CBS, Myrt and Marge aired their backstage serial drama in which Myrt played a crusty vaudevillean keeping a protective eye, as she does here, on young Marge - her real-life daughter. Among the cast was the first unabashedly gay character of the era, the costume designer Clarence [Ray Hedges] Tiffingtuffer. He, Myrt, and Marge all reprise their roles for the film which follows Marge's entry into show business, her romance with the talented Eddie [Foy], and her harassment by Jackson, the conniving, unreliable producer. This romantic triangulation takes place amidst musical rehearsals, road trips, and an elaborate New York finale, all assisted by four stage hands - Healy and his Stooges.

The addition of Healy and his Stooges to the cast was not accidental. Competing with MGM, Universal's Carl Laemmle was signing both stage and radio stars in 1933, and, thanks to producer and friend Bryan Foy [Eddie's older brother], Healy signed with the company after their MGM deal ran out. This new studio contract called for Healy and the Stooges to appear in four features, including 1934's star-filled *The Gift of Gab*, but *Myrt and Marge* was the only film they actually made.

Myrt and Marge gives Healy and the Stooges more screen time than any pre-Columbia feature film. They appear in 17 of 25 scenes and visually dominate two scenes: the four of them stretch across the screen in the hotel lobby and they are featured at the loading dock. They do five extended routines, giving us our longest look at their comic dynamics. Healy is in charge, though not always successfully. He makes fun of all three Stooges and Bonnie, but he dishes out physical punishment to Curly at will. Curly, his physical talents beginning to emerge, bristles and looks menacing, but never hits Healy back; he is too busy looking ignorant and misunderstanding things. Larry and Moe play tough guys, though of the two, Moe is the one usually dishing out slaps, preparing himself, as it were, to step into Healy's role. Bonnie plays the chief annoyance, a role played by Fred Sanborn in *Soup to Nuts* and both Curly and Bonnie in *Plane Nuts*. *Myrt and Marge* also offers ample footage to confirm what the modern viewer already suspects from the stage acts in *Soup to Nuts* and *Plane Nuts*: Healy's concept of foursome and fivesome humor depends on off-key jokes and puns punctuated by slaps, gouges, shoves, and verbal threats. The jokes are strung end to end, as is each line with an introductory "Well," "Oh," "Say," or "You know." The punchlines are hardly hilarious, but the gag patterns are insistent, intriguing, and dependable, especially with our three seasoned comedians supplying energetic gestures, well-timed entries, and their unique kind of comic sincerity. In a few months the Stooges will separate from Healy. The type of slapstick and gag humor will remain the same, but the Stooges will expand their slapstick repertoire greatly. Writers will offer them more polished and completed verbals gags, and the presentation format will be drastically overhauled into compelling narratives starring the Stooges as various characters unified as a dynamic trio.

VISUAL HUMOR: In *Dancing Lady* and *Meet the Baron* , Curly was rarely isolated as the comic butt. Here, for the first time he is the chief clown, particularly at the Chinese restaurant and in the cobra mechanism scenes. Because the concept of the film is essentially radio visualized on film, the slapstick is accompanied by vivid sound effects: wood blocks for bonks and even a plink for a nose tweak. Both of these will be used in the Columbia films, although the latter combination will not be used until the 1940s. When Healy slaps Curly in the

Chinese restaurant booth, we hear a slap and BONK sound effect simultaneously. Many physical comedy gags used here will reappear in later films, although Moe takes the part of Healy: Healy playing the lazy supervisor (*3 Dumb Clucks*); Healy asking Curly to cut a deck of cards ("You don't trust me, eh?"); Larry blowing into Curly's ear, Moe getting it from the other ear (*Goofs and Saddles*); Curly asleep on the job (*Violent Is the Word for Curly*); sleeping three in a train berth; a serviette gag; Curly being slapped by Moe and then turning to be slapped/bonked by Healy (*A Pain in the Pullman*); and Curly getting slapped by a large woman (*Hoi Polloi*). Curly pretends to kiss Moe, which will be varied in *Calling All Curs* and later films. This is basic comedy, of course, but such a hint of homosexuality may have something to do with the presence of Clarence (Healy: "This is not Mrs. Jackson. It's Mullins! You think I'm a sissy or somethin'?"). Marge does a gymnastic dance (as will Flo, Mary, & Shirley) in *Gents Without Cents*. Variations: walking through a scenery door (*Soup to Nuts*, *Dancing Lady*); and each Stooge playing a musical instrument (*The Big Idea*).

VERBAL HUMOR: Ignorance is an essential component of a Stooge's make-up, and Curly here is characterized as particularly ignorant for the first time (Bonnie: "I got a contract to join this show." Curly [looking at the piece of paper]: "The manager's name is 'towel!'" Healy: "That's no contract. That's a laundry list."; Healy: "It's too bad we can't get the mother to acquiesce." Curly: "Maybe she does. Why don't you ask her?"; Healy: "Savvy Confucius?" Curly: "Why bring sex into this?"; and Healy: "Two introductions, piano in forty, then we segue, and we give a little staccato, and then we modulate." Curly: "Yeah, but what do I do with the piano?"). Moe is no genius either ("Don't you think you ought to consult the 'consecutives'"; "You shoulda did it previously"; and Healy: "In Altoona, I'm gonna issue the alma mater." Moe: "Not 'alma mater,' *ulta* mater!").

Curly gives a rudimentary "Nyah, nyah, nyah" when he says, "That's marvelous – that's the funniest story I ever heard"; he made a similar sound in *Plane Nuts*. He speaks without falsetto when he says, "Congratulations! That's my idea of a great story". Three pattern (Larry: "Professional people get paid." Moe: "Always mercenary." Curly: "That's from drinkin' too much coffee!"). Four-pattern (Healy: "We got this act last summer – at the Fireman's Ball." Larry: "We was the hit of the show." Curly: "Of course, there was only three acts." Moe: "And the other two was detained elsewhere!"). The Stooges played at a 'Fireman's Ball' in *Soup to Nuts*.

Stooge verbal firsts: Substituting Moe for Healy: "Rih-cede, will ya'? Rih-cede" (*Pardon My Scotch*); Jackson: "Who are these gentlemen." Healy: "Gentlemen?" (*Horses' Collars*); Healy: "Now you're startin'!" ("You gonna start that again!" in *False Alarms*); Healy: "You know what a burden is, don't ya'?" Larry: "Yeah, a 'burden' the hand's worth two in the bush'" (*A Bird in the Head*); Healy: "Are you an Oxford man?" Moe: "Yeah." Healy: "Go back to high shoes" (*Ants in the Pantry*); Healy noticing Curly eating with a knife: "What would Emily Post say?" (*Uncivil Warriors*; *Hoi Polloi*); Healy: "Mammy, here's your big boy Sammy. He's back from Alabammy. Put on those eggs and hammy. Don't flim-flam me, mammy" (*All The World's a Stooge*); and "What is this - a haunted house?" ("Gee, the joint is haunted" in *Men in Black*).

Healy's verbal threats ("I'll hit you in the head with that truck in a minute!") are more ominous than Moe's "I'll murder you guys!" and "Remind me to kill you later!" in future years. Other threats (Healy: "You know you're gonna regret these sarcastic remarks some day?" Curly: "Startin' when?" Healy: "Startin' now." [SLAP]) are very Moe-like. As in *Meet the Baron*, Moe makes an attempt at becoming the boss. Typical Healy humor includes set jokes (Moe: "Hey, how old are you?" Bonnie: "The last time I was home, I hopped on my mother's knee and said, "Daddy, how old am I?" Moe: "You call your mother 'Daddy'?" Healy: "This may be a personal question, but what do you call your Daddy?" Bonnie: "Oh, we don't call him. He has an alarm clock!"; and Healy: "If it gets after twelve you should be in Washington." Bonnie: "But Washington is dead!"); puns (Bonnie: "This gentleman always writes his contracts on laundry lists." Curly: "To prove the show is clean?"; Larry: "You're liable to get arrested for petty larceny." Bonnie: "I'm not petting!";

Healy: "You know I never attended a strawberry festival, but I attended a meat ball!"; Healy: "Does your father have a queue?" Girl: "He doesn't play billiards."); and insults (Moe: "Give me a three letter word meaning 'rat.'" Healy [pointing to Curly]: "Him!"; and Healy: "Do you know the 'Road to Mandalay'?" Moe: "Yeah, you want us to play it?" Healy: "No, I want you to take it!").

Not only are there gay jokes at Clarence's expense: (Myrt [handing him plumes]: "Put that in the trunk and don't wear it!" Clarence: "Selfish!"; Clarence: "I hope you stick this lovely coat in your assets." Grady: "You wouldn't wear it unless it had lace on it." Clarence: "I'd wallop him if I wasn't afraid of rubbing the polish off my fingernails!"; and Clarence: "Are you girls having a good time?" Chinese Girl: "Yes, ma'am!"). There are two hair jokes at Larry's expense: (Eddie: "Why don't you get a haircut? That'll get a load off your mind!"; and Curly: "I'm so tired, I need a rest." Healy: "Why don't you get some old clothes and spend a couple of weeks in his [Larry's] hair!").

References: Healy's singing impersonation is of Al Jolson, the star of the first "talkie" picture, *The Jazz Singer* (1927), and – as Healy's lyrics suggest – *Mammy* (1930). Larry's "Chevalier" is Maurice Chevalier, the French singer, in Hollywood since 1929. Healy's "Joe E. Brown" refers to the wide-mouthed vaudevillian who appeared in films from the late 1920s and would appear along with the Stooges in *It's a Mad, Mad, Mad, Mad World.* Curly's "John L. Sullivan" refers to the 1882-1892 heavyweight boxing champ. Healy's "Canero" refers to Primo Carnera, the heavyweight boxing champ in 1933/1934 (who later played the mythological Antaeus in *Hercules Unchained* [1959]). Moe's "The Cat and the Canero" refers to John Willard's play, *The Cat and the Canary*, which was made into a 1927 Universal silent film – the prototype of spooky house 'scare comedies' like *Spook Louder* and *The Hot Scots.* Clarence's "It looks like King Kong wore it to a masquerade" makes reference to RKO's *King Kong,* which had been released just the year before. Moe calls Larry "Gable," i.e. Clark Gable, with whom they had just worked in *Dancing Lady.* Healy's "queue" is the term for a [Chinese] pig tail, and "Bo-hunk" was slang for an East-Central European peasant.

As the Stooges close out their early film career in Universal's *Myrt and Marge* (1934), they complete two busy years of co-starring in short films, making cameo appearances in minor feature films and playing minor characters in a number of scenes in major feature films at three different studios. They impressed and delighted a good number of critics and producers and acquainted themselves with dozens of actors. But they were still inseparable from Ted Healy (and Bonnie Bonnell), and they worked from one short-term contract to the next. Many other stage/vaudeville comedians also appeared in films during this period; many of them were not to be heard of thereafter. But the Three Stooges were about to separate from Healy, charm the beastly Harry Cohn and find a spot in Columbia's short-film unit, which would provide them with employment and international exposure for more than three decades (not including a brief hiatus in 1958).

OTHER NOTES: The credits are accompanied, as often in films of the early 1930s, by short film clips of each of the principle actors. The Stooges, in a brief slapping sequence, appear fifth. The warrant for Eddie's arrest is dated Sept. 20, 1938. The projects at Universal that never came to fruition included, according to the *Scrapbook* [65], *Going Hollywood* (1933) with Bing Crosby and *Unemployment Agency*, a feature designed to make the Stooges "filmdom's successors to the Marx Brothers". Bryan and Eddie Foy were two of "the seven little Foys," the famous vaudeville family. Director Boasberg had also directed Moe and Curly (without Larry) in the (now lost) 1934 MGM short *Jailbirds of Paradise. Myrt and Marge* ran on CBS radio until 1945. Myrt makes an ironic comment to apologize for the Stooge's cantankerous slapstick: "I want you to understand that as a rule, we're usually more friendly than this."

"JIMMIE" RAY APPLEBY
"SANFIELD" REGINALD KNORR
"MISS FOLSON" VIOLET LE CLAIR
COLUMBIA
"BILLIE" ELEANOR RELLA
MYRT and MARGE
BOBBY BROWN-DIRECTOR
"SLIM" CHARLES CALVERT
"JACK ARNOLD" VINTON HAWORTH
"CLARENCE" RAY HEDGE
"LAURA" MARGE EVANS
"GWEN" PATRICIA ANN MANNERS
WRIGLEY'S
"PAT" KARL WAY
HARLOW WILCOX-ANNOUNCER
MYRT and MARGE

1933-1959
COLUMBIA SHORTS

1934

Woman Haters • Punch Drunks

Men in Black • Three Little Pigskins

#1 - WOMAN HATERS

Studio: MGM

Released: May 5, 1934

Running Time: 19"18'"

Credited Production Crew:

Directed by:	Archie Gottler
Story by:	Jerome S. Gottler
Photography:	Joseph August
Film Editor:	James Sweeney

Credited Cast:

Moe Howard	Tom
Larry Fine	Jim
Curley Howard	Jackie
Marjorie White	Mary

Uncredited Cast:

Bud Jamison	Chairman, Woman Haters Club
Monte Collins	Mr. Zero
Jack Norton	Justice of the Peace
A. R. Haysel	Mary's father
Dorothy Vernon	Mary's mother
Walter Brennan	train conductor
Snowflake Fred Toones]	porter
George Gray	husband on crutches
Stanley "Tiny" Sandford	cop, brother of Mary
June Gittelson	Mary's sister
Don Roberts	wedding guest
Les Goodwin	
Charles Richman	
Gilbert C. Emery	

PERSPECTIVE: President Harry Cohn brought Columbia from its original Poverty Row status to being one of only two profitable studios during the Depression. A frugal tyrant insisting on short-term contracts and tight budgets, Cohn developed a short film unit much like the one he and his brother Jack had formed in 1919. With musical comedies becoming all the rage in 1933, Paramount, Goldwyn and RKO were paying large salaries to such East Coast stage celebrities as Eddie Cantor [*Roman Scandals*], the Marx Brothers [*Duck Soup*] and Wheeler & Woolsey [*Diplomaniacs*]. Reluctant to pay such salaries, Cohn designed his short subject department to produce low-budget, money-making musical comedies. He had producer Zion Myers hire director/songwriter Archie Gottler to make nine "Musical Novelties," coincidentally just as Moe, Larry and Curly had finished their contractual obligation at MGM and decided to split with Ted Healy once and for all. On March 19, 1934, Cohn signed them to a $1,000 contract for one film with an option to make eight per year. Not wasting any time, the next week "Howard, Fine and Howard" made Gottler's sixth "Musical Novelty," and soon after its release in May, *Woman Haters* was such a success that Cohn decided to exercise the option.

As one of Gottler's "Musical Novelties", *Woman Haters* is unlike any other Stooge film. It is accompanied by music throughout - mostly variations on his 'My Life, My Love, My All.' The dialogue consists entirely of rhymed verse, as were the recitatives preceding 'On the Boulevard' in Wheeler and Woolsey's *Diplomaniacs*. These continuous musical lyrics do not allow for any Healy-like interruptions, puns, or extended gags, and, unlike the expensive MGM shorts, the plot is not interrupted by musical production numbers. Even the slapstick, though still crude and mean spirited as part of their Healy legacy, is incorporated into the plot: when Marjorie White slaps the Stooges it turns them into woman haters forever.

Separating from Ted Healy and becoming a trio without a boss forced the Stooges to search for a new group dynamic. Here they play three competing individuals who each pursue the same woman but are ultimately rejoined in a fitful reunion. Moe [Tom], who joked later, "I took over Healy's role; I was no fool," has already begun to emerge as the boss; Curly [Jackie] continues to act tough and defiant, as he had in *Fugitive Lovers*; and Larry [Jim] plays an outcast, as he would in their last film, *Kook's Tour*. Womanizing, a motif in many Stooge films but the centerpiece of *Woman Haters*, accentuates this inter-Stooge isolationism. It will take a few more films before the Stooges develop their trademark cantankerous triadic unity and their personae within the trio, but here we see an emerging unity as they combine forces in the opening scene, at the bar, in the train compartment, and in the delightful slapstick denouement.

VISUAL HUMOR: When Mary knocks them out the window, the plot is brought to its conclusion, demonstrating how slapstick will often be used as an integral part of Stooge plots at critical junctures. The slapstick is of the same variety the Stooges had

Although this is just a publicity still from *Woman Haters* (1934), it demonstrates the flexibility that a comic trio has in front of a camera, here expanding vertically to encompass the train bunks.

presented in their Fox and MGM films. They fall over as a trio [*Beer and Pretzels*]; Moe and Curly dance with linked arms [*Plane Nuts*]; and a woman slaps them [*Meet the Baron*]. Their arsenal includes the nose tweak [*Meet the Baron*], a naturally exploding celery stalk [*Dancing Lady*] and the uppercut, headlock slap [*Soup to Nuts*]. The primary movements are still the forehead and cheek slaps and the gouge. In fact, the gentle gouge used for the Woman Haters Club initiation was obviously tailor-made for them. It will be very rare in the future that a non-Stooge gouges a Stooge, e.g. *The Yoke's on Me*. Stooge firsts: Curly's derby machine gun; Curly trying to hide only his head; Larry sliding across a floor; using a seltzer bottle as a weapon; and the Stooges toasting and shattering glasses; also: Moe slapping Curly back and forth like a punching bag; and two Stooges (Moe and Larry) slapping each other several times in succession, shrugging their shoulders, and then forgetting about it. This latter routine was part of their stage act. Later, they will conclude the routine by hitting the third Stooge behind them [*Start Cheering*]. Another Stooge first: Moe and Curly crowding each other and bouncing off a doorjamb. The bearded creditors squeezed through a doorway in *Soup to Nuts*, but the Stooges will not jam into a doorway until *Saved By the Belle*. Joe Henrie, Columbia sound man for these early films, used the ratchet sound effect for the initiation arm-bending and the POUND [kettledrum]. Both will become staples, but the many other sound effects that will enhance and palliate the violent slapstick are not yet developed. In the private room, the slap sound [a cracked whip] is used for a BONK. In 1934, while mixing the Walter Catlett [*The Captain Hates the Sea*] short *Get Along Little Hubby*, producer Jules White convinced his boss that short films needed cartoon-like sound effects. Typical early Stooge period clothing: Curly's bursting jacket and Moe's "dapper" white shoes.

VERBAL HUMOR: The rhymed dialogue leaves no room for puns or most other types of verbal gags. In carrying the plot, some of the rhymes are forced, e.g. W-H Chairman: "Please, at ease, relax, relax!...I didn't tell you to break your backs!". A Stooge first: the "Woob-woob-woob!" Curly emits when Moe bites his toe. This may have been an outgrowth of the Indian "Woo-woos!" in *Nertsery Rhymes*. Stooge fans who fail to find the humor in Shemp's, Joe Besser's or Joe DeRita's films should keep in mind that it took Curly several years to find his true persona, not to mention all of the noises that help to express it. The lyrics to 'My Life, My Love, My All': [They vary each time the song is sung.]

For you, for you, my life, my love, my all,
Each evening when the twilight's falling.
I'll come home to you.
Falling for you-oo-oo-oo-oo-oo.
I'll croon a little song about the Moon,
And when I'm finished with my crooning,
On my knees I'll fall,
My life, my love, my all.

OTHER NOTES: Columbia released this film on May 5; MGM released their last Stooge short, *The Big Idea*, on May 12; and MGM put out the feature *Hollywood Party* on June 1. "Curley" will be the official spelling until *Disorder in the Court* (1936). Archie Gottler began his career playing piano in silent movie theaters; he later composed Broadway shows [*Ziegfeld Follies of 1918*] before becoming a pioneer in early sound films. Writer Jerome Gottler was his son. The seventh of Gottler's "Musical Novelties" featured the young Betty Grable. According to Okuda [3-6], Zion Myers was Harry Cohn's second choice to head the unit; he first hired White, who left after one month without making a film and returned to Columbia in 1934. According to White's own recollection (Bruskin 64-65), Myers was hired first, worked with White to set up the unit, left to take a job at RKO and then made White (with Cohn's approval) his successor. White remained its head until the unit closed in 1958/1959. Myers, White's boyhood friend in Edendale, later wrote several Stooge shorts, including *Heavenly Daze*. Moe [63-67] says that on the day they left MGM, he met with Columbia agent Walter Kane – who introduced him to Cohn, who then signed the Stooges to make *Woman Haters*. That same day, Larry met with Joe Rivkin, who introduced him to Carl Laemmle, who signed the Stooges to a Universal contract. Because the Columbia contract was signed a few hours earlier, the Universal contract was voided. The Columbia "sparkle" logo will be used until *Disorder in the Court*, as will hand-drawn title screens. Woman Hater Monte Collins [Mr. Zero] would serve as a Stooge writer as well. Sound engineer Ed Bernds would years later direct many important Stooge films. Bud Jamison [Chairman], who had played supporting roles for Chaplin, Buster Keaton, Harold Lloyd and others, would play in more than three dozen Stooge films until 1944. Thirty-year-old Walter Brennan plays the train conductor. *Moe* [78] recalled that Brennan had trouble memorizing his lines, but in two years Brennan would win the first of three Oscars. Moe also recalled that Larry broke a finger when he fell out of the train berth, the first of numerous minor on-set injuries the Stooges sustained. The "blue eagle" and logo "We Do Our Part" of the N[ational] R[ecovery] A[dministration], ('N[icholas] R[estaurant] A[cropolis] in Curly's 1934 MGM short *Roast-Beef and Movies*), was created in June 1933 as part of Roosevelt's New Deal legislation but then declared unconstitutional in May 1935. The music for "My Life, My Love, My All' was a recycled Columbia tune; for an analysis of the music, see Richard Finegan, "Woman Haters: Music Score Identified at Last," *The Three Stooges Journal* 86 [1998] 10 & 13. The Stooges make a memorable entrance in the first scene; this will become a constant. The scenes are separated by wipes. The last scene, in which the elderly Moe gouges the elderly Curly, contains this irony: in the 1960s, PTA groups applied such pressure to television stations that the elderly Stooges no longer used the eye gouge. Three Stooges will each compete for the same woman again in *Corny Casanovas*.

Jules White's Columbia short film unit would eventually hire a number of minor actors who appeared repeatedly in Stooge films. But in 1934, the unit was new, and for *Woman Haters* [1934] even the Stooges were as yet just temporary hires. So many of these extras would not appear with the Stooges again, and very few of them are credited.

- To the right of Larry is the 26-year old Marjorie White, starlet of the previous year's Wheeler & Woolsey tunefest *Diplomaniacs*, which had the same kind of musical recitative the Stooges croon in 1934's *Woman Haters*; she died tragically the following year in an automobile accident.
- Between Larry and White is Jack Norton [1882-1958], who would play in such important comedies as Wheeler & Woolsey's *Cockeyed Cavaliers* [1934] and, as A. Pismo Clam, in W. C. Fields' *The Bank Dick* [1940]. He would return to Stooge comedy as the insane Mr. Boyce in *Rhythm and Weep* [1946].
- Mary's brother [the large policeman] is played by Stanley "Tiny" Sandford [1894-1961], who would play "Big Bull" in Charlie Chaplin's *Modern Times* [1936].
- Mary's parents are played by A. R. Haysel [1887-1954], who would play the dandruff patient in 1937's *Dizzy Doctors*; and Dorothy Vernon [1875-1970], who had bit parts in dozens of films from 1919 to 1953.

#2 - PUNCH DRUNKS

Studio: Columbia

Released: July 13, 1933

Running Time: 17"29'"

Credited Production Crew:

Directed by:	Lou Breslow
Screen Play:	Jack Cluett
Story:	Jerry Howard, Larry Fine & Moe Howard
Photography:	Henry Freulich
Film Editor:	Robert Carlisle

Credited Cast:

Moe Howard	
Larry Fine	
Curley Howard	
Dorothy Granger	Curley's girlfriend

Uncredited Cast:

Al Hill	Killer Kilduff
Arthur Housman	timekeeper
Casey Columbo	Mr. McGurn, restaurant owner
Larry McGrath	referee
William Irving	Kilduff's manager
Billy Bletcher	ring announcer

PERSPECTIVE: Harry Cohn had insisted on a sixty-day waiting period before Columbia had to exercise its option to sign a long-term contract with the Stooges. Not wanting to wait, Moe developed this project called "A Symphony of Punches," which he had been thinking about for some time. He wrote the nine-page treatment, redrafted it with Larry and Curly and convinced Cohn to give them their seven-year, eight-films-per-year contract. Filmed in May and released in July, *Punch Drunks* was the first film in which the group was officially billed as "The Three Stooges." The screenplay credited to Jerry Howard, Larry Fine, and Moe Howard would turn out to be the only one written by the Stooges themselves. Its real importance lies not so much in the authorship as in what the Stooges accomplished. Their previous films had been plotless Healy creations, filmed stage acts or musicals. But with *Punch Drunks* Moe created the kind of goal-oriented plot that gives the Stooge comedies form, direction, and narrative energy. So it was Moe who invented the format that would make their next 188 films so successful.

With Larry running down deserted streets to the strains of "Pop Goes the Weasel," *Punch Drunks* beautifully incorporates the musical element so essential to previous Healy/Stooge films. The image is memorable. With the fully orchestrated song blasting incessantly in our ears, editor Robert Carlisle underscores Larry's determination to find another musical source by interspersing the fight sequences twelve times, with long shots isolating Larry's winged coattails, fast motion running, sidewalk sliding, and madcap driving. With all of this and the kid vs. timekeeper subplot effectively punctuating the boxing scene, Larry brings the whole thing to a climax by crashing the radio truck through the wall.

Larry's quest for the music is so engaging, we almost forget its critical purpose: it turns Curly into, well, Curly. After a dozen films, this is the first time Curly performs his signature revving: churning his legs, flailing his arms and rubbing his face, all the while woob-woob-woobing in a physical explosion of insane energy. This was Moe's idea, too. And by making his little brother go crazy when he sees or hears something – later it will be mice and tassels, and cheese will be the cure – his genius is finally unleashed. Again (but for the last time), the film

begins with the Stooges characterized as three distinct individuals:

Moe as fight manager.
Curly as waiter.
Larry as violinist.

But they are all united within the first four minutes, and had it not been for this separate characterization, perhaps the idea would never have struck Moe to have Curly go independently insane. Other characteristic comic motifs like Curly's iron skull, ability to chew non-foods, frustrations with inanimate objects, and shyness with women will develop later. This is still the same angry Curly we saw in the MGM films; a less crazed version of Curly's anger was displayed in his solo film *Roast-Beef and Movies*, but slapped by Healy, George Givot, Moe, and even Larry, the Curly we will come to know is literally being beaten into formation. As his film persona develops at Columbia, his emotions will blossom into delightful

displays of movement and noises, not angry stares, vain threats, and a punch in the nose.

VISUAL HUMOR: Knocking Moe and Larry out at the end establishes an important precedent. In most films, the final gag will make sure the Stooges get knocked out, shot at, chased out of town, or abused one more time in some way. This is the first film in which Curly changes expression in rapid succession. When the woman sitting ringside smiles at him and Moe gives him a pound/bonk, Curly in just a few seconds runs through a range of emotions: surprise, anger, defiance, worry. Yet he still has the energy to flirt. Other Stooge firsts: moving the comedy beyond the camera frame (when Curly knocks McGurn up to the fan); Larry's hat with a separate brim; and Curly's swollen hand. Variations: Curly revved his legs (only), and we saw the first pound/bonk in MGM's *The Big Idea*. Larry's slide on the sidewalk resembles his wedding slide in *Woman Haters*. We hear a sound almost like the familiar wood block when Moe bonks Curly on the forehead and a ratchet sound when Larry and Curly pull Moe's toe out from under the car by yanking his neck. But there are no sound effects for the punches and gouge Curly receives in the restaurant, nor any guzzling sound for drinking water. When Curly slaps the corner man with his glove, the sound effect is that of a skin slap. Cinematographer Henry Freulich opens the training scene with a Hitchcock-like camera angle showing each Stooge separately from ground level. A sequence in which Larry rises out of the water with a frog on his head was edited out of the final version.

VERBAL HUMOR: Stooge firsts: Moe: "You nervous?" Curly: "Nah, only in that leg"; the tapeworm gag ("Burnt toast and a rotten egg.... I got a tape worm and it's good enough for 'im"); and Curly's "I'm a citizen". Curly's first sign of ignorant self-confidence: "Don't worry about me, dear; I'm a man without feelins". Variations: "I'm a victim of circumstance (*Beer and Pretzels*); and making music by punching Curly's shorts (*Nertsery Rhymes*). Occasionally, Larry's characterizations lean toward false sophistication, as in "I lost my ba-lànce". Reference: McGurn's 'Beau Brummell' refers to the nineteenth-century dandy who popularized trousers and fine clothing.

OTHER NOTES: The Stooges' new contract increased their salary to $7,500 per film to be divided equally. This was more than the $1,000 Cohn paid Buster Keaton and the $1,250 paid to Harry Langdon, but the Stooges' salary was never increased again during their 24-year tenure at Columbia. There is a photocopy of Moe's original manuscript and the second, typed draft in *Scripts* 128-33. The film is quite different from the original treatment. Moe was to be called "Bangs" and Larry "Fuzzy"; Moe spelled "Curly" as "Curley" and vice-versa. (The Stooges will now typically use their own names, except in costumers ['Duck, Dodge, Hyde' in *Uncivil Warriors*] and multiple-role films [*Self-Made Maids, A Merry Mix-Up*]). Larry was to play "The Stars and Stripes Forever," but "Pop Goes the Weasel" (attributed to W. R. Mandale and dating from the 1850s) was substituted because it was in the public domain and did not cost Columbia a copyright fee. Director Lou Breslow had worked at Fox in previous years, assisting on *Soup to Nuts*. In the late 1920s, he often worked with Raymond McCarey, director of *Men in Black* and *Three Little Pigskins*.

Dorothy Granger worked in many comedy films at Hal Roach Studios and Educational Pictures alongside W. C. Fields, Laurel & Hardy, and Leon Errol; she appeared in more than 150 films, including *Raintree County* (1957).

Mack Sennett veteran Billy Bletcher [ring announcer] would provide his voice for several more Stooge films. He had already provided the voice for the Big Bad Wolf in Disney's *Three Little Pigs* (1933). Larry actually played the violin rather well. He began taking lessons as a child after his arm was accidentally burnt by his father's metallurgical acid. A doctor prescribed the violin as therapy to strengthen the injured muscles. He played a number of instruments, but it was the violin act that Healy saw in 1925, reportedly offering Larry "$90 per week, $100 if he threw away the fiddle." The tune Larry plays in the locker room is "Let's Fall in Love," the title song from Columbia's 1934 film starring Edmund Lowe and Ann Sothern. The song was written by Harold Arlen, best known later for his songs in *The Wizard of Oz*. Archie Gottler's "I Thought I Wanted You," which the Stooges played in *The Captain Hates the Sea* and would be used again for *Men in Black*, is heard over the opening credits, but yields to "Pop Goes the Weasel" at the finale. Jack Cluett, who rewrote "A Symphony of Punches" into the present screenplay, was brought to Columbia by Zion Myers [*Woman Haters*]. Curly suffered a bloody nose and cut his lip during the boxing sequences. The stunt man who took that great fall off the back of the radio trunk reportedly broke his arm; and Larry reported almost drowning during the training sequence. As in *Woman Haters*, all three Stooges are interested in the same woman, but romance is only secondary in this film despite Dorothy Granger's featured billing. In a solo effort, Shemp remade this film in 1945 as *A Hit With a Miss* in which he plays a waiter who goes crazy every time he hears the tune. Like Curly, Oliver Hardy goes berserk when he hears horn blasts in *Saps at Sea* [1940], although Chaplin's *Modern Times* may have been an intermediary influence. The Stooges will enter the ring again in *Grips, Grunts and Groans*; *Fright Night* [and *Fling in the Ring*]; and *The Three Stooges Go Around the World in a Daze*.

This is the aftermath of the initial restaurant scene in which Curly loses himself in a wild rage and pulverizes boxing champs and managers alike. The bottom of the screen is filled with destruction, and in *Punch Drunks* [1934] itself one knockout victim is swirling on the ceiling fan. This is a significant turning point in the history of The Three Stooges. When Curly becomes overstimulated, he revs up his legs, arms and voice alike. He begins to blossom as an extraordinary physical comedian right here in this scenario invented by his brother, Moe Howard.

Here Curly is about to turn his latent destructive skills on Killer Kilduff, played by Al Hill [1892-1954], who in a few years will portray Filthy McNasty in W. C. Fields' *The Bank Dick* [1940]. Hill, who ultimately played in over 190 films, will also return to Stooge films as a crook in *A Gem of a Jam*. Timekeeper Arthur Housman [1889-1942] began his career in silent films in 1912. He played a drunk in the 1932 Harold Lloyd/Clyde Bruckman classic *Movie Crazy* and continued to specialize in playing drunks into the early 1940s.

#3 MEN IN BLACK

Studio: Columbia

Released: September 28, 1934

Running Time: 18"02"

Credited Production Crew:

Directed by:	Raymond McCarey
Story & Screen Play:	Felix Adler
Photography:	Benjamin Kline
Film Editor:	James Sweeney

Credited Cast:

Moe Howard
Larry Fine
Curley Howard

Uncredited Cast:

Dell Henderson	Dr. Graves, Superintendent
Bobby Callahan	messenger
Phyllis Crane	Anna Conda
Jeanie Roberts	hiccuping nurse
Ruth Hiatt	OR nurse
Charles King	OR anesthesiologist
Billy Gilbert	dangerous patient
Little Billy	'woman' in a coma
Bud Jamison	Little Billy's doctor
Irene Coleman	
Arthur West	
Joe Mills	
Joe Fine	
Carmen Andre	
Helen Splane	
Kay Hughes	
Eve Reynolds	
Eve Kimberly	
Lucile Watson	
Billie Stockton	
Betty Andre	
Arthur Rankin	
Neal Burns	
Charles Dorety	

PERSPECTIVE: Archie and Jerome Gottler wrote *Woman Haters* and the Stooges themselves wrote *Punch Drunks*, but this and all subsequent scripts would be written by Columbia staff writers. *Men in Black* was the first of many written by Felix Adler, a Max Sennett/Hal Roach veteran with a vast repertoire of gag scenarios; he will write over sixty Stooge films in three decades. One of Adler's signature approaches was parody, and this film parodies MGM's Clark Gable/Myrna Loy film *Men in White* (1934). Besides the title, Adler parodies both the somber scene in which doctors swear the Hippocratic oath and the incessant ubiquitousness of the hospital's public address system. Audiences loved *Men in Black*, as did film makers: it received a nomination for an Academy Award in the Short Subject category - the only Stooge film to receive a nomination.

Men in Black has its detractors, including both Leonard Maltin ("The Stooges seemed restrained and inhibited in front of the camera; it did not achieve the success of their later hospital films.") and Jeffrey Forrester ("The short is virtually plotless and the wild sight gags are silly, rather than funny.") who prefer the shorts Del Lord would begin directing in 1935. But the film exudes constant movement and reaches non-stop mayhem as the Stooges scurry into, out of, and through Graves' office door and ride through the hallway on a variety of vehicles. Like *Punch Drunks*, *Men in Black* is energized by a repeated refrain, not 'Pop Goes the Weasel' but "DR. HOWARD! DR FINE! DR HOWARD!" which is blasted more than half a dozen times over the loud speaker. Spurred on by this and their oath to 'Duty and Humanity,' not to mention Aristotle's preference for unity of place and time, the Stooges dash about tormenting doctors, nurses, patients, and the custodian who has to reset the glass in the superintendent's office - everyone but the giggling nurse, who as just recompense annoys them and us but elicits Curly's first genuine 'Nyuk, nyuk, nyuk.' Ultimately the Stooges do to the loudspeaker what they did to the radio and sound truck in *Punch Drunks* - destroy it in return for the chaos it inspires them to create.

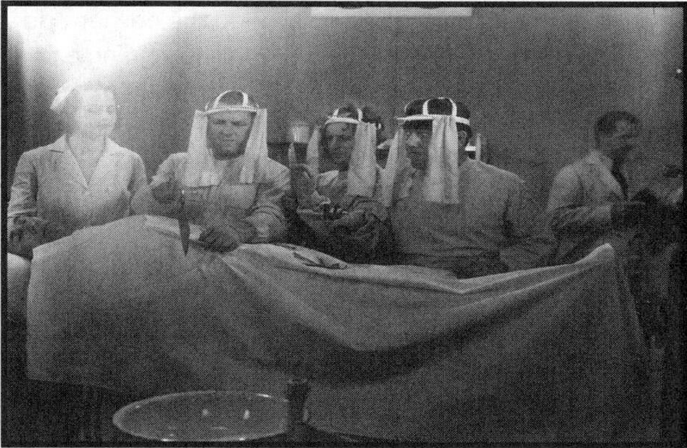

Into this *perpetuum mobile* Felix Adler inserts numerous set routines - Anna Conda's arrest, the telegraph messenger, the giggling nurse, the phone answering routine, the comatose and madman patients, and the operating scene - all setting important precedents. For the first time we see the Stooges unleashing their well-intentioned but destructive energies in a workplace, abusing innocent bystanders, employing telephones for a game of verbal tag, mixing nonsense chemicals, using a stethoscope and a variety of other tools, and riding odd forms of transportation. Most important is that now, finally, for the first time the Stooges begin and end the film as a triadic unit, not the separate characters but an organic entity energized for decades to come. It took a dozen previous Stooge films, years of stage experience with Ted Healy, Adler's Mack Sennett know-how, and director Raymond McCarey's Hal Roach know-how, but in this break-through film Adler, McCarey, and the Stooges create a new kind of Stooge unity as well as a number of concepts from which scores of future comic sequences will be concocted.

VISUAL HUMOR: Stooge firsts: administering an 'anesthetic'; and looking behind themselves—not in response to anyone calling them "gentlemen" but to the comatose midget's "Gee, the joint is haunted!". The slapstick still relies on the basic slaps and gouge as well as the more recently adopted POUND/BONK. Proper sound effects accompany the POUND/BONK and hitting the doctor on the head with mallets, but when Moe gouges Curly there is no PLINK, which will not be developed for years. Ted Healy had double slapped Moe and Curly in *Dancing Lady*, but when Moe double slaps Curly and Larry here ("My Nell!") it is a filmed first for him. Moe does a memorable take when the "giant green canary" lands on his shoulder. His acting talents are often overlooked because of his bossy characterization. The set camera allows characters (Curly, Anna Conda) to come into it and out of focus. Variations: the Stooges fainting after the apple gag (*Beer and Pretzels*, *Woman Haters*); Curly disappearing around the corner and then walking into view (*Meet the Baron*); and riding a tandem bicycle (*Meet the Baron*). Many comedies of the period have someone swallow a lit cigar in excitement; Graves swallows the combination to the safe instead and puts the lit cigar in his pocket!

This advertisement for *Men in Black* (1934) mentions neither 'The Three Stooges' nor 'Curley' Howard. Ingenue Jeannie Roberts (the 'hiccuping nurse') had a short-lived, if diaphragmically active, career.

VERBAL HUMOR: For a photocopy of the script, see *Scripts* 71-125. Major differences between the script and the released film include a baudy interview with a fan dancer; several extended gag sequences with (and a triple slap from) Little Billy (e.g. Moe: "What's the difference between a hill and a pill?" Billy: "One's hard to get up, and the other's hard to get down!"); Larry's "When I'm ready!" gag, which was ad-libbed (filmed first in *Plane Nuts*); and the scripted ending, in which the Stooges take 'their gal' Nel - Siamese triplets [a Siamese Cyclops will appear in *The Three Stooges Meet Hercules*] - into the operating room and emerge as three couples. Stooge firsts: annoying as the nurse's 'apple pie' joke is, she gets Curly to deliver the earliest, and one of the longest strings of 'nyuk, nyuk, nyuk'; he had given a preliminary version of it in *Plane Nuts*. His "Certainly!" is the first on film; the "certainly" in *Meet the Baron* has a different emphasis. When Curly delivers nearly 40 "woob-woobs" on the gurney, it is one of the longest strings in the entire Stooge film corpus. Other firsts: Moe: "Give!"; Moe's train station announcer response: "On track 13, all aboard for Philadelphia, Chicago, and points west!"; and the phone mayhem. Larry gets some of the best lines: "We graduated with the highest temperatures in our class!"; "Let's plug him and see if he's ripe!"; and "Let's make an excursion like this!" His "We'll split this three ways, fellas" is one of many throw-away lines we will hear over the years. Shemp was a master at this. Three-pattern (Patient: "Say doctor, do really think I'm gonna get better?" Moe: "I'm very sorry but I'm afraid you are." Larry: "We'll go right downstairs to the presidents office and—" Curly: "We won't say a word about it!"). An interlocking three-pattern (Graves: "How'd you find the patient in 66?" Moe: "Under the bed!" Graves: "How'd you find the patient in 72?" Larry: "Up on the chandelier!" Graves: "What did you do for him?" Curly: "Nothin'! What'd he ever do for us?!"). Part of the Healy legacy was using insults; the Stooges insult each other and a non-Stooge. Here they exchange insults with the transvestite midget (Patient: "Gee, the joint is haunted!" Larry: "How old are you?" Patient: "35!" Curly: "You couldn't get that fresh in 35 years!"). Other variations: Curly: "Just a victim of circumstance!" (*Beer and Pretzels*); Moe: "Spread out!" (*Plane Nuts*); and Midget: "Gee, the joint is haunted!" ("What is this - a haunted house?" in *Myrt and Marge*).

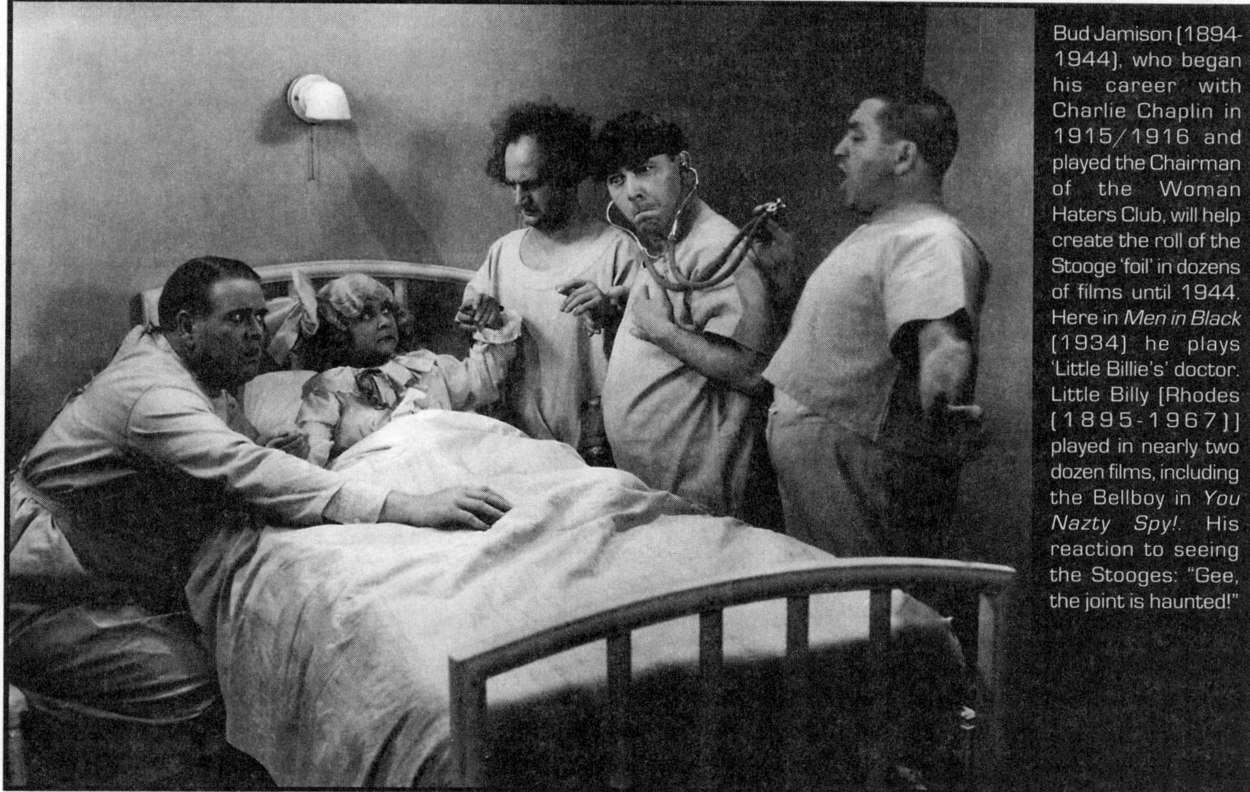

Bud Jamison [1894-1944], who began his career with Charlie Chaplin in 1915/1916 and played the Chairman of the Woman Haters Club, will help create the roll of the Stooge 'foil' in dozens of films until 1944. Here in *Men in Black* [1934] he plays 'Little Billie's' doctor. Little Billy [Rhodes [1895-1967]] played in nearly two dozen films, including the Bellboy in *You Nazty Spy!*. His reaction to seeing the Stooges: "Gee, the joint is haunted!"

References: The 'Schnapps!' gag parodies a radio commercial for the Dutch liquor, which was used for home medical remedies as well. 'Sodium amatol' is a powerful explosive containing TNT. 'Anaconda' was a copper mining stock; in a Depression economy the Stooges "sell" a stock when it is down. Larry croons "ba-ba-ba-boo" into the stethoscope à la Bing Crosby, whose fame was established by the early 1930s; the Stooges almost appeared in a Universal film with him in 1933/1934. Larry's "I ain't got no body," refers to the popular song written by Spencer Williams, Roger Graham, & Dave Peyton in 1916. The song 'Oh Lee, Oh Lady' was a novelty song. The name 'Nellie,' to be used again in *Horses' Collars*, had been a staple since at least 1929's *A Night in Venice*, in which "three of the frowsiest numskulls ever assembled sing...a ballad about that dress that Nellie wore" [J. Brooks Atkinson, *New York Times* May 22, 1929, 30:2]. The plot of *Men in White* forces Clark Gable to choose between his dedication to the medical profession and marrying a rich woman; this was before medical doctors were paid as well as they are in the later years. Perhaps this relates to why the underpaid operating room nurse "lost her voice asking for a raise."

OTHER NOTES: The film was shot in August 1934. It premiered at Los Angeles' Cathay Circle Theatre. Jules White [*Okuda* 61] recalled the response: "I never knew people could laugh so hard.". Though nominated, *Men in Black* lost the Oscar to RKO's *La Cucaracha*, the first Technicolor short. Director Raymond McCarey would also direct *Three Little Pigskins*; with multi-Oscar winning brother Leo he had worked at the Hal Roach studios on Laurel & Hardy, Charlie Chase, and Our Gang films. Felix Adler occasionally wrote for Laurel & Hardy and Abbott & Costello. Jules White attributed much of the Stooges' success to Adler [*Bruskin* 67; photo after 109]. Billy Gilbert [crazy patient] supplied the voice for Sneezy in Disney's *Snow White*. In his introduction to Maltin's *Movie Comedy Teams* [ix], Gilbert describes Shemp as "about my dearest friend". Bobby Callahan [messenger] worked with Curly in MGM's *Roast-Beef and Movies* [1934]. *Moe* [78] says during filming they were cut by flying glass from Dr. Graves' door. The song ['I Thought I Wanted You'] used for the opening credits was used for *Punch Drunks* and in *The Captain Hates the Sea*.

The 'Los Arms Hospital' is the Cedars of Lebanon Hospital, now a Church of Scientology. Moe's daughter Joan [Maurer] gave birth to Moe's grandchildren there.

#4 - THREE LITTLE PIGSKINS

Studio Columbia

Released: December 8, 1934

Running Time: 18"25'"

Credited Production Crew:

Directed by:	Raymond McCarey
Story & Screen play:	Felix Adler & Griffin Jay
Photography:	Henry Freulich
Film Editor:	James Sweeney

Credited Cast:

Moe Howard	
Larry Fine	
Curley Howard	
Lucille Ball	Daisy
Gertie Green	Lulu
Phyllis Crane	Molly

Uncredited Cast:

Walter Long	Joe Stack
Joseph Young	Pete
Milton Douglas	Joe's other henchman
William Irving	photographer
Charles Dorety	photographer
Robert ('Bobby') Burns	'How you fixed for money?' man
Johnny Kascier	'Gun without bullets' man
Lynton Brent	Hamburger man
Joe Levine	
Harry Bowen	
Alex Hirschfield	
Jimmie Phillips	

PERSPECTIVE: This second Felix Adler script establishes the prototype for Depression shorts. The film begins with the now unified Stooges playing jobless bums, or what were known at the time as 'forgotten men,' in realistic exterior scenarios that give the street-walking Stooges opportunities to encounter a variety of characters at the outset of the story. These encounters create variable interactions between the three of them and potential employers, alms-givers, and cops. From such humble beginnings, this type of narrative will develop into a two-part structure, for these intial encounters inevitably lead the Stooges off the street and into a job or other situation for which they are completely untrained. No one ever seems to check their credentials, but once the Stooges enter this second scenario, Stoogeness takes hold and leaves everything in chaotic shambles. This will become the most common narrative format for Stooge shorts of the 1930s, whether they begin as unemployed 'forgotten men' (*Pop Goes the Easel*, *Cash and Carry*) or unskilled workers (*Hoi Polloi*, *Three Little Beers*). As in the first two Columbia shorts, the sidewalk scenario isolates each Stooge as he fails to get money. Moe the self-proclaimed boss then groups them together, but as a trio they again fail miserably, first having to check the lapel of a man they already bothered, then lousing up the placard-carrying job he offers them. Failing miserably even as 'forgotten men' is the result of ignorant incompetence and an insistence that they are neither ignorant nor incompetent - all essential Stooge qualities.

When Lulu leads them into the second scenario, the three Stooges interact with three women for the first time; in previous films they vied for the same woman (and this is still three years before the first set of rhymingly-named women). And then they encounter their first mobster. The criminal element, which will become the staple of Shemp films a decade later, allows the Stooges to develop their trademark cries of "Nyaggh!" and "Whoah!" and various means of cowering, fighting, escaping, and, in later films, winning. In this particular film the second scenario then leads to a third, wherein the Stooges expand their physical humor into the largest

exterior setting to date while ruining not just Stack's bet but an entire football game. Understandably, Stack shoots the fleeing Stooges in the rear.

This becomes the archetype of a commonly employed Stooge ending. It serves nicely because as the Stooges run/ride/canoe off into the distance we laugh at their escape and at their adversary's frustration. Their incompetence is brought to closure without the Stooges being ultimately punished for the destruction or mischief they have caused, and we are reassured that they are merely running off so they may return to entertain us in another adventure. Interestingly, the gun-shots-in-the-rear ending was not how the original script ended. There was to be a denouement in which Moe, Larry, and Curly were to sit in their living room with their look-alike children in their laps: as the Stooges tell the kids what happened at that football game, the kids were to break out in a slapping fight.

VISUAL HUMOR: An important Stooge first: The first 'fist game': Moe holds out his right fist, hits the top of it with his left hand, circles it all the way over his head and comes down on Curly's head. Of all their slapstick moves, this 'fist game' will have the most variations. The seltzer battle is a first, although it derives from *Woman Haters*, as is the Stooges dressing in drag. Other firsts: Curly giving the woman a 'finger-wave'; and Curly drumming his fingers across his cheek [with a modest sound effect]. Curly dances a bit like a chicken but with his head still on, and Larry falls over attempting a Cossack-dance. Moe is almost fully entrenched as the boss in the first scene. Standing in the middle, he slaps/backwards-slaps the others and sets himself up for abuse, as when Curly clocks him with his placard. Much will come of this in subsequent films. The literally understood "Go *that* way! *that* way!" football gag is a prelude to the classic "Do exactly as I do" dance lesson in *Hoi Polloi*. Running with the cameras and shooting with the football, instead of vice versa, resembles Graves' swallowing the combination to a safe and putting a lit cigar in a pocket in *Men in Black*.

VERBAL HUMOR: Stooge firsts: The use of Pig Latin [Igpay Atin-lay]; the number 'H^2O^2'; and Curly stuck at the end of a three-pattern, saying "Low man again!". Epithet: Moe calls Curly "slacker," Larry calls Curly "apple-head," and later the same term is used for Larry. These are the first names the Stooges call each other, although Ted Healy twice referred to Moe as "hatchet-head" [*Plane Nuts*; *Meet the Baron*]; even a Stooge staple like "porcupine" will not appear until 1935. One of the ramifications of Moe acting as boss is the occasional rebellion Larry and Curly mount against him. In the second scene we see an example [Moe to Larry: "Got anything?" Larry: "Nah." Moe: "Layin' down, eh?" [SLAP] Moe to Curly: "Did you get anything?" Curly: "No." Moe: "Oh, slacker!" [SLAP] Larry: "Wait a minute! Did *you* get anything?" Curly: "Yeah, did ya'?" Moe [menacingly]: "No, does it make any difference?" Larry and Curly give in, mumbling separately: "No, not really."]. This pattern of rebellion, reassertion of authority, and yielding is of the same form as the 'When I'm ready" gag used in *Plane Nuts* and *Men in Black* [Larry: "I'll take it when I'm ready!"

Raymond McCarey, director of 1934's *Three Little Pigskins*, and his crew ponder the logistics for filming three adult and three child Stooges, but this ending was ultimately omitted. As for almost every film production, the scripts of Stooge short-films went through several drafts, and then the film itself could be changed considerably during both shooting and the editing part of the post-production process.

Moe: "Are you ready?" Larry [yielding] "Yeah, I'm ready."]. It is used here again just a few seconds later when the man offers them a job (Larry: "Is it honest work?" Man: "Does it make any difference?!" All three lower their heads: "No, not really."). On the other hand, Curly stands up to the football ref by wiggling, snapping his fingers, and saying: "So, professional jealousy, eh?" (a variation from the MGM feature *Fugitive Lovers* and Curly's 1934 MGM short *Roast-Beef and Movies*). In later films Curly will "Rruff!" instead, but he has not developed that sound yet. Another pattern, the one in which Moe gives directions punctuated thrice by a nonchalant "okay" from Larry, is unique. In *Men in Black* the Stooges looked behind themselves when the midget patient said "Gee, the joint is haunted"; here they look behind themselves when Joe mentions "losing your amateur status." In the first scene Lulu did not know what "amateur status" meant either. This kind of ignorance continues to be quintessential in defining Stoogeness. Stooge ignorance often borders on irony (e.g. Moe: "If you get there first, put a check mark." Larry: "Suppose you get their first?" Moe: "Then I'll rub it out!"; and Curley: "You told me to go up from the barber shop to the red light, didn't ya? .. well that red light was a bus going to Boston!"). This film gives us Curly's most polished "gnyah, gnyah, gnyah" to date... Moe's bicarbonate gag ("Say, buddy. let me have a dime for a hamburger." Man: "Go on! You can get a hamburger for a nickel any place." Moe: "I know, but I need the other nickel for a bicarbonate of soda!") is the second (*Soup to Nuts*); there will be over a dozen more. References: The Stooges are confused for 'The Three Horsemen,' i.e. the 'Four Horsemen of Notre Dame,' so named by famed sportswriter Grantland Rice in the 1920s. The game between the 'Cubs' and 'Tigers' sounds more appropriate to baseball, but in 1934 a number of NFL teams had 'baseball-type' nicknames like the Cincinnati Reds and Pittsburgh Pirates. There is no 'Boulder Dam College,' but this film was shot (October, 1934) while Hoover Dam - known as 'Boulder Dam' until 1947 - was being built (1933-36).

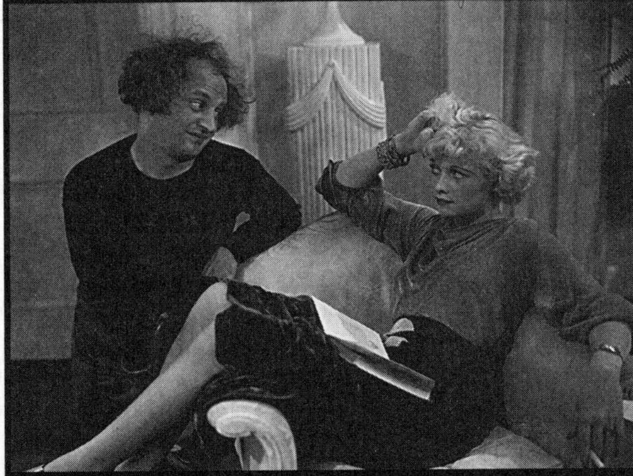

Lucille Ball's appearance is a landmark in Stooge lore. In James Gregory's *The Lucille Ball Story*, she is quoted as saying, "I didn't know what I was getting into with the Three Stooges! They were very nice. But that pie in the face and seltzer up the nose - you know, you can take just so much of that!" Ed Shifres (*The Three Stooges Journal* #67 [1993] 8) records: "The only thing I ever learned from them was how to duck!" But *Okuda* (8) records: "Working with Leon Errol and the Three Stooges was my first training in slapstick and real physical comedy. And I very much appreciated training with some real greats."

OTHER NOTES: Like *Men in Black*, this film has another parody title, now at the expense of Disney's *Three Little Pigs* (1933). In *Fugitive Lovers* Moe said: "Who's afraid of the big bad wolf?" also from *Three Little Pigs*. As in the previous three films, theme music appropriate to the film - in this case, it is a march - accompanies the introductory credits. The same theme will be used a few months later for a Columbia feature with a college-setting, *The Most Precious Thing* (released June 5, 1934); it was probably written for that film. It should be remembered that at the time film-scoring was in its infancy, Harry Cohn's Columbia had precious few dollars to spend on newly composed music, and the short-subject unit had even less. For a detailed study of the music in these early Stooge shorts, see a series of articles by Richard Finegan in *The Three Stooges Journal* in 1998.The football sequence was shot at Gilmore Stadium, then home of the Los Angeles Bulldogs and now the site of CBS Television Studios. The football players were members of the Loyola University team, for whom Director McCarey used to play. As promised, the stadium was empty of fans - not to preserve the amateur status of the 'Three Horsemen' but because Columbia would not pay for any extras; in fact, the second joke about 'amateur status' was inserted to account for the empty stadium. Moe recollected that the Stooges stubbornly refused to shoot the sequence in which they and the photographers are tackled by the entire defensive squad. Director McCarey argued that the Stooges knew how to take falls and that they had never used stunt doubles before, but the trio stood its ground. When the scene was shot, two of the stunt doubles sustained broken legs and the four original photographers each sustained broken limbs. Because the Curly double had to wear so much padding, he was uninjured. Larry [erroneously] recollected that Curly broke his leg in the dumbwaiter sequence and that Joseph Young [Pete] broke Larry's tooth when he punched him. Molly is played by Phyllis Crane, who played Anna Conda in *Men in Black*. Walter Long [Joe Stack] played villains in D. W. Griffith's *The Birth of a Nation* and *Intolerance* and opposite Rudolph Valentino and Laurel & Hardy. The scene with the Stooge children was edited out of the conclusion, but we will see Stooge children again in several later films—*Creeps* and *Outer Space Jitters*. Billy Wolfstone played the young Curly. We never see what happens to the car after the Stooges release its parking brake and send it rolling down the hilly street.

1935

Horses' Collars • Restless Knights • Pop Goes the Easel

Uncivil Warriors • Pardon My Scotch

Hoi Polloi • Three Little Beers

#5 - HORSES' COLLARS

Studio: Columbia

Released: January 10, 1935

Running Time: 18"01'"

Credited Production Crew:

Directed by:	Clyde Bruckman
Story & Screen play:	Felix Adler
Photography:	John Boyle
Film Editor:	James Sweeney

Credited Cast:

Moe Howard	
Larry Fine	
Curley Howard	
Dorothy Kent	Nell Higginbottom
Fred Kohler	Double Deal Decker

Uncredited Cast:

Fred Kelsey	Hyden Zeke
Leo Willis	Lobo
Allyn Drake	dancer
Charles 'Slim' Whitaker	cowboy
Nelson McDowell	bartender
Milton Douglas	waiter
June Gittelson	Larry's dancing partner
Alice Dahl	dancer
Nancy Caswell	dancer
Bobby Callahan	drunk

PERSPECTIVE: This first 1935 release repeats the basic concept Moe invented for *Punch Drunks* – Curly over-responds to stimulus, but Felix Adler developed it into a precedent-setting milestone. The first of many Columbia Stooge shorts to take place in a location other than Los

Angeles, *Horses' Collars* begins with the Stooges as detectives in the East and then sends them to impersonate cowboys in the West. It is structurally the first bi-partite, or two-part, short. *Woman Haters* had a circular ring composition (beginning and ending at the Woman Haters club). *Punch Drunks* developed in linear fashion from restaurant to training to boxing ring, *Men in Black* was episodic, and *Three Little Pigskins* had three parts (street, apartment, football game). The advantage of the two-part structure of *Horses' Collars* is that it establishes the Stooges in one comic scenario from the outset, and once that setting is milked for its relevant humor, it leads to a second and completely new scenario which takes its perspective by either depending on or contrasting with the first. Ambitious beer delivery men can turn into inept golfers, crude carpenters can produce explosive Scotch, and Eastern detectives can become Western cowboys. Stooge comedy has many facets, but this new kind of absurdly juxtaposed scenario couples will provide many reliable narrative foundations for comic settings in the future.

Horses' Collars is also the first film in which the Stooges rescue a damsel-in-distress, the lynchpin that unifies the two scenarios here. The Stooges have flirted with women in almost every film thus far, but rescuing a damsel-in-distress gives the story direction and climactic focus. In the unique sequences at Decker's saloon, the Stooges illustrate how confident and competent they can be for once. Usually they are utterly inept, but here they outdraw Decker with their pistols, burn Lobo's chaps and retrieve Decker's wallet. Then their luck and their talents run short, so they get conked, beaten, and strung up. Now any true hero suffers adversity before the ultimate triumph. What distinguishes Stooge heroes is that as they work toward their rescues they busily encumber themselves with idiocy and fall victim to their own incompetence. Paradoxically, it is both despite and because of their ignorance, physical oddities, and inability to be together for more than a minute without hitting one another that they ultimately triumph. Here, they have a mission to accomplish. And thanks to Moe and Larry getting knocked unconscious, Curly's acute myophobia and the wrong arm in the wrong sleeve, they crack the safe in Decker's office and rescue Nell and her I.O.U.

By inventing the prototype for the Stooge heroic triumph, Felix Adler also creates some of the quintessential tensions underlying Stooge comedy. While the Stooges bungle their way towards a rescue and make us laugh at their incompetence and imbecility, they remain serious about themselves, insufferably confident in their competence and intelligence, and focused on their mission. But they ultimately triumph, thereby reaffirming their unique, endearing, heroic stature.

VISUAL HUMOR: This film is a showcase for Curly's expanding repertoire of quirks and physical movements. Besides his myophobia, Curly acts tough ("Sort of a toughie, eh?") to Decker (*Three Little Pigskins*); gives a finger wave to Decker; shakes his leg when Decker shoots at him; whisks his hand by his ear (*Nertsery Rhymes*) at the second shot; and gives his first full-fledged handwave when Decker walks off with Nell. He experiments, too. When Moe bonks him he quickly spirals down and up. And after he smells the Limburger, he shakes his legs in the air and moves backwards on his elbows and shoulders – a prototype of the chicken-with-its-head-cut-off gag. Decades later, Moe explained that Curly often invented such movements when he forgot his lines and ad-libbed. The two-men-in-the-coat routine, a Stooge first, is enhanced by speeding up the film, adding clear and crisp punching sounds, and dubbing in Curly's repeated "Woob-woob-woobs," the longest string to date. Larry usually offers at least one excellent solo per film. Here he takes Decker's $5 gold piece and walks off: although Moe grabs his hair, Larry keeps his body going. Moe's slaps now often occur with a verbal exchange, e.g. when Larry flips the spoon: "I missed!" Moe: "I didn't!" (SLAP); and Larry & Curly: "It's Nell!" Moe: "Miss Higgin-bottom to youse guys!" (DOUBLE SLAP) For Moe slapstick serves mostly as punctuation; it works well because his timing is so good and his hands are so fast. Many of the Stooges signature routines evolved gradually. In *Myrt and Marge*, for instance, Ted Healy had a verbal response to Jackson's "Who are these gentlemen?" Healy: "Gentlemen?" In *Men in Black*, the Stooges looked behind themselves when the comatose midget said, "Gee, the joint is haunted." In *Punch Drunks*, they looked behind themselves when Joe Stack mentioned "loosing your amateur status." Now here, finally, they look behind themselves when Nell calls them "Gentlemen"; this will become the standard Stooge response. The Stooges continue to develop unison and patterned movements. This is the first Stooge bar scene, and after they take their drink they all gasp, grimace, wriggle, fall backwards onto the floor (*Woman Haters*; *Men in Black*), rise again and brush each other off. Other Stooge firsts: Their heads appearing one above the other from around a corner; one Stooge asking another Stooge's dancing partner if he can cut in but then dancing off with the Stooge instead of the partner; making fun of a man with a toupee; flinging something (in this case the toupee) onto a seated drunk; and gunplay at a bar. Making fun of ugly and fat women will become a staple throughout the Stooges' tenure at Columbia. Here they do both: Moe ridicules the photograph of Heyden Zeke's wife (Moe: "Which is her face?"); and Larry asks a fat woman, apparently sitting in a chair, to dance, but when she stands we see there is a man sitting underneath her, who wipes his forehead in relief. Those trademark sound effects that make the Stooges' slapstick humorously silly instead of sympathetically painful, are beginning to be heard with every contact. One of the new effects for the dance routine is the kettle drum used when Larry's rotund partner (June Gittelson) bounces him off her belly. On the dance floor Moe and Curly back into each other, Moe slaps Curly, Curly smiles and shakes Moe's hand, Moe slaps Curly again, so Curly turns around to resume dancing but gets slapped by his partner. This sort of dynamic, with a non-Stooge slapping a Stooge, originated in the Healy days (*Plane Nuts*). Curly turning the radio dial instead of the safe lock derives from the Marx Brothers' *Duck Soup* (1933). Other variations: Curly hiding himself in the safe (the couch in *Woman Haters*); and using celery as a weapon (*Dancing Lady*; *Woman Haters*). John Boyle's photography varies the Stooges' screen persona by panning from face to face when they explain their plan to Nell.

VERBAL HUMOR: Just as the camera pans from Stooge to Stooge, Felix Adler's script is separating verbal gags into triadic patterns, creating several Stooge firsts, including the 'Yes! yes!' routine (Moe: "Now you listen to me." Curly: "Yes." Moe: "Decker's wallet has a chain on it." Curly: "Yes! yes!" Moe: "Tell Larry." Curly: "Why, certainly!"), a variation of the "yes, yes, yes, yes, yes" Curly says on the phone in *Men in Black*. Adler's script also includes an internal rhyme (Hyden Zeke: "*My* wife!" Moe: "*My* error!") and puns (Nell: "Are you good detectives?" Curly: "You see that 'heel'? I ran that down!"; Larry (about to be hanged): "You guys are stretching this too far!"). This is the first Columbia Stooge short to use humorous signs, especially at the beginning of a film ('HYDEN ZEKE,' 'FREE LUNCH - 25¢ A PLATE' and 'DOUBLE DEAL'S FIVE 'D' DELIGHT - DICE, DANCING, DAMES, DRINKING, & DUNKING'). Other firsts: Moe complementing another Stooge's ignorance (Moe: "Sometimes you got brains." Larry: "Don't let 'em go to your head!"); a favorite bar

Curley will call on Moe and Larry often, but this "Moe! Larry! Cheese!" in *Horses' Collars* (1935) is both the first and classic example. This sequence, modeled after the over-stimulation motif Moe invented for *Punch Drunks*, demonstrates how the Stooges and the Columbia staff excelled at not only developing new gags but varying and enhancing them in subsequent films. In this case the cheese gag masks the narrative success of the film, casting the Stooges as the most unlikely and incompetent of heroes. The camera here isolates the trio amidst a simple but convincing final destruction.

gag (Larry: "It's a tin roof." Curly: "It's on the house!"); and the dance small talk (Moe: "You know, you're not a bad dancer." Curly: "Ahh, I'll bet you tell that to all the boys!"). Dancing is usually accompanied by small-talk exchanges like the ones here (Curly: "You know, you're not a bad dancer yourself." Moe: "Are you insinuatin'?" Curly: "No, just dancin'... I'm not much on leadin', you know... I'll bet you tell that to all the boys!"). The hanging scene offers a physical/verbal three-pattern (Lobo grabs Moe: "That's silk, you know!" Larry: "I gotta go home!" Decker stares at Curly: "Wait for me!"). Moe speaks laconically to Hyden Zeke ("Go on boss, your story's gripping me!") just as Larry said lazily "Okay...okay" in *Three Little Pigskins*. Nell was also the name of the (unseen) woman in *Men in Black*; the name was also used for their stage act in *A Night in Venice*. In *Plane Nuts*, the Stooges started using "rat" as an insult; here we get an exchange (Larry: "Every time he sees a mouse, he goes crazy." Zeke: "Why?" Moe: "Because his father was a rat!"); in later films we will get variations. A yielding gag à la *Three Little Pigskins*: (Curly: "If you was alone I'd punch you right in the nose." Moe: "Well, why don't you do it?" Curly: "Well, I'm with ya'!") . Other variations: Moe: "Spread out!" (*Plane Nuts*); Curly: "Nyang, nyang, nyang" (the telegram sequence in *Men in Black*); Curly's 'nyuks' away from the bar (the 'pippin' joke in *Men in Black*); and the song 'You'll Never Know' (*Soup to Nuts*).

OTHER NOTES: Like most of the Columbia shorts, this one was shot in four days. And although the shooting was in late November, 1934, the film was not released or copyrighted until January, 1935. The typical lag time from shooting to release ranged from three to six months. Director Clyde Bruckman had worked with Buster Keaton, co-directing the classic *The General* (1927), as well as with Harold Lloyd, Laurel & Hardy, and W. C. Fields, including *The Fatal Glass of Beer* (1933). This is the only Stooge film Bruckman directed, but he would write over two dozen Stooge scripts, the last in the 1950s. Fred Kelsey [Hyden Zeke] began in films in 1909, worked with Laurel & Hardy and then in the Columbia short-subject unit, and continued acting in shorts and features well into the 1950s; he often played policemen, as here. Leo Willis [Lobo] was also a graduate of Hal Roach Studios. The stunt doubles were Johnny Kascier (Moe), Bert Young (Curly), and Ed Brandenberg (Larry). The photo of the Stooges (in bathing suits) that Dorothy Kent looks at in the saloon is an [unautographed] copy of the photo the Stooges sent to Jules White from Atlantic City, pictured in *Larry*, 155. The photograph of Hyden Zeke's wife is of Louise Carver, whose gloriously hideous face we will see in later films, e.g. *Dizzy Doctors*. There is a Chicago connection: Decker's wallet has a note from Chicago, and the radio in his office picks up WGN. The bartender changes the chalkboard from "Decker 115" to "Decker 117," but when the Stooges have their drinks at the bar later the tally is still "Decker 115." Also, it is Moe who tosses the quarter in the air for Decker to shoot; when he picks up the change from Decker's five-dollar gold piece, he says to Larry, "Here's your quarter." Lastly, when Curly draws his half gun in the final scene, the pommel and trigger mechanism are clearly made of wood, and when Moe knocks him out a few minutes later, sawdust pours out of Curly's pocket; the wooden pistol is never explained. Fourteen Stooge shorts will be set in the American West, as will their feature films *4 for Texas* and *The Outlaws Is Coming*.

Along with the verbal banter and punctuating slapstick, the Stooges frequently called upon their extensive theatrical/vaudevillean experience, creating memorable moments by singing their triadic harmonies ("You'll Never Know What Love Means / Till You Cry Like You Made Me Cry")

In addition, their tenure at Columbia matched them with several fabulous dance partners, one of the best of which was the generously distributed June Gittelson dancing with Larry here on the left. But, like the "Moe! Larry! Cheese!" gag, all of this serves to move the plot and bring the damsel-in-distress to safety.

#6 - RESTLESS KNIGHTS

Studio: Columbia

Released: February 20, 1935

Running Time: 16"11'"

Credited Production Crew:

Directed by:	Charles Lamont
Story & Screen play:	Felix Adler
Photography:	Benjamin Kline
Film Editor:	William A. Lyon

Credited Cast:

Moe Howard	
Larry Fine	
Curley Howard	
Geneva Mitchell	Queen Ann of Anesthesia

Uncredited Cast:

Walter Brennan	father
George Baxter	Prince Boris of Anesthesia
Stanley Blystone	Captain of the Guard
Chris Franke	Court Crier
Billy Franey	attendant
James Howard	wrestler
Bud O'Neill	wrestler
Ernie Young	henchman
Lynton Brent	court guard
Bob Burns	court guard
William Irving	court guard
Jack Duffy,	guard
Al Thompson	prison guard
Bert Young	prison guard
Joe Perry	
Dutch Hendrian	
Marie Wells	
Eadie Adams	
Corinne Williams	
Dorothy King	
Patty Brice	

PERSPECTIVE: *Restless Knights* is set in the mythical kingdom of Anesthesia, the first of many comical geographical names spanning the globe from the Hot Sea/Tot Sea to Anemia. Its structure is like that of *Horses' Collars*; a brief introduction charges the Stooges with their mission, and then the rest of the comedy takes place in an exotic location, follows the Stooges as they successfully rescue a damsel-in-distress, and concludes as all of them fall unconscious. But Felix Adler stretches this film beyond the temporal and geographical parameters of *Horses' Collars* by setting the story back in time and across the sea in a European world of castles and royalty, thus creating the Stooges' first historical film. Historical settings will do well for the Stooges, taking them away from the familiar streets and trades of southern California and plunking them down in atmospheric sets where they can dress in silly costumes, take strange implements in their hands, confront other odd characters and struggle against wicked but farcical princes, magicians, emperors, and the like.

A short film has only a limited amount of time to spin its comedy. But whereas Laurel & Hardy take just a few gags and build them with slow burns, the Stooges, especially in these early years, move at a much brisker pace and cram many more physical and verbal gags into two reels. Rapid pacing begins right from the outset. The Stooges hit the ground running twice – first popping out from under their father's bed and then literally hitting the ground and sliding on the rug into the Anesthesian throne room. Because the expository talk with their father [Walter Brennan] and interview with the queen are physically stationary, these scenes are filled out with Adler's rapid-fire puns and the Stooges' expanding repertoire of slapstick, facial and hand gestures and

noises. By comparison, the ensuing wrestling sequence seems to move slowly; the physical nature of the wrestling diminishes the effect of the slapstick, which loses its surprise element since in wrestling you are *supposed* to slap one another, sort of. But this minor pause may be intentional, for when they finish — the queen is missing!

This leads to the multi-corridor chase scene, another important Stooge first. The scene bustles with energy, and the chase itself is quite engaging, which is particularly remarkable when one realizes how much chasing, taunting, fighting, and falling is accomplished in just three small dungeon rooms. Sets are quite important in historical settings, but despite the limited budget Columbia allotted to Stooge productions the sets for *Restless Knights* turn out to be the perfect size for Stooge action. Already in *Soup to Nuts*, it was evident how much of a stage the diminutive Stooges could fill with movement, and now they have developed the ability to scurry down ten-foot corridors and fill every inch of them with wild motions and sounds. Add a ruse, like the one that divides and conquers the three armored guards

The final scenes of *Restless Knights* (1935) offered the Stooges their first opportunity for a multi-corridor chase, a scenario that utilizes effectively their ability to scurry in small spaces and fill the screen with body movements, hand gestures, facial expressions and group postures and rearrangements. That's not to mention a variety of human noises and sound effects. They will find themselves in such tight quarters frequently. Nonetheless, victorious as these inept heroes are in this and many films, there is usually a final negative reversal; here it comes from their own clubs.

here, and you have a basic formula for rescuing damsels-in-distress, capturing crooks, and escaping ghouls and beast-men in future films. No comic actors ever mastered the multi-corridor/multi-door chase as did the Stooges.

VISUAL HUMOR: The motion that emerges from the efficiently compact bed upon which their father lies, and the triple slap their father gives them - the first in a Columbia film - is the most efficient and compact slapstick of all. This is the first Stooge film (but one of the only ones) in which every scene ends in a slapstick exchange. The final gag, the Stooges knocking each other out, is a first but will not be repeated as such. First-time Stooge director Charles Lamont is quoted in the *Scrapbook* [231] as saying, "I made them follow the script. I was never a great admirer of ad-libs," but this cannot apply to the slapstick here. At the end of the sword fight, for instance, Curly falls, handwaves, sticks out his tongue, etc. The effect of this is to keep the physical humor buzzing throughout. Curly is developing his ability to string many looks, gestures, and sounds in rapid succession. To his father he gapes, says "Woob-woob," handwaves, rubs his fingers 'tsk-tsk,' and cups his ears in eagerness. In the throne room he bends Moe's arm the *right* way - a Columbia first – handwaves, and makes faces, finally stroking the queen's hand. Other Curly firsts here include sticking out his tongue, and pivoting around one foot. Another first: getting a sword in the rear; here it is used twice for effect (Larry ducks under a thrust, so Moe gets the sword point in his rear; they shift opponents, and again Larry ducks and Moe gets that point in his rear, too). Moe rips out Curly's chest hair, which is unique, but later he will frequently rip out Larry's hair. Enhancing the slapstick is the greatest array of sound effects used to date: SLAP, SCRATCH, BONK, THUMP, SLAP, CRASH, GONG, WHIRL, AND WHISTLE. One visual gag does not involve the Stooges. "Calling All Guards!" echoes through the chain of command, and then a lone elderly man [Chris Franke] with a lonely crossbow responds: "Did you call me, your majesty?". The head butt Moe gives Larry in the stomach will be repeated (*Dizzy Detectives*). The Stooges will do more wrestling in *Grips, Grunts and Groans* and *The Three Stooges Go Around the World in a Daze* (Sumo wrestling). The coin flip in the dungeon reprises those from *Men in Black* and *Soup to Nuts* ("I never beat those guys!"). Other variations: the triple slap (*Hollywood Party, Meet the Baron*); Curly's finger snaps (*Three Little Pigskins; Horses' Collars*); the coin flip (*Men in Black*); and eating the apple before execution (*Punch Drunks*). The royal spittoon, fittingly, wears a crown.

VERBAL HUMOR: Felix Adler excelled at writing verbal gags relevant to the setting and plot. Here he makes fun of European titles (Father: "Years ago I was the royal chamberlain of the Kingdom of Anesthesia." Curly: "And mama?" Father: "She was the royal chambermaid!"; Father: "You [Larry] are the Duke of Durham, and you [Moe] are the Count of Fife." Curly: "And I the Count of Ten?!" Father: "No, you are Baron of Gray Matter."; and the Crier: "The Duke of Mixture, the Fife of Drum, and the Baron of Brains!"), the three-pattern motto à la the Three Musketeers [also varied (thrice)] (Moe: "One for all!" Larry: "All for one!" Curly: "Every man for himself!"; Moe: "One for all!!" Larry: "All for one!" Curly: "I'm for myself!"; and Moe: "One for all!!" Larry: "All for one!" Curly: "I'll take care of myself! Woob-woob!"), executions (Larry: "Maybe they'll miss us." Curly: "That'll be 'a narrow' escape!"; and Curly: "I'd rather be burned at the steak... I'd rather have a hot steak than a cold chop!"), archaic language (Larry: "Didst thou call us. m'lord?" Moe: "Yes, didst?"), and European culture (Queen: "From whence came you?" Larry: "Paris." Curly: "Show her the postcards." [French 'postcards' were considered risqué at the time]; and Queen: "And what were you doing in Paris?" Moe: "Looking over the Paris-sites!"). Stooge historical comedies almost always include anachronistic gags. Three here are automobile anachronisms: "Calling All Guards!" is a variation of the police broadcast "Calling all cars" (cf. *Calling All Curs*); 'Aoogah' was the sound of a car horn; and the three-pattern (Larry: "I'll take the blonde." Moe: "I'll take the brunet." Curly: "I'll take the black and tan!") is a reference to the Black & Tan Taxi Company which rivaled the Yellow Cab Company. Two involve bridge: Larry: "Father we shall do your bidding: two clubs!" Moe: "I double." Larry: "I redouble." Curly: "I triple!" (the three-pattern from *Meet the Baron*) and later "Maybe he trumped [the queen]!" Another bet makes fun of European currency ("Three thousand guineas." "That's a fowl bet.").

The dialogue is particularly rich. Most memorable are the repeated three-pattern oath, the longest string of "Woob-woobs" in the entire corpus [in the wine-cellar chase Curly gives out over fifty consecutive 'woob-woob's without any other human sounds intervening], Curly's very first "Rruff-Rruff!", and a splendid variation of the 'I'll get it when I'm ready!' gag (Curly: "Not me! [SLAP] Not me!" [SLAP] Moe: "Now ya comin'?" Curly: "Soitenly!"). When Moe slaps Larry and Curly, the father yells "Stop!", and Larry says, "You're too late," this is one of the rare comments made by a Stooge to a non-Stooge about inter-Stooge slapstick. The gag based on Stooge ignorance ("The guards have been lax." Moe: "We have not! We've been wrestlin'!") recalls the "losing your amateur status" gag in *Three Little Pigskins*. When Curly tells the (intentionally) worst pun of the film ("That'll be 'a narrow' escape!"), he adds "Nyuk, nyuk, nyuk, nyuk," just as he did for the intentionally horrible 'Pippin' pun in *Men in Black*. Other variations: Father: "You!" Stooges [in unison]: "Yes!" Father: "You!" Stooges: "Yes! Yes!" (*Men in Black; Horses' Collars*); Larry: "We'll guard you well, Annie." Moe: "Queenie to you!" (Larry & Curly: "It's Nell!" Moe: "Miss Higginbottom to youse guys!" in *Horses' Collars*; and "Hiya, pop!" (*Beer and Pretzels; Men in Black*; and the title of *Hello Pop!*). "One for all! ,"All for one!", "Everyman for himself" is borrowed by Clark Gable and Franchot Tone in *Love on the Run* (1936).

OTHER NOTES: The film was the last one shot in 1934 (December). The music used for the introduction of Queen Ann was the same used for the credits; Richard Finegan ['Notes on Stooge Film Music,' *The 3 Stooges Journal* 79 (1996) 4] traces it to the Columbia feature *Whirlpool* (1935), although the release date of the latter (April 10) postdates this film by two months. Music was also heard for the wrestling "dance". Director Charles Lamont, who had been directing comedies since the silent era, directed one other Stooge film, *Playing the Ponies*. He later worked at Universal directing Abbott & Costello and Ma & Pa Kettle features. Unlike *Horses' Collars*, the plot is not worked out: Prince Boris never gets punished; only his minions are knocked out.

#7 - POP GOES THE EASEL

Studio: Columbia

Released: March 29, 1935

Running Time: 18"17'"

Credited Production Crew:

Directed by:	Del Lord
Story & Screen play:	Felix Adler
Photography :	Henry Freulich
Film Editor:	James Sweeney

Credited Cast:

Moe Howard
Larry Fine
Curley Howard

Uncredited Cast:

Robert 'Bobby' Burns	Professor Fuller
Jack Duffy	man looking for clay department
Ellinor Vanderveer	woman hard of hearing
Phyllis Fine	girl playing hopscotch
Joan Howard	girl playing hopscotch
Phyllis Crane	model in tights
William Irving	man with boy
Leo White	French painter
Al Thompson	man in car

PERSPECTIVE: *Pop Goes the Easel* brings Stooge short-film comedy to a new plateau thanks to the advent of director Del Lord, who would also direct all the remaining 1935 Stooge film releases and nearly three dozen more, in addition to a number of non-Stooge Columbia shorts, until 1948, when he left the unit to make feature films. Lord's early training came as a driver for Mack Sennett's Keystone Cops, and he then directed a number of classic silent comedies starring Billy Bevan in 1925/1926. When Jules White hired him at Columbia in 1935 (Sennett had gone bankrupt in 1933; White found Lord selling used cars on Ventura Boulevard), Lord immediately began to infuse into Stooge comedy some of the visual mayhem that characterized Keystone Cops comedy. We see this already in the sidewalk chase through buckets and hopscotch game, and in Larry falling out the window, but there is no better example than the spectacularly paced clay fight - a Stooge first - which flames out from an inter-Stooge squabble to a full-scale riot among an unlikely but appropriate assemblage of character types.

The incredible energy in this climactic scene is the result of a cop chasing the Stooges into an art school. Thanks to this simple premise based on coincidence, the Stooges move from Depression-oriented street begging (*Three Little Pigskins*) to an enclosed interior, the sort of space in which they often do their best work. We do not know if writer Felix Adler can be fully credited with its invention, but by this point the character-type of the Stooge adversary – the angered, determined, vengeful bully like Joe Stack in *Three Little Pigskins*, Double Deal Decker in *Horses' Collars*, and the nameless cop here - is almost fully developed. A critically energizing non-Stooge character in countless films, the Stooge 'foil' swears to "get those guys" for something the Stooges do early in a film, thereby giving form to the rest of the comedy and motivation to the Stooges. It works in both ring composition and two-part narrative formats: the adversary threatens the Stooges who run away, duck into a building (as here) or room or the back of a truck, and in this way enter the second part of their narrative; often the adversary finds them at the end of the film for the climactic gag sequence. The only thing the Stooge adversary role requires now is the individual talents of Bud Jamison and Vernon Dent.

Between Curly's expanding physical and verbal repertoire and Del Lord's recollective Mack Sennett library of visual and physical gags, Stooge slapstick reaches previously unseen levels of variety here. We see for the first time a gouge block, one Stooge mesmerizing another before hitting him, Curly's first double fingersnap/cheekroll, a fist-game variation ("See this?"), and a classic gouge game ("Pick two!"), not to mention the overflow of Stooge slapstick into innocent bystanders: that poor French painter takes quite a shot to the jaw from Curly's hand as a byproduct of Moe smacking Curly, and in the clay fight every time a Stooge ducks someone else gets hit (WHAM!).

VISUAL HUMOR: Moe's delayed retributions are now becoming elaborate, thereby creating a very different sort of comic timing. Two classic examples are his "Pick two!" before a gouge, and his "See this?" before

The Stooges' triadic dynamic distinguishes them from other great solo and duet comedians. A trio has a wider variety of movements, and one can always play against the other two.

the fist game; the former is a Stooge first, the latter is the first variation of the prototype (*Three Little Pigskins*). The longest example is after the 'pair of drawers' gag, where Moe's gouge awaits lengthy strings of ironic utterances: ("Nyuk-nyuk-nyuk-nyuk-nyuk–nyuk–nyuk-nyuk-nyuk." Moe: "Heh-heh-heh-heh-heh-heh-heh-heh." Curly: "Nyuk-nyuk-nyuk-nyuk-nyuk-nyuk-nyuk-nyuk-nyuk.") (For the third consecutive occurrence, Curly says his "Nyuks" after a bad pun.) Moe delays again early in the clay fight when Larry pleads, "It was an accident," a phrase which will become a staple, and after the gouge block when Moe seems to give up, hands Curly the brush and bucket, and then gouges him. When Larry says "It was an accident," notice how quickly Moe backhands the clay into his face without giving the slightest hint that this is what he was planning to do. Much of the success of Stooge slapstick is owed to Moe's quick hands. Other Stooge firsts include knocking the adversary out by knocking him against the wall and having something fall on his head; knocking him down by having one Stooge

kneel behind him and another pushing him over; Larry squatting down to avoid the clay [or a pie] but Moe squatting down and slamming him; and the light spot on the painting. Another is mesmerization, where Moe tosses the kerchief, Curly bends over to watch it, and Moe knocks him down with both hands. Curly will not develop his trademark handwave mesmerization for a few years.

The costumes are wilder than ever, with Larry dressing as a swami and all three Stooges dressing in drag, one step beyond the furry negligees they wore opposite Lucille Ball in *Punch Drunks*. Larry in particular seems to take well to drag roles. The sound effects enhance particularly the sign thrown from the car onto Moe's head (KLINK), the clay fight (WHAM, WHOMP), and the "Look at the grouse!" gag, which would be impossible without the BONK sound effect. Despite the development of the gouge block and "Pick two," the gouge still has no accompanying sound effect. Other variations: taunting and tripping the cop at the entrance to the school building, and Moe's more-than triple slap (*Restless Knights*). Slapping the whole semicircle of people standing behind him, Moe gives the most elaborate multi-person slap in all of Stoogedom.

VERBAL HUMOR: The physical humor replaces the many puns of *Restless Knights*, but verbal retorts are connected with slapstick ("Pick two!"; "See this?"), props ("Give me the bird!"; "Look at the grouse!"), and gags ("Is this the clay department?"; "I said 'come in!'"). In early films the Stooges mix slapstick and an interrogation à la Ted Healy (Moe: "How do spell 'chrysanthemum'? Oh, ignorant, eh?" [SLAP] Moe to Curly. "How do you spell it?" Curly: "C-h-r-y-s-a-n-t-h-e-m-u-m." Moe: "Why weren't you here a minute ago?!" [SLAP, ARMBEND]. The grouse exchange (Curly: "I don't see any grouse." [KICK] Moe: "See any now?" Curly: "No." [KICK] Moe: "See any now?" Curly: "No." [BONK] Curly: "Oh! Look at the grouse!") is of the same verbal/slapstick pattern as the 'Are you stayin' exchange in *Three Little Pigskins* (Curly: "Not me! I'm stayin'!"[SQUIRT] I'm still stayin'!" [SLAP] Moe: "Are you stayin' now?" Curly: "I don't know now."). Both are variations of the 'yielding' motif. Curly's classic line, "Look at the grouse!" is used twice, as was the Musketeer motto thrice in *Restless Knights*. Repeated also is Moe's "Always clowning!".

Among the plot related gags are two easel puns (Curly: "You know the old saying: 'Easel come, easel go!'"; Moe: "Easel out of here!"), four brush gags (Larry [holding a double brush]: "I'm in a hurry!" Moe [holding a brush with a curved handle]: "I can get around the corners with this!" Moe: "What do you expect to do with that?" Curly [holding a small brush]: "Paint the cracks!"; and Fuller: "I'm Professor Fuller." Moe: "Oh, we've been usin' some of your brushes!"), and two 'drawing' puns (Painter: "Gentlemen, I am an artist!" Larry: "I am an artist, too!" Curly: "Oh, a pair o' drawers!"; and Moe: "You know, my old man used to draw." Curly: "Sure, he drew twenty years with one stroke of the pen!"). A Stooge first is using fake languages and accents. Moe uses French and Irish accents, and Larry lapses from swami Stooge nonsense ("Anacanapanasana-alla, cama-cama-cama-cama") into Yiddish; Larry used Yiddish in his solo stage act in the 1920s. When the cop asks Curly, "What kinda language is that?" Curly spins his fingers in loops, moves his hands back and forth, does a DOUBLE FINGER-SNAP-AND-CHEEK ROLL and a HANDWAVE. After Curly makes his hand gestures, their verbal exchange (Cop: "Oh, deaf and dumb, eh?" Curly: "Soitenly!") recalls the telegram gag ("Curly: "Nyang!" Larry: "Is that it?!" Curly: "Certainly!") in *Men in Black*. Curly also uses pig-Latin ("Ix-nay ackin'-cray; it's the op-cay.". Other firsts: During the clay fight, Curly's "Backbiter!... That's a coincidence!...Nyaggh! ya' missed me!"; "How! And how!" is used for the first time here, but in reference to Sitting Bull, not as a toast. The American slang expression 'And how!' had surfaced only in 1928. Moe will commonly use "Come on! Break it up! Get to work! Get busy here!" to end slapstick routines. Also, Moe blames Larry for falling out the window, showing an apparent lack of sympathy that is an essential part of his characterization. Moe's "I christen thee sasparilla" will turn up in *3 Dumb Clucks* as a 'sasparilla frapini." Sarsaparilla was a popular non-alcoholic root beer. Other variations: Curly: "I'm a victim of circumstance!" and Larry: "Say, if he thinks I'm going to paint this floor, I hope you drop dead" (*Beer and Pretzels*); "Gentlemen!" and "The heel has no soul" (*Horses' Collars*); "Hiya, Professor!" (*Men in Black*); "It all depends...when the king is expected home...bridge expert!" (*Restless Knights*); and the use of pig Latin (*Three Little Pigskins*). The street exchange (Man: "How long have you been starving?" Curly: "Mister, I haven't tasted food for three days." Man: "Well I wouldn't worry about it. It still tastes the same!") was a common Depression joke. References: "Oh, we've been usin' some of your brushes!" refers to the Fuller Brush Company. "The bird!" (a nose blow) was the equivalent of 'the raspberries.' Rembrandt is the famous seventeenth-century Dutch painter. Einstein, the German physicist, had emigrated to America just a few months before this film was made. 'Sittin' Bull' was the Lakota Sioux Chieftain who defeated Custer at Little Bighorn in 1876; he was known to Hollywood as part of Buffalo Bill's Wild West Show, and Moe will make reference to Buffalo Bill later in the year. Curly's "How are ya, tall and handsome? I'm glad ya' come up ta' see me!" is his imitation of Mae West's famous line in *Goin' To Town*, also produced in 1935. And Larry's Yiddish expression "Hak mir nit kain tsheinik" means 'Don't bother me' [literally: 'Don't bang on the tea kettle.']

OTHER NOTES: The song 'Pop Goes the Weasel' is used for the introductory credits. Del Lord was Mack Sennett's chief director in the 1920s. For a biography, see *The 3 Stooges Journal* 77 (1996) 6; for a photograph, see Forrester *Chronicles* 42. The girls playing hopscotch on the sidewalk are none other than Joan Howard, Moe's daughter, and Phyllis Fine, Larry's daughter. This was the only appearance they made in their fathers' Columbia films. Ellinor Vanderveer [hard of hearing woman] often played a wealthy matron in Laurel & Hardy and Mack Sennett films. The painter of 'September Morn' had a French accent, the unspoken assumption being that an abstract painter is French and that his painting is worth nothing unless they ruin it first. The painter is a fool, of course, and the Stooges often need a fourth fool to abuse. The actor who played the part, Leo White, also worked with Moe and Curly in the1934 short *Jailbirds of Paradise*. Because the Stooges in drag flirt with the op-cay, the female interest is much reduced here; there is only the flirting with Phyllis Crane at the door of the school. As in *Restless Knights*, the conclusion gets swallowed up in the comic chaos: the cop rather unobtrusively gets knocked out during the clay fight. Again the film ends with the Stooges being knocked out.

Director Del Lord, who had worked with Mack Sennett and directed several classic Billy Bevan comedies in 1925/1926, infused several important elements into Stooge comedy, particularly the visual mayhem that characterized Keystone Cops comedy. As we can see in his first Stooge film, *Pop Goes the Easel* (1935), he was fond of exterior chases (the sidewalk chase), hanging jeopardies (Larry on the window ledge), and pie fights. In this case it is the spectacularly paced clay fight which flames out from an inter-Stooge squabble to a full-scale riot among an unlikely but appropriate assemblage of character types.

#8 - UNCIVIL WARRIORS

Studio: Columbia

Released: April 26, 1935

Running Time: 19"33'"

Credited Production Crew:

Directed by:	Del Lord
Story & Screen play:	Felix Adler
Photography :	John Stumar
Film Editor:	Charles Hochberg

Credited Cast:

Moe Howard
Larry Fine
Curley Howard

Uncredited Cast:

James C. Morton	Union general
Bud Jamison	Colonel Buttz
Phyllis Crane	Judith, Buttz's daughter
Celeste Edwards	Clementine, her friend
Theodore Lorch	Major Filbert
Lew Davis	officer
Marvin Loback	officer
Billy Engle	officer
Ford West	officer
Si Jenks	officer
Lou Archer	soldier
Charles Dorety	soldier
Heinie Conklin	soldier
Jack Kenny	soldier
Hubert Diltz	soldier
Charles Cross	soldier
George Gray	soldier
Harry Keaton	soldier
Jack Rand	soldier

PERSPECTIVE: The Stooges portray crack Union spies who sneak across enemy lines and impersonate Confederate officers in this second of three Del Lord/ Felix Adler 1935 releases. As in *Horses' Collars*, the Stooges are sent on a mission which broadens their characterization: they still have to be stupid enough for Curly to burn up the espionage information and for Moe to bring in the wrong color baby, but they also have to be clever enough to sneak past two sentry posts [using the "Charlie-who-walks-like-this" gag] and avoid the intimidating scrutiny of an inquisitive Major Gilbert. Not quite the confident, smirking gunslingers of *Horses' Collars* but no longer playing the utterly confused, unadulterated idiots of *Three Little Pigskins* either, the Stooges now use their unique triadic unity - walking the thick line between genius and stupidity as they trick the enemy brass into revealing their troop strength and then eat a pot holder. When their espionage is discovered because they try to pawn off the black child as their own, they run and hide in what looks like a hollow tree, but Lady Fortune, the mother of Surprise and Comedy alike, turns the tide in their favor: blasted out of what turns out to be a huge Confederate cannon, the Stooges end up back in the Union camp, bringing the ring-composed plot to a heroic conclusion.

Although it is a historical film set during the Civil War, *Uncivil Warriors* introduces two exterior situations the Stooges will exploit for decades - saluting a superior officer while slapping each other, and traipsing through the woods while smacking each other with swinging branches. Both these gags depend entirely on triadic timing. In contrast, the film also introduces two classic interior scenarios - chewing inedible food and cooking in the kitchen - which will provide the Stooges with some of their finest moments, whether eating crab shells, walnut shells, tamales, or feathers, or preparing a stuffed turkey, can-a-peas, alum-laced punch, or an exploding birthday cake. None of these depend on rapid timing because they are 'slow-burn' gags; they cause us to laugh twice - first at the Stooges' determined ignorance in thinking this thing will be 'edible,' and then at how they or others react when actually eating it.

Uncivil Warriors also shows us how capable the Stooges are of embellishing their already innovative slapstick introduced in previous films. The 'fist game' is a mystery every time we see it. Will Moe hit it down, circle it around and hit Curly on top of the head? Will he hit it up and hit Curly's forehead? Will he ask for Curly's hand and hit that into Curly's head? Will he ask for Curly's hand, ignore it, and slap Curly anyway? Will Curly offer his own hand? All of these variants occur in this film, and they create an anticipation that is always rewarded because Moe's hand is quicker than our eye. In general Moe's paybacks are taking longer and longer to build more anticipation. Moe does nothing about it the first time Larry and Curly hit him in the face with the swinging tree branch. Why not? We find out the second time: Curly asks innocently, "What happened?" and only after Moe says "Nothin'!" and lets them relax does he give them a double slap. Stooge slapstick is not a static art. Gags are continually being discovered, explored, developed, blended, and varied.

VISUAL HUMOR: Besides the branch swinging and fist game variations, the other slapstick setup has Moe pointing to his stripes before bonking Curly. Stooge slapstick firsts: the nostril lift; the nose bite; the ear ratchet [the ratchet sound effect was already used in *Woman Haters* and *Punch Drunks*]; all three Stooges bowing and bonking heads [Larry and Curly bumped heads while eavesdropping in *Woman Haters*]; slapping after saluting; and Larry looking to Moe looking to Curly looking to no one and then looking back at Moe who looks back at Larry. They will use this last gag as late as in *Have Rocket — Will Travel,* and you can find it in *Young Frankenstein* (1974) as well. Another Stooge first: the smashed cigar. After Moe makes the joke about his father being "short," he laughs roundly with a wide open mouth and slit eyes. It is a face we rarely see from him. The sound effects are now consistently crisp, poignant and varied, even in combination routines, although a slapping sound is still used for the nose tweak. The horse replete with life-saver, rope-ladder, and anchor, is an elaborate variation of the vehicles used in the hallways of *Men in Black.* Curly raises his fingers à la Emily Post, the first Stooge reference to the etiquette guru in a Columbia short; (in *Myrt and Marge* Ted Healy noticed Curly eating with a knife and said: "Here! What would Emily Post say?"). As in one of the hallway scenes in *Men in Black,* Curly runs from the woods with a dubbed "woob-woob."

VERBAL HUMOR: Curly gives his first high-pitched "Hmm!" when he salutes Filbert, but it is quite meek. In the kitchen scene there is a brief sequence in which the camera shows us only the cake being frosted while we hear Curly's pun ("I quit that job at that bakery. I got sick of the dough and thought I'd go on the loaf. [SLAP] OW!"). This experiment will influence subsequent films. Adler offers the most memorable internal rhyme in all of Stoogedom in the classic three-pattern (Moe [Southern accent]: "I wondah if this is the right place, lieutenant." Larry: "I reckon this is the place, Captain. What do you all say, Major?" Curly: "Well if there's no other place around the place, I reckon this must be the place, I reckon!"). Adler's script also contains exchanges with puns for punchlines (Moe: "My father? Is he still as tall as ever?" Filbert: "No, he's rather short." Moe: "Well, he can't borrow any money from me, sir!"; General: "What happened to Operator 13." Curly: "He swam across the river and died of

Critics claim the Stooges do only slapstick, but nothing could be further from the truth. Slapstick serves most often merely as punctuation for the Stooges, and it often moves the plot. The Stooges had the advantage of working with skilled but clever writers at Columbia, who created interesting, compelling narratives, and terrific dialogue tailored to the trio concept. Here in *Uncivil Warriors* Felix Adler pens this enjoyable, internally rhymed three-pattern:

Moe: "I wondah if this is the right place, lieutenant."
Larry: "I reckon this is the place, Captain. What do you all say, Major?"
Curly: "Well, if there's no other place around the place, I reckon this must be the place, I reckon!"

Potomac poisoning!"; Larry: "Excuse me gentlemen, I have to take care of a weak back." Filbert: "How long have you had a weak back?" Larry: "Oh about a 'week back'!"; Filbert: "Tell me, captain: Is your wife a blonde or brunette?" Moe: "When she first married me, everybody

accused her of being very lightheaded!"; Moe: "What all did you say the name of this cake was?" Judith: "Southern Comfort." Moe: "Tastes like Southern Comforter!"; and Moe: "How's yours taste?" Curly: "Like a mattress." Moe: "Want mine?" Curly: "I'm stuffed now!"], one-liner puns ["Let's have a Nip and Tuck. One nip and they tuck you away for the night"; "I used to work in a bakery as a pilot...I use to take the bread from one corner and 'pile it' in the other"; and "I got sick of the dough and thought I'd go on the loaf"], literal interpretations [Moe: "Do you know what that paper was?" Curly: "Hot?"; and "He can smell a spy a mile away." Curly: "I'm glad he can't smell 'em any closer!"], anachronisms ["I left my horse parked in a safety zone!"; "All Union soldiers are now wearing Union underwear!"], absurdities [Curly: "I was lost! All by myself!"; Buttz: "Uncle Tom?!" Curly: "That's short for 'pappy'!"; "I baked a cake once, but it fell and killed the cat!"; and Moe: "There, there, Dixie Lou. I'll get him." Filbert: "*Him*?" Moe: "Her." Filbert: "*Her*??" Moe: "It!?"], setups to sight gags [Curly: "It ain't deep!"] as well as responses to sight gags [Curly: "If I hadn't-a helped bake it, I'd-a never known it was a cake!"; Moe: "He's molting!"; Larry: "He's been eating raw chickens!"]. The names 'Duck! Dodge! Hyde!' [originally 'Greps, Burp, and Belch!'] inspire physical gags. Moe makes some Curly-esque sounds for the first time in a Columbia short when he salutes in the beginning of the film. As in the previous *Pop Goes the Easel*, the Stooges use accents, e.g. Moe: "How deep is this h'yere river, Majah?"; and Curly: "No, you're the wrong Charlie. The Charlie we're lookin' for walks like-a this-a!". In *Soup to Nuts* Moe told Larry: "Lay down! You wanna make a fool out of the doctor?!"; here we have another joke said by a supposedly unconscious Stooge [Colonel: "She has fainted. Get her a glass of water." Curly: "No, whiskey!"]. Other variations: "Gentleman of the South, "Hallelujah! Hallelujah!" [*Plane Nuts*]; saluting in sequence and Curly saying "That's a coincidence!" and "I'm a victim of circumstance!" instead of "Low man again!" [*Three Little Pigskins*].

OTHER NOTES: The film was shot in mid-March, 1935. The working title was *Operators 12, 14 and 15.* The credits begin with 'Dixie,' yields to 'The Battle Hymn of the Republic,' and returns to 'Dixie' for the close. Film Editor Charles Hochberg had worked for Jack White at Educational Pictures and taught editing to Jules White. Hochberg grew up near the White [Weiss] family in a Hungarian Jewish enclave in Edendale, CA. The Stooges' next Civil War film, *Uncivil Warbirds* [1946], will be influenced by *Gone With the Wind.* Curly ate inedible objects in the 1934 MGM short *Roast-Beef and Movies*, where he devoured an ink well, a live goldfish, and a film canister. This is the first Stooge appearance for Ted Lorch [Major Filbert] and James C. Morton [Union General], both of whom would create a number of memorable Stooge roles in the 1930s. Lorch played in a number of adventure serials, most notably as Ming's high priest in *Flash Gordon*; Charles Middleton, who played Ming himself, will appear with the Stooges in *Spook Louder*. Morton had a long career in film comedy, working with Hal Roach [Laurel & Hardy, Charley Chase, 'Our Gang'] and W. C. Fields and Mae West [*My Little Chickadee, Never Give a Sucker an Even Break*]. A policeman used a nostril lift on Gus Shy in Vitaphone's *I Scream* in 1934. The African American baby gag is often edited for television broadcast. But many ethnic groups and minorities are used as the butt of jokes in Stooge films, including the Stooges own Jewish and Russian heritage. In this film, it is the impossibility of two white [male!] parents having that child that is the essence of the irony, not the child's race.

Director Del Lord poses with Larry and Moe during the filming of *Uncivil Warriors* in March, 1935. Lord was one of twelve directors who worked on Stooge short films at Columbia. He directed almost three dozen Stooge films between 1935 and 1948. This was his second, and in this photo he was forty years old; Larry was thirty-two, and Moe was thirty-seven.

#9 - PARDON MY SCOTCH

Studio: Columbia

Released: August 1, 1935

Running Time: 18"39'"

Credited Production Crew:

Directed by:	Del Lord
Story & Screen play:	Andrew Bennison
Photography:	George Meehan
Film Editor:	James Sweeney

Credited Cast:

Moe Howard	
Larry Fine	
Curley Howard	
Nat Carr	J.T.'s supplier
James Morton	J.T. Walton

Uncredited Cast:

Al Thompson	Jones, the druggist
Billy Gilbert	Signor Louis Bolero Cantino
Grace Goodall	Mrs. Walton
Barlowe Borland	Scot
Scotty Dunsmuir	Scot
Gladys Gale	Mrs. Martin
Wilson Benge	butler
Alec Craig	bagpiper
Symona Boniface	party guest
Pauline High	party guest
Ettore Compana	singer
Nena Compana	accompanist
Billy Bletcher	

PERSPECTIVE: Although the action of *Pardon My Scotch* takes place the day before the repeal of Prohibition on December 5, 1933, it was shot in April of 1935 and reflects the economy of 1935. By that year, the Depression economy had improved enough to take the Stooges off the streets (*Three Little Pigskins, Pop Goes the Easel*) and put them to work. They had not yet played tradesmen in a Columbia two-reeler (they played Healy's assistant plumbers in *Meet the Baron*), so first-time writer Andrew Bennison belongs in the Stooge Hall of Fame for creating a role type which would put so many hammers, chisels, and saws in the dangerously unskilled hands of the Stooges. The classic carpentry scene that opens this film was so highly regarded that it was one of the first Stooge sequences to be reused in a later film (*Dizzy Detectives*).

We saw the Stooges and a free-standing door in *Dancing Lady*, but who would have thought it could fare so well as a comedy prop? While we are busy listening to the druggist's phone conversation, it seems to float across the floor. The Stooges emerge one by one each time Jones says 'Hello' into the malfunctioning telephone, and in rapid succession the "left-right-left-right" cadence takes the door and the Stooges upstairs where they get their tools ("What tools?"), confuse themselves about which direction is "right," and saw the table Moe is standing on in half. Within seconds Curly collapses the door frame onto Moe ("Give it to me!'"), saws through the ceiling, and sends Moe all the way to the floor below. The scene helps solidify what will become a standard inter-Stooge relationship: Moe is the bossy foreman who puts himself in terrible jeopardy every time he orders the other two to "get busy." Moe really pays for his superior status; if you think Moe is too bossy, put yourself in his shoes - working with two knuckleheads who saw in half the table you are standing on, slam a door frame on top of you, stand on it, put a circular saw blade two inches from your nose, and rescue you by sending you plunging fifteen feet to the floor below. And when one of them waves defiantly at you and says, "We got you out, didn't we?", wouldn't you bonk their heads together, too?

There are many Stooge 'firsts' here, including the Stooges' introductory theme music - a version of the second chorus of 'Listen to the Mocking Bird,' ending an exploit with an explosion, Larry being called "porcupine" and Curly "grape-head," the Stooges imitating Scotsmen, and mixing up their own impossible recipe for booze. Most important for Stooge development, though, is that this is the first time the Stooges are invited to a society party, a scenario where they can fully exploit "eccentric" manners, cultural ignorance, shocking behavior, their penchant for destruction and tangible disdain for aristocratic propriety, and mores. When J.T. Walton's elegant home explodes with 'Vat 106-Plus' of the Stooges' ersatz scotch, the message is clear: moneyed society is filled with self-important beings so desperate to maintain their wealth that they ask Stooges to supply their commerce, and so poor at judging people's true mettle that they invite the Stooges into their homes. It is no accident the next film will be *Hoi Polloi*.

VISUAL HUMOR: The 'door on the right' gag illustrates how important the third person is to Stooge humor. Moe and Curly each point to the right and do wonderful takes turning their heads in stages back towards the left, but then, like Jocasta in *Oedipus Rex*, Larry ("Porcupine") comes into the argument and points in a third direction, utterly complicating the dual duel. On a more mundane level, so do the two-handed slaps Moe gives Curly and Larry. Moe bonking Curly's and Larry's heads together is a Stooge first, although previously George Givot had bonked Curly's ['Jerry Howard'] and Bobby Callahan's heads together in the 1934 MGM short *Roast-Beef and Movies*].

Other firsts: Curly being bitten by his sandwich; shooting fruit into a singer's mouth; using a Bentwood chair as a comic prop (here a strainer); and Curly acting

Whether upright or fallen, the door provides a multi-faceted prop in 1935's *Pardon My Scotch*. This is the first great tool sequence in the corpus of Stooge films.

Even though Moe broke a few ribs during shooting, the scene was so successful that it was one of the first major sequence reused in a later film - 1943's *Dizzy Detectives*.

shy when confronting a woman. We also see the Stooges' best dancing to date, including the first filmed example of the 'Curly shuffle'; two of the next three films, *Hoi Polloi* and *Ants in the Pantry*, contain some of their classic dance routines. Two other routines, the Stooges following the frantic druggist around his shop, and Larry doing a pantomime in long sleeves while eating a flower [à la Harpo Marx] will not be repeated. A number of comedians at the time, e.g. Chaz Chase and Harpo Marx, ate inedible objects for comic effect. Here Larry bathes his eye in a finger bowl, eats a flower, cuts the stem with scissors, and prepares a plate. When Moe says "Get a saw," fine editing has one whirring away in Curly's hand in a split second. The close up of Moe's horrified face as the saw whirs by is also a first, but this close-up camera position in a small interior space will not be exploited fully until 1940's *Boobs in Arms*

Curly's roll dance is modeled after a similar sequence in Charlie Chaplin's *The Gold Rush* (1924); Curly does not have the grace to match Chaplin's dancing potatoes, but then again Chaplin never gouged anybody's eyes with his. When we only hear the pineapple hitting the singer [Billy Gilbert] in the next room, it derives from the off-camera slapstick we heard during the kitchen scene in *Uncivil Warriors*. There are many other parallels with *Uncivil Warriors:* the final Scotch explosion and the final cannon blast, the society dinner party and the feather-filled, Southern Comforter tea party, the Stooges squeezing a 'Hallelujah' into their 'hoot-man' variations, and James C. Morton playing J. T. Walton here and the Union general in the previous film. The mixing scene is also derivative (*Men in Black*), but special effects expand this repertoire staple into a seething, bubbling, exploding drink. Other variations: reacting physically to a powerful drink (*Horses' Collars*); using tools (*Meet the Baron*; *Men in Black*); slapping the bread back and forth (*Woman Haters*); and walking through the unattached door (*Soup to Nuts*; *Dancing Lady*).

VERBAL HUMOR: Curly's characterization has fully evolved. What used to be an angry defiance with Ted Healy and then Moe has now become an innocent defiance. In the 'door on the right' gag, Curly says softly, "Wait a minute. The man said the door goes on the right," and after Larry points in the third direction Curly again says softly, "See?!" Similarly, he lightens up on his delivery of "What are you doin' down there?" and "I think he wants to talk to ya'." This pattern develops along with his childlike persona. The script is filled with such pattern jokes as "Hello...Hello...Hello...Hello" and "Yes...yes...yes" to the druggist, "Left! Right! Left! Right!" as they carry the door frame, "Get me a board!. Get me a board!" and "Make it six inches. Make it six inches" as they do their carpentry work, "Over the river...Skip the gutter...Ver geharget!" as they toast Martin, "McSniff, McSnuff, and McSnort" and "Hoot, hootman, Hootie hoot-hoot-hoot" at the party, and "A little faster! A little slower! A little faster! A little slower!" to the musicians. Dual exchange jokes are mostly ethnic verbal plays dependent on Stooge ignorance (Moe: "We ain't much on the Highland Fling, lady, but we sure knock 'em dead with our Lowland Shin!" Curly: "Yeah, it's the same as a fan dance only you do it in kilts!"; "Are you laddies by any chance from Loch Lomand?" Curly: "No, we're from Loch Jaw!"; and "The gentlemen are going to do their native dance." Curly: "I ain't gonna take my clothes off for anybody!") and puns about drinking (Martin: "Mix me a pick up." Curly: "He wants a derrick!"; and Moe: "This ought-a pick him up." Curly: "And lay him down too!"). Moe saying "Recede!" (as they all reach for the fruit) is a Stooge first, although Ted Healy used "Rih-cede, will ya'? Rih-cede!" in the hotel lobby sequence of *Myrt and Marge*. Other firsts: Stooge toasts (Moe: "Over the river." Curly: "Skip the gutter" Larry: "Ver geharget!"); and Curly saying "We'll have you out of this in a jiffy!" Later Moe tells Martin: "Sure, we'll have you fixed in a second!"... "Get me a board!" leaves Curly without a receiver; it and the party nudging routine that ends in "Low man again!" are variations of the "low man again" routine of *Three Little Pigskins* and the saluting routine of *Uncivil Warriors*; the "Hello" and "Yes" patterns were first seen in Dr. Graves' office in *Men in Black*. Other variations: "Get the tools!" (*Meet the Baron*); and "A winner every time!" (*Men in Black*).

References: Larry's "Lay on Macduff!" is Shakespeare *Macbeth* (5.7.63: "Lay on Macduff/And damned be him that first cries, 'Hold, enough!'"). The name of 'Signor Louis Bolero Cantino' is an ethnic parody that uses musical ('bolero') and quasi-musical ('cantino') terms to name an Italian tenor; this was an era of great Italian tenors, e.g. Caruso. The Scotsman's "It's a broad, bracht, moonlacht nacht tonacht" ("It's a broad, bright, moonlit night tonight") will be reused in *The Hot Scots*. His 'Loch Lomond' is the largest lake in Scotland and a traditional song; 'Lockjaw' is a form of Tetanus. 'Vat 106-Plus' parodies the whisky 'Vat 69.' The toast 'ver geharget!' is Yiddish for 'Drop dead!'

OTHER NOTES: The title parodies the expression 'Pardon my French'. The 'Listen to the Mocking Bird' theme will be used until 1938/1939 when 'Three Blind Mice' will replace it in *Flat Foot Stooges*, permanently with *We Want Our Mummy*. Symona Boniface plays her first of eighteen Stooge roles. The distributor is named 'Mr. Martin' in the script, but his name is not used in the film. When Moe plunged onto the table, he broke several ribs; as he stands up he is clearly in pain. Professional and committed Stooge that he was, Moe still managed to answer Curly's "What happened" with "Nothin!" and deliver a double slap. Then, we hear, he fainted and had to be hospitalized. When the guests are being seated, you can see Curly already doing his roll dance.

Pardon My Scotch is also the first film to place the Stooges in direct conflict with high society. During the Great Depression of the early 1930s, the average moviegoer despised the rich culture of the upper class, so the Stooges were the perfect trio to puncture their hoity-toity bubble. Turning an elegant party, with its own code of sophisticated manners, into a riotous brawl was to become a Stooge specialty - hence the next film, *Hoi Polloi*. The confrontation of Stooges versus society and wealth provides just one example of how the Stooge films record four decades' worth of the history of popular culture in the mid-twentieth century.

#10 - HOI POLLOI

Studio: Columbia

Released: August 29, 1935

Running Time: 18"08"'

Credited Production Crew:

Directed by:	Del Lord
Story & Screen play:	Felix Adler
Photography:	Benjamin Kline
Film Editor:	John Rawlins

Credited Cast:

Moe Howard
Larry Fine
Curley Howard

Uncredited Cast:

Harry Holmes	Professor Richmond
Robert Graves	Professor Nichols
Bud Jamison	butler
Grace Goodall	Mrs. Richmond
Betty McMahon	Nichols' daughter
Phyllis Crane	Nichols' daughter
Geneva Mitchell	dance instructor
Kathryn 'Kitty' McHugh	Curley's blond partner
James C. Morton	toupeed party guest
William Irving	party guest ("Are you dancing?")
Blanche Payson	Curley's brunet partner
Arthur Rankin	party guest
Robert McKenzie	party guest
Celeste Edwards	party guest
Harriet DeBussman	party guest
Mary Dees	party guest
George B. French	party guest
Gaile Arnold	party guest
Don Roberts	party guest
Billy Mann	party guest

PERSPECTIVE: In *Men in Black*, Felix Adler parodied the contemporary film *Men in White*, but now he advances Stooge art to a higher level by creating the first film parody of *Pygmalion*, George Bernard Shaw's 1912 play which would only later inspire two Oscar-winning films - *Pygmalion* (1938) and *My Fair Lady* (1964). Making the lowly Stooges subjects of an experiment to see whether environment or heredity was more important in forming social breeding was a brilliant match. The previous *Pardon My Scotch* had juxtaposed the Stooges and high society for the first time in a Columbia film, but there the Stooges were utter outcasts from the start. Here the idea is to integrate them into society, even if success in cultivating Shaw's Liza Doolittle is hardly the same as trying to cultivate these three. Liza does not at first wish to be cultivated because she is content with her low social status, but the Stooges are downright proud of it ("It would disgrace us for life!"). And unlike Liza's gradual enculturation, the Stooges' is slow not only because they are recalcitrant students (Moe: "Has the deer a little doe?" Curly: "Certainly! Two bucks!"), but because a bee flies down their dance instructor's dress and they cannot get along even with one another, let alone in high society. As they enter the society party Moe slaps both his comrades "in case" they do something wrong, and from that point on, after Curly pulls a thread and ruins Moe's jacket, their whole metamorphosis begins to unravel.

But it is not the society people who reject the Stooges. Except for Prof. Nichols, they all actually embrace the plebeian Stooges - laughing at their antics and even slapping and gouging each other at the end of the film. The greatest metamorphosis that takes place here is turning high society into a bunch of 'rowdies' while the Stooges themselves try to exit with top hats, canes, and stuffy accents. In this ironic reversal the Stooges ultimately learn (too late) to eschew their inter-Stooge violence while the society members learn to slug each other. Even the two professors and butler indulge in the final physical retribution against the Stooges—the ultimate act of Stoogeness. So environment wins out over heredity after all: the hoity-toity learn how to be hoi polloi.

According to this film made in the spring of 1935, members of society need to 1) eat politely, 2) have a basic education, and 3) dance correctly. As for the first, Curly almost forgot to pick up his pinkies while dunking at the feathery tea party in *Uncivil Warriors*, they all battled with celery in *Punch Drunks*, and the banquet in *Pardon My Scotch* ended up on the floor. As for the second, Moe could not spell 'chrysanthemum' in *Pop Goes the Easel* and he slapped Curly for being 'ignorant' when he could not distinguish right from left in *Pardon My Scotch*. As for the third, the Stooges did the Fox Trot in *Horses' Collars* and the Highland Fling (or Lowland Shin) in *Pardon My Scotch*. The concept of Stooge incompatibility with high society has already been developing in the last three films. But now in this third of three 1935 Lord/Adler collaborations, the Stooges have become the perfect force to unleash among the wealthy and refined. What a joy this must have been to see during the Depression.

VISUAL HUMOR: The dance lesson is one of the most famous, often shown segments from any Stooge film. Geneva Mitchell sets the scene with her graceful 'one-two-three-dip' movements back and forth across the screen, in contrast to which the Stooges crash into each other like clumsy oafs. Editor John Rawlins then cuts to the bee flying from the plant onto her chest and down her dress as she delivers the immortal, ominous line: "Now follow me closely and do exactly what I do." From a social perspective, the graceful dance instructor, like the members of high society at the end of the film, is reduced to mere Stoogedom when she loses control.

The Stooges' slapstick has developed considerably in their ten Columbia films. From simple slapping and gouging without sound effects we now regularly see slaps, gouges, bonk, pounds, ear ratchets, hairpulls, and kicks in various combinations involving all three Stooges as well as other people, many of the routines now with dialogue lead ins ("See this?") and accompanied by sound effects. This film offers even more slapstick variations, some of them Stooge firsts: Moe twice takes precautionary measures by hitting Larry or Curly before they do anything wrong (as did Ted Healy did in *Nertsery Rhymes*); the fist game gains two new wrinkles when Moe bounces Curly's fist off the table, and when Curly swings his arm around four times and then hits himself the fifth time (thanks to an additional head slap from Moe); the professor rips some of his own hair out à la Larry; Moe cutely pinches Larry's cheek before slapping him; Moe uses the gouge to get Curly's hand out of the vase; Larry walks over to become the third member of the punchbowl slapstick; a bonk on Curly's head produces stolen silverware; Curly and his large partner exchange slaps, shrug, and resume dancing; Moe kicks champagne spray out of Curly's pocket; and Curly's arm-bends are now accompanied by a fairly distinctive "Hhmm!". The supreme combination sequence comes near the conclusion where Curly offers his fist, Moe hits it and bonks Curly, Moe gouges Curly, Larry gets hit twice for asking "Where's your dignity?", Larry slaps Moe back, Moe turns and hits Curly, and then Moe beats Curly to the ground, all of which makes the professor give up and write his check to Nichols. In subsequent films we will continue to see slapstick combinations and innovations regularly integrated with turns in the plot.

Other Stooge firsts: two clothing sight gags (pulling the thread and ripping Moe's jacket, and Larry's toeless socks); Curly shaving (which also introduces the plucked string sound effect); Moe slapping Larry "in case" he might do something (twice); and Curly sitting on the couch spring and then dancing with the spring attached to his rear, the sound effect (SPRONG) for which is particularly appropriate. This gag was used by Ben Turpin in *Asleep at the Switch* (1923). Hitting someone 'in case' is found in a contemporary film, Vitaphone's *Serves You Right* (1935), starring Shemp. Other variations: Curly raising his fingers à la Emily Post (*Uncivil Warriors*); Curly fighting with the short fellow behind the curtain and out of view (*Uncivil Warriors*; *Pardon My Scotch*); hearing "Gentlemen!" and looking behind themselves (*Horses' Collars*); making fun of strange, ugly, or fat women (*Men in Black*, *Horses' Collars*); Moe slapping Larry, Larry slapping Moe back, Moe shrugging and turning to hit Curly (*Woman Haters*); and both a chain reaction fight and the Stooges getting hit to conclude the film (*Pop Goes the Easel*). Larry pretends to eat beans with a knife, a common gag in the 1930s.

VERBAL HUMOR: The Stooges do improve their manners, which allows for comic juxtapositions when they resort to their old ways. Curly properly swallows his food before speaking but then ruins it by saying the incongruous: "Say, you ain't got a toothpick on you, have you, bud?" Moe and Larry enter the final party to prove their new social status, but they have this ignoble exchange (Moe: "No liquor, no foolin' around, et cetera." Larry: "Are we allowed to smoke?" Moe: "You don't see any signs around, do ya'?"). Besides three-patterns (a gag distributed to all three Stooges), many Stooge films provide one or more sequences in which each Stooge has a line of dialogue, e.g. when Professor Richmond makes his offer (Moe: "You know it would break the old man's heart." Larry: "It'll disgrace us for life." Curly: "I won't be able to look my children in the face.") or during the reading lesson (Larry: "Oh-see-the-cat. Does the mouse see the cat? Yes, the dirty rat!" Moe: "Oh see the deer. Has the deer a little doe?" Curly: "Why certainly! Two bucks!" Curly spells 'cat': "Soitenly! K-I-T-T-Y 'pussy.'"). In *Horses' Collars* the Stooges exchanged verbal patter while dancing; here there is a most fetching exchange with a non-Stooge (William Irving) (Irving: "Pardon me, are you dancing?!" Larry: "Are you asking?" Irving: "Yes, I'm asking." Larry: "Then I'm dancing!"). Moe has his first rapid-fire passage: "I don't mean to mister-represent you and cast my law and jurisdiction upon you by usin' such high influential language, but—" Larry explains: "He means, 'It's okay'". Stooge ignorance (Curly: "It ain't the dippin'; it's the countin' that's got me!"; Blonde: "Your dancing is atrocious." Larry: "Oh, thank you!; I couldn't dance a step last year!"). Yielding gag: Richmond: "Are you ready for your lesson in table etiquette?" Curly: "*Soitenly!*..Sure.". Depression expressions: Curly: "You're all canned up!"; Moe: "Now you're all bottled up!"; and Larry: "Brother, can you spare a Nichol?" that parodied the 1932 song

'Brother Can You Spare a Dime?' written by Jay Gorney and E. Y. Harburg for the stage show *Americana*. Other references: 'Rubbish' was what was collected in the days before recycling cans and bottles. "The mystic powers of Brahma, the eternal spring" refers to Hinduism's creative force of the universe. Curly's "Maskazino cherry" is a Maraschino cherry. A Stooge first: pattern snoring, although sleeping in one bed goes back to *Nertsery Rhymes*. Another variation: Curly's "A backbiter, eh?" (*Pop Goes the Easel*).

OTHER NOTES: The film was shot in early May, 1935 and was released just four weeks after *Pardon My Scotch*. Visible in the left background of the initial exterior street scene are movie theater canopies featuring *Mississippi*, starring Bing Crosby, and *Laddie*, starring John Beal; both films were in release that spring. Dance music plays almost continuously during the party sequence, the closest to a musical soundtrack the Stooges have had since *Woman Haters*. The same music was used in a previous Columbia feature, *Broadway Bill* (1934). Mrs. Richmond actually likes the Stooges. When she says to her husband, "Nice gentlemen you brought into our house," she means it, and she defends the 'rowdies.' In *Ants in the Pantry* a whole room-full of high society people will like the Stooges. In his book Moe (88) describes how Grace Goodall got a thrown cream puff jammed in her throat, partially blocking her windpipe. But there is no cream puff fight in *Hoi Polloi*. The remake, *Half-Wits Holiday*, concludes in a creampuff fight; similarly, the photo (82) of *Hoi Polloi* is from *Half-Wits Holiday*. The incident Moe recalled took place during the shooting of the cream puff fight in *Three Sappy People*. Continuity: the short fellow, whose coat Curly took by force, has it back on for the final scene. There is an unsubstantiated rumor that Helen Howard, Moe's wife, sold the original story to Columbia. Perhaps not coincidentally, a German film version of *Pygmalion* was made in 1935. *Hoi Polloi* is based on a Shaw play, but Laurel & Hardy had parodied several operas in *Rogue Song* (1930) and *Fra Diavolo* (1933). The dance footage will be reused in *In the Sweet Pie and Pie* (1941); the story will be remade as *Half-Wits Holiday* and *Pies and Guys*.

The "new darlings of society" in *Hoi Polloi* (1935) are finally advertised as 'the 3 STOOGES'; the names 'Howard, Fine and Howard' are omitted now that they are no longer necessary.

Stooge slapstick is ever inventive. This detailed publicity photo from *Three Little Beers*, the final release of 1935, demonstrates how adept Moe was at using human appendages as a means of getting one's attention and changing their direction. Considering how many humans have existed on this planet and never considered using hands and noses this way, Moe and his colleagues were uniquely creative in using God's instruments as a means of rough comedy.

#11 - THREE LITTLE BEERS

Studio: Columbia

Released: November 28, 1935

Running Time: 16"16'"

Credited Production Crew:

Produced by:	Jules White
Directed by:	Del Lord
Story & Screen Play:	Clyde Bruckman
Photography:	Benjamin Kline
Film Editor:	William Lyon

Credited Cast:

Moe Howard	
Larry Fine	
Curley Howard	
Bud Jamison	A. Panther

Uncredited Cast:

Harry Semels	groundskeeper
Jack 'Tiny' Lipson	Jones, the foreman
Eddie Laughton	second desk clerk
Frank Terry	golfer
Nanette Crawford	golfer
Eve Reynolds	golfer
George Gray	caddy
Lew Davis	golfer
Frank Mills	golfer (lost ball)

PERSPECTIVE: In *Three Little Beers*, director Del Lord and writer Clyde Bruckman use their Mack Sennett and Buster Keaton experience to liberate the Stooges and let them roam free as never before or since. They may sacrifice plot in favor of Stooge antics on the golf course, but the Columbia unit has by now learned how to place plotless Stooge antics into a larger structure. *Men in Black* simply began and ended with Stooge antics in the hospital, but then *Pop Goes the Easel* brought the Stooges into their art school antics via the introductory street scene/police chase. Now Lord and Bruckman neatly wrap two beer-barrel episodes around the featured golf game, shooting it in non-studio California exteriors that give the film a different look and turn it into a Sennett/Keaton-like romp indeed.

The first act is confined to the loading dock where the vertical stacking and dropping of beer barrels provides the physical comedy while the film's plot develops. By the time the Stooges drop a barrel on A. Panther's head, they actually have two goals: deliver the beer and win that hundred bucks. Driving into and away from the brewery sign takes the Stooges into the center of the comedy which spreads horizontally from the 'Rancho Golf Club' lobby and locker room interiors out across the golf course where each Stooge destroys a different area - Curly the rough, Larry the green, and Moe the fairway. The last shot we see, the long shot of a frustrated Moe, dozens of divots between him and us, throwing a golf ball into the misty, almost horizonless distance, is the most expansive view in all of Stoogedom (prior to their outer space films, of course) and contrasts wonderfully with the verticality of the first act. Spatially and narratively, the Stooges have reached the end of the golf episode. They flee by driving to another beer-barrel scene which blooms horizontally, vertically, and diagonally when barrels roll down and up the hills of Edendale [Silver Lake], scattering people and cars, and leaving the Stooges confined and horizontal in wet cement.

Though its impact is easily ignored, spatial arrangement is such a critical element in Stooge films that it often dictates the style of comedy. Here horizontal expansion on the golf course extends so widely that it separates the Stooges, temporarily subduing the noise of the film. Without inter-Stooge puns, insults, slaps, gouges, or triadic unity, the Stooges cease to be the 'Stooges' and become three separate comedians. This gives Curly the opportunity to shake, rev, and "Hhmm!" himself into a tornado of frustration the likes of which we have not yet experienced; it puts Larry into that silent, determined, professorial mood we see periodically; and it gives Moe the chance to play the simplemindedly optimistic ignoramus who assumes his golf stroke is getting better because his divots are getting smaller. What unifies the Stooges at the end of this sequence? The Italian groundskeepers scurrying about, shouting in funny accents, and overreacting to the Stooges' false bravado. And in the finale, too, the Stooges get scattered by the rolling barrels and then unified by wet cement. Now as confined as they were separated earlier, even with Moe's hand being 'stuck,' together again they return to 'normal' Stoogedom with one good slap to the face.

VISUAL HUMOR: The incredible range of vertical and horizontal movement and the structured variations

between confinement and expansion make this film one of the more visually memorable Stooge episodes: the golf course and barrel-rolling sequences offer Stooge physical comedy its widest and steepest backdrop. The finale was shot in hilly Edendale because Del Lord knew the lay of that land from his Mack Sennett days (the Sennett Studios were very near), and beer trucks and rolling barrels had been used in Buster Keaton's *What No Beer* (1933). The camera angle expands the perspective in which we see this broad comedy. When the Stooges show their PRESS-PRESS-PULL buttons, the camera shows us the clerk's point-of-view and gives us a close-up of Curly's finger wave. The film editing quickens the pace in which the comedy unfolds when Moe swings the broom like a golf club at the loading dock, when Moe swings three clubs at a time on the fairway, and when the Stooges abruptly appear from the lounge with their PRESS-PRESS-PULL buttons. The slapstick exchange at the 7th tee is a carefully planned, well executed ballet requiring three men to perform sixteen different slapstick movements in ten seconds. This is the most elaborate slapstick combo to date:

> Moe slaps Larry and goes to gouge him, so Curly grabs his arm, Moe turns to Curly and gouges him instead. He goes back to Larry who covers his eyes. Moe slaps him in the forehead, and when Larry holds his forehead Moe goes back for the eye gouge. They do this twice, at which point Curly nyucks. Curly now protects himself by putting one hand on over his eyes and the other on his forehead, but Moe pounds him in the stomach and bonks him in the head. Moe makes a fist, Curly slaps it down, and it circles around to slap Larry in the upswing and bonk Curly.

Stooge firsts: Moe saying his arm is stuck before striking; and Moe slapping Larry's neck too far in one direction, then slapping it back to normal. The latter is unique. As for the former, the contemporary Vitaphone film, *Serves You Right* (1935) contains a similar motif at its conclusion when Shemp's enemy is stuck: once Shemp says, "That's all I want to know!" he gets even with him. Moe blames first Larry and then Curly for the ball that hits them all on the head, just as he blames Larry for falling out the window in *Pop Goes the Easel*. Other variations: Moe bonking Curly to make contraband fall out of his jacket, and the use of a truck lever to create a larger physical gag (*Hoi Polloi*); Moe waving Larry on, Larry waving Curly on, and Curly waving on no one (*Uncivil Warriors*); and the Stooges looking behind themselves when the clerk says "gentlemen" (*Horses' Collars*).

VERBAL HUMOR: In *Hoi Polloi*, Stooge ignorance was an integral part of the plot; here it thrives because Bruckman packs the script with plot-related ignorance, i.e. what the Stooges do not know about golf. (Curly: "What

The extreme verticality of the beer-barrel scenario...

do we have to do?" Moe: "Shoot golf." Curly: "Ohhh, hunting!"; Golfer: "I shot a birdie yesterday." Moe to Curly: "Say, Jasper, what did you shoot yesterday?" Curly: "I shot seven yesterday but they wouldn't give me the money!"; Golfer: "Hey you! Fore!" Curly: "Five!" Larry; "Six!" Moe: "Seven!"; Curly: "'Trap?' What do they catch around here?" Golfer: "Pests!" Curly: "Oh, they got them around here, too?"; Larry: "This looks like a kids' game: they're wearin' short pants!"; Moe: "Whadya know! We're right in the middle of one." Larry: "The middle of what?" Moe: "A golf place!" Curly: "I don't see any golfs. [BONK] Look at the golfs!"; Curly: "Wait! How we gonna shoot golfs without guns?"; Golfer: "Quiet, please!" Moe: "Oh, ya got secrets, eh?"; Golfer: "You're supposed to follow us." Curly: "We don't follow nobody!" Moe: "I should say not! Come on, fellas, a lot of open ground around here. Let's go this way!"; Moe to Larry: "Grab a bag of bats, killer!"; Curly: "A washin' machine! I didn't know it was Monday!"; and when Moe's ball rolls into the hole: "Just my luck!". This utter ignorance of the game of golf is counterbalanced by the confidence they exude (Larry: "Those guys are just beginners"; Moe: "It's a cinch to win that hundred bucks!"). The Stooges have not exuded this much confidence since *Horses' Collars*, although there they really were competent (at times). A different plot-related gag is the first 'press' gag' (Clerk: "Are you members of the press?" Curly: "I used to be, but I didn't do any pressin'. I went through the pockets. Sort of a dry

...contrasts thoroughly with the extreme horizontality of the golfing scenario. To enhance the spatial contrasts, the three individual Stooges spread themselves all over the course–a rare moment when the separated Stooges are equally effective as the grouped trio. This exterior publicity still has remained popular for decades.

cleaning!"). Columbia firsts: Curly singing to himself, although it is not yet a full 'La-dee!'; and Moe: "Oh, gettin' personal, eh?" (Ted Healy used the latter in *Nertsery Rhymes*). References: Larry's "Washee shirtee?" imitates a Chinese launderer; Moe's 'Lady Godiver' [Lady Godiva] was the 11th-century wife of Leofric, earl of Mercia, famous for riding naked through the streets of Coventry [England] to win tax relief for the citizens; the Stooges will meet her in *The Ghost Talks*. The silverware-producing head bonking from *Hoi Polloi* now becomes a golfball-producing head–bonking accompanied by cleverly vague dialogue: (Curly: "Oh I did not!" Moe: "You did not what?" Curly: "I still didn't!") This pattern is the defiant Curly at his best. Another clever use of language helps them exit the golf sequence (Curly: "He's pointing to where you are." Moe: "You mean he's pointing to where I *was*!"). Other variations: "Sold to the man with the spittoon haircut" (*Plane Nuts*); and "Look at the golfs," referring to 'Buffalo Bill,' and using two ethnic accents [Chinese and Italian] (*Pop Goes the Easel*).

OTHER NOTES: The film was shot in mid-October and released in late November, 1935, but the date on the golf flyer is, curiously, December 1935. The title screen of *Three Little Beers* contains three drunken bears, referencing the Mother Goose origin of the film's title. This is the first Stooge film to have producer Jules White listed in the credits. Bud Jamison is listed in the credits for the first time as well, even though his role in the film is not central. Writer Clyde Bruckman, who directed *Horses' Collars*, would go on to pen over 30 Stooge shorts. This is the first of over two-dozen Stooge roles for the British born Eddie Laughton; Laughton also toured with the Stooges, playing their straight man in live performances. A few years later W. C. Fields shot an extended golfing scene in *The Big Broadcast of 1938*. Moe also wore his 'dapper' white shoes in *Woman Haters*. Continuity: the shot of the Stooges running up the hill towards the barrels has Curly on the right, but running down he is on the right, too.

1936

Ants in the Pantry • *Movie Maniacs* • *Half-Shot Shooters*
Disorder in the Court • *A Pain in the Pullman* • *False Alarms*
Whoops, I'm an Indian • *Slippery Silks*

#12 - ANTS IN THE PANTRY

Studio: Columbia

Released: February 6, 1936

Running Time: 17"39'"

Credited Production Crew:

Associate Producer:	Jules White
Directed by:	Preston Black [Jack White]
Story & Screen Play:	Al Giebler
Photography:	Benjamin Kline
Film Editor:	William Lyon

Credited Cast:

Moe Howard	
Larry Fine	
Curley Howard	
Clara Kimball Young	Beulah Burlap
Douglas Gerrard	Lord Stoke Bogis

Uncredited Cast:

Harrison Greene	A. Mouser
Hilda Title	secretary
Bud Jamison	Professor Repulso
Isabelle LeMal	Eleanor
Vesey O'Davoren	Gawkins, the butler
Anne O'Neal	matron
Phyllis Crane	debutante with mouse on her back
Al Thompson	her partner
Helen Martinez	maid
Robert "Bobby" Burns	dancing guest
Lynton Brent	his companion
James C. Morton,	guest
Arthur Rowland,	guest
Charles Dorety,	guest
Bert Young,	guest
Lew Davis,	guest
Ron Wilson,	guest
Arthur Thalasso,	guest
Elaine Waters,	guest
Althea Henly,	guest
Idalyn Dupre, ,	guest
Stella LeSaint,	guest
Flo Promise, ,	guest
Gay Waters,	guest
Eddie Laughton,	guest

PERSPECTIVE: In recent films, the Stooges have tended towards mischief rather than heroics, and in *Ants in the Pantry* they are at their most mischievous. Playing exterminators who will be fired if they do not solicit work, they inject pests into an aristocratic home and offer themselves for hire. This method of motivating the Stooges by giving them 'one last chance' at their job is credited to two new principals, writer Al Giebler and director Preston Black (a.k.a. Jack White, Columbia short film department boss Jules White's older brother), and it will be used in a number of films. This plotline's advantages are that it immediately establishes the Stooges as incompetent, creates tension between them and their angry, threatening boss, and then gives the film a driving comic momentum to meet the boss's ultimatum. Comedy often thrives when ultimata and time limits are imposed. In this case the victim is the home of a woman trying to impress her wealthy guests; in *Pardon My Scotch* and *Hoi Polloi* the Stooges had wreaked havoc in wealthy homes, but in neither film was the reason for their havoc so compelling. Now it is fear of losing their jobs that energizes the Stooges to destroy Beulah Burlap's lovely home.

When the Stooges enter a wealthy home they usually insult the upper class. Not here. After pestifying the house, the Stooges chase a mouse from guest to guest, do wild dances (introducing the 'Cossack Dance'), pound on feet with a hammer, and, after cats meow to Professor Repulso's rendition of a Strauss waltz, dismantle a piano in the destructive climax. But the guests all laugh at this!

By having the guests laugh, Giebler and White sacrifice a central element of Stooge comedy - tension between the Stooges and their victims. Usually Stooge destruction angers onlookers and makes them huff, puff, fume, and threaten, and this tension increases the comedy. In *Hoi Polloi, a* few guests laughed at the Stooges' antics, but there the point was to turn the Stooges into gentlemen and gentlemen into Stooges, so the guests began to act like Stooges. Here and in general, *we*, and not the other cast members, are usually the ones laughing at Stooge destruction. But Giebler and White change the formula as well as the direction of the plot. Because the gossipy Eleanor embraces the Stooges' 'vaudevillean entertainment,' the pretentious Beulah Burlap, desperate to conceal her pest problem from Eleanor, must now also laugh even though the Stooges are ruining her house. Never mind the moths in the closet and the mouse on Lord Stoke Bogis' foot. What is essential for Mrs. Burlap is that her sophisticated guests think highly of her, her home, and her party. Since her guests think the Stooges are entertaining, she finds herself in the unlikely position of rewarding them for ruining her house, and so she invites them to participate in the hunt. As viewers we get to enjoy both the Stooges' destructive antics as well as Beulah Burlap's folly, and our amusement is confirmed by her guests' laughter.

Leaving behind the pest-removal premise and eliminating the initial narrative tension, Giebler and White move the denouement out of the house entirely and hastily offer two new conditions. One is that suddenly and unaccountably Curly has a cold, perhaps the most abruptly introduced personal condition in the entire Stooge corpus, the sole purpose of which is to have him blow his nose like a hunting horn. The other is Curly's inability to distinguish a fox from a skunk, one last confirmation that these Stooge exterminators do not know their pests. The Stooges - and their horse - faint and make a quick exit.

VISUAL HUMOR: The man falling from the ladder descends from above the camera frame, increasing the comic surprise. [A similar technique was used when Curly punched McGurn up and out of the camera frame in *Punch Drunks.*] Without a word, the same fellow takes the ladder back and causes the unexpected fall for Curly

and Moe, which is then blamed on Larry. The 'Cossack Dance' is filmed here for the first time. Larry made an individual attempt at one in *Three Little Pigskins*, but he failed and the others did not join in. Larry combined violin playing and a 'Russian' dance for his stage act until 1925, when he joined Ted Healy, Moe, and Shemp. Other Stooge firsts: one Stooge kissing another Stooge by mistake (Moe: "I'm poisoned!"); and Moe trying to grab Curly by the hair. (Moe also makes a verbal gag about Curly's baldness: "Brush the hair out of your eyes and get goin'!"). Result shot: Larry emerging from the piano with his head covered by strings and hammers. Giebler uses one plot-related prop: Larry holds a bear trap, so Moe gives him "a bear hand" slap. The lunacy is restrained audibly. The sound effects are dull when Larry hits Curly (and others) with a hammer, when Moe tweaks Curly's tongue and nose, when Moe gouges Larry's eyes, and when Curly's hand gets caught in the suitcase. There are no mouse sounds, no cake stuffing sounds, even the piano destruction scene is rather muted, and there is not one "woo-woo" in the film. A new variation of the fist game: Moe uses Larry's fist to circle around and hit Curly. "Cutting the cards" with a cleaver derives from the Marx Brothers' *Horse Feathers* (1932). Other variations: Larry losing his pants (*Restless Knights*); Moe stuffing cake in Larry's face for laughing about the cake stuffed into Curly's face (the clay fight in *Pop Goes the Easel*); Moe blaming Larry for something someone else did (*Three Little Beers*); and ending the film with the Stooges smelling a foul odor and fainting (*Horses' Collars*).

VERBAL HUMOR: Stooge firsts: a reference to Napoleon (Moe: You got a head like Napoleon!"); Larry: "I can't see! I can't see!" Moe/Curly: "What's the matter?" Larry: "I got my eyes closed!"; Larry: "It was a great fight! What happened?"; and Moe: "What does this room remind you of?" Larry: "The reform school!" (Ted Healy made a passing reference to a reform school in *Nertsery Rhymes*). We hear the first 'nonchalant' joke, a joke delivered by the Stooges trying to act inconspicuous (Larry: "Say, whatever happened in 1776?" Curly: "What street?" Larry: "Skip it!"); the joke itself, but not the nonchalant delivery, was used in *Nertsery Rhymes*. Stooge ignorance takes center stage when the boss, who has "a head like Napoleon," calls the Stooges "dumbkopfs," and in the extended conversation with the butler, which uses Moe's first malapropism ('conspicerous') to set up Curly's Latin neologism ('No-canna-spic-angulus') and the old Oxford gag used previously in *Myrt and Marge* (Moe: "What school did you go to?" Curly: "Oxford!" Moe: "Well you better go back to high shoes!"). Yielding patterns (Curly: "What does he think I am, a rat?" Moe: "Yeah, what about it?" Curly: "Well, he doesn't have to tell everybody"; and Curly: "Not me! (NOSE TWEAK) I'm not goin'! (TWO-HANDED SLAP; KICK) A hunting we must go!"). A verbal version of the 'eating inedible things' motif: (Curly: "I never felt better in my life." Larry: "I knew it! I didn't put enough rat poison in this cheese!"). Moe correcting Curly with a familiarity of his own (Curly: "You can depend on us, toots!" Moe: "Whadya mean gettin' familiar with the dame? [to Mrs. Burlap] Don't pay any attention to him, babe!") goes a step beyond Moe's "Miss Higginbottom to youse guys!" in *Horses' Collars*. Other variations: Moe: "Lend a hand!"

Curly: "Which one?" (*Punch Drunks*); Mrs. Burlap saying "What are these?" and making the Stooges look behind themselves ("Gee, the joint is haunted!" in *Men in Black*); Curly's fondness for "Camembertie" (*Horses' Collars*); and Moe calling Larry "Rain in the Face" ("Chief Belch in the Face" in *Nertsery Rhymes*). Epithet: Moe calls Curly "puddin'-head". References: A 'broadtail coat' is made of very soft unborn lamb skin. 'Oxford' is the famous English university; 'oxfords' are low shoes. Rain-in-the-Face killed General Custer. The secretary's reference to the New Deal ("They're in there talking politics. I just heard one of them say 'Let's have a new deal.'") is their first joke about contemporary politics. Franklin Roosevelt announced the 'New Deal' when he accepted the Democratic presidential nomination in 1932, but 1936 was the year in which Roosevelt's programs came under heavy fire from opposition leaders, members of his own party, and the Supreme Court. This film was shot in mid-December, 1935. The Stooges will continue to satirize contemporary politics for four decades.

OTHER NOTES: The release title is an 'expression parody' of "ants in the pants." The working title was *Pardon my Ants*. Director Jack White, like his brothers Jules and Sam, grew up in Edendale near the Mack Sennett Keystone Studio; Jules and Jack worked for Sennett as child actors (Jules recollected [Bruskin 39] the irony of being a Jewish child cheering the KKK in *The Birth of a Nation*), but Jack was already directing at age 18. 'Jack White Comedies' became nationally recognized, but with the advent of sound films he quit Educational Pictures and never attempted to regain his former prestige. He worked periodically as a director and writer for younger brother Jules at Columbia until the 1950s. He used the pseudonym 'Preston Black' until *Back to the Woods* (1937); in the midst of a divorce, he made the name change to hide his income. Clara Kimball Young [Beulah Burlap] and Douglas Gerrard [Lord Stoke Bogis] were both silent screen regulars. Gerrard mostly played support, but Young was so successful as a leading lady between 1912-1925 that she started her own production company. In 1935 she was attempting a comeback. The same plot concept will be used in 1951 for *Pest Man Wins*. The Stooges were seen smoking cigarettes previously in *Three Little Pigskins* and, to a lesser extent, in *Uncivil Warriors*; they played cards in *Meet the Baron*. In his book, *Moe* [81] says that during filming a container of red ants broke open in his pocket. He "scratched and squirmed and slapped" himself as the ants bit him, but the director thought it looked great on camera.

One of the routines Larry Fine brought to the trio was the 'Cossack Dance,' first filmed in 1936's *Ants in the Pantry*. In vaudeville Larry played the violin while doing a 'Russian' dance at the same time. The story is, that when Ted Healy asked Larry to join Moe and Shemp in 1925, Healy offered him $90 per week, "or $100 if you forget the violin." In MGM's *Dancing Lady* (1933) Larry played the piano, and in 1934's *Punch Drunks* he played the violin that drives Curly crazy. It is obvious in these and even later years that Larry had very quick feet.

#13 - MOVIE MANIACS

Studio: Columbia

Released: February 20, 1936

Running Time: 17"13'"

Credited Production Crew:

Produced by:	Jules White
Directed by:	Del Lord
Story and Screen play:	Felix Adler
Photography:	Benjamin Kline
Film Editor:	William Lyon

Credited Cast:

Moe Howard	
Larry Fine	
Curley Howard	
Mildred Harris	leading lady'
Kenneth Harlan	leading man'
Bud Jamison	Fuller Rath
Harry Semels	Director Cecil Z. Swinehardt

Uncredited Cast:

Lois Lindsey	sound stage girl
Althea Henly	sound stage girl
Antrim Short	cameraman
Jack Kenny	studio employee
Charles Dorety	studio employee
Elaine Waters	studio employee
Hilda Title	script girl
Bert Young	assistant cameraman
Eddie Laughton	grip
Eve Reynolds	

PERSPECTIVE: In the wake of the archetypal *42nd Street* (1933) and 1934's *Dancing Lady*, the 'backstage' musical became such a popular film genre that it spawned sub-genres. The year after *Movie Maniacs*, David O. Selznick's *A Star is Born* earned an Oscar for its rendition of a Hollywood 'backlot' drama, so Del Lord's and Felix Adler's *Movie Maniacs* should now be recognized as one of the first 'backlot' comedies. It is a parody, but whereas *Men in Black* parodied the contemporary film *Men in White*, *Movie Maniacs* satirizes the entire gamut of film studio personnel – from studio executives and their staff to dictatorial European directors to melodramatic actors to lot guards and even studio lions. In 1936 there may have been a lot of chuckling among actors and raised eyebrows among executives as Moe says, "There's a couple thousand people in pictures now know nothin' about it. Three more won't make any difference."

In running the Carnation Studio the Stooges assume the same exaggerated bravado they used in *Horses' Collars*, *Pop Goes the Easel*, and *Three Little Beers*, where their group confidence enabled them to defy villains, insult experts, and challenge authority. In the saloon scene of *Horses' Collars*, though, the Stooges really were expert shots. It was in *Pop Goes the Easel* (Larry: "I'll show you guys a picture what is a picture!") and *Three Little Beers* (Larry: "Those guys are just beginners!") that they fully developed their bungling personae and began to demonstrate how utterly inept they could be at what they boast as an area of expertise. Stooge viewers may agree with Moe ("Colossal!") in preferring the Stooge version of that romantic film being shot on Stage 7, but virtually everything the Stooges do is wrong - walking onto a live set, lighting a match on an actor's leg, replacing the lead actor and actress, and treating the director so insultingly that he quits (or is fired - it is hard to tell which). But true Stooges are determined; they always assume the rest of the world is wrong. Moe says it best: "I think our genius ain't appreciated here." So they carry on, proving that they are so ignorant of even the studio lot that they run into the lion enclosure.

The Stooges play would-be masters of a film world they hardly dominated. Their perennial box-office successes and Academy Award nomination for *Men in Black* the year before had not earned them even a pay raise. They were studio players at Columbia, nothing more. In fact, the short film unit was across the street from the main lot. The parody of *Movie Maniacs* is then doubly ironic: the Stooges, intimidated by Columbia President Harry Cohn, would never get a pay raise, let alone run the studio.

Perhaps it is just as well. In *Movie Maniacs* the more they take control of the Carnation Studio the worse things get for the Stooges themselves. By the end of the film they are physically chased off the lot and end up being chased and maybe even eaten by a studio lion. But what delicious irony! Three actors who made a career of making Stooge films ruin the film-within-the film by being stooges. The success of *Movie Maniacs* is, paradoxically, that the Stooges ruin the film.

VISUAL HUMOR: An important Stooge first is the pattern in which Moe senses something behind him but blames it ("What are you growlin' about?") first on Curly, then Larry, and only then finds out the truth. This pattern will be used frequently when confronted with large animals, beast men, and criminals. Other Stooge firsts: sleeping at the opening of a film; a pancake hanging from the ceiling; their gas stove hopping into the air when ignited; the pencil/larger pencil/huge pencil gag; Moe catching Curly's extended tongue between his teeth; ironing (i.e. ruining) pants; Moe 'correcting' his slap ([Moe slaps Curly on the back of the head] Curly: "You wouldn't hit me like that if I was Gable, would you?" Moe: "No, like this!" [Moe hits him on the forehead]); and Moe telling Curly, "Use your head" but then kicking him in the rear. Beginning with *Cookoo Cavaliers*, Curly will literally "use his head". Curly is beginning to use his arms more expressively. We see this when he stands behind the actress and

'plays' her part with his arms; and for the first time he does an 'x-wave' - waving his hand back and forth like a checkered flag.

Del Lord was particularly fond of extended slapstick routines. Here in a well rehearsed routine, Bud Jamison [Fuller Rath] offers his hand to Curly who is tipping his hat, Curly puts his hat back and offers his hand, but Rath has already withdrawn his, so Rath then reoffers his hand to Curly, but Curly is tipping his hat again. This type of routine, at least as old as Buster Keaton, will have its apotheosis with Curly's swearing-in scene in *Disorder in the Court*. Also well orchestrated is the champagne drinking scene: Curly drinks directly from the bottle, so Moe grabs it from him and drinks while Curly 'machine-guns' him with his derby. Curly takes back the bottle and drinks. Moe slams the derby onto Curly's head, which makes Curly squirt the champagne all over Moe. The latter is a Stooge first. Visual subtleties: the studio guard silently opens Rath's door and realizes the Stooges are welcome guests; a 'fooler opening' (when the camera pulls back from the pedicure close-up to reveal Curly in drag); Moe slaps the wig off Curly's head, but Curly immediately catches it; Larry knocks on the door and then goes *out*. Variations: sleeping in one bed (*Nertsery Rhymes*); Curly's finger-snaps (*Pop Goes the Easel*); posing the studio guard, and Curly in drag (*Pop Goes the Easel*); Curly kissing Larry (*Ants in the Pantry*); the derby machine-gun (*Woman Haters*); and running away to conclude the film (*Three Little Pigskins*).

VERBAL HUMOR: Like the carefully orchestrated slapstick, Felix Adler deftly created two intricate, triadic verbal exchanges (Moe: "Do you suppose that puddin'-head kicked us?" Larry: "How could he? He's sound asleep." Curly: "Certainly I'm still asleep." Moe: "Then how come you're talkin'?" Curly: "I'm talkin' in my sleep!"; Swinehardt: "I quit!" Larry: "You can't quit!" Swinehardt: "And why not?" Moe: "'Cause you're fired!" Curly: "You can't fire him!" Moe: "Why not?" Curly: "He quit!").

Many gags refer to Hollywood films and filmmakers. The name 'Cecil Z. Swinehardt' parodies Cecil B. DeMille and Eric von Stroheim; 'Fuller Rath' parodies a tyrannical film executive (e.g. Harry Cohn); and 'Carnation Pictures - from Contented Actors' applies a well-known commercial slogan ('Carnation Milk - from contented cows') to an industry in which the "cows" were anything but contented under the studio system. Curly's "Mutiny on the boxcar" refers to MGM's *Mutiny on the Bounty* (1935), and Larry's "Kiss me, my Calaban!" refers to the character in Shakespeare's *The Tempest*, also the name of a film starring John Barrymore in 1927. Larry's "A bad beginning is a good ending" sounds like a Hollywood studio motto; it plays on two proverbs, "A good beginning makes a good ending" [Heywood] and "A bad beginning is a bad ending" [Euripides]. Rarely are punchlines given to non-Stooges, but because of the Hollywood setting Adler could not resist one exchange (Rath: "Prepare an office and see that they have every thing they may possibly want." Assistant: "Yes, sir! I'll order three blond secretaries!"). Curly's "If at first you don't succeed, keep on sucking 'til you do suck-ceed" adds a California touch when it is punctuated by smashed citrus. This line also parodies a well known expression (as do film titles like *Disorder in the Court* and *Oil's Well That Ends Well*). Other references: Curly's "The face from the barroom floor" derives from Hugh D'Arcy's famous poem 'The Face upon the Floor' (1887); the phrase was also the title of a popular song. The kissing sequence uses three baseball metaphors: "hit-and-run type," "sort of a stolen base idea," and "with me it's a sacrifice." Moe's "I wanna look the berries when I go into the movies" is 1930s slang. Curly's "I used to be a corker" is a pun; a 'corker' refers to something remarkable, and

it follows close after the 'toast' pun ("I don't like toast. That black stuff gets in my teeth!")

Stooge firsts: Moe: "Tell me your name so I can tell your mother." Curly: "My mother knows my name"; Curly singing "Lah-lah" (while making the pancakes); Curly delivering a punchline in an annoyed tone of voice ("I'm talkin' in my sleep!"); Moe asking Curly a question but silencing him before he can respond (Moe: "Tell him what we know about kisses... That's enough!"); and Curly plucking his eyebrows (with pliers) while saying "He loves me; he loves me not". The exchange about the train furniture (Larry: "I wander who lent us this furniture without knowin' it." Moe: "If the cops get us you'll find out.") assumes some sort of criminal activity, like the reform school gag in *Ants in the Pantry.* Curly first used "Hhmm!" in the saluting sequences of *Uncivil Warriors*. It has now become a regular part of his non-verbal vocabulary. Epithets: "porcupine" and "puddin'-head". Other variations: Larry's "It was a great fight" (*Ants in the Pantry*); "Pick two!" (*Pop Goes the Easel*); Curley's "I'll bet you tell that to all the girls!" (*Horses' Collars*)

OTHER NOTES: *Movie Maniacs* was released February 20, 1936, just two weeks after *Ants in the Pantry.* It was shot, however, in late October, 1995, two months before *Ants in the Pantry.* In one draft the script had an alternate ending: the Stooges burn down the studio. The title screens contain art deco lettering and Hollywood searchlight beams. No longer will the title screens include a figured cartoon as in all the previous shorts. The two credited leads in the romantic drama are Kenneth Harlan, who often played leading men in the silent era, and Mildred Harris, who is best remembered as Charlie Chaplin's first wife (played by Milla Jovovich in 1992's *Chaplin*). *Ants in the Pantry* also featured two stars from the silent era. As for the reference to Clark Gable in the beginning of the film, the Stooges had acted with Gable at MGM two years earlier in *Dancing Lady* (photo of the Stooges on Gable's lap in *Moe* 54) and recently parodied Gable's *Men in White* (1934). Also, Gable's *It Happened One Night* (1934) was a Columbia production. This is the only Stooge 'backlot comedy' set in Hollywood; *Three Missing Links* involved movie making on location. Nothing ever comes of the baking powder in the pancake except the big bubble. The actress Curly kisses calls him "Mr. Howard". Curly and Larry, not stunt men, break the chair. The kissing sequence is often edited out for TV broadcast, as is Curly putting the paper money down the actress's dress. The lions' den may have been inspired by 1933's *Roman Scandals.*

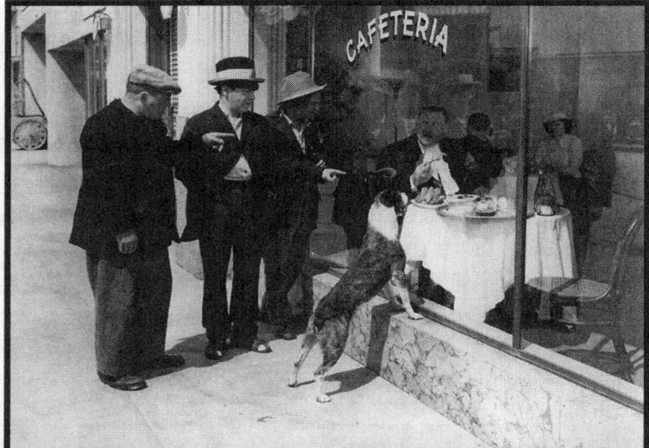

These photographs from *Half-Shot Shooters* also illustrate wonderfully the ability of Stooge writers and directors (here Clyde Bruckman & Jack White) to move the plot while the Stooges perform their inimitable type of physical comedy. Their antics outside the restaurant window anger Dent, so he comes out to slug them, and off they go into the army for the next scenario. This not only gives the film a change of venue for Stooge comedy, it also brings the narrative full circle back to the army and the vengeance of Stanley Blystone's sadistic Sergeant McGillicuddy.

Enter Vernon Dent (1895-1963). Gaining most of his film experience with Harry Langdon at Mack Sennett Studios, Dent brought his talents to more than five dozen additional Stooge shorts. His characterizations ranged from tyrant to simpleton, and his emotions flashed as quickly as his takes from dead pan to surprise to anger. Along with Bud Jamison and a few other actors, Vernon Dent helped solidify the unity of the Stooges by giving them a common foil. *Half-Shot Shooters* (1936) is his first appearance in a Stooge film.

#14 - HALF - SHOT SHOOTERS

Studio: Columbia

Released: April 30, 1936

Running Time: 18"35'"

Credited Production Crew:

Associate Producer:	Jules White
Directed by:	Preston Black [Jack White]
Story & Screen Play:	Clyde Bruckman
Photogrpahy:	Benjamin Kline
Film Editor:	Charles Hochberg

Credited Cast:

Moe Howard	
Larry Fine	
Curley Howard	
Stanley Blystone	Sergeant McGillicuddy
Vernon Dent	man in restaurant

Uncredited Cast:

Harry Semels	officer hit by tomato
Edward LeSaint	examining officer
Johnncy Kascier	soldier hit with Curly's salute
Charles 'Heine' Conklin	officer
Lew Davis	recruiting officer
Eddie Laughton	man leaving recruiting office
Bert Young	soldier

PERSPECTIVE: In three films [*Horses' Collars*, *Restless Knights*, *Uncivil Warriors*], the Stooges have already played a self-contained trio which ultimately, however unorthodox their methods, defeats the bad guys. *Half - Shot Shooters* is the first and only film in the entire corpus in which the Stooges are themselves the victims of the bad guys and do not triumph in the end. It is a credit to the Columbia short film unit that the Stooge corpus contains many experiments; the Stooges would never have become so successful if they did allow for experiments. But in the sense that the Stooges are beaten, tortured, and killed, this a painful film to watch. To see the Stooges receive black eyes, a broken arm, and damaged ear drums; to find them intentionally starved; and then to see that they have been ultimately blown to smithereens by a ten-inch artillery shell shot at point-blank range tests the gray area between slapstick comedy and sadism.

Tipping the balance towards sadism is the stark plot which proceeds merely in series of retaliations: the sergeant kicks, punches, and bends the Stooges into two black eyes and a broken arm as retaliation for sleeping on the job; the Stooges retaliate by ripping, gouging, slugging and kicking the sergeant with their bare hands, a board with protruding nails, and a French-speaking mule; a restaurant diner retaliates for a stolen chicken by slugging Moe twice and thumbing Curly in the eye; and then later the sergeant retaliates by deafening, starving, and then killing the Stooges. Another sadistic element is the enjoyment everyone finds in inflicting pain. The diner laughs as he tricks the Stooges into enlisting, the Stooges thrill at slamming nails into the sergeant's rear and getting him kicked by a mule, and the sergeant laughs at his detonation test torture and smiles as he lowers the artillery at the Stooges.

It is not uncommon for comic protagonists to suffer such violence. Cartoon characters receive this kind of abuse all the time and even end up on crutches and in bandages from head to toe. Chaplin, Buster Keaton, and Laurel & Hardy also find themselves on the short end of violent treatment; the latter's *Two Tars* [1928] is a fine example of this type of retaliation comedy, even if their cars suffer the most damage. But there are significant differences between the violence in *Half-Shot Shooters* and all other Stooge films, especially the effect and duration of the violence. The typical Stooge slap, bonk, or gouge is virtually painless and lasts only a second. Any retaliation is equally brief and benign; Curly and Moe will have retaliation bouts with slaps, arm-bends, gouges, and hand-waves with downward thrusts, but any apparent anger is immediately dissipated as the plot quickly reasserts itself. But Sgt. McGillicuddy dishes out real and lasting pain. There is nothing ephemeral about a broken arm, and breaking that arm was a mean-spirited act, as were the punches, board swipe, mule kick, gun shot, and artillery execution. Real harm was meant with every blow. And these acts of violence are not secondary to the plot; they *are* the plot. Moe's broken arm is particularly illustrative of comedy's gray area. To quote the comedy expert [Alan Alda] in Woody Allen's *Crimes and Misdemeanors*, "If it bends, that's funny. If it breaks, that's not funny." The sergeant bends Moe's arm the wrong way, and it breaks. In other films an angry Curly bends Moe's arm the *right* way, and we take it as an intentionally harmless, silly delight.

VISUAL HUMOR: The sadistic coloring leads the Stooges into new ground which they will visit again. This film offers the first example of a non-Stooge bonking Stooge heads together, and of things [rifles] falling onto Stooge heads. The mean-spirit of the film plays havoc with Moe's characterization. He is meek and submissive in several scenes - he does not even slap the restaurant diner [Vernon Dent] back - and yet while in the trenches and the recruiting office he slaps at Larry and Curly with evil intent. His role as boss is upgraded here to something more sinister. The group work around the big gun is energetic and cleverly orchestrated, Curly makes some fine gesture/noise combinations throughout the film, and Larry in trying to remove the spittoons from his hands (after the 'result shot') does some accomplished clown work.

Moe and Curly knocking themselves out is a first, although in *Restless Knights* Moe and Larry knocked each other out. Moe offering the sergeant his hand and then attacking him dates back to *Pop Goes the Easel* and to Ted Healy in *Plane Nuts*. As the previous film comes to a close, the Stooges may be about to be eaten by the lion, but we cannot be sure and it would be off camera. The only other examples of the Stooges getting killed at the end of a film are the anti-Nazi films.

Curly snapping his fingers on the sergeant's lapel is unique, as is Larry giving the sergeant a kiss, though Bugs Bunny often kisses his adversaries. The Stooges sleeping while standing by the gun is a first, although the Stooges start the film sleeping and Curly slept on the job in *Punch Drunks*. Shemp was knocked out of his shoes in Vitaphone's *Serves You Right* (1935). Other variations: the Stooges sleeping at the opening of the film, the collapsing bench, and the 'fooler opening' (the camera pulling back from the foreground recruiting poster) (*Movie Maniacs*); shoes and socks with holes (*Hoi Polloi*); Stooges begging on the street (*Three Little Pigskins*); and doing the saluting gag twice (*Uncivil Warriors*).

VERBAL HUMOR: Clyde Bruckman wrote several gags to set up the violence, e.g. (Sergeant: "So! You're still yellow!" Curly: "Not me! I'm in the pink!" Sergeant [punching Curly in the eye]: "Now you're in the black!"; Curly: "I'm a stowaway." Moe: "Well stow this away!"; and Curly: "For two cents I'd punch you right in the face!" Diner: "Well here's the two cents." Curly : "Well, I raised my price!"). The latter is a 'yielding gag,' as is (Larry: "Pipe down you guys, you're spoilin' the whole war for me." Moe: What of it? Larry: "Nothin', I was just sayin'."). The aiming sequences are varied by singing a triadic 'Gun Range Okay,' shouting "left"-"right," and imitating football signals (*Three Little Pigskins*) and an auction bidding ("Sold to the man with the Curly-locks!" (*Three Little Beers*). Stooge firsts: Curly: "His mother and my mother were both mothers!"; and Moe's "I'll murder ya'!" Moe's "No bullet's goin' through that skull" is the first reference to the thickness of Curly's skull. Also, Moe hitting Larry and saying, "Then go back to sleep and keep quiet!" will lead soon to "Wake up and go to sleep!".

References: The 'New Deal' joke from *Ants in the Pantry* has its first offspring: (Officer: "Would you fight for this great republic and—" Moe: "Republican, nah, I'm a democrat." Curly: "Not me! I'm a pedestrian!"). Of political orientation also is Moe's "Every time you think you weaken the nation," although baseball manager John McGraw was known to say "Don't think - you weaken the team!" Historical is Curly's 'Lafayette we have come,' from a speech given by Charles Stanton for General Pershing during World War I (July 4, 1917) on behalf of the A.E.F. (American Expeditionary Forces). French gags (Moe: "Vive la France!" Curly: "Bon soir, monsieur!" Larry: "Bon-seur, mon-soir!" and Moe's "Jete a pied! ['Kick him'] Give!" to the polyglot mule). Curly's "I'm in the pink" was a popular expression of the period; it means "to feel good." Moe's "Time marches on!" became a popular expression from Westbrook Van Voorhis' narration for *The March of Time* newsreels which commenced showing in 1935; the NBC radio version began in 1930. One of the less successful comic rou-tines the Stooges use on occasion is to have characters mishear each other. Here the deafened Stooges confuse 'born,' 'torn,' 'horn,' and 'corn.' Also weak is Curly's forced "expec-to-rate in the army". Moe's "I don't know where that one landed, but I hope you didn't hit the pool room!" recalls Ted Healy's "Now the pool rooms are empty" from *Plane Nuts*. Other variations: mixing French with Yiddish (*Pop Goes the Easel*); "Right!" "Right!" "Everything all right?" (*Dancing Lady*); and 'You'll Never Know' (*Soup to Nuts*; *Horses' Collars*).

OTHER NOTES: Printed versions of the title contain a hyphen ("Half-Shot Shooters"), but the title screen of the film itself does not. The film was shot in mid-March, 1936. The title screen has a geometrical sunrise pattern; the production credit screen looks like a geometrical target. For the last time the names of the Stooges appear one after another. This is the first Stooge short that does not have a significant female presence, which may intensify the retribution violence. Continuity: Moe's broken arm works fine when the Stooges beat the sergeant shortly after their discharge; the pistol blast deafens them for the interview with the other officer, they hear him say "Attention!" perfectly at the outset - so they can do their saluting routine. Later the starving Stooges are brought a box of tomatoes which serves little purpose other than to supply a missile for the sergeant to throw in the general's face. Its only narrative purpose is to set up the spittoon scene. Moe's white-brimmed hat seems to be his looking-for-work hat. He wore it when portraying a 'lost man' in *Three Little Pigskins* and *Pop Goes the Easel*. In *Buck Privates* (1941), Abbott & Costello 'accidentally' enlist in the army, and one of the recruiting office sergeants is Stanley Blystone.

#15 - DISORDER IN THE COURT

Studio: Columbia

Released: May 30, 1936

Running Time: 18"01'"

Credited Production Crew:

Associate Producer:	Jules White
Directed by:	Preston Black [Jack White]
Story and Screen Play:	Felix Adler
Photography:	Benjamin Kline
Film Editor:	William Lyon

Credited Cast:

Moe Howard
Larry Fine
Curly Howard

Uncredited Cast:

Susan Kaaren	Gail Tempest
Bud Jamison	defense attorney
Harry Semels	prosecuting attorney
James C. Morton	bailiff
Edward LeSaint	judge
Eddie Laughton	assistant defense attorney
Dan Brady	juror
Bill O'Brien	juror
Hank Bell	clerk
Nick Baskovitch	man in hallway
Arthur Thalasso	man in hallway
Ed Mull	man in hallway
Al Thompson	policeman
Solomon Horwitz	audience member
Tiny Jones	

PERSPECTIVE: After the previous experiment in retaliatory violence, this well-known Jack White/Felix Adler film breaks new ground by putting the Stooges into a courtroom parody, bringing them back to the more harmless style of comedy that had been so successful for them in the mid-1930s. Courtroom parody was a natural choice. Adler had already written parodies of hospital (*Men in Black*) and 'backlot' films (*Movie Maniacs*), and courtroom dramas were already a staple of Hollywood films: MGM's very first all-talking film was the courtroom drama, *The Trial of Mary Dugan* (1929).

Perhaps the direct inspiration for this plot was Paramount's *The Canary Murder Case* (1929), which Adler brightens with the question 'Who killed Kirk Robbin.' Childish nursery rhymes find their way periodically into Stooge films (as already in MGM's *Nertsery Rhymes*), and this easily recognized variation on 'Who Killed Cock Robin' sets the entire film into motion. The murderer in the original version is the sparrow 'with my bow and arrow,' so later in the first scene of the film we meet a second ornithological character - Polly, the parrot, who insists "Read the letter!" It is this same parrot who in the final scene will reveal the real killer, 'Buck Wing,' a name which hints at both the nursery rhyme and bird imagery as well as the dancing nightclub milieu the Stooges bring into the courtroom. Felix Adler skillfully leads his narrative from the nursery rhyme to the Stooges playing childish games, and from the swinging 'vernacular' of the jazzy set to the letter press to the pistol back to the parrot and Buck Wing's confession: "I killed Kirk Robin, and not with my little bow and arrow." Keeping it light-hearted and airy, Adler/White add several Stooge sequences involving non-Stooges, most notably Curly's swearing-in procedure.

The latter captures Curly at his most brilliant, demonstrating how effectively he portrays mental confusion, natural shyness, a whining temper, and hand-waving defiance. In this set piece lasting over two minutes, Curly has the rare opportunity for a slow burn, and because Moe and Larry are not involved, he has no option but to do what he is told despite the contradictory instructions to "raise your right hand!" and "take off that hat!"

This is just one example of how this setting gives the Stooges an opportunity to play swinging musicians who have no respect for courtroom procedure but a sure sense of justice. That justice prevails only after the

Stooges play tic-tac-toe on the D.A.'s rear, launch a bass bow, shoot a toupee, swallow a harmonica, bonk half the jurors on the head, and soak a parrot with a fire hose, is precisely what makes this film work. It maintains its narrative focus within unities of space and time while allowing the Stooges to abuse the normally somber courtroom atmosphere. Nothing and no one stands in their way, not the 'judgie-wudgie' who tries to establish protocol, not the DA who tries to object, and not the 'intellectual' jury. A triumphant ending results from the determination and energy the Stooges put into their efforts to prove Gail Tempest innocent. Once again they prove to be the unlikely heroes and, despite their behavior, save the damsel-in-distress.

VISUAL HUMOR: Stooge firsts: Curly defiantly waving his hand from atop his head; shooting a smoking streak across someone's scalp; and using chewing gum and a fire hose. Moe putting Curly's head in the letter press is an interesting carry over from the violence of the previous film. The hardness of Curly's head will continually be developed as a comic motif. To create the effect here, a rubber head was used as a prop.

Two of the basic elements for the swearing-in scene derive from such recent films as *Movie Maniacs* (the hand-shake/hat-tipping routine in Fuller Rath's office) and *Half-Shot Shooters* (the collapsing chair in the sergeant's office). The Stooges have already danced in many films; they used musical instruments in *The Big Idea*. The number slapstick sequence (Moe: "Well here's two-sies! [GOUGE] Here's five-sies!" [SLAP]) derives from "Pick Two" in *Three Little Pigskins*. Curly falls over the gate as he did the ropes in *Punch Drunks*). Other variations: the press wheel flying into the air and bonking Curly on the head (the rifles in *Half-Shot Shooters*); Moe telling Curly to grab his ear and then pulling him (the nostril lift in *Uncivil Warriors*); Moe trying to grab Curly's hair (*Ants in the Pantry*); Curly rapidly knocking a number of people out, and Larry losing his violin (*Punch Drunks*); Moe putting his hand under Curly's chin and bonking him on top of the head, and Curly's x-wave (*Movie Maniacs*); a toupee (*Horses' Collars*); Curly's derby machine-gun (*Woman Haters*); and making fun of an unattractive female (the midget in *Men in Black*, the photograph in *Horses' Collars*).

It is in 1936's *Disorder in the Court* that Curly's head first becomes a featured prop. In this photograph it forms a duet with his derby to perform his 'machine gun' routine as the parrot, the judge [Edward LeSaint], Larry, Moe, Susan Kaaren, and Bud Jamison look on. Curly also uses his "doiby" in the masterful swearing-in routine.

VERBAL HUMOR: The script offers a variety of language styles. The 'swing' lingo (Curly: "We were tearin' up some hot swing music in the 'orchester.' Gail over there was swingin' her fans. Her sweetie, Kirk Robbin, was inhalin' a bottle o' hooch at a table, and a hoofer by the name o' Buck Wing was gettin' ready to shake his tootsies!") is contemporary; we will hear jive and bebop in *Spooks!*, *Musty Musketeers*, and *Space Ship Sappy*. Courtroom jargon, e.g. the bailiff's "Do you promise to tell the truth..." sounds like "double talk" or "pig Latin" to Curly; the Stooges use gangster jargon (Moe: "I wasted five good slugs!"); and diminutives ("two-sies," "five-sies," "courtie," "judgie-wudgie"). In contrast the judge is wonderfully deadpan ("Gentlemen, you must control your killing instincts.")

Besides the swearing-in sequence, there is another interwoven exchange (Attorney: "Address the judge as 'Your Honor.'" Curly: "Well, it was like this, My Honor—" Attorney: "*Your* Honor, not '*my* Honor!'" Curly: "Why? Don't you like him?" Judge: "Allow the witness to proceed. The court understands him." Curly: "Thanks, Courtie! You're a pal!") and a classic gag based on Curly's ignorance ("Kindly speak English and drop the vernacular." Curly: "Vernacular? That's a *doiby*!") Four-pattern (Judge: "If there are no objections." Attorney: "No objections." Defense Attorney: "No objections." Curly: "No objections [DOUBLE FINGER SNAP] Nyuk, nyuk, nyuk!"). Yielding gag (Attorney: "The action of this pistol is so hard, it would take the strength of a mule to pull the trigger." Curly: "I'm no mule!" Moe: "Nah! Your ears are to short!" [GOUGE] Curly: "So I'm a mule!"). The nursery rhyme motif appears again when Moe plays 'Did You Ever See a Lassie'.

Stooge firsts: a reference to double talk; calling a strange object "a tarantula" (later "octopus"); the parrot saying "What a night!"; and the 1776-gag (Moe: "What comes after 75?" Larry: "76." Moe: "That's the spirit!"). The bailiff's rapid, slurred delivery of "Do you swear to tell the truth, the whole truth, and nothing but the truth" recalls Ben Turpin's delivery of wedding vows in Laurel & Hardy's *Our Wife* (1931). Other variations: "I'm a victim of circumstance!" (*Beer and Pretzels*); the nonchalant delivery of the 1776 gag (*Ants in the Pantry*); the juror telling the attorney to call "Broadlane 9972 ah-fter five" ('When in Chicago call Stockyards 1234 and ask for Ruby' in *Horses' Collars*); and pig Latin (*Three Little Pigskins*).

References: 'Shuffling off to Buffalo' is the title of the well known song from the acclaimed 1933 musical *42nd Street*. 'Stradivarius' is a violin, which Larry could not possibly afford, named after the Italian craftsman c. 1700. As for Tarzan, MGM had by 1936 produced three Tarzan films starring Johnny Weismuller; Jimmy Durante played 'Schnarzan' in 1934's *Hollywood Party*.

OTHER NOTES: The film was shot in early April. The working title was *Disorder in the Courtroom*. Beginning with this film Curly's name is now spelled 'Curly,' it appears to the left (previously it was Moe's), and the title screens are redesigned: the 'sparkle Columbia' is replaced, and all three Stooge heads (l-r: Curly, Larry, Moe) appear at once in photo-drawings. This basic format will be used until 1940's *You Nazty Spy!*. Curly plays spoons, as he did in nightclubs in the early 1930s; he also tore table cloths in time to the music. Because an oversight allowed the copyrights of this film, *Malice in the Palace*, and *Sing a Song of Six Pants* to lapse without renewal, they were bundled into prerecorded video cassettes as the home video market took hold in the 1980s. These tapes (and late-night TBS broadcasts) were instrumental in keeping the Stooges visible during a period in which local television channels were playing their films less regularly and before more recent syndication on The Family Channel and then American Movie Classics. As in *Hoi Polloi* and *Ants in the Pantry*, the courtroom audience laughs at the Stooges' antics.

During the harmonica swallowing incident, Sol Horwitz, father of Moe, Curly and Shemp, makes his lone film appearance; he is the fifth person from the left. When Moe says, "I shot five holes in a divot," he should know; he created dozens of them in *Three Little Beers*. Parrots will appear again in later Stooge films walking into skulls and cooked turkeys. 'Gail Tempest' recalls 'Gale Storm' [Josephine Cottle], who was beginning her career at this time?

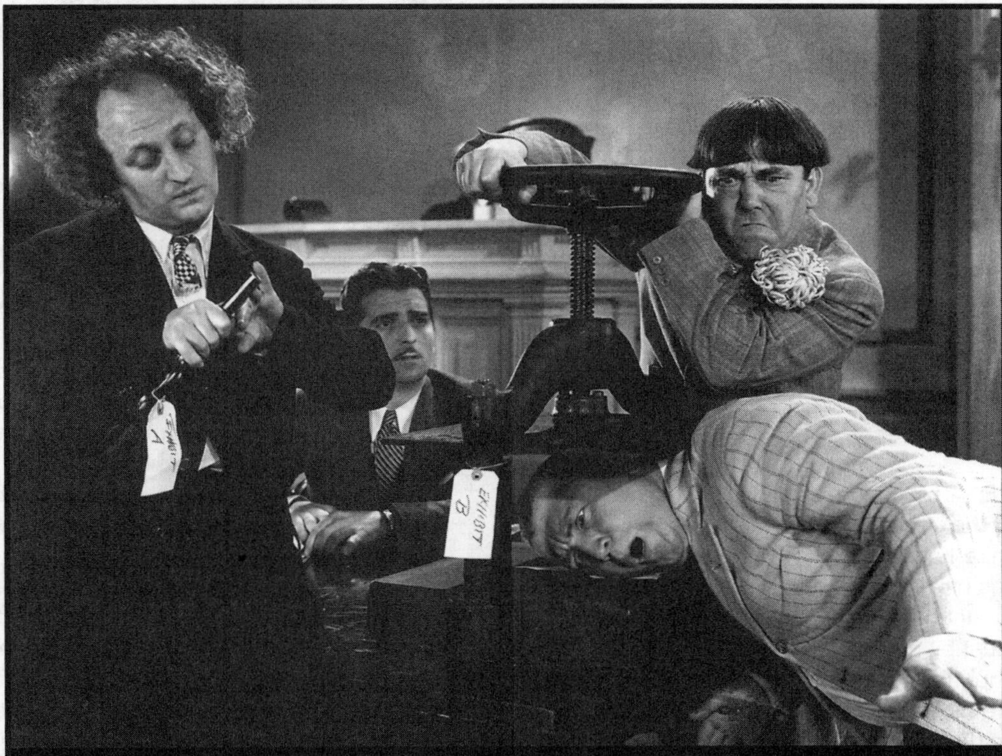

This is the first example of the impenetrability of Curly's head, a motif that will develop fully in subsequent films. Modern viewers should remember that it was only in 1934 that the Stooges began making short films at Columbia, and in 1935 that Curly (then still 'Curley') became the featured Stooge. Now in the next year, the Stooges and the Columbia artists are expanding the parameters of reality by creating an unbelievable prop that only Curly, with Moe's help, can sell on camera.

#16 - A PAIN IN THE PULLMAN

Studio: Columbia

Released: June 27, 1936

Running Time: 19"46"'

Credited Production Crew:

Associate Producer:	Jules White
Written & Directed by:	Preston Black [Jack White]
Photography:	Benjamin Kline
Film Editor:	William Lyon

Credited Cast:

Moe Howard	
Larry Fine	
Curly Howard	
Bud Jamison	Johnson
James C. Morton	Paul Pain

Uncredited Cast:

Isabelle LeMal	landlady
Mary Lou Dix	Karen, Paul Pain's companion
Hilda Title	herself, 'Shorty'
Eddie Laughton	train conductor
Phyllis Crane	sleeping woman
Robert 'Bobby' Burns	himself, man in berth
Ray Turner	porter
Loretta Andrews	show girl
Ethelreda Leopold	show girl
Gale Arnold	show girl

PERSPECTIVE: This is the first Stooge film written and directed by the same person, Jack White (a.k.a. Preston Black). White had directed the previous two releases, but this was his first Stooge script and the only one he would write until the next decade. This much control by one individual by definition limits creative input, so the 'plot' is simply this: three unemployed musicians and a monkey are hired for a traveling show but become so irritating to the manager and star that they are thrown off the train. White, who had been a very successful comedy writer/director as a teenager two decades earlier, had used a similar wild-animal-on-a-train scenario in his very first silent two-reeler, *Roaring Lions and Wedding Bells* (1917). Nonetheless, he fills out the story with 'snappy' dialogue, fast-paced Stooge scurrying, and two set pieces - the crab sequence and the sequence in which the Stooges climb into the sleeping car berth, the latter generally recognized as a classic.

Most of the previous Stooge films had been written by Felix Adler or Clyde Bruckman, so we might expect something noticeably different. One striking new approach is to have the Stooges play not salesmen or soldiers or tradesmen or doctors, but The Three Stooges. The telephone call from the Goldstein-Goldberg-Goldblatt-and-O'Brien Booking Agency is for 'The Three Stooges,' and at the train depot Moe introduces himself and his companions as 'The Three Stooges.' They recognize themselves not as movie actors but as actors doing 'comedy, singin', dancin', and snappy dialogue,' in other words, like the 'real' Stooges who continued to play live performances at least four months a year when they

were on hiatus from shooting their Columbia films. *A Pain in the Pullman* teases the viewer with what could have been a glimpse of the real Stooges' act, an updated, Ted Healy-less version of the stage performance filmed three years earlier in *Plane Nuts*. Instead, the Stooges play an unsuccessful version of themselves. What the viewer sees is a comedy troupe just happy to get a job and go on the road but not orthodox enough to get along with the romantic lead ('the heart-throb of millions') or his bruised-foreheaded business manager ("Johnson!"). But *A Pain in the Pullman* was never intended to be a documentary or a realistic portrait of road life with the Stooges. It is a fantasy of what the Stooges could do if put on a train with a monkey and a stereotyped collection of theatrical types. If the Stooges can play incompetent exterminators, artists, golfers, and detectives, they can play incompetent actors, too, as they will in several subsequent films.

Drawing on a comedy scheme of the silent era, White plays his part in developing the importance of the Stooge foil. During the past two years the angry foil has been developing as part of the Stooge formula. In *Men in Black* a variety of patients and hospital staff were Stooged upon; in *Horses' Collars* it was treacherous Double Deal Decker and his gang; and *Half Shot Shooters*, which Jack White directed, concentrated mostly on the cruel sergeant who gets so fed up with the Stooges he ultimately kills them. *A Pain in the Pullman* is another 'antics comedy' like *Men in Black*, but White concentrates Stooge foolery on two foils, actor Paul Pain and manager Johnson, and turns them into fools. The

monkey rips off Pain's toupee twice, the Stooges eat his lunch, and then the monkey climbs into his pajamas. "Johnson!" he yells six times, and "Johnson!" is woken up six times, each time smashing his head into his berth's low slung ceiling. Thanks to Jack White, now we have three Stooges and two comics foils, not to mention a monkey, a drunk, a large woman, and a toitle.

VISUAL HUMOR: In White's previous directorial efforts Moe said "No bullet's goin' through that skull!" [*Half Shot Shooters*] and then got hurt after putting Curly's head in the letter press [*Disorder in the Court*]. The toughness of Curly's skull is now well established, so we have no difficulty believing that Moe can crack a crab on it. Along with the hardness of his head, Curly's strength and mule-like potential are developing. For the first time we see him carrying a very heavy load - the trunk.

The Stooges play themselves in 1936's *A Pain in the Pullman*, and Hilda Title and Bob Burns also go by their real names as they step onto the train. Here, Curly flirts with Hilda by tickling her chin and calling her "Shorty." Interestingly, Jules White [Bruskin 81] recollected that when traveling East by train, Curly used to call infamously tyrannical Columbia president Harry Cohn 'Shorty.'

Other Stooge firsts: Curly flirting by a hand wave under the chin; an animal tail protruding through a curtain; a black porter fearful of animals; eating a shell and throwing away the edible part; putting one Stooge's leg inside another Stooge's clothes; one Stooge getting an elbow in the face from another; and cooking a shoe. Slapstick choreography: notice in the first scene how quickly and effortlessly Curly slaps Moe's fist, turns back to Pain while Moe circles his arms and hits him, and then turns back to Moe in surprise.

Variations: bowing and bonking heads, and eating inedibles [*Uncivil Warriors*]; removing a toupee [*Horses' Collars*]; the Cossack dance [*Ants in the Pantry*]; the Stooges sleeping together [*Nertsery Rhymes*]; dropping the serviette [*Pop Goes the Easel*]; and train travel [*Woman Haters*]. Repetition of previously used gags reinforces familiarity, and much of the reason for the Stooges' multi-decade popularity is that audiences feel familiar and comfortable with their routines. But then seeing these routines slightly varied delights viewers with surprise and increases their appreciation for their seemingly limitless comic ability. When the Stooges pack their trunk, the only contents are three hats. Curly flirts with Shorty but then acts shyly to Phyllis Crane in the sleeping car.

VERBAL HUMOR: The Stooges deliver their gags in a variety of styles, including nonchalant gags [Larry: "Say, nice shirt you got on. How long you wear a shirt like that?" Curly: [pointing to his thighs] "Oh about down to there." Larry: "Ahh, three or four days, eh?"], throw away puns ("fillet of sole and heel"; "You wanna give me 'berth' marks?"), understated exaggerations (Curly: "How far do I carry it [the trunk]?" Moe: "Just down to the depot."), misunderstood instructions ("Drop the whole thing"), mumbled submissions [Larry's "Sorry, G-man"], intentional misdirections (Johnson: "What's that I hear?" Moe: "You shouldn't believe everything you hear, Mr. Johnson."], and nicely timed dialogues (during and after the phone call, and about the crab ("It's a spider"/"*toitle*"). Other extraordinary sounds include the landlady yodeling "Telephone for The Three Stoo-ges," O'Brien's heavy Yiddish accent, and six repetitions of "Johnson!". Ethnic humor: The Yiddish/Irish firm of Goldstein-Goldberg-Goldblatt-and-O'Brien'; and Larry's "Hak a tsheinik for me too." ('Hak mir nit kain tsheinik' in *Pop Goes the Easel*).

Stooge firsts: Johnson saying "What do you mean by invading the star's drawing room?" and then Moe turning to Curly and yelling: "What do you mean by invading the star's drawing room?" [SLAP]; in *Half-Shot Shooters* Moe hit Larry and told him to go to sleep; now he says the paradoxical "Wake up and go to sleep!".

Curly's "Come in!" when Moe taps on the crab shell derives from Prof. Fuller in the *Pop Goes the Easel* clay fight. Curly's "Jealous, eh?" and "Oh, a cheapie, eh?" we heard in *Fugitive Lovers* and *Three Little Pigskins*. There are two-pattern gags by the phone (Curly: "Hello!" Larry: "Hello!" Moe: "Hello!" Curly to Larry: "Hello!"; and Moe [into the phone]: "Yes, yes, yes!" Larry & Curly: "Yes!" Moe [into the phone]: "Yes, yes, yes!" Larry & Curly: "Yes!" Curly: "What is it? What is it?" Moe: "Yes!" Curly: "Oh boy! YES! [running up the stairs]... Wait! 'Yes' what?" Moe: "A job!"), both variations from *Men in Black*.

Other variations: Curly: "What to you think I am, a mule?" ("I'm no mule!" in *Disorder in the Court*); Curly: "I'm a victim of circumstance!" (*Beer and Pretzels*); and "Meet The Three Stooges - comedy, singin', dancin', and snappy dialogue!" (*Plane Nuts*). The sign in the opening sequence has a verbal gag ('Rates $400 per Week Up - Mostly Up') and a gag name ('Hammond Eggerly'). Paul Pain seems to have lent his last name to name of the film. Reference: O'Brien's 'The Panics of 1936' parodies such musical shows/films as *Gold Diggers of 1933/1935/1937* and *Fashions of 1934*; soon the Stooges would appear in Broadway's *Scandals of 1939*.

OTHER NOTES: The film was shot in late April/early May, 1936. At 19'46", this is the longest of the Stooge Columbia shorts. This is the first of nine Stooge appearances by former model Ethelreda Leopold. Discovered from a photo in a lipstick ad, she played bit parts in hundreds of films, including Chaplin's *The Great Dictator* (1940) and Hitchcock's *The Birds* (1963). This film bears some resemblance to *Show Business* (1932), directed by Jules White and starring Thelma Todd and Zasu Pitts.

The Stooges also portrayed show business people in two of the last three films (*Movie Maniacs*; *Disorder in the Court*). The script and stock footage will be reused in the 1947 Columbia film, *Training for Trouble*, starring Schilling & Lane. The steer-riding getaway ending will be reused in *A Ducking They Did Go*. In his autobiography *Moe* (81-82) says he hated crab so much he made the prop man make him a mock claw of sugar and coloring, and that Curly cut the inside of his mouth chewing on the real claw. A banana gag was apparently edited out. As director Jack White recollected [Bruskin 180]: "Once they brought a gag to me in which the Stooges are on a train. Curly decides to peel and eat a banana. He throws the banana away and eats the peel. The train conductor slips on it and throws a tray in to the air. I said, 'No, that's not funny. Any goddamn fool would know the difference between a banana peel and a banana. I'll make you a small bet.' I went to the preview at the theater and lost the bet. The audience screamed at it. You never can tell for sure."

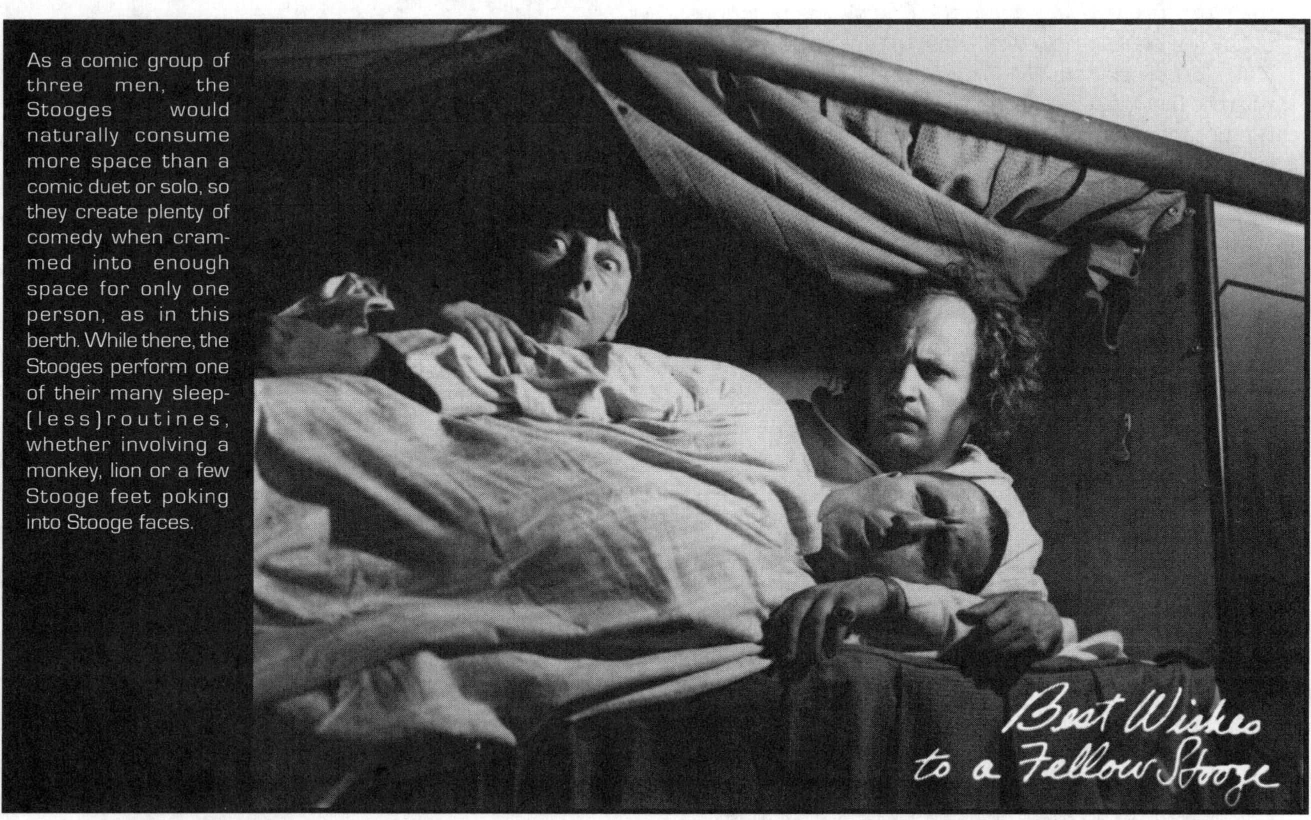

As a comic group of three men, the Stooges would naturally consume more space than a comic duet or solo, so they create plenty of comedy when crammed into enough space for only one person, as in this berth. While there, the Stooges perform one of their many sleep(less)routines, whether involving a monkey, lion or a few Stooge feet poking into Stooge faces.

#17 - FALSE ALARMS

Studio: Columbia

Released: August 16, 1936

Running Time: 16"48"

Credited Production Crew:

Associate Producer:	Jules White
Directed by:	Del Lord
Story & Screen Play:	John Grey
Photography:	Benjamin Kline
Film Editor:	Charles Hochberg

Credited Cast:

Moe Howard
Larry Fine
Curly Howard

Uncredited Cast:

Stanley Blystone	Captain
June Gittelson	Minnie
Johnny Grey	first fireman
Nert Young	car deliveryman
Eddie Laughton	passerby

PERSPECTIVE: Mack Sennett produced scores of comedies from 1912 to 1930. Best remembered for silents featuring the Keystone Cops and Charlie Chaplin, he virtually invented fast-paced, car-chase films that established comedy shorts as a film genre. Some of his most characteristic comedy elements, especially pie fights, were to reappear in Stooge films. In the case of *False Alarms,* writer John Grey and director Del Lord had both worked for Sennett in the 1920s, and no other Stooge film so poignantly features a wild, fast-motion car ride with near collisions and last-minute turns - the kind of exterior action that was a trademark of Sennett films. Nonetheless, this is a Stooge film and not a Sennett silent, so inside the car we hear verbal chatter and see characteristic Stooge slapstick, both of which humanize the exterior vehicular comedy, as does June Gittelson's memorable characterization of the boy-loving, food-loving Minnie ("Let's go places and eat things!"). Stooge slapstick itself becomes the subject of self-referential gags when Moe asks Larry "Are you gonna start that again?" and variations abound when Minnie, Moe, and Curly play the fist game in a veritable 'What's this?' extravaganza. This film is a unique blend of comic styles. Even the fire station pole is used three different times in three different ways.

Although every film thus far (except *Half Shot Shooters*) has included a Stooge attempt at flirting with women, this is one of the few films in which girls actually compete for a Stooge. Maisy and Minnie both vie for Curly, and when he visits the girls he is physically separated from Moe and Larry. The Stooges work best as a trio, but it always pays to observe how separation creates new comedic opportunities for them. Separation creates Moe and Curly's 'phone-slapstick,' and with Moe and Larry working as a duo, Moe gets both to yank Larry's hair and feed him head first into the drain. Curly's isolation, as in *Punch Drunks* and *Horses' Collars*, allows him to flourish as a featured star. Even in the opening confrontation with the captain Curly gets a disproportionately large amount of dialogue while Moe and Larry stand relatively silent behind him, and the entire subplot involving Minnie concerns Curly and not the other two Stooges. Indeed, while the captain looms as a threat to the Stooge trio, Curly's chief adversary is neither the captain nor Moe but Minnie.

John Grey's plot is buried under incessant Sennett-like mayhem, a plus because it is not so much a plot as a narrative premise colored by two subplots. As in *Ants in the Pantry*, the premise is that the Stooges have 'one last chance' to keep their jobs but fail miserably. But in *Ants in the Pantry* the Stooges were rewarded for their failure because they were entertaining; here they have to run for their lives. The subplots involve Minnie's romance and the captain's brand new car, and by the end of the film Minnie gives up on Curly and the captain's car is wrecked. Appropriately it all terminates in a unified narrative crash: Minnie loses her boyfriend; the captain loses his car; and the Stooges lose their jobs.

VISUAL HUMOR: Another legacy from Sennett are the great falls: when Minnie pushes Curly over at the party, Curly's fall is spectacularly sudden and replete with loud sound effects. Curly's fall head first into the cake is well edited, first with the shot of the hot water bottle on the truck, then of Curly keeping pace, then of Curly's

In 1936's *False Alarms*, the Stooges name three of the fire hose pieces "Marie, Annette and Yvonne" - after the Dionne quintuplets born in Canada in 1934. Stooge films are filled with such contemporary references.

struggles [close up], and then of the fall. Another great fall occurs when Larry and Moe slide across the floor atop the broken door, onto the pole hole, and down one flight. When Curly later slides down the pole onto Moe and Larry, there is no sound effect.

Stooge clothing tends to be exaggerated in the 1930s short films. We have seen Moe's white shoes in previous films, but Curly's broad-striped T-shirt and skin-tight overalls emphasize his comical physique. Out on the street [after the quintuplets joke] when Moe slaps Curly, Curly gives an awe-inspiring, pseudo-threatening glare which is greatly enhanced by his curvilinear posture outlined in that overstuffed outfit.

Stooge firsts: Curly's back-and-forth hand wave [with an up-thrust] to Moe; Moe thinking Larry is *in* the sink until the camera pulls back and shows us he is under

it; Moe gouging Curly through the phone; and Moe pulling Larry up the fire pole by the hair. Slapstick combination: When Curly ruins the last piece of hose under a streetcar, Moe asks him if he has any more hose in his hands: Curly sticks out his empty hands, Moe gouges him, slaps him on the back of the head and presses his hands into the wash tub rollers; Larry and Moe then spank Curly with the smaller segments of hose.

Fist game variations: Curly telling Moe they do not have time for the fist routine because the captain is coming, and Curly losing the fist game to Minnie, then to Moe, and then to himself. Other variations: sleeping late [*Half-Shot Shooters*]; jamming Curly's hands into the hose washer [the letter press in *Disorder in the Court*]; Curly waving his hand under Maisy's chin [*A Pain in the Pullman*]; stuffing Larry into the sink [the piano in *Ants in the Pantry*]; Curly getting bleach on the Captain's suit, and driving away at the end of the film [*Movie Maniacs*].

VERBAL HUMOR: Stooge firsts: the poetic Stooge motto ["We gotta come through for the captain/And the crew!"/"And alma-mamie, too"/"Woob-woob-woob-woob-woob, woob-WOO!"]; Curly's "Women and children first!"; and Moe's "Why don't you look before you fall!". Plot-related verbal gags include a three-pattern [Moe: "We'll put out a fire single handed!" Larry: We'll put out two fires double handed!" Curly: "We'll even start a fire and have you put it out!"] and wisecracks [Captain: "Just why did you three halfwits join the fire department?" Curly: "So we wouldn't have to buy any tickets for the fireman's ball!"]. Non-plot-related gags include a military joke [Captain: "If this were the army I'd have you shot at sunrise!" Curly: "We don't get up that early!"], a non-Stooge three-pattern [Minnie: "I'm Minnie!" Mimi: "I'm Mimi" Curly: "I'm hungry!"], and insults [Minnie: "I grow on people." Curly: "So do warts!"; Curly: "Come on, Hercules!"], and some self-deprecation [Moe: "You wouldn't turn us out into the cold, cruel world." Curly: "Yeah, it'd be cruelty to animals!"].

In *Half-Shot Shooters* the Stooges could not hear because of the Detonation Test. Here there are blind and deaf jokes as well, including Curly having soap in his eyes ["I can't hear ya!"], Larry twice not being able to hear Moe "on account of the bell," and Curly's crack about the blind date ["She may be a little hard of hearin'."]. Also reminiscent of the previous film are the names the Captain calls the Stooges ["those three chuckleheads," "three half-wits"].

Moe's "You gonna start that again" is a Stooge first, but derives from Ted Healy's "Now you're startin'!" [*Myrt and Marge*]. Curly's phone conversation ["Yes. Yes. Yes. The line's busy!" Maisy: "Busy?" Curly: Yeah! I'm talkin'!"] follows those in *Men in Black* and *A Pain in the Pullman*. Other variations: a Stooge liking unappetizing food [Curly: "Plenty of pig's knuckles smothered in garlic"], and Moe: "Is there any gas in the tank?" Larry: "The arrow points half way. I don't know if it's half empty or half full!" [*Soup to Nuts*]; Curly's "Ohh, ungrateful, eh?" [*Three Little Pigskins*]; Curly's "It'd be cruelty to animals!" [the mule jokes in Disorder in the Court and *A Pain in the Pullman*]; Curly's "It's haunted!" [*Men in Black*]; and Curly's swing lingo in "We was our shakin' tootsies with the girls last night" [*Disorder in the Court*].

References: Marie, Annette, and Yvonne were three of the much publicized Dionne quintuplets [with Cecile and Emilie] born in Canada in 1934; they appeared in two 1936 films, *The Country Doctor* and *Reunion*. In reference to Minnie's size Curly mentions Hercules, the strongman of ancient Greek mythology.

OTHER NOTES: The film was shot mid-May, 1936. June Gittelson [Minnie] had a non-speaking role in *Woman Haters*. The captain brags that he would have the Stooges shot at sunrise if this were the army; this is the same actor [Stanley Blystone] who played the sadistic sergeant in *Half-Shot Shooters*. Eddie Laughton is a sidewalk passerby before the Stooges and girls drive off in the car; he is also there at the end to help them out of the trunk. Another brief car 'chase' will be found in *Oily to Bed, Oily to Rise*.

#18 - WHOOPS, I'M AN INDIAN

Studio: Columbia

Released: September 11, 1936

Running Time: 17"12'"

Credited Production Crew:

Associate Producer:	Jules White
Directed by:	Del Lord
Story:	Searle Kramer & Herman Boxer
Screen Play:	Clyde Bruckman
Photography:	Benjamin Kline
Film Editor:	Charles Hochberg

Credited Cast:

Moe Howard
Larry Fine
Curly Howard

Uncredited Cast:

Bud Jamison	Pierre
Bob McKenzie	Sherriff Higgins
Al Thompson	deputy
William Irving	bartender
Eddie Laughton	Pierre's sidekick
Blackie Whiteford	
Lew Davis	
Elaine Waters	
Beatrice Blinn	

PERSPECTIVE: The energy and pace of *Whoops, I'm an Indian* are dazzling. The Stooges are exposed as swindlers in the very first minute, run away from Pierre and the sheriff, and continue on the lam until they ultimately lock themselves in jail in the very last minute.

In between, they knock the sheriff over; climb up and fall down from a tree; hook, club, and shoot fish; hide in a cabin; disguise themselves as Indians; ride a three-seat bicycle; look down the barrel of a pistol; watch Curly get married; hide under a bed; survive a knife attack; and run again. The impetus for all this commences with the chase premise of the first scene, and is enhanced throughout by fast-motion, sharp editing, innovative and bright sound effects, and a cornucopia of accents, disguises, vehicles, weapons, and foils. Curly gets to explore all his tempers in the woods, in buckskins, and in drag, and Bud Jamison [Pierre] offers one of his most memorable and persuasively menacing roles.

A fine sampling of this film's artistry appears during a relatively calm moment: Curly's fishing sequence. After hooking himself on the rear, he runs club in hand to Moe and asks for chewing tobacco for the fish: "When they come up to spit I'll get him on the head with my club!" Moe smashes the club over Curly's head. Curly: "You broke my club!" After a hand-wave, he runs back to his spot on the shore, pulls out a fly swatter, kills a fly, throws it into the water, turns around to get his club and misses the fish leaping out of the water, 'hides' behind a little branch, and fails again. [WIPE] He marches into the water with a gun, submerges himself, and after two submarine blasts emerges singing 'La-la' and carrying a string of fish tied to his gun barrel. This is compact, densely textured physical comedy. Even though it involves only two Stooges and simple props, the timing, camera effects, and Curly's ability to make non-human objects come alive fill the sequence with life and movement. Clearly Del Lord as well as Moe and Larry felt comfortable giving Curly the opportunity to display his unique physical and verbal talents in such scenes. Decades later, from a historical perspective, we see Curly developing from Shemp's kid-brother replacement into a comic genius.

Searle Kramer, in his first of several exotic/historical story lines for the Stooges, developed *Whoops, I'm an Indian* into what is essentially a seventeen-minute 'chase film.' Although most of the Stooge Columbia short films to date have begun with an initial premise that drives the rest of the comedy, be it catching bad guys [*Horses' Collars*], making money [*Punch Drunks*], or saving their jobs [*Ants in the Pantry*], *Pop Goes the Easel* is the only previous film that could be labeled another 'chase film.' But when the Stooges ducked into that art school the initial chase motif was mostly forgotten during their art antics and completely forgotten by the end of the clay fight. Kramer's *Whoops, I'm an Indian* stays true to its premise, circles widely, but closes its ring composition with the Stooges back at the saloon and, finally, in jail. The only loose end: Curly's divorce from Pierre.

VISUAL HUMOR: Scenes set in the woods, as in *Uncivil Warriors*, provide the Stooges with cozy pockets of exterior space punctuated by tree branches. Here we see them vary the original Stooge weapon, the slap, high up on a tree branch: Moe slaps Curly, who falls, but grabbing the tree branch with his knees, circles the branch in a 360º spin. At another point, Moe swings a log at Curly, misses, and the branch bounces off the tree and bonks Moe. Moe does not usually get his own rebounds, but here it happens twice: Moe knocks on the cabin door; a board swings down and hits him on the head. The Stooges doing isolated antics in the woods recalls their separate golf antics in the exteriors of *Three Little Beers*. The incredible hardness of Curly's head is again the focus of a gag when Moe breaks the club over it; all Curly can think of is: "You broke my club!" This may also be the first film in which Curly's exhaling is used as a weapon. The sound effects are very appropriate, particularly the deep string sound used for the bow around Curly's neck. The GLUG-GLUG sound, used when Pierre drinks whiskey at the saloon, and the CRUNCH sound, used when Moe bites Curly's ear, are Stooge firsts and will become staples. Columbia sound man Joe Henrie created the GLUG-GLUG sound effect by pouring water out of a one-gallon glass bottle, the CRUNCH by cracking walnuts.

Other Stooge firsts: the series of pine cones landing on Larry's head; Larry chopping wood which flies into the air and lands on his head; and Pierre throwing an ax which bounces and knocks the lamp down onto his head. All three will have many variations in future films. The pine cones falling from the air onto Larry's head derive from the rifles in *Half-Shot Shooters*. Curly turns with his gun on his shoulder and hits Larry in the face with the fish string much like their gun-work in *Half Shot Shooters*. Moe's 'H^2O' warpaint derives from *Three Little Pigskins*, where it was H^2O^2; Wheeler & Woolsey wore question marks on their faces as part of their Indian 'war paint' in *Rio Rita* (1929). Other variations: the Stooges locking themselves in the wrong place (*Movie Maniacs*); Curly flirtatiously waving his arm underneath someone's chin (*A Pain in the Pullman*); tic-tac-toe (*Disorder in the Court*); Curly's back-and-forth handwave (*False Alarms*); the three-seater bike (*Meet the Baron; Men in Black*); two Stooges running away from and then bumping into each other (*Ants in the Pantry*); and the Stooges appearing from around a corner with one head above the other (*Horses' Collars*).

VERBAL HUMOR: Searle Kramer composed the story, but Clyde Bruckman scripted puns (Pierre: "You keep my wigwam?" Curly: "You keep your own wig warm!"), jokes about dressing in drag (Curly: "I ain't wearin' this [dress]. It's last year's model! Hey there's only one leg in this!"; Pierre: "She's a *he*!"), ethnic humor (Pierre: "Hey, Mr. Just of the Peaces"; Sheriff: "You see three paleface 'round here?" Curly: "Me no verstehe." [Yiddish: "I don't understand"]), double talk (Larry as "Big Chief Apopthegrimineh"), contemporary references (Moe: "Now you go up and get a moose and a few meeses. I'll run down an elk." Curly: "I'll try to find a Knights of Columbus" [The Benevolent & Protective Order of Elks,

The scene by the lake in 1936's *Whoops, I'm an Indian* gives Curly the opportunity to demonstrate how adept he is at making comedy with a variety of physical objects. This is a skill he will develop considerably over the next five years. Publicity photos like this one rarely show that sort of comedy, though: publicity photos required two or more Stooges to create a different gag for the still camera; they are not 'snapshots' from the film itself.

and the Knights of Columbus]), and gags based on Stooge ignorance (Moe: "What did you do with the money?" Curly: "I threw it away so I could run faster!"; Curly: "What's that for?" Moe: "That's for what you was thinkin'!" Curly: "I ain't thinkin'!").

The previous film, *False Alarms*, reused the "I can't hear you on account of the bell!" gag twice; *Whoops, I'm an Indian* uses the Indian greeting "How!" in three different scenes, twice in four-patterns and three-patterns (Sheriff: "How!" Larry: "How!" Moe: "How!" Curly: "And how!"; and Moe: "How!" Larry: "How!" Curly: "How we doin'?")... As in recent films, puns accompany slapstick (Moe: "Oh! Deer!" Curly [sweetly]: "I didn't think you cared!" Moe: "I don't!" [POUND/BONK]; Curly: "Maybe a knock would be better." Moe: "Maybe it would!" [BONK]; and Moe: "Maybe you'd like an ermine wrap. [SLAP] There's the 'rap'!). A Stooge first: using the rhythm of 'Shave and a Haircut - Two bits'. Curly's "Hhmm! Hhmm! Hhmm!" (after Moe makes him put on Fifi's dress) is the loudest and angriest in the entire Stooge film corpus.

The hat sequence (Moe: "Take off your hat; you're gettin' conspicerous." Curly: "I'm frozen to the bone." Moe: "Well, put on your hat." Curly: "Oh, thanks!") is a simplified variation of the swearing-in routine in *Disorder in the Court*. The exchange about thieving (Moe: "Where'd you get all this stuff, steal it?" Larry: "What do you think I am, a crook? I just took it.") derives from *Movie Maniacs* ("I wonder who lent us this furniture without knowin' it"). Handwritten notes advanced the plots of *Horses' Collars* and *Movie Maniacs*, as here with Fifi's note. Moe silencing Larry before he can answer (Moe: "Where you been?...Never mind!") derives from Moe's "Tell him what we know about kisses. That's enough!" in *Movie Maniacs*. The Stooges hold an auction (Moe: "We pay ten-to-one." Curly: "Twenty-to-one!" Moe: "Thirty!" Curly: "Forty! ") as in *Three Little Beers* and *Half-Shot Shooters*. Other variations: Curly: "What's that for?" Moe: "That's for what you was thinkin'!" (*Hoi Polloi*); Moe: "Give!" (*Men in Black*); Curly's "I didn't think you cared!" ("Captain!" in *False Alarms*); Moe's "conspicerous," and "Chief Rain-in-the-Puss" (*Ants in the Pantry*); Curly's "An eel!" ("tarantula" in *Disorder in the Court*, "spider/ turtle" in *A Pain in the Pullman*); and Moe: "Hold still, Daniel Boone!" ("Come on, Buffalo Bill" in *Three Little Beers*).

OTHER NOTES: The film was shot in early June, 1936. The working title was *Frontier Daze*. The fast-motion canoe footage will be reused in *Back to the Woods*.

Cast photos were commonly taken on the set. Here is a cast photo from *Slippery Silks*, the final release of 1936. The models, unfortunately, are not wearing those lovely, utilitarian gowns which Larry designed for them.

#19 - SIPPERY SILKS

Studio: Columbia

Released: December 27, 1936

Running Time: 17"15'"

Credited Production Crew:

Associate Producer:	Jules White
Directed by:	Preston Black
Story & Screen Play:	Ewart Adamson
Photography:	Benjamin Kline
Film Editor:	William Lyon

Credited Cast:

Curly Howard
Larry Fine
Moe Howard

Uncredited Cast:

Vernon Dent	Morgan Morgan
Symona Boniface	Mrs. Morgan Morgan
Eddie Laughton	Manager of Madame de France
William Irving	Mr. Romani
June Gittelson	friend of Mrs. Morgan
Hilda Title	fashion show assistant
Elaine Waters	woman at fashion show
Beatrice Blinn	woman at fashion show
Martha Tibbetts	woman at fashion show
Beatrice Curtis	woman at fashion show
Mary Lou Dix	model
Gale Arnold	model
Loretta Andrew	model
Ellinor Vanderveer	woman on turntable
Gertrude Messenger	models' assistant
Jack 'Tiny' Lipson	Missing Persons Bureau officer
Blackie Whiteford	policemanguard
Bert Young	arresting policeman
Lew Davis	legal representative

PERSPECTIVE: Sixty years after its release, *Slippery Silks* is best remembered for Larry's bizarre dress designs with their functional drawers and ponderous rectangularity. And this is as it should be. Far surpassing the old gag of wearing a barrel, these fashions are some of the most incongruous and inappropriate images ever filmed. Besides the clunky, absurdly pragmatic designs themselves, one of the reasons these dresses strike such a memorable image is that they are presented on stage in an atmosphere of unbroken sobriety, coming just after the longest intentionally humorless sequence in all of the Stooge films. Five normal fashion designs — a traveling ensemble, a hunting habit, a bathing suit, lingerie, and a wedding dress - are presented to musical accompaniment for almost two minutes, during which there is only one interruption for Stooging. It is all so abnormally calm, but then we are confronted with the 'modes modernistique' all the more astounding by the contrast.

The film contains another bit of spectacular incongruity when the woman on the street whom Moe and Larry knock over not only smashes them with her package, but runs after and tackles them and then bonks their heads together. Women in the Stooge films thus far have been known to slap Curly, and having a very large woman in the cast - June Gittelson here and in *False Alarms* - has become a regular motif, but we are taken completely by surprise when that woman leaps after Moe and Larry. It reminds us that Stooge comedy often thrives on strong and determined adversaries, and this film has six of them - the Stooges' boss (Romani), Mr. Morgan, the woman, and the three women who clock the Stooges in the final scene. Few Stooge films have so many different individuals angry at the Stooges, and perhaps we should regard this as a barometer of how badly they screwed up in both the furniture and fashion businesses.

Just as the previous film ended where it began, so, too, the plot of *Slippery Silks* comes full circle. Early in the film the Stooges anger Vernon Dent [Morgan Morgan] by destroying his priceless Chinese cabinet, and at the end he rediscovers them as fashion designers. During the interim he is not heard from. This narrative pattern, in which the Stooges do something to a foil early in the film, go somewhere else, and then are found by the foil at the end of the film, will continue to be a dependable formula. *Slippery Silks* marks the initial attempt at redefining the two-part narrative first seen in *Three Little Pigskins* and *Pop Goes the Easel,* and this redefined foil pattern will be used effectively in such films as *An Ache in Every Stake* (1941) and *Listen, Judge* (1952). Vernon Dent, who had slapped Moe and poked his thumb in Curly's eye in *Half-Shot Shooters*, will often play this foil. Hard edged, quick to anger, and a master of a take, Dent is an essential part of the Stooge film corpus.

VISUAL HUMOR: Larry was a furniture designer, so his dresses are utilitarian: a vanity table which allows the model to open a drawer, withdraw a powder puff and a mirror, and powder her chin; and a living room shelf with clock, radio, books, and a vase of flowers. The editing and a liberal use of close-ups enhance the box sawing sequence. The camera angle shows the box coming towards us and the saw. Speeding up the film makes Mr. Morgan's punching Curly eight times more effective as well. Stooge slapstick thrives on unexpected action and immediate reaction. Here you see Moe about to be hit with a falling 10-foot board, yet he keeps talking until the moment of impact, the unexpected action. As for immediate reaction, Curly's response to getting slapped by the spring-loaded mannequin arm is priceless; he gives eight different hand or facial gestures in eight seconds.

In the fist game, Curly slaps Moe's fist, and this time it circles around and hits Larry; Larry does a fine take, again increasing the element of surprise reaction. Since *False Alarms* each film has used a gag or two twice or more. Here the 'put your right hand on your hip' gag (*Plane Nuts*) is used twice, as are the spring-loaded mannequin arm and the 'pick-two' gags. The second time the latter is used Moe 'breaks' his fingers against the back of Curly's head, raises two limp fingers to a laughing Curly, and then gouges him. This is a Stooge first.

Other Stooge firsts: trouble with glue, and getting boards glued to the feet; objects stuck in the rear needing to be pried out; Moe grabbing ears/nose with scissors; plunging scissors into someone's rear; Curly spinning Mrs. Morgan round and round on the turntable; Larry directing artillery with binoculars; and the girls pointing their fingers under their chins and curtsying. Curly sits nonchalantly as Moe hammers two boards resting on Curly's head. His skull will now be perennially, superhumanly hard, a concept developing since *Half-Shot Shooters*. Sound effects: the sound of nails being pried out of a wooden board (for prying nails out of Curly's rear) is a Stooge first and will be used often. There is no sound effect when Curly plunges scissors into Moe's rear; 'PLINK' will not be used until 1941. In *Movie Maniacs*, we were led to assume the Stooges have been in trouble with the law; here when the policemen enter the shop the Stooges hide behind boards. Moe's role as boss is effective when he pretends to be brave, but sends the other Stooges ahead of him (Moe: "You can't do that to my pal. [to Curly] He can't hurt us. Go ahead!"). He learned this from Ted Healy (*Beer and Pretzels*). In *Pop Goes the Easel*, the Stooges had a clay fight; *Slippery Silks* marks their first cream dessert fight, which includes several gags from the clay fight: a cream puff hitting a seated woman, Curly trying to throw but getting hit, and Curly saying "A backbiter, eh?" and "You missed me, nyaah!" New are Curly cleaning with seltzer spray, Moe grabbing Larry's hair and hoisting his head over the counter, and the spring-loaded mannequin arm. Moe launching a cream pie into Curly's face recalls the tree branch gag in *Uncivil Warriors*. Other variations: the Stooges as carpenters (*Pardon My Scotch*); Moe attempting to grab Curly by the hair (*Ants in the Pantry*); getting soaked by street water (*Three Little Pigskins*); a non-Stooge bonking Stooge heads together (*Half Shot Shooters*); and the women bonking the Stooges over their heads with mannequin legs (*Pop Goes the Easel*).

VERBAL HUMOR: First-time Stooge writer Ewart Adamson creates several firsts: the 'V-8' gag; Moe's "By the time we through with that its own mother won't be able to tell 'em apart"; using the word 'putrid' as a positive (Moe: "Isn't that scrumptious?" Curly: "Umm! putrid!"); and one Stooge saying to another: "Say somethin', say a few syllables!" The latter varies a line in *Movie Maniacs:* "Tell me your name so I can tell your mother!". Adamson's plot-related gags include puns (Romani: "Mr. Morgan wants an exact duplicate of this cabinet." Larry: "I get it — a twin!"), insults (Moe: "I always wanted to make a cabinet like that. The idea's been in my head since I was 10 years old." Curly: "Oh, sort of aged in the wood!"; Fat woman: "I think I'd look stunning in that riding habit." Curly: "I think there'd be trouble figuring out which one was the horse!"; and Moe to Miss Eisenbottle: "Bring the tape measure... the thing with the numbers!"), internal rhymes (Moe: "What in creation is wrong with the creation?"; Mrs. Morgan: "Could you create something individual for me?" Moe: "Lady, you're practically created!"); a three pattern (Moe: "A trifle too much train." Curly: "I think there's two box cars and a caboose too many." Larry: "The cow catcher is dragging."), gags based on Stooge ignorance (Morgan: "Are you sure this work will be in competent hands?" Curly: "We're all incompetent!"; Customer: "I'd like to see your hose. Curly [showing his]: "Certainly! Whadya think of 'em?"), and ethnic humor (Chinese 'Hi Lee, Hi Low'; Yiddish "Plotz, please"; and French '*Pinces Soir*' - a Stoogization of *peau de so* [a silk fabric]. The 'Hi Lee, Hi Lo' sequence is intricate; it begins with a pattern joke (Larry: "That's a genuine Ching Hi Lee." Moe: "Chow Mein Hi Lo." Larry: "Hi Lee." Moe: "Hi Lo.") which develops into a song (Curly sings 'Hi Lee, Hi Lo'; Larry adds falsetto 'boop-boops' on the second and third beats) which develops into slapstick (Moe: "Hi Lee? Hi Lo? Boop-boop?" [DOUBLE SLAP]). The song was a popular 1923 novelty recording by Billy Murray & Ed Smalle.

As in recent films, the Stooges get insulted (Officer: "He probably took a look at the picture and couldn't stand the shock!"; Romani: "We're not as dumb as we look around here!"; and Woman [bonking their heads together]: "They don't look so dangerous to me!"), and a pun is used to accompany slapstick as Moe hammers the nails into Curly's rear: "You need some iron!". Other variations: "We're pedestrians," and falsetto "La-la-la-la!" (*Half-Shot Shooters*); and answering phones in sequence (*Men in Black*). Reference: 'aeroplane' fell out of use in World War II.

OTHER NOTES: The film was shot in mid-June, 1936. Ewart Anderson, who wrote six Stooge films, worked with Lord in the 1920s. In 1926 Jules White made a '*Slippery Silks*' for Sunshine Comedies. Director Jack White learned pie throwing from Fatty Arbuckle at the Sennett studios; he attributed its origins to Daddy Nichols, others to Mabel Normand and Ben Turpin. *Moe* [88, 95] discusses Stooge pie/cream puff fights. "Say somethin'; say a few syllables" was adapted by Quentin Tarentino in *Pulp Fiction* (1994).

1937

Grips, Grunts and Groans • Dizzy Doctors • 3 Dumb Clucks

Back to the Woods • Goofs and Saddles • Cash and Carry

Playing the Ponies • The Sitter Downers

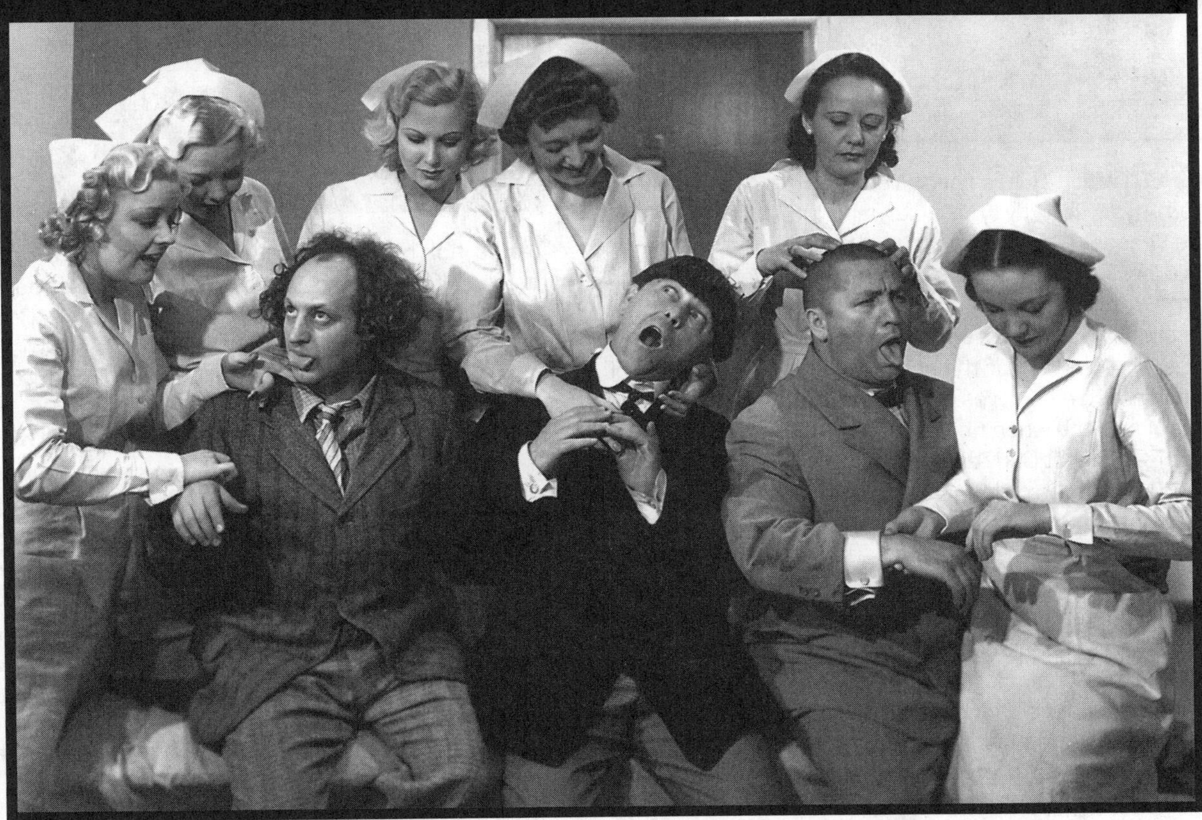

#20 - GRIPS , GRUNTS AND GROANS

Studio: Columbia

Released: January 15, 1937

Running Time: 18"44'"

Credited Production Crew:

Associate Producer:	Jules White
Directed by:	Preston Black
Screen Play:	Clyde Bruckman
Story:	Searle Kramer & Herman Boxer
Photography:	Benjamin Kline
Film Editor:	Charles Nelson

Credited Cast:

Curly Howard
Larry Fine
Moe Howard

Uncredited Cast:

Harrison Greene	Ivan Bustoff
Casey Columbo	Tony, his manager
Blackie Whiteford	his assistant
Lew Davis	Tony's betting advisor
Herb Stagman	Kid Pinkie
Chuck Callahan	Ironhead
Elaine Waters	Bustoff's girl
William Irving	head waiter
Cy Schindell	waiter
Eva McKenzie	woman on street
Tony Chavez	
Bud Fine	
Sam Lufkin	
Everett Sullivan	
Harry Wilson	

PERSPECTIVE: This is the third time Curly has suffered from hypersensitivity to external stimuli like 'Pop Goes the Weasel' (*Punch Drunks*) and mice (*Horses' Collars*). This personality disorder drove the comedy in *Punch Drunks*, but *Grips, Grunts and Groans* is one third over before we see Curly smell Wild Hyacinth for the first time. He smells it for the second time only at the end of the film, when he saves the day, much as Popeye finds a can of spinach when he needs it most. By now we take it for granted that Curly can have this sort of hypersensitive condition, so it is no longer the dominant comic element. Stooge films may repeat gags and scenarios, but they always repackage them.

What propels the comedy in *Grips, Grunts and Groans* instead is its compact, relatively complex plot. This is the second and last script prepared by the team of Searle Kramer, Herman Boxer, and Clyde Bruckman, and as they did in *Whoops, I'm an Indian*, they give this film its initial momentum by putting the Stooges on the lamb right from the outset as Depression vagrants running from cops. This scenario forces them to duck into a gym (cf. the art studio in *Pop Goes the Easel*), where Moe and Larry get Curly a job as a sparring partner; there they also befriend Bustoff, whom they must keep sober or face certain death from Tony the manager. This second energy boost uses the recently developed 'one last chance' idea (*Ants in the Pantry*, *False Alarms*) that the Stooges will be fired if they louse up their jobs one more time. But keeping their jobs has become a matter of life and death now, no longer running from the cops but from a gangster who twice points his pocketed pistol in Moe's direction, thus increasing the kind of threats and pressures on which comics thrive: if the Stooges cannot keep Bustoff from drinking, they have to wake him up; if they cannot wake him up, Curly will have to fight; and if Curly cannot win the fight, they will be killed. That's where the Wild Hyacinth becomes the magical elixir.

The Stooges bungle every opportunity they have for success. By Moe's own admission they could have remained on the train if Curly had not opened the door. If they were not in such desperate need of money they

would not have forced Curly to become a sparring partner. If Curly were not so ignorant he would have kept Bustoff from drinking "only Tequila, Vodka, and Cognac," and if Curly had not knocked the dumbbells and the locker onto Bustoff's head, he would not have had to fight Ironhead himself. This is comedy, of course, so it is better that they bungle their opportunities, but all that happens is not entirely by accident. Curly himself announces his theory about what is happening after the dumbbell incident: "We're toys of fate. It's Kismet!" And indeed, Dame Fortune and the concept of Fate will begin to creep more and more into Stooge films. Just as Curly's skull is becoming hard and his strength Herculean, some of the events which unfold in their films will now take on a magical, almost mystical quality that depends on luck either good or bad. After all these years, the phrase "I'm a victim of circumstance" begins to take on new meaning.

VISUAL HUMOR: There is a Stooge slapstick first when Moe hits Curly in the forehead with a dumbbell and sets off a 'chain reaction': the dumbbell bounces off Curly and hits Moe, whose head hits Larry's. Such 'chain reaction' head bonks will occur frequently in subsequent films. Larry then runs into the iron bars on the window, another Stooge first. Both events are accompanied by five sound effects [four clangs and a thud] in four seconds. There are other examples of extended slapstick series when the Kid knocks out Moe and Larry and then Curly, and also when Larry and Curly tear Bustoff's pants, whose head then gets slammed with the door. Some of the slapstick is quite compact, as when Moe and Larry give Curly a slap, stomp, kick, ratchet, bonk, and choke while convincing him to fight. And there is only one gouge and not a single fist game. Other Stooge firsts: twisting Curly's ankle round and round; Curly getting caught up in the ropes; Curly asking Moe to feel his muscle but Moe rubbing Curly's belly instead of his biceps; Curly running circles around the lockers; and Curly knocking himself out at the end of the film. The CLANG sound effect itself is a Stooge first, as is the TWEET sound effect. Jules White whistled bird chirps to create the latter; the former was the sound of a hammer striking a radiator. Result shot: Curly's feet sticking up from between two rows of seats accompanied by 'woob-woob' for eight seconds.

The editing enhances Moe's "He's just warmin' up, see?" We see Ironhead swinging Curly around in circles. Fast motion is used a number of times, even more so than in the previous film. Experiments: When Curly runs around the lockers, a voice-over is added, and when Larry and Moe beat Curly in the gym much of the sequence is focused on Curly's face. Neither was particularly successful. Notice how Curly treats the dummy much in the same way Moe treats him - he ratchets the dummy's ears; must be learned behavior. Curly's healthy appetite is becoming a characteristic motif: here he eats a sandwich both in the boxcar and while leaning out of the wrestling ring. Also, Curly hitting the dummy and getting hit back by it, like the mannequin arm in *Slippery Silks*, are just the beginning of many magnificent confrontations between Curly and inanimate objects.

As in *Movie Maniacs*, there are baseball motifs. Curly wears catcher's equipment, and his warm-ups end in a pitcher's motion. Other variations: the rail yard cops hitting each other with clubs [*Restless Knights*]; ducking into a door while running from cops, and Curly's fingersnap/cheekroll combination [*Pop Goes the Easel*]; breaking celery over Curly's head [*Woman Haters*; *Dancing Lady*]; Larry taking off his hat, the brim staying on his head [*Punch Drunks*]; Curly's semi-sockless right foot [*Hoi Polloi*]; the dumbbells falling on Bustoff [the pine cones in *Whoops, I'm an Indian*]; a mule kicking someone [*Half-Shot Shooters*]; and Moe grabbing Larry and Curly by the hair [Curly slips away], and pulling off pants [*Ants in the Pantry*].

VERBAL HUMOR: The physical nature of the plot decreases the opportunity for set verbal gags, but does allow for quick exchanges [Cop: "Who's in there?" Curly: "Nobody, just us horses!"]. Most keep the plot moving, the best example being Curly's "Wait a minute! If I'm gonna get beat up I wanna get paid fer it!" After the Stooges realize they are trapped in the locker room, energetically delivered lines drive the plot: Curly: "We're toys of fate. It's Kismet"; Moe: "It's better for one to die than three, so we decided on *you*"; Curly: "A victim of circumstance! But I'll do it!". Stooge firsts: Moe to Larry, "Ohh, we're in trouble and you want a drink" [when it was actually Bustoff who said "I want a drink"] and then doing a take; Moe's "Man the lifeboats!"; and Moe's "We're trapped!" [but not yet "like rats"].

The Stooges reading Bustoff a bedtime story about Indians recalls the Indian tale in *Nertsery Rhymes*. Curly's denial [Moe: "You mean you hit him with the locker too?!" Curly: "I didn't do it! The locker did!"] recalls Curly's "I didn't, I still didn't!" in *Three Little Beers*. Other variations: Curly: "I double." Larry: "I redouble." Curly: "I triple!" [*Meet the Baron*; *Restless Knights*]; "Say a few syllables!" [*Slippery Silks*]; "Victim of circumstance!" [*Beer and Pretzels; Punch Drunks*]; "Women and children first" [*False Alarms*]; and Moe: "What's the matter, kid? You nervous?" Curly: "Naahh, I'm scared" [*Punch Drunks*]. Epithet: Larry calls Curly "puddin'-head". References: The 'Little America' decal on their suitcase is the base in Antarctica where the polar explorer Richard E. Byrd had just spent 5 months in total isolation; 'Duck soup' was a 1930s expression meaning 'very easy'; 'Kismet,' a Turkish word meaning 'fate,' was also the title of an Edward Knoblock play about Arabian Nights which had been filmed twice in the early 1930s.

OTHER NOTES: The film was shot in November, 1935. The copyright date is 1936; it was released in January - three weeks after *Slippery Silks*. The title parodies the expression 'gripes, grunts, and groans'. Harrison Greene [Bustoff] played A. Mouser in *Ants in the Pantry* and with Moe and Curly in the 1934 MGM short *Jailbirds of Paradise*. His fall after being hit by the dumbbells is not convincing; he falls on his hands first. This film marks ex-boxer Cy Schindell's first of many Stooge roles. There are two notable editing glitches in the locker room scene. Some of the films involving Fate are *Cash and Carry*, *Healthy, Wealthy and Dumb*, *So Long, Mr. Chumps*, and *Oily to Bed, Oily to Rise*. This is the first Stooge film in which they encounter con[fidence] men; there will be many more, e.g. *Cash and Carry*.

#21 - DIZZY DOCTORS

Studio: Columbia

Released: March 19, 1937

Running Time: 17"41'"

Credited Production Crew:

Associate Producer:	Jules White
Directed by:	Del Lord
Screen Play:	Al Ray
Story:	Charlie Melson
Photography:	Benjamin Kline
Film Editor:	Charles Nelson

Credited Cast:

Curly Howard
Larry Fine
Moe Howard

Uncredited Cast:

Vernon Dent	Harry Arms
Bud Jamison	policeman
June Gittelson	Moe's wife
Eva Murray	Larry's wife
Ione Leslie	Curly's wife
Louise Carver	ugly lady next to car
Ella McKenzie	desk nurse
Harlene Wood	ward nurse
Cy Schindell	orderly
Jack 'Tiny' Lipson	shoe-shine victim
Al Thompson	surgeon
WIlliam Irving	surgeon
Robert 'Bobby' Burns	man in wheelchair
A. R. Haysel	dandruff patient
Frank Mills	Dr. Bright
Lew Davis	man in car
Bert Young	traffic cop
Eric Bunn	
Wilfred Lucas	
Betty McMahan	
Charles Dorety	
Frank Austin	

PERSPECTIVE: *Dizzy Doctors* is a three part comedy which characterizes the Stooges as lazy-bum husbands in their domestic quarters, inept salesmen in the street, and misfit fugitives in a hospital. The continuity from scenario to scenario is smooth and believable: their wives order them out to become salesmen, and bungling that they hide in the back of a van which takes them to a hospital, the perfect place for medicine salesmen. Hiding in the back of the truck is a clever variation of the comic device used in *Pop Goes the Easel* and *Grips, Grunts and Groans*, in which the Stooges were being chased and ducked into doorways that took them and the comic narrative into a change of scenarios. For the Stooges this is a particularly effective device since changing the course of the narrative midway thickens the plot, increases the number of comic scenarios, and justifies the transitional action. Transportation is important later in the film as well: the sailing gurney carries them back to their neighborhood to dive through the window back into bed, bringing the story back full circle to where it began (as in *Whoops, I'm an Indian*) - at home with their wives.

The Stooges have not been married in previous films (except Larry in *Woman Haters*), but in two of the last three films (*False Alarms*; *Slippery Silks*) strong, bossy, and large women have been more integral to the comedy. This stereotype comes to full bloom here as the Stooges are each bossed around by wives, June Gittelson being the most memorable of the three. In contrast, when the Stooges play the part of Brighto salesmen, they bring an enthusiasm to the job quite unlike the laziness they portray in the first scene. In *Slippery Silks* they were industrious (if dangerous) workers in both the furniture and clothing shops, so we as onlookers can apparently accept the Stooges in either guise - as lazy or hard working. The enthusiasm they have for their work is particularly energetic in this film since they have two 'one last chance' situations: in *Ants in the Pantry* and *False Alarms* they had one last chance to save their jobs, but in *Dizzy Doctors* they have one last chance to save their marriages AND one last chance to save their Brighto jobs.

The hospital scenario may seem similar to the one in *Men in Black*, especially since both are located in Los Arms Hospital, but almost every comic aspect is fresh and thoroughly rethought. The Stooges are salesmen, not doctors; they knock over and break the display table at the Brighto shop, not Superintendent Graves' glass door; they now speak over the PA system instead of hearing their names paged incessantly; Anna Conda in

Dizzy Doctors offers an innovative variation of the PA-system gags introduced in 1934's *Men in Black*. Instead of being repeatedly paged over the PA, the Stooges themselves talk into it, and then, remarkably, the whole hospital as well as the audience *hears* their slapstick without seeing it.

the wheelchair becomes a man accused of drunk driving; and even the comatose midget in *Men in Black* is transformed into a falsetto male trying to break Rip Van Winkle's record. One of the keys to producing 190 Stooge comedies at Columbia was having each film maintain a proper balance between newly created gags and scenarios and familiar, dependable gags and scenarios that were thoroughly varied and refreshed.

VISUAL HUMOR: Director Del Lord and photographer Benjamin Kline offer a different point-of-view when the Stooges abuse the hospital PA system. We *see* the doctors and nurses in the hallway while we *listen* to Stooge slapstick. The sound effects and Curly's verbal reactions are so familiar that the slapstick – usually a visual commodity - can work without being seen. Voice-overs are used as well in the final stretcher chase (Curly: "I can't find the clutch!") and as the Stooges run around the streets yelling 'Brighto.' The film is sped up frequently, especially during the hospital chase, the most intricate interior chase since *Restless Knights*.

An important Stooge first: shooting, hitting the light, and having it fall on the cop's head, which derives from

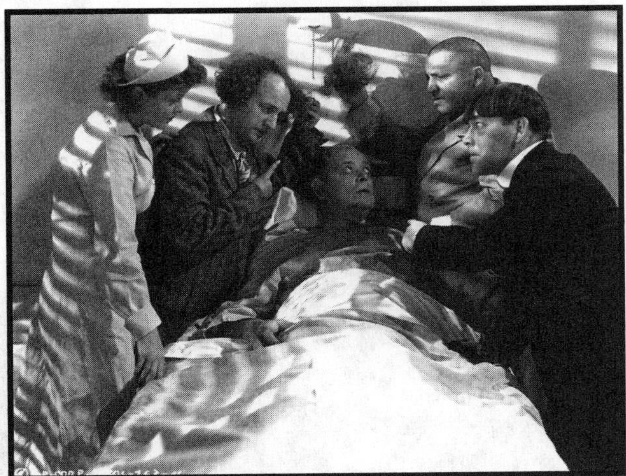

the ax gag in *Whoops, I'm an Indian.* Other Stooge firsts: Curly hoisting an umbrella while still sleeping; Moe grabbing someone's nose and slapping it; Curly slapping someone else's scalp; and zipping off nighties to reveal clothes underneath. A quadruple take: the Stooges and Harry Arms [Vernon Dent] recognizing who they are. The man in the car gouges Curly; in early films this was more common, e.g. *Woman Haters.* Larry is particularly enjoyable when selling Brighto by the fence. He delivers his lines crisply and shows great hand and head movement. When Moe bonks him for saying "One way or round trip," his head hits the wall, his hands fly, and his face screws up. The one-leg gag was used the next year by Laurel & Hardy in *Blockheads* (1938).

Stepping on one another to move the elevator arrow recalls the formation they used to knock the policeman over in *Pop Goes the Easel.* Other variations: eating inedible stuff [soap] (*Uncivil Warriors*); hats in the ice box (hats in the trunk in *A Pain in the Pullman*); Curly making a wrong turn in the hallway (*Men in Black*); sleeping with exaggerated exhaling (*Whoops, I'm an Indian*); pattern snoring (*Hoi Polloi*); and kissing the wrong wives and then 'shifting,' and the anesthetic with a mallet (*Men in Black*).

VERBAL HUMOR: Columbia staff writer Al Ray's screenplay is filled with a variety of verbal patterns, including one liners, whether socially relevant (Curly: 'We looked for a job one day last year; there isn't any!"), prop-related (Curly: "Keep a cool head, that's me!"; Larry: "I think I got somethin'! Or somethin's got me!"), or internal rhymes (Moe: "Here we are: three of the best salesmen that ever 'saled!'"; "If you've got a knickknack with a nick in it, we'll knock the nick out of the knickknack with Brighto."). He also writes numerous simple exchanges appropriate to the domestic scene (Curly: Why can't our wives get our breakfast?" Moe: "Our wives can't get breakfast and work at the same time?"; Moe: "Cheese? That's soap." Curly: "I thought it taste kind-a strong!"; and Larry's wife: "I haven't had a new dress since we've been married." Larry: "Well we're only married five years!") and the hospital (Moe: "Just as I thought: drunk drivin'. Write him a ticket." Larry: "One way or round trip?"; and Moe: "I see a coat!" Curly: "Where's the vest?").

Some exchanges are tailor-made for the telephone (Curly: "A man wants to know what to do for inflammation." Moe: "Tell him to dial 'inflammation.'") and the stethoscope substitutes for a telephone (Curly: "Line's busy!" Moe [pulling it from Curly's ears]: "Now you're disconnected!" Curly: "Give me back my nickel!" Moe: "Here's five!" [SLAP]). The latter is still another example of a number gag ("Pick two!") integrated into slapstick. There is also the more elaborate double exchange (Man. "Want a ride?" Curly: "No. Want to buy

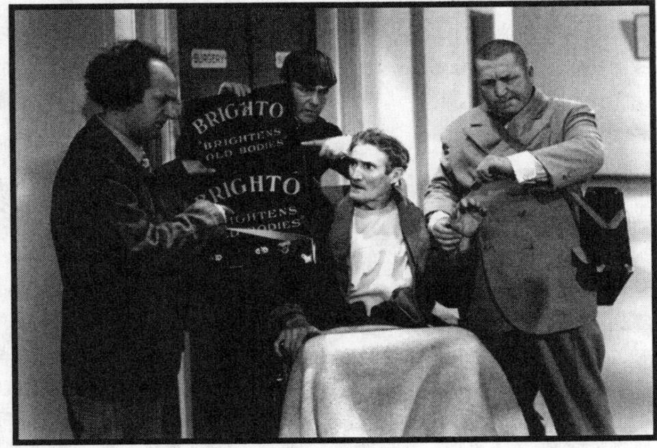

a bottle of Brighto?" Man: "No." Curly: "Then I'll take a ride!". Pattern gags also include a three-pattern (Owner: "Have you ever sold anything?" Larry: "Have we ever sold anything!" Moe: "Have we ever sold anything!" Curly: "Have we?"), a 'Yes! Yes!' variation à la *Restless Knights* (Man: "Brighto. Stooges: "Yes!" Man: "The savior of a nation!" Stooges: "Yes! Yes!" Man: "The scientific marvel of the age!" Stooges: "No!" Man: "Yes!"), and a rhythmic chant à la *False Alarms* (Moe: "Brighto, Brighto, It makes old bodies new!" Larry: "We'll sell a million bottles!" Curly: "Woob-woob-woob-woob-woob-woob-WOO!").

Stooge firsts: Curly going "Rruff!" but getting hissed in return; and the Stooges [unison]: "Jeez, BOOM, Cookoo!". Other variations: Curly hollering "Brighto", but Moe slapping Larry by mistake (*Grips, Grunts and Groans*); Curly's "Line's busy" (*Men in Black*); "Rruff!" (*Restless Knights*); Larry crooning (*Woman Haters*); Larry: "Why it's a cleaner, you chump." Curly: "I know, it's auto polish!" ("spider/turtle"-crab in *A Pain in the Pullman*); "Right!" "Right!" "Right!" (*Dancing Lady*); Curly: "Be a regular guy!" (*Ants in the Pantry*); Curly: "Low man again!" (*Three Little Pigskins*); and Moe to Curly: "Why didn't you think of that?!" [SLAP] Curly to Larry: "Why didn't you think of that?!"; and Moe: "Why don't you say somethin'?!" Curly: "That's enough!" (*Movie Maniacs*). Names: "chuckle-head," "sleeping hyenas," "weasel-faced porcupine."

OTHER NOTES: The film was shot in mid-December, 1936. The secretary at Brighto Medical Company says "Since prosperity's back everybody's working," yet the Stooges complain to their wives that there are no jobs (Curly: 'We looked for a job one day last year; there isn't any!"). 1937 was a turning point in US economic history, and these Stooge contradictions

It is too often forgotten that the 'Three Stooges' were actors. But they were entirely convincing as actors playing stooges, particularly as a trio. They developed a large vocabulary of gestures, expressions, and postures, perfected their triadic timing, and, so armed, they enlivened the scripts Columbia studios provided them eight times a year for one quarter of a century. In *Dizzy Doctors* (1937), after they are threatened by their wives, they obtain employment as Brighto salesmen and proceed with tremendous enthusiasm. They run about the streets shouting and harassing anyone and everyone, proving that they are indeed "three of the best salesmen who ever saled."

The Stooges' great enthusiasm is tempered only by their incompetence and ignorance, so when in *Dizzy Doctors* they energetically attempt to clean Vernon Dent's once shiny car with Brighto, they strip the paint. This in turn sets them up for one of their patented escapes which takes them to a new comic scenario–in this instance, a hospital. The time spent in their metamorphosing from sleeping bums to beleaguered husbands to Brighto salesmen to fugitives is a scant nine minutes. Such condensed narrative development, both intensified by and expanded with verbal and physical gags and slapstick punctuation, makes the Stooge films unparalleled in the history of the cinema.

reflect this turning point between the Great Depression and 'Prosperity'; or the secretary is being sarcastic. Separating the Stooges into individual Brighto salesmen uses the same spatial arrangement as the two mid-Depression job-seeking films, *Punch Drunks* and *Hoi Polloi*. Turning the hospital P.A. system into a radio broadcast was appropriate in late 1936, when soap operas (Moe's Brighto ad), prize fights (Curly's lines), and variety shows (Larry's crooning) were regular broadcast formats. The next year radio quiz shows would become popular, whence *Healthy, Wealthy and Dumb*. The voice-over used when Harry Arms recognizes the Stooges in his office ("Get 'em, boys!") is not Vernon Dent's voice. The sailing gurney footage will be reused in *From Nurse to Worse*.

#22 - 3 DUMB CLUCKS

Studio: Columbia

Released: April 17, 1937

Running Time: 16"49'"

Credited Production Crew:

Associate Producer:	Jules White
Directed by:	Del Lord
Screen Play:	Clyde Bruckman
Photography:	Andre Barlatier
Film Editor:	Charles Nelson

Credited Cast:

Curly Howard
Larry Fine
Moe Howard

Uncredited Cast:

Lucille Lund	Daisy
Eddie Laughton	Chopper, Daisy's boyfriend
Frank Mills	his henchmen
Frank Austin	guard
Lynton Brent	hat salesman
Al Thompson	butler
Cy Schindell	wedding guest
Charles Dorety	wedding guest

PERSPECTIVE: The Stooge family is branching out in 1936/1937. First their Uncle Pete left them his Fifth Avenue shop in *Slippery Silks*, then Stooge wives bossed the trio around in *Dizzy Doctors*, and now they have a mother and father in *3 Dumb Clucks*. In real life, Moe, Curly, and Shemp were brothers, of course, but Larry was unrelated, and it was only in *Restless Knights* that the Stooges first played brothers. In that film, they had a common dedication to do good at the request of their beloved parent. And here in *3 Dumb Clucks*, it is not one last chance at keeping a job or fleeing from the authorities that motivates the Stooges; it is again filial duty. Consequently, it is imperative that their buffoonery not only be funny but work out successfully in the end. Their mother is counting on them not to conclude the film by being blown out of their boots or knocking themselves out.

To have the Stooge father look like a member of the family, Curly doubles as the father, making this the first film in which a Stooge plays a double role. Curly makes it easy to differentiate himself from his father. When playing the father he speaks with sobriety, lowers his voice, and tones down his screen presence so that we are never confused which Curly is which. (The double used for Curly's back shots is also unobtrusive.) Using two Curlys gives the film a different look, particularly in the climactic chase. Curly gets twice as much screen time, and to leave the real Curly unidentifiable to the

thugs, Moe and Larry cannot appear because they would give away the ruse. The scene may last only two minutes, but for those two minutes of a 'Curly only' short, Curly rewards us with incredible physicality. He runs down the stairs and up the stairs - at the top he gives us his first 360-degree, tip-toe pivot turn - and then he runs again down the stairs, and up the stairs, "Rruffing" along the way. Finally, he plows into Moe and Larry, spilling their champagne, and ending his solo duet sequence.

Director Del Lord and photographer Andre Barlatier made this film look different in other ways as well. Besides the stunning 'stop action' used to emphasize the staleness of Moe's self-supporting socks and the fast motion used to enhance Curly's 'using his head' to crash through the prison wall, there is the pre-*The Lady from Shanghai,* Wellesian mirror setup in the hat shop, derived in part from Buster Keaton's *Steamboat Bill, Jr.* (1928). During this unique scene we see Curly from three different angles with a full-length mirror behind him and a vanity mirror to the left. The scene sounds different, too, with very little dialogue and few sound effects. The scene plays rather calmly though underneath there is plenty of subtle activity. This was no doubt another experiment: in the previous film (*Dizzy Doctors*) there was the innovative hospital scene where we heard slapstick sound effects over the PA system but did not see the slapstick; here we see the physical comedy but do not hear it. Sixty-four years later, the hat shop scene may not be considered a Stooge landmark, but it represents the kind of experimentation that kept the Columbia Stooge film corpus vibrant for 24 years.

VISUAL HUMOR: This film differs from most of its immediate predecessors in having no fist game or eye gouge. Moe has his fingers poised for a gouge at the wedding, but this is just before Curly overhears the plans to kill his father and all slapstick comes to a halt for a minute. This clever use of aborted slapstick leads to an important plot development, one of many such instances to be used in future films. As for the fist game, the iron bar gag outside Popsie's gate is more or less a variation where Moe says "Look what you did to my hand," Curly looks, and Moe bangs him on the skull. Sometimes a new gag is introduced and then reused with variations in the same film. Butting Curly's head through the prison wall is the innovation, and then the variations are where Curly almost butts his head against his father's iron gate and where Moe and Larry shove him head first through Popsie's window. Another example is Curly's 360-degree, one-legged pivot turn, which he performs both at the wedding and just inside Popsie's window before he crashes through.

Other important Stooge firsts: one Stooge squirting another because he is having difficulty squeezing a liquid out [of the oil can]; Moe saying "Use your head" and Curly taking him literally; one Stooge hitting both the other two with the backswing and foreswing of a mallet or hammer; and Moe acting lazy (smoking a cigar on his prison bunk) while the other two work. All will become staples... Other Stooge firsts: the 'Men At Work' sign; Larry shaking a few drops onto his head and massaging his scalp and hair; Moe whacking Curly over the head with a silver tray; and the Stooges marching arm on shoulder prison style. Moe uses an electric razor, indicating how popular that item had become since mass marketed in the early 1930s. The Stooges will often incorporate modern gadgetry into their films.

Being suspended atop a high building was a silent comedy standard, most often associated with Harold Lloyd (*Safety Last* [1923]). This is the first time the Stooges are in prison, except for a brief moment at the

end of *Whoops, I'm an Indian*. The woman hissed back at Curly in the previous film, *Dizzy Doctors*; here the detective barks back when Curly goes "Rruff!". Mixing the 'sarsaparilla frappini' recalls the mixing sequences in *Men in Black* and *Pardon My Scotch*. Other variations: a 'fooler opening,' i.e. opening the film with the camera pulling back from a close-up (*Movie Maniacs*) which intentionally misleads the viewer; Curly trying to get out the small jail window with his head (*Woman Haters*); Moe's socks standing still (the base bow in the bailiff's mouth in *Disorder in the Court*); the chain reaction head bonk, and being threatened by thugs (*Grips, Grunts and Groans*), and Curly stealing silver (*Hoi Polloi*).

VERBAL HUMOR: It was an advantage for the screenwriter to have three mouthpieces, the first two 'setting up' the third in three patterns. Here Clyde Bruckman writes pattern gags for the encounter between the escaped convict Stooges and their wealthy father at the dinner table (Larry: "Hiya, pop!" Moe: "Hiya, dad!" Curly: "Mmm! Food!"; and Moe: "Nothin' doin'. You can't bribe me!" Larry: "Me neither!" Curly: "Me, too!"), and for when the Stooges overhear the thugs planning whether to shoot, strangle, or push the groom out the window (Larry: "I'm sure glad they made up their minds." Moe: "They had me worried." Curly: "I'm *still* worried!"). There is a nice irony in Moe criticizing Curly for taking their father's money ("Give it back!") and then taking it himself ("You would, eh?")

A Stooge first: Moe: "Think of something'!" Curly: "I got an idea in the back of my head." Moe: "Well bring it out front." (BONK) Curly: "You knocked it clear out!". Curly's "And I aim to do it too! That's what I aim to do. I aim!" recalls his classic "I reckon this must be the place" speech in *Uncivil Warriors*. Other variations: Guard: "What's going on here?" Moe: "Termites!" ("Just us horses" in *Grips, Grunts and Groans*); "What tools?" (*Meet the Baron*); Moe: "Please say somethin'." Curly (waking up): "Somethin'!" (*Slippery Silks*); the song 'Oh, lee, oh lady' (*Men in Black*); "I'll get married when I'm good and ready" (*Plane Nuts*; *Men in Black*); "Low man again!" (*Three Little Pigskins*), and Moe: "What are you shakin' about?" Curly: "I don't know! I'm in a hurry all over!" (Moe: "You nervous?" Curly: "Only in that leg" in *Punch Drunks*). Reference: Curly's "After the Thin Man!" refers to the 1937 sequel to MGM's *The Thin Man*, the successful film adaptation of Dashiell Hammett's novel about rich, alcoholic sleuths Nick [William Powell] and Nora [Myrna Loy] Charles.

OTHER NOTES: The film was shot in early February, 1937. Of the sixteen Stooge films which employ the word 'three' in the title, *3 Dumb Clucks* is the only one to use number '3'. No 'story' credit is given. Curly's double is a little obvious when Curly smashes through the prison wall. Also, at the conclusion of the hat shop scene, Moe asks, "How much do we owe ya'?" and there the scene ends - an awkward cut. This film was remade as *Up in Daisy's Penthouse* in 1953. *Moe* [101] relates how Curly was injured when he fell down the elevator shaft and cut his scalp on a protruding board. In real life, Moe and Curly's father, Solomon Horwitz, was very happily married to their mother, Jennie.

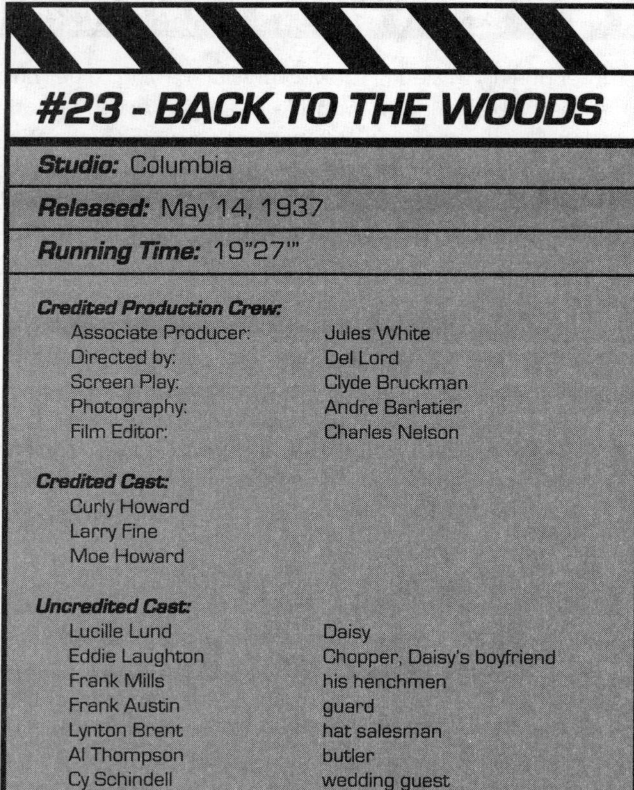

#23 - BACK TO THE WOODS

Studio: Columbia

Released: May 14, 1937

Running Time: 19"27'"

Credited Production Crew:

Associate Producer:	Jules White
Directed by:	Del Lord
Screen Play:	Clyde Bruckman
Photography:	Andre Barlatier
Film Editor:	Charles Nelson

Credited Cast:

Curly Howard
Larry Fine
Moe Howard

Uncredited Cast:

Lucille Lund	Daisy
Eddie Laughton	Chopper, Daisy's boyfriend
Frank Mills	his henchmen
Frank Austin	guard
Lynton Brent	hat salesman
Al Thompson	butler
Cy Schindell	wedding guest
Charles Dorety	wedding guest

PERSPECTIVE: *Back to the Woods* is the fourth Stooge film set in the historical past and the first to contain footage from a previous Stooge film, demonstrating how successfully old material can be reused and rearranged. The Stooges have been located in the American frontier, dealt with Indians, used the name 'Rain in the Puss,' and made jokes about lodges before [*Whoops, I'm an Indian*]; they have said "One for all!... All for one! Every man for himself!" and defeated enemies by having Curly draw them away one by one before [*Restless Knights*]; Curly and Larry have swung branches at Moe before [*Uncivil Warriors*]; and the Stooges have all escaped in a high-speed canoe before. In fact, it is the canoe footage from *Whoops, I'm an Indian* that is re-employed here. But after 22 films, Columbia and the Stooges already know well how to refurbish older gags.

In *Restless Knights*, for example, Curly [then still 'Curley'] distracted one guard at a time to be knocked out by Moe and Larry. Here Moe is not there to help him, so Curly gouges, kicks like a mule, revs up, and ultimately throws his own fat body on his victim. Later that same ploy is varied again when the Stooges omit the clubbings and shovel hot coals down the Indians' pants instead. Another example is the borrowed canoe footage. In *Whoops, I'm an Indian* the Stooges wore fur caps, so they have to wear those same caps here to match up with that footage. The change from the colonial three-cornered hats to these fur hats is treated as a disguise, and it makes for some silly comedy: Curly gives us a variation of the "Rruff! Rruff!" barking he has been doing in the previous few films by having his skunk hat bark at Moe; then he pets it to calm it down. Similarly, in *Uncivil Warriors* Moe got a branch in the face, but here the swinging branch turns into an important new kind of Stooge weapon.

The Columbia short film department collectively knew all the plot-types, scenarios, and visual and verbal gags developed for/by Mack Sennett, Buster Keaton, Laurel & Hardy, and others, and they had an expanding repertoire of gags they were creating for/with the Stooges themselves. With such an array of comic colors on their palette, writers like Searle Kramer, Clyde Bruckman, and Felix Adler and directors like Del Lord and Jack White were able to create combinations and variations that made each new film appear fresh. And after the scripts were prepared for shooting, the skillful Stooges gave each gag a new epiphany. The importance of this process, which first evidences itself here in the borrowed canoe footage, cannot be overstated. The Stooges would eventually make more two-reel comedies than any comedy team in history, and creating this extraordinary output would not have been possible without reusing footage and repeating gags and scenarios. But the Columbia unit and the Stooges turned comic variation into an art. Whether simply variations of the fist game or of "Say a few syllables," or more complex refurbishings of whole films [in the Shemp era], repetition and variation were essential for keeping the Stooge film corpus artistically vibrant as well as

perennially profitable for Columbia.

VISUAL HUMOR: Stooge firsts: Banging a rifle on the ground and accidentally shooting down a bird; and scooting along a burning rear. Both these will reappear often. Other firsts: chasing the enemy in a circle and clubbing them; the woodpecker landing on Larry's head; and Curly tripping with the water bucket. A new technique is to whirl the camera from all the 'NO XXX-ing' signs to the last sign which says 'SCRAM.' Another camera effect: the governor yelling "*Quiet*!" at the music box. Unique is Moe and Curly pulling Larry's crotch into the tree trunk. Real mule kicks were used in *Half-Shot Shooters* and *Grips, Grunts and Groans*; here Curly kicks like a mule.

We have seen one Stooge knock another with something carried on his shoulder as early as the street scene in *Three Little Pigskins*, but the Stooges offer us three different episodes of turning, clanging, and clubbing in *Back to the Woods* with muskets and branches. Other variations: the 'Cossack dance,' and fearing a skunk (*Ants in the Pantry*); Curly heading off twice in the wrong direction (*Men in Black*); bowing and bonking heads (*Uncivil Warriors*); and the 'Shave and a Haircut' rhythm (*Whoops, I'm an Indian*). With the 'Cossack dance' in England and the minuet with Hope, Faith, and Charity, there is as much dancing in this film as in any Stooge short. Reference: the finger-waving dance was known as the 'Shag' and 'Suzie Q.'

VERBAL HUMOR: Venturing linguistically well beyond *Restless Knights*, Andrew Bennison fills a historical screenplay with pseudo-archaic suffixes, pronouns, and phrases ("You see-eth, it was like this-eth"; "Wouldst?"; "Giveth them the works!"; "Why does thou not lookest where thou smackest?"; "I'll be back before thou can say Ticonderoga, if thou can say Ticonderoga!") as well as anachronistic gags (Chief Rain in the Puss: "Ug! Good down payment. Take mortgage on balance. Interest 6%"; the Indians' warning sign: 'SCRAM'; Moe: "We best take the ozone"; Judge: "Order!" Curly: "I'll take a ham sandwich!" Judge: "Hold thy tongue!" Curly: "Not tongue! Ham!"; and calling the horse race). The puritanical simplicity of the governor's daughters makes particularly endearing their unison chant "We shall perish of hunger. Oh woe is us! Oh woe is us!" - a Stooge first. Other firsts include four Stooge classics: Curly yelling "Hey Moe! Hey Moe!"; the epithet "numskull"; the realization: "We're trapped like rats!" Moe: "You gettin' personal?"; and three women with similar (but not rhymed) names - 'Faith, Hope, Charity'. Epithets: besides "numskull," "quince-head".

The script includes a pun (Curly: "I just love corned beef and savage"), a Stooge motto ("Ta-TA-ta, ta-TA-ta, ta-TA-tahh; A hunting we must goeth"), internal rhyme (Curly: "How I shall gobble this gobbler!"), and a literal gag (Moe: "Fire at will." Curly: "Which one is Will?"). The three-pattern (Moe: "I shall bringeth the moose." Larry: "And I shall bringeth the elk." Curly: "I'll bring a couple of odd fellows") makes reference to two benevolent societies (The Benevolent and Protective Order of Elks, The Independent Order of Odd Fellows) as in *Whoops, I'm an Indian.* In *A Pain in the Pullman* and *Dizzy Doctors,* Curly made fun of Paul Pain's and the dandruff patient's baldness. Here Curly jokes about his own baldness (Moe: "They'll scalp us alive!" Curly: "Not me! Nyuk, nyuk, nyuk!").

We heard auctioning in *Three Little Beers*, but Curly's bidding up the number of years he will be sentenced is a first to be imitated later (*Booby Dupes*). Other variations: Larry ad-libbing "Hallelujah" and "Yeah, babe!" gospel style (*Plane Nuts*); "Give him the bird" (*Pop Goes the Easel*); calling the horse race (*Nertsery Rhymes)*; and "Say a few syllables" (*Slippery Silks*). Other references: 'Baloney watch time' parodies the 'Bulova Watch Time' ads of the 1930s; Larry's "I need not Charity. I'm on the W.P.A." refers to the New Deal 'Works Progress Administration,' formed after May 6, 1935; 'odd fellows' are non-club members; Moe's "take the ozone" was a 1930s expression meaning to "run away"; Curly's "Keep a stiff upper chin" parodies the expression "Keep a stiff upper lip," (which derives from Phoebe Cary's nineteenth-century poem of the same name).

OTHER NOTES: The film was shot in early March, 1937. At 19'27" this is one of the longest of the Columbia shorts. The Stooges began the previous film as prisoners, too. The dance with Hope, Faith, and Charity is a minuet, appropriate for the early seventeenth century Colonial period. But they dance to Beethoven's *Minuet in G* which was not written until about 1800. The Stooges come by the epithet 'numskull' honestly. In 1929 *The New York Times* review of *A Night in Venice* called the Stooges (Ted Healy, Moe, Larry, Shemp) "the frowziest numskulls ever assembled". This would be the last (of seven) Stooge films directed by Jack White (Preston Black). Years later he told *Okuda* (24): "The Stooges had a set way or working and you had to work that way. The three of them would go into a huddle and hold discussions. My brother Jules might have helped them invent some of the things they did, but on the whole I was glad to just finish the job." After this he served in the army and returned to Columbia (as a writer) in 1942 (*What's the Matador?*).

#24 - GOOFS AND SADDLES

Studio: Columbia

Released: July 2, 1937

Running Time: 17"10'"

Credited Production Crew:

Associate Producer:	Jules White
Directed by:	Del Lord
Story and Screen Play:	Felix Adler
Photography:	Benjamin Kline
Film Editor:	Charles Nelson

Credited Cast:

Curly Howard
Larry Fine
Moe Howard

Uncredited Cast:

Stanley Blystone	Longhorn Pete
Ted Lorch	General Muster
Sam Lufkin	colonel
Hank Mann	Lem
Eddie Laughton	bartender
Lew Davis	gambler
Joe Palma	stretcher carrier
Hank Bell	
Ethan Laidlaw	
George Gray	

PERSPECTIVE: In *Goofs and Saddles* the Stooges portray good guys on a mission sponsored by the United States government. They were sent on such a mission in *Uncivil Warriors*, and now for three films in a row they have portrayed devoted sons (*3 Dumb Clucks*) or redeemed prisoners (*3 Dumb Clucks*; *Back to the Woods*) fighting against thugs, Indians, and cattle rustlers. In all these films, as in the World War II films to follow, the Stooges must succeed: Stoogeness must somehow prevail, whether it takes a lucky fourteen-story fall from a flagpole, or a shovel, hot coals, and a fast canoe in the middle of a woods, or a meat grinder that shoots bullets. This is positive Stooge productivity.

These heroic scenarios stretch our ability to believe, and this is an important precondition for silly, absurd comedy. When the Stooges are street bums or prisoners or inept employees, we need little convincing that they are real characters. But when these men who cannot tell that a stagecoach has ridden over their heads are said by General Muster to be the army's "best scouts" ("If *they* can't handle the situation, nobody can!"), that is too much to believe. But it is the very absurdity of the characterization that propels the comedy. We hear the silly bugle call echoing the last phrase of the Stooge theme song, we see them dressed as nineteenth-century cavalry scouts reconnoitering from a tree limb, and the seductive power of the cinema is already beginning to take hold. When these scouts then bump heads, fall off a tree limb, crash onto the general's table, make an elaborate and well choreographed salute, and present themselves as "Buffalo Billious, Wild Bill Hiccup, and Just Plain Bill," we find ourselves genuinely interested in them. And when they engage in a 'Yes! No! Yes!' exchange with the general, get their orders, salute, and run off to do their duty, we are now fully immersed in their task and are ready to follow them through thick or thin. Once we cross that bridge, once we accept the Stooges as unable, but delightfully eccentric scouts, then believing they can reconnoiter a valley while disguised as trees and that outlaws would not notice these trees moving around is easy. In fact, the more absurd it is, the funnier it becomes. That is the very essence of this 'disbelief system,' and the Stooges' inimitable determination, sincerity, energy, and enthusiasm makes the comedy all the more convincing and enjoyable.

This brings us to the set piece and the climactic chase and battle. A set piece has been integral in a number of recent films (the cabin scene in *Whoops, I'm an Indian*, the furniture fashion show in *Slippery Silks,* the hat scene in *3 Dumb Clucks*, and the minuet in *Back to the Woods).* Here the card game provides a peaceful interlude in which frantic, physical slapstick is reduced in a scene so quiet that a perfectly annoying foot-scratching sound and Curly's angrily sung "La-DEE-da-dah" can be highlighted and cherished for their simplicity. The subsequent chase and battle have been an integral part of Stooge films since *Restless Knights*, and here the film reaches its climax, as in any great American Western, with a gun battle, the arrival of the US Cavalry, the defeat of the bad guys, and a monkey manning a meat-grinder Gattling gun.

VISUAL HUMOR: Stooge firsts: Curly on a leash acting like a blood hound; and the mousetrap in the pocket. Curly's exhaling is becoming a trademark. It enhances the card shuffling finger-snaps as well as his mugging upon entering the bar (after he turns the brim of his hat). Similarly, his idly singing 'La-Dee' has become more expressive, here identifying his frustration at being handed [footed] the wrong cards. Slapstick turns the plot when Curly's gluttony ("Oh! Eats!") leads to the discovery of the meat-grinder Gattling gun. Because of the plot and Western setting there are similarities to *Uncivil Warriors* and *Horses' Collars*. Replacing the cheek-knocking salute of the former is the elaborate interlocking salute in *Goofs and Saddles*, and the Stooges' tough-guy entrance into Pete's Saloon is derived from the latter. But, after all the dancing in the previous film (*Back to the Woods*), there is no hint of the dance scene from *Horses' Collars*. Other variations: blowing the mud through Moe's head (the oil can in *3 Dumb Clucks*); toasting and breaking glasses (*Woman Haters*); a monkey (*A Pain in the Pullman*); a pigeon (the parrot in *Disorder in the Court*); toeless socks (*Hoi Polloi*); and Curly catching his hat immediately after it is knocked off (*Movie Maniacs*).

VERBAL HUMOR: A Stooge first: the toast "Here's how!...I know how!". The set piece has some wonderful writing (Larry: "Oh! I just had four kinks in my back." Moe: "You know, when I get kinks in my back, I generally go to the desert." Curly: "The desert?" Moe: "Yeah, desert. Oasis! Oasis!" Curly: "That's nothin'! I been to the desert twice." Moe: "Me, too!"). Adler wrote several single lines to emphasize Stooge incompetence and ignorance (Curly's "I think we lost 'em"; "Look! Wagon tracks... and they're fresh, too!"; and Curly's "Do you feel a draft?"). The last is a Stooge first. The three-pattern gag is filled with intentionally incongruous nautical terms (Moe: Aye-aye, sir!" Larry: "Ship Ahoy!" Curly: "Shiver my timbers!"). Moe 'knocking' on Curly's bush, and Curly responding "Who is it?" is a variation of the knocking/'Who is it?' gag in *Whoops, I'm an Indian*. Other variations: "This must be the place all right!" (*Uncivil Warriors*); General Muster's "And remember!" (Superintendent Graves' speech in *Men in Black*); their 'scout call' includes the last few measures of their theme song (DEF#EF#Dd) and 'Shave-and-Haircut' (*Whoops, I'm An Indian*); the "Yes!-No!-Yes!" exchange with Muster we heard with the Brighto salesman in *Dizzy Doctors*; and the Tarzan yells derive from Larry's in *Disorder in the Court*. Along with 'Buffalo Billious,' 'Wild Bill Hiccup,' and 'Just Plain Bill,' the pigeon was named 'Bill,' too. Reference: The 'pigeon express' parodies the Pony Express.

OTHER NOTES: The film was shot in mid-April, 1937. As in *Uncivil Warriors*, getting a note back to the cavalry is of prime importance. Sam Lufkin [colonel] played in many Laurel & Hardy films. Kudos for the spills and takes by Hank Mann [Lem], the cowboy assigned to investigating the Stooges in the bushes. Mann was one of Mack Sennett's favorite actors, and he had a long career, appearing with Charlie Chaplin, Abbott & Costello, Jerry Lewis, and others. The chase sequence will be reused in *Stop! Look! and Laugh!*; the Gattling gun sequence in *Pals and Gals*.

#25 - CASH AND CARRY

Studio: Columbia

Released: September 3, 1937

Running Time: 18"21'"

Credited Production Crew:

Associate Producer:	Jules White
Directed by:	Del Lord
Screen Play:	Clyde Bruckman & Elwood Ullman
Story:	Clyde Bruckman
Photography:	Lucien Ballard
Film Editor:	Charles Nelson

Credited Cast:

Curly Howard
Larry Fine
Moe Howard

Uncredited Cast:

Harlene Wood	Jimmy's sister
Sonny Bupp	Jimmy
Eddie Laughton	bank teller
Al Richardson	President Roosevelt
Lew Davis	conman
Lester Dorr	
John Ince	

PERSPECTIVE: Portraying the Stooges as penniless ignoramuses, this quintessential Depression film combines innovative slapstick, an internally consistent verbal banter, heartwarming melodrama, and New Deal politics. Stooge slapstick takes a new direction and reaches new heights down in that pit with Curly and Larry poking, picking, and bashing Moe with their shovel and pickax blades and handles, and the dialogue offers us ample proof that the Stooges are intellectually challenged. Yet through it all, the Stooges maintain their motivation to find money for an operation that will allow a young boy to walk without his crutch. This motivation is strong enough to have the Stooges not only break federal law; but to take them in an extraordinary ending face to face with the President of the United States, Franklin D. Roosevelt, who ultimately offers them executive clemency.

Script co-author Elwood Ullman, who begins here an association with the Stooges that will last through the feature films of the 1960s, helped to flesh out Clyde Bruckman's story by consistently delineating the Stooges as ignoramuses throughout the film. Yes, the Stooges always play stooges, but they are not always this dumb. In previous films Curly could spell 'chrysanthemum' and Moe knew that when Anaconda reached 95 1/8 it was time to sell, but here none of them can add six and six, and they confuse denominations of hundreds, thousands, and millions. They do not know when they are being conned, they do not know how to read a map, and they cannot even tell when they have broken into a U.S. Treasury vault. In an intellectual sense the Stooges are disabled even more than Jimmy is physically. He may well grow up and get a job; they have not been able to do even that. And yet once they feel they can help the young lad, they typically pour all their energies into succeeding.

The Stooges are assisted by sheer felicity. They are lucky to find Jimmy's money in the first place, lucky to be (so gullible to be) duped by the crooks in the bank, lucky to find the vault, and lucky to be pardoned, particularly by the president himself. It may be that their occupation as prospectors helps them: they drive home as prospectors in the beginning of the film, they act as prospectors looking for more money in the junk yard, and they act as prospectors looking for Captain Kidd's kid's treasure in the unoccupied house. Prospectors need good fortune to come across a rich find, and the Stooges' luck changed the moment little Jimmy came into their lives. They did not get wealthy - they only received a pardon from FDR - but they enriched their humanity, demonstrating that while the Stooges remain inept ignoramuses they can also follow an admirable quest. The Stooges already made two films (*Horses' Collars*; *Restless Knights*) and would make more than a few more (e.g. *Oily to Bed, Oily to Rise*) in which they defend and rescue the helpless, and this was a concept in vogue at the time. Heart-tugging films about lost men and orphaned children abounded in the Depression (e.g. Wallace Beery and Jackie Cooper in 1931's *The Champ*), and if any American president was admired in his day, it was FDR in 1937 when he had been recently reelected by a landslide. *Cash and Carry* gives us a whole new side of Stoogery.

VISUAL HUMOR: The tool abuse sequence in the hole works so well in part because of its fine pacing between hits and in part because of the sound effects. Sound distinguishes each poking and picking and gives each a sudden visual and aural impact on two of our senses. Then comes the final hit from the shovel blade, and the final CLANG gives the routine a final exclamation point. There are two additional silent touches: after Moe slaps Curly ("A tooth for a tooth!"), Curly opens his eyes wide and nods as if he gave Moe a silent message, smiles, and returns to digging; and then the camera angle from above the hole offers us Curly's subjective view. In contrast to these silent gags, the sound effects that accompany the dynamite explosion in the hole and the collapsing floor are some of the loudest and longest to date. The crashing floor moves the plot along, as does Curly's struggle with an inanimate object: when Curly hits the tire stuck in the pile of cans with the stick, it bounces back and hits Moe on the head, so Moe picks up a can to

throw at him, but it turns out to be Jimmy's can of coins.

Other Stooge firsts: Moe sprinkling dirt on Curly's tongue; Curly filling a bag with gold but ripping out the bottom trying to pick it up; putting a sledge hammer through a wall. Bonking heads twice as they bend to pick up their shovels is unique. When Curly drops the tools on Moe's foot in the foyer, Moe hops up and down rhythmically, but no 'Cossack dance' develops; we are reminded of this later when they "drop the gold," as ordered, on the police chief's foot. Variation of the fist game: Moe: "What's that?" Larry: "An eye!" (GOUGE). Other variations: Curly clanging Larry in the face with the backswing of his hammer and Moe in the chest with the foreswing (*3 Dumb Clucks*) of a golf swing (*Three Little Beers*); the stick hitting the tire and bouncing back at Curly and then Moe (the club bouncing off the tree in *Whoops, I'm an Indian*); Curly falling down the stairs (the elevator shaft in *3 Dumb Clucks*); and Moe blaming Curly and Larry for the cans Sis and Jimmy throw at him (the second ladder sequence in *Ants in the Pantry*).

VERBAL HUMOR: Stooge ignorance includes a spectrum of deficiencies: math (Jimmy: "How much is 6 and 6?" Curly: "Don't tell me. Box cars!"; Curly: "Five hundred dollars! That's almost a million!"; Crook: "How would you like to get in on a deal where you can make thousands?" Curly: "That ain't enough; we gotta make 500 dollars."), physics (Moe: "The idea is to get the dirt out of the hole. We gotta dig a hole to put that dirt in!"), verbal (Crook: "So long, chumps!" Curly: "Chumps!? He don't even know our names!"; FDR: "I find it possible to extend to you executive clemency." Curly: "Oh no! Not that!"), reading (Curly: "I didn't know they put money up in cans! [pointing to the 'Canned Corn' label] See! 'Canned Coin!"), and map reading (Curly: "'Walla Walla'. It's in the walla." Moe: "But there's two 'wallas.'" Curly: "Certainly! There's a walla, and there's a walla over there." Larry: "Which one is it buried in?" Moe: "It don't make a difference. We'll each take a walla."); the latter is one of the most extended puns in any Stooge film. Other gags make use of spatial elevations (Larry: "Did ya' find anything?" Curly: "Yeah! I found that first step everyone tells you to watch out for!"; Moe: "I'd murder you if I had you down here!" Curly: "But I ain't down there!"; and Curly tumbling onto Moe and Larry: " I just dropped in!") and their jalopy (Moe: "We've been diggin' for six months and all I got is blisters!" Curly [looking at his rear]: "I'm still gettin' blisters!"; and Moe: "Bring the key; the car ain't insured!").

Of the human drama, Moe's white lie to Jimmy ("We made a mistake. This ain't our house. We didn't have any curtains.") is very kindhearted. The kindly relationship the Stooges have with Jimmy precludes any love interest or even a "Hey! Toots!" to a passing woman. An innovative dialogue feature is the repeated use of internal rhyme (Moe: "Go on, stranger. You strangely interest me!"; Moe: "Grab that chisel, chiseler!"; and Crook: "The treasure buried by Captain Kidd's kid." Curly: "No kiddin'!") and wordplay (Crook: "$200 or nothin'." Curly: "We'll take it for nothin'!"; and Larry: "Now Jimmy can get his operation!" Curly: "There's enough here for all of us to have an operation!").

Stooge firsts: Moe: "Remind me to kill you later!" Curly: "I'll make a note of it"; and starting the engine with "Contact!". Moe silencing Larry ("And when you take it out, they give you some more! I had a dollar once—" Moe: "That's enough!") was used first in *Movie Maniacs*. Curly's reference to craps ("Box cars! Looks like two little pieces of sugar with small pox—") recalls a similar one in *Three Little Beers*. Other variations: Curly's "Time marches on" (*Half-Shot Shooters*); and "Bbrrrrt! Pptttt! Ahhhhh!" ("Jeez, BOOM, Cookoo" in *Dizzy Doctors*).

References: "If we knew you was comin' we'd-a baked a cake" derives from a popular expression, not the song of the same name which was not written until 1950; we will hear the expression thrice in 1952's *Corny Casanovas*. The mule's sit-down strike reflects one of

In one of the most extraordinary conclusions to any Stooge film, *Cash and Carry* ends up at the White House with the Stooges facing the President himself. Co-writers Clyde Bruckman and Elwood Ullman wrote this rather astonishing denouement, no doubt influenced by FDR's recent landslide victory in the 1936 election. FDR here is played by Al Richardson, Jimmy by Sonny Bupp [see below], and his sister by Harlene Wood (who also played Faith in *Back to the Woods*). Delightfully ignorant, Curly utterly misunderstands FDR's offer of "executive clemency." This, along with New Deal politics and heartwarming melodrama, not to mention innovative slapstick and wordplay, makes *Cash and Carry* the quintessential Depression comedy in the Stooge corpus.

organized labor's most powerful weapons during the Great Depression, when workers would literally take over and live in their factory until their demands were met. The longest sit-down strike was by GM workers in Flint, Michigan from December, 1936 to February, 1937, and *Cash and Carry* was filmed in early May, 1937. Two films hence the Stooges will have their own sit-down strike in *The Sitter Downers*. Sit-down strikes were declared illegal by the Supreme Court in 1939. The political leaning towards the New Deal is notable. They call FDR "a swell guy" and salute him, and Moe even gets mad when Curly jokes about how banks used to freeze funds (Jimmy: "Will the bank give it back to us?" Curly: "They didn't used to, but now they do."). Previous remarks about the 'New Deal' (the card game in *Ants in the Pantry*, and Larry's W.P.A. gag in *Back to the Woods*) were non-committal.

OTHER NOTES: The film was shot in early May, 1937. The working title was *Golddigging in the Treasury*, a parody of the 'Golddiggers' films of the mid-1930s. When Screen Gems, Columbia's television subsidiary, released this film in the late 1950s, the title had been modified to *CA$H AND CARRY*. The story was later remade with Andy Clyde as *A Miner Affair* (1945) and *Two April Fools* (1954). Jules White hired Elwood Ullman in 1936. His background was not in film writing - he had been a newspaper and magazine humorist - so White paired him with such experienced screenwriters as Al Giebler and Searle Kramer for a few years. His first solo efforts for the Stooges were the classics *A Plumbing We Will Go* and *How High is Up?*. The teller says it would take "104 years, 6 months, and 17 days" for $62 to become $500, but it would take about 36 years (at Chief Rain in the Puss's interest rate of 6%). Continuity: Where did Curly get that coin he pulled out of his pocket with his handkerchief? They're supposed to be completely broke.

Mayer 'Sonny' Bupp played a number of child roles from 1934-1943, most notably Kane's son in *Citizen Kane*. He retired from acting soon after and eventually became a manager at a Ford Motor Company factory.

As in the finale of the door sequence in *Pardon My Scotch* (1935), the Stooges thrive when breaking through walls and floors, thereby changing the spatial parameters of a scene and expanding the comic surprise. *Cash and Carry* (1937), continually breaks new ground both literally and figuratively, not to mention politically.

#26 - PLAYING THE PONIES

Studio: Columbia

Released: October 15, 1937

Running Time: 17"07'"

Credited Production Crew:

Associate Producer:	Jules White
Directed by:	Charles Lamont
Screen Play:	Al Giebler, Elwood Ullman & Charles Melsen
Story:	Irv Frisch and Will Harr
Photography:	Allen G. Siegler
Film Editor:	Charles Hochberg

Credited Cast:

Curly Howard
Larry Fine
Moe Howard

Uncredited Cast:

Lew Davis	conman
William Irving	customer with dog plate
Jack 'Tiny' Lipson	customer with food stains on tie
Charles Dorety	customer who eats peperinos
Billy Bletcher	announcer

PERSPECTIVE: As the number of Stooge films grew, the Columbia short subject unit kept developing new ideas for subject matter, inter-Stooge activity, and narrative structure. *Playing the Ponies* is indeed a different sort of Stooge film, even if Stooge devotees differ as to whether this difference is a plus or a disappointment. The subject matter, horse racing, was in response to the Marx Brothers' *A Day at the Races* which was released in 1937. Shot just two weeks after *Cash and Carry*, the Stooge variant was written and directed by six different artists, only two of whom (writers Al Giebler and Elwood Ullman) were Stooge regulars. Three of the writers (Charles Melsen, Irv Frisch, and Will Harr) never worked on another Stooge film, and director Charles Lamont directed only one previous Stooge film (*Restless Knights*) and none after. The result is a film with a very different feel.

They structured the film by dividing it into two eight minute halves. The first-half is unlike any other in Stoogedom in that the Stooges work together in the confined space of a restaurant while rarely interacting or exploiting their polished inter-Stooge timing or dysfunctional relationships. They work in isolated areas, Curly in the kitchen, Larry behind the register, and Moe at the tables. For Stooge interaction Moe merely yells orders back to Curly and glances over Larry's shoulder to make sure he is not pocketing any coins. Otherwise Curly makes chicken soup and fishes for mackerel and sole by himself; Larry deals with three dissatisfied customers by himself; and Moe confronts four other disgruntled customers by himself. Besides these repeated encounters with seven customers, still other repeated gags fill up the scene: Curly catches fish twice and grabs for salted peanuts five times, Larry tries to pocket coins twice, and Moe bangs into the swinging doors thrice. Finally, the last peanut grab - as in *Goofs*

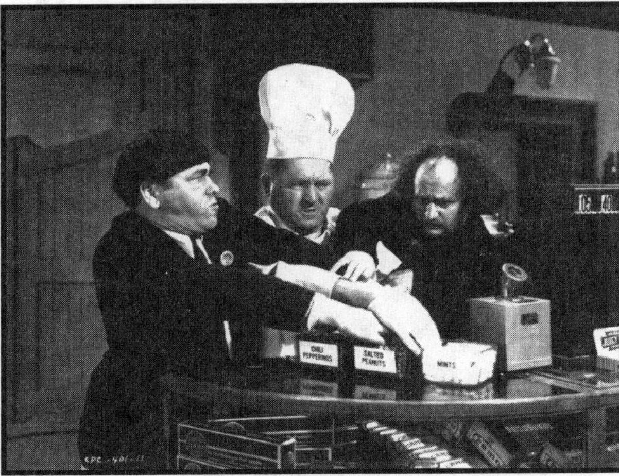

and Saddles, Curly's gluttony leads to a plot development - and the last two customers lead the plot out of the restaurant to the second-half of the film at the race track.

The pre-race scenes depend on a developing Stooge motif: Curly's equine strength. He was compared to a mule in *A Pain in the Pullman* and *Disorder in the Court*, and now he has the opportunity to out-race a race horse not so thoroughly bred. The second scenario, Larry mounting his ride, derives from the berth sequence in *A Pain in the Pullman*, and the third scenario adapts several other motifs - companionship with an animal (the mule in *Cash and Carry*, the monkey in *A Pain in the Pullman*), ingesting strong 'foods' (*Uncivil Warriors*, *Pardon My Scotch*), and reacting strongly to external stimulus

(*Punch Drunks*; *Horses' Collars*) - and turns the horse race into a Stooge horse race. The writers decided upon the elaborate prop gag that has Moe and Curly man the sidecar with the water bucket while Larry rides the horse, but this again serves to separate the Stooges and eliminate the kind of interaction to which we have become accustomed. The finale then concentrates not so much on the Stooges and Stooging as on the horse, who deserves that silver bowl of oats.

VISUAL HUMOR: New gags: Larry's head crashing through the top of the stable door; using a pitchfork as a comic prop; and the quick recipe for chicken soup. The latter is a Stooge first. Moe's being hit by the swinging doors three times is an experiment at role reversal; usually this sort of individual struggle between an isolated Stooge and a physical object will be left to Curly, e.g. where he tries to pull the tire out of the can heap in the previous film. Perhaps Moe's isolated falls are an extension of his taking the shovel beating in the previous film, *Cash and Carry*. He will not often play the clown. Certainly inspired by the shovel and pickax scene in *Cash and Carry* is Curly taking the handle of the pitchfork in the face three times. Curly spills the bucket of water just when it is most needed, as in *Back to the Woods*. Other variations: Curly trying to shake hands to close the deal (*Movie Maniacs*); Moe keeping his hat and coat in the bread box (*Dizzy Doctors*); and the camera panning across the table to Thunderbolt (the 'SCRAM' sign in *B*ack to the Woods).

VERBAL HUMOR: The restaurant scene inspires a sign mocking gourmet food ('Today's Double Feature' - Lobster with Frog's Legs - 35¢'], several exchanges with the customers (Customer: "What is this: pork or veal?" Moe: "Whadya' order?" Customer: "Veal." Moe: "Then it's veal."; Customer: "What's this dog growling at me for?" Moe: "Don't mind him. He's mad 'cause you're eatin' out-a his plate."], and two gag orders (chicken 'soup'; and "two eggs on toast" [Moe: "Adam and Eve on a raft!"] "scrambled" [Moe: "Wreck 'em!"]). The equine scenario produces three notable ironies: Curly: "He must have slept under a lumber pile"; Curly: "You told me to 'race him' around the track, and I beat him!"; and Moe: "Pipe down. You wanna make Thunderbolt and us nervous?". The Stooges' marked ignorance in the previous film is featured only thrice: the Stooges are duped again by two crooks, and Larry is perplexed by "Why don't catfish have kittens?". Stooge firsts: Curly's "Oh shut up! I don't have to!" and "That's a goiter"; and Moe's "Not him, the other horse!". Variations: "Contact!" and Larry's "How time flies!" ("Time marches on" in *Cash and Carry*); and the "H_2O" on Thunderbolt's saddle blanket (*Whoops, I'm an Indian*). Epithet: "puddin'-head."

OTHER NOTES: This film was shot in mid-May, 1937, one week after *Cash and Carry*. The eight-and-a-half-minute opening scene is one of the longest in any Stooge short. Director Charles Lamont left Columbia and later directed Abbott & Costello films: "I had an intense hatred of [Harry] Cohn, so my stay at Columbia was a brief one!". The crooks are played by the same two actors as in the previous film; Lew Davis is the thin, mustached one. Columbia had released a successful horse-racing film, *Broadway Bill*, in 1934; it was directed by Frank Capra, who was much admired by Jules White. The article in the newspaper (to the left) says 'Total on Strike in State is Estimated at 100,000'; cf. the mule's sit-down strike in *Cash and Carry*. The newspaper seems to be from Pennsylvania.

The Stooges usually perform as a trio, but in a number of films they encounter either a foil, like the Bud Jamison and Vernon Dent characters, or are joined by a fourth Stooge. Here in *Playing the Ponies* (1937), the role of the fourth Stooge is played by 'Thunderbolt.' But the unique assemblage of writers for this script opted to separate the conventional trio first, thus diluting the effect.

#27 - THE SITTER DOWNERS

Studio: Columbia

Released: November 26, 1937

Running Time: 15"34'"

Credited Production Crew:

Associate Producer:	Jules White
Directed by:	Del Lord
Story & Screen Play:	Ewart Adamson
Photography:	George Meehan
Film Editor:	Charles Nelson

Credited Cast:

Curly Howard
Larry Fine
Moe Howard

Uncredited Cast:

Betty Mack	Dorabell/Corabell
June Gittelson	Corabell/Florabell
Marcia Healy	Florabell/Dorabell
James C. Morton	Mr Bell
Robert McKenzie	sheriff
Jack Long	Justice of the Peace
Bert Young	Truck Driver [SB]

PERSPECTIVE: Though it was filmed the same month as *Cash and Carry* and *Playing the Ponies* in a rush to complete the final three 1937 releases, *The Sitter Downers* is regarded as one of the classics of the Stooge corpus. It showcases Moe at his most dominant, Curly at his most defiantly vulnerable, and Larry in one of his most extensive physical scenes. It thrives on the essence of Stoogeness: try to do what is right, never do it right, and be proud of it. Walls collapsing, dynamite exploding, pipes bursting, and Stooges hit with two-by-fours and flung into tree tops keep the physical comedy surging throughout, and all of it stems from an underlying socio-economic parody of contemporary sit-down strikes.

What makes the physical comedy particularly successful is that exterior construction projects are harmful to the incompatibly matched Stooge family. Following the ground-breaking carpentry scenes in *Pardon My Scotch* and *Slippery Silks* and the shovel/pickax scene in *Cash and Carry*, the Stooges have another chance to work with tools. But they do it outside. No longer confined to a room or an earthen pit, the Stooges have a whole acre lot to run around, send a barrel soaring above, and set off a couple sticks of dynamite below. (It *is* a good thing that dynamite "always blows down.") This exterior lot has no thugs, cops, or disgruntled Brighto customers to pursue the Stooges. Here the great chase is merely Moe in hot pursuit of Larry, but keeping the violence within the Stooge family makes bricks, boards, and dynamite sillier and more comical. When one Stooge hits another, we know very well it is just Stooge squabbling, even if Moe's pursuit of Larry leads to Curly's being knocked out, dynamited up into the tree, and knocked down by his wife – which in turn leads to her being knocked out. Characterizing the Stooges as newlyweds turns all this into an innocent, if destructive and ranging, family spat. Moe bosses people around, Curly believes everything Moe tells him, Larry cannot wait to get even, and the wives are just beginning to learn how inept their loving husbands are.

What caused the whole concatenation of exterior events? Larry tried to pull a board out of a pile and accidently rammed it into Moe. That's all it took to get something like this started. But the ultimate cause, the reason the Stooges had a house to build and a lot to build it on in the first place, was the national outpouring of sympathy for their sit-down strike. The film's title and the references to unions and strikes reminds us that union membership had become a vital element of the American economy during the first few years of the Roosevelt administration when union membership grew from 3 to 8 million strong. Curly had joked that his mule was on a 'sit down strike' in *Cash and Carry*, but now we have a whole film based on two sit-down strikes. First the Stooges strike against Mr. Bell (Cora-/Flora-/Dorabell's father), and then they strike against their wives. Socio-economically speaking, the Stooges represent the ultimate union laborers: family men who work hard and quarrel amongst themselves but remain united as a group, even if their labor skills are not perfected.

VISUAL HUMOR: Stooge firsts: tossing a harmful object onto a chair to await someone's rear; Curly's lip quivering with light gasps (when he sits on the knitting needles). Using a long pole to remove an above-ground Stooge is unique. The cement-shoes sequence is the first of a series in which Moe and Larry work on Curly stuck in a physically confining predicament; we will see more in *Healthy, Wealthy and Dumb* and *How High is Up?*. When Moe stops the scooter, it is not Curly or Larry who is jolted forward - it is the dog. Put a stop watch on Curly's legs revving in the cement. Because of the rushed filming schedule, many of the sight gags are variations, but they are varied with clever and appropriate improvements and changes: having a dog companion (*Playing the Ponies*), dusting each other off (*Horses' Collars*), hitting Moe by with an opening door (*Whoops, I'm an Indian*); Curly getting knitting needles in the rear (roofing nails in *Slippery Silks*), fading back the camera to show Curly fishing (the opening shot of *3 Dumb Clucks*); using a newspaper headline to move the plot (*Playing the Ponies*); trying to pull a board out of a pile (*Cash and Carry*); messing up freshly laid cement, and making sure Moe is stuck before hitting him (*Three Little Beers*); messing something up several times (Graves' door in *Men in Black*); using dynamite, and a collapsing house (*Cash and Carry*); and exterior chases (*Back to the Woods, Goofs and Saddles, Playing the Ponies*). The water bucket gag from *Back to the Woods* and *Playing the Ponies* is nicely varied: instead of Curly dropping it he first sprinkles water from it and then tosses the contents at Dorabell, cement and all. Moe cooks eggs *without* the shell.

VERBAL HUMOR: Writer Ewart Adamson gives Moe and Curly ten different exchanges during the cement sequence, and in each Moe intimidates and Curly acts appropriately defiant, vulnerable, or gullible (e.g. Curly: "Somebody hit me with a keg of nails." Moe: "I knew I missed a keg of nails!" Curly: "But it didn't miss me!"; Curly: "Dynamite? You're not gonna blast?!" Moe: "What would you do?" Curly [yielding]: "I'd blast."; Curly: "Listen, I don't want to butt in, but you don't you think half a stick is enough?" Moe: "No! Besides, dynamite always blows down." Curly: "Oh, I didn't know that."). Some of the best of Adamson's dialogue sets up or reacts to visual gags (Moe's "He was right: a half a stick would-a been plenty"; Larry's "Whadya let go for?; Curly's "Don't be so mean!"; and Dorabell's "Come down outta there, Tarzan!").

Important Stooge firsts: three similarly named women (Corabell, Dorabell, & Florabell, daughters of Mr. Bell); and the premature eulogy (Larry: "Gee, he was a swell guy." Moe: "You know, I think I'll let him keep that dollar he owes us... Forget what I said about that dollar!"). Both have predecessors, though, the latter from *Soup to Nuts* ("Lay down! You want to make a fool out of the doctor?"), the former from the non-rhyming names in *Back to the Woods* (Hope, Faith, Charity). Another innovative moment occurs when we hear Curly cooing off screen while Moe chases Larry; it holds the Stooges together even when Curly is not visible. Other variations: the reference to Tarzan, and Curly's "I think it's an octopus" (*Disorder in the Court*); Curly's "Say somethin' - not too much - but say somethin,'" and Moe's "Tell him a few syllables" (*Slippery Silks*); Larry's "Are you sure? That's all I want to know!" (*Three Little Beers* and Shemp's Vitaphone film, *Serves You Right* [1935]); and the Stooges' 'Shave and a Haircut' knock (*Whoops, I'm an Indian*). Epithets: Curly is referred to as 'Puddin'-head' three times. References: Curly's "I get Stetson!" refers to the famous hat manufacturer. Curly's quip to Mr. Bell about "not interfering with interstate commerce" refers to the 1937 Supreme Court decision (NLRB v. Jones & Laughlin Steel Corp.) which granted the federal government the power to regulate all interstate commerce. Always ominous words: Moe's "Don't worry. We'll have that stuff off ya' in a jiffy."

Thousands of letters arrive in support of the Stooges' sit-down strike in the appropriately named *The Sitter Downers* (1937). In this film, the Stooges are the consummate union laborers...except that they lack any labor skills whatsoever. Contemporary audiences delighted in the Stooges who were both completely in line with current economic politics and just as completely out of line with the work-related abilities of the common man.

OTHER NOTES: For sit-down strikes, see also *Cash and Carry*. The strike material is worked into a scenario derived from Buster Keaton's *One Week* (1920). Because of its many union pickets, this film wins the prize for having the most signs. This is the second film in which all three Stooges are married; June Gittelson ("I'll bring 'em down!") reprises her role from *Dizzy Doctors*. A scene has been edited out: the girls mention starting a fire before they go shopping, and Moe later says "If that puddin'-head hadn't burned up the plans—". In the opening scene Moe, Larry, and Curly greet the girls in order and call June Gittelson 'Corabell,' Marcia Healy 'Florabell,' and Betty Mack 'Dorabell.' When they later draw names out of the hat, Gittelson is 'Florabell' (we see a close up of her name pin), Mack 'Corabell,' and Healy 'Stetson''Dorabell.'. Contagious Stooging: When Curly says "I get Stetson," notice how Moe's fiancée's facial gesture becomes the same as Moe's. Next to the newspaper headline about the Stooges is an article with a gag headline: '10,000 Chinese Living in Trees As Result of Flood.'

"Come down outta there, Tarzan!" says Marcia Healy as she maneuvers a twenty-foot beam to poke husband Curly out of a tree in one of the most memorable, complex and ironic sequences in *The Sitter Downers*. The Stooges ineptly engage in the construction of their home, and in the process Curly freezes his feet in cement. Moe convinces him that "dynamite always blows down," but here is proof that it does not. When Florabell/Dorabell knocks him down with this beam, he lands on her and knocks her out. Benevolently trying to revive her with a bucket of water, she is struck instead with a piece of the cement that had blown into the water. This is complex physical comedy that makes full use of its exterior setting and the hostile relationships between the Stooges and the Bell daughters. Adding poignancy to the sequence is that Marcia Healy (Marcia Elizabeth Nash) was the sister of Ted Healy, the original patriarch of the Stooges' act. This was her only appearance in a Stooge film, and it was her only film credit. Ironically, *The Sitter Downers* was shot in late May/early June 1937, and Ted would be murdered on September 12.

Though they were by no means rich by Hollywood standards, the Stooges were certainly comfortable in the mid-1930s. Each Stooge earned $20,000 per year from the Columbia contract alone. They each made additional money from stage appearances during their annual four-month hiatus. Unfortunately, they were not given a raise at any time in their twenty-four-year association with Columbia, so inflation ate away at their salary. On the other hand, when television revived their popularity in the late-1950s they did much better, though neither Curly nor Shemp lived long enough to enjoy that latter-day prosperity and neither Moe nor Larry received television residuals from the Columbia shorts.

1938

Termites of 1938 • Wee Wee Monsieur • Tassels in the Air

Flat Foot Stooges • Healthy, Wealthy and Dumb

Violent is the Word for Curly • Three Missing Links • Mutts to You

#28 - TERMITES OF 1938

Studio: Columbia

Released: January 7, 1938

Running Time: 16"33'"

Credited Production Crew:

Associate Producer:	Charley Chase & Hugh McCullum
Directed by:	Del Lord
Story & Screen Play:	Elwood Ullman & Al Giebler
Photography:	Andre Barlatier
Film Editor:	Arthur Seid

Credited Cast:

Curly Howard
Larry Fine
Moe Howard

Uncredited Cast:

Bess Flowers	Muriel Van Twitchett
Bud Jamison	Lord Wafflebottom
Dorothy Granger	Mabel Sturgeon
Symona Boniface	guest
Beatrice Blinn	guest
John Ince	

PERSPECTIVE: Major structural and personnel changes took place in the Columbia short-subject department in 1937 which profoundly affected the 1938 Stooge releases. Maintaining a policy of hiring otherwise unemployed silent comedy veterans, Jules White hired the talented, likable Charley Chase, who had been a successful director/writer for Mack Sennett, Hal Roach, and Jack White, to direct, write, and act. Also, apparently under some pressure from Harry Cohn, White 'promoted' Hugh McCollum, who had been hired at Columbia in 1929 as Cohn's secretary, to the level of producer. White had made him business manager of the department at its inception in 1934, and now he divided all the films between two production units, one headed by himself, the other by McCollum. This arrangement would last until 1952. Apparently White never thought highly of McCollum's artistic ability since McCollum did not have the silent-era training of most of White's hires, but McCollum more than made up for this by giving his co-producers and directors, notably Ed Bernds in future years, more freedom than White allowed his. The McCollum-Chase team would make five of this year's eight Stooge releases.

By the fifth year of Stooge Columbia releases, experiments were more important than ever to keep each film fresh and innovative, and *Termites of 1938* certainly sounds and looks different. Chase & McCollum assigned Elwood Ullman (*Cash and Carry*) & Al Giebler (*Ants in the Pantry*) to write it. Each of their previous films had been innovative, and Giebler's *Ants in the Pantry* introduced the very plot elements - high society, pests, and the Stooges as exterminators - reassembled here. But in *Ants in the Pantry* the Stooges deceived the hostess, brought in pests, bungled the extermination, and were accepted by members of high society. Now in *Termites of 1938* the Stooges are accidentally invited in by the hostess, find the pests inadvertently, bungle the extermination, and are chased away and blown up.

Into this reformatted plot the two new associate producers inject new elements. Chase, who had sung in some of his own Hal Roach comedies, filled *Termites of 1938* with music. The Stooges theme song - not the 'Three Blind Mice' introduced later this year but the 'Listen to the Mocking Bird' used since *Pardon My Scotch* - is used when we first see the Stooges. Curly later plays a bit of 'I Dream of Jeannie' on his piccolo, the Stooges chant their business motto twice, background music plays throughout the dining scene, and the Stooges pretend to play instruments while playing a record. In contrast, the dining scene is noted for its absence of dialogue. Once the meal begins, nothing is said. Visually the film is equally experimental in its elaborate gadgetry

sequence, and in emptying and refilling the camera frame thrice - when Curly gets out of the driver's seat, walks out of the frame, and returns to slap Clayhammer's hand and remove the car door; when Curly disappears and reappears to reclaim his stogie and then disappears again; and in the extraordinary climax when the empty set is suddenly filled by Arthur entering the shot from behind the camera, Moe from the left, and Curly and Larry from the right, while Muriel's head juts out from the staircase!

The background music is appropriate for the society party, but when Moe announces 'Remownodie Sequadnie by Liederkranz,' the frivolity of the wealthy class - one of underlying themes Al Giebler imported from *Ants in the Pantry* - is brought home. Unflinchingly polite members of high society cannot distinguish pretense from reality, and because the Stooges are thought to be college chaps (since they could not hear on the phone because the mouse shot the cannon at them because they were lousy exterminators), Lord Wafflebottom, the hostess, and all the guests listen to absurd band music, applaud the name Liederkranz, and eat peas and mashed potatoes with a knife. Although to members of 1930s 'higher' society nothing was 'lower' than ignorant day-workers, these members of high society are unable to spot them in their midst. Ironically, it takes mice to reveal the Stooges for what they really are: classless exterminators deserving a thoroughly appropriate gopher-bomb extermination.

VISUAL HUMOR: Stooge firsts: Curly's 'chicken-with-its-head-cut-off'; and pretending to make music while playing a record. Though not a first, innovative Stooge gadgetry becomes important for the first time since *Soup to Nuts*. The first experiment with out-of-frame gags was in *Punch Drunks*. There have been fishing gags in the previous two films; here Larry gets slammed into the wall just as Curly was slammed into the window in *Playing the Ponies*. The WHISTLE sound effect accompanying it is atypical. The variation of the fist game here has Moe's fist rebounding from the floor. Other variations: the Stooges called 'Howard, Fine, and Howard' (*Men in Black*); being shot at by an animal (*Goofs and Saddles*); the stethoscope giving a 'busy signal' (*Dizzy Doctors*); the Stooges playing a trio of musicians (*Disorder in the Court*); and the silence during the dinner scene (the hat scene in *3 Dumb Clucks*).

VERBAL HUMOR: One Healy-like gag pattern was used in *Soup to Nuts* (Moe: "Did you see a large female moth. fly through here?" Curly: "Was it a white one?" Moe: "Yeah." Curly: "No I didn't see it!"). The cannon blast makes the Stooges temporarily deaf, as in *Half-Shot Shooters*, but the confusion their deafness causes is used here to get the Stooges into where they are not supposed to be - a society party. Other variations: a Stooge motto (*False Alarms*); double talk (*Whoops, I'm an Indian*); calling Clayhammer "Sledgehammer" ("Pigheart" for "Swinehardt" in *Movie Maniacs*); Lord Wafflebottom's name (Nell Higginbottom in *Horses' Collars*); Larry being characterized as a thief (*Movie Maniacs*); calling a (tall!) woman 'Shorty' (*A Pain in the Pullman*); Moe's "Sometimes I think you got part of a brain!" (*Horses' Collars*); and the Stooges checking their pants when the Englishman says "Ripping!" (looking behind when someone says 'Gentlemen'). Epithet: "Jug-head". References: Liederkranz is a strong cheese; Robert Browning's 'The Pied Piper of Hamelin' was written in 1845. 'Pie-eyed' ("If a pie-eyed piper can call them out then I guess I can be sober") is 1930s slang for 'drunk.'

OTHER NOTES: The title parodies *Gold Diggers of 1937*; cf. 'The Panics of 1936' in *A Pain in the Pullman*. The film was shot in mid-October, 1937, after the Stooges' annual four-month hiatus. It was adapted later for Shemp Howard & Tom Kennedy as *Society Mugs* (1946). For a biography of Dorothy Granger [Mabel Sturgeon], see Richard Finegan, *The 3 Stooges Journal* 73 (1995) 12-13. Richard Finegan ['Notes on Stooge Film Music,' *The 3 Stooges Journal* 79 (1996) 4] identifies some of the dinner music as derived from Victor Schertzinger's score for the 1933 Columbia feature *Cocktail Hour*. The bag of gopher bombs is visible in the background of the first Stooge scene. Stooge motto: "At your service day and night, we do the job and do it right, *A-C-M-E*!". The address of Acme Exterminator Company: '2851 Hill Drive'; Mrs. Sturgeon's address: '1320 Laurel Canyon Drive'. The plot is nicely circular, with Arthur coming to the rescue at the end. Notice the irony in that he is a hunter/fisherman. This film is also the first of a sequence of films which will not use the Stooges in the very first scene. Why is there a saw on the piano?

Bess Flowers [Muriel Van Twitchett] was the 'Queen of Hollywood Extras,' appearing in hundreds of films between 1922-1964, some half dozen of which were Stooge films.

#29 - WEE WEE MONSIEUR

Studio: Columbia

Released: February 18, 1938

Running Time: 17"23'"

Credited Production Crew:

Associate Producer:	Jules White
Directed by:	Del Lord
Story and Screen Play:	Searle Kramer
Photography:	Andre Barlatier
Film Editor:	Charles Nelson

Credited Cast:

Curly Howard
Larry Fine
Moe Howard

Uncredited Cast:

Vernon Dent	Tsimmes
William Irving	captain
Bud Jamison	sergeant
Harry Semels	landlord
John Lester Johnson	Nubian guard
Ethelreda Leopold	toidy-toid girl

PERSPECTIVE: *Wee Wee Monsieur* takes the Stooges overseas to Paris and the Sahara Desert for a free-wheeling romp through two distinct but nearly contemporary Old World settings. Writer Searle Kramer, who had co-written the equally free-wheeling frontier parodies *Whoops, I'm an Indian* and *Back to the Woods*, accomplished this in his first sole-authored Stooge script by dovetailing two classic European romances. He models the opening after Puccini's much-beloved 1896 opera *La Boheme*, which commences in a Parisian loft with four starving artists: a painter, a poet, a philosopher, and a musician. Here, Moe plays a sculptor instead of a poet or philosopher since neither lends itself as readily to physical comedy as a sculptor with a chisel. The opera opens with the artists practicing their arts and singing about their poverty; the Stooges parody this by practicing their arts and singing their 'Lollipop' song. In the opera the first visitor to their loft is the landlord who comes to collect the rent; the artists make fun of him and quickly usher him out. This is pretty much what the Stooges do to their landlord, too, although in the opera the artists are so cold they burn pages of the poet's writings to keep warm, while in the Stooge parody Curly smashes his painting over the landlord's head.

The second part of the film is modeled after *Beau Geste*, the 1924 P. C. Wren romantic adventure novel about the French Foreign Legion. Paramount had first adapted the novel into a silent film in 1926 and was already preparing to shoot (in the dunes outside Yuma) the now well-known sound version with Gary Gooper. Searle Kramer found a clever way to append the Beau Geste parody to the Boheme tale by having the Stooges run from their Bohemian Parisian loft just down the street to the Foreign Legion office where an interesting linguistic confusion leads them to the Algerian desert.

Although these two French settings depend on non-Stooge models, the comedy itself depends on a cleverly assembled combination of Stooge narrative formulae. Like this film every recent Stooge film since *Playing the Ponies* (except *Termites of 1938*) has had a two-part structure; the Stooges played penniless bums recently in *Cash and Carry* even if they were not exactly pillars of the economic community in *The Sitter Downers* either; they were in trouble with the law recently in both *Cash and Carry* and *3 Dumb Clucks*; they were chased by a cop in *Dizzy Doctors*; they signed up for the military by accident previously in *Half-Shot Shooters*; and the 'one last chance' scenario originated *Ants in the Pantry*. The 'one last chance' scenario sets up the conclusion: the sergeant had threatened to throw the Stooges to the lions, but after being given their one last chance they accidentally run into a lion's den anyway. Unlike the similar scenario in *Movie Maniacs*, this time the Stooges tame the lion and have him draw their wagon. Not only that, usually Curly's "Rruff!" fails to intimidate other people, yet here it apparently intimidates a lion. Ironically, and perhaps unintentionally, Moe concludes, "I guess we showed him who's boss," to which Curly responds, "Whadya mean '*we*'? Oui, monsieur.

VISUAL HUMOR: As in the previous *Termites of 1938*, the Stooges have two different musical numbers - one song, one dance. The dance sequence puts the Stooges in drag again, this time with pull-chord veils à la *Men in Black*. When the graceful Stooges kick Tsimmis in the jaw, the dance scene advances the plot, as does the blindfolded Curly when chasing a woman. One slapstick bit was carried out offscreen: Moe clanging Curly's head while we see Larry at the piano, a gimmick perfected in *Dizzy Doctors*; the lion was tamed off screen as well. The policeman bouncing off the door jamb too narrow for his barrel is a fine variation of door-jamb collisions we have seen since *Woman Haters*. The visual/verbal three-pattern routine in which the sergeant asks "Why didn't you guard the captain?" and then Moe turns and asks the same of Larry, Larry turns and asks the same of Curly, and Curly turns, and has no one to blame, derives from *A Pain in the Pullman* ("What do you mean by invading the star's drawing room?"). Notable head bangings: Moe hitting Curly with the chisel; all three Stooges ramming into the gate in the Legion office (a variation from *Grips, Grunts and Groans*); and Curly knocking the urn onto the servant's head. The latter is a

Searle Kramer was one of the most imaginative writers at Columbia. Here for *Wee Wee Monsieur* he models the first scenario after Act 1 of Puccini's 1896 opera, *La Boheme*...

...and the second after P. C. Wren's 1924 novel, *Beau Geste*.

Stooge first, as are the rifle drill, and Larry unfolding a pre-set dinner table from the piano. This is the fourth film in a row a Stooge has gone fishing. Other variations: the Stooges kissing each other (*Half-Shot Shooters*); piling up one Stooge on top of the other (*Dizzy Doctors*); the Stooges sticking their heads around the corner one above the other (*Horses' Collars*): Curly walking in large, strange shoes (*The Sitter Downers*); the blindfolded Curly chasing a woman (*Three Little Pigskins*); ripping off the cop's pants (*Ants in the Pantry*); 'laundry' consisting of merely two socks (*3 Dumb Clucks*); and clanging heads with gun barrels (*Back to the Woods*).

VERBAL HUMOR: The film's most distinguishing verbal feature is the foreign language component. At the Foreign Legion office the hard-of-hearing gag which was strained in *Half-Shot Shooters* (after the Detonation Test) and *Termites of 1938* (the phone call after the cannon blast) works neatly when the French-speaking desk sergeant hears the English word "home" as the homonymous French word "hommes" and enlists these three "hommes" ['men'] for the Legion. The Stooges do not speak a word of French (other than 'Vive la France' and 'Oui! Oui!'), which gets them their five year term in the Foreign Legion, but then, too late, they find out the Legion recruiter speaks English just fine. In addition there is the play with a Brooklyn accent and a Yiddish term (Curly: "Where you been all my life, toots?" Blonde: "Down at toidy-toid and toid avenoo. I just got ovah." Curly: "Oh, a landsman!"). There are two art-related gags for the La Boheme scene, the ironic exchange between Curly and the landlord [Harry Semels] (Curly: "This'll be worth a fortune after I'm dead." Landlord: "I should kill you now and find out!"). and the landlord's "Masterpiece?! Fui!".

The search for the captain produces an interesting three pattern (Larry: "Captain! Here, Captain!" Curly: "Calling all captains!" Moe: "Oh Captain! Oh Captain!"). Larry calls as if for a dog, Curly as if on a police radio, and Moe offers the first line of the Walt Whitman poem of the same name. Other references: the 'Bastille' was the famous Parisian prison, destroyed at the outset of the 1789 French revolution; a 'sou' was a coin worth 5 centimes, 1/20th of a franc; Tsimmes is Yiddish ('a big nothing'), as is landsman ('fellow countryman'); 'Curly Van Dyke' parodies the name of the Flemish painter Anthony Van Dyke (1599-1641), who in the 1930s was more commonly known than now, in part because of the type of goatee named after him; Curly's "I bet you a buck we bring 'em back alive" refers to Frank Buck's *Bring 'Em Back Alive*, filmed by RKO in 1932; the "Oh, there ain't no Santa Clause" sounds like the famous pun on "sanity clause" in the Marx Brothers *A Night at the Opera* (1935). There are two references to the Y.M.C.A. and the Y.W.C.A., and the reference to the W.P.A. is now the second (*Back to the Woods*). To Curly's "Your mother and my mother are both mothers" (*Half-Shot Shooters*), Moe now adds "On his father's side!". Other variations: Curly: "There's nobody home" (*Grips, Grunts and Groans*); "Chiseler!" (*Cash and Carry*); Moe: I'll take the blonde." Larry: "I'll take the brunette." Curly: "I'll take the black and tan!" (*Restless Knights*); and "Lafayette, here we come!" (*Half-Shot Shooters*). This last line is intentionally backwards; it is supposed to be said when arriving in France, not leaving. One of Curly's most defiant responses: "You hit Santy Claus!"

OTHER NOTES: The working titles were *We We Monsieur* and *The Foreign Legioneers*. Laurel & Hardy starred in *Beau Hunks* (1931), their own version of *Beau Geste*. As for the Stooges' hope that the French Foreign Legion would honor their association with the American Legion, the American Legion *was* founded in Paris after World War I, but it had no relation at all to the French Foreign Legion. Curly's painting shows cubist-primitive abstract expressionistic-surrealistic influences. The Santa Clause footage will be reused in *Malice in the Palace* (1949).

#30 - TASSELS IN THE AIR

Studio: Columbia

Released: April 1, 1938

Running Time: 17"09'"

Credited Production Crew:

Associate Producers:	Charley Chase & Hugh McCollum
Directed by:	Charley Chase
Story and Screen Play:	Al Giebler & Elwood Ullman
Photography:	Allen G. Siegler
Film Editor:	Arthur Seid

Credited Cast:

Curly Howard
Larry Fine
Moe Howard

Uncredited Cast:

Bess Flowers	Maggie Smirch
Bud Jamison	Thaddeus Smirch
Vernon Dent	Building Superintendent
Vic Travers	elevator man

PERSPECTIVE: For the fifth time, the Stooges begin a two-part film as tradesmen and end up encountering the upper classes. But every Stooge film is unique, and this one not only offers the classic pig-Latin lesson and gives the Stooges their greatest opportunity to work with paint brushes, it also exposes the upper class as frauds who warrant punishment from the lower class Stooges. In *Hoi Polloi*, *Slippery Silks*, and *Termites of 1938*, the Stooges brought the upper class down to their level by luring them into a slapping fight; a creampuff fight; and eating mashed potatoes and peas with a knife. But the Stooges are ultimately punished. In *Pardon My Scotch*, the Stooges soaked everyone in hooch suds, so we can presume they are punished afterwards there, too. Only in *Ants in the Pantry* are the Stooges fully appreciated by the upper class, but this was because the hoity-toity party guests were so gullible as to believe those bungling, home-wrecking exterminators were vaudeville entertainers. Now here in *Tassels in the Air* the Stooges once again encounter the rich, but for once it is the Stooges' turn to punish them.

Of course, neither the Smirches nor Mrs. Pendle is really upper class. Mr. Smirch makes it clear he was until recently a letter carrier, and Mrs. Smirch's only concern is achieving entry into a country club and *Who's Who*. The Smirches are nouveau riche, nothing more. Even their butler has a sign on the back of his tails that says 'NOT RESPONSIBLE FOR HATS AND COATS.' Mrs. Pendle is taking kickbacks and worries about owing Mrs. Smirch $3.60, so her social standing is in question as well. And then we find out that the great Parisian designer Omay is in thick with these frauds.

The Stooges finally have a chance to get even with members of the upper class, but the sad conclusion is that after making every door sign on an entire floor incomprehensible and unsafe and ruining the decorations in a private home, they are then also unable to teach a lesson to Louella who genuinely deserves some embarrassment. They single out the fraudulent Louella for punishment but end up punishing themselves. And why not? They bungle every other job they have - stenciling doors, painting the table, clock, and chairs, and even eating lunch - so why should they be able to catapult paint cans successfully? As so often the final gag of the film is at the expense of the Stooges, and so maybe Louella gets off relatively easy only because it is the Stooges' turn to be the comic butts. But when you step back and look at the Smirch house after that bridge game, Louella is exposed, she and her friends are mortified and have chairs stuck to their rears, Omay is insulted and cheapened, Mrs. Smirch has had everyone stare at her ripped dress, Mr. Smirch (who is the only person in the film comfortable with his lower class origins) spends an entire afternoon at the futile task of trying to mix up a batch of spotted paint, and the Stooges have paint buckets on their heads. Sometimes the most successful Stooge films are those in which everybody is made to play the Stooge, whether they belong to the silly rich or the lower classes or are the Stooges themselves. This was a good day's work.

VISUAL HUMOR: Many of the gags depend on the Stooges' inability to paint. This is the first time we have seen them in this line of work since *Pop Goes the Easel*, and the variety of gags is astounding. Even when they concentrate on their work, they paint rear ends and faces; dip their

brushes into and drink paint out of coffee mugs; eat brushes and paint with sandwiches instead; step on flooring they have just painted; paint a cuckoo clock only when it strikes; paint chairs that stick to peoples' rears; and catapult buckets of paint onto their own heads. When they are not painting they use the paint cans to play checkers on the floor and kick them to start a 'Cossack dance,' get a retired postal worker to mix spotted paint, and then a paint brush is the tool Moe uses to calm Curly down from a tassel frenzy.

The tassel frenzy is Curly's fourth and final over-stimulus gag (*Punch Drunks*, *Horses' Collars*, and *Grips, Grunts and Groans*), and calming Curly down with the wet paint brush is a fine variation, as is using a chunk of Larry's hair as a substitute. This is the first time Moe has pulled out a clump of Larry's hair. (Professor Richmond ripped out his own hair in *Hoi Polloi*, and Moe ripped out Curly's chest hair in *Restless Knights*). After Moe reprimands Curly at the cuckoo clock, Curly silently juts his head back and forth (like a walking pigeon) into Moe's face. This is a first, although in the pit of *Cash and Carry* Curly silently stuck his face in Moe's and raised his eyebrows at him. Other variations: the 'Men at Work' sign, and falling down an elevator shaft (*3 Dumb Clucks*); and Curly sleeping on the job (*Punch Drunks*). Photographer Allen G. Siegler lined up a very interesting shot just after Mrs. Smirch stood up and ripped her skirt: with the butler occupying the entire left side of the screen and holding steady, both Omay in the mid-ground and Mrs. Smirch in the foreground lean in to survey the damage, with Mrs. Smirch finally bringing her hand up to her mouth that stands agape.

The pig Latin lesson in 1938's *Tassels in the Air* is a true masterpiece that demonstrates the skill of Columbia's writers - here Al Giebler & Elwood Ullman - and the Stooges' facile, but precise delivery. As usual, the 'Moe/O-may' gag advances the plot, making 'Moe' the alter ego of the temperamental 'Omay.'

Moe: My name is Moe. In Pig Latin that's 'Oe-may.'"
Larry: "My name is Larry. Now what's that in Pig Latin?"
Curly: "Oe-may?" Larry: "It's Arry-lay!" Moe: "Boy are you umb-day!"
Curly: "I'm umb-day in Pig language?"
Moe: "You're umb-day in any language!"...
Larry - 'Arry-lay,' Moe - 'Oe-may,' Curly? Curly: "Curly-que!"...
Mrs. Smirch: "Omay?"
Curly: "Oh, you're wise to it, too, eh? Oe-may's inside. I'm Umb-day."

VERBAL HUMOR: French is spoken by Omay and Mrs. Smirch, when she says '*recherché*'; Moe confuses the latter just as he did '*homme*' in the previous film and 'inconspicuous' in *Ants in the Pantry*. But in this film the important second language is pig Latin, the pre-World War I schoolyard form of back slang formed specifically by transferring an initial consonant or consonant cluster to the end of a word with the vocalized syllable 'ay' added to it. Besides the hilarity of the pig Latin lesson itself, the plot of the film works only because 'Omay' is confused with 'Oe-May,' just like the '*homme*' gag in the previous film. Putting up the wrong room signs leads to the second part of the film as well. This demonstrates what an important role Stooge ignorance plays in this film: Larry and Curly argue about 'left' and 'right,' Moe confuses which side is which and thinks carrying Larry down the stairs will save the paint job, Curly cannot understand pig Latin, Moe French, and Larry the importance of a Louis XVI antique ("second hand, eh?"). They are all Umb-day in any language. Appropriately, Moe says: "I'll explain it so even you can understand it" (*Pardon My Scotch*) and "You're gettin' to be a mental giant!" There is also this three-pattern (Moe: "That's pig Latin." Larry: "Anybody can understand it; it's very simple." Curly: "Well, I can't understand it, and I'm simple!"). Curly is now regularly using "Rruff!" for dominance. References: the 'Ritz,' 'Waldorf,' and 'Biltmore' are all high-class hotels in New York; *Who's Who* is a popular register of important people, first published in 1899 and well established in the 1930s; 'Rembrandt' is the seventeenth-century Flemish artist whose name will appear again in Stooge films; 'Golden Bantam' was a type of premium corn.

OTHER NOTES: The *Scrapbook* points out that this is a partial reworking of *Luncheon at Twelve* (1933) with Charley Chase, who directed and co-produced *Tassels in the Air*. This was the second Stooge film made by the McCollum/Chase production unit. Many films since *Ants in the Pantry* have depended on the Stooges getting 'one last chance.' Here, Larry asks the superintendent to give them another chance, but before he can answer, he falls down the elevator shaft.

#31 - FLAT FOOT STOOGES

Studio: Columbia

Released: May 13, 1938

Running Time: 15"37'"

Credited Production Crew:

Associate Producers:	Charley Chase & Hugh McCollum
Director:	Charley Chase
Photography:	Lucien Ballard
Film Editor:	Arthur Seid

Credited Cast:

Curly Howard	
Larry Fine	
Moe Howard	
Dick Curtis	Fred Reardon
Chester Conklin	Fire Chief Kelly
Lola Jensen	Cricket Kelly, daughter of the chief

Uncredited Cast:

Charlie 'Heine' Conklin	policeman
Al Thompson	net holder

PERSPECTIVE: Apparently written, scripted, directed, and co-produced by Charley Chase, *Flat Foot Stooges* looks and proceeds like no other Stooge film, for no other Stooge film was ever so entirely under the artistic control of one person. When Charley Chase left Hal Roach and joined the Columbia short film department in 1937, he brought with him over twenty years of experience as actor, writer, and director and a well honed approach to short film comedy. He tended to concentrate on developing a complex story more than tagging brief and unrelated gags together, so a trademark of his films was a slow build up to an explosive payoff. In *Flat Foot Stooges*, his style evidences itself in the rather complex tale of a salesman sabotaging a fire station's outmoded horse-drawn pump so he can replace it with the modernized equipment he is selling, but during the act of sabotage a duck eats some of the gunpowder he spills, lays an egg, and starts a fire that jeopardizes both the salesman's life and that of the fire chief's daughter who had caught the villain in the act of sabotage. The Stooges are incidental to the plot – a rarity – and the other characters find themselves in more jeopardy than in the typical Stooge film. We see this in not only the thug chasing the chief's daughter and her lying unconscious in the midst of a blazing fire but also the fight between the dog and the mouse and Reardon's leap from the window. Everything works out well, of course, but these situations are more like silent film 'girl-tied-to-the-railroad-tracks' situations and reminiscent of Chase's days with Mack Sennett in 1914-1916.

Also Sennett-like are the exterior chase sequences, especially since they do not at all require the Stooges' presence. There are plenty of extras to carry the chief's wagon, and the chief's wagon does not really have to be taken to the fire in the first place since no one attempts to put the fire out; the only equipment they need is a net, and there is no net on the wagon. Similarly, the scene at the Turkish bath, although it does involve the Stooges, has no bearing on the plot at all. And then there are all the animals - horses, a mouse, a dog, a duck. There is nothing like this in previous Stooge films.

Chase's characteristic slow build towards an eventual gag payoff begins when Curly mentions his invention in the first Stooge scene, continues in the next scene when Curly nags Moe to pull the string, and culminates in the ninth scene when the apparatus fails, falling on the Stooges instead of the horses. In Stooge comedies, which often have a dozen gags a minute, this long setup seems overplayed and slows the pace of the film. The last major Stooge invention, Moe's mouse catcher in *Termites of 1938*, consumed only one scene and led directly to the next stage of the plot. But readers should view this perspective as more analytical than negatively critical, for there are certainly enjoyable moments in the film, and it brings up an interesting question: what kind of film might the Stooges have made if they had gotten a chance to work with Chaplin or Keaton or Sennett? *Flat Foot Stooges* at least shows us how different a Stooge film could be when directed and written by the veteran Charley Chase.

VISUAL HUMOR: The scene in which Larry slides down the pole into Moe's punch is new, a fine use of vertical space and the camera frame. We have seen the Stooges move into the picture from outside the frame as recently

as *Termites of 1938*, but coming from the top was startlingly different. There is a nice variation where Moe pulls Larry by the hair *up* the fire pole - as he did in *False Alarms* - and then bonks Curly *down* the pole. Also new is where Moe winds his arm around twice to punch Larry *up* the pole. This is a fun idea, but Moe never winds up to throw a punch, let alone twice, for good reason: he slaps, pokes, or gouges quickly because his fast hands are an essential ingredient in Stooge slapstick. The WHISTLE sound effect slows the slapstick further; Stooge sound effects work best when they magnify the sound of the hit, not when they make fun of it. Such experiments help us appreciate the 'normal' Stooge approach. Other 'different' bits of slapstick include spitting at each other with the word 'petunia,' and Curly's reactions to Moe's abuse ("You said it! You said it!"; "It's...you know!"). The exploding egg is a Stooge first, reused later in *The Yoke's on Me*. Other variations: sleeping at the opening of a film (*Movie Maniacs*); Moe punching Larry into Curly (*Grips, Grunts and Groans*); and Curly covering his face and squatting to avoid Moe (*Pop Goes the Easel*).

VERBAL HUMOR: Chase's tendency to build to a big finish is reflected verbally in the repetition of the phrase "I have an idea!" We hear the phrase when they go to the Turkish bath and when they try to catch the mouse. The finish comes when they find a way to fix the wagon: all three of the Stooges say "I have an idea!" simultaneously. Related is another exchange (Moe: "This is my brain child." Curly: "You're not even married!"). Another noticeable verbal difference is twice using the 'I mean' pattern (Curly: "Horses falls on the harnesses [pause] the harnesses fall on the horses."; and Moe: "What did you expect a firemouse, I mean, uh, a firehouse mouse to smell like?"). Chase offers fine examples of verbal silliness: Larry: "I forgot to turn it off. I feel so silly"; Moe: "Do you smell anything?" Curly: "No - especially smoke."; and Cop: "Where do you think you're going, to a fire?".

Larry says "I'm a victim of circumstances!"; usually this is Curly's phrase. Another variation: Moe: "We can't have any rats around the firehouse." Curly: "Don't get personal!" (*Back to the Woods*). Reference: Curly's "We're doin' a Corrigan!" refers to Douglas 'Wrong Way' Corrigan, an ephemeral folk hero who bought a used plane for $310 and planned to fly it across the Atlantic from New York; authorities declared his plane unsafe, so Corrigan said he would fly home to Long Beach but landed in Ireland 28 hours later on July 18, 1938: "My compass froze. I guess I flew the wrong way." He never changed his story, even on his death bed in 1995. He appeared in an autobiographical film, *The Flying Irishman* (1939).

OTHER NOTES: There is some confusion about the date of the film. The *Scrapbook* records shooting dates of Oct. 25-28, 1937, the week after #28 *Termites of 1938* (Oct 19-23) and two weeks before #29 *Wee Wee Monsieur* (Nov. 12-17, 1937) which was released earlier (Feb., 1938). But the reference to 'Wrong-Way' Corrigan must post-date his flight of July, 1938, suggesting that *Flat Foot Stooges* could not have been released in May, 1938, let alone shot in Oct., 1937. But the Corrigan reference is voiced-over and could have been added after the film's initial release. Internal evidence that the film might have been altered, is the introductory 'Three Blind Mice' theme, which would not be used again or regularly until *We Want Our Mummy*, released Feb. 24, 1939. The *Scrapbook* reports variant release dates of May 13, Nov. 25, and Dec. 5, (Okuda has May 13) and Larry, although sometimes wrong, lists this film after *Mutts To You* (Oct. 14, 1938) and just before *Three Little Sew and Sews* (Jan. 6, 1939). Most Stooge releases were separated by 3-8 weeks, so it is less likely that *Flat Foot Stooges* was released May 13, just one week before *Healthy, Wealthy and Dumb* (May 20, 1938), and the Nov./Dec. release would have allowed for the 'Corrigan' voiceover and the 'Three Blind Mice' theme to have been added during post-production. Besides 'Three Blind Mice,' the credit screen photos of the Stooges are matted differently, and some of the actors are credited, as they had been in films until *A Pain in the Pullman*. This is the only Stooge film not to give credit to its writer. The consensus is that Chase wrote it; working with the Hugh McCollum production unit, he was given creative freedom to write, produce, and direct two-reelers, and act in them as well. This is the first of a dozen Stooge roles for Dick Curtis [Fred Rardon], often cast as a villain in his films, which included *King Kong*. This is the first of five Stooge roles for silent star Chester Conklin; his brother Heinie also worked in a number of Stooge films. As in *Tassels in the Air*, the Stooges do not succeed in punishing 'the bad guy', but again injure themselves in the attempt. When the Stooges try to put their pants on together, it is not clear what they 'bonk' together.'

Douglas 'Wrong Way' Corrigan is introduced to a cheering New York crowd by Mayor Fiorello La Guardia in 1938.

#32 - HEALTHY, WEALTHY AND DUMB

Studio: Columbia

Released: May 20, 1938

Running Time: 16"24'"

Credited Production Crew:

Associate Producer:	Jules White
Director:	Del Lord
Story & Screen Play:	Searle Kramer
Photography:	Allen G. Siegler
Film Editor:	Charles Nelson

Credited Cast:

Curly Howard
Larry Fine
Moe Howard

Uncredited Cast:

Lucille Lund	Daisy
Jean Carmen	Marge
Erlene Heath	Lil
James C. Morton	hotel manager
Bud Jamison	house detective
Robert 'Bobby' Burns	room service waiter

PERSPECTIVE: Money has been a major concern in recent films. Whether the money was in the possession of the wealthy class [*Termites of 1938*] or the nouveau riche [*Tassels in the Air*], or whether the Stooges had a scheme to make it [*Cash and Carry; Playing the Ponies*], they have never had any. In *Healthy, Wealthy and Dumb* we finally see what the Stooges would do if they actually became wealthy. As we might expect, they wear tuxedos and top hats, drink champagne, smoke fat cigars, and rent the most expensive suite in the 'Hotel Costa Plente.' So far they are much like the rest of us. But they have come to the top from much lower down the class and evolutionary scales, so the comedy exploits the paradox inherent in any Stooge visits to the penthouse. Larry calls a bathtub a "rowboat" and takes his bath buoyed by a balloon flotilla that he pops with his cigar. Curly calls champagne "Sodie pop" and drinks it from the bottle until it comes out his ears. Who else would think a canopied bed had an upper berth? Who else would compare the bed "that goes back to Henry the Eighth" to one "that went back to Sears Roebuck the third"? Their ignorance is superb. Being the nouveau-est of riche, the Stooges have no class or understanding of manners, elegance, or high culture. But the greatest irony of all is the ultimate result of their ignorance: they not only fall prey to con-(wo)men but surrender their entire fortune to New Deal taxation.

The introductory radio quiz scenario reflects contemporary media developments. *Professor Quiz* debuted in 1936, and soon after radio quiz shows became quite the rage. And beginning with the amateur-contest radio craze of 1934, shows began offering prizes to program listeners who could complete the last line of an advertising jingle "in twenty-five words or less." But, as in *The Sitter Downers*, Curly does not win the radio contest through intelligence. He wins through stubbornness and luck, and luck is a theme writer Searle Kramer consciously explores in this film. When Larry beats Moe at cards he admits "it must be beginner's luck"; Moe is frustrated that "every day you have beginner's luck." And when Luck is present, it is often joined all too soon by its evil cousin, Bad Luck: Larry claims luck at cards but ends up being slapped in the head; Moe claims luck at winning Larry's breakfast but ends up with his mouth glued shut; and Curly's lucky access to the contest winnings of $50,000 turns into a huge hotel bill, a huger tax bill, and a potential cleaning by three attractive golddiggers.

The ancient Greeks, shrewd observers of the vicissitudes of human existence, wrote tragedies about heroes like Oedipus, whose life progressed from being an abandoned child to a triumphant king but then plummeted to being a blind, exiled beggar. Here the Stooges progress from the lower class to wealth and the penthouse only to return to being beaten paupers with a huge debt. This is not to say that *Healthy, Wealthy and Dumb* is a Greek tragedy, but it does exploit a similarly wide range of human vicissitudes. In this case, the progression from triumph to decline leads not to tragedy but to comedy. How close those two opposites can become when we laugh at someone else's tragedy!

VISUAL HUMOR: A Stooge first is the struggle with the glue, adapted from Buster Keaton's first Fatty Arbuckle film, *The Butcher Boy* (1917). Moe and Larry helped Curly out of his cement shoes in *The Sitter Downers*, but that was mostly between Moe and Curly; here for

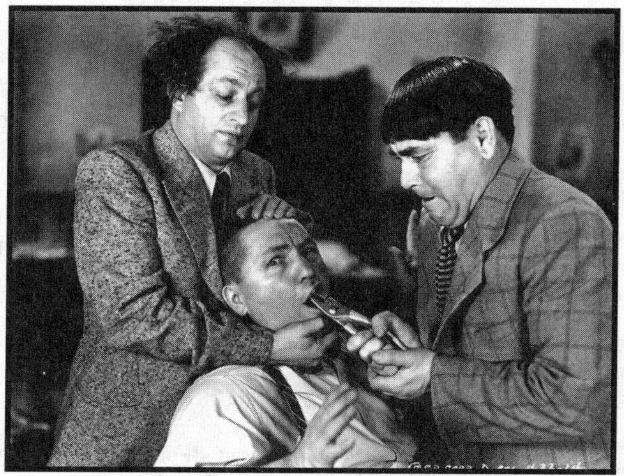

the first time Moe and Larry work together to get Curly's mouth unglued. Having both Moe and Curly glue their mouths together in succession is an oddity: usually just one Stooge suffers each idiocy. Other Stooge firsts: the collapsing 'bunk' bed (although its predecessors are the collapsing floor in *Cash and Carry*, the collapsing house in *The Sitter Downers*, and the collapsing [regular] bed in *Whoops, I'm an Indian*); piling the Stooges three high under a costume or blanket (an extension of their mounting upon one another in *Dizzy Doctors* and *Wee Wee Monsieur*); and having a liquid [champagne] spray out of a Stooge orifice [ears].

Moe blames Curly for breaking something (the spoon), which he himself broke; this may be a variation of Moe blaming Larry for removing the ladder in *Ants in the Pantry*, but it has become a regular feature. Other variations: Mistaking glue for syrup (paint/coffee in *Tassels in the Air*); a monkey moving the plot (*Goofs and Saddles*), and hiding in pants (*A Pain in the Pullman*); Curly hitting Moe (with pliers) who hits Larry (*Grips, Grunts and Groans*). Moe's punching, gouging, and slapping Curly through the broken top hat is most innovative. The final gag - getting knocked out by the three gold diggers - is of the same type as in *Pop Goes the Easel* and *Hoi Polloi:* the Stooges are caught and punished, but we have to assume what happens next.

VERBAL HUMOR: Searle Kramer's script includes a pun (Curly [squirting ink into the detective's eye]: "I just dotted his eye!"), insults (Larry's "Why don't you play cards and improve your mind - what there is of it"; Curly: "What's that monkey got that I ain't got?" Moe: "A longer tail!"), ironies (Moe: "Why didn't you bring me a softer board?!"), a gag about incompatible foods (Curly: "Pie à la mode with beer chasers!"), and a fine, understated line by an extra (Curly: "Did you say 'millions'?" Woman: "Yes, just a few"). The Stooges sang triadic harmony in *Nertsery Rhymes* and *Half-Shot Shooters*, but this is the first time they sing a triadic greeting ("Come in!").

The gag about the taxes deducted from Curly's winnings, a complaint about New Deal taxation, is in stark political contrast to the smiling salute they gave FDR in *Cash and Carry* the previous year. Having a voice on the radio speak back was a popular 1930s gag. Similarly, "Maybe it's somethin' he ate!" varies from the common 1930s complaint: "Maybe it's something I 'et'". Other references: The name of the monkey, 'Darwin,' parodies Charles Darwin's theory of evolution, i.e. that humans are descended from apes. "Quiet, Cleopatra!" refers to the first-century BC Queen of Egypt but is applied to any woman with a high opinion of herself. Moe intentionally says "habus corpus" for the Latin legal phrase "*habeas corpus*". We hear "Curly Howard" on the radio; we last heard a Stooge last name in *Termites of 1938*, which also had the previous Yale reference. Other variations: The "How!" gag (*Whoops, I'm an Indian*); Moe's "Let's go places and buy things" ("...eat things" in *False Alarms*); Moe's "Look! The joint is haunted!" (*Men in Black*); Moe's "sugar bowl haircut!" ("spittoon haircut" in *Three Little Beers*); "Give 'em the ozone" (*Back to the Woods*); and "Oh! This is so sudden!" said in unison by three extras ("Oh woe is us" in *Back to the Woods*).

OTHER NOTES: The title parodies Ben Franklin's 'Early to bed and early to rise, makes a man healthy, wealthy, and wise'; the former half of the expression will be parodied in a future title. Working title: *Cuckoo Over Contests*. When this film was remade later with Shemp as *A Missed Fortune* (1952), the quiz program was updated by adding a phone call to the Stooges, a feature that dates back to the 1939 NBC-Red radio quiz show 'Pot O' Gold'. Jean Carmen [Marge] often used the stage name Julia Thayer, and was best known for her roles in B Westerns and serials (*The Painted Stallion*). Continuity: When Moe slaps Larry and knocks him backwards, we never see where or how he ends up. Also, when Curly collapses the bed, Moe never gets caught inside; nonetheless, we see him caught in the following result shot.

Stooge humor frequently vacillates between the pain of slapstick and the joy of laughter. But Searle Kramer's *Healthy, Wealthy and Dumb* (1938) ranges widely from the good fortune of getting rich *via* a radio quiz program to the double tragedies of getting conned and then taxed back into poverty.

#33 - VIOLENT IS THE WORD FOR CURLY

Studio: Columbia

Released: July 2, 1938

Running Time: 17"37'"

Credited Production Crew:

Associate Producers:	Charley Chase & Hugh McCollum
Director:	Charley Chase
Story & Screen Play:	Al Giebler & Elwood Ullman
Photography:	Lucien Ballard
Film Editor:	Arthur Seid

Credited Cast:

Curly Howard
Larry Fine
Moe Howard

Uncredited Cast:

Gladys Gale	Mrs. Katsby
Marjorie Deanne	daughter
Bud Jamison	gas station boss
Eddie Fetherstone	professor
Al Thompson	professor
John T. Murray	professor
[Pat Gleason	professor]

PERSPECTIVE: Some of the most pleasant Stooge films are those where the inept trio happens upon some opportunity which they ruin but which leads them to another opportunity -- which they also ruin but inadvertently make right. The Stooges are rarely rewarded for a positive outcome, but for them at least not being shot at or chased down the street is, relatively speaking, a reward. *Violent is the Word for Curly* is just such a film. They begin at a service station, and on their first day they annoy three customers and blow up their car, run away, take the job those customers were supposed to have, louse that up, and then get those customers back to their rightful jobs. As always, they leave a trail of destruction behind them, and then they are off to their next episode. Not exactly great adventurers like Don Quixote, Ulysses, or the Star Trek crew, the Stooges nonetheless bounce through life in 190 Columbia episodes, a vast collection of tales, each worthy of being told.

The plot of the film depends on tremendous irony and coincidence. Why should it be that Larry manages to take the professors' academic robes out of the car just before Curly and Moe combine to blow it up? Why should it be that the professors are blown back into the college by the very bomb they created? And why should it be that the gas station owner would leave his station in the hands of three men he had never seen work before? If this were a picaresque novel or a heroic epic, concepts like 'Fate,' 'Dame Fortune,' and 'Divine Intervention' would be used to answer such questions. One would think those concepts are too profound to apply to Hollywood studio comedies of the 1930s, but we saw the beginnings of this in *Grips, Grunts and Groans*, and in the next film after *Violent is the Word for Curly* [*Three Missing Links*], B.O. Botswaddle will say specifically that "Fate must have sent" Curly. Absurd coincidence is the comic equivalent of epic fortune and divine intervention.

This is the third film produced by the new McCollum/Chase team and written by the Al Giebler/Ellwood Ullman duo [*Termites of 1938*; *Tassels in the Air*], and in all three the plot ties together neatly in the end. In *Termites of 1938*, the gopher bombs we see in the first scene end up exterminating the Stooges in the final scene, and in *Tassels in the Air* the highfalutin Mrs. Smirch and Louella Pendle of the first scene are exposed in the final scene. In *Violent is the Word for Curly*, the German professors we hear about on the campus of Mildew College in the very first scene and are blown up in the second scene are then blown back over the wall onto the campus at the conclusion of the film. And just as the real social standing of the society types and the ethnic Omay are so well delineated in the first two films, these German professors should not be relegated simply to the stock of comic character-types either. When this film was shot in mid-March of 1938, the Nazis had already forced or frightened a number of intellectuals out of Europe and into the United States or Russia. You would not know it from the film's characterization of Drs. Feinstein, Frankfurter, and Von Stupor, but the political gloom on the European horizon would darken the film shot the very next week - *Three Little Sew and Sews*.

VISUAL HUMOR: The gas station scene has as much energy and variety as any sequence in Stoogedom. Some of the humor depends on the passive professors who make such wonderful targets for Stooge abuse, some on inter-Stooge abuse, and the rest on the Stooges' having trouble with inanimate objects. Curly's wrestling match with the hose is his best battle with an inanimate object to date. Typical of director Charley Chase's work, the scene builds to a big close which features a sharply ironic contrast between the huge explosion, the bewildered professors, and the still sleeping Curly. Other inventive, well executed, effectively edited visual gags include the struggle to free the pickle from Curly's mouth (like the glue sequence in *Healthy, Wealthy and Dumb*); Moe ramming Gladys Gale's [Mrs. Katsby] elbow into Curly's throat; Larry's absolutely blank stare on stage; and the sequence in which Katsby extends her arms and calls out to the Stooges, "Welcome to Mildew!": they stop, look behind themselves as they do when called "Gentlemen," and then push and shove trying to get into the car. Other variations: the 'Men at Work' sign, and the electric razor (*3 Dumb Clucks*); Curly sleeping on the job (*Punch Drunks*); the Stooges rushing for the food before anyone else (*Pardon My Scotch*); and Curly jumping into the stream to cool himself off (*Back to the Woods*).

VERBAL HUMOR: The song 'Swinging the Alphabet' is a Stooge classic. *Okuda* [27] attributes the song to director Charley Chase, who featured music in his first Stooge film, *Termites of 1938*. The lyrics ("B-A-Bay, B-E-Bee, B-I-Bicky-bi, B-O-bo, bicky-bi-bo-be-u-bu, bicky-bi-bo-bu; C-A-cay") are a bit below college level, but the harmonized and jazzed-up choruses make it more musically complex. On 'C' Larry and Curly join in; on 'D' Moe asks the girls to join in; on 'G' the camera frames a happy chorus of seven girls singing a jazzy harmony; by 'J' Curly and Larry are dancing; Curly sings 'K' and 'L' - the latter finishing with the chorus' "Curly's a dope." After 'M' the Stooges play instruments (*Disorder in the Court; Termites of 1938*) - Larry the violin, Curly the spoons, and Moe a piece of cloth. The Giebler/Ullman script includes a fine insult (Katsby: "Mildew has a lovely student body." Moe: "Yours wouldn't be so bad either if you took off about twenty pounds!"), a three pattern (Moe: "What this college needs anyway is athletics - football!" Larry: "—and basketball!" Curly: "I can do very nicely with a high ball!"), and gags based on Stooge ignorance (Curly: "I'll meet you in the gymnasium next to the dumbbells; you'll know me - I got a hat!"), Curly-esque gluttony (Katsby: "We have a grand day planned: first a visit to the classrooms, then a reception and a buffet luncheon." Curly: "I never ate a buffet but I bet you got somethin' there!"), and mishearing à la *Half Shot Shooters* (Von Stupor: "Tonight we return to Hamburg on the Clipper." Curly: "I never heard of such a thing. He's gonna get a hamburger with a zipper!"). Curly's "Swing it!" derives from *Termites of 1938*, but this is its first use as an isolated expression. According

Violent is the Word for Curly (1938) depends on an ironic paradox: stooges make intellectuals look like stooges, while these same stooges (*the* Stooges) pose as intellectual college professors and teach class.

to *Moe* [59], Curly used this expression regularly when spending many a late night out at clubs; Curly also used to rip table cloths in time to the rhythm, as does Moe here. Other variations: "Right! Right!" (*Dancing Lady*); "I'll explain it so that even you can understand" (*Pardon My Scotch*); and "Just a little: about one quart" (Curly: "Did you say 'millions'?" Woman: "Oh just a few." in *Healthy, Wealthy and Dumb*). References: 'Seabiscuit' was voted Horse of the Year in 1938 and was the top money-winner in 1937. Curly's "knee action" refers to a contemporary shock absorbing mechanism.

OTHER NOTES: The film was shot March 14-17, 1937. This is the first film title that has little bearing on the film's plot. The title is a parody of *Valiant is the Word for Carrie*, an RKO melodrama released in 1936. It told the story of a woman devoting her life to helping orphans, which would have been more appropriate to *All The World's a Stooge*. The introductory theme music blends from the credits into the body of the film as the college girls are playing ball. This technique will be used again for several more films. Two of the professors are played by Eddie Fetherstone and John T. Murray, both of whom had long-standing film careers from the silent era. Sound man Ed Bernds recalled later in interviews that Curly suffered some scorching while strapped to the spit above the open flame; he was so heavy the stage hands had difficult lifting him. Some footage will be reused in *Stop! Look! and Laugh!*. This was one of three (*You Nazty Spy!*; *Yes, We Have No Bonanza*; *Violent is the Word for Curly*) Stooge films Columbia collected along with Buster Keaton and Vera Vague shorts and released to theaters in 1974 as *The Three Stooges Follies*.

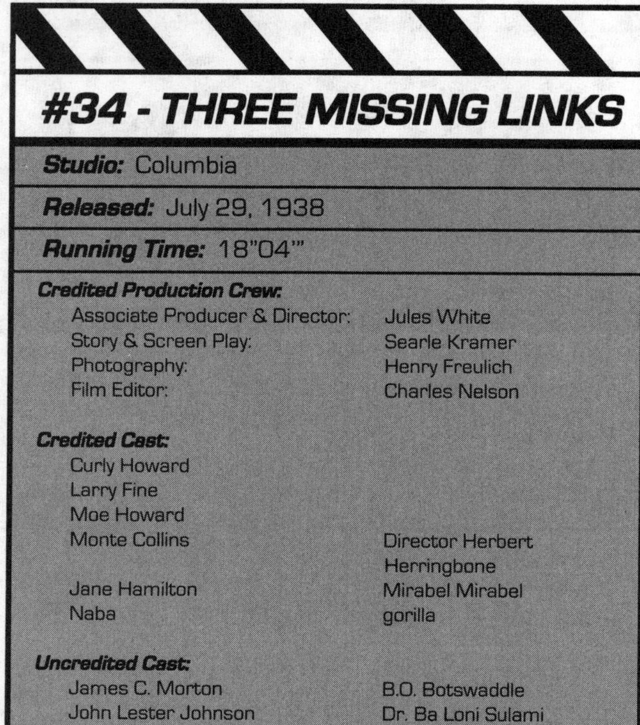

#34 - THREE MISSING LINKS

Studio: Columbia

Released: July 29, 1938

Running Time: 18"04"'

Credited Production Crew:

Associate Producer & Director:	Jules White
Story & Screen Play:	Searle Kramer
Photography:	Henry Freulich
Film Editor:	Charles Nelson

Credited Cast:

Curly Howard	
Larry Fine	
Moe Howard	
Monte Collins	Director Herbert Herringbone
Jane Hamilton	Mirabel Mirabel
Naba	gorilla

Uncredited Cast:

James C. Morton	B.O. Botswaddle
John Lester Johnson	Dr. Ba Loni Sulami

PERSPECTIVE: The recent tendency to omit the Stooges from the opening scene begins with *Termites of 1938* and was used in three of the last five films (*Tassels in the Air*, *Flat Foot Stooges*, and *Violent is the Word for Curly*). This technique, which allows for immediate exposition of the plot and then brings the Stooges into the plot by accident, reaches new heights in *Three Missing Links*, the second film the Stooges made about making a film (*Movie Maniacs*). If the Stooges had not entered Botswaddle's office to clean it, Curly's 'talent' as an animal impersonator would never have been discovered. Curly and Larry sandwich Moe with their broom handles, and Larry and Moe dole out vengeance upon Curly for wiping his seltzer-bottle sprayed glass cleaner all over them, so B. O. fires them, which should be punishment enough; but when the Stooges in a 'one last-chance' scenario claim to be actors and Curly plops to the floor to impersonate a chicken-with-its-head-cut-off, director Herbert gets ready to kill him, too! Curly snarls, and pounds his chest, and Herbert and B. O. agree: "The fat one - Fate must have sent him - he's the dead image of the missing link!" This concatenation of events, all punctuated with rapid slapstick, establishes Curly as a credible gorilla actor.

While plot design was improving film after film, so were the physical gags. We saw an early version of the 'chicken-with-its-head-cut-off' when a mouse-chasing Curly spun on his shoulder in *Termites of 1938*, but now Curly expands the movement and validates it with a name. The Stooges wrestled with inanimate objects in *Cash and Carry* (Curly pulling the tire), *The Sitter Downers* (Larry pulling a board out of a pile), and *Violent is the Word for Curly* (Curly wrestling with the air hose), but here this kind of gag blossoms into a 150-second sequence in which Curly wrestles with the tent stakes. Similarly, animals have been popping up recently with the monkey in *Healthy, Wealthy and Dumb* and the horses, mouse, dog, and duck in *Flat Foot Stooges*. But now we have two gorillas playing lead roles. Much of this rapid physicality can be attributed to the experienced hands-on producer but first-time Stooge director Jules White, and, as often, White made the physical comedy convey the plot: Curly shakes the wet tree and runs from Moe, but as he turns to avoid a slap he suddenly discovers— Dr. Ba Loni Sulami's hut and the love candy.

These three ingredients - two gorillas and a bowl of love candy - create genuine identity crises for both Curly and the gorilla. When Curly sees the real gorilla he challenges him for the right to play the gorilla role in the film. (Sure, he thinks it is Moe in that suit, but how often does Curly kick Moe in the rear?) As for the gorilla, when he sees Curly pulling off his gorilla head he tries to do the same with his own head. Even Moe and Larry cannot

tell which is the 'real' gorilla, and for that matter, neither can we since the costumes look the same. The whole identity crisis is epitomized beautifully in Curly's classic ungrammatical declaration: "Hey! I'm not me!" But then Curly swallows the love candy and falls in love with the gorilla, solving the identity crisis and bringing the film to a conclusion we have not yet seen in a Stooge film and will barely see again: Curly chases the gorilla off into the horizon. Ain't love grand?

VISUAL HUMOR: Some often used Stooge slapstick firsts: the nose bonk Moe delivers in the opening sequence; and two Stooges opening the door to a beast after the third Stooge has knocked but runs away in fear. It is impossible to apportion how much of this slapstick innovation should be credited to the writer, director, or the Stooges themselves. The 'new blood' here is Jules White; at least this was the first Stooge film he directed - the first of over 100 - and he prided himself on rapid activity. For him, crucial to creating effective Stooge physical comedy was triadic timing (Moe's initial encounter with Larry's and Curly's broom handles), quick, effective reactions (Larry's fearful gesturing while the medicine man contemplates eating him), and constant movement (the hut sequence continuously buzzing with Stooge scuffling).

The sequence in which a beast breathes on the Stooges from behind, making the Stooges accuse each other (Moe: "Hey quit breathin' on me, will ya'?" Larry: "Cut it out, puddin'-head!"). We first saw in the lion enclosure of *Movie Maniacs*. The medicine man is the African equivalent of the Indian chief in *Back to the Woods*: a savage who speaks poor English yet knows plenty about modern commerce ("Customer always right!"). The fist game variation is an energetic one, with Curly acting as if he is boxing. This is the first time Moe gets hit with Curly's fist. The WHISTLE sound effect (*Flat Foot Stooges*) is used for the tent stakes popping up. Curly drinking the ink cordial and getting it on his chin recalls having his chin painted black in *Tassels in the Air*; the pay off is nicely set up at the beginning of the scene. Shemp drank ink in his first Vitaphone short *Saltwater Daffy* (1933). Other variations: Larry sleeping against the tent post (Curly sleeping on the car fender in *Violent is the Word for Curly*); Curly hitting Moe's hand with the sledge hammer (*3 Dumb Clucks*); and Moe and Larry shooting at each other from opposite sides (clubbing in *Restless Knights*).

VERBAL HUMOR: There is tremendous irony in Curly's "I'm not me!" For once, his logic is better than his grammar, but that makes Moe's complaint about Curly's grammar even more ironic: the gorilla is the problem, not Curly's grammar. Earlier he had warned him to mind his "Ps and Qs". Writer Searle Kramer fills the script with other ironies (Larry: "I stayed up all last night to see if I snored, and I didn't!"; Curly [drinking the ink]: "Darkest Africa!"; and Larry: "We'll be quiet as a mouse." Curly: "Yeah, a deaf and dumb mouse!") as well as a pun (Herbert: "I wonder where that safari is." Curly: "Maybe they're safari away we'll never catch 'em!"), and three-pattern (Moe: "We're terrific!" Larry: "We're colossal!" Curly: "We're even mediocre!"). This three-pattern is a Stooge first; its punchline is dependent on Stooge ignorance. Other Stooge firsts: Curly's 'cha-cha-cha-cha-cha'; and Moe's "What was the number of that truck?!". Epithets: "turnip-head" and "bubble-brain".

This is the second time the Stooges have been placed in a 'back lot' setting, and as in *Movie Maniacs* there are gags about the film industry (Mirabel Mirabel: "Why go clear to Africa? The studio alone looks like Africa!"; B. O.: "Haven't we got anyone under contract that even looks like an ape?" Mirabel: "No, not even your relatives!"). The ensemble pattern response (Director: "As the scene opens, you're kneeling at her feet. [Moe & Larry: "Yes!"] That's where Curly comes in. You grab your clubs and you fight him. [Moe & Larry: "Yes!"] He knocks you down [Moe & Larry: "Yes!"] Do you understand? [Moe & Larry: "No."]) most closely resembles a pattern in *Dizzy Doctors*. Other variations: comparing the Stooges to Neanderthals (MGM's *Hollywood Party*); Moe: "Well just watch your 'P's' and 'Q's'" (*Beer and Pretzels*); "Oh, ungrateful, eh?", and "Women and children first!" (*False Alarms*); "Wake up and go to sleep!" (*A Pain in the Pullman*); and Curly: "You mean they fffft?" Herbert: "Yes, they ffft!" ("P-tunia" in *Flat Foot Stooges*). References: Curly's "I'm the Robert Taylor type!" refers to the 1930s dashing leading man under contract with MGM, where the Stooges had worked half a decade earlier. 'The

missing link' was a hypothetical species physical anthropologists believed bridged 'cavemen' and apes; since the 1930s scientists have discovered many species of pre-human hominids and abandoned the term.

OTHER NOTES: The film was shot in early April, 1937, the fourth of four in a tight schedule to finish the year's filming [Mar. 14-17 (*Violent is the Word for Curly*), Mar. 22-25 (*Three Little Sew and Sews*), Mar. 30-Apr. 2 (*Mutts to You*), and Apr. 7-12 (*Three Missing Links*)]. The *Scrapbook* says the release date is also given as September 2; in either case, it was released in 1938, the year before *The Gorilla*, starring the Ritz Brothers. Director Jules White learned to edit from childhood Edendale friend Charles Hochberg, whom he later hired at Columbia. Ironically, Monte Collins starred in some of White's earliest directorial projects at Educational Pictures. White attributed 90% of his directorial education to learning the editing process, though his idol was Columbia's Frank Capra, not Educational's Del Lord (whom White also hired at

Columbia). For his early career, see *Bruskin* 49-66. Later White described his Stooge work: 'My theory was to make those pictures move so fast that even if the gags didn't work, the audience wouldn't get bored." Critics accuse him of using excessively cruel, unnecessarily violent gags, but White considered the Stooges to be "caricatures". They weren't for real, so you couldn't take anything they did seriously" [*Okuda* 24-25]. John Lester Johnson [Dr. Ba Loni Sulami] was a professional boxer turned actor; he once boxed Jack Dempsey. He may be best known for his memorable catch line in Our Gang's *The Kid From Borneo* (1933): "Eat 'em up, Yum! Yum!". When the Stooges escape from the medicine man and run into the tree, Moe's high-pitched voice is either sped up or voiced-over by Curly. There is a similar effect during the chase sequence in *Mutts to You.*

Although Curly's battle with the air hose in *Violent is the Word for Curly* was an important predecessor, here in *Three Missing Links* he battles some feisty tent stakes for two-and-a-half minutes. Now in his fifth year of short film production at Columbia, Curly in 1938 is capable of making an inanimate object come alive–like Fred Astaire with a freestanding coat rack, only much less graceful and much more comical. The frustration he exhibits is the result of being isolated from his fellow Stooges, but when they come to assist him they inevitably pay a severe price. This, in turn, causes Curly more pain but this time at the hands of a very animated object - Moe. In several subsequent films, Curly's struggles with inanimate objects will be developed further, reaching a zenith in 1939's *Oily to Bed, Oily to Rise.*

#35 - MUTTS TO YOU

Studio: Columbia

Released: October 14, 1938

Running Time: 18"02'"

Credited Production Crew:

Associate Producers:	Charley Chase & Hugh McCollum
Director:	Charley Chase
Story & Screen Play:	Al Giebler & Elwood Ullman
Photography:	Allen G. Sigler
Film Editor:	Arthur Seid

Credited Cast:

Curly Howard	
Larry Fine	
Moe Howard	
Bess Flowers	Mrs. Manning

Uncredited Cast:

Lane Chandler	Doug Manning
Bud Jamison	Officer O'Halloran
Vernon Dent	Landlord Stutz
Cy Schindell	policeman

PERSPECTIVE: This is the first Stooge script to be pulled out of the Columbia archives. In 2001, we rarely see or even hear about the other two-dozen comedy series Jules White's Columbia short film department produced between 1933 and 1957. But most of the same producers, writers, directors, and actors that worked on Stooge films belonged to the Columbia staff and worked on these other series. *Mutts to You* is based on *Ten Baby Fingers* (1934), a two-reeler made by the comedy team of [George] Sidney and [Charlie] Murray, and the same story was filmed again as an Andy Clyde short called *My Little Feller* (1937). None of these Columbia stories/scripts were ever just re-shot, though. *Mutts to You* is a McCollum/Chase production, so gadgetry and music are added: the dog-wash and baby hamper gadgetry are adapted from the harness apparatus in their *Flat Foot Stooges* and the mouse catcher in their *Termites of 1938*, and the music accompanying the final baby-washing sequence recalls the background music of their *Termites of 1938*.

The plot depends on a number of mistaken identities and judgments. The Stooges think the baby is an abandoned one, Mrs. Manning thinks the baby has been kidnapped, Mr. Manning thinks taking the dog to Palm Springs is a good idea, Mr. Stutz cannot find the baby in the laundry hamper, and the Irish policeman thinks the Stooges are Irish or Chinese and that Curly is a woman. As in most of the films written by the McCollum/Chase and Giebler/Ullman teams, almost everyone is a Stooge at some point in the film. Three of them just happen to be much sillier, energetic, and physical than the rest. No one else puts ice cream in their pocket or sponges in their stockings or runs down the street dressed as Chinese launderers.

The ultimate statement about misjudgment is Moe's: "I don't know; it was my idea but I don't think much of it." This unique line uttered by Moe as Curly loads the Manning child into the car turns out to be the first and one of the very few soliloquies in a Stooge film. Of course, it was a bad idea to take the child from the Manning door stoop, especially in the shadow of the Lindbergh kidnapping trial two years earlier. Of all the mistaken identities and judgments in the film, this is perhaps the worst. But Moe's momentary reflection is subtly yet utterly hilarious. These guys do just about everything wrong, and almost every idea they have backfires whether or not the original idea was a good one. Picking up the baby turned out to be a bad idea, and putting sponges in Curly's nylons turned out to be not a particularly good idea. Come to think of it, hiding the baby in a rolling laundry basket turned out to be not such a great idea either. Bad ideas or good ideas that turn sour produce comedy, and that is the goal. But that is why Moe's soliloquy is so ironic: if the Stooges did everything right, they would not be Stooges. Moe is not supposed to admit that; he is not even supposed to know it. He's a Stooge.

VISUAL HUMOR: It is precisely when Curly's mechanical check up concludes in a joke (Moe: "Did you ever have your valves ground?" Curly: "Certainly! With onions!") and Moe grabs Curly's nose and prepares for a gouge that Moe observes the baby on the stoop. This very effective technique of interrupting a slapstick event to drive the plot onwards was used successfully in the previous film when Curly in mid-slapstick espied the cabin of Dr. Ba Loni Sulami. The car-pushing scene has a pedigree that dates back to the jalopies in *Cash and Carry* and *Termites of 1938* and to Curly taking on mule-like strength (*A Pain in the Pullman*) and equine speed (*Playing the Ponies*); in *Three Missing Links* Curly plays a

gorilla - a wild animal - and here in this film he plays, in a sense, a car engine - a mechanical devise. And yet, when he touches the dog-wash mechanism at the end of the film, he completely screws it up. The water ruining Curly's sponge-filled stockings and the radiator melting the ice cream in Moe's pocket are quite similar in form. They are both Chase-like silent gags that need no verbal accompaniment. A Stooge first: using the cash register as a slot machine. Moe slaps Larry because "if you were over here I'd give you this!" This is a variation on the slap Moe gives Curly "for what you was thinkin'!" in *Whoops, I'm an Indian.* We have already seen Moe blame/slap the wrong person, but here the paperboy throws the newspaper and hits Moe, Moe blames and slaps Curly, and then Curly blames the baby. Other variations: a solo Curly in drag (*Whoops, I'm an Indian*); and using a stethoscope (*Men in Black*).

VERBAL HUMOR: Giebler and Ullman wrote specific gags for the Curly-as-machine sequences (Curly [pedaling the dog-wash bicycle]: "I'm gettin' sick and tired of this job. I ain't gettin' anywhere!"; Moe: "You know the old engine ain't what it used to be." Larry: "Listen to that exhaust!"; and Moe: "Why don't you close your cutout? Turn her over. Just as I thought! Two cylinders missin'!") and the baby sequences (Moe: "We'll take him over to the police station." Curly: "You're going to have him arrested for loitering?"; Curly: "That was little-bitsie me you heard talkin'." Moe: "Baby want a cracker? [he smashes it on Curly's forehead; to Stutz] He's spoiled!"), including two three-patterns (Larry: "Maybe someone's tryin' to get rid of it." Curly: "You mean it's being adopted." Moe: "'Abandoned,' ya' lug!"; Larry: "He's a cute little rascal, ain't he?" Curly: "I'd like to keep him and raise him up myself." Moe: "Nothin' doin'! It ain't fair to the kid!"). Two of Curly's gag lines - "I like babies. I was one myself once!" said with the greatest enthusiasm, and "I don't feel like a mother," said quite softly - demonstrate the emotional range he brings to his roles.

Decades before the concept of political correctness became the norm, ethnic humor played a regular role in Stooge comedy. Whether imitating or making fun of Chinese-Americans (as here in *Mutts to You* [1938]) or German, Irish, Jewish, Italian, African-Americans or other groups, the Stooge films can hardly be accused of insulting any of them considering that the Stooges themselves played utterly inept imbeciles. Almost everyone was fair game for their humor: fat people, bald people and – in this case – babies, dogs, Chinese Americans, women, policemen and middle class white males.

Two of the car gags ("two cylinders missin'!" and "Sounds like a carbon knock to me!") follow upon the one ("Knee action") in *Violent Is the Word for Curly.* Just as in *Pop Goes the Easel* and *Wee Wee Monsieur*, there are plenty of ethnic accents here for comic effect, including Chinese, Irish, and Yiddish, and Moe saying in a Chinese (toned) accent one of their old standby phrases: "Okay, Larry. Give!" The Chinese box in *Slippery Silks* Larry called 'Ching Hi Lee'; here the Chinese laundry is 'Wong Hi Lee'. The flea execution, an early exploration into Stooge sadism that will thrive in some of the WW II films, is clever from the moment Larry begins inspecting the Dalmatian ("the one with the freckles") to the flea's "Oh, they got me," the latter recalling the immortal last line of the radio tube in *Men in Black.* Curly's chatter while doing the Dalmatian's nails ("Did anyone ever tell you you have pretty paws? But you shouldn't bite your nails!") improves on the manicure he gave to the horse in *Flat Foot Stooges.* Other variations: Larry's "Somethin' I et!" (*Soup to Nuts*; *Healthy, Wealthy and Dumb*); the Yiddish "Hak mir nit kain tsheinik," and "Backbiter!" (*Pop Goes the Easel*); and Moe: "Mind your 'Ps' and 'Qs' (*Beer and Pretzels*).

OTHER NOTES: The film was shot in late March/early April, 1938, the week before *Three Missing Links.* The title parodies the popular insult 'Nuts to you!'; the working title was *Muts to You.* Three of Sidney & Murray's six 1934 scripts were used for Stooge films. Besides this one, *Plumbing for Gold* was the basis for *A Plumbing We Will Go*, *Vagabond Loafers*, and *Scheming Schemers*, and *Back to the Soil* was remade as *Yes, We Have No Bonanza.* The concept of *Mutts to You* will be reused for 1942's *Sock-A-Bye Baby.* Bess Flowers has now played a society woman in three films. "The Queen of the Extras" appeared in hundred of films during her four-decade career. Here she is given credit on the title screen. Lane Chandler [Doug Manning] appeared in over 400 films, including everything from bit parts to supporting roles in DeMille films and leading roles opposite the likes of Garbo. Cleaning up the baby in the final scene is an elaboration of the offer to clean up the nitro-glycerinated professors in *Violent Is the Word For Curly.* Landlord Stutz' bicarbonate remedy of three heaping teaspoons of baking soda has about 16,000 mg. of sodium.

Gadgetry has long been a part of Stooge films. Their very first film, Fox's *Soup to Nuts* (1930), was written by the famous gadget-designer Rube Goldberg, and Stooge short film director Charley Chase loved inserting gadgety into his comedies. The harness gag in 1938's *Flat Foot Stooges* as well as the mouse catcher in *Termites of 1938* are predecessors, but of all these films this dog-cleaning machinery in the final release of 1938 - *Mutts to You* - remains the most vibrant some sixty years later. The machinery fits very well into the narrative because it serves to frame the ring-composed story: the opening sequence only tantalizes the viewer with the dog-cleaning machinery, so the final denouement with the baby inserted into the dog-machinery brings the tale to a satisfying conclusion.

1939

Three Little Sew and Sews • We Want Our Mummy

A Ducking They Did Go • Yes, We Have No Bonanza • Saved By the Belle

Calling All Curs • Oily to Bed, Oily to Rise • Three Sappy People

#36 - THREE LITTLE SEW AND SEWS

Studio: Columbia

Released: January 6, 1939

Running Time: 15"47"'

Credited Production Crew:

Associate Producer:	Jules White
Director:	Del Lord
Story and Screen Play:	Ewart Adamson
Photography:	Lucien Ballard
Film Editor:	Charles Nelson

Credited Cast:

Curly Howard	
Larry Fine	
Moe Howard	
Phyllis Barry	Miss Olga
Harry Semels	Count Alfred Gehrol

Uncredited Cast:

James C. Morton	Admiral H.S. Taylor
Bud Jamison	policeman
Vernon Dent	guest at party
Ned Glass	[sailor who gives admirals pants?]
Cy Schindell	prison guard
John Tyrell	

PERSPECTIVE: This innovative film creates for Stooge comedy a new world of geo-political territories, spatial dimensions, and satirical tones. Writer Ewart Adamson had a penchant for creating elaborate scenes, huge venues to play them in, and innovative and rough slapstick with plenty of hardware. We saw a fine example of this in the construction sequence of his *The Sitter Downers*, where the Stooges have an entire lot in which to run around and fall from house frames, get dynamited up into trees and knocked down again with a 20-foot board, all because of a sit-down strike - front page stuff of national political importance. With Europe on the brink of war, Adamson expands his political horizons to international scope and places the Stooges in the mythical European kingdom of Televania, where, outfoxed by a Mata Hari-like spy, they upgrade that lumber and dynamite for a prototype-type submarine, biplanes, bombs, and 10-inch shells, and have the whole sea as the setting for their chase sequence.

Besides the mythical setting, the international espionage and the cutting-edge war machines that make this film grander in scope than the previous Stooge films and, for that matter, almost any 1930s Hollywood comedy, the wild submarine ride expands the boundaries of Stooge physical comedy. Consider the vehicles the Stooges have ridden in their films to date - everything from a reindeer-drawn sleigh to a sail-boat hospital gurney - and then consider how they not only ride in a submarine here but ride it in 360° circles both horizontally and vertically as it spins and leaps in and out of the ocean like a dolphin. We see this in not only model shots but also interior shots with the Stooges spinning upside down and around. It is as if previous films have confined Stooge movements to a two dimensional world, while this one sets them free to explore and abuse a three dimensional world defying laws of earthly and nautical physics. It will be seventeen years before the Stooges explore outer space in *Space Ship Sappy*, but the final sequence of *Three Little Sew and Sews* finds them being chased through the stratosphere in a world without a horizon.

Like the previous Ewart Adamson films [*Slippery Silks; The Sitter Downers*], this one falls into two distinct parts. The first part shows the Stooges bragging about women and shore leave in a scene devoid of a comic

focus, and then Curly impersonates an officer, throws his military buddies in the brig, and bribes them for 5 bucks. All this amounts to little more than atypical enlisted-men comedy, a genre of comedy different from previous Stooge military comedies like *Uncivil Warriors* and *Half-Shot Shooters*, but one which all comedians will exploit during the war years. These scenes exhibit Stooge normalcy only where their triadic powers are allowed to flourish, as when Curly kicks Moe who kicks Larry who kicks the guard [Cy Schindell] who kicks Curly, or where Curly marches down the hallway forwards in the wrong direction and backwards in the right direction. In his own little way, Curly's spatial and directional use of that hallway is as expansive as the submarine in the sea and the angelic Stooges in the air.

VISUAL HUMOR: The chase around the periscope, with Curly hitting Olga with the backswing and the count with the foreswing, derives from the chase around the tree in *Back to the Woods*, but there is a lasting innovation: this is the first time a Stooge knocks out two enemies with the backswing and foreswing of the same blow. This kind of movement dates back to when Curly hit Larry with the backswing of a sledge hammer at the gate in *3 Dumb Clucks* and in the pit in *Cash and Carry*; in *Healthy, Wealthy and Dumb* Moe broke the $5000 vase with the backswing of a board. Director Del Lord includes three other 'chain reaction' gags: the admiral's uniform is passed from the sailor to Moe to Larry to Curly ("Cleaned and pressed for the admiral in a hurry!" à la *A Pain in the Pullman*); the Stooges and the prison guard enact the sequential 'kicking an officer' routine; and when at the finish of the party scene Curly leans down to take a taste of the cake Larry holds behind his back, the count stops, Larry smashes into him, and Curly's face goes right into the cake.

Few Stooge films to date contain extended beatings. One or two slaps, gouges or kicks usually completes a sequence. But here the extended beating Moe and Larry give Curly drives the plot. It puts Moe and Larry in jail, gives Curly a chance to do his window antics, allows him to bribe Moe and Larry, and gives them the idea of masquerading as the admiral and his companions, which gets them to the party. Curly's full-body movements are becoming even more elaborate, as when he quivers, slips, falls, and sits after kissing Olga and struggles to get away from the couch with the spring attached to his clothing. No sound effects are used in the 'kicking an officer' routine. The large shell whistling by Curly may derive from the Marx Brothers' *Duck Soup* (1933). Other variations: the spring gag (*Hoi Polloi*) and the nose bonk (*Three Missing Links*, although *Three Little Sew and Sews* was actually shot two weeks earlier).

VERBAL HUMOR: Larry's "He's an old sew and sew" is the first title gag to be used internally in the dialogue of a film. We hear two new Stooge voices: Moe mimics Curly in a semi-falsetto ("*Join the navy and see the world. No more smelly sweat shops. Beautiful girls in every port. Woo-woo!*"), and in the brig scene Curly whispers in his lower, normal voice. Their voices in the submarine sound occasionally distant. Adamson scripted a few gags for the initial dressing sequence; they emphasize repellent Stooges (Moe changing his socks: "What an experience!"), repellent Stooge dates (Larry: "You should see that bearded lady in the circus. Is she a beaut' when she gets a shave!"), alcohol (Curly: "You know gasoline don't taste so good since prohibition...They ain't so careful like when they use it for makin' gin... but it ain't bad."), and a prop joke after Moe sits on Larry's curling iron and clips it on Larry's nose ("I always wanted to see how you look with a permanent wave!"). The submarine sequence includes appropriate periscope gags (Curly: "A microscope! I can see!" Moe: "What?" Curly: "Water!"; Curly [hearing meows]: "A school of catfish just went by!"; and Moe: "Get to your post!" Curly: "What post? I don't even see a street lamp!"). Curly makes threats ("Put these men on rations of bread and water! On second thought, plain water! [GOUGE] Salt water!"), and defiant responses to threats (Moe: "We'll be shot at sunrise for this." Curly: "Maybe the sun won't come out tomorrow: it might rain!"; Olga: "One move out of you and I'll kill you." Curly: "If you do I'll never talk to you again!"). Epithet: "chuckle-head" (*Half-Shot Shooters*). As in *Mutts to You*, Moe has a self-reflective line: "Whadya think we're in the movies?".

Curly's lament about beans ("You see, they feed you beans every day, except on Sunday. That's when you get bean soup *and* beans!") recalls the only dialogue Moe [27] could remember from his first vaudeville performance with Shemp in 1916: "All they do is give you beans. Beans for breakfast, beans for lunch, and beans for dinner. Why they even send you to war with a bean shooter!". Using gags based on mishearing (Larry: "We'd still be all right if you hadn't blabbed off about us being tailors." Curly: "Well don't 'tailor' sound like 'sailor'?") began in *Half-Shot Shooters*. Other variations: "Ha-cha-cha-cha-cha!" and "bubble-brain!" (*Three Missing Links*; although this film predates that one); Larry: "We're trapped like rats!" Moe: "Speak for yourself!" (*Back to the Woods*); Moe calling Curly 'bloodhound' (*Goofs and Saddles*); thinking the 'aerial bomb' is a pelican ('tarantula' in *Disorder in the Court*; 'octopus/spider' in *A Pain in the Pullman*; Curly offers up Moe as a 'pelican' to Dr. Ba Loni Sulami in *Three Missing Links*). Reference: 'Old Taylor' was a brand of whiskey, a Stooge favorite.

OTHER NOTES: The shooting dates (late March, 1938) predate those of *Three Missing Links* (early April, 1938). Two working titles: *Three Goofy Gobs* and *Submarine Behave!*. The angel Stooges at the conclusion of the film are accompanied by the 'Listen to the Mocking Bird' theme; the same music introduced the Stooges' first scene in *Termites of 1938*. Columbia pioneered submarine films with Capra's initial *Submarine* (1928), remade as *Fifty Fathoms Deep* (1931) and *Devil's Playground* (1937). Stock footage of the sub at the sea bottom is from the latter; it will be reused in *They Stooge to Conga*. This may be the first submarine comedy; *Born to Dance* (1936) was the first musical set, in part, on a submarine. Just before filming the final process shot, Larry screamed while suspended by piano wire. [Forrester, *Trivia* 45]. *Restless Knights* was set in a mythical country, but here the Stooges wreak havoc in a contemporary mythical country. The name 'Televania' was probably inspired by 'television' to be used in *A Plumbing We Will Go* one year hence.

#37 - WE WANT OUR MUMMY

Studio: Columbia

Released: February 24, 1939

Running Time: 16"27'"

Credited Production Crew:

Associate Producer:	Jules White
Director:	Del Lord
Original Screen Play by:	Elwood Ullman & Searle Kramer
Photography by:	Allen G. Siegler
Film Editor:	Charles Nelson

Credited Cast:

Curly Howard
Larry Fine
Moe Howard

Uncredited Cast:

Bud Jamison	Dr. Powell
James C. Morton	Curator
Dick Curtis	Crook
Robert Williams	Prof. Tuttle
Ted Lorch	claw-handed mummy
Eddie Laughton	taxi driver

PERSPECTIVE: The greatest legacy of ancient Egyptian civilization has been its awe-inspiring, deeply religious belief in an eternal afterlife. But in the wake of 1922's highly publicized discovery of Pharaoh Tutankhamen's ('King Tut's') burial site and the mortal curse associated with it, Hollywood would regularly assign most films involving ancient Egyptian afterlife to the horror genre. Universal Studios, after its initial 1931 beast-man type horror films, *Dracula* and *Frankenstein*, established this tradition in 1932 with its creepy and mysterious hit, *The Mummy*. In 1935, the great vaudevillean Eddie Cantor (whose films would influence Stooge comedies more than once) turned this concept into farce by setting a large portion of his *Kid Millions* amidst haunted ancient tombs in modern Egypt. Now it was the Stooges' turn. Searle

Kramer had already placed the Stooges in historical or exotic settings in *Back to the Woods*, *Wee Wee Monsieur* and *Three Missing Links*. For this second of the 1939 releases he and co-writer Elwood Ullman adapt Cantor's concept and take the Stooges not to ancient Egypt but to the in-between world of Egyptian archaeology, combining the exotic desert of modern Egypt and the mystery of ancient Egypt.

The desert setting evokes a transoceanic taxi ride

and the fine 'mirage' sequence, but it is the 'the curse of King Rutentuten' that makes this film ground-breaking. Many degrees spookier than the castle corridors of *Restless Knights*, the subterranean Egyptian setting teems with underground passages, secret vantage points, trap doors, a hidden well, mummies, skeletons, claw hands, knives thrown from nowhere, and spooky voices and echoes. Each of these horrors sets the Stooges off in a different direction, and the Stooges never walk in any of them. They scurry, fall, climb, or step slowly backward, and no film comedians were ever so adept at filling the camera frame and generating so much chaotic movement scurrying back and forth between confined passageways and close-ended rooms in compact, well-orchestrated movements. In addition, every time the

Stooges change direction the plot takes a turn as well. Each new fright brings them into a more complex scenario. They separate, frighten each other, describe the frightening thing they have seen, and then run from another fright, all the while yelling "Whooaah!" or "Woob-woob-woob." And every scene progresses quickly into a slapstick finish or someone yelling "Look!" to advance to the next scene.

It is significant that the Stooges for the first time here find themselves in a haunted situation. With many permutations and combinations, such 'scare comedies' will occur again and again in the next decade, particularly after Shemp rejoins the trio, providing endless occasions for beast-man chases and physical comedy that extends out beyond inter-Stooge slapstick and usually ends with the Stooges capturing the bad guys. Both in terms of plot and physicality, haunted corridors will provide an excellent setting for Stooge comedy.

VISUAL HUMOR: Stooge firsts: looking at Larry's hair/scalp through the telescope ("We're comin' to a jungle! I can see the tunneled underbrush, and camels walkin' through it!"); the delayed soaking from a well; Curly shaking off water like a dog; Curly's metallic sounding teeth chatter; and covering a hole with the carpet. Curly fought a gorilla in *Three Missing Links*; this time it is an alligator. Film editor Charles Nelson deserves credit for editing the bite sequence. The alligator is real; Curly's rear end (in the close up) is not. The movements in Curly's swimming pantomime are of the same vintage as his wrestling with the air-hose in *Violent is the Word for Curly* and the tent stakes in *Three Missing Links*; and dressing as a mummy is of the same vintage as his appearances as a gorilla. When Curly says "Follow me!" to Moe, he has that same confident, twinkling-eyed look he had in the pit in *Cash and Carry*. Curly's fist movement when he says "Hey Hey" is a development from the office scene in *Three Missing Links*. Queenie hid in a mummy coffin in *Soup to Nuts*. The first entrance the Stooges made in a Columbia film (*Woman Haters*) was backwards, as is their entrance here. Other variations: Curly smashing the other two with the box he is carrying (*A Pain in the Pullman*); Curly as a disguised detective (*Horses' Collars*); the taxi with the nautical equipment (*Uncivil Warriors*); the 'Shave and a Haircut' knock (*Whoops, I'm an Indian*); falling to the basement, and throwing the rope and urn at Curly (*Cash and Carry*); Curly getting hit in the belly and spitting water in Moe's face (*Movie Maniacs*); and liquid squirting out of Curly's ears (*Healthy, Wealthy and Dumb*).

VERBAL HUMOR: Verbal gags abound. Besides the mummy gags (Curly: "He's all unraveled!"; [three-pattern] Moe: "We'll make a mummy out of you." Curly: "I can't be a mummy: I'm a daddy!" Larry: "All right, so you'll be a daddy mummy!"), Egypt-related gags include gags about Egyptian kings (Tuttle: "This is Rutentuten. He was a midget." Moe: "All this trouble for a shrimp like that!" Curly: "What a small world!"; Powell: "We will never find the missing king." Curly [pulling a playing card from his pocket]: "How'd you know the king was missing?" Moe to Curly: "That's how you won my thirteen cents!"), parodies of multi-syllabic ancient Egyptian names (Rutentuten, Hotseetotsee), puns on North African geography (Curly: "I'd rather go to Tunis. Then we could have Tunis-sandwiches for lunch!"; Curly: "I got an uncle in Cairo. He's a Cairo-practor!"), an anachronism (Larry: "Maybe we're in the subway."), and an insult to the Stooges (Curator: "If the curse does strike them, it would be a blessing to humanity!").

The modern Egyptian desert setting evokes the spectacularly ignorant argument about the word 'mirage' (Curly: "It's the ocean!" Larry: "Ocean nothin'. That's a mirage ['MEER-ij']." Moe: "A mirage ['MEER-ij'] is somethin' you see yourself in. That's a mirage ['mir-AHJ]. Curly: "Mirage?! ['mir-AHJ] That's where you keep your automobile!:" Moe: "I said a 'mirage' ['mir-AHJ]." Curly: "mirage ['MEER-ij'], mirage ['mir-AHJ'], whatever it is, I'm goin' swimmin'!"); the idea of one dolt teaching another recalls the 'inconspicerous' sequence in *Ants in the Pantry* and the pig Latin lesson in *Tassels in the Air*. Another set piece is the exchange between Curly and the Echo (Curly: "Where are you?" Echo: "Where are you?" Curly: "I'm here; where are you?" Echo: "I'm here; where are you?" Curly: "I asked you first. Where are you?" Echo: "None of your business!").Non-plot specific gags include literal jokes (Moe: "Weigh the anchor!" Curly: "40 pounds!"; "He's the real McCoy!" Larry: "McCoy? I thought his name was Rutentuten?"; and "Take a grip on yourselves." [Curly grabs Moe]), and four more three-patterns (Moe: "For science!" Larry: "For science!" Curly:

"For 5000 bucks!"; Moe: "I'll take that end." Larry: "I'll take this end." Curly: "I'll take the end of the middle!"; Larry: "Hmm!" Moe: "Hmm!" Curly: "Hmm-hmm-hmm-hmm-hmm, hmm-hmm!" [*Whoops, I'm an Indian*]; and Curly: "We'll start in the basement!" Moe: "To the basement!" Larry: "To the basement!" All [unison]: "To the basement!"].

Stooge firsts: "Who came in?" in response to "Gentlemen!"; and the first Stooge use of the word 'imbecile'. As in the previous film, there are some strange sounds: Moe's voice used as an echo; and Curly's gorilla sounds when he sees the first mummy. The classic "Being as there's no other place around the place, I reckon this must be the place, I reckon," and the use of nautical terminology derive from *Uncivil Warriors*.

The 'beast behind' pattern [Voice: "This is the tomb of the mighty King Rutentuten!" Moe to Curly: "How do you know?" Curly: "I didn't say anything. Larry: "Neither did I"] derives from *Movie Maniacs*. Other variations: "Bring 'em back alive" [*Wee Wee Monsieur*]; "The joint is haunted!" [*Men in Black*]; "I'll go when I'm ready!" [*Plane Nuts*]; a Stooge motto [*Termites of 1938*]; the commercial radio announcement [*Dizzy Doctors*]; and "They're octopus!" [*Disorder in the Court* and *The Sitter Downers*]. Moe telling Curly, "You take it easy or we won't let you carry it at all," represents a typical inter-Stooge dynamic: Curly works, Moe supervises and criticizes, Larry looks over the shoulder.

References: In the 1938 World Series the Yankees swept the Cubs; the film was shot in November, about one month after that Series; 'Rutentuten' is modeled after 'Tutankhamen,' who died in c. 1340 BC.; 'Hotsee-totsee,' contemporary slang, may have been inspired by Hatshepsut who lived a generation before Tutankhamen; 'Excelsior!' is from the 1842 Longfellow poem of the same name; 'Michaelmas Day' is the Feast of St. Michael [September 29]; 'Ali Ben Woodman and his Swinging Bedouins' makes reference to Benny Goodman, "King of Swing"; and 'It's a good thing I'm an old tailor' refers to Old Taylor whiskey [*Three Little Sew and Sews*].

OTHER NOTES: 'Three Blind Mice' is the theme song for this and the rest of the 1939 releases; it will be used, with several variations, until 1959. The front credits still overlay a grayish background, as since 1936, but only for the rest of the 1939 releases. Moe provides the voice for the radio announcement and its echo, confusing the latter. Most, not all, ancient Egyptian mummies are older than "2000 years". Motto: 'At your service night and day. If we don't get 'em you don't pay. Excelsior!". The Stooges visit ancient Egypt in *Mummy's Dummies* (1948).

We Want Our Mummy (1939) is the first Stooge 'scare comedy.' Cinematic horror and macabre settings grew their roots during the silent era in the United States and Germany, and after Universal Studios released *Frankenstein* and *The Mummy* in the early 1930s, the genre was well established in the sound era as well. This genre was perfect for Stooge comedies. Inexpensive to produce, scare comedies required only narrow passageways, hidden closets and doors, and frighteningly silly beast-men. The Stooges' ability to scurry around the passageways and react - or not notice and then react - to the beast-men would develop for more than a decade into the Shemp era.

#38 - A DUCKING THEY DID GO

Studio: Columbia

Released: April 7, 1939

Running Time: 16"16'"

Credited Production Crew:

Associate Producer:	Jules White
Director:	Del Lord
Orginal Screen Play by:	Andrew Bennison
Photography by:	Lucien Ballard
Film Editor:	Charles Nelson

Credited Cast:

Curly Howard
Larry Fine
Moe Howard

Uncredited Cast:

Lynton Brent	Blackie
Wheaton Chambers	crook
Bud Jamison	Chief of Police
Cy Schindel	fruit vendor
Vernon Dent	vegetarian customer
Al Seymour	policeman
Victor Travers	policeman; member of club

PERSPECTIVE: To be a Stooge requires being gullible, simple-minded, incredibly fortunate, and above all, ignorant and incompetent, but all these qualities are often contagious for those who come into contact with the trio. As this narrative unfolds, the jobless Stooges louse up their nicely orchestrated attempt at stealing a watermelon when an incompetent Larry throws (and an inept Curly misses) a high pass which lands on a policeman's head. They are fortunate enough to escape thanks to the policeman's incompetence, but they louse up this escape by gullibly trusting a conman. They simple-mindedly attempt to sell a hunting club membership to first their boss, then a vegetarian and then that same policeman. They run from him and louse up this second escape by incompetently running into a police station, but there they are fortunate enough to sell all their memberships to the gullible police chief and the mayor. Ultimately they louse up the hunting expedition by being ignorant and incompetent enough to steal prize ducks and shoot holes in their own boat.

Andrew Bennison, who wrote the early classic *Pardon My Scotch*, helped to define these qualities. There the Stooges loused up their job as incompetent, simple-minded ("The door goes on the right") carpenters, were simple-minded enough to think they could concoct a pick-me-up, lucked upon a great formula, and showed their ignorance at the party by blowing the booze all over the place. The actual plot of *A Ducking They Did Go* is quite different, but Bennison puts the Stooges through similar changes in what seem to be just the typical vicissitudes in a day in the life of the Stooges. This is Bennison's method of producing compact, energetic, and relentless comedies. Comedy often thrives on escalating predicaments, and the comedy here snowballs through the first eight episodes. The watermelon episode starts things off with its physicality and closing chase, and this yields to the verbal silliness of the encounters with the bosses and the vegetarian. Another chase leads to the second verbal encounter, this time with important people as gullible as the Stooges themselves. (It makes for good comedy to make the mayor and police chief into bumpkins; conmen, on the other hand, work much better when they play it straight and allow the comedy to develop in spite of them.)

The final few minutes change course rather drastically. Put on the artificial lake set built for them in Columbia Stage #6, the diminutive Stooges all of a sudden have a very large, hollow set to fill, and the formerly compact story spreads them out, separating them from the hunting party and each other for most of the scene. The intensity of the earlier scenes is replaced by a solo Curly trying to shoot a water-spouting duck, a solo Larry trying to shoot a duck off Moe's back, and Larry and Moe trying to shoot a duck off Curly's head. Previous solo scenes, e.g. Curly wrestling the air hose in *Violent is the Word for Curly* or the tent stakes in *Three Missing Links*, come in the midst of their plots. Solo work like this late in a film tends to diffuse the intensity established earlier in the film.

VISUAL HUMOR: Stooge firsts: This film has the first of many egg smashings in a Stooge film; after Curly shakes hands with Blackie and smashes an egg into his hand, the take lasts a full twelve seconds. Another first is Larry trying to shoot a duck off Moe's back. For the first time in several years, the 'fist game' is just the original fist game without variation. Other variations: beginning a film hungry and jobless (*Three Little Pigskins*); watermelon and a policeman (*Wee Wee Monsieur*); shooting into the air and hitting the street light, and Curly marching into the water (*Whoops, I'm an Indian*); having the Stooges characterize themselves as thieves (*Movie Maniacs);* coming to a sliding, screeching halt, and Curly shaking himself off like a dog (*We Want Our Mummy*); Moe getting a branch in the face (*Uncivil Warriors*); and marching backwards into the wall (*A Pain in the Pullman*).

VERBAL HUMOR: Curly varies Blackie's sales pitch with great enthusiasm, rendering "Every red-blooded man is a potential hunter at heart. Why there's one in every office." first as "Every blooded he-man is a potentate hunter. There's one in every office." and then as "Is your blood red? Are you a potent hunter? What about a duck? There's one in every office!". Other gags include a 'mis-hearing' gag (Blackie: "Have you ever sold anything?" Curly: "Why certainly: whatever we can lay our hands on." Moe: "The gentlemen said 'sold' not 'stole.'), internal rhyme (Curly: "We'll be back in a quack with a quack, and I do mean quack!"), and Stooge ignorance (Curly: "My mind's a blank"). A Stooge first: Moe whispering plans into Larry's ear inaudibly to us. Variations: "Three of the best salesmen who ever saled!" (*Dizzy Doctors*); "To the hunt, to the hunt!" (*We Want Our Mummy*); "Well, that's for what you was thinkin'!," and the 'Shave and a Haircut' rhythm (*Whoops, I'm an Indian*); Curly's "Certainly, old chiefie, old kid, old chief old kid!" (*Wee Wee Monsieur*); the song 'You'll Never Know' (*Soup to Nuts*; *Horses' Collars*); and "You've heard of the Pie-eyed Piper of Hamelin, ain't ya'? Well, I figured if he could pipe rats pie-eyed, then I could pipe ducks sober!" (*Termites of 1938*).

OTHER NOTES: There is no hyphen ('A-Ducking') in the title. The working title was *Never Duck a Duck.* This is the second film containing footage from another Stooge film. In both instances the footage was used for the ending, but here the steer footage from *A Pain in the Pullman* is utterly inappropriate. In comedy 'inappropriate' sometimes translates into hilarity, sometimes it just means being out of place.

A Ducking They Did Go was shot in mid-November, 1938, two weeks after *We Want Our Mummy.* Visible on the top of the magazine stand is the Nov. 14, 1938 issue of *Life*; on the cover is Brenda Frazier, the very debutante Brenda of 'Brenda & Cobina' parodied in the Stooge feature-film, *Time Out for Rhythm* (1941)

Particularly in the later years, Stooge film sets were modest, as was the size of the supporting cast. Columbia spent more money than usual on 1939's *A Ducking They Did Go*, building an artificial lake on Stage #6 and hiring a large cast. But in the film's final scenes the vacuum is too large for the Stooges, the rest of the cast and the ducks to fill.

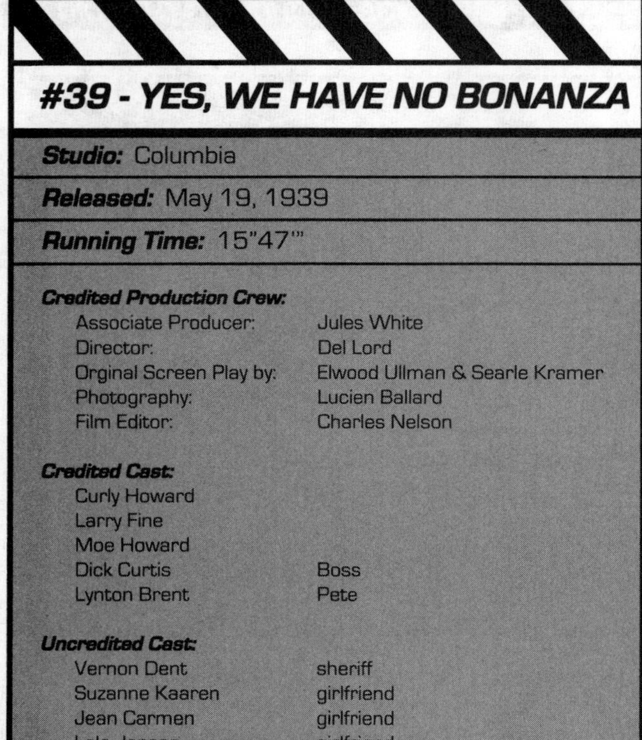

#39 - YES, WE HAVE NO BONANZA

Studio: Columbia

Released: May 19, 1939

Running Time: 15"47'"

Credited Production Crew:

Associate Producer:	Jules White
Director:	Del Lord
Orginal Screen Play by:	Elwood Ullman & Searle Kramer
Photography:	Lucien Ballard
Film Editor:	Charles Nelson

Credited Cast:

Curly Howard	
Larry Fine	
Moe Howard	
Dick Curtis	Boss
Lynton Brent	Pete

Uncredited Cast:

Vernon Dent	sheriff
Suzanne Kaaren	girlfriend
Jean Carmen	girlfriend
Lola Jensen	girlfriend

PERSPECTIVE: This film combines some of the most successful Stooge scenarios and gags. Those include a Western setting; singing and dancing; prospecting; working with tools; handling dynamite; traveling with animals; trying to help damsels in distress; defeating crooks; stumbling upon a treasure; and being involved in a wacky chase scene. All these elements are blended together in a well-crafted narrative by Elwood Ullman and Searle Kramer, the former of whom had co-written the prospecting scenario of *Cash and Carry*, the latter of whom had written the camping sequences in *Whoops, I'm an Indian.*

Causality is an essential part of any human endeavor. Knowing the cause for something makes it comprehensible and believable, even in comedic narrative. But comedy can exaggerate, too, and Ullman & Kramer break new ground by extending the comedic causality in this film. Their basic plot is simple: in a Western saloon the Stooges need money to rescue three women co-workers from a crooked boss. And to find the money Ullman & Kramer have the Stooges simply go prospecting, but they do that only because Pete unintentionally showed them a gold piece, and they would not have found the gold had not Larry chopped the wood badly, had he not thrown the rock at Curly, had Moe not at that very moment tossed a rock behind him, had not Curly thrown the rock and hit Moe, had not Moe thrown the dynamite next to the burro, had not the dog carried the dynamite into the food stores, had not Curly been preparing ribs for dinner, had not Curly had that silly dream, had not Moe hit him because of it, had not Curly landed on that tooth. What an amazing string of coincidences! And they all depend, of course, on the Stooges being in the same part of the hills as the Boss's stash in the first place. As these coincidences unfold, they all advance the plot, energize the scene, and give the Stooges plenty to fight and joke about.

There are some extraordinary moments up there by the lake, the same set the Stooges used for the duck hunting sequence in the previous film. One of these moments is the near creation of a trademark slapstick gag (the bent pickax and "Oh! Oh! Oh! Look!"), for which see the next section. The other is the 'exploding' burro, Yorick. His name comes from Shakespeare's *Hamlet,* and that this reference was conscious on the part of the writers is clear from Moe's lament: "Alas, poor Yorick. I knew him well." Hamlet himself offers this line during a scene (V.1.201) in which grave diggers, using pick-axes, come upon the skull of Yorick, the deceased court jester. And now we hear not only the great modern jester Moe quoting *Hamlet*, but another jester, Curly, has a dream about Yorick: "Yorick told me he liked me, and any time somebody tells me they like me something always happens!" Well something does happen: Moe knocks Curly down and he finds the gold nugget. It is as if Yorick, a four-centuries old Shakespearean jester and one of the earliest comedians whose name we know, befriended and benefited the Stooges on behalf of some sort of Shakespearean comedic brotherhood. And people say the Stooges are ignorant and uncouth!

VISUAL HUMOR: The hardness of Curly's skull reaches a new degree in this film: Curly dents the pickax with his head, a forerunner to the classic saw routine coming soon in *Oily to Bed, Oily to Rise*. Essential ingredients of the gag are the close up of the damaged tool (earlier in the film Larry dents his ax on a rock and we see a close up), and for Curly to holler "Oh! Oh! Ohhhhl*ook*!" Here Curly says this when he falls on the gold tooth, but his voice does not blend the "Oh!" and the "Look!" together just yet. The phrase develops from the recent tendency to have the slapstick turn the plot when someone about to get hit says "Look!" (*Three Missing Links*). Stooge firsts: the boss bending the tray over Curly's head (in *3 Dumb Clucks* Moe merely clanged the silver tray over his head); and the large ice tongs. The slapstick following Curly's description of his dream (GOUGE, BACK-AND-FORTH HAND-WAVE with an up finish, SQUIRT, GOUGE, TWO-HANDED SLAP) is an extended series, perhaps in part ad-libbed; extended slapstick series will become more common in future films.

Several other motifs have been developing recently and have by now become standard. One is for one Stooge to be hit by another and think he has been hit by the third, which actually goes back to the Ted Healy days. We saw it recently in *Three Missing Links* when Curly dumped water on Larry and Moe, who then blamed each other. We see it here when Larry throws the rock at Curly; he thinks it was Moe. Each precedes an important turning point in the plot. Similarly, Curly has been doing a lot of long takes in the previous few films. He trails on for quite a few words before realizing he is doing the wrong thing to the wrong person. A forerunner was Curly's take when the watermelon Larry threw landed on the policeman's head in *A Ducking They Did Go*; the best example here is Curly asking the Boss to hold the tray while he describes how he will stand up to the Boss.

Also from *A Ducking They Did Go* are plans whispered in secret, Curly describing a vision, and objects tossed like footballs. Other variations: Curly entering the saloon with his hat brim staying on his head, and pulling his apron out from his clothes (*Punch Drunks*); the camera pulling back in a 'fooler opening' to show Curly on his bike (*Movie Maniacs*); Larry chopping wood (*Whoops, I'm an Indian*); a hornet's nest (*Back to the Woods*); digging like dogs (*Cash and Carry*); eggs turning into chicks (*Wee Wee Monsieur*); and Moe and Larry grabbing a bucket of water and running in opposite directions (*Ants in the Pantry*). Moe knocking Curly and the pack all the way over the burro is one of the best punches in Stoogedom.

One of several extraordinary moments in *Yes, We Have No Bonanza* (1939) is the Shakespearean scene when the Stooges' mule Yorick becomes both the subject of an important reference and one of the keys to discovering the gold. That this was conscious on the part of writers Elwood Ullman and Searle Kramer is clear from Moe's lament: "Alas, poor Yorick. I knew him well!" This is a common variant of a line Hamlet offers during the very scene (V.1.201) in which grave diggers using pickaxes unearth the skull of Yorick, the deceased court jester - just as the jester Stooges use pickaxes and unearth the gold in this scene. The Shakespearean Yorick is one of the earliest comedians whose name we know, and here he benefits the Stooges over three hundred years later on behalf of some sort of historical comedic brotherhood.

VERBAL HUMOR: The complexity of the plot precludes too many verbal gags, but there are two based on Stooge ignorance (Larry: "Whoever heard of gettin' bonds out of the ground?" Moe: "Why not? Them is gold bonds!" Curly: "Gee! Ain't nature wonderful!"; Moe: "Where's the eggs?" Curly: "On top of the burro so they'll be nice and fresh in the sun!") and two puns (Moe: "If a dumb guy like that can dig up gold, so can we!" Curly: "We're gonna be gold diggers!"; Moe: "And 14 carats!" Curly: "Carats? That don't look like a vegetable to me!" Moe: "I'll give you a cauliflower ear!"). The latter leads to slapstick, as does Curly's dream and more ignorance ("I can see it now. I come home after a hard day's work. I whistle for the dog, and my wife comes out. Me - with my own wife and children - dozens of them!" Moe: "Dozens of them? How many is that?" Curly: "Two!" [GOUGE]). A Stooge first: calling eggs "Hen fruit".

Variations: Moe: "Say somethin'! Say somethin', kid!" (*Slippery Silks*); and Moe's "Recede!" (*Pardon My Scotch*). References: Moe's Shakespearean "Alas poor Yorick. I knew him well" is a common misquotation; the original is "Alas poor Yorick. I knew him, Horatio." Immediately after Moe's quotation, Curly ("Gone with the Wind. Fffft!") makes reference to *Gone with the Wind*, the film version of which was released the same year as this film. Curly's 'horse' 'Silver' ("Whoa, Silver! I couldn't help it. Silver had a flat tire!"), was the name of the ranger's horse in *The Lone Ranger*, on radio since 1933. The phrase "Yes, we have no bonanzas" was popularized by the Frank Silver/Irving Cohn song 'Yes, We Have No Bananas' recorded by Billy Jones in 1923. For Curly's "We're gonna be gold diggers!" see *Cash and Carry* and *Termites of 1938*.

OTHER NOTES: The film was shot in late November/early December 1938, two weeks after *A Ducking They Did Go*. The working title, *Yes, We Have No Bonanzas*, was reportedly the result of an ad-lib by Curly. It is one of the last lines of the film. This was one of three Stooge films (*You Nazty Spy!; Yes, We Have No Bonanza; Violent is the Word for Curly*) Columbia collected along with Buster Keaton and Vera Vague shorts and released to theaters in 1974 as *The Three Stooges Follies*. The plot itself is a remake of Sidney & Murray's *Back to the Soil* (1934), and was in turn remade with Andy Clyde as *Gold Is Where You Lose It* in 1944 and *Pleasure Treasure* in 1951.

#40 - SAVED BY THE BELLE

Studio: Columbia

Released: June 30, 1939

Running Time: 17"22'"

Credited Production Crew:

Associate Producers:	Charley Chase & Hugh McCollum
Directed by:	Charley Chase
Story by:	Searle Kramer & Elwood Ullman
Photography by:	Allen G. Siegler
Film Editor:	Arthur Seid

Credited Cast:

Curly Howard	
Larry Fine	
Moe Howard	
LeRoy Mason	Joe Singapore
Carmen LaRoux	Senorita Rita

Uncredited Cast:

Gino Corrado	General Casino
Vernon Dent	Mike
Al Thompson	mule-cart driver

PERSPECTIVE: Not every Stooge films lends itself to thematic analysis, but this one is clearly a tale of Fortune, a story of three men who frequently run into the most extreme cases of good and bad Luck. They are unlucky enough to be placed as salesmen in this sleepy country, but then they are lucky enough to hit upon the idea (Curly: "I don't believe it!") of selling earthquake shock absorbers.

They are then unlucky enough to be arrested as possible spies but lucky enough to be let free because Rita vouches for them. Then the "good luck" parrot brings them bad luck again, and once in jail the earthquake is the good fortune that frees them. They are lucky enough to find the map, unlucky enough to lose it, and lucky enough to find a car to take them out of town. When the car is found to be resting on blocks, Larry observes: "Just our luck!" And so on until the end in which they are lucky enough not to be executed, unlucky enough to be in a munitions truck, lucky enough to be saved by the horse after the explosion, and then unlucky enough to fall off. Other Stooge films move the stars in and out of trouble and good fortune, but none has all the vagaries that this film has, and none has "the parrot that brings good luck."

Such previous films as *Cash and Carry* and *Healthy, Wealthy and Dumb* used Luck and Fortune as explicit or subtextual themes, and the writers of *Saved By the Belle*, Searle Kramer and Elwood Ullman, worked on both of them. They also wrote *We Want Our Mummy*, which like this film has an exotic setting. Director and co-producer Charley Chase, ever fond of gadgetry, no doubt delighted in the earthquake shock absorbers. Such a combination of talents demonstrates how effective a Stooge production can be when the co-producer, director, and writer(s) contribute their various ideas which they have introduced and developed from previous films. What the viewer may perceive as mere repetition or variation is better understood as artistic development and variation .

One of the factors that makes the vicissitudes of Fortune so unpredictable, variable, and frequent in this film is the setting in a fictional 'tropical' country that has a sleepy population, a political revolution, seismic instability, and even a cosmic irregularity. Anywhere the Stooges live and work is already a place that has wider tolerances than real places on earth, but Valeska is by design an extremely odd location where extraordinary things can and do happen. This is not a tropical paradise, nor is it a never-never land; it is a land structured perfectly for a Stooge comedy and allows them to plow ahead with all their energies and idiocies. When things get beyond them, nature takes over. Earthquakes make them money and free them from their appointed death by firing squad. And when they are trapped in a tire-less car, a sudden, miraculous sunrise helps them understand where they are. As Curly remarked in Kramer and Ullman's *Yes, We Have No Bonanza* when he found gold bonds in the ground: "Gee! Ain't nature wonderful!"

VISUAL HUMOR: Recent films are beginning to contain more elaborate Stooge slapstick battles. An example from the previous film is the gouge/ seltzer-bottle battle; in this film both the battles at the map table (NOSE BONK, TEETH CHATTER, NOSTRIL LIFT) and the GOUGE/KICK/ SLAP on the way to their execution provide examples. (Keep in mind that the battles between Moe and Curly in this film are in part motivated by Moe's jealousy.) Larry even gives Curly a gouge, a rarity. Stooge firsts: trying to fit through a doorway all at once; and the gag in the hotel hallway, including the Stooge whispers before Joe starts banging on the door. Patterns: the search in Casino's office (where the guard substitutes for Larry); falling off the horse in unison; and dropping their utensils, covering their eyes, taking one more look at the meatless bone, and covering their eyes again in unison. The stationary car upgrades the stationary cigar-store horse in *Yes, We Have No Bonanza*. The earthquake shock absorber pillow is a low-tech version of the gadgets in Charley Chase's *Mutts to You, Termites of 1938*, and *Flat Foot Stooges*. The pineapple hand grenade is the most recent non edible food-stuff. Other variations: a talking parrot (*Disorder in the Court*); knocking with the hard bread, causing Curly to say "Come in!" (*Pop Goes the Easel*); Curly picking up his pinkies as a sign of good manners (*Hoi Polloi*); and the triple tandem bicycle (*Men in Black*).

VERBAL HUMOR: The writers give most of the punchlines to Curly, be they puns ("Commissions? Not me! Straight salary or nothin'!"; "...General Casino." Curly: "But we don't play casino. How about a little rummy?"), ironies (Curly: "I'm tryin' to make the alarm work." Moe: "What for?" Curly: "We're gonna be shot at sunrise and I wanna make sure we don't oversleep!"), literal gags ("What kind of fool do you take me for?" Curly: "Why? Is there more than one kind?"; Curly: "Won't you sit down and pick a bone with us?"), mis-hearing gags ("eat, drink, and be merry!" Curly: "Where's Mary?"), or throw-away lines ("Hmm! Woodpeckers!"; "Have you got a shoe horn?"; "Hey, keep an eye on those samples, will ya'?"; "I hope they give me a double breasted suit. I'd look much thinner!"; "We signed contracts with six month options"). Moe has a few insults for Curly (Curly: "You know I'm temperamental!" Moe: "Yeah! 95% temper and 5% mental!"; "You've almost got a brain!"), and, as often, Larry has one great line: "Our clothes are fresh - you can still smell the ocean!". As a unit the Stooges have a three-pattern at the hotel (Moe: "You wait here. I'll get it." Larry: "I'll help him!" Curly: "I'll help *him*!") and another when they confuse "Hallo" for the French "allons" (à la *Wee Wee Monsieur*); but in the prison the guard has a Spanish accent, confusing "soap" and "soup".

A Stooge first occurs when Curly helps the enemy by saying what he should not (Rita: "But general, the fat one does not look like a spy. He looks very innocent." Curly: "Oh I dunno. I been around!"). Another is Curly's "taking me too illiterately!". "Take these warrants to General LaGrandee. He'll take care of you in a large manner" is a pun on 'grandee,' an important person. When Curly corrects himself ("Don't you harm a feather in his bed, I mean, head") and when Moe restates "If the boss don't send us some dough, we'll be stranded" to the boss as "I was just tellin' my pal here this is lovely country and I'm glad we landed," they are both cumbersome gag styles that were used earlier in *Half-Shot Shooters* and Charley Chase's *Flat Foot Stooges*. Curly was called "the fat one" earlier in Searle Kramer's *Three Missing Links*. Curly calling the horse "a four-legged V-8" derives from "he looks like a V-8" from *Slippery Silks*. Other variations: Curly: "Do you feel a draft?" (*Goofs and Saddles*); language misunderstandings ('present wardrobe'/'President Ward Robey') (*Wee Wee Monsieur*); and 'Ffft! (*Three Missing Links*). Epithets: "ignoramus," "puddin'-head," and "dummies."

The Stooges are soon to face a firing squad in Charley Chase's final Stooge film, *Saved By the Belle* (1939), a unique story set in a mythical country ablaze with revolution. Thematically the Stooges rise and fall, succeed and fail, live and die (almost) along with the vicissitudes of Fortune and Luck.

OTHER NOTES: The film was shot in mid-December, 1938, but the cablegram from Moe's boss is dated January 2, 1938, the hotel bill 'Jan 4'. The title parodies the boxing expression 'saved by the bell'. This was the last film Charley Chase directed for the Stooges. He died of a heart attack on June 20, 1940. The use of the William Tell Overture as background for their 'horseback' ride is derived from *The Lone Ranger* like the 'Silver' reference in the previous film.

Carmen LaRoux's French accent is natural; she is the first of several French-speaking actresses who will act in Stooge films over the years. The Valeska flag includes an arm holding a mallet, the sleeve rolled up. This Communist icon and the name 'Valeska' suggest more of an Eastern European state, although most of the inhabitants look as if they belong in a Hispanic country in the Western hemisphere. The laziness of the inhabitants becomes a comic motif is several subsequent films set in Mexico (e.g. *What's the Matador?*). About to be 'shot,', Curly says he will "send a photo home to Elaine," the name of his real (second) wife (1937-1941), Elaine Ackerman.

#41 - CALLING ALL CURS

Studio: Columbia

Released: August 25, 1939

Running Time: 17"19'"

Credited Production Crew:

Associate Producer & Director:	Jules White
Screen Play by:	Elwood Ullman & Searle Kramer
Story by:	Thea Goodan
Film Editor:	Charles Nelson

Credited Cast:

Curly Howard
Larry Fine
Moe Howard

Uncredited Cast:

Lynton Brent	dognapper
Cy Schindell	dognapper
Willa Pearl Curtis	housekeeper
Beatrice Blinn	nurse Thomas
Beatrice Curtis	nurse
Dorothy Moore	nurse
Robin Raymond	nurse
Ethelreda Leopold	nurse

PERSPECTIVE: Unlike the five previous films which depend on complex plots in mostly exotic locations, *Calling All Curs* is delightfully simple: the Stooges play veterinarians who have to retrieve a kidnapped dog. This puts the Stooges into some familiar territory: they get to act as doctors, work with animals, abuse a hospital and the home of a well-to-do woman, chase crooks on the street, and have a final battle in the kidnapper's hideout. These scenarios offer plenty of sight gags, slapstick, puns, and jokes, some old, some revised, and some new. Compared to the enormity of the problems the Stooges have faced in the last few films - retrieving a 2000-year old mummy, defrauding a mayor and police chief, stealing $40,000 from crooks, and facing a firing squad during a third-world revolution - this plot is relatively simplistic. But long-time associate producer Jules White, directing only his second Stooge film (*Three Missing Links*), would rarely in 24 years run short of gags or the ability to let the inner core of Stooge humor flourish.

The Stooges squirt things in each other's faces, flirt with nurses, give double-talk names to medical tools, pull each other's extremities with those tools, bonk heads, play around and in the loud speakers, sing, make jokes about animal ailments, invent a gadget, dine with dogs, try to think, disguise a mutt as a pedigreed dog, get into a fist fight, and much more, culminating in the birth of puppies. When you tally the number of comical lines and movements, there are about eight dozen physical gags and gestures, and another four dozen verbal jokes, puns, and comical expressions in these sixteen and one-half minutes, or on average one every six seconds. Since the plot does not take long to develop or explain, the film runs end-to-end gags which culminate in a successful, in fact productive, conclusion. This film more than any other illustrates Jules White's approach to Stooge comedy - stringing gags end to end, one after the other.

One of the liabilities of filling out a simple plot with so many gags is that some of the gags will necessarily not be as successful as the others, and in gag comedy very often one 'stupid' or 'unfunny' gag can disproportionately affect the viewer's opinion. Howard Hawks once remarked that what made a good film was "three good scenes and no bad scenes." In comedy, one 'bad joke' can almost spoil the whole bunch. This is because comedy depends heavily on the mood of the viewer (the "comic climate"), and if the one 'bad joke' sours the viewer's mood, even another dozen good jokes might not restore it fully. This film, for instance, breaks the 'comedy rule of three' by containing one too many squirting scenarios, four instead of three: the soap dispenser squirts soap, the rigged garbage can squirts water, and the seltzer bottle squirts seltzer twice. By the fourth squirt the comic mood definitely begins to sag, and it is not until the Stooges get back out onto the street that it picks up again. This is not a condemnation of the film. It is an observation and should serve as a guide for viewers who might dislike a particular episode because of one or two bad jokes: enjoying gag humor rests in part in the viewer's willingness to find the sixty or seventy pleasing gags and ignore as best as possible the few that do not work quite so well.

VISUAL HUMOR: In a gag film the opening is important for getting the audience into the right mood. The Stooges are introduced as 'the world's greatest specialists' and plunge immediately into an energetic "To the operation!" ("To the hunt!" in the previous two films). Soon after, Curly takes a fall - one of his best - to the floor as he makes eyes at the nurse and misses the glove she holds. Right from the outset we notice a most notable innovation - role reversal. Larry washes his socks (Curly's role in *Three Little Beers*); Curly says "What do you think you're doin'?" and slaps Larry with the wet socks (usually Moe's role); and Curly says "I can't see! I can't see...I've got my eyes closed," (usually Larry's role). Stooge firsts: trying to knock on a door but knocking on some one's head instead; putting on a gas mask; having the dog tail signal them from around the corner; and knocking down a door on top of someone. The photographer is not credited, but there is an innovative sequence: in Mrs. Bedford's house Curly rides the mutt-pulled drink cart closer and closer to the camera and then beyond its frame, after which we hear it crash and see Mrs. Bedford faint onto the floor. Animals have appeared in a number of Stooge films recently, but here seventeen dogs empty out [fast motion] into the hospital corridors and eat at the dining room table. Jules White's greatest pre-Stooge successes were the *Dogville Comedies* he made at MGM in 1930/31.

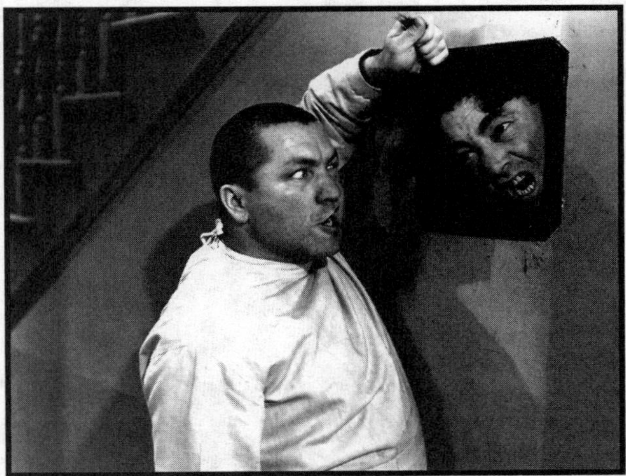

Moe gets his head stuck in the wall, as in *Cash and Carry* and *The Sitter Downers*, and Curly verifies it ("Are you sure?") as in *Three Little Beers*. Other variations: giving an anesthetic with a mallet (*Men in Black*); Moe pulling Curly by the ear with forceps (*Slippery Silks*), playing brass instruments (*The Big Idea*), playing Reveille (*Uncivil Warriors*); Curly flirting by tickling the nurse's chin (*A Pain in the Pullman*); the garbage-can gizmo (*Termites of 1938*); a sandwich biting Curly's nose (*Pardon My Scotch*); Moe ripping out a clump of Larry's hair (*Tassels in the Air*); the 'Cossack dance' (*Ants in the Pantry*); Curly hitching up an animal and saying "Mush!" (*Wee Wee Monsieur*); spraying seltzer (*Three Little Pigskins*); Curly kicking like a mule (*Back to the Woods*); and the two-men-in-a-coat routine (*Horses' Collars*).

VERBAL HUMOR: Unlike *Men in Black* and *Dizzy Doctors*, the Stooges engage in a three-pattern with the loud speaker: Dr. Curly is to "See a man with a dog's diet"; Dr. Larry is to treat a "dog chasing its tail; bit itself"; and Dr. Moe is to treat a Pomeranian with "a coat on its tongue." They combine this with the physical gag where Larry hits Moe's protruding head and the additional verbal silliness of "She loves me, she loves me not" (*Movie Maniacs*).

The verbal gags come fast and furious and, in contrast to the previous film, the punchlines are distributed among all three Stooges, including internal rhyme (Moe: "Listen, if you got any pointer in ya', you better start pointin' and point out those dog-nappers, get the point?"; Larry: "He suffers from acute alcoholism." Curly: "Ain't he a cutie?"; and Curly: "He looks more like Garçon than Garçon!"), grammatical play (Larry: "Do you think it's serious, Dr. Curly." Curly: "Yes indeed, to say the least, if not less."), neologistic, pseudo-technical language (Curly: "My proboscis!"; Moe: "The perambulation of the pedal extremity is impeded by the insertion of a foreign botanical offshoot"; "Looks like a botanical offshoot in the upholstery!"; 'G.C.M.'; .his "Garbage Can Moocher" suffers from "scavengeritis"; Moe's "anacanpahn... pittel-dittel-tah"), puns (Reporter: "Will it hurt its carriage?" Larry: "I don't know about his carriage, but it is going to raise Cain with his wagon"; Speaker: "A Pomeranian in Ward 6 has a coat on its tongue. What should we do?" Moe: "Give him the pants, a vest, and take him for a walk!"), prop gags (Curly [holding Garçon's collar]: "It ain't so serious. All we have to do is refill it!"; Larry: "Instruments!" Curly: "Instruments!" [The nurse brings two trumpets]); and other literal interpretations (Moe: "Since when do I look like a dog?" Curly: "I don't know. I ain't seen ya' lately"; Larry: "I didn't know you had it in ya'." Curly: "I didn't. She did!").

There are plot-related dog and cat puns ("He's a lap dog...lapped up two cases of beer. A bad case"; Curly: "He must be a Point Setter!" Moe: "Quiet, you Hot Airedale!") and gags (Moe: "We're lookin' for a dog." Curly: "He had four legs and a tail"; Curly: "One little kitten lost its mitten— how careless!"; Moe: "A cat with operatic tendencies — he likes to sing opera on back fences"; Curly: "Hey that nurse [apparently meowing] must've eaten catnip!"). The Stooges even make jokes talking to the animals (Curly [to a barking dog]: "Quiet! This is my argument!"; Larry [to the St. Bernard with an ice bag on his head]: "Keep a cool head, kid." Curly [the dog hiccups]: "Gesundheit!"; and Curly [as if a police radio call]: "Calling all curs, calling all curs! Dinner is ready. Come to the dining room. That is all!"). Moe has two notable exhortations ("I'll tear your esophagus out!"; "On your toes, you heels!").

All three join in shouting "Success!" twice and "the instruments!" once. Three-pattern (Larry: "We have none." Moe: "We have none." Curly: "Oh yes we have!"). Stooge first: Curly beating his dog biscuit sandwich "into submission". New epithet: Moe calls Curly an "onion-head".

This film offers one of the classic exchanges illustrating Stooge ignorance (Moe: "Start thinkin', if possible." Curly: "I'm tryin' to think but nothin' happens!"). The gag derives from *A Ducking They Did Go*, where Moe slaps Larry ("I didn't say nothin'!"), says "Well that's for what you was thinkin'!" and then looks menacingly at Curly, who smiles: "My mind's a blank!". Other variations: Curly: "We'll bring him back - alive!" and "Santa Claus will hear of this!" (*Wee Wee Monsieur*); "To the operation!"

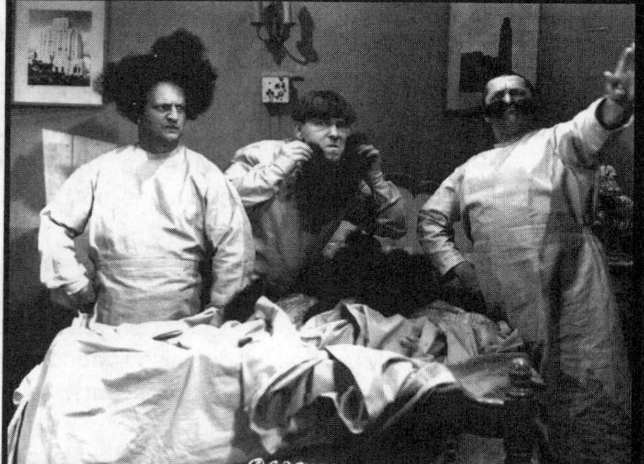

This fascinating photo was shot apparently during a break in filming *Calling All Curs* (1939). Clowning around with the mattress stuffing the Stooges will glue onto the ersatz-Garçon, Curly has made himself a Hitlerian mustache and gives a left-handed Nazi salute. This film was shot in late December, 1938, at which point Hitler had recently taken over the Sudetenland. At the time, the United States government was officially neutral, and so was Hollywood. Charlie Chaplin would not begin filming *The Great Dictator* until nine months after this, and even the Stooges' own *You Nazty Spy!* was still one year away. Of course, in the Stooges' World War II films, it will be Moe who plays Hitler.

(*We Want Our Mummy*); "She loves me, she loves me not," and "Mutiny as not on the Bounty" (*Movie Maniacs*); "Gesundheit!" (*Violent is the Word for Curly*); "Mazzeltov!" (*Half-Shot Shooters*); and "It had dandruff!" (*Dizzy Doctors*).

OTHER NOTES: The film was shot in late December, 1938. The release title parodies the police radio call 'Calling all cars!' The working titles were *Call a Doctor* and *Dog Hospital.* Charlie Chase had now finished his final Stooge production, so Jules White will direct and produce five consecutive films. Besides there being one squirt scene too many, in the first scene the soap starts shooting out at Curly before Moe hits the container. Some of this footage will be reused in *Stop! Look! and Laugh!*. An 'airedale' also meant a worthless race horse or person.

#42 - OILY TO BED, OILY TO RISE

Studio: Columbia

Released: October 6, 1939

Running Time: 18"13'"

Credited Production Crew:

Associate Producer & Director:	Jules White
Orginal Screen Play by:	Andrew Bennison & Mauri Grashin
Photography by:	Henry Freulich
Film Editor:	Charles Nelson

Credited Cast:

Curly Howard
Larry Fine
Moe Howard

Uncredited Cast:

Dick Curtis	Mr. Clipper
Eddie Laughton	crook
Eva McKenzie	Mrs. Jenkins
Linda Winters [Dorothy Comingore]	daughter [April]
Lorna Gray [Adrian Booth]	daughter [May]
Dorothy Moore	daughter [June]
Richard Fiske	farmer
Victor Travers	Justice of the Peace

PERSPECTIVE: Curly's uncanny luck at making his wishes come true makes this film unique. He wishes for a car and finds one that says 'FREE AUTO.' He wishes for a cigar and finds some in the glove box, and then he wishes for a chicken meal and apple pie and beautiful girls and gets all three. He also wishes to get his hands on the crooks, which he does, and he finally wishes for a justice of the peace, who walks in the door. These wishes-come-true transform the comedy after its ground-breaking initial slapstick segment into a magical odyssey that leads to riches, heroism, and love. For once the Stooges get what they want, do the right thing, save the damsels-in-

distress, and ultimately triumph with the money and the damsels, taking them to a higher level of achievement, all the while, of course, making us laugh. Humor is the common element in every Stooge film whether they ultimately fail and get shot at, blown up, or run out of town, or whether they save the innocent and strike it rich. Clearly it is not what the Stooges achieve or fail to do, nor is it how they end up that determines the comic mood. It is the method and the means with which they face every challenge. They are, after all, stooges. Stooges win, stooges lose, but stooges remain stooges. And these are The Three Stooges.

The writers did not invent this concept from scratch. In previous films the Stooges had visions of wives and domestic happiness [*Yes, We Have No Bonanza*] and a run of good and bad luck [*Saved By the Belle*]. But *Oily to Bed, Oily to Rise* takes a step forward that makes luck the essence of the narrative. If the Stooges had not stolen the crooks' car, the crooks would have recorded the Jenkins deed, and then there would have been no oil. And bad luck still plays an important role as well: when the Stooges do achieve success they tend to forget themselves and make disastrous errors. When the Stooges sit in the back seat of the car and relax, they brush with death. Heading out of control towards a cliff, Curly says with plenty of calm: "Hey! I think we're going to be killed!"

It is not clear what cosmic mechanism allows Curly to achieve his wishes. The film does not give him an auspicious start. At first he merely dreams of roast chicken and dumplings and gets slapped by Moe "for not dreamin' enough for the both of us!" Shortly after, Curly plummets to what must be his lowest emotional point ever, lower than when he cried at the end of the previous film, and even lower than his frustration with the tent stakes in *Three Missing Links*, when he four times fails to close the bottom door of the wood wagon and backs into a pitch fork. He collapses, weeping on the floor, pounding his hands, kicking his feet, shaking his head, calling for his two only friends, and admitting "I'm so aggravated!" In the very next scene, though, one of the crooks [Eddie Laughton] wipes the mud off his feet with the 'FREE AUTO' sign, tosses it onto the car, and everything from that point falls into place for Curly's wishes. Moe is slow to believe in Curly's power ["Wishin'! Always wishin'! What does it getcha? Nothin'!"], but eventually he is milking him for more, including quintuplets.

VISUAL HUMOR: Two classic Stooge firsts: One is Curly ruining a saw with his head and saying "Oh! Oh! Oh! Ohhhhl*look*!" His head ruined the pickax in *Bonanza*, and he said "Oh! Oh! Oh! Oh!" and "Look!" when he found the tooth, but he did not put them together before. The other is the Stooges trying to jam into a doorway simultaneously. They were dragged as a trio backwards through a narrow doorway in *Saved By the Belle*, but this film shows the Stooges trying to fit laterally through a doorway frontwise; in fact, they try to fit through the Jenkins door that way twice. [There is a similar but non-Stooge prototype in *Soup to Nuts*].

The entire saw sequence is remarkably varied; you would not know you could do so many things with saws: Curly and Larry pull the two-man saw with the teeth facing up, Curly pulls the saw and Larry's head into the log, Curly gets under the saw and ruins its teeth with his head, Curly rolls off the blade and slams it into Moe's belly, Curly and Larry try to break it but Larry wangs Curly in the face, Curly completely wears away the blade trying to saw the large saw in half with a little saw, and the routine ends with a fine internal rhyme ("I'm sawin' a saw in half with a saw, see?") and an irony ("Don't get excited! You can still use it for a cheese knife!").

When Curly winks to the camera at the end of the film ("We'll honeymoon in Canada") this is the first time a Stooge has broken through the formal barrier between their antics on film and our watching them. A precursor may have been the cart riding towards the camera in *Calling All Curs*. A variation of Curly's finger-snapping: he finishes it off by pulling a match from behind his ear and lighting it on his scalp. The sound of Curly's chicken imitation is particularly loud.

Role reversal [*Calling All Curs*]: Curly gives Moe a nostril raise. Result shot: the camera pans to reveal the egg in Moe's face [*A Ducking They Did Go*]. In *False Alarms* Curly told Moe he did not have time for slapstick, as he does again here. Other variations: Curly backing into the door [*A Ducking They Did Go*]; smashed cigars [*Uncivil Warriors*]; clanging others with a crow bar over the shoulder, then getting hit by the spinning crowbar [*Three Little Pigskins; Back to the Woods*]; Curly in drag [*Pop Goes the Easel*]; the pitchfork stab [*Playing the Ponies*]; and Curly kissing Moe by mistake [*Calling All Curs*].

VERBAL HUMOR: As in *Pardon My Scotch* and *A Ducking They Did Go*, Andrew Bennison (with Columbia staff writer Mauri Grashin) complements most of the visual gags with appropriate punchlines ("I'm sawin' a saw in half with a saw, see?") and fills moments of physical relaxation with plot-related gaglines about wishing ("Never look a gift horse in the puss"; "The guy is haunted!") and driving ("Hey don't look now, but I think we're about to be killed!"), puns for the pump fixing sequence (Moe: "You mean a 'crow bar.'" Curly: "Don't a rooster crow?"; Moe: "How could there be a bear down there?" Curly: "It's barely possible!"), and Stooge ignorant word play for the oil discovery (Larry: "It's an inkwell!" Moe: "Inkwell nothin'! Why that's earl, coal-earl!" Curly: "You mean oil! It's a geezer!" Curly: "Look, I'm a successful cork! I'm an unsuccessful cork! Uncork me!"; "It's a geezer right on the piazza!"; "The oily boid catches the woim!").

Epithets for Curly: "onion-head" and "Plymouth Rock"; both refer to his head. Moe also makes two animal references: "Playin' possum, eh?" and "you half-brother to a weasel"; Curly's response ("On behalf of the weasel I resent that!") is a Stooge first. Moe also unloads a double conditional insult to Larry: "You know if I wasn't so weak from hunger I'd bat your brains out if you had brains!". A Stooge first: "Took me illiterately!".

Curly's "I am consecratin'! But nothin's happenin'!" is a step beyond "I'm tryin' to think but nothin' happens!" from *Calling All Curs*. In *Pop Goes the Easel* Curly could spell 'C-H-R-Y-S-A-N-T-H-E-M-U-M,' but here he can say only "Chrysanthemumumumum". Other variations: "hen fruit" [*Yes, We Have No Bonanza*], Moe: "Tell me your name so I can tell your mother." Curly: "My mother knows my name!" [*Movie Maniacs*]; "Backbiter!" [*Pop Goes the Easel*]; the Stooges looking behind themselves when they are called 'Gentlemen' [*Horses' Collars*]; the 'Shave and a Haircut' rhythm [*Whoops, I'm an Indian*]; "A pumping we will go" [*A Ducking They Did Go*]; and the names "April, May, and June" ("Hope, Faith, and Charity" in *Back to the Woods*). For Moe's closing reference to Canada's Dionne quintuplets, see *False Alarms*.

OTHER NOTES: The title parodies Ben Franklin's 'Early to bed and early to rise, makes a man healthy, wealthy, and wise'; the latter half of the expression was already parodied in *Healthy, Wealthy and Dumb*. For all the squirting in the previous film, the squirting pump here advances the plot. Curly sitting on top of the oil geyser is one of the visual icons of Stoogedom. It will be repeated in the 1958 remake with Joe [*Oil's Well That Ends Well*]. Lorna Gray [May] now plays in four consecutive Stooge films. She later changed her name to Adrian Booth and starred in Republic westerns.

Linda Winters [April] would later change her name to Dorothy Comingore and act in feature films, including the memorable role of 'Susan Alexander' in *Citizen Kane* (1941). This film marks the first of Richard Fiske's seven Stooge appearances. Dick Curtis' character seems to be called both Mr. 'Clipper' and Mr. 'Clifford.'; cf. Corabell/Florabell in *The Sitter Downers*. Some of the driving footage will be reused in *Stop! Look! and Laugh!*

Several 1939 films were thematic. Here in *Oily to Bed, Oily to Rise*, the theme is Curly's uncanny luck in having his wishes come true. He wishes for a car, he wishes for three beautiful girls, and here they are. One of these Stooge girls, April (Linda Winters) - (center) would soon play Kane's wife in RKO's *Citizen Kane* (1941).

#43 - THREE SAPPY PEOPLE

Studio: Columbia

Released: December 1, 1939

Running Time: 17"17'"

Credited Production Crew:

Associate Producer & Director:	Jules White
Orginal Screen Play by:	Clyde Bruckman
Photography:	George Meehan
Film Editor:	Charles Nelson

Credited Cast:

Curly Howard	
Larry Fine	
Moe Howard	
Lorna Gray [Adrian Booth]	Sheri Rumsford
Don Beddoe	J. Rumsford Rumsford
Bud Jamison	Williams

Uncredited Cast:

Ann Doran	countess
Richard Fiske	guest
Eddie Laughton	painter; party guest
Victor Travers	party guest
Beatrice Blinn	party guest

PERSPECTIVE: The popular view of psychiatry in the 1930s included several stereotypical motifs that play an integral role in this comedy, including Germanic names like 'Ziller, Zeller & Zollar' and the odd neurological testing procedure the Stooges employ. Nearly two minutes of the film explore the comic ramifications of testing a person's knee reflexes, which for the Stooges translates into an opportunity to have physical contact with each other and total strangers. Curly at first is unable to evoke a normal response, as is Moe until he slugs Curly in the stomach. This causes Curly to kick Moe back (in the head) and then it is open season - not only on a man with a wooden leg and a replica of *The Thinker*, but by the end of the scene every one at the party is chopping away at a knee. Director Jules White seems to have designed this concept after the saw sequence in the previous film, where one physical concept - sawing - was used, reused, and modified in many ways for several minutes.

Another spillover from the popular view of psychiatry was that it was only the wealthier classes of people who would employ a psychiatrist. As often for Stooge comedy, this means an opportunity to visit the home of a wealthy person, but for once it also means the high fees the Stooges receive at the end of the film. $1500 is a long way from the thirteen cents Moe and Curly fought over in *We Want Our Mummy*, and after the oil well they discovered in the previous film (*Oily to Bed, Oily to Rise*), the Stooges are on quite a win streak. They achieve what they set out to do - get money for Curly's Gertie who is "expecting." (In the previous film the Stooges won wives; now Curly is to be a father?!) In fact, not only do they get the money they need, they also solve Sheri Rumford's psychological problem, or at least what her husband perceived as her problem. Ultimately the Stooges are so successful in this film that it is Sheri Rumsford, not the Stooges, who takes the physical abuse and comeuppance at the conclusion of the film. That is three films in a row now in which the outcome has been favorable for the Stooges.

As evidenced by her penetrating and persistent laughter, Sheri Rumsford's psychiatric problem is her inability to maintain stable social and familial relationships because her egotistical appetite for diversion is excessive. She does not even look forward to a birthday party her husband has prepared for her. Friends and important people are there, and the festivities include an alcoholic punch, champagne, a special-ordered meal, cream puffs, and a huge cake, but she would rather go on a whimsical submarine ride. Fortunately, her substitute psychiatrists, telephone repairmen by training, indulge her addiction to fun and thrilling entertainment and thereby cure her. In *Ants in the Pantry* the Stooges were unintentionally amusing to wealthy guests and were rewarded with an invitation to the hunt. Here they are unintentionally amusing to a wealthy woman who needs ample, healthy, domestic laughter. This really was the perfect job for the Stooges.

VISUAL HUMOR: A most notable tendency in this film is to use the visual 'result shot' – that is, a setup shot showing the result of a fall or thrown object. We see it first when Sheri tosses her fur and hat onto the stationary butler and then again when Curly falls into the paint cans, when the Stooges knock William's tray onto the countess, when Curly shoots the champagne cork into Moe's eye, and when Curly blows powder on the countess' face. The technique was used just once in the previous film - when Moe ended up with egg on his face. Stooge firsts: Rodin's *Thinker* (c. 1880) coming to life, the first inanimate object to come to life in a Stooge film; and playing trains. Both will be varied in the next film. The nine bonks Moe gives Curly after the champagne spray is a record. Although the knee reflex test is a filmed first here and will be varied in the future, there was a reflex gag cut out of *Men in Black* [*Scripts* 109]. This film finds still more uses for a stethoscope and a toupee, two of the Stooges' most reliable and durable props. When Curly bonks Moe, it is another example of the role reversals we have seen in the previous two films. Curly's turning the ladder in the opening sequence builds on the oil pump crow bar (*Oily to Bed, Oily to Rise*), shovels (*Cash and Carry*), and guns (*Back to the Woods*) in previous films. Other variations: Curly eating the powder puff (*Uncivil Warriors*); antics by the punch bowl and raising the pinkies (*Hoi Polloi*); pulling out three increasingly larger pencils (*Movie Maniacs*); pulling the telephone wire and someone's head (the two-man saw in *Oily to Bed, Oily to Rise*); an electric razor, and breaking out of a jail cell (*3 Dumb Clucks*); and falling off their triple-tandem bike (*Saved By the Belle*).

VERBAL HUMOR: Plot-related food gags depend on Stooge ignorance (Curly's tamale: "It don't know whether it's comin' or goin'!"; [Curly sneezes] Sheri: "Hors d'oeuvre?" Curly: "No, hay fever."; Rumsford: "Let me tell you a little about Sheri." Moe: "Oh don't bother, I'll take Scotch!" Larry: "Make mine Rye." Curly: "I'll take Gin smothered in Bourbon!" [three-pattern]), and ethnic humor (Sheri: "I hope you gentlemen will like my Spanish dinner." Curly: "I'm just crazy about Spanish food - especially corned beef and cabbage!"). The script also includes an insult based on Stooge ignorance (Moe: "Why don't you get a toupee with some brains in it?"), an insult to a non-Stooge (Moe to the secretary: "Never mind the wise cracks, toots"), an ironic line by an extra ("The king shall hear of this!" said by the countess hit by a cream puff), and internal rhymes (Moe: "We'll be there in a flash in the flesh!"; Moe: "There's an impatient patient waiting!").

Stooge firsts: a triadic "Ah-ah-ah rats"; and Moe's "War-ses-ter-shire". The exchange (Moe: "Remind me to kill you later." Curly: "I'll make a note of it") was used in *Cash and Carry* - also written by Clyde Bruckman - but the pencil gag derives from *Movie Maniacs*. The three-pattern (Larry: "A marvelous accomplishment!" Moe: "A prodigious achievement!" Curly: "You said it! It's putrid!") derives from a prototype in *Three Missing Links*. Curly's tapeworm joke (Curly: "Bring me back a piece of burnt toast and a rotten egg! I got a tape worm and it's good enough for 'em!") dates back to *Punch Drunks*, the only script the Stooges wrote. Other variations: the names "Ziller, Zeller, Zoller" (Dorabell, Corabell, Florabell in *The Sitter Downers*); "Eats!!" (*Goofs and Saddles*); and "I'll take Gin smothered in Bourbon." (eggs smothered in steak in *Yes, We Have No Bonanza*). Epithets: "puddin'-head" (twice).

References: Sheri's "The last one in is a Republican!" reflects the resounding defeat of the Republican Party in the previous national election: in 1936 Franklin Roosevelt defeated Republican candidate Alf Landon 523 electoral votes to 8, the greatest landslide in U.S. history; the party was so devastated, the 1940 Republican candidate for the presidency, Wendell Willkie, had previously been a democrat. Moe mentions 'Emily Post" (*Myrt and Marge*); in the 1920s and 1930s, Emily Post wrote numerous books on etiquette and also had a radio program. An 'infernal machine,' popularized in Jean Cocteau's 1934/1936 play of the same name, was an archaic name for a bomb. The sign 'POST NO BILLS' was common on fences or walls, but not on a wooden leg!

OTHER NOTES: The film was shot in early April, 1939. The title parodies the song 'Two Sleepy People' written the previous year (1938) by Hoagy Carmichael and Frank Loesser for the Bob Hope film *Thanks For the Memory*, the title song of which became Hope's theme song. The working title was *Three Sloppy People*. This was the only Stooge role for Ann Doran (the countess), but her career included roles in such important films as *Mr. Smith Goes to Washington* and *Rebel Without a Cause* (as James Dean's mother). The prototype for the Stooges getting a job by accident is *Three Little Pigskins*. The wooden leg gag is sometimes edited out for television broadcast.

Of all the thrown clay, creampuffs and whatever in Stooge comedies, the bull's eye into Sheri Rumford's loud, laughing, open mouth is perhaps the most perfect shot. Moe, as almost always, threw the creampuff. There is an anecdote that it became so deeply lodged in actress Lorna Gray's mouth that she needed emergency medical attention. However, Ms. Gray told the author that she was never in danger but that an overly concerned Jules White almost ruined the take.

1940

You Nazty Spy! • *Rockin' Thru the Rockies* • *A Plumbing We Will Go*

Nutty but Nice • *How High us Up?* • *From Nurse to Worse*

No Census, No Feeling • *Cookoo Cavaliers* • *Boobs in Arms*

#44 - YOU NAZTY SPY!

Studio: Columbia

Released: January 19, 1940

Running Time: 17"59'"

Credited Production Crew:

Producer & Director by:	Jules White
Story & Screen Play by:	Clyde Bruckman & Felix Adler
Director of Photography:	Harry Davis
Film Editor:	Arthur Seid

Credited Cast:

Curly Howard
Larry Fine
Moe Howard

Uncredited Cast:

Richard Fiske	Ixnay
Lorna Gray [Adrian Booth]	Mattie Herring
Dick Curtis	Onay
Don Beddoe	Amscray
Florine Dickson	Miss Pfeffernuss
Little Billy	Gestapo midget
John Tyrrell	Minister of Umphola
Bert Young	storm trooper
Joe Murphy	peasant
Eddie Laughton	Delegate Vance Rippemup
Al Thompson	

PERSPECTIVE: Despite Mussolini's attack on Ethiopia in 1935 and Hitler's successive conquests of Austria, Czechoslovakia and Poland, the United States had remained officially neutral towards European politics since 1935. But in November, 1939, Congress revised its policy, ending U.S. isolation and allowing the sale of supplies to benign European countries like England and France. Until then, the U.S. film industry had also remained neutral, hesitant to antagonize the totalitarian Nazis and Fascists. But despite a formal complaint by the German consulate, Warner Brothers filmed *Confessions of a Nazi Spy*, a semi-documentary exposé. Its release in September, 1939 caused one reviewer to remark: "The Warner Brothers have declared war on Germany!" The Stooges' *You Nazty Spy!* was shot a few weeks later (the first week of December, 1939) and released in mid-January, 1940, making this the first film to satirize the Nazis and the Fascists. Charlie Chaplin had already begun production on his satire of Hitler, *The Great Dictator*, in mid-September, 1939, but he did not complete and open the film until October, 1940, nine months after the Stooge release.

The Hungarian born Jules White (Weiss), was of Eastern European, Jewish origin, as were the Stooges. At least according to Moe's daughter, Joan, the prime motivation for making this film was indeed ethno-political, and it is certainly no accident that the first unison words out of the Stooges' mouths here are "Sholem aleichem." The previous June they had released *Saved By the Belle* satirizing an imaginary country with an invasive police force, but now *You Nazty Spy!* was making film history as the first satire of the genuine tyranny in Europe.

Much of the satire reflects recent current events: Hitler's acquisition of the Sudetenland (September, 1938) to protect German minorities is satirized by the Minister of Umphola's objection to "making our majorities minorities"; the Munich conference (September, 1938) and its 'appeasement' are satirized when Larry saws a 'square' table and Curly 'appeases' the delegates with golf balls; the Nazi-Soviet Pact of Non-aggression (November, 1939) is satirized in Larry's being given 'Mikey Finlen' and in Curly's pun about 'Stalin'; the Polish Corridor and the Blitzkrieg against Poland (September, 1939) are satirized in Moe's planned corridor through 'Double Crossia' and his 'Blintzkrieg with Sourkrieg'; and the problems in Bohemia-Moravia are satirized in the name 'Moronika.'

Much of the rest of the satire reflects the American public's knowledge of European, particularly German, political events and characters: Hitler's failed Beer Putsch, the book burnings, Gestapo storm troopers, Mussolini and Goering (Curly), Goebbels (Larry), and the World War I spy Mata Hari. Since filmed newsreels of Hitler's public rallies were giving the American public striking images of the Nazi regime, and since Moe could be easily made to look like Hitler, the film naturally caricatured Hitler's public speaking style. Standing on the balcony with his propaganda minister Pebble (i.e. Goebbels), who holds up cue cards to the mob, and a general who looks like Mussolini, 'Moe Hail!-Hail!-Hailstone' lies about acquiring neighboring lands and inspires the people to believe that "Moronika is for Morons!" They all certify "Ya!," but Larry poignantly turns the final "Ya!" into a gospel-like "Yeah, man, Hallelujah!" And then it is not just a silly conclusion or merely another chance for the Stooges to get on a loud speaker, when Larry and Curly announce that the station is "N-U-T-S" and that it is "3:00 Boloney-a Watch Time." This is exactly the message Jules White and the Stooges were trying to get across.

VISUAL HUMOR: Purely visual political satire includes Curly imitating Mussolini, Larry holding up the cue cards, 'storm troopers' in rain gear goose-step kicking each other in the rear, and Curly using his epaulet for a hypnotizing hand-wave in Moe's face. There are two variations on the eye gouge and one on Curly's derby-machine gun: Moe takes Curly's machine-gun fingers and gouges Curly's own eyes with them, and then when Curly takes "Notre Dame and 2 points" he gets gouged again.

You Nazty Spy!, the first release of 1940, was efficiently written, shot and released in less than two months - making it the first Hollywood film satirizing Hitler. The Stooges spent the summer of 1939 in Europe and were sensitive to its politics, as was Hungarian-born Jules White. All four were of Jewish European heritage and were proud of this courageous film.

The golf bag club is one of the largest hand weapons the Stooges use. A Stooge first: holding each other's hands - instead of a woman's - under the table. As in the previous film, a statue moves when Curly approaches. Also from *Three Sappy People* is the train imitation by all three Stooges. Other variations: the Stooges not fitting through the door (*Oily to Bed, Oily to Rise*); a funny salute (*Uncivil Warriors*, *Goofs and Saddles*); and lions (*Movie Maniacs*).

VERBAL HUMOR: To effect the satire the Bruckman/ Adler script changes the Stoogified Musketeer motto ("One for all!" "All for one" "Every man for himself") from *Restless Knights* and *Back to the Woods* to 'One for all and all for me!' Also satirical are Curly's "I'd like to take him up to the roof and over-throw him," Hailstone's motto to his countrymen ("Make our country safe for hypocrisy!"), Ixnay's description of a dictator ("He makes love to beautiful women, drinks champagne, enjoys life, and never works. He makes speeches to the people, promising them plenty, gives them nothing, then takes everything!"), the 8-ball exchange (Moe: "Why that's an 8-Ball!" Mattie: "Sit right down behind it."), the salute "Hail! Hail! Hailstone! Wa-Hoo!" (a farcical version of 'Sieg Heil!'), and "a concentrated camp". There is also the extended exchange about how to kill a treasonous peasant who had a chicken (Midget Soldier: "I caught this man walking down the street with a chicken." Curly: "Blonde or brunette?" Moe: "Where'd you get the chicken?" Peasant: "From an egg." Larry: "Where'd you get the egg?" Peasant: "From a chicken." Curly: "A vicious cycle. We must kill it. Remind me to kill a cycle." Moe: "Throw him to the lions!" Curly: "But we have no lions. How about the Tigers or the Cubs?" Larry: "Or the Giants?"), which ends with an all-American baseball reference.

Political puns include Curly's definition of propaganda ("A papa ganda marries a momma ganda and they raise a lot of little goslings"), a multi-geo-political pun (Larry: "If I take Mikey Finlen I'd better be Russian." Curly: "Then quit Stalin!"), a string of puns about Mata Hari ('Mattie Herring'; "Marinate her and send her in."; "Ah, my favorite dish!"; and "You'd have been in some pickle with that Herring!"). Non-political puns include Moe's "And you shot me in the excitement" (i.e. his rear); Moe: "Just hold her arm; she's a spy!" Curly: "She's a spy all over, isn't she?"; and Moe: "How can you shoot her with dice?" Curly: "They're loaded!". Non-political Stooge firsts: 'Herman the Sixth and Seven-Eighths'; and the 'Fleur de Skunk' cologne. The map gag names derive from politics (Double Crossia, South Starv-vania), drinking (Mikey Finlen, Hang Gover, Asperin, ScrewBall Key, Gin

Rickia], puns [Bay of Window, Bay of Rum], and familiar doublets [Razzle Lake & Dazzle Lake, Look Sea & See Sea]. Nux Vomika is both a poison and a medicinal cardiac stimulant; for the equine shaped 'Sea of Biscuit,' see on Seabicscuit [*From Nurse to Worse*].

Other references: The 'Beer Putsch' refers to Hitler's unsuccessful coup d'etat in 1923; Mata Hari, the prototype for Olga in *Three Little Sew and Sews*, was a World War I figure, executed for espionage in France in 1917; Moe's order to Curly: "Get a confession from a nasty spy and shoot her!" refers to Warner Brothers' *Confessions of a Nazi Spy*, the conductor announcing "Syracuse!" and Moe's "The boy's from Syracuse!" refer to the Rodgers & Hart *The Boys From Syracuse*, a musical adopted from Shakespeare and Plautus that ran on Broadway in 1938/1939 and became a Universal film in the following year; Moe's evil laugh into the microphone sounds like 'The Shadow'; 'Beblach' is Yiddish for 'beans'; a 'niblick' is an 8-iron; 'Pfeffernuss' is a German peppery cookie; 'Queen of the May' refers to a role in an old English folk dance; and 'behind the eight-ball,' a sign of bad luck, was an expression that had surfaced recently in 1932 and used in 1938's *Bringing Up Baby*. Curly sounds: After the statue moves, Curly's "Nyuk, nyuk, nyuk, nyuk. Nyaggh! Woob-woob-woob!" is a rare combination. When Hailstone looks at Curly's address book, it is the first and only time we see 'Woob! Woob! Woo!' in writing; it is a good thing Curly pronounces it correctly for us. Curly's definition of propaganda is followed by a [loud] goose imitation worthy of his chicken imitation in *Oily to Bed, Oily to Rise*. Other variations: the toast "Here's how!" "I know how!" [*Goofs and Saddles*]; pig Latin names [*Tassels in the Air*]; P.A. nonsense [*Dizzy Doctors*]; 'Boloney-a Watch Time' [*Back to the Woods*]; "Concentrate!" and "You got asthma?" [*Oily to Bed, Oily to Rise*]; and "Hallelujah!" [*Plane Nuts*].

OTHER NOTES: The 1940 releases offer a new format for the credit screens: the Columbia image remains on the left for all three screens, the title of film is in a different lettering style, with or without actor credits, and the credits last only twenty seconds. This format will be used until *Idiots Deluxe*, a 1945 release. Jules White is now credited as 'Producer,' and 'Photography [by]' now becomes 'Director of Photography'. Shot Dec. 6-9, the film was released just five weeks later, an extraordinarily compressed schedule; most shorts were released 6-12 months after shooting. Don B. Morlan ['The Three Stooges Contribution to World War II Propaganda: Moe Hailstone & Adenoid Hynkel's Race to the Screen,' *The 3 Stooges Journal* 64 [1992] 8-9, 14; see also *The New York Times*, July 10, 1994, IV, 7:1] researched and confirmed the amount of time by which *You Nazty Spy!* preceded *The Great Dictator*. The working title was *Oh, You Nazty Spy!*. This film marks the first of some two dozen Stooge appearances by John Tyrrell [Minister of Umphola], formerly a vaudeville dancer.

Adolph Hitler reportedly once worked as a paperhanger - a profession that fits into the Stooges' resume as well. Their various characterizations as tradesmen gave them entrance to numerous mansions, offices, and assorted places they did not belong: the more ironic the juxtaposition the more effective the comedy.

Three years earlier, an African-American, Jesse Owens, embarrassed Hitler by defeating his master race at the Berlin Olympics. One wonders if this had anything to do with Larry's "Hallelujah!". The stock footage of the rally seems to be of the Piazza Venezia in Rome, where Mussolini held his most famous balcony rallies. The Stooges had just made an 8-week tour of England, Scotland, and Ireland during their 1939 hiatus, but the tour was cut short either by the political storm or their touring schedule; according to Larry's autobiography [112-114] it was only four days after the Stooges arrived home on the Queen Mary that Germany declared war on England, but the Stooges were already under contract to appear on Broadway in George White's *Scandals of 1939*, which opened on August 28 and ran for 120 performances. According to Forrester *Chronicles* [51], the Stooges developed satirical impersonations of Axis dictators for that act. 'Moronika' is spelled with a 'K' on the flag but with a 'C' on the note from the king. Maybe that is why he was forced to abdicate; then again, it is a land of Morons. We are given a full thirty seconds to read the map. Television broadcasts often edit out Mattie Herring's disrobing scene and any evidence of Curly being devoured by the lions. This was one of three [*You Nazty Spy!*; *Yes, We Have No Bonanza*; *Violent is the Word for Curly*] Stooge films Columbia collected along with Buster Keaton and Vera Vague shorts and released to theaters in 1974 as *The Three Stooges Follies*. Joan Maurer, Moe's daughter, reports that this was one of Moe's, Larry's, and Jules White's favorite Stooge films. She herself published the script in *Scripts* 179-222. Two of the more interesting differences between the script and the final release are an omitted paper hanging scene in which Curly papered the wall, floor, opposite wall, and ceiling with one roll [Hitler reportedly once worked as a paperhanger], and the dialogue the lions were supposed to deliver: "Ach! Dot taste awful!" "Yah! I got indigestion!" "Me too! Phooey!"

#45 - ROCKIN' THRU THE ROCKIES

Studio: Columbia

Released: March 8, 1940

Running Time: 17"24'"

Credited Production Crew:

Producer & Directed by:	Jules White
Story & Screen Play by:	Clyde Bruckman
Director of Photography:	Henry Freulich
Film Editor:	Arthur Seid

Credited Cast:

Curly Howard	
Larry Fine	
Moe Howard	
Linda Winters	[Daisy]
Dorothy Appleby	[Tessie]
Lorna Gray	[Flossie]
Kathryn Sheldon	Nell

Uncredited Cast:

Dick Curtis	Chief Growling Bear
Bert Young	indian

PERSPECTIVE: It is hard to believe that anyone would knowingly hire the Stooges to guide them on a trek from Kansas to California, but this is actually the fifth time the Stooges have been hired as scouts or sleuths [*Horses' Collars, Uncivil Warriors, Goofs and Saddles, We Want Our Mummy*], and the fourth time they have been, literally, in the woods. The feature attraction of the woodland setting is that it gives the Stooges an opportunity not just to louse up their scouting or sleuthing but to do it while encountering outlaws, Indians, wild animals, and the harsher elements of nature. In most of these films the Stooges rescue damsels-in-distress, and while the bulk of *Rockin' Thru the Rockies* suggests that the Stooges are failing miserably, when all is said and done they do shoot several ducks, ward off a bear, catch a large fish [besides the one that looks like Moe], save the women from the hostile Escrow Indians tribe, and sail off on their prairie schooner.

The Stooges enter the film in the second scene, as they have done for six films in a row. This technique that fills us in on the plot and raises our anticipation that the Stooges will greet us with new costumes, new jobs, and an inter-Stooge squabble that will pay off almost immediately. Here we see the Stooges in explorer outfits scouting in the woods as Curly and Larry whiz a few branches just over Moe's head. We are already in eager anticipation, and when the third one clocks Moe in the face, the comedy is off and running. From there the gags continue to dovetail, just about every one of them enhanced by a prop or accompanied by a verbal counterpart, and some of them leading to a shift in plot direction. The branch gag leads to grabbing each other by the back of the shirt, which leads to Nell's head bonk, which leads to Curly's peanut vendors union joke, which

leads to Curly kissing Moe, which leads to the corn beef can opening, which leads to the ax cheer, which leads to the ax disaster, which leads to shooting Moe's toe, which leads to the Sitting Bull jokes, which lead to the Escrow Indians, who introduce a whole new set of jokes, pose a threat, and force the Stooges to spend the night in the

makeshift cabin, and so on. A number of these gags and jokes include two or three different punchlines or actions, and there are plenty of Stooge hits, threats, and insults to fill any voids. As with *Calling All Curs*, this is characteristic Jules White Stoogedom with wall-to-wall gags in this, the fifth consecutive Stooge film he has directed.

All of this happens in one place - a make-shift campsite somewhere within five months of Kansas and two months of San Francisco - in one twenty-four hour period from one afternoon to the next. Aristotle considered such a unity of time and place to be ideal for drama; it intensifies this particular comedy by confining its physical and temporal parameters. Within a 100-yard radius of where the Stooges are camped, Indians, ducks, and bears lurk about, cold weather brings snow from the roof and ice cubes from the pump, and a frozen

lake contains at least one very smart fish. That is all that is required for seventeen minutes of comedy. There is no need for a gold mine, the cavalry, or much else. Just Stooges, foils, and props.

VISUAL HUMOR: A Stooge slapstick first: pulling the back of each other's vests and jackets to get to dinner. This is the kind of rhythmic, weaving movement the Stooges had developed for their live act; in essence it is a non-architectural adaptation of their trying to squeeze laterally through a doorway in *Oily to Bed, Oily to Rise*. Other firsts: opening the door to charging attackers; and wearing clothes underneath their pajamas. (In *Flat Foot Stooges* they put their clothes over their pajamas.). This is the first film with a bear in it, although the Stooges are no strangers to large animals. All three animal scenes conclude effectively - the bear runs when Curly goes "Rruff!"; the duck incident has the echo tag "Look at the ducks. Look at the horses. Look at the ducks!"; and the ice fishing culminates with Curly's "Hey! This fish looks like Moe!". Unlike the previous film, the camera pans to only one 'result shot' - the canned corn beef on the faces of Moe and Larry. A slapstick variation: Moe pounds Curly in the belly, Larry bonks him on the forehead, Moe holds Curly's nose, and Larry bonks it.

From cement (*The Sitter Downers*) to watermelons (*Wee Wee Monsieur*), Curly's footwear collection is growing; here he wears two guitars for snow shoes and skates with them. Yanking the crossed fishing lines is similar to yanking the switch board lines in *Three Sappy People* and the two-man saw in *Oily to Bed, Oily to Rise*. Curly kissed Moe at the conclusions of *Calling All Curs* and *Oily to Bed, Oily to Rise*; it is a throw-away gag here as well. Again Curly is frustrated by an inanimate object (the corned beef can) to the point of tears, but here it results in shooting three ducks. The rigged sail is reminiscent of the Stooges' gurney in *Dizzy Doctors*. Other variations: the swinging branch (*Uncivil Warriors*); shooting a bird inadvertently (*Back to the Woods*); Curly shaking himself off like a dog (*We Want Our Mummy*); Nell bonking the Stooges' heads together (*Slippery Silks*); Larry asking Nell to "Dish it out!" (Moe's "Give it to me!" in *Pardon My Scotch*); Curly waving his hand up and down like a ship on water and making himself seasick (*Wee Wee Monsieur*); sprinkling something on Curly's tongue after he goes "Nyaggh! (*Cash and Carry*).

VERBAL HUMOR: Clyde Bruckman's busy script features word plays (Larry: "Here's your water." Moe: "These are ice cubes!" Larry: "So it's hard water!"; Chief: "No pale face allowed." Curly: "We ain't pale. We're sunboint!"; Moe: "You picked a fine time to go sailin'!" Curly: "Sail! If we only had a department store we could have a rummage sale!"; Larry: "We thought you was a fish." Moe: "Do I look like a sucker?"; and Moe: "Use the bear skin!" Curly: "Bare skin? How can I use my bare skin?"["bearly possible" in *Oily to Bed, Oily to Rise*]), verbal manipulations ("Sitting?! Bull!!"; Moe: "You keep a sharp lookout." Curly: "I'll keep two sharp lookouts!"; Curly: "A lizard, I mean a blizzard, an avalanch-ee."), understatement (Moe: "We only left Kansas five months ago!"), and a climaxing sequence (Curly: "It's a midget. It's a whale. Hey! This fish looks like Moe!"). The internal rhyme ("Start rummaging, rummy!") and the union gag (Curly: "We don't belong to the peanut vendors union!") recall similar gags in *Cash and Carry*, also written by Bruckman. Stooge firsts: Curly's "Tote that barge! Lift that bail!" and "Whadya' takin' a bath for? It ain't Saturday!". Curly's barking is getting ferocious; he barks in his sleep, he scares the bear away, he even shuts Nell up (Moe: We'll use the scenery!" Nell: "Oh no you don't!" Curly: "Oh yes we will!" Nell: "Oh no you won't!" Curly: "Well, we'll have it your way — we will! Rruff! Rruff!").

The latter is just one example of some intricate exchanges, another preceding slapstick (Curly: "I'm sick and tired of lookin' for Indians. Let 'em look for us for a change!" Larry: "Yeah, let 'em look for us for a change." Moe [pulling back the branch]: "Won't you look for one little one for me?" Larry: "A little one?" Moe: "Yeah, one with a fat stomach?" Larry [smiling]: "Just one? Okay?" Moe lets the branch go, Larry ducks, so it hits Moe in the face: "Ohh!" Larry: "Did you see one?" Moe whacks Larry in the face with the branch: "Yeah!"]. At the end of *Oily to Bed, Oily to Rise* Curly winked at the camera. Here Curly says "That's enough" to Moe in his natural voice to break the barrier between the audience and the film (Moe: "Ship Ahoy! Forward on the poop deck, shiver my timbers—" Curly: "Hey that's enough! Come on!"].

Curly helps the enemy (Nell: "The only thing that keeps me from killin' you birds is I'm short of bullets." Curly: "Oh I have plenty of bullets! I'd be glad to lend you some!"] as he did in *Saved By the Belle*. "Look at the ducks!" is like "Look at the grouse!" in *Pop Goes the Easel*; it is used four times here. Curly's "Give 'em the ax!" cheer follows chants/cheers in *You Nazty Spy!*, *A Ducking We Will Go*, *Oily to Bed, Oily to Rise*, and *Termites of 1938*. Other variations: the three-pattern (Chief: "How!" Moe: "How!" Larry: "How!" Curly: "How do you do?"), an Indian using slang ("Scram!"; "You make-um 23 skidoo!"), and Curly conscious of his baldness: "The barber got mine!" (*Back to the Woods*); Moe: "What's the big idea?" Larry: "You said come and get it!" Nell: "Well you got it!" (*Pop Goes the Easel*); "Takin' me illiterately, eh?" (*Oily to Bed, Oily to Rise*); "Say a few syllables."... "I hate you!" (*Slippery Silks*); "To the corned beef!" ("To the hunt!" in *We Want Our Mummy*); Curly calling a woman "Shorty" (*A Pain in the Pullman*); "Quiet, Airedale!" (*Calling All Curs*); "Get over there and quit neckin'!" (the "necking" address in *You Nazty Spy!*.) and "Swing it!" (*Violent is the Word for Curly*). "This country's good enough for us!" is intentionally patriotic. Epithets: "apple-head" and "bloodhound".

Epithets for the Stooges: "good-for-nothin' loafers"; "dumb clucks"; "three, flat-footed, broken down hoofers"; "sun-baked hams". The Escrow Chief calls Nell "Hatchet-Face". References: "We have met the enemy and the situation is well in hand" is a paraphrase of Oliver Hazard Perry's dispatch from the US Niagara after the Battle of Lake Erie in 1813. Sitting Bull, the Sioux chief who defeated Custer in 1876, was referred to in *Nertsery Rhymes*.

OTHER NOTES: The film was shot in early November, 1939. The working title was *Nell's Belles*; the opening banner reads "Nells Belles" [sic]. It has the same type of opening credit screens as *You Nazty Spy!* - plus four actor's credits. Dorothy Appleby, a former 'Miss Maine' who would appear in six more Stooge films, worked with Moe and Curly in the 1934 MGM short *Jailbirds of Paradise*; her feature credits include *Stagecoach* (1939) and *High Sierra* (1941). Ed Bernds recounted years later how Larry scared Lorna Gray, who was terrified of the bear on the set: getting on his hands and knees, Larry growled and grabbed Gray's leg; she fainted.

In this scene from *Rockin' Thru the Rockies* (1940), Curly's reference to the "walls of Jericho" parodies Columbia's 1934 multi-Academy Award-winning film *It Happened One Night*, starring the Stooges' old friend Clark Gable and Claudette Colbert. Colbert spends a night reluctantly in the same room as Gable, and the "wall of Jericho" is a hanging blanket that divides the room in two. Robert Young had been the first choice for the Gable role but turned it down because the plot involved a bus trip; Young had just made *Fugitive Lovers* (1933) which also involved a bus trip - and supporting roles by the Stooges.

#46 - A PLUMBING WE WILL GO

Studio: Columbia

Released: April 19, 1940

Running Time: 17"31"

Credited Production Crew:

Produced by:	Del Lord & Hugh McCollum
Directed by:	Del Lord
Story & Screen Play by:	Elwood Ullman
Director of Photography:	Benjamin Kline
Film Editor:	Arthur Seid

Credited Cast:

Curly Howard
Larry Fine
Moe Howard

Uncredited Cast:

John Tyrrell	judge
Bess Flowers	his wife
Bud Jamison	Officer Kelly
Dudley Dickerson	cook
Eddie Laughton	prosecutor
Monty Collins	Professor Bilbo
Symona Boniface	guest
Al Thompson	store owner

PERSPECTIVE: This is the sixth film in which the Stooges have wrecked someone's home, and they are obviously getting better at their work. They ruined their own home in *The Sitter Downers*, and here the damage is much more extensive than in *Pardon My Scotch, Ants in the Pantry, Termites of 1938*, or *Tassels in the Air*. They ruin the basement, the upstairs bathroom, the kitchen, the living room, and the lawn, and they destroy the plumbing as well as the electrical, telephone, gas, and steam lines. They did not mean to do this originally; they were just trying to find something to eat. Maybe the judge should not have let the Stooges out of court in the first place, maybe Officer Kelly should have arrested them instead of punching Curly, and maybe the butler should not have let them into the house, but whoever is to blame the Stooges - guilty of theft, grand theft-auto, fishing without a license, and avoiding arrest - destroy an expensive home.

The house destruction generates the comedy for the last thirteen minutes of the film, and the unrelenting pace of the gags, lines, and special effects intensifies as the film heads toward its conclusion. Editor Arthur Seid and director Del Lord guide the comedy along by carefully organizing the chaos caused by three different Stooges doing three different types of destruction in three different parts of the home. In some recent films separating the Stooges has been effective (the dynamite sequence in *Yes, We Have No Bonanza*; the fishing scene in *Rockin' Thru the Rockies*) in tying together three distinct Stooge activities, and here the editing is particularly skillful where Seid connects each area of the Stooges' catastrophic service call: Moe's pipes screw up the kitchen faucet; Curly's misunderstanding of the difference between a water pipe and electrical conduit ruin the kitchen clock and living room television - the Niagara Falls surprise is one of Stoogedom's most memorable moments - and his upstairs bathroom fiasco soaks Moe and plunges the judge into the basement; and Larry's trench forms a conduit through which the Stooges, judge, cops, and even motorcycles can exit this neatly constructed film of a mess.

Usually Stooge victims know very well who is ruining the house; in this film the judge, Officer Kelly, and the butler know or find out what Stooges they are dealing with, and Mrs. Casey knows that plumbers are wrecking the house. Only the chef is left in ignorance. When he sees the sink faucet turn upside down and fall off, when water mysteriously squirts in his face, when the kitchen clock goes haywire, and when water comes out from the oven, he has no idea what is causing any of this. He is isolated, completely unaware of the Stooge forces at work behind the kitchen walls. As in many classic 'Negro' roles of the period, Dudley Dickerson's character was supposed to be confused, scared, and amazed, but Dickerson goes beyond the call of duty to create what might be the greatest non-Stooge solo comic performance in the entire corpus. He puts on a raincoat and attempts valiantly to turn off the water, performing fine takes and pratfalls, and saying one of Stoogedom's most often quoted lines: "This house is sho' goin' crazy!"

It is not just the plumbing scenario, which is simply a reworking of Sidney & Murray's *Plumbing for Gold* (1934), but a new behind-the-scenes chemistry that is responsible for the success of this film. It is the first co-production by the Hugh McCollum/Del Lord team, the latter returning to Stooge films after a hiatus of almost a year. Lord brings with him the same Mack Sennett bravado he introduced five years earlier into such films as *Pop Goes the Easel, Hoi Polloi*, and *Three Little Beers*, some of the gag scenarios and spatial elements of which are recast for this film. Jules White will rely on this team repeatedly after Charlie Chase's fatal heart attack, and in the next four years they will make such other classics as *No Census, No Feeling* and *An Ache in Every Stake*. This is also writer Elwood Ullman's first solo effort after three years of development as a Stooge co-author. This new production chemistry was so effervescent, it created a Stooge zenith in *A Plumbing We Will Go*, without question one of the most memorable comedy films ever made.

VISUAL HUMOR: Del Lord conjures up a number of new physical gags: Curly tries to get his fingers to snap in the policeman's face as part of a three-pattern which ends with the cop's surprise kick to Curly's rear; and Curly beats up the dummy cop and has the real cop turn his face so he can punch him, but the cop slugs Curly. A two-Stooge innovation, based on the hypnotizing hand-wave, occurs where Curly and Moe rapidly move their heads up and down during the Jack and Jill hydraulic lesson. Conversely, a slow, silent beauty is Larry squeezing his head up through the sod, disappearing, then grabbing his hat from below ground level. Notice how many gestures and faces Curly makes as he sits on the edge of the tub to think about solving a problem. When he finally builds his labyrinthine pipe structure, he is, as often, struggling on his own against an inanimate object Film historians write about Fred Astaire dancing with a clothes tree and making it seem graceful; Curly makes pipes and tools take on a life of their own. Stooge firsts: appearing in a magic box; and a television gag.

The first production by the Lord/McCollum team and writer Elwood Ullman, *A Plumbing We Will Go* (1940) features brilliant physicality from isolated Stooges and Dudley Dickerson, and a surprise, gushing climax from a television set, all helping to make this one of the most memorable comedy films ever made.

The initial ventriloquism sequence was inspired by the frequent film appearances of Edgar Bergen, Charlie McCarthy, and Mortimer Snerd in 1938-39, following Bergen's special Oscar in 1937. Curly's crash through the floor is the best massive fall since the floor collapses in *Cash and Carry* and *The Sitter Downers*. Covering the hole with the carpet derives from *We Want Our Mummy*. The Stooges are fishing again, as in *Rockin' Thru the Rockies*; they fished in a tank in *The Sitter Downers*. Other variations: running from a cop [*Pop Goes the Easel*, *A Ducking They Did Go*]; a court scene [*Disorder in the Court*]; the cement trough [*Three Little Beers*]; escaping in a truck [*Violent is the Word for Curly*]; stealing food [*Wee Wee Monsieur*]; the camera panning across the court and to the fish tank [*Three Sappy People*]; and breaking something outside the camera frame [the drink cart in *Calling All Curs*].

VERBAL HUMOR: Preferring ironic reactions to set jokes, Elwood Ullman does not interrupt the pace of the physical comedy but complements the visual gags. This happens in the fishing sequence [Curly: "A barrie-cudie, and what a cutie!"]; the magician's box [Moe: "There's no room for an argument in here!"]; while fixing the steam pipe with a corset [Larry: "A straight jacket." Moe: "A perfect 36!" Larry [referring to the garter clips]: "Ya' swing on 'em, you know."]; while in the upstairs bathroom [Curly: "Bahth, bath, bahth - you gotta get outta here!"]; in the kitchen ["This house is sho' goin' crazy"]; or as an exit line [Curly: "Don't mind me! I'm only the plumber!"]. Three-pattern: Moe: "Where's the leak, boy?" Butler: "In the basement." Larry: "Where's the basement?" Curly: "Upstairs!" Moe: "To the basement!".

Curly's "Why don't you call your stops?" varies the common line "Why don't you call your shots?!". Epithets: "lame-brain" and "egg-head". The yielding-gag [Moe: "What are you gonna do about it?" Curly: "Get another piece of pipe."] derives from "Are you ready?"/"Yeah, I'm ready" [*Plane Nuts*], but the circumstances and sentence structure resemble more an exchange [Moe: "What would you do?" Curly: "I'd blast"] from *The Sitter Downers*. Other variations: "Dandruff," "A barrie-cudie, and what a cutie!" [*Calling All Curs*]; "Three of the best plumbers who ever plumbed a plumb" ["Three of the best salesmen who ever saled!" in *Dizzy Doctors*]; "To the basement!" and "You imbecile!" [*We Want Our Mummy*]; a nursery rhyme ["Jack and Jill went up the hill to fetch a pail of water"] [*Nertsery Rhymes*]; and "Give me a hand" [*Punch Drunks*].

OTHER NOTES: There is no hyphen in the title. Columbia's Sidney & Murray short-film, *Plumbing for Gold* (1934), was remade again as *Vagabond Loafers* (1949) by the Stooges (with Shemp), as *Pick a Peck of Plumbers* (1944) with El Brendel and Shemp, and as *Scheming Schemers* (1956) with the Stooges; the original story involves searching for a lost ring, as in *Sheming Schemers*. Footage from *A Plumbing We Will Go* will be used in *Vagabond Loafers*, *Scheming Schemers*, and *Stop! Look! and Laugh!*. In 1940 Laurel & Hardy had a house go haywire, too, in *Saps at Sea*. The television broadcast on 'WX21' from Niagara Falls is not sheer fantasy. In February, 1940 - just months after this film was shot (mid-December 1939) - NBC transmitted the first official network television broadcast from New York City to station W2XBS in Schenectady. How ironic that this wonderful scene should involve the same electronic medium that would make the Stooges so popular when televisions began to broadcast Stoogedom into American living rooms in the 1950s. This is the second new appliance incorporated into a Stooge film, the first being the electric razor in *3 Dumb Clucks* and *Tassels in the Air*. Moe [107] offers an anecdote about how Del Lord created a shadow on the rushes by nervously twirling his hair. in his fingers.

#47 - NUTTY but NICE

Studio: Columbia

Released: June 14, 1940

Running Time: 17"45"

Credited Production Crew:

Produced & Directed by:	Jules White
Story & Screen Play by:	Clyde Bruckman & Felix Adler
Director of Photography:	John Stumar
Film Editor:	Mel Thorsen

Credited Cast:

Curly Howard
Larry Fine
Moe Howard

Uncredited Cast:

John Tyrrell	Dr. Lyman
Vernon Dent	doctor
Ned Glass	Mr. Williams
Lynton Brent	Spike
Bert Young	police detective
Ethelreda Leopold	hostess
Johnny Kascier	beer man
Lew Davis	first man on street
Charles Dorety	hot foot victim
Cy Schindell	crook (and man on street)
Eddie Garcia	

PERSPECTIVE: Two film genres would become characteristic in the 1940s. One was the war film, and we have already seen the Stooges on the forefront of this movement with *Three Little Sew and Sews* and *You Nazty Spy!*. The other was what the French labeled 'Film Noir' - "black films" that featured dark settings, gangster crime, human disillusionment, and loner heroes. The greatest early film noir productions would be John Huston's *The Maltese Falcon* (1941) and Michael Curtiz' *Casablanca* (1942). Lo and behold, here the Stooges are in 1940 with their film being very *noir*. *Nutty but Nice* concerns heartless gangsters committing robbery and kidnapping, a sad, disillusioned little girl, and heroes whose stoogeness separates them out as loners. Curly even delivers a 'death-bed speech' filled with tragic pathos, and for the climactic battle the film actually goes "black" five times! If there were such a genre as 'comedy noir,' *Nutty but Nice* would be the prototypical example.

Nutty but Nice will become a model for many subsequent Stooge films, for dark interiors were a common part of contemporary films, not to mention that they were easy on the budget, and underworld goons make great foils who rough up the Stooges, but get beaten by them in the end. Shemp films will glory in such mobster scenarios, which fuel a multiplicity of sight gags. By their sheer numbers these gangsters increase the mass of the physical chaos and bring about more impressive triumphs once the Stooges finally overcome two, three, or even four of them. The mattress sequence here, for example, is relatively easy to stage and inexpensive to produce, but it produces continuous and compact comedy, placing three mobsters, three Stooges, a hostage, a mattress, a door, and a book all within the space of twelve square feet, creating no end to confusion by hitting the wrong person and then helping the wrong person. The basement scene similarly thrives on the confusion caused by three Stooges, Mr. Williams, and three mobsters all doing battle - in utter darkness!

There is an interesting variation in the plot in that the Stooges are requested as amateur comedy experts to cheer up a young girl. At the outset their characterization is established when the Stooges tell jokes in the restaurant and are laughed at by the customers (contrary to the norm since typically the Stooges anger people with their antics), and then the doctors ask the Stooges to cure young Betty Williams specifically because they are funny, a new twist on the premise of *Uncivil Warriors* and other films in which the Stooges are supposed to be 'experts,' and of *Three Sappy People* where they cheered up their patient despite not being doctors or comedians. We know the Stooges as professional comedians, but usually the characters in their films do not. In *What's the Matador?* and *A Pain in the Pullman* they played comic actors, but they were mostly unsuccessful. Here as amateur comedians the Stooges are asked to brighten the *noir* life of a young girl, and they actually do help the child (*Cash and Carry*) despite some rather unorthodox methods and a few bumps and bruises along the way.

VISUAL HUMOR: Stooge firsts: Curly holding a lit light bulb; knee biting to disarm an assailant; punching through

Ned Glass and Cy Schindell introduce the bentwood chair into Stooge comedy in *Nutty but Nice* (1940), the first of their 'noir' comedies. The final battle is completely 'dark.'

a wooden door; framing some one's head with a bentwood chair; a hot foot; and the blackouts. There are both elaborate physical sequences (a 'Cossack dance' complete with "Hoot-ta-hah! Hoot-ta-hey!") and more

subtle ones (Curly doing his nails with an iron file). As in the previous film, extras are given feature gags. Johnny Kascier as the beer man takes tremendous spills; Cy Schindell [Butch] makes cuckoo faces when he is knocked out. Another of the elaborate sequences occurs when Curly yodels outside the building. In the previous film Moe moved over each time he got wet from the holes Curly drilled into the bathroom floor. Curly moves over here each time he yodels; first he is hit with water, then again with water, and finally with a flowerpot - with some concern about a "loose piano". In *Oily to Bed, Oily to Rise* Curly ruined the saw and said "Oh! Oh! Oh! Ohhhl*look*!" Here he gets bonked and pounded, says "Oh! Oh! Ohhh!" and leads into the Lollipop Song (*Wee Wee Monsieur*). Also in *Oily to Bed, Oily the Rise* we saw the camera panning to result shots, as here it pans to Butch with the iron bed frame on his head. A number of variations derive from early Stooge shorts: knocking out the enemy, as well as fellow Stooges, and reviving the enemy with spilled water (*Back to the Woods*); the dumbwaiter gags, and the Stooges harassing passers-by on the street (*Three Little Pigskins*); and knocking the detective over by kneeling behind him (*Pop Goes the Easel*). When Moe pokes Curly's belly with the metal arrow, the sound effect is oddly inappropriate.

VERBAL HUMOR: Curly's elaborate, tragic death scene ("I'm stabbed. I'm dead, I'm murdered. I'm killed, I'm annihilated! What'll the world do without me? What'll I do without myself? I'm slaughtered, I'm annihilated, I'm destroyed, I'm barbecued, I'm done for [to Moe] Can you think of anything else?") is one of the most extraordinary innovations in the script. A Stooge first: Curly counting "One. Two. Two-and-a-half!". Two set jokes are used in the opening scene to establish the Stooges as known comedians (Doctor: "What have you today, boys?" Curly: "Well, doc, I got a terrific pain right here. Every time I squeeze my Adam's Apple, I can taste cider."; Larry: "A train going to Kansas City 120 miles an hour, what's the engineer's name?" Moe: "I don't know." Larry: "Pat McCartny." Moe: "How do you know?" Larry: "I asked him!"). The three pattern (Moe: "No bonds." Larry: "No identification!" Curly: "Oh yes there is. He's a boyscout!") moves the plot along when the Stooges run from the detective

Curly's yielding gag ("Then we can blast") is reminiscent of his "I'd blast" in *The Sitter Downers*. Curly's "This soup is a marvelous accomplishment; it's a prodigious achievement! You're going to love it! It's putrid." was a formulated as a three-pattern in *Three Sappy People*. Other variations: Williams: "The dumb waiter!" Curly: "I resent that!", "chysanthemumumum" (*Oily to Bed, Oily to Rise*);"He's haunted!" (*Men in Black*) "P-tunia (*Flat Foot Stooges*); "We're trapped like rats!" (*Back to the Woods*); and "Who's there?"/"Termites!" ("Who's in there?"/ "Nobody, just us horses" in *Grips, Grunts and Groans*). The Stooge version of 'Yankee Doodle': "Our Yankee noodle soup is good. You'll find it is no phony. If you don't have the noodle soup we'll serve you macaroni."

OTHER NOTES: The title on the screen is a mixture of capital and small letters: *NUTTY but NiCE*; the phrase parodies the 1939 Warner Brothers musical, *Naughty But Nice*; the same year, Warner Brothers issued a Sniffles cartoon with the same title. Both Johnny Kascier and Cy Schindell appear as passersby on the street and as crooks in the apartment building. Curly's, "Well ya' break the arm off about there...Then we can blast!" it is the first time his high pitched voice sounds like a mere falsetto.

#48 - HOW HIGH is UP?

Studio: Columbia

Released: July 26, 1940

Running Time: 16"26"

Credited Production Crew:

Produced by	Del Lord & Hugh McCollum
Directed by:	Del Lord
Story & Screen Play by:	Elwood Ullman
Dirctor of Photography:	Allen G. Siegler
Film Editor:	Arthur Seid

Credited Cast:

Curly Howard
Larry Fine
Moe Howard

Uncredited Cast:

Vernon Dent	Mr. Blake
Bruce Bennett	worker
Edmund Cobb	worker
Bert Young	worker
Cy Schindell	Blake's assistant

PERSPECTIVE: The comedy in this masterful short winds through five scenarios: 1) the Stooges sleeping; 2) working on their car; 3) dressing/undressing; 4) drumming up business; and 5) being atop a skyscraper. All of these are scenarios we have seen before, but they illustrate the ability of co-producer Hugh McCollum, co-producer/director Del Lord, and writer Elwood Ullman to build previously established gags into a new comedy. The Stooges began *Movie Maniacs* sleeping in a train and *Dizzy Doctors* sleeping in their bed, but here the 'fooler opening' scenario moves to the street. This is bizarre enough, but when the water flows they lower their 'Men At Work' sign and remain sleeping as they float down the street to their rendezvous with a truck and a policeman. The Stooge day has begun.

The car scenario recalls their slogan-covered vehicle in *Termites of 1938* and the jalopy of *Cash and Carry*, but the misplaced salami patch episode combines the discarded pot holder in *Uncivil Warriors* and Ullman's prospecting scene from *Yes, We Have No Bonanza*, where the dog carried the dynamite. The flat tire has little bearing on the plot, but Moe's back-swing anchor clanging on Larry's head and Larry's "What tools?" - both often used but ever effective gags - carry the scene to one of the most outstanding set pieces the Stooges ever filmed - the sweater sequence. Lasting over three minutes, this epic struggle takes Curly's well-established difficulties with inanimate objects to a new level in that he must struggle with not only the sweater but with Moe and Larry. Once Moe says the ominous "We'll have you outta this in a jiffy," the scene flows with more CLANGs and CLINGs than have ever been grouped together, each accompanied by a different physical reaction from Curly and the music of incidental Stooge chatter: Larry's wisecracks ("He looks like a V-8"; "He's only got two ears, you know!"), Moe's threats and unswerving confidence, and Curly's mounting frustration ("Don't mind me! *Don't mind me*!").

The second half of the film takes the Stooges into a world of factory and construction workers they have not visited before. It would have cost too much to place the Stooges in a fully manned factory or construction site, so McCollum/Lord solved the problem by placing them in first the lunch area and then on the 97th floor of an unfinished building. The lunch-pail-puncturing tool which creates a problem to drum up business is the child of adding pests to the house in *Ants in the Pantry*, and the skyscraper sequence is a fabulous blend of the fall from a skyscraper flagpole in *3 Dumb Clucks*, eating inedible objects (*Uncivil Warriors*), the construction disasters of *The Sitter Downers*, and the off-camera crash of *Calling All Curs*. All this makes for a new look - Stooges sleeping in the street, sitting on the running board, and constructing a skyscraper - even though the gag concepts are mostly refurbished. Del Lord excelled at making old dogs learn new tricks, salami patch or not.

VISUAL HUMOR: Two Stooge firsts: Curly finishing off his hypnotizing hand wave with an up thrust and a head bonk; and the 'V-8' gag (Larry: "He looks like a V-8!' Moe: "Did you ever hear of a 'V-5'?" Larry: "What's that a new car?" Moe: "No it's an old sock!" [SLAP]). A 'fooler opening' is one in which the camera shows us a limited view, then pulls back to show us the comedy of the situation. This film opens with a classic example. We have seen sleeping gags with a lion (*Three Missing Links*), a monkey (*A Pain in the Pullman*), and wives (*Dizzy Doctors*), but this is the first with a bug. Curly has often been hit on the head, but when Moe bangs him to get the sweater off, this is the first time Curly reacts by checking his upper teeth. Then again, he eat rivets with those hard teeth, just as he filed his nails with an iron file in the previous *Nutty but Nice*. The sweater sequence makes great improvements over a lengthy, relatively tedious sequence in *Be Big*, a 1930 Laurel & Hardy three-reeler, in which Laurel spends a full reel trying to take Hardy's boots off. Other variations: the 'Men at Work' sign (*3 Dumb Clucks*); Curly cooling off his burning rear in water (*Back to the Woods*); Curly drawing back his arm to prepare for a jab (*A Plumbing We Will Go*); the anchor (*Uncivil Warriors*); and the Stooges running from behind other men to take a job (*Men in Black*).

VERBAL HUMOR: The sweater sequence depends on Curly's obesity, so at the beginning of the sweater scene we hear one of the occasional fat jokes Curly makes at his own expense ("I didn't have any trouble, but since then I might-a put on a little weight!"); the most recent was physical, where he repeatedly turned the drill handle into his belly in *A Plumbing We Will Go*. Curly also has a moment of self-deprecation for his looks (Moe: "Was your mother frightened by somethin'?" Curly: "Yeah, by me!"). A Stooge first: Moe: "Did that sweater have a pink bow?" Curly: "No!" Moe [to Larry]: "Ya cut his ear off!". Two 'yielding' gags: Curly: "What are *you* going to do?!" Moe: "I'm gonna see if the horn works." Curly: "I just thought I'd ask"; and Larry [to Curly]: "Yeah, get busy! [Moe looks at Larry] I'm gonna help him". Moe's "Am I gonna have trouble with you, too?!" is a variation of his "You gonna start that again?" in *False Alarms* and Ted Healy's "Now you're startin'!" in *Myrt and Marge*. Other variations: "What tools? Oh those tools!" and Larry: "Wait a minute! You want to kill 'im?" Curly: "Why don't you mind your own business? (*Meet the Baron*); "Give me a hand" (*Punch Drunks*); "Three of the best riveters that ever riveted!" (*Dizzy Doctors*); "Weeee fix 'em!" (said like "Swing it!" in *Violent is the Word for Curly*); Curly: "I'm surrounded!" (*A Plumbing We Will Go*); Curly: "I think he means us" (*Pardon My Scotch*); and Curly: "A bonanza!" Moe: "Stop thinkin' of food and get to work!" (*Yes, We Have No Bonanza*). The word "buckaroo" is used here to mean a "rivet"; it was a currency in *You Nazty Spy!*.

OTHER NOTES: The title on the initial screen is capitalized thus: *How High is Up?*. The Stooges work on the 97th floor of the skyscraper; at that time the Empire State Building, completed in May, 1931, was the only building in the world that had that many floors (102). Bruce Bennett, the tall, first lunch pail victim, had a long career in Tarzan, Lone Ranger, and other action pictures; his name at birth was Herman Brix. Footage from this film will be used in *Stop! Look! and Laugh!*.

One of the most outstanding set pieces the Stooges ever filmed is the sweater sequence in *How High is Up?* (1940). Lasting over three minutes, this epic struggle takes Curly's well-established difficulties with inanimate objects to a new level in that he must struggle with not only the sweater but also Moe and Larry. Beware: when Moe says the ominous, "We'll have you outta this in a jiffy!" - you know the trouble is just beginning.

#49 - FROM NURSE TO WORSE

Studio: Columbia

Released: August 23, 1940

Running Time: 16"43"

Credited Production Crew:

Produced & Directed by:	Jules White
Directed by:	Jules White
Screen play by:	Clyde Bruckman
Story by:	Charles L. Kimball
Director of Photography:	Benjamin Kline
Film Editor:	Mel Thorsen

Credited Cast:

Curly Howard
Larry Fine
Moe Howard

Uncredited Cast:

Lynton Brent	Jerry
Vernon Dent	Dr. D. Lerious
John Tyrrell	anethestetician
Dorothy Appleby	receptionist
Cy Schindell	policeman
Marjorie 'Babe' Kane	woman in office
Joe Palma	assistant surgeon
Al Seymour	orderly
Al Thompson	head orderly
Dudley Dickerson	hospital orderly
Blanche Payson	tall nurse
Poppie Wilde	assistant surgeon
Charles Phillips	assistant surgeon
Johnny Kascier	attendant
Bert Young	photographer
Ned Glass	dog catcher
Charles Dorety	dog catcher

PERSPECTIVE: The story of *From Nurse To Worse* by one-time Stooge writer Charles L. Kimball hinges on a clever mirror-image variation of an old formula in which the Stooges louse something up in the early scenes, create an apparently unrelated havoc in the middle scenes, and then are recognized in the finale and are punished/chased by the person they encountered in the first scene. The classic example thus far is *A Plumbing We Will Go*; the judge and the cop appear in the outer scenes while the inner scenes involve only the destruction of the house. In *From Nurse To Worse* the roles - but not the sequence - are reversed. In the early scenes, the Stooges do not get into trouble but actually take advantage of an opportunity, an insurance scam. They succeed so thoroughly in convincing Dr. D. Lerious that Curly is crazy that the middle of the film is spent trying to avoid brain surgery; ironically, just as the house was the victim of the middle havoc in *A Plumbing We Will Go*, the Stooges are the victims of the middle havoc in *From Nurse To Worse*. In the finale the Stooges chase and punish the person who offered them the opportunity in the first scenes, a mirror-image of the norm.

This means the hospital chase scenes are not mere fillers to transport the Stooges from one scenario to the next. The chase scenes are the middle havoc of the film, and that is why there are so many gags attached to them - 'Charlie who walks like this,' the man with the tray, making faces at the infants, the fake gurney made of crutches, the man with the tray again, Curly escaping from and running back into the operating room, the wig-mop disguises, the confusion with the anesthesia, Dudley Dickerson being spooked, the man with the tray again, and the escape on the sailing gurney. We have toured hospitals with the Stooges previously in *Men in Black*, *Dizzy Doctors*, and *Calling All Curs*, but the energy in all these gags derives from a genuine desire on the part of Dr. D. Lerious to cure or sedate Curly.

The mirror-image structure also brings a reverse emphasis to the second scene. In *Men in Black*, *Dizzy Doctors*, and *Calling All Curs* it was the Stooges who examined weird patients, but now Curly is the weird patient, and this will not be the last time Curly will be the subject of a doctor's examination. He makes a great comic patient. Unlike patients the Stooges examine, Curly can make noises, faces, and gestures, not to mention wise cracks and eyes at women. Similarly, the sailing gurney in the finale takes on a different purpose. The footage is from *Dizzy Doctors*, but its purpose is not merely to provide escape for the Stooges: it conveys them to Jerry, who, although he is not a terrible villain, is the object of the Stooges' anger. They punish him for giving them this 'opportunity' to take out an insurance policy. Ironically, they give him the same treatment the cop in *A Plumbing We Will Go* got - a dumping into a cement trough. Poor Jerry: is it really his fault that Curly turned into such a believable canine? Rruff!

VISUAL HUMOR: Curly's dog impersonation has its predecessors: he created a (live) chicken impersonation for *Oily to Bed, Oily to Rise*; his chicken-with-its-head-cut-off and his gorilla in *Three Missing Links*; and his brief goose imitation in *You Nazty Spy!*. He has been barking "Rruff!" since *Restless Knights*, but in the van we get a frightening close up of Curly's barking face. *Restless Knights* was also the first film in which scratching - with the proper sound effect - became part of Stoogedom, and two highlights in *From Nurse To Worse* are Curly's vigorously scratching himself in the doctor's office and the shot of all three Stooges scratching in the van with the help of (real) dogs. Moe's smile is particularly photogenic; he has not sported a smile that big since saluting FDR in *Cash and Carry*. There is a new sound effect introduced here - the washing machine sound from inside Curly's head. There is a sound effect missing the first time or two Moe's elbow hits Curly's face while trying to pull out the dollar. The nose tweak Moe then gives Larry is very muted as well. When the Stooges slip out the other side of the taxi, it is just a prelude to the clever chase in the hospital.

Curly's locked purse is a variation of the sweater gag from the previous film, but it is a first in that we will see locked garments/accessories in future films. Curly entering on a leash from behind the camera is the mirror image of his exiting towards the camera in another dog film, *Calling All Curs*. The hospital orderly [Dudley Dickerson] seeing the Stooges lift the cover sheet, raises his hands, screams, and leaps out the window varying his fright-reaction role in the recent *A Plumbing We Will Go*. Other variations: Moe grabbing Curly's nose with a scissors (*Slippery Silks*); stepping on the sheet to unmask the multi-Stooge gurney disguise (*Healthy, Wealthy and Dumb*); imitating "Charlie, the fella who walks like this" (*Uncivil Warriors*); the 'Shave and a Haircut' rhythm (*Whoops, I'm an Indian*); and the abuse of a stethoscope (*Men in Black*).

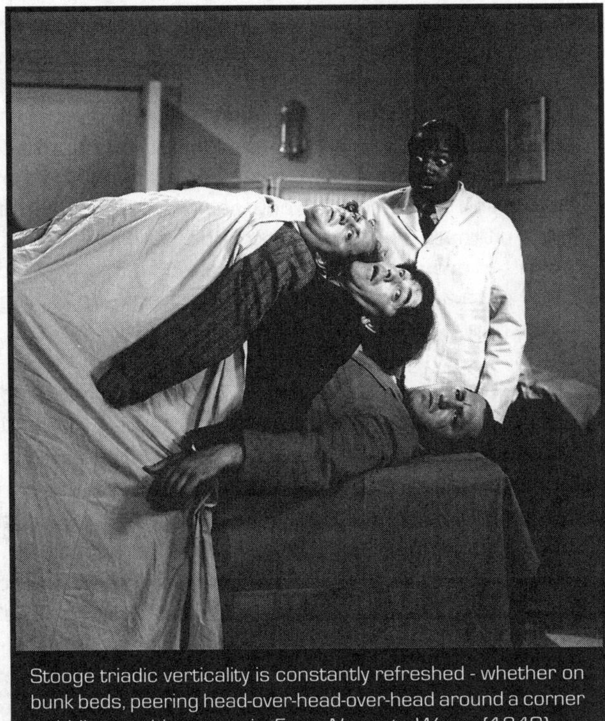

Stooge triadic verticality is constantly refreshed - whether on bunk beds, peering head-over-head-over-head around a corner or hiding on this gurney in *From Nurse to Worse* (1940).

VERBAL HUMOR: The canine subject matter breeds a number of animal gags (Moe: "If you had played your part like a Pekinese instead of a Wolf Hound, our plan would-a worked!"; Curly: "Hit a dumb animal, would you?"; Two of Moe's names for Curly, "Bowser" (Curly: "Yowsir!") and "Hydrophobia," are apt for his canine personality. Stooge ignorance is also crucial to the plot (Moe: "Where's the key?" Curly: " In the purse!" Moe: "What's it in there for?" Curly: "So I won't lose it!"; Curly [running in circles]: "This is the longest room I've ever seen!"; and Doctor [rattling Curly's head]: "There's something loose inside." Moe: "Oh you're wrong, doctor. *His* head is empty."). This also occasions the first use of the classic Stooge epithet "nitwit". The insurance scam inspires one 'yielding' gag (Jerry: "Which one do you want to insure? Moe & Larry: "Him!" Curly: "Not me! [SLAP] I refuse! [HEAD SLAP] I still refuse! [Moe grabs his nose with a scissors] I surrender!") and a money gag (Curly: "That's my favorite dollar. I raised it from a cent!").

Moe's "You mean he may go from mad to worse?" is a pun echoing the title of the film, as in *Three Little Sew and Sews*. The gag from *Uncivil Warriors* (Larry: "You know Charlie, the fella who walks like this") is varied by Moe's "Yeah, he's got a bad case of ingrown heel. He starts out like this—". Other variations: Curly saying "Come in" when his head is knocked (*A Pain in the Pullman*); Doctor: "Now let's see, the heart—" Curly: "Two spades!" Larry: "I double." Moe: "I redouble!" (*Meet the Baron*); and Curly: "$500 a month! It's a banana!" Moe: "Bonanza!" Curly: "Bonanza, banana, bandanna- as long as we don't have to work any more!" (*How High is Up?*). References: the initials on Dr. D. Lerious' door: M.D. [Medical Doctor], C.C.C. [Commodity Credit Corporation, a New Deal lending institution established by Congress in 1935], F.H.A. [Federal Housing Administration], W.P.A. [Works Progress Administration; see *Back to the Woods*], A.W.O.L. [Absent WithOut Leave - a military acronym]. Moe calls Curly "Seabiscuit," Horse of the Year in 1938 and the top money-winner in 1937. The same horse was mentioned in *You Nazty Spy!* ('Sea of Biscuit' on the map) and *Violent Is the Word for Curly*. As usual, Moe dubs the radio voice.

OTHER NOTES: The correct capitalization of the title is *From Nurse To Worse*.

#50 - NO CENSUS, NO FEELING

Studio: Columbia

Released: October 4, 1940

Running Time: 16"29"

Credited Production Crew:

Produced by:	Del Lord & Hugh McCollum
Directed by:	Del Lord
Story & Screen Play:	Harry Edwards & Elwood Ullman
Director of Photography:	Lucien Ballard
Film Editor:	Arthur Seid

Credited Cast:

Curly Howard
Larry Fine
Moe Howard

Uncredited Cast:

Symona Boniface	hostess
Marjorie 'Babe' Kane	woman on street
Max Davidson	store owner
Vernon Dent	party guest
Ellinor Vanderveer	Larry's bridge partner
Bruce Bennett	football player
John Tyrrell	home owner
Bert Young	referee
Frank Austin	

PERSPECTIVE: As in *How High is Up?* the Stooges wake up in the late morning and soon find a policeman hot on their tails. The string of Jules White films that opened with expository scenes ended with *Rockin' Thru the Rockies*, and since *A Plumbing We Will Go*, Del Lord has had the Stooges begin their antics right from the outset. Here they pour out of that awning to face a new day of running from authorities, annoying people, and running again. But being in trouble like this is good for the Stooges: it rushes them effectively into their mid-film havoc where they can best express their superior lack of all talents except comedy. The Stooges thrive where they are not supposed to be, and all it takes is an open truck door, a desperate homeowner or butler, or an undiscriminating manager to take them into an as-yet untainted environment to destroy. The Stooges are not supposed to be sleeping in that awning, and as a by-product of one of their typical inter-Stooge squabbles they damage the shop owner's dishes, so the cop chases them, and this leads them into City Hall. Now they are somewhere else they do not belong, and here it is the faceless bureaucracy of the federal government that gives them three Census Bureau ledgers and promises 4¢ per person— enough motivation for them to pester the rest of us.

There really was a national census taken in 1940, and characterizing the Stooges as census takers was a brilliant stroke, enabling them to engage in a number of clever verbal Q & A sequences and physically pursue a variety of victims on the street, in a home and at a football game. It is not just the wealthy whom the Stooges disturb; they bother everybody. These Stooges disturb construction workers, football players, policemen, and shop owners - average men and women - as well as the rich. And let us not forget, the Stooges are always disturbing each other. They may alumize the punch and rip the pants off two linemen, but no one else gets a Census ledger on the head or a grated cheek just because they say they were born in Lake Winnepesaukee.

No Census, No Feeling exposes the Stooges to a broad spectrum of humanity, and just as *How High is Up?* took the Stooges from the depths of a soaking wet gutter to the 97th floor of a skyscraper and back down again to the gutter in a kind of vertical-spatial ring composition, *No Census, No Feeling* takes the Stooges spatially not up but out. They unroll from the awning, run down the street, crowd through the City Hall doors, spread out to interrogate three separated Census victims, run again, and reunite in a home and then in a football stadium from which they run one last time. Thanks initially to the Mack Sennett know-how of Del Lord [*Three Little Beers*], the Stooges have always and will continue for years to explore various spatial arrangements. They will find themselves in such confined spaces as telephone booths and garbage cans, and they have already spread out in three different parts of a house and all over a golf course. It is no accident that their ultimate spatial goals will be outer space, time travel, an around the world voyage, and a fantasy land in each of their five Columbia feature films some twenty years hence.

VISUAL HUMOR: Stooge firsts: Moe holding one hand in pain while punching with the other hand; Curly acting like a calculator; twisting one's own foot around and around. In the 'fooler openings' of *Movie Maniacs* and *3 Dumb Clucks*, the camera pulled back to show us the 'joke,' that is, where the Stooges were. Now it is a change of camera angle: one angle shows us Moe talking to a man lying under a newspaper, the next shows us that it is Larry lying on a living room couch; the first angle shows us Moe's perspective, the second Larry's. This same technique was used in Director Del Lord's most recent Stooge film, *How High is Up?*, where the changed camera angle showed us that the sleeping Stooges were lying under a truck parked in the street. The job of collecting census information dictates that this is predominantly a verbal comedy, but three physical stunts are noteworthy: Curly's fall off the kitchen table [similar to his missing the glove in *Calling All Curs*], the amazing fall the stunt man takes down the City Hall steps, and the cop being hit by the shop owner's broom. Curly makes some particularly creative movements and facial gestures after Moe grates his face, especially when he tries to reopen his own eye. Result shot: the punch bowl spinning on Curly's head; it is one of the better result shots in Stoogedom.

Inter-Stooge slapstick developments: Curly slapping Moe four times without much retaliation; Larry protecting himself with a pot; and a new variation on the gouge: Moe points with one finger, then two, and then gouges. Throwing ice cream at a football game derives from the Marx Brothers' *Horsefeathers* (1932.). The alum-laced punch is one major comic ingredient beyond the Tabasco concoction they made in *Three Sappy People*. Shemp had accidentally put alum into a sugar bowl in his 1934 Vitagraph short *A Peach of a Pair*. Other variations: hitting Larry and Curly with the backswing and foreswing of the Census ledger (recently the anchor in *How High is Up?*); setting up a slap with "Would you take five?" (the "V-8" setup in *How High is Up?*); twisting a foot around (*Grips, Grunts and Groans*); and being run out of a football stadium (*Three Little Pigskins*).

VERBAL HUMOR: The most remarkable elements in the (first-time Stooge writer) Harry Edwards/ Elwood Ullman (*A Plumbing We Will Go; How High is Up?*) script are the plot-related, Census-taking patterns. The first Census subject is the victim of a three-pattern (Moe: "What's your name?" Larry: "And your address?" Curly: "And what's more important, what's your phone number?"), but then a classic double two-pattern interloculatory expands into three and interlocking confusion (Moe: "How old are you?" Larry: "What address is this?" Woman to Larry: "One Hundred and Two—" Moe: "You don't look a day over 80." Woman: "Young man, I'm 29!" Moe: "Oh yeah?" Woman: "Well how do I look?" Moe: "You look like a million!" Larry: "Ah she can't be that old!"). There is also a solo delay-pattern (Moe: "Are you married or happy?" Wife: "HEN-REE!" [CRASH] Moe: "Married!"), the football signal patterns (Curly. "How old are you?" Quarterback: "27-!" Curly: "Now we're gettin' some place!" Quarterback: "19!-83!-27!-22!" Curly: "Why don't you make up your mind?!"), and the inter-Stooge Q & A (Moe: "Where were you born?" Curly: "Lake Winnepesaukee." Moe: "Lake Winn— How do you spell that?" Curly: "W-O...Woof! Make it Lake Erie - I got an uncle there!" Moe: "What was your family decomposed of?" Curly: "Well I'll tell you. There was a litter of three, and I was the one they kept!") which is later varied with a similar sequence between Moe and Larry.

The exchange (Moe: "You take the right end! I'll take the left end. [to Curly] What'll you take?" Curly: "I'll take vanilla!") is like a three-pattern, only Moe takes Larry's line. Of all Stooge three-patterns, none is more memorable than (Larry: "Quarterback!" Moe: "Halfback!" Curly: "Hunchback!"). Other plot-related gags depend on Stooge ignorance of the Census (Moe: "We get four cents a name for takin' the census." Larry: "Where we gonna get the census?" Curly: " Yeah, where we gonna get 'em?"; and Moe: "We're working for the Census." Curly: "Ya' mean Will Hays?").

"Well have some!" is used before two head blasts - Moe getting a cane over the head from the man of the house, and Curly getting the ice cream cone in the forehead. The phrase is the derivative of "Give it to me" (recently in *Oily to Bed, Oily to Rise*). Similarly, two scenes with the 'yielding' gag, the first before heading to the stadium (Moe: "To the census! Where you goin'?" Curly [yielding]: "To the census."), the second before breaking the dishes and heading for City Hall (Moe: "What are you gonna do with that?" Curly [yielding]: "Get rid of it."). Epithets: "flat-head" and "knuckle-head".

The Napoleon gag (Moe: "You got brains like Napoleon!" Larry: "Napoleon's dead." Moe: "I know it.") was used in *Ants in the Pantry*, but there it was incomplete. Other variations: Moe: "To the census!" ("To the basement!" in *We Want Our Mummy*); Moe: "I bubble." Hostess: "Rebubble." (*Meet the Baron*); and "Roses are red, and how do you do./ Drink four of these and woob-woob-woob-woo!" ("woob-woob-woo!" rhymes with "crew" in *False Alarms*).

References: 'Jiggers!' was a 1930s expression of alarm. Curly mentions 'Will Hays' because he confuses "census" and "censor"; Will Hays was the President of the Motion Pictures Producers & Distributors from 1922-1945, overseeing the self-implemented 'Production Code" (Hays Code) of censorship. Similarly, Moe ("Little heavy on the 'Angora' Bitters...that goat walked right through it") confuses the mohair-producing "angora" goat with "Angostura" bitters, a flavoring created only a decade earlier in Angostura, Venezuela. As for Curly's "Look what they did to Thanksgivin'," for the three years from 1939 to 1941 Thanksgiving was changed to the third Thursday in November instead of the fourth. Curly's "Sold! American!" is from a contemporary tobacco company advertisement. Lake Winnepesaukee is in New Hampshire; it was a prime vacation spot for New Yorkers in the 1930s.

OTHER NOTES: The working title was *No Answer, No Feeling*. The Census of 1940 turned up 132,164,569 Americans, almost half of the population in the 2000 census, although Moe's, Larry's, and Curly's ledgers were never turned in. This was the first census to survey housing conditions in the US, so we can also wonder if the residents of the Square Deal Swap Shop awning were counted. When Symona Boniface calls Moe and Larry "Gentlemen," they actually respond to her instead of looking behind themselves.

#51 - COOKOO CAVALIERS

Studio: Columbia

Released: November 15, 1940

Running Time: 17"24"

Credited Production Crew:

Produced & Directed by:	Jules White
Story & Screen play by:	Ewart Adamson
Director of Photography:	Henry Freulich
Film Editor:	Arthur Seid

Credited Cast:

Curly Howard
Larry Fine
Moe Howard

Uncredited Cast:

Lynton Brent	Pedro Ruiz
Dorothy Appleby	Rosita
Bob O'Connor	Manuel Gonzalez
Blanche Payson	fish customer in window
Anita Garvin	

PERSPECTIVE: The Stooges damage just about everything - dinners, tools, cars, houses, offices, jail cells and skyscrapers. They have squashed a 2000-year old mummy, interrupted 100,000 spectators at a football stadium, and blown up a submarine. They have humiliated cops and clobbered thugs, embarrassed a gorilla, drugged a horse, and glued mattress stuffing onto a dog. And they have beaten, gouged, and abused each other. The one thing they have not damaged yet is a young, beautiful woman - other than a cream puff in the face and such - but *Cookoo Cavaliers* closes down that category once and for all. The Stooges start with the lovely Rosita, rip off her hair, pack cement on her face, cut off her long nails, spray paint what squared-off stubs she has left, and then hammer her face with a mallet. Next!

The Stooge palate of comic elements has long contained a blob or two of old-fashioned misogyny. Their very first Columbia film, *Woman Haters*, seems to say it all in the title, but even that film is not so much about hating women as it is about desiring a single woman. Typical of films in the 1930s and 1940s, the Stooges pick up women on trains, in houses, along the road, in the country, and in the city. No one ever considered this to be inappropriate at the time, and Hope, Faith, and Charity thought their advances were fun and cute. But ugly women (like the one who flying tackled Larry and Moe in *Slippery Silks*), fat women (like June Gittelson in *False Alarms*), shrewish women (like Curly's wife [Ted Healy's sister] in *The Sitter Downers*), and even silky, elegant, European spies (like Mattie Herring in *You Nazty Spy!*) get laughed at, as do African-American, Chinese and Yiddish characters, and as do the Stooges themselves. Stereotyping was not thought to be 'politically incorrect' by the generation born when Teddy Roosevelt was president. We in the 21st century can accept Stooge chauvinism in Pagliasque terms: ALL men are stooges; these are the only three honest enough to admit it.

Surprise is an essential comic element, and the goal here was to turn Juanita's, Conchita's, and Pepita's good looks into a horrible, comical surprise. The element of surprise recently made that great television moment in *A Plumbing We Will Go*, and now here in *Cookoo Cavaliers* uglified women were to make the climactic moment. The senoritas are like that poorly plumbed house in that they are victims of Stooge stupidity: the Stooges do not know the difference between a 'saloon' and a 'salon,' spray painting and a manicure, or mud and cement any better than they knew the difference between water pipes and electrical conduit. While the Stooges work through a number of physical gags, we and the girls are being set up for the biggest laugh of all, only this time the surprise is not Niagara Falls pouring out of a television but that amazing moment when with great fanfare ("Presto! Change-o! Domino!") the Stooges in unison fling off the towels and reveal Juanita, Conchita, and Pepita to be completely bald! More concentrated than the build-up gags of Laurel & Hardy and in Charley Chase's *Flat Foot Stooges*, this surprise creates one of the most unforgettable images in Stoogedom.

VISUAL HUMOR: Moe and Larry beat Curly mercilessly in the salon, another in the line of beatings in recent films. In the previous film we saw Curly deliver slap after slap to Moe's face, and before that Jerry the insurance salesman took quite a beating to conclude *From Nurse to Worse*. Moe gets hit with his own fist in the 'fist game' for the first time since *Three Missing Links*. The purpose here was for Moe to get angry, throw the hair remover, and depilate the "poochie," but the result shot has apparently been edited out. A Stooge first: using a clothes pin as a 'gas mask'. The predecessor of Curly's bartending pantomime is the foodless table etiquette lesson in *Hoi Polloi;* the twist he gets in his eyes derives from the lemon-gag in the previous film (*No Census, No Feeling*). We would like to have more footage of Curly dancing à la Mexicana; it is even more impressive than when he wiggles his ears, an illusion accomplished by the use of very thin threads. The sleepiness of the Mexican town recalls the ethnic stereotyping of the fantasy land in *Saved By the Belle*. Just as in *From Nurse To Worse*, a dog is used as a comic when he rolls over from "Tarpon monoxide!" Even the flowers play their part right and wilt on cue. The Stooges hawk wares as they had in *How High is Up?*. This is the first shooting exit

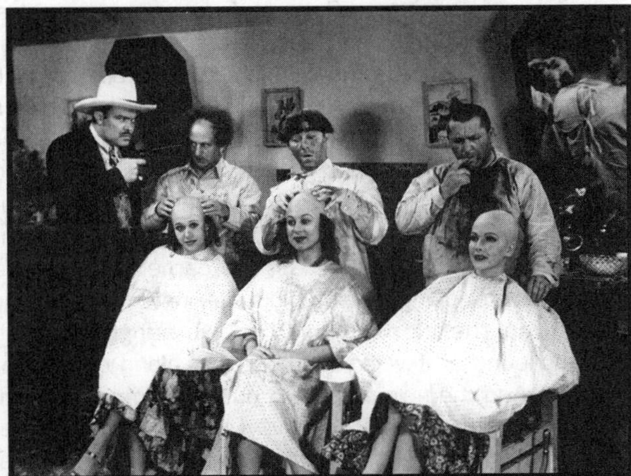

Essential to many Stooge comedies is the Stooges' ability to damage valuable objects, whether as small as a Chinese box (*Slippery Silks*) or as large as a house (*A Plumbing We Will Go*). In *Cookoo Cavaliers* (1940), the Stooges damage three beautiful women. Director Jules White and writer Ewart Adamson paced this routine carefully, leaving the unveiling of Juanita's, Conchita's, and Pepita's coiffures for a grand, surprise finale. In giving the narrative a dynamic structure, this kind of comic motif also provides the owner of the valuable object - in this case the girl's father (Bob O'Connor) - with a convincing motive for revenge.

since *A Ducking They Did Go*. Other variations: Moe trying to hair-pull Curly (*Ants in the Pantry*); Curly kissing Moe (*Calling All Curs*); Curly "using his head" to batter open the salon door, and Moe hitting Larry on the backswing and Curly's hand with the foreswing (*3 Dumb Clucks*); and dulling the drill bit on Curly's head with "Oh! Oh! Oh! Ohhllook!" (*Oily to Bed, Oily to Rise*).

VERBAL HUMOR: Ewart Adamson creates some different verbal patterns. The fish 'rap' ("We have rock cod, sea bass, albacore and pickerel, / sand dab, yellow tail, tuna fish and mackerel, / blue fish, sail fish, tarpon, carp and if you wish / swordfish, white fish, and herring and gefilte fish, / and that ain't all!") is unlike any previously heard forms of Stooge music, poetry, chant, or cheer; it derives from Laurel & Hardy's *Towed in the Hole* (1933). The standard three-pattern (Larry: "Where's the bar?" Curly: "Where's the pretzels?" Moe: "Where do they keep the Mickey Finns?") is expanded to six (Gonzalez: "Adios!" Moe: "So long!" Curly: "Good- bye!" Larry: "Skip the gutter!" Curly: "Tootle-oo!" Moe: "Break a leg!" [*Pardon My Scotch*]). The Stooges repeating and mimicking Gonzalez's advertisement ("We know: 1410 South American Way - no cover charge, anytime!. Glad to meet me!") is a first, too.

The latter is a type of ethnic sarcasm. Similarly, the Mexican accents of Gonzalez and the girls are made fun of, especially when Rosita speaks with a Brooklyn accent, the latter recalling "toity-toid" in *Wee Wee Monsieur*. But Curly's observation about their names ("They must be hungry; they all end in '-ita'!") is equally the result of Stooge ignorance. The Stooges cannot spell 'saloon' (Moe: ""S-E-L-U-N-E!" Curly: "You don't even know how to spell 'saloon.' Any sap knows you spell 'saloon' with a 'C'."), and they do not know the Spanish word "Si" (Curly: "'C' girls. Mermaids! You know the thing with the brush on the bottom—"); Larry is ignorant of basic science ("And you nearly talked us into buying ice! - just to put on the fish!") and what "henna" is ("Henna color at all, kid" [a Stooge first]), and all three Stooges are unable to smell a rat when Gonzalez tells them "You give me $300, I give you the business." The Stooges have misunderstood languages before to their chagrin, as in signing up for the Foreign Legion in *Wee Wee Monsieur*. Scenario-related fish puns (Moe: "That's a week fish." Woman: "Smells strong to me!"; Woman: "Do you have a haddock?" Curly: "I don't have a haddock, but I get a little attack here every time I eat too much."; and Moe: "What's the matter with him?" Curly: "Tarpon monoxide!").

Other variations: three (or four) like-named women (*The Sitter Downers*); 'Fleur de Skunk[ie]' (*You Nazty Spy!*); Curly's operatic singing (*Calling All Curs*); Moe mimicking Curly in the opening scene (*Three Little Sew and Sews*); and Curly: "Your English is atrocious!" Pepita: "Thank you, señor!" (*Hoi Polloi*). References: the 'Gas attack' gag (*From Nurse to Worse*, *Calling All Curs*) harks back to World War I. Curly's "All quiet on the fish front!" refers to Erich Maria Remarque's novel about World War I trench warfare, *All Quiet On the Western Front* (1929), made into Universal's Oscar-winning film in 1930. 'B-girls' used to hang around bars encouraging male customers to buy drinks.

OTHER NOTES: The working title was *Beauty à la Mud*. Curly says "You can't blame me this time," but he is the one who used the word "beauty" to Ruiz and caused the confusion (Curly: "It's got to have class, and it's got to have beauty." Ruiz: "Oh! You want to buy a 'beauty saloon.'"); of course, no one else caught the mistake either, and Gonzalez is in this respect no different from the swindlers in *A Ducking They Did Go*. When Curly says "I know how to bleach hair. My last wife used to bleach her own," this is the second reference Curly has made to a wife (*Three Sappy People*) or ex-wife without explanation. In real life, Curly's second wife, Elaine, left him in 1940.

#52 - BOOBS IN ARMS

Studio: Columbia

Released: December 27, 1940

Running Time: 17"55"

Credited Production Crew:

Produced & Directed by:	Jules White
Story & Screen Play by:	Felix Adler
Director of Photography:	John Stumar
Film Editor:	Mel Thorsen

Credited Cast:

Curly Howard	
Larry Fine	
Moe Howard	
Richard Fiske	Mr. Dare
Evelyn Young	Mrs. Dare

Uncredited Cast:

Lynton Brett	man with cigar
Eddie Laughton	man at apartment door; officer
Charles Dorety	trainee; guard
Johnny Kascier	guard
John Tyrrell	enemy officer
Cy Schindell	enemy soldier

PERSPECTIVE: The final release of 1940, *Boobs in Arms* depends structurally on a number of previously used scenarios thoroughly rethought and recombined. From *Cookoo Cavaliers* and *How High is Up?* comes the street hawking scene, from *Half-Shot Shooters* and *Wee Wee Monsieur* come the Stooges enlisting in the military unknowingly, from *No Census, No Feeling* and *How High is Up?* comes lining up for a 'job' while running from someone, from Shemp's solo film *Salt Water Daffy* (1933) comes the arms drill, and from *Half-Shot Shooters* come the ideas of having the Stooges sleep on the front lines and being punished in the military for beating up their sergeant in civilian life. The laughing gas routine is at least as old as Laurel & Hardy's *Leave 'Em Laughing* (1928) and Eddie Cantor's *Roman Scandals* (1933), and the shelling scenes are reminiscent of both the Stooges' own *Three Little Sew and Sews* and the Marx Brothers' *Duck Soup* (1933). As Stooge viewers know well, complete originality is not a requirement for humor, and *Boobs in Arms* succeeds on many levels - from knocking on doors and foreheads to performing the manual of arms and doing about faces to experimenting with a fourth-stooge foil, Richard Fiske, who takes as many blows as Moe, Larry, and Curly.

Besides the addition of a veritable fourth Stooge, what distinguishes *Boobs in Arms* from every previous Stooge film is the work of photographer John Stumar, who broadens the visual scope of the film and offers us new ways of seeing the Stooges. From the opening close-up of the sign, the pan to Larry's face, and Moe's card slapping Larry in the nose, this film looks different. The camera focuses in on the Stooges waiting in line and pans quickly to the 'RECRUITMENT' sign, just as it focuses in on the Stooges sitting on a bench and then hurriedly pans across to Sergeant Dare. When the Stooges are laughing hysterically and captured by the enemy, they are walked to and right past the camera. When their platoon is skipping, we see it leisurely in a long shot, which sets up the close-up of the drill sergeant in the foreground, as if we do that huge take along with Richard Fiske. And then we see the Stooges inside the bayonet bags. Stumar's visual creativity introduces the concept of viewing each Stooge inside an enclosed space as a blade comes through just under his nose or chin. This perspective will be used often in the future, although the circular saw close-up in *Pardon My Scotch* was its distant predecessor.

The sound is sometimes different as well, particularly in the raucous climax. The Stooges laugh almost non-stop for the final two minutes of the film, but most of the laughter is dubbed, giving it a lack of immediacy. In addition there is the oddity of hearing the Stooges laugh. They make us laugh all the time, and occasionally, as in *Ants in the Pantry* and *Nutty but Nice*, an audience within a film laughs at the Stooges, but they themselves rarely laugh. Curly 'nyucks' when proud of himself, Moe laughs sarcastically before striking, and when Larry can sneak out a quick laugh ("He looks like a 'V-8!') he gets slapped. So hearing the Stooges laugh for almost two minutes is indeed an odd sound. This will not set a precedent. In itself Stooge laughter is not as funny as when the Stooges take their mini-crises seriously.

VISUAL HUMOR: Though it was used in Universal's *Myrt and Marge*, the PLINK sound effect, created by plucking a violin/ukelele string twice and recording the sounds a frame or two apart, is a Columbia Stooge first. Other Stooge firsts include Moe pulling Curly by the lip; and Larry getting himself a drink instead of giving it to the victim. Curly did his first 'shuffle' in *Pardon My Scotch* but here he offers one of his best forwards-backward shuffles, the next coming in the very next release, *So Long, Mr. Chumps*. Mr. Dare [Richard Fiske] cries twice out of frustration, much as did Curly in *Oily to Bed, Oily to Rise* and *Three Missing Links*. Besides making Fiske into a veritable fourth stooge, Evelyn Young [Mrs. Dare] has a brief Stooge moment when seltzer comes squirting out both her ears (*Healthy, Wealthy and Dumb*).

The Stooges themselves have several role reversals: it is Curly who orders Larry to drop something and has it dropped on his foot, usually Moe's role (e.g. *A Plumbing We Will Go*). Also, Curly's "What's the

Richard Fisk, tall, lean, and quick to anger, played the foil so well he was a veritable 'fourth Stooge' in *Boobs in Arms* (1940). Such Stooge foils as Fiske, Vernon Dent, and Bud Jamison, while creating unforgettable characters in films that have lasted six decades, usually earned only $75-100 per day in one to four days of shooting. Sadly, after playing an army drill sergeant and being driven to distraction by the inept Stooges in this film, Fiske was killed during World War II at LeCroix, France, in August, 1944.

idea goin' swimmin'? We got work to do!" is usually Moe's line. Being kicked in the rear and shooting a bird was introduced in *Rockin' Thru the Rockies*, but *Boobs in Arms* offers a fine variation. Other variations: hitting one Stooge, whose head bonks another - thrice in the opening scenes (*Grips, Grunts and Groans*); Moe daring Dare to hit Curly once more (*Yes, We Have No Bonanza*); Curly's two head butts (*Restless Knights*); knocking on the door/ someone's forehead (*Calling All Curs*); shooting down a light fixture onto one's head, and the 'Shave and a Haircut' knock - nicely varied when the knocker answers 'Two Bits' (*Whoops, I'm an Indian*); Larry moving his arms as if they were Mrs. Dare's (*Movie Maniacs*); Curly doing the Manual of Arms "just like" Dare does it (*Hoi Polloi*); and flying in the clouds (*Three Little Sew and Sews*).

VERBAL HUMOR: A Stooge first: the Stooges numbering their card types; many years hence they will number their slapstick in *The Three Stooges Go Around the World in a Daze*. When Curly calls the woman on the street a "snob-ess" it is a neologism, a sign of linguistic sophistication, in contrast to the persistent Stooge ignorance of the previous film. Moe's rhythmic chant ("Adirondack! / One zell, two zell, three zell, zam—") was a common pattern of the time; it recalls the fish-hawking chant in *Cookoo Cavaliers*. Another contemporary pattern is heard in Fiske's "Hippity Hop at the Barber Shop!". Reference: Curly's "He don't pay my salary. It's a guy with a beard," refers to Uncle Sam. Epithet: "pumpkin-brain"; Moe reprises "Nitwit" (for Larry) from *From Nurse to Worse*. Other variations: card number "H2O" (*Three Little Pigskins*; *Whoops, I'm an Indian*); and 'O'Brien' (on Curly's deli ad) (Jewish names), and (Voice: "That's what you think!" Moe to Curly: "That's what I said! What about it?" Curly: "I didn't say anything!" Voice: "But I did!") (*Movie Maniacs*).

OTHER NOTES: The release title parodies that of the Rodgers & Hart backstage musical, *Babes in Arms*, which in 1939 MGM made into an Oscar-nominated film starring Judy Garland and Mickey Rooney. The working title was *All This and Bullets Too*; the ad on Curly's army uniform includes 'All this and Herring, too'. Richard Fiske and Evelyn Young are credited on the title screen. Fiske will now become a Stooge regular for a few years until his death in World War II. The stock footage of World War I trench warfare is the same used for *Half-Shot Shooters*. This is particularly interesting because this film is made just before World War II escalated, so the memory of World War I is still vivid both here and in the 'gas mask' gag of the previous film. It is significant that the Stooges confuse a recruitment line with a bread line in this film. The Depression era was changing into the World War II era; cf. "Join the army and see the world or what's left of it" and Curly's quick imitation of Mussolini. Some of the drill footage will reappear in *Dizzy Pilots*. Laurel & Hardy played greeting card salesmen and encountered a jealous husband in *The Fixer Uppers* (1935), and Shemp and Jack Haley parodied army drilling and used the "Go that way" gag in their first Vitaphone film, *Saltwater Daffy* (1933).

1941

So Long, Mr. Chumps • Dutiful but Dumb

All the World's a Stooge • I'll Never Heil Again • An Ache in Every Stake

In the Sweet Pie and Pie • Some More of Samoa

#53 - SO LONG, MR. CHUMPS

Studio: Columbia

Released: February 7, 1941

Running Time: 17"32"

Credited Production Crew:

Produced & Directed by:	Jules White
Story & Screen Play by:	Clyde Bruckman & Felix Adler
Director of Photography:	Barney McGill
Film Editor:	Mel Thorsen

Credited Cast:

Curly Howard
Larry Fine
Moe Howard

Uncredited Cast:

John Tyrrell	B. O. Davis
Vernon Dent	desk sergeant
Eddie Laughton	Percy Pomeroy
Dorothy Appleby	young woman
Robert Williams	blind man
Bruce Bennett	prison guard
Bert Young	policeman
Lew Davis	laughing man

PERSPECTIVE: Some Stooge films examine a recurring theme. In *Oily to Bed, Oily to Rise* it was the concept of wishing. In *Saved By the Belle*, as its title suggests, it was the alternation of good and bad luck. The title of *So Long, Mr. Chumps* suggests that this first release of 1941 is a comic study of honesty and trust, and the Stooges do indeed spend the entire film on the long and short ends of putting trust in their fellow man. As a result of their cantankerous attempt at ridding San Francisco's streets of stray newspaper, the Stooges find bonds which belong to B. O. Davis. They return the bonds to him and are rewarded for their honesty with some money "on account" and promised an even greater reward of $5,000 if they can find an honest man. They search but find only a faker and a thief. The faker gets away with the cash ("That faker is no faker. He's a crook!"), but the thief is punished by having his pants blown off him: dishonesty pays only once. When a dog brings the wallet to Moe, he has to conclude: "The only honest man we've found all day, and it's a dog." This concept is so crucial to the theme of *So Long, Mr. Chumps*, that Moe repeats it a minute later to the woman who owns the dog. But she disagrees. Her sweetheart is an honest man — "He's honest, honest... He's honest!" — but he is in jail. Moe concludes: "Maybe all the honest men are in jail!"

This may be an inverted assumption to anyone but a Stooge, but their sampling of passersby failed to turn up an honest man, here was a seemingly honest woman who used the word "honest" three times in the same sentence telling them there is an honest man in jail, and B. O. Davis has sent them on a quest for an honest man. So, to help her out, earn their bonus, and prove Moe's point, the Stooges make three failed attempts to get into jail. The attempts fail because 1) the Stooges are too honest - they move out of the policeman's line of sight to offer themselves up, 2) they encounter 'Gyp the People,' who is more dishonest than they could ever be, and 3) they tell a lie about a crime which turns out to be the truth. And when they do get arrested, it is because they nobly try to help a policeman escape being hit by a falling light fixture. Ancient Diogenes held up a lantern to find an honest man. The Stooges use a falling light fixture.

It is in prison that they find their honest man, but they have to be dishonest to get him out. In a physical

representation of the ultimate dishonesty, they paint themselves up as something they are not. They sneak out but run into B. O. Davis, the same man who sent them out to search for an honest man in the first place, and they learn that he has dishonestly taken an alias and, as "the biggest bond swindler in America," is the most dishonest man of all! At the close of the film the Stooges stretch the concepts of honesty and trust even further by admitting that the rocks Moe breaks over Curly's head are fake. In a rare moment they are honest enough with us to admit that they themselves are dishonest, that what we see on film is not the truth, and, incidentally, that Curly's skull is not made of iron after all.

VISUAL HUMOR: Telling us about the fake rock at the conclusion of the film piggybacks on several recent incidents - Curly winking at the camera at the conclusion of *Oily to Bed, Oily to Rise*, and Curly's "That's enough" in his normal voice in *Rockin' Thru the Rockies*. The camera, of course, is by nature dishonest and intended to deceive us. In the opening scene Larry starts after a flying newspaper, invades the area the camera is hiding beyond the frame, and pokes Moe in the butt. Stooge comedy will always flourish when paint brushes are around. Here they paint their uniforms [Laurel & Hardy painted prison uniforms white in *The Second Hundred Years* [1927]] and Curly paints a sandwich, a fire extinguisher, and a guard's face. All these painting gags move the plot along. A Stooge first is Moe painting Curly's protruding tongue. Painting also gives us the most understated sight gag of the film: the striped horse. Slapstick firsts: Moe mirror-imaging Curly as he raises up and down on his toes and moves his head forwards and backwards; Curly thrusting his hand down hard after a hypnotizing hand-wave; and Moe dishing out a double-double slap. Other Stooge firsts: the Stooges weaving in and out past each other; hiding dirt under grass (or a carpet); fly paper; and all three Stooges weeping.

The impeccable timing of Curly missing the huddle in prison recalls the missed handshake in *Movie Maniacs*. Slapstick variations: Curly sticking his tongue out at Moe and pushing it back into his mouth, and all four prisoners bonking heads in the huddle. Moe hitting the insect with the sledge hammer recalls the opening of *How High is Up*. The PLINK sound effect was introduced in the previous film, *Boobs in Arms*. Other variations: the dog pointing a directional tail (*Calling All Curs*); the camera panning to open the film, and Curly doing two shuffles back for every two pushes forward (*Boobs in Arms*); "Oh! Oh! Ohhhh*look*!" (*Oily to Bed, Oily to Rise*); eating the banana peel and not the fruit (*A Pain in the Pullman*); Curly backing into the door jamb (*Woman Haters*); pulling out a cigar, a bigger cigar, and an even bigger cigar (*Movie Maniacs*); the electronic WOLF-WHISTLE sound effect (*Nutty but Nice*); the falling light fixture (*Whoops, I'm an Indian*); Moe hitting his fist himself, and the 'NBC' chime (*Back to the Woods*).

VERBAL HUMOR: From this point on, Moe will often take the noun Curly or Larry just used and turn it into a transitive verb and a threat. Here when Curly says: "Maybe he's the warden," Moe responds: "I'll warden you!". Another Stooge first: Curly's "So it shouldn't be a total loss I'm takin' a bath!". New epithets for Curly: Moe's "Great Dane" and Larry's "mallow-head". The Bruckman/Adler script offers internal rhyme ("He's honest, honest... He's honest!"; Curly: "A hornet's trying to horn in on me!") and a Stooge slogan ("We're on our way for an honest man. / We'll bring him back as fast as we can. / Excelsior!"); "Excelsior" was used in *We Want Our Mummy*. Two simultaneous conversations between three people worked twice in *No Census, No Feeling*, and here it works well when Curly asks for the keys from the prison guard who is speaking on the phone promising something else to the warden.

Other variations: "Tote that barge, lift that bail, and *swing* it!" and "We have met the enemy and they belong to us!" (*Rockin' Thru the Rockies*); "6 7/8" (*You Nazty Spy!*); "H2O" (*Whoops, I'm an Indian*); Larry: "That's a coincidence!" (*Pop Goes the Easel*); Moe's "Remind me to have you stuffed" ("Remind me to kill you later!" in *Cash and Carry*); "Have this refilled" (*A Pain in the Pullman*); Curly's "Sergeant, oh sargie" (*Wee Wee Monsieur*); and the reference to "Cock Robin," and Curly thinking the exhaust plug was "a bumble bee" and that the falling light fixture was "mosquitoes!" (*Disorder in the Court*).

OTHER NOTES: The first title screen has a full-sized Columbia logo with no accompanying music; the next two screens are the same as they were in 1940, for a total of 30 seconds. The release title parodies the Oscar-nominated *Goodbye Mr. Chips*, a 1939 MGM film based on the James Hilton novel of the same name. The working title was *So Long, Mr. Chump*. Just as *Cookoo Cavaliers* was set in San Diego to provide easy access to the town of Cucaracha, this search for honesty is set in San Francisco because it is a financial center. Bond swindlers would be more apt to feed in a city with its own exchange, and the San Francisco area also offered Larry the breeze that blew the newspaper he chased, not to mention a federal prison, although this one is not identifiable as Alcatraz. The desk sergeant [Vernon Dent] makes reference to the great 1906 earthquake. The Stooges give some genuine smiles after the final gag. Also relatively relaxed is the sprinkler sequence, which serves no narrative purpose. Why is Larry carrying gun powder in the pocket of his fur-collared coat? Then again, why is Curly carrying a pistol?. Some of the prison footage will be reused in *Beer Barrel Polecats* (1946).

The 1941 releases open with an extraordinary, internally consistent film, *So Long, Mr. Chumps*. Co-written by the two veterans Clyde Bruckman and Felix Adler, the film is a comic study of honesty and trust, and takes the Stooges through a series of encounters with a fraudulent millionaire, a faker, a thief, and a woman whose husband is in jail ("honest...Honest, he's honest!"). In a unique ending to the film, the Stooges break the 'dramatic illusion' by using a non-fake stone on Curly's head - admitting that what the film's audience has just seen on screen is fake and dishonest.

#54 - DUTIFUL but DUMB

Studio: Columbia

Released: March 21, 1941

Running Time: 16"47"

Credited Production Crew:

Produced by:	Del Lord & Hugh McCollum
Directed by:	Del Lord
Story & Screen Play by:	Elwood Ullman
Director of Photography:	Benjamin Kline
Film Editor:	Arthur Seid

Credited Cast:

Curly Howard
Larry Fine
Moe Howard

Uncredited Cast:

Vernon Dent	chief editor of *Whack*
Bud Jamison	sergeant
Fred Kelsey	Colonel
Eddie Laughton	officer
Chester Conklin	waiter
Marjorie Deanne	bride
Stanley Brown	groom
Bruce Bennett	messenger
Harry Semels	Vulgarian citizen
Bert Young	guard

PERSPECTIVE: The trade in which the Stooges are employed at the outset of a film has varying degrees of relevance for the rest of the film. Often their trade leads them accidentally into another vocation, as in *Three Missing Links*, where their jobs as custodians turn into jobs as actors. Other times they leave a vocation temporarily, as in *Mutts To You*, where they are dog cleaners who spend much of the film baby-sitting, only to return to their dog cleaning at the end. In other films they continue in their vocations throughout the film, as in *Termites of 1938*. In *Dutiful but Dumb* their photographic 'skills' carry the comedy from the antics inside and outside a movie star's hotel room, through a dark room scene, back into the editor's office, and into Vulgaria and its penal system. That is, the Stooges are given scenarios in which they are to sneak a domestic 'gossip' photo, print a photo, publish a photo, and take an international political photo. Forget the stethoscopes, shovels and rifle barrels, the Stooges have a new comic tool - the camera and its accouterments.

Their final insult to the world of photography, not to mention to Vulgarian technology, is employing the Vulgarian 'invisible ray' as a camera and leaving Moe and Larry standing there in their boxer shorts. The gun shots caused by the ray camera/gun bring the Vulgarian brass back into the Stooge's grasp, and the Stooges capture them and strip them of their uniforms. Now the 'bad guys' are in their shorts. To photographers who live in a country which guarantees the right of a free press and went to extreme means to photograph an unphotographable movie idol, the idea of not being allowed to take pictures is an outrage. As they do every so often, the Stooges right a wrong here. In this case they punish an oppressive European government. Just as they made a comical attack on Nazi book burnings in *You Nazty Spy!*, so here they make a comical defense of the right of the news media to have free access to the truth. The Stooges are comedians, of course, but political humor comes in many forms: here it starts at the Vulgarian frontier which, the sign said, was 'subject to change without notice.' With Hitler on the loose, this was the condition of central European politics.

Ultimately the Stooges are recaptured because of Curly's foolery with a nasty little oyster, which has nothing to do with the photography or political oppression themes. As in *A Ducking They Did Go*, the final scenes virtually abandon the plot and focus on an isolated Curly in a battle against a feisty pest. The oyster soup bit was an old gag, at least as old as Billy Bevan's *Wandering Willies* (1926), also directed by Del Lord. Curly (and the oyster) perform the gag well; it is yet another fine moment in which Curly does battle against an inanimate, or in this case inhuman, object. In future films (*Shivering Sherlocks* and *Income Tax Sappy*) this gag will be placed in the middle of the film where it does less damage to the narrative continuity.

VISUAL HUMOR: Frequent screen insertions (the newspaper, the clock on the wall, the screen title, and the Vulgarian signs) assist in establishing the plot. Similarly, the clock, the long cigar, and Curly's four watches combine to create a minor theme: the passing of time. This is unusual; since most Stooge comedies take place within a day's work, the passing of time tends to be of relatively little importance. Much of the visual humor is electronic or gadget oriented: the camera hood and miner's hats, Curly playing four musical instruments inside the radio, and Moe impersonating a floor lamp. When Curly hides in the radio, the interior shots recall the bayonet bag sequence in *Boobs in Arms*. There are several choreographed gags: the intricate marching when disguised in Vulgarian uniform, the interweaving escape from the firing squad (which might have been better used at the conclusion of the film), and the "Heave! Ho" routine. Curly is isolated in three scenes - under the movie star's silver dome, inside the radio, and in the battle against the oyster. Stooge firsts: the domino-like easels, the camera hood, and two clothing firsts: Moe and Larry in their boxers, and pulling jackets over their heads.

Two moments break the 'dramatic illusion,' as at the end of *So Long, Mr. Chumps*: when Curly stops playing but the music continues, and when Curly looks right at the camera thinking he has defeated the dark bottle. Other variations: the long cigar and Curly jutting his head forward when butting Moe with his miner's hat [*So Long, Mr. Chumps*]; two Stooges under an overcoat [*Healthy, Wealthy and Dumb*]; running into jail on their own [*Whoops, I'm an Indian*]; kicking Curly and turning him alternately [*Boobs in Arms*]; the light bulb working without electrical contact [*Nutty but Nice*]; Moe ratcheting Curly's ears for a specific purpose ("Ya' forgot to turn the winder!" - wringing water from Curly's ears in *We Want Our Mummy*); and Curly stopping Moe from hitting him because there is no time ("Ya' ain't got time. I hear footprints!" in *False Alarms*).

VERBAL HUMOR: Elwood Ullman characterizes the movie star with simple brush strokes (Star: "Oh my public!" Bride: "Darling, have you forgotten all your other wives?" Movie Star: "Completely, except on alimony day, but this is Wednesday!"). For the dark room discussion he creates an interwoven plot-related set joke (Larry: "I can't find the negative." Moe: "How about the positive?" Curly: "I'm positive about the negative, but I'm a little negative about the positive." Moe: "Oh, negative, eh?" Curly: "No I'm positive the negative is in the developer."), which ends, as often, in an insult (Moe: "Your brains need developin'!"). Another dark room set joke, a Stooge first, is telling time with three-watches ("This one runs ten minutes slow every two hours; this runs twenty minutes fast every four hours; the one in the middle is broken; it stopped at 2:00. I take the ten minutes on this one and subtract it from the twenty minutes on that one, then I divide by two in the middle." Moe: "What time is it now?" Curly [pulling out an oversized pocket watch]: "Ten minutes to four.").

Plot-related jokes emphasize how long it takes the Stooges to realize how undemocratic Vulgaria is, building on the same sort of Stooge dimwittedness that makes them slow to realize a lion or gorilla is standing behind them. This begins the Vulgaria sequence (Local resident: "Read the sign!" Curly: "We ain't gonna park here!") and blossoms when the execution party comes around the corner (Curly: "Oh boy! A parade!" Larry: "Let's shoot some pictures of it!" Moe to the sergeant: "We wanna shoot a picture. You look important, Stand in the middle." Curly: "You're coverin' the little fella!" Moe: "Tilt your hat; your shadin' your face!" Curly: "Hey I got a new idea! Put this gun to his head." Sergeant: "That man shoot pictures. Now we shoot heem!" Larry: "An execution!" Moe: "Hey can we shoot a picture of it?" Sergeant: "Yeah! You shoot the picture, and we shoot you!" Stooges: "Thanks! Nyah-ah-ah!"). Epithets: "nitwit," "frog-head," "numskull," and "dimwit". The Vulgarian sign translating itself was a

technique used previously by Cecil B. DeMille in *Sign of the Cross* (1932). Continuing the motif from *Termites of 1938*, and, recently, *Boobs in Arms*, the Stooges have a chant: Larry: "Vulgaria!" Curly: "Vulgaria!" Moe: "Viva Vulgaria!" All three Stooges: "A veevo, a vivo, a veevo vivo vum." Moe: "A bum-cat-a rat-cat-a pit-a-pat-a-cat-a!" All three: "Rah-Rah-Rah Vulgaria! Ya-hoh!". Other variations: the trio of names 'Click, Clack, Cluck' (Ziller, Zeller, Zoller in *Three Sappy People*); "Eats!!" [*Goofs and Saddles*]; the name 'Vulgaria' ('Moronika' in *You Nazty Spy!*); Curly's "We always bring 'em back alive!" [*Wee Wee Monsieur*]; and Curly: "Ya missed me, nyaah!" [*Pop Goes the Easel*].

OTHER NOTES: The title of the film on screen is capitalized as *Dutiful but Dumb* (as was *Nutty but Nice*). The oyster gag was used by Stooges three more times and by numerous other comedians, including Abbott & Costello this same year in *Keep 'Em Flying* (1941). Years later Stooge writer/director Edward Bernds recalled: "If you think a cat has nine lives, just take a look at comedy routines. For example, the man who's eating a bowl of oyster stew and an oyster comes up and takes his cracker - I don't know how many times *that* bit has been used. But you must remember that these pictures were meant to be seen weeks, months, even years apart from one another. Only through television reruns has this repetition become apparent." [Okuda 35].Three times after a gag a Stooge says "What happened?". The 'de Puyster' name will be used again in *Heavenly Daze*. Continuity: The photo Curly takes of the newlyweds is not the photo that sticks to his face; (he forgot to turn the winder). Entering the cafeteria they knock over someone, but we do not see whom; we hear a thud and a groan, and Curly gives him a hand-wave. The sign on their Vulgarian motorcycle says *Focus Magazine*, not *Whack*. And does Curly's pistol hold sixteen rounds?

#55 - ALL THE WORLD'S A STOOGE

Studio: Columbia

Released: May 16, 1941

Running Time: 16"03"

Credited Production Crew:

Produced by:	Del Lord & Hugh McCollum
Directed by:	Del Lord
Story & Screen Play:	John Grey
Director of Photography:	Benjamin Kline
Film Editor:	Arthur Seid

Credited Cast:

Curly Howard	
Larry Fine	
Moe Howard	
Lelah Tyler	Mrs. Bullion
Emory Parnell	Ajax Bullion

Uncredited Cast:

Richard Fiske	Dr. I. Yankum, dentist
John Tyrrell	building superintendent
Bud Jamison	policeman
Olaf Hytten	Barters, the butler
Symona Boniface	guest
Gwen Seager	guest
Poppie Wilde	guest
Ethelreda Leopold	guest

PERSPECTIVE: There seems to have been no end to the number of characterizations and scenarios the Columbia producers and writers could invent for the Stooges wherein they could work their havoc. They have not been characterized as dentists before - an occupation rife with damaging possibilities and tailor-made for comedians who excel at graying the line between physical pain and comedy. The circumstance that allowed the Stooges to act as dentists was, to quote Curly, "A coincidence." They happened to be cleaning those particular windows on that particular floor, and Moe and Larry pulled Curly back up from a fall just as the dentist opened his window and allowed himself to be soaked. The dentist leaves his office, and in walks a desperate patient. The Stooges look behind themselves when he addresses one of them as "Doc," and Moe tries to explain, but the patient insists. How could he have known that the Stooges would pull the wrong tooth, cement his mouth solid, and blast it with dynamite but still achieve perfect results? All this is incredible coincidence, but it is the kind of coincidence the Columbia writers and directors have arranged for the Stooges consistently, year after year.

The other scenario of the film is also based on coincidence, but someone who is not discriminating often ends up hiring or allowing the Stooges into the scenario in which they will create their havoc. In this case it is ultimately the bubbling, almost unflappable Mrs. Bullion [in the script her first name is 'Lotta'] who is to blame. Just as her husband's desperation leads to his dental disaster, her desperation to adopt a refugee child irritates her butler, her husband, and apparently even her cat. Her social position is very much like that of Maggie Smirch in *Tassels in the Air*, for just as Mrs. Smirch wished to hire the interior decorator Omay to get into *Who's Who*, Mrs. Bullion wishes to adopt a child because "It's quite the thing socially!" Contemporary war-torn Europe was filled with the refugees she wanted to adopt, but she got the Stooges instead. This is social, not political satire.

Contrast is another important comedic element, so the hard-boiled Mr. Bullion, like Mr. Smirch, counterbalances his spouse's social climbing. He lets the Stooges into his home not so much because dynamite blew up in his mouth as because he sees those 'refugees' hiding in his car as a coincidental opportunity to cheat his wife of the foreign waifs she so desperately desires. The Stooges had played children previously in *Nertsery Rhymes* and *Nutty but Nice*, but in both films they were confined to one room and either controlled by Ted Healy or the little girl. Here they get eight minutes to wear kids' clothes, throw food, and much more. Curly does his great 'Mammy' routine, recites a poem, catches a cold, gets mothered, and sits in a woman's lap. Their mom loves them, as do the guests, except for Curly's Limburgered halitosis. All the while their childlike activities are contrasted with their adult slapstick, dice playing, and cigar smoking. We laugh at the contrast: we know the Stooges are not children. But in the film only their 'dad' knows they are not, which is where his ax comes in handy.

VISUAL HUMOR: This film introduces new Stooge props: glasses, which Curly needs to operate; and fake teeth, which they use to great effect with Curly's chattering teeth, his dance, Moe landing on them, putting them on Curly's nose, and, in a great finish, with the teeth barking back at Curly. When the teeth bark back at Curly, this is the first time someone/thing has barked back at Curly since *3 Dumb Clucks*. Two sets of parallel gags: early in the film the teeth land on the sofa, and then later the burning cigar is hidden under the chair cushion; and Curly ("Cute") and then all three Stooges ("Doc") look behind themselves twice in the film. When Mr. Bullion splits the tree, it is one of the more supernatural special effects in the corpus. In *So Long, Mr. Chumps* Curly belly-bumped Moe; here Moe bounces Curly against the wall and gives him a gouge when he bounces back. The PLINK sound effect which we hear when Symona Boniface sticks a pin in Curly's rear is being used more frequently (the Bismarck helmet in *Boobs in Arms*, the paper-picker in *So Long, Mr. Chumps*). Other variations: the 3-watch gag (*Dutiful but Dumb*); sitting on a burning cigar (*Three Little Sew and Sews*); delivering 'anesthetic' (*Men in Black*); Curly's flamenco dance (*Cookoo Cavaliers*); tossing water but missing (*Back to the Woods*); and stepping on the edge of a blanket disguise (*Healthy, Wealthy and Dumb*).

VERBAL HUMOR: A Stooge first: the reference to "sleepin' Venus". Someone, be it producer, director, or the Stooges themselves, had Curly's poem ("Little fly upon the wall") added to Columbia staff writer John Grey's (*False Alarms*) script; Moe had recited it in MGM's *Nertsery Rhymes*. Also from *Nertsery Rhymes* are the Indian whoops. Grey himself wrote: Curly: "I didn't do nothin'!" Moe: "That's why I slugged ya'! Do something'!"; and Curly: "Can I help it if I was born dizzy?" Moe: "I'll dizzy you!" The latter is another example of Moe making a transitive verb out of an adjective (*So Long, Mr. Chumps*). Curly's "I relent that" varies "I resent that" (*A Plumbing We Will Go*). Other variations: "Eats!" and "Heave! Heave!" (*Dutiful but Dumb*); Curly's "Put 'em back alive!" (*Wee Wee Monsieur*); "An octopus!" and "serviette" (*A Pain in the Pullman*); "That's a coincidence!" (*Pop Goes the Easel*); and Curly's "I'll bet you tell that to all the interns!" (*Horses Collars*). Epithets: Moe calls Curly a "nitwit" twice, and Larry calls him an "apple-head" once. References: Curly's Al Jolson imitation ('Mammy') derives mostly from the 1930 film of that name; Ted Healy used the same impersonation in *Myrt and Marge*. Moe's "Hey Nijinsky! Give me those clickers!" refers to Vaslav Nijinsky, the ballet legend who had retired from the Stage some twenty years before this film was made. 'Jack the Ripper' was the notorious London serial killer in 1888-91. Curly's 'Paddy dee Fwah-grah' is goose-liver pate (*pate de foie gras*). Moe mistakes an order for it in *Beer and Pretzels*.

OTHER NOTES: The title parodies Shakespeare's 'All the world's a stage,' (*As You Like It* II.vii.139). Curly's shorts reveal his thin left leg which he injured accidentally shooting himself with a .22-rifle during the summer of 1916. It frequently caused him to limp and feel pain. Both Lelah Tyler [Mrs. Bullion] and Emory Parnell [Ajax Bullion] had long careers as character actors. The previous year Tyler had been in *Babes in Arms* with Judy Garland and Mickey Rooney, and Emory Parnell would act well into the television era, when he played Riley's boss in *The Life of Riley* (1953-58).

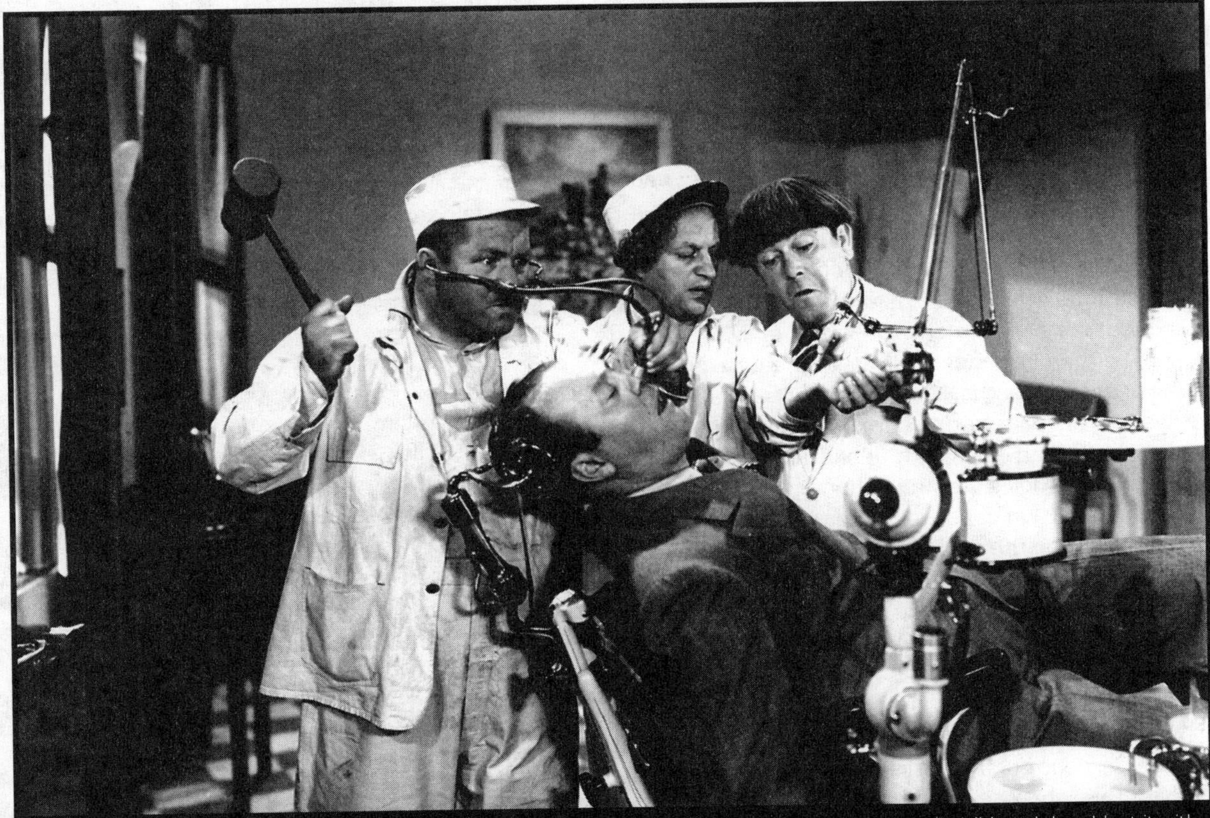

In *All the World's a Stooge* (1941) the Stooges pull the wrong tooth, cement their patient's mouth solid, and then blast it with dynamite. In real life, of course, this would be a) painful and b) fatal, not to mention c) actionable. But real-life pain becomes fuel for Stooge comic routines, and dentistry, with its accompanying fear, is tailor-made for these actors who excel at regularly and effortlessly graying the line between physical pain and comedy.

#56 - I'LL NEVER HEIL AGAIN

Studio: Columbia

Released: July 11, 1941

Running Time: 18"09"

Credited Production Crew:

Produced & Directed by:	Jules White
Story & Screen Play by:	Felix Adler & Clyde Bruckman
Photography:	L. W. O'Connell
Film Editor:	Jerome Thoms

Credited Cast:

Curly Howard
Larry Fine
Moe Howard

Uncredited Cast:

Mary Ainslee	Gilda
Vernon Dent	Ixnay
Bud Jamison	Umpchay
Lynton Brent	Amscray
Johnny Kascier	Napoleon
Jack 'Tiny' Lipson	Bey of Rum
Duncan Renaldo	Japanese representative
Cy Schindell	Chizzilini
Don Barclay	Russian representative
Bert Young	guard
Robert 'Bobby' Burns	royal attendant
Al Thompson	valet

PERSPECTIVE: Although the slapstick and verbal repartee is not as thickly packed as in the previous year's *You Nazty Spy!*, this virtual sequel is the most daring and globally significant of any Stooge film. Its humor is delivered in a package bordering as close to genuine political satire as Germany to Poland or Moronica to Pushover, for it satirizes specifically the developments of the previous months. Moe Hailstone *is* Adolph Hitler: he wears an arm-band, sports a mustache ("My personality!"), and allies with Japan and Italy. His Axis conference parodies the Anti-Comintern Pact signed by Germany, Italy, and Japan in September, 1940. Russia is represented at the conference - the thickly mustached emissary is named 'Bawlin,' i.e. Stalin, in the script - because Germany and Russia were still operating under the Nazi-Soviet Pact of Non-Aggression, ironically, until this very summer. By the time viewers saw the film, the Nazis had broken the pact and invaded Russia. In the fall of 1940 Mussolini ('Chizzilini') had invaded Greece with 200,000 troops but failed miserably, and Curly reminds Larry of this when he goes to "wipe out" the "greece" under the "turkey." The 'Bey of Rum' represents the Albanian puppet government the Nazis employed for their own invasion of Greece just before this film was made. When Curly describes the air war, he may read ball scores and horse-race results, but he also reads how many hospitals and schools they bombed because Hitler had launched his failed massive air assault, the 'Battle of Britain' ('Great Mitten') during the summer of 1940. And when Moe asks if he has taken the "dikes of Holland," Curly's "Certainly! And the Van Dycks of Amsterdam and the Updikes of Rotterdam, and the Hunchback of Notre Dame!" satirically describes Hitler's rapid conquests of Holland and France in May/June 1940.

Some aspects of the satire are allegorical. The 'turkey' sequence is stuffed with statements of political appetite ("I still want a piece of turkey"), and when the two-dimensional painting of Napoleon comes to life and runs with the turkey into a veritable fourth dimension unreachable by Hailstone, he bursts into tears. The real Turkey was to remain neutral until 1945, but the message must be that Hitler's hopes of becoming a historically respected conqueror like Napoleon were physically impossible. The film concludes with the struggle for another allegorical symbol - the globe. Moe grabs it from the other Axis powers, who play football and do the rumba: "The world belongs to me!" When his field marshal smashes it on his head, Hailstone laments: "You shattered my world!"

The allegory concludes with the demise of the Axis powers. Italy is defeated both by Germany's betrayal and being hit on the head with the very world it desires; photo-maniacal Japan knocks itself out; Germany blows itself up after first destroying the world it wanted; and the Moronican beasts are beheaded and stuffed like common game trophies with which they share immortality on the wall of the hunting lodge of King Herman the Sixth and Seven-Eighths.

VISUAL HUMOR: Larry and Curly are always squabbling with Moe, but some of the quarreling in this film emphasizes the dictator's detestable nature; the 'fear of Moe' takes on a greater meaning. Curly even gouges Moe, and see what happens when they laugh at Moe after he hits himself with his shaving cream brush. Curly has two particularly special moments: when he struggles with another inanimate object (the hookah tube), and when he bounces off the wall and returns perfectly into Moe's arms to dance off to lunch. Stooge firsts: the painting coming to life, particularly ironic in that the point of the Napoleon references in *Ants in the Pantry* and *No Census, No Feeling* was that Napoleon was dead; and dancing the rumba, which was the latest fad (cf. *Time Out for Rhythm*).

The image of Hell and the devil images are a Stooge first; we saw angels in *Three Little Sew and Sews*. Curly looks into the camera to say: "They're nuts!"; later he kicks the globe right at the camera (*Calling All Curs; So Long, Mr. Chumps*). Other variations: shaving cream coming through the phone (*False Alarms*); the 'Shave and a Haircut - Two Bits' knock (*Whoops, I'm an Indian*); the Russian representative landing upside down against the wall (*Restless Knights*); the metal tray under Larry's shirt (*3 Dumb Clucks*); Curly lining up a punch (*A Plumbing We Will Go*); using a pool cue to stop Moe's gouge (the rope in *Three Little Beers*); and the initial disclaimer (*You Nazty Spy!*). The WHISTLE sound effect is used for the wood in the air.

VERBAL HUMOR: When Vernon Dent looks to the heavens and says, "Can't you take a joke?" he is talking to God or Fate. Umpchay and Amscray look up, too, suggesting that putting Hailstone in place was an acceptable error, but even Fate or God - in a Stooge film - punishes the wicked by bonking them on the head. Felix Adler's & Clyde Bruckman's pool-table gags include political jokes about "too much English" and "the Brenner Pass"; the latter is the lowest pass leading from Germany into Italy, and so it is located in the 'pocket'. Other political gags include the party at Belcher's Garden, a corollary to Curly's joke about the 'Beer Putsch' in *You Nazty Spy!*; "Stunka [i.e. Stuka] bombers"; "What a blitzkrieg!" (*You Nazty Spy!*); and Moe: "Put it down or I'll take away your medals!" Curly: "They're not yours. I bought 'em in a hock shop!". German language pattern jokes include Moe lapsing into imitation Hitlerian German rhetoric; Moe and Curly's variation of 'Alouetta' ("Ist dass ist a submarine? Curly: "Ya dass ist a submarine." Moe: Ist dass ist a trolley car?" Curly: "Ya dass ist a trolley car." Moe: "Submarine, trolley car."); "Gesundheit" (*Violent is the Word for Curly*); and Moe's Yiddish "Plotz" (*Slippery Silks*).

Adler/Bruckman wrote non-political gags, as well, including extended department store puns (Gilda: "I am your new astrologer, the Seeress of Roebuck! Larry: "Oh, was your father the Seer of Roebuck?" Gilda: "Oh no. I was raised by Montgomery." Curly: "Montgomery's ward!" [a Stooge first]) and the movie 'star' puns (Moe: "You must help me get in touch with the stars." Larry: "Me, too. I'll take Lamarr." Curly: "I'll take Lamour." Moe: "I'll take Lazonga with six lessons."). The latter is a three-pattern. Another is the triadic "Come in - come in - come in. Ya!".

Though there are similarities and duplications, the map is not the same as the one used in *You Nazty Spy!*. This one uses geographical puns (Jug O'Slavia, Inseine River, Bulge-Area, Great Mitten, Hot Foot [shaped like Italy]), drinking references (Straights of Rye, Corkscrew Straights), food references (Lake o Lamb, Starvania), verbal doublets (Hot Sea, Tot Sea; Atisket, Atasket), conjugations (I Ran, He-Ran, She-Ran, They-Ran; Also-Ran), puns (Rubid Din, Cant Sea), ethnic gags (Yum Kippers, Toot Sweet), and Stoogisms (Jerkola, Woob-woob, Slap Happia). Other variations: Larry's "Yeah, man, I'm from the south, Ya, Ya, Yeah, man" and "Herman the Sixth and Seven-Eighths" (*You Nazty Spy!*); reveille (*Uncivil Warriors*); Moe's "Somebody dropped a bomb!" (*Pop Goes the Easel*); and 'Cofferdale cigarettes' ('Coffin Nails' in *Healthy, Wealthy and Dumb*).

References: "This morning they took Paregoric" - paregoric is not a country but an opiate anti-diarrhetic; the stars 'Lamarr' and 'Lamour' refer to Hedy Lamarr and Dorothy Lamour, both of whom had begun their Hollywood careers in the late 1930s; Moe's "I'll take Lazonga with six lessons" makes reference to Shemp's recent solo film, Universal's *Six Lessons from Madame Lazonga*; 'Seabiscuit' was Horse of the Year in 1938 (*Violent Is the Word for Curly; You Nazty Spy!*); and 'Gallahadeon' is a variation of Challedon, Horse of the Year in 1939 and 1940. The previous film had two Greco-Roman allusions to Venus and Cleopatra (rolling up a woman inside a carpet); this film has, "It contains enough high explosives to blow Hailstone and his henchmen to Hades."

OTHER NOTES: The title parodies the song title 'I'll Never Smile Again' written by Ruth Lowe just the previous year (1940). Duncan Renaldo, the camera-happy Japanese representative, later starred in the *Cisco Kid* on -56). We get 50 seconds to look at the map. Only Morons would omit an umlaut in the 'über' of 'Moronica Über Alles.'

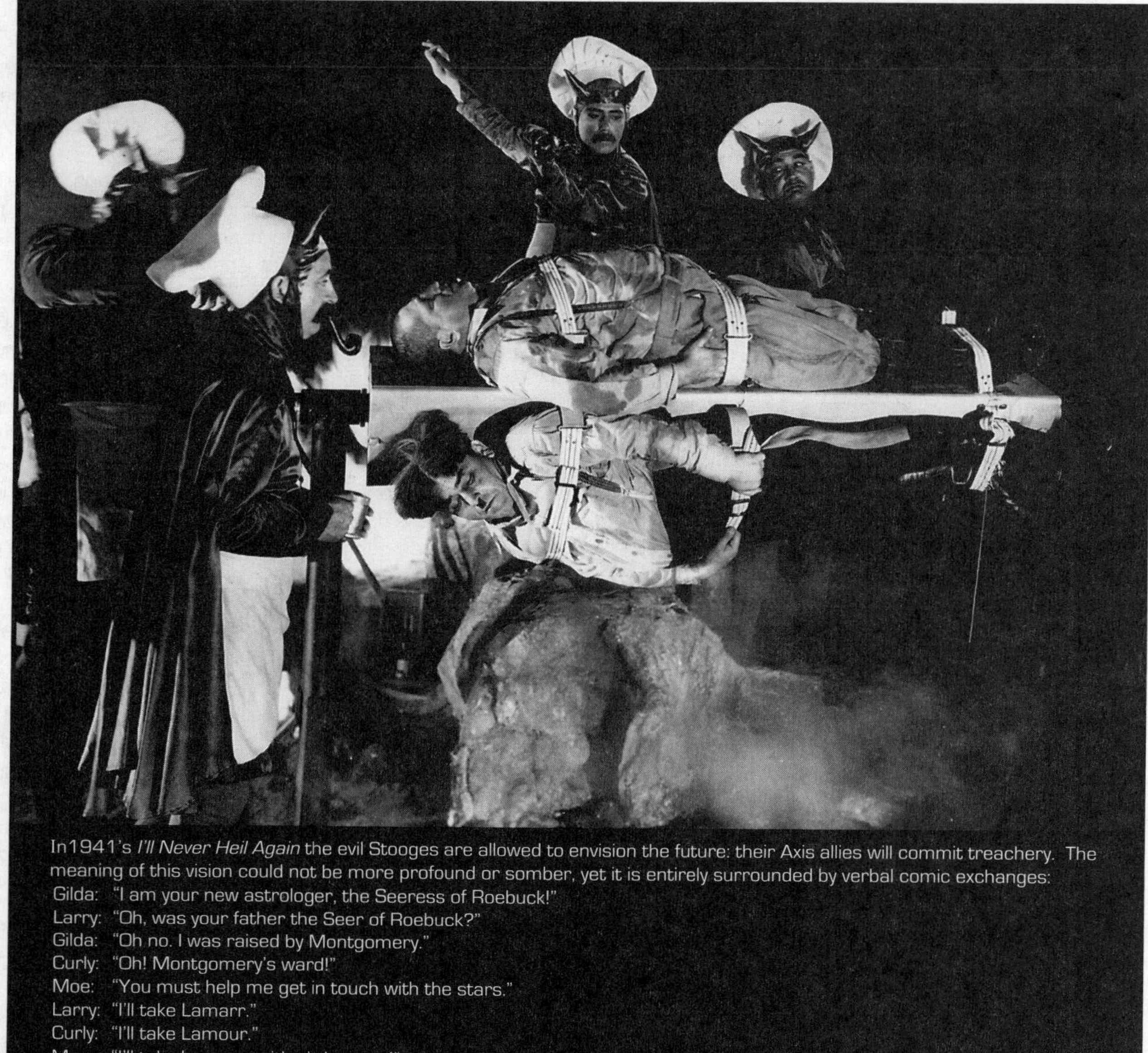

In1941's *I'll Never Heil Again* the evil Stooges are allowed to envision the future: their Axis allies will commit treachery. The meaning of this vision could not be more profound or somber, yet it is entirely surrounded by verbal comic exchanges:
Gilda: "I am your new astrologer, the Seeress of Roebuck!"
Larry: "Oh, was your father the Seer of Roebuck?"
Gilda: "Oh no. I was raised by Montgomery."
Curly: "Oh! Montgomery's ward!"
Moe: "You must help me get in touch with the stars."
Larry: "I'll take Lamarr."
Curly: "I'll take Lamour."
Moe: "I'll take Lazonga with six lessons!"

#57 - AN ACHE IN EVERY STAKE

Studio: Columbia

Released: August 22, 1941

Running Time: 18"05"

Credited Production Crew:

Produced by:	Del Lord & Hugh McCollum
Directed by:	Del Lord
Story and Screen Play:	Lloyd A. French
Director of Photography:	Philip Tannura
Film Editor:	Burton Kramer

Credited Cast:

Curly Howard
Larry Fine
Moe Howard

Uncredited Cast:

Vernon Dent	home owner
Bess Flowers	his wife
Bud Jamison	baker
Gino Corrado	chef
Blanche Payson	his assistant
Symona Boniface	guest who gets 'prizes'
Victor Travers	man waiting for icemen

PERSPECTIVE: What makes the first part of this Stooge classic unique is juxtaposing the incompatible inhuman elements of heat, ice, height, and distance. For the comedy to work, these elements need to be interdependent: the heat of the day is not funny without the ice gags, the ice gags would be very limited without the distance the ice has to be carried, and the distance the ice has to be carried turns to comedy because of the height of the steps. Ice melting on a hot day is not funny, but carrying a large melting block up a long flight of steps - twice - is. Of course, once the top of the steps becomes attainable, then a comic Sisyphus is needed to tumble back down again. That Sisyphus is the Vernon Dent character, 'Poindexter Lawrence' in the script.

The Stooges mess things up in every film. Sometimes they mess things up for a variety of people (*No Census, No Feeling*), and sometimes they mess things up for the same person in both the beginning and the end of the film (*A Plumbing We Will Go*). This last type of plot, a ring composition, flourishes with the addition of an effective performance from a tormented, frustrated, angered, threatening, and vulnerable Stooge foil, and Vernon Dent's performance here is a classic example. While the Stooges fill almost all of the eighteen minutes of film with their ice and cooking gags, Dent falls face first into two cakes, is chased and knocked down a flight of steps by an ice box, is bumped three times by a dancing, springing Curly, and blows up his birthday cake by making a wish. His total screen time is less than one minute, and yet he is the glue that holds this comedy together and gives it its memorable dramatic tension. Stooge slapstick in a film is amusing to the film viewer but not to either the Stooges themselves or their fellow Thespians (with a few notable exceptions). It takes an external audience to enjoy Stooge slapstick, and it is all the more enjoyable when they can follow the progress of a fourth person. This arrangement develops most noticeably from the mean-intentioned sergeant (Stanley Blystone) in *Half-Shot Shooters* to another angry drill sergeant, the Richard Fiske character in *Boobs in Arms*. Bud Jamison (Pierre in *Whoops, I'm an Indian*) helped develop the type in a non-military situation, but Vernon Dent would be the actor who would perfect the fourth stooge/Stooge foil role in civilian life.

The rest of the comedy involves food. The Stooges had practice making pancakes in *Movie Maniacs* and punch in *Three Sappy People* and *No Census, No Feeling*, but here they prepare and serve a whole meal for the first time. They injure the chef, louse up the turkey stuffing, never do get ice into the punch, and screw up serving even the ice water. After a little spring dancing, their cake turns out to be a bomb, which reminds Dent of who the cooks are - the ice men, boobs who earlier in the film could master neither heat, freezing, distance or height and who now at the end of the film cannot master heat and gas. First and only time Stooge writer Lloyd A. French seems to be telling us that what ruins Poindexter Lawrence's birthday is the Stooges' ignorance of basic chemistry and physics.

VISUAL HUMOR: Two sequences, carrying the ice up the stairs and the turkey preparation, put this film into classic status, but neither is more extraordinary than Curly shaving the ice. Film historians have praised Fred Astaire for making even inanimate partners seem to dance gracefully, so Curly should receive similar credit here for metamorphosing an inanimate block of ice into a 'being' capable of having a shave and a conversation. Usually, he gets frustrated with an inanimate object, but

here he is in total control. Inspiration for the scene came in part from Moe Hailstone's shaving sequence in the previous film. Stooge firsts: Curly getting pinned by a knife and 'bleeding' ketchup; and Moe pulling Curly by the tongue. There are two result shots besides the final explosion: Dent under the wagon, and Moe with icing on his nose. The exhaled gas fire that singed the Bey of Rum's beard in the previous film fed the comic fuel that led to the Stooges' gas gags here. Bending the chisel back to its original shape by hitting Curly with it a second time is a variation of the 'Oh! Oh! Oh! Ohh*look*!' routine from *Oily to Bed, Oily to Rise*. Curly had bowled with a prison leg-chain ball in *So Long, Mr. Chumps*, but here he keeps score and gets slapped because he needs "another strike". The chef is bombarded from an overhanging shelf as was Bustoff in *Grips, Grunts and Groans* and Gonzalez in *Cookoo Cavaliers*. Other variations: the spring dance, and exchanging slaps with a dance partner, shrugging, and continuing dancing (*Hoi Polloi*); everyone smiling while eating something horrible (*Uncivil Warriors*); sleeping at the beginning of a film (*Dizzy Doctors*); ice tongs (*Yes, We Have No Bonanza*); and Curly wiggling his head in Moe's face (*So Long, Mr. Chumps*).

VERBAL HUMOR: The verbal humor is also most notable in Curly's ice shaving routine and in the cooking sequences. In the former Curly creates speech with a block of ice, and in the latter the Stooges have to pantomime their misinterpretations of the recipes they read aloud. Curly's "Tell me, is it as warm in the summer as it is in the country, or vice versa?" derives from an old vaudeville act known as 'Moss and Frye'; Moe in his autobiography (27-28) admits to borrowing the line for his first vaudeville performance in 1916. Larry also misinterprets instructions when he "takes" the gas tube (just as he responded to "Get a drink of water!" in *Boobs in Arms* by pouring one for himself). Three- pattern and a Stooge first: Woman: "You will?!" Stooges (in unison): "Will we?". Larry: "Do we know how to cook?" Moe: "DO we!" Curly: "Do we?". Another first: Curly's "My father died dancing on the end of a rope!". Moe has some fine throw-away lines ("A frozen dainty!"; "We forgot to allow for shrinkage!"; and "Pump in a four more slices!") as do the extras (Bud Jamison: "I told you to be careful!"; Vernon Dent: "I'm *wearing* it!"). The "Here's your lip" gag stems from the sweater scene in *How High is Up?*, as did the ice block stuck on Curly's head.

Other variations: "Whadya' roll over in your sleep for?" (*No Census, No Feeling*); "A frozen dainty!" (*Violent is the Word for Curly*); "I'll kill you later, personally!" (*Cash and Carry*); "When I want your advice I'll ask for it!" (*A Plumbing We Will Go*); and Curly: "Say, did you have a pink tie on? No? Well here's your lip." (*How High is Up?*). Epithets: "chuckle-head," "numskull," "turnip-head," "grape-head," and "ignoramus". Reference: Moe's "Don't do anything until you see the white's of my eyes!" parodies William Prescott's immortal words at Bunker Hill (June 17, 1775): "Don't fire until you see the whites of their eyes."

OTHER NOTES: The film opens not with the usual sign but a thermometer, immediately establishing the heat motif. Carrying ice up the stairs derives from Billy Bevan's *Ice Cold Cocos* (1926), also directed by Del Lord. The stairs go from 2200-2258 North Fair OakView Terrace in the Silver Lake area of Hollywood. Laurel & Hardy carried a washing machine (*Hats Off* (1927)) and piano (*The Music Box* (1932)) up nearby stairs, (932-935 Verdome St.) the latter film winning an Oscar, commemorated today by a plaque on the third step. The concept of angering a victim and later ending up unknowingly in his home was used earlier in Shemp's 1934 Vitaphone short *Corn on the Cop*; from a basement window Shemp hits a cop on his foot 'corn' and turns up later in the cop's home posing as his nephew. This film was partially remade as *Listen, Judge* (1952). The protective pad on Curly's rear is quite visible when they pull him out of the ice wagon.

As in any art form, comedy is built upon the teachings of the past. No artist invents or creates something entirely new; there are always artistic predecessors and influences: Shakespeare learned and borrowed from Marlowe, and Marlowe from Chaucer, and Chaucer from Boccaccio, and so on.

Comedy short films were no different. Many of the Stooge directors worked for Mack Sennett in the silent-film era, and this classic turkey-stuffing sequence from *An Ache in Every Stake* (1941) is not new with this film. Hiring cooks/servers by accident was used in the 1934 Vitaphone short *A Peach of a Pair* in which Shemp Howard "separates" two eggs, "dices" two potatoes, "cleans" oysters, "soaks" the bread, and leaves his watch in the stuffed turkey. After spilling alum on the grapefruit (cf. *No Census, No Feeling*), Shemp uses a gasoline drum instead of a wine barrel to fill a pitcher; this leads to a final explosion. Lloyd French, who wrote this Stooge film, also directed the Shemp film, and Shemp, of course, was the older brother of Curly and Moe, so an ever-renewed supply of comic inspiration must have been flowing into and around Columbia.

Some of the most respected comedians of the mid-twentieth century - Milton Berle, Sid Caesar, and Steve Allen - were all unabashed in joking that they 'stole' material from each other and other comedians. It was not a matter of inventing a gag or routine or plot, it was a matter of how it was adapted and performed. The Stooges and their Columbia staff constantly reinvented and adapted older comic material for the trio-format of the Stooges, and stuffing a turkey became one of their own signature recipes. And in the new millennium many of the comedians from whom they borrowed are generally forgotten, their films warehoused or lost, while the Stooge films are still seen and admired by each subsequent generation.

#58 - IN THE SWEET PIE AND PIE

Studio: Columbia

Released: October 16, 1941

Running Time: 17"25"'

Credited Production Crew:

Produced & Directed by:	Jules White
Screen Play by:	Clyde Bruckman
Story by:	Ewart Adamson
Director of Photography:	George Meehan
Film Editor:	Jerome Thoms

Credited Cast:

Curly Howard	
Larry Fine	
Moe Howard	
Dorothy Appleby	Tiska Jones
Mary Ainslee	Taska Jones
Ethelreda Leopold	Baska Jones

Uncredited Cast:

Richard Fiske	Diggins
Symona Boniface	guest in black dress
Vernon Dent	senator
Geneva Mitchell	dance instructor [stock footage]
Eddie Laughton	hunter
Lynton Brent	prison vendor
John Tyrrell	butler
Al Thompson	warden
Bert Young	prison guard
Victor Travers	Justice of the Peace
Lew Davis	prisoner

PERSPECTIVE: This film depends on an absurd premise that unites three ambitious young women with three convicted murderers. It is difficult to imagine two groups of humans more different in economic class, intellectual capacity, and social status. But it is specifically because Tiska, Taska, and Baska are ambitious, gold-digging women of status that they agree to use the Stooges to get what they want. Like their heartless attorney Diggins [Richard Fiske], they expect to feel no remorse at deceiving three men the day before their execution. Usually a justice system offers condemned prisoners one last wish, but the Jones girls and Diggins not only deny the Stooges any last minute dignity whatsoever, they *want* them dead and even taunt them.

Ironically, it is characters more depraved than the Stooges who save them. Mickey Finn and his gang confess their guilt and release the Stooges into the Jones mansion. There they face three successive challenges. The first, the physical challenge, does not at the outset look promising - the wives punch the Stooges onto the floor - but immediately the Stooges turn the tables by giving their wives a judo flip. The second is the challenge to advance themselves socially in the eyes of their superior wives; the wives had determined that to get "rid of them. All we do is insist they take dancing lessons, fencing, baths." But the Stooges succeed in this challenge very nicely, too. Despite a poor night's sleep, they wake up to attend their dance lesson, doing "exactly" as their instructor does in the classic footage from *Hoi Polloi*. We see them at their toilette twice, which may not be "ten baths a day" as Tiska says, but it gets the point across. The Stooges are determined to hold the social status they have achieved to this point, so the wives turn to Diggins one more time to establish the third and most difficult challenge - that the Stooges have to be fully accepted in society. The trio may get off to a false start by coming out to the party in their underwear and watching Curly drop his cuff into the punch, but they ultimately triumph. The woman in the black dress - Symona Boniface, who symbolizes society in her many Stooge appearances - comes to their defense in the pie fight and helps punish real evil in the forms of the calculating attorney and the bribed butler. We saw the Stooges win society's laughs in *Ants in the Pantry*, and we saw them win $1,500 from the rich in *Three Sappy People*, but here they win the great challenge to be accepted in society with the help of society itself.

The comic climax to this inspirational story is the most elaborate pie fight in Stoogedom. The title of the film alone suggests that the story glories in this Mother of All Pie Fights. Unlike the clay fight in *Pop Goes the Easel*, this fight has everything to do with the plot. In fact, the last pies thrown are not at the Stooges but at the wicked attorney. No running away in this film; in seventeen minutes the Stooges move from the gallows to society, from the accused to the punisher, and from the condemned to the triumphant.

VISUAL HUMOR: George Meehan's camera controls our access in several scenes. It turns the initial newspaper photograph into a real-life scene, it shows us the hole in the floor before it shows us the bunk beds, it shows us the shaking lamp and an empty mattress before it shows us the snoring Stooges clumped together on one mattress, and it shows us the Stooges in tuxedos before it shows us that they are not wearing pants. Slapstick punctuates each scenario of this socially significant story. The physical challenge requires the punch and judo flip, the social advancement test includes the classic dance lesson footage with Geneva Mitchell from *Hoi Polloi* and is preceded by the bunk-bed routine [a Stooge first], and then their social acceptance hinges on the pie fight. The dance lesson footage has been re-edited to emphasize "do exactly what/as I do" twice; the newly written introduction to the dance lesson - the wake-up scene - joins the old footage. The prison scenes include Curly "thinking" against the wall and their saw gags: sawing

Curly's scalp, sawing against his chin, and the saw-sword fight. We saw saw routines in *3 Dumb Clucks* and *Oily to Bed*. The sound effect of Curly "thinking" against the wall is thunderous and makes it easy to believe he has "a terrific headache".

The Stooges rarely close a scene with purposeless slapstick after the scene's dialogue has come to a close, but here, like the sprinkler scene in *So Long, Mr. Chumps*, there is a slapstick barrage after the 'married' Stooges are closed up in jail. The Stooges appear in underwear, as they have several times recently. In contrast to scenes in *Calling All Curs* and *Oily to Bed, Oily to Rise*, Moe and Curly kiss intentionally. Other variations: Curly admiring his looks (*Movie Maniacs*); Curly hiding a hammer in his clothes, and getting elbows in the jaw (*3 Dumb Clucks*); Curly covering the hole in the floor with a carpet (*A Plumbing We Will Go*); Moe crying like a baby (*I'll Never Heil Again*); the 'Shave and a Haircut' knock (*Whoops, I'm an Indian*); and pulling Curly by the lip (*Boobs in Arms*).

VERBAL HUMOR: The physical part of the saw routines is enhanced by Clyde Bruckman's rhapsody puns ('I Hear a Ripsody' and 'A Rhapsody in the Kisser') and internal rhyme (Curly: "Let a guy that can saw, see, saw?!". Stooge firsts: Larry: "They say strawberries are good for a cold." Warden: "Strawberries won't be in season for six months.' Stooges [in unison]: "We'll wait!"; and Moe: "You going to eat that entire chicken alone?" Larry: "No. Maybe if I wait I'll get some potatoes!". At society parties Stooge dialogue usually ranges from puns based on Stooge ignorance (Woman: "Are you familiar with the Great Wall of China? Curly: "No, but I know a big fence in Chicago!") to ignorant malapropisms (Larry: "Ain't she hospital!") to imitating high society snootiness, Moe's specialty (Moe: "I say, Jasper. How's your tape worm?" Curly: "It took the Blue Ribbon at Madison Square Garden last week." Moe: "'Fahncy' that!" Curly: "You 'fahncy' that!").

Curly's vocal inventiveness in "I fall down" may owe something to Oliver Hardy's "I fall down" [into a cake] from *The Hollywood Revue of 1929*. The phrase used to be a common expression: L&H starred in a film, albeit silent, *We Faw Down*, and the the vaudevillean Bob Burns wrote the hit song 'I Faw Down and Go Boom'. Moe's most startling admission: "For once I agree with you guys!". The execution announcer offers another Stooge abuse of airwaves (the loud speakers in *Three Punch Drunks*; the P.A. system in *Men in Black*). His presentation features gallows humor: "Hangemall Prison," "Edam Neckties," and "jerk-by-jerk." Treating the Stooges as "contestants" is another reference to radio quiz show programs, as in *Healthy, Wealthy and Dumb*. 'Fleur de Stinkum' is still a favorite Stooge essence (*Cookoo Cavaliers*; *You Nazty Spy!*). Diggins whispering his plans to the butler recalls a similar plan-whispering moment in *Yes, We Have No Bonanza*. The title of the 1879 song, 'A Tisket, A Tasket' was also used on the map in *You Nazty Spy!*.

References: Curly's 'I Hear a Rhipsody' parodies the 1940 popular song 'I Hear a Rhapsody' written by Jack Baker, George Fregos, and Dick Gasparre. Moe's "I am the Shadow" parodies the Columbia serial *The Shadow* (1940); the radio show debuted in 1930, but the Lamont Cranston character became popular on Mutual Radio in 1936. As for calling the Stooges "Frankensteins," between 1931, when Universal's *Frankenstein* was released, and *In the Sweet Pie and Pie*, two Frankenstein sequels had been made, *Bride of Frankenstein* (1935) and *Son of Frankenstein* (1939), and this same year (1941) *Ghost of Frankenstein* was being made.

OTHER NOTES: The title parodies the song 'In the Sweet Bye and Bye' written in 1902 by Harry Von Tilzer and Vincent Bryan for the show *The Wild Rose*, starring Eddie Foy. The working title was *Well, I'll Be Hanged*. This is the first of several Stooge plots attaching a time constraint to receiving an inheritance. Notable will be *Brideless Groom*. The concept dates back to Buster Keaton's *Seven Chances* (1925). In the script the Symona Boniface character is named 'Mrs. Gotrocks'. Eddie Laughton's lion-hunter characterization is his longest and most elaborate filmed Stooge appearance. Moe's "I've been sabotaged!" is a war reference; the judo flip reflects contemporary interest in Japan, and notice the irony that Tom, Dick, and Harry are in the Navy and going to Honolulu - in October 1941!. The sawing footage will be reused in *Beer Barrel Polecats* (1946); the pie footage will appear in *Half-Wits Holiday* (1947) and *Pest Man Wins* (1951). For a summary of great film pie fights, see William K. Everson, *The Complete Films of Laurel & Hardy* (55-56). This is the final Stooge appearance, other than in stock footage, for Richard Fiske. He was killed in World War II. For a biography, see Bill Cappello, *The 3 Stooges Journal* 64 (1992) 6-7 and 14.

#59 - SOME MORE OF SOMOA

Studio: Columbia

Released: December 4, 1941

Running Time: 16"40'"

Credited Production Crew:

Produced by:	Del Lord & Hugh McCollum
Directed by:	Del Lord
Story & Screen Play by:	Harry Edwards & Elwood Ullman
Director of Photography:	L. W. O'Connell
Film Editor:	Burton Kramer

Credited Cast:

Curly Howard
Larry Fine
Moe Howard

Uncredited Cast:

Symona Boniface	Mrs. Winthrop
Mary Ainslee	nurse
Tiny Ward	king
Louise Carver	king's sister
John Tyrrell	gardener
Robert Williams	Winthrop
Duke York	Kingfisher

PERSPECTIVE: One of the oldest stories in the world is the quest for the magic fruit. Almost 5000 years ago in ancient Mesopotamia Gilgamesh searched for it, found it, and then had it stolen by a serpent. Over 2000 years ago in ancient Greece, Hercules searched for it in the Garden of the Hesperides at the world's end, and it, too, was guarded by a serpent. In ancient Israel Adam and Eve found it in the Garden of Eden, listened to the serpent, and even took a bite out of it. Now the Stooges search for the sacred fruit. This is not to say that the writers intentionally or knowingly created a mythical tale to make the Stooges part of the ancient mythological and biblical traditions, but it reminds us that great stories are timeless and can be retold countless times in countless ways.

The first part of the film introduces a magical theme. Curly injects Vitamin P.D.Q. into a tree and gets it to grow and bear fruit in a matter of seconds. Then he accidentally injects himself and almost doubles his height. In their repartee Curly and Moe turn immediately to the world of myth and legend: Curly: "I'm a giant!" Moe: "Well, I'm a giant killer and my name ain't Jack!"

The Rhum Boogie portion of the film introduces a number of the ancient story's mythological elements. Just as the Biblical and Greek versions locate the plant in a mythical paradise at the world's end, the Stooges trace the plant to the end of their world. In the previous film [*In the Sweet Pie and Pie*] the radio announcer at the hanging described the three corners of the world as "Alaska, Antarctica, and Pago Pago," and presumably Rhum Boogie lies somewhere near Pago Pago - perhaps beyond - in the South Pacific. All great mythological heroes make grand journeys - Jason in quest of the Golden Fleece, Ulysses seeking his homeland in Ithaca, and the Stooges in search of the puckerless persimmon in Rhum Boogie, even if they travel by a boat which Moe "rowed every step of the way." Another mythological element appears when Curly tries to take the plant from the totem. Resembling the Hindu God Siva, the multi-arm totem moves, breathes, makes horrible noises, and, fittingly, slaps, clubs, and bonks its violators, so Curly defeats it appropriately by whacking it on the nose. Still another mythological element is the alligator. Nearly all the ancient versions of the myth associate the sacred plant with a serpent, and the Stooges indeed battle a large reptile, the largest reptile and one of the longest battles with any beast the Stooges will have until they encounter the Siamese Cyclops in *The Three Stooges Meet Hercules*, another mythical tale. The final element of the ancient saga is the hero ultimately losing the sacred fruit. The fruit represents eternal happiness, not a gift ancient gods wished humans to acquire, so Gilgamesh, Hercules, and Adam & Eve all failed to achieve this eternal earthly bliss. Gilgamesh lost his prize because a serpent stole it and took it to the bottom of the sea. In a last heroic attempt to retrieve it, Gilgamesh tied stones to his feet so he could dive after it, but he was unsuccessful. Maybe he should have tried sinking in a leaking boat.

VISUAL HUMOR: A Stooge first: this is Curly's first full 360-degree turn around his leg, and he does it twice. A previous version takes place near the elevator in *3 Dumb Clucks*. The flower hopping up and down on Curly's head is unique, although it is not entirely unlike Moe's hair standing on end. Other notable physical gags: Larry 'picking up' footprints, Curly pushing the chef into the stew pot [in fast motion], and the take Moe and Larry do when they see the natives surrounding them. The Stooges offer us a different bumping strategy as they enter the plant room in the Winthrop house.The confusion caused by working on two patients simultaneously is a Stooge first and filmed convincingly so that Mrs. Winthrop and the nurse believe Mr. Winthrop's "limbs" are being cut off.

Curly has two 'heroic' battles, one with the alligator, the other with the totem. The duel with the alligator is even more comprehensive than the battles with the gorilla in *Three Missing Links*. Curly daring Moe to hit him again with the mallet derives from *Yes, We Have No Bonanza*, but here Curly adds "That's not the same," walks off camera and gets hit off camera: "*That's* the same!". Other variations: hitting Moe with a two-man saw (*Oily to Bed, Oily to Rise*); a branch in the face (*Uncivil Warriors*); the Rhum Boogie dance ("Viva Vulgaria" in *Dutiful but Dumb*); the operation on the tree with "Cotton!" and "Hike!" (*Men in Black*); and Moe and Larry blaming each other for grunting before they see the natives (*Movie Maniacs*).

VERBAL HUMOR: The script by the same Harry Edward/ Elwood Ullman team that wrote *No Census, No Feeling,* produced a number of plot-related botanical puns (Curly: "I don't like the sound of its bark!"; Curly: "Just a little thing I picked up to make big trees outta little saps." Larry: "Don't look at me!"; and Moe: "This poor thing is pining away for a girlfriend." Curly: "Or maybe a boyfriend") and a three-pattern: Larry: "Looks like Aphis." Curly: "Ephus." Moe: "Iphis"). There are medical puns (Curly: "Transfusion is less confusion!'; Curly: "I'm back to normal." Moe: "You'll never be that." Curly: "Oh, I bet you tell that to all the sturgeons!"); gallows humor, as in the execution sequence in the previous film ("Cheer up! We kill or cure! We won't muss up the joint. We'll even burn up the trimmings."); gambling humor (King: "Every time a natural!"), cannibalistic jokes ("Short rib. Pork Chop. Soup bone!"; Larry: "Where do we come in?" King: "In the stew!"; and the menu sign "ROAST STOOGE"); and dialogue appropriate for a battle with an alligator (Moe: "You put your foot on his lower." Larry: "I'd rather take the upper." Curly: "I'll take a compartment!" Moe: "You'll take the lower and you'll like it." Larry: "I'll take the lower but I won't like it"; Curly: "I don't know if it's the tree or his tonsils!"; and Larry: "I lost the end of my shoe!" Moe: "The end of a shoe ain't important!" Larry: "Well this one is - I think it had my toes in it!").

Like a stethoscope and a saw, the phone is a great tool for the Stooges. The pattern here is derived from the phone sequence in *A Pain in the Pullman.* The Rhum Boogie dance is their motto/ slogan for this film. Other variations: the ugly woman surprise (*Slippery Silks*; *Cookoo Cavaliers*); reference to a mermaid (*Cookoo Cavaliers*); "Milk From Contented Coconuts' ('Carnation Pictures - from Contented Actors' in *Movie Maniacs*); and nonsense medical names (*Men in Black*).

References: the imitation of 'Amos 'n Andy' is from the radio show that ran from 1928; 'Lightnin' was the janitor, and, ironically, their lodge was the 'Mystic Knights of the Sea.' Moe's "Dr. Deadrock, I presume" refers to the greeting, "Dr. Livingstone, I presume," best known from the film *Stanley and Livingstone* (1939). Curly's "Well, beat me, daddy, down to the floor" is from the song 'Beat Me, Daddy (Eight to the Bar),' written by Don Raye and Hughie Prince for the 1940 film *Down Argentine Way*, that same year they wrote the song 'Rhumboogie' for the Andrews Sisters in the Ritz Brothers' comedy film, *Argentine Nights*; the following year they wrote '*Boogie Woogie Bugle Boy*' for Abbott & Costello's first feature film, *Buck Privates*, in which Shemp Howard also appeared. 'Rhum Boogie' is the first Stooge reference to 'boogie-woogie' music, which had become popular in 1938. An 'aphis' is a plant louse; and an 'ephus' is a trick baseball pitch. "Szibill" seems to refer to a turn-of-the-century musical by Miksa Brody. Epithets: "iron-head" and "imbecile."

OTHER NOTES: Louise Carver, who plays the king's sister, specialized in 'ugly' roles. We saw her photograph in the opening scene of *Horses' Collars* and her face (by the car) in *Dizzy Doctors*. When Curly puts his head in the bag to answer the phone, he starts whining before Moe actually closes the bag on his neck.

For the final release of 1941, writers Harry Edwards and Elwood Ullman take the Stooges on a long mythological voyage in quest of the magical fruit. *Some More of Samoa* tells a story as old as the Mesopotamian tale of Gilgamesh, and in doing so the Stooges travel to the never-never land of Rhum Boogie to do battle with a multi-armed divinity and a wild beast, in this case an alligator. Unfortunately for the beast in this posed publicity photo, it is attacking the least vulnerable part of Curly's body.

1942

Loco Boy Makes Good • Cactus Makes Perfect

What's the Matador? • Matri-Phony • Three Smart Saps

Even as IOU • Sock-A-Bye Baby

#60 - LOCO BOY MAKES GOOD

Studio: Columbia

Released: January 8, 1942

Running Time: 17"24'"

Credited Production Crew:

Produced & Directed by:	Jules White
Story & Screen Play by:	Felix Adler & Clyde Bruckman
Director of Photography:	John Stumar
Film Editor:	Jerome Thom

Credited Cast:

Curly Howard	
Larry Fine	
Moe Howard	
Dorothy Appleby	'Shorty,' Waldo Twitchell's date
John Tyrrell	Waldo Twitchell

Uncredited Cast:

Bud Jamison	landlord
Vernon Dent	Balbo the magician
Eddie Laughton	drunk
Robert Williams	Mr. Scruggins
Ellinor Vanderveer	guest of Twitchell
Al Thompson	man with seltzer bottle
Bert Young	man in hotel lobby
Symona Boniface	dancer with mouse
Lynton Brent	bearded diner
Vic Travers	his companion
Robert 'Bobby' Burns	dancer
Heinie Conklin	dancer

PERSPECTIVE: Stooge writers were capable of creating films in which the Stooges louse up everything but still save someone in distress and catch the bad guys. In this first release of 1942, just as in *Oily to Bed, Oily to Rise*, they do almost everything wrong but have enough good luck to achieve their altruistic goal - to help 'the old lady.' Their luck first turns on being thrown out of their hotel: in the gutter they find a newspaper article that gives them the idea of slipping on a bar of soap and suing. Their luck turns again when Curly picks up the magician's coat by mistake.

Wait! The Stooges read an article that gives them the idea of slipping on a bar of soap and suing for damages? There is probably no more patently absurd premise in any Stooge film. The hotel defense attorney would play all fifty-nine previous Columbia films to demonstrate that these guys fall down all the time, that Curly has an iron head capable of withstanding blows from chisels, saw blades, and sledge hammers, that Curly trips over a bar of soap four times, the last time laughing hysterically, and that the third time Moe bonks him on the head, making Curly admit: "You know I'm not normal!" How would you like to be their lawyer? The comic message is clear: the Stooges are such stooges, they do not even know they *are* stooges.

In the second turn of fortune, Curly puts on Balbo's coat. A master of disguise in many films, Curly unknowingly brings magic to the doomed hotel, transforming a disaster into - to use Larry's words - "a riot." He makes Twitchell, 'Shorty,' and everyone else laugh uproariously. In this sense, the magic he brings is the magic of silly laughter.

In between is almost pure Stoogeness except for the hotel lobby scene with Scruggins. This is one of those occasional scenes, like the initial bar scene in *Horses' Collars*, in which the Stooges seem to know what they are doing. They talk tough, act tough, do good things for a good person, and do bad things to a bad person - steal his money, steal his watch, shove him out the window, and throw something at him. By the end of the film, they have prevented him from dispossessing Mrs. Brown. In being so competent, they cease to be stooges temporarily, and by sending Scruggins out the window, they make a stooge of him. The Stooges only do this sort of thing rarely, and their competence in this scene is very quickly counter-balanced in the next with Moe and Curly's idiotic discussion of which way a nail should point. Even Moe makes a fool of himself in this next scene, quickly reestablishing their stoogeness, which is, after all, the most important aspect of their screen presence. It is no coincidence that in this film Moe has one of those rare moments in which he realizes out loud that he is being a stooge: "Tote that barge! Lift that Bail! Zoot! What am I doin'?" And in the same scene, Moe and Larry have an exchange in which they use their real voices:

Larry: "Well would it be possible for us to—?"

Moe: "I don't think it would be possible!"

They are such stooges, whatever they try will not be possible. Even the dog is amazed at how stoogelike the Stooges are.

VISUAL HUMOR: Curly stands in front of Scruggins to steal his money and watch. This different camera framing is designed to distract us as well as Scruggins. After Curly slides into Moe, they indulge in a slapstick extravaganza with seven consecutive acts of silly violence, and an eighth just a moment later. Then Moe and Curly have more extended slapstick in the linoleum sequence. This is essentially a Stooge first since similar multiple slapstick sessions will become common in future films. Curly yells at the linoleum, then blows it away, then cries - a classic example of his frustration with inanimate objects. You can punch him, hit him over the head with a board, or hammer a nail in with his head, but do not beleaguer him with an inhuman object. In contrast, Curly makes a deal with one inanimate object when he says to the bar of soap: "Now you work with me, and I'll see that you're put in the tub and nobody uses you!". When Moe breaks a board over Curly's head instead of using a saw and then nails the wood to the wall using Curly's head instead of a hammer, we see how Curly's iron head has finally become a tool - not for thinking but for woodworking.

Embellishing the scene in which Curly's head is used as a hammer, three times he cries "Oh!" in pain, but when the nail is in and Curly turns around to see it, he says a happy "Oh!" This is a variation on "Oh! Oh! Oh! Ohhhl*look*!" from *Oily to Bed, Oily to Rise*. Moe and Curly toss Larry into the large trough, but this kind of bath is usually reserved for a non-Stooge (*A Plumbing We Will Go; From Nurse to Worse*). Curly pats his head at Moe as he did in *In the Sweet Pie and Pie*. The musical interlude offers us some intriguing piano work from Larry, the first since *Dancing Lady*; notice how quickly Moe's hand moves to shut the lid à la Ted Healy. A laughing audience saved the day in *Ants in the Pantry*, too, and in the same film we saw mice as well as a skunk. Other variations: riding on the drink cart (*Calling All Curs*); carrying their trays in interwoven patterns (*So Long, Mr. Chumps*); a Stooge in his underwear (*Dutiful but Dumb*); Curly eating soap (*Dizzy Doctors*); Curly making a muscle with his arm but Moe feeling his belly instead (*Grips, Grunts and Groans*); Curly characterized as a thief (*Three Little Beers; Hoi Polloi*) and ending with a skunk (*Ants in the Pantry*).

VERBAL HUMOR: Moe ("I don't think it would be possible?") had a moment of self-reflection earlier in *Mutts to You* ("I don't know; it was my idea but I don't think much of it."). The printed signs have been clever in recent films. In the previous film it was 'Roast Stooge'; here it is 'Free Showers When It Rains'. A variation on "Say a few syllables" is "They're the *wrong* syllables". The magician here is named 'Balbo'; in *A Plumbing We Will Go* the magician was 'Professor Bilbo'. Other variations: "Do you have 'paté du foie gras?": Larry: "I'll see if the band can play it." (*Beer and Pretzels*); Curly: "Don't you *dare* hit me in the head. You know I'm not normal!" (*Hello Pop!*)

"Lift that barge! Tote that bail! Zoot!" (*Rockin' Thru the Rockies*); 'Chisel Inn Hotel' (Chizzelini in *I'll Never Heil Again?*); and "Get my other pair of socks; they're standin' behind the stove" (Moe's socks in *3 Dumb Clucks*). Epithets: "nitwit," "dimwit," and "blubber-head".

References: 'Waldo Twitchell' parodies the well-known columnist Walter Winchell, who appeared in several movies in the late 1930s. 'Shylock' was the Jewish usurer in Shakespeare's *The Merchant of Venice*, one of many Shakespearean references in Stooge films. Curly's "And Major Bowes said I had talent!" refers to the *Major Bowes and His Original Amateur Hour* radio show, which searched for new young talent (and discovered Frank Sinatra in 1937). Curly's "It's sabatoogee!" is another bit of evidence that the European war is having its influence in Hollywood. Moe used the phrase "I been sabotaged!" in *In the Sweet Pie and Pie*. Characteristically, Moe turns the word into a verb: "I'll saba-toogie you!" Although released in January, 1942, this film was made before the Japanese attacked Pearl Harbor in December, 1941.

OTHER NOTES: The release title parodies the newspaper-headline expression 'Local Boy Makes Good'; the working title was *Poor but Dishonest*. In March, 1946, four years after the release of *Loco Boy Makes Good*, Harold Lloyd filed a $500,000 suit against Columbia for violation of copyright. The court found the script for Lloyd's *Movie Crazy* (1932), which Clyde Bruckman had directed, virtually identical with Bruckman's script for *Loco Boy Makes Good*. Columbia lost the suit. Universal was later sued for similar violations in several Bruckman scripts, costing them several million dollars in damages. In 1955 Bruckman, penniless and an alcoholic, borrowed a pistol from old friend Buster Keaton and committed suicide. This is John Stumar's first film as Director of Photography since *Boobs in Arms*, but there is nothing experimental here as there was in that film.

Loco Boy Makes Good (1942) offers an extreme contrast. In the hotel lobby scene, the Stooges are competent, confident and utterly dominant over Scruggins. In the ensuing linoleum sequences, however, they are more Stooge-like than ever. Director Jules White emphasizes their ignorance and extends slapstick sequences, a trademark of his films.

#61 - CACTUS MAKES PERFECT

Studio: Columbia

Released: February 26, 1942

Running Time: 17"18"'

Credited Production Crew:

Produced by:	Del Lord & Hugh McCollum
Directed by:	Del Lord
Story & Screen Play by:	Elwood Ullman & Monty Collins
Director of Photography:	Benjamin Kline
Film Editor:	Burton Kramer

Credited Cast:

Curly Howard
Larry Fine
Moe Howard

Uncredited Cast:

Monty Collins	mother
Vernon Dent	prospector
Ernie Adams	prospector
Eddie Laughton	con man

PERSPECTIVE: The opening scene of *Cactus Makes Perfect* establishes a motivation that impels the Stooges on their wayward course through the entire film: their mother kicks them out of their house. They spend the first five minutes of the film in their mother's house simply (and comically) waking up and preparing themselves in the bathroom, as they have done presumably every day of their lives. But it is on this particularly day that she kicks them out and they leave to find their fortune. This is an interesting variation on a Depression-type film like *Three Little Pigskins*, which began with the jobless Stooges walking the streets and *Dizzy Doctors*, which began with them mooching off their wives. Now they are mooching off mom. But once she kicks them out, they do not last very long out in the cruel world. Right across the street from their house they are swindled.

They have been swindled before, but in all the previous films they acted so Stoogely that they turned being conned into success. In *Playing the Ponies* they just happened upon the peperinos; in *Cash and Carry* they just lucked into dynamiting through the treasury wall; and in *A Ducking They Did Go* the Stooges accidently found the police station and Curly accidently found the ducks. Here in *Cactus Makes Perfect* it takes getting Curly's head stuck in the wooden mine entrance and some painful digging, but they succeed in finding the gold because Curly actually created an invention that worked. Curly, to whom Moe complained in the previous film, "Why don't you do things right?" actually did something right. A far cry from the backfiring mouse trap in *Termites of 1938*, Curly somehow managed to produce a valuable gadget. How was this possible?

In the context of this film, it was possible because of his loving mother's inspiration. When the Stooges (finally) wake up in the morning, they hurry to get ready because their mom wants them to. When they find the gold later in the film, their first and only thought is to use the gold to get "mom" out of the kitchen. It is not that she had anything to do with the invention itself - except to be shot by it - but clearly the Stooges wish to please her, perhaps even to prove that they are not utterly lazy, useless loafers. Their mom, played by Monty Collins the actor who had worked with them already in *Woman Haters* and Monty Collins the writer who understood Stooge shtick, displays character traits that seem genetically connected to her Stooge sons: she gets frustrated like Curly, she slaps like Moe, she even gets her hair ripped out like Larry. She is cheap, too, saying: "You WOULD take it!" Her attitude towards her boys is wonderfully natural. She is a good, old-fashioned mom who loves her sons yet disciplines them physically and calls them denigrating names. After meeting their Curly-esque father in *3 Dumb Clucks*, we now have a further clue to understanding why the Stooges are the way they are. Only a gene pool like this could have produced such Stooges.

VISUAL HUMOR: Associate Producers Del Lord & Hugh McCollum, and writers Ellwood Ullman & Monty Collins designed five very abusable scenarios for physical gags: the whirling bed, the bathroom, the mine entrance, the mine shaft, and the safe. The whirling bed embellishes the opening sequences of *Dizzy Doctors* and *How High is Up?*, but in addition to sleeping through noise, motion, traffic, and wives, now we have an additional wrinkle: the Stooges are whirled around, tossed out of the bed, and piled up on the floor - still sleeping - in the result shot.

What makes the bathroom scene take a few steps beyond the toilette scene of *In the Sweet Pie and Pie* is the closeness of the Stooges jammed into a 2' x 4' room. They move like a well-oiled, internally quarrelsome machine with such simple 'tools' as a toothbrush, hairbrush, shaving brush, and razor. The scene begins well with Curly squeezing himself in and then comes to a magnificent finish with Curly telling Moe to say "Ah," Curly getting the shaving brush knocked into his own open mouth, and then Moe pointedly saying "Ah." (Shaving scenes in recent films include *I'll Never Heil Again* and *An Ache in Every Stake*).

When Curly gets his head stuck in the mine entrance, we watch head-on as Curly's nose, eyes, mouth, cheeks, and ears are all poked, slapped, squished, and pulled. In addition to the ear-catching sound effects, Curly offers an amazing array of noises and faces. This scene is the interior bayonet bag view in *Boobs in Arms* meets

The real Stooge matriarch, Jennie Horwitz, mother of Moe, Shemp and Curly. She had the sharp business acumen Moe inherited. She spoiled baby Jerome, thereby helping to shape the character we know as 'Curly.'

prying the sweater off in *How High is Up?*. The mine shaft scene puts the Stooges in an enclosed space with digging implements again, very much like the prototype scene in *Cash and Carry*, which also led to a dynamite scene. Getting the pick stuck in Moe's clothing is derived from *A Plumbing We Will Go*.

Other variations: Curly turning the skunk tail hat towards Moe [*Back to the Woods*]; wearing pajamas with clothes underneath [*Rockin' Thru the Rockies*]; the arrow pinning mom to the wall [*An Ache in Every Stake*]; bonking Curly, whose head bonks Moe's, whose head bonks Larry's [twice] [*Grips, Grunts and Groans*]; Curly calculating and pulling a tape from his mouth [*No Census, No Feeling*]; Curly hiding money on his chest [*From Nurse to Worse*]; Moe sprinkling dirt on Curly's tongue [*Cash and Carry*]; Curly getting cactus needles in his rear [*Slippery Silks*]; Curly's surprise appearance from behind the hotel desk [*Some More of Samoa*]; and Curly's cheerfulness when the jackpot hits him [when he slips on the soap for fourth time in *Loco Boy Makes Good*]. A Stooge first: the taxi 'pick up'. Special kudos to Vernon Dent for his take when he sees the dynamite next to him. There is good dummy work in both the previous film [Larry falling into the paste trough] and this one [Curly flying into the gold mine head first]. Visual reference: the cactus that grabs Larry is a saguaro cactus, indigenous and exclusive to the Sonora Desert of Arizona and northern Mexico.

VERBAL HUMOR: A Stooge first: "Where men are men are men are men are men are men—and they're glad of it". The 'young' Stooges glory in their stupidity. First, Curly thinks 'J-e-r-k' spells 'Jack,' and then they all think "utterly incomprehensible" is a complement. Shortly after Curly says "He don't know I got another fifty" too loudly. Ullman/Collins also offer gallows humor [Moe: "You're leavin' the ends in him!" Larry: "Well, they don't show!"; and Larry: "This ain't gettin' us no place; we'll have to blast." Moe: "Maybe we can pry him out." Larry: "It'll take longer but go ahead."], an insult [Moe: "For two pins I'd bat your brains out." Curly: "I ain't got any pins!" Moe: "You haven't got any brains either!"], internal rhyme [Curly: "It's safe in the safe"], and a Stooge chant ["Gold! Gold! We want gold! Zoot!"]. We heard the boogie-woogie word 'zoot,' which became popular in 1942, for the first time in the previous film ["Lift that barge! Tote that bail! Zoot!."]. Epithet: "marble-head". Mom offering five dollars and then accusing "You would take it!" we heard, ironically, in *3 Dumb Clucks* where Moe said it in front of the Stooges' father. Other variations: Moe: "What's the idea of rollin' over in your sleep?" [*False Alarms*]; Curly: "You ain't got time. We gotta find the gold!" [*False Alarms*]; Curly: "Termites! I think a termite bit me!" [*3 Dumb Clucks*]; and Curly's "Hhmmm! BOOM! Cookoo! Fourth of July!" [*Dizzy Doctors*; *Cash and Carry*].

References: 'I shot an arrow into the air, and where it lands I do not care" is adapted from Longfellow's 'The Arrow and the Song' [1845]. 'William Tell' was the legendary Swiss marksman who shot an apple placed on the head of his son; the legend was further commemorated in Rossini's final opera [1829], the overture of which was used as 'The Lone Ranger' theme song. A 'safety zone' was what today is known as a crosswalk.

OTHER NOTES: The title parodies the ancient proverb 'practice makes perfect'. When Curly flies through the air with the arrow we hear "Whooaah!" for twelve seconds. Both of Curly's long yells [19 seconds total] build, sustain, and conclude appropriately. Curly calculates a huge sum again. In *No Census, No Feeling*, taxes were a small part of the joke, but this time, as in *Healthy, Wealthy and Dumb*, the New Deal taxes are the butt of the joke. 100,000 tons of gold at $35 an ounce is actually $112 billion - less taxes. Monty [often spelled 'Monte'] Collins had minor roles in *Woman Haters* [Mr. Zero], *Three Missing Links* [Director Herbert] and *A Plumbing We Will Go* [Prof. Bilbo]; this the first of six Stooge films he would write. He began his career acting in silent films, including Cecil B. DeMille's *The King of Kings* [1927]. In the 1920s, he was teamed with Vernon Dent to make one-reel comedies for Jules White at Educational Pictures.

Ironically, in real life Curly, the youngest of five Horwitz sons [Irving, Jack, Shemp, Moe], was very close to his loving, but domineering mother. She called him 'Babe,' tried to prevent him from entering show business, and broke up his first marriage. When she saw him on the screen for the first time in *Nertsery Rhymes*, she is reported to have exclaimed, "Moe, you no goodnik! That's your baby brother, Babe, you're smashing. For this I slaved all my life - so my sons should be movie stars! Feh!" [*Curly* 78-79] Jennie Horwitz died in September, 1939 after the Stooges returned from their tour of Great Britain; they were still in New York performing in George White's *Scandals of 1939* and were unable to attend the funeral. Over the next few years Curly became increasingly solemn, often a loner, finding refuge in buying cars, houses and puppies, dating frequently, and marrying several more times.

#62 - WHAT'S THE MATADOR?

Studio: Columbia

Released: April 23, 1942

Running Time: 16"16'"

Credited Production Crew:

Produced & Directed by:	Jules White
Screen Play by:	Jack White & Saul Ward
Story by:	Jack White
Director of Photography:	L. W. O'Connell
Film Editor:	Jerome Thoms

Credited Cast:

Curly Howard	
Larry Fine	
Moe Howard	
Suzanne Kaaren	Dolores
Harry Burns	Jose
Dorothy Appleby	Receptionist

Uncredited Cast:

John Tyrrell	Shamus O'Brien
Don Zelaya	"Good-bye" man
Bert Young	Mexican passerby
Eddie Laughton	telegraph office clerk; bull ring worker
Cy Schindell	bull ring worker

PERSPECTIVE: In this film, the Stooges literally bring their act to Mexico. They refer to themselves as 'The Three Stooges' in their telegram to Mexico City, where the comedy involves Spanish speakers, a Latin temper, and a mock bull fight starring "those loco Americanos comedians, The Three Stooges." The last time they played 'The Three Stooges' was in *A Pain in the Pullman*, which, not coincidentally, was the last film written by Jack White. Both of his scripts portray the Stooges as an unsuccessful song/dance/comedy trio working through a German Jewish/Irish booking agency. In *Pullman* they got a job only because other actors were sick; here in *What's the Matador?* they get a job because they send a fraudulent telegram. In both films getting a gig sends the rest of the comedy into motion - there on an overnight train ride, and here on a bus to Mexico - but the similarities end there. In *Pullman* we see the Stooges rehearsing; here they actually perform their act in public, and while the train ride in the earlier film dead-ended their careers on the backs of galloping steers, here their Mexican performance brings them great success. The reason for this is as usual mostly accident and coincidence, for their arrival in Mexico brings them at first only a tussle with a jealous husband who ends up with the suitcase containing their costumes.

Retrieving their suitcase from a man who has threatened to kill them changes the middle portion of the film into a 'comedy of manners,' a type developed in Restoration England just before 1700 and brought to the screen most famously by Ernst Lubitsch in the 1920s and 1930s. Comedies of manners usually involve bedroom settings, hidden lovers, duplicitous wives, and jealous husbands, all elements of the bedroom scene here. In fact, the viewer will notice very little slapstick by the Stooges in this scene. The comic protagonist is the jealous husband who runs into the wall, puts his head through the door, spinelessly refers to his wife as a "tangerine" and "avocado," gapes at not one, not two, but three different hidden lovers running out the bedroom door, and generally plays the buffoon.

Once the Stooges retrieve their suitcase they become 'The Three Stooges' again and perform in the Plaza de Toros. The audience laughs at their act, and when Moe and Larry jump out of their bull outfit and hide from the real bull, the audience continues to laugh, even if some of it could be at their expense. The audience laughs some more as Curly defeats the bull with his impenetrable iron head, and then they carry off the victorious Curly in a swell of fan appreciation. As Curly

explains to the bull, it took the Stooges three months to get this gig, but now they are a rousing success. They lied to get the gig, lost their luggage, had to deal with a crazed husband and an angry bull. But they persevered, performed, and evoked laughter by unintentionally screwing up the act. They overcame practical roadblocks, succeeded in the comedy of manners, scored in their bullfighting act, and then excelled in an ad-lib struggle. In the context of the film's narrative, this is a complete Stooge comedy triumph.

VISUAL HUMOR: The camera offers some humor of its own when it frames the Stooges' rears in a bull's-eye matte. When they dance their 'Mexico dance,' Curly moves right into the camera, as we saw first in *Punch Drunks*. As in *Three Missing Links* and *Some More of Samoa*, the climax of the film is designed around Curly confronting a large animal; this time he barks him away and butts him into submission. As in *Three Missing Links*, Moe and Larry dress as the fake animal, and when they see the real one, they do a take by hopping. Curly's bull ride contains dummy work, as have the previous two films. When Curly leans on the "locked" door, he takes one of his great falls, reminiscent of the kitchen fall in *No Census, No Feeling* and the missed glove fall in *Calling All Curs*. Gouge variation: Curly: "Have you got new ones?" Moe [lifting two]: "What are these?" Curly: "Those are the old ones." Moe: "They'll do!" [GOUGE]. Other variations: Curly and Larry crashing through the glass door [*Men in Black*], the triple slap from another person, which is the seventh they have received since *Restless Knights*; and Curly's 360-degree turn [*Some More of Samoa*].

VERBAL HUMOR: Much of the verbal humor is ethnic, predominantly at the expense of Mexicans, but with the added mixture of Jewish and Irish names in 'Goldstein, Ginsberg, Rosenberg, & O'Brien' and 'Shamus O'Brien'; the Stooges had made fun of English-speaking Mexicans in *Cookoo Cavaliers* ("Pleased to meet me") but here they use a bilingual pun ("see Esther"/"siesta"), confuse "Hello" and "Good-bye," gesture for forty seconds while the Mexican gives directions in Spanish, and make their newest chant: "Mexico here we come! Gah!" The hot chili powder is appropriate for the Mexican setting as well. Moe makes a presumably sarcastic comment about Mexicans being dishonest ("The door's open. Must be honest people in this country!"), and Mexicans are characterized as cheap ("Money is no object, as long as it's cheap."). One of the names Moe calls a Mexican character, "Tamale," is politically incorrect in the new millennium, but Moe calls his best friends and business associates worse names than that all the time. In that sense, Moe is always politically incorrect. His insult, "I'll bet he eats soup with a knife," could be applied to anyone, but here it seems more mean-spirited. His "There must be honest people in this country" is particularly interesting considering how many con men the Stooges have run into in California. Then again, the lengthy passage in Spanish is insulting to the Stooges: "Go down this street three blocks, turn right and go two more blocks, turn right, cross the square, and turn right. Walk down that street until you find an alley, but keep walking. Go down that street until you find another alley, but don't enter that alley either. Turn right. There you will find a river. Do me a favor: jump into the river and drown yourself!".

Along with his other produce-oriented terms of endearment, Jose offers a flighty: "I am flying, my little tangerine. I am flying too fast!". A Stooge first: Moe: "Haunt that house." Curly: "How many rooms?" Moe: "Seven." Curly: "With bath?". When Curly asks Dolores: "What is it makes me so irresistible to women?" it is hardly his shy aspect. He uses both but at different times. The three-pattern (Curly: "It's phenomenal!" Larry: "It's sensational!" Curly: "It's terrific!" Moe: "It's even mediocre!") derives from *Three Missing Links*. Other variations: "Skip the gutter." [*Pardon My Scotch*]; and Curly: "Hey! What are ya doin' over there when you belong over here?" [*Three Missing Links*].

The genre known as 'comedy of manners' has a long pedigree extending back to Restoration England. Its typical elements - bedroom settings, hidden lovers, duplicitous wives, and jealous husbands - are all found in the bedroom sequences of 1942's *What's the Matador?*. As a result there is very little slapstick by the Stooges in this scene. The comic protagonist is the jealous husband, who runs into the wall, puts his head through the door, and gawks at three different hidden Stooge lovers running out the bedroom door. Harry Burns [1885-1948], who played two dozen ethnic roles in other films, plays the husband - 'Jose.' His wife 'Dolores' is played by Suzanne Kaaren, who also appeared in *Yes, We Have No Bonanza*.

OTHER NOTES: The working title was *Run, Bull, Run*. The film will be refurbished as *Sappy Bull Fighters* (1959) with Joe Besser. Some of the bull-fight footage will be reused in *Stop! Look! and Laugh!*. Writer Jack White returned to Columbia from the service after a 5-year hiatus. He would now stay until 1946, but then he would depart again until 1952. Harry Burns [Jose] often played character roles, recently in Cecil B. DeMille's *Northwest Mounted Police* (1940). Suzanne Kaaren [Dolores] had played in a number of films in the 1930s; this very year she married actor Sidney Blackmer. Eddie Laughton plays two rolls, as he did in *Boobs in Arms*. The Three Stooges do not capitalize their name in the telegram, but generally they cannot spell, or add, for that matter.

#63 - MATRI-PHONY

Studio: Columbia

Released: July 2, 1942

Running Time: 17"10"'

Credited Production Crew:

Produced by:	Del Lord & Hugh McCollum
Directed by:	Harry Edwards
Story & Screen Play by:	Elwood Ullman & Monty Collins
Director of Photography:	George Meehan
Film Editor:	Paul Borofsky

Credited Cast:

Curly Howard	
Larry Fine	
Moe Howard	
Vernon Dent	Emperor Octopus Grabus
Marjorie Deanne	Diana

Uncredited Cast:

Monty Collins	Grabus' assistant
Cy Schindell	guard
Ralph Dunn	guard

PERSPECTIVE: The Stooges have visited imaginary countries like Vulgaria and Moronica, an Egyptian tomb, the colonial *Back to the Woods* and a medieval castle. But they have never gone this far away or this far back in time. 'Erysipelas' is essentially ancient Rome. The tunics, togas, and military costumes look Roman, the names 'Mohicus,' 'Larrycus,' and 'Octopus Grabus' have Latin endings, 'Curly-que' is ungrammatical pig Latin [*Tassels in the Air*], and the imperial governmental system resembles that of ancient Rome. However, since DeMille's *Cleopatra* (1934) and RKO's *The Last Days of Pompeii* (1935), no Hollywood films had been set in ancient Rome, nor would any until MGM's epic *Quo Vadis?* in 1951.

There were two different models for *Matri-Phony*. One was the well-known Rodgers & Hart Broadway musical 'The Boys From Syracuse,' which was set in ancient Syracuse, whence the Greek-sounding 'Erysipelas.' It was made into a film by Universal already in 1940, and it was referred to in *You Nazty Spy!*. The other model was Samuel Goldwyn's *Roman Scandals* (1933) starring Eddie Cantor, whose *Kid Millions* set the modern Egyptian stage for *We Want Our Mummy*. In *Roman Scandals* Cantor plays the wine taster for Emperor Valerius, disguises himself in the women's quarters, and gets poked aplenty with spears, all of which reoccurs here with the Stooges.

Harry Edwards, who directed Harry Langdon and Billy Bevan shorts for Mack Sennett in the 1920s and co-wrote *No Census, No Feeling* and *Some More of Samoa*, directed a number of setting-related gags in *Matri-Phony*: the swinging shop sign, the clay 'cigar,' the large pot, the proclamation on the wall, the weaponry, and the imperial buffet. On the other hand, some of these and several other gags depend on anachronistic ironies for their humor: Larry lighting his clay cigar with a lighter, the emperor wearing glasses, and Curly joking about income taxes. These anachronistic gags use the ancient Greco-Roman setting more as a historical straight man, as it were, than as a subject for humor. Both types of gags require the Greco-Roman setting for their effectiveness.

The plot line – the Stooges help a damsel-in-distress threatened by powerful royalty - resembles that of the first historical Stooge film, *Restless Knights*, and it, too, contains an effective chase scene, although this one is highlighted by the Stooges shaking the head of the unconscious guard, Curly dressing in drag and flirting with the emperor, the buffet scene, and the wine tasting sequence. Ironically, whereas we have seen Curly do battle recently with a large alligator and a bull, in the final buffet and wine-tasting scenes Curly confronts an aggressive little crab who bites Curly on the nose, keeps the emperor from drinking the poison, and then gives Curly the longest CRU-U-U-NCH in Stoogedom. That little crab is even feistier than *Dutiful but Dumb*'s stew-dwelling oyster, no doubt its cinematic ancestor.

VISUAL HUMOR: Stooge firsts here include the crab crunch; shaking the unconscious guard's head; and getting stabbed by a sword shoved through a door. What makes this crab sequence different from the crab sequence in *A Pain in the Pullman* or the eating sequence in *Uncivil Warriors* is that the crab is alive, anxious to fight back, and even capable of spitting out an olive pit, a bit of fine detail. Shaking the unconscious guard's head goes back at least to the 1920s and *Fluttering Hearts*, in which Charley Chase manipulates a store dummy to seduce a (pre-Stan Laurel) Oliver Hardy. As usual, the gag is changed considerably. Although Director Edwards missed a few beats and directed only one other Stooge film, he directed Curly in some new physical movements when he bumps his head in every conceivable way against the sign outside their shop, bumps the top of his head while hiding under the bench, and dances his 'graceful' flutter from the couch to the buffet when Grabus tries to kiss him. Curly also does two 180-degree left-foot spins [*3 Dumb Clucks*] in the final chase sequences.

Edwards experimented with sound effects, successfully for the crab CRU-U-UNCH-ing and the extensive PLINK-ing for every the spear-point and agave-plant jab, less so for the WHISTLE sound effect accompanying the initial gag where Moe sticks the paint brush down Larry's throat, hits the palette on Curly's face, and shoves the clay cigar into Larry's ear. The multiple slapstick session that takes place behind curtain has now become a regu-

In the 1940s, none of the major studios would make a dramatic film set in the ancient world. But Jules White and the Columbia staff were forever reinventing places and periods in which to insert the Stooges. Eddie Cantor's musical farce, *Roman Scandals* (1933), and Universal's filmed version of Rodgers & Hart Broadway musical, *The Boys From Syracuse* (1940), were the most immediate comic predecessors for *Matri-Phony* (1942) – originally called *Roamin' Romans*. Ruling the sickly kingdom of Erysipilas, Emperor Octapus Grabus [Vernon Dent] finds that this alluring woman's bite is worse than her bark.

lar feature; the first was in *Loco Boy Makes Good*. When Moe slaps Curly seven times, the slap is more of a slapping claw and a face rub with the palm. The Stooges flip onto spears at the end of this film as they did onto bayonets at the end of *Dutiful but Dumb*. Other variations: blowing the clay cigar from Larry's ear into Moe's face (*Goofs and Saddles*); playing tic-tac-toe (*Disorder in the Court*); and the squirting pickle (*Violent is the Word for Curly*).

VERBAL HUMOR: A Stooge first is Curly's truism: "Every time you take care of it, I get it!". Another first is the gobble sound Curly makes when hit on the head by the sign. He also reveals a new and different voice when he menacingly says "the back of the drapes. Yeah!" to the Roman guard. Pig Latin (Moe's "Ix-nay. I ut-pay the oad-bray in the ase-vay!") is a *sine qua non* in a film set in a veritable ancient Rome. So are anachronisms ("We used to be bill pasters for Barnum & Bailey!").

Curly's 'Rasbanyshatiyafuchi-yakanikarunji' was first heard in the 1941 feature *Time Out For Rhythm* and will be reprised in *Three Little Pirates*. Grabus' pet names for Curly ("My little sardine, my little halibut") resemble the terms of endearment used by Jose in the previous film; similarly, because Curly dresses in drag Moe delivers the absurd line: "Go on, get sexy.". In *Some More of Samoa* we had 'Vitamin P.D.Q.'; here we have "Vitamins A, B, C, D, E, F, Gee! I like food!". Other variations: "Oh gentlemen!" and "I bet you tell that to all the boys, er, girls." (Horses' Collars); Larry's "It's a royal Mickey!" ('Mikey Finlen in *You Nazty Spy!*); and Curly's "A tarantula!" (*Disorder in the Court*). Epithet: "Turnip-head"... References: 'Erysipelas' is an infectious skin disease, whence "the *rash* emperor Octapus Grabus." Curly's "This will put a pot in every palace" parodies "A chicken in every pot," an old proverb attributed to Henri IV of France, but used as an American presidential campaign promise in 1928. Curly's "10th-century" pot is too early (BC) or too late (AD) for the Roman period. Curly's insult to the Roman guard, "Can I interest you in a new mug?" depends on the contemporary slang term 'mug,' i.e. face.

OTHER NOTES: This fourth release of 1942 is the first film to use the more rapidly paced, 'driving' version of 'Three Blind Mice' as the introductory theme song; it replaces the slower, sliding-violin version but lasts nearly one second longer. This introductory music will be used until the end of the 1944 releases. The final screen has also changed; the Columbia image no longer splits 'THE END,' and the 'driving' theme is reprised. This screen will be used until the comic mask is introduced in *Idiots Deluxe* (1945). The same closing music, with variations, will be used for all the remaining Columbia shorts. The working title of this film was *Roamin' Romans*. Eddie Cantor's *Roman Scandals* has other Stooge connections: its laughing gas scene influenced the one in *Boobs in Arms*; Louise Carver, recently playing the king's hideous sister in *Some More of Samoa*, appeared as a hideous and unwanted slave in *Roman Scandals*; and there is a giant alligator in both *Some More of Samoa* and *Roman Scandals*. Also, scenes filmed with starlets playing beauty contest winners were cut from the final release; this would be in keeping with *Roman Scandals* as well. The emperor's written proclamation may derive from DeMille's *Sign of the Cross*, as did the sign in *Dutiful but Dumb*.

#64 - THREE SMART SAPS

Studio: Columbia

Released: July 30, 1942

Running Time: 16"40'"

Credited Production Crew:

Produced & Directed by:	Jules White
Story & Screen Play by:	Clyde Bruckman
Director of Photography:	Benjamin Kline
Film Editor:	Jerome Thoms

Credited Cast:

Curly Howard	
Larry Fine	
Moe Howard	
Bud Jamison	Moe's first rumba partner
Barbara Slater	Curly's rumba partner
John Tyrrell	Mr. Stevens

Uncredited Cast:

Ruth Skinner	Stella
Julie Gibson	Della
Julie Duncan	Bella
Sally Cairns	dancing partner
Vernon Dent	man with tailor
Eddie Laughton	prison guard
Victor Travers	Justice of the Peace
Lew Davis	card player
Frank Terry	man on the street
Frank Coleman	cop

PERSPECTIVE: This time, the Stooges are indeed "three smart saps," for saps by definition are gullible and trusting. And in a romantic venue, they fall head-over-heels in love. The word "smart" does not often apply to the Stooges, but these three smart saps devote their collective intelligence to acquiring the hands of Stella, Nella, and Bella and actually succeed. Such a success is not unique. In *Cactus Makes Perfect*, Curly created a successful invention which allowed them find their fortune, and all three Stooges best the unintelligent Jose in the comedy of manners portion of *What's the Matador?* Now in *Three Smart Saps* the Stooges have a few more moments of intelligence and cleverness. They outsmart the doorman at the dining hall party, steal another suit, successfully mingle with the guests so they can get their photographs, and escape unharmed.

What makes this comedy particularly striking is all the idiocy that precedes, punctuates, and comments upon these brief forays into intelligence. The Stooges plan to get arrested (*So Long, Mr. Chumps*) by kicking a cop but get their heads bonked instead. They plan to get arrested by throwing rocks through a window, but they knock out Moe instead. Curly 'uses his head' to break that same window but dives through the wrong window. They try to hide behind a half-filled wire trash can and are, not surprisingly, seen. They twice try to enter the jail by knocking the secret knock, but get punched both times. But as happens so often in Stooge films, someone slips up - hires them or gives them a job that they will regret later - and in this case the doorman leaves his post. In falls Curly, literally (uttering the inimitable "Let a guy who knows how to knock knock knick, knack, knyuk, nyuk, nyuk!"), and their brains go to work. In between their serious efforts are silly dances, ripped clothing, and a drunken Larry, but somehow they get the job done.

We all daily walk the delicate line between intelligence and stupidity, oscillating between praising and berating ourselves for our cleverness or lack thereof. Nearly every scene in the film exploits this human trait as comic interplay. After Curly recognizes that "We aren't ordinary people. We're morons," the Stooges think up strategies for rescuing their fiancée's father. Moe thinks up the idea of kicking a cop but Curly beats himself for being a "dumbbell"; Larry thinks up the rock-throwing idea but Moe's head is said to make "a hollow sound." They see iron bars on jail windows and query: "How do they expect anyone to get in?" After stupidly crashing through the prison door Moe compliments Curly by saying "That's usin' your head." Seconds later the pinball ("marble") machine goes CUKOO and hypnotizes them, Curly utters the malapropism "Maybe he's in resolitary refinement," and Curly shoots a camera backwards. The Stooges know themselves, tell themselves, even beat themselves for how unintelligent they are. But despite all this reinforced self doubt their cleverness ultimately triumphs and allows them to win their brides. Good fortune and success come to those who persevere, and no one perseveres more than Stooges who happen to be smart saps in love.

VISUAL HUMOR: The door to the prison opens up opportunities for the Stooges just as did the door to Dolores' house in *What's the Matador?*. Director Jules White gives the Stooges plenty of time to display their considerable physical talents. The exit from their fiancée's house is extended with two attempted hair pull variations and Curly crashing into the door jamb. When Curly beats himself it sets up an extended slapstick exchange with Moe before they waltz off together face to face. The dance sequence lingers for Curly's multifarious steps, and then the scenes near the curtain give an inebriated Larry and an amorous Curly ample opportunity to play off each other, culminating in Curly's slipping down the chair and saying the memorable "Can't ya see I'm fallin' for ya?!" The final scene lingers again for Curly, but the single-camera view, the dark background, the dearth of dialogue, and a persistent battering by thrown objects limit Curly to creating reactions rather than actions. The Stooges always react well, but actions speak louder (and funnier) than reactions. Stooge firsts: the dancing partner barking at Curly before Curly barks at her; and throwing shoes (and rice) to celebrate a wedding. The unbreakable glass falls into the 'gadget' category, as does the pinball machine which drives them 'cuckoo'; pinball machines became popular during the Depression years (1932/33). Another variation: Curly responding literally to Moe's "Use your head" (*3 Dumb Clucks*).

VERBAL HUMOR: The wedding song is a Stooge first, although Curly has been saying "Swing it!" since *Violent is the Word for Curly*. Another Stooge first: with an eggshell on his nose, Curly imitates Jimmy Durante ("I got a million of 'em. Am I mortified!"); the Stooges worked with Durante in *Hollywood Party, Meet the Baron*, and *Start Cheering*. The script also offers a Stooge insult (Moe: "'T. B.'...Two Bellies"), Larry at his subtle best ("Hmm! Spirits!"), and Moe making his most elaborate noun into a verb ("I'll Venus de Milo you!"). Three word plays depend on contemporary developments. The military build up for World War II inspired two of them (Moe: "I said right face!" Curly: "This is my right face!"; Woman: "Do you feel a draft" Moe: "No. I was exempted."), and a newly popular dance inspired the other (Woman: "Do you rumba?" Curly: "Only when I take bicarbonate!"); the Stooges began making rumba references in 1941. Moe 's "Ya gotta have a snoot suit" plays on the 'Zoot suit' popular in 1942 and is the third reference we have heard to the word "zoot" (*Loco Boy Makes Good*; *Cactus Makes Perfect*). Curly's extraordinary verbal transition ("Let a guy who knows how to knock knock knick, knack, knyuck, nyuck, nyuck") morphs one word into another as in "Ohhhll*look*!". Other variations: Curly's "I don't care!" and "Listen you. " (*Loco Boy Makes Good*); GOBBLE-GOBBLE (*Matri-Phony*); "Say somethin'." "I hate you!" (*Rockin' Thru the Rockies*); "Are you dancing?" "Are you asking?" (*Hoi Polloi*); three rhyming female names (*The Sitter Downers*); and "My father died dancing on the end of a rope!" (*An Ache in Every Stake*).

OTHER NOTES: The working title was *Father's in Jail Again*. In that the Stooges prepare for marriage at the conclusion of this film, it begins a Stooge family trilogy, with Stooge 'children' appearing in the next two films. Even though these are the very people who are going to be caught and put in prison, the people at the party laugh at the Stooges and particularly at Curly. Moe and Larry starred in a non-extant MGM short, *Jailbirds of Paradise* (1934) which took place in a luxurious prison. Notice here the federal prison pennants from 'Sing Sing,' 'Joliet,' and 'Alcatraz'. This is John Tyrrell's first credited appearance despite fine roles as the judge in *A Plumbing We Will Go*, B. O. Davis in *So Long, Mr. Chumps*, and many others. Bud Jamison had received credit in *Three Sappy People*. What was supposed to happen with that prison chain belt and key?

Writer Clyde Bruckman drew from Harold Lloyd's *The Freshman* (1925) for the dancing sequence in *Three Smart Saps* (1942). But Curly used to lose sleeves regularly as part of the band conductor act he performed for Orville Knapp in 1932, before he joined Moe, Larry, and Ted Healy in 1933.

#65 - EVEN AS IOU

Studio: Columbia

Released: September 18, 1942

Running Time: 15"37'"

Credited Production Crew:

Produced by:	Del Lord & Hugh McCollum
Directed by:	Del Lord
Story & Screen Play by:	Felix Adler
Director of Photography:	L. W. O'Connell
Film Editor:	Paul Borofsky

Credited Cast:

Curly Howard	
Larry Fine	
Moe Howard	
Ruth Skinner	dispossessed mother
Stanley Blystone	ventriloquist con man

Uncredited Cast:

Wheaton Chambers	con man
Vernon Dent	driver
Bud Jamison	policeman
Charles 'Heine' Conklin	turnstile guard
Jack Gardner	doctor
Billy Bletcher	voice of Seabiscuit
Bert Young	winners window attendant

PERSPECTIVE: Animals have appeared in Stooge films with increasing frequency since the pests of *Ants in the Pantry*. But even more so than the magician's coat in *Loco Boy Makes Good*, *Even As IOU* is littered with a menagerie: a race horse, a family of goats, a large fish, a hungry cat, a wooden dog, a wooden fish, a piggy bank, Sea Basket the Wonder Horse and a talking pony, not to mention a human child. Such an assortment of pedigreed, game, domestic, barnyard, manufactured (and human) animals is unheard of in a Stooge film and will hardly be seen again. Comedians have always been wary of co-starring with animals and children, who tend to upstage the adults and evoke a pathos counterbalancing the comic effect. But in this experimental film Del Lord and Felix Adler substitute the multiple animal encounters for the Stooges' more customary encounters with tools, and drive the narrative, albeit in spurts, with the noble goal of helping a poor child, as in the Depression-era classic *Cash and Carry*.

The narrative development moves smoothly from the opening horse-racing scenario, which, as ever, the Stooges screw up, so they get chased into their encounter with the child, which in turn brings about the sequences with the goats, fishes, cat, and dog. When Curly steals the child's piggy bank, it takes the final third of the film to the race track where the Stooges encounter the race horse and the conmen, and this leads to a final surprise - Curly giving birth to a pony! Stooge films only rarely conclude with final surprises (usually the climax terminates in one last blunder), but throughout his twenty-three year Stooge career Felix Adler excelled at developing thematic concepts, and here his grand concept is motherhood, that is, bringing things to life. Earlier in the film Curly brought a clothing dummy to life by attaching it to a policeman, another came to life as a fugitive, a fake house front was brought to life by setting up a home inside it, a sousaphone was brought to life by blowing into it, a wooden fish was brought to life by cooking and 'eating' it, a wooden dog was brought to life when Curly offered to feed it, and an unconscious Curly was brought to life when Moe brought a doll to life by leaning on it, so *Even As IOU* depends on not only animals and a child for its comedy but also a strange biology that allows Curly to give birth to a talking pony.

The secret? Vitamin Z, a magical, hitherto unknown panacea. To modern viewers this may seem a mere throw-away gag, but the idea of using synthetic vitamins as dietary supplements was innovative and exciting in the early 1940s, replacing the dreaded Castor Oil of earlier generations. The first Stooge references to vitamins appear in 1941's *Some More of Samoa* (the growth 'Vitamin P.D.Q.') and 1942's *Matri-Phony* (Curly: "Vitamins A, B, C, D, E, F, & G-ee I like food!"), and with good reason: it was just the year before, 1940, that the National Research Council of the National Academy of Sciences had begun issuing its 'Recommended Dietary Allowances' (RDA) of vitamins and nutrients. This was new science, but little did anyone know vitamins would inspire the birth of an equine Stooge child.

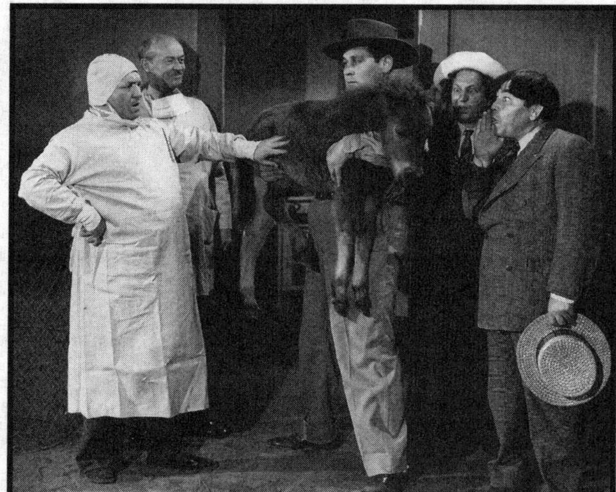

VISUAL HUMOR: Because the narrative is of such a different concept, there is a noticeable diminution of inter-Stooge slapstick from the immediately previous films, but two sight gag extravaganzas (Curly being hit in the head by a speeding car; the cop dragging the dummy alongside) help take its place. A Stooge first: swallowing the horse pill. The 'ma-ma' doll gag, another Stooge first, had been used recently in Laurel & Hardy's *Saps at Sea* (1940). The dummy-coming-to-life was used in Vitaphone's *I Scream* (1934).

A fine variation of the rhythmic snoring introduced in *Hoi Polloi* is the Stooges snoring in rhythm with the horse - a snoring quartet. The goat butt derives from the bull sequence in *What's the Matador?*. Other variations: confusing a cop for a dummy (*A Plumbing We Will Go*); appearing in the open house-front door one head over the other (*Horses' Collars*); slapstick behind the house-front which is heard but not seen (*Dizzy Doctors*); Curly appearing separately after a chase (*Some More of Samoa*); Curly running around the ticket-betting windows (*From Nurse to Worse*); and Moe turning his head to Larry, who turns his head to Curly, who turns his head, and doing it in the reverse order, all with a ratchet sound effect (*Uncivil Warriors*).

VERBAL HUMOR: Audible humor becomes dominant in the domestic sequences: Curly fooling with the 'bazoony,' the ratchet sound accompanying sequentially turning Stooge necks, the child bleating like a goat, Curly playing the 'scales' of the fish, and the doll saying "mama." This lays the path to different sorts of sounds later in the film: the ventriloquist's voice for the horse ("I beat Filly Mignon in the Porterhouse stakes!") and the voice for Curly's pony child. As in the previous film, we hear Curly use new accents and speech patterns when he tells the policeman, "Now I've got to go!" and when he says to Moe at the door: "Pardon me, but I'm working my way through college—". A Stooge first: the delay pattern in the banter about betting the child's money (Moe: "Why you cheap crook - stealin' a baby's bank!" Curly: "It's only a lend-lease. I figured I'd bet on a 50-1 shot and double the baby's money." Moe: "Why you imbecile! Why don't you pick a 100-1 shot and triple it?!". A Moe malapropism: "A sort of a del-eye-cacy". The word "sap" was used in two different scenes; it was used for the first time in the title of the previous film.

When Curly hugs the pony and cooks the wooden fish he uses the giggle-laugh he has been employing in the last few films; we first heard it when he fell on the soap for the last time in *Loco Boy Makes Good*. The doll gag gives birth to the new variation on "Say somethin'". Other variations: "press, press, pull!" (*Three Little Beers*);the horses 'Bicarbonate' (*Soup to Nuts*; *Three Smart Saps*) and 'Nip-N-Tuck' (*Uncivil Warriors*); and Moe: "What kind of fish you say this was?" Larry: "Saw." Curly: "See? Saw." Moe [picking up a saw]: "Saw!" Curly: "See?" (*Oily to Bed, Oily to Rise*).

New Deal references: 'An FBI loan' is Stooge ignorance for an FHA [Federal Housing Administration] loan. Curly's "It's only a lend-lease" refers to the hotly debated Lend-lease Law passed by Congress in March, 1941, which authorized the US to 'Send Guns, Not Sons' to our allies overseas to fight the Axis powers. Other references: the milk gag (Moe: "Jersey?" Curly: "No. New York!") refers to Jersey cows. 'Seabasket' is a parody of Seabiscuit, for which see *From Nurse to Worse*. Curly's phone call ("Give me Ripley - yeah, believe it or not!") refers to the newspaper feature 'Ripley's Believe It or Not,' nationally syndicated in 1929. 'Filly [filet] Mignon' and 'Porterhouse' are both cuts of steak. And Larry's "I wouldn't have him as a gift" refers to the old proverb about "looking a gift horse in the mouth" which he rephrased as "Never look a gift horse in the puss" in *Oily to Bed, Oily to Rise*.

OTHER NOTES: The title screen does not use periods after the letters of 'IOU'. Billy Bletcher, who supplied the voice of Seabiscuit, had a long history in comic films, from Mack Sennett's Keystone Cops (with Del Lord) and Hal Roach's 'Our Gang' comedies (as Spanky's father) to Wheeler & Woolsey's *Diplomaniacs*. He also provided the voice for the Big Bad Wolf in Disney's *Three Little Pigs* (1933). The previous film, *Three Smart Saps*, ended with the Stooges getting married, and now they have a 'child.' The next film, featuring the Stooges as parents, will be the third film of a domestic trilogy. The movie poster partially visible in the background of the tuba sequence is for Columbia's *The Girl Friend* (1935), starring Ann Sothern (*Swing Parade of 1946*) and written by Benny Rubin, later an actor in several Stooge shorts of the 1950s. A number of animals will appear in two subsequent Stooge shorts - *The Yoke's on Me* and *Sweet and Hot*.

#66 - SOCK-A-BYE BABY

Studio: Columbia

Released: November 13, 1942

Running Time: 17"45'"

Credited Production Crew:

Produced & Directed by:	Jules White
Story & Screen Play by :	Clyde Bruckman
Director of Photography:	Benjamin Kline
Film Editor:	Jerome Thoms

Credited Cast:

Curly Howard
Larry Fine
Moe Howard

Uncredited Cast:

Bud Jamison	policeman
Julie Gibson	Mrs Collins
Clarence Straight	Mr. Collins
Baby Joyce Gardner	Jimmy
Dudley Dickerson	road worker

PERSPECTIVE: *Sock-A-Bye Baby* revives the Columbia scenario in which the protagonists take care of an abandoned baby. It was first filmed by Sidney & Murray in *Ten Baby Fingers* (1934) and refurbished by Charley Chase, Al Giebler, and Elwood Ullman as the Stooges' *Mutts to You* (1938). *Sock-A-Bye Baby* is therefore of particular interest as the first remake of a previous Stooge film, especially since there will be so many refurbishings in the Shemp and Joe eras. In most of these the plot stays the same while the gag scenarios are changed. In this film, too, the plot resembles that of *Mutts to You*: the baby is left on a doorstep because his parents are quarreling; the Stooges find him and resign themselves to parenthood; they bungle their attempts at providing the infant's basic needs; they learn the child has been kidnapped, are discovered by the police, and are chased; and in the end the baby is returned to its parents, who are reconciled. The gag scenarios are different: the dog-cleaning gadgetry, which consumed large portions of Charley Chase's *Mutts to You*, as well as the suspicious landlord sequences are absent, and in their places are the feeding and diapering scenes. The police encounter is transformed from a discovered-disguise scenario to slapstick hide-and-seek, and the chase scene is expanded from a laundry hamper on an urban sidewalk to a mechanized tent-mobile on a rural road.

During this period, producer Jules White seems to have had Stooge domestic situations on his mind. *Sock-A-Bye Baby* appears to be a logical extension of the previous film, *Even As IOU*, in which the Stooges set up a make-shift home and then Curly, through the magic of Vitamin Z, has a child, albeit a pony. It is as if we have the pregnancy and delivery of a Stooge child in one film and its nurturing in the next. In *Three Smart Saps*, the film immediately preceding *Even As IOU*, the Stooges earned the right to marry their wives and then finished the film leaving for their honeymoon, so *Three Smart Saps, Even As IOU*, and *Sock-A-Bye Baby* form a unique domestic trilogy of films which explore Stooge courtship, marriage, childbirth, and parenting.

Bringing up a child presents Stooges with a quintessential comical problem: being ignorant Stooges themselves, how do they provide for and relate to an ignorant child? They buy foods more befitting a cocktail party (celery, radishes, artichokes, herring, Limburger, bicarbonate, beer, and nipples), and pay for their mistake when the infant uses the artichokes and olive pits as comic props while Curly misuses the celery, beer, and nipples. Having an infant throw food in Moe's face means there can be no slapstick retort, no verbal insults to accompany it, and none of that impeccable Stooge timing that carries so much of their comedy. This temporary shift in comic style continues what we saw in the previous film where there was a relative lack of inter-Stooge slapstick. They have been too busy with children and animals to pay attention to each other. Such is the way of family men, and 1942 in general was a year of sentimentality in films (*Bambi, Mrs. Miniver, Pride of the Yankees, Yankee Doodle Dandy, Now, Voyager*). But the United States has now entered the World War, and in the 1943 releases the war effort is going to call upon the Stooges' triadic services and redirect their comedies.

VISUAL HUMOR: Despite the relative absence of inter-Stooge slapstick, there are fine moments. The scene in which Curly scrunches Moe's face into their truck's horn just as they are trying to keep quiet is well choreographed, as is the sequence in which Moe forces out Curly's tongue with his tie and then grabs it. Probably the most unexpected sight gag, and a Stooge first, is the out-of-control ironing board sequence, where a cop sneaks into the kitchen, pulls a closet open, and out comes Larry [in fast motion] on the folding ironing board which opens onto the policeman's head - twice. Another first: hanging celery up to dry. The tent-mobile is one of their more elaborate vehicles, recalling the gurney sailboat in *Dizzy Doctors* and the prairie schooner in *Rockin' Thru the Rockies*. Much of the final chase sequence writer Clyde Bruckman adapted from Harold Lloyd's *Professor Beware* (1938). Other variations: Larry sending the scissors into Moe's rear, and Moe grabbing Larry's nose and Curly's ear with the scissors (*Slippery Silks*); spitting out an olive pit (*Matri-phony*); the Stooges all crying at once, and Curly's hand wave with a down-thrust (*So Long,*

Mr. Chumps]; Larry getting flour all over his face [the facial powder in *Three Sappy People*]; and hiding in haystacks [*Goofs and Saddles*].

VERBAL HUMOR: This is the first Stooge film offering evidence that the US had already entered World War II. Filmed after December 7, 1941, the dialogue contains a number of phrases relative to the war effort: "Ptoo on the Japanese," "Nazi onion," "eternal triangle," and "fit for an airplane worker." The 'eternal triangle' actually dates from 1907 [anonymous]; 'The Japanese Sandman,' was a Richard Whiting/Raymond Egan song written in 1920. A plot-related Stooge insult: "When you were born you were delivered by a buzzard!". The Stooges sleep in a 'choo-choo' train-like rhythm in the opening of the film, and later they have a different method; both these follow upon the snoring quartet of the previous film.

The 'pin/scissors' routine derives from the "Cotton!" routine in *Men in Black* and *Some More of Samoa*. For Moe's vitamin gag ("Now you're gettin' your vitamins, starch, vegetables, hypochondriacs"), see *Even As IOU*. Curly's 'artichoke' variations ("a smarty-coke, a party-smoke, a okey-doke, this feathered apple") recall his "A lizard, I mean a blizzard, an avalanch-ee" in *Rockin' Thru the Rockies*. Other variations: Moe's "Zip! Boom! Cuckoo!" [*Cash and Carry*]; Moe's chant about the food offerings [the street-vending scene in *Cuckoo Cavaliers*]; Moe's "For once you're showing a slight trace of brains!" [*Horses' Collars*]; Larry's "6 7/8" [*You Nazty Spy!*]; and Moe's "A perfect 36!" [*A Plumbing We Will Go*]. Epithets: "bunion-head" and "grape-head."

OTHER NOTES: The release title parodies the lullaby 'Rock-a-Bye Baby.' The working title was *Their First Baby*. As in *Nutty but Nice*, the Stooges have an inability to make kids laugh. This is an utter paradox when compared to their live act which for decades delighted thousands upon thousands of children. The Stooges own a refrigerator now instead of delivering ice for an ice box, as in *An Ache in Every Stake*; the home refrigerator had become popular already in the 1920s. For once a Stooge does his math correctly when Larry realizes: "Oh I forgot! I'm one-third of a father!". Some of the baby-care footage will be reused in *Stop! Look! and Laugh!*.

1942 produced such sentimental films as *Bambi*, *Mrs. Miniver* and *Now, Voyager*. *Sock-A-Bye Baby* is the third in a series of three family-oriented Stooge films which closed out the 1942 releases. The Stooges were married in *Three Smart Saps* and had a 'child' in *Even As IOU*. Now *Sock-A-Bye Baby* revives the old Columbia scenario in which the protagonists take care of an abandoned baby, previously refurbished by Charley Chase, Al Giebler, & Elwood Ullman as the Stooges' *Mutts to You* [1938]. Amidst the ineptitude and quarreling, Stoogedom allows for sentimentality, too.

1943

They Stooge to Conga • Dizzy Detectives • Spook Louder

Back From the Front • Three Little Twirps • Higher Than a Kite

"I Can Hardly Wait" • Dizzy Pilots • Phony Express • A Gem of a Jam

#67 - THEY STOOGE TO CONGA

Studio: Columbia

Released: January 1, 1943

Running Time: 15"32'"

Credited Production Crew:

Produced by:	Del Lord & Hugh McCollum
Directed by:	Del Lord
Story & Screen Play by:	Elwood Ullman & Monty Collins
Director of Photography:	George Meehan
Film Editor:	Paul Borofsky
Art Director:	Carl Anderson

Credited Cast:

Curly Howard
Larry Fine
Moe Howard

Uncredited Cast:

Vernon Dent	Nazi spy
Dudley Dickerson	chef
Lloyd Bridges	phone caller
Julie Duncan	phone caller
John Tyrrell	phone caller
Stanley Brown	pilot

PERSPECTIVE: This first 1943 release is the third Stooge film involving World War II. The Stooges play repairmen who obliterate a 'rats nest' of Axis spies, a dramatic shift from 1942's closing trilogy of domestic films. But as we saw in the previous film in phrases like "Ptoo on the Japanese," "a Nazi onion," and "fit for an airplane worker," the United States has by this time officially declared war on Germany and Japan after the attack on Pearl Harbor. With recruiting posters visible on the back wall of the opening scene, *They Stooge to Conga* was the first Stooge film to focus specifically on the US war effort. It moves beyond mere parodies of Nazi "papa-ganda" (*You Nazty Spy!*) and appeasement conferences (*I'll Never Heil Again*), so no longer do the Stooges impersonate Axis leaders. Now they play Stateside patriots in a politically sweet revenge comedy which interrupts Axis communications, blows up their submarine, and bonks spies on the head, all the while making fun of Germans and Japanese.

The Stooges do not abandon their handyman tradition in favor of their anti-espionage activity. They remain bungling tradesmen who bring mass destruction to a house and perform outrageous slapstick routines. In fact, commentators have often decried the boot-spike incident in this film as violent and tasteless. We observed in *Half-Shot Shooters* that there was a fine line between comic slapstick and sadistic violence, so some think the spike sticking into Moe's scalp, eye, and ear crosses that line. Unlike the arm-breaking and pistol detonation scenes in *Half-Shot Shooters*, though, the spike has no lasting effect. Moe simply pulls it out of his scalp (THWUMP), bites Curly's foot, shoe and all, and then gets even by scorching Curly's rear with a flame-throwing acetylene torch. A little later Curly electrocutes himself, and the finale sees explosives going off in a room with six people in it. While all these violent acts are, well, violent, we should remember that 1942 and 1943 were particularly demoralizing war years. Pearl Harbor produced 2403 American casualties, and it was not until the Pacific battle of Midway in June, 1942; Allied victories in North Africa in the fall of 1942; and the German surrender at Stalingrad in February, 1943 that an Allied victory looked likely. Compared with the prospect of global subjugation by aggressive, evil tyrants, what was a harmless spike in the eye of a civilian Stooge?

Similarly, the idea of a German U-boat attacking an American harbor was not so preposterous in early 1943. Throughout 1942 German U-boats had been sinking freighters carrying millions of tons of US cargo in the Atlantic, and it was not until later in 1943 that they were neutralized. Declassified government documents show that the FBI even thwarted at least one U-boat incursion into the St. Lawrence Seaway. The Stooges are heroes here. Just as they achieved personal successes recently in *Loco Boy Makes Good* and *Three Smart Saps*, now they succeed in a great political triumph and save our harbors. This is one of the few times the Stooges get to punish someone else when the film fades to black.

VISUAL HUMOR: The outrageous slapstick here makes up for the relative absence of slapstick in the previous few films. Their tools are bigger and meaner than ever, and now they add electrocution to the mix. New tools include the huge wire wrench, Curly's climbing spike, an acetylene torch, and a belt sander, and the chef gets a waffle iron on his rear. The frequency is intense as well. Curly hits Moe twenty times with a hammer, Moe hits Curly four times with a small board, and the Axis spies get myriad bonks in the final scene. Stooge firsts: ripping wires out through plaster and wall paper; and the ominous woman at the entrance of the spy house. The mind reader is a new gag as well. Yanking Moe through the wall is a fine extension of a similar sequence in *Cash and Carry*. Curly looks at and speaks to the camera when he finds a second wire, as in *So Long, Mr. Chumps*. Other variations: going through a door blocked by Larry's sandwich board (*Saved By the Belle; Soup to Nuts*); Curly pulling the radio (the springing pickax in *A Plumbing We Will Go*); Curly as a conductor of electricity (*Nutty but Nice*); Moe playing Hitler and a poster come to life (*You Nazty Spy!; I'll Never Heil Again*); Moe street hawking (*Cookoo Cavaliers*); and Moe punching with his left hand while holding his right in pain (*No Census, No Feeling*).

VERBAL HUMOR: Insults to Hitler and the Nazis abound ("Sabatoogees! Column Fives" [spies], "rogue's gallery," "Schicklgruber" [Hitler's mother's name], Moe's fake German, and use of the actual German words *Schweinhund*, *Dumbkopf*, and *Dumbköpfe* (the plural used by the U-boat commander). As for the Japanese, the Japanese officer says "So!" several times, the Nazi uses it once, and Larry uses it once; then the Japanese officer is quickly depicted as a coward (Nazi: "If we see them we shoot them between the eyes!" Japanese Officer: "No! In the back!").

Writers Elwood Ullman and Monty Collins use radio for the most elaborate set (and prop) joke of the film blended with slapstick (Announcer: "The $64 Dollar Question!" Moe (behind the radio): "Why can't a chicken lay a loaf of bread?" Curly: "She ain't got the crust!" Moe: "You win!" Curly: "Gimme! Gimme!" [CLANG] Curly pulls the radio wire so far it snaps back into Moe's face, so Moe approaches Curly with the radio. Curly: "Short wave?" Moe: "No. Permanent!" He smashes it over Curly's head and turns his eyes and nose like dials.). The "short wave...permanent" gag derives (without slapstick) from *Gold Diggers of 1935*. Curly made an 'FBI' joke ("an F.B.I. loan") in *Even As IOU*; here he has another (Nazi: "F.B.I., eh?" Curly: "No! I.B. Curly!"). We have heard about dandruff (*Dizzy Doctors*) and termites (*Nutty but Nice*), but here Curly thinks Moe is "A termite with dandruff!". A Stooge motto/slogan is replaced here with the simple sung phrase "And that ain't all". Other variations: the three-pattern Moe: "Can we fix it! Larry: "Can we fix it!" Curly: "Can we?" (*An Ache in Every Stake*); "Zoot" (*Loco Boy Makes Good*); "You know I get dizzy in high places!" Moe: "You're dizzy in low places!" ("You were born dizzy" in *All the World's a Stooge*); and "Hello, Ma! Hello, Pa! It was a great fight!" (*Ants in the Pantry*).

References: 'Fifth Column,' sympathizers and supporters of resistance against the Axis tyranny, was an expression left over from the Spanish Civil War and applied to WW II espionage and sabotage as well. The quiz show Curly wants to listen to on the radio (*Healthy, Wealthy and Dumb*) is *The Lone Ranger*, which ran for 22 years from 1933 to 1954; there was a previous reference to 'The Lone Ranger' in *Yes, We Have No Bonanza*. Instead Curly hears *The $64 Question*, radio's predecessor to television's more lucrative *The $64,000 Question*.

OTHER NOTES: The title parodies a well-known Eighteenth-century stage comedy, *She Stoops to Conquer* (1773), by Oliver Goldsmith; the 'conga' was a form of rumba, for which see on *Time Out For Rhythm*. This first release of 1943 is the first Stooge film to credit an art director. Lloyd Bridges, who would have a long career in film and television and father of actors Jeff and Beau Bridges, plays the second frustrated caller ("Operator! Operator! What's the matter?"). The montage of operators, callers, and phone switches is a different method of plot exegesis for a Stooge film. The submarine footage is from *Three Little Sew and Sews* (1939). That was another film in which the Stooges played unlikely military heroes, a narrative concept developed already in *Uncivil Warriors*. Jules White was the Stooge director most often accused of using excessively violent gags, but this film is directed by Del Lord and produced by Lord and Hugh McCollum, not White. For a discussion of the violence, see *Okuda* 24-25. The radio program *The $64 Question*, was originally titled *Take It Or Leave It*, debuting on CBS in 1940.

#68 - DIZZY DETECTIVES

Studio: Columbia

Released: February 5, 1943

Running Time: 18"32'"

Credited Production Crew:

Produced & Directed by:	Jules White
Story & Screen Play by:	Felix Adler
Director of Photography:	Benjamin Kline
Film Editor:	Jerome Thoms
Art Director:	Carl Anderson

Credited Cast:

Curly Howard
Larry Fine
Moe Howard

Uncredited Cast:

John Tyrrell	Mr. Dill
Bud Jamison	Police Commissioner
Lynton Brent	Bonzo's handler
Dick Jensen	crook

PERSPECTIVE: *Dizzy Detectives* opens with the classic door-installation segment from *Pardon My Scotch*, even if carpentry has nothing to do with the rest of the plot; then again, carpentry had nothing to do with the Scotch-making in the original either. But reusing older material is becoming more common recently: the previous film, *They Stooge to Conga*, contained submarine footage from *Three Little Sew and Sews*, and the film before that, *Sock-A-Bye Baby*, readapted the accidental kidnapping concept from *Mutts to You*. Reuse of old footage and scenarios will increasingly become an integral part of Stooge films, particularly in the 1950s, but we of the television era should remember that movie theater audiences in the winter of 1943 would not have seen this carpentry segment since its original release eight years earlier, if at all.

There are few Stooge films more widely appreciated than this one. After opening with one of their best tradesmen routines, the ensuing police station scene offers some clear plot exposition while Curly makes his own background music by noisily cracking and eating walnut shells and drinking a glass of water. Larry concludes the sequence with one of his most memorable lines ("That Dill sure has the chief in a pickle!"), and then all three Stooges perform one of their best phone bits. They spend most of the final eleven minutes of the film being afraid, a comical emotion the Stooges have not had the opportunity to explore for any length since their first 'scare comedy,' *We Want Our Mummy* (1939). And this is one of their best early scare comedies. Far from being confined to mere reaction, the Stooges are proactive: they stay close together, bump into each other, turn sharp corners and jump into each other's arms. Fear in Stooge films establishes quiet anticipation followed by sudden bursts, as we see in the cat-tail/rocker sequence where Curly murmurs assurances to himself when fearful and then explodes when frightened, where Moe acts tough ("A dummy can't hurt ya!") but switches to transparent bravado ("I'll lead the way...Go ahead!"), and where Larry turns suspicion ("Say, for a dummy she sure gets around!") into excitement ("That's no chimp, ya' chump! That's a gorilla!"). In this particular film fear even gives Larry a second verbal gem when Curly reports that he was clawed by a woman. Larry [straightening his tie] smiles and says: "Is that bad?"

In the finale the fear of the unknown develops into a struggle of Good over Evil, and the weapon of Good turns out to be Curly's head-butt, which he has perfected recently. Last year he bested a bull and a goat, and now he is called upon to head-butt human foes. Needing no cheese or tassel stimulus to get him revved up, he triumphs over human criminals and a huge animal much as he emerged triumphant over the Axis spies in the previous film. But fear not. Curly has not ceased being a Stooge or become entirely competent: he almost cuts his own head off in the guillotine, knocks out Larry and Moe, takes ten blows to the chin and another to the belly, and ultimately blows up the entire antique shop they were supposed to be saving from a mere burglary.

VISUAL HUMOR: A sound effect has been added where there was none in *Pardon My Scotch*. When the Stooges all say "Make it six inches," Larry bumps his elbow into Curly's belly [POUND]. Stooge firsts: the use of a guillotine; hiding in a large box; and the wrench bouncing off a tire hanging on the wall. A unique and indescribable Curly face appears when Moe puts the clothes pin on his tongue; the Stooges first used a clothes pin as a comic prop in *Cookoo Cavaliers*. The use of fast motion when Bonzo's handler [Lynton Brent] punches Curly ten times establishes visually a frustration so intense it inspires Curly to rev up and use his two most extreme fighting skills, head-butting [*Restless Knights*; *Boobs in Arms*] and mule-kicking [*Back to the Woods*]. The nitro-glycerin explosion parallels the final explosion in the previous film.

Moe acting tough but then pushing the others ahead was originally a Ted Healy gag which we saw in *Beer and Pretzels*. A frightened Moe and Larry both jump into Curly's arms; we saw Larry alone jump into Moe's arms in *Oily to Bed, Oily to Rise*. Larry's thinking Curly is beheaded recalls the wife who thought the Stooges were amputating her husband's legs in *Some More of Samoa*. The ape opening the door while Curly searches for the key varies the door opening gags in

What's the Matador? and *Three Smart Saps*. Other variations: the 'chicken-with-its-head-cut-off' (*Movie Maniacs*); holding a finger like a gun in the pocket (*Time Out for Rhythm*); Curly shaking a loaded gun in Moe's face, and Curly making a muscle and pointing to it (*Grips, Grunts and Groans*); backing into a sword (*Matri-Phony*); hitting the wrong guy in a rolling tussle (*Three Little Sew and Sews*); Curly's 180-degree turn (*3 Dumb Clucks*); the cat tail under the rocker (the curling monkey tail in *A Pain in the Pullman*; the curling dog tail in *Calling All Curs*); and Curly swallowing his cigar (the opposite of Graves swallowing the combination to the safe and putting the lit cigar in his pocket in *Men in Black*). The gorilla roar at end of the film (like the pony in *Even as IOU*) appropriately deflates the Stooge victory, as is necessary to close the film.

VERBAL HUMOR: Felix Adler's verbal wit is especially important for scary scenes. He delineates Moe's transparent bravado ("I'll lead the way - Go ahead!"; "Don't be scared! Don't be scared!...Just run!"; "That woman's a dummy like you!...a dummy can't hurt ya!"), Larry's explosiveness ("That's no chimp, ya' chump! That's a gorilla!"), Curly's ignorance ("It's real! A real 'chimanee-panzee'!"; Moe: "There's somethin' rotten in Denmark and we're gonna find it!" Curly: "Oh boy! We're goin' to Denmark!"), childlike fear ("I'm not afraid...Babies are afraid...I'm not a baby."), and his own false bravado ("Remember my big toe? [snapping his fingers] Shot off!...Almost."; Moe: "You stand guard while we frisk the joint!" Curly: "Me?!" Moe: "You!" Curly [meekly]: "Me."). Adler makes Curly's speech in the guillotine a Cartesian self-discovery, a comical-philosophical awakening: "I don't want to be dead! There's no future in it...How can I be dead: I'm talkin'? That's a coincidence.".

Adler, as always, includes plot-related gags and insults (Dill: "This ape man is making a monkey of the police department." Curly: "That ox can't call me a monkey!" Moe: "Shut up, ya' baboon!"), and enhances several physical gags with verbal exchanges (Moe: "Next time you handle a gun shoot yourself in the head." Curly: "I'll make a note of it!...How do you spell 'head'?" Moe: "B-O-N-E! 'Head.'" [Moe bonks him with the gun] Curly: "Oh! Oh! Oh! Ohh-*look*!" [The pistol butt is crushed]) and punchlines ([After Curly's 10-punch face-pounding]: "Wait a minute! This is gettin' monotonous! [The crook slugs him in the belly.] That's different!" [cf. "That's not the same...*That's* the same!" in *Some More of Samoa*]). The Stooges have been doing phone gags since their Healy days and *Men in Black*, but here we get a triadic "Hello" (*Some More of Samoa*) as well as a thrown phone. Moe's "I'll lead the way - Go ahead!" recalls his "Tell him a few syllables" in *The Sitter Downers*. Other variations: Curly's "I'm dyin' and you start a quiz program" (*Healthy, Wealthy and Dumb*; *They Stooge to Conga*); Moe: "Shadup, Tarzan. You're all wet!" (*Disorder in the Court*); and "I'm poisoned!" (*Ants in the Pantry*).

OTHER NOTES: The working title was *Idiots Deluxe*, which will actually be used for a 1945 release. This script was reworked twice with Joe Besser, *Fraidy Cat* (1951) and *Hook a Crook* (1955). The belly bumping segment is where the transition occurs from the stock footage to the new. The Stooges hearing suddenly that they have been accepted as cops is a bit extreme, even for a Stooge plot. Transitions between old and new footage will become much smoother in future years.

There is personal irony when Curly shoots the hat resting on his foot; he had shot himself in the foot as a teenager, which made his left leg permanently thinner and caused him to limp in pain for his entire life. 'Bonzo' was the name of the chimpanzee featured in 1951's *Bedtime for Bonzo*, starring future US president Ronald Reagan. As in *They Stooge to Conga*, there is a US Savings Bond poster in the background of the opening scene (behind the man downstairs)

Like Ted Healy before him, Moe bossed his fellow Stooges around. But Moe had more depth, and while he sounded very brave, he tempered this with a delightful cowardice: "What are you, cowards? *I'll* lead the way!......GO AHEAD!"

#69 - SPOOK LOUDER

Studio: Columbia

Released: April 2, 1943

Running Time: 15"59'"

Credited Production Crew:

Produced by:	Del Lord & Hugh McCollum
Directed by:	Del Lord
Story & Screen Play by:	Clyde Bruckman
Director of Photography:	John Stumar
Film Editor:	Paul Borofsky
Art Director:	Carl Anderson

Credited Cast:

Curly Howard	
Larry Fine	
Moe Howard	
Stanley Blystone	Head Spy (undertaker)
Lew Kelly	J. Ogden Dunkfeather, special investigator

Uncredited Cast:

Symona Boniface	drenched customer
Ted Lorch	Mr. Graves, inventor of death ray
Charles Middleton	butler

PERSPECTIVE: Along with the previous two films, *They Stooge to Conga* and *Dizzy Detectives*, *Spook Louder* makes the third film of a 1943 Stooge mystery trilogy coinciding with the extreme popularity of the mystery genre in contemporary feature-length B-movies. Such basic mystery elements as a narrated flashback, a haunted house, a mad doctor, dismembered body parts, Axis spies, mysterious screaming, and the gorilla of *Dizzy Detectives* can all be found in such individual films of the era as the Ritz Brothers' *The Gorilla* (1939) and Abbott & Costello's *Hold That Ghost* (1941), and in such film series as 'Charlie Chan' (1934-49), 'The Falcon' (1941-49), 'The Lone Wolf' (1935-49), 'Henry Aldrich' (1943's *Henry Aldrich Haunts a House*), 'Mexican Spitfire' (1942's *Mexican Spitfire Sees a Ghost*), and Columbia's own 'Crime Doctor' series (1943-49), one entry of which was *The Crime Doctor's Strangest Case* (1943). This last title is particularly significant because in this Stooge film Professor Dunkfeather says this is the "strangest case!" And no wonder - the Stooges are involved.

Of the previous Stooge mysteries the most similar to *Spook Louder* is their first 'scare comedy,' *We Want Our Mummy*. It contained a number of the elements we see again here: kidnappings, hidden doors, and hands reaching out; even a mummy appears in the inventor's den of *Spook Louder*. But unlike any previous Stooge film or any previous film of the B-mystery/horror genre, this film offers a new kind of villain: an invisible pie thrower. Indeed, this is the film's real mystery, the question *Times* reporter Wallace keeps asking Dunkfeather: "Who threw those pies?"

During the narration of the story three pies are thrown. The first is thrown just as the undertaker is about to shoot the Stooges, the second is thrown just as Moe is about to strike Curly with a club, and the third is thrown just after the Stooges throw their bomb at the end of the film. It looks as if the pie thrower is a pacifist. But then the eccentric Professor Dunkfeather confesses that he threw the pies. This makes no sense; he was not even in Grave's house. He could simply be lying, of course, but Dunkfeather's confession can be dismissed conclusively since he himself is struck with a pie. The pie thrower cannot be one of the Stooges who are standing right there, nor can it be one of the blown up spies, for they are dead. Eliminating both the piano-playing cat and the cuckoo-clock parrot, the only two humans unaccounted for in the four pie-throwing episodes are Dr. Graves and his butler. Could the 'Death Ray' that Graves was going to sell the government really be a pie-throwing apparatus? No, probably not. Apparently there is some supernatural force that throws these pies. If you find this an unsatisfactory solution to the mystery, keep in mind that the film itself tells you that this is the "strangest case" and that Stooge films almost never conclude with all their loose ends tied up. Running away from their pursuers, lying amidst the rubble of an explosion, the Stooges often leave us hanging. *Spook Louder* turns out to be a whipped cream-covered cliff hanger.

VISUAL HUMOR: This film contains one notable Stooge first: Moe's hair standing on end. A few minutes before, the middle of Larry's hat stands up in fear. Most of the physical humor consists of variations of gags used in the previous two films of this mystery trilogy. The fearful

running, mass explosion, the rocking chair, Curly accidently aiming a loaded gun at people, and animal fright (the live monkey and the stuffed bear) derive from *Dizzy Detectives*. When Wallace hears that the door-to-door salesmen flashbacks have nothing to do with the mystery, the parallel is the irrelevant carpentry scene insertion to *Dizzy Detectives*. The door-to-door hawking, the tall woman at the door, Curly's shaking with the reducing machine (as he did when he was electrocuted), and Curly mistaking Moe for the villain ("Was that you?") derive from *They Stooge to Conga*. The collapsing awning water is unique in Stoogedom. Moe hitting Larry when someone else (in this instance, the voice at the door) speaks we first saw in *Grip, Grunts and Groans*.

VERBAL HUMOR: Stooge firsts: Larry: "I just saw a ghost!" Curly: "Was it a fat one?" Larry: "Yeah!" Curly: "That was ME!" Also, when the Morse code message is interpreted, this is the first time we hear a Stooge be too literal when asked "What did he/it say?" Curly and Larry answer: "Eh-eh-eh-eh-eh." Connected with this communications joke is Moe's second 'short wave' gag - the first was in the first film of the mystery trilogy, *They Stooge to Conga*. The introductory war bonds joke ("Do you want us to be patriotic and buy war bonds, or do you want us to be unpatriotic and pay the rent?") is appropriate for the spy motif, as is Curly's reaction when asked if he is "a Jap".

The Stooge short films provided acting opportunities for young actors just beginning their careers (Lucille Ball, Walter Brennan) as well as older actors too energetic and professional to retire. Ted Lorch [1873-1947] and Charles Middleton [1873-1947] appeared in nearly 300 films during their careers. Both had significant roles in the *Flash Gordon* series of the 1930s as the High Priest and Ming the Merciless, respectively. They also had both appeared in two different versions of *Showboat*. Lorch created a number of memorable roles in Stooge films, including Chief Rain-in-the-Puss and General Muster in *1937's Back to the Woods* and *Goofs and Saddles*.

Story/screenwriter Clyde Bruckman offers several notable responses and exchanges: Curly, after hearing the Russian clock 'sing' at 5 o'clock: "Hey, let's come back at twelve o 'clock and hear the whole song"; Larry: "Did he say 'blood'?" Curly: "I'm anemic"; and Curly: "There's nobody there!" Moe: "Let's sneak up on him!" Twice Bruckman uses 'mis-hearing/cover-up' gags (*Half Shot Shooters*); the second (Moe: "He meant 'sap,' not 'Jap.'") is less clumsy than the first (Moe: "Make that seventy-five." Woman: "What's that you say?" Moe: "I said 'It's great to be alive!"). Curly's "But we're not— [a look from Moe]— Yes we are!" is a variation of the gag used when getting their job in *They Stooge to Conga* (Moe: "Can we fix it! Larry: "Can we fix it!" Curly: "Can we?"). Other variations: "She had dandruff...proving a case of suicide!" (dandruff was treated as a disease in *Dizzy Doctors*); Moe: "Let's sneak up on him...Go ahead!" (*Dizzy Detectives*); Curly: "An octopus!" (*The Sitter Downers*); Moe: "Say, you're not a bad dancer!" Curly: "I'll bet you say that to all the boys!" (*Horses' Collars*); Moe: "You'd be but you got your legs on backwards!" (*Nutty but Nice*).

References: Selling war bonds was a patriotic occupation for Hollywood. 'Rachmaninoff's *Prelude*' refers to a piece by Russian born Serge Rachmaninoff, one of the best known classical piano composers and performers of the period; he actually published two collections of preludes in 1901 and 1910. Ironically, the clock in the foyer is also Russian, and Rachmaninoff died on March 28, 1943, just a few days before *Spook Louder* was released. Spooky!

OTHER NOTES: The film was shot in mid-July, 1942. The script is a refurbishing of Mack Sennett's *The Great Pie Mystery*, which was also directed by Del Lord. The prototype of all spooky house comedies was the Universal silent film, *The Cat and the Canary* (1927). Charles Middleton [the butler] is best known for his role as 'Ming the Merciless' in the Flash Gordon serials. We saw the 'Death Ray' concept previously in *Dutiful but Dumb*.

#70 - BACK FROM THE FRONT

Studio: Columbia

Released: May 28, 1943

Running Time: 17"41'"

Credited Production Crew:

Produced & Directed:	Jules White
Story & Screen Play by:	Jack White & Ewart Adamson
Director of Photography:	John Stumar
Film Editor:	Edwin Bryant
Art Director:	Carl Anderson

Credited Cast:

Curly Howard
Larry Fine
Moe Howard

Uncredited Cast:

Vernon Dent	Lt. Dungen
Bud Jamison	Nazi petty officer
Stanley Blystone	Nazi captain
Charles 'Heine' Conklin	Nazi sailor
Johnny Kascier	Nazi sailor (wrestling)
Al Thompson	Nazi sailor (wrestling); Nazi officer
George Gray	Nazi sailor
Jack 'Tiny' Lipson	large Nazi sailor
Harry Semels	Nazi guard

PERSPECTIVE: This is the fifth World War II film, if you include *Spook Louder* and its "Jap spies." In both *Spook Louder* and *They Stooge to Conga* the Stooges went about their trade as repairmen and accidently stumbled upon Axis spies. But here in *Back From the Front*, significantly, they enlist in the Merchant Marines. Not that they are dedicated patriots just yet. Their motives are questionable when they dance and sing "We're off to sea, to see what we can see," and it is only after a bout of sea sickness, a painting squabble, hitting a torpedo they think is a beached whale, being blown up with their ship, hitching their dog to their survival craft, and climbing aboard the *SS Schicklgruber* that they realize they are confronted with Germans. As in the earlier films, they still accidentally stumble across the enemy; it just takes more time, a longer journey, and a lot of water.

In *Spook Louder* and *They Stooge to Conga*, the Stooges broke up land-based espionage rings and made our harbors safe. Now they move off shore and join the Merchant Marine in a new war venue. The timing was not accidental. In summer/fall 1942 the battle for the North Atlantic was still furiously fought and vital to win. Hitler's ultra-modern fleet of U-boats sank 111 merchant ships in June, 1942 alone, some 500 for the entire year. These 'undersea raiders,' a contemporary term Moe uses, were eventually defeated by RADAR, air patrols, and aerial bombing, but it would not be until June of 1943, months after this film was made.

In the spirit of the nameless, faceless civilian heroes of the Merchant Marine who defied Hitler's 'wolf packs,' the Stooges are given the common nicknames of Inky, Winky, and Dinky. These names are not at all important for the plot of the film; we only hear them once. But they are important for the message of the film and the spirit of the times. In the previous film we heard a pitch for buying war bonds. Now as enlisted Merchant Marines the Stooges portray (relatively) regular Americans and represent the average American giving himself to the war effort. When the Nazi captain is puzzled at being defeated by only three men, his officer tells him, "But Heir Capitan! These are Americans!" And when we consider how many Americans are more competent than the Stooges, viewing this film may have made the war effort seem less bleak than it looked in 1942-1943. To bolster morale, the comedy in *Back From the Front* comes less from political satire than from making fun of Nazi incompetence, beating Nazis up with clubs, pulleys, nets, and oil, calling them "Ratsies" and "Limburger Destroyers," and sneezing Hitler's mustache off. The Stooges turn "Heil Hitler!" into "Hang Hitler!"; and they even get a Nazi to say "We are Nazis. We have no brains!" Imagine, three merchant marines names Inky, Winky, and Dinky, who look and act suspiciously like The Three Stooges, getting the enemy to admit that they have no brains! So much for Americans being intimidated by the German armed forces.

VISUAL HUMOR: Stooge firsts: the sea-sickness sequence, highlighted when Moe comes back for the mop; the swinging pulley; and a slapstick reversal - the first time Moe waves his hand and Curly follows it with his face. Curly's set piece with the port hole - another Stooge first - is one more chapter in his struggle against inanimate objects, although his quip "That's not the same day!" stems from his telling the crook in *Dizzy Detectives* that being punched ten times in a row is getting "monotonous".

Curly has Larry look out the port hole without incident just as Larry looked at the bookshelf without incident in the previous film (*Spook Louder*). The painting sequence has several new wrinkles, especially Curly knocking Dungen out of his hammock and then shuffling back into Moe. The gun swab is the longest handle with which the Stooges get to knock someone.

Moe plays the "see those" [fingers] with a Nazi and gouges him just as he gouged the Hitler poster in *They Stooge to Conga*. The slippery oil on the deck is reminiscent of the slippery sidewalk in *Loco Boy Makes Good*. Other variations: Curly head-butting Dungen (*Dizzy*

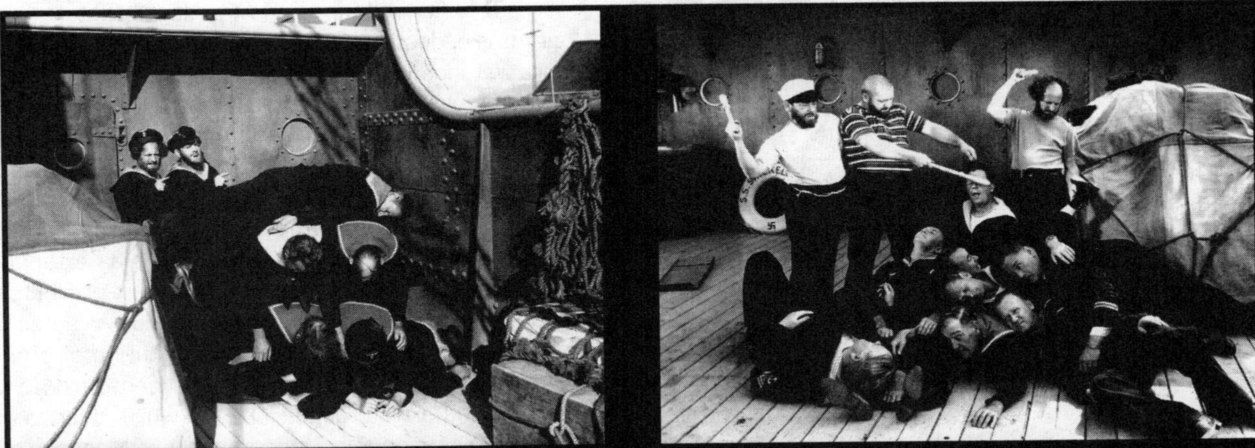

Back From the Front (1943) is a historic film. As members of the merchant marine, the Stooges do their part to win the desperate struggle for secure shipping lanes in the North Atlantic. They not only uncover and utterly defeat a Nazi force; they also humiliate them, as demonstrated by the two on-set publicity photos shown here. Heroic acts fit easily into the Stooges' group persona: for years now they have been handling weapons, confronting thugs and beasts, and rescuing helpless victims. Their *modi operandi* may be unconventional, which is where the comedy lies, but the Stooges work very convincingly as heroes who enjoy their triumph and bolster the chauvinistic spirits of theater-going audiences.

Detectives); the vase falling from the wall onto the captain's head (*Pop Goes the Easel*); and the splash from the Nazi's falling into the sea hitting the Stooges (*We Want Our Mummy*).

VERBAL HUMOR: Most of Curly's noteworthy punch lines, retorts, and puns in this film express logic: "Hey fellas, I can't hear a thing!" Moe: "Why not?" Curly: "I'm not listenin'!"; Moe: "If we're discovered, we're lost!" Curly: "You're crazy. If we're discovered, we're found!"; Moe "We gotta use strategy." Curly: "We can't use nobody! There's only three of us!"; Curly: "You better have it or we'll get it!"; and Curly: "Hoarders is hoarders!". This does not mean he has a great brain, though. He asks the seasick Moe and Larry: "Where'd ya get the suntan?" He also has to ask Moe: "What comes after '1'?". Internal rhymes: Curly: It's a whale of a whale!"; Moe: "We better scram before he gets back." Curly: "I'd like to scramble some breakfast. I'm starved!"; and the fear gag (Larry: "Something tells me we better take a walk." Moe: "Yeah, but run!"), a variation of Moe's "Don't be scared...Just run!" in *Dizzy Detectives*. Curly's "Hey fellas, I can't hear a thing...I'm not listenin'!" is the aural equivalent of "I can't see...I have my eyes closed". Moe refers to Hitler's mustache as his "personality," as in *I'll Never Heil Again*. Other variations: the initial disclaimer (*You Nazty Spy!*); 'Schicklgruber' (*They Stooge to Conga*); the rhyming names Tizzy, Lizzy, and Dizzy (*The Sitter Downers*); Larry: "A hoarder, eh?" and Curly: "Hoarders is hoarders!" ("Girl hoarders, eh?" in *Matri-Phony*); Curly: "You better have it or we'll get it!" ("Every time you 'take care of that,' *I* get it!" in *Matri-Phony*); Curly's "I don't care! I'm gonna eat!" (*Loco Boy Makes Good*); "smother the whole thing in fried chicken" ("eggs smothered in steak" in *Rockin' Thru the Rockies*); Curly's misidentifying the torpedo as "a whale!" (*Disorder in the Court*); and the references to beans (Curly: "You see, they feed you beans every day, except on Sunday. That's when you get bean soup...*and* beans!" in *Three Little Sew and Sews*); cf. Larry: "We gotta use the old bean." Curly: "I couldn't look another bean in the face!".

References: Moe's "This is the beginning of the second front" refers to plans for launching an Anglo-American, anti-German offensive from the West after the German loss at Stalingrad in the fall of 1942; such an offensive was nigh unto impossible until the Atlantic was cleared of German raiders. "Ersatz" beans are "substitute" beans, using a German psychological term, as parodied by Profs. Ziller, Zeller, and Zoller in *Three Sappy People*. "We're off to sea, to see what we can see!" parodies either 'The Bear Went Over the Mountain' ["to see what he could see"] or a contemporary Irving Berlin song 'We Saw the Sea' ["We Joined the Navy / to see the world / And what did we see? / We saw the sea."] written for the 1936 Fred Astaire film *Follow the Fleet*. "We forgot our duffel, bags!" uses the slang term 'bags' for women/wives.

OTHER NOTES: The working title was *A Sailor's Mess*. Johnny Kascier and Al Thompson rarely have any lines; here they speak with German accents. It was the Stooges' dog that gave them away to the Nazis, although he powered them in the sea.

#71 - THREE LITTLE TWIRPS

Studio: Columbia

Released: July 9, 1943

Running Time: 15"27'"

Credited Production Crew:

Produced by:	Del Lord & Hugh McCollum
Directed by:	Harry Edwards
Story & Screen Play by:	Monty Collins & Elwood Ullman
Dirctor of Photography:	John Stumar
Film Editor:	Paul Borofsky
Art Director:	Carl Anderson

Credited Cast:

Curly Howard	
Larry Fine	
Moe Howard	
Chester Conklin	circus worker
Stanley Blystone	Herman

Uncredited Cast:

Bud Jamison	detective
Duke York	Sultan of Abadaba
Charles 'Heine' Conklin	Louie, circus attendant
Al Thompson	ticket salesman

PERSPECTIVE: Charley Chan had made his circus film in 1936, and the Marx Brothers made theirs in 1939. So this is the Stooge entry into an established comedy film scenario. A circus is certainly an appropriate place for a Stooge comedy. Circuses have costumes, animals, freaks, bosses, workmen, plenty of tools and weapons, crowds for hawking, and hiding places, and the Stooges make ample use of all of these elements. Circuses also usually have clowns, of course, but clowns might have competed with the Stooges' own 'clowning around,' to use Moe's phrase, so there are no clowns. Besides, Stooge physical comedy is rapid and intense, while clown physical comedy tends to build slowly and then become exaggerated, which would clash with the Stooges' style.

The Stooges begin the film, as often, as tradesmen and, as usual, they screw up. But in this instance instead of running from their employer they scalp the free tickets he gives them on the circus midway, and this brings about a full-fledged chase scene, which leads in turn to Curly's confrontation with the bearded lady, the Chester Conklin horse-shooting interlude, and the Stooges' capture. As punishment they face a 'firing squad,' a.k.a. the spears of the Sultan of Abbadabba, but they escape, and a second chase sequence takes Curly not only to the topmost part of the Big Top but plunges him down well into the earth. In fifteen minutes the Stooges cover a lot of circus ground and air.

This final chase winds up, appropriately, in two circus-like, death-defying acts - knife throwing and high-wire walking. The Sultan of Abbadabba triumphs in both. In terms of the narrative this is in stark contrast to the Stooge heroism of the previous few films and the relative tranquillity of the domestic trilogy previous to those. In terms of the physical comedy, this circus-act climax constrains the Stooges' physicality. When a non-Stooge is punishing the Stooges, especially for as extended a sequence as the final tight rope scene, it prevents the Stooges from employing all their physical talents. They are limited to running, hollering, or gesturing, all of which they do very well, but they are prevented from inter-Stooge and extra-Stooge slapstick, which they do even better. The comedy in Stooges-in-jeopardy scenes often relies on visual/aural gimmickry and the comic effectiveness of the tormentor. In this finale Director Harry Edwards creates the comedy with the mysterious rope that captures the Stooges by itself, the antics of Duke York as the Sultan, the giant swings of the high wire, and the plunge to earth. As in the scene in which Chester Conklin attempts to shoot the Larry/Curly horse, the special effects, editing, and sound effects are competent, and Duke York and Chester Conklin are both seasoned comic actors, but the results, which look quite different from any of the recent Stooge releases, tend to be relatively flat. As in his previous Stooge film, *Matri-Phony*, Harry Edwards, a Mack Sennett/Harry Langdon veteran, had an elaborate vision worthy of his training, but it beat differently from the pulse of typical Stooge comedy. Edwards would never direct another Stooge film.

VISUAL HUMOR: Larry gives Curly a unique look after he says: "I'll play the head and shoulders; you play the other part!" The Stooges do not make too many off-color jokes. Several Stooge antics are new: Herman and the policeman follow Curly's hands with their faces, and then Moe and Larry bonk them; we have not seen Curly pulling out Larry's hair before either, although we have seen other role reversals. For all the mule kicks we have seen, this time it is done by Larry in the back half of a horse outfit. A new sound effect is Curly's plunging like an airplane from the high wire; with World War II in progress and the US building its air force, airplanes would become increasingly common in Stooge films, as we will see in the next film.

We have seen Curly cause Moe and Larry as well as himself to pass out before (*Horses' Collars*), but it was always at the end of a film. Larry and Moe wore a horse suit in *What's the Matador?*, but putting Curly up front allows us to enjoy that unmistakable pivot with the left foot. Curly's wolf impersonation is highly energetic, the cousin of his chicken impersonation in *Movie Maniacs*. We saw something similar to Curly's hopping hat in *Some More of Samoa*. Other variations: Curly getting his hat pinned by the spear [*Cactus Makes Perfect*]; hiding in a large trunk [*Dizzy Detectives*]; the interior view of the knife inside the horse [*Boobs in Arms*]; deliberately putting the Stooges in a dangerous situation (sending them to Vulgaria in *Dutiful but Dumb*); falling into a hole in the ground [*Flat Foot Stooges*]; and the dust cloud rising from the hole (the water splash in *We Want Our Mummy* and *Back From the Front*).

VERBAL HUMOR: The dialogue by Monty Collins & Elwood Ullman [*They Stooge to Conga*] offers some Stooge irony when Moe remarks: "Boy! What some people will do to earn a living!" and when Larry insists: "We've got no time for kibitzers". They have Curly insulted by a non-Stooge (Herman: "That wild man looks uglier every time I look at it!") and by Moe (Curly: "I haven't been to the circus since I got out of the fourth grade." Moe: "Yeah, that was last year!"), but Curly dishes it out, too, when he tells the bearded lady, "You remind me of a girlfriend in Detroit, but you look more like her stepfather!" and responds to her "You kill me!" with "You're not doin' me any good!". Moe works in the name "twirps" ("Now snap it up, you twirps") in the opening scene, a rare reference to the title of a film in its dialogue. Moe's "Let him have it! We're right behind ya!" derives from *Dizzy Detectives*. Other variations: "Swing it!" [*Violent is the Word for Curly*]; Larry & Curly "Right!" "Right!" Moe: "Wait a minute. Everything all right?" Larry & Curly: "Right!" [*Dancing Lady*]; "Hhmm, I resemble that!" ("I relent that!" in *All the World's a Stooge*); and Larry's "That's my asthma." [*Oily to Bed, Oily to Rise; Fugitive Lovers*].

OTHER NOTES: Monty Collins & Elwood Ullman also wrote *Matri-Phony*, the first Stooge film directed by Harry Edwards. Edwards tends to over-produce contrived gags, e.g. the clay cigar incident in *Matri-Phony* and the opening scene and the rope sequence here, and he was one of the more controversial directors at the Columbia short-subject unit. Barbara Jo Allen, who starred in the long-running, Vera Vague series (1943-1952) which earned an Academy Award nomination for *The Jury Goes Round 'N Round* (1945), absolutely refused to work with Edwards after 1944. According to *Okuda* (28), the Stooges requested that they never work with him again either; he was fired ultimately. Nonetheless, he did co-author such Stooge classics as *No Census, No Feeling* and *Some More of Samoa*. Also, editor Paul Borofsky was the least admired of the Stooge editors, and awkward moments here or sequences that last too long should have ended up on the cutting room floor. Borofsky also edited Edwards' *Matri-Phony*.

The movie poster the Stooges cover over in the first scene is for Columbia's *The Man Who Returned to Life* (1942). The background march music during the ticket sequence we heard briefly in *Termites of 1938*; it will be used again for Curly's trombone playing in *Idle Roomers*, for the radio-in-the-sink sequence in *Gents in a Jam*, and elsewhere. It is the 'Frederic March,' [pun intended] written by Columbia staffers Howard Jackson and Raphael Penso; for details, see Richard Finegan, "The Three Stooges Meet Frederic March," *The Three Stooges Journal* 89 (1999) 5.

Three Little Twirps (1943) sets the Stooges inside a circus. But the clown humor of a circus and the directing of Mack Sennett veteran Harry Edwards made for an atypical Stooge comedy, as was Edwards' *Matri-Phony* (1942).

#72 - HIGHER THAN A KITE

Studio: Columbia

Released: July 30, 1943

Running Time: 17"28"'

Credited Production Crew:

Produced by:	Del Lord & Hugh McCollum
Directed by:	Del Lord
Story & Scree Play:	Elwood Ullman & Monty Collins
Director of Photography:	Benjamin Kline
Film Editor:	Paul Borofsky
Art Director:	Victor Greene

Credited Cast:

Curly Howard
Larry Fine
Moe Howard

Uncredited Cast:

Dick Curtis	Marshal Bommel
Vernon Dent	Marshal Boring
Duke York	Kelly, Colonel Henderson's chauffeur

PERSPECTIVE: For this sixth World War II film writers Elwood Ullman & Monty Collins take the Stooges to the next stage of the war. In *You Nazty Spy!* and *I'll Never Heil Again* the object of the political satire was Hitler, the Axis powers, and their takeover of Europe. In *They Stooge to Conga* and *Spook Louder* the Stooges captured spies in the United States, and in *Back From the Front* they enlisted in the Merchant Marine and battled Nazis in the Atlantic. And now with the Atlantic shipping lanes cleared of Nazi U-boats the Stooges are ready to fight overseas, but their attempt at flying for the RAF hits a detour in the motor-pool garage. As usual they make a horrible mess of each other and the job they are supposed to complete, so they run, and, as often, hide in a 'vehicle' which takes them to the next leg of their comic odyssey. This time the 'vehicle' is a bomb, which drops them behind enemy lines, reflecting the recent British bombing at Cologne, Germany, in May, 1942. In addition to the usual foolery, the Stooges steal the Führer's battle plans and presumably - one rarely knows for sure at the end of a Stooge episode - make it back to "somewhere in somewhere" as victorious heroes.

By this time the Nazi salute has become a regular part of Stooge slapstick. They goose-stepped in *You Nazty Spy!* and saluted "Hang Hitler!" while slapping each other's foreheads in *Back From the Front*, but this time the idolatry of Hitler and the accompanying 'Heil' salute is the direct cause of the Stooges' victory and the Nazi failure to stop them. When first seeing Boring and Bommel Curly salutes them, drags his hand under Boring's chin and twiddles his lips in great disrespect. When Larry emerges as the lovely 'Moronica,' he gives a falsetto "Heil!" that drips of irony in its meekness. After Larry leaves with Boring, Moe and Curly have a whole slapstick exchange based on the 'Heil' salute, highlighting the absurdity of the whole thing. Then in the finale Curly escapes because the Nazis cannot resist saluting 'Heil' every time they see the Führer's picture. The only people with any sense about the whole 'Heil" business are the Stooges and the dog, and what did that say to contemporary audiences about the intelligence of people who mindlessly salute a photo of the Führer?

The Nazis appear in only the final third of the film, so it is interesting to observe how Stoogeness is comically heroic when let loose on the Nazis but simply comical when let loose on the RAF. After all, the Stooges ruin the colonel's car in this film, in *Back From the Front* they blew up the *US Dotty* by striking a German torpedo with sledgehammers, and in *They Stooge to Conga* they rewired and confused the entire Los Angeles telephone system. There are two reasons why this double-standard of destruction works. One is simply that Stooge destruction is comical destruction and is funny to everyone except the person who owns what they are destroying. The second is that the war effort was already demanding sacrifice on every one's part, and if the Stooges needed to ruin an automobile, a ship, and a telephone system in order to win the war, so be it. They would have ruined them anyway.

VISUAL HUMOR: A number of laughs rely on the element of surprise: when Kelly backs the car into the Stooges; when the Stooges knock Kelly into the water; when the vacuum, jack, and exhaust attack Moe's face; when the tire spins Moe backwards; when Curly barely notices his head being tapped with a wrench; when we see the Swastikas on the Nazi underwear; and when Bommel feels compelled to salute the photograph of Schicklgruber. When Moe's head is stuck in the pipe section, the photography is necessarily confined by that enclosed space. Previous enclosed shots of this sort had a little more room for maneuvering (the bayonet bag in *Boobs in Arms*, the gold mine in *Cactus Makes Perfect*, and the horse's head in the previous film). By contrast, the scene in which Moe's neck stretches is all the more expansive. And the spiral grease marks are a nice touch. When Moe gouges Curly (in the car), the sound effect is a HONK. Another innovative sound effect here is that produced when Curly's head is banging against the inside of the bombshell.

Of the many battles between Curly and inanimate objects, this one with the car hood is a good one ("Rruff!"). The Stooges have not done this much damage to a car since *Violent is the Word for Curly*. Other variations: Boring slapping Bommel ("Dumbkopf!") who slaps Moe ("Dumbkopf!") who slaps Curly ("Dumb-kopf!") who slaps no one (*Pardon My Scotch*); this gag is used twice with a variation; the feathers and dust blowing out of the vacuum into Moe's face (the oil can in *3 Dumb Clucks*); and limb stretching (Curly's tooth in *All the World's A Stooge; Some More of Samoa*).

VERBAL HUMOR: A variety of verbal gag types include a set joke (Curly: "I'm hungry!" Moe: "Don't tell me you want to eat more of those sawdust frankfurters?" Curly: "They weren't bad with mustard." Moe: "Yeah, but that wasn't mustard!"), puns ('navigator' - Curly: "Crawls in a swamp until it becomes a suitcase"; 'hand grenade' - Curly: "An avocady's uncle!"; and a 'squeak' - Larry: "They're usually a small little—"), an alliterative internal rhyme (Moe: "We'll squelch that squeak in nothin' flat!"), Larry's (Moronica's) insulting, seductive prattle ("Heil!...What lap?...I love every chin on your face!"), and throw-away lines (Curly's "He got my bait!" and "Wings for the Beagle"). Anti-German propaganda is put into the mouths of the Germans themselves, making them look even more ironic and cowardly (Bommel: "Don't you listen to our radio? Don't you know a German soldier never runs?"; Boring: "No wonder we are retreating!"; Boring: "We Germans never get stuck!")...

References: The locations of airfields in Britain were still secret in 1943, hence 'A FLYING FIELD SOMEWHERE IN SOMEWHERE.' Marshals 'Boring' and 'Bommel' parody Hermann Göring, engineer of the Battle of Britain, and Erwin Rommel, the 'Desert Fox,' recently defeated by Montgomery in North Africa in late 1942; Boring sees the map with the "28th Division in the Red Sea and the African Core in the North Pole," referring to the North African campaign in the fall. 'Edelweiss' is a flower native to the Swiss Alps. The orders "from the Führer. He got some from a new astrologer" satirizes Hitler's interest in astrology. "Schicklgruber" (*They Stooge to Conga*) was Hitler's mother's name; his father's name was unregistered. Boring: "Dumbkopf! I only got an E Card!" refers to the rationing that Americans were experiencing at home during rearming; fuel ration cards ranged from 'A' to 'E'. Larry's drag name 'Moronica' is that of Moe Hailstone's country in *You Nazty Spy!* and *"I'll Never Heil Again*, but with his fruit headdress Larry looks like Carmen Miranda, the 'Brazilian Bombshell' who debuted in 1940's *Down Argentine Way*, when Larry has his hair in a peak-a-boo look, he mimics Veronica Lake, the peak-a-boo girl who became popular on screen in the early 1940s; the name 'Moronica' accidently blends 'Miranda/ Veronica.' Curly's "Wings for the Beagle" parodies Warner Brothers' *Wings for the Eagle* (1942) which focused on the war effort and aircraft workers.

All three Stooges give raspberry Edelweiss to Schicklgruber in *Higher Than a Kite* (1943), their only World War II film in which they penetrate into German territory. The inspiration for a European setting was that the 8th Bomber Force of the United States had begun bombing Germany in August, 1942. But the Stooges join the RAF instead of the USAF because such films as *A Yank in the RAF* (1941) and *Eagle Squadron* (1942) had placed Americans in the British war effort.

Epithets: "gophers" and "jug-heads". Other variations: Curly to Moe "Whadya doin' down there?" (*Pardon My Scotch*); "Switch on!" (*Cash and Carry*); and "Orders is orders!" ("Hoarders is hoarders" in *Back From the Front*).

OTHER NOTES: The auto mechanic footage will be reused in *Stop! Look! and Laugh!*

#73 - "I CAN HARDLY WAIT"

Studio: Columbia

Released: August 13, 1943

Running Time: 18"27'"

Credited Production Crew:

Produced & Directed by:	Jules White
Story & Screen Play by:	Clyde Bruckman
Director of Photography:	John Stumar
Film Editor:	Charles Hochberg
Art Director:	Victor Greene

Credited Cast:

Curly Howard
Larry Fine
Moe Howard

Uncredited Cast:

Bud Jamison	Dr. Yank
Lew Davis	Dr. Tug
Adele St. Mara	receptionist
Al Thompson	dental patient

PERSPECTIVE: Goliath was felled by a pebble, Achilles had his heel, and Curly has a bad tooth. The comedy of *"I Can Hardly Wait"* derives from the anxiety Curly feels before visiting a dentist (particularly an old fashioned dentist) and in his trying to extract the bad tooth prior to going to the dentist. Of course it is absurd that Curly the "numskull" should feel pain, especially considering how often Curly takes punches, slaps, and gouges to the face, iron tools to the skull, head-butts from a goat, a bull, and a speeding car, not to mention how he willingly throws away walnut meats to munch on the shells. But absurdity is central to Stooge comedy, and the absurdity of his feeling pain finds happy companions in the absurdity of his biting a fishing line as if he were a huge marlin and thinking a doorknob is his tooth.

Curly's pain and anxiety were clearly the focus of the film, for in the one previous Stooge dentistry sequence (*All the World's A Stooge*) it was the Stooges who operated on a patient; Curly may have had his tooth stretched a few inches by accident, but he was not the one with the real toothache. Now in *"I Can Hardly Wait"* Curly's own toothache and tooth extraction gives him the chance to howl, cry, and moan. We have often seen Curly frustrate himself while struggling with inanimate objects, but now the object is his own tooth so it must be twice as frustrating. The tent stake in *Three Missing Links* made him call for Moe and Larry and kick his feet; the wood wagon in *Oily to Bed* made him cry; but now he has his own internal pain to deal with, and as Moe tries to extract the tooth, Curly's pain soars to a level far above normal - even for a Stooge. And then in the great reversal

at the end of the dream sequence, Curly's pain is comically diverted by the yanking of Moe's tooth. The resulting anger Moe displays at Curly begins with one of the great Stooge takes - it takes 18 seconds for Moe to revive and focus on Curly holding the tooth in his hand - and the punching Curly dreams of is horrific - the kind of beating he gets only from crooks, as we saw in *Dizzy Detectives*.

Throughout the film Moe is lovingly abusive. In the previous film Larry and Curly poked, ripped at, burned, submerged, stretched, and twisted Moe when he was caught in the pipe section, so here in a kind of payback Moe shoves Larry's nose in boiling water and leads Curly through many tortures. But all the while he is genuinely trying to help Curly. Sure he yells at him to go to sleep, but when Curly makes it clear how much his tooth hurts, Moe offers him his own bed. The hot-water bottle puts an end to that, so in the ensuing dream sequence Moe begins a series of attempts to extract the tooth. Perhaps the greatest irony of the film is its fitting conclusion: Moe simply socks Curly in the jaw and knocks the problem tooth out. That brings them back to a normal Stooge pain level, the 'nightmare' - that is what the dream sequence portrays - is over, and everyone can go to sleep happy to prepare for a new day of Stoogedom and battling the Axis powers.

VISUAL HUMOR: The plot calls for painful physical comedy, and there are many gleefully unbearable moments, including using Curly's head for sandpaper, burning Larry's nose in hot water, exploding a firecracker in Moe's pajamas, and Moe bouncing along the floor on his rear (a Stooge first). Jules White often equated comedy short-films to cartoons, whence the unabashed violence of his gags. In contrast, there are many moments in which we watch Curly's physical representation of fear, as in his falling off the chair in the dentist's reception room. It is amazing how much comic mileage they get out of a ham steak - searching for it in Larry's hair, tossing it onto Curly's head, spreading mustard on Moe, scrubbing it on the washboard, wringing it dry, ironing it (somewhat like the celery in *Sock-A-Bye Baby*), and having the bone break Curly's tooth and end up in Moe's eye. The ham steak also brings Moe to set up Curly's elbow on his knee so he can kick his foot, a Stooge first. Another Stooge first: Curly swimming in the water he dumps on himself. Moe's bossy nature literally backfires when Curly tries to warn him about the firecracker in his pajamas; when Moe says "Shad-up!" Curly just lets the inevitable happen. Variations: collapsing beds (*In the Sweet Pie and Pie*); Larry bumping his head after being boosted into an upper berth (*A Pain in the Pullman*); pattern snoring (*Hoi Polloi*); Curly neighing like a horse (*Three Little Twirps*); and the chicken-with-its-head-cut-off (*Movie Maniacs*).

VERBAL HUMOR: Clyde Bruckman focused on Curly's fears and preoccupation with his pain to produce several fine exclamations ("Look at that tooth [the doorknob]! It's a whopper!"; "Somethin' tells me I shouldn't do this"; and "You got 'em all! You got me bald-headed in the mouth!"). Elsewhere he plays with language in literal puns (Moe: I got an idea that will revolutionize dentistry!" Curly: "I never knew this would start a revolution!"; Moe: "Why don't you look where you're walkin'?" Curly: "Whadya' expect me to have eyes in my feet?"); a double conditional statement (Curly: "Say if I belonged to the Elks I'd wear this on my watch chain...if I had a watch chain," resembling Moe's double conditional insult to Larry ["You know if I wasn't so weak from hunger I'd bat your brains out, if you had brains"] in *Dutiful but Dumb*); and an internal rhyme and a neologistic verb made from a noun (Curly: "Feels like gremlins are gremling in it".

The latter is just one of several references to the military buildup ('HEEDLOCK AIRPLANE CORP.,' i.e. 'Lockheed'; Moe's "We're defense workers. If you want to cut down on absenteeism, yank this guy's tooth. He won't let us sleep. He's sabotaging the war effort!"; and "...the shades are down...If those Japs ever knew how many planes we turned out today, their yellow jaundice would turn green!") and the domestic rationing of 1942/1943 (Larry: "I'm so hungry I could eat a horse!" Moe:

"What do you guys think you've been eatin' for the last month?"; the set joke (Larry: "Say, sugar: How'd you like to come over to my house tonight and see my coffee? Receptionist: "Fresh!!" Larry: "Oh yeah! Ground today!"); and the end of Curly's song "...I'll cut myself a nice big slice of her cauliflower ear! 'Cause that ain't rationed."). Another reference: Moe calls Curly 'Man O'War,' the name of the near triple crown winner of 1920 and sire of many other thoroughbred racers.

A Stooge first: Curly's "Oh my poor little, sweet little, cute little tooth!" and "My poor little, sweet little, adorable, lovable, sweet little putchy-wutchy tooth!". Epithets: Moe calls Curly "empty-skull," "chuckle-head," "numskull" (twice), and "pumpkin-head"; Curly calls Moe "cabbage-head". Curly says "I can hardly wait," the title of the film (cf. *Three Little Sew and Sews*). Other variations: Moe: "Clean this ham!" Curly: "I'll clean it when I'm ready!" (*Plane Nuts; Men in Black*); Moe: "One!...Two!.." Larry: "Two and a half!" (*Nutty But Nice*); "At last you got a hunk a brain." Larry: "Yeah? Where'd I get it?" (*Horses' Collars*); the professional's door with multiple initials: 'D.D.S., Ph.D., C.O.D., F.O.B., P.D.Q.' (*From Nurse to Worse*); badge '6 7/8' (*You Nazty Spy!*) and 'H2O' (*Whoops, I'm an Indian*); Moe: "I got it!" Curly: "Every time you got it, I get it!" (*Matri-Phony*); Curly: "I just love bonanzas and cream!" (*Yes, We Have No Bonanza*); and Curly: "What are you doin' down there?" (*Pardon My Scotch*).

OTHER NOTES: The title screen sets the title of the film in quotation marks. The working title was *Nothing But the Tooth*. Curly tries to stop the dentist from pulling Moe's tooth just as the Stooges tried to stop Kelly from driving the engine-deficient car in the previous film.

#74 - DIZZY PILOTS

Studio: Columbia

Released: September 24, 1943

Running Time: 16"45'"

Credited Production Crew:

Produced & Directed by:	Jules White
Story & Screen Play by:	Clyde Bruckman
Director of Photography:	Benjamin Kline
Film Editor:	Charles Hochberg
Art Director:	Victor Greene

Credited Cast:

Curly Howard
Larry Fine
Moe Howard

Uncredited Cast:

Harry Semels	Sky Aircraft Company rep.
Al Thompson	Sky Aircraft Company rep.
Judy Malcolm	girl in hangar
Sethma Williams	girl in hangar
Richard Fiske	drill sergeant [stock footage]
Charles Dorety	soldier [stock footage]

PERSPECTIVE: While contemporary America is producing 300,000 aircraft to fight the war, *Dizzy Pilots* takes the Stooges back into the air. Rising above *Higher Than a Kite*'s bomb sequence, Larry and Curly float Moe into the air, shoot him down, and toss him off a propeller, and all three 'Wrong Brothers' fly their plane without a rudder, flip it over, and plunge to earth. Unlike other Hollywood air-war films of 1941/1943 (e.g. Warner Brothers' *Dive Bomber*), this innovative short-film entertained contemporary audiences by featuring not the glory of the air war but the panic of being airborne when you do not belong there and have no idea how to fly.

Those audiences knew the Wrong Brothers would have to make their own rubber: the Japanese had cut off the US-Malayan rubber trade in 1942. But what they did not know was that Moe would get covered in it, or that Larry and Curly would use a pole, lasso, circus act, and a shotgun to rescue him, continuing the recent pattern of one Stooge in physical jeopardy being rescued by the other two. The pattern derives from the sweater-removal and head-extraction sequences of *How High is Up?* and *Cactus Makes Perfect* and has been developed recently in the pipe- and tooth-extraction sequences of *Higher Than a Kite* and *I Can Hardly Wait*, invariably demanding the liberal use of tools, each one geared for a particular failure which causes the victim a previously unfathomable sort of physical torture. Stoogeness comes to full bloom with facial contortions, repeated painfully tasteless insertions of crowbars and such into ears, nostrils, and mouths, creaking, croaking, yanking, and clanging sound effects, and an assortment of non-verbal cries and verbal threats. Viewer fascination, as long as the jeopardy is believable, is at a peak. We might recoil, as with the boot-spike in *They Stooge to Conga*, but we laugh when we see that the Stooge in jeopardy just gets angry, not hurt. No comedy team ever worked scenes like these so convincingly. The jeopardy itself, the tools and attempted extractions, and the cries and threats vary widely; some of the sequences involve Moe, others Curly, and some of them end happily, some not. *Dizzy Pilots* takes the pattern to its extreme: after all the effort of getting Moe out of the rubber suit, he is flung by the propeller back into the rubber-filled bathtub. We do not need to see the second extraction; we feel secure in knowing just how Stooge-esque the Wrong Brothers are.

Super weapons like the 'Death Ray' in *Dutiful but Dumb* and *Spook Louder* often played a role in early World War II comedies, and the Stooges have a history of creating inventions (e.g. Curly's gold finder in *Cactus Makes Perfect*). What makes the invention in *Dizzy Pilots* different is a time limit: the letter from the 'Republic of Cannabeer Draft Board' requires them to finish their 'Buzzard' within thirty days or they will be drafted. The Stooges have not become unpatriotic; (they live in 'Moronica,' not the US). This superimposed time limit is just an old, often used comedy twist that adds urgency to a plot. In this narrative sense, the 30-day deadline simply ties the plot together and therefore justifies the insertion of the 3.5-minute, *Boobs in Arms* infantry sequence after the Stooges' invention fails.

VISUAL HUMOR: Moe's voice-overs help sell the floating rubber-suit sequence; his voice sounds appropriately distant and as if his lips are coated with the rubber. A Stooge first: Moe attaching a plunger to Curly's scalp. A Stooge most: Moe never rips out more of Larry's hair (about 10 inches) than he does with the rubber-dipped oar here. Reusing the boot-camp footage from *Boobs in Arms* continues a recent trend; older footage was reused in *Dizzy Detectives* and *They Stooge to Conga*. Moe's fingers being almost too broken for a gouge derives from the 'new fingers' gag in *What's the Matador?*. When Larry shoulders the oar, turns, and whacks Moe, who sees Curly with his mallet, the situation resembles that in the previous film (*I Can Hardly Wait*) when Moe sees Curly holding the tooth the dentist extracted but blames Curly. Also from the previous film, Curly warns Moe and Moe refuses to listen before he "throws out the clutch," just as Curly tried to warn Moe when the dynamite went down Moe's pajamas. The water splashes up from the well and soaks Curly and Larry, as in *We Want Our Mummy*, but here they plunge into the well a second

In 1942, the Japanese cut off Malaysian rubber exports to the U.S. So the Stooges make their own in 1943's *Dizzy Pilots*. Audiences found this sort of Stooge ineptitude a great release from domestic sacrifices.

time and soak the two aircraft company representatives. Curly's plunge to earth recalls the end of *Three Little Twirps*.

VERBAL HUMOR: As in the previous film, Clyde Bruckman's script gives Curly a variety of postures. He claims a moral innocence ("Vice? I have no vice. I'm as pure as the driven snow!") and pedantically corrects Moe's grammar (Moe: "Don't saw the wings! You saw the garage!" Curly: "I *see* the garage, but I don't *saw* the garage. You are speaking incorrectly! You are moidering the king's English...et cetera! See? Saw? See?"), but he also can be completely ignorant ("One!...What comes after one?"; Moe: "It's the gas, you idiots!" Curly: "Shall I get you some bicarbonate of soda?"). Bruckman includes aeroplane puns (Larry: "Contact!" Moe: "Contact!" Curly: "Hey wait a minute! I wanna 'contract,' too!" Moe: "You'll get a contract! Step right on the dotted line!"; and Larry: "A cabin job!" [passenger planes were a recent invention]) and new gag names ('Cannabeer,' 'Stincoala,' 'Joe Strubachincoscow' [Moe: "What a moniker!"], and the 'Wrong Brothers'). From the latter he derives the exchange (Moe: "Anything the Wright Brothers can do, the Wrong Brothers can do, right!" Larry: "Right!" Curly: "Wrong!...Brothers!") finishing with a pattern that echoes Curly's "See? Saw? See?". Larry's delay gag ("Don't you know any better than to use a rifle?! You might miss him!...Use the shotgun!") uses a pattern we saw earlier in *Even As IOU*. Epithets: "nitwit," "idiots," and "muttonhead".

When in the airplane Moe says "We're losin' altitude! We gotta get rid of some weight!" and Curly responds: "Whadya lookin' at me for?", the pattern resembles one in *Some More of Samoa* (Curly: "Just a little thing I picked up to make big trees outta little saps." Larry: "Don't look at me!"). When Curly offers Moe, "Shall I get you some bicarbonate of soda?" he borrows from many Stooge gags about bicarbonate, the most memorable in *Three Smart Saps* (Woman: "Do you rumba?" Curly: "Only when I take bicarbonate"). Other variations: "A flying we will go!...Zoot!" (*Back to the Woods*, *Cactus Makes Perfect*); Larry: "Gas on...Gas off!" (*An Ache in Every Stake*); Curly: "Hey Moe! Whadya doin' up there?" (*Pardon My Scotch*); "What comes after one?" Larry: "P-two!" (*Back From the Front*); "That ain't Moe!" (*Rockin' Thru the Rockies*); Curly: "Don't you dare hit me in the head! You know I'm not normal!" (*Loco Boy Makes Good*); Curly: "The arrow points half way. I dunno if it's half empty or half full!" (*Soup to Nuts*); and Curly: "...just some little ol' wire that broke loose from some little ol' lever" (*"I Can Hardly Wait"*).

References in Curly's "We're great inventors: Robert Fulton, Thomas Edison, Alexander Graham Bell, Don Ameche and us!": Robert Fulton invented the steamboat in 1807; Thomas Edison perfected the light bulb and invented the phonograph and moving pictures in the late nineteenth century; Alexander Graham Bell invented the telephone in 1876; and actor Don Ameche played Bell in *The Story of Alexander Graham Bell* (1939).

OTHER NOTES: The working title was *Pest Pilots*. This is first Stooge film since *Pop Goes the Easel* and *Uncivil Warriors* for which the director and writer are the same as those of the previous release.

#75 - PHONY EXPRESS

Studio: Columbia

Released: November 18, 1943

Running Time: 17"09'"

Credited Production Crew:

Produced by:	Del Lord & Hugh McCollum
Directed by:	Del Lord
Story & Screen Play by:	Elwood Ullman & Monty Collins
Director of Photography:	John Stumar
Film Editor:	Paul Borofsky
Art Direction:	Victor Greene

Credited Cast:

Curly Howard	
Larry Fine	
Moe Howard	
Shirley Patterson	Lola
Bud Jamison	Red Morgan

Uncredited Cast:

Victor Travers	newspaper editor
Snub Pollard	sheriff
Chester Conklin	bartender
John Merton	Red's assistant
Blackie Whiteford	gang member
Joel Friedkin	Doctor Abdul
Sally Cleaves	dancing partner
Gwen Seager	dancing partner

PERSPECTIVE: Ever since *Horses' Collars* (1934), Western and frontier settings have provided the Stooges with inspirational, prop- and plot-loaded scenarios that involve guns and shootouts, horses and wagons, girls and dancing, saloons and drinking, and sheriffs and outlaws. *Phony Express* uses all of these and fills them with both fresh ideas and cleverly varied gags, even if it moves abruptly from one scenario to the next after appropriate gags use up a their comic energy allowance. In the end, *Phony Express* provides a fine example of a Stooge film in which a rapid-fire pace negates plot diversions, loose ends, and weaknesses. Comic continuity gives the film the appearance of plot unity.

The Stooges begin as vagrants chased by a sheriff and miraculously appear from behind a tree. They run to their next comic event, Doctor Abdul's Medicine Show, which gives them the chance to get a slapstick bout out of their system and to mix one of their infamous, bubbling concoctions. They offer this to a sheriff, but his violent reaction to their combustible panacea necessitates their next escape, not to mention an explosion, which apparently takes them into Peaceful Gulch to be mistaken for lawmen. They themselves do not know this, so they apply for the porter job, which gives them the chance to be perceived as tough even though they are not (unlike *Horses' Collars*, where they really were tough). It also means they can drink, dance, and fight without knowing what they are doing, and shoot once they do know what they are doing. Deputized, they clunk each other with rifle barrels, completely screw up the holdup, and mistakenly arrest the bank president, but they ultimately retrieve the money because Curly is a bloodhound and accidentally steps on a floorboard. It may not be utterly clear, but the Stooges triumph in the end: first they consciously set traps to capture four of Red's gang, and then Curly's bullet-belts shoot at Red and one other gang member. This is about as successful as the Stooges get in films like these. The purpose, after all, is to end with a triumphant gag, not a jocular triumph.

The transitions between these scenes are minimal. This seems to be intentional; at least it is consistent throughout the film. The appearance from behind the tree seems to be the key to understanding how this film works, for these 'vagrants' seem to come from nowhere and go to nowhere. They concoct an explosive liquid that blows their wagon to bits and leaves them in an extraordinary Delacroix-like tableau of tattered clothes, spinning wheels, passing sky and trees, and invisible galloping horses. We never learn what town they were in, and once in Peaceful Gulch they do not know who they are thought to be. When they screw up the robbery, it is not at all made clear that they need to retrieve the money. To do so, Curly becomes a bloodhound, gets his rear caught in a bear trap, and hides himself in a stove that becomes a weapon. Nothing is what it seems; everything becomes something else.

Moe began his career as an actor, not a comedian. He developed considerable vocal skills, including the rapid delivery of a hawker.

VISUAL HUMOR: The mysterious appearance from behind the tree is another innovative idea realized by photographer John Stumar (*Boobs in Arms*), as is the post-explosion tableau, one of the finest result shots in Stoogedom. It has a romantic, heroic air about it, making it all the more ironic. Their initial slapstick bout is a variation on some of their standard moves: (GOUGE-BLOCK, POUND, GOUGE, POUND, "Rruff!", NOSE BONK), but there is a significant Stooge first: the gouge is accompanied by the PLINK sound effect. In *Dizzy Pilots* we heard a HONK for the gouge; in earlier Stooge films there was no sound effect used for a gouge. The sheriff's spinning mustache is unique. There are other interesting movements, e.g. Larry rushing to the bar when Red says "Have a drink on me!" and Curly fighting a skunk, acting like a bloodhound, eating moth balls, yet simply stepping on a floorboard, hitting Moe in the chin, and discovering the loot. His cross-eyed look at the pistol is precious. Curly smashes his beer mug in the faces of the gang members before he knows he is supposed to be Hiccup.

Curly spilling the beer and imitating his partner's wriggles seems to be derived from the *Hoi Polloi* dance. When Curly gives Red a hand-wave and rips his finger along his upper lip, it is a variation of the wave he gave to Boring in *Higher Than a Kite*. Other variations: the bullets in the stove (the monkey-Gattling gun in *Goofs and Saddles*); shooting a toupee (*Disorder in the Court*); the cap flying into Moe's eye (the ham bone in *I Can Hardly Wait*); dusting each other off (*Horses' Collars*); shooting down the light fixture onto Red's head (*Whoops, I'm an Indian*); clanking Moe with rifle barrels (an echo of *Boobs in Arms*); Curly as a bloodhound (*Goofs and Saddles*); branches in the face (*Uncivil Warriors*); Curly's horse sounds (*Three Little Twirps*); Curly's not noticing that he has been hit on the back of the head [Moe: "How does that feel?" Curly: "What?"] (*Dizzy Pilots*); and the skunk-skin hat with a tail in Moe's face (*Back to the Woods*).

Larry at age 40. Although he rarely headlined, he was an integral part of the Stooges triadic dynamic, as here in *Phony Express*:
Larry: "Do you know anything about mixing medicine, doctor?"
Curly: "Why certainly, professor. All you gotta do is mix a little of this and a little of that."
Larry: "We got plenty of 'this.'"
Curly: "Then I'll try 'that.'"

VERBAL HUMOR: Writers Elwood Ullman and Monty Collins offer wordplays (Moe: "Get in there and make some more while I do some spielin'!" Curly: "I think you did enough spielin' already!"; Larry: "Do you know anything about mixing medicine, doctor?" Curly: "Why certainly, professor. All you gotta do is mix a little of this and a little of that." Larry [picking up a bottle]: "We got plenty of 'this.'" Curly: "Then I'll try 'that.'"; and Moe: "I got it! The traps!" Curly: "You mean: *I* got it the traps!" Moe: "Get the rest of 'em!" Curly: "Shut your trap!"), insults (Moe to Curly: "Why don't you change that face of yours - you scare people!"), and ironies (Curly: "Buy me a bottle. I can't sleep." Moe: "Whadya mean? You sleep 12 hours every night." Curly: "But I'm wide awake all day!"; and [after Red points out that the bank is open only from 10 to 3] Moe: "Oh we're sorry, we'll be back in the morning."). Moe again turns a noun into a verbal threat (Curly: "I think you did enough spielin' already." Moe: "I'll spiel you!").

A succinct Curly offers two gaglines by using just one word (When Moe clunks him with the rifle barrel and asks how it felt: "What?"; and when he sees the large hole in the bank wall: "Termites!". The latter reprises gags in *3 Dumb Clucks* and *Cactus Makes Perfect*. Recently there have been a number of diminutives ("avocadie" in *Higher Than a Kite*). Here we have "Peppermenthies" and "colleag-ees". Epithets: "lump-head" and "cabbage-head". Moe's "Hey! Looks like you guys are goin' to work" is another example of Moe's laziness at the other two's expense. Other variations: Red: "Here's how!" Curly: "And how!" (*Pop Goes the Easel*); "You dance like you got your legs on backwards" (*Nutty but Nice; Spook Louder*). References: 'Lumbago' is an old fashioned word for lower back pain. Moe's "There's gold in them thar hills!" is an old Western movie cliché.

OTHER NOTES: The Stooges are not introduced until the second scene, a technique we have not seen since *Spook Louder* and *Cactus Makes Perfect*. Snub Pollard [Sheriff] and Shirley Patterson [Lola] both specialized in B Westerns during the 1940s. Pollard's career spanned fifty years from 1912, including more than 100 silent comedies in 1919-1927; he will appear in four more Stooge roles. This was the last of nine Stooge films in which Monte Collins was involved as an actor or writer. After this film the art director is credited under 'Art Direction' for several more films. Part of the premise and some stock from this film will be reused in *Merry Mavericks* (1951).

#76 - A GEM OF A JAM

Studio: Columbia

Released: December 30, 1943

Running Time: 16"27'"

Credited Production Crew:

Producer:	Hugh McCollum
Written & Directed by:	Del Lord
Director of Photography:	John Stumar
Film Editor:	Paul Borofsky
Art Direction:	Victor Greene

Credited Cast:

Curly Howard
Larry Fine
Moe Howard

Uncredited Cast:

Dudley Dickerson	watchman
John Tyrrell	Joe, wounded crook
Al Hill	crook
Fred Kelsey	cop
Al Thompson	cop

PERSPECTIVE: This final release of 1943, the first of three films both written and directed solely by Del Lord, offers a different recipe for some common Stooge ingredients. The Stooges start as janitors, but because they are janitors in a doctor's office they have some new paraphernalia to play with. Not only that, because they are in the doctor's office two crooks make them operate on their wounded companion; the Stooges try to explain that they are not the doctors, as they had as non-dentists in *I Can Hardly Wait*, but threats prevail. After a lost body, suspected murder, and a police pursuit send the Stooges, crooks, security guard, and cops into a six minute chase scene filled with some fine fear/sneak/scream/run 'scare comedy' routines, the likes of which we have not seen since *Spook Louder*, Lord gives the Stooges even more opportunities for prop gags by setting that doctor's office in a building which contains some warehoused department-store equipment. In the midst of all this the Stooges capture or lead to the capture of all three crooks, but the last two are pinched with two minutes left in the film. What follows is a fright-filled denouement. *A Gem of a Jam* is ultimately a hodgepodge, but as in the previous *Phony Express* the pace of the unrealistic narrative flow and the combination of comic ingredients create genuine humor in their absurdity.

Unique in this film is the way Curly is used inside and out. When he swallows the fish and stands behind the fluoroscope we see something we have not yet seen: Curly's strange anatomy. We know he eats very strange items and has an iron head, and in *From Nurse to Worse* a doctor found his head to be empty, but only now do we see a fish swimming around in his belly. As if in an echo of this scene, shortly afterwards he is on the operating table undergoing the knife ['Hema-glober'] and cut open, "taken apart," and "picked clean." Once he has been fully examined and dismantled on the inside, the final scenes have his exterior completely covered with mannequin wax. No one recognizes him as human, not even Moe and Larry, and so we spend the first half of the film focusing on Curly's insides, the second half on his outside.

Covered with wax (as Moe was covered with rubber earlier this year in *Dizzy Pilots*), Curly cannot maneuver very well, nor can we see his facial expressions. He just stands or walks slowly and says an occasional line. But because Stooge comedy often requires - and will continue to do so for a few more years - Curly's energetic voice patterns and his quick, funny movements, he has to be replaced in these scenes. The replacement is Dudley Dickerson, who had created that brilliant kitchen scene in Del Lord's *A Plumbing We Will Go*. He screams, makes

faces, and even does battle with Curly twice, once with the door knob and once in the thumb wrestling contest that brings the film to its conclusion. In this sense he does not play the fourth Stooge as Richard Fiske and Vernon Dent have done before; he actually substitutes for Curly in as significant a comedy role as any other comedian has had thus far in a Stooge film.

VISUAL HUMOR: In the recent *Dizzy Pilots* we were led to believe at the outset that the Stooges were airplane mechanics; this film, too, opens with a deception: the Stooges acting as if they are doctors. The THWUMP sound effectively accompanies Curly stepping out of the wax trough. This gag resembles one used in Laurel & Hardy's *The Live Ghost* (1934). Fishing in Curly's belly parallels the fishing for Curly's tooth in the recent *I Can Hardly Wait*. Operating on Curly underneath the sheet allows the Stooges to combine their operating shtick (*Men in Black*) on the outside and a single Stooge in an enclosed jeopardy (*Pardon My Scotch*; *Boobs in Arms*) on the inside. Other variations: the Stooges rinsing their hands like doctors (*Calling All Curs*; *Some More of Samoa*); Hitler imagery (*You Nazty Spy!*); the 'Cossack

dance' (*Ants in the Pantry*); the fish bowl on Curly's head (the pot in *How High Is Up?*); Moe and Larry trying to climb into a large box (*Matri-Phony*); Larry jumping into Moe's arms (*Oily to Bed, Oily to Rise*); Larry hitting Moe and thinking it was one of the crooks (*Spook Louder*); and the Stooges at the end of the hallway going in every direction (*Dizzy Doctors*).

VERBAL HUMOR: Del Lord gives Moe and Curly some unique medical opinions (Curly: "Have I got somethin'?" Moe: "Nothin' that we can't catch."; Crook: "Whadya give him?" Curly: "Hammer-itis!"; Moe: "When we get through with him he'll be a different man!"; and Curly (looking at the pistol): "It looks like a case of life and death!") and antagonistic banter (Moe: "Give me an anesthetic, doc." Curly: "What color?"; Curly: "Hey have you got a fishing license?" Moe: "No." Curly: "Then give me back my fish!" Moe: "Here's one!"). Other variations: a silly rendition of a word "Flower-scopee" (*Higher Than a Kite*; *Phony Express*); the Latin neologisms "spectus-on-the-floorus" ("in-canna-spic-angulus" in *Ants in the Pantry*) and "sulpha-thia-sote" (*Men in Black*); and "I'll cut off your zoot suit!" (*Three Smart Saps*). When he backs into a mannequin, Dudley Dickerson says "I'm losing my mind!" (a Stooge first), but this line is often muted for television broadcasts.

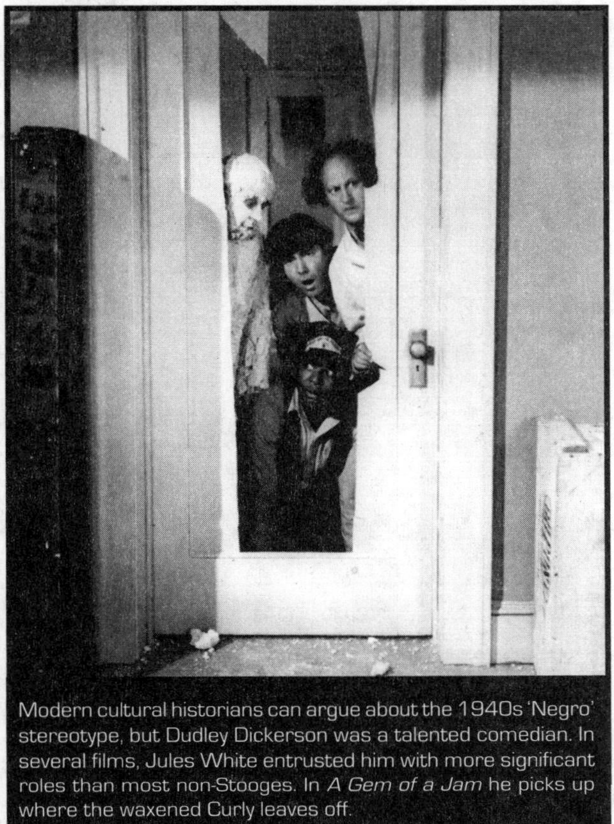

Modern cultural historians can argue about the 1940s 'Negro' stereotype, but Dudley Dickerson was a talented comedian. In several films, Jules White entrusted him with more significant roles than most non-Stooges. In *A Gem of a Jam* he picks up where the waxened Curly leaves off.

OTHER NOTES: This is the first film written and directed by the same person (Del Lord) since Charley Chase's *Flat Foot Stooges* and Jack White's *A Pain in the Pullman*. It is the first film produced by Hugh McCollum without Charley Chase or Del Lord, although Lord's impact is considerable. 'Mac' will go on to produce over thirty more Stooges shorts before his departure in 1952. The "Flower-scopee" is actually a 'fluoroscope,' predecessor to the X-ray machine. The bust Curly dusts off and slaps seems to be of Hippocrates, the Father of Medicine. This is the tenth release of 1943, more than in any other year.

1944

Crash Goes the Hash • *Busy Buddies* • *The Yoke's on Me*

Idle Roomers • *Gents Without Cents* • *No Dough Boys*

#77 - CRASH GOES THE HASH

Studio: Columbia

Released: February 5, 1944

Running Time: 17"36'"

Credited Production Crew:

Produced & Directed by:	Jules White
Story & Screen Play by:	Felix Adler
Director of Photography:	George Meehan
Film Editor:	Charles Hochberg
Art Direction:	Charles Clague

Credited Cast:

Curly Howard	
Larry Fine	
Moe Howard	
Dick Curtis	Prince Shaam of Ubeedarn
Bud Jamison	Flint, the Butler
Vernon Dent	Fuller Bull

Uncredited Cast:

Judy Malcolm	secretary
Symona Boniface	Mrs. Van Bustle
John Tyrrell	reporter
Johnny Kascier	reporter with broken foot
Wally Rose	reporter
Victor Travers	guest covered with canapés & potatoes
Beatrice Blinn	party guest
Ida Mae Johnson	party guest
Elise Grover	party guest

PERSPECTIVE: The Stooges are commonly mistaken for someone else. Ever since Felix Adler's *Three Little Pigskins*, the fourth Columbia Stooge film and Adler's second Stooge script, the Stooges have often gotten their mid-film, havoc-creating jobs by being mistaken for someone else. In *Movie Maniacs*, *Tassels in the Air*, and numerous other films this sort of misrepresentation serves as the means by which the Stooges are let into a situation they can then destroy through their incompetence. In the previous film [*A Gem of a Jam*] they were mistaken for doctors who would "pick [the patient] clean," and in the film before that [*Phony Express*] they were intentionally misrepresented as lawmen instead of vagrants. The present film offers another example of this plot device, but it has been cleverly developed here as an ever-present running theme. As in Shakespeare's *A Comedy of Errors*, this comedy depends upon repeated misrepresentational confusion: the Stooges are other than they seem, the prince and butler are other than they seem, and in one of the best loved Stooge sight gags, the turkey is not what it seems either. This is developing into a favorite Stooge concept, and years hence, in 1957, Adler would write the script for *A Merry Mix-Up*, which indeed is actually based on Shakespeare's *A Comedy of Errors*.

To make this type of misrepresentation comedy work the audience must be notified as to who is who even if the characters themselves do not know, and Felix Adler and Jules White have done this with great variety: they show us the entire back of the 'Star Cleaning Pressing Co.' truck while Fuller Bull only sees half ['Star Press']; Flint the butler does not know that the Stooges are not a cook and two butlers, but we do; nor does he know those three men to whom he says, "Such levity! You remind me of The Three Stooges!" really are The Three Stooges, but we do; no one knows the parrot has climbed into the turkey except us; and we find out that the prince is not a prince before the Stooges do.

Amidst this medley of misrepresentation the Stooges once again capture the bad guys and win out despite their incompetence. As in the previous *A Gem of a Jam*, they capture the crooks long before the end of the film, but the denouement here contains a new twist: they are not chased away or blown up; they beat each other up. We have seen occasional extended slapstick routines with as many as seven or eight exchanges [*Three Little Sew and Sews*; *Loco Boy Makes Good*], but this film concludes with seventeen slapstick events, yes, seventeen. Those who know the inter-Stooge temperament know that this means they are in a good mood and celebrating their success. This is particularly significant because it is in the midst of the misrepresentations - when the Stooges are pretending to be a chef and butlers while still pretending to be newspaper reporters - that the butler - who is pretending to be a good guy but is actually a thief along with the crook pretending to be a prince - says "Such levity! You remind me of the Three Stooges." He thinks they are like the Stooges even though they *are* the Three Stooges playing cleaners playing reporters playing domestic workers!

VISUAL HUMOR: Stooge firsts: the parrot climbing into the turkey, Moe getting his nose caught in the hinge side of a swinging door; Larry having the grand piano lid smash on top of his head; and a bent-over Larry having the hot turkey put on his back. Stooge role reversal: Moe substitutes for Curly in the 'two-men-in-the-coat' routine [*Horses' Collars)* Non-Stooge role reversals: the butler and Mrs. Van Bustle combination bonk and triple slap the Stooges; Moe shaves mashed potatoes from Victor Travers' face; and the butler knocks Curly out with the foreswing and Larry with the backswing. Stooge records: Curly revs up for ten seconds, and he walks backwards all the way from the buffet table to the kitchen. Sound effects: a xylophone is used twice for the GOUGE; the TWEET is revived from *Grips, Grunts and Groans*; there is no sound effect when Curly bites into the dog biscuit; and the sound effects are limited when Curly sharpens his knife. We have seen many cigar gags (*Men in Black*; *Uncivil Warriors*; *So Long, Mr. Chumps*), but here squashing Curly's cigar is a running gag. Other variations: a deceptive introduction to the Stooges' occupation (*Dizzy Pilots*); Curly taking Moe's pointing arm and dancing off with him (*I'll Never Heil Again*); Curly's Mexican dance, although it is a different dance (*Cuckoo Cavaliers*); Curly turning the wrong way in the hall (*Men in Black*); the Stooges poking their heads into the kitchen, one above the other (*Horses' Collars*); cooking a turkey (*An Ache in Every Stake*); large ice tongs (*Yes, We Have No Bonanza*); stepping on the edge of a dress (*Healthy, Wealthy and Dumb*); Moe blowing the prince down (*Punch Drunks*); one Stooge knocking out two others with both a foreswing and backswing (*3 Dumb Clucks*; *Three Little Sew and Sews*); and leading a Stooge into the wall/door jamb (*Three Smart Saps*).

VERBAL HUMOR: Felix Adler's first solo script since *Dizzy Detectives* contains numerous puns early in the film (Larry: "I've been runnin' my legs off all morning till my cuffs are frayed." Moe: "'Fraid of what?"; Moe: "What are you doin'?" Curly: "Listenin' to the [cigar] band."; Bull: "I want to find out if he really intends to press his suit." Curly: "He ought to. A man can't get married in baggy pants."; Larry: "Don't you know what 'bonus' is?" Curly: "Soitenly! Spanish! Bonus Naches! Si, si, senor!"; and Flint: "Are you good on stews? Curly: "Certainly, he's always half stewed!"). A fine self-denigration is this exchange (Van Bustle: "Fool!" Curly: "So am I!")... These prepare us comically for the canapés jokes, all eight of them (1) Moe: "Canapés? Oh, you mean the toast with the lace curtains!"; 2) Curly: "Now what would he want with a can o' peas?"; 3) Larry: "'Canapés' - 'canapés'? One of us is crazy and it's not you!"; 4) Moe: "Canapés! Hors d'oeuvres!" Curly: "Which one? Can o' peas or 'derves'?"; 5) Moe: "You put 'em on crackers. They give you an appetite like a horse!" Curly: "Oh! animal crackers!"; 6) Moe to Larry: "Go on, make the canapés." Curly: "With animal crackers!"; 7) Curly: "Yeah, a candid picture of can o' peas."; and 8) Prince: "Why my dear, these capers turned green. It's mildewed." Curly: "That's no calves' ear. It's can o' peas!". Epithets: for the first time Moe calls someone "mongoose"; Moe and Flint each use "feather-brain" to which Curly responds "I think you're right. I'm startin' to get chilblains." [cold sores]. Moe turns another noun into a verbal threat: Curly: "It's the gypsy in me." Moe: "I'll gypsy you later!". Roll reversal: Larry uses Curly's "I fall down" from *In the Sweet Pie and Pie*. Other variations: Curly's "It's haunted!" (*Men in Black*); "I just gave you the bird!" (*Pop Goes the Easel*); "We're colossal! We're stupendous! We're terrific! We're even superlative!" (*Movie Maniacs*); "Orders is orders!" (*Back From the Front*); and Moe's "Don't shoot until you see the bags under his eyes" (*An Ache in Every Stake*). The parrot's "Jeepers creepers! What a night!" combines the 1930's slang euphemism for 'Jesus Christ' (made into the Johnny Mercer song 'Jeepers Creepers, Where'd You Get Those Peepers' in 1938) and the parrot's "What a night!" from *Disorder in the Court*.

OTHER NOTES: The 1944 releases preserve the same credit screens and music as the previous year. This was the last of three dozen Stooge roles for Bud Jamison; for a list, see Forrester, *Trivia* 33-34. He passed away in September, 1944 at the age of 50. This is the first of eight Stooge appearances for Judy Malcolm [secretary]. This was a remake of [Monty] Collins and [Tom] Kennedy's *New News* (1937), directed by Charles Lamont (*Restless Knights*) and employing many Stooge-familiar Columbia actors at the dinner party (Stanley Blystone, Bud Jamison, Harry Semels, Lynton Brent, Lew Davis, William Irving, Bert Young, Eddie Laughton, Al Thompson, and Symona Boniface, who is in the Stooge version as well). The plot requires the Stooges to get a photo of a celebrity, as in *Dutiful but Dumb*. Daniel Volk (*The Films of the Stooges* [1988]) rates this as the "last great Stooges short."

Crash Goes the Hash (1944) is Felix Adler's and Jules White's cleverly concocted study in misrepresentation.

#78 - BUSY BUDDIES

Studio: Columbia

Released: March 18, 1943

Running Time: 16"42"'

Credited Production Crew:

Produced by:	Hugh McCollum
Directed by:	Del Lord
Story & Screen Play by:	Del Lord & Elwood Ullman
Director of Photography:	George Meehan
Film Editor:	Henry Batista
Art Director:	Charles Clague

Credited Cast:

Curly Howard
Larry Fine
Moe Howard

Uncredited Cast:

Vernon Dent	restaurant customer
Victor Travers	soup customer
Fred Kelsey	pie salesman
Eddie Gribbon	milking champ
Eddie Laughton	Sellwell rep
John Tyrrell	referee

PERSPECTIVE: The Stooges have been triumphant in most of the eleven films since early 1943. They have had victories over crooks, Western outlaws, spies, Nazis, and a gorilla, and they even took Curly's tooth out by themselves. Before *Busy Buddies* the only recent defeat the Stooges suffered was in the circus film, *Three Little Twirps*, and the narrative patterns of *Three Little Twirps* and *Busy Buddies* are similar: the Stooges begin as workmen who need money just to stay afloat, dream up a fraudulent scheme of making that money, and therefore go to a circus/carnival where they are soundly defeated by a large, mean-looking man. Producer Hugh McCollum and writer Elwood Ullman worked on both films, but the most significant reason for the similarity may be that 1943 and 1944 were years in which financial, social, and political factors sapped creativity from non-war films. Mysteries, crime dramas, romances, scare comedies, and Westerns became repetitive fare. Three days before *Busy Buddies* was released, *Casablanca*, a war romance, won the Academy Award for 'Best Picture,' and of nine nominees, four were war films, one a Western, and two religious fantasies.

In *Busy Buddies* the Stooges begin as entrepreneurial restaurant owners. This is just about the most ambitious form of employ they have had since *Playing the Ponies*, and in retrospect we can assume it resulted from the economic boom barely evident in the late 1930s, but now in full force since early in 1942. These are not unemployed 'lost men' from the Depression any more. They have become private businessmen who happen to serve lousy food and cannot pay their bills on time. The humor of the restaurant scene relies on how badly they treat and serve their customers and their providers. Their failure in this venture forces them to find another job to pay off their debt, and in these relatively prosperous times they do not seem to have any trouble at all finding a job as bill posters. But they abandon this second job for a long shot. Their choice raises a question: why did they think they could win a milking contest if they could not even tell the difference between a bull and a cow?

The answer, of course, is that they are Stooges, and the same Stoogeness that puts Curly in the bull pen three times also allows Moe and Larry to believe that they can impersonate a cow at a rural county fair. They pulled off something similar in Mexico in *What's the Matador?*, but here their opponent is smarter than a bull and their audience within the film more demanding. The humor in these middle scenes depends on Curly battling the bull, the cow chart, and the gas/milk analogy, not inter-Stooge work. And continuing this decrease in inter-Stooge slapstick, the finale requires the audience watching the film to appreciate the absurdity of the situation and Stooge pretense, not the actual physical activity of the Stooges. The audience *within* the film boos the Stooges roundly, which dehumorizes the end for the audience *watching* the film: if *they* don't buy it, *we* don't buy it. The Stooges had a bad idea, cheated, and lost. Sometimes being a Stooge means being a Stooge and paying the consequences.

VISUAL HUMOR: Stooge firsts: the two fried eggs on Moe's eyes; and the paint brush tapped on the tongue, although we have seen them paint chins and tap faces with paint brushes before (recently in *Back From the Front*). Other new sight gags in this visually inventive film include Curly removing corn kernels with wire cutters, tying Curly's apron to the shelves, Curly being launched by the spring and sliding into the cash register which rings up 'No Sale', turning the fence upside down instead of the poster, having Curly bang his head against the telephone pole repeatedly while bouncing on his suspenders, and the cow ringing the bell to signal the end of the round. The comedy of the bull scene depends on the camera not focusing on Curly. Instead, we see Curly forced to enter the pen, we watch Moe and Larry as we hear CRUNCH, and then we see the Curly dummy flying over the fence. And then Moe blames Curly. The sequence was cheap to produce, but effective. Tying the stool to the tail was used the previous year in Abbott & Costello's *Ride 'Em Cowboy*. Curly does a teeth-chatter without the metal sound effect. The cow map recalls the maps in *You Nazty*

A number of still photographs were taken during Stooge film production, many of which are reproduced in this book. Most of these stills were gag shots to be used for publicity - posters, lobby cards, etc. Very few of them were production shots, as is this one from *Busy Buddies*, the second release of 1944. Here, the crew is setting up the sequence in which Curly becomes entangled in the phone lines high above Moe, Larry and a cow.

Spy! and *I'll Never Heil Again*. Other variations: Moe and Larry wrapping the blanket around the tree and crashing into each other (*Some More of Samoa*); hot cakes and feathers (*Uncivil Warriors*); confusing coffee and paint (*Tassels in the Air*); the leaping stove (*Movie Maniacs*); the cow costume (*What's the Matador?*); the chicken soup recipe (*Playing the Ponies*); the hot soup landing on Moe's back (the turkey in *Crash Goes the Hash*); cooking egg shells (*"I Can Hardly Wait"*); Curly calculating (*Cactus Makes Perfect*); Curly being caught in the ring ropes (*Punch Drunks*); Curly suddenly gaining consciousness (*Even As IOU*); and Larry taking a drink when Curly calls for water (*Boobs in Arms*).

VERBAL HUMOR: The verbal gags demonstrate Curly's different plane of comprehension. He issues malapropisms ("Are you casting asparagus on my cookin'?!"), has reading difficulties ([looking at the upside-down poster] "Hey, what kind-a language is that?!"), and shows a lack of understanding of both bovine behavior (Moe: "I thought I told you to get some practice!" Curly: "Well the cow didn't know that. He threw me out!") and Vernon Dent's complaint about drinking paint (Dent: "This coffee tastes like paint!" Moe [tasting it]: "I just drank some paint!" Curly: "That's silly. I always drink coffee!"). The bull sequence brings out his defiant side (Curly: "It won't happen again!" Moe: "No?" Curly: "No! I'm not goin' in there again!"; and Moe: "What's the idea of crossin' us up?" Curly: "Didn't you hear me comin'?"). Moe uses both "Verify it" and "Rectify it".

There is a new sound effect (BOINK) for Vernon Dent's bent fork and for the usual 'bonk' sound. We heard the word "zoot" first in 1942's *Loco Boy Makes Good*; now the 'Jive Cafe' offers the following jive lingo on the sign at the end of the counter: 'Jive Dinners: Bloop Soup, Reat Meat, Jake Cake, and Hava Java'. Variations: The pie man's "Give 'em to me!" (*Three Sappy People*); Moe: "You nervous?" Curly: "Just in that knee." (*Punch Drunks*); "That's the trouble we have with help nowadays!" (*Crash Goes the Hash*); and "Sabatoogee" (*They Stooge to Conga*). References: 'Steinmetz' is Charles Steinmetz, the great electrical engineer and inventor, who worked from the 1890s to the 1920s. 'Reclaimed rubber' is another war-time phenomenon; the Stooges synthesized their own rubber in *Dizzy Pilots*.

OTHER NOTES: The title *Busy Buddies* was used for a Laurel & Hardy film of 1933. Eddie Gribbon (the milking champ) was a Mack Sennett regular in the 1910s, made features in the 1920s, and comedy two-reelers in the 1930s. Curly calculates that earning $97 from 25 posters a day at one cent per poster will take until 1992; actually from March, 1944 25¢ a day would come to $97 in just over a year, unless you factor in taxes, and at the standard Stooge rate that would take until...yes, 1992.

#79 - THE YOKE'S ON ME

Studio: Columbia

Released: May 26, 1944

Running Time: 16"08'"

Credited Production Crew:

Produced & Directed by:	Jules White
Story & Screen Play by:	Clyde Bruckman
Director of Photography:	Glen Gano
Film Editor:	Charles Hochberg
Art Direction:	Charles Clague

Credited Cast:

Curly Howard
Larry Fine
Moe Howard

Uncredited Cast:

Bob McKenzie	pa
Eva McKenzie	ma
Emmett Lynn	Mr. Smithers
Al Thompson	sheriff
Victor Travers	deputy

PERSPECTIVE: No Stooge film so profoundly disturbs modern viewers as this one. Many local television markets and such nationwide cable channels as TBS and The Family Channel have even blacklisted it. The problem with *The Yoke's on Me* is that it focuses on six 'Japs' who have escaped from a local relocation center and are ultimately killed. In doing so, this film reflects a dark chapter in American history: hoping to prevent Japanese espionage and fearing even a full-scale Japanese invasion, President Roosevelt confined over 40,000 resident Japanese and 70,000 Japanese-Americans at ten West coast relocation centers by executive order in March of 1942; the Supreme Court upheld the order in 1944. In their eagerness to explore the comic side of the war, the Hollywood-based Columbia short film staff, who had already made a number of films about Nazis in Europe and Nazi espionage in the U.S., turned now to this West Coast phenomenon.

While decades later this chapter in American history is not one of which we are proud - in 1988 the US government officially apologized and compensated each survivor with $20,000 - it is fascinating to see it through Stooge eyes. Even though many relocated Japanese were US citizens, the Japanese are not permitted to speak in the film, and their very identity takes on an eerie alienation when they inexplicably put pumpkins on their heads, a visual insult in Stooge terms since Moe and Larry often call Curly "pumpkin-head." The escapees actually cover their faces with Jack-o-lanterns, and in doing this they lose their identity as 'Japs.' This is particularly interesting since in anti-Nazi films the Nazis have to be identifiable by their accents and/or swastikas. But Japanese did not need attributes for identification; their faces were their attributes, so why cover their faces? Were the Japanese being made into dehumanized faceless demons and that much easier to kill? Were they considered so sinister that Californians in 1944 were supposed to suspect the Japanese of using any kind of sneaky disguise to infiltrate the West Coast? Or was this just supposed to be silly, just one step beyond the parrot stepping into the turkey in *Crash Goes the Hash?*

It may seem odd that Japanese prisoners and an ostrich just happen to escape on the same day, but Stooge successes typically depend on chance. Their triumph in *The Yoke's on Me* depends on the Stooges being unfit for military service, on buying a farm the same day six Japanese and one ostrich escape from confinement, and on the ostrich eating blasting powder. These coincidences lead to Moe tossing that ostrich egg, and the most horrifying tableau in all of Stoogedom and, for the matter, in any World War II comedy, is the aftermath of this ostrich-egg explosion: we see a DeMillean tableau of six lifeless Japanese in tortuous poses scattered about the debris of the explosion which killed them. This is difficult to watch in the twenty-first century. These people may well have been American citizens. But in 1944 most Americans thought of the Japanese as bitter enemies, and many would have found this scene triumphantly patriotic and humorous in its triumph.

VISUAL HUMOR: Despite the cloud that hangs over this film, there are many sight gags that have nothing to do with politics, particularly the entry sequence into the farm house. It finds the picket fence falling piece by piece like dominoes as the Stooges walk up the path; the loose floorboard on the stoop; and Curly leaping through the window with the pail over his head and then reentering by knocking. Another interesting comic ploy is the block and tackle running gag. The Stooges do not usually rely on running gags, but we recently saw one with Curly and his cigars in *Crash Goes the Hash*. Two bits are enhanced by fast motion: Moe being kicked into the wall by his pa, and Smithers driving the car away. Larry's best fall comes when he is knocked off the box by Curly. One of the politically incorrect gags is notable: when the three 'Japs' in pumpkin-heads gouge the Stooges, this is the only time three non-Stooges gouge the Stooges at once. The PLINK sound effect has now become the regular sound effect for the eye gouge. Another new sound effect is the BOINK/THUMP combination used when Moe jabs Larry in the belly and when Curly tests the ax. There are a number of animal gags: Curly's seal imitation, filling the 'water hole' for the duckling, the goose biting Curly's nose and making him strike his own head with the ax, and Curly's ostrich-tail fan dance.

Of course, the main gag is the exploding ostrich egg, which derives from the exploding duck egg in *Flat Foot Stooges*. Other variations: water from the knee (the squirting turkey in *Crash Goes the Hash*); Curly stepping on a loose board which hits Moe in the head (*Phony Express*); the goose on Curly's back (*A Ducking They Did Go*); Curly following Moe's arm with his nose (*Time Out for Rhythm*); a non-Stooge gouging a Stooge (*Woman Haters*); Larry and Curly in harness (*Mutts to You*); and the two 'Japs' swinging clubs and knocking each other out (*Restless Knights*).

VERBAL HUMOR: It is hard to imagine that there are more goose puns anywhere, but 'papa-gander' (*You Nazty Spy!*), 'Mahatma Gander,' and 'Goose-Stapo' are perfect political word plays for 1944, as is Curly's 'Picket duty.' Moe typically uses the latter as a verb ("I'll picket you"). The immediately Stooge prototype for this many puns in sequence is the 'canapés' scene in *Crash Goes the Hash*. The former was Felix Adler's creation; this is Clyde Bruckman's. Epithets: "squash-brain," "nitwit," and "dummy". Non-political exchanges (Larry: "I don't see a single cow." Curly: "I don't even see a married one!"; and Moe: "If you don't stop, I'll give you a pop." Curly: "What flavor?"). When Curly says "What do I know about blasting powder? I'm a horse?" he should think back to *Disorder in the Court* where he declared "I'm no mule...So I'm a mule!". Other variations: Curly: "Oh! Termites!" (*3 Dumb Clucks*); Curly's nonchalant "Pardon me, is the lady of the house in?" (*Even as IOU*); and calling the ostrich a 'pelican!' (*Disorder in the Court*). References: 'Mahatma Gander' is Mahatma [Mohandas] Gandhi, the non-violent revolutionary leader of the movement for Indian independence from Great Britain. 'MacArthur' is General Douglas MacArthur, who in the spring of 1944 was attempting to remove the Japanese from the Philippines.

OTHER NOTES: The release title parodies the expression 'the joke's on me'; the working title was *Fouled by a Fowl*. Bob McKenzie [Pa] was married in real life to Eva McKenzie [Ma]. Their real-life daughter Ella, who played the desk nurse in *Dizzy Doctors*, married Billy Gilbert, who played the insane patient in *Men in Black*. Shemp Howard was a close friend of Billy Gilbert.

The Yoke's On Me (1944) was one of the most controversial World War II films ever made, for the enemies are not Nazis or Japanese soldiers, but escapees from a California Japanese internment camp. These were the same group of people to whom the US government officially apologized and compensated financially in 1988. The film, which concludes with an explosion and the death of the escapees, is rarely broadcast on television.

#80 - IDLE ROOMERS

Studio: Columbia

Released: July 16, 1944

Running Time: 16"49'"

Credited Production Crew:

Produced by:	Hugh McCollum
Directed by:	Del Lord
Story & Screen Play by:	Del Lord & Elwood Ullman
Director of Photography:	Glen Gano
Film Editor:	Henry Batista
Art Direction:	Charles Clague

Credited Cast:

Curly Howard	
Larry Fine	
Moe Howard	
Duke York	Lupe, the Wolf Man
Christine McIntyre	Mrs. Leander
Vernon Dent	Mr. Leander

Uncredited Cast:

Eddie Laughton	hotel clerk
Joanne Frank	young woman
Esther Howard	sleeping woman

PERSPECTIVE: This film pushes Stoogedom to new frontiers of locomotion. They have recently ridden in a crazy plane (*Dizzy Pilots*), a bomb (*Higher Than a Kite*), and a blown-apart Western wagon (*Phony Express*), but in *Idle Roomers* the form of locomotion is the elevator. Yes, they ran in and out of and controlled an elevator in the hospital chase sequence of *Dizzy Doctors*, but here the elevator is again and again the focus of the film. At the very outset, the Stooges rise from their deep sleep and flip for the right to escort a woman into the elevator; Moe cheats Larry and Curly and walks her to the elevator, but Larry outsmarts Moe and smashes his nose in the elevator doors; while Larry rides with the woman, Moe runs up eight flights of steps, arrives before the elevator, and smashes Larry's head in the elevator doors; and in the final chase sequence they return to the elevator several times, ultimately riding it into the stratosphere.

Idle Roomers pushes Stoogedom to new frontiers of zoology as well. When the Stooges are not in the elevator, they deal largely with the Wolf Man, a strange beast who is neither a fraud nor a genuine monster. He is a beast who is "absolutely harmless...except when he hears music: then he goes insane!" After the bull of *What's the Matador?*, the talking horses of *Even as IOU*, and the gorilla of *Dizzy Detectives*, the writers were looking for a bigger, smarter animal, and combining that desire with the successfully frightful corridors of such films as *Spook Louder* and *A Gem of a Jam*, the Wolf

Man emerges as the perfect solution. He is real but unrealistic, scary but insane. In short, he is a very silly beast who frightens the Stooges and makes them act excessively Stooge-like. In some ways the Wolf Man reminds us of an animalistic version of Curly. Like Curly in *Punch Drunks*, the Wolf Man goes insane when he hears music. Their similarity and dissimilarities are most ironic in the sequences in which they both appear. When the woman is pointing and shouting "Wolf! Wolf!", Curly thinks she is referring to him, but moments later when the hairy Wolf Man literally mirrors the bald Curly, Curly is perplexed: "I need a shave but I don't feel any whiskers!" Most extraordinary is the peculiar moment when the silly wolf-beast is confronted with an even sillier beast - Curly with the buzzing radio on his head.

Del Lord and Elwood Ullman interwove both locomotive and zoological experiments to form the matrix for the otherwise enigmatic conclusion to this scare comedy. Larry closes the elevator doors on Moe and Curly who bounce off the doors back into the room with the beast. Trying to run from him, they panic as they push the elevator button and wait for their ride to safety. But after they enter the elevator and ride away, the Wolf Man makes them come back to the same floor by moving the outside dial - something the Stooges had done in *Dizzy Doctors*. Finally they are all in the elevator together and ready for the climactic moment, so the Wolf Man abuses now the inside controls to make the unlikely craft burst through the roof and soar into the air (*Three Little Sew and Sews*). From ground to clouds, the Stooges and a Stooge-esque beast turn an elevator into a comic means of locomotion.

VISUAL HUMOR: Another parallel between Curly and the Wolf Man: the beast evokes a screaming response from the sleeping woman much as Curly evoked a screaming response from Dudley Dickerson in *A Gem of a Jam*: her hair stands on end, as did Moe's in *Spook Louder*. And speaking of hair, the Wolf Man examines Larry's hair as if it thinks Larry might be one of him. Stooge firsts: Curly carrying the trunk on the carpet pulled by Larry; and one Stooge opening a door for another Stooge who is no longer there and letting the beast in instead, the latter to become a staple in indoor chase sequences. Being knocked backwards may look like mere slapstick but it also advances the plot. Here Moe and Curly get knocked back from the elevator into the room to confront the beast for the first time, just as Larry got knocked backwards to free the parrot from his cage in *Crash Goes the Hash*. The trombone music ('The Frederic March') is the same as the sousaphone music in *Even as IOU* and the circus music in *Three Little Twirps*.

The METAL TEETH-CHATTER sound effect, usually for intimidating some one, works well when Curly sees the monster. The Wolf Man throwing something [the radio] and hitting Moe beyond the ducking Curly is as old as the clay fight in *Pop Goes the Easel*, but the radio on Curly's head looks similar in concept to the pumpkin-head Japanese in the previous film. Other variations: Curly's foot spinning back by itself after Moe twists it (*Grips, Grunts and Groans*); the Stooges sleeping at the outset of the film (*Movie Maniacs*); Mrs. Leander stepping in the way, as Moe usually does, to get kissed by Curly (*Ants in the Pantry*); Curly knocking on Moe instead of the door (*Calling All Curs*); Moe's nostril pull with a hammer (*Uncivil Warriors; Even As IOU*); and the 'Shave and a Haircut' rhythm (*Whoops, I'm an Indian*). The mirror sequence is a gag as old as Charlie Chaplin's *Floorwalker* (1917), best known perhaps from the Marx brothers' *Duck Soup* (1933). Reactions: Notice Larry's response when Moe says to him in the elevator, "Whadya' growlin' about?"; and the face Vernon Dent makes when describing how the Wolf Man "goes insane."

Because one of the most important elements of comedy is suspension of reality, special effects are often required to differentiate what the audience sees on the screen from what they recognize as real. The conflict between the two creates the required irony. Here wires assist Curly in lifting more than a dozen trunks and suitcases in *Idle Roomers* (1944), a film which features expansive and unreal spatial frontiers.

VERBAL HUMOR: The Del Lord/Elwood Ullman script includes a notable word play (Curly: "Wait a minute! I want my tip!" Moe: "Well, I'll give you one: get out!") and an ignorant Stooge method of double-locking a door (Curly: "Once this way [clockwise] and once this way [counterclockwise]"). Larry's most ironic lines are both said in the elevator: "O captain, O captain! (derived from Walt Whitman's poem; used in *Wee Wee Monsieur*) and "There's no place to go here!". Other variations: "How can you be you when you just went out the window?" (*Three Missing Links*); Moe's always ominous "What are you growlin' about?" (*Movie Maniacs*); Curly's "I resemble that remark!" (*Three Little Twirps*); and Moe's "I always said your face scares people. Why don't you throw it away?" ("Why don't you change that face of yours - you scare people" in *Phony Express*). References: The Stooges visited 'Rhum Boogie' in *Some More of Samoa* and have made several references to "zoot," "zoot suit," and "jive," the last with the 'Jive Cafe' in *Busy Buddies*; here Curly calls a radio 'a boogie-woogie box.' 'Pyorrhea' is a gum disease. 'Lupe,' the Wolf Man's name, is derived from the Latin word for "wolf."

OTHER NOTES: Esther Howard [no relation] does a significant take, a rarity for a woman in a Stooge film. This film marks the debut of Christine McIntyre, who would play in nearly two dozen Stooge shorts. Her appearance here with the beast and Curly might have suggested some sort of beauty and the beast theme, but it did not, except for Curly's ("Wolf! Wolf!") momentary self-reflective concerns that he does not look good ("Hey I ain't that ugly...or am I?"). Curly's voice is clearly beginning to deepen.

#81 - GENTS WITHOUT CENTS

Studio: Columbia

Released: September 22, 1944

Running Time: 18"58'"

Credited Production Crew:

Produced & Directed by:	Jules White
Story & Screen Play by:	Felix Adler
Director of Photography:	Benjamin Kline
Film Editor:	Charles Hochberg
Art Direction:	Charles Clague

Credited Cast:

Curly Howard	
Larry Fine	
Moe Howard	
Lindsay [Bourquin]	[Flo]
Laverne [Thompson]	[Mary]
Betty [Phares]	[Shirley]

Uncredited Cast:

John Tyrrell	Manny Weeks
Lynton Brett	lieutenant in 'At the Front'
Judy Malcolm	secretary
Robert 'Bobby' Burns	audience member
Eddie Borden	

PERSPECTIVE: To entertain domestic factory workers and troops overseas during the war, Hollywood studios made a number of films featuring both well-known contract stars and eager new acts performing musical numbers and military comedy skits. Some of the best known of these studio extravaganzas were Paramount's *Star Spangled Rhythm* (1942), Warner's *Thank Your Lucky Stars* (1943) and *Hollywood Canteen* (1944), and MGM's *Thousands Cheer* (1943). *Gents Without Cents* is the Stooge entry into this category. The previous year they had filmed the 'Niagara Falls' routine for a Columbia feature, *Good Luck, Mr. Yates* (1943), but their scene was edited out before release. Now in a continuous offering of music, dance, and sketch comedy the Stooges perform 'Niagara Falls' in their own apartment, watch Flo, Mary, and Shirley dance upstairs, perform 'We Just Dropped In To Say Hello' to the delight of no one in Manny Weeks' office but then redeem themselves with 'Ratattootily-day-day.' This earns them the chance to perform 'Niagara Falls' at the shipyards - working in the earlier footage – and gives the girls another number and the Stooges themselves the chance to perform the comedy skit 'At the Front.' From the freshly syncopated music of the opening credits and the opening Stooge number everything is performed with the zesty, bright attitude that usually characterized such quickly produced wartime musicals.

When the Stooges portray themselves as entertainers they do not hesitate to make fun of themselves. Characters in the film who watch the Stooges' act often do not laugh at them, whether it is the snotty Paul Pain in *A Pain in the Pullman*, the saddened little girl in *Nutty but Nice*, or Manny Weeks in this film. There are two reasons for this. One is that the Stooges louse up all their jobs one way or another; they play bad plumbers, bad doctors, and bad carpenters, why should they not play bad entertainers? The other is that it was common in backstage musicals to portray movie stars as struggling entertainers desperate to get a 'break,' conniving to get that break, and then winning over both audience and producer for the tuneful, danceful finale. Ultimately performing their act with Flo, Mary, and Shirley before the appreciative crowd of 'Noazark Shipbuilding Company' workers, the Stooges move from rags to riches and find love along the way.

A 'backstooge' musical is a little different, though. The Stooges perform their 'Niagara Falls' act well, but always have an accident when they get to "inch by inch." At one point such an accident leads them to the wonderful bathtub ad-libbing. At the conclusion of the film it takes on a broader significance, for by this point they have moved out of the world of backstage musicals and into the real world. That is, their theatrical world behind them for the moment, they and the girls get

married and are going on their honeymoon in Niagara Falls! Being on hiatus from the theater does not stop Moe and Larry from reacting to the words 'Niagara Falls,' and even their wives join in. Singing and dancing may be something the Stooges do for a living in this film, but screwing up and beating up is something they do quite naturally. They take no vacation from Stooging. All the world's a stooge.

VISUAL HUMOR: The live stage act, which even the on-stage musicians enjoy very much, gives us the flavor of the Stooges actual live act which they performed long before their tenure at Columbia and continued to perform throughout their careers. Like the Marx Brothers' *Cocoanuts*, *Gents Without Cents* successfully transfers a live act to the screen. In fact, even the bathtub scene is clearly ad-libbed as if it were live; (it also demonstrates what a basic tool Curly's head is)...

Because this film is of a different genre, the visual humor is limited mostly to the skits. New slapstick gags are of modest proportions: Curly spinning his head while looking at the record, the Stooges taking a bath together, and Curly hanging a lantern on his coat tail. The latter two are Stooge firsts. Variations are limited as well, although there are two of the 'fist game': the first with the baseball bat, the second with Moe showing Curly his fist ("See that?"), Curly slapping it, then Moe slapping it and bonking Curly on the head.

Curly backs into the bath as Larry had backed into the parrot cage (*Crash Goes the Hash*) and Moe and Curly had backed into the room with the Wolf Man (*Idle Roomers*). Other variations: Curly's hand caught in the spittoon, and the Stooges snoring together (*Hoi Polloi*); and Larry imitating a Japanese person, Curly Mussolini, and Moe Hitler (*You Nazty Spy!; They Stooge to Conga*). Sound effects: the eye gouge is now regularly accompanied by the PLINK sound (*The Yoke's on Me*). The "woob-woob-woob" is dubbed in the second time Moe turns to Curly on stage and says "Niagara Falls!"

VERBAL HUMOR: The verbal gags are also limited because it is a 'revue' type of film, but standouts include Curly's infamous misreading of the 'Go Slow' sign; Shirley's "Oh what an awful lump!"; the stage exchange (Moe: "Every time I hear it it tears me apart." Curly: "It don't do me any good either!"); and the camera panning down to read 'Berlin Soon'. Moe uses a comic delay twice. The first is when he says "I'll handle this: I'll break their necks, I'll bash their noses in. And if it's a big muscular guy in there...[to Curly]...you handle him!" The second precedes the bathtub sequence ("A bath!...Move over."). This pattern recalls that used recently in *Even As IOU* and *Dizzy Pilots*. Curly took a bath "so it shouldn't be a total loss!" previously in *So Long, Mr. Chumps*. Other variations: the name of the Stooges' act, 'Two Souls and a Heel' (a cut of beef ['Filet of Sole and Heel'] on the cow map in *Busy Buddies*); and "I fall down! (*In the Sweet Pie and Pie*).

References: Just as Flo, Mary, and Shirley dance to a boogie-woogie version of a bugle call in this film, in the last film Curly had referred to the radio as "a boogie-woogie box"; Boogie-woogie gained its popularity in 1938, and by 1944 the Andrews Sisters, certainly the inspiration for Lindsay, Laverne, and Betty ('Flo, Mary, and Shirley'), had made 'Boogie Woogie Bugle Boy' into a smash hit. Larry imitates a Japanese person with "So solly, prease. Bomb Tokyo!" Curly Mussolini with "Ratat-tootily-poosh-em-up!" and Moe Hitler with "Ratat-tootily-Ya-Voll-Invasion!" The verbal gags in the show sign include 'NOAZARK Shipbuilding' and 'Castor and Earle,' i.e. Castor Oil.

OTHER NOTES: The shooting dates were in mid-June, 1944. The working title was *Tenderized Hams*. The introductory Stooges' musical theme is syncopated because of the jazzy subject matter; after the next release (*No Dough Boys*) the syncopation will be used regularly. The performance at the shipyard was typical of wartime shows put on by the USO, which had been founded in 1941. Many of the Stooges' actual USO performances were sponsored by Coca-Cola. Gymnastic jazz dancing was popular in 1943-44, e.g. Busby Berkeley's *The Gang's All Here* (1943). In the stage version of 'Niagara Falls,' Larry blows his line and says "inch by inch" before "step by step" the last time around. Abbott & Costello used the routine in *Lost in the Harem* (1944). The gag, not always using 'Niagara Falls' as the trigger, originated in Burlesque and dated back several decades. This is the last of seven Stooge appearances by Robert 'Bobby' Burns [dancer], best remembered as Professor Fuller in *Pop Goes the Easel*. He is not to be confused with Bob Burns, the singer/dancer vaudeville comic.

#82 - NO DOUGH BOYS

Studio: Columbia

Released: November 24, 1944

Running Time: 16"54'"

Credited Production Crew:

Produced & Directed by:	Jules White
Story & Screen Play by:	Felix Adler
Screen Play:	Felix Adler
Director of Photography:	George Meehan
Film Editor:	Charles Hochberg
Art Direction:	Charles Clague

Credited Cast:

Curly Howard	
Larry Fine	
Moe Howard	
Vernon Dent	Hugo, Nazi spy
Christine McIntyre	Delia Zwieback

Uncredited Cast:

Kelly Flint	Amelia Schwarzbrot
Judy Malcolm	Celia Pumpernickel
John Tyrrell	director
Brian O'Hara	restauranteur

PERSPECTIVE: This final 1944 release offers a unique anti-Axis satire in which all three Stooges impersonate Japanese soldiers. Previously we have seen the camera-happy Japanese representative [Duncan Renaldo] in *I'll Never Heil Again*, the "So!" spy in *They Stooge to Conga*, Larry's "So solly, prease. Bomb Tokyo!" in *Gents Without Gents*, and the six relocation center escapees in *The Yoke's on Me*, but here the Stooges themselves dress and talk like Japanese. They wear buck teeth, repeatedly say "ah so!" "prease," and "vely," make fun of Japanese misused participles ("Maybe going into conference"; "Ah to getting me out, prease!"), noun prefixes ("Mit-chewie!") and suffixes ("Come backie," "My mistackie," the name 'Waki'), speak calmly about blood, brains spilling out, and broken bones, and offer a jujitsu demonstration.

Incorporated into this scenario are four Nazi spies, three of whom are the "well bred" Amelia Schwarzbrot, Celia Pumpernickel, and Delia Zwieback. This is a narrative wrinkle adapted from the Flo, Mary, and Shirley of the last film as well as the various rhyming female triplets of earlier films (e.g. Dorabell, Corabell and Florabell in *The Sitter Downers*). This combination of seven spies is a lot for three men, let alone Stooges, to tackle on their own. In fact, other than the collection of Nazi sailors they defeated and stacked up in *Back From the Front*, this is the largest complement of Axis enemies the Stooges will have to face. But as in *Back From the Front*, the large number of adversaries makes the Stooges that much more heroic. It allows them to have both the jujitsu struggle with the women early on and then the final lights-out battle adapted from *Nutty but Nice*. By defeating the Nazi women, the Japanese spies, and the swastika-print underweared Hugo [Vernon Dent], the Stooges in a symbolic sense win both theaters of the war all by themselves.

It is not clear at the outset what profession the Stooges are malpracticing in this film, but the reason Hugo the Nazi thinks the Stooges are Japanese is that they are dressed as Japanese soldiers for a photographic shoot. When Moe later mentions their 'acrobatic act,' it becomes clear that they are showmen by profession, just as they were showmen in the previous film (*Gents Without Cents*). This means that The Three Stooges are playing 'The Three Stooges,' so it is 'The Three Stooges' who round up this nest of Axis spies. There is another similarity with the previous film, also produced, directed, and written by Jules White and Felix Adler. *Gents Without Cents* ended with the Stooges maintaining their theatrical roles even in real life; the phrase 'Niagara Falls' endangered Curly in his non-theatrical married life just as much when he was on stage. Here the Stooges step off the photographic set, keep their uniforms on, and play their roles in a non-theatrical experience. They defeat the spies because they can act, look and talk like Japanese, and do acrobatics like Japanese. The Germans may see through their disguise, but it is the play acting that allows the Stooges to survive until the final battle. All the world is still a stooge.

VISUAL HUMOR: There are new wrinkles where Moe surreptitiously puts his elbow next to Curly's belly and then rams his fist into it, and where Curly makes a face, a noise and wiggles his pinkie finger in his ear in front of Hugo. He offers another series of gestures and noises in the hallway. After all this time there is a new variation on the gouge (Moe: "Watch your Ps and Qs." Curly: "Don't forget to dot the 'I's." [GOUGE]; Moe's 'Ps and Qs' we heard in *Three Missing Links*. Other slapstick variations: when Curly is introduced as 'Waki,' he gives his longest finger-snap to date, and, in role reversals, all three Stooges perform at least the floor-crawling part of the chicken-with-its-head-cut off. The secret door that leads from the restaurant to the second part of the plot is a stationary variation of the 'unknown transfer' (e.g. the back of a truck) the Stooges often employ to move the plot to a different scenario.

The swastika underwear is a nicer print than that used in *Higher Than a Kite*. Curly pulls out a cigarette, cigar, and pipe as he does pencils in *Movie Maniacs*. Smoking an imaginary pipe was used in Laurel & Hardy's *Way Out West* (1937). Speaking with bread stuffed into their mouths recalls the alum sequence in *No Census, No Feeling*. Other variations: Moe having trouble with the swinging door (*Playing the Ponies*); bending a metal tray around someone's head (*Yes, We Have No Bonanza*); the bird pecking at Curly's head (*Back to the Woods*); Curly's head smashing through to the other side of a wall (*Cactus Makes Perfect*); the Stooges saluting 'Heil' and slapping a Nazi's forehead (*They Stooge to Conga*); cooling a burning rear in a tub of water (*How High Is Up?*); champagne squirting out the ears (*Healthy, Wealthy and Dumb*); Moe rapping on Curly's forehead and Curly saying "Come in!"(*From Nurse to Worse*); the seltzer fight (*Three Little Pigskins*); smashing a globe over a Nazi's head (*I'll Never Heil Again*); and making Curly bend over, hitting him on the back of the head, and knocking him to the ground (*Pop Goes the Easel*).

VERBAL HUMOR: Moe utters a classic line when he unknowingly bangs Larry's head on the floor and says, "Whadya' doin' in my hands?". Curly offers a political pun: "Through the 'ally'". The Stooges have done phone answering gags since *Men in Black*, but here the "Shut up you idiots...I don't mean you, sir. I mean these other idiots," derives from *What's the Matador?*. "Yes" is a word the Stooges have often had fun with, but this is the most extreme case (Director: "Hello...yes!...ohh, yes...yeesss...yes, yes, yes, yes, yes, yes, yes." Stooges [in unison]: "yes, yes, yes, yes, yes, yes, yes, yes!"). Epithet: when the bird pecks on Curly's head, Moe calls him a "numskull".

Moe's pun on the women's names ("They are all vely well bred!") is a variation of "She was well bred up in Kentucky" (*Loco Boy Makes Good*). The closing "Ist dass not a swastika?" chant is from *I'll Never Heil Again*. Moe's "pesseristic" for "pessimistic" recalls his "inconspicerous" malapropism in *Ants in the Pantry*. The 'yielding' gag (Curly: "I'll give you—" Moe: "What?!" Curly [yielding]: "The meanest look.") is like the "I'd blast" exchange in *The Sitter Downers*. Moe: "Hello there!" Curly: "Hello there!" Moe: "Where are you?" Curly: "Right here!" resembles Curly's echo encounter in *We Want Our Mummy*. References: the sign 'VAN DYKE RUBEN' refers to two great Flemish painters, Anthony Van Dyke (*Wee Wee Monsieur*) and Peter Paul Rubens. The names 'Pumpernickel,' 'Schwarzbrot' [black bread], and 'Zwieback' [twice baked] are all types of German bread.

OTHER NOTES: There is no comma in the title *No Dough Boys*. The expression "dough boys" means 'GIs.' It may derive from certain pre-Civil War uniforms on which buttons were as large as dumplings ("dough boys"). The term was used by the British to describe U.S. soldiers in World War I, replacing the term '[Uncle] Sammies'. The working title was *The New World Odor*, a phrase Hugo uses in the final scene.This is the last of only six releases in 1944, the fewest since their first year at Columbia; the following year there will be only five.

In consecutive films - the previous *Gents Without Cents* and here in *No Dough Boys* (1944) - the Stooges play performers who involve themselves in the war effort. In the former, it is in the USO. But in *No Dough Boys*, the Stooges play and maintain their roles as Japanese soldiers so they can defeat a nest of Axis spies. This is the last time they will have to encounter Nazis, for the war in Europe is reaching a conclusion six months after D-Day. But the war in the Pacific continues.

1945

Three Pests in a Mess • Booby Dupes • Idiots Deluxe

If a Body Meets a Body • Micro-Phonies

#83 - THREE PESTS IN A MESS

Studio: Columbia

Released: January 19, 1945

Running Time: 17"41'"

Credited Production Crew:

Produced by:	Hugh McCollum
Directed & Written by:	Del Lord
Director of Photography:	Benjamin Kline
Film Editor:	Henry Batista
Art Director:	Charles Clague

Credited Cast:

Curly Howard	
Larry Fine	
Moe Howard	
Christine McIntyre	secretary
Brian O'Hara	I. Cheatham
Vernon Dent	Philip Black

Uncredited Cast:

Snub Pollard	watchman
Charles 'Heine' Conklin	devil
Victor Travers	patent office man

PERSPECTIVE: This first release of 1945 recombines three frequently used plot elements from previous Stooge films - gadgetry, conmen, and spooks - but rearranges the first two and reassigns the third. As in *Termites of 1938*, the Stooges have invented a better mouse trap. This time it is a fly catcher that exploits the fly's nosy nature to tempt him up eight flights of fly steps and his competitive nature to make him see his reflection in a mirror, think it is another fly, and plunge to his death. A simple calculation of how many flies it will take at a penny a fly to earn $100 catches the ears of the three conmen across the hall. The writers separate out Curly and the secretary for a few minutes of private silliness. Then, the six actors reconvene in the hallway and the next office for a few minutes in a neat, compact interior chase sequence which has the Stooges running out the door twice into the conmen, reversing, and fleeing back, each time knocking a rifle down onto their own heads. With one of those rifles, Curly inadvertently shoots the hat off an innocent passerby and then 'murders' a mannequin. As the Stooges flee out the window with their bagged victim, the narrative events of the first half of the film, as rarely happens, come to a finite conclusion. The conman element is utterly terminated when the secretary discovers the Stooges have no money; the joke about the winner's taxed earnings bringing both the gadgetry and conmen portions of the film to a decidedly final close. The one loose end is the cop who chases the "murderers," and although we do not hear from the cop again this secondary chase forces the Stooges to the gates of the cemetery for the 'scare comedy.'

This third element is connected to the first half of the film in several ways. It was while hiding from the conmen that the Stooges murdered the mannequin in the first place, so they bring it to this spook scenario, unique in that unlike previous examples [*Spook Louder*, *A Gem of a Jam* [also written and directed by Del Lord], *Idle Roomers*] the scare comedy takes place not in interior building rooms and corridors but in a dark exterior cemetery. Also, an animal cemetery is an appropriate place for those who would have killed 100,000 flies. And then there is the persistent theme of the film - death.

Death follows the Stooges throughout. Early on Moe and Curly relish talk about the death of the fly [Moe: "He jumps down, lands on his stomach and knocks his brains out." Curly: "It's a beautiful sight!"], not unlike the Japanese sadism in *No Dough Boys* ["If falling are smashing head, spilling brains and blood. Vely beautiful."] Then the mannequin dies, and personified Death deals Curly as much physical abuse as it can. The mannequin corpse slaps him, the caretaker pretends to be a corpse and kicks him, and at the end of the film Curly has a corpse thrown at him. When the Undertaker [=Death], the Devil [=a tormentor of corpses], and the Skeleton [=a corpse "picked clean" [*A Gem of a Jam*]] rise out of the grave, it scares the Stooges so much that they run away. They may be able to defeat Axis spies and even 100,000 flies, but they cannot defeat Death...not until *Heavenly Daze*.

VISUAL HUMOR: Stooge firsts: water spraying out of holes in Curly's scalp; the Stooges' socks springing up; the Stooges jumping out of their shoes; and the Stooges running run out from behind a door just as the conmen are about to break in, which they do twice. The latter is one of many door gags that will develop in future films. One of the techniques used in almost every scare comedy is to isolate the individual Stooges so each can be scared, scare the other two when he runs into them, leave another stranded outside a door, and reconvene with the other two for a final plan. Here in the cemetery Moe runs away after knocking on the door, and by the time Larry opens the door, the devil has reached the same spot. This gag sequence we saw in *Three Missing Links* and *Idle Roomers*, but here Larry slams the door on him and then backs into the skeleton. The door, interestingly, leads nowhere; it is open on Moe's side, open on Larry's, and it sits in the middle of an exterior location. Doors are important for spatial separation in a chase sequence, so this door is a barrier, not an exit/entrance.

One of the advantages of being a comedy trio is having three heads, six arms, three bodies, and six legs to work with, not to mention tools and gadgets as extensions. In this shot from 1945's first release, *Three Pests in a Mess*, the Stooges posture their heads in unison but choreograph their hands and arms variously in an attempt to convince a patent office worker [Victor Travers] that their Fly Catcher is a worthy invention. The permutations are many, complex, and ever-changing.

Curly often takes a beating, but not at the hands of a lovely woman. Previously he has been slapped, hit, and barked at by women, but Christine McIntyre really manhandles him, leading up to the beating in the next film and the one she gives Shemp in the classic *Brideless Groom*. The multiple sound effect of knitting needles sticking in Curly's head matches the multiple holes they make; another appropriate sound effect is the knocking sound we hear when the skeleton scratches his head. The 'aoogah' horn sound effect was first used in *Restless Knights*. Knocking on a forehead instead of a door we have seen since *Calling All Curs*, but here Moe honks Curly's nose as well. Other variations: Curly's multi-layered wardrobe, and calculating a large sum reduced by heavy taxes (*Cactus Makes Perfect*); Curly turning to Moe ("What is it?") who turns to Larry who turns to Moe ("Nothin'!") who turns to... (*Uncivil Warriors*); Moe stopping Larry, then Curly with "That's' enough!" (*Movie Maniacs*); sitting on knitting needles (*The Sitter Downers*); the Stooges losing their shoes (*Half-Shot Shooters*); Curly beating his vest like Tarzan (*Disorder in the Court*); Curly ducking so the ink hits Moe (recently in *A Gem of a Jam*); and water spraying out of a bodily orifice (*Healthy, Wealthy and Dumb*).

VERBAL HUMOR: Del Lord wrote fine lines for Christine McIntyre, including a fractured nursery rhyme ("I went to the cupboard to get my poor self a bone. But when I went there, the cupboard was bare, not even a bottle was there!") which makes the Stooges cry (*So Long, Mr. Chumps*), and a pitiable line ("They tried to drown me...As a matter of fact they did!"). He gives Curly and Larry characteristic ignorance (Larry: "Why can't we bury him out in the street?" Curly: "What? And have someone run over him and kill him again?"; Curly [describing tumble weed]: "a man running on his hands and knees...he had a big head and long curls—"), and Moe uncharacteristic sarcasm (Larry: "You gonna hit him with the water?" Moe: "No, I'm gonna throw the water away and hit him with the bucket!").

References: Curly's "Call for Philip Black" mimics the popular 'Call for Philip Morris' cigarette commercials of the day. Larry calls the ink-faced Moe "porter" and "mammy," the latter making reference to Al Jolson (*All the World's a Stooge*). Curly's "I ain't got no body! I lost it!" refers to the popular song, as in *Men in Black*. Epithet: "numskull". Other variations: Secretary: "Look what you did to my knitting needles!" Curly: "They didn't do me any good either!" (*Gents Without Cents*); Curly: "Why don't you make up your mind? Are you a yo-yo?" (*No Census, No Feeling*); and Moe: "What are you yellin' about?" Curly: "That wasn't me." Larry shakes his head no. (*Movie Maniacs*).

OTHER NOTES: The music for the opening credits, re-recorded for the first three 1945 releases and for 1946's *Three Loan Wolves*, has a sustained bassoon note over the driving 'Three Blind Mice' theme, a jazzy, syncopated middle and a xylophone featured at the end. The latter half of the film is a reworked version of El Brendel's *Ready, Willing but Unable* (1941), which was also directed by Del Lord; the cast included Dudley Dickerson and Bud Jamison. The concept dates back at least to Laurel & Hardy's *Habeas Corpus* (1928). Lord also wrote and directed the previous scare comedy, *A Gem of a Jam* (his second of three solo efforts), and directed both *Spook Louder* and *Idle Roomers*. It would take 10,000 flies to earn $100.

#84 - BOOBY DUPES

Studio: Columbia

Released: March 17, 1945

Running Time: 17"02"'

Credited Production Crew:

Produced by:	Hugh McCollum
Directed & Written by:	Del Lord
Director of Photography:	Glen Gano
Film Editor:	Henry Batista
Art Direction:	Charles Clague

Credited Cast:

Curly Howard	
Larry Fine	
Moe Howard	
Rebel Randall	Captain's girl
Vernon Dent	Captain

Uncredited Cast:

John Tyrrell	man with boat
Dorothy Vernon	customer
Snub Pollard	ice cream vendor
Wanda Perry	bather
Geene Courtney	bather
Lola Gogan	bather

PERSPECTIVE: The Stooges have abused many elaborate forms of aquatic transportation from acrobatic submarines to Nazi freighters, but now they purchase a small boat in what would turn out to be the Stooges final World War II film. To develop the story, Hugh McCollum and Del Lord revive the Stooges' fish peddling scenario from *Cookoo Cavaliers* and combine it with the fishing exploits from *Whoops, I'm an Indian* and several military motifs - impersonating an officer, picking up women, and surviving an air raid - from *Higher Than a Kite* and the pre-war *Three Little Sew and Sews*. Curly wears an officer's uniform and picks up a girl at the beach, which leads into the struggle with the officer since Curly has taken both his clothes and his girlfriend. As in the conman scenario of the previous film (*Three Pests in a Mess*), this initial scenario ends rather abruptly. And again as in the previous film, there is little carryover into the rest of the film, except the realization that they need a boat. One subtle but important carryover, though, is that Curly saves his 'radio,' that is, the Victrola.

The Stooges are about 50-50 with conmen; sometimes they win, sometimes they lose. In this case they indulge in a disastrous auction in which Curly and Larry stupidly jack up the price. And when they finally purchase the boat from the swindler, they laugh because they think they have duped him, but he laughs because he knows he has indeed duped them. In truth, we are the winners in this transaction since preparing the dilapidated boat requires the Stooges to use tools on it and each other, and once they get it out onto the water they end up destroying it through their incompetence - first jettisoning the anchor and the steering mechanism, then chopping holes in the bottom and drilling more to let the water out - much as they destroyed their own plane in *Dizzy Pilots*. Fortunately a plane flies overhead just in the nick of time, but unfortunately to send an SOS Moe uses a flag with a splotch of red paint that makes it look as if they are 'Japs.' (They were recently confused for Japanese spies in *No Dough Boys*.) They barely escape with their lives, saved by an [unexplained] extra boat and Curly's Victrola.

This terrible SOS blunder is just one of the many incidents in this film in which Moe takes more abuse and indulges in dumber stunts than usual. He gets blasted by a horn in his ear and hit with a boomeranging record on the back of his head, he sits on a fish bone, Curly steps on his head, he gets nails in his feet, his pants ripped up by the propeller, his head conked by the mast and hit with the metal "sinker," and then he throws the steering wheel overboard. Curly even challenges his authority when he demands to be made captain. Fear not, though; the pants presser puts an end to that, and several times Moe slaps Larry simply to reassert his authority. Perhaps it has something to do with Curly's failing health, but it also may be Del Lord's plan for Moe to be challenged and ultimately triumph. After all, it was Moe's bright idea to wave the Japanese flag in the first place, but he also came up with the idea of using the Victrola to escape.

VISUAL HUMOR: The truck 'radio' is another Curly gadget, as was the fly catcher in the previous *Three Pests in a Mess*. Also from the previous film (where Christine McIntyre manhandled Curly) are the girls hitting Moe and Larry, Moe sitting on the fish skeleton (like Curly sitting on the knitting needles), and Curly making a foghorn sound (the 'aoogah' car horn). Laurel & Hardy had a similar type of car 'radio' in *Busy Bodies* (1933). Vernon Dent wearing Curly's clothes is quite a sight. The boat-

for-car exchange recalls the car-for-farm exchange in the recent *The Yoke's on Me*. Curly's fight with the fish is an expanded, exterior version of his battle with the feisty oyster in *Dutiful but Dumb*. Curly insists he is not the tailor - another example of someone assuming the Stooges run a business just because they are in the office. Vernon Dent is knocked into the ice cream cart much as he went head first into his birthday cake in *An Ache in Every Stake*. Reference: the paint-stained flag Moe waves looks like the Japanese 'rising sun' flag.

VERBAL HUMOR: Del Lord included many appropriate maritime puns (Larry [saluting]: "Aye aye, captain!" Moe [saluting]: "Aye!" Larry [hit in the face]: "Aye!"; Moe: "Bail out!" Larry: "I haven't got my parachute!"; and Curly [holding a fish eaten by cats]: "A skeleton fish!";), insults (Larry: "Shut up!" Moe: "Are you talkin' to me?" Larry: "No, I'm talkin' to the fish!" Moe: "Don't call me a fish!"), ironies (Curly [when their boat is still tied to the dock]: "It's a little slow, ain't it?"), and ignorant neologisms: Curly calls the drill "a water-letter-outer!" and the bomb blast a "flying fish". Lord also inserted several military puns (Moe: "They're finding the range!" Curly: "I wish I was at home on the range!"), ironies (Girlfriend: "If he finds me here with you he'll kill you!" Curly: "If he finds me here in this suit he'll do worse than that!"), and insults (Girlfriend [seeing her fat boyfriend i]: "My! What a uniform does cover up!". Moe shouts, "Hey! It's the Stooges!" They have played themselves in three of the last four films.

After all these years Moe finally mimics Curly's "Nyuk, nyuk, nyuk"; he had mimicked Curly's falsetto in *Three Little Sew and Sews*). Moe said "That's enough!" (*Movie Maniacs*) twice in the last film and once here to Curly when he botches up his explanation of why they should get a fishing boat. Moe's "The better to see us, my dear!" is a nursery rhyme reference; there was one in *Three Pests in a Mess*. Other variations: the auction sequence (*Three Little Beers*); "She loves me; she loves me not" (*Movie Maniacs*); "My! What a beautiful head of bone you have!" (*Whoops, I'm an Indian*); "I'll bet you tell that to all the boys!" (*Horses' Collars*); singing "catfish" as a major triad (various); and Curly: "I reckon this must be a good spot, I reckon" (*Uncivil Warriors*). Epithets: "mallet-head," "lunk-head," and "nitwit". References: 'Boogie-woogie' has been referred to in the previous few films. Here the Stooges listen to big band jazz on their 'radio' and mention Harry James, the popular trumpeter/band leader (and husband of Betty Grable) who starred in several feature-length musical revues of the *Gents Without Cents* variety. Every once in a while Moe issues a profound truism (e.g. *Calling All Curs*): "When you didn't know what you were talking about, you really had something!"

OTHER NOTES: Laurel & Hardy's *Towed in a Hole* (1933) includes similar gags - selling fish, blowing a horn, buying a boat (Billy Gilbert played the boat salesman) - but L&H never make it to the water, and while Laurel saws a mast down onto Hardy's head, the slapstick characteristically advances at a much slower pace. The boat scene must have been too costly to reshoot, for a number of mistakes are visible: the fish leaps out of the boat into the water and then leaps back into the boat; Curly hits Larry in the middle of the back with his ax; Curly swims out of the shot; and there is no explanation for the second boat.

"Tuna fish, cod fish, smelt fish,dogfish! First tuna, second tuna, barracuda, bass!"

The Stooges give one of their rhythmic chants during the intial scenario of *Booby Dupes* (1945). This is the third and final film both written and directed by Del Lord (*A Gem of a Jam; Three Pests in a Mess)*. Lord had directed more than three dozen Stooge shorts to date, but he would not direct another until 1948's *Shivering Sherlocks*. And that would be his last.

#85 - IDIOTS DELUXE

Studio: Columbia

Released: July 20, 1945

Running Time: 17"28'"

Credited Production Crew:

Produced & Directed by:	Jules White
Story & Screen Play by:	Elwood Ullman
Director of Photography:	Glen Gano
Film Editor:	Charles Hochberg
Art Direction:	Hilyard Brown

Credited Cast:

Curly Howard
Larry Fine
Moe Howard

Uncredited Cast:

Vernon Dent	judge
Paul Kruger	policeman
Al Thompson	courtroom audience member

PERSPECTIVE: If the legal climate of today existed in the Stooge era, one Stooge would have taken another to court for "intent to commit mayhem" a long time ago. But as it was, this film came at an interesting point in the Columbia series. In the previous film, it was Curly's idea to buy their own boat and cut out the middleman from their fishmonger business, so he insisted: "I wanna be captain!"; Moe quickly terminated this rebellion by grabbing Curly's nose and putting his head in the pants presser. Now in *Idiots Deluxe,* Moe's authority is so challenged that Curly and Larry take him to court. In addition, in the previous film Moe's increased bullying was balanced with a greater vulnerability. Now he is so challenged and annoyed with his "roommates" that he goes after them with an ax, and he is so close to being at wit's end with them that he is reduced to a nervous breakdown, a regimen of pills and vitamins, and bed rest for six months. In terms of vulnerability, this is the low point for Moe's character in all the Stooge films. His dominant postures and aggressive acts have apparently ceased to have any effect. Ironically, in real life it is Curly who had experienced several small strokes by this point and was the vulnerable one, hence Moe's becoming the comic butt.

The courtroom scene is the structural frame of the film. It establishes the flashback (the first since *Spook Louder*) to the camping trip which is the essence of the film. Once there, the narrative of the camping trip itself is very simple, a return to simplification after the involved plots of the previous few films: the Stooges go camping to calm Moe's nerves, the bear eats their food, they hunt him and think they have killed him, but then he wakes up, drives their car and crashes it.

The bear generates most of the humor, more so than the bear in *Rockin' Thru the Rockies* and more so than their fear of the gorillas in *Three Missing Links* and *Dizzy Detectives*, the alligator in *Some More of Samoa*, and the Wolf Man in the recent *Idle Roomers*. We see this in their takes when they see the bear and in their ineptitude in trying to shoot, capture, and escape the bear: when Moe accuses the others of eating his food, when he is first swiped by it, when Larry jumps into the window in fast motion, when Curly bounces back into the trap, when Moe tries to convince Larry to go back outside, when Larry and Curly walk in the direction opposite of where the bear was seen, when Larry and Curly confuse Moe for the bear, when the bear keeps hitting Curly and Larry in the car, and when the bear drives the car and makes a turn signal. Although Stooge action is usually preferable to Stooge reaction, the Stooges are clearly expanding their repertoire of reactions to fear, threat, and surprise and turning these reactions into destructive, comical actions that bring out some of their finest comic qualities: suspecting each other of causing a problem, inventing silly solutions to the problem, and hurting each other while trying to eliminate the problem, all the while yelling, running, and gesturing in groups of one, two, or three Stooges in a *perpetuum mobile* of comic movement and gestures.

VISUAL HUMOR: Curly and Larry have help: even the cat's footsteps disturbs Moe. Heads at risk: Curly hitting Larry's with the shovel; Moe hitting the cop's with the ax; and Curly hitting Moe's with his rifle barrel. In *Busy Buddies* Curly cooked eggs and their shells; here he cooks them with a hammer. The end of the pill-taking scene is ad-libbed, as was the bathtub scene in the recent *Gents Without Cents*. In *Three Pests in a Mess* a door served as a comic prop in an exterior setting; here the substitute is the shutters through which Larry leaps in fast motion and into which Curly crashes. Banging the rifle on the floor and shooting a duck derives from *Back to the Woods*; Curly holding out his hands and "waiting for the dressing and the cranberry sauce" is a fine verbal addition. The previous court film (*Disorder in the Court*) also included an instrumental musical number. Other variations: Moe putting the duck beak on Curly's nose (the clothes pin in *Dizzy Detectives*); Curly taking the pills that Moe needs (the water in *Boobs in Arms*); bear traps (*Rockin' Thru the Rockies; Flat Foot Stooges*); a wrapped-around trombone (*Idle Roomers*); Curly and Larry cooking (*I Can Hardly Wait!*); the spaghetti on Moe's head (*Sock-A-Bye Baby*); swinging branches (*Uncivil Warriors*); and Curly blocking the gouge with his rifle (the rope in *Three Little Beers*).

VERBAL HUMOR: Elwood Ullman included a number of jokes based on fear of the bear (Moe: "You want the bear to eat him alive? Go out there and help him!" Larry: "That bear don't need no help!"; Moe: "Go on out and save him." Larry: "I'll go but my heart ain't in it"; Moe: "What's stoppin' you?" Curly: "The bear!"; Moe: "If I wasn't afraid - I mean, if I wasn't sick - I'd help ya' too"; and Curly [thinking the bear is dead]: "If you don't believe me put your head on his chest and listen to his heart." Larry: "I'll take your word for it."). Some involve internal puns (Curly: "Come on you cowards! He's a coward, too."; Moe: "I'd go with you but my nerves are shot." Curly: "I ain't got the nerve either!"; Larry: "Woe is Moe!"; and Curly: "I saw the bear in person I tell ya'. I saw him with my eyes, I heard him with my ears, and his trap got me by the tail!"). A few are of the same sort as in Adler's *Dizzy Detectives* (Larry: "Don't be afraid; I'm right behind you."). Other gags depend on Stooge ignorance (Curly: "You mean moider!" Larry: "Yeah, and he tried to kill us, too!"; Judge: "You mean you have something to say in extenuation?" Moe: "Oh not that! No! No, your honor. You see I had a good reason!"; Judge: "Were you ever indicted?" Moe: "Not since I was a baby!"; Larry: "There ought-a be plenty of shooting around here...I just saw a sign that said 'Fine For Hunting'"; and Larry: "Do you know a taxidermist?" Curly: "Certainly, my cousin Willy from Pittsburgh: he drives a taxi!"). The judge calling Moe "Mr. Moe" is a first, as is Moe's "Oh that's a bum job. That's like hem stitching with a picot edge!". Curly issues one of the longest GOBBLE-GOBBLEs ever.

'Vitamins A-P-U' [i.e. smelly] are bottled by the Shtunk [i.e. smelly] Manufacturing Company]. Other variations: "If there's anything I like better than honey and ketchup, it's bologna and whipped cream!" (*Soup To Nuts*); the wolf jokes (*Three Little Twirps*); 'NO SMOKING, NO HUNTING, NO FISHING, NO NOTHING - GO HOME' (*Back to the Woods*); "How could you hit me over here if your hands are in your lap?" (*Three Missing Links*); Moe: "I think you got a little piece of brain now" (*Horses' Collars*); and "106 7/8" (*You Nazty Spy!*).

OTHER NOTES: The title screens change with this film: the Columbia logo is no longer on the left side as it had been since *You Nazty Spy!*, so there is no longer a divided screen; the background, which now has an ancient Greco-Roman comic mask in the upper left-hand corner, remains for all three screens; and 'The Three Stooges' in the first screen is in cursive script. With variations (at *Monkey Businessmen* the first screen begins not to have the mask), this format will remain through the end of the Shemp films (1956). The final screen also contains the comic mask; this will remain the basic format of the final screen for all remaining Columbia shorts. The release title *Idiots Deluxe* was formerly the working title of *Dizzy Detectives*. The release title parodies the title of the Robert Sherwood play/film *Idiots Delight*, a 1939 MGM offering starring former colleague Clark Gable. The working title of this film was *The Malady Lingers On*. Laurel & Hardy went on a retreat in *Them Thar Hills* (1934), but this plot is a reworking of Collins & Kennedy's *Oh, My Nerves!* (1935). It will be reworked again with Joe Besser as the 'third Stooge' in *Guns A Poppin!* (1957). The Stooges have played musicians or showmen in three of the last five films. The bear licks the honey jar for 41 seconds. 1945-1946 were productive years for producer/director Jules White, who earned Academy Award nominations for *The Jury Goes Round 'N' Round* (1945) and *Hiss and Yell* (1946), both Vera Vague shorts made by his unit at Columbia.

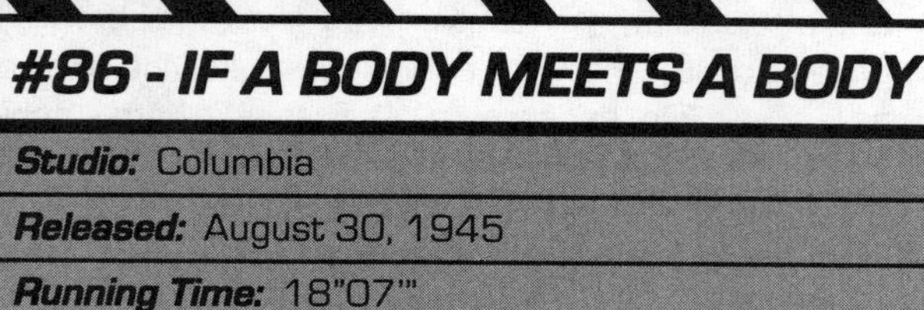

#86 - IF A BODY MEETS A BODY

Studio: Columbia

Released: August 30, 1945

Running Time: 18"07'"

Credited Production Crew:

Produced & Directed by:	Jules White
Screen Play by:	Jack White
Story by:	Gil Pratt
Director of Photography:	Benjamin Kline
Film Editor:	Charles Hochberg
Art Direction:	Charles Clague

Credited Cast:

Curly Howard	
Larry Fine	
Moe Howard	
Ted Lorch	Jerkington
Fred Kelsey	Detective Clancy

Uncredited Cast:

Joe Palma	housekeeper
Victor Travers	Link relative
Al Thompson	Bob O. Link
John Tyrrell	deceased attorney

PERSPECTIVE: This film continues exploring the power struggle between Moe and Curly that we have seen in the previous few films, with Moe forcefully reasserting his dominance. The Stooges are unemployed and broke, and when Curly goes to the store to buy dinner he ends up buying horse meat and cooking it along with a horseshoe. This time Moe and Larry literally kick Curly out of the house - as if the other Stooges are better cooks. But this is simply a plot device engineered to bring Curly back stronger than ever when Moe and Larry see that he could be their ticket to becoming millionaires.

Although it is in keeping with the way the Stooges' interrelationships were being reinvented at the close of the war and as Curly's energy continued to wane, the idea of having Moe and Larry treat Curly as an outcast only to reclaim him when they find out he is heir to a fortune ("the missing Link") comes from *The Laurel & Hardy Murder Case*, which was produced by Hal Roach in 1930. The Stooges had already been heir to a fortune in *Slippery Silks*, but the Laurel & Hardy model supplied the murder mystery aspect of the plot, the guilty cross-dressed butler, and even the flying-parrot skull which in the former film was a bat flying around in a pillow case. There is a common source for both films, the prototypical *The Cat and the Canary* made by Universal in 1927.

The Stooges have been involved in mysteries before [*We Want Our Mummy*, *Spook Louder*, *Dizzy Detectives*], but this is their first murder mystery, a staple of feature films since the late 1920s. A darkened natural setting has its roots in traditional theater and is as old as Seneca and Shakespeare - even Macbeth and Hamlet had to face ghosts - but this particular type of mystery, known as a 'thunderstorm mystery,' had been particularly popular in the 1930s. It almost always included stormy weather, secret internal passages, hidden bodies, clutching hands, and a butler who was discovered to be guilty at the end of the film. The Stooges parody the first of these motifs at the outset by soaking the butler with their raingear and by having Larry wear boots under his pants and carry a stripped and completely useless umbrella. Then the atmosphere of fright begins with the murder and literally darkens when the mysterious hand shuts off the lights. The frightening atmosphere is given verbal reinforcement when the butler wishes the Stooges a "Illllonnnnggg sleep," and then, as if nature itself frowns upon the evening, the wind picks up and frees the parrot from his cage. The Stooges spend the rest of the film seeing, disbelieving, and running from various frights, using skills and gimmicks developed in a number of recent films, particularly *Idle Roomers* and *Three Pests in a Mess*. But thunderstorm mysteries also tend to be gruesome, which not only accounts for the first pun of the film [Curly: "The morbid the merrier!"], but also the tableau with the family lawyer sprawled in a supine position across a table, a dagger emerging from his chest. There is nothing quite so graphic in the previous Stooge films, except of course for the Japanese bodies strewn about in the final and often censored tableau of *The Yoke's On Me*. But that was a war film.

VISUAL HUMOR: There are two scenes with dressing/undressing oddities, the first with the rain gear in the foyer, the second in the bed room where Curly pulls out his nightshirt and puts his jacket back on. After Larry then calls Curly "a 'fraidy cat" for sleeping with his clothes on, Larry and Moe look at each other, shrug their shoulders, and climb into bed with their clothes on, too. This recreates the setup used before climbing into the bathtub in *Gents Without Cents*. Besides being modeled on the Laurel & Hardy bat, the flying skull also derives from the parrot walking in the turkey carcass in *An Ache in Every Stake*. Stooge firsts: the corpse standing in the closet; Larry pulling his own hair; and the nose tweak accompanied by the PLINK sound effect. Curly jumping high and backwards is a new gimmick, and the special effects work well at masking Curly's slowing condition. Larry, a master of reacting, has a particularly fine reaction when he sees the parrot skull. The horse-shoe soup is not much less meaty than the chicken soup Curly last made in *Busy Buddies*. Other variations: pants rolling up in fear [*Three Pests in a Mess*]; Moe's hair standing on end [*Spook Louder*]; Curly's "Rruff!" exchange with

the detective, and the Stooges marching with their arms on each other's shoulders (*3 Dumb Clucks*).

VERBAL HUMOR: Stooge firsts: the gag British-type name 'Jerkington'; Curly's "I was born awfully young"; and the three-pattern: Curly: "I'm hungry!" Larry: "Me too!" Moe: "Me three!" The latter, one of the most distinctive Stooge patterns, was used first in the 1938 Columbia feature *Start Cheering,* but lay dormant for seven years. Another first is "or reasonable facsimile thereof," a phrase borrowed from radio advertisements. Most memorable are Jack White's puns on the Link family name ("Quff Link," "Bob O. Link," "Curly Q. Link"; "Link Sausage, Mink Sausage, and Pink Sausage"). Because of Curly's deteriorating condition, White gives him mostly short silly outbursts ("What knicky-nackies!"; "The spook spoke!" [internal rhyme]), while giving Moe throw-away lines ("I can see the darkness!"), another non-verb turned into a verb ("It's a fine time to be Hello-in'!"), and fear lines ("I ain't scared, but lets get the heck outta here!"; "You guys go first. I'll be right behind you!") à la Adler's *Dizzy Detectives*, new threats ("If you so much as breathe I'll tear your tonsils out and tie 'em around your neck for a bow tie!"; Larry: "What's the idea of hittin' me on the head?" Moe: "I didn't hit you on the head...yet!"; Moe: "Let me give you a little advice." Larry: "What?" [SLAP] Moe: "That!") and insults ("Ya' got nothin' to worry about: if he stabs you in the head he'll wreck his knife!"; "You're a sleep wrecker!"). Larry gets his one line: "He's probably the kind-a guy that would put water in his soup!". Curly's "The morbid the merrier!" pun takes on additional meaning once we enter the murder-mystery portion of the film, as does Moe's reference to Lucretia Borgia, the infamous Renaissance mistress of intrigue.

Other references: 'Harmitoonionian rugs' refer to the Armenian-American rug trade. 'The missing link' refers to the species of hominid that is ancestor to our own species. A 'bobolink' is an American songbird, a member of the blackbird family. 'Somnambulas' are sleep walkers. A 'piker' is 1940s slang for a stingy person, 'Moola' for "money." Moe's "Thanks, Dracula" was probably inspired by the four recent Dracula films (*Son of Dracula* [1943], *Return of the Vampire* [1944], and *House of Frankenstein* and *House of Dracula* [1945]). Stooge chant: "Let's go and get the moola!". The countersign gag (Curly: "Halt! Who goes there?" Moe: "Friend or enemy?" Larry: "Give the countersign!" [TRIPLE SLAP] Stooges: "Pass, friend!") is a variation from *Uncivil Warriors*. The exchange (Larry: "We're filthy with dough!" Moe: "You're filthy without it!") has the same structure as one in *They Stooge to Conga* (Curly: "You know I get dizzy in high places!" Moe: "You're dizzy in low places!"). Larry's "Reminds me of reformatory!" and Moe's reference to Oxford hark back to *Ants in the Pantry*. Other variations: "nice soup from a nice juicy bone!" (*Some More of Samoa*); and Moe: "I'm gonna have trouble with you, too!" (*How High is Up?*). Epithets: "numskull" and "lunk-head."

OTHER NOTES: The working title was *Nearly in the Dough. The Laurel & Hardy Murder Case* also featured Fred Kelsey as the detective. The new introductory music recorded for the initial 1945 release has 'Three Blind Mice' and sliding strings at the outset, a jazzy, syncopated middle, and a slower ending. This recording will be used until 1947's *Hold That Lion*, with two exceptions (*Uncivil War Birds; Three Loan Wolves*). We met Curly's father in *3 Dumb Clucks* and mother in *Cactus Makes Perfect.* Curly's voice is noticeably deeper and slower here.

#87 - MICRO-PHONIES

Studio: Columbia

Released: November 15, 1945

Running Time: 16"45'"

Credited Production Crew:

Producer:	Hugh McCollum
Directed & Written by:	Edward Bernds
Director of Photography:	Glen Gano
Film Editor:	Henry Batista
Art Director:	Charles Clague

Credited Cast:

Curly Howard	
Larry Fine	
Moe Howard	
Christine McIntyre	Alice Van Doren
Symona Boniface	Mrs. Bixby
Gino Corrado	Signor Spumoni

Uncredited Cast:

Sam Flint	Mr. Bixby
Fred Kelsey	Boss Dugan
Chester Conklin	drunk pianist
Bess Flowers	party guest
Lynton Brent	Don Allen
Ted Lorch	Bixby butler ("Masters")
Heinie Conklin	studio pianist
John Tyrrell	recording engineer
Judy Malcolm	woman in hallway

PERSPECTIVE: The image of Curly as Señorita Cucaracha singing in that delicate, acrobatic soprano voice while wearing an absurd Spanish outfit makes this a delightful enterprise and a grand masquerade. Moe listed *Micro-Phonies* as one of his favorite films, and it is often one of the most popular choices at Stooge film festivals. Most of its success should be attributed to the influence of rookie Stooge writer/director Edward Bernds, who had served since 1930 as a Columbia sound engineer but left his position as the studio's top sound man in 1939 to write and direct films for the McCollum unit. This was one of his first directorial projects, and he would direct many more Stooge films, including many of the 1960s feature films. In these early years, Bernds tried to streamline his short-film comedies by designing coherent, uncomplicated tales that came to a logical conclusion without loose ends and without irrelevant gag sequences, and this is what he accomplished in *Micro-Phonies*.

Bernds could see that Curly's genius was flagging, so he constructed a film relying more on Curly's sheer screen presence than on his weakened energies and failing voice. In fact, it is specifically Curly's *bad* voice that is the focus of the comedy. From the moment he begins mouthing the words to 'Voices of Spring,' Curly's physical genius takes on an audio dimension not seen or heard before. The Stooges always do their own singing, as in the recent *Gents Without Cents*, and at most Curly will blow into a sousaphone [*Even as IOU*] while we hear the sound of a whole band. But here the Stooges, with Curly as the lovely soloist, resort to what they do best - doing something badly - and sing terribly. Of the many fine moments in this film, perhaps the most astounding occurs when Spumoni pulls the plug on the Victrola and the Stooges are left 'singing' the operatic aria by themselves. Their voices are untrained and straining, so they quickly rush to the Señorita to mask their charade. Having put them in real jeopardy, Bernds leads the Stooges from here to their redemptive act of valor: Alice [Christine McIntyre] forces them to mouth 'Voices of

Spring' once more while she proves her worth as the singer behind the curtain; Spumoni figures out what is happening just as the song is ending; and when he shoots that banana into Curly's open mouth it tells everyone that Curly's voice is a sham.

The comedy is conveyed with music in ways entirely different from *Punch Drunks* or *Gents Without Cents*. The Stooges mouth Strauss's 'Voices of Spring' at the radio station, they shoot cherries into Signor Spumoni's operatic mouth, they holler Donizetti's 'Sextet From Lucy,' Curly mouths to Alice's singing, and Moe even "hears an angel singing" when he bangs his head on the radiator. With the war and its steady demand for war films coming to an end, 1945 became a year for comedy teams to innovate; Abbott & Costello even made two films in which they did not play a team. As for the Stooges, from the death-theme of *Three Pests in a Mess* to the murder mystery of *If a Body Meets a Body* to the music of *Micro-Phonies*, these innovations came just in time - before Curly's health ultimately failed in 1946.

Ed Bernds' first directorial release, *Micro-Phonies*, was a huge success, but not because of traditional Stooge slapstick. He was proud to substitute purer narrative types as well as different kinds of physical and verbal gags. In time, though, the indomitable Stooge slapstick would rise once again to the surface, but it was forever changed.

VISUAL HUMOR: The Stooges are always intense and sincere about their humor, and they treat their music the same way; the musical comedy works so well here because the Stooges mouth and play in earnest. In his early films as a director Bernds intentionally avoided excessive slapstick, so there is relatively little inter-Stooge slapstick in this film. The physical gags in the first scene involve Curly and Larry pulling the wrench and Moe slipping, falling, and banging his head. Their are no slaps, reprisals, or gouges. Bernds particularly objected to the gouge, so none appear in his films (except gouge-blocks in *Monkey Businessmen and Vagabond Loafers*). The glove antics - Moe pulling them off one finger at a time, Larry pulling and pulling them - are a Stooge first. Bernds introduces the Stooges by letting us hear a strange sound and then showing us what that strange sound is, as in Del Lord's dentistry/window cleaning introduction to *All The World's a Stooge*. Spumoni and the Stooges shoot fruit as they had in *Pardon My Scotch*. The boss's getting stuck, bitten, and banged under the piano lid is a variation of Larry's piano problems in *Crash Goes the Hash*. Other variations: pretending to play music while a record is playing (*Termites of 1938*); Moe destroying the record (the boat's steering wheel in *Booby Dupes*); the pianist having a bigger "Rruff!" than Curly (recently in *If a Body Meets a Body*); and the Stooges exchanging kisses (*Half-Shot Shooters*).

VERBAL HUMOR: Bernds' script includes gags based on silly ignorance of spelling (Moe: "'Gritto' spelled sideways is 'Atrig—g-gah'"), music (Moe: 'Sextet From Lucy' - Can you sing it?" Curly: "I can't even say it!"), and anatomy (Moe: "Short eyeballs, eh?"; Mrs. Bixby: "What is it? Laryngitis?" Moe: No, fallen arches!") and literal responses (Moe: "You lost your voice!" Curly: "Where?"; Moe: "Oh! A micro-phony!" Curly: "And a phony at the mike!") and insults (Moe: "Oh no: she always looks like that!"). Bernds unifies the verbal and physical humor when he has Moe remark "Boy! Right on the head!" just before the violinist smashes his violin over Moe's head. There are several radio gags, as in Moe's "And now Gritto's own story of Susan Sandpile in 'Here's Mud in Your Eye..." and the "Crispy Crunchy Program," the latter referring to a commercial, as did 'or reasonable facsimile thereof" in the previous film. Moe's Gritto commercial at the microphone recalls his 'Brighto' PA announcement in *Dizzy Doctors*. Curly's impaired vocal ability does allow him one memorable falsetto sequence: "My! nyuk, nyuk, nyuk, Ain't she pretty?!' Moe: "You can say that again." Curly; "My! Nyuk, nyuk, nyuk, Ain't she pretty?! [SLAP] You said I could!".

Spumoni's "You break-a my glasses! You break-a my violin!" is reminiscent of Billy Gilbert's "What you try to make for me, a fruit salad?" in *Pardon My Scotch*. Other variations: Larry: "Reminds me of the reform school" (*Ants in the Pantry*); and Moe: "You're gettin' half a brain in your skull, now, huh?" (*Horses' Collars; Termites of 1938*). Epithets: "jug-heads," "numskulls," and "imbeciles". References: Allen's "Simple like radar" reminds us that radar had just been developed during the war. The 'Sextet From Lucy' was not written by the drunken pianist ("Know it?! I wrote it!"), but is the sextet from Gaetano Donizetti's 1835 opera, *Lucia di Lammermoor*, a technically complex, deservedly admired piece of the operatic repertoire, but hard to listen to with a straight face once one has seen this film. The other music includes Johann Strauss's 'Voices of Spring' [*Frühlingsstimmen*] - which was disliked at its 1883 debut because of "excessive" coloratura! - and the traditional Italian aire, 'Den' ti des ta Fanciulla la luna,' the first line of which is 'Vieni sul mar.' 'Señor Mucho' and 'Señor Gusto' refer to the Spanish expression *con mucho gusto*. 'Cucaracha,' the title of a well known song, means "cockroach."

OTHER NOTES: Bernds' recollection [*Okuda* 65-69] was that *Micro-Phonies* was filmed after *A Bird in the Head* and *Three Troubledoers*, and that McCollum opted to release *Micro-Phonies* first so that Ed Bernds' directorial debut would be as successful as possible. [According to the *Scrapbook* the production numbers are in the order *A Bird in the Head* [#4043], *Micro-Phonies* [#4044], *Beer Barrel Polecats* [#4045], and *Three Troubledoers* [#4046]]. Bernds recollected that Curly's condition was 'up' for this film, and that it was after *A Bird in the Head* that Producer Hugh McCollum asked him to write a script to display Christine McIntyre's singing voice: "I wasn't even aware that Christine McIntyre was a singer!" [Forrester *Chronicles* 59]; [Gloria Jean had sung 'Voices of Spring' in 1941's *Never Give A Sucker An Even Break*]. The actors who worked with both Bernds and Jules White relate that White, who would act out the parts and show the actors what he wanted them to do, was more autocratic than Bernds, who often left the actors to develop a part on their own. Also, Bernds recollects that he liked shooting gags from several different angles to give some flexibility in the editing

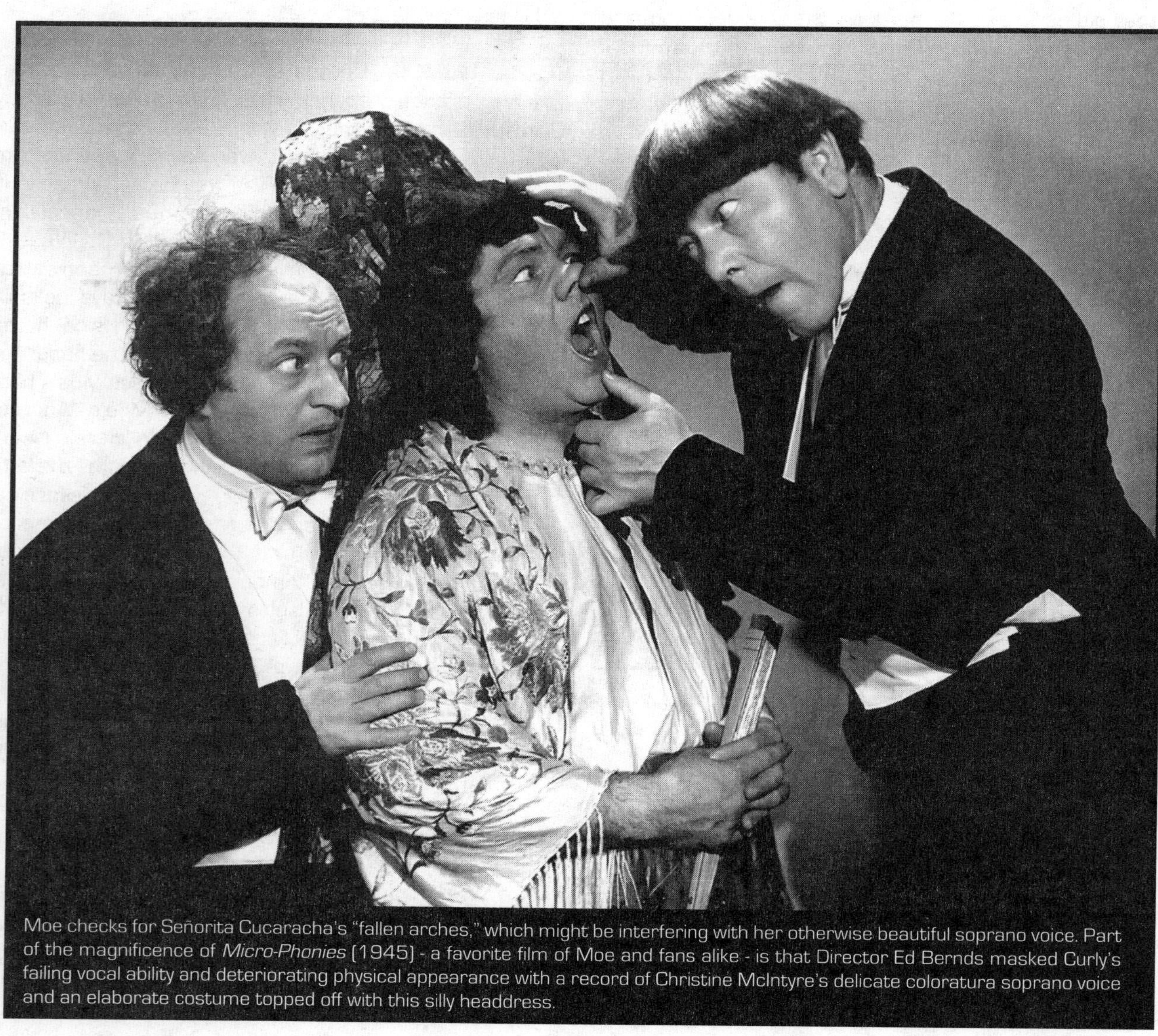

Moe checks for Señorita Cucaracha's "fallen arches," which might be interfering with her otherwise beautiful soprano voice. Part of the magnificence of *Micro-Phonies* [1945] - a favorite film of Moe and fans alike - is that Director Ed Bernds masked Curly's failing vocal ability and deteriorating physical appearance with a record of Christine McIntyre's delicate coloratura soprano voice and an elaborate costume topped off with this silly headdress.

process, he liked to let the camera roll to allow for spontaneous gestures and ad-libbing, and he did not believe in radical adjustments to the script on the set; he preferred to do his rewriting at night: "Many of our gags required a great deal of planning - breakaway props, wire-belt rigging, the use of stunt doubles - all these things involved a lot of advance preparation. With our limited budgets and schedules, it was foolish to throw these sort of things into a picture at the last minute." *[Okuda* 31]. For a summary of Bernds' work, see Brent Seguine, *The 3 Stooges Journal* 79 (1996) 8-10. Bernds had been Columbia sound engineer, and in this film we see a sound engineer in the recording studio. Desiring to become a director, Bernds was encouraged by Frank Capra, for whose films he had served as chief sound mixer.

There is a similar plot in *Hot Sports* (1929), starring Monte Collins and directed by Jules White. For Señorita Cucaracha's relationship to Carmen Miranda, see *Time Out for Rhythm* [Other Notes]. Jerry Lewis did a similar imitation in *Scared Stiff* (1953). Lynton Brent [Don Allen] here plays his last of 16 roles in Stooge films. He was also a painter, as illustrated in *Okuda* 203. If the underlying theme of *Micro-Phonies* is music, then the medium to carry the music is radio. In the previous film Moe and Curly use the common radio expression "reasonable facsimile thereof," and in earlier films the Wolf-Man saw Curly with a radio smashed over his head (*Idle Roomers*) and Curly won money from a radio contest (*Healthy, Wealthy and Dumb*). Some footage will reappear in *Stop! Look! and Laugh!*.

This is the fifth of only five 1945 releases, the smallest Stooge output of any year at Columbia (except for the final year, 1959, by which time the Stooges' contract with Columbia had already been terminated).

"You break-a my glasses! You break-a my violin!" Another accomplished musician in *Micro-Phonies* is the Italo-American Signor Spumoni, here played brilliantly by Gino Corrado. Stooge comedy, based in vaudeville and bas humor of the 1930s, often exploited Italian, Chinese, Japanese, German, and other ethnic types. Gino Corrado created a memorable character in this film, one of the best in the Stooge Columbia corpus. His career highlights also include roles in such important films as *Casablanca, Citizen Kane, The Ten Commandments* (1923) and the Marx Brothers' *A Night at the Opera*.

1946

Beer Barrel Polecats • A Bird in the Head • Uncivil War Birds

Three Troubledoers • Monkey Businessmen • Three Loan Wolves

G.I. Wanna Home • Rhythm and Weep • Three Little Pirates

#88 - BEER BARREL POLECATS

Studio: Columbia

Released: January 10, 1946

Running Time: 17"21'"

Credited Production Crew:

Produced & Directed	Jules White
Story & Screenplay by:	Gilbert W. Pratt
Director of Photography:	George Kelly
Film Editor:	Charles Hochberg

Credited Cast:

Curly Howard	
Larry Fine	
Moe Howard	
Robert Williams	guard
Vernon Dent	warden

Uncredited Cast:

Al Thompson	photographer
Joe Palma	tripping convict
Blackie Whiteford	convict
Eddie Laughton	convict #41144 [stock footage]
Bruce Bennett	guard [stock footage]
Emory Parnell	painted guard [stock footage]

PERSPECTIVE: In the previous film Edward Bernds successfully masked Curly's deteriorating condition by having him mouth the words to Christine McIntyre's singing, thereby creating a new type of Stooge comedy. In *Beer Barrel Polecats*, the first 1946 release, director Jules White masks Curly's condition by inserting six minutes of prison-break footage from *In the Sweet Pie and Pie* and *So Long, Mr. Chumps*, films made in 1941 when Curly was more energetic and still had command of his falsetto. These film supplements provide enough humor and energy to carry the present Curly through the new scenes.

Writer Gilbert Pratt, whose first and only other Stooge assignment had been to adapt a Laurel & Hardy

film for *If A Body Meets a Body*, now needs to piece together two story elements - beer-making and its criminal consequences. The beer-making relies on the proven Stooge motif of ineptly following a recipe (*An Ache in Every Stake*), and fittingly any Stooge hopes for a steady supply of home-made hooch explode with the oven-heated beer bottles. Curly's limited shooting schedule prevented Pratt from including a scene depicting an arrest, so the next thing we know the Stooges are in prison; we hear only that Curly sold a bottle illegally: "How did I know he was a detective?" Lacking a different inspiration, Pratt duplicates his first plot device by having Curly's contraband barrel of beer explode from the heat of the photography lights. This lands the Stooges in a different jail cell where we now see the sawing sequence from *In the Sweet Pie and Pie.* That attempted jail break has no consequence, so Pratt added the ice cream cone scene which unfortunately reveals just how limited Curly's physical actions have become as he winds up to knock out the perpetrator and hits the warden instead. Hitting the warden puts them out on the rock pile, and that is where the *So Long, Mr. Chumps* footage applies.

Pratt never explains why the Stooges are looking for convict #41144, but in piecing these footages together Pratt, the director, and the editor create a new kind of plot structure in which the Stooges descend into a series of ever-worsening predicaments. Usually the Stooges screw up something which leads to a second situation in which they catch crooks and spies, help someone in distress, or fail miserably. In this film their predicament of not being able to find a single bottle of beer gets them deeper and deeper into trouble from bootlegging in their kitchen to a holding jail and from there into prison and from there to the rock pile to a botched escape to another rock pile and to old age. This series of ever-worsening predicaments develops because the old footage contains these ever-worsening predicaments. Previously old footage had been used because a scene warranted repeating (the carpentry sequence of *Pardon My Scotch* reused in *Dizzy Detectives*] or was too expensive to recreate [the submarine footage of *Three Little Sew and Sews* reused in *They Stooge to Conga*]. In *Beer Barrel Polecats* the purpose of the borrowed footage was to give Curly relief from the usual four-day shooting schedule and mask his condition on the screen.

VISUAL HUMOR [NEW FOOTAGE ONLY]: With Jules White back at the helm, there is a little more slapstick than in the previous Edward Bernds film. It includes a variation of the fist game, a mop-handle sequence, and two eye gouges. The only innovative scene is where Curly punches the warden, for which his skills are failing. Larry being knocked back into the bathtub of beer has its forerunners in *Dizzy Pilots* and *Gents Without Cents*. We first saw aged Stooges in the denouement of *Woman Haters*.

VERBAL HUMOR [NEW FOOTAGE ONLY]: Pratt devised two parodies of expressions, Curly's "Ahh, stop cryin' over spilt beer!" and "Be still, my heart!". We have heard 'brain' gags since *Horses' Collars*. The new version here is an exchange [Curly: "Here's my brainchild." Larry: "At last you got a brain, child!"]. The pattern is a Stooge first. Curly's voice is failing him, so Larry has to correct Moe's pronunciation of "hops" and "crock," which is usually Curly's job ["You are moiderin' the king's English" in *Dizzy Pilots*]. As Curly mops the floor, he can barely sing "La-dee". Moe has often taken others' ideas. Here the exchange [Curly: "I got an idea!" Moe: "Shadup!. What is it?"] resembles that in the previous film [Curly: "I don't know who did, but I wanna get out-a here!"...Moe: "Hey, I got a great idea! We better get out-a here!"]. 'Panther Pilsner' was the brand used in *Three Little Beers*, and 'Hot-sie Tot-sie' was on the map as the 'Hot Sea' and 'Tot Sea' in *You'll Never Heil Again*. Other variations: Larry's "Burnt toast and a rotten egg. I got a tapeworm and it's good enough for him!" [*Punch Drunks*]; and "Goiter!" [*Playing the Ponies*]. Epithet: Larry calls Curly "imbecile."

OTHER NOTES: The film was shot in 1945 and copyrighted 'MCMXLV.'. The release title parodies the song title 'Beer Barrel Polka'; the working title was *Three Duds in the Suds*. No art director is listed in the credits, perhaps because of all the stock used. The Robert Williams [guard] credited here, who will play in the next two releases also, is not the same Robert Williams who played in several 1939-1942 Stooge films. Beer was scarce domestically in 1945 because of the war. The film uses the prison sequences from *In the Sweet Pie and Pie* and *So Long, Mr. Chumps*; there were also prison breaks in *3 Dumb Clucks, Three Little Sew and Sews*, and *Saved By the Belle*. Moe had thrown Curly out in the opening scene of *If a Body Meets a Body*, but he brought him back when he realized Curly was worth a fortune. In this film he finally does get rid of him by sending him back into jail. Ironically, Curly would not be a Stooge at all in the following year.

In 1945/1946 Curly's ability to perform was inconsistent and unpredictable. For *Beer Barrel Polecats*, the first release of 1946, Curly was unable to endure the four-day shooting schedule, so director Jules White used stock footage for part of the film. Where Curly was called upon to perform physical comedy, his body did not respond with its accustomed flexibility, nor could his face or voice produce the gestures and sounds that made him unique. In this scene he perfunctorily spills a bucket of sand on Vernon Dent.

#89 - A BIRD IN THE HEAD

Studio: Columbia

Released: February 28, 1946

Running Time: 16"54'"

Credited Production Crew:

Produced by:	Hugh McCollum
Written & Directed by:	Edward Bernds
Director of Photography:	Burnett Guffey
Film Editor:	Henry Batista
Art Director:	Charles Clague

Credited Cast:

Curly Howard	
Larry Fine	
Moe Howard	
Vernon Dent	Professor Panzer
Robert Williams	Mr. Beedle, landlord
Frank Lackteen	Nikko

Uncredited Cast:

Art Miles	Igor, the gorilla

PERSPECTIVE: This is Edward Bernds' second Stooge release, but reportedly the first Stooge film he directed. As would be his aim in writing *Micro-Phonies*, he composed a coherent script, this one concentrating on a mad doctor's desire to transplant a small human brain into the skull cavity of his gorilla. Gorillas are nothing new to Stooge films [*Three Missing Links; Dizzy Detectives*], and the Stooges already met a mad doctor wanting to perform brain surgery on a nearly canine Curly in *From Nurse to Worse*. But to these elements Bernds adds one other Stooge motif, a room-to-room chase, which we have seen in such 'scare comedies' as *We Want Our Mummy* and *Spook Louder*. Bernds neatly combined these three Stooge elements to wind the tale of *A Bird in the Head* tightly around a unifying, triangulating factor - that both the mad doctor and the gorilla desire the same thing: Curly.

The timing is apt. Curly has always been the (very) odd man out, but twice in the last three films we have seen Moe literally throw Curly out of the group. Bernds gives Curly's isolation a different twist: Curly has the only brain the mad doctor wants, and Curly has the only looks and personality the gorilla likes. Bernds focuses on Curly's fine interior and his internal qualities, so the viewer barely notices Curly's deteriorating condition. This is accomplished in several other ways as well. For one, Curly is given a half dozen good punchlines that do not require his special falsetto intonation ("Breathe down my neck...onions, too!") or exclamations that are easy for any falsetto range ("Eeeeeeeeeeeeee!") The doctor takes on a lot of the humor, too. His eccentricity, his way of admiring Curly's head, his 1945 German sadism, and that maniacal laugh of his we hear three times keep the story together and the enjoyment mounting. Even the gorilla becomes a comical and likable character. When Curly brings him into the lab, Moe asks: "Ya' monkey! Why did you bring that ape in here?" Curly: "He's my pal!" The ape hugs Curly and he tickles his 'beard': "Five o'clock shadow. Remember, you're gonna shave in the morning!" From this point on, we cannot help but take a liking to the gorilla who has taken a liking to Curly and become his "pal." This new partnership means Curly does not have to act wildly or be the comic protagonist. The gorilla does it for him.

Even better, the gorilla protects Curly from Moe, and since director Bernds tried to downplay inter-Stooge slapstick, what better gimmick to use than a comic gorilla who protects Curly from Moe's punishing blows? Towards the end of the film the gorilla also protects Curly from the mad doctor, and by picking up the machine gun he - instead of Curly or the other Stooges - becomes the star of the final action gag, a heroic, giant-sized version of the Gattling-gun monkey of *Goofs and Saddles*. Curly may not be in his top form, but these last few Curly films made by Ed Bernds show us how well the Columbia staff worked around Curly's condition. In fact, having the doctor and the gorilla take a special liking to Curly gives him as much charm as ever. They make Curly lovable and allow the gorilla to be the clown.

VISUAL HUMOR: Even landlord Beedle [Robert Williams] adds to the comedy and temporarily takes the spotlight with his "No, no, no. no, no, no..." and fast motion slide across the room on the wallpaper paste. Bernds reuses his non-confrontational slip-on-a-bottle, fly-into-the-air gag from *Micro-Phonies*, but even Bernds could minimize Stooge slapstick for only so long. A unique slapstick move has Moe holding his fist next to Curly's face and calling his name so that when Curly turns he punches himself on it. A Stooge first is where Moe tells his slapstick plans while demonstrating on Larry (Moe: "We'll ambush him! [RATCHET], 'infilterate' him [FOREHEAD SLAP], then we'll give him the old pinces movement! [SLAP]". Of many paint brush gags, this is the first time Moe double brushes Curly and Larry. There are two new sound effects, one of which is complex and given a lot of attention after first the gorilla and then Curly take shots of grain alcohol and just stand there while we hear the DRINKING sound effect, the second, a spring/sprong-like sound, is heard when Moe illustrates the "pinces movement" in the hallway alcove.

Panzer hearing a rumba through his stethoscope while Moe and Larry dance to it derives from *I'll Never Heil Again*. Other variations: the wall paper that keeps

Director Ed Bernds and the Columbia staff found a variety of ways to cover for Curly's deficiencies in 1946. In *A Bird in the Head* Bernds used both the mad Germanic doctor and his gorilla - with the gorilla taking special care of Curly.

rolling back up [*Loco Boys Makes Good*]; the wallpaper badly applied [*The Sitter Downers*]; the falling plank, and Moe grabbing Curly's nose with the scissors [*Slippery Silks*]; the fluoroscope [*A Gem of a Jam*]; Dr. Panzer landing on a set of teeth [*All the World's a Stooge*]; Moe wiping the brush on Curly's and Larry's tongues when they stick their tongues out [*So Long, Mr. Chumps*]; the gorilla breathing down their necks, and ending the film with Curly and the gorilla [*Three Missing Links*]; walking away from a door just before it opens [*Dizzy Detectives*]; the jar crashing down from the shelf onto Panzer's head [*Cookoo Cavaliers*]; Moe and Larry trying to squeeze out of the alcove at the same time and Moe ordering "Recede!" [*Oily to Bed, Oily to Rise*; *Pardon My Scotch*]; and Curly emitting something (smoke) from his ears [*Healthy, Wealthy and Dumb*].

VERBAL HUMOR: Bernds' verbal humor depends often on the German Dr. Panzer's eccentricity ("Bee-yoo-tiful!"; Curly: "Suppose we don't live long?" Moe: "Quiet, stupid, or I'll knock your brain out! [to Panzer] Did you hear what he said? Silly, wasn't it?" Panzer: "Yes, silly! Ha! Ha! Ha! Ha! Ha!!"), which causes Stooge fright (Curly: "It's silly to be scared...Boy am I silly!"; Moe: "As long as we...As long as we...Let's get out-a here!?"; and Curly: "Eeeeeeeeeee!" Moe: "Shadup! This is no time to be singin'!"), and gorilla gags (Moe: "Have you got a fur coat on?" Curly: "No, but he has!"; "Five o'clock shadow! Remember, you're gonna shave in the morning!"). There are several plot-related 'head' gags, too (Moe: "If he's a head hunter, he's huntin' small game!"; and "Practically unoccupied"). To the frequently used Stooge line "I'll bet you do that to all the boys," Curly adds "especially if you're gonna get their brain!". Other gags are ironic ("We can use a job. We just resigned!"), associated with show business (Larry: "Lucky guy! Gets a screen test!"; "You going to make a Quiz Kid out of him, doc?"; and Curly: "It ain't the Crooner!") or puns (Panzer: "Gentlemen, here are your quarters." Curly: "Oh! Two bits a piece!"; Larry: "It's a bird!" Moe: "Sure! A bird in the head's worth two in the bush!"). The latter is used for the title of the film [*Three Little Sew and Sews*]. An earlier version was used in *Myrt and Marge* (Healy: "You know what a burden is, don't ya'?" Larry: "Yeah, a 'burden' the hand's worth two in the bush!'). Moe turns a noun into a transitive verb ("I'll plank him!"), and offers a malapropism ("infilterate"). Epithets: "monkey," "stupid," "wise guy," and "bird-brain".

References: Curly's "Have you got a permit from the O.P.A.?" refers to the Office of Price Administration and Civilian Supply, the forerunner of the Consumer Protection Agency. Larry asking "Are you going to make a Quiz Kid out of him?" refers to the popular *Quiz Kid* radio show, in which kids ages 6-14 fielded difficult questions; 'the Crooner' was Bing Crosby, then host of radio's *Kraft Music Hall*. Other variations: Moe's "You fall down!" [*In the Sweet Pie and Pie*]; "pinces movement" [*pinces soir* in *Slippery Silks*]; Curly: "This face looks like Moe!" Larry: "It *is* Moe!" [*Rockin' Thru the Rockies*]; and Moe's "You won't know the joint when you get back!" [*Cookoo Cavaliers*].

OTHER NOTES: Although the film was copyrighted in 1945, producer Hugh McCollum held release until February 28, 1946 so that *Micro-Phonies* could be released first; he wanted Bernds' first directorial release to be well received and could see that *Micro-Phonies* was the superior product. The film was shot April 9-13, 1945, but shooting was discontinued on April 12 out of respect for the death of President Roosevelt. Director Bernds was grateful for the brief hiatus, for it gave him some extra time to consider how to shoot around Curly's condition [*Okuda* 65]. *Larry* [171] incorrectly remembered the day of Roosevelt's death as the day of Curly's major stroke, but that would occur weeks later on May 6. Ironically, Curly's stroke-addled brain in real life is what is troubling him, and yet his brain is what the doctor wants from him in the film. The drinking scene is sometimes edited out for television broadcast. Art Miles [the gorilla] also played, interestingly enough, in the Ritz Brothers' *The Gorilla* (1939).

#90 - UNCIVIL WAR BIRDS

Studio: Columbia

Released: March 29, 1946

Running Time: 17"16'"

Credited Production Crew:

Produced & Directed by:	Jules White
Story by:	Clyde Bruckman
Director of Photography:	Philip Tannura
Film Editor:	Charles Hochberg
Art Director:	Charles Clague

Credited Cast:

Curly Howard
Larry Fine
Moe Howard

Uncredited Cast:

Faye Williams	Mary Belle
Marilyn Johnson	Lulu Belle
Eleanor Counts	Ringa Belle
Ted Lorch	Union colonel
Robert Williams	Union Lieutenant
John Tyrrell	Union sergeant
Lew Davis	Confederate soldier
Vic Travers	Justice of the Peace
Blackie Whiteford	Union officer
Maury Dexter	Union soldier
Al Rosen	Union soldier
Joe Palma	Union soldier
Cy Schindell	Union soldier

PERSPECTIVE: It had been over ten years since the Stooges made *Uncivil Warriors*. In the intervening decade, two major events fundamentally changed the way in which Hollywood could make a Civil War comedy. The first was the publication of Margaret Mitchell's Pulitzer Prize-winning *Gone With the Wind* in 1936 and its much heralded, lavish MGM film version of 1939. The second was the entry of the United States into World War II two years later. The former gave Civil War films a new perspective: that of landed Southern gentry, Confederate patriots, and romantic entanglements interrupted by the war. The latter made the enmity between North and South almost immaterial; we-all had a new enemy now. Compared with the enmity that existed between the U.S. and Germany and Japan, any bitterness that still existed eighty years after the completion of the Civil War was considerably muted. *Uncivil War Birds* was subject to both of these influences.

The opening credits are accompanied by a rendition of 'Dixie,' and then the film opens like *Gone With the Wind* with Southern gentlemen frolicking on the lawn of a Southern plantation, only in this case the frolickers are a Southern version of the Stooges. They are dressed as Southern gentlemen, they speak with Southern accents, and they use '-all' as an ever-present pronominal suffix. We sense the romantic element immediately as they play jacks and sit on a see-saw and swing, and as in the beginning of *GWTW* they ask their 'belles' Mary Belle, Lulu Belle, and Ringa Belle to marry them. As at the outset of *GWTW* and other films of the genre (e.g. *Jezebel*), the Stooges foolishly think the war will be over quickly (Mary Belle: "How long do you reckon it's gonna take y'all to win?" Moe: "Oh about a week, I reckon. You know it takes time to win a war!"), and their family will be divided between Union and Confederate loyalties. Later in the film there are more Southernisms; the Stooges sing a version of 'Dixie' and Curly appears in black face as a 'mammy.' Of course, leave it to a Stooge to wipe off his own blackface disguise.

Because *GWTW* was set in the South, and because World War II gave America such vivid modern enemies, it did not matter much whether the North or South won the skirmish (unlike *Uncivil Warriors* which made sure the North won). In fact, during *Uncivil War Birds* the plantation changes hands several times, and this drives the comedy by forcing the divided Stooge family to fight together to preserve itself against both armies. It does not matter whether the Stooges fight for the North or South in this film, and for a while at least they fight for both. What distinguishes this film is the loyalty the Stooges feel towards each other no matter on behalf of which side they might be fighting. This is one of the recognizable touches of writer Clyde Bruckman (*The Yoke's on Me*) and it is one of the most positive: the Stooges stick together, win their part of the war, and marry their Belles so they can live happily ever after...except for a little strangling.

VISUAL HUMOR: This films offers us a minor revival of the physical comedy we had become used to before 1945. There are two cleverly set up eye gouges, and we see an ants-in-the-pants gag similar to the one in *Ants in the Pantry*. Curly's mobility is still limited, of course, but he fakes his death very well and even offers us one last chicken-with-its-head-cut-off; the officer brags, "Now that's the way to kill a man!", but he really should be

reacting to Curly's fall and saying "Now that's the way to pretend you are dying!". We have seen other actors taking over some of the physical comedy in recent films,

and we see this here when the Union colonel [Ted Lorch] slams the door into three of his men and knocks them 'cookoo' twice. In fact, when Larry knocks Lorch silly with his banjo, you can still see those three in the background. As in the previous film, there is a new sound effect: the SKY-ROCKET is used for Larry kissing his beau. Curly sang 'Mammy' in *All the World's a Stooge*. Other variations: Moe and Curly pulling a sleigh (*Flat Foot Stooges; Wee Wee Monsieur*); Moe clubbing the enemy and Larry with his backswing (*Back to the Woods*; *Three Little Sew and Sews*); Curly holding a rifle backwards (*Three Pests in a Mess*); and soldiers rubbing their rears along the ground (*I Can Hardly Wait*).

VERBAL HUMOR: The film itself does not contain a credit for the screenwriter. It attributes only the story to Bruckman and the production and direction to White. The *Scrapbook* reports that White wrote the script, which would make this the first and only script he wrote for a Stooge film. Southernisms like "Wait you-all, it's me-all!" create a unique sound for the film, as does the South Brooklyn version of Dixie. (The Howard family grew up in Brooklyn).

With Curly ailing, Larry and Moe are given a much larger portion of the verbal gags, including a fine variation of Curly's "I reckon" speech from *Uncivil Warriors* (Larry: "Well I reckon that this is the place, and he ain't around the place, I reckon he must be some other place, I reckon." Moe: "No, I'm wreckin'!"); the exchange now even concludes with a gouge. Also from *Uncivil Warriors* is the ruse that gets them past a guard (Larry: "You-all don't know who General Grubblebump is? He walks like this—" Moe: "General Grubblebump don't walk! He *runs*!"). Curly is given mostly short responses, for instance when he challenges the Union officer (Lieutenant: "Forward march, you fools! [Curly does not move] What's the matter with you?" Curly: "I'm no fool!" Lieutenant: "Forward march, you *idiot*!" Curly: "That's different!"); we first heard that pattern in *Grips, Grunts and Groans* (Bustoff: "That's not alcohol; it's just tequila, vodka and cognac." Curly: "Ohh! That's different!"). Curly's "I'll be more than a colonel, I'll be a corporal!" belies his ignorance of the chain of command.

Three-pattern (Larry: "If we-alls can get that map down to headquarters, we-alls can win this war." Curly: "Than we-alls can get married." Moe: "Brother, you-all ejaculated a mouthful. We-all is gonna get that map!"). Another three-pattern is a variation: (Larry: "I'm gonna join up!" Moe: "Me, too!" Curly: "Me, three!" [*If A Body Meets a Body*]). Larry 's solo throw-away line ("This war's gonna be over before we change our clothes!") recalls Ted Healy's "It takes so long the burglar's liable to die of old age before he's caught!" in *Soup to Nuts*. Other variations: Moe: "A fine time to take a nap!" (*Punch Drunks*); and Larry: "We-all are Union men!" Colonel: "Well you belong to the wrong union!" (*The Sitter Downers*).

References: Little did the playwrights Beaumont and Fletcher suspect in the early seventeenth century that their dramatic line "Kiss till the cow comes home" would be used 330 years later (Lulu Belle: "For such a man as you-all I'd wait till the cows come home." Larry: "But we haven't got a cow." Lulu Belle: "Then we-all'll get a cow." Larry: "Right! Well, good-bye, cow...Lulu Belle, I mean—"). Curly's "Keep the home fires burnin', Ringa Belle" derives from Lena Ford's 1915 World War I song (music by Ivar Novello).

OTHER NOTES: The correct title has three words: *Uncivil War Birds*. The working title was *Three Southern Dumbbells*. 'Dixie' provides the introductory music for the front credits - it was used also for *Uncivil Warriors* - and continues as background music for nearly twenty seconds into the opening scene. The closing screen returns the regular 'driving' version of 'Three Blind Mice'. The stock shot of the union lieutenant on horseback with his battalion of eight comes from a Buster Keaton film, *Mooching Through Georgia* (1939); *Okuda* (88) calls the Stooge version a 'remake'; Clyde Bruckman later reworked it as a telescript for *The Abbott and Costello Show*. This is the last of 24 Stooge roles for John Tyrrell; for a biography, see *The 3 Stooges Journal* 76 (1995) 10.

#91 - THREE TROUBLEDOERS

Studio: Columbia

Released: April 25, 1946

Running Time: 17"04'"

Credited Production Crew:

Produced by:	Hugh McCollum
Directed by:	Edward Bernds
Story & Screen Play by:	Jack White
Director of Photography:	George Kelley
Film Editor:	Henry Batista
Art Director:	Charles Clague

Credited Cast:

Curly Howard	
Larry Fine	
Moe Howard	
Christine McIntyre	Nell
Dick Curtis	Badlands Blackie

Uncredited Cast:

Blackie Whiteford	henchmen
Ethan Laidlaw	henchmen
Hank Bell	townsman
Budd Fine	townsman
Steve Clark	townsman
Joe Garcia	waiter
Vic Travers	Justice of the Peace
Judy Malcolm	bar girl

PERSPECTIVE: From *Horses' Collars* and *Restless Knights* (1935) through *Even As IOU* (1942), the Stooges made a number of films in which the prime focus of the plot was their aiding a damsel-in-distress. Since 1942 they have been absorbed in winning the war, running from spooks and beasts, seeking wealth, and getting into trouble. *Three Troubledoers*, the first solo Jack White script since *A Pain in the Pullman*, returns them to that earlier damsel-in-distress plot formula which calls for the Stooges to be romantically and shyly heroic while defending and rescuing an otherwise defenseless woman and confronting, resisting, and annoying the heck out of a pompously tyrannical villain.

Dick Curtis brings a tremendous helping of silly villainy to his Badlands Blackie character. A menacing gorilla with a soft spot in his heart for Curly recently took center stage in *A Bird in the Head*, and now we have a menacing outlaw with a soft spot in his heart for Nell, whom Curly wants to marry. His huge soft spot for Nell actually controls the plot: he has kidnapped Nell's father and will release him only if she consents to marry him. He bellows throughout all his scenes with deep-voiced Westernisms like "Never mind that palaver! Let's get-a goin' here!" and "Sit down, Mrs. Blackie, and put a smile on y'er purty face." Physically he stands a foot taller than everyone else, and he looks just as threatening pulling his two six shooters as he looks plain silly falling backwards into the watering trough. He plays a wonderful foil to Curly who seems relatively well in this film - he snaps his fingers in Blackie's face, makes a few Curly-esque noises and exhalations, plays set jokes, takes a crowbar and hammer to the face and head, and even gives us a 360-degree pivot. Curly's face looks wearied, and a comparison between the crow bar extractions here and in 1942's *Cactus Makes Perfect* reminds us of how many facial poses and strange noises Curly used to be able to create in just a few seconds. But we have come to expect and are now satisfied with less. After making this film he will get a seven-month hiatus.

The directors of the most recent Stooge films have found various ways to vary the physical humor in climaxes. For *A Bird in the Head* a gorilla picks up a machine gun, for *Beer Barrel Polecats* stock footage is used, and for *Micro-Phonies* a simple banana shot across the room into Curly's mouth suffices. Here Edward Bernds with the help of film editor Henry Batista cranks the action up two notches by interweaving two parallel scenes - the wedding of Nell and Blackie, and the Stooges riding their bicycle. The Stooges ride in fast motion to strains of the 'William Tell Overture,' fall off their bike, and knock Moe off behind them as the wedding comes closer and closer to completion. Although this is a tried and true narrative technique for B-Westerns, it is a first for a Stooge film - even if it is somewhat reminiscent of

the rousing 'Pop Goes the Weasel' hunt in *Punch Drunks*. We will see it again next year in the first Shemp Western, *Out West* (1947). A brief gun battle with some high explosives brings the comedy to a successful conclusion, although Curly does not get to marry the girl. His father would "rather be dead." Maybe he was dry-gulched in that hole too long.

VISUAL HUMOR: Ed Bernds invented the non-violent group gag in which Curly shoves Moe and Larry out of way, snaps his finger in Blackie's face, and then pushes Moe and Larry back together to protect himself. More violent is the exchange reminiscent of the hallway alcove sequence with Moe and Larry from the recent *A Bird in the Head:* (Curly: "I'll get that scum, Blackie." Moe: "Like this? [SLAP] or like this?" [POUND]). Moe's gadget does not work as well as he hoped, but of all the Stooge gadgets it seems to have the most staying power, and it makes for good comedy: first the gunpowder backfires into his face, then a spring hits him in the eye, and finally it sends out a rocket that blows Blackie out of the picture. Bernds gets plenty of mileage out of the toupee: Curly tries to grab the Justice of the Peace but gets the toupee instead; Curly wears it; it shakes loose; and everyone knows it except Blackie, who does a great take. Moe said "Oh! Superstitious, eh!?" as long ago as *Three Little Pigskins*, but this time Blackie is holding a 'good luck' horseshoe and clangs it on the heads of Moe and Larry. The bullets in the gun belt are heated by the fire just like the beer bottles in the recent *Beer Barrel Polecats*; they fire like the monkey Gattling-gun in *Goofs and Saddles* and the stove in *Phony Express*, two previous westerns. From the first Stooge Western, *Horses' Collars*, comes Curly's pistol stuck in the holster, the toupee gag, and the shooting contest - here with balloons and crackers; the glasses gag is from *All the World's a Stooge*. Moe wielded the club in the previous film; in this film it is Larry wielding the hammer. Other variations: the sun moving quickly (*Saved by the Belle*); Larry knocking out Blackie and henchman with foreswing and backswing of his sledge hammer (*Three Little Sew and Sews*); the waiter falling into the wedding cake (*An Ache in Every Stake*); the three-seater bicycle (*Men in Black, Meet the Baron*); Curly pretending to be a dog (*From Nurse to Worse*); the nails of the horseshoe stuck in Curly's rear (*Slippery Silks*); and Blackie backing into the watering trough (*Gents Without Cents*).

VERBAL HUMOR: Blackie's exaggerated Western accent comes on the heels of the exaggerated Southern accents of the previous release, *Uncivil War Birds*. A functional Curly delivers several punchlines (Moe: "While Gladys is wettin' her whistle we'll see about gettin' her a pair of new shoes, too." Curly: "She could use a pair of bedroom slippers, too."; Moe: "Who told you you need glasses?" Curly: "An obstetrician!"; [reading from a farm catalogue]: "Do you take this horse collar for your lawful wedded harness?"; and Moe: "Were you lookin' where you were goin'?" Curly: "No, I was goin' where I was lookin'"). The latter is a Stooge first, as is (Moe: "Are we mice or men?" Curly & Larry: "Mice!"); Moe's response, "Don't get personal," dates back at least to *Three Little Beers*. Other variations: "You got an ounce of brains!" (*Horses' Collars*); "Hello old poppy old pappy old kid!" (*Wee Wee Monsieur*). A throw-away line by an extra: (Curly: "Oh boy! I'll be able to get married!" Town elder: "I told you he was brave man!"). Epithets: "dummy," "porcupine," and "mashed potato muscles"; Curly calls himself "Coney Island Curly". "Dry gulch" originally meant to hide in a gulch before ambushing a passerby.

OTHER NOTES: The film was shot at Columbia's Providencia Ranch in mid-May, 1945, previewed in Compton, California on January 11, 1946, and released April 25, 1946. It was filmed after *A Bird in the Head*, but before *Micro-Phonies*. The special effects man loaded up Moe's weapon with too much powder, and some of it blew up under his eyelids, causing some temporary concern that Moe had been blinded. An accident that occurred when Moe was an infant actually did blind him for 11 months. This would be Jack White's last work at Columbia until 1952 (*A Missed Fortune*). In the interim he worked at Fox and elsewhere.

Dick Curtis and Christine McIntyre - as Badlands Blackie and Nell - carry the plot of *Three Troubledoers* (1946). Curtis towers over everyone and delivers one 'purty' Western cliché after another. He had played in Westerns since the early 1930s and ultimtely amassed nearly 200 movie credits.

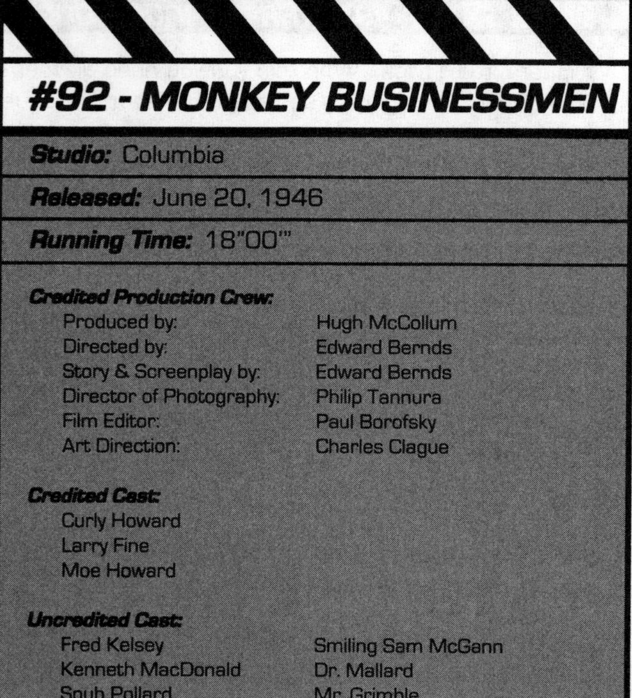

#92 - MONKEY BUSINESSMEN

Studio: Columbia

Released: June 20, 1946

Running Time: 18"00"'

Credited Production Crew:

Produced by:	Hugh McCollum
Directed by:	Edward Bernds
Story & Screenplay by:	Edward Bernds
Director of Photography:	Philip Tannura
Film Editor:	Paul Borofsky
Art Direction:	Charles Clague

Credited Cast:

Curly Howard
Larry Fine
Moe Howard

Uncredited Cast:

Fred Kelsey	Smiling Sam McGann
Kenneth MacDonald	Dr. Mallard
Snub Pollard	Mr. Grimble
Jean Donahue	Nurse Shapely
Cy Schindell	nurse
Rocky Woods	nurse
Wade Cosby	George

PERSPECTIVE: After the annual seven-month production hiatus, *Monkey Businessmen* benefits from a revitalized and even frantic Stooge energy. They bang and smack each other and anyone who comes within their reach; ruin an office complex and a sanitarium; and run from and get the better of four con artists. And they do this in random acts as well as in orchestrated routines both as a trio and in separated arrangements. They chase women, bang the bad guys, make puns and perform surgery. Ironically, this is the second film (*Idiots Deluxe*) in which a Stooge takes a long rest for his health, and all is insanely well again in Stoogedom with Curly performing at 80% of his former capacity.

The Stooges have not had very many tool-abuse sessions since the previous year's *Booby Dupes*, largely because it took a while before former sound man and now writer/director Ed Bernds felt comfortable with the violence inherent in giving the Stooges so many potentially destructive weapons. In *Micro-Phonies* they barely used a wrench and a piece of pipe, but in *A Bird in the Head* the Stooges explored the world of paper hanging. Now in Bernds' third film they begin as inept electricians, and though they have never served as electricians before, as plumbers and telephone repairmen they did dabble with wiring in *A Plumbing We Will Go* and *Three Sappy People*. The common element in each of these and still other films (*Pardon My Scotch; Cash and Carry; Termites of 1938*) are the walls, doors, and ceilings that separate rooms. When the Stooges work in your home and office, walls, doors, and ceilings cease to be significant barriers. Walls, doors, and ceilings allow the Stooges to burrow, drill, chop, and rip; they provide corridors for heads, arms, fists, whole bodies, and inanimate objects; they give the non-Stooges on the other side of the wall or door a false sense of security, whether they are on the phone, standing idly by, or making a cake. In *Monkey Businessmen* the Stooges pull McGann's phone through the wall, get punched by McGann's fists through the wall, burst out of two different doors at Mallard's, and pull the exercise machine out of the wall. Barrier destruction is the tradesman's equivalent of throwing cream pies at the wealthy, for both of them break through barriers we normally would not think were capable of being penetrated.

The frames within the film often explode with this kind of barrier destruction, and the look of the film is therefore quite different from the recent spook-and-hide films of the last few years. Scare comedies necessarily depend on doors, curtains, closets, and walls to keep the parties separate and thus create the comic surprises. In breaking through these kinds of barriers, *Monkey Businessmen* turns its comic focus not on the chasers but on the chasees - the Stooges, who are once again acting rather than reacting. Creating chaos is one of their specialties, and in this renewed two-part film they create chaos twice. But even though they are blazingly fired from their first job and then destroy Mallard's Sanitarium, they end up curing a hypochondriac and earning $1000 - not a bad Stooge day's work.

VISUAL HUMOR: The revitalized physical comedy appears throughout. A good example of complex, one-leads-to-another, extended slapstick has the Stooges pantomiming Mallard's schedule, Moe knocking off Curly's hat, prettying themselves for the nurses, Curly banging his head against the metal lamp shade, Larry taking his temperature, Curly eating the thermometer, picking his teeth, bonking himself, and then Larry and Curly hugging the nurses. The finest orchestrated routine has Curly sliding one way down the operating table to avoid the saw and then sliding off the other way. In the best Stooge fashion, some of it moves the plot along: Curly cannot move the pulleys, so Moe and Larry remove them, knocking the nurses woozy, and accidentally getting them to utter the truth about Mallard's scam. The special effects improve the barrier destructions. The fast motion used for Curly's pulling the pulleys off the wall is particularly eye-catching. There are two close-ups: McGann being electrocuted and Curly having his nose squeezed with pliers. Two other sequences also offer interesting variations of camera angles: when Mallard's and George's arms reach out and grab Moe and Larry, and when Curly runs at the camera to close the film. Bernds allows an eye gouge, but it is tempered by a real barrier: the glass door. Stooge firsts: closing the door on Larry's nose; and Curly disappearing behind a door, after which we hear a scream and a "How dare you!".

The Stooges struggled with alarm clocks in *Saved By the Belle*, *In the Sweet Pie and Pie*, and elsewhere; here Curly drops the clock into the pitcher of water. Other variations: Sam punching his fists through the wall (*Nutty But Nice*); Curly trying to snap his fingers unsuccessfully (*A Plumbing We Will Go*); wearing clothes underneath their nighties (*Dizzy Doctors*); getting electrocuted (*They Stooge to Conga*); feeling Curly's 'muscle' (*Grips, Grunts and Groans*); breathing fresh air and coughing (*Idiots Deluxe*); pantomiming while someone else speaks (*What's the Matador?*); Moe gouging Curly without contact, but hurting him anyway (*False Alarms*); Curly running towards the camera at the close (*Punch Drunks*); and Curly trying to tell Moe the nurses are right behind him (*Movie Maniacs*).

VERBAL HUMOR: This is Ed Bernds most gag-filled script to date. He offers two plot-related electrical jokes ("The line is busy!"; "A live wire!"); many plot-related sanitarium jokes (Curly: "What'll we eat?" Mallard: "Vitamins and calories." Curly: "With cream gravy!"; Curly: "What are you all steamed up about?"; Larry: "Don't get better - we'll be right back"; Grimble: "Will you examine me?" Moe: "You look terrible!"; Nurse: "Whadya' think you're doin'? Moe: "We're breathin'!" Nurse: "Well, cut it out! It ain't on the schedule!"; Curly: "We'll fool that guy! We'll cut through your skull so fast he won't know the difference!" Curly: "What about me?" Moe: "You won't know the difference either!"; Moe: "What's his temperature?" Larry: "Ninety proof!"); puns (Curly: "We'll get some grease, spread it on the floor, and slip by!"; Larry: "That Mallard's nothing but a quack!"; Moe: "Shh! The patient is in a transom!"; Moe: "What did you give him?" Curly: "Ether!" Larry: "Ether?" Curly: "Yeah - e[i]ther the bottle or the hammer!"; and Moe: "Dr. Windbag, I presume?" Larry: "Well blow me down!"); prop jokes (Curly [with an umbrella]: "I got somethin' put away for a rainy day!"); a tongue-twisting absurdity (Moe: "We better get busy before he finds out we were breaker-uppers at a peanut brittle foundry!"); romance jokes (Moe: "Take it easy, bloodhound, I'm runnin' a fever myself!" Larry: "I ain't freezin'!"; Curly: "I can take hint!"); ironies ("Five o'clock! That's the time you get up to get shot at sunrise!"; Moe: "You snore so loud my ears are ringin'"; Curly: "I know, a nice big bowl of milk." Mallard: "Oh no! No milk. You drank it all for lunch!"; and Mallard: "I wasn't expecting you." Moe: "That makes us even: we weren't expecting you either!"); and a contemporary economic reference: "The man power shortage is supposed to be over!".

Several dozen or more publicity photos were taken for most of the Columbia Stooge short-films. Publicity photos were often taken on the set, and since most films were efficiently shot in four days or less, there was not much time allotted for this purpose. Also, most of them are posed gags which may or may not be used in the film. But this particular photo is different in that the publicity department took the time to create a special effect so it looked as if Curly and Moe were being electrocuted. The negative-scratching process was simple, but no other Stooge publicity photo has a similar special effect.

The incredible racket at the beginning sets the maniacal tone of the film, as does Jordan's sped-up phone voice that fires them and bursts into flame. For the first and only time, a non-Stooge (George) understands every word of Moe's patented medical double talk ("tracto-hobo-lactometer" and "hamma-deepa-seena-fern"). Epithets: "pebble-brain," "nitwits," "porcupine," "grape-head" (and "Like a nanny goat!"). A Stooge first, and one of Moe's future favorite lines: "I'll get a cheap lawyer!". Variations: Nurse: "Gentlemen—" Larry: "Who came in?" (*We Want Our Mummy*); Moe: "Well, partners, it looks like we resigned" (*A Bird in the Head*); Fleur de Polecat!" (*You Nazty Spy!*); I'm a citizen!" (*Punch Drunks*); Curly: "I'm still hungry!" Moe: "You gotta tapewoim!" (*Beer Barrel Polecats*); Moe: "A thousand bucks!" Larry: "Nearly a million!" (*Cash and Carry*); and Moe: "Dr. Windbag, I presume?" (*Some More of Samoa*).

OTHER NOTES: The film was shot in late January/early February, 1946. It had two working titles: *Sanitarium Stooge* and *Monkey Business*. This is the first film with the MCMXLVI copyright date on it. The first title screen from this point on no longer has the comedy mask. The plot is a remake of Smith & Dale's *Mutiny on the Body* (1938). This is Kenneth MacDonald's first Stooge role; he would have one dozen more. In most of them he plays a crook, but he is also known for his appearances as a judge in *Perry Mason*. He appeared as well in such well known features as *The Cain Mutiny* (1954) and *The Ten Commandments* (1956). Ed Bernds' recollection was that Curly's condition was so bad during filming that Moe had to coach Curly line by line. When Moe says "Well, kid, we accept your apology," Curly never gave one. The Stooges were paid more ($1500 instead of $1000) for curing a patient in *Three Smart Saps*.

#93 - THREE LOAN WOLVES

Studio Columbia

Released: July 4, 1946

Running Time: 16"40'"

Credited Production Crew:

Produced & Directed by:	Jules White
Story & Screen Play by:	Felix Adler
Director of Photography:	George Kelley
Film Editor:	Edwin Bryant
Art Director:	Charles Clague

Credited Cast:

Curly Howard	
Larry Fine	
Moe Howard	
Beverly Warren	Molly
Harold Brauer	Butch McGee

Uncredited Cast:

Wally Rose	henchman
Joe Palma	henchman
Jackie Jackson	boy

PERSPECTIVE: This film gives Larry a chance to step into the limelight for the first time in over a decade of Columbia films. He is the one who takes in the worthless musical instruments and plays the guitar and tuba; he is the one who is left alone to mind the shop (and the screen); he is the one who takes in the baby; he is the one who calls himself its "mother,"; he is the one who takes the lion's share of Moe's verbal and physical abuse; he is the one who gets most of the camera time in the final fight; he is the one who gets spanked at the end; and he is the one on whom the camera isolates when he mixes a three-spirit cocktail with turpentine, tries to make the baby laugh, tells the baby the 'Three Bears' story, and throws the water out the window. In the on-going attempt to adjust Stooge comedy to fit the new reality of Stooge ability, Larry steps into the Curly role as chief clown and comic butt.

Originally a vaudevillean musician/dancer/comic, Larry is not Curly. He is quite gifted, but he is a different kind of physical comic: he reacts better then he acts, and he suffers better than he bullies. He takes slaps beautifully: his head turns sharply, he grabs his crooked hat, his hair flies, his elbows rise, and his arms and shoulders recoil and wobble; he holds his cheek and assumes an angry or confused look. He makes faces during Moe-Curly dialogue and slapstick, and participates in every scene even if silently. Often he is the innocent bystander who happens to be so close to the argument between Curly and Moe that he becomes part of it, taking one side or the other. His presence is always vital. The third man gives the group its trademark dynamics and intensifies the relationships between Moe and Curly, or between all three Stooges and a foil, or between all three Stooges and a trio of women. And usually once a film he delivers a classic line like "I'll show you a picture what is a picture!" He is in sum a grand clown, but not a headliner.

In *Three Loan Wolves* Larry steps right up and says "Millions for defense, but not one cent for tribute!" to the face of the crook. This is a bold step for Larry, but even when he does this and when he narrates the three bears story and attempts to throw the water out the window, he creates a kind of gentle, soothing pace and tone that we rarely associate with a Stooge film. This relatively relaxed pace fits the plot appropriately: the entire play, a 'box comedy,' takes place within the walls of their pawn shop and within the framework of a flashback. It calls not for the kidnapping Stooges to run in a frantic chase to keep away from the authorities (*Mutts to You*) but for the Stooges to watch over a kidnapped baby (*Sock-A-Bye Baby*) and to explain to the grown child how he came into the Stooge family. The Stooges returned to their save-the-damsel-in-distress formula two films previously, and in the previous film they harassed a scam artist. Here they stick a thug into a baby carriage, more than appropriate for three Stooges featuring gentle Larry and riding on a good-guys' streak. In a familial sense, they are as triumphant in saving their shop and family from thugs as in any endeavor. The kid leaves them, but Larry's spanking is the most appropriate ending for this film.

VISUAL HUMOR: This film includes plenty of slapstick activity, which, parallel to the pre- and post-flashback scenes with the boy, is found most intensively at the beginning and end of the flashback scenes. Moe shows Butch how tough he is, Butch punches Curly, and the

Three Loan Wolves (1946) is a landmark for two reasons. It was the first film in which Larry was the featured comedian. Jules White and Felix Adler tried this as another way to diffuse the spotlight from the ailing Curly, who is particularly pitiable in this film. It was also the first Stooge 'box comedy' in which all the actors and action come in to where the Stooges work. This requires a set of only one or two rooms, so it is relatively inexpensive to produce.

Stooges beat Butch up in the first two minutes, which is balanced in the finale by the roll-top desk/seltzer bottle/press/hot coal battle with Butch and the two thugs. There are a number of new and unique physical moments as a result of Larry's new role and Curly's limited abilities: Larry blocking an eye gouge; Curly getting his nose pressed like a door buzzer with the DOOR BUZZER sound effect; Curly fiddling a piece of plywood; and rolling up the thug in a roll-top desk.

Stooge firsts: Moe ordering Larry to "Drop what you're doin' and give me a hand!" and Larry therefore dropping the china; and the henchman [Joe Palma] literally losing a tooth; Shemp will soon spit out loosened teeth. Curly's boxing steps are as meek as they were in *Beer Barrel Polecats*, but the three jujitsu falls [by stunt man, Danny Craig] look good, and this leads into more physical comedy when he head-butts the thug and knocks him into the bowling-ball jeopardy. In the series of eight hits Moe gives Curly early on, the POUND sound effect is changed. Curly's faces to the baby are not accompanied by sound effects. Pawn shops traditionally are identified by the spheres hanging outside - but not with Stooge images. One of the faces Moe makes to amuse the baby is a "Jappy" face; Germans were parodied recently in *A Bird in the Head*. Shooting the light fixture and having it land on Moe's head we last saw in *Phony Express* and *Boobs in Arms*. Other variations: rubbing one's painful rear along the floor (*I Can Hardly Wait*); putting hot coals down someone's pants (*Whoops, I'm an Indian*); Moe dumping powder on Larry, and spraying shaken beer (*Sock-a-Bye Baby*); using a press on someone's head (*Disorder in the Court*); the baby crunching a cheek (the crab in *Matri-phony*); the sound effect used when Larry drinks the cocktail (*A Bird in the Head*); Moe conking a customer with the backswing (*3 Dumb Clucks*); and Curly wiggling his ears (*Cookoo Cavaliers*).

VERBAL HUMOR: Felix Adler gave Larry the majority of the gag lines, though Larry's forte is not in offering punchlines, but silly vocabulary ("An offspring!"; "Fire water!"), emotional support (Molly: "Even his ring was a fake!" Larry: "The phony!"), a scatterbrained tale ("I mean the kid walked in and asked for a match. I said, 'I don't smoke!'— Look, it's cute!"), and irony ("How dare you strike a mother with an infant in his arms?!"). His 'three bears' story is a pleasant concoction of references and verbal plays on the noun 'bear,' the verb 'bear,' and the adjective 'bare' ("Once upon a time, there were three bears: Max Baer, Buddy Baer, and Bugs Bear. Now bear in mind, these bears were never bare because they ran around in their bear skins - but, with their bare feet!") culminating in the pseudo-archaic, frothy, internally rhyming "so the three little bears went skipping and frolicking hither, tither, and yither without their mither and fither!".

References: Brothers Max and Buddy Baer were both fighters turned actors. Buddy fought Joe Louis twice, then played in MGM's *Quo Vadis?* and later in *Snow White and the Three Stooges*; (Max Baer, Jr. would years later play Jethro in *The Beverly Hillbillies*). Bugs Baer (unrelated) was a little older and had played in silent films. Other references: The sign 'HERE TODAY, PAWN TOMORROW' parodies the phrase "Here today, gone tomorrow" by the seventeenth-century English playwright Aphra Behn. 'Millions for defense, but not one cent for tribute!' was said by Robert Harper to French emissaries, who tried to bribe Charles Pinckney in 1798. The exchange (Larry: "I was just about to play 'Comin' Through the Corn!' Curly: "You mean 'Rye'!" Larry: "The way I play it, it's 'Corn'!") makes fun of the traditional song 'Comin' Through the Rye' and the slang meaning of "corn," i.e. corny. Samuel Woodworth's lyric, 'The Old Oaken Bucket,' was supplied with a melody in 1826. Moe's "These two bullies were attacking me with poison gas!" is slang for "bad talk." Larry's "a genuine Stratosphere!" refers to a Stradivarius, for which see on *Disorder in the Court*; Felix Adler adds a pun (Moe: "Play some air(e)"). This reference is very contemporary: the stratosphere, which sits some seven miles above the earth's surface, had only recently been identified and explored; cf. "Simple like RADAR" in *Micro-Phonies*. Adler wrote hip talk for the boy, e.g. "I want the low down. Now come clean!".

Larry's "Hold it for thirty days!" was used in *Uncivil Warriors*, but here they really are in a pawn shop. Other variations: Larry: "So it shouldn't be a total loss, I'll drink it myself" (*Gents Without Cents*); Curly's "Wait a minute! [Thug: "What for?"] So I can hit you!" (*Dizzy Detectives*); and Moe: "Now you've got a sliver of a brain!" (*Horses' Collars*). Epithets: "nitwit," "two-ounce brain," and "apple-head!" the latter said seconds apart to both Larry and Curly.

OTHER NOTES: The working title was *In Hock*. The introductory music of this film reverts to the bassoon/jazzy/xylophone version used for the first three releases of 1945. The *Scrapbook* credits assistant director Tommy Flood. This is Harold Brauer's [Butch] first Stooge film; he played in Shemp's first Stooge short, in *Quiz Whizz* (as 'Bill Brauer') with Joe, and in the feature *The Outlaws Is Coming* (as 'Tiny Brauer') with Curly-Joe; he and Emil Sitka were the only actors who worked with all four Stooge configurations. Felix Adler will more fully exploit this kind of 'box comedy' in next year 's *Sing a Song of Six Pants*. This is the fourth film in which we meet members of the Stooge family - dad in *3 Dumb Clucks*, mom in *Cactus Makes Perfect*, and a pony child in *Even As IOU*. This count does not include members we hear about but do not see, e.g. Uncle Bob O. Link in *If a Body Meets a Body*, Curly's wife Gertie in *Three Sappy People*, or, for that matter, Uncle Tom in this film.

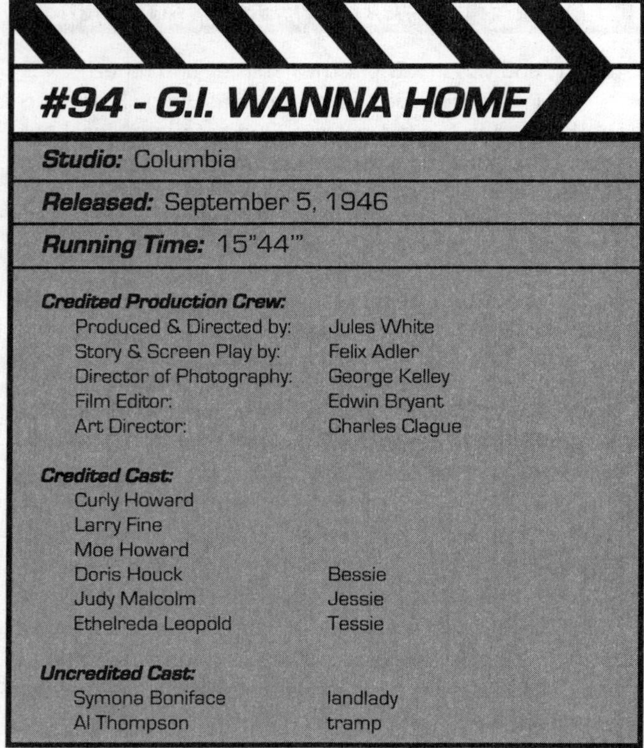

#94 - G.I. WANNA HOME

Studio: Columbia

Released: September 5, 1946

Running Time: 15"44'"

Credited Production Crew:

Produced & Directed by:	Jules White
Story & Screen Play by:	Felix Adler
Director of Photography:	George Kelley
Film Editor:	Edwin Bryant
Art Director:	Charles Clague

Credited Cast:

Curly Howard	
Larry Fine	
Moe Howard	
Doris Houck	Bessie
Judy Malcolm	Jessie
Ethelreda Leopold	Tessie

Uncredited Cast:

Symona Boniface	landlady
Al Thompson	tramp

PERSPECTIVE: Stooge films often consciously reflect contemporary changes in American politics, economics, and popular culture. From Depression to New Deal to World War II and 'boogie-woogie,' many Stooge films have had plots and gags appropriate to current events and trends, and the roles the Stooges play change accordingly. Now no longer needed to capture Nazi and Japanese enemies, the Stooges are discharged from the service to find an America not quite ready to accommodate them, the very concept of this year's Oscar winning *The Best Years of Our Lives*. In *G.I. Wanna Home* we see the effect the return of nearly fifteen million soldiers had on the American economy.

In *Monkey Businessmen* we heard an angry Smilin' Sam McGann yell, "I thought the manpower shortage was over!" and indeed the G.I. Bill of Rights (1944) had provided for job reinstatement, training, and education for eight million veterans. Getting a job or at least job training was relatively easy; finding a place to live was not. The G.I. Bill enabled the Veterans' Administration to guarantee some $16 billion for home and business loans, but there would be no major Housing Act until 1949, and the great American suburbs were still on the drawing board. In this sense the Depression that preceded the war had not yet disappeared, particularly in 1945-47 during a two-year let down from the over-extended war-time economy. It is no wonder Tessie exclaims that getting dispossessed "is a new American custom!" or that Moe says "It's gettin' so nowadays that a person can't enjoy the comfort of their own domicile."

Since the comedy simply parodies post-war cultural economics, it is necessarily limited in scope. The focus is not getting hired for and screwing up a job or two, something on which many Stooge films depend, but on searching for a home and living without one. The opening scenarios all fit into this focus: the Stooges try to hitch a ride, find their fiancées dispossessed, move their possessions, and locate an apartment. Finally, without explanation, they have moved into/onto someone's lot. The narrative connection is not as important as the various post-war domestic scenarios. Even romance plays a secondary role to the housing shortage, for we barely see Tessie, Jessie, and Bessie again. In two words, *G.I. Wanna Home* is in name (cf. 'G.I. Bill') and essence a contemporary satire.

Living in this same world, audiences of 1946 would have thought it was delightfully ludicrous yet completely understandable for the Stooges to maintain their illegal home by cleaning the grass floor with a lawn mower and a horn-equipped vacuum, reap "spinach" for dinner by collecting lawn grass, steal the neighbor's eggs, shoot at his chicken, and ultimately get chased out by the fast-motion tractor driven by the faceless lot owner. To fill the cracks Felix Adler inserts a number of gags, and we get a few minutes of a Stooge favorite (*Crash Goes the Hash*; *If a Body Meets a Body*) - the live parrot in the cooked bird, suggesting maybe that the parrot is just trying to homestead like the Stooges.

The denouement consists of one last post-war scenario. The year the war ended produced a record number of marriages as returning G.I.s and their beloveds got hitched and initiated what would become known as the 'baby boom' generation. The Stooges had a pre-baby boom child in the previous film, but here the couples are just starting out in their lives together. After being unhoused and then housed outside improperly, the

Densely packed Stooge tableaux often tell a story. This exaggerated and comical shot represents a genuine socio-economic problem in 1946: finding work and homes for returning veterans and their young families.

Some Stooge films in the 1930s reflected the Great Depression among both the unemployed and high society alike, and many Stooge films in the early/mid-1940s featured the war effort whether at home or abroad. Now in *G.I. Wanna Home* (1946) the Depression has diminished and the war is over, so the Stooge writers and producers turn their attention towards the lack of housing and jobs back home. One of the aspects that makes the Stooge corpus of films so remarkable is not just its longevity but its reflection of American society through four decades.

Stooges and their wives finally squeeze into a two-room apartment where Curly climbs to the top of a triple bunk bed, whence gravity takes over.

VISUAL HUMOR: The most consistent feature here is Felix Adler's accompanying slapstick gags with an appropriate response, verbal challenge, or quip. Many of them are refurbished gags with variations. Examples include Moe and Larry pounding and bonking Curly, grabbing him by the ears, and escorting him towards the camera, as in *Monkey Businessmen*, but now adding: "I'm budgin'! I'm budgin'!"; Curly pulling the car (*Mutts to You*) but now pulling out that huge sandwich: "If I'm gonna work like a horse, I'm gonna eat like one!"; Curly shaving the potatoes (*An Ache in Every Stake*) but now putting on aftershave and asking: "Did I get some in your eye?"; the man slamming the door into Moe's nose (*Monkey Businessmen*) with Larry asking: "Did he break your nose?" Moe: "No." Larry: "That's too bad!"; the parrot laughing when Larry tickles the carcass, and Curly feeding it crackers; the hot pan on Larry's back (*Crash Goes the Hash*) but here Moe dusts off the dirty bird carcass with a whisk broom; and Curly falling through the bunk bed (*I Can Hardly Wait*), but now saying "Whadya know! I didn't get hurt!" with Moe adding "Oh yes you did!" and punching him. Other variations: the fight over the gun (*Three Loan Wolves*); shooting the 'duck' (*Back to the Woods*); the 'AYOOGAH' horn (*Three Pests in a Mess*); Curly slapping Moe after saluting him (recently in *Booby Dupes*); knocking on the manager's forehead (*Calling All Curs*); Moe slapping his own face with an egg (*Loco Boy Makes Good*); the parrot crunching Larry's nose (the crab in *Matri-Phony*, the boy in *Three Loan Wolves*); and Moe kissing Larry and saying "I'm poisoned" (*Ants in the Pantry*). The duffel bag hitting is a Stooge first, to be reused, for example, in *Stone Age Romeos*.

VERBAL HUMOR: Other than the verbal additions to the physical gags, this film includes a rare off-color poem: 'Nothing to buy./Nothing to sell./ We've gone fishing./ You can go— Fishing too'. The Stooges display a particularly silly brand of ex-G.I. speech patterns: "fian-sees," "some doilies for the goilies," and "How you do dat?". The Stooges' own version of the G.I. Bill ("After we're married, we'll get 'em the best jobs they ever had!") derives from *Dizzy Doctors*. Other variations: 'GINSBERG, ROSENBERG, GOLDSTEIN, and O'BRIEN REAL ESTATE' (*A Pain in the Pullman*); "Hey fellas! Duck!" (*Uncivil Warriors*); "What would Emily Post say?" (*Hoi Polloi*); Symona Boniface: "No dogs allowed." Curly: "Rruff!" Landlady: "Meow! Psst!" (*3 Dumb Clucks*); and Moe insisting "That's an order!" Curly: "Aye-aye, sir!" (*Three Loan Wolves*). Epithets: "porcupine," "onion-head," and "lame-brain". Reference: "418 Mishugena Avenue" - *meshugeneh* is Yiddish for 'crazy.'

OTHER NOTES: The correct title is *G.I. Wanna Home*, not *G.I. Wanna Go Home*". During the Depression the Stooges lived outside in *Even As IOU*.

#95 - RHYTHM AND WEEP

Studio: Columbia

Released: October 3, 1946

Running Time: 17"37'"

Credited Production Crew:

Produced & Directed by:	Jules White
Story & Screenplay by:	Felix Adler
Director of Photography:	Philip Tannura
Film Editor:	Edwin Bryant
Art Director:	Charles Clague

Credited Cast:

Curly Howard	
Larry Fine	
Moe Howard	
Gloria Patrice	Wilda
Ruth Godfrey	Tilda
Nita Bieber	Hilda
Jack Norton	Mr. Boyce

PERSPECTIVE: The Stooges have played frustrated, unsuccessful musicians previously in *A Pain in the Pullman*, *What's the Matador?*, and *Gents Without Cents* as well as their second MGM short *Beer and Pretzels*. Here in *Rhythm and Weep*, having been tossed out of more than two dozen theaters, the Stooges decide to commit suicide. Meeting a trio of equally frustrated female entertainers who are also about to leap from a tall building does not deter them. When even beautiful young women do not give the Stooges the will to live, you suspect a miracle is about to happen. What could save the Stooges? A saw and a stethoscope or another favorite Stooge toy? No, it is only music that can save them: a lively pianistic rendition of 'Turkey in the Straw' and the promise of a Broadway musical production. Overjoyed, the Stooges begin dancing while still standing precariously on the ledge, as if they are fearless and utterly oblivious to how close they stand to death. Curly summarizes this oblivion when he says: "You know a guy could get killed from up here!"

Unfortunately, as the self-deluded millionaire producer runs out of his insane freedom and is led away, the plug is pulled on both trios, so the Stooges go insane with frustration. With artists incapable of doing their art, there is little left but insanity. The frustration that often accompanies artistic genius too often leads to insanity and suicide, Vincent Van Gogh and Kurt Cobain providing nineteenth- and twentieth-century examples. Similarly, artistic producers and agents are not always to be trusted and often trump up their accomplishments. Ask almost any painter, actor, or musician. Take these commonalities of the artistic world and give them Stooge treatment, and you end up with the tragi-comical framework of *Rhythm and Weep*.

The rest of the film is filled with two more Stooge musical numbers, some Stooge sketch comedy, and two dance routines by the female trio. More so than the gymnastically vigorous female trio in *Gents Without Cents*, this trio is quite versatile, equally adept at tap and ballet, and their numbers do not run too long. While the girls give their scenes a serious and artistic presence, the Stooges create continuous mirth with their violin and base-bow work in the rooftop number and their ballet moves in the rehearsal segment. In fact, the Stooges' incidental musical antics are as interesting as the actual sketch they perform, which must have been of the sort they performed in their live engagements during the war and just after, judging by the military uniforms Moe and Larry wear and comparing it with the military sketch in *Gents Without Cents*. The limited scope of this film and the previous two (*Three Loan Wolves* and *G.I. Wanna Home*), all three of which were directed by Jules White and written by Felix Adler, is noted but ends here. The final two Curly films and the first few Shemp films will seek broader horizons. 1946-1947 were not Hollywood's most creative years in any genre. The sudden absence of war-focused films had left a creative vacuum.

VISUAL HUMOR: Jules White created numerous visual antics to accompany the musical numbers and fill in the thin plot: Curly leans 45º off the building ledge, nails his shoes to it, drops the hammer and hits an unseen victim below, blows paint from the sax, and dances in a tutu; Larry plays 'Yankee Doodle' on the clarinet "by ear" and gets his head caught in Curly's suspenders; and Moe gets hit with bows from each side. The bow work derives from *Disorder in the Court*, as does Curly's taking off and replacing his hat in the military sketch. The Stooges make ballet look so natural and easy; their grace is hard to mask even in their silliness. In contrast, 'Swingaroo Joe' is the first time we have actually seen the Stooges playing boogie woogie.

The Stooge films were in transition in 1946. Curly's abilities had diminished, the postwar economy was repressed, and the world in general – including the film world – had not yet refocused. The background city-scape painting from *Rhythm and Weep* reveals the measure of financial restraint under which the Columbia short-film unit was operating. Nonetheless, cinema is all about illusion, and the camera and its viewers pay more attention to Curly's precariously oblique, suicidal lean atop a skyscraper than the restricted conditions under which *Rhythm and Weep* was made.

Long fades have not been used often except at the ends of films; *Rhythm and Weep* uses a long fade to conclude the rooftop scene. This sort of abrupt conclusion recalls the tractor-destruction sequence in the previous film, *G.I. Wanna Home.* We have seen Curly turn to the camera and speak to us before (*So Long, Mr. Chumps*), but not Larry. Here Larry kisses his girl, looks at us, and adds: "This I like...And I get paid for it, too!" Another striking role reversal occurs when Larry runs up the bidding like an auctioneer ("Lady, will you make it three?" Tilda: "No, two!") and she gouges him. Other variations: the multiple wrist watch gag (*Dutiful but Dumb*); Curly heading off stage in the wrong direction but being whistled back in a normal walk, and the Stooges going insane from frustration (*Men in Black*); and Curly picking up the saxophone with his right hand incorrectly placed on the top (*The Big Idea*).

VERBAL HUMOR: Felix Adler injected a stage-sketch type of dialogue into the theatrical parts of the film, with vaudevillean banter and punchlines (Moe: "This is the twenty-sixth theater we got thrown out of this month. What is there left for us?" Larry: "Four more theaters!"; Moe: "Where were you born. Curly: "In a hospital." Moe: "Why?" Curly: "I wanted to be with my mother!"; Larry's ["Do you happen to be musicians?"] "Oh sure! I play in five flats and get thrown out of all of 'em!"). Adler adds a number of ironies connected with death and suicide (Moe: "Come on! We got some croakin' to do!"; Curly: "You know a guy could get killed from up here!"; Curly: "They're my uncles!" Moe: "They look like a[u]nts!"; Curly: "I took a short cut"; Moe: "If you're gonna bump yourself off, what's the idea of eatin' pie?" Curly: "So I can 'di-gest' right!"; and Moe: "I gotta be at the cleaners at two o'clock"), and a typical Stooge insult (Larry: "Simple, isn't it?" Moe: "Yeah, so are you!"). We heard a gag similar to the exchange (Moe: "How old are ya', bub?" Curly: "I'm 26." Moe: "Nah, you couldn't get that homely in 26 years!") in *No Census, No Feeling.* Other variations: Moe's "I'll get myself a cheap lawyer" (*Monkey Businessmen*); a name like 'Mr. Smellington' (*If a Body Meets a Body*); and Curly's "Swing it!" (*Violent is the Word for Curly*). Epithet: "porcupine."

OTHER NOTES: The release title parodies the card-game expression 'Read 'em and weep'; the working title of the film was *Acting Up.* The crazy-man producer gimmick was used in Curly's 1934 MGM short *Roast-Beef and Movies* (1934). We will see this motif again in *Pardon My Clutch.* Jack Norton made a career of playing incoherent types, most notably in *Cockeyed Cavaliers* (1934) and *The Bank Dick* (1940). Ruth Godfrey [White], who plays Tilda, was Jules White's daughter-in-law. This was her first of over one half-dozen Stooge appearances; she later appeared in *To Kill a Mockingbird* and *Midnight Cowboy*, and won an Emmy. The music includes the traditional 'Turkey in the Straw,' the boogie-woogie 'Swingaroo Joe' ('Chambers Boogie' by Tommy Chambers), Anton Rubenstein's 'Melody in F' (1883), Mendelsohn's 'Spring Song,' and the overture to Franz von Suppé's *Poet and Peasant.* The skyscraper footage is of the RCA building in Rockefeller Center in New York, home of NBC. The pill gag was originally written to have Curly pop the pills into his own mouth, but his physical coordination was so poor that the gag had to be changed.

#96 - THREE LITTLE PIRATES

Studio: Columbia

Released: December 5, 1946

Running Time: 17"51'"

Credited Production Crew:

Produced by:	Hugh McCollum
Directed by:	Edward Bernds
Story & Screenplay by:	Clyde Bruckman
Director of Photography:	Philip Tannura
Film Editor:	Paul Borofsky
Art Direction:	Charles Clague

Credited Cast:

Curly Howard	
Larry Fine	
Moe Howard	
Christine McIntyre	Rita Yolanda
Robert Stevens	Black Louie
Vernon Dent	Governor of Deadman's Island [Enchilada]
Dorothy DeHaven	his woman [Chiquita]

Uncredited Cast:

Ethan Laidlaw	henchman
Joe Palma	henchman
Jack Parker	soldier
Larry McGrath	soldier
Al Thompson	pirate
Cy Schindell	pirate

PERSPECTIVE: This is one of the classic Stooge episodes, largely because it features Curly's last great costume characterization, the very wise Raja of Canarsie. The Stooges visited the south seas in *Some More of Samoa* and Africa in *Three Missing Links* and they have portrayed everything from French artists to Chinese launderers. But the magi-like robes and turbans, the polyglottal exchanges, and the promise of rare gifts from wayfarers create an exotic grandeur far above the level of any other Stooge costumer. The exotica commences right from the outset when the Stooges are interviewed in the elegant palace of the tyrannical governor of Deadman's Island and escape from a prison lined with human skulls. From that point the 'Maha!' ["Aha!"] and the 'Gin of Rummy' do their magic.

The Stooges themselves wrote the Maharaja scene, played it on stage, and filmed it first in the 1941 Columbia feature *Time Out For Rhythm*. There the 'Chow Mienian Raja' offered more physical comedy and normal speech than here, since it was more a gag sequence than an exotic interview. In *Three Little Pirates* Curly's language becomes stranger and more dominant. He speaks in a pseudo-Russian double talk which may have ultimately derived from the Howard family's Lithuanian background, but Moe had been honing his skill at creating imitation languages and foreign accents with the Hitlerian German speeches in *You Nazty Spy!* and *I'll Never Heil Again*, the French and Irish phrases in *Pop Goes the Easel*, and his frequent double talk names for medical tools and chemicals. Curly's delivery is very effective, even when he runs out of breath on his second "Oh, shut up I don't have to!" Perhaps because of his failing health he could not vary his style of speech as much as he did in *Time Out For Rhythm*, but that may have turned out for the best. In his limited range he consistently whines "Aha," rolls off the proem "Razbanyas yatee benee futch ah tinney herongha," emphasizes "parah*NEE*keemahheehah," and then lapses into a non-accented "I'd like to see some babes myself!" The thick glasses cover his wearied face, and the two spills he takes from his chair are convincing. Director Bernds marveled later at how well Curly performed during production.

Sandwiching this memorable scene are the prison and barroom scenes, the former reviving one of the Stooges' most reliable scenarios - having an array of tools in a small enclosed space; in fact, this particular prison closet is so small the slapstick depends mostly on ricochets. The brawl in the pirate saloon with its oriental decor consumes more space and time and expands the comic possibilities. It begins with the knife-throwing from the Maharaja routine in *Time Out For Rhythm*, greatly enhanced by one of the more memorable characters in the Stooge films - the smiling, intimidating, bullying Black Louie [Robert Stevens]. The brawl then finds the Stooges confronting more adversaries - nearly a dozen - than usual, and they are able to use some bizarre means of knocking out pirates, including a chandelier, a four-dimensional painting, and a huge, tilting pinball-machine mallet.

VISUAL HUMOR: In the confining prison closet there are a dozen blows struck in just 40 seconds; the tightness of space recalls similar scenes in *Cash and Carry* and *Cactus Makes Perfect*. The prison break concludes with a slapstick free-for-all, suggesting that Stooge physical comedy dominated the artistic criteria of Edward Bernds more than the other way around. In contrast to the small prison closet, the pin-ball mallet is the largest mallet in Stoogedom; its inspiration may have been the Rube Goldberg burglar alarm mallet in *Soup to Nuts*. A Stooge first: Curly sitting with legs crossed but standing up to cross them first. Knocking down the chandelier onto two pirates does the shoot-the-light-fixture-down-on-some-one's-head gag [*Whoops, I'm an Indian*] one better. In the previous film [*Rhythm and Weep*] Tilda takes a Stooge role and gouges Larry; here Moe would slap Curly but the tall soldier holds Moe's arms and slaps Larry himself.

We have not seen a painting come to life since *I'll Never Heil Again*, but in *Three Little Pirates* the painting comes alive twice. Other variations: Curly giving a flirtatious chin wave [*A Pain in the Pullman*]; the glasses test [*All the World's A Stooge*]; a woman helping the Stooges break out of prison [*Saved by the Belle*]; tools hidden under a prison mattress [*3 Dumb Clucks*]; a pinball machine [*Three Smart Saps*]; and Moe challenging the tall soldier to shove him again [*Half-Shot Shooters*].

VERBAL HUMOR: The Maharaja scene, dictated by Moe to script writer Clyde Bruckman, is the most elaborately written and lengthy verbal exchange in any Stooge film. There are plenty of silly-sounding phrases ("The Ruby de Lollipopskia"; "No leak-a dat?"; "Hello, doll!"), one-liners (Moe: "He had some bubble gum, but I think he swallowed it!"), exchanges (Governor: "You may choose the manner in which you will die!" Larry: "Oh that's easy! Old age!"; Moe: "Guaranteed forever!" Larry: "You should live so long!"; Moe: "You got some slick chicks?" Curly: "Oh, a wolf!"), set jokes (Governor: "I don't believe they're sailors..." [Rita enters in a strapless dress; the Stooges whistle] They're sailors, all right!"; Curly: "It's raspberry!" Governor: "What fire! I have been given many pigeon-blood rubies, but never have I been given the raspberry!"), and poetic descriptions ("The Raja says that in his domains on the islands of Coney and Long, there are some fair chickadees who prowl through the meadows day and night. If you give us 'til sun up, we shall bring some back by sundown!").

The pseudo-Russian lingo includes a little Yiddish ("ingenzommen," also used the previous year in *Rockin' Thru the Rockies*) and several New York geographical references: Bay Meadows, Canarsie, Flatbush, Long Island, and Coney Island. These references are appropriate to three 'sailors' shipwrecked off a New York City Garbage Scow. Elsewhere this Clyde Bruckman screenplay features gallows humor about the skulls in the prison room (Moe: "If that guy don't stop starin' at me I'll knock his block off!" Larry: "Somebody beat you to it."; Rita: "Just a couple of men who tried to help me escape"; Rita: "She'd split your throat for two doubloons!" Moe: "We got a barber at home would do it for two bits!") and in the pirate bar ("You have nothing to worry about: if either one of us hits you, we lose!"; Curly: "We better call the cops." Moe: "We better call the Marines!...Let's not lose our heads." Curly: "Yeah! Let's not!"). Bruckman adds plenty of silliness as well ("Oh! The west wall!"; "Eenie, Meenie, Mynie, Moe. You can't go wrong with Moe!"; and the atmospheric 'Ye Olde Tilt'). Epithets: "pickle-puss" and "frog-head". The Governor watches the Raja doing a finger-snap and slapping Moe's chin and then the Gin of Rummy doing a finger-snap and slapping Larry's chin, and says: "Can we dispense with the formalities?"!

References: Larry in the Maharaja scene is introduced as "our valet, Rudy," referring to stage and screen star Rudy Vallee, who co-starred in and was on screen with the Stooges during the Maharaja scene in *Time Out For Rhythm*. The governor refers to "winged feet," a classical reference to the god Hermes; there is also a classical bust on the bureau behind him. Curly's "burning at the steak... because a hot steak is better than a cold chop!" was used in *Restless Knights*. Other variations: I fall down!" [*In the Sweet Pie and Pie*]; Moe: "*Will* we!" Larry: "*Will* we!" Curly: "Will we?" Larry: " We *will*!" [*An Ache in Every Stake*]; singing a triad [*Half Shot Shooters*] of "Contact!" [*Cash and Carry*]; and "a Mickey Finn" [*Cookoo Cavaliers*].

OTHER NOTES: The *Scrapbook* records that Edward Bernds says Moe dictated the scene to Bruckman "crazy syllable for crazy syllable" at the writers' conference in early April. A printed transcription can be found in *Okuda* (36-41). The Maharaja scene will appear again with Curly-Joe in *The Three Stooges Go Around the World in a Daze*. The script names the other characters 'Rita Yolanda,' 'Governor Enchilada,' and his girl 'Chiquita'. 'Robert Stevens' was the screen name of Robert Kellard early in his career. Bernds recollected later [*Okuda* 66-67] that Curly's condition was 'up' for the last time: "I guess I should be thankful that Curly was in one of his 'up' periods, because it was strange the way he went up and down. In the order I shot the pictures, not in the order they were released, he was down for *A Bird in the Head* and *Three Troubledoers*, he was up for *Micro-Phonies*, way down for *Monkey Businessmen* and then up again, for the last time, in *Three Little Pirates*." Mostly because of Curly's condition, although also in part because of a general Hollywood malaise, 1946 turned out the weakest grouping of Stooge releases.

1947

Half-Wits Holiday • Fright Night

Out West • Hold That Lion • Brideless Groom

Sing a Song of Six Pants • All Gummed Up

#97 - HALF - WITS HOLIDAY

Studio: Columbia

Released: January 9, 1947

Running Time: 17"29'"

Credited Production Crew:

Produced & Directed by:	Jules White
Story & Screenplay by:	Zion Myers
Director of Photography:	George Kelley
Film Editor:	Edwin Bryant
Art Director:	Charles Clague

Credited Cast:

Curly Howard	
Larry Fine	
Moe Howard	
Vernon Dent	Professor Quackenbush
Barbara Slater	Lulu
Ted Lorch	Professor Sedlitz

Uncredited Cast:

Emil Sitka	Sappington the Butler
Symona Boniface	Mrs. Smythe Smythe
Al Thompson	party guest (first pie target)
Johnny Kascier	party guest (councilman)
Helen Dickson	Mrs. Gotrocks
Victor Travers	seated, sleeping party guest

PERSPECTIVE: It is hard to believe that the gentle "Hhmm!" Curly gives Moe when he takes the pie from him in this first release of 1947 was the last "Hhmm!" we will hear from this comic genius. During the shooting of this film on May 6, 1946, Curly suffered a stroke so debilitating that he could not continue his career, let alone the film. When canvasses were being put up on the set before filming the pie fight, Curly's absence was noticed by the extras, but Moe, Larry, and Jules White told no one how serious his condition was. He could not and did not appear in the pie fight, which he indirectly started by stealing that pie off Sappington's tray. What a fitting, ironic conclusion to more than a dozen years of brilliant Stooge film production: subconsciously refuse to become a gentleman, steal some silverware, champagne and a pie, which starts a pie fight and creates chaos among wealthy society, and then retire.

The film itself is a remake of Felix Adler's classic *Hoi Polloi*, the 1935 attempt at transforming the Stooges into gentlemen. These two Pygmalion films look very different, though. The most obvious addition is the pie fight; and because the dance scene from *Hoi Polloi* had already been reused in *In the Sweet Pie and Pie*, it is omitted here, and that leaves a second hole in the film in addition to Curly's absence from the pie fight. To the reading lesson has been added Moe reading upside down, no doubt a variation of those brilliant neologisms ("Razbanyas yatee benee futch ah...") we just heard in *Three Little Pirates*. The table etiquette lesson now has too many courses, however, and because the imitation food by nature creates long silences without support from Curly's multiple expressions of past years, the scene has a slower pace than viewers normally find in Stooge films.

Despite Curly's absence, some very special moments come during the pie fight, especially when the 'Sword of Damocles' pie is hanging from the ceiling over Moe and Mrs. Smythe Smythe [Symona Boniface]. The humor here comes visually from the anticipation that we and Moe know about the dangling pie while the cultured, earnestly interested Mrs. Smythe Smythe does not, and verbally by Mrs. Smythe Smythe's educated references to Moe's "metamorphosis" and the "Sword of Damocles." Another great moment is created for Emil Sitka, who comes along here just in the nick of time to act in his first Stooge film just as Curly is departing. After he is hit with a pie, he says calmly and with the proper reserve as befits his role as butler: "Pardon me, madam." Still another is the sledge hammer scene by the fireplace. Not only is the timing impeccable, the sound effects crisp and variegated, and the banter deliciously Stooge-like (Larry: "Don't worry, we always fix it right the second time!"), we see Curly hit on that iron head for the last time. After one early Paramount short, eleven MGM shorts and features in 1933, one 1934 Universal feature, and 97 shorts and 5 features filmed for Columbia between 1934 and 1946, the film career of Jerome Howard, save a brief cameo in *Hold That Lion,* comes to and end.

VISUAL HUMOR: Many of the gags from *Hoi Polloi* are still here: hiding, kicking, spraying champagne, stealing silverware, doing "exactly" as the teacher does (although at the dinner table), and Quackenbush ripping his hair out. New is Curly trying to put the ripped out hair onto his own scalp. Stooge firsts include the result shot showing us footprints all over Sappington [Emil Sitka], Moe washing off in the punch, Curly biting the diamond off the woman's ring, and pulling the rug with the man standing on the other end of it on the other side of the curtain. Curly has eaten many inedible objects since *Uncivil Warriors*. Here his last bad meal is lipstick. The hammer and chisel by the fireplace is a variation of the prison scene in the previous film, but a new wrinkle is hitting the professor in the stomach. Other variations: the reflex tests (*Three Sappy People*); Curly hitting Larry on the backswing and Moe's hand with the foreswing (*3 Dumb Clucks*); Curly howling like a wolf (*Three Little Twirps*); Moe tipping ashes into Curly's mouth (*Cash and Carry*); holding hands under the table (*You Nazty Spy!*); biting Curly's nose (*Uncivil Warriors*); hitting a sleeping man with a pie, and Larry and Moe stooping in a fight (*Pop Goes the Easel*); and a pie sticking to the ceiling (*Movie Maniacs*).

VERBAL HUMOR: The beginning of Moe's upside-down reading: "Tar ytrid eht, sey" is "Yes, the dirty rat" backwards, a variation on "the dirty rat" reading in *Hoi Polloi*. Replacing the "k-i-t-t-y" spelling is this exchange (Larry: "Oh see thee pretty cat. Does thee pretty cat have chickens?" Quackenbush: "That's 'kittens.' A cat does not have chickens." Larry: "Oh no? Well I had a cat that got in the chicken house, and that cat had chickens!"). Also added, but to the fireplace sequence, is the classic Stooge set joke (*Nertsery Rhymes*): Sedlitz: "If I gave you a dollar and your father gave you a dollar, how many dollars would you have?" Larry: "One dollar." Sedlitz: "You don't know your arithmetic." Larry: "You don't know my father!" The Stooge father is brought up, as in the original, albeit indirectly, in an exchange (Larry: "There ain't been a gentleman in our family for fifty generations." Moe: "Quit braggin'!"). First time Stooge writer Zion Myers wrote fine lines of verbal pomposity for the professors (Quackenbush: "It is completely illogical, preponderantly impracticable, and moreover, it stinks." Sedlitz: "Tutt-tutt and poof-poof, to say nothing of piffle!") They mention "three missing links" (cf. *Three Missing Links* and *If a Body Meets a Body*), and Darwin, so they might be a little smarter than Prof. Richmond in *Hoi Polloi*, who wagered $9,000 more than Quackenbush that he could educate the Stooges. Their language is more current, too: the phrase 'hubba hubba' had recently (1944) come into American English during World War II as a Japanese loan-word; Moe calls Lulu "the Hubba-Hubba kid". Myers wrote the bulk of the best dialogue for Moe, including inept pick-up lines ("What a lulu...Toots, I'd love to cover you with furs and automobiles...Only the best furs: mink, skunk, porcupine..."), Stooge etiquette instructions ("You don't eat peas with a knife. You mix 'em with the mashed potatoes. Then you eat 'em with a spoon!"), a self-correcting malapropism ("I wish I had some 'Worcester-cester-sheer-sheer-shire Sauce. I just can't say Worcestershire!"), a pun ("That's neither hair nor there"), and some pomposity of his own (Mrs. Gotrocks: "You disgraceful vagabonds!" Moe: "Who do you think you're talking to?"). Two malapropistic three-patterns (Larry: "Delighted!" Moe: "Devastated!" Curly: "Dilapidated!" Larry: "Enchanted!" Moe: "Enraptured!" Curly: "Embalmed!"). The Moron cheer is no longer tasteful, but Monty Python played 'twits' in the 1970s.

References: The 'Sword of Damocles' refers to the fourth-century BC Sicilian tyrant Dionysius I, who taught his courtier Damocles how unhappy a tyrant's life is by feasting him beneath a sword suspended from the ceiling by a thread. The inspiration for the 'Amalgamated Association of Morons' was a revived labor movement in 1946; without wartime price controls, prices soared, so four million Union members attempted to equalize the inflation with work stoppages. The name 'Smythe' in the 1940s was a sophisticated variant of the name 'Smith,' so 'Smythe Smythe' is even more so, which is why Moe was "very very happy happy" to meet her. "Delighted!... Devastated!..."Dilapidated!" parodies Cole Porter's "It's delightful, it's delicious, it's de-lovely" (*Red, Hot and Blue* - 1936). Moe's "It's a good thing Kilroy wasn't here" refers to the common WW II graffito: 'Kilroy was here'. Epithets: Moe's "dummy," "petty-larceny Stooge," "feather-brain," "wise-guy," "lunk-head," and "flat-top"; Sedlitz calls Larry "You with the mattress head". 'Sappington' is another stuffy name like 'Jerkington' in *If a Body Meets a Body*, but here we first hear the '-ngton' suffix added to a Stooge name and more (Moe: "Oh Curlington!" Curly: "Yesington?"). Other variations: Larry's reference to the reform school (*Ants in the Pantry*); "Local 6 7/8" (*You Nazty Spy!*); and Moe's baseball metaphor: "I'll do the pitchin'; you do the catchin'!" (*Movie Maniacs*). Curly's last burst of blissful ignorance: Quackenbush: "There is definite evidence of Vacancy of the Cranium." Curly: "Gee, thanks!"

OTHER NOTES: Shooting dates were May 2-6, 1946, although Moe [145-149] recollects the date of Curly's stroke as May 14; his account of Curly's last moment on the set is touching. *Larry* [171] recollected the day as April 12, the day Roosevelt died. White [*Okuda* 67] recollected that Curly had difficulty even with the malapropistic three-patterns (Larry: "Delighted!" Moe: "Devastated!" Curly: "Dilapidated!"). The working title was *No Gents — No Cents*. The plot will be remade with Joe as *Pies and Guys*. The pie-fight footage, the most re-used in the corpus, will reappear in *Pest Man Wins, Scheming Schemers, Pies and Guys*, and *Stop! Look! and Laugh!*. The slow pace of the etiquette scene is also due to Edwin Bryant's editing. In the early 1930s Zion Myers with boyhood friend Jules White co-directed/produced MGM's *Dogville* 'barkies,' canine spoofs of contemporary feature films (*All Quiet on the Canine Front*). Myers ran the Columbia short-subject unit in 1933/1934; he hired Archie Gottler to produce the 'Musical Novelties' (e.g. *Woman Haters*). Like Hugh McCollum, who had been secretary to Columbia's Harry Cohn, Myers began as Carl Laemmle's secretary at Universal. Myers' sister, Carmel, was a starlet in the silent era, playing the wicked Iras in MGM's *Ben-Hur* (1925). Emil Sitka, who played in over three dozen Stooge films, would perform also with Shemp, Joe, and Curly-Joe in all four Stooge configurations. In 1971 Moe asked him to join the group to replace the loss of Larry. Sitka agreed, but Moe was taken ill shortly after. The *Scrapbook* assigns the idea for the 'Sword of Damocles' and the original *Hoi Polloi* to Helen Howard.

#98 - FRIGHT NIGHT

Studio: Columbia

Released: March 6, 1947

Running Time: 17"41'"

Credited Production Crew:

Produced by:	Hugh McCollum
Directed by:	Edward Bernds
Story & Screenplay by:	Clyde Bruckman
Director of Photography:	Philip Tannura
Film Editor:	Paul Borofsky
Art Direction:	Charles Clague

Credited Cast:

Shemp Howard	
Larry Fine	
Moe Howard	
Dick Wessel	Chopper Kane
Claire Carleton	Kitty Davis

Uncredited Cast:

Harold Brauer	Big Mike
Cy Schindell	Moose
Tommy Kingston	Chuck
Stanley Blystone	cop 1
Dave Harper	cop 2
Charles 'Heine' Conklin	Gorilla's trainer

PERSPECTIVE: Although the screenplay for *Fright Night* was originally written for Curly, Shemp took his place in the 'third Stooge' role he had abandoned just before the team signed with Columbia in 1934. The opening sign reads 'The THREE STOOGES Props,' and the opening shot frames the three of them together with Shemp in the middle; Shemp gets the first gag line and receives the first slapstick blow. This makes it clear from the first seconds of the film that these are indeed 'The Three Stooges,' even if one Howard has replaced another. Stooge fans forever compare Curly and Shemp, matching an instinctive genius with a more accomplished professional. It may be that "ee-bee-bee-bee" cannot replace "nyuk, nyuk, nyuk" and that fluid boxing steps are no real substitute for a chicken-with-its-head-cut-off. But there was no choice at the time: the intensity Curly used to instill in every scene had been missing for more than a year, and after the May stroke Curly was too ill to perform at all. So Shemp stepped in. Not only was he Moe and Curly's older brother, he was a seasoned veteran who had appeared in eight dozen Vitaphone, RKO, and Columbia films either solo or with the likes of W. C. Fields. And he knew the Stooge act, which he had left mostly because his wife could not stomach Ted Healy's shenanigans.

Shemp brings to Stoogedom an inimitable physicality and comedic delivery. He has an infinite number of tones, facial gestures and bodily gyrations, none as magnificent as Curly's perhaps but an impressive and fascinating repertoire with which he seems completely comfortable. A good actor, he takes on roles convincingly, whether as tough guy or sap, simpleton or trickster. In *Fright Night* he does his boxing steps [inspired by his Vitaphone Joe Palooka short-films], has his head rammed into a door, is slugged by Chopper, and takes slaps from Moe. He delivers throw-away lines ["What's good for a fractured skull?"], enlivens set jokes [I'll call the police.! I'll call the fire department. I'll call the Marines! I'll—" Moe: "Shut up!" Shemp: "That's what I mean, I'll shut up."], and defeats the crooks.

What this film and Shemp's reentry demonstrate is that Stooge films are not simply vehicles for Curly's movements and noises. Stooge films are two reels of slapstick and verbal comedy set within a compact narrative frame stretched to capacity by a trio of well synchronized Stooges perpetually joking, hitting, running, yelling, separating, and reuniting while interacting with odd characters in crisis situations. Stoogedom is larger than the individual Stooges, and it became clear during Curly's waning months that an alternative energy source was required. Shemp would go on to make another 76 short films with Moe and Larry at Columbia. In the broader perspective of the history of film and American popular culture, these additional films would transform the Stooges from an oddly likable trio making films in the 1930s and early/mid 1940s into the widely recognized comedy institution that spanned three decades into the television era of the 1950s.

VISUAL HUMOR: The first scene displays Shemp's great variety of physical movements, especially his unique foot-and-hand work [getting his body caught in the ropes and his hand tied to a rope, walking blindly into the post, taunting Chopper, and boxing the dummy [compare this sequence with Curly's effort in *Three Loan Wolves*]] and body range [getting his body knocked all over the ring, and getting his head stuck in the bucket]. Ed Bernds' directing and Philip Tannura's camera frequently supplement the visual humor, from the opening gag [Shemp: "Bring up your right hand!" The camera shows Chopper lying on a bed, lifting a tiny dumbbell with his right hand] to the "there goes Shemp!" gag to the warehouse chase around crates which we see from a camera set about twenty feet above. The chase is marvelously chaotic with Big Mike crawling and sneaking over a crawling and sneaking Shemp, Shemp bashing Larry hiding in a trash can, and Larry confusing Moe for a crook. The Shemp films will produce a number of wonderful chase sequences. Pointing and silent takes are used twice - when Moe and Larry point at Shemp to be the sparring partner, and when Big Mike points at

Shemp to be the battering ram. Two particularly clever sound effects: the CRUNCH when Chopper puts his big glove on Larry's face, and the BLONK when Shemp walks into the post.

Stooge firsts: a bucket handle strangling a Stooge; slipping on the mothballs; Chopper shoving Shemp's own cream puff into Shemp's face; and, of course, Shemp's boxing steps. Inspired by Shemp's footwork, Larry does a nice little tap dance, as he had in his previous film with Shemp (*Soup to Nuts*). This is set up by a verbal three-pattern (Moe: "You'll spar a little with the Chopper and exchange some love taps." Shemp: "Taps?" Larry: "Yeah, taps."). The unconscious Cy Schindell [Moose], himself an ex-boxer, whose head Moe turns and controls, also played the unconscious guard in *Matri-Phony*. In 1934 Shemp played in Gus Shy's *I Scream*, which included a battering ram sequence similar to the one here. Other variations: Shemp knocked upside down against the ropes (*Restless Knights*); Big Mike standing behind the Stooges before they know it (*Movie Maniacs*); the Stooges pointing to each other and saying: "He is!" (*Three Loan Wolves*); Shemp confusing red paint for blood (*An Ache in Every Stake*), and Larry unknowingly clubbing Moe, who retorts: "That was *me*!" (*Spook Louder*).

VERBAL HUMOR: Clyde Bruckman wrote a barrage of lines to supplement the boxing and chase sequences, including dual exchanges that emphasize Shemp's cowardice (Moe: "You can start on the dummy." Shemp: "He means the other dummy!"; Chopper: "Don't be a baby. It's all in fun." Shemp: "I hate fun!"; Moe: "Think of the dough." Shemp: "I'd rather think of my health!"), set gags (Moe: "There goes Shemp with a left jab! There goes Shemp with a right uppercut! There goes Shemp with a haymaker!...There goes Shemp!"; Shemp: "They can't do this to us! I'll call the police. I'll call the fire department. I'll call the Marines! I'll—" Moe: "Shut up!" Shemp: "That's what I mean, I'll shut up"; Shemp: "I got a father, I got a mother, I got a grandmother...I got a little sister - ee-bee-bee-bee - I got a little brother this high, I got a little brother this high..."; Moe: "The poor kid! And I owe him five bucks!" Shemp: "Wait a minute! I heard that!"), and throw-away one-liners [or ad-libs] by Shemp: "I bruise easy!"; "If I only had some coffee!"; "I got a soft skull!"; "What's good for a fractured skull?"; "That's a good idea! I'm glad I thought of it!"; "You're bendin' the stripes!"; "Now I know how a gopher feels!"; "How do you like that guy — busted a perfectly good cream puff!"; "You're crushin' my eyebrows!"; and "I batted 1000 percent in the racket league!"). Several staff members at Columbia are on record saying that Shemp was the funniest of all the Stooges when it came to ad-libbing. Other notable one-liners: Chopper [about cream puffs]: "My favorite fruit."; and Moe's "Any blood - ignore it!".

Larry supplies some verbal fill when he tries to remove the bucket from Shemp's head ("I got a system!"), and when he offers Shemp a face guard ("We don't want the Chopper to hurt his hands"). A Stooge first: Moe: "What does your watch say?" Shemp: "Tick, tick, tick". Shemp told a sob story in the beginning of *Corn on the Cop* in the same way he tells his "I got a little brother this high..." story in this film. Other variations: Moe: "Lay down! You wanna make a fool out of the doctor?" (*Soup to Nuts*); Shemp's "I'm too young and good lookin' to die...Well, too young" (*In the Sweet Pie and Pie*); and Moe: "Ya' nervous?" Shemp: "Just my left hand" (*Punch Drunks*).

OTHER NOTES: On the title screen 'Fright Night' is written in wavering, shadowed lettering. Dick Wessel [Chopper] played in a number of Stooge shorts and such well-known features as *On the Town*, *Gentlemen Prefer Blondes*, and *Around the World in 80 Days*. Shemp's footwork in the 1934 Vitaphone short *Corn on the Cop* - when he is 'cured' of his foot ailment - looks much like the boxing moves here. 7.5 minutes go by before Moe slaps his 'new' Stooge partner. Shemp was born 'Sam,' but his mother had a thick Lithuanian-Jewish accent and called him 'Shemp'. The Stooges previously explored the ring world in *Punch Drunks* (boxing), *Grips, Grunts and Groans* (wrestling), and *Busy Buddies* (milking). This film will be refurbished as *Fling in the Ring* (1955).

The script that was originally planned for shooting after *Half-Wits Holiday* was *Pardon My Terror*, but because of Curly's illness *Pardon My Terror* was filmed with Schilling & Lane, also directed by Edward Bernds and including Dick Wessel and Emil Sitka in the cast. This same script resurfaced in 1949 as the Stooges' *Who Done It?*. No official press release explained Curly's retirement; film exhibitors had to inquire "Whatever happened to the fat guy?". Bernds recollected [*Okuda* 69]: "Curly was a genius in his own right, but Shemp's performances had more depth. Shemp was a better actor, ...a great improviser. Many times when I was directing him I would actually delay cutting a scene just to see what he would do. He used to bowl me over with the things he'd dream up." *Jules White* (71): "Don't get me wrong. I loved working with Shemp and thought he was a naturally funny guy, but when Curly left the Stooge comedies were never the same. We made a few good ones after that, but they were nothing like the Curly's."

Stooge watchers eternally ponder whether Curly or Shemp was 'better,' but in 1946 Curly could not continue any longer. Shemp stepped back into the 'third Stooge' role he had played in the 1920s and early 1930s and revitalized their films. The Stooge act was bigger than its separate parts, and it was always in a state of development and transformation.

#99 - OUT WEST

Studio: Columbia

Released: April 24, 1947

Running Time: 17"32'"

Credited Production Crew:

Produced by:	Hugh McCollum
Directed by:	Edward Bernds
Story & Screenplay by:	Clyde Bruckman
Director of Photography:	George F. Kelley [sic]
Film Editor:	Paul Borofsky
Art Director:	Charles Clague

Credited Cast:

Shemp Howard	
Larry Fine	
Moe Howard	
Christine McIntyre	Nell
Jack Norman	Doc Barker
Jacques [Jock] O'Mahoney	Johnny, the Arizona Kid

Uncredited Cast:

Stanley Blystone	colonel
Vernon Dent	doctor
George Chesebro	Quirt, Barker's henchman
Frank Ellis	Jake
Charles 'Heine' Conklin	Bartender
Blackie Whiteford	cowboy

PERSPECTIVE: The comic narrative of *Out West* moves with driving conviction. The doctor who diagnoses an "enormous vein" in Shemp's leg recommends a therapeutic trip out West, and a fade immediately transports the Stooges out to the Red Dog Saloon. There the sinister Doc Barker mistakes the diagram of Shemp's vein for a map to a gold mine while the distressed Nell asks the Stooges to free the Arizona Kid so he can notify the US Cavalry. These two diverging goals focus the comedy on a decisive poker game in which a) Barker aims to win the map from Shemp, and b) the Stooges aim to get the jail key out of Barker's coat. Barker cheats, Shemp wins, and Moe's 'Ickey-may' terminates the game, making Barker so thirsty for water that Shemp soaks him with a fire hose to strip his coat. Key in hand, the Stooges let the Kid out to retrieve the cavalry, who ride in a frantic, tightly edited climax as Nell sings, the Stooges clang and clatter, and Barker chases the Stooges. By the end of the film, the Stooges, who do not even know they have a lit stick of dynamite in their possession, have once again rescued a damsel-in-distress through silly plans and memorable bungling.

Clyde Bruckman concocted this clever plot by stitching together rather seamlessly the motif of a sick Stooge requiring some R & R from *Idiots Deluxe*, the shooting contest from *Horses' Collars*, the showdown poker game from *Goofs and Saddles*, and the abbreviated chase around the crates from the previous film, *Fright Night*. Within each scene the Stooges perform some very sturdy comic routines: as they enter the bar Shemp gets to act tough and challenge rugged cowboys to a shooting match, reducing a large coin to small change; at the outset of the poker game Moe and Larry use their special mixological skills; in the middle of the game are Shemp's sockless toes; at the end of the game Shemp's stunt double does one of the best of his body stunts when he flips over the taut fire hose; Larry's subsequent imprisonment gives the newly configured Stooges their first chance to work with tools; and the climax sets them loose for another chase scene and another Western dynamite stand-off [*Cactus Makes Perfect*].

There is a time-honored Stooge theme: confusion yields success. The doctor in the opening scene is not confused; he makes his diagnosis so clear he draws a map, but this map sends everyone else into a series of confusions. Nell and the other doctor, Doc Barker, are confused about Shemp's 'vein,' Doc Barker's card partner is confused as to whom he was handing those aces, Moe is confused as to which drink goes to which player, and Shemp is so confused he 'bluffs' Barker by holding a piece of dynamite he does not even know is lit. Fomenting this sense of confusion is the interconnected climax highlighted by fast motion and lively background music ['The William Tell Overture'] à la *Three Troubledoers*. The confusion yields such utter success that the Stooges do not even need the US Cavalry, and it is so infectious it can make even horses run backwards-all because of Shemp's bad leg.

VISUAL HUMOR: Stooge firsts: Shemp reacting to an alcoholic drink; the FIREWORKS sound effect; and the Stooges ramming a pipe through a floor to knock someone on the chin. Mixing drinks derives from *Pardon My Scotch* and other films, but adding paint and paint remover is new, as is the fire hose chaser. 'The William Tell Overture' and the inter-edited fast motion scenes are more numerous and complex than those in *Three Troubledoers*. Moe does a fine take when he sees Barker and his gang ["We don't need any help, fellas"] When Barker and his three men appear from around the barrels just after Moe says, "We'll be forty miles away by the time those yokels wake up. "Nyagh!/Whoa!" this is the same take-pattern used in the Curly era mostly for beasts [*Three Missing Links*] and natives [*Some More of Samoa*]. The RATCHET sound effect for Shemp's bad leg is an old comedy standard. The blown-up crooks draped over the bar are reminiscent of the ostrich-egg bombed 'Japs' in *The Yoke's on Me*. Other variations [Shemp substitutes for Curly in this and all subsequent films]: Shemp heading off in the wrong direction [*Back to the Woods*]; toeless socks [*Hoi Polloi*]; Moe hitting Shemp in the head with his backswing of his mallet and Larry in the hand with his foreswing [*Cash and Carry*]; lighting the fuse with the nearby lamp [*Spook Louder*]; and the Stooges in sequence each turning his head to the next [*Uncivil Warriors*]. The backwards cavalry is the comic conclusion, while the genuine hug between Nell and Johnny brings the melodramatic romance to its logical conclusion, as was Edward Bernds' intent.

VERBAL HUMOR: Stooge firsts: 'Old Homicide' [i.e. 'Old Granddad'] whisky; and Shemp: "I ain't gonna lose my leg, am I, doc? I've had it ever since I was a little kid." The former is a comic enhancement of the 'Old Taylor' gag used first in *Three Little Sew and Sews*. Writer Clyde Bruckman had no shortage of double entendres to expand the vein confusion verbally: "twenty men with picks and shovel," "dynamite," "big operator," and "they won't have a leg left to stand on". He also included a prop-related pun (Moe [sawing Shemp's ear]: "What is that, a cross cut?"), an irony (Nell: "You're angels." Shemp: "Not yet we ain't"), and a gag about the motion picture industry (Colonel: "Son, never in the history of motion pictures has the United States Cavalry been too late!"). His set joke about "How long to you wear a shirt like that" is from *A Pain in the Pullman*, but Moe's add on, "What a brain, should be on the meat counter," is new. The 'yes' pattern (Nell: "I have a plan...[Stooges: "Yes!"]...If we can just a get the key to this door...[Stooges: "Yes! Yes!"]...We can let Johnny out and he can ride for help." Stooges: "Yes! Yes! Yes!") derives from *Horses' Collars*. Moe's "Why don't you look where I'm goin'?" echoes a gag in *Three Troubledoers*. "Ickey-may" is pig latin for 'Mickey Finn'. Larry shows great expression when he says to the (first) doctor, "We're headin' West!". References: "The Stooges have landed and have the situation well in hand!" mimics a famous military quote. The Stooges referred to themselves as "The Three Stooges" in the previous film as well; there still seems to be a need to emphasize that this combination of three actors is indeed 'The Three Stooges.'

OTHER NOTES: This film is a reworking of Harry Langdon & El Brendel's last Columbia comedy short, *Pistol Packin' Nitwits* (1945), which also included Christine McIntyre. The baby-faced Langdon had been a silent film star in the 1920s. *Out West* was also the name of a 1918 Buster Keaton/Fatty Arbuckle film. Jock O'Mahoney will appear again as the Arizona Kid in *Punchy Cowpunchers*. Not coincidentally, he began his career as stuntman for 'The Durango Kid' - Charles Starrett, with whom the Stooges played in *Start Cheering*. Later Mahoney would go on to play Tarzan roles in the late 1950s/early 1960s. Actress Sally Field is his stepdaughter. George Chesebro [Quirt] was an old hand at Westerns, playing with Gene Autry and Tex Ritter. Extensive footage from *Out West* will be reused in *Pals and Gals* (1954), although Jack Norman is billed there as Norman Willes.

Of the dozens of set routines the Stooges developed and varied over the years, the mixology gag was one of the most dependable. The mixing itself always blends verbal and visual comedy, and it usually serves to further the plot by drugging someone, in this case - for 1947's *Out West* - the villain. Their Ickey-may recipe:

> Pour Old Homicide into a bucket, add old beer, molasses, Tabasco, seltzer, two eggs (broken on a forehead), and paint. If you add too much paint, add some paint remover. Shake in a large boot, and serve to your worst enemy.

#100 - HOLD THAT LION

Studio: Columbia

Released: July 17, 1947

Running Time: 16"27'"

Credited Production Crew:

Produced & Directed by:	Jules White
Story & Screenplay by:	Felix Adler
Director of Photography:	George F. Kelley
Film Editor:	Edwin Bryant
Art Director:	Charles Clague

Credited Cast:

Shemp Howard	
Larry Fine	
Moe Howard	
Kenneth MacDonald	Icabod Slipp
Emil Sitka	Attorney Poole
Dudley Dickerson	porter

Uncredited Cast:

Charles 'Heine' Conklin	conductor
Vic Travers	bearded man on train
Blackie Whiteford	passenger
Curly Howard	barking train passenger

PERSPECTIVE: *Hold That Lion* contains as many memorable, even lovable, scenes as any Stooge film: the battle with the filing cabinet, Icabod Slipp knocking out each Stooge in sequence, Shemp speaking in the fish bowl and Larry imitating him, Curly's cameo appearance,

the lion on the train, and Dudley Dickerson's posterior "Help! I'm losin' my mind!" Traditional Stooge slapstick is revitalized with over two dozen gouges, slaps, and clangs punctuating every sequence, most of it set up or accompanied by clever exchanges (Shemp: "I can't see without my glasses." Moe: "What's this?" Shemp: "Two dirty fingers." [GOUGE]; Larry: "My right palm itches. What's that a sign of?" Moe: "Your hand's dirty!" [SLAP]). As a unit the Stooges run ("WHOAH!") and react ("NYAGGH!") in harmony, and they are confronted with two believable antagonists - Icabod Slipp and a growling lion.

These many delights help us forget that the plot seems to derail once the Stooges board the train. Felix Adler has been criticized for writing terrific gags but treating a plot as if its only purpose was to string gags together. This is a deficiency only in some of his films - certainly not *Dizzy Detectives* - and for those films which are plot-deficient, for instance *Pop Goes the Easel*, the gags are so compelling that audiences hardly notice. Technically speaking, the story of the-Stooges-finding-Icabod-Slipp-to-regain-their-inheritance does seem to fade from view once the Stooges board the train. They board the train specifically to find Slipp, so the incidents with Curly, the bearded man, the conductor, and the lion certainly seem to delay the action as they search. But as an artist Adler is equally entitled to the assumption that he had an inspired and well thought out design, and what the lion sequences in particular offer to the plot is a magnificent coincidental symmetry that allows the Stooges to encounter the lion while searching for Slipp and then encounter Slipp while running from the lion. Characterizing the Stooges as not doing anything right except by accident, Adler has Moe simply knock Slipp out with an inadvertent hammer throw to bring the plot to a conclusion. MacDonald's Slipp is so villainous, he may have deserved a more heroic challenge. But Stooge comedy often depends on absurdity, and Adler's symmetrical plot design would not seem so strange except in comparison to the more logical ones developed after the arrival of Ed Bernds. Fifty years later, we may assume that Adler's Slipp/lion/Slipp symmetry belongs to a higher art, as the working title, *The Lion and the Louse*, suggests.

A historical marker should be placed here for Curly's cameo. We see an uncharacteristic head full of short hair but hear two of his patented sounds ("Woo-woo-woo"; "Rruff!"). And as we look at his visage one last time, his big brothers speak lovingly about him, too (Shemp: "What's that, a cocker spaniel?" Moe: "I think it's just a spaniel."). This is Stooge love at its most heartwarming, appropriate for the only footage in which Moe, Shemp, and Curly Howard appear together. Precious stuff.

VISUAL HUMOR: In the first scene the Stooges have a major slapstick exchange (SLAP, DOUBLE POUND, DOUBLE BONK, NOSE BONK), the most comprehensive thus far in a Shemp film. Shemp's boxing steps deserve to be admired again and again; he is very light on his feet, agile, and varies his moves well; he threatens, challenges, and seems so confident, and then he is so suddenly and easily knocked out. A file cabinet gag scene was used in the Marx Brothers' *Go West* (1940), a lion in the train in Jack White's *Roaring Lions and Wedding Bells* (1917). This is the third consecutive film with a chase around crates and boxes.

Moe's conked-out look is very convincing, and it is enhanced with the TWEET sound effect. Sound effects are abundant throughout. The lion scenes are enhanced visually by fast motion and audibly when the lion laughs like a hyena, followed by Moe's infectious laughter. The lion sequences borrow from the lion scenes of both *Three Missing Links* and *Movie Maniacs* (licking the feet; breathing from behind), as well as, from the gorilla scenes in *Dizzy Detectives.* The Stooges had confronted lions previously as well in *You Nazty Spy!* and *Wee Wee Monsieur*, they encountered a monkey on a train in *A Pain in the Pullman.* When Moe picks up Shemp's knee, hits Larry, and then kicks Shemp, it is a variation of the set-up kick in *I Can Hardly Wait.* Shemp featured a glasses gag in his Vitaphone short *Dizzy and Daffy* (1934); cleaning glassless glasses resembles the cleaning of a non-existent windshield in *Higher Than a Kite.* Teasing the conductor into the woman's room and tripping him expands upon the similar action in *Pop Goes the Easel.* Other variations: Shemp saying "Never felt better in my life!" but falling over (*Out West*); Moe slapping Larry's hand into his face (Chopper shoving the cream puff into Shemp's face in *Fright Night*); Slipp blowing Moe over (*Punch Drunks*); Moe's white socks that start above the ankle and end at the ankle (*Hoi Polloi*); and ducking, making the Stooges hit each other (*Restless Knights).*

VERBAL HUMOR: The writing offers internal rhymes with Slipp's name (Moe: "We'll slap slip with these 'subpoenees'"; Larry & Shemp: "No slippery guy named Slipp..."), set-up gags (Shemp: "Them's fightin' words in my country!" Slipp: "All right! Let's fight!" Shemp: "Well we're not in my country"; Moe: "We search the train carefully and give everybody a close uh...uh...say, what's a good word for 'scrutiny'?" Shemp: "Scrutiny."), throw-away lines (Moe: "Poor kid must have indigestion"; Shemp: "I feel like a piece of French toast"), support for the visual humor (Moe: "It's a matter of principle with me. I'm gonna shut that drawer if it's the last thing I do!"; "Moe: "Stop breathin' down my neck!" Shemp: "I ain't breathin'!") and slapstick ("Fine time to play hopscotch!"). We also get Larry's literal repetition of Shemp's indecipherable words from within the fish bowl and Dudley Dickerson's silent scream. A number of lines have to do with brains and intelligence (Moe: "See? You have to use your brains! [He hits his head on the drawer]; Moe: "Now you're using a bit of your brain!" [*Termites of 1938*]; and the porter's "Help! Help! I'm losin' my mind!" [*A Gem of a Jam*]). Epithets: Moe: "pickle brains" and "goose-brain"; Larry calls Shemp a "nitwit".

Shemp was such a naturally talented ad-libber that many of his Stooge films will end with a final reversal. Here in *Hold That Lion* (1947) he gets egged, but the publicity department captured something we rarely see...

...a photo of Shemp washing the egg out of his hair after a take. The Stooges make their slapstick and physical gags look simple to perform; they were, for the most part, performed without artifice or special effects. They did use stunt doubles, padding, and rubber implements, but the Stooges did suffer several injuries over the years - and a lot of dirty hair and faces.

This film offers the first chant in a Shemp film: "We'll get the filthy lucre, the moola, the geetis./No slippery guy named Slipp/is ever going to cheat us!/A-zoot, a-zoat, a-zoe!" We first heard "zoot" in *Loco Boy Makes Good*. The berth scene has a reprisal of "Wake up and go to sleep," the first coming from the berth scene in *A Pain in the Pullman*. References: Larry's "Here's where we beard the lion in his den" derives from a line by Sir Walter Scott; Larry's itching palm refers to getting money; "geetis" is slang for 'money'; Shemp's "Rome wasn't built in a day, and neither was Syracuse" refers not to Syracuse, NY so much as to ancient Sicilian Syracuse, the setting of Rodgers' and Hart's *The Boys From Syracuse,* the musical they referred to in *You Nazty Spy!*. Other variations: Moe to Larry: "Why don't you take a bicarbonate of soda?" [*Soup to Nuts*]; and "Say a couple-a adjectives!" [*Slippery Silks*].

OTHER NOTES: The title parodies the expression 'hold that line'. The introductory theme music has been re-recorded; it now uses the 'driving,' quicker tempo introduced in *Matri-Phony* and discontinued in 1945. But now it leads into a jazzy, syncopated middle section, and ends with a solo flute. This recording will be used intermittently through 1948; thereafter it will be used for all the remaining Columbia shorts, with variations, particularly at the advent of the Joe era in 1957. The train footage will be reused in *Booty and the Beast* [1953], the Icabod Slipp sequences in *Loose Loot* [1953]. Jules White [*Okuda* 69] recalled later that Curly just happened to be visiting the set, and that he waved at White from behind a newspaper; this inspired White to develop the cameo. Moe looks towards the camera in Slipp's office and says "It's gettin' dark," as if the window is on our side of the room. Moe notes that Slipp "gave us the business" and behind him is a statue of Mercury, Roman God of Business.

After the Stooges tear the sleeping car curtain down, we can hear an unemotional extra's voice saying "Hey look, a lion!". The newspaper in the opening scene prints the name of the executor as 'Elmer Slipp,' not 'Icabod Slipp'. Emil Sitka [*Scrapbook* 45] reported that Shemp was so afraid of the lion that he insisted that a glass plate be put between him and the animal, even if the lion "was so sickly he would fall asleep in the middle of a take." For a more complete accounting of Shemp's phobias, see *Besser* [154-155].

After his debilitating stroke in 1946, Curly returned for this lone cameo in *Hold That Lion* [1947]. When Shemp left the act in the 1930s, Curly joined, and when Curly left in 1946, Shemp rejoined. This was the only time all three Howard brothers performed together on film. Curly retired and lived until 1952. Shemp would continue with the Stooges until his death in 1955.

#101 - BRIDELESS GROOM

Studio: Columbia

Released: September 11, 1947

Running Time: 16"36'"

Credited Production Crew:

Produced by:	Hugh McCollum
Directed by:	Edward Bernds
Story & Screen Play by:	Clyde Bruckman
Director of Photography:	Vincent Farrar
Film Editor:	Henry DeMond
Art Director:	Charles Clague

Credited Cast:

Shemp Howard	
Larry Fine	
Moe Howard	
Dee Green	Fanny Dinkelmeir
Christine McIntyre	Lulu Hopkins
Doris Colleen	former girl friend

Uncredited Cast:

Nancy Saunders	former girl friend
Emil Sitka	Justice Benton
Johnny Kascier	bellhop

PERSPECTIVE: There is a timeless myth about the divine musician Orpheus: he sang so beautifully that even wild animals came to hear his woodland odes, but insanely jealous Bacchic women tore him to pieces or stoned him to death. Although there is no evidence that *Brideless Groom* is a conscious modernization of this tale [as was Tennessee Williams' *Orpheus Descending,* originally published just two years earlier in 1945], Shemp's characterization as an Orphic figure is nonetheless an integral part of this Clyde Bruckman masterpiece. Bruckman had used the same theme two decades earlier for Buster Keaton's 1925 [silent] short, *Seven Chances*, in which an army of women do indeed throw stones at Keaton, and Shemp is now cast as a musician. His musicianship establishes the homely Fanny as a self-proclaimed love interest and provides the opening comedy bits for Larry at the piano and Fanny with her shrill voice ("too fortissimo, too allegro, too Cointreau!"). His characterization as a musician returns later when the wedding ring flips inside the piano: with Moe shoving his head into the piano strings, the musically trained Shemp notices: "I think the piano is out of tune." And although no woodland animals come to hear him sing, the most memorable line from this entire film [and of Emil Sitka's career] is, "Hold hands, you love birds."

The idea of having a Stooge inherit money was just used in *Hold That Lion*, though the plot here reverses that of *In the Sweet Pie and Pie* in which three women had to marry the Stooges to preserve their inheritance. In those films the Stooges were willing to undergo any trials necessary to inherit the money, but here there is a major road block. Shemp does not want to get married, and we see why: the women he knows are either homely and overbearing, gold-digging, or rough and bully-like. He ignores Fanny's adoration, gets his head crushed by the brunette, and the one woman he seems to like, Lulu Hopkins [Christine McIntyre], slaps him, bonks him, and slugs him in the jaw. The Stooges have been making fun of ugly women since the first scene of *Horses' Collars*, but this is payback. Advocates of strong roles for women in film should find at least some compensation in Christine McIntyre slapping Shemp in rhythm to the words "poor, weak, helpless woman," the brunette pressing a proposal out of Shemp's head, and the two women smashing rifles over Larry's and Moe's heads.

This Bacchic frenzy develops in intensity after an atypical initial scene which does not even include a third Stooge. After Moe enters and introduces both the marriage and the time-limitation elements, there are two moments when time stops, as it were, for Shemp and

Moe to be wrapped up in the phone booth and for Shemp to be tied up by the piano wire, yet the pace intensifies and pressure builds as Shemp tries to shave in a hurry, Lulu beats him up, and a genuine brawl breaks out at the wedding ceremony. The brawl is beautifully directed by Ed Bernds and effectively edited by newcomer Henry [Hank] DeMond. And then, unlike the previous two films, the final gag is brief and appropriate. In fact, it may well have been that Orpheus' last words were, like Shemp's: "Help! Help!"

VISUAL HUMOR: Some combination movements: Larry backswings the rifle butt into Moe's face, so the woman grabs the rifle and smashes Larry over the head with it; Shemp looks behind him before "fainting" into the chair; and Moe takes advantage for the first time of one of the major differences between Curly and Shemp: he grabs Shemp by the hair. In contrast, the scene with Moe and Shemp in the phone booth is another enclosed circumstance like the pit scene in *Cash and Carry*, the mine scene in *Cactus Makes Perfect*, and the prison scene in *Three Little Pirates*, though here without tools. When a Stooge or two has to work in an enclosed space, physical movement contracts to such gags as dialing another's face, biting one's own hand, and simply making a face against the glass. We see Shemp's face, his nose broadened against the phone booth glass, and the phone wires pulling his mouth down into a deep frown. The woman screams and slaps Larry because Shemp looks particularly ugly, another victory for women in this film. Larry's sedate comedy thrives at the piano, as in *Loco Boy Makes Good*, and outside the phone booth where he nervously bites and spits out his nails. Some of the physical gags are designed to bring a scene to a close, as when Moe sits on the iron and knocks the basin of shaving water all over Shemp; the hair pull serves the same purpose. Shemp perfected his rapid shaving in the 1933-4 Vitaphone shorts *Here Comes Flossie* and *Smoked Hams*. Two variations from the previous film, *Hold that Lion*: Moe trying to entice one of the women [like the conductor] to chase him, and Moe smashing his head through the drawer [the file cabinet sequence]. Hearing beautiful singing without seeing the victrola derives from *Termites of 1938* and *Micro-Phonies*.

VERBAL HUMOR: Bruckman's dialogue enhances Shemp's take when he learns of his inheritance ("He's a louse and a weasel....That old skinflint... Five hundred thousand bucks...[Moe: "Yeah, well he just died and left you 500,000 bucks!"]...Poor Uncle Caleb! Like I was sayin', he was a swell guy...He'd give you the shirt off his back and throw in the buttons, too."] and his negative reaction to women ("Your little dream boat is sailing: wooo!"; "Gargle with old razor blades!"; and [Fanny: "I know you wouldn't want anything to happen to my throat."] Shemp: "Except to have somebody cut it!"). Bruckman wrote effectively for the women, e.g. Doris Colleen [the tough brunette]: "That was before I read the papers. Now I accept!... Okay, toots, let her rip!" and Christine McIntyre: "taking advantage of a poor, weak, helpless woman!" Completing his variegated characterizations are the quivering words of Emil Sitka: "Join/Hold hands, you love birds!". Part of Shemp's reluctance to marry is due to his own poor looks ("No woman is interested in me!"), but Moe reinforces this self-deprecation (Shemp: "You want to spoil my looks?" Moe: "Impossible!"; Shemp: "There I am! - pretty as a picture!" Moe: "Yeah, of an ape!")... Moe telling Larry, "You wouldn't hit a lady with that?...Use this, it's bigger!" derives from *Dizzy Pilots* (where Curly was going to shoot at the rubberized Moe with a rifle instead of a shotgun) and earlier prototypes. Other variations: Fanny: "Oh, professor, you want it more like a bird!" Shemp: "That's it, give me the bird!" (*Pop Goes the Easel*); Shemp: "I ought-a—" Moe: "You oughta what?" Shemp [yielding]: "I oughta be a little more careful" (*Dizzy Detectives* et al.); "You're married, kid! Say somethin'!" ("Say a couple-a adjectives" in *Hold That Lion*); Shemp [in the vice]: "I'm gettin' a headache!" ("You're crushin' my eyebrows!" in *Fright Night*); and Larry calling the bear trap as an "octopus" (*The Sitter Downers*). References: "Too *fortissimo* ["loud"], too *allegro* ["fast"], too *Cointreau* [an orange-flavored liqueur]." Larry's "You sure look funny with a Buster Brown collar" refers to a type of rounded shirt collar.

This publicity pose of Shemp and Christine McIntyre represents the kind of gracefully sly characterizations she brought to a number of Stooge films in the late 1940s. Like the best film comediennes of the 1930s and 1940s, she had a stunning visage, a shapely figure, and a wry wit. In addition, though, she had the magnificent singing voice immortalized in *Micro-Phonies* (1945) and *Squareheads of the Round Table* (1948).

OTHER NOTES: The working title was *Love and Learn*.The idea of having a Stooge inherit something was used in *Slippery Silks* and *If a Body Meets a Body*. The *Scrapbook* credits Carter DeHaven as assistant director. *Besser* (175) offers Shemp's account of filming the 'Cousin Basil' sequence; he had to coach Christine McIntyre because she was being tentative: "Honey, if you want to do me a favor, cut loose and do it right. A lot of half-hearted slaps hurts more than one good one. Give it to me, Chris, Just let it rip!" After his encouragement she ultimately gave him the hard slaps and authentic looking slugs we see here on film. *Brideless Groom* will be refurbished as

Husbands Beware in 1956. In Quentin Tarantino's *Pulp Fiction* (1994) Eric Stolz's character is introduced watching footage of *Brideless Groom*; Emil Sitka is given a screen credit as "Hold hands, you love birds." A few minutes later Stolz brings Uma Thurman to consciousness saying "Say something!" Thurman says, "Something!" (perhaps derived from "Say something!" Moe: "Numskull!" in *Who Done It?*).

Brideless Groom (1947) is one of the best of the Shemp films. His rejoining the trio for the 1947 releases inspired the whole production staff, and many of the scripts and gag scenarios in 1947 and 1948 were first rate - some of them expanding into thematic narratives. In this film Shemp's quest for a bride confronts the Stooges with women fore and aft, and then the conclusion turns into a bacchic frenzy replete with high priest Emil Sitka as the minister ("Hold hands you love birds!"). The scene was used decades later as background sound and sight for Quentin Tarentino's *Pulp Fiction* (1994). *Brideless Groom* will in some ways be improved upon in the 1956 refurbishing *Husbands Beware*.

Left is Emil Sitka (1914-1998), who played a number of kooky eccentrics in Stooge films from the 1940s to the 1960s and worked with Curly, Shemp, Joe, and Curly-Joe, recites the immortal refrain, "Hold hands, you love birds!" Next to him is Dee Green, who will play an undesirable woman again in *I'm a Monkey's Uncle* ('Baggie'). She actually had a beautiful soprano voice and retired from film to tour with an opera company and teach voice.

#102 - SING A SONG OF SIX PANTS

Studio: Columbia

Released: October 30, 1947

Running Time: 16"54'"

redited Production Crew:

Produced & Directed by:	Jules White
Story & Screenplay by:	Felix Adler
Director of Photography:	Henry Freulich
Film Editor:	Edwin Bryant
Art Director:	Charles Clague

Credited Cast:

Shemp Howard	
Larry Fine	
Moe Howard	
Virginia Hunter	Flossie
Harold Brauer	Terry Hargen
Vernon Dent	Officer Sharp

Uncredited Cast:

Phil Arnold	little man
Cy Schindell	torpedo
Johnny Kascier	torpedo

PERSPECTIVE: The notability of this film is its unity of location in the Pip Boys' tailor shop. Every Columbia Stooge short to date (except *Three Loan Wolves*) has put the Stooges in at least two different venues. From offices, apartments, and sidewalks to rich houses, trains, hospitals, and football stadiums, from the loading dock to the golf course, from the streets of Paris to the North African desert, and from an English airfield to Nazi Germany, Stooge narratives most often begin by establishing the Stooges in a trade or situation which leads them intentionally or accidentally into the comic juxtaposition of a second venue - unlikely places like society parties or spooky hallways. In contrast, *Sing of Song of Six Pants* is centrifugal. The Stooges remain focused as the center of comic gravity while the rest of the comic characters and narrative are attracted to them in their tailor shop. Within the setting of the shop the Stooges have plenty of room to do their physical magic and possess an array of great tools - an iron, ironing board, scissors, whirling clothes tree, hot press, needle and thread, and carding comb. It may well be simply that the budget was limited, but Felix Adler deserves credit for developing this type of 'box' comedy for the Stooges.

The Stooges have been tailors before in *Slippery Silks* and *Three Little Sew and Sews*, but those plots scattered in different directions. This 'box comedy,' like the experimental *Three Loan Wolves*, brings the plot into the Stooges' shop and keeps it there. First the Terry Hargen character comes in to hide from the police, then the police officer comes in looking for Hargen, then Hargen's moll comes in to retrieve the combination to a safe, then Terry Hargen reenters to retrieve the combination, and then the police officer comes back to take Hargen to jail. All the while the combination to the safe stays with the Stooges, but they do not leave to use it; come to think of it, they do not even know what safe it belongs to. The only thing that concerns them is the lapel money, and Hargen brings that in to them as well...twice!

The plot, like many of these early Shemp films, is relatively simple: it pits the Stooges against rough opponents, concludes happily with the Stooges beating them up, and inserts into every scene a major visual and/or verbal gag. But in addition, *Sing of Song of Six Pants* is aptly named, for the Stooges play tailors very convincingly and consistently throughout the film. If shredding a suit coat, rubbing a hole in a pair of pants, pressing a man's head, and kicking another man from the revolving clothes tree are not 'unaccustomed tailoring' and 'altercations,' as advertised on the Pip Boys' front window, then what is? All of the comic gags and narrative early in the film derive from the tailoring motif: Larry struggles with the spot and drinks the cleaning fluid, Shemp battles the curled pants and the recalcitrant ironing board, and all the while Moe is efficiently developing the plot by reading the letter from the 'Skin & Flint' Finance Corporation. In *Sing of Song of Six Pants* Felix Adler accomplished perfectly and comically Aristotle's dictum for the unity of place and time.

VISUAL HUMOR: Almost all the visual gags are related to tailoring: Shemp reaches through a sleeve and grabs the fifty dollar bill out of Moe's hand; Larry gives a characteristic 'dumb' look and scratches his head when he picks up a mannequin's, i.e. Terry Hargen's, foot. Although the Stooges have made pancakes in several films, cooking them in a pants press is a first. Most of the other tailoring gags are variations: the fast motion ironing board sequence is more complicated than the piano wire sequence in the previous film (*Brideless Groom*) and recalls something similar in *Even As IOU*; the stubbornly curled pants are like the linoleum rolls in *Loco Boy Makes Good*; Larry works on pants as in *Movie Maniacs* and *Three Little Sew and Sews*, but the light spot is from *Pop Goes the Easel*; Moe's crunching Shemp's nose with the scissors derives from *Slippery Silks*; Shemp's fight from the circular clothes tree is a variation of the "two-men-in-a-coat" routine (*Horses' Collars*), particularly interesting since there were so many coats in the store. Pulling Shemp by the broom handle in his mouth is a Stooge first (to be varied next in *Baby Sitters Jitters*), but in *Slippery Silks* Moe pulled Curly several times with scissors.

Shemp takes a page or two from Curly's book. When wrestling with the curled pants, he makes a "Hhmm!" sound and does a kind of 360-degree spin; and when the closet door swings open the last time he makes a "Rruff!" sound. He also adds and pulls the tape from his mouth like Curly in *No Census, No Feeling*. Other variations: the Stooges fainting in unison [*Beer and Pretzels; Woman Haters*]; and the torpedo tickling Moe (the lion in *Hold That Lion*); we saw a beard gag in that same film.

VERBAL HUMOR: Felix Adler's script offers a variety of tailor jokes, with Shemp getting the bulk of the punch lines: set puns (Shemp: "Where did you ever get this mess?" Officer: "I bought it here." Shemp: "Oh, what a beautiful mess-terpiece!"; Flossie: "I'd like to have this dress dyed...henna color." Shemp: "Henna color at all?"), single puns (Shemp: "It's 200% wool...these sheep led a double life!"; "This is the store where your dollars have more cents!"), throw away lines (Shemp: "He had a loose baste!"; Flossie: "Do you dye?" Moe: "That's his natural expression!"; Shemp: "Henna color." Larry: "You mean brown reddish?" Shemp: "Yellow turnip, blue cucumbers, anything"), an internal rhyme (Larry: "What he wants is a pair of our slick slacks"), and two magnificent pattern gags with non-Stooges (Policeman: "I don't want a coat. I don't want a coat! I don't want a coat!!" Stooges [in unison]: "Oh! He don't want a coat!"; and Shemp: "Ya mean the one with the numbers on it.? Hargen: "That's it! That's it!" Shemp: "And the letters LRLRLRL?" Hargen: "Yes! Yes! Where is it?!" Shemp: "I never saw it."). Adler also closes several scenes well, with the man's wife being "crazy about" the shredded coat and Shemp's "How'd that [fifty dollar bill] get in there?" ending the film; the later gag was used previously by Bob Hope in *Road to Zanzibar* (1941). A number of gags emphasize Stooge ignorance: Moe: "We're going to be paupers, paupers!" Shemp: "We're not even married!"; the three-pattern (Shemp: "$411, but there's a sale today." Larry: "You get ten percent off." Moe: "Makes it $42.50"); Flossie: "H - E - N - N - A; it's a kind of a brown reddish." Shemp: "I ain't never had a brown radish"; and Shemp's reading of 'L-R-L-R-L-R-L.' Somewhere between puns, ignorance, and silliness are the supplements for 'TH': Larry: "Thomas Hedison"...Shemp: "Teddy Hoosevelt?".

References: The latter refer to the inventor Thomas Edison and former president Teddy Roosevelt, but Moe's response, "You're wrong, Quiz Kid," refers to the *Quiz Kid* radio show [*A Bird in the Head*]. In response to the letter ('Dear Gentlemen—') Shemp's "That ain't for us. We're not gentlemen" and Moe's "Speak for yourself!" are a combination of the usual Stooge response to "Gentlemen" (looking behind themselves) and "We're trapped like rats!". Other variations: 'Skin and Flint Finance Corporation, I Fleecem, President' ('Cess, Poole, & Drayne' in *Hold That Lion*); Shemp's pleading "Please, officer. I got six wives and two kids..." ("I got a brother this high..." in *Fright Night*); Shemp's "I'm too young to worry and get wrinkles on my pretty little face" (I'm too young and good lookin' to die" in *Brideless Groom*); "No-Burpoline...the only gasoline con-taining bi-carbonate of soda" (various); "Henna color at all" [*Cookoo Cavaliers*]; and Larry: "Genuine import - smell the ocean?" [*Saved By the Belle*].

OTHER NOTES: The title makes a pun on 'pence' and 'pants' from the anonymous nursery rhyme, 'Sing a Song of Six Pence,' turned into an elaborate production number in *Nertsery Rhymes*. The working title was *Where the Vest Begins*. The film will be reworked in 1953's *Rip, Sew and Stitch*, and several segments are featured early on in the 1985 feature film *Stoogemania*. Jules White provided the voice of the radio announcer.

Sing a Song of Six Pants (1947) is the first great 'box comedy' in the Stooge corpus; *Three Loan Wolves* (1946) was the prototype. The concept is to keep the Stooges confined and bring the story into them. This particular box comedy features both inter-Stooge quarreling and the ultimately triumphant Stooge struggle with the crooks.

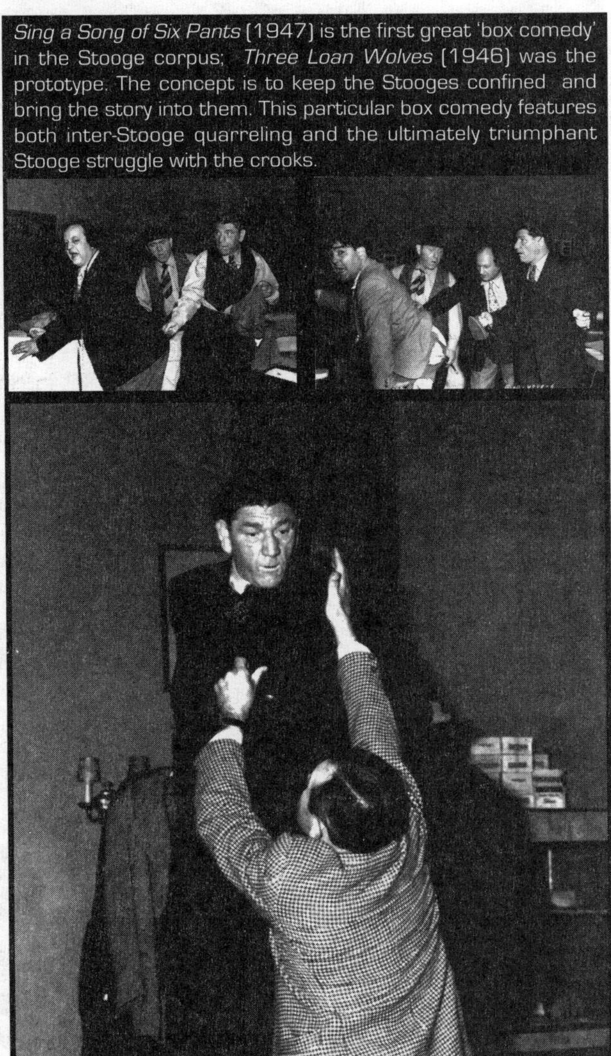

#103 - ALL GUMMED UP

Studio: Columbia

Released: December 18, 1947

Running Time: 18"07'"

Credited Production Crew:

Produced & Directed by:	Jules White
Story & Screenplay by:	Felix Adler
Director of Photography:	Allen Siegler
Film Editor:	Edwin Bryant
Art Director:	Charles Clague

Credited Cast:

Shemp Howard	
Larry Fine	
Moe Howard	
Christine McIntyre	Cerina Flint
Emil Sitka	Amos Flint

Uncredited Cast:

Al Thompson	first customer
Judy Malcolm	second customer
Cy Schindell	customer with prescription
Victor Travers	bubble gum customer
Symona Boniface	skirtless woman

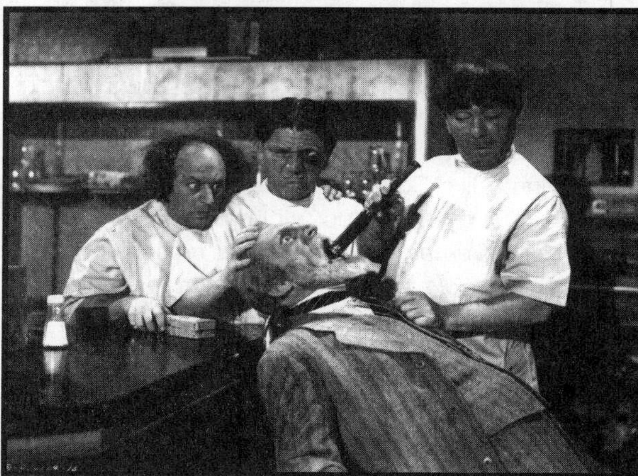

PERSPECTIVE: This is a modest 'centrifugal' or 'box comedy' which even more so than the previous film (*Sing a Song of Six Pants*) remains in one location. This technique, easy on the art director, shooting schedule and production budget, demands that the plot intrigue be brought into the Stooges, but it will by nature tend to produce a slower paced film: only so much can unfold in one place at one time. In the previous film, there were plenty of tailoring gags to fill the void, but in *All Gummed Up* the Stooges are given separate drug store customer gags and do not interact at all in the opening and final scenes. The only slapstick to be found is when they concoct and force-feed their potion, when they dance with the newly revitalized Cerina, and when they discuss icing the cake. There are only two moments of heightened energy - Cy Schindell's entrance/exit, and the Stooges' escape from the shrinking Mr. Flint.

This plot technique requires that the characters who bring the plot into the Stooges be eccentric and ripe for humorous treatment. This is why the film opens with the three customers, one to allow each Stooge to do a comic bit. Larry gets ink on his face; Moe lights a bulb in his hand; and Shemp rips a skirt off a female customer. Then Cy Schindell runs in with a medical emergency so severe the doctor had to write the prescription on his shirt. He exits by leaping over the landlord, and this brings us to the central, two-part motivation for the Stooges - to keep their lease with Mr. Flint and to help Mrs. Flint. They spend some time cranking Mr. Flint up and down both to ease his lumbago and torture him with a horseradish plaster, and then they do their most elaborate mixing routine to date, a routine we first saw earlier in *Men in Black* and *Pardon My Scotch*. Finally they kill two birds with one stone: their 'fountain of youth' both makes Mrs. Flint youthfully happy and reduces Mr. Flint to a crying infant - after he signs the building over to them. Felix Adler's plot develops clearly and is resolved neatly, but it consumes only twelve of the film's eighteen minutes.

That leaves the Stooges and Cerina time to celebrate, and the last two and one-half minutes of the film are devoted to the bubble-gum draped 'Marshmallow Jumbo.' Even more than in the closing sequences of three of the first five Shemp films (the ketchup/doctor sequence in *Fright Night*, the egg sequence in *Hold That Lion*, counting the money in *Six Pants*), the Stooges are left to their own devices to close out the film. The concept seems to have been devised to give Shemp and the other two Stooges the opportunity to improvise, so here they make faces and blow bubbles. Structurally speaking such a scene is a denouement: it follows the conclusion of the plot and lacks dramatic purpose. But then in this film it also lacks the usual inter-Stooge slapstick barrage. It is supposed to be simply a display, and as a display it works pretty well. The Stooges do enough with their bubbles - Larry's face alone is remarkable - to make it worth watching. But it is a much more passive type of comedy than the trademark Stooge comedy we are used to seeing, particularly at the conclusion of a film. This passivity was not lost on Jules White: he will refurbish the film as *Bubble Trouble* in 1953 and make the necessary adjustments.

VISUAL HUMOR: Sitka falling over his pant legs, Larry jabbing the fork into Shemp's rear to force him to open his mouth, Shemp tossing the cotton (*Men in Black*) off camera and getting it tossed back at him, and, of course,

Cerina's transformation provide the most surprising physical moments of the film. Shemp cutting in but dancing with Moe is a Stooge first, although Curly cuts in in *Loco Boy Makes Good* and dances with Moe in *Time Out for Rhythm*. The bubble gum scene has in its family tree: the feather-cake of *Uncivil Warriors* and the alum punch of *No Census, No Feeling*, though these were used in mid-film. The Stooges' mixing boot (*Pardon My Scotch*) is getting larger, and now it has learned to rumba. Other variations: Moe lighting the bulb (*Nutty But Nice*); the board on the counter as an accidental catapult (*Pop Goes the Easel*); the squirting fountain pen (*Healthy, Wealthy and Dumb*); catching something other than fish with a fishing pole (*I Can Hardly Wait*); hitting Shemp to extract the idea from the back of his head (*3 Dumb Clucks*); and Moe shoving Larry's icing-filled hand into his face (*Fright Night*).

VERBAL HUMOR: Stooge firsts: Shemp: "Does marshmallows got pits?"; and calling someone's name ("Mrs. Flint") in a musical triad. The Stooges offer their most extensive use of neologistic ingredients in two different sessions: zem-dayphis, mishugaz, ireecon, ingenzommen, and ana-canna-panna-san. They even make real ingredients like "le-mon, spices, onion, and cackle fruit" sound as if they are extraordinary. Ingenzommen (*Rockin' Thru the Rockies*), ana-canna-panna-san (*Pop Goes the Easel*), and cackle fruit ("Hen fruit" in *Yes, We Have No Bonanza*) we have heard previously. Larry's politeness with Shemp ("After you, doctor." Shemp: "Why certainly, professor.") resembles the horse-mounting sequence in *Rockin' Thru the Rockies* but is briefer. When Larry says Cerina's Marshmallow Jumbo "tastes more like Marshmallow Gumbo," it recalls Felix Adler's "Southern comfort[er]" gag in *Uncivil Warriors*. Other variations: The three-pattern: Moe: "It's tremendous!" Larry: "It's colossal!" Shemp: "It's putrid!" (*Three Sappy People*); 'Cut Throat' Drug Store (a play on 'cut rate' - *You Nazty Spy!*); "The mortar the merrier" ("The morbid the merrier" in *If a Body Meets a Body*); "filet of sole...and heel" (*Busy Buddies*); Moe: "You're not a bad dancer!" (*Horses' Collars*); Shemp's "Come back with that bait." (*Higher Than a Kite*); "Track clear!" (*Back to the Woods*). Epithet: "nitwit".The customer's "That's no 'lady,' that's my mother-in-law" varies the old vaudeville gag, "That's no lady; that's my wife!". Reference: a 'horseradish plaster' is a hotter version of a mustard plaster.

OTHER NOTES: The working title was *Sweet Vita-Mine*. The Stooges first worked in a drug store in *Pardon My Scotch*, and there, too, they concocted a miraculous potion. As in the previous film, *Sing a Song of Six Pants*, the Stooges run their own establishment.

All Gummed Up, the final release of 1947, is the third box comedy. Unlike most previous Stooge short-films, this one completes its narrative prematurely and leaves a purposeless denouement for playing with bubble gum - not one of the Stooges' best comedy props. In 1953 Jules White would rearrange sequences and repair the damage in *Bubble Trouble*.

1934 - 1951
MIDDLE FEATURE FILMS

The Captain Hates the Sea • Start Cheering

Time Out for Rhythm • My Sister Eileen • Rockin' In the Rockies

Swing Parade of 1946 • Gold Raiders

THE CAPTAIN HATES THE SEA

Studio: Columbia

Released: October 22, 1934

Running Time: 17"41'"

Credited Cast:

Victor McLaglen	Schulte
Wynne Gibson	Rosalynn Jeddock ('Goldie')
Alison Skipworth	Mrs. McGruder
John Gilbert	Steve Bramley
Helen Vinson	Janet Grayson
Fred Keating	Danny Checkett, alias Faraday
Leon Errol	Layton, Chief Steward
Walter Connolly	Captain Helquist
Tala Birell	Gerta Klargi
Walter Catlett	Joe Silvers, bartender
John Wray	Bernard Jeddock
Claude Gillingwater	Judge Griswold
Emily Fitzroy	Mrs. Griswold
Geneva Mitchell	Miss Hockson
Donald Meek	Josephus Bushmills
Luis Alberini	Juan Gilboa
Akim Tamiroff	Salazaro
Arthur Treacher	Major Waringforth
Inez Courtney	Flo
The Three Stooges	musicians

Uncredited Cast:

Heine Conklin	assistant bartender
Lew Davis	deck steward

Credited Production Crew:

Producer & Director:	Lewis Milestone
From the novel by:	Wallace Smith
Screen Play:	Wallace Smith
Photography:	Joseph August
Film Editor:	Gene Milford

PERSPECTIVE: The Stooges' contract with Columbia granted them a hiatus of twelve weeks per year. Much of this 'free' time was spent touring and giving live performances on stage, but while their Columbia contract stipulated that they could not do any film work for other studios, they were allowed, and no doubt encouraged on occasion, to take small parts in other Columbia films. Their brief and rather insignificant appearance here in *The Captain Hates the Sea* is their first in a Columbia feature film. There will be five more.

We know from Moe's biography that he was eager for the Stooges to appear in features, and this was a period when they were happy to get any film work offered to them. They could make extra money, gain additional exposure, and expand their business and artistic horizons. After all, they had been the *sans*-Healy 'Three Stooges' for only a few months, they had been at Columbia for an even shorter amount of time, and they could hardly have imagined they would still be making short films at Columbia two decades down the road and only then making feature films for a decade or so after that. Within the past eighteen months they had made feature and short films at MGM, Paramount, and Universal, and signed a long-term contract with Columbia to make short films. By the time *The Captain Hates the Sea* was released in October, 1934, just weeks after the release of their third and soon-to-be Academy Award nominated short *Men in Black*, the Stooges must have felt that their film career was accelerating in leaps and bounds.

Although none of the leads in the film are household names now, all were well-known actors of the day. John Gilbert [Steve] was one of the most successful romantic leads in the 1920s, and Victor McLaglen [Schulte] would win an Oscar the next year for his work in *The Informer*. As for the production team, Director Lewis Milestone

This was silent-film star John Gilbert's [Steve] last film; he died in 1936 at age 41. His decline, hastened by alcoholism, began when 'talkies' replaced silents, and was memorialized in Robert Carson's Academy Award-winning screenplay for *A Star is Born* (1937). Reportedly Gilbert drank heavily while shooting this film, as did McLaglen, Errol, Catlett, and Connelly. Harry Cohn wired: "Hurry! The costs are staggering." Director Milestone wired back: "So is the cast!"

had already won Academy Awards for the comedy *Two Arabian Nights* (1927) and the drama *All Quiet on the Western Front* (1930). This was not an accidental assemblage of talents. Columbia was enclosing an all-star cast within an ocean liner just as MGM had put an all-star cast in its prototypical, Oscar-winning *Grand Hotel* in 1932, with each character having his or her own particular agenda, shady past, or personal associations. In this case, it all happens aboard a ship manned by a captain who hates the sea.

Incidental to all of this, the Stooges play musicians performing for the passengers in the dining room of the S.S. San Capeador. They had appeared in this sort of film before. One year earlier, when they first joined MGM, they made a cameo appearance in *Turn Back the Clock* as turn-of-the-century songsters, and towards the end of their tenure at MGM they made the all-star revue film *Hollywood Party*. Actually their role in *The Captain Hates the Sea* is very similar to the role they played in *Turn Back the Clock* in that in both films they play musicians, neither plot gives them much dialogue at all let alone verbal comedy, and neither calls for any slapstick. Nonetheless, there is something of interest here for Stooge viewers: the first tune they play ('Are You Mine' by Charles Rossoff) is the same one used for the dance sequence in *Horses' Collars*, the second is the tune used as the introductory theme ('I Thought I Wanted You' by Archie Goettler & Edward Eliscu) to both *Punch Drunks* and *Men in Black*, and later they play the tango ('Oh, Che Con Me Tango' by Constantin Bakaleinikoff & J. H. Woods) we hear in the first part of the saloon scene in *Horses Collars*. All four of these films were made at about the same time, in the middle of 1934.

VISUAL HUMOR: There is none intended. In fact, Moe holds his sax correctly, unlike the comical posture in *The Big Idea* and, later, *Rhythm and Weep*. The Stooges appear in two different combinations, the first with Larry at the piano, Curly on drums, and Moe on sax. The second, for the wedding march, has Curly at the cello, Moe at the violin, and Larry again at the piano.

VERBAL HUMOR: Danny calls Larry "Mocksin" by mistake; 'Mocksin' was the name on the drum. Larry tells him: "We picked the drum up in a hock shop and the sign was on it already."

OTHER NOTES: The Stooges would appear in four more Columbia feature films in the Curly era (1934-1946), six more with Curly-Joe after 1959. Geneva Mitchell [Miss Hockson] would again work with the Stooges and carve her niche in film history as the dance instructor in *Hoi Polloi* and Queen Ann of Anesthesia in *Restless Knights*. Alison Skipworth [Mrs. McGruder] appeared in several comedies with W. C. Fields. Archie Goettler's 'I Thought I Wanted You' was originally written for one of his Musical Novelties; cf. *Woman Haters*. For the identifications of the music, see Richard Finegan, "Stooges Music: More Swell Numbers Identified," *The 3 Stooges Journal* 93 (2000) 8. The exterior footage of the San Capeador, shot in San Pedro Harbor, will be reused for *Dunked in the Deep*.

Leon Errol (1881-1951), who plays Layton, the alcoholic chief steward, made four two-reeler comedies at Columbia in 1933/34, quit after an argument with the studio bosses, and went on to make a series of comedy shorts at RKO. This lobby card is for a 1946 Joe Palooka film in which he played Knobby Walsh - the same character Shemp had portrayed in 1936's *For the Love of Pete*.

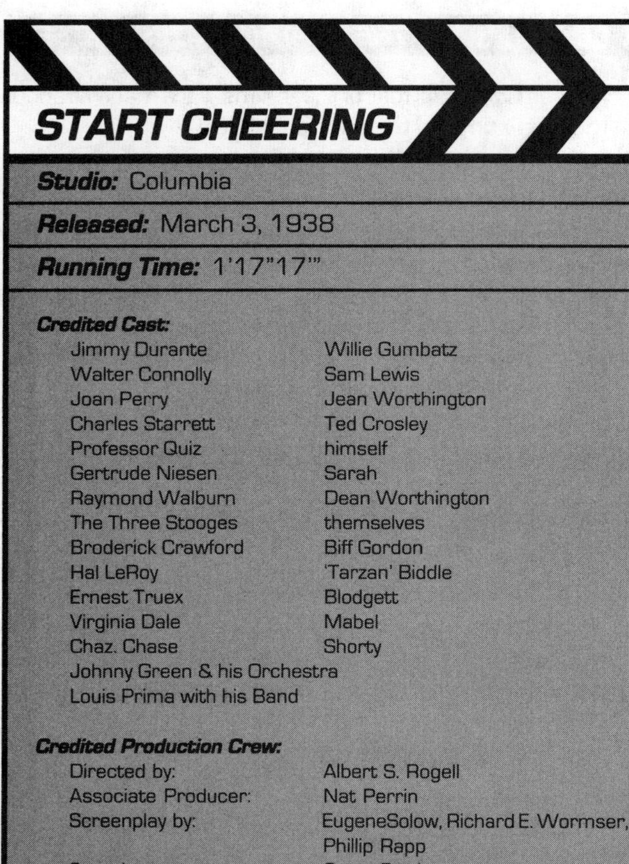

START CHEERING

Studio: Columbia

Released: March 3, 1938

Running Time: 1'17"17'"

Credited Cast:

Jimmy Durante	Willie Gumbatz
Walter Connolly	Sam Lewis
Joan Perry	Jean Worthington
Charles Starrett	Ted Crosley
Professor Quiz	himself
Gertrude Niesen	Sarah
Raymond Walburn	Dean Worthington
The Three Stooges	themselves
Broderick Crawford	Biff Gordon
Hal LeRoy	'Tarzan' Biddle
Ernest Truex	Blodgett
Virginia Dale	Mabel
Chaz. Chase	Shorty
Johnny Green & his Orchestra	
Louis Prima with his Band	

Credited Production Crew:

Directed by:	Albert S. Rogell
Associate Producer:	Nat Perrin
Screenplay by:	EugeneSolow, Richard E. Wormser, Phillip Rapp
Story by:	Corey Ford
Music:	Johnny Green
Lyrics:	Ted Koehler
Musical Director:	Morris Stoloff
Photography:	Joseph Walker
Editor:	Gene Havlick

PERSPECTIVE: *Start Cheering* is Columbia's contribution to the 'college musical' genre established by Paramount's *College Humor* (1933) and MGM's *Student Tour* (1934). College musicals were usually pleasant films that combined youthful romance, singing and dancing, football, and a smattering of education in a college campus setting. They often served as vehicles to showcase young talent. *College Humor* was one of the vehicles that helped to launch Bing Crosby's career, and *Student Tour* did the same for Betty Grable. This particular Columbia college musical sends a young movie star [Charles Starrett] to college where he falls in love with a coed [Jean Worthington], antagonizes the members of the football team, leaves college dejected, but returns - after a car/train chase - in time to sing the finale. Though Starrett never became a huge success, his tenure at Columbia, like the Stooges', turned out to be a long one. He remained under contract there until 1952 where he played in mostly B Westerns as 'The Durango Kid.' [Jock O'Mahoney would play 'The Arizona Kid' in two Stooge shorts, *Out West* and *Punchy Cowpunchers*.] *Start Cheering* also serves as a Jimmy Durante vehicle, as had MGM's *Hollywood Party* four years previously, so this is the third film the Stooges made with him.

Where do Stooges fit into this college-musical formula? In *Meet the Baron* they played workman at Cuddle College. But in this second of their non-starring roles in a Columbia feature the Stooges have two different cameo appearances, the first as college football players, the second as firemen/policemen at the college. The first is particularly interesting in comparison with their earlier Columbia short *Three Little Pigskins* (1934). In that short they had no idea how to play football; the humor depended on their misunderstanding signals, formations, and even the direction of play. Here they know the game very well. They even have their own plays. It is just that they do not execute well. After getting knocked over by charging linemen [Coach: "We've got the wrong dummies!"], they run their own plays, get confused, and end up slapping one another. Then they try again but while calling signals ("Hip! Hip!") they just bump into each other, which induces them to revive their 'which way is right?' routine from *Pardon My Scotch* (1934). As always, the Stooges vary a routine, so here they have a 'fourth' Stooge, Chaz. Chase, point to *his* right so that now we have actors pointing in all four directions. Chase's reward for appearing with the Stooges is getting slapped by all three of them simultaneously. It is indeed a rarity for the Stooges to slap a non-Stooge simultaneously.

The second Stooge scene has them entering the women's dorm as firemen searching for a man in hiding. They enter the matron's room, whereupon Curly barks at her, Larry jokes with her, and Moe asks her to find him a girl friend. The scene moves briskly and culminates with the dean bursting into the room and exclaiming: "This is a fine how-do-you-do!" With that impeccable tone and timing he brings to at least one moment each film, Larry shouts back "Fine! How do you do!"

VISUAL HUMOR: When the Stooges appeared in feature films and television there was a tendency to cram in as many of their standard gags as possible, not always with the same effect they had in the short films. Here the pace of the 'point-to-the-right' gag is more brisk than in *Pardon My Scotch*, and Curly twice exchanges barks with women. When Moe gives Curly a POUND/BONK, the sound effect we hear is merely a slap. Also, when all three Stooges slap Chaz. Chase, only two slapping sounds are heard.The gas station scene is reminiscent of the Stooges' 'Super Service' sequence in *Violent is the Word for Curly*, which was made in the same year as *Start Cheering*. When Larry searches for the man in the matron's room, he looks first and only under a small fruit basket on the coffee table. The Stooges will get involved in a football game in 1940's *No Census, No Feeling*.

VERBAL HUMOR: Another addition to the 'point-to-the-right' routine is an exchange [Moe: "Do you know your right from your left?" Larry: "I used to." Moe: "Close enough!"]. This is the first screen appearance of a Stooge trademark exclamation: "Me, three!" Remarkably, it will not appear in a Columbia short film until 1945's *If a Body Meets a Body*. By nature "Me, three!" requires a previous "Me, too!" in a three-pattern. Shouting "Right! Right! Right!" would appear again this very year in *Violent is the Word for Curly*. It originated in the Healy days [*Dancing Lady*]. For Moe's reference to the Four Horsemen, see on *Three Little Pigskins*, where the Stooges were confused for the 'Three Horsemen'. Curly-esque irony comes as a response to the dorm matron saying "There's no man in this room!" Curly: "No? What about us?". Moe says an interesting and uncharacteristic line to Larry: "You're even dumber than I am!" They did not have their usual writers for feature film appearances. Because the Stooges had only a cameo role, they were not given the opportunity to be students in a classroom where they could have displayed their marvelous ignorance. Durante is given the chance to do that instead. In the library, when shown the book *Roman Empire*, he remarks "Who wants a book about baseball?"

OTHER NOTES: The working titles were *College Hero* and *College Follies of 1938*. Louis Silver's 'Eastmoor College March' used in the film is the same used for the introductory music to *Three Little Pigskins*. Charles Starrett reportedly played professional football in the 1920s; his first film was *The Quarterback* (1926). Chaz. Chase [Shorty] was known for his omnivore routine; he is not to be confused with Charley Chase, the silent film star who went on to direct and/or co-produce a half dozen Stooge shorts in 1937-38. Curly had played an omnivore in his non-Stooge 1934 MGM short *Roast-Beef and Movies*. Professor Quiz [Dr. Craig E. Earle] was the star of a radio quiz show of the same name. The show debuted on CBS in mid-1936 and is now recognized as the prototype for the radio quiz shows that appeared in 1937-38; cf. *Healthy, Wealthy and Dumb*. Walter Connolly [Sam Lewis] also played the captain in the Stooges' first Columbia feature, *The Captain Hates the Sea* .Raymond Walburn [dean] played in Columbia's Oscar-nominated *Mr. Deeds Goes to Town* (1936). Ernest Truex, who had a long film and TV career, played Blodgett, a studio representative aptly named: in *A Star is Born* (1937) the starlet's original name was Esther Blodgett.

The Stooges played in a handful of Columbia features, often in cameos. This lobby card from the 1938 'college musical' *Start Cheering* pictures the scene in which the Stooges play fireman and burst into the women's dorm. Dean: "This is a fine how-do-you-do!" Larry: "Fine! How do you do?!"

TIME OUT FOR RHYTHM

Studio : Columbia

Released: June 5, 1941

Running Time: 1'14"45'"

Credited Cast:

Ann Miller	Kitty Brown
Rudy Vallee	Daniel Collins
Rosemary Lane	Frances Lewis
Allen Jenkins	Off-Beat Davis
Joan Merrill	herself
Richard Lane	Mike Armstrong
The Three Stooges	
Brenda & Cobina	themselves
Six Hits and a Miss	themselves
Stanley Andrews	James Anderson
Eddie Durant's Rhumba Orchestra	
Glen Gray and His Casa Loma Band	

Credited Production Crew:

Directed by:	Sidney Salkow
Produced by	Irving Starr
Screen Play by:	Edmund L. Hartmann & Bert Lawrence
Story by:	Bret Granet
Based upon a play by:	Alex Ruben
Musical Numbers Directed by:	LeRoy Prinz
Lyrics and Music by:	Sammy Cahn & Saul Chaplin
Musical Director:	M. W. Stoloff
Director of Photography:	Franz F. Planer
Film Editor:	Arthur Seid

PERSPECTIVE: *Time Out for Rhythm* was made during a transitional period for the Hollywood film industry. 1939 had been a great year (*Gone With the Wind, Stagecoach, Wuthering Heights*) drawing weekly audiences of 85 million people, but the next two years brought domestic and international problems. Legal action by 11,000 independent theater owners and federal anti-trust laws ended the era in which studio-produced films gained an automatic screening in studio-owned theaters, and eleven hostile and war-torn European countries banned English-language films or limited the amount of profits that could be exported. Looking for new markets in South America, Twentieth-Century Fox and Warner Brothers filled the screen with the colorful, tuneful image of the 'Brazilian Bombshell,' Carmen Miranda with her trademark fruit-filled headdress.

As the larger studios acquiesced and sold off their theater networks, smaller studios like Columbia and Universal appealed the governmental ruling but with limited finances found themselves producing mostly low-budget films: B-Westerns, thrillers, and musicals. Columbia designed these formulaic films specifically for double feature bookings and relied heavily upon distribution guarantees. This was the period in which *Time Out for Rhythm* was made, and it dictated its musical form and backstage content. As for the cast, this was a year in which top a radio star like Orson Welles (*Citizen Kane*) was brought to Hollywood, so radio pioneer and crooning idol Rudy Vallee was a natural as the headliner for *Time Out for Rhythm*.

Columbia was finding itself increasingly dependent on the consistent profits derived from the Stooges' short films, so they injected the reliably popular trio into six different scenes. The Stooges play three nameless, unemployed actors, as they had in *A Pain in the Pullman* (although there they were 'The Three Stooges') eager to find a gimmick that will get them a radio spot. In fact, Moe tells Danny (Rudy Vallee) "I got rid of those two mugs," suggesting that Curly and Larry were new hires. Shortly after that in their first scene the three of them introduce the Maharaja knife-throwing routine (Moe: "Maja!" Curly: "Aha!") better known from and more fully developed version in Curly's last complete film, *Three Little Pirates*. In their second scene they do a variation of the Ted Healy 'foreclose-on-the-mortgage' routine from their stage act, filmed earlier in MGM's *Plane Nuts*. In the third they are hired to be tough guys wearing black trench coats and sinister hats, and they pretend to have guns in their pockets. All three of these "new acts" fail in getting the Stooges the radio time they are seeking. In their fourth scene they deliver a telegram to Danny, but Curly rips it up and they have to piece it together. The plot turns on this scene, for it sets up the film audition in which, after they fill their fifth scene by proudly declaring their ignorance, they dance a final rumba number ('The Rio De Janeiro') and win over, believe it or not, three beautiful women. For the rumba number Curly "has to have fruit," so he bursts into the dining room, steals a bowl of fruit, and wears it on his headdress, thus imitating the Carmen Miranda image and dancing the South American rumba so popular in the early 1940s.

VISUAL HUMOR: In 1941 the Stooges with Curly were at their zenith of quickness and timing, so a number of their familiar slapstick movements are showcased in this feature film: the gouge (with the "pick two" setup, not used since 1936's *Slippery Silks*), hair pulls, a tongue pull, a nose tweak, slaps, a double slap, belly bumps, an ear pull, a hand-wave with a downthrust, Curly banging into a door jamb and doing a chicken-with-its-head-cut-off [seen from above]. Stooge firsts: Moe pointing his arm and Curly running his nose along it; and pretending to have guns in their pockets. A most elaborate physical/verbal three-pattern has Moe crossing over to give Curly an additional slap and then stopping Curly from slapping him back (Moe: "You heard what he said: later!" [SLAP] Larry: "You heard what he said: later!" [Larry slaps Curly]

This was the Stooges' first rumba, no surprise since Hollywood was looking south of the border in 1940 while Xavier Cugat ("the man who made America rumba-conscious") was becoming the rage. The Stooges parody the new fad with a three-pattern (Moe: "We rumba!" Larry: "We rumba!" Curly: "We rumba! Hey, what's rumba?"), and Larry brags, "We're rumba experts." Curly makes fun of the dance by merely shuffling in his socks, and when the Stooges sing the 'Rio de Janeiro' they work Curly-esque hand snapping into the rhythm.

The Stooges would first use the dance in a Columbia short-film in *I'll Never Heil Again* of the same year. One of these two Stooge rumba scenes seems to have had some impact, for the very next year in MGM's animated *Hollywood Steps Out* the Stooges are depicted doing a slapstick rumba. The following year in *Three Smart Saps* the Stooges offer us another verbal gag:

Woman: "Do you rumba?"
Curly: "Only when I take bicarbonate!"

Along with Xavier Cugat, the 'Brazilian Bombshell' Carmen Miranda became increasingly popular in the early 1940s, hence Curly's costume. Actually, Curly seems to have lost his banana headdress for the last few minutes of the dance, but in four years Curly will revive the characterization, with a different use for the fruit, when he plays Señorita Cucaracha in the classic *Micro-Phonies* (1945).

Curly: "You heard what he said—").

Other new visual movements include Moe raising himself up on his toes while Larry and Curly imitate him; and Curly ("Not me!") prancing back and forth, hands on his hips, and wiggling his shoulders. Curly as the Maharajah does a fine job falling over the table and then falling onto the floor when he misses his chair. He punctuates his knife throwing with a new sound: "Oy-yah!". Larry creates such an unusual visual impression when he enters in an oriental outfit and turban, that Davis asks: "What is it?" Another odd visual look is the (unrecognizable) Stooges as three menacing, dark figures in overcoats and hats and smoking cigarettes. Even odder is Curly beating Moe and Larry in coin flipping; cf. *Restless Knights* and *Soup to Nuts*. The Stooges originally developed the Maharaja knife-throwing gag for vaudeville. Other variations: tick-tack-toe chalked onto the floor (*Disorder on the Court*); Moe and Larry marching backwards and forwards while Curly cannot keep pace (*We Wee Monsieur*, *Boobs in Arms*); Curly mouthing and mimicking the words to the 'telegram speech' (the Spanish directions in *What's the Matador?*); and Curly dancing with a taller woman, and getting his belt decoration caught like a couch spring (*Hoi Polloi*).

VERBAL HUMOR: The Stooges' use of language is quite variegated throughout the film. The pseudo-Russian Maharaja lingo ("Razbanyas yatee benee futch...") is juxtaposed with contemporary slang (Curly: "Razbanyas Gimme a fish cake, daddy-y-y!"; Moe: "That's a knife which you're gonna pitch it?" Curly: "That's a knife which I'm gonna chuck it"), double talk (Moe: "His royal Chow Mienian Highness, the Maharaja of Minti-tikh-stabach and his not so Royal Assistant Spielenikatz-Klahviahtch"), neologisms (Moe: "Give him a raw-dition!"; Curly: "A maskazini cherry!" ['Maskazino' in *Hoi Polloi*]), and excessive literalness (Moe: "At this time the Raja says he will throw the razor edge daggers at random." Larry: "Are you 'Random'?" [Moe: "Fire at will!" Curly: "Which one is Will?" in *Back to the Woods*]). Later in the film comes the wonderfully confused reading of the ripped up telegram (Moe: "What have you got that's fresh....Wednesday" Curly: "Stop" Davis: "Want nothing" Curly: "Stop" Danny: "Hollywood" Curly: "Stop" [Moe bonks Curly] Curly: "Stop!"). More contemporary slang: Larry: "It's a sort of a kind of our own like." Curly's "It's an orig!" is similar to the bar-speak ("Don't be ridic!") in the Oscar-winning *The Lost Weekend*; Moe's "Stand where you are, see? Right where you are, see?" is a pattern often associated with Edward G. Robinson; "Up, Sadie!" is a typical address for a performing elephant.

Contemporary Stooge shorts, e.g. *An Ache in Every Stake*, have three-patterns as does this feature (Moe: "Your worries are over!" Larry: "Yeah, they're over." Curly: "Are they?"; and Moe: "I take half." Larry: "I take half." Curly: "I get the rest!"). Another three-pattern is their laughter while wearing the dark coats: (Moe: "Ha! Ha!" Larry: "Ha! Ha!" Curly giggles). Similar are this exchange in the Maharaja routine (Curly: "Who does that?" Moe:

"You do!" Curly: "Do I?"], this exchange with Davis [Moe: "That's great!" Larry: "Colossal!" Davis: "Putrid." Moe: "He liked it!" [*Three Sappy People*]] and this extended version [Larry: "Hollywood here we come!" Moe: "Let's rush home and pack!" Curly: "Woob-woob-woob-woob!... [calmly]: "We're packed"]. As it is for slapstick, a feature film is a place to reuse standard verbal gags: Larry: "I'll take it when I'm ready!" Moe: "Are you ready?!" Larry: "Yeah, I'm ready." [*Plane Nuts*; *Men in Black*]; and Curly: "Not me!" [*Three Little Pigskins*]. Stooge ignorance is celebrated: Davis: "Stupid!" Larry: "Stupidity?" Moe: "We're technical experts." Curly: "I'm *ignorant*!"; Moe: "This is 'it' with a capital 'E'; Frances: "These men are gangsters." Mike: "Why these dopes aren't even men!"; Davis: "How would you like to join the biggest act in town? 52 consecutive weeks without a layoff? They even supply the costumes." Moe: "Where?" Davis: "Bartlett Building, number 248: local draft board." Larry: "Let's hurry up before somebody beats us to it!".

Writers Edmund L. Hartmann & Bert Lawrence penned several notable exchanges, one inter-stooge [Curly: "Muck." Larry: "Mire!" Curly: "Oh, Hiya, Mire." Larry: "Hiya, Muck"], one with Davis and Danny [Moe: "We have an important message for you." Davis: "How do you know?" Curly: "We read it!" Danny: "What did it say?" Curly: "You think I'm a stool pigeon?"] and a unique exchange with comediennes Brenda and Cobina [Cobina: "Is it possible?!" Curly: "If you're possible, we are too!" Brenda: "This place is beginnin' to look like the chamber of horrors." Cobina: "Oh I remember you! I never forget a face." Moe: "Well you better go home, sister, 'cause you forgot it today!"]. One liners: Moe: "Spread out: make it look like a big act!"; Moe: "Are you sufferin' from clean underwear?"; and singing in a triad: "Telegram for Mr. Collins!". Epithet: "You over-stuffed davenport". Reference: Moe's "Laughing-yet we are here" parodies "Lafayette, we are here!" [*Half-Shot Shooters*].

OTHER NOTES: The working title of the film was *Show Business.* The rumba began surfacing as early as 1931 ('Cuban Love Song'), but it did not become popular until 1940/1941. Jerry Lewis co-starred with Carmen Miranda and, like Curly in *Micro-Phonies* [1945] lip-synced her music to a record player in *Scared Stiff* [1953]. Rudy Vallee was host and producer of 'The Fleischmann Hour' which introduced such stars as Edgar Bergen, Milton Berle, and Carmen Miranda. The Stooges had appeared with him in *Hollywood on Parade.* Ann Miller, who was featured in numerous musicals in the 1940s and 1950s, had made her film debut recently in 1937. During their 1939 hiatus the Stooges worked with her in George White's New York stage hit, *Scandals of 1939.* Brenda [Blanche Stewart] and Cobina [Elvia Allman], who parody real-life society girls Brenda Frazier and Cobina Wright, were regulars on Bob Hope's *Pepsodent Show* which aired Tuesday evenings on CBS from 1938-1955. [A photograph of 'Debutante' Brenda Frazier on the cover of the Nov. 14, 1938 issue of *Life* is visible on the magazine stand photo in *A Ducking They Did Go*]. This is one of the few solo appearances by Priscilla Lane, one of the three Lane sisters. Editor Arthur Seid worked on many Stooge shorts from 1937. Columbia contract players and frequent Stooge extras abound: Eddie Laughton plays the uncredited sound engineer, Bess Flowers the receptionist, and Bud Jamison the lunch counter waiter.

MY SISTER EILEEN

Studio: Columbia

Released: September 24, 1942

Running Time: 1'36"38"'

Credited Cast:

Rosalind Russell	Ruth Sherwood
Brian Aherne	Robert Baker
Janet Blair	Eileen Sherwood
George Tobias	Mr. Appopolous
Allyn Joslyn	Chic Clark
Grant Mitchell	Walter Sherwood
Elizabeth Patterson	Grandma Sherwood
June Havoc	Effie Shelton
Frank Sully	Jenson
Gordon Jones	'Wreck' Loomis
Richard Quine	Frank Lippincott
Donald MacBride	Officer Lonigan
[Miss] Jeff Donnell	Helen Loomis
Clyde Fillmore	Ralph Craven

Uncredited Cast:

The Three Stooges	construction team
Arnold Stang	newspaper room worker
Dudley Dickerson	porter

Credited Production Crew:

Produced by:	Max Gordon
Directed by:	Alexander Hall
Based on the play by:	Joseph Fields & Jerome Chodorov
Adapted from the stories by:	Ruth McKenney
Screen Play by:	Joseph Fields & Jerome Chodorov
Director of Photography:	Joseph Walker
Film Editor:	Viola Lawrence
Musical Director:	M. W. Stoloff

PERSPECTIVE: Although original screenplays and adaptations of novels provided the stories for most films, theatrical producers and writers also found a niche in Hollywood when the sound era began. Along with Robert Sherwood and Eugene O'Neill, the team of Joseph Fields & Jerome Chodorov regularly found their stage plays transferred onto film. Produced by Max Gordon both as a New York play and as a film, *My Sister Eileen* provided the type of comedy Hollywood was so fond of in the early 1940s. It contains the wacky characters (Appopolus, Effie) and absurd situations (an apartment frequently shaken by subterranean blasting for a new subway route) essential to contemporary screwball comedies as well as the all-American types (Eileen, Grandma Sherwood, 'Wreck' Loomis) glorified in Preston Sturges comedies and the Mickey Rooney/Judy Garland Andy Hardy musicals. The story is a product of the Hollywood Dream Factory: two Columbus, Ohio sisters come to New York to establish themselves as a writer and actress; they find little success but plenty of annoyances; and just when they are about to give up they get a contract, a husband, and promises of success; even the subway blasting ceases, if only to be replaced with pneumatic drilling - by The Three Stooges.

The Stooges' cameo is uncredited and unannounced, and, judging from the original studio sources, it seems that their presence in the film was a last-minute addition. Nonetheless, it helps bring the screwball comedy to a delightful, unexpected, and even screwier close, and not because of Curly's sole line of dialogue ("Hey Moe! I think you made the wrong turn!") or any slapstick action on their part; there is none. The humor is in the absurdity of having subterranean workers accidentally drill up through the apartment floor and having these workers turn out to be the most recognizably screwy people around. Indeed, it is the recognition that these intruders into the oft-intruded upon apartment are The Three Stooges that is significant. By 1942 those famous profiles are recognizable everywhere; in the previous year their caricatures had appeared even in Warner's animated *Hollywood Steps Out*.

Though the Stooges appear for just a few seconds at the very end of the film, there is much in the rest of the film that Stooge viewers will find familiar from the early 1940s Stooge shorts, namely, such contemporary situational elements as young people setting out on their own (*Cactus Makes Perfect*), ephemeral apartment-living (*Loco Boy Makes Good*), and men innocently protecting females in distress (*So Long, Mr. Chumps; Even As IOU*). Such scenarios were common in Depression and post-Depression situational comedies, and the early war years were psychologically still suffering from a Depression economy. Some of the characters are familiar to us, too, particularly a quirky landlord (*Loco Boy Makes Good*), unmarried young people thrilled by the prospects of marriage (*Three Smart Saps*), and a dopey football player (*No Census, No Feeling*). And then, of course, there is the conga (*They Stooge to Conga*).

OTHER NOTES: Rosalind Russell won the Best Actress Oscar for her role as Ruth Sherwood. In 1955 Columbia made *My Sister Eileen* into a musical with Betty Garrett, Janet Leigh, Jack Lemmon, and Bob Fosse. It was directed by Richard Quine, who acted the role of Frank Lippincott in this version. In 1960 it was turned into a TV sitcom with Elaine Stritch (Ruth) and Shirley Bonne (Eileen). Frank Sully (Jenson) played in six 1950s Stooge shorts in a variety of roles, e.g. 'Big Mike' in *Fling in the Ring* and the waiter in *A Merry Mix-Up*. He played supporting roles and bit parts in hundreds of features. The previous year director Alexander Hall earned an Oscar nomination for *Here Comes Mr. Jordan*, the film parodied in *Heavenly Daze*. Arnold Stang works in the newspaper room in the opening scene; he will appear along with the Stooges in *It's a Mad, Mad, Mad, Mad World*. Dudley Dickerson plays a porter at the bus station.

ROCKIN' IN THE ROCKIES

Studio: Columbia

Released: April 17, 1945

Running Time: 1'07"25'"

Credited Cast:

The Three Stooges	
[Moe Howard	Shorty Williams]
[Jerry Howard	Curly]
[Larry Fine	Larry]
Mary Beth Hughes	June McGuire
Jay Kirby	Rusty
Gladys Blake	Betty
Tim Ryan	
Tom Trove	
The Hoosier Hotshots	
The Cappy Barra Boys	
Spade Cooley, King of Western Swing, [and His Orchestra]	

Uncredited Cast:

Jack Clifford	Sheriff Zeke
Forrest Taylor	Sam Clemens
Vernon Dent	Mr. Stanton, owner of the Wagon Wheel Cafe
Lew Davis	roulette wheel operator
John Tyrrell	

Credited Production Crew:

Directed by:	Vernon Keays
Produced by:	Colbert Clark
Story by:	Louise Rousseau & Gail Davenport
Screen Play by:	J. Benton Cheney & John Grey
Director of Photography:	Glen Gano
Film Editor:	Paul Borofsky
Art Direction:	Charles Clague
Set Decorations:	Fay Babcock

PERSPECTIVE: To entertain the fighting men overseas as well as the rest of the population on the home front during World War II, the major studios produced a number of comedy/musicals. These were modest in scope but served the purpose well and were cranked out with the same kind of efficiency that was to produce tens of thousands of airplanes and tanks in just a few years. A typical setting for such a film was the contemporary American West, and some of the most notable of these Western war-era musicals include Universal's *Ride 'Em Cowboy* (1941) with Abbott & Costello, *A Lady Takes a Chance* (1943) with John Wayne, and *Can't Help Singing* (1944) with Deanna Durbin. One of Columbia's entries was the B-film *Rockin' In the Rockies* which featured The Hoosier Hotshots and the Cappy Barra Boys with The Three Stooges receiving top billing. This was the first time the Stooges starred in a feature film.

Not to be confused with and bearing almost no resemblance to the 1940 short *Rockin' Thru the Rockies, Rockin' in the Rockies* ignored many of the ingredients that were making contemporary Stooge short-films so successful. Writers Johnny Grey and J. Benton Cheney, who had barely written for the Stooges before, separated the Stooges and left Moe to act solo, included very few slapstick exchanges, and omitted an effective foil whom the Stooges could abuse or frustrate. At one point Moe has words with and almost strangles Betty (Moe: "Jasper [the mule] and I are alike in a lot of things." Betty: "Only your ears are shorter." Moe: "I resemble that last remark!"), which is exactly the sort of personnel combination in which the Stooges do not succeed. Normally the Stooges either rescue a damsel-in-distress or are beaten up by tough, ugly, or overweight women. Here, instead of a heroic rescue or a slapstick exchange, Moe has to pull back his hands, Betty has no verbal or physical comeback, but later she gives Moe a kiss. This film may headline the Stooges, but it is not a Stooge film.

Either the writers/director did not understand what the Stooges were all about or they consciously tried to create a new kind of vehicle for them. Characterizing Moe and Curly as wiseguy tricksters fails because the writers were unable to make them either tricky or clever liars. Often in their mid-career feature films the Stooges are called upon to "do" their old gags and cram as many of them as possible into a few minutes, but here they simply recycle old gags without the kind of improvements *Time Out for Rhythm* achieved, and the dialogue is so limited that although the stag, horse and mule all talk, they actually have very little to say. Larry and Curly speak in an uncharacteristically courteous dialogue as they mount the horse, and at one point the creativity is so lacking Moe calls Curly merely, "You silly so-and-so." Even the sound effects are anemic or inappropriate. For the physical gags Curly's ailing health is apparent, and Moe is rarely around to cover for or interact with him. This leaves Larry as the toughie - not his best persona. Larry even has to run the "when-I-say-go-we-all-point-to-the-right" routine. When Curly and Larry finally mount the horse, when Larry rides on top of Curly, and when Larry uses a sledge hammer on Curly's head, there is a real absence of either franticness or even the basic Stoogeness that makes them elsewhere so successful. Ultimately the entertainment in *Rockin' in the Rockies* derives from its wacky and upbeat musical acts. As always the Stooges give it all the energy they can muster, but when the writing divides them into a duo and a solo, they lose their comic dynamic.

VISUAL HUMOR: New gags: Curly putting gum on his shoe to pick up the roulette chip; Larry riding on Curly; Larry measuring the saddle with his hands; and tossing dynamite back and forth. The most successful new gag has Curly ramming his head into the fence post and bouncing backwards into Larry.

The most interesting variation happens when Curly holds his ear and is pulled by Moe (*Hoi Polloi*), stops to take a pebble out of his shoe, regrabs his ear and continues on. Old standards include a double slap and Curly's chicken-with-its-head-cut-off. Other variations: Larry boosting Curly over the horse (*Playing the Ponies*); Curly picking Larry up by the hair (*False Alarms* - paralleling Curly leaving Larry suspended from the moose's antlers); Larry and Curly throwing their hats on the hat rack, falling after drinking, and brushing each other off (*Horses' Collars*); pointing "to the right" (*Pardon My Scotch*); Moe playing the xylophone on Curly's head, and Curly trying to sing but Moe and Larry covering his mouth (*Time Out for Rhythm*); Curly dressed as a Señorita (*Time Out for Rhythm*; and *Micro-Phonies*, which was made this same year); Moe seeing "a million of 'em" in the back of Larry's scalp (*We Want Our Mummy*); Curly on a leash (*From Nurse to Worse*); Moe grabbing Curly by the 'hair' (*Ants in the Pantry*); Moe slapping Larry in the chest ("Get busy and close that trunk!"), Larry doing the same to Curly, and Curly slapping no one: "Hmm! Low man again!" (*Punch Drunks*; *Pardon My Scotch*); Curly and Larry hiding in a large trunk (*Dizzy Detectives*); Larry daring Moe to hit Curly again (*Yes, We Have No Bonanza*); Curly stabbing Moe in the rear while cutting the upholstery (*Slippery Silks*); Larry using a sledge hammer on Curly's head, Moe trying to stop them, but Curly objecting: "Why don't you mind your own business?" (*Meet the Baron, How High is Up?*).

VERBAL HUMOR: The best series of exchanges comes in the termite routine ("Seam lizards." Moe: "'Seems' like they ought-a be in there"; Trove: "Stop it! I'm goin' crazy!" Moe: "Don't brag. We're nuts already!"; Moe: "How dare you stab me in the back when I ain't lookin'!") and in June telling Larry: "Get this horrible thing [the moose head] out of here!" Larry slaps Curly: "Get out-a here! You're scarin' the lady!". Weaker exchanges: Curly: "I wish I had a hamburger with onions." Larry: "Quiet, you know I don't like onions!"; and Moe: "We wanna see if we got pay dirt." Betty: "You mean people actually pay for this dirt?" Moe: "No, they pay for the metal that's in the dirt." Betty: "Oh, well if they pay for the metal, why fool around with the dirt?!". New gags: Dealer: "Double 'O'" Curly: "Uh-oh"; Curly & Larry: "Oh no we won't! Quote!" [They snap their fingers] Moe: "Unquote!"; Larry: "Our slightest desire is your wish!"; Moe: "Before somebody else gets a chance to cheat you!"; and Larry: "That horse'll say he won the Kentucky Derby." Curly [tipping his derby]: "He's lucky. I had to buy mine!" (cf. the 'Filet Mignon' gag in *Even As IOU*). Epithet: "Cabbage-head". A Stooge first: Moe's "ingenzommen". Additions to the "Which way is right" routine: Curly: "I told you you were wrong which way was right." Larry: "Right!" Curly: "Two rights don't make a left, or vice versa!". Other variations: "That's a tin roof" (*Horses' Collars*), "mooses...meeses" (*Whoops, I'm an Indian*), "I resemble that last remark" (*Three Little Twirps*), "Every time you got it, I get it" (*Matri-Phony*), "Use your head" (*3 Dumb Clucks*), Moe: "You better rock this thing before I forget I'm a miner." Betty: "Ah, you're older than that" (*Three Little Pigskins*); Larry: "Are you serious?!" Rusty: "Yes, I'm serious!" Larry [yielding]: "That's what I thought." (*Plane Nuts*); "For two pins I'd toss you over that fence" (*Meet the Baron*), "Gentlemen!" Larry: "Who came in?" (*We Want Our Mummy*); singing a triadic "Come in" (*Healthy, Wealthy and Dumb*); and "Before you can say Ticonderoga" (*Back to the Woods*).

OTHER NOTES: The Hoosier Hotshots (Paul 'Hezzie' Trietsch, Ken Trietsch, Frank Kettering/Gil Taylor, and Otto 'Gabe' Ward) became popular as radio's "highest paid novelty musicians" on NBC radio's 'National Barn Dance' program in 1933 (broadcast live from Chicago) and 'The Uncle Ezra Show' in 1934. They were one of the best known of the Country/Western bands in an era which considered Country/Western music as merely a novelty. Here they play mostly Western swing. Columbia used them in 14 films between 1944 and 1948. Mary Beth Hughes' [June] best-known role was in 1943's *The Ox-Bow Incident*. The song 'Somewhere Along the Trail' was introduced in 1941 for Columbia's *Go West, Young Lady*. Film Editor Paul Borofsky edited a dozen Stooge shorts in 1942-1947. Art Director Charles Clague worked on over forty in 1944-1950. Director of Photography Glen Gano worked on five in 1944-1945. Set Decorator Fay Babcock worked on two in 1957. Vernon Keays never directed another film.

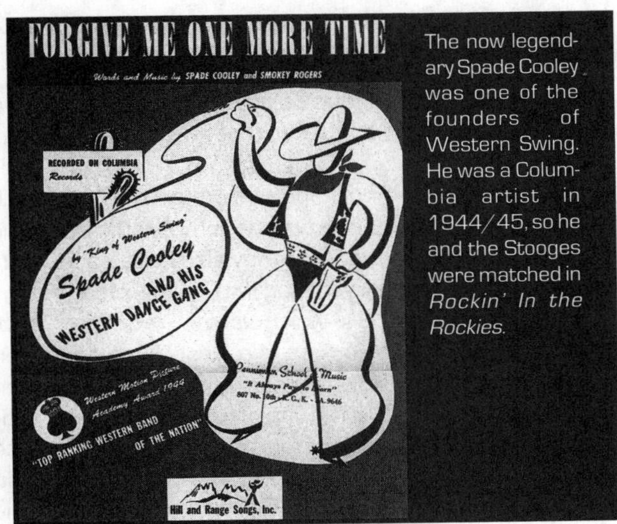

The now legendary Spade Cooley was one of the founders of Western Swing. He was a Columbia artist in 1944/45, so he and the Stooges were matched in *Rockin' In the Rockies*.

SWING PARADE OF 1946

Studio: Monogram Pictures

Released: March 16, 1946

Running Time: 1'14"01'"

Credited Cast:

Gale Storm	Carol Lawrence
Phil Regan	Danny Warren, Jr.
The Three Stooges [Larry Fine] Jerome Howard Moe Howard]	kitchen helpers
Connee Boswell	herself
Edward S. Brophy	Moose
Mary Treen	Marie Finch
Russell Hicks	Daniel Warren, Sr.
Windy Cook	himself
John Eldredge	Bascomb, Warren's assistant
Leon Belasco	Pete Welsh
Jack Boyle	dancing partner
Will Osborn & His Orchestra	
Louis Jordan & His Tympany Five	

Credited Production Crew:

Directed by:	Phil Karlson
Executive Director:	Trem Carr
Produced by:	Lindsley Parsons & Harry A. Romm
Screenplay by:	Tim Ryan
Original Story by:	Edmond Kelso
Additional Dialogue:	Nicholas Ray
Musical Director:	Edward Kay
Production Numbers Staged by:	Jack Boyle
Photographed by:	Harry Neumann
Supervising Editor:	Richard Currier
Art Director:	Ernest R. Hickson
Set Decorations by:	Charles Thompson & Vin Taylor

PERSPECTIVE: The contract the Stooges signed with Columbia in 1934 stipulated that they make eight short films per year within 40 weeks, with 12 or more weeks per year free for them to pursue other employment. The Stooges spent their free time at home with their families or on the road touring, but they also used some of this time to play secondary roles in five Columbia feature films, the most demanding of which were *Time Out for Rhythm* and *Rockin' in the Rockies*, the least demanding being their cameo in *My Sister Eileen*. Their original contract prevented them from making films for other studios, but in 1946 they were permitted - the exact circumstances are unknown - to play a secondary role in this production from Monogram Pictures. Monogram, the poorer half of Allied Artists which was in the process of reorganization in 1946, specialized in B-films, particularly comedies, crime dramas, and Westerns. 1946 was a banner year for the company because it was the year they launched their Bowery Boys series, and here they were allowed to include the Stooges in a musical feature as well.

For aficionados of the golden days of early television, it is a treat to see the young Gale Storm, future star of *My Little Margie* (1952-1955) and *Oh! Susanna* (1956-1958; retitled *The Gale Storm Show* for 1958-1960), in a leading musical role. The plot casts her as a hard-luck kid trying to break into show business, and after a rejection at the front door of the club she finds some encouragement from the Stooges in the kitchen and meets Danny, the son of the wealthy businessman who is trying to close the club. Of course a narrative formula has control of the outcome, so by the end of the film Carol is accepted, Danny's father acquiesces, and the film ends with a production number. As at the end of *Time Out for Rhythm*, the final is so joyous the Stooges even end up with beautiful, smiling women.

The script confronts the Stooges with other characters perfectly tailored to Stooge requirements. Carol is the damsel-in-distress, Danny is the nice guy they try to help and impress, Moose is the tough guy who yells at them, slaps them, and ultimately finds himself over his head in the basement they flooded. Unlike the contemporary *Rockin' in the Rockies*, *Swing Parade of 1946* places the Stooges in roles guaranteed to let them thrive. Working as a trio they play loyal assistants to the male lead much as they did in *Time Out For Rhythm*. This allows them to do several different things, and since it was a feature film lasting more than an hour, the more flexible their role the better. The Stooges take turns cooking, serving, waiting on tables, playing bouncers and confidantes, and, unfortunately for Moose and the building, plumbing. They glory in their ignorance, with plenty of puns followed by slapstick tags.

Although none of them records the very best of Stooge comedy, this is the sixth feature film in which Curly plays the third Stooge. The debilitating stroke he suffered in May, 1946 terminated his film career prematurely, and the Stooges would make only one feature-film during the Shemp years.

VISUAL HUMOR: New gags: washing the single dish and passing it around Moe's back; Curly walking off with the wrong dancing partner; and being introduced from behind newspapers. The directing puts the Stooges in many of their favorite postures, poses, and positions: peering around a corner with one head above the other, getting their heads bonked and their faces triple slapped by Moose, sleeping, snoring, and getting kissed. When Moose bonks their heads together, though, the sound effect is muted. Other variations: Larry stuffed into the drain, and gouging through the phone (*False Alarms*); creating a labyrinth of pipes (*A Plumbing We Will Go*);

Moe slamming the piano lid on Curly's hands (*Dancing Lady, Loco Boy Makes Good*); Moe and Larry grabbing Curly by the ears (*How High is Up?*); Curly and Larry being told to "Drop every thing!" and therefore dropping their piles of dishes onto the floor (*Three Loan Wolves*); and the flooded basement (*Meet the Baron*).

VERBAL HUMOR: Script writer Tim Ryan makes Curly's ignorance quite impressive. He cannot read (Moose: "I'll see that you get a type-written transcript of the conversation." Curly: "But we can't read!"; Man in restaurant: "We can read!" Curly: "Oh, a showoff!"), and he does not understand 'financial success' ("Not only that, but we'll make some money, too!"), 'impetuous' ("Careful: there's a lady here!"), or 'attachment' (Moe: "She's got an attachment for Danny." Curly: "I knew it! I knew it was love at first sight!"). All three Stooges fail to see through Danny's or Moose's sarcasm, and Moe cannot figure out that Larry is under the drain. Curly is characterized not only as ignorant, but also as ugly (Moe: "If you hadn't looked at her she'd a never fainted!" [SLAP]; cf. in *Rockin' in the Rockies*: "Get this horrible thing [the moose head] out of here!" Larry to Curly: "Get out-a here! You're scarin' the lady!"). Danny and Moose show appropriate respect for the Stooges' disaster potential: (Moose: "But they couldn't—" Danny: "Oh I know what you mean, but what else can we do?"). Curly's circular exchange (Man: "Waiter! Let's have something to eat." Curly: "Yeah! Don't mind if I do!...What do you want?" Man: "A menu! I wanted to see what you had to eat!" Curly: "I didn't eat yet!") is of the same form as "I quit!"...You're fired!"...You can't fire him, he quit" from *Movie Maniacs*. The exchange (Larry: "A wrench?" Moose: "Monkey." Curly: "Don't get personal!") derives from a classic exchange in *Back to the Woods* (Larry: "We're trapped like rats." Moe: "You gettin' personal?"). Moe answering the wrong number on the phone varies the many phone gags dating from *Men in Black* and even earlier in *Soup to Nuts*. Other variations: Curly: "Oh, superstitious, eh?" (*Three Little Pigskins*); Moe: "Quiet, feather-brain!" (*Dizzy Pilots*); Moe: "Recede! Line forms on the right! Curly: "Right!" Larry: "Right!" (*Myrt and Marge*; *Dancing Lady*); and Moe arguing with the customer about roast beef (*Beer and Pretzels*).

OTHER NOTES: Gale Storm's real, unweathered name was Josephine Cottle. Edward S. Brophy [Moose] played the tough guy also in *Beer and Pretzels* and *Hello Pop!*. Russell Hicks [Daniel Warren, Sr.] played with the Marx Brothers in *The Big Store* (1941) and with Shemp in the 1934 Vitaphone short *My Mummy's Arms*. Leon Belasco [the dance director] played in the TV-series version *My Sister Eileen*. Nicholas Ray, who wrote 'Additional Dialogue,' went on in the next year to begin an acclaimed directorial career (*Rebel Without a Cause*). When Moe looks down the drain, he says "Third dimension," offering perhaps some verbal corroboration that films like *Three Little Sew and Sews* and *I'll Never Heil Again* make conscious use of multi-dimensional space.

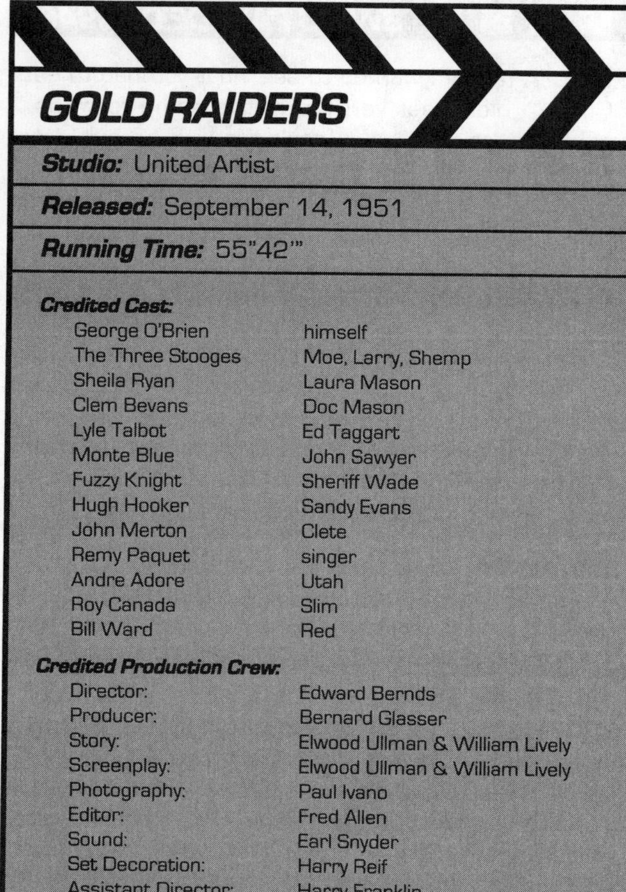

GOLD RAIDERS

Studio: United Artist

Released: September 14, 1951

Running Time: 55"42'"

Credited Cast:

George O'Brien	himself
The Three Stooges	Moe, Larry, Shemp
Sheila Ryan	Laura Mason
Clem Bevans	Doc Mason
Lyle Talbot	Ed Taggart
Monte Blue	John Sawyer
Fuzzy Knight	Sheriff Wade
Hugh Hooker	Sandy Evans
John Merton	Clete
Remy Paquet	singer
Andre Adore	Utah
Roy Canada	Slim
Bill Ward	Red

Credited Production Crew:

Director:	Edward Bernds
Producer:	Bernard Glasser
Story:	Elwood Ullman & William Lively
Screenplay:	Elwood Ullman & William Lively
Photography:	Paul Ivano
Editor:	Fred Allen
Sound:	Earl Snyder
Set Decoration:	Harry Reif
Assistant Director:	Harry Franklin
Music:	Alex Alexander & June Starr

PERSPECTIVE: United Artists released this Bernard Glasser production, making *Gold Raiders* the second of two feature-films the Stooges filmed with a different production company while bound by their contract with Columbia, but it is the only feature-film Shemp made during his 1946-1956 tenure with the trio. (He made *Soup to Nuts* twenty one years earlier in 1930; and he took time out in 1949 to make *Africa Screams* with Abbott & Costello.) It was not designed as a Three Stooges vehicle; top billing goes to George O'Brien, a former military boxing champion turned stunt man and then cowboy actor, whose 40-year film career was even longer than the Stooges' to date, beginning in the silent era with a break-through role in John Ford's *The Iron Horse* in 1924. (Moe had appeared in Vitagraph silents as early as 1909, but he appeared only as a teen-age extra.). O'Brien spent the middle part of his career as a successful, B Western matinee idol listed among the top five money-making Western stars every year between 1936-1940. After a hiatus, he returned to the screen in 1947 and played major character roles again for John Ford in *Fort Apache, She Wore a Yellow Ribbon*, and other Westerns. By 1951 his film career was in decline again, so pairing him with the Stooges was a means of combining two different box-office attractions. Apparently United Artists planned two more features (*Tucson Joe*; *Gasoline Alley*), and in the final scene of *Gold Raiders* O'Brien and the Stooges promise the folks of Red Mesa that they "will all be back." No sequel was ever made, though. In fact, this will be the last Stooge feature film appearance until after their Columbia two-reeler contract was terminated and they finally got the opportunity to star in their own features with 1959's *Have Rocket - Will Travel*.

In *Gold Raiders* O'Brien plays an insurance salesman who cleans up the Western town of Red Mesa to make it safe for miners (and insurance policies). He foils the Taggert Gang's gold-ore robberies, defeating them in the final saloon brawl. The Stooges work in and around the plot but play secondary roles and appear less in the latter third of the film.

As in *Swing Parade of 1946*, the Stooges receive co-star billing and appear throughout much of the film. But unlike *Rockin' In the Rockies*, the Stooges work together as a trio. This was to be expected since Ellwood Ullman, the long-time Stooge writer, co-wrote the script, and Edward Bernds directed. As a result this is one of the few pre-1959 feature films in which the Stooges play the feuding but ultimately helpful trio they portray so successfully in their annual output of short-films. Ullman and Bernds vary the comedy effectively, at times concentrating on intra-Stooge gags (performed while sitting on the wagon bench, unloading their wares, loading the gold, and figuring out how George punches), at times providing a tough guy foil (peddling their glasses, and Shemp pretending to be 'Tex,'), and once giving them a helpless victim to abuse (in the medical examination).

VISUAL HUMOR: As in many of their pre-1959 feature films, the Stooges reuse gags from their earlier features: Moe and Larry slap each other, shrug, and then hit Shemp (*Start Cheering*); they surround a helpless victim in a chair (Trove in *Rockin' In the Rockies*); and they drop china dishes (*Swing Parade of 1946*). The 'Tex' routine debuted recently in 1948's *Pardon My Clutch*, but it will be used again in another Western feature, *4 for Texas*. Also as in many of their pre-1959 feature films, they vary gags from their contemporary short-films: cheering George on during the fight (*Fright Night*); holding up 'glasses' to avoid being hit, and Shemp punching himself silly after the fight (*Crime on Their Hands*); selling their wares like conmen, with Shemp pretending to be an elderly customer (*Mummy's Dummies*); Larry trying to challenge Moe's authority but immediately yielding (*Who Done It?*); Moe telling Shemp to put his chin on his fist, his knee to his elbow, then kicking the bottom of his foot (*Hold That Lion*); and Shemp spitting out teeth (*Squareheads of the Round Table*).

Stooge participation in the final battle, unlike in the contemporary Western *Punchy Cowpunchers*, is limited: Moe uses a bottle to knock out first a bad guy and then Shemp sticks out a hat, says "The coast is clear," and gets conked. New gags: Shemp banging his head repeatedly against the back of the wagon; Shemp reading the eye chart even though Taggert's gunman rolled it up; and throwing explosive cigars. In the medical routine, Shemp misuses the headband reflector and the tongue depressor; when they ask the patient to say "Ahh," they sing a triad; the patient, still unconscious, conks his head on the table; in testing his reflexes, the patient twists up his legs (Shemp: "He must-a swallowed a corkscrew!"); and then Larry gets his head caught between the patient's knees. A similar combo of improper patient care, blinding glasses, and Western setting appears in *The Tooth Will Out*.

VERBAL HUMOR: Elwood Ullman's and William Lively's dialogue is superior to that of most other pre-1959 Stooge features. It portrays the Stooges as fast-talking conmen (Larry: "If you can't go shoppin' in the big city, we're gonna bring the big city to you!"; Moe: "Anybody can wear these glasses no matter what your vision: 40/30, 30/20, or 23/Skidoo!"), ignoramuses (Larry: "Firecrackers?" Moe: "That's shootin', you ignoramus!; George: "Do you know what insurance is?" Larry: "Greatest stuff in the world!" Shemp: "Ha! Ha!...What's insurance?"; George: "No bandits would ever expect three irresponsible peddlers." Moe: "You hear that? We're 'irresponsible'! He likes us!"; Larry: "They guarantee delivery to the smeller." Moe: "You mean 'the smelter'!" Larry: "Ain't you ever smelt one?"), and cowards (Moe: "The men out here are rough and tough and they love battles." Larry: "Well I'm weak and soft and I love the Bronx!"; and Larry: "There must be some mistake." Moe: "And we made it: stayin' out West!"), and provides for insults (Shemp: "He's got horse sense!" Larry: "Too bad you ain't a horse." Moe: "Whadya wanna insult the horse for?") and false bravado (Laura: "Let's let bygones be bygones, shall we, gentlemen?" Larry: "'Gentlemen'! That's us!").

The dialogue also sets up and accompanies slapstick (Moe: "Let's get some goods in the saloon and sell it or we don't eat tonight." Larry: "Hey, we didn't eat last night!" Moe: "Last night was yesterday." Shemp: "Every day is 'yesterday' with this guy, except February which has 28." Moe: "Here's 29!" [SLAP] Shemp: "Lucky it didn't have 30; he'd-a killed me on 30"; [Shemp lets an exploding cigar go off in his hand] Moe: "You wanna give away our position?!"; and Larry: "We still have this tin plate left." Moe [to Shemp]: "Look what you're doin' to his hat!" Larry removes his hat to look, so Moe slams the tin plate over his head).Twice the dialogue/slapstick combination reflects the Stooges trying to disguise O'Brien's decoy plan (Shemp: "That gold's sure heavy! [KICK] That *gravel's* sure heavy!" [SLAP]; and Shemp: "You mean that old— [POUND] that wonderful Doc Mason". Shemp's other throw-away lines: [about the guitar] "You got it out of tune!"; [wearing glasses and bumping into a cowboy] "Pardon me, madam!"; and [about the stone-faced cowboy] "Who let you out without a muzzle?". Stooge firsts: Larry: "Paganini." Moe: "'Paganini'? That's 'page nine'!"; Moe's "Abandon ship!". The Stooges sing in triadic harmony about 'Mary' and 'Just Plain Jane' and during the medical examination. Variations: Larry & Shemp: "Right! Right!" Moe: "Wait a minute! Everything all right?" Larry & Shemp: "Right!" (*Dancing Lady*); "23/Skidoo!" (*Rockin' in the Rockies*) - these two from feature films; Shemp: "I resemble that remark!" (*Three Little Twirps*); Moe: "Fire at will!" Larry: "Which one is 'Will'?" (*Back to the Woods*); and "I'm the roughest, toughest, rooten-est, shooten-est hombre!" (*Punchy Cowpunchers*).

OTHER NOTES: Made in late December, 1950, the film was originally scheduled for a 12-day shoot, but producer Glasser's financial difficulties reduced the schedule to just five days; the film cost merely $50,000. Director Bernds: "I'm afraid the picture shows it." It was released in Los Angeles in June 1952, just as Bernds left Columbia; local reviews were so poor, Bernds had trouble securing new employment. It was released overseas as *The Three Stooges Go West*. The Stooges were Western peddlers in *Phony Express* (1943). Both the Sheriff and the Stooges blame themselves for staying in the West. Larry's "I love the Bronx" is ironic: the Howards were from Brooklyn; Larry from Philadelphia.

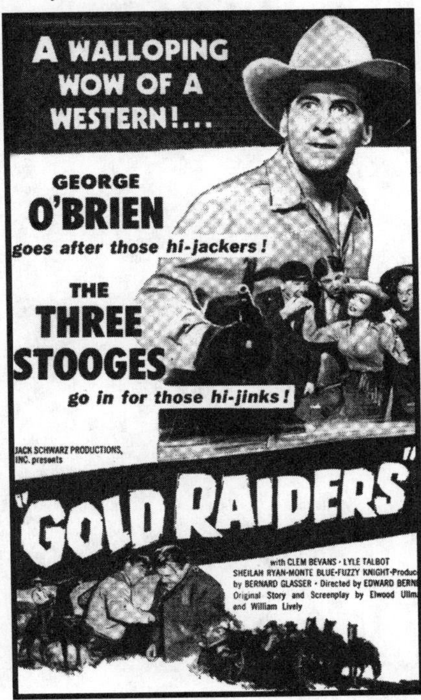

1948

Shivering Sherlocks • *Pardon My Clutch* • *Squareheads of the Round Table*

Fiddlers Three • *The Hot Scots* • *Heavenly Daze*

I'm a Monkey's Uncle • *Mummy's Dummies* • *Crime on Their Hands*

#104 - SHIVERING SHERLOCKS

Studio: Columbia

Released: January 8, 1948

Running Time: 17"17'"

Credited Production Crew:

Produced by:	Hugh McCollum
Directed by	Del Lord
Story & Screenplay by	Del Lord & Elwood Ullman
Director of Photography:	Allen Siegler
Film Editor:	Henry DeMond
Art Director:	Charles Clague

Credited Cast:

Shemp Howard	
Larry Fine	
Moe Howard	
Christine McIntyre	Gladys Harmon
Vernon Dent	Captain Mullins
Kenneth MacDonald	Lefty Loomis
Frank Lackteen	Red Watkins
Duke York	Angel

Uncredited Cast:

Stanley Blystone	short-ribs customer
Cy Schindell	policeman

PERSPECTIVE: Del Lord had not directed a Stooge film since *Booby Dupes* (1945), and for the first time in three films he and Elwood Ullman free the Stooges from the confines of the tailor shop (*Sing a Song of Six Pants*) and drug store (*All Gummed Up*) and take them from a garbage can to a police station to a cafe to a haunted mansion for a climactic multi-room chase. The Stooges always produce good energies in the spooky corridors of a large building, and this is the first time Shemp, who performed well in the crate-and-barrel chases of *Fright Night, Out West*, and *Hold That Lion*, is put into a 'scare comedy.' Lord and Ullman knew their craft here. They had been involved with *We Want Our Mummy* and *A Gem of a Jam* and had co-written *Idle Roomers*, all Stooge prototypes of the genre, and now Shemp is part of the mix. Some moments of surprise in these scare comedies elevate multi-room corridor chases ("Pardon me...Nyaggh!"; "Did you see that big guy outside? Whoah!") to high comic art. In the process the Stooges continue to rid the land of crooks. Constituted with Curly, the Stooges often won by accident; with Shemp they seem to do it with clearer intentions in the spirit of late-1940s crime dramas. Breaking out and going to different locales in *Shivering Sherlocks*, the Stooges exploit their comic skills in taking a lie detector test, cooking, painting, eating, running, hiding, being scared by a beast-man, scaring each other ("That guy out in the hall looked like Shemp!"), and ultimately snatching victory from Angel's beastly jaws of defeat.

In a spatial sense, the Stooges expand as the film unfolds. They begin in the most confining container they have ever been in - a single garbage can. Their initial attempt at extreme confinement was the classic pit sequence in *Cash and Carry*, and it was revived in the telephone booth sequence three films ago in *Brideless Groom*. That scene also contained a foot gag and a biting gag, but it involved only Moe and Shemp. Now all three are in the tiny, 10-cylindrical foot volume, and it is hard for us (and them) to tell whose foot is whose. Out of the garbage can, they are held within a five-foot radius at the police station, with two of them confined to 'the hot seat' and the lie detector. From there they are given three areas of the Elite Cafe in which to roam, and they even intentionally spread out at Moe's request so Larry and Shemp cannot get at the crackers fast disappearing from his soup .

By the time they reach Glady's property/Lefty's hideaway, they can spread around the outside of the house, run through its interior halls, separate, reassemble, scare each other, and run from and towards Angel as well as towards and from the two crooks. Ironically the conclusion of the film brings more confinement, but this time it is Angel and the two crooks who are confined in barrels and then taken by the police for incarceration. The Stooges are hit with a barrel but not confined within it. Even the powdery flour flies from Larry's unrestrained hair into the air without any bounds. Victorious over the crooks and released from suspicion, the police station, and the garbage can, the Stooges have solved a major crime 1940s style.

VISUAL HUMOR: The slapstick is elaborate, with several two-handed slaps, two-handed pounds, two-handed bonks, Moe slapping Shemp's own hands into his face (like the cream puff in *Fright Night*), Larry coming *out* the front door to give Moe a crowbar to get *in* ("Can you use it? Moe: "And how!" [CLANG]), and the cafe customer throwing the plate at Larry. Most of these events reinforce Moe's position as boss, as does his slapping Larry and Shemp when they discover that Moe had signed a large number of cafe checks. Similarly, when Moe sends Larry behind the counter and Shemp into the kitchen, he adds: "If it's absolutely necessary, I'll go to work, too." Moe is periodically characterized as the lazy boss. One of the physical gems of the film is Shemp's reaction to seeing that the statue (of "Washington") has walked away. He uses many different motions in rapid succession one after the other. In this sense he moves his body as much as Curly used to move his face. Speaking of Curly, just as Shemp felt compelled to say

"Hhmm!" and "Rruff!" at the ironing board in *Sing a Song of Six Pants*, Moe here makes a number of Curly-esque sounds and gestures when frustrated by the live clam soup. Curly did the live-crustacean-in-the-soup routine in *Dutiful but Dumb*, but Moe adds additional slapstick by blaming Shemp and Larry. (Also, this 'clam' is a mussel!). Many of the room-and-corridor 'spook' routines derive from *Idle Roomers*, which also included a beast-man. Other variations: the chicken soup, the hopping stove, and the fried egg mask (*Playing the Ponies*); the paint/coffee mix up (*Tassels in the Air*); Shemp thinking his head is gone (*Brideless Groom*); and squirting ink into someone's face (*Healthy, Wealthy and Dumb*). The Stooges are brave when they think the wooden chair in the police station is the electric chair (Larry: "The hot seat!" Moe: "Be brave kid: it'll be over in a minute." Shemp: "And we'll see that you get a nice sendoff" [three-pattern]), but when the detective tells them it is a lie detector, they panic and try to pull away.

VERBAL HUMOR: Elwood Ullman wrote a number of effective exchanges, particularly for the police station sequence, some supporting visual gags (Moe: "What's that on the stool?" Shemp: "Must be a stool pigeon!"; Mullins: "Have you got any visible means of support?" Larry: "I got suspenders!") and some changing the direction of the scene (Captain: "Now then, I have a couple of questions I want to ask you." Moe: "And so have I! [to Shemp] Did you or did you not take that quarter out of my shoe last night?"; Mullins: "What were you doing at eleven o'clock last night?" Shemp: "I don't know...What were *you* doing at eleven o'clock?" Captain: "Uh, I was at a lodge meeting."[WOOB-WOOB]). It is important to open with some mood-elevation to set the proper comic climate, and these jokes do just that. Vernon Dent's lie brings the scene to a fine close.

Ullman features Stooge ignorance thrice: (Moe: "You had a hallucination." Shemp: "No I had a hunk of pipe!"; Moe: "Now you're showin' intelligence." Larry: "Am I?"; and when, grabbed by Angel, Larry tries to say something to Moe but is completely inarticulate. Ullman's one-liners include insults (Moe: "If the customers can stand to eat your cookin' so could you!") and ironies (Shemp:("It *is* paint!...ee-bee-bee...*This* is better"). Moe turns a plot-related noun into a verb (Shemp: "This joint gives me the creeps." Moe: "Well start creepin'; we gotta find Gladys"). The "Just garbage!" gag in the garbage can derives from the train sequence in *Grips, Grunts and Groans* ("Just us horses").

Reference: Shemp's conclusion about the statue ("Oh it must be Washington. He slept everywhere.") refers to the title of the recent Kaufman & Hart play, 'George Washington Slept Here' (1940), made into a Warner Brothers film starring Jack Benny in 1942, and featuring, like *Shivering Sherlocks*, a deserted country house.

OTHER NOTES: Bill O'Connor was the assistant director. Born in Asia Minor (Turkey), Frank Lackteen (Red Watkins) played ethnic types in feature films, e.g. *The Charge of the Light Brigade* (1936). The film has plot similarities with *Taxi Spooks* (1928), directed by Del Lord and co-written by Del Lord and Ewart Adamson. *Shivering Sherlocks* was the last of 39 Stooge films directed by Lord, who since *Pop Goes the Easel* had directed such classics as *Uncivil Warriors, Hoi Polloi, Three Little Beers, Cash and Carry, A Plumbing We Will Go, How High is Up?*, and *No Census, No Feeling*. The remaining two decades of his professional career were unremarkable. The *Scrapbook* reports that the film was shot at the Columbia ranch. *Shivering Sherlocks* will be refurbished as *Of Cash and Hash* (1955).

Del Lord returned from a three-year hiatus to direct his last Stooge film, *Shivering Sherlocks*, the first release of 1948. The flour-covered Stooges break out of the box- comedy format with a vengeance, though this comic study in spatial arrangements begins and ends with barrel confinements.

#105 - PARDON MY CLUTCH

Studio: Columbia

Released: February 26, 1948

Running Time: 15"16"'

Credited Production Crew:

Produced by:	Hugh McCollum
Directed by:	Edward Bernds
Story & Screen Play by:	Clyde Bruckman
Director of Photography:	Allen Siegler
Film Editor:	Henry DeMond
Art Director:	Charles Clague

Credited Cast:

Shemp Howard	
Larry Fine	
Moe Howard	
Matt McHugh	Claude Finkle

Uncredited Cast:

Emils Sitka	lunatic professor
George Lloyd	gas station attendant
Alyn Lockwood	Petunia (Shemp's wife)
Doria Revier	Marigold (Larry's wife)
Wanda Perry	Narcissus (Moe's wife)
Stanley Blystone	Dippy, the attendant

PERSPECTIVE: This uncharacteristic diversion unfolds in a string of loosely connected situational gag-scenarios which, like the Stooges R&R trip, never quite reach their goal, illustrating that Stooge comedy thrives on tension-driving plots rather than Laurel & Hardy-like gag situations. The prototype for the trip-that-never-gets-underway was in fact Laurel & Hardy's *Perfect Day* (1929), which also contained the model for the tire-changing sequence. This alone creates an interesting situation, for although by nature the Stooge *trio* usually creates comedy very unlike that of the Laurel & Hardy *duo*, here Moe leaves to get the spare tire while Shemp and Larry struggle with each other in a slapstick duo. But *Pardon My Clutch* derives from a variety of sources: a sick Stooge needing medical attention and peaceful recuperation in the country was the premise of *Idiots Deluxe*; the knee reflex test we saw recently (with Curly) in *Half-Wits Holiday* and previously in *Three Sappy People*; and the tooth extraction is a much abbreviated version of *I Can Hardly Wait*, but now with a fourth Stooge. Also, models for a madman duping the Stooges were the recent *Rhythm and Weep* and the earlier *Roast Beef and Movies*, the 1934 MGM film Curly made with two other Stooge-types. Nonetheless, despite an aimless plot, each of the sequences has its pleasantries, and the tent sequence is remarkable as one of Stoogedom's most elaborate setups.

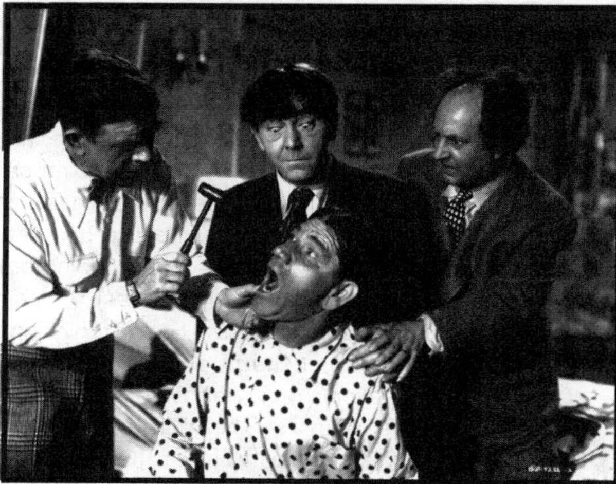

As in several 1947 releases where the comedy is brought into where the Stooges work, here we see a modified type of 'box comedy' which demands that the characters who accompany or visit the Stooges carry much of the comedic burden. The wives are terrific - classic Stooge women who boss the Stooges around and slug them at will (*Brideless Grooms*). Of the outside characters who come in, Matt McHugh (Claude) is the first, and there are moments when he seems to reprise the Ted Healy role by taking charge, yelling at the Stooges, and cheating them. The second is the gas station attendant, whom they actually visit briefly; his only purpose is to allow each Stooge to challenge him, and he obliges by hitting them with his mallet and ultimately getting 'tired' himself. This brings us to the mad professor, who like an eccentric angel appears to save the Stooges from the terrible situation Claude has created for them. As always, with that quavering, insecure voice, the sunken, angular face that emits it, and the seemingly frail body that supports it, Emil Sitka gives the role the sprite insanity it requires.

The insertion of these three fourth-Stooge types serves the purpose of adding comedic roles but also diminishes the comic roles for the Stooges, rendering them relatively passive. There are moments in the bedroom when Moe and Larry stand idly by while the comedy is left entirely in the hands of McHugh - never a headliner - and Shemp. But then Moe takes over the tooth extraction, and the tent scene uses all six Mr. and Mrs. Stooges beautifully. By the end of the film the Stooges have won out over Claude, the professor, and the gas station attendant and taken possession of a car, and Moe has taken control of Larry and Shemp. Now, they can go fishing, but they have run out of time.

VISUAL HUMOR: Clever directing spreads the tent-crashing sequence to four different spots in the room. Larry's wife opens the door, the collapsing tent takes Moe's wife with it, the lamp falls on Moe's head, and the vase crashes onto Shemp. Then Larry's wife slams the door on Larry's nose, Shemp tries to comfort his wife, but she slaps him. Moe intercedes with: "He's my brother!" Shemp's wife: "Yeah, well he's my husband!" She slaps Moe. Moe's wife joins in, saying "Wait a minute, he's my husband!" and slaps Moe. Larry runs in the middle and is promptly slapped by both wives. This is a fine sextet of slapstick. Just before the collapse, there is another fine exchange with Moe ramming the tent beam into Larry's face and vice versa. Because of the added characters, there is less inter-Stooge slapstick than in the previous film.

Stooge firsts: the 'Tell him, Tex' routine - to be used as late as in *4 For Texas* (1963) - although Moe shoving Shemp towards a fight dates back to Ted Healy in *Beer and Pretzels*; the rope catching Larry by the throat; and pulling the window shade down onto Claude's head. Moe walks into the door jamb, as was Curly's wont. Other variations: klinking each tooth until the bad one makes a different sound (*All the World's a Stooge*); Larry's ringing the service station attendant with a tire (the barrels in *Shivering Sherlocks*); Shemp and Larry tossing their stuff beyond the car onto Moe (*Hoi Polloi*); Shemp's feet on the pillow and his head at the bottom of the bed (*Movie Maniacs*); and Shemp thinking the doorknob is his tooth (*I Can Hardly Wait*).

VERBAL HUMOR: Clyde Bruckman created several new exchanges playing on Stooge ignorance (Larry: "You know fish is great brain food." Moe: "You know, you should fish for a whale!"; and Claude: "A rash...can be caused by excessive use of the gray matter of the brain." Moe: "It must be somethin' else!"; and Shemp's "All trimmed with chrumumbelium"), the 'Columbus' (Larry: "What is it?" Claude: "A Columbus." Shemp: "Never mind who you bought it from, what make is that?" Moe: "I thought he came over in a boat."), drinking (Moe: "Get some water!" Shemp: "No, champagne!"; and Shemp: "All right fellas, let's get loaded." Larry: "Wait a minute, you know I don't drink."). He also penned a one-line deception (Claude: "Ah ha!...["What is it?"]...Nothin'"), a one-line insult (Larry to his wife: "Next time you come in, knock first, and then don't come in!"), and a throw-away line (Moe: "We must-a left the root in there!").

Taking the phrase "Take the pill and skip an hour" too literally is used in W. C. Fields' *The Bank Dick* (1940). Epithets: "nitwit," "imbecile," and "pickle-puss". Waking Shemp to take the second pill so he can sleep is a physical variation of "Wake up and go to sleep". Other variations: Moe: "Remind me to murder you later!" Larry: "I'll make a note of it." (*Cash and Carry*); Shemp saying "I feel like a million bucks" but swooning (*Fright Night*); "Ticonderoga, if thou canst say 'Ticonderoga'" (*Back to the Woods*); Moe: "You gotta use your brain!" (*Hold That Lion*); the impromptu Hollywood love scene (*Movie Maniacs*); Moe: "Raise that pole! Lift that tent!" (*Rockin' Thru the Rockies*); and Moe: "Give him a hand." Shemp: "Which one?" (*Punch Drunks*).

OTHER NOTES: The introductory music has been re-recorded, most noticeably rewriting the final solo flute. This new arrangement will be used, with minor variations and exceptions, for the for the rest of the Shemp films. Matt McHugh was the brother of well-known Warner Brothers' actor Frank McHugh. Moe had worked with them in his youth when he was traveling around as a dramatic, sometimes even Shakespearean, actor. Their sister, Kitty, also appeared in Stooge films.This film will be refurbished in 1955 as *Wham-Bam-Slam!*

During the 1947 production season, Ed Bernds noticed, while strolling across the backlot, a castle built for Columbia's 1946 feature *The Bandit of Sherwood Forest*. Inspired, he obtained permission to write several scripts to shoot in the castle. The next three films, *Squareheads of the Round Table*, *Fiddlers Three*, and *The Hot Scots*, are the result - not to mention the three 1954 refurbished versions, *Knutzy Knights*, *Musty Musketeers*, and *Scotched in Scotland*. Sets were rarely of paramount importance in Stooge comedies because the focus was on the trio itself. But they always fill a room with energy, and here they have a whole castle in which to romp.

#106 - SQUAREHEADS OF THE ROUND TABLE

Studio: Columbia

Released: March 4, 1948

Running Time: 18"06'"

Credited Production Crew:

Produced by:	Hugh McCollum
Written & Directed by:	Edward Bernds
Director of Photography:	Allen Siegler
Film Editor:	Henry DeMond
Art Director:	Harold MacArthur

Credited Cast:

Shemp Howard	
Larry Fine	
Moe Howard	
Christine McIntyre	Elaine
Phil Van Zandt	Black Prince
Jacques O'Mahoney	Cedric
Vernon Dent	king

Uncredited Cast:

Robert Stevens	guard
Joe Palma	guard
Harold Brauer	Sir Satchell
Douglas Coppin	soldier
Joe Garcia	executioner; trumpeter

PERSPECTIVE: Using the spacious, intricately designed castle built for Columbia's 1946 feature *The Bandit of Sherwood Forest*, first-time Stooge art director Harold MacArthur gives *Squareheads of the Round Table* a rich visual texture for fine triadic singing, armored dancing, two tool-abuse scenes, a carefully interwoven multi-door chase sequence, brisk slapstick, and a romance that fills the air between ground and balcony. Writer/director Edward Bernds fleshes out this physical and visual expanse with a compelling, if inconsistent, save-the-damsel script glorying in the most memorable pseudo-operatic song lyrics ("Oh Elaine, Elaine come out, babe") in any Stooge film, self-conscious anachronisms (Moe: "Turn on the radio." Larry: "This is ancient times." Moe: "This is an ancient radio!"), and a fusillade of puns and insults. There are also several bright moments which seem to be carried by Stooge ad-libbing. The result is a Stooge classic - perhaps the best historical short film the Stooges ever produced and certainly one of the most beloved.

The film maintains such balance between all these elements that the viewer never knows what to expect next - slapstick, romance, a verbal gag, plot development, tools, or music. Juxtaposing so many different types of fun keeps the viewer in gleeful anticipation of a very high Stooge energy level, and the scenes which require intense action, the multi-door chase scene in particular, step up the pace even further. In several instances either the song lyrics or the slapstick advance the plot, as in Elaine's [Christine McIntyre] tuneful "Flee, but flee, the Black Prince is looking iiiiiinnnn / IIIIIII will rai-aise the shade, the lovely shade, when the coast is clear," and when Moe whacks Shemp on the head with the heavy, rattling bread (Shemp: "The princess should-a used more yeast in it!"), making the others realize it contains the tools they need to escape.

The plot revolves around the characterization of the Stooges as troubadours. Shemp begins by saying they are on their way to entertain King Arthur, but he digresses by explaining how their armor protects them from fruit thrown by their "critics." As in *A Pain in the Pullman, Rhythm and Weep*, and *Gents Without Cents*, they play the role of lousy musicians, but it never keeps them from singing, and this time they have their armor to protect them. So they sing for the guards, they sing for Cedric and Elaine and pledge themselves to aiding them against the Black Prince. Then they dance for the king to give Elaine time to free Cedric, and they finish, appropriately, as if in some sort of bad-music ring composition, with some thrown fruit. Ironically, it is ultimately the Stooges who get to be the critics: they throw fruit not at poor musicians like themselves but at court trumpeters whose music would signal the death of Cedric and/or the king. The plot is not flawless - we never learn why Cedric is to be killed before the king, or what "proof" Elaine has - but *Squareheads of the Round Table* is one of the high water marks of Stooge costume comedy.

VISUAL HUMOR: A classic corridor chase: fast-motioned, relentless and varied, it relies on a T-shaped hallway leading into four rooms. In the first sixteen seconds the guards chase the Stooges in seven different combinations. The film offers a steady stream of crisp slapstick, prop gags, and stunts: Moe slapping Shemp in the helmet, the guard [Robert Stevens] triple slapping the Stooges in rhythm, Shemp's accordion cheek punching and Larry's bow in Moe's mouth, Larry's rock hitting the king in the head, Shemp hiding underneath and flipping the bed over (a Stooge first), and the king falling off the trellis. Uncharacteristic but effective, six gags are repeated early and late in the film: first Cedric and then, later Elaine crunch the Stooges' hands; twice two guards hit each other over the head; twice Stooge clang each other on backswings; twice the Stooges stick their heads out around a corner in vertical succession; twice they put their hands together to swear; and twice Moe ("Hold this!") tells Shemp to remove his helmet so he can slap him. The latter is just one of several armor-related jokes: Moe raises Larry's visor to give him a nose bonk, and there are various armor antics in the 'Swannee River' soft shoe dance. The jail break/tool scene progresses from Larry hitting Moe in the head with his small hammer, Moe hitting Shemp's face on a backswing, Moe chiseling Shemp's teeth, and Moe hitting Shemp's head and Larry's hand with the sledge hammer. The scene ends with an ad lib; in fact, you can see Moe smiling as Shemp prepares to hammer a nail into his head. In the first scene of the film Moe bends Shemp over an anvil, rears back with a sledge hammer, hits Larry in the face with the backswing, and then hits Shemp in the head. Throwing fruit into the trumpets resembles the fruit-throwing plot device in *Micro-Phonies*. The bedroom scene with the king and Shemp recalls the bedroom sequence with Larry and the jealous husband in *What's the Matador?*. Other variations: Shemp spitting out teeth (*Three Loan Wolves*); lining up a hammer stroke but hitting someone with the backswing (*3 Dumb Clucks*); Moe lining up Shemp's head on the chisel (*Three Little Pirates*); and two guards swinging at the Stooges but hitting each other on the head (*Restless Knights*).

VERBAL HUMOR: Bernds featured anachronistic jokes about armor (Moe: "How'd you get in that thing on?" Shemp: "I was always poppin' rivets so I had my tailor spot weld me!"; Shemp: "I found some shin guards"; Radio: "Are you short of money? Are you still wearing last year's rusty old armor? Then see the Scowling Scotsman today!") and decapitation (Shemp: "It's sharp medicine, but it's a sure cure for all diseases." Moe: "I'll take penicillin!"; and Shemp: "Maybe they give him the big haircut already!"), puns (Guard: "The king commands your presence!" Shemp: "We ain't got any presents. The stores were all closed!"; Moe: "Three restless knights." Shemp: "Our days ain't too hot either!"; King: "My daughter marry a Smith?" Shemp: "Millions of women marry Smiths every year!"), insults (Moe: "The way we sing, sometimes they throw rocks!" Guard: "I can believe that"; Shemp: "Come out on your front porch." Moe: "Balcony you knot-head! Ain't you got no romance?"), ironic statements (Black Prince: "You'll forget all about love when I marry you"; Larry: "There's a draft in here." Shemp: "No wonder! The door is open!"), internal rhyme (Moe's "Dance, you dunce" and "We're gonna make that Black Prince feel mighty blue!"), silly song lyrics ("Sooo weee stuck our little tootsies in the wa-ter / And we ducked under the waves we did - Ha! Ha!"), scene-ending throw-aways (Shemp: "And I gotta write a letter." Larry: "I'll never be able to write under water" [a Stooge first]), and a record seven three-patterns (1) Larry: "I'd hate to be in his shoes!" Shemp: "I'd hate to be in his collar!" Moe: "I'd hate to be him!"; 2) Larry: "What does he want Cedric's head for? Ain't he got one of his own?" Shemp: "Ya dope: two heads are better than one!" Moe: "He's going to have a haircut down to here!"; 3) Moe: "We can get into the palace, see?" Larry & Shemp: "See?" Moe: "See?"; 4) Larry: "She's a good lookin' kid." Shemp: "Must take after her mother—" Moe: "—on her father's side!"; 5) Larry: "Charmed!" Shemp: "Pleasure!" Moe: "Indeed!"; 6) Moe: "You know that Black Prince character, the guy that tried to kill our pal Cedric?" Larry & Shemp: "Yes!" Moe: "Well he's gonna kill the king." Larry & Shemp: "No!" Moe: "Yes"; 7) and Moe: "I gotta get a cheap lawyer!" Shemp: "And I just bought two new hats!" Larry: "I can't die! I haven't seen *The Jolson Story*!").

References: *The Jolson Story*, a Columbia film, was released in 1946. The melody of 'Oh Elaine' is, like the 'Sextet from Lucy' in *Micro-Phonies*, from Gaetano Donizetti's opera, *Lucia di Lammermoor*. Moe's "I'll take penicillin!" is interesting since penicillin use had just become common in the early 1940s. Moe's "Jiggers!" was 1940s slang for "Wait! Someone's coming." The introductory 'In Days of Old When Knights Were Bold...' was a standard, limerick-like ditty that had various endings. From *Fright Night* come Shemp's characterization as cowardly and ugly (Larry: "They must have guards all over the place." Shemp: "Well then let's go home!...[Moe, Larry, and Cedric look at Shemp to climb the trellis]...Wait a minute, fellas...I get dizzy!...How do I know the babe won't scream her head off when she sees me?"), Larry's resurrection (Moe: "If we could only bring him back, I'd never hit him again." Larry [coming out from hiding]: "No kiddin'?" [SLAP]), and Shemp's "Look what he did to my feather!" ("busted a perfectly good cream puff"). Other variations: Moe: "One for all!" Shemp: "And every man for himself!" (*Restless Knights*); Shemp: "Yeah, singin', dancin'..." (*Plane Nuts*); Moe: "I gotta get a cheap lawyer!" (*Monkey Businessmen*); Moe: "This is a fine how-do-you-do!" Shemp: "How do you do?!" (*Start Cheering*); Shemp: "Must take after her mother—" Moe: "—on her father's side." (*Wee Wee Monsieur*); and Moe: "Always clownin' around!" (*Pop Goes the Easel*).

OTHER NOTES: The title screen is in Gothic script; the introductory music reverts to the 'sliding stings' version of 'Three Blind Mice'; and there is an introductory fanfare after the credits. This is the first of almost a dozen Stooge roles for Philip Van Zandt. Previously the Dutch actor played in features, including *Citizen Kane* (1940). Van Zandt is the fourth Stooge actor to have played in Welles' landmark film; the others are Sonny Bupp (*Cash and Carry*), Dorothy Comingore (*Oily to Bed, Oily to Rise*), and Gino Corrado (*Micro-Phonies*). Charles Clague had been the art director for the previous nineteen films (since *If a Body Meets a Body*). *The Bandit of Sherwood Forest* was a Robin Hood adventure, starring Cornel Wilde. When a set from a Columbia feature was available, Jules White would send a writer to a set to create a story and basic gag scenarios and submit them to White or McCollum; if approved, the writer developed the gags, although their final form was the director's responsibility. The Stooges were involved in the process at several points, particularly in finalizing the gags. This film will be refurbished as *Knutzy Knights* (1954).

#107 - FIDDLERS THREE

Stuio: Columbia

Released: May 6, 1948

Running Time: 17"06'"

Credited Production Crew:

Produced & Directed by:	Jules White
Story & Screenplay by:	Felix Adler
Director of Photography:	Allen Siegler
Film Editor:	Edwin Bryant
Art Director:	Charles Clague

Credited Cast:

Shemp Howard	
Larry Fine	
Moe Howard	
Vernon Dent	King Cole
Virginia Hunter	Princess Alicia
Phil Van Zandt	Mergatroyd the Magician

Uncredited Cast:

Sherry O'Neill	woman-in-the-box
Cy Schindell	guard
Joe Palma	guard
Al Thompson	cup bearer

PERSPECTIVE: The second of two historical films set in the European castle originally built for Columbia's *Bandits of Sherwood Forest* (1946), *Fiddlers Three* written by Felix Adler and directed by Jules White makes for an interesting comparison with *Squareheads of the Round Table* written and directed by Edward Bernds. Each film has its own sub-genre - *Squareheads* being a save-the-damsel musical, *Fiddlers Three* a save-the-damsel nursery rhyme.

From the beginning, *Fiddlers Three* looks like a Stoogified nursery rhyme rather than a historical adventure like *Squareheads of the Round Table*. It begins with the Stooges singing to a nursery rhyme character, Old King Cole [Vernon Dent], and this develops into a unique sequence in which the viewer hears the Stooges play and sing three nursery rhymes - Jack Be Nimble, Little Miss Muffet, and Simple Simon - while seeing the Stooges act them out. The sequence looks almost like mini-videos of nursery rhymes, much simpler than the elaborate production numbers in MGM's *Nertsery Rhymes*. The theme continues when the Stooges go to the blacksmith's shop where they read that he has "gone to rest under the spreading chestnut tree," a quote from Henry Wadsworth Longfellow's 'The Village Blacksmith.' This poem may not be a nursery rhyme, but it is part of the same literary reference pool. Yet if this poem is only tangentially a nursery rhyme, the entire horse-shoeing sequence is only tangentially related to the main plot. Nonetheless, with one kick of the horse the Stooges are right back in the hunt for the princess. Larry suggests they scour the kingdom on horseback, but no need - after "shoeing Sue," Sue herself kicks them over the railing and down to the very place where the princess is being held.

The woman-from-the-box changes the direction of everybody and everything, and at first glance she seems to disturb the whole nursery rhyme scenario, too. As the guards capture the Stooges, the woman-from-the-box leads the guards astray, leaving the Stooges to recover the princess and expose the evil magician. Then, just as the Stooges capture the magician, the woman-from-the-box leads *them* astray as well. Since the 1950s there has been a tendency to think of the Stooge films as made for children, but they were not, not until well into the 1950s. Drinking, gambling, and womanizing were a regular part of their comic repertoire. In the latter day world of political correctness and gender equality, the woman-from-the-box scenes may shock or embarrass the modern viewer as much as the blown-up Japanese in *The Yoke's on Me*. But to audiences of 1948, wolf-whistling men following the woman-from-the-box was a funny anachronism and normal, albeit silly, male behavior. This was the era in which Betty Grable's legs were insured for $1,000,000. Looking at the film in the context of 1948, the woman-from-the-box and her long legs lead the guards, the magician, the king, and even the Stooges out of the court, up the steps, and into a comical, adult, human version of the Pied Piper of Hamlin, one more nursery rhyme to bring this Stooge fable to a close.

Fiddlers Three (1948) is a Stooge fairy-tale, with King Cole as its monarch, 'Will Edge' (i.e. Village) as its blacksmith, and several extraordinary 'videos' like this one for 'Jack Be Nimble.' In an appropriately harmonious conclusion, the Stooges and everyone else follow a very leggy 'Pied Piper.'

VISUAL HUMOR: Of the three nursery rhyme 'videos,' the second ends in total surprise with Larry screaming à la Fay Wray and being pulled up out of the camera frame; the crown flying off the king's head is a faint echo of this. The fist game ("See this?") is played with a hammer that ends up on Shemp's head. The initial song ending with a rhythmic "Ha! Ha! Ha! Ha!" followed by BONK, BONK resembles the rhythmic triple slap by the guard in the previous film, *Squareheads of the Round Table*; similarly, suddenly breaking out from the magician's box resembles Shemp flipping the king's bed over. Letting the viewer see the Stooges inside the magician's box derives from the bayonet bag sequence in *Boobs in Arms* but with very clever variations: the saw on Larry's head and butt, swinging the saw blade back and forth, the sword bent into a zig-zag, and ripping off the boxer shorts, all with appropriate sound effects, particularly the cymbal crashes for the banging saw. Other variations: the long stretch of laughter (*Boobs in Arms*); the horse's tail, with hammer attached, hitting Moe's face (*Busy Buddies*); water squirting out the holes in Shemp 's chest (*Three Pests in a Mess*); Moe squeezing out water from the "stuck" bellows (*3 Dumb Clucks*); whispering an inaudible plan into the villain's ear (*Yes, We Have No Bonanza*); the Stooges appearing in a magician's box (*A Plumbing

We Will Go*); cooling off a burning rear by sitting in water (*Back to the Woods; How High is Up?*); and the train-step with Larry as caboose going "woo-woo" (*Three Sappy People*), although the latter may also derive from *Road to Rio* (1947) with Bob Hope and Bing Crosby.

VERBAL HUMOR: Unlike *Squareheads of the Round Table*, the script is filled with archaistic speech, e.g. "Nay I have not the heart to beat a dumb shoe," highlighted by adding the suffix '-eth' to as many words as possible: "Shempeth," "Larryeth," "shaketh thy leg," "button-eth up thy lip," "okay-eth," and "scrammeth." Such archaisms highlight the lone three-pattern (Moe: "Shemp-eth, Larry-eth! Spring is just around the corner. We must get the princess back or we cannot be wed." Shemp: "Quite so!" Larry:

Moe: "Our steed is not shod. Sue has not a shoe."
Shemp: "Then we will shoe Sue, for if Sue has no shoe, a shoeing Sue we must do!"

"Quite quite!") and the sibilant-twister about shoeing Sue: They also set up the anachronistic 'FBI': Flan-nigan, Brannigan and Iskevitch'. The 'Beeee-Ohhhh' horn gag is new; it seems to be based on a radio commercial ("Your best friend should tell you.").

References: "Give us the gate" is 1940s slang for "getting rid of" us; "Will Edge, Blacksmith" is a pun on Longfellow's 'The Village Blacksmith'. 'Coleslaw-vania' and 'Prince Gallant III of Rhododendron' are two new entries into the series of Stooge geographical and royal joke-names. When Moe blames Shemp for letting him drive a nail into his foot, Moe's "Thou hath made me shoe the wrong mule" is reminiscent of his treating Curly like a mule in past films. Epithets: "Idiot" and "lame-brain".

Moe's inability to say "strategy" is a variation of the "scrutiny" gag from *Hold That Lion*. As in the previous film, Shemp is again characterized as cowardly (Shemp: "Let me at 'em. I'll tear 'em limb from limb!" Moe: "Well, what's keepin' ya'?" Shemp: "Me!"). Other variations: Shemp: "I got it!...A terrific headache!" (*In the* Sweet Pie and Pie); Moe: "Time marcheth on!" (*Half-Shot Shooters*); the screen title: '...A small kingdom in ye old country where ye men are men and ye women are glad of it' (*Cactus Makes Perfect*); and "Flannigan, Brannigan, and Iskevitch" (mixed ethnic names as in *A Pain in the Pullman*).

OTHER NOTES: As in the previous film, the title is in Gothic letters; the introductory castle-painting screen is accompanied by a bit of a musical background. The final music is played at a very rapid tempo. Besides *Nertsery Rhymes, Disorder in the Court* was another film in which the Stooges used nursery rhymes, several films have been named after nursery rhymes, e.g. the recent *Sing a Song of Six Pants*, and the Stooges' theme song was 'Three Blind Mice.' In the future they will release a Cinderella-UFO hybrid in *Flying Saucer Daffy* in 1958 and then the feature *Snow White and the Three Stooges* (1961). *Fiddlers Three* will be refurbished as *Musty Musketeers* (1954).

#108 - THE HOT SCOTS

Studio: Columbia

Released: July 8, 1948

Running Time: 17"16"'

Credited Production Crew:

Produced by:	Hugh McCollum
Directed by:	Edward Bernds
Story & Screenplay by:	Elwood Ullman
Director of Photography:	Allen Siegler
Film Editor:	Henry DeMond
Art Director:	Harold MacArthur

Credited Cast:

Shemp Howard	
Larry Fine	
Moe Howard	
Herbert Evans	The Earl
Christine McIntyre	Lorna Doone
Charles Knight	Angus
Ted Lorch	McPherson

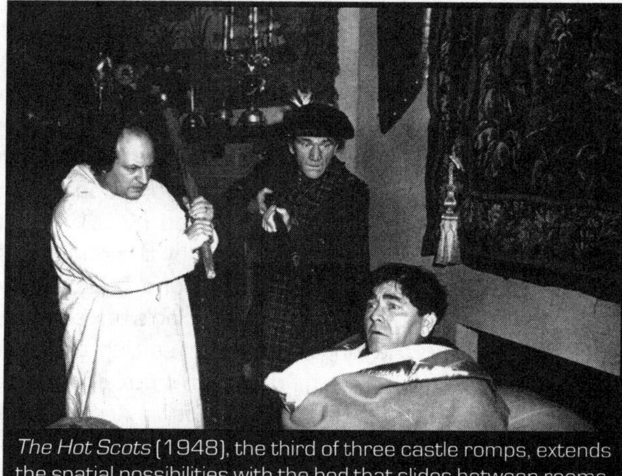

The Hot Scots (1948), the third of three castle romps, extends the spatial possibilities with the bed that slides between rooms.

PERSPECTIVE: For the third consecutive film the Stooges romp through the large-scale castle built for Columbia's 1946 feature *The Bandit of Sherwood Forest*. Set in contemporary Scotland, this particular castle romp does not follow the historical damsel-in-distress formula but the *The Cat and the Canary* (spend-a-night-in-a-spooky-castle—scurrying—room-to-room—frightened-by-spooks—who-turn-out-to-be-crooked-servants) type. At the outset the Stooges, trained by the 'A-1 Correspondence School of Detectin',' take on two sleuthing assignments. In the first scenario they "locate some missing papers" in Scotland Yard's yard, reprising the butt-plinking opening of *So Long, Mr. Chumps*, and this leads to the second - guarding the valuables at Glenheather Castle. As usual the Stooges are neither properly trained for, let alone legitimately assigned to, this task, but what they find in the castle is not so much crooks as spooks...for whom they are equally ill prepared.

The sliding bed, traceable back to the 1914 Keystone Comedy, *Cursed by his Beauty*, is the most notable addition to the Stooge spook-genre 'scare comedy' repertoire. More than just a prop, the sliding bed adds literally a new dimension - the ability to move between rooms without going into the hallway. The hallway in *Spook Louder*, *Idle Roomers*, and other scare comedies was the central vector for Stooge movement, frights, and confusions, but use of the hallway reached a zenith in the recent *Squareheads of the Round Table*. The sliding bed moves the action from the hallway into the adjoining rooms, concentrating movement and even more confusion into a differently configured space. In the first few Shemp films the Stooges flourished when confined to small areas (the garbage can in *Shivering Sherlocks*; the telephone booth in *Brideless Groom*). Now the sliding bed and adjoining rooms allow Shemp to save Larry from being stabbed, but confuse the masked figure with Larry; they allow Shemp and Larry to conk Moe on the head unknowingly; and they allow all three Stooges to pin the spooks' heads to the wall and rip off their disguises. Meanwhile, downstairs the crooks steal valuables by using another entrance to this intra-mural dimension - the portrait of the Arab - and at the conclusion of the film the Stooges and the earl leap out the window, bursting through the castle walls once and for all.

Recalling that the Stooges began the film wearing disguises and speaking in false accents, we might reconsider their suitability for this security assignment. They convince the Scottish earl that they are Scottish, even if Shemp is from below the 'McMason-McDixon' line, and they withstand the terror of the spooks and ultimately unmask them. They may run and yell and hit each other accidentally, and one or more of them might be knocked unconscious or held captive, but the Stooges use their incompetence well. They somehow master crooks who seem intelligent and organized until they run into the unintelligent, totally disorganized Stooges, who not only capture the crooks and turn them over to the authorities but get frightened half to death once they have finished.

VISUAL HUMOR: Further enhancing the multi-dimensional comedy space is the variation between upstairs and downstairs action, with Moe downstairs dealing with the painting while Shemp and Larry are upstairs dealing with the sliding bed. Because both areas are active, the separation of the Stooges works rather well here. Perhaps Jules White was inspired in this by the sheer size of the castle set. Inter-Stooge slapstick punctuates

several of the sequences where all three Stooges are together, with Moe twice grabbing Larry by the hair, and once pulling Shemp by the nose with his hands and once with the hedge clippers (à la scissors in *Slippery Silks*). In one instance the slapstick is enhanced by a clever verbal setup (Moe: "What would you rather have: a shoe full of dollar bills or two socks of five?" Shemp: "I'll take the two socks." Moe: "You got 'em!" [SLUG]). This type of slapstick setup resembles the "Did you ever hear of a V-5...an old sock" from *How High is Up?* and even "Pick two!" from *Pop Goes the Easel*. Fast motion is used thrice, and in the final bed sequence director Bernds, originally a sound engineer, speeds up the sound of the film for comic effect.

A Stooge first: Shemp setting up the bowling ball above the door, although many objects have fallen from above onto people's heads previously. Other variations: the painting-come-to-life (*I'll Never Heil Again*); the Stooges wearing sleuth disguises (*Horses' Collars*); and movements that accompany the three-pattern (Moe: "Get the bag!" (SLAP) Larry to Shemp: "Get the bag!" (SLAP) Shemp to no one: "Get the-" (*Uncivil Warriors*).

VERBAL HUMOR: The previous film added the archaic '-eth' suffix for comic effect, and here writer Elwood Ullman calls for a Scottish brogue. The Scottish exchange with the earl is a classic and surpasses its model in *Pardon My Scotch*. Moe's skill in comic dialects comes across with his convincing "It's a broad, bracht moonlacht nacht tonacht," which is supplemented immediately with two three-patterns (Shemp: "Nachten benacht!" Larry: "And today too!"; Moe: "Meet McLarry, McShemp, and I'm McMoe." Shemp: "Hiya, mac!" Moe: "Hiya, mac!" Larry: "Glad to MacMeet ya'!") and a third three-pattern later (Moe: "Aye." Shemp: "Aye." Larry: "Aye-aye-aye!"). The latter is expanded later with Moe and Lorna (Moe: "How about me and you making with a conversation?" Lorna: "Aye." Moe: "Oh, me too!" Lorna: "You too?" Moe: "Aye.").

Much of the script's Scottish content is pun material (Larry: "And what might your name be, lass?" Secretary: "Perhaps you've heard it— 'tis Lorna Doone." Shemp: "Hi, Lorna, how ya' doin'?"; Earl: "I'm off to a gatherin' of the clan!" Shemp: "Oh, a clan bake, eh?"; Moe: "Through these veins flow some of the finest Scotch in the world"; and the screen title: '...the Bonny Banks of Scotland...But 'tis late and the Bonny Banks are Closed'... Stooge sarcasm to the Earl's 'snifter' of Scotch: Shemp: "When he said 'snifter' he wasn't kiddin'...No thanks, I gotta drive." Earl: "It's 150 years old." Moe: "With a little luck it should get to be 250!". Shemp's "McMason-McDixon line" and "McYowsir" recall the 'Ted Healy and His Southern Gentlemen' routine of twenty years earlier.

The dialogue for the Scotland Yard scenes features double entendre (Inspector: "Your assignment is to locate some missing papers"), disgruntled Stooges (Larry: "This is humiliatin'."), and a sight gag that leads to the Glenheather assignment (Shemp: "If there's any more paper in this yard, I'll eat it." Moe: "Here comes your lunch!"). Moe at one point becomes uncharacteristically aware of his humor ("Clean as a whistle! So let's blow!...not bad!" Larry: "Not good."); this is a Stooge first that will be varied in several subsequent films. Shemp is again characterized as cowardly: "I ought-a take something for my nerves." Moe: "Like what?" Shemp: "A trip home!". References: Lorna Doone, besides being a shortbread cookie, was the title character in R. D. Blackmore's 1869 Scottish romantic novel. The Earl running for the taxi to save a few pennies parodies proverbial Scottish frugality. Shemp's "Yowsir, that's what the man said!" recalls "He said, that's what the man said, he said that" in *The Big Sleep* (1946). Epithet: "dough-heads". Having the Stooges trained at 'A-1 Correspondence School of Detectin'' gives them a kind of bogus diploma, as in *Men in Black* ("We graduated with the highest temperatures in our class"). Other variations: Inspector: "What can I do for you gentlemen?" Moe: "Before we answer that I want to prove we're not gentlemen!" (*Hoi Polloi*); Shemp: "Gimme my lip, will ya'?" ("Your crushin' my eyebrows" in *Fright Night*); Larry: "What are *you* gonna do?" Moe: "Nothin'! What about it?" Larry [yielding]: "Nothin'. I just thought I'd ask." (*Ants in the Pantry*); Moe: "[Highland Fling] - tis a rumba with kilts." (cf. *Time Out for Rhythm*).

OTHER NOTES: The working title was *Scotland Yardbirds*. The title is laid out in plaid-filled lettering; the introductory music reverts to the 'sliding strings' version of 'Three Blind Mice'. The T-shape upstairs hallway of the set is clearly the same used in *Squareheads of the Round Table*. When the Earl knocks the butler over, papers fly into the air, as they did in Scotland Yard. The high-pitched voices in the semi-final scene seem to have been designed to quicken the pace. Stooge films when prepared for television broadcast are often run at faster than normal speed, but this seems to be an aberration on the Columbia master copy. The Scotland Yard footage will be reused in *Hot Ice* (1955); the script will be reworked for *Scotched in Scotland* (1954). Long-time Stooge actor Ted Lorch [McPherson] passed away November 12, 1947, and would have to be worked around in *Scotched in Scotland*. Everyone in the cast is credited.

#109 - HEAVENLY DAZE

Stuio: Columbia

Released: September 2, 1948

Running Time: 16"47'"

Credited Production Crew:

Produced & Directed by:	Jules White
Story & Screenplay by:	Zion Myers
Director of Photography:	Allen Siegler
Art Director:	Charles Clague
Film Editor:	Edwin Bryant

Credited Cast:

Shemp Howard	
Larry Fine	
Moe Howard	Moe; Uncle Mortimer
Vernon Dent	lawyer
Sam McDaniel	Spiffingham

Uncredited Cast:

Vic Travers	Mr. De Peyster
Symona Boniface	Mrs. De Peyster
Marti Shelton	Miss Jones, the angel

PERSPECTIVE: One of the biggest hits of 1941 was Columbia's *Here Comes Mr. Jordan*, which told the story of a young prizefighter who dies in a plane crash, is taken to heaven by mistake, and then returned to earth to inhabit a new body. This film had a weirdly calming effect on audiences newly preoccupied with war and death. Given Academy Awards for both its original story and screenplay and nominations for director Alexander Hall [*My Sister Eileen*] and actor Robert Young [*Fugitive Lovers*], *Here Comes Mr. Jordan* was a huge financial success and inspired such adaptations as *A Guy Named Joe* (1944), *The Horn Blows at Midnight* (1945), *Angel on My Shoulder* (1946), and Columbia's own (despite Harry Cohn's general dislike of fantasy films) *Down to Earth* (1947) and the remake, *Heaven Can Wait* (1978). *Heavenly Daze* is the Stooge contribution to this list, a natural choice in that the plot follows an old Stooge formula giving the Stooges one last chance to redeem themselves, a formula dating back to 1936's *Ants in the Pantry* and *False Alarms*.

To create a Stooge version of *Here Comes Mr. Jordan*, director Jules White and writer Zion Myers had to create a major shift in Stooge triadic dynamics: one of the Stooge 'cousins' (Shemp) had to be dead like *Mr. Jordan*'s Joe Pendleton and therefore separated from the other two, and one of the Stooges (Moe, appropriately) had to double up to play the Claude Rains' role, here named Uncle Mortimer, as the heavenly supervisor. Shemp's isolation necessarily creates some oddly static moments while the realization slowly comes upon Larry and Moe and later Spiffingham that an invisible, spiritual Shemp may be present. But these calm moments are immediately followed by wildly active demonstrations - blowing the money off the desk, shifting it between pockets, punching Moe across the room, making the painting come alive, spilling drinks, haunting coats and hats, and increasing the speed of the mix master in the classic whipped-cream sequence.

The whipped cream sequence deserves its fame. Descended from the better mouse traps of *Termites of 1938*, *Three Pests in a Mess*, and Rube Goldberg's *Soup to Nuts*, the invention intrigues us as delightfully impractical and disastrously messy. But unlike its predecessors which interested no buyers, this particularly absurd Stooge product earns an aura of grandeur when we hear that it has attracted sophisticated investors like the De Peysters, and few people take cream in the face better than Symona Boniface (cf. "Young man, you act as if the Sword of Damocles is hanging over your head!" [*Half-Wits Holidays*]). Years later the scene moved into legendary status when it was learned that Larry was injured during filming, the pen actually penetrating into his forehead. Though the film offers a variety of Stooge gags and situations - cream-puff fights, gadgetry, satirizing the wealthy, and fearing the supernatural - the whipped cream sequence is the moment everyone remembers, deliciously topped off with the dream-explanation denouement (*I Can Hardly Wait*) and Shemp's letter to "Dear Ma..."

VISUAL HUMOR: Visual gags are appropriate to the various scenarios: heavenly scenes (Shemp's wings rising up when he sees Miss Jones, running into the rain

A musical Ten Commandments sequence was edited out of the final release by order of the Hays Office; in the 1955 refurbishing, *Bedlam in Paradise*, a devilish musical scene is substituted.

cloud, and getting the lightning bolt in his rear), Shemp's earthly demonstrations of his spiritual presence (blowing the money, slugging Moe, poking Moe and Larry in the rear with his lapel pin, spilling drinks on Moe and Larry, and cranking the mixer), Moe and Larry's wealthy airs (Larry's foot-long cigarette holder and Moe's two-cigar holder), and the fiery denouement. Bell sounds accompany the heavenly introduction and Shemp addressing Uncle Mortimer. The train whistle sound effect we first heard in *Nutty but Nice*. Moe and Larry wringing out their soaked handkerchiefs on a flower pot and growing the plant is a Stooge first, although we saw a tree grow quickly from a vitamin injection in *Some More of Samoa*. The flower pot falling off the wall onto a victim's head is an elaboration of the horseshoes which fell on Larry two films ago (*Fiddlers Three*), and the flower pot falling onto a Nazi's head in *Back From the Front*. This gag will become standard over the next few years. The previous film (*The Hot Scots*) used an active painting, but we saw the Arab portrait first. Here the cowboy is three-dimensional from the outset. Other variations: Shemp bouncing his burning rear along the floor (*I Can Hardly Wait*); extinguishing his burning rear in water, and Larry dumping the water on Moe instead of the target (*Back to the Woods*); the false teeth (*All the World's a Stooge*); and pulling each other back by the coat tails (*Rockin' Thru the Rockies*).

VERBAL HUMOR: The heavenly scenes include several divine gags about death (Shemp: "Get me a pitch fork and a red union suit and I'll go."...'Good-bye,' she says. If I leave now, that proves I'm dead...I'll reform that Moe and Larry if it kills me. Hey...I'm already dead," the latter being a self-conscious joke, like Moe's "Clean as a whistle, so let's blow...Not bad!" in the previous film. We hear the first Stooge jokes about California (Shemp to the rain cloud: "What's the idea? You think you're in California?"; "All aboard the Heavenly Express bound for the Big Dipper, the Little Dipper, Earth, Mars, Venus, Cucamonga, Anaheim") since *Movie Maniacs*; Larry made a train announcement in the previous film's castle setting. With Shemp 'dead,' Larry takes on name calling ("Shemp...was such a sweet stinker...that fat-head") and jumps at the chance to make money ("*Money*!" [BONK] "It's a good thing you hit me with money or I'd resent that"; and "I had some airmail stamps"). A major part of Stooge characterization is that they are not only ignorant and quarrelsome but also destitute.

The same fate met a switchboard scene with Judy Malcolm.

Speaking of ignorance, Zion Myers has a fine grasp of Stooge logic: (Larry: "Why would anybody want a fountain pen that writes under whipped cream?" Moe: "A fellow could be in the desert where there ain't any water to write under, can't he?"); Larry mentioned writing under water in *Squareheads of the Round Table*. Vernon Dent's shyster lawyer character reprised Kenneth MacDonald's in *Hold That Lion*; the name 'I Fleecem' was used in *Sing a Song of Six Pants*. Sam McDaniel, brother of *Gone With the Wind*'s Hattie McDaniel and a master of 'Negro' comic posturing and dialogue has more lines than were ever given to Dudley Dickerson: "That's funny, I'm sure I heard that doorbell ring...Uh-oh, if someone's in here, how come I can't see him? And if they ain't in here, then this hat and coat is out for a walk by itself"; "Who am I gesundheitin'?"; "Says which?"; "Feet, why

don't you get goin'?...I'm goin, but my heart ain't in it"; "Mister, you don't know the half of it". The repetition of "Thank yaw" was used by the Marx Brothers in *A Day at the Races* (1937). Counting out money, interrupting one's self, and then resuming counting at a higher number was a vaudeville gag. It will appear again in *A Funny Thing Happened On the Way to the Forum*. The names 'Moeington,' 'Larryington,' and 'Spiffingham' derive from 'Jerkington'" in *If Body Meets a Body*. Moe's "Plotz" we heard in *Slippery Silks*.

OTHER NOTES: The working title was *Heaven's Above*. Beginning with this film the Art Director is credited before the Film Editor. This is not the first time a Stooge [Moe as Uncle Mortimer] has played a second role; Curly played their father in *3 Dumb Clucks*. Uncle Mortimer warns Shemp: "I hope you brought your asbestos suit"; Shemp must have worn one to shoot the final fire scene. *Here Comes Mr. Jordan* earned seven Academy Award nominations.

#110 - I'M A MONKEY'S UNCLE

Studio: Columbia

Released: October 7, 1948

Running Time: 15"56"'

Credited Production Crew:

Produced & Directed by:	Jules White
Story & Screenplay by:	Zion Myers
Director of Photography:	George F. Kelley
Art Director:	Charles Clague
Film Editor:	Edwin Bryant

Credited Cast:

Shemp Howard	
Larry Fine	
Moe Howard	
Dee Green	Baggie
Virginia Hunter	Aggie
Nancy Saunders	Maggie

Uncredited Cast:

Cy Schindell	caveman
Joe Palma	caveman
Charles 'Heine' Conklin	milkman

PERSPECTIVE: In the silent era D. W. Griffith made the first caveman film, *Man's Genesis* (1912), and comic versions followed in 1914 with Chaplin's *His Prehistoric Past* and Laurel & Hardy's *Flying Elephants* (1927). For actor/director Buster Keaton's first feature film, *The Three Ages* (1923), writer Clyde Bruckman parodied Griffith's *Intolerance* (1916) by satirizing three historical eras, including the stone-age. Nearly twenty years later, in 1940, Hal Roach produced *One Million B.C.*, a prehistoric adventure/romance starring Victor Mature and several enlarged lizards acting as dinosaurs. *One Million B.C.* was still memorable enough two years after *I'm a Monkey's Uncle* to spawn a sequel, *Two Lost Worlds* (1953), so it seems that the same kind of adaptive inspiration that satirized 1941's *Here Comes Mr. Jordan* as the previous Stooge film, *Heavenly Daze*, also inspired Jules White to adapt *One Million B.C.* as *I'm a Monkey's Uncle*. White used the same writer, Zion Myers, who specialized in such adaptations; White and Myers had also adapted *Hoi Polloi* into *Half-Wits Holiday* the previous year. Apparently the time had come for Hollywood's most uncivilized film trio to turn their talents towards a Stooge-ification of our paleolithic ancestors.

Because Stone Age existence was devoid of almost everything except daily survival, *I'm a Monkey's Uncle* concentrates on the Stooges' sleeping, waking, bathing, fishing, hunting, shopping, cooking, eating, and dressing. The humor derives from an assortment of approaches - silliness (Shemp blowing ash all over himself and being tickled to make butter, Larry pretending to bathe, the dogfish gag, and using clothes pins for skunk gas-masks), exaggeration (defoliating a tree by snoring), incompetence (shooting at the duck but hitting Moe), and pre-Flintstone gadgetry (an ax for a razor, a fish skeleton for a comb). Anachronism plays an important part in all of this, especially with the cave-to-cave milkman, Shemp's rock lighter, Moe's 'N-B-C' alarm clock, and the use of large leaves as towels. Indeed, there is a great multi-millennium chronological irony in Larry's: "Hang up my towel to dry *and don't wrinkle it*!"

The daily survival scenario yields to dramatic tension only near the end of the film. The Stooges court three girls with huge clubs, although 'Baggie' ends up

clubbing the reluctant Shemp. This leads to the finale - the fight with the rival cavemen in a primitive save-the-damsel sequence, but the absence of a dinosaur battle à la *One Million B.C.* leaves us wondering what memorable footage we might have had if the Stooges had been confronted with a giant reptile. Despite victorious struggles with gorillas and beast-men in previous films, the stingy Columbia budget did not allow for such an expense. Neither did history, for that matter, since dinosaurs became extinct sixty million years before humans evolved. But never mind: there was a long-standing cinematic tradition (which still continues) of pitting men against dinosaurs. Stooge viewers would just have to wait for the large lizard in *Space Ship Sappy* and the gigantic Siamese Cyclops in *The Three Stooges Meet Hercules*.

VISUAL HUMOR: Many of the gags befit the primitive scenario, notably tickling Shemp to make butter, the club alarm clock, and the girls saying "Let's just ignore them" even though the Stooges bonk them over the head thrice. Director of Photography George F. Kelley varies the look of the film. In the opening shot the camera dollies to inside the Stooges' cave; dissolves are used twice to set up the result shots - the snore-defoliated tree and the finished butter brick; and first stop action and then fast motion enhance the final skunk gag. Another result shot: the eggs and nest. Larry's reaction to Moe ripping his hair out is masterful. As if any of us could stand that even once, Larry shows incremental surprise, discomfortable amazement, and then fully realized pain. He retaliates only after the third batch, and then plays the Moe role, giving Moe a nose-bonk and saying: "Wake up and go to sleep!". In other role reversals, both Moe and Shemp do Curlyisms - Shemp uses "Rruff!" twice in the butter sequence, and Moe repeats "Hhmm!" during his struggle with the duck.

The wood chopping gag derives from *Whoops, I'm an Indian*, although Shemp adds the appropriate "kindling!". Most of the gags in Moe's duck hunt derive from *A Ducking They Did Go*. Other variations: clothes pin gas masks (*Cookoo Cavaliers*); being taken down by a flying tackle (*Slippery Silks*); the branch catapult and skunk, the NBC chimes, and the bird pecking on Moe's head (*Back to the Woods*); the turtle attached to Larry's nose (the teeth in *Heavenly Daze*); and Shemp's face covered in ash (*Higher Than a Kite*).

Of the many narrative types the Stooge writers introduced into the Columbia short film, one of the most consistently inspirational was the historical comedy. With a pedigree reaching well back into the silent era, this sub-genre fit the Stooges well. In 1948 releases alone there were four (*Squareheads of the Round Table, Fiddlers Three, I'm a Monkey's Uncle, Mummy's Dummies*), with another set in a foreign castle (*The Hot Scots*). Part of any historical comedy relies on anachronism, attributing to the historical world something modern. Here Moe and Larry tickle Shemp so he can 'churn' their butter. Cows, of course, were not domesticated in the stone age period, which may be as much as part of the gag as the silly method of churning butter. Then again, maybe they didn't know...

VERBAL HUMOR: Anachronisms involve modern processes ("Homogenized!" [milk]; "Oh boy! Grade A!" [butter]), home products (Moe: "Did you take a bath?" Shemp: "Is there one missin'?"), futuristic concepts (Larry: "She's a delicious dish." Shemp: "Dish! Yowsir; she's a flying saucer!"), and 1940s slang (Moe: "Hiya, toots!" Aggie: "Oh, Hello, Moe. Whadya know?" Stooges: "We just got back from a dinosaur show. Ya!"). Other gags include puns (Shemp: "A dogfish!" Larry: "I hope he ain't got fleas!") and insults (caveman: "You stole our girls, you horse thieves!"). As for the latter, the hideous Baggie is the opposite of the attractive woman-from-the box in *Fiddlers Three*. Shemp's insults ("Did you come from behind that rock or under it?"; "What would you charge to haunt a cave?"), far from being chauvinistic in the context of 1948, serve to make Baggie giggle and think Shemp is cute; she wins him over in the end. Epithet: "pussy-willow brain".

Moe likes to push another Stooge into his fight, as in the "Tell him, Tex!" sequence in *Pardon My Clutch*. Here he says: "I'll protect those girls to the last drop of *your* blood". Shemp used "yowsir" as a southern Scot two films previously. The Stooges first divided words for gags in *Beer Barrel Polecats* (Curly: "Here's my brainchild." Larry: "At last you got a brain, child!"); here (Shemp: "Wait a minute! I wanna smell good!" Moe: "Don't worry, you smell...good!"). Other variations: Moe: "Talk respectful when you're talkin' about my tomata'" ("Whadya mean gettin' familiar with the dame?...Don't pay any attention to him, babe" in *Ants in the Pantry*); 'Lilly of the Alley' ('Fleur de Skunk' in *You Nazty Spy!*); and "I bet you say that to all the cave girls!" (*Horses' Collars*). References: The dogfish is a type of shark. The 'Darwin' in the opening screen title is Charles Darwin, the father of modern evolutionary science. Moe's "I'll give you the most beautiful cave in Mesopotamia" is anachronistic; bronze age civilization flourished there thousands of years after the Stone Age.

OTHER NOTES: Dee Green [Baggie] also portrayed successfully the undesirable woman in *Brideless Groom*. Her role in the next film is perhaps her best 'ugly' role. This film will be refurbished as *Stone Age Romeos* (1955).

#111 - MUMMY'S DUMMIES

Studio: Columbia

Released: November 4, 1948

Running Time: 15"49'"

Credited Production Crew:

Produced by:	Hugh McCollum
Directed by:	Edward Bernds
Story & Screenplay by:	Elwood Ullman
Director of Photography:	Allen Siegler
Art Director:	Charles Clague
Film Editor:	Henry DeMond

Credited Cast:

Shemp Howard	
Larry Fine	
Moe Howard	
Vernon Dent	King Rootentooten
Ralph Dunn	Rhadames, Chief of the Palace Guard
Phil Van Zandt	Tutamon
Dee Green	Princess

Uncredited Cast:

Suzanne Ridgeway	female attendant
Virginia Ellsworth	female attendant
Wanda Perry	princess

PERSPECTIVE: Three of the previous five films [*Squareheads of the Round Table, Fiddlers Three, I'm a Monkey's Uncle*] were historical in nature, and the fourth [*The Hot Scots*] was set in an old European castle. Having not yet exhausted the possibilities of historical satire, producer Hugh McCullum, director Edward Bernds, and writer Elwood Ullman set this Stooge comedy in ancient Egypt during the reign of the imaginary Pharaoh Rootentooten. This is the same production team that created *The Hot Scots*, and the plot marries the Stooges-capturing-an-inside-ring-of-thieves concept of *The Hot Scots* to the Stooges-brought-before-the-king concept of 1942's *Matri-Phony*, the only other Stooge short set in the ancient Greco-Roman-Egyptian world. This plot combination is ideal for the Stooges to engage in another chase through multi-roomed corridors adjoining large, luxuriously appointed spaces. Interestingly, the choice of an exotic, Pharaonic Egyptian setting predates by one year the prototype of the Hollywood Biblical spectacles of the 1950s that commence with Cecil B. DeMille's *Samson and Delilah* in 1949. Once again, the Stooges are on the cutting edge.

The plot develops efficiently and rapidly. Playing shyster used-chariot salesmen, somewhat like the shyster all-weather pen salesmen in *Heavenly Daze*, the Stooges anger Rhadames, Chief of the Palace Guard. Sentenced to death by a king suffering from a toothache, the Stooges manage, in an amazing display of incompetence, to pull everything but the king's distressed tooth yet somehow relieve him of his pain and are given a life of leisure as a reward. Again as in *Heavenly Daze*, Stooge luxury is a paradox, so we watch a slave plop two grapes into Larry's mouth and then a pear onto his face, and we see Shemp hold up a banana, ordering: "Boy, have this peeled and brought back as soon as possible." Their leisure leads them to the wine cellar where, because they cannot determine their right from their left, they happen to overhear the king's corrupt aids, and the chasees become chasers as the Stooges once again capture the crooks and become heroes. As usual, though, something goes wrong at the end, and Shemp finds himself betrothed to the extremely unattractive princess [Dee Green]

The Stooge crew engineers some fine action throughout the film, often spinning concatenations of gags unfolding one after another as if the physics of the comedy universe can be described with the formula: cause = infinite effect. As Tutamon, for example, runs towards the basket, Larry springs up like a Jack-in-the-Box so Moe can clang Tutamon, who stumbles backwards onto a lit flame, recovers, and rushes Moe and Larry with his sword, misses, and plunges through the basket top and the curtain behind, puncturing the rear of the king who tosses his wine mug into the air, and, while it crashes onto his head, Moe clangs Tutamon cold. Resurrecting as well such reliable Stooge activities as painting and dentistry, *Mummy's Dummies* remains half a century later the finest comedy ever set in ancient Egypt.

VISUAL HUMOR: Another string of physical gags: the guard closes the mummy case, knocking dust onto Shemp's nose, making him sneeze, which causes the guard to open the case and get clanged by Shemp's sledge hammer; Moe jumps up from the basket and smashes a vase over the other guard's head, and when Moe frees Shemp, Shemp clangs him, too. Another: Rhadames puts his hand in the wet paint, steps through the floorboard, then watches the tire fall off and the whole chariot collapse onto the ground. In contrast the chase climax focuses on only one continuous event: Shemp spinning and spinning and spinning out of his mummy wrappings à la Mrs. Morgan in *Slippery Silks*. The basket scenes are descended from the magician's box in *Fiddlers Three*; every basket episode is fresh, especially when Rhadames tries to sit on the basket after it has moved and when the periscope does a take.

Stooge firsts: the 'SMILING EGYPTIANS' sign flipping to read 'CLOSED'; the board spiking Rhadames with a nail; Moe throwing a vase at Shemp ("Comin', Moe!") from off camera; and the slave pinching the king's cheek with him shaking his head 'No'. The sooty dust cloud recalls Shemp's ash cloud in the previous film. Other variations: Shemp putting on a disguise to fool Rhadames (*Pop Goes the Easel*); Moe dividing the money unequally (*Heavenly Daze*), Moe painting Larry's protruding tongue (*So Long, Mr. Chumps*); Shemp wearing glasses (*Hold That Lion*); Shemp backing into the agave (*Matri-Phony*); Moe and Larry arguing about 'right' and 'left' (*Pardon My Scotch*); Shemp inside the mummy case and Moe and Larry inside the basket (the bayonet bag in *Boobs in Arms*);.Moe and Larry taking a step back to volunteer Shemp (*Gents Without Cents*); ending the film with Shemp about to marry an ugly woman (*Brideless Groom*); and Moe and Larry throwing rice and shoes (*Three Smart Saps*).

The budgets for Stooge films were very restrictive. But the invariably simple decor and costuming matched the simplicity of the narrative settings. In many instances Stooge films are metaphorical - more suggestive than they are realistic. This can be true for the decor and costuming as well as the slapstick and verbal humor. It is easy to overlook some of this simplicity. For instance, the natural short stature of the Stooges shown in this publicity still from *Mummy's Dummies* (1948) immediately differentiates the three of them from the taller thugs who manhandle them, allows them to scurry away from them with all the more agility, and creates an ever-present fundamental comic juxtaposition of good vs. evil.

VERBAL HUMOR: The film glories in ancient Egyptianisms, as when the Stooges are referred to as "sand fleas." The name 'Tutamon' was inspired by the multi-syllabic name of the Egyptian Pharaoh Tutankhamen, as was 'Rootentooten' ([spelled 'Rootentootin' in the script], although his name also suggests Yosemite-Sam-like, American 'Western' slang], and 'Madman Ramesses' uses the name of a dozen or so pharaohs of the same name; the Egyptian bull-form oracle Shemp impersonates ("They went that-a-way, and that ain't no bull!") is the ancient god 'Apis'; 'Rhadames' is a lead role in Verdi's opera, *Aida*, also set in ancient Egypt; 'Put-N-Take-It' sounds Egyptian but was a popular 1940s game; Moe calls Shemp 'Painless Papyrus'; and then there is the 'Sphinx' perfume (Shemp: "Some perfume, sister. What brand do you use?" Servant: "Sphinx." Shemp: "I know, but what brand do you use?"). In most historical films, there are verbal anachronisms, as in Moe's "The cops! Scram!" and "Don't shoot!".

Most of the verbal humor is meant to accompany the physical, either to set up a one-blow gag (Shemp: "I think this tire needs a recap." Moe: "So does your head! [BONK]; Shemp: "I didn't know it was you!" Moe: "A natural enough mistake, m'lad. You know it now!" [CLANG]; and Moe threatening "an even split" of Shemp's head with an ax), set up a longer routine (Shemp: "Something in a nice, clean used chariot?"; Guard: "Poor old Put-N-Take-It; he sure was an ugly old cuss!"), or finish it off (Moe: "If that chariot doesn't do everything we claimed for it I wouldn't be a bit surprised"; Shemp: "Did you see him hit a Royal Chambermaid?"). One-phrasers and one-liners punctuate the dentistry scene (Moe: "Oh! A rear bicuspidor!"; Shemp: "Whadya know! A vacancy...I'll put it back"; Shemp: "King size!") and the luxury scene (Shemp: "Be careful! That's me under that nail."). Larry is occasionally singled out as a thief (*Movie Maniacs*), as here (Moe: "How do you do, sir? I'm Honest Moe, that's Honest Shemp, and that's...that's Larry"). Moe's "Oh, ambidextrous, eh?" varies the "which way is right" gag.

Other variations: Shemp: "We'll cross that bridge when we come to it...not bad!" Moe: "Not good!" (*The Hot Scots*); Moe: "I'm gonna get myself a cheap lawyer!" (*Monkey Businessmen*); and the Stooges: "Right!...Right!...Right!" (*Dancing Lady*).

OTHER NOTES: Tutamon's excuse that there was "a flood on the Nile" will not wash since ancient Egyptian crops grew *because* the Nile river flooded; also, as for Moe's "It belonged to an old couple in Babylon; all they did was drive it up to the Temple of Isis once a week," Isis was an Egyptian goddess, not Babylonian. This marks Suzanne Ridgeway's first of nine appearances in Stooge films. Dee Green reprises her ugly role from *I'm a Monkey's Uncle*. This was the only one of the 1947-1949 Stooge releases that was not refurbished in the 1954-1956 releases. The reasons for this no doubt include the cost of rebuilding the sets and the contemporary release of *Abbott and Costello Meet the Mummy* (1955).

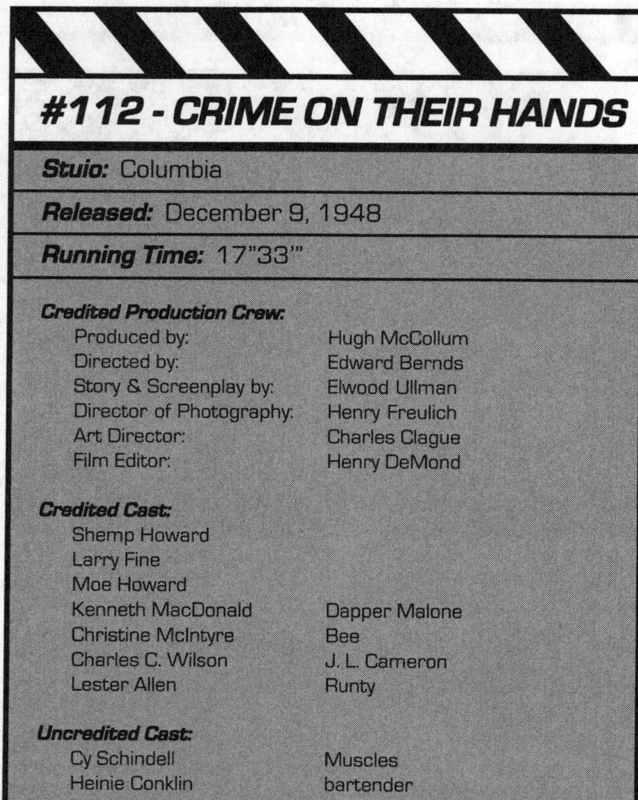

#112 - CRIME ON THEIR HANDS

Stuio: Columbia

Released: December 9, 1948

Running Time: 17"33'"

Credited Production Crew:

Produced by:	Hugh McCollum
Directed by:	Edward Bernds
Story & Screenplay by:	Elwood Ullman
Director of Photography:	Henry Freulich
Art Director:	Charles Clague
Film Editor:	Henry DeMond

Credited Cast:

Shemp Howard	
Larry Fine	
Moe Howard	
Kenneth MacDonald	Dapper Malone
Christine McIntyre	Bee
Charles C. Wilson	J. L. Cameron
Lester Allen	Runty

Uncredited Cast:

Cy Schindell	Muscles
Heinie Conklin	bartender
George Lloyd	McGuffey
Blackie Whiteford	thug
Bud Fine	thug

PERSPECTIVE: The press had for decades played a major role in Hollywood films. Such classics as *The Front Page* (1931) and its remake *His Girl Friday* (1940) blend city desks, zealous reporters, and crime-solving with comedy, and like those feature films, *Crime on Their Hands* manages to maintain its humor while offering a thoroughly gritty feel for 1940's realism. After the last few historical/fantasy films, the Stooges return to a 1940s urban environment with a vengeance. The early scenes contain a bloody beating, a murder, stock footage of a rolling press, an editor's door without a funny name, and an editor who is devoid of humor. In the first scene the Stooges satirize contemporary movies about newspapers, with Shemp getting a rare opportunity to slap Moe while demonstrating how "in the movies the reporter always talks back to the boss." Moe bonks him with the telephone receiver and menaces Larry: "Say,

you didn't by any chance see that picture, too?" This is Stooge realism.

Besides the visual realism inherent in the genre, Kenneth MacDonald [Dapper] gives the film an intimidating, hard-boiled villain. Whether preparing to operate on Shemp (Shemp: "Cut it out!" Dapper: "'Cut it out,' that's *just* what we're doin'!"), throwing Moe and Larry in the closet, or softening only enough to allow for an anesthetic (Muscles: "Aren't you even gonna put him to sleep?" Dapper: "Oh you're gonna get technical, eh?"), MacDonald plays the criminal Dapper as relentlessly vicious, and this allows the Stooges in stark contrast to be relentlessly silly. While Moe and Larry attempt to extract the diamond from Shemp's stomach by holding his feet and banging his head on the floor, Dapper sits quietly, as if this were an acceptable method; and then when Moe tries a pair of ice tongues, Dapper applauds the Stooge-to-Stooge cruelty: "Now you're getting smart!" Dapper is so mean, so determined, it is only fitting that he ultimately gets his way when he demands of Muscles, who has been replaced by the gorilla: "Anesthetic...Come on, come on! Give it to me!" [CLANG].

The comedy develops into two interlocking parts: the Stooges battle both the evil Dapper and the terrifying gorilla. Unlike the expansive castle-setting films, the finale of *Crime on Their Hands* takes place in only three rooms, but the clever juxtaposition of the operating room, closet, and gorilla cage creates a neatly compact farce. While Dapper works on Shemp, Larry frees himself from the adjoining closet only to find himself in the next room's gorilla cage. In one of his greatest scenes, a dazed and frightened Larry is shoved back and forth between the powerful gorilla and Moe's sarcasm ("You afraid to go by yourself? All right, I'll take you by the hand, little boy!") which the woozy Larry is prepared to accept at face value. When Moe discovers the gorilla, he, too, performs a terrific take. At one point photographer Henry Freulich even scares *us* by filming the gorilla from Shemp's point-of-view; and soon after the gorilla is tossing humans about with reckless abandon. From beginning to end, this is a hard-hitting, comedy-crime-drama.

VISUAL HUMOR: The introductory realism disallows any humor for the first minute, but it prepares the atmosphere for Shemp to pretend he is a reporter talking back to the boss. The first gag, when from outside the office we hear Cameron say, "This'll be a tough assignment. Do you think you can cover it?" and then see that he is talking to the Stooges, who will fix the 'cover' of his chair cushion, is similar to the opening detective gag in *Shivering Sherlocks*. Plot-related gags: Moe pressing Shemp's ears with books ends ("Stop the presses!"); making the Stooges flip coins and bend their hat brims; and Shemp and Larry acting afraid after Moe says: "If anybody wants to turn back, now is the time". The sequential slapstick (Moe drops his coin, Shemp scrambles for it under the table, Moe steps on his hand, Shemp rises in pain, knocks over the table, and soaks one of the men with beer; and Dapper gets hit on the head and throws the knife in the air, which lands next to Shemp's cheek) is like that recently featured in *Mummy's Dummies*, as is sawing through the wall into the gorilla's rear similar to Tutamon's running his sword into Rootentooten's rear through the basket. The McCollum/ Bernds/Ullman production team made both films.

Bee (Christine McIntyre) giving the Stooges a huge triple slap is reminiscent of her slugging Shemp in *Brideless Groom*. Moe slamming the wire waste basket onto Shemp's head recalls Curly wearing the waste basket in *Micro-Phonies*. Other variations: a gorilla befriending a Stooge (*Three Missing Link*); Shemp's using a faucet handle for a 'Press' pin (*Three Little Beers*); Shemp drinking the water meant for the fainted Bee (*Boobs in Arms*); Moe hitting Larry "for absolutely nothin'!" (*Nertsery Rhymes*); Muscles tapping Shemp with a hammer (BONG, BONG) and finally hearing TINK (recently *Pardon My Clutch*); Moe doing a take when seeing the gorilla: "How do you like this guy? —Nyaggh!" (*Out West*); Dapper saying "Anesthetic. Come on, come on! Give it to me!" and then getting "it" (*Pardon My Scotch*); Shemp knocking on Bee's forehead instead of the door (*Calling All Curs*); and Shemp holding up glasses so he will not be hit (*Three Little Pirates*).

The Stooges begin *Crime on Their Hands*, the ninth and final release of 1948, playing newsmen...well, not actually newsmen but custodians. In a typical 'fooler opening' we hear from outside the manager's door, "Well, men, this'll be a tough assignment. Do you think you can cover it?" but soon we see that the manager is asking his custodians to fix the "cover" of his chair cushion. Inevitably someone is negligent enough to give the Stooges an opening, and once the phone rings, they are on they case. This effective method of dividing Stooge short-films into two parts and getting them involved in activities for which they are ill-equipped dates back to the mid-1930s (*Three Little Pigskins, Horses' Collars*). The fooler opening itself they first used in Del Lord's *Movie Maniacs* (1936).

VERBAL HUMOR: The gritty realism pervades the script and works particularly well for Moe while he tries to extract the diamond from Shemp (Moe: "He's just bein' stubborn...Must be caught on somethin'." Larry: "Maybe it's his appendix?" Moe: "We'll soon find out...Not even a tonsil!"). Elwood Ullman, as often, conjured up a variety of simple-minded puns (Larry: "Evidence! Let's weigh it"; Moe: "Use a fine-tooth comb." Larry: "I haven't got a comb. Will a wire brush do?"), fear gags (Dapper: "Darling. You better wait outside. This is no place for a weak stomach." Shemp: "I got a weak stomach!"), insults (Bee: "He thinks I'm lying. Any half-wit can see I'm telling the truth." Shemp: "Yeah, I can see you're tellin' the truth"), slapstick accompaniment (Shemp [tossing and swallowing mints]: "With oranges it's much harder"; Moe [when Bee faints]: "She must-a got a good look at you!"; Moe: "Where'd you get the tools?" Larry: "On the head."; Moe: "Hit the lock, hit the lock!" [Larry hammers Moe's hand] "Does that look like a lock?!"), and even a pick-up line (Moe: "We're lookin' for a guy named 'Dapper.'" Bee: "Dapper? I never heard of him.. I'm all alone." Moe: "Good! I mean, uh, we'll check on that!") as well as gags based on Stooge ignorance (Moe: "You know, porcupine, for a guy without brains you're a genius!"; and Larry misreading 'Museum' in the headline). Three-pattern (Moe: "Boy, what a dive." Larry: "I wonder which one of these guys is Dapper?" Shemp: "No one looks 'dapper' in here!"). Reference: Moe's "You look like a bird in a gilded cage!" derives from Arthur Lamb's *A Bird in a Gilded Cage* (1900). Epithets: "porcupine" and "nitwit".

The opening scene contains two phone gags (Shemp saying "Hello" to Moe repeating "Hello," and Shemp: "Yes! Yes! Yes! No! No." Moe: "What was it?" Shemp: "Wrong number"), recalling those in *Men in Black* and *Swing Parade of 1946*. Another variation: Larry: "We're trapped like rats!" Moe: "Speak for yourself!" (*Nutty but Nice*).

OTHER NOTES: The title parodies the expression 'time on their hands'. On the title screen the word 'crime' is written as if painted with a broad brush. The film is a remake of the Andy Clyde film, *All Work and No Pay* (1942). It will be refurbished as *Hot Ice* (1955). The Stooges had previously played press photographers in *Dutiful but Dumb*. This marks the last of Cy Schindell's two dozen Stooge appearances; he died of cancer on August 24, 1948. Shemp says the 'Punjab' Diamond has 50 carats; the Hope Diamond at the Smithsonian has 44.5. Continuity: the gag Dapper stuffs into Shemp's mouth becomes a tied gag; and the Stooges never had a chance to notify the police.

1949

The Ghost Talks • *Who Done It?*

Hokus Pokus • *Fuelin' Around* • *Malice in the Palace*

Vagabond Loafers • *Dunked in the Deep*

#113 - THE GHOST TALKS

Stuio: Columbia

Released: February 3, 1949

Running Time: 16"07'"

Credited Production Crew:

Produced & Directed by:	Jules White
Story & Screenplay by:	Felix Adler
Director of Photography:	M. A. Anderson
Art Director:	Charles Clague
Film Editor:	Edwin Bryant

Credited Cast:

Shemp Howard
Larry Fine
Moe Howard

Uncredited Cast:

Nancy Saunders	Lady Godiva
Phil Arnold	voice of Tom

PERSPECTIVE: In 1943 Jules White and Felix Adler created *Dizzy Detectives*, a classic spook film, and in their only Stooge production of 1948 they teamed up again to create the nursery rhyme farce, *Fiddlers Three*. For *The Ghost Talks* they inject both spooks and fabled characters into the castle scenario used so successfully in 1948 to create a comedy of the hauntingly strange. Smorgasbord Castle offers up real spooks, not villains in disguise, and the 'damsel-in-distress' turns out to be the headless, armor-bound spirit of Peeping Tom, saved, ironically, by not the Stooges but the legendary Lady Godiva whose naked ride through the streets of Coventry had cost him his freedom in the first place. Previous scare comedies tended to have elaborate plots, but here the viewer's disorientation begins with a very simple premise: the Stooges enter Smorgasbord Castle to remove three items for, as we find out later, the A to Z Express Company. Never mind the usual introductory motivational scene, White and Adler chose to submerge the Stooges into the strangeness as quickly as possible.

Parodying the contemporary radio mystery show *Inner Sanctum*, Shemp prophesies "Strange things will happen in this mysterious castle," and thus the series of weirdnesses proceeds: the umbrella gets stuck and dumps water on Moe, Shemp frightens himself in the mirror and has a shield fall on his head, and Larry is shot in the rear with a crossbow released indirectly by of the wind. This last incident lures the Stooges towards the suit of armor, and the Peeping Tom sequence leads to more oddities: armor talking, smoking, and drinking; skeletons walking, talking, and playing chess; and a skull flying about. Except for the arrow in Larry's rear, the Stooges are not harmed and should not be frightened by any of this strangeness. Tom is just waiting to be freed from his 1000-year imprisonment and taken away by Lady Godiva, and the skeletons just want the Stooges to leave them alone: "Go away, boys. You bother me!" The film's conclusion brings in some final, weird moments, with Lady Godiva [in a one-piece bathing suit] riding on her horse 'Tiger' through the interior of the castle and the Stooges becoming part of a 1000-year old, shutter opening, pie-throwing mystique, very much as in *Spook Louder*, the prototype for this sort of Stooge weirdness.

Two years earlier Adler and White created *Sing a Song of Six Pants* and *All Gummed Up*, two of the films that pioneered the centrifugal 'box comedy' concept of confining the Stooges within a single area and bringing the plot in to them. The final release of 1948, *Crime On Their Hands*, had successfully made economical use of three adjacent rooms, and *The Ghost Talks*, too, despite being set in a castle, has been shrunk down to three adjacent, doorless rooms. For this type of film it is effective to confine the weirdnesses and the Stooges into a small space. Like Peeping Tom, the Stooges do not mean to look at things they are not supposed to, but their space is so limited they cannot avoid seeing the skeletons, who do not want the Stooges to look at them, or Lady Godiva, who costs them three pies in their faces.

VISUAL HUMOR: As in the previous two films, slapstick mishaps are chained together in sequence: Shemp turns, sees his reflection in a mirror, screams in fright, backs up against the wall, causing a large shield to fall onto his head; and the wind blows a shutter which hits a suit of armor which has a cocked cross bow which shoots its arrow which lands in Larry's rear. Similarly, visual gimmicks are now often compounded: the visor bounces up and down twice, causing Larry's hat to hop off his head and spin around; Larry runs back towards the split table and slams one half into the other, catching Moe's neck in between; and Shemp hollers, jumps, does mule-like leg kicks, and spins [in fast motion] like a chicken-with-its-head-cut-off. The latter is Curly's move, as is Moe's trying to butt the door open with his head. Another role reversal is Moe taking the conk from the 'slot machine' armor. Two visual three-patterns: each Stooge going one after the other to examine the armor; and Moe tossing the skull to Shemp who tosses it to Larry who tosses it onto the easy chair. The flashback in Tom's story resembles the nursery rhyme 'videos' in *Fiddlers Three*; from the same film is the bent pin Shemp jabs into Moe. *Spook Louder* is the prototype for Moe's hair standing on end as well as the mysterious pie in the face. The frog in the hat and the owl in the skull both derive from the parrot in the turkey in *Crash Goes the Hash*, also written/directed by Adler/White. Other variations: the shield falling on Shemp's head [*Restless Knights*]; the wind-inverted umbrella [*If a Body Meets a Body*]; Moe leading Shemp by the nose [*Nutty but Nice*]; Shemp tapping the quarter to the rhythm of 'Shave and a Hair Cut,' the armor responding with the 'Two Bits' [*Whoops, I'm an Indian*; *Oily to Bed, Oily to Rise*]; Moe and Larry bashing Shemp's head against the door like a battering ram [*Fright Night*]; Moe flicking ashes on Shemp's protruding tongue [*So Long, Mr. Chumps*]; and the 'N-B-C' sound effect [*Back to the Woods*].

VERBAL HUMOR: Adler's script employs internal echoes [Shemp: "What happened?" Larry: "Strange happenings." Shemp: "That's strange"; Larry: "That was just a coincidence. [The arrow hits Larry] What happened?" Shemp: "Just a coincidence."], retorts [Larry: "'If the British march, hang a...hang a..." Moe: "I'll hang one!"; Shemp: "Six lions were tearin' me apart! Six lions!" Moe: "You're lyin'!"; Shemp: "You're awake!" Moe: "Yes! But *you* won't be for long!"; Owl: "Who? Who?" Moe: "Us, you lame-brain."], and repetitions [Shemp: "Oh, I don't have to, Nyaahh!" Moe: "What did you say?" Shemp: "I don't have to, Nyaahh!"]. Puns are found even in a three-pattern [Tom: "That confounded shutter! " Shemp: "I shutter to think of it!" Moe: "Shutter up!"].

Adler uses misdirected sounds and voices before the Stooges learn the armor talks, and when the frog lets out a loud croak, Moe says to Shemp: "Why don't you watch your manners?". The dialogue for Tom [cf. the talking gorilla in *Crime on their Hands*] tends to be polite and archaic ["Please don't take me away, I beg of you...I beseech you!...Gentleman, I warn you...Heed my warning!"]. Two jokes depend on his age [Tom: "I haven't had a smoke in a thousand years." Shemp: "Think you're old enough to smoke?"; and Moe: "Remember what happened to Peeping Tom." Larry: "That was a thousand years ago."]. Larry's is the voice of reason, an interesting recovery from his wooziness in *Crime on their Hands*; he is so rational ["What we need is a harder head"], he even tries to speak with Tom in other languages, although his 'Irish' ["Sprechen Sie Irish?"] is German. Shemp, on the other hand, lies twice ["Six lions were tearin' me apart!"; [when Shemp hits Moe and Larry with the broom]: "It's a lucky thing I took it away from him or he'd-a killed you both." As in *Dizzy Detectives*, Moe excels at being scared, convincing Larry and Shemp to be courageous, as in "Don't be afraid now, boys, but LET'S GET OUTTA HERE!"; and the verbal three-pattern [Shemp to Larry: "I think you better go get the armor." Larry to Moe: "Moe, I think you better go get the armor." Moe: "Wait a minute, I think we all better get the armor. Let's not be afraid, come on...Go ahead!"]. The Stooges and Tom even have a four-pattern [Moe: "I gotta have a drink!" Larry: "Me, too!" Shemp: "Me three!" Tom: "Make it four!"] This is a Stooge first. Role reversal: Larry's "Cut out the clownin'! We got work to do!" is usually Moe's line. Epithets: "nitwit," "fraidy cats," "lame-brain," and "dumbbell". References: Lady Godiva was the 11th-century wife of Leofric, earl of Mercia; she rode naked through the streets of Coventry [England] to win tax relief for the citizens. Peeping Tom was a Coventry tailor who became blind after 'peeping' during her famous ride. Shemp's "This is Desmond of the Outer Sanctorum" parodies the introduction to the radio mystery *Inner Sanctum* ["This is Raymond, your host, welcoming you in to the Inner Sanctum"] which debuted in 1941. Larry's "If the British march, hang a...hang a..." borrows from Longfellow's 'Paul Revere's Ride'; [Longfellow was quoted also in Adler's *Fiddlers Three*]. Shemp's "Oh, Red Skeleton" refers to the radio, film, and [later] TV star Red Skelton, who had just recently starred in *Merton of the Movies* [1947] and *Fuller Brush Man* [1948]. Larry's "Parlez vous Française?" means "Do you speak French?" "Smörgasbord" is a Scandinavian buffet. "Go away, boys. You bother me!" was a popular slang phrase, attributed to Mae West.

Moe has been using "A fine..." since *Punch Drunks*, but here "A fine time to take a nap!" was used in *Uncivil War Birds*. Shemp's "Shut up! Oh I don't have to!" was Curly's line in *Three Little Pirates*. Other variations: Tom: "Hootman!" [*The Hot Scots*]; Tom: "Thank you." Moe to Shemp: "What are you thanking me for?" Shemp: "I wasn't thankin' you for anything." Moe to Larry: "Then why were you thanking me." Larry: "I didn't say a word." [*Movie Maniacs; Three Missing Links*] Moe: "One of us is nuts and it can't be you!" [*Crash Goes the Hash*]; Shemp: "Say a few syllables!" [*Slippery Silks*]; Shemp: "Wait a minute, fellas. I think it's crackin'." Larry: "What, the door?" Shemp: "No, my head." [*In the Sweet Pie and Pie*]; and Tom: "In the days of old, I was a tailor—" Larry: "Oh, Old Taylor!" [*Three Little Sew and Sews*].

OTHER NOTES: The working title was *That's the Spirit*. The title screen is written in 'ghostly' letters. 'Smorgasbord Castle' is described verbally, not with a sign. The cast of this film consists of the Three Stooges, Nancy Saunders in a cameo, and the voice of Phil Arnold. Several more 1949 releases will have very small casts. Phil Arnold had previously played the little man with the shredded suit in *Sing a Song of Six Pants*. The last time we saw the Stooges smoking cigarettes was in *Heavenly Daze*. *The Ghost Talks* will be refurbished as *Creeps* [1956].

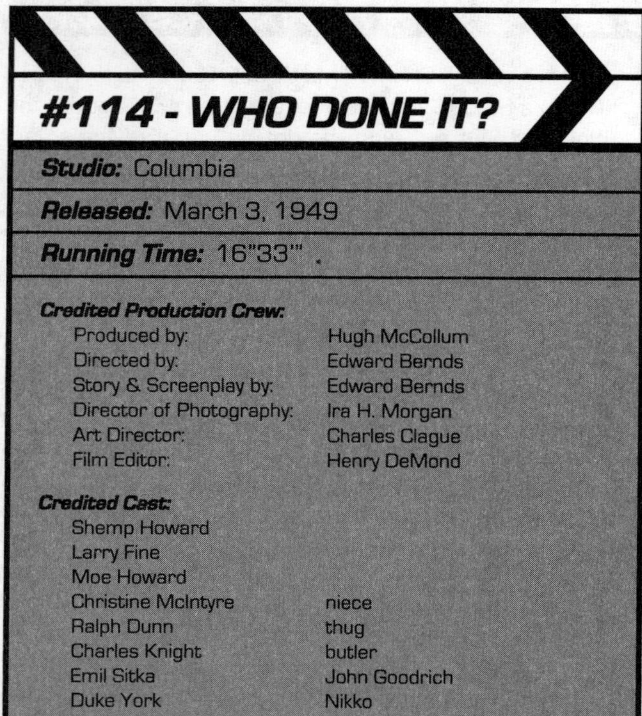

#114 - WHO DONE IT?

Studio: Columbia

Released: March 3, 1949

Running Time: 16"33'"

Credited Production Crew:

Produced by:	Hugh McCollum
Directed by:	Edward Bernds
Story & Screenplay by:	Edward Bernds
Director of Photography:	Ira H. Morgan
Art Director:	Charles Clague
Film Editor:	Henry DeMond

Credited Cast:

Shemp Howard	
Larry Fine	
Moe Howard	
Christine McIntyre	niece
Ralph Dunn	thug
Charles Knight	butler
Emil Sitka	John Goodrich
Duke York	Nikko
Dudley Dickerson	janitor

PERSPECTIVE: Writer/director Ed Bernds blends a variety of familiar Stooge comedy elements here: the Stooges save a kidnap victim, outwit a femme fatale, defeat a beast-man, and capture two crooks. They do it with cowardly incompetence while cowering and fleeing through a multi-room house teeming with secret passageways, trick paintings, and intermittent lights. Bernds originally wrote the script in 1946, inspired by Walter Catlett's *You're Next* (1940); in fact, "You will be next" is the message attached to the rock thrown through John Goodrich's window in the first scene here. Bernds was ready to shoot the film after *Half-Wits Holiday*, but when Curly suffered his stroke Bernds had to quickly rewrite the script for two other Columbia comics, [Gus] Schilling & [Richard] Lane, the former playing a combined Curly/Larry role, the latter playing Moe's. The Schilling & Lane version appeared in 1946 as *Pardon My Terror*, and included Christine McIntyre and Emil Sitka in its cast.

Bernds later admitted the script was ill-fitted to Schilling & Lane, for this well-balanced mixture of physical abuse, verbal banter, and emotional surprise is particularly vibrant even for a Stooge film. In previous films we have seen a beast-man, lion, or gorilla stand behind the Stooges while Moe accuses Larry and Shemp of breathing heavily or some such, then doing a fine take when he sees what is behind them. Here, though, Nikko emerges from the secret panel, Shemp 'ee-beeps' (Moe: "Shadup! This is no time for singin'!") and Larry screams, so Moe bonks Larry, so Nikko bonks Moe, so Moe slaps Shemp, so Nikko slaps Moe, so Moe slaps Larry, so Nikko slaps Moe, so Moe turns— and *then* sees Nikko. Similarly, the scene in which the niece [Christine McIntyre] and Shemp point out their favorite paintings while switching the drugged drink elegantly builds to a climax unparalleled in all of Stoogedom with forty seconds of Shemp wheezing, 't-k'-ing, meeping, shuttering, flipping, flopping, chicken-with-its-head-cut-off-ing, and then slamming his legs on the ground in near rigor mortis. As often in Stooge short-films, such sequences mark important narrative turns: when Shemp and Larry run in, they realize who the crooks are, and when Larry refuses to answer the phone - earning him two slaps, a pound, and a bonk - it is the important phone call from Goodrich that Moe beats him into answering. Perhaps more importantly, the Stooges' ability to hit, duck, and take a blow in such encounters makes their ability to emerge triumphant from the crazy fight at film's end all the more believable. Ultimately, *Who Done It?* is one of the finest Stooge films of its type.

In 1949 America stood on the brink of the television revolution, but radio was still king. Both this and the previous film begin with radio-like introductions, the villains are murderous radio-like crooks, and Goodrich laments: "They tied me up and made me listen to singing commercials!" The finale might as well be a radio drama: it ends in the dark. This intermittent 'film noir' produces striking visual close-ups for us to see, but it also requires us to use our visual imagination for what we cannot see. Turn the lights out, and whether it is film or radio, the vision is supplied by the audience. As in *Dizzy Doctors*, we know Stooge humor so well we do not even have to see it to understand it.

VISUAL HUMOR: The hide-away closets and movable paintings expand the interior space. We see this as Nikko twice emerges from secret panels (first missing Shemp and then bonked as Moe blindly hoists the tripod over his shoulder), in the moving paintings and the scary face behind the painting, in Goodrich's body falling out from the closet, and when the Stooges burst through a door. (Moe injured his leg bursting through the breakaway door and had to limp in the remaining scenes.) The surprises continue in the hallway chase: Moe and Larry come around opposite corners and scare each other, and Moe thinks Nikko's long hair is Larry's. Sleuth-related props include the magnifying glass (Moe pulls Larry with it, looks at his scalp, and smashes it over Shemp's derby) and the camera (Shemp shoots Moe and Larry with the butler, squeezes fluid out of the shutter bulb, uses the camera hood to sniff for fingerprints and ogle at the niece, and is frightened looking at Moe's face). Role reversal: Moe uncharacteristically rammed his head into the door in the previous film; here he fails to outwit Larry and

Shemp with the head-bonking painting lever, they circle their fingers to suggest he is "goofy," and he cries "Hmm!" and calls "Shemp, Larry!" à la Curly. Shemp's 40-second death dance after drinking the poison is an expanded version of his complex reaction in the previous film, *The Ghost Talks* (when the frog slides down his back). Also from that film is the shield falling from the wall onto a Stooge head. Goodrich putting a match in his mouth and trying to strike his cigar recalls Graves cigar/safe combination reversal in *Men in Black*. The opening painting substitutes for the 'action' paintings in *The Hot Scots*. The close-up of the gorilla in *Crime on Their Hands* paved the way for the close up of Moe's face in the camera. The glasses gag (*Crime on Their Hands*) now includes a glass-breaking sound effect. Other variations: the fight in the dark (*Nutty but Nice*); Shemp knocking himself out to end the film (*Grips, Grunts and Groans*); Moe looking through his magnifying glass at Larry's scalp (*We Want Our Mummy*); the leaning corpse in the closet (*If a Body Meets a Body*); Shemp extending out the camera hood (*Dutiful but Dumb*); running into a room, barring the door with furniture, and without looking hitting a fellow Stooge (*Idle Roomers*); and pulling one another back from the lead (*Rockin' Thru the Rockies*).

VERBAL HUMOR: Bernds complements many physical gags with ironic tag lines and vice versa, as when Goodrich says: "I feel a lot safer all ready" just before Nikko emerges from a wall panel to strangle him, when Moe kicks Shemp ("Don't you raise your hand to me!"), when the 'ALERT DETECTIVE AGENCY' is literally gagged and "tied up," when Shemp says: "What could happen?" just before Nikko emerges, when Moe assures Shemp "Nothin's gonna happen, absolutely nothin'!" and smashes the magnifying glass over his derby, and when Moe smashes Shemp's glasses (Shemp: "I'm framed!"). The Stooges embellish even the classic "I'll answer it when I'm ready...I'm ready" gag with two slaps, a pound/bonk, and a threatened punch. This is particularly true in the hallway chase when Moe and Nikko pass by Shemp ("He got away from you, didn't he—Whoa!"), and when Shemp and Nikko pass Larry (Shemp: "That thing, the goon! He's comin'!" Larry to the goon: "Hey, what'd he say?—Yeoww!"). In addition to complementing the physical humor, verbal gags include internal rhyme (Shemp: "The niece is nice!"; Moe: "We're here on business." Shemp: "I mean business!"), excessive literalness (Moe: "There must be a secret panel. You take that wall." Shemp: "Where to?"; Moe: "What does your watch say?" Shemp: "It don't say nothin'; you gotta look at it."), fear jokes (Larry: "Who was that guy?" Moe: "I dunno, but he don't like us!"), and jokes about Stooge ignorance (Moe: You're nothing but a nitwit." Larry: "Oh thank you!"; Moe: "We're in a tough spot, men." Larry: "Yeah, it's gonna take brains to get us outta here." Moe: "That's why I said we're in a tough spot!"). In contrast, Shemp's lines about the moving painting are gentile ("So natural it looked like the trees moved...Oh charming, charming!"). This is because the niece [Christine McIntyre] speaks so sweetly, even though her intent is deadly ("sleeping pills - the permanent kind!"; "Short life and a merry one!"; "Now don't you go get yourselves murdered!"). Beginning in a soft voice she tells the Stooges how her uncle disappeared: "He was sitting right over there. Suddenly, I HEARD A SCREAM!" In contrast, Emil Sitka speaks, as usual, in a shaky voice. Camera-related lines: Shemp: "Stop down a quarter of a mile. Somebody left some hypo in there"; ['hypo' (sodium thiosulfate) is a fixing agent]. Moe has one touching line [after Larry hits him with the shovel]: "Don't you know? You been around me many years! Don't you know what I look like?". As in *Crime on Their Hands*, the Stooges make internal references to movie making, here in a patterned fear gag (Moe: "We're private detectives, ain't we? [Larry & Shemp: "Yeah."] In the movies does a private eye ever give up? ["No."] But you softies want to quit like cowards just because you might get killed. ["Yeah."] That's a great idea! Let's go!"). Other variations: Shemp's answer to "What's your watch say?" ("tick, tick, tick" in *Fright Night*); and Larry: "I'm sorry....Say something'!" Moe: "Numskull!" ("I hate you!" in *Three Smart Saps*).

OTHER NOTES: This is the second time that every cast member is credited. Walter Catlett played the bartender in *The Captain Hates the Sea*. *Pardon My Terror* was one of eleven comedy shorts Schilling & Lane made at Columbia between 1945-1950. *Who Done It?* will be refurbished as *For Crimin' Out Loud* (1956), the last film Shemp made before his death.

Beast-men appear in several Stooge films. Beast-men effectively tower above the Stooges, sneak up from behind them, scare them silly, allow them to mistake him for each other, and generally establish a climate of sheer panic. Ultimately and ironically, though, the Stooges always find a way to defeat them. Nikko here in *Who Done It?* was played by Duke York [Charles Everest Sinsabaugh - 1908-1952], who among his ninety-plus roles also played the prototypical Wolf-man in *Idle Roomers* and Angel in *Shivering Sherlocks*.

#115 - HOKUS POKUS

Studio: Columbia

Released: May 5, 1949

Running Time: 16"08'"

Credited Production Crew:

Produced & Directed by:	Jules White
Story & Screenplay by:	Felix Adler
Director of Photography:	Vincent Farrar
Art Director:	Robert Peterson
Film Editor:	Edwin Bryant

Credited Cast:

Shemp Howard	
Larry Fine	
Moe Howard	
Mary Ainslee	Mary
Vernon Dent	Insurance adjustor
Jimmy Lloyd	Cliff

Uncredited Cast:

David Bond	Svengarlic
Ned Glass	agent

PERSPECTIVE: After the Gottlers wrote *Woman Haters* and the Stooges themselves wrote *Punch Drunks* in 1934, Felix Adler was the first Columbia staffer to write Stooge films. In 1935's *Uncivil Warriors* he continued to develop what was to become a common type of Stooge format that begins with one scenario, moves abruptly into a second for the body of the film, and then returns to the original scenario for a denouement, bringing the narrative full circle. Fifteen years later, Adler's thirtieth Stooge comedy, *Hokus Pokus*, follows the same 'ring composition' pattern - starting and ending with the disabled Mary's bogus insurance claim but sandwiching a Stooge encounter with the magician Svengarlic in between.

Adler and producer/director Jules White, who had made six films together since Shemp joined the trio in 1946, apparently looked at their seventh Shemp venture as an opportunity to experiment with some different arrangements for inter-Stooge dynamics. In 1947's *Sing a Song of Six Pants* and *All Gummed Up*, they had experimented with centrifugal narrative space and brought external characters into the Stooges who were themselves confined to a single shop, and earlier this year in *The Ghost Talks* they had experimented with combining such non-Stooge characters as spooks and legendary figures. In *Hokus Pokus* they seem to be experimenting with role reversals, having Larry boss Moe around ("Break it up. We got work to do!"), giving Moe a Curly-esque hand-wave with a down thrust and insulting himself ("What stupid, imbecile, fool put that—...I did! Boy am I dumb!"), having Moe circle a hammer around and hit himself on the head and sing a Curly-esque 'La-Dee' while the insurance adjuster [Vernon Dent] gives Larry an eye gouge, and having Shemp order Moe to "Take a powder" and get so frustrated by the inanimate card table à la Curly that he cries, stomps his feet, and says "Rruff!" Such gags surprise a Stooge viewer used to seeing Moe as the boss giving out gouges, hitting, and insulting others, Larry as the recipient, and Shemp doing, well, Shemp things. For Adler and White as well as the Stooges this was healthy innovation; no artist likes to be too repetitive even if the public tends to want more of the same.

Adler filled out the plot line with a half-dozen set-gags: the Morse-code hammer banging, the circular shaving, the little dance after dressing, the folding table sequence, the paste-brush handle gag, and the hypnotism ('Sing Sing') gag. Although criticized for creating strings of gags in search of a plot, Adler has the first four gags establish the subservient relationship between the Stooges and Mary with code communications and the elaborate preparation and presentation of breakfast, and the other two establish the Stooges' introduction to Svengarlic. Cumulatively these gags reveal how Mary uses the Stooges as "saps" for her insurance scam and Svengarlic as subjects for his publicity stunt. Adler suggests that when the Stooges are perceived to be stooges, they get treated like

stooges, yet when all is said and done, these genuine Stooges reveal Mary's scam, free themselves from Svengarlic's trance, and emerge victorious...except for an obligatory, film-ending 'N-B-C' bonking.

VISUAL HUMOR: Other role reversals: Shemp hitting Moe in the gut with the long paste brush handle, making him swallow his cigar, and Moe grabbing Larry by the hair and banging him into the wall. Interesting introductions: we first hear about the Stooges as "the three saps living downstairs," much as we heard in the previous *Who Done It?* that they were the 'Alert Detective Agency'; and a quickly panning camera brings Svengarlic into view for the first time, a visual technique not used since the camera panned to the Stooges atop a tree branch in *Whoops, I'm an Indian*. There are a number of new gags in both the domestic scenes (Shemp bending over to touch his toes; Shemp asking Moe: "Help me up!" and Moe kicking him flat on the floor; Shemp keeping hot towels in the fridge; and Shemp almost strangling himself tightening his tie) and the hypnotism sequences (Svengarlic having two extra eyes on his palms; a hypnotized Larry becoming a cat; Shemp becoming a monkey and picking through Larry's hair for lice; and Shemp hanging by Moe's feet and pulling his pants down).

The card table gag derives from a Harpo Marx routine, but with much variation. In the previous film Shemp looked at an enlarged Moe in the camera and Moe looked at enlarged Larry's scalp in the magnifying class; here the repeated/varied routine is Shemp getting in the way of Moe's hammer and then Larry getting in way of Moe's paste brush. Shemp's boxing routine is one of his smoothest. The morning shaving routine derives from the opening of *Cactus Makes Perfect*, although the Stooges have elsewhere dusted (*Horses' Collars*) and bathed (*Gents Without Cents*) each other. The falling flower pot, which will become common in the following dozen films, probably derives from the falling shields in *The Ghost Talks* and *Who Done It?*, the previous two films, although we saw it previously in *Restless Knights* and *Heavenly Daze*. We most recently heard the 'N-B-C' gong in *The Ghost Talks*. The breakfast preparation scene - Moe putting eggs through a coffee grinder and a pint of lard in the frying pan - is reminiscent of the meal preparation scene in *I'm a Monkey's Uncle*.

The sequence in which Shemp and Moe show each other how hard Moe hit Shemp with the hammer (Moe: "All I did was hit you like this (BICK)." Shemp: "It was harder than that." Moe: "Well at the most it was only like this (BICK)." Shemp: "It was much harder than that. I'll show ya' [He hits himself with the hammer (BANG)] See?") derives from the Ted Healy/Bonnie Bonnell slapping discussion by the bar in *Hollywood on Parade*. Other variations: multiple clangings (*They Stooge to Conga*); the Stooges on a flagpole (*3 Dumb Clucks*); the Stooges hanging a poster (*Three Little Twirps*); Shemp thinking he has lost a finger (his head in *Brideless Groom*); the Stooges sleeping, turning, and snoring in unison (*Hoi Polloi*); Shemp 'swimming' on the floor (*We Want Our Mummy*); the fried eggs flipped onto Moe's eyes (*Busy Buddies*); the Stooges shifting ('Hike!') and throwing towels in each others' faces after the three-pattern "Towel...towel" ("Cotton!" in *Men in Black*); being covered in white powder (flour in *Sock-a-Bye Baby*); Shemp turning and hitting Moe with the long handle (*Three Little Pigskins*; *Back to the Woods*); and yawning, stretching, and punching Larry in the face (*G.I. Wanna Home*).

VERBAL HUMOR: Adler's script offers one major new routine (Shemp: "Look me in the eye. Hokus-pokus, hokus-pokus, alacadabra. Ftt! Ftt! Ftt! You are now in Los Angeles." Moe [monotone]: "I am now in Los Angeles." Shemp: "You are now in New York." Moe: "I am now in New York." Shemp: "You are now in Sing Sing." Moe holds up a bentwood chair: "I am now in Sing Sing." Shemp: "You are now in Boston." Moe: "I am now in Sing Sing." Shemp: "NO! You are now in Boston!" Moe: "I am now in Sing Sing." Larry: "You can't get this guy outta Sing Sing." Shemp: "Good! That's just where he belongs!"). It also features several new insults (Shemp: "Does my head look like a steam pipe?" Moe: "No, a steam pipe doesn't have ears!"; Moe: "Your face is too sharp!"; and Shemp: "I have an idea." Moe: "You?"), a three-pattern (Larry: "Powder!" Moe: "Powder!" Shemp to Moe: "Take a powder!"), threats (Moe: "Listen, halibut! I'll fillet you!"), puns (the poster: 'The Great HYPNOTIST SVENGARLIC - He'll Steal Your Breath Away'), and throw-away lines (Shemp [to Moe with the eggs on his eyes]: "Where'd you get the sunglasses?"; Shemp [hanging from Moe's pants]: "You're inside out!"). Epithets: "barracuda," "numskulls," and "blithering idiots!".

References: 'Svengarlic' is a play on John Barrymore's well-known film role as the hypnotist in *Svengali* (1931); 'Shlemiel Number 8' parodies 'Chanel Number 5,' one of Coco Chanel's most famous and best selling perfumes introduced in the 1920s. 'Shlemiel' is Yiddish for "fool, loser". The Stooges have snored and wheezed in unison and sung together, but they have never before sighed or snored in major triads. The eggs are called both "cackle fruit" (*Busy Buddies*, *All Gummed Up*) and "hen fruit" (*Yes, We Have No Bonanza*). The three-pattern (Larry: "Towel!" Moe: "Towel!" Shemp to no one: "Towel.! Low man again!") derives from *Three Little Pigskins*. Other variations: Larry: "Break it up. We got work to do!" (*Cash and Carry*); "I feel a draft" (*Three Smart Saps*); "hotcakes smothered in vinegar" ("pig's knuckles smothered in garlic" in *False Alarms*); and Shemp: "This thing is haunted" (*Men in Black*).

OTHER NOTES: The working title was *Three Blind Mice*. The *Scrapbook* reports that the stock shot of the flagpole cracking is from Buster Keaton's *The Taming of the Snood* (1940). This is the only Stooge role for David Bond [Svengarlic], although he will reprise his role in the refurbished version, *Flagpole Jitters* (1956). As an actor he played Seurat in *Lust for Life;* as a writer his work was produced on Broadway; and as a director/producer he founded the Hollywood Shakespeare Festival. Ned Glass [Svengarlic's agent] was the husband of Kitty McHugh (*Listen, Judge*).

#116 - FUELIN' AROUND

Studio: Columbia

Released: July 7, 1949

Running Time: 16"40'"

Credited Production Crew:

Produced by:	Hugh McCollum
Directed by:	Edward Bernds
Story & Screen Play by:	Elwood Ullman
Director of Photography:	Vincent Farrar
Art Director:	Robert Peterson
Film Editor:	Henry Batista

Credited Cast:

Shemp Howard	
Larry Fine	
Moe Howard	
Christine McIntyre	Hazel, Snead's daughter
Emil Sitka	Professor Snead
Vernon Dent	Anemian general
Philip Van Zandt	Captain Rork
Andre Pola	Colonel Clutz
Jacques O'Mahoney	guard

Uncredited Cast:

Harold Brauer	Leon

PERSPECTIVE: This is the first Stooge film since *Booby Dupes* (1945) to satirize a political enemy. After the surrender of Germany in 1945, the USSR established a communist sphere of influence in eastern Europe. In the initial years of the ensuing Cold War, the U.S. countered with democratic 'missionary diplomacy,' defending European democracy by establishing the National Security Council and CIA in 1948 and NATO in 1949. An arms race developed as well - it was feared the Soviets would acquire their own 'A-bomb' by 1952, but they did so just three months after the release of *Fuelin' Around* - demanding the acquisition of accomplished scientists to build more sophisticated weaponry. One such piece of weaponry would be the ballistic missile, hence the Anemians' quest for 'super rocket fuel.' Enter for the first time the Stooges into the Cold War. This was serious stuff: when Shemp suggests admitting they are impostors, Moe explains: "If they find out we're only carpet layers, they'll go back and grab the real professor. And not only that, they'll shoot us. Now we gotta fool 'em, savvy?" Once again the Stooges are called on to save the free world, and as always, they deliver.

The Stooges were minding their own business - being inept, squabbling, flirtatious carpet layers working in an otherwise quiet American suburb. Yes, also for the first time, after so many recent films set in castles, spooky mansions, and urban shops, the Stooges find themselves in 1949 working for the expanding, post-war middle class. It just so happens, though, that they are doing this installation in the new home of the brilliant American rocket scientist, Professor Snead [Emil Sitka]. As so often, all it takes is for one careless person to confuse the Stooges for someone else. Here, Anemian spies confuse Larry for the scientist known, as was Einstein who lived then in a similar style home in Princeton, for his distinctive, unkempt hair. For once Larry's hair comes in handy for something other than ersatz dog fur, mattress stuffing, flower petals ("She loves me"), or Moe's grasp.

The post-war era gave the Stooges opportunities for new comedy situations. The housing boom popularized wall-to-wall carpeting, and by crawling under the carpeting Moe enters a subterranean dimension castles and Depression-era offices never offered, inspiring such gags as grabbing Larry's nose with sheers, snapping the measuring tape into Moe's face, and yanking a runner from under Shemp's feet. Once the Stooges are put into the Anemian laboratory they can blend their unique mixological magic with political satire. Despite being confounded by the most elementary chemistry, they develop a Cold War-winning fuel and trick their captors with double talk. It is Larry, "the most intelligent imbecile," whom the Anemians confused with Professor Snead in the first place, who then suggests that the prisoners use their acidic rocket fuel to engineer a jail break. Shemp ("just-an-imbecile") takes over from there, fueling the jeep so they can bring the real professor back to the free world while stripping the aptly named Anemian military down to their powder-burnt long johns. Better living through chemistry developed by a patriotic ersatz Einstein and his able assistants.

VISUAL HUMOR: As in the previous year, the Bernds/ Ullman team tends to string gags together (the measuring tape flies into Moe's face, Moe yanks the carpet runner and slams back into the door, Shemp flips upside down over a chair, a carpet roll topples over on him, and a vase rolls off the shelf, crashing onto his head; Moe grabs Leon's pistol by the barrel, bangs Shemp over the head with the handle, and hands the pistol back to Leon, points the gun away from himself and towards Larry, who points it away from himself; Jacques Mahoney bangs his head into the lamp, gets hit by the swinging lamp, and then falls around the corner) and punctuate verbal exchanges with slapstick (Larry: "*I'm* the professor!" Moe: "Sorry, professor." [SLAP]; Moe: "With that stuff a plane can go 1400 miles an hour." Shemp: "In low gear." [SLAP]). A visual five-pattern (the General slaps Rork with his gloves, Rork grabs the gloves and does the same to Larry, Larry to Moe, Moe to Shemp, and Shemp to no one), a Stooge first, includes two Anemians. This sequence gets a very elaborate setup: outside in the previous scene the general gives Rork a medal, then in this scene he removes it, adding: "One moment, Captain Rork - ha-ha, stupid of me - *Private* Rork....I was in error giving you this, but not *this*!" Several other sequences involve the Anemians in physical gags (downing Shemp with a flying tackle, stretching Shemp in the hole, and Shemp's two fists punching them in their faces from down in the hole).

Stretching Shemp between floors derives from Moe being stretched in *Higher Than a Kite*, although Shemp was hanging from Moe on the flagpole in the previous film, *Hokus Pokus*. Also from the previous film are role reversals (Larry: "My men'll have this job done in a couple of hours." Moe: "Who's men?" Larry: "*Us* men."), Moe thinking his toes are gone (Shemp's finger [but also *Some More of Samoa*]), Morse code signals, the vase rolling off the shelf onto Shemp's head (the flower pot), Larry slapping Moe while explaining how he should "Put out your hand when you go up a side street" (Moe explaining how he hit Shemp with the hammer), the professor's daughter opening the door onto Shemp's head thus making him swallow the tacks (Moe swallowing the cigar), and the clever introduction of Rork - when the fuel cork pops across the room into his eye.

Other variations: Stooges pacing in an interwoven pattern (*Loco Boy Makes Good*); Shemp getting his nose caught in the door (*Crash Goes the Hash*); Moe rasping Shemp's face with the stretcher (*No Census, No Feeling*); Larry cutting the toes off Moe's shoes (*Some More of Samoa*); Shemp putting the funnel in Moe's sleeve (*All Gummed Up*); soldiers reduced to underwear (*Dutiful but Dumb*); twisting Shemp's feet around, and the Stooges banging their heads on iron window bars (*Grips, Grunts and Groans*); Moe pulling the carpet runner (*Idle Roomers*); Moe stuck under the carpet (the door in *Pardon My Scotch*); and spraying a fire extinguisher into Moe's face (*So Long, Mr. Chumps*).

VERBAL HUMOR: A notable feature of Ullman's script is the number of solo wisecracks he wrote for each Stooge, for Shemp (when he knocks a jar onto his head: "How'd that mule get in here?"; when he sees Moe under the carpet: "a noisy wrinkle"; when his derby blinds his eyesight: "How did I get in this cellar here?"; when he hears the professor has a short memory: "I've got a little booklet here: *How to Train Your Memory in Five E-Z Lessons*"; when he tries to "take a look around town...I'm back" [some of these are no doubt ad-libs], Larry ("Our duty to posterior" [i.e. posterity]; "Drop us a line and let us know how you come out."; "Did I give you carbolic acid?...I'd love to!"), and Moe ("This ain't no reform school. It's a theater...[a general walks past]...There goes the doorman!"). Ullman wrote several worthy exchanges (Moe: "How many feet you got?" Shemp: "Two"; Shemp: "Moe! You was that lump!" Moe: "And you'll be the next one!"; Larry: "Pardon me, do you have any idea what we're doin'?" Moe: "Now that you mention it, no"; Moe: "Top of the morning to you, Captain." Shemp: "And the rest of the day for myself!"; Moe: "With that stuff a plane can go 1400 miles an hour." Shemp: "In low gear!"; Leon: "Call the guard!" Shemp: "What's the guard's name?". Moe has one internal rhyme ("You don't know my sleeve from a jug, you jug-head!") and assesses Stooge ignorance beautifully ("He's the most intelligent imbecile I ever saw!" Shemp: "Hey, how about me?" Moe: "Ohh, you're much smarter: you're just an imbecile"). Epithets: "jug-head," "skillet-head," and "good-lookin'".

Perhaps the highlight of the dialogue is the round-robin, three-pattern, double-talk formula for the fuel (Moe to Larry: "Tell him, professor." Larry to Shemp: "Uh, tell him!" Shemp: "First you put in a half a pint of ekta-whosis." Larry: "No, no. Ekta-whatsis." Moe: "And four grams of alca-bob, then you pour in the shish-ka-bob, then you fold in the jigger of saskra-phonia." Shemp: "Put down a squid of haratan. Spelled sidewords it's 'ta-hara-titn-tk-tk-tk.'" Captain: "Uh, how you spell this 'tk-tk-tk-tk'?" Shemp: "That's right. Put it down!").

"Tk" we just heard in *Hokus Pokus*; we also heard "Low man again," the old Curlyism. The Morse code/knock-knock routine derives from the Morse code of *Hokus Pokus*. 'Anemia' is a Stooge geographical name of the sort we saw in *You Nazty Spy!*. Shemp's "I've got a little booklet here: *How to Train Your Memory in Five E-Z Lessons*" is the same sort of aid-the-enemy gag used in *Rockin' Thru the Rockies*. Other variations: Larry's fish-bowl sound imitation (*Hold That Lion*); Moe: "Give me that tape!" ("Give it to me!" in *Pardon My Scotch*); Larry: "Reminds me of the reform school" (*Ants in the Pantry*); and Shemp's "My neck! You're killin' me!" ("You're crushin' my eyebrows"), and watch imitation ("tick-tick-tick") (*Fright Night*). References: Carbolic acid is toxic and corrosive, but also has antiseptic properties. Pyrogallic acid is used as a photographic developer; cf. the 'hypo' in *Who Done It?*

OTHER NOTES: The quest for the super rocket fuel is one weapon-generation after the Televanian M-9 submarine from *Three Little Sew and Sews* (1939). It precedes the Stooges' sci-fi/outer space films by almost a decade. Colonel Clutz, who helped capture Snead, chastises Rork for it later. This film will be refurbished as *Hot Stuff* (1956).

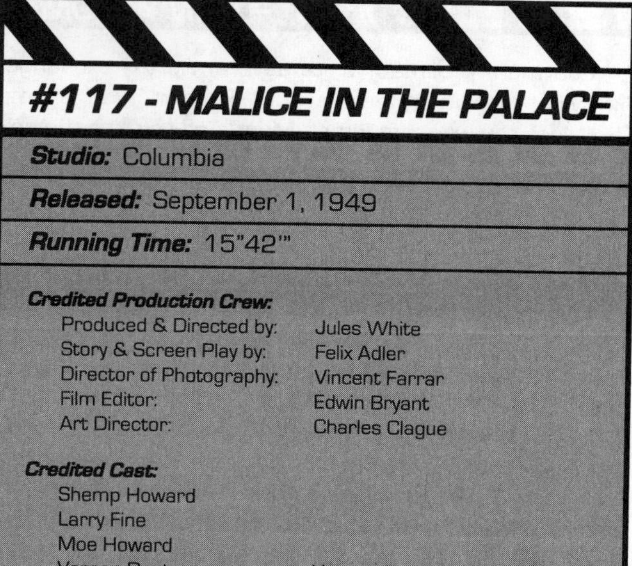

#117 - MALICE IN THE PALACE

Studio: Columbia

Released: September 1, 1949

Running Time: 15"42'"

Credited Production Crew:

Produced & Directed by:	Jules White
Story & Screen Play by:	Felix Adler
Director of Photography:	Vincent Farrar
Film Editor:	Edwin Bryant
Art Director:	Charles Clague

Credited Cast:

Shemp Howard	
Larry Fine	
Moe Howard	
Vernon Dent	Hassan Ben Sober
George Lewis	Ghinna Rumma
Frank Lackteen	Half Adollar

PERSPECTIVE: In their 1949 releases, Felix Adler and Jules White are turning out low-budget but imaginative creations. *The Ghost Talks* and *Hokus Pokus* are devoid of chases but full of mystery and magic with ghosts, skeletons, and a four-eyed hypnotist. The comic narrative in both films steps from gag to gag until it reaches a visually stimulating and surprising climax. *Malice in the Palace* follows this same pattern: the exotic, musically introduced Middle-Eastern setting offers us humorously named, dagger-wielding desert weasels who consume most of the Stooges' time until the film climaxes in a rolly-polly potentate's grand palace cooled by an elegant fountain and guarded by a huge, turbaned Nubian wielding a four-foot scimitar.

The palace climax consumes only the final four minutes. The rest of the film unfolds in a restaurant where the Stooges play waiters who spill food all over the customers and break plates on each other - and that is *before* the customers order. What follows is a classic scene (derived from *Playing the Ponies*) in which everyone believes Larry is cooking a cat and a dog. The gag builds for a long time with Laurel & Hardy-type timing while the animals are seemingly butchered in the kitchen and sneeze and fight under the table as the Stooges, Hassan Ben Sober, and Ghinna Rumma try to eat the *tabu*. The ensuing chaos leads to the discovery that the self-proclaimed aristocrat, Hassan Ben Sober, is a

costumed fraud, merely the doorman at the Oasis Hotel. In a memorable moment of final narrative resolution, Moe and Shemp proclaim: "You mean to tell me you're only a doorman? Well there's the door, man!"

Even the plots of ancient Greek tragedies changed direction when messengers arrived, and the dagger-delivered message leads the Stooges - they have an accurate map to get them over the Giva Dam - to the palace of the Emir of Shmow, a one-room set elegantly decorated by Charles Clague. The outside of the palace looks familiar since it is the Santa Clause footage from *Wee Wee Monsieur*. (This would be unremarkable except that the next film, *Vagabond Loafers*, uses footage from *A Plumbing We Will Go*.) The elaborate costumes - billowing pantaloons, sashes, and turbans - set the stage for ironic paradoxes: the Emir of Shmow giggles as he reads the funny papers, believes the pyramided Stooges are a real spirit, and obeys them by sticking his head in the fountain until he reaches total saturation. The imposing Nubian guard is no less gullible. Round 1: a leap frog game leads to a scimitar crowning, reducing him to skipping fool. Round 2: after the priceless threat "I weel *keel* you!" he takes grapefruits in the face and a banana in the mouth. Round 3: a huge bronze vase is pulled down onto his head (GONG-NG-NG-NG). The ineptitude of all four, silly-named Arabs differs from the competence of such Adler-created opponents as Peeping Tom and Svengarlic. Stooge Arabs, like Stooge Indians, generally make for silly opponents. Being a Stooge usually means acting like a stooge, but sometimes it means defeating stooge-like adversaries with creativity and cleverness. When it comes to being "intelligent imbeciles," Moe, Larry, and Shemp are the cat's meow.

VISUAL HUMOR: Just as anachronisms are appropriate for historical films, ethnic and cultural ironies are appropriate here, so the Stooges dress as Santa Clause in an Islamic desert kingdom and the Emir of Shmow reads the funny papers. The Stooge introduction is innovative; They weave intricately with their trays (*Loco Boy Makes Good*; the previous film, *Fuelin' Around*), but then Shemp knocks everything over. Ghinna Rumma holding out his knife ("Would you give me five for this?" Moe: "No, but I'll give you two!") and Moe gouging him is the first time this routine has been done with a non-Stooge; Vernon Dent gouged Larry recently in *Hokus Pokus*. Other new gags: the hot dog licking Shemp's cheek; the round and round handshake; Moe pulling a fork and a lit candle out of Hassan Ben Sober's beard; Shemp hand-waving Moe to the floor and making him bonk his head against the floor; and Shemp pulling scarf after scarf from within his shirt. Slapstick sequence: the Arabs slap Shemp's hot dog to the ground, so the dog and cat fight over it, causing the table to be knocked over and the Stooges to entangle themselves; when they see the animals Moe slaps Larry, slaps and pounds Shemp for telling him to leave Larry alone, and puts Larry's fist on Shemp's chin and socks Larry's elbow, then Larry and Shemp in unison give Moe hand-waves with a downward thrust, so Moe pounds their bellies and bonks their heads.

Shemp exhales on the knife à la Curly. Larry tends to eat with delight whenever he is given the opportunity, as in *Three Sappy People*. Shemp and Moe cry a lot, and later Hassan Ben Sober does, too.

Sound effects: TWEET (*Grips, Grunts and Groans*) when the Nubian gets clanged with the scimitar blade; and the 'COO-KOO' sound (*Soup to Nuts; Uncivil War Birds*) when the guard gets clanged into the sack. Both the Santa Clause routine and the bronze vase were used in *Wee Wee Monsieur*. The final throw away gag - the fountain squirting the Stooges - is of the same sort as the final gag in *Hokus Pokus*. Other variations: stepping on a cat's tail (*Dizzy Detectives*); spitting in Moe's face (*Hoi Polloi*); Hassan Ben Sober looking at Ghinna Rumma's upside-down fez for relief (*Back From the Front*); Ghinna Rumma spinning in his sash (*Mummy's Dummies*); spaghetti landing on Ghinna Rumma's head (*Sock-a-Bye Baby*); dressing as a giant by piling on top of one another (*Wee Wee Monsieur, Healthy, Wealthy and Dumb*); and flinging fruit in a guard's face (*Squareheads of the Round Table*) and a banana in the mouth (*Micro-Phonies*).

VERBAL HUMOR: Felix Adler worked on both *You Nazty Spy!* and *I'll Never Heil Again*, so the map here includes the same style of drinking jokes (Corkscrew Straights, Straights-of-Rye, Hang Over, Mikey Finland), double names (Hot Sea, Tot-Sea; Atisket, Atasket; Snowland, Noland, Shmowland), puns on real geographical names (the Inseine River; Great Mitten; Egypt, Ugypt; I-ran, He-ran, She-ran, They-ran, Also-ran), word plays (Slap Happia, Double Crossia), puns (Cant Sea, the Bay of Window, Rubid-Din, Giva Dam), and Stooge-isms (Woo-Woo, Jerkola). The Arab names 'Hassan Ben Sober,' 'Ghinna Rumma,' 'Omagosh,' and 'Half Adollar' are of the same sort. 'Shmow' is a Stooge favorite, as in the name 'The Emir of Shmow,' Moe's "The Shmow is flooded," and the working title of the film (*Here We Go Shmow*); the word will appear again in *A Train Named Shmow*, the working title of *Cuckoo on a Choo Choo*. There are two four-patterns with internal word plays (Larry: "What'll you have?" Hassan Ben Sober: "We want—" Moe: "We don't have anymore!" Larry: "All we got left is rabbit and hot dogs." Hassan Ben Sober: "Rabbit." Ghinna Rumma: "Hot dog." Larry: "Hot dog! They'll take rabbit"; Larry: "A thousand pardons!" Moe: "This would degrade you." Hassan Ben Sober: "'Tis true! I am an aristocrat! I am Hassan Ben Sober!" Shemp: "I had a few too many myself!"). Twice (once before the meal, once after), Moe concedes at knife point; he says "You talked us into it!" and "You convinced us!". Shemp is again characterized as a coward: "That Emir of Shmow is a cutthroat. Suppose he cuts my throat?" Larry & Moe: "Well?!". Shemp throw-away lines: "Well there's the door, man!"; "That's government property!"; and, when he snips Ghinna Rumma's spaghetti, "People don't know if you're comin' or goin' with this on." "There's the door, man," belongs to the divided-word pattern first heard in *Beer Barrel Polecats* (Larry: "At last you got a brain, child!").

Moe's "Our bus boy's out" is a throw-away line for wiping Hassan Ben Sober's beard. When Moe calls him "spinach chin," he reprises his metaphor from *Hollywood Party* ("Come out from under that spinach, Gable"). Other variations: Shemp's "100 carats! He sure knew his onions!" (Curly's "That don't look like a vegetable to me!" in *Yes, We Have No Bonanza*); and Hassan Ben Sober: "Gentlemen!" Shemp: "Who came in?" (*Monkey Businessmen*).

References: the 'Casbah' is the famous old section of Algiers; 'Black Sheep...Bah-bah-bah' parodies the Rudyard Kipling (and song) lyrics: 'We are poor little lambs who've lost our way, baa-baa-baa/We're little black sheep who've gone astray, baa-baa-baa'; 'Get the gate' is slang for to be eliminated from contention; Larry refers twice to Hollywood, once with sarcasm "Boy! With that kind of money [$50,000] we could rent a one-room apartment in Hollywood...maybe," and once to the "Oasis Hotel." A favorite Hollywood hotel/apartment/hangout at the time was 'The Garden of Allah' at Sunset Blvd. and Havenhurst St. The currency of 'chilblainers' parodies the word 'chilblain,' a cold sore.

OTHER NOTES: There is a rumor, based on a publicity-type photograph, that Curly was originally cast as the chef, and that the sequence was inexplicably deleted from the final release. See Volk, *The Films of the Stooges* (130); the photograph is in *Okuda* [70] and *Larry* [198]. Curly's face looks different, particularly in profile, but after a stroke and drastic weight reduction, Curly looked more like his father; see *Curly* 108 and 144-146. Unlike *Mummy's Dummies*, the script spells 'Rootentooten' as 'Ruttin' Tuttin'. The most recent Stooge film to begin with a musical introduction was *Fiddlers Three*.

The Stooges visited a Middle-Eastern setting in *Wee Wee Monsieur* and the two mummy films. Abbott & Costello made *Lost in the Harem* in 1944; their *Abbott and Costello in the Foreign Legion* appeared the year after *Malice in the Palace*. The 100-carat diamond tops the 50-carat Punjab diamond in *Crime on Their Hands*. We get thirty seconds to look at the map. This film will be refurbished as *Rumpus in the Harem* (1956). As with *Disorder in the Court* and *Sing a Song of Six Pants*, the copyright for this film lapsed without renewal decades ago.

#118 - VAGABOND LOAFERS

Studio: Columbia

Released: October 6, 1949

Running Time: 15"51'"

Credited Production Crew:

Produced by:	Hugh McCollum
Directed by:	Edward Bernds
Written by:	Elwood Ullman
Director of Photography:	Vincent Farrar
Art Director:	Charles Clague
Film Editor:	Henry DeMond

Credited Cast:

Shemp Howard	
Larry Fine	
Moe Howard	
Christine McIntyre	Mrs. Allen
Kenneth MacDonald	Mr. Allen
Symona Boniface	Clarabell Norfleet
Emil Sitka	Walter Norfleet
Dudley Dickerson	Henry, the chef
Herbert Evans	Wilks, the butler

PERSPECTIVE: This film marks an important turning point in Stooge film-making. It is the first Shemp film to refurbish a previously used Stooge script, and this will become common after 1951's *Pest Man Wins*. It is not an entirely new procedure: several Stooge films have reused stories from older, non-Columbia comedies (*If a Body Meets a Body* was derived from *The Laurel & Hardy Murder Case*) or reworked scripts written for other Columbia short subject productions (*Three Pests in a Mess* was a reworked version of El Brendel's *Ready, Willing but Unable; Idiots Deluxe* was a reworked version of Collins & Kennedy's *Oh, My Nerves!*; Sidney & Murray's *Ten Baby Fingers* was reworked as Andy Clyde's *My Little Feller*, in turn reworked as *Mutts to You* and *Sock-A-Bye Baby*), and when Curly was ailing during the 1945 shooting of *Beer Barrel Polecats*, director Jules White masked Curly's condition by piecing together six minutes of footage from *In the Sweet Pie and Pie* and *So Long, Mr. Chumps*. Also, in just the previous film some of the Santa Clause footage came from *Wee Wee Monsieur*. But a fully refurbished Stooge script is something revolutionary in the Shemp era.

The McCollum/Bernds unit chose to refurbish *A Plumbing We Will Go*, the classic tool-abuse, Stooges-as-tradesmen, destroy-a-wealthy home film. Because the original starred Curly, only non-Curly footage could be reused, that is, the scenes with Dudley Dickerson slipping and sliding in a kitchen that is "sho' goin' crazy," and Larry digging out in the yard. In reworking the script writer Elwood Ullman, who had written the original for the first Lord/McCollum production, updated the scenario and transferred the plot into a contemporary Shemp-type. No longer Depression-era, penniless bums running from the cops, as they often were in Curly-era films, the Stooges now have their own business, as they do in *Sing a Song of Six Pants* and five of this year's films. In many Shemp-type films the Stooges capture crooks, and that is what is written into this old plumbing script. Instead of running away at the finale, the Stooges are rewarded for capturing the crooks, even if Shemp's refusal to move into a higher tax bracket causes much of the basement plumbing to suffer a serious relapse.

The refurbishing is artful, turning the hole in the bathroom floor into an integral part of the plot which calls for Allen to be captured and the painting to be recovered down below. The wet kitchen now causes the chef to rescue a bag of flour which turns Larry into the spook-like figure that scares the crook. Thus Larry's isolation out in the yard has turned him into the hero who recaptures Allen when he is holding everyone else at gun point. Thanks to the flooded kitchen, the hole outside, a bag of flour, and a frightened chef, for once it is a Stooge who does the haunting. Editor Henry DeMond sequenced the episodes involving the Allens and the chef, Shemp and Mr. Allen, Shemp and Mrs. Allen, and Larry and the chef, so we can follow the bathroom, basement, and hallway activities as they culminate with the entire cast assembling in the basement for an Agatha Christie-like, crime-solving climax.

VISUAL HUMOR (NEW MATERIAL ONLY): An important visual element is the water itself; it comes out hard and fast. Trickles are not nearly as funny as huge gushes. Compare the Stooges being sprayed by the fountain towards the end of the previous film with the geysers that soak everyone in this film. Slapstick sequences: Larry dropping the tool bag onto Moe, sliding down the pole and hitting the jeep's accelerator, and then Shemp missing the jeep; the Stooges swinging the pipes, knocking a table, causing the butler to drop his tray in order to save a vase, then Moe clanging Wilks in the head and causing him to drop the vase onto the floor; and Larry igniting Moe's rear, causing him to step into a bucket of water, causing Larry to pull his leg out, causing Larry to get kneed in the jaw and Moe to back into Shemp, causing Shemp to pull the wrench off the leak and hit Moe in the head. Result shot: Allen draped over the trash can, his head in a bucket.

Stooge firsts: the phone on an accordion arm which punches Moe thrice; and Larry sitting and reading the newspaper, tipping over the bucket full of leak water, putting the bucket back in place, and reading the paper again. When Mrs. Norfleet demands "Give me what you have in your hand!" and Shemp puts a blow torch in her hand, this is an embellishment of the usual "Give it to me!" (*Pardon My Scotch*).The barrage Moe gives Larry for saying "Wet, ain't it?" (GOUGE-BLOCK, POUND, BONK, WET SLAP) is as complex as the post-meal barrage Moe gave Shemp and Larry in the previous *Malice in the Palace*. This is Larry's first perpendicular-handed gouge block; interestingly, it occurs in a film directed by Ed Bernds, who did not like the gouge. Other variations: Moe reading the plumbing textbook (chemistry textbook in *Fuelin' Around*), the pull-chain bed dumper (*Idle Roomers*); Shemp hitting Allen with the pipe and Moe with the backswing (*Three Little Sew and Sews*); the sack of flour (the talcum powder in *Hokus Pokus*); and Moe's swinging and destroying the basement as the final gag (*The Sitter Downers*).

VERBAL HUMOR (NEW MATERIAL ONLY): The new arrangement of scenes declimaxes the previously important water-gushing TV set, but Ullman enhances the sequence with Emil Sitka's verbal quip: "It's realistic, isn't it darling?" Also enhancing the physical humor of the water damage is Larry's "Wet, ain't it?"; Dudley Dickerson's "Sorry, folks. Dinner's postponed on account of rain!"; Shemp's "Moe! Larry! I'm trapped by the risin' water. I'll be drowned like a rat" (a variation of "We're trapped like rats" [*Back to the Woods*]); and the chef's response to Mrs. Allen's "Just looking for a drink of water": "Turn on anything, you'll get it!". Many gag lines accompany visual gags (Shemp's "Gotta get a longer jeep!" when he slides down and misses it; Moe's "What's the idea of droppin' in without a calling card?" when Shemp falls through the hole; Mr. Norfleet's "Short circuit, no doubt!" when the lamp is sliding up and down the wall; Allen's: "If I took that picture, may I be struck by a bolt from the blue!" just before Shemp drops the pipe onto his head; and Larry and Shemp sleeping after we see the sign: 'DAY AND NITE PLUMBERS - WE NEVER SLEEP'. Different is Moe's cry when everyone assumes the plumbers stole the painting: "Take it easy, folks! I'm just a beginner!" He thinks it is his bad plumbing.

The hoity-toity accents of Mrs. Norfleet and Wilks, the butler, ("Look h-yere, you menn!") are particularly snotty, making the Stooges' mimicry and vulgar language (Moe: "Now take it easy, lady. Don't blow a fuse!") all the more comical by contrast. The Stooges are irreverent to Allen as well (Larry: "Well lead on, pal!" Mr. Allen [indignant]: "Pal!"). Replacing Curly's "Bath, bahth" gag is Shemp's literal response to Mr. Norfleet's "Well I say!" Shemp: "Never mind what you say!". Other variations: Moe: "You're a very intelligent imbecile" (*Fuelin' Around*); Moe: "What would you charge to haunt a house?" Larry: "How many rooms?" (*What's the Matador?*). Epithets: "slugs," "oyster-brain," and "dimwit". Stooge time measurement: Moe's "We'll be over in two shakes of a martini.".

References: The Dutch 'van' part of the artist 'Van Brocklin' may echo the the seventeenth-century Flemish painter Anthony van Dyck referred to in *Wee Wee Monsieur* and *I'll Never Heil Again*, but Norm van Brocklin, the rookie quarterback of the L.A. Rams, had led the team to the NFL Championship game just four weeks before the film was shot in late January, 1949; the Rams lost to the Cleveland Browns in the final 28 seconds of that game, but this was the first NFL Western conference championship the Rams had won after moving to L.A. from Cleveland in 1946. The painting itself is no doubt Flemish and predates 1749. There are two references to the inflation America was experiencing at the time: the otherwise wealthy Mr. Norfleet complains about the cost of the painting ("He only died in poverty; from now on I'll have to live in it!"), and Larry and Shemp's final complaint about a higher tax bracket, expressed in a three-pattern in which Moe turns a noun into a verb: Larry: "We don't want no more money." Shemp: "No, it'll put us in a higher tax bracket." Moe: "I'll bracket your head!"

OTHER NOTES: Changes in the front credits: the cast credits (introduced by 'with') now appear on a second screen, and Ullman's credit is given as 'Written By' for the first time instead of 'Story and Screenplay By'. The title parodies the romantic expression 'vagabond lovers'; *The Vagabond Lover* was a Rudy Vallee/Marie Dressler film of 1929, and a Rudy Vallee/Leon Zimmerman song ('I'm Just a Vagabond Lover'), of which Vallee sings the first line in *Hollywood on Parade*. *The Vagabond King* (1930) was the first Technicolor feature film. Shemp had teamed with El Brendel in *Pick a Peck of Plumbers* (1944), an earlier, non-Stooge version of *A Plumbing We Will Go*, which in turn was a reworking of Sidney & Murray's *Plumbing for Gold* (1934). Another Stooge version will be *Scheming Schemers* (1956), one of the four 'Shemp films' made after his death. This was Dudley Dickerson's final role in a Stooge film. It was also Symona Boniface's last of eleven Stooge roles. Both will appear in stock footage. For a brief biography, see Bill Cappello, *The 3 Stooges Journal* 66 (1993) 6-7.

#119 - DUNKED IN THE DEEP

Studio: Columbia

Released: November 3, 1949

Running Time: 16"46'"

Credited Production Crew:

Produced & Directed by:	Jules White
Written by:	Felix Adler
Director of Photography:	Vincent Farrar
Art Director:	Charles Clague
Film Editor:	Edwin Bryant

Credited Cast:

Shemp Howard	
Larry Fine	
Moe Howard	
Gene Roth	Bortch

PERSPECTIVE: In 1948 Winston Churchill identified the 'Cold War,' and with the creation of the CIA the trenchcoated war of espionage began to capture national attention. President Truman's Loyalty Review Board investigated 3 million federal employees, and Richard Nixon led a highly publicized investigation of Alger Hiss in the House Committee on Un-American Activities. While *Dunked in the Deep* was being produced, eleven New York communists were imprisoned; three months later Joe McCarthy began his infamous Senate hearings; and then later Julius and Ethel Rosenberg were to become the only Americans executed for espionage during peacetime. Hollywood, itself under HUAC investigation, entered this world of intrigue, suspense, and anti-American operatives already in 1948 with Fox's *Iron Curtain*, followed in 1949 by Republic's *The Red Menace* and RKO's *The Woman on Pier 13*. Move six piers over to Pier 7 and you will find this second Stooge Cold War film. As in their early World War II anti-Nazi efforts, the Stooges were the avant garde at incorporating ominous political winds into their satire, beating by two years a slew of 1951 spy films. Unlike the earlier *Fuelin' Around, Dunked in the Deep* concerns not a neo-science super rocket fuel but a single, despicable spy carrying microfilm in plugged watermelons. Microfilm, not coincidentally, was the main evidence Richard Nixon used to convict Alger Hiss of perjury – and it was found stuffed into a pumpkin!

The narrative follows the interaction between Stooges and spy. At the outset we viewers see that Bortch is a foreign agent, but even when Bortch offers his gullible friends the harsh, paper-peeling, acidic 'pre-war' hooch, it fails to raise the Stooges' suspicions. Finding themselves involuntarily stowed away aboard a freighter, the plucky Stooges can only snatch a meal out of the stingy European during the salami-slicing sequence [modeled in part after the nut-crushing gag in *Dizzy Detectives*]. It is only after they steal their second meal in the morning that they unplug Bortch's espionage from a watermelon, and their immediate reaction is to "turn him over to the authorities." The end of the film becomes a battle between the Stooges and the spy highlighted by a cinematically enhanced chase scene that employs, in contrast to every previous Stooge chase scene, only two actors; the last five films have each pitted all three Stooges against two or more adversaries. In fact, the entire film has only the Stooges and the one other actor [Gene Roth] playing the spy. The inspiration for this may have been that Cold War espionage films prescribe solitary spies and their dark, confined hideaways. Then again, Jules White's budget may have been depleted at the end of the year: the previous release used stock footage, and this film uses just the one actor.

The rest of *Dunked in the Deep*, the final 1949 Adler/White release, like *The Ghost Talks*, the first Adler/White 1949 release, contains characteristic inter-Stooge work with plot-related paraphernalia, namely

the sea-sickness/water bucket, the hammock, the porthole, the tackle and pulley, and the dynamite cargo box on Pier 7. The latter is a particularly masterful scene that reminds us, like the dynamite sequence in *Yes, We Have No Bonanza*, of how destructive inter-Stooge dynamics can be when the Stooges are left to squabble amongst themselves near a substance as unstable as they are.

VISUAL HUMOR: For the chase sequence, Shemp stands and watches in regular motion while Bortch runs around behind him in fast motion. This method of blending normal and fast/slow motion was utilized the previous year for a Fred Astaire dancing sequence in *Easter Parade* and the same year for the famous Hades sequence in Jean Cocteau's *Orfée*. Adler and White often work from a fundamental simplicity and avoid elaborate narrative setups: the dynamite scene unfolds from the simple desire to crack a Brazil nut, the salami sequence from simple hunger, and the hammock scene from Shemp's simple desire to go to sleep. They then make the scenes more elaborate, adding the machine parts to the salami scene, and a cigarette, stock footage (a ship in a stormy sea), and the rolling, burning trash can to the hammock scene. Slapstick firsts: Moe giving Shemp a double nose bonk and then bonking Larry with the back of his fist; and Shemp taunting with "Nyaah-nyaah!".

Shemp took his first drink in *Out West*, and had his longest reaction in *Who Done It?*; here he has another great reaction to booze that burns through wood, spins his tie, pops his hat, makes him 'ee-bee,' and peels wall paper. The sea-sickness and porthole scenes, the latter reprised at end the film ("Land! Land!"), derive from *Back from the Front*; we recently saw a 'vomit gag' with a fez as the bucket in *Malice in the Palace*. Other variations: Moe's egg in the hand, and Moe and Larry waking up, stretching, and punching each other in the face (*G.I. Wanna Home*); the pepper/sneezing gag (*Malice in the Palace*); watermelon shoes (*Wee Wee Monsieur*); Stooges dusting each other off (*Horses' Collars*); Bortch hearing metal in his belly (*Men in Black*); hearing a mysterious sound, peeling back layers of tarp, and finding Shemp 'ee-bee-beeing (Curly 'woob-woobing' on the gurney in *Men in Black*); breaking a watermelon over Shemp's head (the crab in *A Pain in the Pullman*); and Bortch groping Larry's forehead instead of the watermelon (Curly under the bed in *Who's the Matador?*).

VERBAL HUMOR: Because of the small cast and Bortch's secrecy, verbal gags are relatively sparse. The most appropriate occurs where Moe and Shemp confuse the microfilm at first for a "seed" and then a "prize". Bortch's dialogue is sarcastically dis-dainful: "My *wisa* has expired. I must leave your *glorious* country". Replacing verbal exchanges are two printed gags on the crate ('DANGER-DYNAMITE CAPS - DO NOT JAR, SHAKE, OR DROP - HIGHLY EXPLOSIVE - DANGER') and the flyer ('Old Holland Cheese in Five Delicious Flavors...Amsterdam, Rotterdam, Beaver Dam, Boulder Dam, and Giva Dam'). We heard Rotterdam/Amsterdam jokes in *I'll Never Heil Again*, and saw Giva Dam on the map in *Malice in the Palace*. Shemp's "We sing for the 'halibut'" is at least as old as the Marx Brothers but a first for a Stooge film. Larry and Shemp sing 'We're off to see the sea/To see what we can see,' [*Back From the Front*], altering the Irving Berlin lyrics ("We joined the navy to see the world,/But what did we see? We saw the sea") written for the Fred Astaire & Ginger Rogers film *Follow the Fleet* (1936). Other variations: Bortch: "That's what you think!" Moe: "That's what I said...Hello!" (*We Want Our Mummy*);

As budgets tightened towards the end of each year's production schedule, Jules White was forced to find methods of cutting costs - but not at the cost of depriving the Stooge-short films from innovative comedy. In *Dunked in the Deep*, the final film of 1949, he designed a narrative that involved just one other actor (Gene Roth) and a few simple sets, and then used the savings to employ avant garde special effects. The efforts for the dramatic chase scene in which Shemp watches while Bortch runs around behind him in fast motion was utilized the previous year in *Easter Parade* and this same year in Jean Cocteau's classic film, *Orfée*.

Shemp [eating salami]: "If only I had some whipped cream!" (*Soup to Nuts*); Moe's "Why, you back-biter!" (Pop Goes the Easel); Shemp's "My dogs are barkin'" (*A Ducking They Did Go*); and Larry: "Me, too." Moe: "Me, three."(*If a Body Meets a Body*).

OTHER NOTES: The stock footage of the S.S. San Capeador is from the Columbia feature, *The Captain Hates the Sea*, in which the Stooges appeared. The film image is shown in reverse. The *Scrapbook* reports that the stock shot of peeling wallpaper is from radio announcer Harry Von Zell's first Columbia short subject, *So's Your Antenna* (1946). Long-time Stooge stunt man Johnny Kascier's face is visible when 'Shemp' burns his rear in the trash can. This is the first of seven Stooge appearances for Gene Roth (Stutenroth), including the feature *The Three Stooges Meet Hercules*. The radio introduction to the espionage crime recalls this year's *Who Done It?* which also began with a radio introduction. (It is coincidence that this same year of the Cold War saw the introduction of Radio Free Europe.) As often, it is Moe's voice on the radio. *The Woman on Pier 13* included a horrific drowning scene by the pier. This film will be refurbished as *Commotion on the Ocean* (1956).

1950

Punchy Cowpunchers • *Hugs and Mugs* • *Dopey Dicks*

Love at First Bite • *Self-Made Maids* • *Three Hams on Rye*

Studio Stoops • *Slaphappy Sleuths* • *A Snitch in Time*

#120 - PUNCHY COWPUNCHERS

Studio: Columbia

Released: January 5, 1950

Running Time: 17"15'"

Credited Production Crew:

Produced by:	Hugh McCollum
Written & Directed by:	Edward Bernds
Director of Photography:	Vincent Farrar
Art Director:	Charles Clague
Film Editor:	Henry DeMond

Credited Cast:

Shemp Howard	
Larry Fine	
Moe Howard	
Jock O'Mahoney	Elmer, the Arizona Kid
Christine McIntyre	Nell
Kenneth MacDonald	Dillon
Dick Wessel	Sgt. Mullins
Vernon Dent	Colonel
Emil Sitka	Captain Daley

Uncredited Cast:

George Chesebro	Jeff
Bob Cason	Black Jeff
Ted Mapes	Red
Stanley Price	Lefty
Heinie Conklin	bartender

PERSPECTIVE: *Punchy Cowpunchers* starts the 1950 releases off with a remarkably hectic pace, especially in comparison to the intentionally isolated, spatially confined climactic chase of the the final film of the previous year, *Dunked in the Deep*. *Punchy Cowpunchers* instead spreads out all over the 'wild West,' bandying back and forth from military fort to saloon to the trail connecting them, and it involves not just the Three Stooges and one criminal or even the usual gang of three or four but a barmaid, the Arizona Kid, three cavalry officers, and a gang of five outlaws. And much of this is accompanied by music, making this a Western of epic scope, Stooge style. Stylistically, there is nothing as grand as this in the Stooge Columbia short-films. Hollywood's epic era (1949-1965) was already beginning with Cecil B. DeMille's *Samson and Delilah*, and *Punchy Cowpunchers* was shot in early February, 1949, shortly before *Samson and Delilah* was released. Again the Stooges are on the cutting edge, limited as their budget was. (Their only appearance in a genuine Hollywood epic will be their silent cameo in *It's a Mad, Mad, Mad, Mad World* [1963]).

Several years earlier Director Edward Bernds created the exciting climax of his first Stooge Western, *Three Troubledoers*, by editing together two different narrative strands - Blackie's wedding and the Stooges riding towards it on a three-seater bicycle - enhanced by fast motion and the strains of 'The William Tell Overture.' In his next Western, *Out West*, Bernds expanded that narrative duet to a brief trio, but now in *Punchy Cowpunchers* he calls for a trio of simultaneous action - the Stooges' crate and barrel chase downstairs, Nell's slugging gang members in the jaw upstairs, and the Kid's riding to and from Fort Scott outdoors while accompanied by screen titles ('HE FELL OFF AGAIN!'). The music is apt for each part of the trio, so in this sense this is a 'horse opera' in which the comedy builds upon each contrasting scenario: von Suppé's 'Light Cavalry March' makes the riding scenes gallant, the turbulent diminished music makes the fight scenes driving and dark, and the violin strains of Mendelssohn's 'Spring Song' turn Nell's scenes into hilarious melodrama where she and the music convince us she is "just a poor, weak woman" as she paradoxically punches out three men.

It is very rare that a non-Stooge character or even the characters played by the Stooges themselves carry from one film to another; Stooge films almost always begin anew with their characters, locations and plots. But ever innovative, the Columbia short-subject team for the first time (other than using Moe Hailstone in *You Nazty Spy!* and *I'll Never Heil Again*) make use of a pair of non-Stooge continuing characters - the Arizona Kid and Nell - from *Out West*. Jock O'Mahoney again plays the handsome, tall, stumbling hero who trips or bumps or forgets something with a grace and bravado that is absent for only the tragic second in which he loses his concentration. He is never discouraged, always polished, and a-rarin' to go, but rarely successful. Never lacking in sincerity, he should live happily ever after with the devoted Nell, so long as he avoids her right cross.

VISUAL HUMOR: Much of the slapstick in this film is implemented by the non-Stooges, as happens only rarely in Stooge films. As in *Out West* and *Fuelin' Around*, former stuntman Jock O'Mahoney's pratfalls are skillfully executed: he falls over the chair and is hit by the opening door; he misses the chair, but falls over a stool, somersaulting, smartly repositioning his guitar, and going out the door; he struggles determinedly to step out of the trash can, doing an amazing, flying spill onto his back when Nell slugs him and an equally astounding flip when she throws the pitcher at his head. One other highlight is when the Kid draws his pistol and shoots— but hits the light. He makes a great pair with Nell, who complains how weak she is each time she decks an outlaw and then helplessly walks over to the bed to swoon; once she faints onto the couch but bonks her head first on the wooden backing. Even the military performs its own slapstick when the captain walks through the door where the sergeant, waiting for the Stooges, wallops him with a huge board. Many extras in this film were Columbia stunt men who make Christine McIntyre's wallops seem that much more effective. Innovative Stooge highlights include the pistol twirling, Shemp bartending and dropping the egg on the cowboy's hand, and the well-choreographed mustache scene culminating with the mustache landing on Dillon's nose. The prop gag with the saddle horn is plot-related (Moe: "That's the backstop; that's to keep you from slidin' off backwards." Larry: "No it ain't; that's the horn." HONK, HONK). An extended slapstick sequence: Shemp hits the horseshoe on the anvil, into the air, and onto the head of the sergeant, who pushes Shemp into the fire, which makes Shemp shove him into the water bucket; from above one, two, three, four, five horseshoes slide off a nail and clang him on the head...and then a sixth, too. The last gag derives from *Grips, Grunts and Groans*.

Tossing dynamite in and out of the safe derives from *Cactus Makes Perfect*, here with the innovation that every time the gang member spins the lock, Shemp on the inside spins it back. Other variations: Moe tossing the saddle towards the horse, overshooting and hitting Sergeant Mullins (*Uncivil War Birds*; *Playing the Ponies*); the crate and barrel chase (*Fright Night*); Larry whacking a gang member with a wood beam while hitting Moe with the backswing (*Three Little Sew and Sews*); empty pairs of boots after the explosion (*Half-Shot Shooters*); the Stooges looking sequentially in one direction and then the other (*Uncivil Warriors*); and Moe opening the bottle on Shemp's teeth (*Three Loan Wolves*). When Shemp takes an alcoholic drink he 'ee-bee-bees,' shudders, and gets out the word "smooth" in eight seconds. The intermittent screen titles give the film a B-Western, serial-film look.

VERBAL HUMOR: With the large cast and cinematic enhancements, much of the humor is visual. Notable in the script, however, are the dialectical contrasts. Most memorable are the Kid's Westernisms (cf. *Out West*): "slingin' lead," "I forgot m' gee-tar," and "I hurt m' knee." The Stooges play on his dialect. Moe's response to the Kid's "I'm hittin' the trail" after hearing him fall outside is, "Sounds like the trail hit him!"; and Shemp's response to the Kid's "W'ar's Nell?" is "In thar!" Shemp offers his own string of Western clichés: "Stand clear, hombres, 'cause I'm rough and I'm tough, yessir! I'm lighting with a shootin' iron, that's what I am...greased lighting!" In contrast, the Stooges parody Western dialect with puns (Moe: "We're desperadoes, see?" Shemp: "I don't feel very desperado!"), anachronisms (Shemp [to the horse]: "What size, madam? We have some lovely ground-grippers—"), or modern double talk ("Just inspecting the counterfram for flaws in the adirussick"). The ultimate anachronism is when Shemp orders his bar drink: "I'll take a milkshake...[everyone stares]...with *sour milk*!". Other cast members speak ominous lines (Colonel: "These men that you select probably will never come back." Sergeant: "I have just the men, sir"; Dillon: "How can those hombres report to Fort Scott...if they're dead?"), but Moe has at least one humorous response (Dillon: "Spying, eh?" Moe: "No... leaving!"). Nell's "I'm just a poor, weak woman!" is a variation of her "poor defenseless woman" in *Brideless Groom*. .The three-pattern (Moe to Shemp: "Show him, Tex!" Shemp to Larry: "Show him, Tex!" Larry to Shemp: "*You're* Tex!") is a variation of the routine first seen in *Pardon My Clutch*. When Moe comments to the sergeant, "They are the laziest bunch of guys I—" he revives a part of his characterization seen as early as *3 Dumb Clucks*.

OTHER NOTES: The film was shot at the Columbia Ranch. As we saw first in *Vagabond Loafers*, the credits include a 'With' screen for all six credited actors. Edward Bernds is credited with the compact 'Written and Directed by.'

Unlike the cast of one in the final release of 1949, the first release of 1950 has a very large cast acting out three simultaneous tales with an equine operatic accompaniment. *Punchy Cowpunchers* is extraordinarily complex and lavish for a Columbia short-film, and perhaps it is no coincidence that this very year Cecil B. DeMille released his luxurious *Samson and Delilah*, the film that began the explosion of epic films in the 1950s. Some of the cast members pictured here, e.g. Jack Chesebro and Kenneth MacDonald, played 'heavy' characters in Stooge films, adding an element of realism that was featured in 1948's *Crime on Their Hands* and 1949's *Dunked in the Deep*.

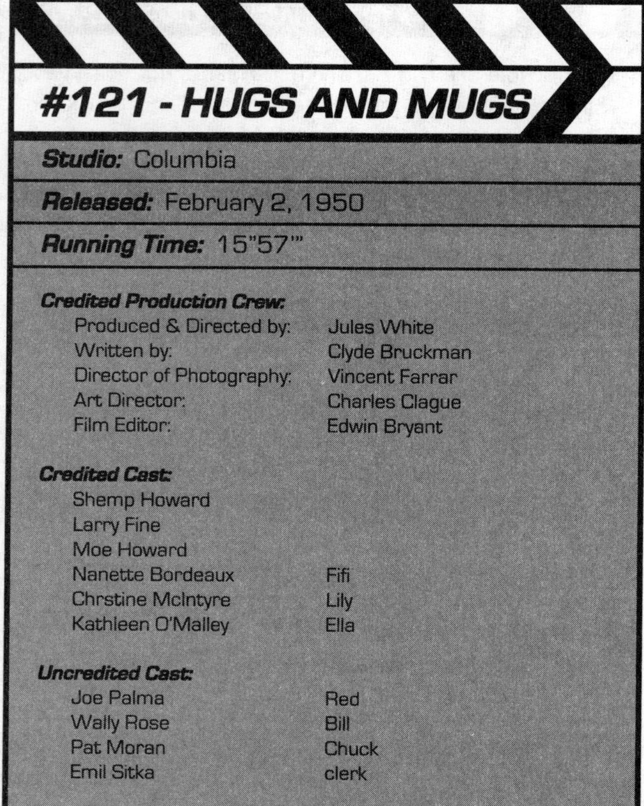

#121 - HUGS AND MUGS

Studio: Columbia

Released: February 2, 1950

Running Time: 15"57"'

Credited Production Crew:

Produced & Directed by:	Jules White
Written by:	Clyde Bruckman
Director of Photography:	Vincent Farrar
Art Director:	Charles Clague
Film Editor:	Edwin Bryant

Credited Cast:

Shemp Howard	
Larry Fine	
Moe Howard	
Nanette Bordeaux	Fifi
Chrstine McIntyre	Lily
Kathleen O'Malley	Ella

Uncredited Cast:

Joe Palma	Red
Wally Rose	Bill
Pat Moran	Chuck
Emil Sitka	clerk

PERSPECTIVE: This film revitalizes the narrative structure of the innovative *Sing a Song of Six Pants*, confining the Stooges to their shop where they are visited by various protagonists. This time the Stooges own a furniture repair shop, and the visitors, as the title *Hugs and Mugs* suggests, include trios of seductive women and tough-guy crooks; as in the previous *Punchy Cowpunchers*, the cast is relatively large. Jules White and Felix Adler invented and developed this kind of narrative structure for Stooge films, but here White, wearing his associate producer hat, assigned Clyde Bruckman to write a script considerably different from such earlier, wild, White/Bruckman romps as *Dizzy Pilots* and *The Yoke's on Me*. To turn shop-confinement into a physical, Stooge-worthy comedy, Bruckman brings a simple bifold plot - a search for stolen pearls - into the shop where elaborate inter-Stooge slapstick, romantic encounters with the three women, and then a plot-related, prop-oriented, pitched battle with an iron in a material bin can flourish.

The Stooges drill, prick, slap, and gouge each other in one of their first extended slapstick- sequence entrances into a film, but to vary the tone Bruckman introduces a trio of women [named 'Fifi,' 'Ella,' and 'Lily' in the script] who play as important a role as any women since *I'm a Monkey's Uncle* [the only other woman trio in a Shemp film to date]. Two brief scenes of exposition establish the women in one fold of the bifold plot, beginning the physical humor with Stooge-like prison-marching from *In the Sweet Pie and Pie* and ink squirting from *Healthy, Wealthy and Dumb*, (both films featuring trios of women). The girls then dupe the Stooges in a romantic interlude amusingly undercut by Lily ripping the easy chair to shreds, followed by a Laurel & Hardy-style scene in which they rip each other's clothes off one article at a time. These scenes were so successful that woman trios were to be reintroduced into two of the next three films as Stooge war brides in *Love at First Bite* and as the very Stooge-like Moella, Larraine, and Shempetta in *Self-Maid Maids*. That is probably why Lily decides to return the pearls to their rightful owners: the 'hugs' have to turn out to be 'good guys' in contrast with the trio of 'mugs.'

Bruckman was adept at making slapstick gags lead to plot shifts, and the romantic scene with Fifi seducing Shemp on the couch - after the couch spring gets stuck on his rear - leads directly to the discovery of the pearls and surprises us with the sudden appearance of fold #2 - the gangsters. An active six-man engagement ensues which begins with well choreographed stomping and punching and climaxes with the use of plot-related props: a board precariously placed on sawhorses, a hot iron, and a material bin. The latter is particularly noteworthy: as if the enclosed space of the shop was not enough, now we have all six men in a 6' x 8' material bin, and as if that was not a small enough place, no one's head rises higher than two feet unless Shemp irons their backside.

In all of Stoogedom, there is no place so small that holds so many people having so furiously silly a fight.

VISUAL HUMOR: Slapstick moves the plot also when Moe slaps Shemp, causing Fifi to hug him, causing Shemp to check on the "beads" in his pocket. In the opening extended slapstick sequence, Moe nose bonks Shemp, who backs into Larry's needle, making him leap forward to drill Moe's rear again. To keep momentum going, Shemp slaps Moe, a previously rare occurrence that becomes more common in the 1950s. Larry thrice slaps Shemp across the cheeks with the box they bought at the auction yesterday. This moves the plot, too. Both Larry and one of the women use foot stomping as an initial attack move, and twice the action concentrates on each Stooge with his woman in visual three-patterns. The film colors the slapstick with a variety of sound effects, including CUCKOO, TWEET, and a piano wire sound.

New gags: Larry aims his hammer at a crook, but the head flies backwards and hits Shemp in the head; and the saw horse routine, more than an elaboration of the saw horse gag in *The Sitter Downers*. Moe and Larry missing the crooks and punching each other in the face is a variation of clubbing each other in *Restless Knights*. In the previous film non-Stooges performed many of the gags; here the women reprise a Stooge gag when they struggle with the filing cabinet à la *Hold That Lion*. The bird cage falling on Shemp's head is reminiscent of the fish bowl falling on his head in *Hold That Lion*; a bird cage was used in *Brideless Groom*. Shemp defeats the crooks with the iron, but then in the usual deflating post-finale he gets his own backside tattered and torn. Other variations: Moe tossing the box onto an easy chair (*All the World's a Stooge*); Moe grabbing Shemp's nose with a pair of sheers (*Slippery Silks*); a mouse trap in the pocket (*Goofs and Saddles*); bowing and bonking heads (*Uncivil Warriors*); the couch spring on the rear (*Hoi Polloi*); Shemp sitting in water to cool his rear (Back to *the Woods*); and blowing Larry over when he is unconscious (*Punch Drunks*).

VERBAL HUMOR: Bruckman's script features verbal duets for each Stooge and his woman. They tend to be complimentary (Ella: "What *gorgeous* hair you have, goldilocks. How do you keep it so nice?" Larry: "I use a home permanent." Ella: "And such a beautiful head of skin in front, too!" Larry: "I polish it with floor wax!"), but some banter turns insulting (Fifi: "You know, cheri, I'll bet you are a regular lady killer." Moe: "Oh sure, the ladies take one look at him a drop dead." Shemp: "Oh yeah? I been asked to get married lots of times." Larry: "Who asked ya'?" Shemp: "My father and mother."). Larry says a punchline without the setup ("So the mouse says to the elephants, 'Wait a minute, fellas. Let's be careful not to tread on each other!' Ain't that a dilly?!"). Moe has one throw-away line ("You should be playing tackle on a football team!").

Shemp offers gag responses (Moe: "You stuff a chair! I'll stuff an ottoman!" Shemp: "I'll stuff a duck!"; Ella: "She's only testing the material." Shemp: "Testin' it? She's makin' noodles out of it!") and an extraordinary number of throw-away lines (when he drills Moe: "I'm sorry, Moe. The bit bit ya'"; when he picks up the iron: "And now for a little flatwork!"; when he kisses the iron: "I got hot lips!"; when the bird cage falls on his head: "What is this, a housing shortage?...Don't you lay an egg on me!"; when Fifi compliments Moe's eyes: "What's the matter with my eyes? They look like halawah?"; when Fifi tries to kiss him: "What if my scoutmaster walked in and caught me?"; when the spring gets caught on his rear: "I'm havin' clutch trouble!"; and when he burns himself with the iron: "I smell somethin' burnin'. Somebody's roastin' a ham...It's me!"). Shemp offers a throw-away line even after each of three eye gouges ("Get me a dog, will ya'?"; "Where's the chair?"; "This one is all right!"), much as he quipped "Give me my teeth back" after Moe opened a beer with them in *Punchy Cowpunchers*. Shemp's "I'll stuff a duck, heh-heh-heh" has a pronounced version of his 'Heh-heh-heh' laugh, which he will use frequently from this point on.

The three-pattern (Lily: "You're not much to look at, but, baby, I go for you!" Ella to Larry: "That goes for me, too, cutie." Fifi to Shemp: "And that goes for me three, baby!") is a variation on the "Me, three!" of *If a Body Meets a Body*. Other variations: Moe's "A toughie, eh!?" (*Horses' Collars*); Moe saying "I'll fight for the woman who loves me! Go ahead! Annihilate him!" while pushing Shemp forward (*Dizzy Detectives*); "And such a beautiful head of skin in front, too!" ("What a beautiful head of bone you have!" in *Booby Dupes*); the Stooges responding in unison to "Which one of you *handsome* men is the proprietor?" with "I am!" (*Three Loan Wolves*); and Larry running to get some water saying, "Don't go away!" (Curly in *Playing the Ponies*).

OTHER NOTES: The film was shot at the Darmour Studios in mid-February, 1949. The *Scrapbook* has Gilbert Kay as the assistant director. This is the first of seven Stooge appearances by Canadian-born, French-accented Nanette Bordeaux [Fifi].

In 1949 Jules White - as the producer of "the 'Stooge' Comedies" - earned the Motion Picture Herald's Laurel Award for 1948, given by the exhibitors of the U.S. and Canada for being in the top-ten of two-reel moneymakers. They would win the award again in 1951, 1953, 1954, and 1955. This 1948 award was presented to White and the Stooges during the shooting of *Hugs and Mugs*.

#122 - DOPEY DICKS

Studio: Columbia

Released: March 2, 1950

Running Time: 15"43'"

Credited Production Crew:

Produced by:	Hugh McCollum
Directed by:	Edward Bernds
Written by:	Elwood Ullman
Director of Photography:	Vincent Farrar
Art Director:	Charles Clague
Film Editor:	Henry DeMond

Credited Cast:

Shemp Howard	
Larry Fine	
Moe Howard	
Christine McIntyre	Professor's assistant
Philip Van Zandt	Professor
Stanley Price	Ralph, Professor's assistant

PERSPECTIVE: El Brendel, who specialized in doing comedy *schtick* in Swedish dialect, made nineteen relatively unsuccessful comedies for the Columbia short subject unit. Searching for a better chemistry, Jules White teamed Brendel with other Columbia contract artists, including Tom Kennedy, Harry Langdon, and even Shemp Howard in *Pick a Peck of Plumbers* (1944), a reworking of the Stooges' *A Plumbing We Will Go*. In the midst of World War II Brendel was teamed with Monty Collins (who had co-written such Stooge films as *Cactus Makes Perfect* and *Phony Express*) to make *Boobs in the Night* (1943), the story of Home Defense workers who encounter a mad scientist seeking a human head for his mechanical man. *Dopey Dicks* employs the same plot but changes the original story considerably. Five years after the conclusion of World War II, the political significance of the 'fiend's' plan to conquer the world with robots was no longer as timely, but Edward Bernds and Elwood Ullman were just the production team to update and Stooge-fy this story: they had recently teamed to write *Fuelin' Around*, the Stooges' first Cold War film, and their most recent collaboration was *Vagabond Loafers*, itself a reworking of *A Plumbing We Will Go*.

In redesigning *Boobs in the Night* as a Cold War Stooge film, Bernds and Ullman generate their own comic essence by adding and substituting familiar Stooge elements. Instead of playing anti-Axis Home Defense workers, the Stooges portray incompetent custodians who in the process of moving a private detective's office manage to drop an armload of equipment, paint each other's faces, and get confused for the real 'Sam Shovel,' a parody of Dashiell Hammett's 'Sam Spade' (Humphrey Bogart in *The Maltese Falcon* [1941]). Bernds and Ullman create this confusion, which is often the means by which the Stooges become involved in some larger intrigue, by introducing the Christine McIntyre character, a typical sort of Stooge damsel-in-distress whose further connection to the mad-scientist plot - she is said to be the professor's assistant - is not developed.

In following her through the thunder and lightning to 275 Mortuary Road, the naive Stooges get spooked in the foyer by the wonderfully ghoulish Ralph, and then one minute later they find themselves scurrying about in a spectacular, eight-minute, multi-room chase. Director Bernds and editor Henry DeMond separate the Stooges, the young woman [named Louise in the script], their two crazed pursuers, and the headless robot into more than twenty different arrangements, frightenings, chases, or struggles - averaging one 'spooking' event nearly every twenty seconds - in perhaps the most complicated multi-room chase in all of Stoogedom. Maintaining a frantic pace, the Stooges run through the lab with a decapitation gadget, the dining room with a two-leafed table, a bedroom with a collapsing bed, a study with both a curtain and a revolving bookcase, a hallway closet with hanging clothes, the hallway itself, the road, and an automobile driven by the headless robot, a scare comedy extravaganza.

VISUAL HUMOR: The Stooges begin their chase mechanisms while still at the office: the woman sees a shadow of a man with a sinister-looking hat and screams, causing the Stooges to get frightened and run into the walls, go out into the hallway, huddle, and bang into the walls again when Moe says "Spread out!". We hear Shemp sneeze from inside the office and then see a 'result-shot': Shemp and his load all over the floor. Although we saw a result shot as early as in *Punch Drunks*, these later years will feature them in almost every film. The Stooges have perfected the comically suspenseful delay (*Movie Maniacs*) while realizing that a fiend/beast is behind them. Here Shemp finds the telephone number (Main-2468), walks to the phone, forgets the number, and has to look it up again as the robot walks up from behind him and leans on his shoulder.

Larry is involved in numerous gags, including sleeping while leaning on the vacuum cleaner and getting a spike-filled planter base caught on his nose. Most of his other sequences are derivative: getting his face painted (*So Long, Mr. Chumps*), acting as a working lamp, and appearing to be decapitated with his head on a table (*Dutiful But Dumb*); and trapping Ralph's head between the table leaves (*The Ghost Talks*). Other variations: the professor stabbing Larry with the sword point through the wall (*Mummy's Dummies*); the professor being

Stanley Price, playing the wonderfully ghoulish, mad-professor's assistant in 1950's *Dopey Dicks*, frightens Moe and Shemp as part of a spectacular, eight-minute, multi-room chase. Director Ed Bernds and editor Henry DeMond separate the Stooges, the young woman, their two crazed pursuers, and the headless robot into more than twenty different arrangements, frightenings, chases, or struggles - averaging one 'spooking' event nearly every twenty seconds - perhaps the most complicated multi-room chase in all of Stoogedom. In contrast to the natural brilliance of many Curly films, many of these Shemp films flourish in their contrivance. In this year alone the releases include a Western extravaganza (*Punchy Cowpunchers*), this scare comedy classic, and, two films hence, a film featuring the Stooges playing themselves *and* their fiancées.

knocked out by the flower pot falling from a shelf (*Heavenly Daze*); the stretching door handle (*A Gem of a Jam*); Moe knocking on the door and then Ralph's forehead (*Calling All Curs*); the revolving bookcase, and Ralph awaiting them outside the window (*Spook Louder*); Shemp watching the action through the keyhole (*Matri-Phony*); and Moe grabbing Shemp and walking him into the wall (*Three Smart Saps*).

VERBAL HUMOR: Elwood Ullman's script offers inspired situations in the office scene, especially when Shemp fantasizes: "Gee, it must be great to be a private eye. You always got a stubby little gun in the top drawer - just in case of trouble...[He sees the drawer full of guns]...This guy's expecting a lot of trouble! ...You could be relaxin' just like this when a beautiful dame rushes in, desperate, not knowin' where to turn." Woman [rushing in]: "I'm desperate, I don't know where to turn!" Dialogue exchanges include: (Woman: "Strange men are following me!" Shemp [looking her over]: "They'd be strange if they didn't!"; Shemp [aiming a gun at Moe]: "I ought-a let you have it." Moe: "Well?" Shemp [yielding]: "You can have it.")... Some of this accompanies slapstick (Moe hits Shemp on the hat. [PUFF] Shemp [looking at his dented hat]: "Look what you did!" Moe: "I'm not finished!" [BONK]). The exchange between Moe and Shemp about where to put the lamp (Shemp: "The wall!" Moe: "The corner!" Shemp: "The wall!" Moe: "The corner!" Shemp: "The wall!" [CLANG] Shemp [yielding]: "The corner.") sounds like cartoon exchanges between Bugs Bunny and Yosemite Sam, but the Stooge version ends with trademark Stooge slapstick. In the mansion Ralph steals the first two scenes with his responses to interrogation ("Young lady...about five-feet two, with golden hair?" Stooges: "Yes!" Ralph: "Blue eyes?" Stooges: "Yes! Yes!" Ralph: "Long, curling lashes?" Stooges: "Yes! Yes! Yes!' Ralph: "Haven't seen her"; [*Soup to Nuts; Sing a Song of Six Pants*]) and his plea to the professor who wants his brain: "But I haven't got any brains. You've told me so yourself, remember?". Ralph forces Moe into bragging ("I'm the brains of this outfit!" Ralph: "Brains! Come with me.") and makes Moe an ignorant Stooge: "This is the best of the lot, professor, which isn't saying very much." Moe: "Thank you, thank you!".

Ullman invokes a number of Moe's characterizations: lazy (Moe: "Boy, am I exhausted!" Shemp: "Hope you didn't strain yourself carrying that duster."), nervously friendly (Professor: "That will be all, Ralph." Moe: "That will be all, Ralph! [to the professor] Weird sort of duck...You're all right."), ironically naive (looking into the decapitation gadget: "What have I got to lose?"; speaking to the robot: "You better beat it, bud. I guy could get his head caught off around here...Nyaggh!"), fearful (Shemp: "I found the girl all right, but she disappeared." Moe: "That's what we gotta do - disappear!"), and vengeful (Shemp: "Moe! Are you okay?" Moe: "Yeah! Pretty good. What did you hit me with...Oh, pewter!" [CLANG]).

One-liners dominate the chase sequence, so Shemp is given the bulk of the lines (to the woman bound and gagged: "What's the matter, kid? You got a toothache?"; when a large knife appears between the curtains: "Nothin''s gonna happen when I'm around!"; when the woman disappears the second time: "Gone again. What makes her so restless?"; at the telephone: "Central Section, Northeastern Section, Western Section. If I don't hurry we'll all be in sections!").

Other variations: Shemp's "Every man for himself!" (*Restless Knights*); Moe's "When you make a right turn, put your arm up!" ("Why don't you put out your hand when you go up a side street?" in *Fuelin' Around*); Shemp's "Heh-heh-heh! Sneezed!" (*Hugs and Mugs*); Moe: "Well, Sherlock, how you gonna handle the case?" Shemp: "Easy! I'll use my wits." Moe: "Now she's really in trouble." (Moe: "We're in a tough spot, men." Larry: "Yeah, it's gonna take brains to get us outta here." Moe: "That's why I said we're in a tough spot!" in *Who Done It?*); and the operator telling Shemp "Look behind you" for the directory (the radio talking to Curly in *Healthy, Wealthy and Dumb*).

OTHER NOTES: The whole cast is credited. The mad doctor in *If a Body Meets a Body* also wanted a 'human' brain - Curly's; he wanted it for his gorilla. In *From Nurse to Worse* the mad doctor wanted merely to operate on Curly's brain.

#123 - LOVE AT FIRST BITE

Studio: Columbia

Released: May 4, 1950

Running Time: 15"54'"

Credited Production Crew:

Produced & Directed by:	Jules White
Story & Screenplay by:	Felix Adler
Director of Photography:	Rex Wimpy
Art Director:	Charles Clague
Film Editor:	Edwin Bryant

Credited Cast:

Shemp Howard	
Larry Fine	
Moe Howard	
Christine McIntyre	Katrina
Yvette Reynard	Fifi
Marie Montiel	Maria

Uncredited Cast:

Al Thompson	Maria's father

PERSPECTIVE: The title of *Love at First Bite* is a phrase Larry offers when describing how he fell in love during World War II, and it leads to flashbacks of romantic Stooge encounters in Italy, Vienna, and Paris. A flashback was used for another film in which the Stooges reminisced about their past, *Three Loan Wolves*, and in both films the use of flashback technique provides still another variant to the narrative structure of Stooge two-reelers. Flashback substitutes for exposition; it takes the first two scenes of, say, *Hugs and Mugs*, and turns them into historical visual comedy instead of a narrative introduction. And because characterization is important in a film about the Stooge family, flashbacks allow the usually triadic Stooges to be reintroduced to us as individuals, that is, charming, light-hearted, ex-G.I. lovers isolated from each other and alone with women who actually like them.

Because the previous film [*Dopey Dicks*] was written for El Brendel during the war, and because *Love At First Bite* has its narrative origins in the aftermath of the war, it is interesting here in 1950 to look back on World War II which we comically fought alongside the Stooges. World War II is no longer a current event, and its Axis enemies are virtually forgotten. Instead we see a part of the war we never saw in the 1940s. As if this comedy is reconfigured by the Marshall Plan, we visit the allied populace in Italy, Austria, and France, and each of the three stories begins with an ethnic stereotype: Italians eat pastas, Austrian frauleins clean their homes and wear pigtails, and the French drink at sidewalk cafes and do not bother to speak English. Felix Adler and Jules White, the latter born in Budapest, turn each of these stereotypical assumptions into a pleasant, little Stooge romance.

But then we come back to the Stooges in their 1950, slapstickful apartment. From the very beginning Larry is conked on the head by the horseshoe that represents good luck for him and his bride. It bounces off his head, and from that point on it seems as if nothing goes right. Moe gets gum all over himself, Shemp makes Larry drop the flowers, Larry smashes an apple on Shemp's head, and they all get so drunk they cement Shemp into a huge basin. This is the drunkest we ever see all three Stooges. They all take occasional drinks [e.g. Larry in *Three Smart Saps*], and Shemp often works taking a belt of liquor into his schtick and will even have hallucinations a few years hence in *Cuckoo on a Choo Choo*, but Stooge comedy demands quick reactions, so this experimental foray into the familiar comic-drunk territory of RKO's Leon Errol [who worked at the Columbia unit with the Stooges in 1934] and the 'Mexican Spitfire' Lupe Velez [with whom the Stooges worked in *Hollywood Party* that same year] will be repeated only that one time. But their day does not end in drunken foolishness, for just as that horseshoe bounced off Larry's head and went back to its proper spot, the Stooges themselves blow themselves up from out of their living room all the way over to the dock where they are embraced by their fiancées. As often, though, there is a little humiliating, extracurricular wetness at the very end of their lucky unlucky day.

VISUAL HUMOR: The opening sequence is filled with traditional Stooge slapstick: Moe gives Shemp a nose bonk, gouge, and two-handed backwards slaps; Shemp blocks a gouge, and Moe comes back to gouge him. Later Shemp tosses some of the smashed apple into Moe's face, so Moe gouges him, Shemp gives him a hand-wave, and Moe slaps Shemp. A minute later Shemp reminds Moe it is their wedding day, so "We should be happy, friendly, not doing this [GOUGE], and none of that [SLAP]". The last is a motif first used in *A Bird in the Head.*

The drunk scene has Shemp falling over, Larry and Moe missing a hand shake and falling over, Larry and Moe sleeping standing up and falling over, a seltzer war à la *Three Little Pigskins*, and Moe and Larry unsuccessfully punching Shemp [Johnny Kascier] much like Shemp vs. the punching bag in *Fright Night.* Bubble gum is not entirely new to Stooge comedy [*Disorder in the Court*; *All Gummed Up*; *Rockin' in the Rockies*], but it has never been used so extensively - on Larry's nose, the phone, Moe's face, and the towel, and it causes Shemp to run into the hanging lamp. Similarly, we have

In *Love at First Bite* (1950), the Stooges get extremely inebriated, which necessitates a very different type of delivery for both their verbal and physical humor. It also excuses all of their actions, attributes them to their drunkenness, not to their Stoogeness.

seen spaghetti thrown and worn in *Sock-A-Bye Baby*, *Idiots Deluxe*, and *Malice in the Palace*, but here a forkload of spaghetti is blown by a fan into a gaping mouth of Al Thompson. For the drinking scene, Moe hits Shemp with his elbow to pull the cork, Moe pours back and forth across the three glasses ("This is the way they do it in Vienna!"), Larry adds barely a dash of soda ("Bottoms up!") and they each drink twelve ounces (GLUG-GLUG), shake, hear car horns, emit steam from their mouths (*A Bird in the Head*), and pass out backwards onto the carpet. Result shots: gum on Larry's nose; and Moe sitting on the freshly scrubbed floor with a bucket over his head. (Shemp had a bucket over his head and was choked by the handle in *Fright Night*). Shemp banging his head twice against the hanging light fixture resembles Jock Mahoney's stunt in *Fuelin' Around*, but here it knocks Shemp and his gummy towel onto Moe's face. Larry and Moe sleeping while standing up against the wall is an elaboration of Larry sleeping on the vacuum cleaner in the previous film (*Dopey Dicks*).

Fruit-smashing had been a part of the Stooges' act since Shemp rejoined Moe and Ted Healy in 1925; here Larry smashes an apple onto Shemp's forehead. Other variations: multiple lipstick smears all over Larry's face (*G.I. Wanna Home*); Shemp and Moe nose to nose (the phone booth sequence in *Brideless Groom*); Moe using Curly's "Hhmm!" (*Shivering Sherlocks*); Maria slapping Larry and Larry slapping her back, and Moe getting his hand stuck in the vase and breaking it on his forehead (*Hoi Polloi*); Shemp thinking a woman is flirting with him under the table (*You Nazty Spy!*); Moe knocking on the fraulein's forehead (*Calling All Curs*); seltzer squirting out Shemp's ears (*Healthy, Wealthy and Dumb*); Moe (twice) stretching out his arms and socking Larry and Shemp (*G.I. Wanna Home*); and Moe, Larry, Katrina, and Maria leaning over and getting soaked by Shemp's and Fifi's splash (*We Want Our Mummy*).

VERBAL HUMOR: The verbal humor uses ethnic stereotyping, particularly Katrina's Germanic "I'm zo glad to zay I'm zorry" and Shemp's pseudo-French "mademoisell-ee" and "Rue de la Pew." [The Looney Tune French character, Pepe Le Pew, was created in 1945 and became popular in the late 1940s.] When Fifi speaks French to Shemp, he responds: "I don't know. A fly went into mine, too. Drink up kid!". Adler gives Larry several puns ("It was in a little restaurant. It was love at first bite. I was stationed in Italy eatin' bread and hot dogs and waitin' to be 'mustered' out."; and Moe: "Let's cremate him." Larry: "We can't do that: we ain't got no cream!").

As in the previous film, Moe's characterization is given several facets; he was a rather good actor and could play a gambler ("He's a favorite?...Fine: 5 to win, 5 to place, and 25 to show...That's 35 cents all together"), romantic fool ("That's more dangerous than a fox hole!...She literally swept me off my feet. Boy am I in love!"), and accusatory boss ("Oh, stallin', eh?"; "Ya' puddin'-head! Ya' put cement in your foot bath instead of salt!"). Because Shemp is under water, the final tag of the film is also given to Moe: "A tidal wave!". Shemp sometimes speaks in childlike diminutives, as in "Remember, palsy-walsy: no slap-sies". When drunk, Shemp challenges Moe to a "drool" and Moe calls the seltzer spray "Eye bullets". Epithets: "puddin'-head" and "mosquito-brain".

The wedding song ['Oh the wedding bells will start to ring, Ding-Dong-Ding/ The birds and bees will start to sing, Ding-Dong-Ding...'] is a variation of the opening song in *Three Smart Saps*. In *Hugs and Mugs* the other Fifi [Nanette Bordeaux] referred to Shemp as "Casanova." Here Shemp says this Fifi [Yvette Reynard] "just couldn't resist the Casanova in me!". Shemp's Parisian puns ("I was anxious to see the Paris sites...One afternoon I was strollin' along the boulevard lookin' for post cards") derive from *Restless Knights*. Other variations: 'OLD PANTHER - BOTTLED YESTERDAY' ('OLD HOMICIDE - BOTTLED MONDAY' in *Out West*); 'Rue de Shlemiel' ('Shlemiel Number 8' in *Hokus Pokus*); Moe's "You know I really fell for ya'!" (Curly's "Can't ya' see I'm fallin' for ya'!" in *Three Smart Saps*); and regarding dynamite - Shemp: "Will it hurt?" Moe: "You won't feel a thing!" (*The Sitter Downers*).

OTHER NOTES: The release title parodies the expression 'love at first sight'; the working title was *New Grooms Sweep Clean*. Unlike previous films released in 1950, the credits read 'Story and Screenplay by' and not 'Written by' for Felix Adler. The melody Katrina sings is 'The Beautiful Blue Danube' by Johann Strauss, Jr.; Moe knocks on the door in rhythm. This film will be refurbished as *Fifi Blows Her Top* (1958) with Joe Besser.

#124 - SELF - MADE MAIDS

Studio: Columbia

Released: July 6, 1950

Running Time: 15"47'"

Credited Production Crew:

Produced & Directed by:	Jules White
Written by:	Felix Adler
Director of Photography:	Vincent Farrar
Art Director:	Charles Clague
Film Editor:	Edwin Bryant

Credited Cast:

Shemp Howard	Shemp, Shempetta, infant
Larry Fine	Larry, Larraine, infant
Moe Howard	Moe, Moella, father, infant

PERSPECTIVE: The Columbia short film unit had no doubt found the previous year's British film *Kind Hearts and Coronets*, in which Alec Guiness played eight different family members, much to their liking. It inspired them to create this film in which the Stooges play multiple family members. Besides giving all three Stooges a chance to dress in drag, this new format allows for the ultimate, improbable Stooge romance - a crowning sequel to the romantic encounters of two recent films [*Hugs and Mugs* and *Love at First Bite*]. Since Stooge comedy almost always requires an adversary, this kind of film gives Moe the additional role of playing the Stoogettes' father, much as Curly had played the Stooges' father in *3 Dumb Clucks*. There are two bonus offerings, too: we get to see the Stooge triplets at the conclusion of the film as well as the formal family painting on the wall in which the husband [Shemp] and wife [Larry] scratch their ant bites. With twelve Stooges in all, this is the most elaborate confusion of Stooges in the entire corpus, at least until we meet three different sets of Stooge triplets and their women in *A Merry Mix-Up* (1957).

Split-screen and matte photographic techniques, used experimentally in *Dunked in the Deep*, determined how this film looks. The split screen technique, used for every scene in which the Stooges and the Stoogettes appear together, necessitated that the Stooges appear on one side of the frame, the Stoogettes on the other [in the art studio and the nursery]. In one instance, when the father reenters the apartment with cake on his face, there were three mattes used. When the Stooges and Stoogettes are physically mingled on the screen [as in their final engagement hug], doubles - always shot from behind - were required to supplement the photographic tricks. This was also the case for all the scenes in which the father and the Stooges appeared together, although when the father was reloading his bullets in the background, there we got a side view of Moe's double. Doubles had often been used in Stooge films for awkward or dangerous stunts, but here it was a matter of how many Stooges were needed to play the parts. When the credit screen claims that 'All parts in this picture are played by The THREE STOOGES,' it does not mean that theirs are the only bodies in the film.

As in *Dunked in the Deep*, the technical requirements make the chase scene choreo-graphically different from the recent multi-door chase scene in *Dopey Dicks*. The need to edit Moe as the Stoogettes' father separately from the Stooges themselves shapes the chase: he laps the apartment seven times [in fast motion] and always seems to be half a lap behind. Editing in 'father Moe' separately also shapes the sequences in which the Stooges hide behind the room dividing curtain, hide and disappear behind the window curtains, and then reappear as a 'couch.' All these gimmicks obviate the need for more complex, sophisticated, and expensive split screens and stand-ins which were reserved for only the sequences in which the Stooges and Stoogettes appear together.

VISUAL HUMOR: The opening, which focuses on Moella finishing at her toilet, Shempetta noticing a run in her stocking, and Larraine fixing her girdle, concludes when the 'girls' hold hands, skip towards the door, and smash into the wall. Similarly, the Stooges themselves appear in the next scene as Moe chisels a statue, Larry sculpts a bust, and Shemp paints a canvas [*Pop Goes the Easel*; *Wee Wee Monsieur*] and then indulge in a slapstick sequence involving clay and Moe's statue [a non-nude Venus *pudica*]. A third slapstick sequence seems to involve four Stooges - Shemp tweaks the father's nose, so the father scrunches both Shemp's and Larry's noses, Shemp rams the whole cake into his face, Larry sticks ice cream down his shirt and then they push him over to the wall, from which a flower pot falls onto his head. But the stand-in for Moe plays a non-active role. The film ends with a fourth arrangement of Stooges, again culminating in a slapstick exchange when the middle Moe baby takes the nipple of the Shemp baby, who squirts milk in baby Moe's face, and then after a gouge the Moe baby hogs both his brothers' nipples and slaps the Larry baby. Laurel and Hardy played infant versions of themselves in *Brats* (1930).

The scratching sequence, in which the Stoogettes scratch their ant bites only when the Stooges are not looking at them, was technically difficult. Although the Stooges appeared in drag as early as *Pop Goes the Easel*, this is the most extensive drag sequence in Stoogedom. Actually, a number of the sequences here derive from early Stooge films: the Stooges appeared as artists, used a gag about the upside down boat, and fought with clay in *Pop Goes the Easel*, ants were itch-inducing in *Ants in the Pantry*, the same film gave us our first strange piano contents - here feathers, there cats; and we saw a bursting thermometer (here burst by love, there by Scotch) in *Pardon My Scotch*. Other variations: the flower pot falling off the shelf (*Heavenly Daze*); using the cigar as a paint brush (Emil Sitka lighting his cigar in *Who Done It?*); characters moving in a painting (*You Nazty Spy!*); the Stooges as Scotsmen (*Pardon My Scotch*); the TWEET sound effect (*Grips, Grunts and Groans*); opening the door for the charging father and letting him run into the wall (*Rockin' Thru the Rockies*); and using tickling to defeat an enemy (*Restless Knights*). A Stooge first: hiding under the curtain and making it look like a couch, although Larry and Moe pretended to be a gurney in *From Nurse to Worse*. Result shot: Larry peels the clay off, but a large piece clings to his nose. He says à la Jimmy Durante: "Am I mortified! It's sabatoogee!" Curly had imitated Durante, with whom the Stooges worked in *Hollywood Party, Meet the Baron*, and *Start Cheering*, in *Three Smart Saps*.

VERBAL HUMOR: Because of the special visual effects, the script has a limited array of verbal gags. As in several of the immediately preceding films, some complement the physical humor (Moe says "We gotta make a *hit* with the girls' father!" just before the father opens the door into them; Shemp says "That'll teach you a lesson - bouncing doors in peoples' faces!" just before Moe opens the door into Shemp's and Larry's faces; and before knocking the head off Moe's statue Shemp says: "What's that on your neck?" Larry: "That's a mole." Shemp: "That mole's walking. Hold on and I'll kill it!"). The Stoogettes talk about the Stooges with silly admiration (Shempetta about Moe: "that handsome, debonair artist"; Larraine: "I'm crazy about the one with the big bags - you know, those folded satchels under his eyes. He really sends me!") and speak once in unison ("Oh woe is us" from *Back to the Woods*): "Papa! Wha' happen'?" The father speaks disparagingly about the Stooges ("bozos" and "gangsters"); this sets up Shemp's ironic line: "Your father will go crazy when he meets us!".

The Stooges have one set pun (Moe: "What are those things?" Shemp: "Eyes, 'boat' of them, get it? 'Boat!'") and imitate medicalese ("der-stich"; "ana-cana-pooner!"); we first heard "ana-cana-pooner" in *Men in Black*. Other variations: Shemp: "Why don't you look where you're goin'?!" Father: "Why don't you go where you're looking?! (*Three Troubledoers*); the Lollipop Song (*Wee Wee Monsieur*); Moella: "Mine has such a *gorgeous* head of skin!" (*Hugs and Mugs*); tempting the father with "nyaah-nyaah!" (*Dunked in the Deep*); and "Sabatoogees" (*They Stooge to Conga*).

OTHER NOTES: The couple arrangement is Larry & Moella; Shemp & Larraine; Moe & Shempetta. The original ending of *Three Little Pigskins* had the Stooges explain their adventures to their young children, though child actors were to be used so there was no split screen planned. Moe's voice ("I got you, rat! Take that!") is looped in, but the father's lips do not move. Also, Moe kicks the shoes behind the curtain before fully exposing them. In 1921 Buster Keaton had played all the parts in the opening scene of *The Playhouse*.

No doubt inspired by Alec Guiness' *Kind Hearts and Coronets* (1949), the Stooges' *Self-Made Maids* (1950) lets them play ten different roles as the Stooges themselves, their three fiancées, their three infants, and their father. More so than in the previous year's *Dunked in the Deep*, where trick photography was used to enhance the chase scene, trick photography is rampant in *Self-Made Maids*. Later in the 1950s the Stooges will play three sets of triplets in *A Merry Mix-Up*.

#125 - THREE HAMS ON RYE

Studio: Columbia

Released: September 7, 1950

Running Time: 15"38'"

Credited Production Crew:

Produced & Directed by:	Jules White
Written by:	Clyde Bruckman
Director of Photography:	Al Ziegler
Art Director:	Charles Clague
Film Editor:	Edwin Bryant

Credited Cast:

Shemp Howard	
Larry Fine	
Moe Howard	
Nanette Bordeaux	Lulabelle
Christine McIntyre	Janiebelle
Emil Sitka	B. K. Doaks

Uncredited Cast:

Mildred Olsen	showgirl
Judy Malcolm	showgirl
Ned Glass	Nick Barker
Brian O'Hara	tall actor
Danny Lewis	shorter actor
Blackie Whiteford	stagehand

PERSPECTIVE: The early 1950s were a period of transition for the film industry. During the Great Depression and World War II, movie-going audiences averaged 80-90 million admissions per week. These audiences enjoyed dramas, comedies, musicals, B-westerns, and inspirational propaganda while supplying the film studios with booming box office receipts, but the end of the war, labor and theater chain disputes, the House Un-American Activities Committee investigations of the film world, and then the advent of broadcast television brought recession to Hollywood. With many film writers, actors, directors, and producers under government scrutiny, televisions in 18% of American homes, and weekly movie admissions averaging barely 60 million, budgets were limited. We see this in the four 1950 releases produced by Jules White; they are relatively modest in scope and execution, and this includes *Hugs and Mugs*, *Love at First Bite*, and *Three Hams on Rye*.

The plot of *Three Hams on Rye* follows the same formula as such previous backstage Stooge comedies as *Rhythm and Weep* and *Gents Without Cents*: 1] the Stooges portray failed actors who cannot break into showbiz; 2] in their attempt they encounter showgirls and a wacky producer; and 3] they ultimately get a break and make the big time, sort of. But *Three Hams on Rye* is not a mere rehash. Writer Clyde Bruckman and producer/director Jules White grafted into the story the great 'southern comforter' gag from Felix Adler's and Del Lord's *Uncivil Warriors* and the critic character, Nick Barker [Ned Glass] à la *Loco Boy Makes Good*. Adding the critic does more than make producer Doaks [Emil Sitka] nervous: it allows the Stooges to shift from their portrayal of actors into inept sleuthing. They must detect and yet hide from the critic, so they have the opportunity of disguising themselves again as they had so successfully as bearded Scotsmen in the previous film [*Self-Made Maids*]. In fact, each of the major non-Stooge characters helps advance the comic narrative: Barker necessitates the disguise scene, producer Doaks motivates the baking scene and plays the fall guy for several slapstick routines, and although they are given much less importance than in previous backstage films, the showgirls inspire Moe and Larry to a paint-brush sword fight and Shemp to do some Shakespeare, to which he will return for the finale.

Just as the Stooges bungled their quasi-entertainment job in *Loco Boy Makes Good* but managed through their idiocy to become popular with the internal audience, so here, too, they bungle every assignment. They make a mess of their painting, they do not keep Barker from entering the theater, they forget to buy the cake and salad, they bake a disastrous cake, and they blow the third act of 'The Bride War Spurs.' But after the unintentional success of the feather scene, Shemp returns to Thespian pursuits and recites the immortal Shakespearean query from *Hamlet*: 'To be or not to be — that is the question." After 350 years, Moe finally has the answer: a pie in the face.

VISUAL HUMOR: The back stage drama establishes a comic matrix brimming with slapstick. As in *Hugs and Mugs*, Shemp stands up to Moe verbally and physically, which creates extended exchanges. As in a number of recent films the opening Stooge scene contains some of the most complex slapstick choreography. Highlights include the painting sword fight and Shemp's struggle with the suit of armor [a variation on the drill/needle opening of *Hugs and Mugs*]. The sound effects are slightly upgraded [TWEET and double slaps with 'N-B-C' tones [an elaboration of the closing gag of *Hokus Pokus*]], as is the verbal accompaniment to the slapstick battles between Moe and Shemp [Shemp: "I'm sorry, Moe; it was just an accident." Moe: "Think nothin' of it, son. Anyone can have an accident. Why only last week I was holdin' a paint brush and suddenly I got a twitch in my right arm like this." [He dabs the brush in Shemp's face.] Shemp: "You know? I gotta itch to twitch, too!" [He gets Moe back]; and when Shemp dumps flour on Moe's head: "I don't know what I'd have done without you, but I do know what I'm going to do with you!" [SLAP, NOSE BONK, FIST GAME, BLOCKED GOUGE (with a bowl over his head), GOUGE] Shemp shakes hands but tosses flour in his face). We even see it when Moe orders "Schnoz!": Shemp grabs Larry's nose, Moe grabs Shemp's, and off they go. Shemp's opening the kangaroo door and getting punched in the face by a boxing-gloved arm looks very much like the McKimson cartoons featuring a boxing kangaroo, e.g. Warner Brother's *Hop, Look and Listen* (1948) starring Sylvester and Hippity Hopper. Result shot: Moe with a grease question mark on his face.

Larry's disguise as the 'black banana' resembles the robot man in *Dopey Dicks*; both hide the actor's head beneath the shoulder level of the disguise, a shape used first in *Dutiful but Dumb*. From the previous film, *Self-Made Maids*: .Shemp's squeezing a tube into Moe's face, and the beating Moe and Shemp give Larry (thinking he is Barker), which resembles the beating the Stooges give the Stoogettes' father. The Stooges have thrown, smashed, swallowed and worn eggs. Here Moe flaps his arms and coughs one up, then Shemp coughs up a fried egg. Other variations: Larry hanging up the lettuce (*Sock-A-Bye Baby*); Moe painting Shemp's protruding tongue (*So Long, Mr. Chumps*); Shemp giving Moe a hand-wave with a downthrust (*Love at First Bite*); the Stooges saluting and hitting each other (*Uncivil Warriors*); Shemp getting hit by a mace held by a suit of armor (*The Ghost Talks*); Shemp hitting Moe with his backswing (*In the Sweet Pie and Pie*); and Moe and Shemp sneaking under Larry who is sneaking past them (*Fright Night*). A notable parallel: Moe gets frightened by the skeleton in his dressing room, the disguised Shemp by his own reflection in a mirror.

VERBAL HUMOR: Several of Clyde Bruckman's theater-related verbal gags are Shakespearean. From *Romeo and Juliet* [2.2.42-43] comes Moe's "A rose by any other name would smell—"; Shakespeare added "as sweet," but Larry substitutes: "And so do you!" Also from *Romeo and Juliet*, although not a direct quotation, is Moe's "Never lived a Capulet that could insult a Montague!" which begins the paint brush fight. The film closes with Shemp's rendition of *Hamlet* 3.1.56: "To be or not to be — that is the question." Other references include Shemp claiming to be "a great Thespian lover...Your eyes are like two limpid pools of fire that burn into my soul. Ah, fair one, come with me to the Casbah-dor." The latter part is a widely used misquotation from the classic romantic drama *Algiers* (1938), starring Charles Boyer and Hedy Lamarr; 'Thespian' refers to the ancient Greek Thespis who is credited with the creation of drama.

On the other hand, the rapid exchange - Larry: "I didn't do it." Moe: "Ya' did!" Larry: "I didn't!" Moe: "Ya' did!" - is a pattern resembling cartoon arguments between Bugs Bunny and Yosemite Sam or Daffy Duck, and there was a similar verbal exchange in *Dopey Dicks*. Cartoons may have also inspired the boxing kangaroo and Shemp's misreading of 'DANGEROUS KEEP AWAY' as "Dann-ger-oos Kip Awah.". This is a reading gag, while Barker's column ("the odor of ham coming from the Mason Theater will smell up Broadway for miles") is a printed gag. We recently saw two printed gags in *Dunked in the Deep*.

Bruckman's prop-related puns come when Shemp and Moe think Larry is "a black banana" and when Shemp complains about the feather cake: "Boy is that cake 'fowl'". Moe's characterizations range from accusatory ("Why did you let me forget [the cake and salad]?!") to submissive ("You wanna crab the show? You gotta eat it: it's part of the plot!"). Epithet: "imbeciles". Janiebelle calling the cake "Old Point Comfort" varies the 'Southern Comforter' gag from *Uncivil Warriors*; Larry adds the variation: "I get the point!" From the same film come Shemp's "They're molting!" and Moe's "You know this cake is as light as a feather!"; Shemp's "Delicious, you all!" is new. Other variations: Shemp: "I'll get busy when I'm ready!" Moe: "Are you ready?" Shemp: "Yeah, I'm ready." (*Plane Nuts*; *Men in Black*); Shemp: "Fine time to take a nap." (*Uncivil War Birds*); Moe: "Remind me to kill you later." Shemp: "I'll make a note of it." (*Cash and Carry*); and "Women and children first!" (*False Alarms*).

OTHER NOTES: The working title, *How Hammy Was My Hamlet*, demonstrates Bruckman's interest in Shakespeare. Some of filmdom's best adaptations of Shakespeare are roughly contemporary, e.g. Olivier's Oscar-winning *Hamlet* (1948) and Orson Welles' *MacBeth* (1948) and *Othello* (1951). Nanette Bordeaux is the top-billed actress, but she appears only in the second scene. In 'The Bride War Spurs' sequence, the Stooges and two other actors sing to Janiebelle in full quintet harmony, a Stooge rarity. One of the two additional actors, (the short, dark-haired one), is Danny Lewis, the father of comedian Jerry Lewis. Jerry Lewis had successfully teamed with Dean Martin first in *My Friend Irma* the previous year (1949), so Jules White, hoping to cash in on Lewis' sudden popularity, signed Jerry's father for this film. We hear anecdotally that Lewis senior had trouble spitting out the feathers; he kept swallowing them. Lewis junior would make a cameo appearance in 1963's *It's a Mad, Mad, Mad, Mad World*, as would the Stooges. Jerry Lewis on the Stooges: "All they do is schtick". Director of Photography Allen C. Siegler is credited as 'Al Ziegler.'

#126 - STUDIO STOOPS

Studio: Columbia

Released: October 5, 1950

Running Time: 16"00'"

Credited Production Crew:

Produced by:	Hugh McCollum
Directed by:	Edward Bernds
Written by:	Elwood Ullman
Director of Photography:	Vincent Farrar
Art Director:	Charles Clague
Film Editor:	Henry DeMond

Credited Cast:

Shemp Howard	
Larry Fine	
Moe Howard	
Christine McIntyre	Dolly Devore
Kenneth MacDonald	Dandy Dawson
Vernon Dent	Captain Casey

Uncredited Cast:

Charles Jordan	crook (Tiny)
Joe Palma	crook (Louie)
Stanley Price	reporter Brown

PERSPECTIVE: This film demonstrates how the innovative McCollum/Bernds/Ullman team can combine two frequently used Stooge premises with a recently popular Stooge scenario and an old gimmick to present a fresh Stooge crime drama. The first premise - confusing the Stooges with someone else - we saw as recently as in *Dopey Dicks*, where a frightened damsel-in-distress - the second premise - confused the Stooges for detectives. As far back as 1934's *Three Little Pigskins* the Stooges were confused for the 'Three Horsemen,' and in 1941's *All the World's a Stooge* they were confused for dentists. In *Studio Stoops* the Stooges are exterminators - as they were in *Ants in the Pantry* and *Termites of 1938* - who merely stand in an office while J. B. Fletcher, President of B. O. Pictures, presumes they are who the office door ('PUBLICITY DEPARTMENT') says they are. Interestingly, the film begins by playing the same deception on us, the viewers. We, like Fletcher, read the door sign and from outside hear Larry saying "It's terrific! It's colossal!" Not until we see the Stooges inside working as exterminators do we know better, but Fletcher never had that opportunity. The Hollywood lingo ("You've been knocking 'em dead!") applies to both film makers and exterminators and serves only to solidify the confusion.

Now given a 'special publicity' assignment, the Stooges have a bad idea for a publicity stunt which leads them into the recently popular Stooge scenario: a multi-room chase of grand proportions. We saw in *Idle Roomers* how a multi-room chase could be spread vertically to several floors of a building, but now the chase extends horizontally not only into several rooms and down the hall but even outside the building via the accordion telephone arm. This is an old gimmick, and it is at least as old as Del Lord's and Billy Bevan's *The Lion's Whiskers* (1925). Moe battled an accordion telephone recently in *Vagabond Loafers*, and we saw the hypnotized Stooges wonder out onto a flagpole in *Hokus Pokus*. But an old gimmick is once again extended to new horizons: Shemp is extended outside the building physically (by the accordion arm and then the rope, which, in fact, becomes crucial to capturing the criminals) and acoustically (by talking on the telephone).

Inside the building the chase encompasses a hotel room, its closet (*Dopey Dicks*), a second room, the hallway outside, the elevator (*Idle Roomers*), the poker game down the hall, and even the bathtub across the hall. It involves not just the three Stooges, but a kidnapped woman, three crooks, and four policemen — a cast even larger than the ones used in their quasi-epic Western *Punchy Cowpunchers* and their Stooge-fest, *Self-Made Maids*. All in all, this is quite a day for three exterminator Stooges. They are given jobs as movie publicity agents, they almost lose Shemp, almost lose their Hollywood starlet, and ultimately capture three kidnappers. As so often, one of their lousy ideas, in this case to fake Dolly Devore's disappearance, turns into a triumphant event. Stooges by nature seem to be lucky.

VISUAL HUMOR: Clever use of the camera alone embellishes the comedy twice: at the beginning by focusing on the 'PUBLICITY DEPARTMENT sign before 'SPEEDY TERMITE EXTERMINATORS,' and later when Shemp says into the phone "*what*??" just before the camera holds a close up of Dolly Devore and then pulls away to reveal the two crooks by her side. The rope provides for a series of new prop gags: as Moe and Devore tug, Shemp's head hits the ledge four times; the crooks break in the door and force them to drop it; a loop catches on Kenneth MacDonald's foot and makes him crash into the wall; Larry ("Woe, Nellie!") loosens the loop and gets pulled almost completely out the window; Shemp is pulled up to the brunette's balcony; and Shemp drops the rope, sending Moe and Larry flying backwards across the hallway and into the bathtub.

Other new gags: the Stooges working at three desks side by side; Moe being struck by Larry's flying typewriter carriage; Moe answering the door when the phone rings; Devore being zipped up in a garment bag; shooting prop guns issuing a pennant saying "BANG"; and jabbing a paper spindle into someone's rear. The latter two are Stooge firsts to be varied several times. The physical humor often moves the plot, where Larry

throws eggs at the four policemen, where the rope pulls one crook into the wall, and where Miss Devore and Moe smash flower pots over the other two crooks' heads. By falling and pulling the rope with him, Shemp saves the day. The rope is the physical opposite of the garbage can in *Crime on Their Hands*, which was a confining space; the rope lets the Stooges spread out and extend outside a building and back into another apartment's bathtub. The typewriter gag, where Shemp types very little for whole sentences, and four carriage returns' worth for "and," was used by the Marx Brothers.

The fights behind closed doors (of the elevator and second room), resemble the 'invisible' fight in the material bin of *Hugs and Mugs* and the lights-out fight of *Who Done It?*, this technique will be reused in subsequent films. When Moe orders Shemp to "Take a letter," Shemp walks effeminately over to Moe, recalling the recent *Self-Made Maids*. Moe bonking Larry and then bonking Shemp with the backswing derives from *3 Dumb Clucks*, but Moe will give a number of backwards bonks in future films. Other variations: the police captain warning Shemp that he will punch, sock, and knock him on the head as he does so (the alcove sequence in *A Bird in the Head*); the finger mouse trap (*Hugs and Mugs*; *Goofs and Saddles*); the multiple wrist watch gag (*Dutiful but Dumb*); the Stooges popping their heads around a hallway corner one above the other (*Horses' Collars*); the vase toppling onto the crook's head (*Cookoo Cavaliers*); being knocked into the bathtub and bathing with suits on while singing versions of 'La-Dee' (*Gents Without Cents*); and hearing the bathtub splash and seeing the water in the air (*We Want Our Mummy*).

VERBAL HUMOR: Elwood Ullman scattered a linguistic array among his characters. Miss Devore is a snob ("How d'you do"), Kenneth MacDonald is typically serious ("Tell them to be here with the dough in an hour or you'll take a dip in the ocean...a one-way dip!"), and the police captain uses slang (calling Shemp "Scoop," i.e. a reporter). Of Stooge lingo, Larry offers a neologism ("It's 'stupendious!"), and Shemp speaks in both pick-up slang ("Hiya, toots. Mind if I drop in?") and Maharaja-speak à la *Time Out For Rhythm* and *Three Little Pirates* ("Ogloon gobble yatibenifuchi-timiny haranja paradeek-man ee-haa June 22"). Moe and Larry have an exchange in pseudo-British accents (Larry: "What happened to my carriage?" Moe: "Your carriage waits without!") reminiscent of the Shakespeare in the previous film, then a pseudo-intellectual exchange nicely undercut by a final punch (Larry: "You better bolt that door in case our adversaries come back." Moe: "'Adversaries?'" Since when did you get so smart?" Larry: "Oh I've been smart all the time, only you didn't know it....Say, when I come back, I'll give you the password. Moe: "Brilliant. What'll it be?" Larry: "'Open the door.'" [SLAP]).

Prop-related puns complement the slapstick (Crook: "Who are you?" Shemp [throwing ashtray sand]: "I'm the sandman!"), especially with Shemp hanging outside and talking on the phone: "I'm hangin' outside the building on the eighth floor ("I guess it's the tenth floor - Would it be too much trouble to send me down a rope?"; "Will I hang on? What do you think I'll do, let go?"; [Moe: "If you fall off, watch out for the traffic."] "The green light's with me!"; "Could you hurry it up a little? It's urgent, and besides, someone wants to use the line!"). Moe bosses the cops ("You're a trifle late, but...clean it up!"), insults Shemp (Shemp: "If ya' ain't got a gun for me, whadya bring me along for?" Moe: "For bait!"), opens himself to insult ("Do I look like a termite? Don't answer that!"), and offers a new epithet: "chowder-head"... Both Larry and Shemp offer punch lines based on fear (Shemp: "Keep your chin up. Mine is down at my knees"; Moe: "This is the Zero Hour, men...If we're not out in five minutes, you better come and get us." Larry: "You better make that 30 seconds").

Ullman's gag names: the 'B. O. PICTURES CORP.'; the reporter's "I'm Brown from the *Sun*"; and Miss Devore's next film, '*Kiss the Moonbeams Off My Elbow*,' which parodies Universal's 1948 film title, *Kiss the Blood Off My Hands*; 'B. O.' was used in another film associated with movie production ('B. O. Botswaddle' in *Three Missing Links*). Other variations: Moe saying "Mmm...mmm...mmm," and when Larry is asked "What did he say?" Larry saying "Mmm...mmm... mmm!" (*Hold That Lion*); Shemp's problems with the telephone operator (*Dopey Dicks*); Moe: "Poor Shemp!" Larry: "And he had his good suit on, too!" (*Fright Night*); Larry: "Hey! This ain't Saturday night!" (*Rockin' Thru the Rockies*); Shemp laughing "Heh-heh-heh" (*Hugs and Mugs*); and Larry's "There was a room marked property, but it didn't say whose property!" (*Movie Maniacs*).

OTHER NOTES: The *Scrapbook* lists Gilbert Kay as assistant director. Continuity: Moe sends Larry for the rope, but it is Miss Devore who returns with it.

#127 - SLAPHAPPY SLEUTHS

Studio: Columbia

Released: November 9, 1950

Running Time: 16"09'"

Credited Production Crew:

Produced & Directed by:	Jules White
Written by:	Felix Adler
Director of Photography:	Vincent Farrar
Art Director:	Charles Clague
Film Editor:	Edwin Bryant

Credited Cast:

Shemp Howard	
Larry Fine	
Moe Howard	
Stanley Blystone	head crook
Emil Sitka	customer
Gene Roth	Fuller Grimes

Uncredited Cast:

Nanette Bordeaux	crook [Louise]
Joe Palma	crook
Blackie Whiteford	crook

PERSPECTIVE: The uniqueness of this aptly named film is its concatenations of slapstick exchanges, that is, slapstick sequences which do not stop after an isolated hit and a reaction but build on themselves and extend to a fourth, fifth, or sixth ricochet. We saw this in the opening Stooge scenes of *Punchy Cowpunchers* and *Hugs and Mugs*, but here it occurs in several scenes, three in the first half of the film alone. In Grime's office, Shemp feels something caught in his teeth, cuts a toothpick with his pen knife, gets hit with the toothpick, has his knife tossed onto the chair, sees Grimes sit on it, gets poked by Moe, pulls a plate out of his pants, builds a sandwich, gets it smashed on his face, and sees Moe wipe ketchup from his face and put it on Larry instead. At the gas station, after going through a whole routine with Emil Sitka's character and the popcorn popping radiator, they go through an inter-Stooge series: attempting to put his coat on (inside out), Shemp socks Moe, knocking him backwards so a tire falls on their heads, Moe gouges Shemp, the cash register drawer hits Shemp in the belly, he catches his fingers in the drawer, drops it on Moe's toe, Larry swallows gas, gets his finger caught in the door lock, socks Moe in the face after pulling it out, and gets his eye gouged. A second later Shemp is down on the ground sniffing a trail of oil...all the way into an apartment building. Despite a common misperception, particularly by those who dismiss Stooge comedy as nothing other than men hitting each other, Stooge slapstick usually serves to punctuate verbal gags and advance the plots of their films.

As usual, it is impossible to determine whose idea this was - that of producer/director Jules White, writer Felix Adler, or the Stooges themselves - but the last several White/Adler Stooge ventures have been very experimental in nature, including *Love at First Bite*, *Self-Made Maids*, and *Dunked in the Deep*. To make room for the extensive slapstick they had to design a streamlined plot by assigning the Stooges a simple sleuthing job (à la *Horses' Collars*) in which they pursue crooks who leave an obvious trail. Indeed, the main crook drives right up to their gas station, robs it, and leaves an oil trail all the way to his apartment door. To get in the apartment is also an easy matter for the Stooges: they just use "the door treatment." For the Stooges, this is a formula as old as *Pop Goes the Easel*, but it gets them into the sight of the final battle and sets up 200 more seconds of still more extended physical exchange.

In contrast to the previous film (*Studio Stoops*), the final battle does not require a chase or an expanse any larger than a single room which is perfect for this type of compact, high-energy, extended-slapstick struggle involving some extraordinarily interlocking punching, misdirected clubbing, inadvertent throwing, body spinning, head crushing, and a super two-men-in-the-coat routine (also from *Horses' Collars*, but this is Shemp's first). As in a Shakespearean tragedy, the final image is of a pile of bodies on the set. Shemp sees this and knocks himself out, adding himself to a pile of bodies in a mock-tragic Stooge suicide.

VISUAL HUMOR: The car service scene offers another extended slapstick sequence using the empty windshield, popcorn coming out of the radiator (filling the customer's hat) and tail pipe, exhaust soot, overinflating the tire, blowing oil from a tube, and the inter-Stooge broom fight. The finale offers another example, with double and fast motion punches, Moe knocking out the crook with the top of his head when he himself is knocked out by an uppercut, the vice, the artillery shell, and the pitcher of water which sets up the two-men-in-the-coat routine. Nanette Bordeaux gets knocked out twice, both times showing wonderfully goofy expressions on her face, as does Emil Sitka after being knocked silly by his car hood. Also, both the head crook [Stanley Blystone] and Larry toss things [a gun, a pipe] in the air and knock themselves out.

Some of theses physical gags are Stooge firsts, for instance Larry handing the crook the phone and saying "It's for you," but shaving the gas customer with "Onion service" derives from the Stooges' "Super Service!" in *Violent is the Word for Curly*. The two-men-in-the-coat routine from *Horses' Collars* uses 29 punches; the 30th is wielded by the main crook, misses Shemp, and hits the woman who was aiming that shell at Shemp's head. Other variations: the painted eyelids (*Horses Collars*); tossing the knife onto a chair (*All the World's a Stooge*); Moe grabbing Larry and Shemp by the nose and leading them away ("Schnoz!" in *Three Hams on Rye*); Shemp confusing 'STOP LEAK' for popcorn (*An Ache in Every Stake*); a crook punching Moe and Shemp in fast motion numerous times (*Slippery Silks*); Shemp squirting himself with the stopped up water hose (*Who Done It?*); Larry getting soaked with oil that Moe blows out with an air tube, and the plate in the back of Shemp's pants (*3 Dumb Clucks*); Shemp tied to a leash and sniffing the oil like a bloodhound (*Goofs and Saddles*); biting the crook in the knee to disarm him (*Nutty but Nice*); and Shemp knocking out Larry and Moe and himself (*Who Done It?*).

VERBAL HUMOR: Though the extended slapstick sequences dominate the comedy, Fuller Grime tests each Stooge verbally, asking Larry if he has been held at gunpoint ("Yeah, but he couldn't shoot me...I had my finger in the barrel!"), Moe if he ever had a commission in the service ("No, just straight salary!" [*Saved By the Belle*]), and Shemp if he is a good detective ("You see this heel? I ran that down!" [*Horses' Collars*]). Stooge ignorance is exploited (Grime: "You fellows are certainly stupid-looking enough, but about being brainy detectives, that's open to conjecture." Stooges: "Oh, thank you!" Shemp: "I'll button mine!"; Moe: "Keep an eye on him!" Shemp: "I'll keep both eyes on him!"; and Shemp picking up the cash register "so we don't get robbed again while we're gone!").More so than in most films, the printed names are all parodies - the gas names 'Ethel' [i.e. Ethyl Alcohol], Becky, and Hazel,' 'Onion Oil' ['Union Oil, whence 'ONION OIL - IN ONION THERE IS STRENGTH'], 'I. M. Greecy,' 'FULLER GRIME,' and the back of Stooges' advertising overalls [Moe's: 'TRY DR BELCHER'S COMPOUND FOR GAS ON STOMACH'; Larry's: 'FEEL TIRED? TAKE STUN. STUN IS NUTS SPELLED BACKWARD'; Shemp's: 'HAVE SORE FEET? TRY TIC-TAC. GOOD FOR THE TOE'].

The song they yodel is a variant of the song we heard in *Men in Black*. Other variations: Shemp: "You ruined my lunch!" (*Fright Night*); Shemp: "You double-crosser, you!" (*Calling All Curs*); Larry: "Why don't you sing 'Mammy'? ("Hey, porter!" in *A Gem of a Jam*); Moe: "Remind me to kill you later!" (*Cash and Carry*); the "Nyaah-nyaah!" taunt (*Dunked in the Deep*); and Shemp saying to the crook in the vice: "Don't go away!" (*Playing the Ponies*; recently in *Hugs and Mugs*).

OTHER NOTES: Nanette Bordeaux is listed as 'Louise' in the script, but not named in the film.

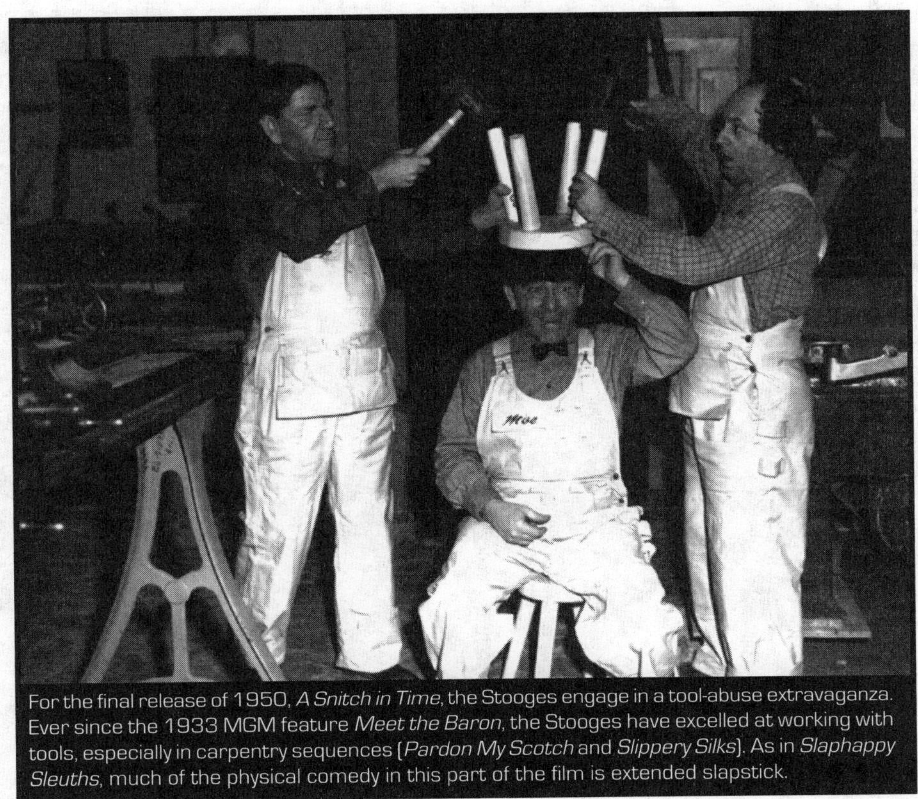

For the final release of 1950, *A Snitch in Time*, the Stooges engage in a tool-abuse extravaganza. Ever since the 1933 MGM feature *Meet the Baron*, the Stooges have excelled at working with tools, especially in carpentry sequences (*Pardon My Scotch* and *Slippery Silks*). As in *Slaphappy Sleuths*, much of the physical comedy in this part of the film is extended slapstick.

#128 - A SNITCH IN TIME

Studio: Columbia

Released: December 7, 1950

Running Time: 16"28'"

Credited Production Crew:

Produced by:	Hugh McCollum
Directed by:	Edward Bernds
Written by:	Elwood Ullman
Art Director:	Charles Clague
Film Editor:	Henry DeMond

Credited Cast:

Shemp Howard	
Larry Fine	
Moe Howard	
Jean Willes	Gladys Scudder

Uncredited Cast:

Bob Cason	Jerry
Henry Kulky	Steve
John Merton	crook

PERSPECTIVE: This final release of 1950 is a nicely blended bi-partite episode which divides into two different scenarios but has some overlap between them. The first scenario establishes the Stooges as furniture builders. One could hardly ask for more. Ever since *Meet the Baron*, the Stooges have excelled at working with tools, especially in carpentry sequences (*Pardon My Scotch* and *Slippery Silks*). Here in *A Snitch in Time* they have their widest variety of tools to misuse - nails, drawers, boards, saws, planers, brushes and glue - in a continuous exercise in skilled inexpertise. As in the previous film, *Slaphappy Sleuths*, much of the physical comedy in this part of the film is extended slapstick, largely because of the multiplicity of tools, particularly after Moe gets glue in his eye, whereupon the comedy unfolds in over a dozen gags with pliers, a chisel, a large screwdriver, a hammer, a brush, Moe's eye, Larry's foot, Moe's stomach, Moe's rear, the circular saw, nails, and a hack saw, all ending with Moe's hands being glued to Shemp's and Larry's faces. The one bit of plot in this six-minute first scenario is cleverly moved: we learn that Moe likes Miss Scudder ("You're just about the cutest bunch of curls I've ever seen!") and promises to bring the new furniture over to her house...even though he saws through the phone line.

The second part of the film develops gradually, first giving the Stooges the opportunity to continue their poor craftsmanship and reprise two of their better tradesmen sequences from *Tassels in the Air* - painting a cuckoo clock, and staining a table while eating lunch, drinking stain, and staining each other. But while they are making a mess of these jobs three crooks terrorize Miss Scudder and soon hold Larry and Shemp at gun point. A confusion of bags - a motif not used since *What's the Matador?* - then leads to a 4 1/2- minute battle and multi-room chase that takes them all over the downstairs of a home perfectly equipped with sticky furniture, a set of sliding doors, a set of china, a hot iron (à la *Hugs and Mugs*), and a bucket-bearing curtain rod.

The crime drama is more realistic and hostile in this film than usual. Kenneth MacDonald always plays his criminal parts to the hilt, but here the crooks tie up

and taunt Miss Scudder roughly, hold the Stooges hostage, and even fire their gun and have a hand-to-hand struggle with the pistol. There is a certain harshness about it, which is paralleled by the way Moe is treated. We have seen Moe being slapped by Shemp in recent films, but here he takes an incredible beating in the opening scene. He took a climber's spike in his eye in *They Stooge to Conga*, but this is one of the more painful looking gags in all of Stoogedom: even Curly, who destroyed many a saw with his skull, never had his face jammed into a whirling circular saw blade. It may be that much of this comic violence results from Moe's paybacks, but the degree of violence is notable, particularly since Director Ed Bernds made it clear when he directed *Micro-Phonies* that the violence was not to be excessive.

VISUAL HUMOR: Before getting his face in the saw, Moe almost cuts his finger off while yelling at Larry. Enhancing the extended slapstick is fine editing with use of fast motion when Larry gets punched through the sliding doors, a large array of sharp, appropriate sound effects, and a few combination hits [Moe double pounding/double bonking Shemp and Larry, and Moe using the bucket to hit Larry with the backswing, Shemp with the foreswing]. A Stooge first: a new type of take for Moe: when struck with the iron, he begins to talk, then passes out.

As in the previous film, there is some doubling of slapstick antics. Shemp's hands get stuck to his nailed glove, Moe's to the board of glue; Moe bends over and gets his hair planed and then his rear stained; and Shemp silently signals Moe about Steve holding him at gun point, and later silently signals the police into the next room. Steve goes flying over the living room chair twice as well. Larry acts effeminately after he shows Moe his drawer [Moe: "Whadya want me to do, kiss ya'?" Larry [smiling]: "Well..." [SLAP]] much like Shemp as secretary in *Studio Stoops*; from the same film come Larry and Shemp acting politely to each other before smashing the china plate over the crook's head, and hearing punching sounds from the next room where a Stooge or two is being beaten up.

Sticking to the chair is another gag borrowed from *Tassels in the Air*. Other variations: wiping off Moe's face with dirty rags, and Moe and Larry repeatedly getting their faces punched [*Slaphappy Sleuths*]; Larry's struggle with the chest of drawers [*Hold That Lion*]; a twelve-foot board [*Slippery Silks*]; a woman gagged and bound to a chair [*Dopey Dicks*]; and Shemp rigging the can of paint on top of the hallway curtain rod [a bowling ball in *The Hot Scots*].

VERBAL HUMOR: Elwood Ullman's script is filled with puns [Shemp: "Camel's hair brush? Must be the hump."]; internal rhymes [Moe: "With these helpers, I'm helpless."]; ironies [Shemp [seeing the glue in Moe's eye]: "This is pretty serious...Larry! Bring the chisel!"]; sarcasm [Moe: "And this time get some stain on the table."]; romantic realism [Moe: "We've got a date!" Shemp: "No you ain't!"]; threats [Moe: "Bring some proper tools here or I'll annihilate ya'!"]; insults [Moe [planing Larry's bald scalp]: "I drew a blank!"; Shemp: "He's stuck again." Moe: "Yeah, with you guys!"]; orders [Moe: "I want that board smooth enough to dance on."]; prideful realizations [Larry [taking over Shemp's job]: "Boy, glue those boards together! Whadya know? I been promoted!"]; and wisecracks [Shemp [about the spitting cuckoo clock]: "How do you like that? He gave me the drippin's!"]. Epithets: "weasel-brain" and "imbeciles". The crooks' speeches are appropriately hard-hearted [Steve: "Boy, you should have seen the old guy shake with a gat in his ribs." Jerry: "Never mind reminiscing."]. The introductory sign extends the archaic final 'e' of 'YE OLDE - Furniture Shoppe' to 'While-U-Waite'.

A radio talking back to Larry ["$5000!" Radio: "That's right!"] we heard first in *Healthy, Wealthy and Dumb*. Other variations: Moe: "You won't recognize the stuff" [*Flat Foot Stooges*]; Moe: "We're in a nest of crooks!" [*Termites of 1938*]; Larry: "Wait a minute! Don't use that - it's got a crack in it" [*Dizzy Pilots*]; Moe: "Does my head look like hardwood?" Shemp: "Well." ["Do I look like a termite? Don't answer that!" in *Studio Stoops*].

OTHER NOTES: The title satirizes the proverbial expression 'a stitch in time'. This is the first film of three without credit for a Director of Photography. Jean Willes [Miss Scudder] signed a studio contract with Columbia in 1949; three years after this Stooge appearance she played Annette, the saloon hostess, in Columbia's *From Here to Eternity*. Coincidentally, Bob Cason [Jerry] played Corporal Paluso in *From Here to Eternity*. Miss Scudder's reference to her tax bill ["I can use the money all right with my tax bill coming due. I almost had to sell the family heirlooms."] precedes *Income Tax Sappy* by a few years. Jerry overhears this line and fills his pockets with jewelry, adding: "Thanks for the tip about the family heirlooms." We saw a similar plot set-up in the previous film when Vernon Dent leaves his grocery bag, thus setting up his return to beat up Shemp.

Henry Kulky [Steve] was once a professional wrestler known as 'Bomber Kulkavich.' He was best known later for playing Otto Schmidlap in the television series *The Life of Riley* [1953-58]

1951

Three Arabian Nuts • *Baby Sitters Jitters* • *"Don't Throw That Knife"*

Scrambled Brains • *Merry Mavericks* • *The Tooth Will Out*

Hula-la-la • *Pest Man Wins*

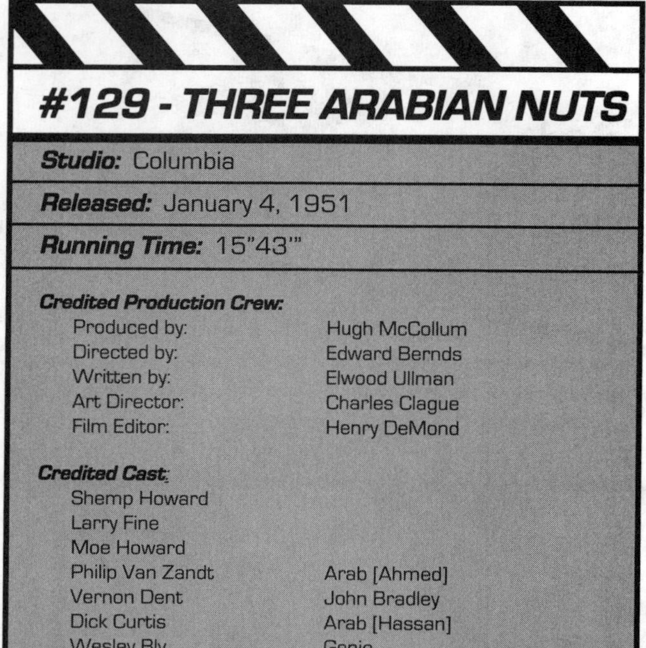

#129 - THREE ARABIAN NUTS

Studio: Columbia

Released: January 4, 1951

Running Time: 15"43'"

Credited Production Crew:

Produced by:	Hugh McCollum
Directed by:	Edward Bernds
Written by:	Elwood Ullman
Art Director:	Charles Clague
Film Editor:	Henry DeMond

Credited Cast:

Shemp Howard	
Larry Fine	
Moe Howard	
Philip Van Zandt	Arab [Ahmed]
Vernon Dent	John Bradley
Dick Curtis	Arab [Hassan]
Wesley Bly	Genie

PERSPECTIVE: Very similar to the final release of 1950, *A Snitch in Time*, this first release of 1951 unfolds in a two-part plot and casts the Stooges in a trade that conveys them to a house ripe for a multi-room chase, although warehousing and Arabs replace carpentry and crooks, and scimitar swinging replaces gun play. There is again some overlapping between the two scenarios since the Arabs are seen first at the warehouse and then follow the Stooges to the Bradley home. Another similarity between the two films is that Bradley comes to the warehouse to get his china delivered that afternoon, just as Miss Scudder called Moe to get her furniture delivered the same day. [In comic narratives it is often desirable to compact as much action into as little time as possible.] One significant improvement is transforming the vicious crooks and damsel-in-distress of the previous film into the silly Arabs and flustered Bradley [Vernon Dent]: instead of watching the bungling but able Stooges stop a real crime in progress, we watch the bungling Stooges compete with the equally inept Arabs, who want the magic lamp, and Bradley, who stupidly gives the lamp up voluntarily.

The biggest difference between the two films is the genie, or as Shemp says, "the genius." A genie was featured in Alexander Korda's Oscar-winning *Thief of Bagdad* (1940), where it was played to the hilt by Rex Ingram, the tall African-American who played in a number of Hollywood epics, and now the Stooges use Wesley Bly in a similar role. Since magic tricks and comic coincidences come from the same aesthetic realm of belief and appearance, the car driven into the apartment in *Slaphappy Sleuths* may well have been a forerunner to the genie's presence, as is Larry's miraculously carrying that huge crate by himself. Nonetheless, even the luck Curly had in *Oily to Bed, Oily to Rise* never had as visible a presence as this. Initially the genie is asked merely to give Shemp a Zoot suit and is soon tossed away, boxed up, and lost in the fireplace. At the end, though, like a *deus ex machina* the genie literally saves Shemp's head and bestows great wealth upon the Stooges. And, as happens only rarely, a non-Stooge bears the brunt of the final gag while the Stooges walk off with women and wealth, although it is probably good that the genie carries the money for them; they drop everything else.

The operative word here is 'breakage.' We already knew right at the beginning that Bradley was in trouble when Moe told him: "Don't you worry. We're gentle as a flock of kittens." By the time they deliver the crates from the warehouse, it is remarkable that there is anything left to deliver. Throughout the film china-breaking sound effects fill our ears as the Stooges drop, toss, bump, and smash piece after piece, and when china is not breaking someone is being clanged, thumped, bonked, or sizzled, or the Genie is going WHOOSH. Even more than in the previous film, the sound effects here are frequent, appropriate, and insistent, with nearly three dozen of them punctuating the film before Vernon Dent clangs himself on the head 28 times to bring the film to a close.

VISUAL HUMOR: Shemp's beating heart is another gimmick that lies between comical perception and magic. As for technical magic, stop camera technique is used to effect the genie's appearance and Shemp's change of clothes in mid-run. The sheer number of physical gags necessitated many new motifs: Moe tickling Shemp so he can get his hands off his head and bonk him; Larry tossing the lamp through a transom window and clanging Moe on the head; Bradley sitting on the hot plate (twice); Moe ripping off the Arab's robe sticking out from the crate; the Arab dropping the scimitar blade on the table and Shemp politely handing it back to him; Shemp swinging the scimitar only to have the blade fly off and stick into the wall behind him; and the final hot potato tossing of the magic lamp. The flow of Arabs is nicely worked out. They appear behind boxes, climb into a crate, climb through a window, and stand behind curtains. Larry confuses one of them for a set of curtains, and Moe confuses one for the Genie. Later, because he has a towel on his head, Bradley gets confused for an Arab.

Because the Arabs spend much of the film lurking, we see several motifs from such scare comedies as *Idle Roomers* and *Dizzy Detectives*, namely the Arabs grabbing at Shemp ("I got a funny feelin' I'm being watched"), and Larry, mistakenly thinking he has Shemp by the hand, leading one down the hall. When he gets his first wish, Shemp wears a snazzy Zoot suit, a broad skimmer, a bow tie, and a long chain; we first heard reference to 'Zoot" in *Loco Boy Makes Good*. Larry does a memorable full-body take when he sees him. When Moe smashes two vases over Shemp's and Larry's heads, they at first remain unaffected (Shemp: "Did you hear a loud noise?" Larry: "Well...") before getting a goofy look and passing out. This new type of take was re-introduced in the previous film when Shemp threw the iron that hit Moe on the head.

Larry mistakenly hits Bradley with the towel over his head just as Larry hit Moe by mistake in *Fright Night*. Other variations: pouring coffee on Larry's hand, then shoving it in his face (*Three Hams on Rye*), handing the phone to an enemy in the midst of a chase (*A Snitch in Time*), running the sword through the wall (*Mummy's Dummies*); seeing the Arab banged around inside the crate, and Moe pulling Shemp by the lip towards the door (*Boobs in Arms*); Shemp dropping the crate onto the ground as Larry pulls the flatbed away (*Vagabond Loafers*); and Shemp spinning face to face with Moe (*Love at First Bite*). The final tableau is somewhat like that in *The Yoke's on Me* but much more pleasant: as the smoke clears we see the two Arabs tied up with thick ropes and the Stooges on the floor next to the fireplace, each reclining next to a beautiful woman. A blonde pats Shemp's cheek, and two brunettes playfully feed Moe grapes and twist Larry's hair. Bradley hitting himself silly on the head twenty-eight times is a record for a Stooge (or any?) film.

Vernon Dent was perhaps the most recognizable foil in the Columbia Stooge short film corpus. Born in California in 1895, he soon took to the theater and was working in film comedy by 1919. From 1923 he worked as a supporting player at the Mack Sennett Studios where he achieved a modicum of fame working in the Harry Langdon and Billy Bevan films. At 5'9" and 250 pounds, he cast quite a figure on the screen, and he excelled at playing the Stooge foil, as in this first release of 1951, *Three Arabian Nuts*. Unfortunately, the dozens of other non-Stooge Columbia short film comedies are rarely seen today.

VERBAL HUMOR: Elwood Ullman's script plays second fiddle to the intensive physical humor, but he writes some fine banter for Moe trying to calm Bradley (Bradley: "Merciful heavens! What was that?" Moe: "Oh it could be any number of a thousand things!"), being attacked by an Arab scimitar ([to Larry and Shemp:] "Now step on it or I'll take your heads off...It's drafty in here!"), and insulting Shemp (Shemp: "How do I look?" Moe: "As ugly as ever.") as well as some charming slang for Larry in the final tableau ("You're my type, baby - a woman!").

The Arabs are made fun of verbally (Larry: "There may be more of these buzzards around here!"; Shemp: "Smack everybody that's wearing a turban!"). Moe adds more ethnic flavor by toning the label on a crate in pseudo-Chinese, adding, as if he understood Chinese, "Oh, knick-knacks!"; later one of the Arabs thanks Shemp by calling him "Sahib." Shemp undercuts this realism by being nonchalant (Genie: "A million? How do you want it?" Shemp: "I wish you wouldn't bother me with details"), calling the genie "genius," and speaking in slang ("Wait'll the dames get a load of me!") and jive ("Hot ziggety!...Hey Amos! Where's the moola?"). 'Amos' refers once again to *Amos and Andy*, which was to be broadcast on television for the first time in the summer of 1951. Epithets: "porcupine," "nitwits," and "lunk-heads"

Moe's "What is this, mutiny?" is an old Ted Healy line (*Meet the Baron*). Moe's "I'd knock your brains out if you had any!" recalls *Cactus Makes Perfect* (Moe: "For two pins I'd bat your brains out." Curly: "I ain't got any pins!" Moe: "You haven't got any brains either!").

OTHER NOTES: The release title parodies 'Arabian Nights'; the working titles were *Genie with the Light Brown Hair* and *Genie Was a Meanie*. The film was shot in early January, 1950, yet was not released until one year later and bears the copyright date of 1951. This is the second of three films that omit credit for the Director of Photography; on the title credit screen there is a gap where this credit belongs, all the actors are credited.

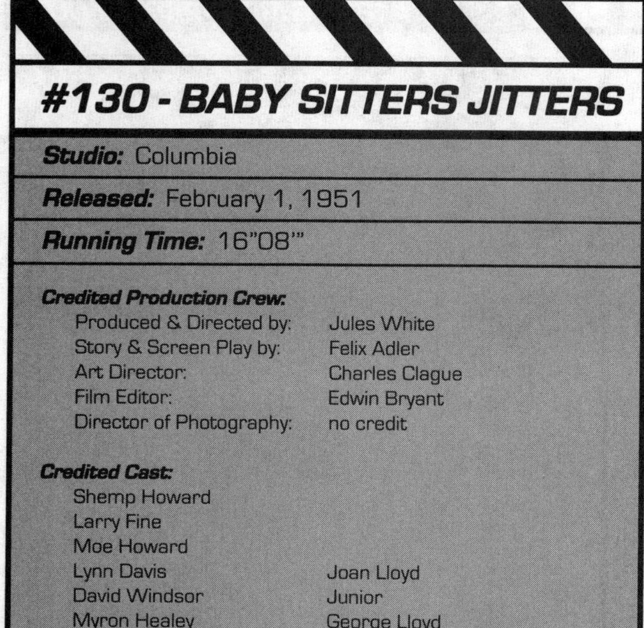

#130 - BABY SITTERS JITTERS

Studio: Columbia

Released: February 1, 1951

Running Time: 16"08'"

Credited Production Crew:

Produced & Directed by:	Jules White
Story & Screen Play by:	Felix Adler
Art Director:	Charles Clague
Film Editor:	Edwin Bryant
Director of Photography:	no credit

Credited Cast:

Shemp Howard	
Larry Fine	
Moe Howard	
Lynn Davis	Joan Lloyd
David Windsor	Junior
Myron Healey	George Lloyd
Margie Lizst	Mrs. Crump

PERSPECTIVE: There is an old saying in show business: never act with animals or children. The reasoning is sound, because audiences by nature tend to find children and animals to be cuter, funnier, and more attractive than the adult star who accompanies them. But an exception to this rule would be when the 'adult ' stars happen to be three imbecilic, childish, and ignorant Stooges who are no more mature than the kid. In fact, a parallel between their levels of maturity is established right from the outset: the first thing we see the kid do is play mindlessly with a gun, and minutes later Shemp mindlessly shoots a strip off of Moe's scalp. So who is more childish - Shemp or the child? Not surprisingly, Shemp is throughout the film characterized as child-like: he has the reading skills of a child, sleeps in the crib like a baby, cries at the end of the film, and look who turns Shemp's infantile tears to laughter - the kid, by standing on his head, the same trick Shemp used to stop the kid from crying earlier. What makes all this even sillier is that Mrs. Lloyd, a 'normal' adult, laughs, too, when Shemp stands on his head, a clear sign that this film takes us into a topsy-turvy universe in which the difference between maturity and immaturity seems to depend on which direction your head is pointing.

The Stooges have baby sat before, and the plot is similar to *Mutts to You* and *Sock-A-Bye Baby* in that all three films end with the married couple reuniting around the Stooges and the child. But there is a significant difference: in *Mutts to You* and *Sock-A-Bye Baby* the Stooges find the child on a stoop; here they are hired and, amazingly, recommended [!] as baby sitters. They have studied the subject in Davenport Seats' book, '*How to Become a Baby Sitter*,' so they should know what they are doing. But one of the quintessential qualities of being a Stooge is genuinely thinking you know what you are doing even when you do not, and one of the narrative requirements for Stooge films is that someone is negligent enough to hire them to do an important job.

Long before we know how unqualified the Stooges really are, the film opens with the Stooges feeding, diapering, and cuddling three babies. Although Larry is using the window shade to diaper his, this all looks perfectly normal and differs from the openings of several previous films which begin with extended slapstick routines. But then in one of the most extraordinary opening surprises in all of Stoogedom, the Stooges throw their babies to each other, Shemp trips and squashes one, and Moe ("Butt out of this, porcupine!") hits Larry over the head with his. In a kind of infantile yet symmetrical justice later in the film, the child in their care, more capable than the infants in *Mutts to You*, *Sock-A-Bye Baby*, and *Three Loan Wolves*, bites Larry's hand, throws a coke bottle at his head, smashes all three Stooges and his father with a hammer, and then imitates Shemp by standing on his head to make everyone laugh. You see, the old warning was right: never act with animals or children because they always win out in the end.

VISUAL HUMOR: Several slapstick routines are particularly well placed in the narrative. Larry begins to shadow box Moe, but Moe ignores him, turns, and kicks Larry through the door across the hall - where they find the kid. In the same scene, Moe kicks Shemp in the rear, and more bubbles come out of his mouth, a reminiscence of the previous scene. Although most of the physical gags are derivative, they are nicely varied. Shemp's boxing steps, for instance, are typically intricate, but he interrupts them in the middle of the routine to amuse the child. And although the Stooges had trouble with a transom in *Dutiful but Dumb*, Moe gets a surprise punch from this one. Similarly, although Curly shot ink through a keyhole in *Healthy, Wealthy and Dumb*, Shemp now gets a key in the eye and nostril as he peeks into this keyhole. An excellent variation of this sort of *paraclausithuron* ['outside the door'] comedy is Shemp peeking under the door just as the occupant is sweeping dust out the bottom.

Speaking of varying old motifs: Moe uses a hand-wave for the first time; Moe pounds Shemp and bonks Larry to grab them both by their open mouths (*Sing a Song of Six Pants*); Moe reaches back to bonk both of them without looking (a variation on *Studio Stoops*); Shemp takes a swig of liquor and Moe pounds him in the belly, making Shemp spit it out on Moe (*We Want Our Mummy*). The best extended slapstick sequence in the film comes after Moe discovers Shemp has stolen silver.

A more subtle Shemp moment is when he looks under the crib mattress for the baby. The bubble blowing borrows several motifs from *All Gummed Up*. Larry puts a nipple on a coke bottle as Curly did with a beer bottle in *Sock-a-Bye Baby;* this is the first Coca-Cola bottle we have seen, and it is put to two good uses. Other variations: christening Shemp over the head (*Pop Goes the Easel*); fly paper (*So Long, Mr. Chumps*); the gun in the child's mouth (*Three Loan Wolves*); cutting a diaper (*Sock-a-Bye Baby*); the tray stuffed in Shemp's rear (*Slaphappy Sleuths*); knocking on a head instead of a door (*Calling All Curs*); shooting off a stripe of Moe's hair (*Disorder in the Court*); Moe smashing an apple on Shemp's forehead (*Love at First Bite*); Shemp stealing silverware (*Hoi Polloi*); Larry saluting ("Aye, aye, captain!") while slapping Moe (*Uncivil Warriors*); and eating walnut shells and not the 'stuffing' (*Dizzy Detectives*).

VERBAL HUMOR: Because an infant is the 'fourth Stooge,' typical dialogue, insults, and threats with him will not work, so Felix Adler substitutes visual verbal gags like the book title and author ('*How to Become a Baby Sitter*' by Davenport Seats; [a 'davenport' was originally a writing desk, but is generally a type of couch or bed]) and Shemp's soliloquy, that is, his memorable reading of the ingredients for "consummated soup" ("Feel Ikes Fay Mouse Consume-triate Soup ['FELIX Famous Concentrated SOAP']..."sag-ee [sage], cay-a-ninny [cayenne] - what no pits in that? - mou-stard [the can, too], gloves [cloves] - Oh! little gloves! - and powdered bacon [baking powder] - what'll they think of next?"). Because the Stooges are supposed to be the adult baby-sitters, Adler wants to emphasize their childlike ignorance - poor reading and grammar (Shemp: "You know I can't read good"), mispronunciations (Shemp: "I'm losin' my ba-lánce!"), poor vocabulary (Shemp: "Eureka!" Moe: "You don't smell so good either!"; Larry: "You couldn't fool me that way!" Moe: "No, you're too much of an ignoramus." Larry: "Yeah, and that goes for my whole family, too!"; Moe: "Nuts." Larry: "Hey!"), childish language (Moe: "Shempie!" Shemp: "Yes-sie"), and childish lies (Shemp: "I was passin' by, a drawer was open, and my sleeve got caught"). To a certain extent they even deny they are adults (Moe: "If the child's crying persists...have some adult stand on his head." Shemp: "If we only could find an adult"; Larry: "Hey fellas, I think I got somethin' that'll keep the little brat quiet." [CRASH] Never mind! He's found somethin' that'll keep me quiet"; later Moe calls Larry "baby face"). Early in the film they are even reduced to saying "Nyaah" and barking at the landlady.

In contrast, there are adult lines about drinking (Shemp: "There's a thousand reasons why I shouldn't drink...But I can't think of one right now"), a pun (Larry: "We work as a unit." Shemp: "We're Unitarians!"), insults (Moe: "I told you to find the kitchen, not steal it!"; "Tastes like a dead horse!"), slapstick banter (Moe: "Say, did you ever see how they launch a ship?" [SMASH] Moe: "What's the matter with you?" Shemp [tottering]: "I'm seasick."), and a transitional three-pattern (Moe: "We're the baby-sitters." Shemp: "I hope that's the baby!" Larry: "Some baby!"). Other variations: Moe: "What does the clock say?" Shemp: "Tick-tick-tick" (*Fright Night*); singing a major triad of "Come in!" (*Healthy, Wealthy and Dumb*). Epithets: "bloodhounds," "nitwit," and "porcupine"; the landlady calls them "no-good loafers."

OTHER NOTES: The correct title of this film has no apostrophe and consists of three words, not two. This is the third consecutive film to omit credit for the Director of Photography, but the first to show the producer/ director credits on a fourth title screen. Recent films have not been using wipes; this film contains one. A landlady will be a stock character in several subsequent films. George Lloyd [Myron Healey] was the actual name of the actor who played in *Pardon My Clutch* and *Crime on Their Hands*. The Lloyd's address was the 'Folger Apartments at 212 Tenth Street'. All the actors are credited.

Writer Felix Adler, ever interested in updating Stooge comedy, penned *Baby Sitters Jitters* for the 1951 releases. As the Stooge corpus moved into the 1950s, the scenarios became increasingly domestic. Interior shooting is, of course, less expensive, but the main impetus for this was television programming, wherein domestic situation comedies were rapidly becoming the prevalent theatrical comedy genre in the popular culture. The following film, *"Don't Throw That Knife,"* makes this even more evident.

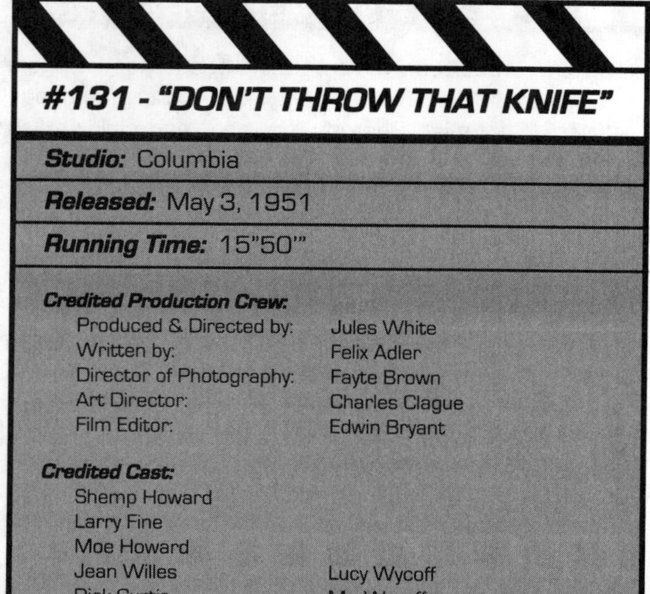

#131 - "DON'T THROW THAT KNIFE"

Studio: Columbia

Released: May 3, 1951

Running Time: 15"50'"

Credited Production Crew:

Produced & Directed by:	Jules White
Written by:	Felix Adler
Director of Photography:	Fayte Brown
Art Director:	Charles Clague
Film Editor:	Edwin Bryant

Credited Cast:

Shemp Howard	
Larry Fine	
Moe Howard	
Jean Willes	Lucy Wycoff
Dick Curtis	Mr. Wycoff

PERSPECTIVE: Just as the 1940 U.S. Census inspired *No Census, No Feeling*, the 1950 census inspired this little romp. Unlike its predecessor, *"Don't Throw That Knife"* does not reach from street to mansion to football stadium but plays in the confines of a single-opening corridor and a two-room apartment. This represents quite a shift from not only the physical expanse and variety of locations used for the 1940 film but also the interior multi-room chases that have climaxed a number of Shemp films. Several of the most recent films have been more modest in scope (*Love at First Bite*), whether limiting the number of players (*Self-Made Maids*) or sets (*Hugs and Mugs*). The previous film, *Baby Sitters Jitters*, was the most modest of all, and that this film, too, is played out entirely in interior apartments demonstrates a major change occurring in Hollywood comedies at the time. *"Don't Throw That Knife"* was shot in June, 1950, and it is no coincidence that *The Life of Riley* had already premiered on television in October, 1949 and that the pilot for *I Love Lucy* would be shot in a few months to usher in the first wave of television domestic situation comedies. The concept of comedy in 1950 was shifting towards modest, less costly interior settings and domestic situations, whether they involved a bumbling husband and his sensible wife, a zany redhead and her emotional Cuban band leader husband, or Stooge census takers and a jealous prestidigitating husband.

Without a multi-room chase and with just a small number of players, Jules White and Felix Adler had to create other ways of filling two reels with comedy, so they combined a variety of new, renewed and revised gags, gimmicks, gadgets, set jokes and slapstick antics. They indulge in the verbal *cine qua non* of the plot - the census Q & A - once among the Stooges and once with Mrs. Wycoff, creating in the first instance an interior variation by having Shemp and Larry disguise themselves. To this they add a number of gimmicks by having Shemp produce a locked safe, a musical powder box, a water-squirting worm, and a disheveled hairdo so that the viewer barely notices that the entire first four minutes of the film take place within a sixty square-foot area.

The second part of the film is a comedy of manners, a bedroom comedy modeled on the middle portion of *What's the Matador?*, and again, in addition to the hot water bottle, aspirin fetching, and hiding routines of the original film, Adler/ White add the 'CRY IN THIS' hanky, thrown shoes, the collapsing chair, Moe impersonating a hopping chair, Shemp talking in Mrs. Wycoff's voice, a trick chair, fun-house mirrors, a false-bottom box, knife throwing, Larry talking in the television - talk about the influence of television! - and an egg cannon. There is no Stooge film that uses so many gimmicks, and then it culminates in an unsuccessful ending, that is, one of those 'run-away' endings we saw more often in the Curly films. In no Shemp film to date have the Stooges run off into the distance pursued by an unvanquished assailant, but in 1950 situation comedy the husband always gets to keep his wife.

VISUAL HUMOR: The safe, musical powder box, and water squirting worm are all connected in an extended slapstick sequence. Other new gags: the false bottom box (a Stooge first); following the woman saying "walk this way"; and trick mirrors. Moe does several solo gags: opening the portfolio into his nose, a full body take and trying twice to sit on the trick collapsing chair ("That chair's got weak knuckles!"). He offers several new or varied moves, including slapping Larry thrice (cheek, cheek, forehead) and biting Shemp's ear. In the previous film we saw a slapstick role reversal (Moe hand-waving Shemp); here Larry tweaks Shemp's nose, and Moe's forward and backward bonks are also a variation of previous film's two backwards bonks. Result shot: three fried eggs clinging to Shemp's eyes and mouth. The skeleton wriggling out of the box is reminiscent of *The Ghost Talks*. Other variations: the safe under the shirt (*Cactus Makes Perfect*); the BANG pistols, and looking out the bedroom window at the street below (*Studio Stoops*); the egg-shooting Gattling-gun (*Goofs and Saddles*); one Stooge biting another (*Uncivil Warriors*); knife throwing (*Three Little Twirps*); emerging from the janitor's closet on three scooters (*Men in Black*); and the Stooges sticking their heads out the closet door one above the other (*Horses' Collars*).

VERBAL HUMOR: Recent films like *Slaphappy Sleuths* and *Three Arabian Nuts* had so much action that little time was left for verbal humor. This film, despite all the

Jean Willes [1923-1989] was a contract Columbia player. After such Stooge short-films as *"Don't Throw That Knife"*, she worked her way into minor [*From Here to Eternity* [1953]] and then major roles in features [*Desire Under the Elms* [1958] and *Ocean's Eleven* [1960]].

gadgetry, reverses that trend, beginning with the disclaimer: 'ANY RESEMBLANCE BETWEEN THE THREE STOOGES AND REGULAR HUMAN BEINGS, WHETHER LIVING OR DEAD, IS A DIRTY SHAME'.

Much of the verbal humor comes in chains of set jokes - verbal parallels to the extended slapstick: the census Q & A in the hall (Moe: "Do you have any children?" Larry [counting nine fingers]: "No children." Moe: "Where were you born, madam?" Shemp: "In the hospital...I wanted to be near my mother." Moe: "Is this your home state?" Shemp: "No, we're from the South." Moe: "What part of the South? Shemp: "Montreal, Canada." Larry: "Mighty pretty country around there. That's the home of the wild gooses, and the mooses, and the mices ['meeses']—" Moe: "And the mouses!"); the 'Wycoff' puns (Woman: "Wycoff." Moe: "A little irritation in the throat." Woman: "Wycoff." Larry: "Because he don't brush his teeth, lady." Woman: "Wycoff." Shemp: "He's got a frog in his throat from eatin' toadstools!"); the magician jokes (Larry: "What does your husband do?" Mrs. Wycoff: "He's an expert in legerdemain." Larry: "Oh, a book keeper." Mrs. Wycoff: "No, he's a prestidigitator." Shemp: "Oh, a pants presser!" Moe: "Are you guys ignorant?...He presses refrigerators!" Mrs. Wycoff: "No, no, no. We do an illusion act in vaudeville. He's a magician. He makes things disappear." Shemp: "I got an uncle who can make things disappear." Moe: "Is he a magician?" Shemp: "No, he's a kleptomaniac!"); Shemp and Larry finding four different ways of saying "Goodbye" (Shemp: "Adios!" Larry: "Toodle-oo." Shemp: "Goodbye!" Larry: "Ver geharget!");

Both Larry and Shemp impersonate women; Larry puts on a woman's hat: "Tell him I'm your aunt." 'Shempetta' was Shemp's female name in *Self-Made Maids*; calling her husband Larry "the rat" derives from "the dirty rat" of *Hoi Polloi*. Shemp's "ear-y-sipelas" was used as the name of Octopus Grabus' kingdom in *Matri-Phony*. Other variations: Larry and Shemp acting "Southern" ("Hallelujah, tote...pull that barge—" [*Dancing Lady*, *Plane Nuts*]; Larry's "Ver geharget!" [*Pardon My Scotch*]; and "In the hospital...I wanted to be near my mother" [*Rhythm and Weep*].

Larry's speech from inside the TV ("Don't you dare! Don't you dare do anything to endanger the lives of others! When you drive, drive carefully!"). Other set exchanges: Shemp: "I wouldn't be his wife!" Larry: "Why not?!" Shemp: "You're not my type!"; Wycoff: "If he finds you here, he'll kill you!" Larry: "If he finds me here, I deserve to get killed!"; Moe: "We're gettin' no place fast." [The husband knocks at the door] Shemp: "We better get some place fast!"; and Shemp: "Money shrinks!" Moe: "So do you, every time you get near a bathtub!" Epithets: "idiots," "fools," "cowards"; Moe also characterizes the Stooges beautifully: "Remember: we're census takers, not *ordinary* idiots".

OTHER NOTES: The film has a 1951 copyright date, but was shot in June, 1950, later than three subsequent 1951 releases (*Scrambled Brains*, *Merry Mavericks*, *The Tooth Will Out*) the title screen has "Don't Throw That Knife". The working title was *Noncensus Takers*; the release title has quotation marks around it. Credit screens now have a diagonal pattern on the third screen (writer, photographer, art director, film editor), the photography credit has been reinstated, and the credit for producer/director Jules White again appears on a fourth screen. The connection with television was even more immediate for the Stooges themselves; they had recently appeared on CBS' *The Ed Wynn Show* on March 11, 1950, the first regular show to be carried live from Hollywood. Their first television appearance had been on an episode of Milton Berle's *Texaco Star Theater*, broadcast on NBC on October 19, 1948. All the actors are credited.

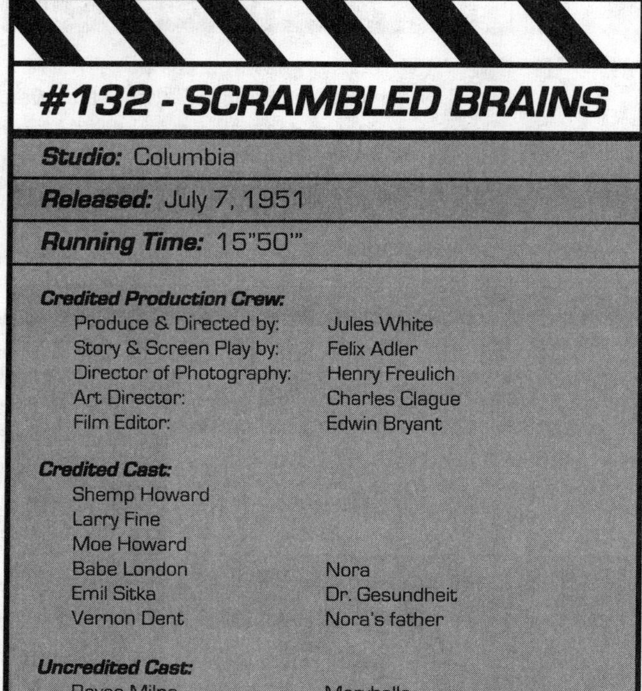

#132 - SCRAMBLED BRAINS

Studio: Columbia

Released: July 7, 1951

Running Time: 15"50'"

Credited Production Crew:

Produce & Directed by:	Jules White
Story & Screen Play by:	Felix Adler
Director of Photography:	Henry Freulich
Art Director:	Charles Clague
Film Editor:	Edwin Bryant

Credited Cast:

Shemp Howard	
Larry Fine	
Moe Howard	
Babe London	Nora
Emil Sitka	Dr. Gesundheit
Vernon Dent	Nora's father

Uncredited Cast:

Royce Milne	Marybelle

PERSPECTIVE: As they have in several of their 1950/ 1951 productions, Jules White and Felix Adler experiment here with a new Stooge concept: alternative vision. Avoiding crooks, spooks, and chases, they replace the sinister elements of contemporary Stooge crime dramas with a brighter look and a different, stranger kind of story. The plot concerns Shemp's mental illness, but unlike other Stooge stories of illness like *Idiots Deluxe* and *I Can Hardly Wait*, this Stooge malady is entirely visual and is cinematically realized through special effects. This means the narrative cannot stray too far from the concept, and although Felix Adler has been accused of writing comedies that merely string one gag upon another, *Scrambled Brains* provides still another example of how Adler was adept at unifying a gag-related concept and a recurring theme.

The narrative of *Scrambled Brains* develops through five scenes: the double visions at the sanitarium, the doctoring at home, the double visions at the piano, the struggle in the phone booth, and the climactic wedding scene. To supplement these five gag scenarios and form them into a story, Adler employs a stock Stooge character he had perfected in the previous decade's *Boobs in Arms*, namely, an intimidating foil whom the Stooges anger early on in the film ("I'll get you guys!") and who returns at the climax, recognizes the Stooges, and brings the film to a close by chasing his nemeses. Adler recreates a character somewhat like the Stoogettes' father [Moe] in *Self-Made Maids*, but the genius who plays this role here is Vernon Dent, the strongest Stooge adversary, whose desire for vengeance is capable of driving new energy into the finale of any film and sending the Stooges down to defeat. As if in an ancient Greek *anagnorisis*, he 'recognizes' the Stooges, does a great take, and chases them off. The television-like ending of the previous film (*"Don't Throw That Knife"*) gave us a prelude to this, though Shemp marrying an ugly, admiring woman derives more directly from the memorable *Brideless Groom*.

Just as he made Luck a recurring theme in *So Long, Mr. Chumps*, Adler makes alternative visions appear and reappear throughout this film. He had happened upon the concept previously, if indeed it is simply an extension of Shemp reading "SOUP" for 'SOAP' in *Baby Sitters Jitters*. But here we are introduced to it in the beginning with Larry's "No more hallucinations!" and Moe's "And no more seeing things that aren't there." But no sooner does Shemp appear than he looks at the hideous, toothless Nora [Babe London] as if she were a beautiful blonde, a hand extends from the fireplace, and later he sees first one and then two more hands playing piano. In each case *we* see these hallucinations, too: we see the beautiful Nora, and the two sets of hands. When all is said and done, the fake hypnosis is in itself a reverse sort of alternative vision, and after seeing the Vernon Dent character twice, a double dose of real vision, Moe and Larry join in Shemp's hallucination and try to jump through the Venetian blind shadow at the film's end. Beauty may be in the eye of the beholder, but a window and a wall are not.

VISUAL HUMOR: Moe draws Venetian blinds at the beginning of the doctor scene, foreshadowing the final visual gag. The camera plays other tricks on our eyes. It closes in on Shemp's face to introduce his first hallucination. Larry swallows the pill and falls out of the camera frame; we hear snoring, and then the camera pans to the sleeping Larry. When Shemp cuts the fingers off with the piano lid it really looks at first as if they are his fingers. Also, we feel intimate with the extended phone booth slapstick because the camera is placed in the interior - until the booth teeters over; then we see it from the exterior. The phone booth sequence involves an elaborate choreography with over thirty interrelated movements from crowding in the door to dialing Dent's mouth. The finale is a triple result shot of Moe, Shemp, and Vernon Dent.

Shemp spitting nickels out of his mouth is just one of several mouth gags: Shemp spitting the pills at Moe, Moe spitting out teeth after walking into the door, and Nora not having any teeth. The fist game between Larry and Moe (Moe shows Larry the fist; Larry hits it; it circles onto Larry's head. Larry shows Moe his own fist; Moe hits it; it circles and bonks Larry) is a simplified version of the one in *Uncivil Warriors*, though it is one of the most elaborate in the Shemp films. A Stooge first: the doctor blowing through his own stethoscope; the ugly woman motif Felix Adler and Clyde Bruckman introduced in *Horses' Collars*. Other variations: the doll under the rocking chair, and taking a pill through a tube [*Even as IOU*]; hypnotizing a Stooge [*Hokus Pokus*]; Shemp's face being covered in lipstick [*G.I. Wanna Home*]; Larry getting eggs on his face, and Dent biting Shemp's ear [*"Don't Throw That Knife"*, though this film was made first]; shoving the cake in Dent's face [*Self-Made Maids*]; Shemp being carried off at the end of the film, his head bumping into the upper door frame [*What's the Matador?*]; hearing a strange sound through a stethoscope [*Dizzy Doctors*]; hearing a rattling sound from a Stooge head [*From Nurse to Worse*]; Moe spitting out teeth [*Three Loan Wolves*]; and playing 'boogie-woogie' [*Idle Roomers*].

VERBAL HUMOR: The essence of this film is visual, so the verbal gags are limited. They include insults about [not *to*] Nora (Shemp: "Ain't she a dream?" Moe: "Dream? She's a nightmare!"; Larry: "You know I think she's uglier than you are?"; and Larry: "I better have another drink. I can still see her face.") and quintessential Stooge ignorance (Shemp: "I've got that usual empty feeling in my head"; Larry "I got a brainstorm." Moe: "Anything in his brain is a storm."; Moe: "And if you're a good boy we're gonna give ya' some C-A-N-D-Y." Shemp: "You know I don't smoke."). There are two name puns ('Dr. Gesundheit,' and the sign: 'DOCTORS HART-BURNS & BELCHER'). Shemp offers two of his patented reactions: when he spits nickels out of his mouth ("I hit the jackpot!") and when Moe spits out his teeth ("His gum came out!").

Shemp's muffled imitation of Dent (Moe: "What he say?" Shemp: "Mph-ph-mmph-phmm!") derives from *Hold That Lion*. Other variations: the trio harmonization of 'Nora, Nora, Today I'll marry Nora/'Cause I'm so in love with No-or-a' (they sang a triad of "Come in!" in *Baby Sitters Jitters*); and trouble with a telephone operator [*Dopey Dicks*]. References: 'Stromboli' is a romantic volcanic island off Italy; it provided the name used for Pinocchio's cruel master in the 1940 Disney film and for a title of a contemporary (1949) Roberto Rosselini film. Shemp makes another Italian reference by comparing Nora to the ancient Roman Goddess of Love: "She's got eyes like stars, a shape like Venus, and teeth like pearls!"

OTHER NOTES: The *Scrapbook* reports that this film was shot in March, 1950, before *"Don't Throw That Knife"*. The working title was *Impatient Patient*. Director of Photography, Henry Freulich, is credited above Felix Adler. The Stooges visited [ruined] a sanitarium in *Monkey Businessmen*. Babe [Jean] London had played in films for decades already, including the classic Mack Sennett comedy, *Tillie's Punctured Romance* (1914), starring Charlie Chaplin, Marie Dressler, and Mabel Normand. In her retirement she accompanied Larry (after his stroke) on his visits to Los Angeles area schools. Dr. Gesundheit - the only thing thicker than his German accent ("Vell, vat zeems to be the trouble?") are his glasses - will be recreated in Moe's Dr. Gansamacher in one of the last Columbia shorts [*Sweet and Hot*]. The mutilated fingers gag is sometimes edited out for television broadcast. The *Scrapbook* reports that this was one of Larry's favorite films - one of the few he had in his personal collection. Critic Leonard Maltin concurs, writing [*Movie Comedy Teams* 202] that this "is among the best work the Stooges ever did."

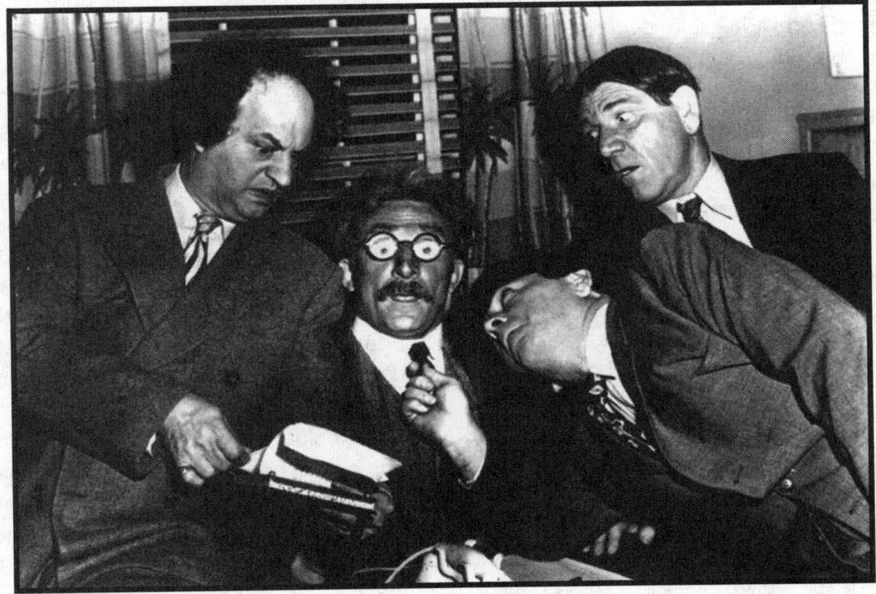

#133 - MERRY MAVERICKS

Studio: Columbia

Released: September 6, 1951

Running Time: 15"46"'

Credited Production Crew:

Produced by:	Hugh McCollum
Written & Directed by:	Edward Bernds
Director of Photography:	Al len Siegler [Ziegler]
Art Director:	Charles Clague
Film Editor:	Edwin Bryant

Credited Cast:

Shemp Howard	
Larry Fine	
Moe Howard	
Don Harvey	Red Morgan
Marion Martin	woman
Paul Campbell	Pete

Uncredited Cast:

Emil Sitka	sheriff
Al Thompson	bartender
Blackie Whiteford	Al
Victor Travers	newspaper editor [stock]

PERSPECTIVE: *Merry Mavericks* is the seventh Stooge short written and directed by Edward Bernds and the first since *Punchy Cowpunchers*, which was also the most recent Stooge western. The original concept Bernds and producer Hugh McCollum had for *Merry Mavericks* in February, 1950 was to set a dentistry sequence in the midst of a Western farce. The dentistry footage previewed very well to a sample audience, but it ran so long that Bernds and McCollum decided to create a second film, and thus was born *The Tooth Will Out* which was to be released four weeks later. This meant making some significant narrative revisions to the original concept of *Merry Mavericks*, particularly in the exposition. Bernds turned to an even earlier Stooge Western, *Phony Express*. He reconfigured its Red Morgan gang, he revised the saloon sequence originally written by Elwood Ullman & Monty Collins, and lifted the non-Curly footage of shooting up the streets of Peaceful Gulch while the newspaper editor and bank president hide behind a desk. To this he then tacked on an initial scene.

Not everything in the resulting narrative is water tight. The first scene serves little purpose except to establish the Stooges as vagrants and give them cause to head 'West.' The Clarence Cassidy character successfully parodies The Arizona Kid of *Punchy Cowpunchers* but has no clear part in the plot. Bank President Higgins inexplicably moves the mine payroll from the security of his bank - the scene of the central scenario in *Phony Express* - to an unsecured haunted cabin. And when the Stooges head for the 'old Horton place' to protect the money, Moe says, "A job's a job," even though no one ever hired them. The only job the Stooges asked for was to be "cleaner uppers," and Moe posed that offer ("Hey, mister, we aim to do a little cleanin' up around here") to the outlaw, Red Morgan.

The second part of the film ends up in the spooky old Horton place and turns into an energetic, multi-room, chase-filled scare comedy in which the payroll money is mentioned only once. Bernds' most important contribution here is the headless Indian chief who comes back to the Horton place periodically to search for his head. The look of this headless wraith is one we have seen before [*Dutiful but Dumb*; *Dopey Dicks*; *Three Hams on Rye*] but every time he appears the element of surprise drives the humor. He swings his tomahawk at an amazed Larry ("I saw his head - where it wasn't...He was eight feet tall, nine feet wide!"), and he ambushes Shemp in a clothes closet. We do not see this struggle except to hear a ruckus from outside the closet door (a gag developed in *Studio Stoops*), but just when it looks as if Moe (by Pete in the chair), Larry (by the woman), and Shemp (by the Indian in the closet) are all captured, Shemp arrives disguised as the Indian ("Ungowah!") and saves the day. Of all the Stooge film climaxes, this ending relies as heavily as any on the element of surprise. To string a few lose ends together, the cowboy faints at the sight of blood, and Larry and Shemp howl at the woman.

VISUAL HUMOR: Because the Stooges are busy combating the Red Morgan gang, there is relatively little inter-Stooge slapstick, but Moe biting Shemp's pointing finger in the first scene is enhanced by two different sound effects (CRUNCH, POP), and the fist game/punch-in-the-eye exchange (Moe: "Oh, you're pretty smart! [holding out his hand] What's that?" Larry: "That's a hand." Moe: "Good. What's that?" [He makes a fist] Larry: "That's a fist." Moe [punching Shemp in the eye]: "Right! What was that?" Larry: "A punch in the eye." Moe: "Right!" [He punches Larry in the eye]) is rather spectacular; the fist game was revived in the previous film (*Scrambled Brains*). Special kudos to the stunt man who does that tremendous fall first forwards and then backwards against a saloon table. Stooge firsts: closing the cell door on Shemp by mistake; and Larry lying down and banging his head on the gun. Moe tapping Shemp on the shoulder, dancing with Shemp ("You dance divinely!"), and kicking his spur into Morgan's rear are all from *Phony Express*. Frequently used chase motifs: the Stooges surprise each other in the hall and run in opposite directions, barricade a door with the fiend behind them, and run to one door and find a fiend, run to another door/window and find another fiend. Other variations: imitating furniture by hiding under upholstery (*Self-Maid Maids*); and the pistol bullet hitting a light fixture which falls and knocks out a person or two (*Boobs in Arms*).

VERBAL HUMOR: The added expository scene requires puns about vagrancy (Larry: "You take a flower, and it smells real nice - that's vagrancy!"), two pattern jokes (Shemp: "We can beat that rap." Moe: "You chowder-head. 'Vagrancy' is when you're a hobo or a tramp." Shemp: "Uh-oh - we can't beat that one!"; and Moe: "There's only one thing left to do [Larry & Shemp: "Yes!"]: we gotta pull up stakes [Larry & Shemp: "Yes!"], get outta town [Larry & Shemp: "Yes!"], and go to work." Larry & Shemp: "No!"), and a long speech (Moe: "Now listen you nitwits: there's a lot-a rocks in this county, and the sheriff just loves to have guys like us to make itty-bitty ones out of great big ones...the birds sing, the bees hum—") which makes Larry and Shemp fall asleep on their feet. Moe twice mentions getting a job, making Larry and Shemp try to flee (Shemp: "You said a nasty word!"). Shemp offers a half dozen throwaway lines to close gags or scenes ("A bee bit me or somethin'"; "Hey bud, you got a calendar?"; Woman: "Hello, handsome!" Shemp: "Did somebody come in?"; "Now I know how a frankfurter feels!"; and Moe: "This 'fraidy cat will stay with me." Shemp: "But Moe, I'm a 'fraidy cat, too!"). When he has trouble getting his Indian sleeve off, he quips: "Get an ax, will ya'?" even though as the Indian he just had one. Larry, as often, gets one featured line: [Moe: "These tin horn outlaws haven't got the nerve to shoot. If they did kill us, they'd all hang. That would make things even."] Larry: "Don't sound very even to me!"

References: The name 'Clarence' Cassidy disappoints the Stooges who expected 'Hopalong' Cassidy, the cowboy star of screen (from 1935), radio (from 1941), and contemporary television (1949-51). "Ungowah" was an all-purpose 1950s ethnic utterance usually used in jungle films. Epithets: "earthworm," "chowder-head," "bird-brain," and "nitwits." Shemp's plea for mercy ("...I got a little gold-haired sister looks just like you. She's *this* high, and a baby brother *this* high—") he used in his first Stooge film, *Fright Night*. Cassidy's speech ("Never hurt none"; "I reckon I'd-a wiped 'em out") and Shemp's imitation ("Don't sound quite right nohow, somehow!") recall the cowboy dialect in *Out West* and *Punchy Cowpunchers*. The exchange (Moe: "You scared?" Larry: "No, just apprehensive!" Moe: "That's a mighty fancy word. What does that 'apprehensive' mean?" Larry: "It means you're scared...with a college education!") derives from *Studio Stoops*. A variation on "You wouldn't hit a lady with that?...Use this, it's bigger" from *Brideless Groom* and other films: Shemp: "All right, sister, get goin' or I'll knock your brains out!" Moe: "Is that any way to talk to a lady?!" Shemp takes off his hat: "All right, sister, get goin' or I'll knock your brains out!" Moe: "That's better!" Moe's "I wish you'd get a new face. You scare people." was lifted from *Phony Express*.

OTHER NOTES: There is some contradictory information about the making of this film. The *Scrapbook* (257) and Okuda (46) record Ed Bernds' statements [c. 1980] that two extra days of shooting were added to make *The Tooth Will Out* as proof that it was extracted from *Merry Mavericks*, but the reported shooting dates for *The Tooth Will Out* were February 19-20, 1950, while those for *Merry Mavericks* were much later, June 13-16, 1950. The *Scrapbook* lists a 'Duke,' who must be the 'Arizona-Kid' clone, and 'Gladys', but neither is named in the film. It is common for script names not to match names used in the final version of the film; in fact, names were often omitted altogether for minor characters. 'Gladys' is played by Marion Martin, a veteran of the Ziegfeld chorus and star of numerous B-films; she also acted in several Marx Brothers and Abbott & Costello features. Here she gets to throw a bottle at Moe, miss, hit the other gang member, and cause him in his woozy state to conk the leader over the head just before he himself passes out. The added exposition ends with a rarely used fade out, a sign that a comic idea was lacking. The poster with the Stooges' picture on it ('WANTED FOR VAGRANCY - REWARD - 50¢ or 3 for $1.00 - Sheriff Merriweather') is only slightly changed from *Phony Express*, where it was 'Sheriff Hogwaller.'

Dick Curtis in the dental chair, *Merry Mavericks*, this scene was re-edited into the next release, *The Tooth Will Out*, resulting in two short films, neither offering the usual narrative unity.

#134 - THE TOOTH WILL OUT

Studio: Columbia

Released: October 4, 1951

Running Time: 15"59"'

Credited Production Crew:

Produced by:	Hugh McCollum
Directed by:	Edward Bernds
Written by:	Edward Bernds
Director of Photography:	Fayte Brown
Art Director:	Charles Clague
Film Editor:	Edwin Bryant

Credited Cast:

Shemp Howard	
Larry Fine	
Moe Howard	
Margie Liszt	Miss Beebe
Vernon Dent	Doc Keefer

Uncredited Cast:

Emil Sitka	Vesuvius Restaurant chef
Slim Gaut	first patient
Dick Curtis	second patient

PERSPECTIVE: Since painless and preventive dentistry was almost unheard of in the first half of the last century, a sudden toothache would conjure up fears of a terrifying visit to a dentist to have the tooth pulled. But comedy, one of humanity's means of dealing with shared fear and pain, to the rescue! Numerous comic films were set in dentists' offices since the Mack Sennett days, most famously W. C. Fields' *The Dentist* (1932) and Laurel & Hardy's *Leave 'Em Laughing* (1928), not to mention the Stooges' *All the World's a Stooge* (1941) and *I Can Hardly Wait'* (1943). *The Tooth Will Out* we know very well was created specifically to incorporate its dentistry sequence. Ed Bernds said so in the very [c. 1980] interview in which he recalled that this and the previous film began as part of the same project. Originally titled *A Yank at the Dentist*, the dentistry sequences had been shot in February, 1950, but were too long to remain in the final cut of *Merry Mavericks*. This, then, is a film made from that footage - a film dedicated to Stooge dentistry.

Several other Stooge Columbia short films had been designed to incorporate a gag popular in their live act (*Gents Without Cents*) or one particular extended gag scenario (*Three Little Pirates*). This is an example of the latter. Dentistry drives the plot beginning to end, the tooth-extraction sequences consuming the entire second half of the film. To set up the dentistry concept Edward Bernds renews the method of exposition used first in *Pop Goes The Easel* where the Stooges run from a failed job to take refuge in a school. But Bernds often takes the Stooges one step beyond: here they lose *two* jobs in *two* minutes, are thrown out on their rears twice [with spectacular tumbles by Johnny Kascier (Moe), Charlie Cross (Larry), and Harold Breen (Shemp)], and then flee into a dentistry school. To flesh out the school scene Bernds uses several plot-related prop gags with false teeth, one created anew (passing the good set of teeth from the case to Shemp to Larry to Moe to the doc), one borrowed from *All the World's a Stooge* (biting Moe's nose), and one adapted from *The Ghost Talks* (the talking teeth). The school scene also has Moe trying to pull Larry's tooth, an odd foreshadowing of the Western dentistry scene.

Like the recent *Scrambled Brains*, the dentistry scene in the second half of the film depends largely on Shemp's ability to maintain a confusion caused by ignorance and incompetence. The glasses gag traditionally (*All the World's a Stooge*) begins with Moe asking Shemp/Curly to compare their vision with/without glasses, but here we simply assume a Stooge doctor wears glasses so he cannot see. The scene also depends on lively support from Moe and Larry and the patients, too, who vary in character from the energetically submissive cowboy to the tough and intimidating but then unconscious lawman. The fugitive ending is abrupt, but it is a reliable part of an old and proven formula in which the Stooges start a film as fugitives and end it that way as well. This is the third fugitive ending we have seen since *Don't Throw That Knife* . When the plot runs out of juice, send the boys out of town.

VISUAL HUMOR: Moe takes the brunt of the pain during the extended slapstick of the false teeth sequence. He has not taken that much punishment since the opening of *A Snitch in Time*. A hammer blow to his head even causes a mouse on his forehead- a Stooge first despite all the previous head blows. Perhaps this realism was inspired by the 'blood' gag at the end of the previous film (*Merry Mavericks*). The exterior chase is one of the longest, most realistic street-chase scenes in years. Ugly women like Miss Beebe [Margie Liszt] or Nora (*Scrambled Brains*) offer an equally humorous alternative to the femme fatales played by Christine McIntyre and Marion Martin (*Merry Mavericks*). In the previous film, Larry and Shemp fled when Moe mentioned "work" or "a job"; here they carry two satchels, a medicine box, a clothes tree, and four hats while Moe carries only a pair of tongs and a small jar of cotton, saying: "Whew! Boy! This is a lot of work, movin' in!" From the previous dentistry films come tapping teeth until they find the right one (KLINK, KLINK, KLINK, THUD), and pulling the wrong tooth. Other variations: the Stooges turning "Go West!" into a rhythmic dance ('Viva Vulgaria' in *Dutiful but Dumb*, 'Rhum Boogie' in *Some More of Samoa*); Shemp and Moe

looking up what to do in a textbook (*Fuelin' Around*); and the pattern operation (Moe: "Metal object!" Larry: "Metal object!" Moe: "Metal object!" Shemp: "Metal object!" Moe: "Ammer-hay!" Larry: "Ammer-hay!" Moe: "Ammer-hay!" Shemp: "Ammer-hay!") (*Men in Black*).

VERBAL HUMOR: The majority are plot-related dentistry gags (Larry: "Hey doc, can you see that tooth?...That's funny, 'cause I can't!"; Moe: "Ain't those choppers done yet?" Shemp: "They gotta cook a little longer. Twenty minutes to the pound!"; Moe: "The mouth is in the front!" Shemp: "They moved it, huh?"; Shemp: "The next step is to sandpaper the chest." Moe: "Must be somethin' new in dentistry." Larry: "Be careful of his tattoo." Shemp: "He had a tattoo?"; Shemp: "He's got that poly-monot-dred-nut with the bicuspid can-a-fran!"; Shemp: "Are you comfortable?" Patient: "No!" Moe: "Who asked ya'?"; and Shemp to the groaning patient: "Save that for later, pal; you'll need it"), and the threats from the tough lawman ("You know what happened to the last dentist who worked on me? He struck a nerve. That's him there...notch number nine." Moe to Shemp: "You better be darn sure you're right with this bird or you'll be notch number ten!"; and "Hold it! Where you goin'?" Shemp: "I'm just takin' a short cut to the bowl"). Shemp's questionable literacy, featured first in *Baby Sitters Jitters*, now includes misreading signs ('DISHWASHER WANTED.' Moe: "You see that sign?" Shemp: "Who's smokin'?!"); Shemp made a similar joke in *Scrambled Brains*. Larry's moment: Moe: "What do you think of this lad as a dishwasher?" Larry [swaggering]: "I can recommend him very highly!" As if a combination of the Shemps who have loved (*Scrambled Brains*) and loathed (*Brideless Groom*) ugly women, Shemp both insults Miss Beebe ("Hi, Miss Buckshot") because of her upper malocclusion and praises her ("Ain't she gorgeous!"). As in *Scrambled Brains* Larry and Moe respond as if he is crazy (Moe: "He's been standin' too close to that oven!"). The Stooges begin the song 'Lucky Strike' ("Bumm-bumm-bumm-bumm") with the same kind of pick up notes they (and Ted Healy) used in *Beer and Pretzels*; the Stooges wrote the song themselves.

The exchange (Shemp: "All I did was pick up one little box." Moe: "And it had ten other boxes full of dishes right on top of it!") recalls the china breaking in *Three Arabian Nuts*. Doc Keefer's graduation speech recalls Dr. Graves' in *Men in Black*, with a fine variation when the Stooges thank him for saying "I will not embarrass them by mentioning their names." Other variations: Moe: "We only have four dollars." Doc: "I'll take it! (*Cactus Makes Perfect*); Moe: "What's the matter, you nervous?" Shemp: "Just in the left arm" (*Punch Drunks*); and Doc Keefer: "Five Dollars apiece, or three for twenty-five!" (the vagrancy posters in *Phony Express* and *Merry Mavericks*). Epithet: "nitwit". References: Horace Greeley, the New York newspaper titan, actually borrowed his famous "Go West, young man!" from John Soule, who wrote it for the *Indiana Express* in 1851. Shemp's mistaken response, "Don't give up the ship," is a common restatement of the fatally wounded James Lawrence's order "not to give up the ship" made on the *Chesapeake* in 1813. Shemp's "George Washington" and chopping motion hints refer to the cherry tree episode.

OTHER NOTES: The release title parodies the proverbial expression 'The truth will out'. Doc Keefer [Vernon Dent] pleads with the Stooges to "Go West," much as in the film *Out West* when Shemp needs an "operation" on his "vein." In *Merry Mavericks* Moe makes a reference to and a joke about this famous phrase, but it fits much better in *The Tooth Will Out* since the Stooges are not yet 'out West' but are already at the beginning of *Merry Mavericks*. This demonstrates again that *The Tooth Will Out*, the later release, was written before the expository material of *Merry Mavericks*. Actor Slim Gaut [first patient] played in some well-known comedies, including W. C. Fields' *The Bank Dick* (1940). This is the last of nearly a dozen Stooge roles for Dick Curtis [second patient]. The Assistant Director was Gilbert Kay.

#135 - HULA - LA - LA

Studio: Columbia

Released: November 1, 1951

Running Time: 16"06'"

Credited Production Crew:

Produced & Directed by:	Hugh McCollum
Story & Screen Play by:	Edward Bernds
Director of Photography:	Henry Freulich
Film Editor:	Edwin Bryant
Art Director:	Charles Clague

Credited Cast:

Shemp Howard
Larry Fine
Moe Howad

Uncredited Cast:

Jean Willes	King's daughter, Luana
Kenneth McDonald	Varanu, the witch doctor
Emil Sitka	Mr Baines
Maxine Doviat	Kawana
Lei Aloha	Armed Idol

PERSPECTIVE: Hugh McCollum ("Mac") had been co-producing Stooge films since 1938, five with Charley Chase [*Termites of 1938*], fifteen with Del Lord since 1940 [*A Plumbing We Will Go*], and finally thirty-two on his own since 1943 [*A Gem of a Jam*]. One year after *Hula-la-la* he would be fired by Jules White, but in this last year of his tenure at Columbia he finally directed a few films. Once Harry Cohn's secretary and by training a business manager, Mac usually made only business decisions and kept out of the creative process except for giving final approvals and making occasional suggestions. But by 1949 he had lost the services of both his directors for the Hugh Herbert series - Del Lord quit the short film unit in 1949; Ed Bernds had quarreled on the set with Herbert in 1946 - and found himself directing Herbert in *A Slip and a Miss* [with Jean Willes] and *Trouble In-Laws*. It was the next year, 1950, that McCollum directed his only Stooge film, *Hula-la-la*.

Ten years earlier, McCollum had co-produced *Some More of Samoa* with Del Lord, and now with MGM's Tahitian *Pagan Love Song* (1950) as recent inspiration and Columbia's *On the Island of Samoa* (1950) for more immediate pickings, producer/director McCollum puts the Stooges for the second time on a south sea island. Following a plot line much like that of *Three Missing Links*, the Stooges are working for a movie company and are sent far away on assignment. Once on the island of 'Rarabonga,' they are captured by head hunters - in *Some More of Samoa* it was 'Rhum Boogie' cannibals - and end up saving a damsel-in-distress, in this case the local princess [Jean Willes], who is not at all as hideous as the king's sister [Louise Carver] in *Some More of Samoa*. The plot actually accords with old Stooge formulas, but neither a Western like *Horses' Collars* nor a medieval romp like *Restless Knights*, *Hula-la-la* is uniquely Polynesian. With bamboo huts, women in leis, a pagan idol, and a crocodile or two creating an island atmosphere, the threat of becoming part of the witch-doctor's head-shrinking collection adds the dramatic tension, and the final Hawaiian musical accompaniment adds charm.

The viewer looking for evidence of McCollum's directorial touch will find it mostly at the beginning and the end. He opens the film by focusing on a chorus line rehearsing, and then pans the camera along the line until it reveals Larry playing the piano, Moe directing, and Shemp, in leotards, dancing; to close the film symmetrically he pulls the camera back to encompass the island dancing lesson: Moe kneels, Larry pounds out a native beat on his head, and Shemp dances too close to the boiling cauldron. The previous film focused on plot-essential dentistry gags, and in this film McCollum offers two more plot-related set-gags: Moe struggling with 'Ol' Four Arms,' and the princess sitting on the bed hiding Shemp and the alligator(s). Both are carefully staged, impeccably choreographed, and smoothly edited. Though both a three-armed idol and a threatening crocodile appeared in *Some More of Samoa*, McCollum's updated versions stride beyond where those episodes ventured. As often in Stooge films of the 1950s, whether they are directed by McCollum, Edward Bernds, or Jules White,

Although involved with dozens of Stooge films as co-producer, Hugh CcCollum directed only one Stooge film, *Hula-la-la*.

refurbished gags are utterly revitalized in their second Stooge coming.

VISUAL HUMOR: The idol looks like the Hindu god Siva (animated by Ray Harryhausen in 1974's *The Golden Voyage of Sinbad*). Although only two Stooges are involved (in *Some More of Samoa* there was just Curly), there are a total of 8 hands, 29 slaps, 10 head bangings, and 1 gouge in the sequence, highlighted by the idol shaking two of its hands and signaling 'OK' with another, and the timed surprise when the idol does nothing to Larry for a few seconds, then slaps him 20 times - many more times than Moe ever hit him at once. McCollum enhances the crocodile sequence by having the mother croc follow its baby up Shemp's pant leg. A third set gag of the film, although intentionally not the focus of its scene, involves Baines [Emil Sitka] and his assistant who moves his chair around behind him, ultimately flirting with a chorus girl and letting Baines miss the chair and fall to the floor. Sitka does a fine fall, and it takes five men to help him up.

Moe breaking the bamboo bars with Larry's head recalls hammering in nails with Curly's head in *Loco Boy Makes Good*. Other variations: Shemp blowing off dust from the stump [Larry in *Merry Mavericks*]; the witch doctor being exploded out of his sandals [*Half-Shot Shooters*]; an animal in a pant's leg [*A Pain in the Pullman*]; Shemp hiding under and flipping the bed over [*Squareheads of the Round Table*]; and Moe slamming the piano lid on Larry's hands [*Dutiful but Dumb; Dancing Lady*].

VERBAL HUMOR: It is hard to determine what exactly was McCollum's input, but much of the verbal humor in Ed Bends' extraordinary script is fully integrated into the physical: when Shemp puts sheet music on the floor and dances oddly ("I'm dancin' from a trombone part!"); before Baines falls to the floor ("I don't want you to fall down on the job!"); while the princess's bed is being bounced by Shemp and the crocodile ("I've never felt this way before...I can't help bouncing for joy!"); when Moe and Shemp discuss the idol's hands (Shemp: "That'd come in mighty handy in case of mosquitoes. You could slap with one hand, scratch with another, and play gin rummy with the other two...or, you could scratch with one and slap with two." Moe: "I think I'll slap with two!" [DOUBLE SLAP]); when Moe says: "You know, for an imbecile you got some brains." Larry: "Thanks! Are they showin'?" (SLAP) Moe: "Not now!"; when the guard jabs a spear into Larry (Moe: "You see the point?" Larry: "No but I feel it!"); and when the princess asks where [the exploded] Varunu went (Moe: "Somethin' unexpected came up, so he went to pieces.")

Bernds included headhunting-related jokes (Shemp: "I wanna keep my head. I've had it ever since I was a little kid"; Shemp: "And to think, I only got a haircut this morning, too!"; Witch Doctor: "We have our hobbies. In your country men collect paintings, rare coins, and postage stamps. I— collect heads." Shemp: "Oh I'd get a big kick seeing you paste heads in an album, doc!"; Witch Doctor: "My warriors bring them from the jungle." Moe: "Oh, sort of finders keepers." Shemp: "Yeah, tails you win, heads they lose!" Moe: "I notice there's vacancies on that shelf there. Who's noggins are you plannin' on puttin' in there?" Witch Doctor: "Yours." Shemp: "I don't wanna be in his collection." Larry: "Hangin' all day like a smoked goose liver." Shemp: "I'd have a terrible headache.") and one about cannibalism ("I am Varanu, witch doctor of this tribe." Larry: "What's cookin', doc?" Moe: "Shadup. Don't give him any ideas!"). The head jokes lead to some about Larry's baldness ("Your skin shines like a lovely pearl....Any man can have hair on his head. This one has lovely skin!"). The opening scene has a dance-related set gag (Moe: "These girls have their rondelets mixed up with their pirouettes, and they got their fortissimos tangled up with the allegrettos." Shemp: "I know, but what's wrong with their dancin'?").

References: 'Pirouettes' belong to ballet lingo; 'rondelets' are song types; 'fortissimos' are general musical dynamics; and 'allegrettos' are tempo designations; cf. *Brideless Groom*. For island coloring, the princess yells at her maidens in a native language; Moe and Shemp make fun of the islanders in British jargon. There are two different "Yes!/No!" pattern jokes (Baines: "B. O. Pictures is in trouble." Stooges: "No!"; Princess: "You help me and I'll help you!" Stooges: "Yes!" Princess: "You save Kuala. I will show you how." Stooges: "Yes! Yes!" Princess: "The walls are thin. Cut your way out. When it's dark, come to my hut." Stooges: "Yes! Yes! Yes!"). Another pattern joke (Princess: "The witch doctor is a bad man." Larry: "You can say that again!" Princess: "The witch doctor is a bad man.") recalls a similar gag in *Micro-Phonies*.

In the previous film Larry said with a swagger: "I can recommend him very highly!" Here he brushes his hair back proudly: "I was carried away!" An elaborate variation of "Are you nervous?"..."Just in my xx": (Moe: "What's the matter, kid. You nervous?" Shemp: "Just the pinkie...[A guard knocks off his helmet, pulls out a hair (PLUNK) and cuts it with his huge, curved blade (PLINK)]...Now I'm nervous all over!"

'B. O. Pictures,' for whom they also worked in *Studio Stoops*, derives ultimately from 'B .O. Botswaddle' (*Three Missing Links*). Other variations: "Southern hospitality" (recently in *"Don't Throw That Knife"*); "ungow" (*Merry Mavericks*); Baines: "Can't you just see it: moonlight on the warm sea, waving palms, natives dancing their native dances?" (Moe's "...where...the birds sing, the bees hum" in *Merry Mavericks*); Moe's "How do you like this guy?" (*Crime on their Hands*); Shemp: "I wanna keep my head. I've had it ever since I was a little kid!" (*Out West*); Shemp's 'Coca-Cola' [Kuala] reference (*Baby Sitters Jitters*); "This one has lovely skin!" (*Hugs and Mugs*); and Moe: "You know, for an imbecile you got some brains" ("He's the most intelligent imbecile I ever saw" in *Fuelin' Around*) Epithet: "egghead"; the witch doctor calls Shemp "the beautiful one". A Stooge first (Witch Doctor: "Why you impertinent swine!" Moe: "Aww, flattery will get you nowhere.").

OTHER NOTES: In the script the witch doctor's name is 'Varana'; he pronounces it as 'Váranu'; the princess as 'Varúnu'. At the end of the film there is Hawaiian music, not the usual Stooge music.

#136 - PEST MAN WINS

Studio: Columbia

Released: December 6, 1951

Running Time: 16"01'"

Credited Production Crew:

Produced & Directed by:	Jules White
Written by:	Felix Adler
Director of Photography:	Fayte Brown
Art Director:	Charles Clague
Film Editor:	Edwin Bryant

Credited Cast:

Shemp Howard	
Larry Fine	
Moe Howard	
Margie Liszt	Mrs. Castor
Nanette Bordeaux	Fifi, the maid
Vernon Dent	Mr. Philander
Emil Sitka	Meadows, the butler

Uncredited Cast:

Helen Dickson

[in stock footage: Symona Boniface, Eddie Laughton, Vic Travers, Al Thompson, Heinie Conklin, Ethelreda Leopold

PERSPECTIVE: Shot in mid-February 1951 shortly after the annual winter hiatus, *Pest Man Wins* is of historical significance within the Stooge corpus since it is the first Shemp film to reuse extensive material from previous films. This was not an entirely new procedure: director Jules White had reused footage from *In the Sweet Pie and Pie* and *So Long, Mr. Chumps* to substitute for the ailing Curly in *Beer Barrel Polecats*; 1949's *Vagabond Loafers* reused footage and script material from *A Plumbing We Will Go*, Santa Clause footage from *Wee Wee Monsieur* reappeared in *Malice in the Palace;* the carpentry sequence from *Pardon My Scotch* was reused in *Dizzy Detectives*; and a bit of *Phony Express* reappeared just recently in *Merry Mavericks*. But *Beer Barrel Polecats* was the result of an emergency situation, *Vagabond Loafers* was only one of five versions of a Columbia staple, and the other borrowings are minuscule. With *Pest Man Wins*, White opens up a new avenue of Stooge film production that will refurbish scripts and footage in 25 of the remaining 38 Shemp films. White's rationale was in part that the Stooge audience of 1951 was now mostly children who had not seen the earlier films and would not be able to differentiate the two stocks; after all, those easily recognizable Stooge silhouettes still looked essentially the same as they did years ago.

The most compelling reason for this major shift in production was cost. Television was increasingly seducing movie-going audiences to stay home, cutting deeply into profits of the smaller film studios. In response Columbia reduced its feature film production from 40 films in 1950, to 29 in 1951, to 15 in 1952, and began to purchase the distribution rights to more independent films. But signing independent producer Stanley Kramer (*High Noon*) to a five-year, $25M contract resulted in only one hit (*The Caine Mutiny*), and the studio floundered. Jules White's short-film unit fell victim, perhaps intensifying personnel problems that would lead to Hugh McCollum's and Edward Bernds' departures before this year's productions were finished. Rising to the challenge, White found this different, cheaper method to make Stooge films, which in the modern world of video replays and TV rebroadcasts may seem unremarkable. But 45 years ago it served as an inexpensive mode of adaptation that kept Stooge films in production for a long time.

To make *Pest Man Wins* White adapted the plot of *Ants in the Pantry* by adding footage from both *In the Sweet Pie and Pie* and *Half-Wits Holiday*. Gone are the office and hunting scenes from *Ants in the Pantry*, the gold-digging women of *In the Sweet Pie and Pie*, and the Pygmalion theme of *Half-Wits Holiday*. The result is a film featuring two classic Stooge motifs - societal infestation and a pie fight - as if White was preparing some mixture of pure, concentrated Stoogedom, a 'Best of the Three Stooges.' The theme of *Ants in the Pantry* is necessarily changed: when Fifi tells Mrs. Castor she has ants and Mrs. Castor replies, "Don't get personal, Fifi," we see that the essence of the film is no longer the Stooges' infiltration into society but the sheer absurdity of introducing pests into a wealthy home to drum up business. The worst thing Mrs. Castor has to lose here is her pastry business, not her place in society. This is a film for audiences of 1951, not 1936.

VISUAL HUMOR (NEW FOOTAGE): Replacing the one-last-chance premise of *Ants in the Pantry*, Moe slaps Shemp for not thinking up Larry's idea, and with that one slap we move right into the infestation sequences, eliminating the need for the original office scene. Mrs. Castor's pastry business accounts for the multitude of ballistic desserts. The bulk of the pie-fight footage is from *Half-Wits Holiday* (the start of the fight, the Sword of Damocles, the butler ["Your drink, madam... Pardon me, madam"], the sleeping man, the "you disgraceful vagabonds!" woman, Larry ducking, Larry biting Moe's finger, and Moe washing off in the punch bowl), and the rest is from *In the Sweet Pie and Pie* (Eddie Laughton as the lion hunter) or new (the final duel with Shemp, the cats licking the Stooges' faces). The recent popularity of the CUCKOO sound may have inspired the cuckoo to be hit with the pie.

Vernon Dent's dance is a new treat, and it

Pest Man Wins, the last release of 1951, is the first Shemp film to reuse extensive material from previous films. Jules White had reused footage to substitute for the ailing Curly, and occasional bits or even whole sequences had reappeared in later films. But now White would begin to make this a common practice, leading to some accomplished refurbishings.

summons up a Stooge 'Cossack dance' (originally in *Ants in the Pantry*) which we have not seen since 1943's *A Gem of a Jam*. The fist game has appeared in three of the last four films. A new variation from *Hoi Polloi*: both Larry and the butler steal the silver. Other variations: pressing Stooge noses against the window (*Brideless Groom*); Mrs. Castor barking back at Shemp (*3 Dumb Clucks*); and banging all three Stooges on the head to the tones of 'N-B-C' to end the film (*Hokus Pokus*).

VERBAL HUMOR (NEW FOOTAGE): Because of the mix of films, there are several different kinds of plot related gags, whether related to exterminating (Fifi: "Madam, there is mouses in the houses!"; Moe: "All the mice we caught we can sell to a furrier to make fur coats"; the suitcase motto: 'Got Ants in your Plants? We'll Kill 'Em'; Shemp's "The poppy seeds are walkin'!"; Larry: "See spots in front of your eyes?" Moe: "Naa! I used to see triangles." Larry: "I knew it! I should-a put more rat poison in there"; and Mrs. Castor: "The guests must not know what you're doing." Larry: "You're a cinch, lady. We don't know what we're doin' ourselves!") or banqueting (Moe's ignorant misstatements: "a ban-kwetty" and "She's very hospital!"; Moe seeing a Dagwood sandwich on Shemp's plate: "Think you're playin' poker? Quit stackin' the deck!"; Moe: "You gonna eat that alone?" Larry: "No, maybe I'll get potatoes!").

Moe criticizing Shemp with "Why you stupid stooge!" is a first, though somewhat similar to the insult Bud Jamison offered in *Crash Goes the Hash*: "You remind me of the Three Stooges!". The exchange (Moe: "What was that?" Shemp: "I didn't hear a thing." Larry: "Neither did I") recalls *Three Little Beers:* (Larry: "Did you pick up the gentleman's ball?" Larry: "Why, no!" Curley: "Oh I did not!" Moe: "You did not what?" Curley: "I still didn't!"). When Mrs. Castor says "Don't get personal, Fifi," the phrase derives from (*Back to the Woods*) but this is the only time a non-Stooge says it. Other variations: Shemp's "What do you think this is, a pinwheel?" ("Do I look like a sucker?" in *Rockin' Thru the Rockies*); Moe: "Why don't you watch what you're doin'?" Shemp: "Why don't you do what you're watchin'?" (*Three Troubledoers*); Larry: "Some cheese?" Moe: "My favorite fruit!" (*Fright Night*). The song Mr. Philander plays is Johann Strauss' 'The Beautiful Blue Danube'; meowing cats respond with the second part of the opening phrase.

OTHER NOTES: The release title parodies the expression 'the best man wins'; the working title was *Mousers in the Trousers*. In 1951 the Stooges again earned the Motion Picture Exhibitors' Laurel Award for making the top two-reel moneymakers.

1952

A Missed Fortune • *Listen, Judge*

Corny Casanovas • *He Cooked His Goose* • *Gents in a Jam*

Three Dark Horses • *Cuckoo on a Choo Choo*

#137 - A MISSED FORTUNE

Studio: Columbia

Released: January 3, 1952

Running Time: 16"06'"

Credited Production Crew:

Produced & Directed by:	Jules White
Screenplay by:	Jack White
Story by:	Searle Kramer
Director of Photography:	Fayte Brown
Art Director:	Charles Clague
Film Editor:	Henry DeMond

Credited Cast:

Shemp Howard	
Larry Fine	
Moe Howard	
Nanette Bordeaux	golddigger
Vivian Mason	golddigger
Vernon Dent	hotel manager

Uncredited Cast:

Suzanne Ridgeway	golddigger
Stanley Blystone	hotel detective

PERSPECTIVE: This first 1952 release reprises previous material, but unlike the final 1951 release, *Pest Man Wins*, which grafted footage from two old films onto an older script, and 1949's *Vagabond Loafers*, which revised an old Columbia story, Jules White here essentially reshoots *Healthy, Wealthy and Dumb*. In the original film, Curly interacted with the three gold-digging girls, the hotel manager, the room-service waiter, and the hotel detective, so none of that footage could be reused. In fact, the only notable Stooge scene that did not include Curly - the luxuriating bathtub sequence in which the cigar-smoking Larry resting on a balloon flotilla reads the funny pages, turns his head, accidentally pops a balloon with his cigar, and plunges into the water - is nearly the only footage reused from the 1938 original. The only two other bits are the bed-collapsing stunt, and the 20-second viewing of the letter from 'A. Gyper' who informs the Stooges that after taxes their $50,000 is worth $4.85. Reusing this letter is rather interesting since the shock of New Deal taxes, particularly the $3000 Unemployment Insurance and $1900 Social Security Tax, was more topical for the 1938 version than for a 1952 audience. But taxes are taxes, and the gag still works even today.

Many of the other memorable moments from the original are recreated and look very familiar. In the monkey-in-the-pants sequence, for example, Larry still wears a striped bathrobe, he still sticks his hand into the wiggling pants to be bitten by the monkey ("My pants bit me!"), Shemp like Curly still tries to throw the expensive vase at the pants, and Moe still breaks the vase with the backswing of a board and yells "Why didn't you bring me a softer board?!" Not only the story and slapstick but also Jack White's script retains more than a handful of verbal echoes from the earlier version: Curly's "I admit the pancakes ain't so good, but the syrup is delicious!"; Curly's "We had a bed that went back to Sears Roebuck the third!' [changed to "the twelfth"]; Curly's "I just dotted his 'eye'"; and Larry on being ordered to take a bath: "But it ain't spring yet!" Jack White had not worked on a Stooge film in six years, but from this point on he will specialize in refurbishing old scripts.

The White brothers expand Searle Kramer's original quiz-show story. The radio contest now includes the 'Bunion Ache' telephone call, parodying a quiz-show gimmick which postdated the 1938 release of *Healthy, Wealthy and Dumb*: quiz-show phone calls originated with the 1939 NBC-Red radio quiz show 'Pot O' Gold. Making this gimmick visible was intended for audiences already seeing popular radio quiz shows on television; NBC, for instance, in 1950/1951 was broadcasting Groucho Marx' *You Bet Your Life* on both TV and radio. To give the quiz-show element more importance than in the original film, the Whites have Shemp compose jingles throughout the film. This makes the poetic conclusion (Shemp: "Roses and red,/violets are blue." Moe: "You crush his skull!/I'll break him in two!") more relevant. The monkey no longer takes the letter detailing the high 1938 taxes to the women. In the new version the angered women hit the Stooges not because the bungling trio has incompetently lost $50,000 - the monkey never gives them that information - but because they have incompetently soaked the women twice with ice water.

VISUAL HUMOR (NEW MATERIAL): A new gag: Larry pulling the hollow cigar from his lips, revealing a lit cigarette inside. The slapstick battle between Moe and Shemp (after the bed collapse) is still extended, as was the original between Moe and Curly, but the moves are different after Moe punches his adversary through the broken top: Moe gouges Shemp, who gives Moe a hand-wave with a downthrust and slaps Moe; Moe grabs his hair and gives him a NOSE BONK, POUND, BONK, GOUGE, and TWO-HANDED SLAPS; then Moe bites his nose. Larry blocking an eye gouge was last seen in *Vagabond Loafers*; the routine in which it appears (where Larry brags, "I fooled him!") is very much like that with Shemp and Moe in *Baby Sitters Jitters*, where we first heard Moe say: "Oh Shempie?"

VERBAL HUMOR (NEW MATERIAL): To maintain a quiz

Kramer's original lines with poetic jingles. Curly admired the bed's softness and did not want a "wake up call 'til Wednesday"; Shemp now recites instead: "How I love this pretty bed / Now I'll rest my weary head." White expands other lines with his own brand of humor; to Curly's "Quiet, I can't hear myself read!" he adds "I'm wearin' my short eyeballs." He puns about the vase: "Ming? Oh, no wonder it would cost so much for a 'Ming' coat". When the manager offers, "If I can be of further service, please call me personally," the Stooges [in unison] respond with a literal joke: "Thank you, Mr. Personally!". Perhaps the "bed that went back to Sears Roebuck the third' has been changed to "the twelfth" because "the third" sounded too much like a genuinely royal ordinal. Larry embellishes his room service call from the original ["Send up a dozen bottles of champagne dozen...dozen!...spell it? Make it twelve instead!"] and adds his patented: "I can't see! I can't see!" Moe: "What's the matter?" Larry: "I had my eyes closed!" [*Ants in the Pantry*]. 'B-U-R-P' radio replaces the 'Coffin Nail Cigarette Contest' of the original, and 'Stick Fast Glue' has been changed to 'STIX FAST GLUE'. Epithet: "cement-head."

OTHER NOTES: Jack White will now remain until the Columbia short-subject unit closes in 1958/1959. When at the breakfast table Moe hits Larry with a hammer, he seems to think that Larry's chiseling the pancake out of his mouth with a hammer was wrong, but his hitting Larry on the head with it is okay!

Because the Three Stooges act was born in the Great Depression of the 1930s, money was often of considerable importance in both their set routines and comic narratives. In a number of films the Stooges make fun of the rich by circumventing snooty butlers, insulting pompous party guests, turning their social gatherings into brawls, or just destroying their homes.

On the other side of the financial spectrum, the Stooges often played unemployed bums, ranging in industry from comfortably lazy to ineptly prepared. The trio made a number of attempts at getting rich, often being swindled before their quarter-hour story was used up. Every once in a while, the Stooges actually make it rich, albeit temporarily, a scenario conceived of first by Searle Kramer in 1938's *Healthy, Wealthy and Dumb*, which is refurbished here with Shemp, Vernon Dent and Stanley Blystone in 1952's *A Missed Fortune*.

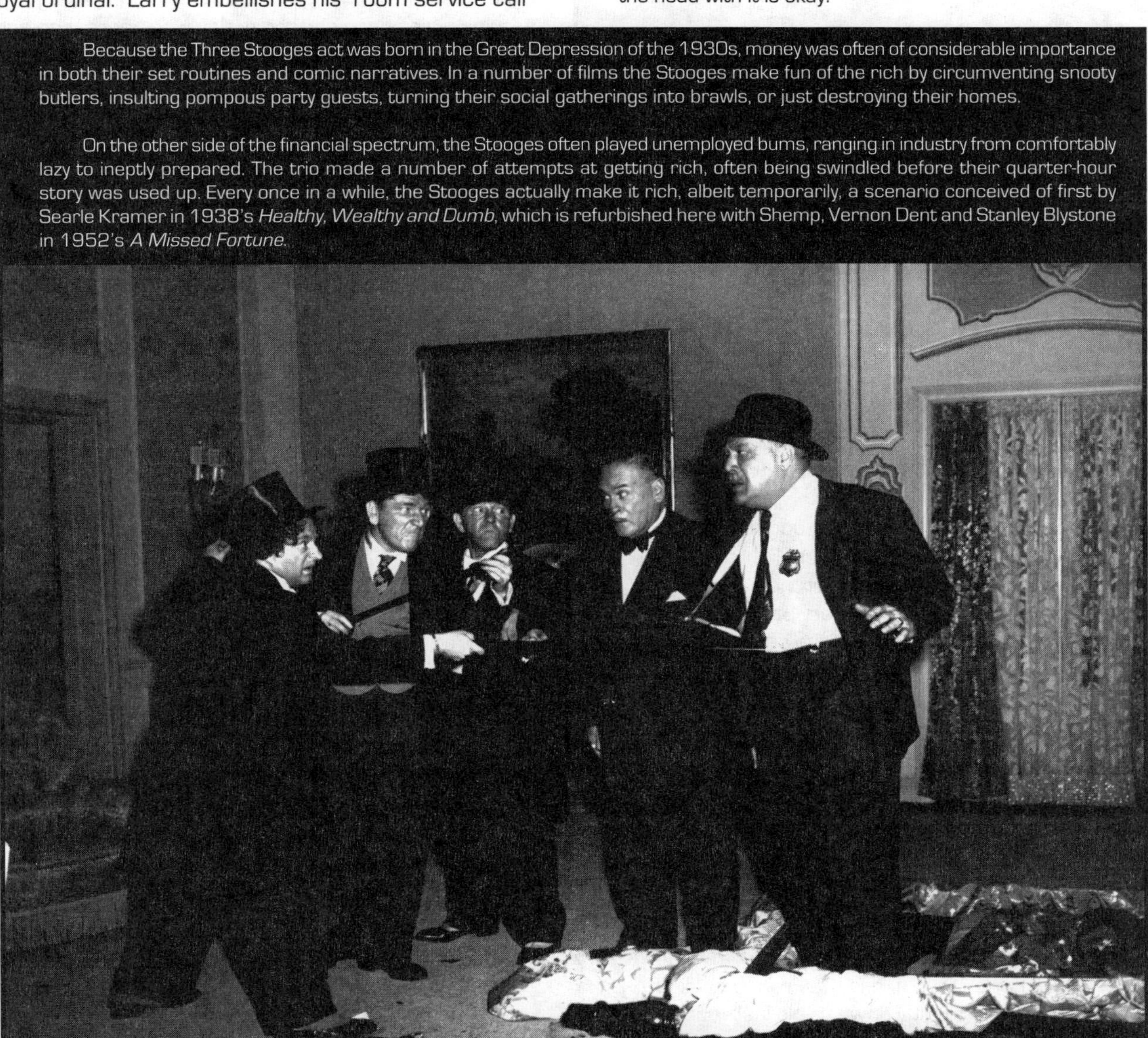

#138 - LISTEN, JUDGE

Studio: Columbia

Released: March 6, 1952

Running Time: 17"01'"

Credited Production Crew:

Produced by:	Hugh McCollum
Directed by:	Edward Bernds
Written by:	Elwood Ullman
Director of Photography:	Ellis W. Carter
Art Director:	Charles Clague
Film Editor:	Edwin Bryant

Credited Cast:

Shemp Howard	
Larry Fine	
Moe Howard	
Kitty McHugh	Mrs. Henderson
Vernon Dent	Judge Henderson
Emil Sitka	the French chef

Uncredited Cast:

Mary Emory	Lydia Morton
John Hamilton	George Morton
Gil Perkins	Officer Ryan
Chick Collins	Officer Casey

PERSPECTIVE: This is the third consecutive film to re-use earlier material, each doing so in a different way. The first blended old footages and scripts, the second remade an old script with minor enhancements and adjustments, but now this one blasts off from the fast-paced courtroom scenario adapted from *A Plumbing We Will Go*, wastes not an instant moving into the doorbell and wall-wrecking scenarios from *They Stooge to Conga*, during which the Stooges hear that their employer desperately needs a cook, butler, and waiter, and this brings them into the kitchen and society party scenarios from *An Ache in Every Stake*. Because all the footage is new, as are most of the sequences except for the turkey and cake preparations, this third film has all the coherent energy that a new production enjoys. Making a new film pieced together from old footage or scripts always runs the risk of lapsing into aimless connections or filler gags lacking in original artistic inspiration. But when made correctly a film of this type can be a revitalized gem as good as or better than any of its original parts. *Listen, Judge* offers this kind of freshness.

The linchpin neatly uniting the doorbell (*They Stooge to Conga*) and kitchen/serving (*An Ache in Every Stake*) portions of the film is the French chef. Emil Sitka plays this role brilliantly down to his last "oui, oui, oui." A brief argument with Moe creates a seamless transition while Sitka bewitches the viewer with his magnificently Gallic snootiness. Similarly, Vernon Dent reprises his role as the angry homeowner in *An Ache in Every Stake*, but writer Elwood Ullman has changed him from the guy shoved down onto his own birthday cake into the judge in the courtroom scene derived from *A Plumbing We Will Go*. This slight change helps tie the first and third parts of the film together. And then there is Kitty McHugh, the judge's wife, who commissions the doorbell 'repair' of the second part of the film and hires the Stooges to prepare the party for the third. The Stooges just keep right on stooging while these three non-Stooges as well as the sandwich board unite the film's three parts. At the end, when the judge reads the sandwich board under which Mrs. Morton has been thrown by the explosion, he finally recognizes the Stooges, pulls all three parts of the story together, and runs for a shotgun - as if ruining his house and reelection was not reason enough to shoot them already.

This is the ninth and final McCollum/Bernds/Ullman production. McCollum and Bernds will make one last Stooge film this year, and Ullman and Bernds will have a fine renascence in the 1960s when the Stooges begin starring in their own feature films. But it is important to observe here the end of an era in Stooge films which gave us some of the finest scare comedies (*The Hot Scots*), crime dramas (*Crime on Their Hands*; *Vagabond Loafers; A Snitch in Time*), extended slapstick sequences (*Mummy's Dummies*), multi-door chases (*Studio Stoops*), and wacky adversaries (*Three Arabian Nuts*) in the entire Stooge corpus, not to mention two forays into the world of the Cold War (*Fuelin' Around*; *Dopey Dicks*).

VISUAL HUMOR: Visually, the film is very rich with a relatively large number of new gags (the judge accidentally banging his gavel on Officer Ryan's hand; spinning Shemp by the tool belt; clanging one another with the hammer from the tool belt; pouring coffee on Larry's foot; Shemp using a turkey baster to fill punch cups; Moe dipping four cups at once into the bowl; sticking the lollipop on Shemp's cheek; and the floating cake), an extraordinary number of result shots (Moe pulled halfway into the wall; Moe pulled out like "a gopher"; the shorted bulb in Shemp's ear; the burnt turkey; Moe's spilled tray; and everyone covered in exploded cake), nearly a dozen variations of old gags [see below], and even Shemp slapping Larry. The camera controls the pacing of the swinging door sequence: we see Larry peer in the door, smile, then yell; the camera moves down to show us Moe pouring the hot coffee on Larry's foot. The sandwich board is a factor at the end of the doorbell sequence: Moe punches it instead of Shemp, so he sneaks around it to grab Shemp's nose; a little later it is flipped over and becomes a 'Men at Work' sign (*3 Dumb Clucks*). There is a subtle whisltle sound effect used for the flying batter.

Bumping into a cabinet and knocking over a vase (Mrs. Henderson: "This vase ['vahz'] is worth $3000!") revisits the Ming vase in the previous film. Other variations: the icing question mark (*Three Hams on Rye*); the officers running into the doors (*Uncivil War Birds*); Moe snapping Larry's suspender (*Shivering Sherlocks*); a painting smashing over Moe's head (*Wee Wee Monsieur*); Moe jamming a plunger in Shemp's face and pulling him (*Dizzy Pilots*); Moe pushing the table and making the chef drop his dish on the floor (*Three Arabian Nuts*; *Vagabond Loafers*); Moe sliding off the table (*Pardon My Scotch*); sweeping dirt under the carpet (*A Gem of Jam*); blowing air through Shemp's ears into Moe's eye, and Shemp "using his head" against the door (*3 Dumb Clucks*); pulling Moe through the wall, thinking he is an animal, and clanging "it" on the head (*Rockin' Thru the Rockies*); and flipping batter onto the chef's head (*A Plumbing We Will Go*).

VERBAL HUMOR: Ullman's script abounds with language gags, including printed signs with spelling errors ('JIFFY FIXERS - We Repare Enything'; 'PLEASE NOCK'), Moe turning a noun into a verb ("I'll gopher both of ya'!"), a malapropism (Larry: "Just like inferior decorators!"), internal rhymes (Larry: "We're in trouble!" Moe: "I'll say you're in trouble!"), and Moe's insults to the chef ("Go on, you French poodle. Your father's got fleas!"; Moe later offers his own French: "Pièce de résistance!"). Elsewhere, the Stooges mimic Mrs. Henderson's pronunciation of "vahz" and speak in British accents. (Shemp: "Do you have a bloater?" Larry: "No, but I have a sardine.") as they did recently in *Studio Stoops* and *Hula-la-la*. In contrast, Moe blasts Mrs. Henderson in Brooklynese "You'll have to beat it, lady. We gotta lot-a work to do!". Elsewhere, the script uses insults (Shemp: "Don't stand around like a bunch of buzzards; there's enough here for everybody!"), puns (Moe: "I've been framed...but you guys are gonna take the rap!"; Moe: "Check those wires for a short." Shemp: "There's nothin' short about this!"; Judge: "They have visible means of support." Larry: "Does he mean our suspenders?"; Moe: "Make that punch and make it 'snappy'!" Shemp: "But the lady said she wanted it 'weak'!"; and Larry about the gas-filled, floating cake: "Moe said 'Make it 'light'"); ironic foreshadowings (Mr. Morton: "My friend Judge Henderson will blow this campaign sky high!"), and Stooge logic (Shemp: "If the doorbell is out of order, how they gonna know we're out here?"; Chef: "This kitchen is not big enough for us both. Either you stay or I go!" Moe: "That let's you out. So long!"; and Shemp: "I only had the dial set at 650 degrees!"). A Stooge first, but an old joke: (Judge: "What's the matter with him?" Moe: "He thinks he's a chicken." Judge: "Why don't you put him in an institution?" Larry: "We can't, we need the eggs!"). Mrs. Morton is given a Stooge-like punch line [coming out from under the sandwich board]: "Is the shooting over?". Ullman repeats and varies the pattern from *An Ache in Every Stake*: (Mrs. Henderson: "Can you fix it?" Moe: "Can we!" Larry: "Can we!" Shemp: "Can we?; later, Larry: "Just like we fixed the doorbell." Mrs. Henderson: "And did you fix it? Moe: "Did we fix it? Larry: "Did we fix it?" Moe and Larry cover Shemp's mouth so he cannot say "Did we?"). Larry's "I just got a flash from the kitchen: you better fill up on these!" resembles Dudley Dickerson's "Dinner is postponed on account of rain" (*Vagabond Loafers*). The literal jokes (e.g. Moe telling Shemp to "shake a leg" and Shemp doing so as he carries out the punch) fall into the same category as the "Mr. Personally" gag from the previous film. Moe's self-deprecating "This looks like a simple job for simple people" parallels Larry's "You're a cinch, lady. We don't know what we're doin' ourselves!" from *Pest Man Wins*. Moe and the chef also have a "Ruff!" exchange as in *Pest Man Wins*. Other variations: Moe: "C-A-N-D-Y' "I don't smoke" (*Scrambled Brains*); Shemp: "I'm gettin' dizzy." Moe: "You were born dizzy!" (*All the World's a Stooge*); and "mazarino cherry" (maskarino' in *Hoi Polloi*). References: the exchange (Shemp: "We'll fill it up...with gas!" Larry: "Now you're cookin'!") parodies the 1940s expression: "Now you're cookin' with gas." Shemp's "Don't worry, where there's life, there's hope" derives ultimately from Cicero's Latin expression *Dum anima est, spes est* [*Att.* 9.10]. The Stooges sing us a harmonized chorus of 'For He's a Jolly Good Fellow'. Epithets: "idiot," "possum-puss," and "imbecile"; there is a play on "imbecile" when the chef searches for the right English word to describe Moe: "You idiot, you!! You— you—" Moe: "Imbecile?" Chef: "Oui, oui, oui. You *imbécile*, you!!" Moe supplying the word for the chef derives from "scrutiny" in *Hold That Lion*. Interestingly, in France *Les Trois Stooges* are also known as *Les Trois Imbéciles*.

OTHER NOTES: This film was shot in November, 1951. The Assistant Director was C. Hiecke. John Hamilton [George Morton] was currently playing *Daily Planet* editor Perry White in the television series *Superman*, which began production in July 1951, but was not broadcast until the fall of 1952, after the release of this film. Elwood Ullman next worked at Allied Artists writing features for the Bowery Boys (1953-1955); he had commented that there was no prestige in writing short-films. There is some apparent ad-libbing when Shemp finishes stuffing the turkey and Moe says (while Shemp walks to the doorbell): "He's known as 'lightning"; and in the awkward exchange: (Moe: "How's that cake?" Shemp: "Wonderful! If we didn't hold it down it would float away!" Moe: "If I want a smart crack I'll make one myself! Put the candles in and get it out there!"). Larry's unmeasured two cups of milk are actually pretty close to being accurate. Larry last said, "I'm a victim of circumstances" in *Flat Foot Stooges* (1938). The Stooges were arrested for vagrancy recently in *Merry Mavericks*.

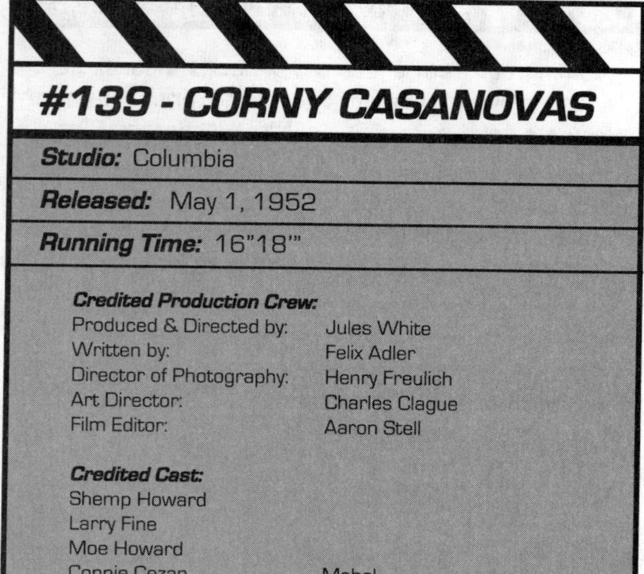

#139 - CORNY CASANOVAS

Studio: Columbia

Released: May 1, 1952

Running Time: 16"18'"

Credited Production Crew:

Produced & Directed by:	Jules White
Written by:	Felix Adler
Director of Photography:	Henry Freulich
Art Director:	Charles Clague
Film Editor:	Aaron Stell

Credited Cast:

Shemp Howard	
Larry Fine	
Moe Howard	
Connie Cezan	Mabel

PERSPECTIVE: This modest romance falls into two distinct parts, a ten-minute domestic scene with the Stooges cleaning and fixing up their apartment and themselves - modeled after the similar opening of an earlier romance, *Love at First Bite* - and a six-minute comedy of manners in which each Stooge in sequence visits their fiancée's apartment, asks her to marry him, and only then discovers that they are all engaged to the same woman in a *ménage a quatre*. Such Stoogesque romantic three-timing is rather atypical of early 1950s Shemp films; this same Jules White/Felix Adler team had created relatively 'normal' romances in *Love at First Bite* and *Self-Made Maids*. But the same concept - the Stooges vying for the same woman - appeared already decades ago in the very first Columbia Stooge film, *Woman Haters*. And the result is the same: in *Woman Haters* Moe and Curly each make an unsuccessful play for Larry's fiancée, and all of them ultimately reject women in the end of the film. *Corny Casanovas* is different in that the woman despises all three of them from the outset and uses them just so she can make off with three (*very* small) diamond rings; but in the end the Stooges still remain womanless after knocking each other out in an unadulterated inter-Stooge rumble.

Since the Stooges always find a reason to quarrel with one another anyway, it is very natural for them to fight over what any closely knit assemblage of men would fight over - a woman. And since these particular men happen to be Stooges, it is not surprising that they are completely unaware either that they are all engaged to the same girl or that the girl does not even like them. From *Woman Haters*, through all the flirting, courting, proposals, and marriages in *Dizzy Doctors*, *The Sitter Downers*, *Oily to Bed, Oily to Rise*, *In the Sweet Pie and Pie*, *Three Smart Saps*, and many other films, part of being a Stooge has always included being a romantic fool, or to use the proper Stooge word, "sap."

This kind of romantic situation exacerbates the Stooges' stoogeness. Ignorant, incompetent, and insolent in film after film, they are very rarely tamed by wealthy dowagers or angry men of authority. But give them a beautiful woman to woo and they become utter saps at an utter loss to cope. This aspect of Stoogery gives the trio an endearing vulnerability that wins our hearts even if they are unable to win their girl's. Just as we root for the Stooges and feel their pain when they are temporarily defeated by crooks or beasts, we feel the same when they are duped by a golddigging woman. Unfortunately, they are such Stooges they are unable to overcome their mutual jealousies and gullibility and, unlike the victories they ultimately win against crooks, they lose this one. Cheated out of three diamond rings, covered with soot and bruises, and knocked silly, they have lost their woman and, insofar as this film is concerned, even their friendship. In this sense, this particular romantic interlude has been a disaster for them, but we viewers thrive on both Stooge successes and disasters. In any event, they never learn. The next two films will find them involved with more romances in an odd sort of latter-day romantic trilogy.

VISUAL HUMOR: The opening domestic scene uses gadgetry (the tack gun, the Murphy bed, the magnet, propelling Larry by his suspenders), special effects (fast motion for the bed, Larry blowing on the sheet), new choreography (wrapping the vacuum cord around the step ladder) and three result shots (the fall off the ladder, the flattened hammer, the bullet shot through Moe's hair [recently in *Baby Sitters Jitters*]). The slapstick offers a few clever new curiosities as well (punches in the knees; Larry breaking a telephone over his head; Moe going to gouge Shemp, Larry grabbing his arm, and Moe gouging Larry with the other arm; and Moe trying to gouge Larry, but Larry ducking so that Moe gouges Shemp). The apartment scenes offer the first boxing match between Shemp and Moe, the first extensive use of bellows as a prop (*Fiddlers Three*), Larry and Moe grabbing each other's hair, and the kitten bristling and growling at Shemp's photograph. Recently Shemp's ugliness has been used more frequently as a comic motif. Slapstick oddities: Shemp spits the shoe polish at Moe and gives him a hard shoe cloth rub in the face. Role reversal: Larry tweaks Shemp's nose; in the previous film Shemp slapped Larry. Sound effects: The CUCKOO sound effect is repeated more than usual at the end of the film. The WHISTLE sound effect accompanies the spreading sheet, as it did the batter bowl in the previous film. Shemp's knock on the door is a marching cadence.

One slapstick setup is adapted from early in the bathtub sequence of *A Missed Fortune*, in turn taken from *Healthy, Wealthy and Dumb* (Moe: "Fix the bed!" Larry: "Who's gonna make me?!" Moe: "*He* is!" [Moe points, Larry turns, Moe launches him towards the bed]). A magnifying glass was used in *Horses' Collars* but not this effectively, enlarging Connie Cezan's eye to many times normal, suggesting that by comparison the diamond is microscopic.

As with the previous film, there are many other variations: Shemp's glasses (*The Tooth Will Out*); yanking the tacks from Moe's rear, and Moe crunching Shemp's nose with a scissors (*Slippery Silks*), the magnet, and the 'Shave and a Haircut' knock (*Whoops, I'm an Indian*); the bullet shot through Moe's hair [recently in *Baby Sitters Jitters*]; Larry's five vests (*"Don't Throw That Knife"*); the result shot with Moe's head in the cleaning bucket (*Fright Night*); Shemp poking Moe in the face with the mop handle (*Cash and Carry; Hokus Pokus*); Shemp bumping his head on an open drawer (*Hold That Lion*); Moe smashing an apple on Larry's head, and Larry banging his nose into the door (*Love at First Bite*); Moe jamming the shaving brush into Shemp's mouth (*Cactus Makes Perfect*); toeless socks (*Hoi Polloi*); the large cake tossed onto the woman (*Three Sappy People*); and the flower pot falling from a loosened shelf onto Shemp's head (*Heavenly Daze*).

VERBAL HUMOR: To set up the confusion about their fiancées, three times Shemp teases Moe and Larry about their women ("What gets me is how you two found anyone who'd marry such house haunters!"; Larry: "'Bribes'? You mean 'brides.'" Shemp: "Any body would marry you two buzzards would have to be bribed!"; and calling Moe's girl "a goon"). Adler helps turn the Stooges into romantic saps by playing on "She loves me...She loves me not" three times. It causes Larry to break the phone over his head, and at the conclusion it causes Shemp to rip out tufts of Larry's hair. The fiancée herself, nameless in the film but 'Mabel' in the script, barely speaks but is memorable for Connie Cezan's repetition of "I knew you were coming, so I baked a cake!".

References: "I knew you were coming, so I baked a cake" derives from an old expression used already in 1937's *Cash and Carry*, but in 1950 Al Hoffman's popular song, 'If I Knew You Were Comin' I'd've Baked a Cake' revived its popularity. Moe's "bells on his fingers and rings on his toes" derives from the nursery rhyme 'Ride a Cockhorse to Banbury Cross'.

Shemp offers a fine pun ("The tacks went in; maybe they're 'income tacks!'), three malapropisms ("bicyclefocals," "presentimental," "that's a coincidental"), a grammatical nightmare ("Oh you shouldn't-a ought-a done it"), and Curlyisms ("Oh! Oh! Oh! Oh! Look!"; "That's a coincidental"). Adler also wrote lines requiring rapid delivery for both Larry and Shemp (Shemp: "Gee, Moe, I'm sorry, Moe. What 'moe' can a fella say? That's all there is; there ain't no 'moe'"; Larry: "...a continuous shooting automatic rifle...I figure if a rivet gun can shoot rivets, this can shoot tacks!". Larry issues an internally rhyming pun ("These tacks will never attack you again!") and throw-away lines ("Move your tonsils...that way!"; and [when cutting Moe's coat] "I must be goin' against the grain!"). Moe's throw-away line: "My luck! I buy a two pants suit, and he ruins the coat!". Epithets: "cement-head" and "titmouse". Shemp called people "buzzards" in the previous film and in *Three Arabian Nuts*; here we hear two references to buzzards (Larry about Moe, and Shemp about Moe and Larry). Moe's "I'm losing my mind!" derives from *Hold That Lion*; later he offers the variation: "You're tearin' my heart out!". Other variations: 'Oh the Wedding Bells Will Start to Ring' (*Three Smart Saps*); Larry: "See if your nose will write under water" (*Heavenly Daze; Square-heads of the Round Table*); Larry: "Me three!" (*If a Body Meets a Body*); Larry: "My poor, poor, little, cute, lovable nose!" (*I Can Hardly Wait*); Moe: "We'll soon have housewives to do the work instead of us!" ("Our wives can't get breakfast and work at the same time" in *Dizzy Doctors*); Moe: "You're getting to be a smart little imbecile" (*Fuelin' Around*); and the 'davenport cover' ('Davenport Seats' - in *Baby Sitters Jitters*)

OTHER NOTES: The working title was *One Won*. All four actors are credited. This is the first of six Stooge appearances for Connie [Consuelo] Cezan. Her last name [Cezon] is misspelled in all of them; her family claims [Stephen Cox, *The 3 Stooges Journal* 62 (1992) 8-9] a distant relationship to artist Paul Cezanne. Her entry into film was as a Bette Davis lookalike. The film will be refurbished as *Rusty Romeos* (1957) with Joe Besser.

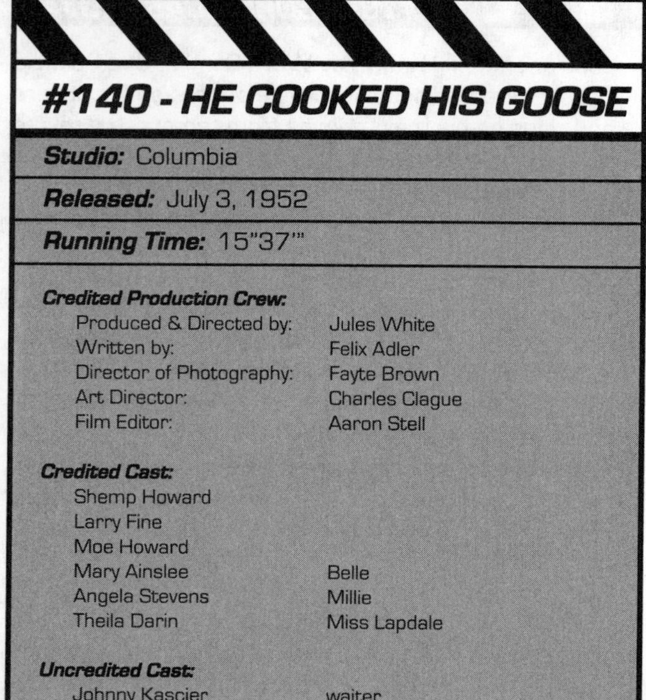

#140 - HE COOKED HIS GOOSE

Studio: Columbia

Released: July 3, 1952

Running Time: 15"37'"

Credited Production Crew:

Produced & Directed by:	Jules White
Written by:	Felix Adler
Director of Photography:	Fayte Brown
Art Director:	Charles Clague
Film Editor:	Aaron Stell

Credited Cast:

Shemp Howard	
Larry Fine	
Moe Howard	
Mary Ainslee	Belle
Angela Stevens	Millie
Theila Darin	Miss Lapdale

Uncredited Cast:

Johnny Kascier	waiter

PERSPECTIVE: The concept of Stooges-in-love was such a rich mine for comedy that romance films were often produced in groupings in the later years. The 1950 releases included a duet of Stooge romances (*Love at First Bite*; *Self-Made Maids*), and this film belongs to a 1952 trio. Romances come in many forms, but the sheer fact that there are *three* Stooges inspires specific mathematical arrangements and plot types. The earliest type, in which the three Stooges vie for one woman, we saw in the first Columbia film (*Woman Haters*) and in the most recent film (*Corny Casanovas*). The next and most familiar type matches the Stooges with three distictively named women, like Faith, Hope, & Charity in *Back to the Woods*, Tiska, Taska, & Baska in *In the Sweet Pie and Pie*, and Moella, Larraine, and Shempetta in *Self-Made Maids*. Now the second of the 1952 trio of romances, *He Cooked His Goose*, develops a more complicated nexus by having two women. Matching three women with the three Stooges and having the Stooges all pursue one woman prescribe the interpersonal relationships. But adding a second woman complicates the plot by separating the Stooges and allowing for a number of narrative permutations and combinations: Larry becomes a philanderer in love with both Shemp's fiancée Millie and Moe's wife Belle, but Moe's wife, who dislikes Moe, does like Larry, whereas Shemp's fiancée does not. Further complicating the relationships within this romantic quintet are that Belle is unaware that Millie even knows Larry, Moe thinks it is Shemp who is cheating with his wife, Larry tells him he used to be a private detective and can prove it, and Belle tries to hide Shemp when Millie comes looking for him.

The driving force behind this involved situation, the most complicated romance in all of Stoogedom, is Larry the philandering porcupine. This is quite a role for him, his most extensive since *Three Loan Wolves* and a prelude to his Brando-esque performance in *Cuckoo on a Choo-Choo* later this year. He appears solo in the very first scene of the film, opposes both Moe and Shemp, goes after two women on his own, has the opportunity to slap, gouge, pound, and kick Moe without recrimination, bites Shemp's fingers, smokes a huge cigar, runs the trained clam gag, and thinks, plans, connives, and plays the bad guy who runs off screen at the end of the film humiliated and shot in the rear.

Of all the activities in which Larry engages, thinking is the most extraordinary. Sure, Moe has been telling him for several years that "You're getting to be a smart little imbecile," but here Larry genuinely thinks. We have seen the germ of this in previous films. In *Corny Casanovas*, for instance, Larry gets the idea of using the rifle for shooting the tacks, and in *Hula-la-la* he thought up an explanation for 'Ol' Four Arms.' But here when he thinks up the ideas of how to win Millie by accusing Shemp of infidelity, and how to divert Moe's jealousy by using Shemp as his "fall guy," he pauses, looks thoughtful, and hears a ringing. For a Stooge, this is deep thought, and it is appropriately celebrated by ringing bells, albeit small ones.

VISUAL HUMOR: Because the Stooges act as separate individuals, there is much solo comedy. Larry does three bits with a golf ball (absent mindedly biting one, throwing it against a wall only to have it bounce back and hit him on the head, and slipping on one) and dials an exhausting fourteen numbers on the telephone (in the days before area and access codes). Shemp steals the flowers through the window, socks himself in the jaw, wrings the dog dry, and models the underwear samples. Moe knocks over the Christmas tree (twice), shoots himself in the foot (twice), and eats bird seed ("It always calms my nerves!").

The ringing sound used for Larry's thinking process is used in *Heavenly Daze*. The CUCKOO and TWEET sounds, also used frequently in recent films, are used to complement Moe's dizziness. Larry demonstrating what to do ("Give him this [SLAP] and that [SLAP] and this [GOUGE] and this [POUND] and this [BONK] and this [NOSE BONK]!") derives from *A Bird in the Head*. Shemp wringing the dog dry is pet humor, following upon the cat bristling at Shemp's picture in the previous film. Other variations: the moving chair (*Hula-la-la*); the trained clam (a more civilized version of the oysters in *Dutiful but Dumb* and *Shivering Sherlocks*); the step ladder and the bellows

[*Corny Casanovas*]; the hand from the fireplace, and spitting teeth [*Scrambled Brains*]; Larry walking into the door with his nose [*Love at First Bite*]; knocking the waiter over [*Brideless Groom*]; the secretary on Larry's lap [*Studio Stoops*]; and a Stooge disguised as Santa [*Wee Wee Monsieur*]. Result shots: Moe with Christmas lights in his mouth and chest, and the silver vase on his head.

VERBAL HUMOR: Much of the script is spent helping the complicated plot unfold, limiting the verbal humor for the most part to sarcasm and abuse from the women [Millie to Larry: "You again!"; Belle: "Careful, Moe dear, you might fall...I hope!"; Belle calling Moe "Clumsy ox" and "Clumsy idiot"], terms of endearment [Larry: "Millie, my little dilly"; Shemp: "Flowers for the fair"], and Stooge threats [Moe: "I'll tear ya' apart, ya' philanderin' porcupine! You keep away from my wife or I'll tear this cucumber off and shove it down your throat!"; Shemp to Larry: "I want you to stay away from Millie, you fuzzy-top Casanova. She's *my* girl!"; and Shemp to the clam: "Listen, you. I'll get you in a chowder one day and look out—"]. Elsewhere there is role-playing silliness [Larry as boss: "To my Siamese representative, Ami: Dear Mi— I—, I—, I—yaye yaye yaye yaye!"; Shemp as Santa Claus: "Helloooo, children. I'm a little early but I got a lot-a runnin' to do. Blitzen's in the kitchen, and 'Prances's got the ants-es in his pants-es!"; Millie and Belle as Stooge women trying to pull the vase off Moe's head: "Shrink your head! Pull in your ears!"]

Shemp offers one irony [Millie: "Wherever did you get the money to buy such a beautiful bouquet?" Shemp: "Think nothing of it. It was practically a steal."] and several throw-away lines ["Is that my gums?" [*Scrambled Brains*]; "Anything to make a dishonest dollar!"; "The latest creation from gay Paris ['Par-ee']"; and [after being squirted by the clam] "Salt water!"]. Larry gets one ["I never saw your wife! I'm engaged to three beautiful girls!"], as does Moe just before knocking the tree and himself over ["Why, Belle, baby, the only one I'd ever fall for is you!"]; using the word 'fall' to joke about a fall has been particularly popular since *Hula-la-la*, although it begins with Curly's "Can't ya' see I'm fallin' for ya'?!" in *Three Smart Saps*. Moe's malapropism "impeturous" resembles his "infilterate" in *A Bird in the Head*

OTHER NOTES: The film was shot in early January, 1952, when Christmas trees were available, but not released until July. When Belle answers the door for Shemp, there is no Christmas tree in sight. The working title was *Clam Up*. The assistant director was Earl Bellamy. This marks the first of seven Stooge appearances for Diana Darrin, sometimes, as here, billed as Theila Darin. Curly, age 48, passed away on January 18, two weeks after the film was shot. Although his health continued to deteriorate during his last 5 years, his fourth wife, Valerie, and daughter, Janie, reportedly made him very happy. His favorite TV comedian was Jackie Gleason, and he enjoyed watching *Benie and Cecil* with Janie. Larry's hair is particularly long and wild in this film. *He Cooked His Goose* will be refurbished as *Triple Crossed* (1959) with Joe Besser.

#141 - GENTS IN A JAM

Studio: Columbia

Released: July 4, 1952

Running Time: 16"12'"

Credited Production Crew:

Produced by	Hugh McCollum
Written & Directed by:	Edward Bernds
Director of Photography:	Fayte Brown
Art Director:	Charles Clague
Film Editor:	Edwin Bryant

Credited Cast:

Shemp Howard	
Larry Fine	
Moe Howard	
Kitty McHugh	Mrs. Magruder
Emil Sitka	Phineas Bowman
Dani Sue Nolan	Gertie Dugan
Mickey Simpson	Rocky Dugan

Uncredited Cast:

Snub Pollard	telegram delivery boy

PERSPECTIVE: For their final Stooge short, Hugh McCollum and Edward Bernds reworked a script they had originally developed for Hugh Herbert's *Hot Heir* (1947). It could not have been better timed, for it fits neatly as the third part of the 1952 romantic trilogy. In *Corny Casanovas* the Stooges were jealous of each other in a romantic quartet; in *He Cooked His Goose* a philandering Larry manipulated Shemp, a jealous Moe, and two women in a romantic quintet. Now the Stooges make another man jealous, combining a new motif with old reliable Stooge motifs. The new motif is the jealous neighbor, which is adapted from Laurel & Hardy's *Blockheads* (1938). The old reliable Stooge motifs include the multi-room chase [*Spook Louder*], the beast-man in the hall [*Idle Roomers*], and the inheriting-a-fortune-from-a-rich-relative motif [*Brideless Groom*]. Almost as complicated as the plot of the previous film, *Gents in a Jam* culminates its romance with a final negative reversal for the Stooges. In this case it turns out to be another romance - the one between their landlady and Shemp's rich uncle which ultimately deprives Shemp of his inheritance.

Several recent Stooge films [*Love at First Bite*; *Corny Casanovas*] have begun with domestic scenarios inspired by contemporary television sitcoms. These scenarios ostensibly allow the Stooges to clean and prepare their domicile but in reality give them ample opportunities to quarrel and use their slapstick. This particular comedy cleverly expands the purpose of the domestic motif by interweaving the slapstick plumbing, radio, and packing gags with entrance sequences for both the intimidating "battle ax" Mrs. Magruder and the rich Uncle Phineas as well as the sweet-but-dangerous Mrs. Dugan and her humongous, jealous husband. The result shot after the trunk mayhem, for instance, leads directly to the discovery of the unconscious telegram delivery man announcing the impending arrival of Uncle Phineas. Similarly, Shemp's cake baking and his spilled batter, itself the result of the vanilla-bottle gag, makes the strongman's wife fall and lose her skirt. As in the previous film when an innocent Shemp has to hide from a jealous Moe, the innocent Mrs. Dugan now has to hide from her jealous husband. This is what then leads to some very clever variations of the multi-room chase and corridor surprises, particularly because of the introduction of another innocent bystander, the just-arrived Uncle Phineas.

Heir to the tray-carrying waiter-in-the-hall of the previous film, the dazed and confused Uncle Phineas suffers from the Stooges' romantic entanglements by getting knocked over, hit on the head, and ricocheted from wall to wall. Always at the wrong place at the wrong time as the Stooges and the Dugans run over, by, and through him, Emil Sitka takes one hilarious spill after another and wobbles in between. But then along comes the *dea ex machina* overwhelming all this foolishness as well as the brute force of the world's strongest man - Mrs. Magruder, who is resurrected from the opening scenes and with one tremendous punch stops all the chaos. Even mightier than Christine McIntyre's "poor, weak, helpless woman" punch in *Brideless Groom*, there is no a single punch like this one in all of Stoogedom.

VISUAL HUMOR: Setting up the great punch are Mrs. Magruder's triple slapping the Stooges early in the film and Rocky picking up Shemp by the head and twisting, shaking, kicking, crushing, crunching, and spinning him in the hallway. New gags: painting around the radio; pulling the radio and its wire so hard the roof antenna bends and snaps back; and the loud rumbling pipes. Moe's backwards rolling pin bonk continues a series of backwards hits which started in *Baby Sitters Jitters*. Result shot: Moe with a table on top of him, an unconscious telegram delivery man underneath. The dough flying from the table derives from *Listen, Judge*. The Stooges hid in a large trunk in *Dizzy Detectives*, but hiding a lady in the trunk may derive from Laurel & Hardy's *Blockheads*. Shemp packs only a toothbrush, a yo-yo, and roller skates; in *A Pain in the Pullman* the Stooges packed only three hats. Other variations: destroying the radio ("You got me!"), and abusing a telegram delivery boy [*Men in Black*]; opening the vanilla bottle with teeth [*Three Loan Wolves*]; spitting teeth [*Three Loan Wolves*]; Shemp throwing the bucket which bounces off a cabinet and hits Moe [the golf ball in *He*

Cooked His Goose]; letting Rocky charge through the unbarred door [*Rockin' Thru the Rockies*]; the swinging door [*A Snitch in Time*]; Rocky crunching Moe's hand while shaking it [*Three Little Pirates*]; Shemp mistakenly crashing a vase over Uncle Phineas' head [*"Don't Throw That Knife"*]; pulling off Mrs. Dugan's skirt by stepping on it [*Healthy, Wealthy and Dumb*]; making a muscle [*Grips, Grunts and Groans*]; and the wolf whistle [*Nutty But Nice*; *Fiddlers Three*]. At the end of the first landlady sequence, the Stooges continue an ad-lib quarrel into a fade.

VERBAL HUMOR: The script features Moe. The opening scene depends on Moe's takes when he learns of Uncle Phineas' millions ("Let him go sponge on somebody else!" Shemp: "Sure! Let him stay at a hotel...He's got six million bucks." Moe: "Sure why should we— *six million bucks*?!], and when the landlady overhears him insulting women ("I'll tell that bitty a thing or two or three...Women! I tame 'em like Frank Buck tames tigers. Some times I'm kind to 'em; some times I crack the whip and make 'em jump...Charm...women swoon when I turn on the old personality. *Stop waving*!...Take Mrs. Magruder—"). The latter ends when Larry and Shemp turn it into a decisive three-pattern (Moe: "Take Mrs. Magruder." Larry: "You take her!" Shemp: "You got her!"). Moe participates in another plot-moving pattern ("Is he so high?" Mrs. Dugan: "Yes!" Moe: "And so wide?" Mrs. Dugan: "Yes!" Moe: "And has he got whiskers?" Mrs. Dugan: "Yes!" [KNOCK KNOCK]. Moe: "That's him!") and a quick cover up (Rocky: "I come down here for my misses." Moe: "I know, I mean, I know all about you!")... The other Stooges have similar kinds of responses to the Dugans (Mrs. Dugan: "Look: if my husband sees me like this all you'll pay for is hospital bills!" Shemp: "Oh that's all right. I got insurance!"; Rocky: "Ya' want me to tear a telephone book in half for ya'?" Shemp: "Ya' can never tell when ya' need it." Larry: "To call a doctor or somethin'!").

Elsewhere, Moe asserts his dominance over Larry (Larry: "How come you give all the orders around here?" Moe: "'Cause I got all the brains around here! Any objections?" Larry: "Yeah!" [SLAP] Moe: "Objections overruled!") and insults him thrice (Larry: "Stupid, isn't he?" Moe: "Look who's talkin'"; Larry: "I had a sure winner." Moe: "Fifty cent parlay player!"; Moe [introducing Larry]: "This is chrome dome." Uncle Phineas: "How do you do, Mr. Chromedome"). There are still two more pattern gags, a four pattern (Moe: "There goes our six million bucks." Larry: "There goes our share." Shemp: "There goes our oil wells." Rocky: "There goes my...TEETH!") and a three-pattern (Larry: "Oh no, Mrs. Battle Ax." Shemp: "Oh no, Mrs. Bitty." Moe: "Oh no, Mrs. Dragon!") which elicits Mrs. Magruder's triple slap and a fine finish (Moe: "That *is* a battle ax." Larry: "I was right!"). Shemp's throw-away line after Moe soaks him with the vanilla: "Lucky for him that I was in the midst of makin' a cake!".

Epithets: "termites" and "imbecile"; Mrs. Magruder to Moe "You worm! You miserable creature!". The setup with Mrs. Magruder recalls Moe talking on the disconnected phone in *A Snitch in Time*. Talking about hitting while hitting a fellow Stooge was used recently in *He Cooked His Goose*. We last heard a reference to Frank Buck in *Wee Wee Monsieur*. Another variation: Larry wanting to get "the eighth race" on the radio [*A Snitch in Time*].

OTHER NOTES: Besides the verbal and visual humor, the radio march music keeps the first few minutes frantic; it is the same 'Frederic March' which freaks Curly out in *Idle Roomers* and is heard in *Termites of 1938*, *Dutiful but Dumb*, *Three Little Twerps*, *Gents Without Cents*, (and 1953's *Pardon My Backfire*). Emil Sitka also played the rich uncle in Hugh Herbert's *Hot Heir*. Kitty McHugh [Mrs. Magruder] played Mrs. Henderson recently in *Listen, Judge* and seems to have been Curly's thoroughly made-up blonde 'shaving' partner in *Hoi Polloi*. She was the sister of the better known Warner Brothers' contract player, Frank McHugh, and Matt McHugh who played Claude in *Pardon My Clutch*. Her husband Ned Glass played Svengarlic's agent in *Hokus Pokus*. Mickey Simpson [Rocky Dugan] played a tough guy in a number of John Ford Westerns and fought Rock Hudson in the famous brawl in *Giant* (1956). After leaving Columbia, Bernds joined Elwood Ullman at Allied Artists to work on Bowery Boys features.

Kitty McHugh, Emil Sitka, the Stooges, Mickey Simpson, and Dani Sue Nolan pose in this cast photo for *Gents in a Jam*, the third of the 1953 romantic trilogy along with *Corny Casanovas* and *He Cooked His Goose*.

#142 - THREE DARK HORSES

Studio: Columbia

Released: October 16, 1952

Running Time: 16"31'"

Credited Production Crew:

Produced & Directed by:	Jules White
Story & Screen Play by:	Felix Adler
Director of Photography:	Henry Freulich
Art Director:	Cary Odell
Film Editor:	Edwin Bryant
Assistant Director:	James Nicholson

Credited Cast:

Shemp Howard	
Larry Fine	
Moe Howard	
Kenneth MacDonald	Bill Wick
Ben Welden	Jim, Wick's assistant

PERSPECTIVE: *Three Dark Horses* is the only Stooge film in which the Stooges assert critical domestic political influence. Yes, they met FDR in *Cash and Carry* and defeated Axis powers in the World War II films and Cold War enemies more recently. But now they not only serve as delegates to a national political convention but even become the swing votes in a presidential nomination. Even more, Moe is chosen to deliver the nominating speech! Writer Felix Adler, always adept at conjoining opportunities for slapstick and verbal gags with a plot and an underlying theme, molds *Three Dark Horses* into a political comedy which begins and ends as a white collar crime drama. Limited by financial constraints, he focuses on back room politics: the crooked campaign manager searches for "three delegates who are too dumb to think," so the Stooges launch into an extended parody of a campaign they "saw on television"; later, during the convention itself, the Stooges accept a larger bribe and change their vote, which the crooked campaign manager learns about from his television. In the best Stooge tradition, the Stooges discover and thwart men attempting to subvert our democratic process. They assumed the Stooges would be too dumb to realize they had been hired to promote the fat cats instead of the working man, but Adler reminds us that the Stooges were at heart members of the working class - albeit inept ones. When they hear a pro-labor campaign promise for a two-day work week, they turn their support to the working man and successfully subvert the punishment the crooks plan for them – saving themselves and their fellow Americans.

The inspiration for this comedy, unique for both its emphasis on politics and its multiple uses of television, was the 1952 presidential campaign, the first to have full television coverage. In fact, in an advertising scheme utterly unaffordable today, television set manufacturers sponsored *full* coverage of the campaigns to promote their products. With Philco buying up all of NBC's time, Admiral ABC's, and Westinghouse CBS's, a marriage between the burgeoning television industry and national political campaigns was established in the July conventions. *Three Dark Horses* was filmed just one month later in August and released in October, a mere three weeks before the 1952 election.

The film lacks any stock footage of convention floor activities, so the Stooges imitate loud speaker announcements and speeches, create spontaneous celebrations and demonstrations, throw confetti, parade their posters, and parody almost every visual, verbal, and otherwise chaotic image of the 1952 televised national political convention. They have to do this within the confines of only a one-room office and a hotel room, but they still generate enough energy both to have their political rally and defeat the bad guys in a final tussle that culminates in the meager square footage of a hotel bathtub. They have also been paid enough money to "buy a yacht" and cast the key votes that elected the best candidate. Like the ancient Roman dictator Cincinnatus who won the war and returned to his simple farm, the Stooges, "so it shouldn't be a total loss," celebrate by taking a bath.

VISUAL HUMOR: Recent films have included extended slapstick exchanges. Here in an extraordinary exchange Shemp blocks a gouge, Moe pounds and gouges Shemp, Shemp gives Moe a hand wave with a down thrust, Moe gouges Shemp in the back of the head, Shemp bites Moe's hang nail while Moe simultaneously bites Shemp's nose, and all this after Moe gives Larry six nose bonks [with a new, duller sound effect]. Another is the toupee sequence, even if Ben Welden is limited in his responses. Throughout the film there are many individual sight gags: Shemp's smoking, barking feet [a variation on Curly barking at his foot 'Fido' in *Oily to Bed, Oily to Rise*]; Larry and Shemp putting sugar, more sugar, and even more sugar in Shemp's coffee [a Stooge first]; Shemp getting a spoon in the eye; Moe slapping the glue brush onto Larry's upper lip; the Stooges running into the doors with their placards; Shemp putting the ringing clock in the bureau drawer; and Shemp collapsing on the table after swinging the ice water container. The celebrations are not fully choreographed.

Variations: the handle in Moe's face [*Hokus Pokus*]; the parrot in the turkey [*Crash Goes the Hash*] eating crackers [*G.I. Wanna Home*]; the animal pepper sneeze [*Malice in the Palace*]; opening the door to onrushing men [*Self-Made Maids*]; pulling each other back by the pants (*Rockin' Thru the Rockies*); swinging clubs from both sides and hitting each other (*Restless Knights*); the Stooges climbing into a bathtub (*So Long, Mr. Chumps*); Moe throwing the sponge but missing the ducking Larry and hitting Shemp from behind (*Idle Roomers*; *Pop Goes the Easel*); the 'Shave and a Haircut' knock (*Whoops, I'm an Indian*); Moe getting hit by "Shoulder arms!" and "About face!" (*Back to the Woods*); Shemp and Moe putting on different sleeves of the same coat (*Horses' Collars*); the vacuum cleaner sucking up Jim's toupee (*Calling All Curs*); gouging a non-Stooge as a getaway move (*Hula-la-la*); and Shemp's take when Wicks is standing behind: "Why don't you mind your own business. Then we'll all—NYAGGH!" (recently in *Hula-la-la*).

VERBAL HUMOR: Adler's script offers a multitude of plot-related gags about political conventions (Shemp: "Go caucus yourself!"; Moe: "Will the sergeant-at-arms please clear the aisles. Order! Order!" Larry: "I'll take a steak and French fries!" Moe: "You're out of order!"; Shemp: "I'm-a demand a recount." Moe: "What's the delegate's name?" Shemp: "Gee-ronimo from Rico Porto!"; and Moe: "Don't be a chump, ya' chump. You can't believe all that stuff. That's a campaign promise!"), candidate names ('Hammond Egger'; 'Don't be a muttonhead: Vote for Abel Lamb Stewer'), campaign slogans ('Hammond Egger wants your vote / Shout his praises from your throat/ You'll eat steak instead of stew/5-4-3-2/3-2-3-2'), political appointments (Moe: "I'll make you [Larry] Secretary of the Offense and you [Shemp] Secretary of the Inferior. And I'll be Toastmaster General."), and governmental phrases (Shemp: "...of the people, by the people, for the people, and against the people!"). Moe's nominating speech consists of a malapropism ("Fellow Degenerates, uh, Delegates") and various types of verbal plays ("What our country needs is tax reform and land reform. Instead, all we get is chloroform!"; "Shall we continue to remain asleep? [Shemp and Larry sleep]); and "in these sordid and morbid times when our national economy is at stake - and 'steak' is three dollars a pound!").

Otherwise Adler fills the small room spaces with other word plays (Shemp: "What's the idea of sponging on me?"; Shemp: "I heard of hot feet but never a hot eye"; Larry: "It's your toupee and your stuck with it!"; "You scalped him!"; Shemp: "No wonder you can't carve it: it's ticklish!"); a parody ("Wash the wall and don't spare the water!" from "Use the whip and don't spare the horses!"); an insult (Shemp: "Here y'ar, Moe: shine up that honeydew!"); and two set-gags, the latter a display of Stooge ignorance (Moe: "We can buy a yacht!" Larry: "And go fishin'." Moe: "You got worms?" Larry: "Yeah, but I'm goin' anyhow"; and Moe: "It must have been an awful job to cut all these little pieces of confetti up with a scissors." Larry: "They don't use a scissors, you dope - a razor blade!"). There are two "Don't look at me!" gags back to back (Moe: "Something smells strong around here." Larry: "Well don't look at me, I changed my socks yesterday!"; Moe: "I could eat a horse." Shemp: "Don't look at me." Moe: "I said a horse, not a jackass!").

Epithet: "porcupine". Moe's "Are you out of your mind? Do you want to punch a hole in this man's toupee?" recalls the shot-gun gag in *Dizzy Pilots*. Several gags derive from early Stooge shorts, e.g. Moe: "Order!" Larry: "I'll take a steak and French fries!", and Shemp calling the horse race (*Back to the Woods*); and Moe's "It's haunted!" (*Men in Black*). Other variations: Moe: "Can't you read the sign?" Shemp: "Who's smokin'?" (*The Tooth Will Out*); and Moe's "Yatibenifuchi-timiny haranja' (*Three Little Pirates*). Moe admits he made a mistake (Moe: "Look at the mess you made!" Shemp: "You made it, too!" Moe: "Well, so I did."); this is to enable the parrot to climb in the window while the Stooges bend, clean up the mess, and exchange the two set-gags.

OTHER NOTES: The working title was *Small Delegates at Large*. All five actors are credited. The photo on the campaign posters is of Bud Jamison. Including this film, the final 48 Stooge Columbia shorts were directed by Jules White. He was a hands-on director, explaining later, "I always added to the scripts while on the set. I would dictate the final shooting script; I was responsible for at least one quarter of every script I directed". He also directed the actors and photographers during publicity photo shoots. Co-workers say he loved to act, too, frequently acting out parts and reciting lines on the set. When asked once why he worked so hard on comedy shorts, White responded: [*Okuda* 25] "What else is there to do? As far as I'm concerned, every one of these pictures is *Gone With the Wind*." Coincidentally, this film is the first to offer a screen credit for an assistant director (James Nicholson).

The Stooges recreate the political convention "they saw on television," inspired by the first coast-to-coast live broadcast of just a few weeks before. On a few occasions Stooge productions were hastened to make their cultural satire more immediate and keep current events current.

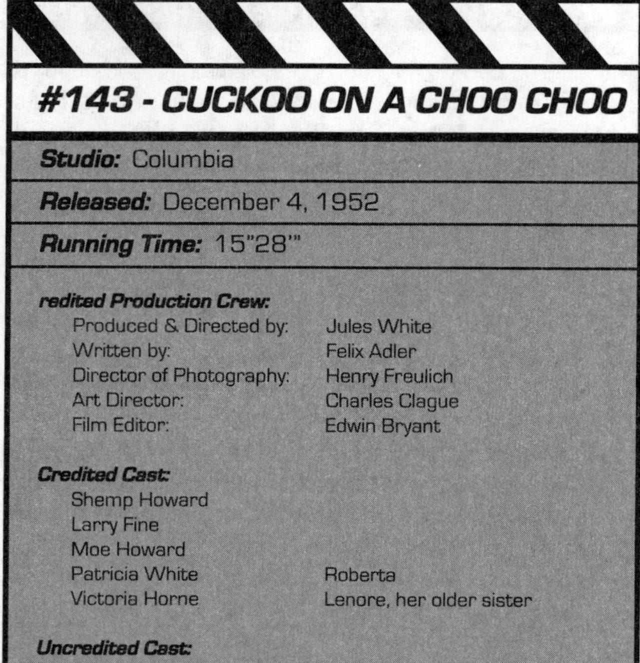

#143 - CUCKOO ON A CHOO CHOO

Studio: Columbia

Released: December 4, 1952

Running Time: 15"28'"

redited Production Crew:

Produced & Directed by:	Jules White
Written by:	Felix Adler
Director of Photography:	Henry Freulich
Art Director:	Charles Clague
Film Editor:	Edwin Bryant

Credited Cast:

Shemp Howard	
Larry Fine	
Moe Howard	
Patricia White	Roberta
Victoria Horne	Lenore, her older sister

Uncredited Cast:

Reggie Dvorack	Carey the canary

PERSPECTIVE: Even the otherwise neutral *The Three Stooges Scrapbook* labels *Cuckoo on a Choo Choo* as "without a doubt, the worst Stooge comedy," but this iconoclastic film with an entirely different concept deserves a second and broader interpretation. From another perspective *Cuckoo on a Choo Choo* should be recognized as one of the most daring, contemporary, and innovative films in the entire Stooge corpus. The working title was *A Train Called Schmow*, which reveals that this film was designed to be a Stooge-ization of *A Street Car Named Desire*, the Pulitzer Prize winning Tennessee Williams play turned into an Oscar winning film by Elia Kazan in 1951. *A Streetcar Named Desire* is a dispiriting tragedy that features the animalistic Stanley Kowalski [Marlon Brando], his wife Stella, and his wife's emotionally unbalanced sister Blanche struggling amidst squandered family wealth, archaic Louisiana customs, and a morality as directionless as "the streetcar named 'Desire.'" Any comedy made from this southern American tragedy would have to establish a different kind of atmosphere, and *Cuckoo on a Choo Choo* is in this respect certainly unique among Stooge films and, for that matter, every Hollywood comedy ever made.

Appropriately, this Stooge parody takes place entirely on "a railroad car named Schmow," made clear with the opening shot and the first five words in the radio news flash. Wearing a dirty T-shirt and speaking in a gravelly voice, Larry mimics Brando's emotive Stanislavsky 'method acting' and from the beginning talks tough to Lenore [Stella], his bride to be. He cannot marry her because the "old family tradition" requires the oldest sister Roberta [Blanche] to marry first, a tradition as quirky as the archaic Napoleonic Code of the original play. Then there is the alcoholic Shemp kissing Larry's fiancée, a Stooge-ization of Stanley Kowalski's brutal but theatrically powerful rape of his sister-in-law.

A Streetcar Named Desire contains no giant canary, of course, but *Harvey*, a popular 1950 film [based on another Pulitzer Prize winning play] featuring an alcoholic Jimmy Stewart and his imaginary giant rabbit named Harvey accounts for Shemp's characterization as well as the 'pooka' bird. This makes *Cuckoo on a Choo Choo* a daring film, first parodying a brooding, disturbing tragedy and then blending it with a batty comedy about an amiable alcoholic and his invisible giant rabbit. Only a Stooge Brando opens a bottle of beer in someone's ear or eats a Limburger sandwich with a skunk on his shoulder, and only a Stooge Jimmy Stewart dances with a giant, partially visible canary. Lost to many modern viewers is the additional irony that Lenore here is played by comedienne Victoria Horne who actually played an important role [Stewart's niece, Myrtle Mae Simmons] in *Harvey*. And then perhaps the greatest and culminating irony of this blended parody is that Shemp ends up romancing not one of the two sisters but the canary! This is clever stuff, if not a typical Stooge comedy; and if it is more clever in its conception than it is humorous in its execution, it is nonetheless just a step or two shy of being Aristophanic.

Within a year or two profound 1950s cinematic dramas would often inspire parodies, but television sketch parodies were in their infancy in 1952, the famous print parodies in *Mad Magazine* would not be produced for four years yet, and turning real drama into filmed comedy shorts was unheard of; indeed, the Columbia short-film unit was nearly the only short-film production unit still in existence. So when the Stooges close out their 1952 releases with this fourth romance of the year, a unique sextet this time, they are putting themselves once again on the cutting edge of American popular culture, and not for the last time.

VISUAL HUMOR: Lenore rips Larry's T-shirt, representing a perfect blend of vulgar Stooge comedy and gritty Tennessee Williams drama, as when Larry uses the same brush for his shoes and his hair. The story does not call for any tools or Stooge paraphernalia, so other than the razor, beer bottle, and whisky jug, much of the slapstick is *a cappella*, i.e. without tools. Shemp bumps his head twice on the sleeping compartment and once on the door, Moe throws the ball at Larry's forehead ["You better play ball with me!"], Shemp kicks Moe several times, and Moe and Larry go to punch Shemp but punch each other instead. Then there is the great slapping

Cuckoo on a Choo Choo, the final release of 1953, was a daring experiment. Felix Adler combined parodies of both the depressing drama *A Streetcar Named Desire* and the delightful comedy *Harvey*. Larry played the Marlon Brando/ Stanley Kowalski role in a T-shirt, and Shemp envisioned not the giant rabbit Harvey but a huge canary. Added to the mix was actress Victoria Horne [upper left] who played in the 1950 film version of *Harvey*.

exchange (derived from *Hoi Polloi*) and the chain reaction in which the dancing kick ends up with smashing the jug over Larry's head. Most of the sound effects for drinking (GLUG-GLUG, chimes playing 'How Dry I Am,' whizzing, whirling fireworks, loud traffic sounds, drums, gongs) we heard in *A Bird in the Head*. They are heard five times, twice off-screen. Result shots: Moe's head stuck through the bottom of a suitcase, a powder box remaining on his head; and the skunk perched on Shemp's head. Shemp's hallucinations resemble those in *Scrambled Brains*, especially since the camera again shows us what Moe and Larry see. Moe tells Shemp to put his fist under his chin and leg under his elbow and kicks the bottom of his foot, as in *I Can Hardly Wait*; here Shemp kicks Moe the second time. Other variations: opening the bottle in Moe's ear (Shemp's teeth in *Gents in a Jam*); the skunk (*Ants in the Pantry*); the sisters with clothes pins on their noses, and Shemp spreading powder on Moe's hair (*Cookoo Cavaliers*); Moe smashing celery over Larry's head (*Woman Haters*); Moe spraying himself with the perfume spritzer (*Three Little Pigskins*); the 'DO NOT DISTURB' sign (*The Big Idea*; *Dizzy Doctors*); Limburger cheese (*Horses' Collars*); and Roberta exhaling smoke after a kiss (*Love At First Bite*).

VERBAL HUMOR: Right at the outset Felix Adler mimics Tennessee Williams' emotional dialogue characterizing the love/hate relationship between Larry and Lenore (Larry: "Ahh, shadup!" Lenore: "Who you tellin' to shut up?" Larry: "You! And furthermore, how'd you like a bust in the nose?" Lenore: "And who's gonna give it to me?!" Larry: "*I'm* gonna give it to you right in the— Baby!" Lenore: "Sweetheart!"). Elsewhere the dialogue parodies the original drama by using name calling (Larry: "You don't think he'd marry this bean pole!" Lenore: "How dare you insult my sister, you- you- porcupine!") and alternating between gutter talk (Lenore: "He's filthy with money." Larry: "Ah, he's filthy with or without!") and emotional ecstasy (Moe: "I've searched the world over and at last I've found her! What thrills! What bliss! What ecstasy! Darling, kiss me!"; Shemp to Lenore: "Baby you send chills up and down my spine...What chills! What thrills!"). An effective exchange occurs where Shemp cannot say the right thing to the jealous Moe (Shemp: "I don't want her." Moe: "She's not good enough for you, eh?" Shemp: "Okay, I'll take her!" Moe: "Oh, tryin' to cut me out again, eh?"). One dramatic question (Moe to Roberta: "Why'd you turn me down? Why didn't you marry me?") we never get answered.

The lower class speech of the Williams parody is at the same level as the drunken patter of Shemp (Shemp: "I'm shot, or half shot, or I ought-a be shot, or I guess I'll have a shot"; "I been robbed!"; Lenore: "Why do you always drink twice too much?" Shemp: "To get rid of my red nose...Drink till it turns blue!"; Larry: "Why don't you sober up and marry Roberta?" Shemp: "No soap, not me!"; calling the skunk "pussy cat") and Moe and Larry (Larry: "That rum-pot thinks he's dancin' with somebody." Moe: "Give me that jug. Maybe I'll think so, too." Larry: "Save a waltz for me!"; and Moe: "Boy, this stuff has really got a kick!"). The post-drinking phrases (Shemp: "Horrible, but I like it," "Horrible, but delicious," Larry: "Horrible, but I needed it") are repeated thrice. It is this sort of drinking dialogue that many viewers seem particularly to hate. References: Shemp names his pooka 'Carey,' blending 'canary' and 'Harvey'; the 'Penciltucky' railroad parodies the 'Pennsylvania Railroad'; and Shemp's' "little brown jug" and the chimed 'How Dry I Am' both derive from drinking song lyrics. A variation on "Me, too"..."Me, three!" is Moe: "Get outta here, you two-timer!" Larry: "You, too, you three-timer!".

Other variations: Moe: "Say a few syllables. Tell me your name so I can tell your mother." Shemp: "My mother knows my name!" (*Oily to Bed, Oily to Rise*); the name 'Schmow' ('Stronghold of Schmow' on the map in *Malice in the Palace*); Moe: "My favorite fruit (*Fright Night*); Moe: "If we only had some applesauce!" (wishing for "bologna and whipped cream" recently in *Idiots Deluxe*); and Shemp: "Oh, you got dandruff" (*Calling All Curs*). There is one other 'regular' Stooge epithet: "imbecile."

OTHER NOTES: Larry was particularly fond of this film during his retirement years. This is one of the few films to show a Stooge's bare back and chest so blatantly. For the eating scene Larry wears a button down shirt. The radio voice is Moe's. Shemp and the canary dance to 'The Blue Danube Waltz,' last heard in *Pest Man Wins*. The Stooges will parody another contemporary film, *High Noon*, in *Shot in the Frontier* (1954). Comedian/actress Victoria Horne [Lenore] also played in *Abbott and Costello Meet the Killer* (1949).

1953

Up in Daisy's Penthouse • *Booty and the Beast* • *Loose Loot*

Tricky Dicks • *Spooks!* • *Pardon My Backfire*

Rip, Sew and Stitch • *Bubble Trouble* • *Goof on the Roof*

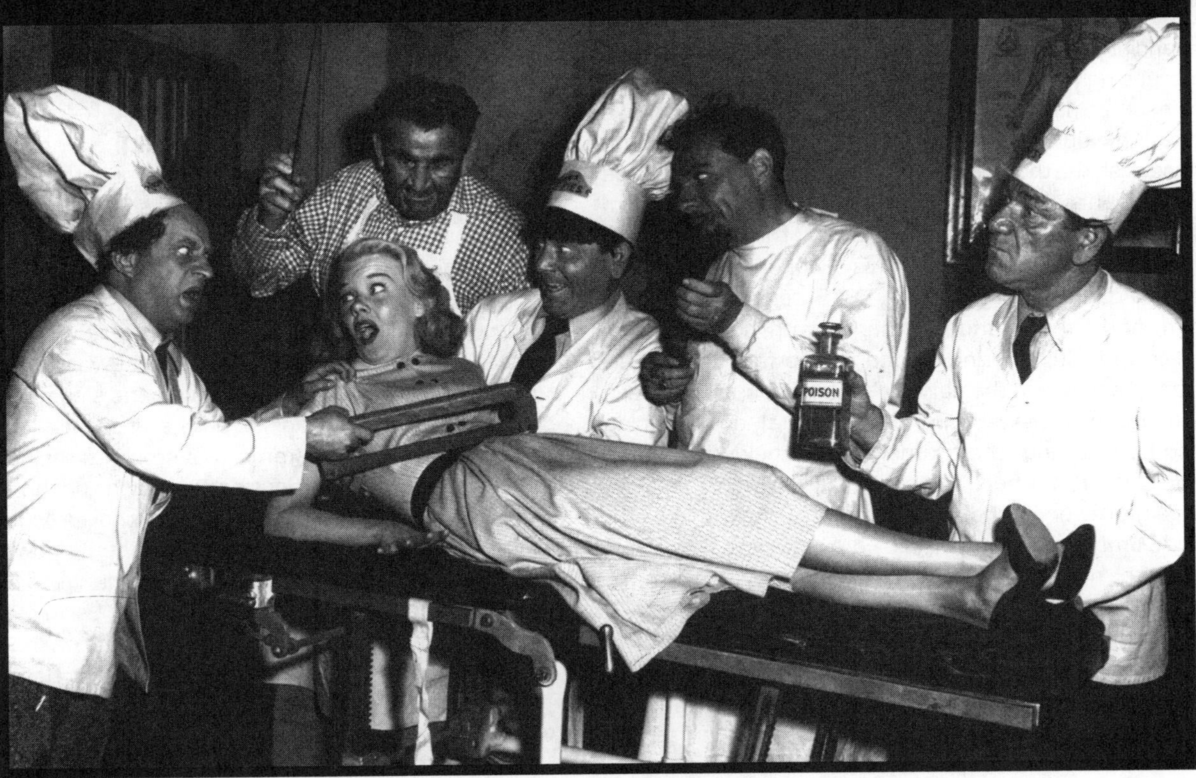

#144 - UP IN DAISY'S PENTHOUSE

Studio: Columbia

Released: February 5, 1953

Running Time: 16"32'"

Credited Production Crew:

Produced & Directed by:	Jules White
Screenplay by :	Jack White
Story by:	Clyde Bruckman
Director of Photography:	Henry Freulich
Art Director:	Charles Clague
Film Editor:	Edwin Bryant

Credited Cast:

Shemp Howard	
Larry Fine	
Moe Howard	
Connie Cezan	Daisy
John Merton	Butch
Jack Kenny	Chopper

Uncredited Cast:

Suzanne Ridgeway	waitress
Blackie Whiteford	detective

PERSPECTIVE: With the departure of Edward Bernds and Hugh McCollum in 1952, Jules White was now the sole producer of Columbia's Stooge short films. Pressed financially and for experienced personnel, White turned increasingly to reworking old Stooge scripts. This first release of 1953 reworks 1937's *3 Dumb Clucks*, a breakthrough film which featured Curly playing both himself as the third Stooge and the Stooges' father. Clyde Bruckman's plot had the Stooges' mother urging them to break out of jail so they could stop their father from marrying the blonde 'Daisy Waisy,' who turned out to be a gang moll planning to marry the Stooges' old man, kill him, and then spend his money with her gangster boyfriend. Culminating in one of the few completely 'happy' endings in the early Columbia films, the Stooges are forced off a skyscraper but land safely on an awning and bounce onto their father whom they whisk off to rejoin their mother. Jules and Jack White had just recently reworked the script of 1937's *Healthy, Wealthy and Dumb* to create *A Missed Fortune* for the first 1952 release; now this first 1953 release is even more thoroughly reworked. It had to be: no footage from *3 Dumb Clucks* could be re-used since it actually featured 'four' Stooges, including Curly's double role as father and son. All the footage of the had to be reshot.

The introductory prison scenario, a popular setting for 1930s comedies, was jettisoned to accord with 1950s tastes and replaced with the unadorned bedroom sequence, moving the film more quickly into the main plot. The reserved few minutes are then used to replace the experimental, subdued hat shop sequence with the boisterous dressing sequence, featuring new kinds of struggles between Moe and Larry at the mirror and outside the closet (while slipping on mothballs), Moe pulling Larry out of the closet, Larry pulling a thread from Moe's jacket, with Shemp's Solomonian decision bringing the whole scene to a close.

As the climax of the original film turned into a virtual Curly short, so the climax of the remake depends largely on Shemp's ability to differentiate his two roles and to build the comedy with his running, yelling, takes, surprise, fear, and panic. It also depends on the ability of the two crooks to act bewildered. All this and the flagpole scene come off without a hitch, but the Jimmy Durante conclusion at first seems a bit abrupt: what is that on Shemp senior's nose and where did it come from? The stand-in who played Shemp senior in this final scene has to be disguised because Shemp is in the scene as well. In *3 Dumb Clucks* Curly senior was dragged off by the feet and we never saw his face, but here the Stooges take the chance of showing us "Pa," even if he has to be disguised as Jimmy Durante. Why Durante? The Stooges had acted with him several times in the 1930s and imitated him later, but Durante had not made a film since 1950 (*The Milkman*). Ah, but in 1950-1953 he was one of four rotating hosts of 'All Star Revue,' an NBC comedy/variety show, and he won the 1952 Emmy Award for Best Comedian. Little did the Stooges know then just how successful they would be on television in the future.

VISUAL HUMOR (NEW MATERIAL): The opening sequence strings together reliable gags: the Stooges sleep together in one bed (*Nertsery Rhymes*), snore rhythmically (*Hoi Polloi*), sing a major triad of "Good morning, ma!" (*Healthy, Wealthy and Dumb*) and unzip pajamas to reveal themselves already clothed (*Rockin' Thru the Rockies*). The sequence in which the Stooges break into their father's house is nicely varied. Not only does Shemp hit Larry and Moe with the sledgehammer, as did Curly in the original, but he drops it on his own foot, too; then Moe hammers Shemp into the house as retribution. Other additions and variations on the original: the father after offering money now shoves Moe's face into the food; while getting dressed Shemp now sprays cologne under his coat's armpit; at the wedding Moe now shakes his head in sympathy with Larry's cocktail shaker; after finding out about the wedding on the phone, father Shemp now grabs his cane and pulls a large floral display over; and while fleeing Shemp now slides up the banister and bangs his head on the wall/ceiling. The NOSE BONK sound effect is once again a slap rather than a bonk. Shemp's fluttering tie is a variation on Moe's blowing hair, of which we see a version in the opening

To expand the cast of the Three Stooges, the writers/producers periodically developed extended family members. Previously they introduced us to the Stooges' mother, father, children, wives, and fiancées. Here in *Up in Daisy's Penthouse*, the first release of 1953, we see Shemp playing the father Stooge, just as Curly had in 1937's *3 Dumb Clucks*. Of course this illusion calls for some photographic effects and a Shemp-double, but it also requires a compelling story. With Jack White rewriting the original story by Clyde Bruckman, we follow the Stooges trying to rescue their father from the clutches of a gangster and his moll [Connie Cezan].

scene. Throwing away the dollar bill is a less wasteful version of throwing the fifty away in the final gag of *Sing a Song of Six Pants*. Other variations: waking up only for breakfast [*Dizzy Doctors*]; slipping on mothballs [*Fright Night*]; pulling the thread out of Moe's sleeve [*Hoi Polloi*]; Shemp trying to remove a light spot from his pants [*Pop Goes the Easel*]; and Moe flying back against the wall, whereupon a vase falls from a shelf onto his head [*Heavenly Daze*].

VERBAL HUMOR (NEW MATERIAL): Parts of the original script are changed slightly: Shemp calls the sledgehammer "a screwdriver"; "Popsie" becomes "Popsie-wopsie"; after the triple slap Moe says "Gee, Pa can still slap!"; at the wedding Moe mixes an "e-nah frappini" ("sarsaparilla frappini" in *3 Dumb Clucks*) with the ingredients "Retta," "Poi Thistle," "Pipic de Menthe," & "Frickle Juice" and adds: "This drink'll put sparks in your hair!"; Shemp adds a squirt of seltzer: "I think you made it a little too strong!"; before the ceremony Moe introduces himself and Larry: "I'm his best man; this is the worst."; Shemp adds: "I won't get married today—[Butch holds a pistol in his face] What are we waitin' for?"; Daisy asks, ironically: "Are you ready for the big leap?"; and while climbing the flagpole Moe and Shemp have an exchange [Shemp: "What do you think I am, a squirrel?" Moe: "No, your ears are too short."]. References: Shemp makes one of the few *Old Testament* references in the Stooge corpus while cutting a pair of pants in half ("King Solomon would give 'em each half; so I'm King Solomon!"); Pa speaks à la Jimmy Durante ("Am I mortified!?"); and Larry's "We'll bring 'em back alive!" is another Frank Buck reference, the most recent heard in *Gent in a Jam*. This one is varied with Moe's tag: "Or in pieces!". The new dressing scene evokes comments on spilling the moth balls [Larry: "You hit the jackpot!" Moe: "Those moths lay a lot of eggs, don't they?"] and on Shemp's pants with a hole in them [Shemp: "A monocle!"]. In response to Moe's "Ma sent us up here to keep you from marryin' that blonde," Larry says: "And I aim to do it, I aim to, I aim." The pattern resembles Curly's "I reckon there ain't no other place around the place, I reckon" [*Uncivil Warriors*] and Shemp's "Yowsir, that's what the man said. He said 'yowsir'!" in *The Hot Scots*. "Indrubitably" goes into Moe's dictionary of malapropisms. Other variations: Moe: "Ain't she hospital?" [*Pest man Wins*]; Larry: "You hit the jackpot!" [*Scrambled Brains*]; Shemp: "Me, too!" Larry: "Me, three!" [*Start Cheering*, *If a Body Meets and Body*]; Moe: "Must be imported material: I smell the ocean!" [*Saved By the Belle*]; Moe: "Somethin' smells awful." Larry: "Whadya lookin' at me for?!"(twice in *Three Dark Horses*]; and the Stooges singing 'The Wedding Bells Will Ring' [*Three Smart Saps*].

OTHER NOTES: The newspaper article the Stooges' mom shows them has nothing to do with their father; it is from the financial pages. As usual, only the headlines are relevant to the plot. *Up in Mabel's Room* was the name of a comedy made in both 1926 and 1944. It has a different plot.

#145 - BOOTY AND THE BEAST

Studio: Columbia

Released: March 5, 1953

Running Time: 15"55'"

Credited Production Crew:

Produced & Directed by:	Jules White
Screen Play by:	Jack White
Story by:	Felix Adler
Director of Photography:	Fayte Brown
Art Director:	Walter Holscher
Film Editor:	Edwin Bryant

Credited Cast:

Shemp Howard	
Larry Fine	
Moe Howard	
Kenneth MacDonald	crook
Vernon Dent	security guard

Uncredited Cast:

[in stock footage:
Vic Travers
Charles 'Heine' Conklin
Dudley Dickerson
Blackie Whiteford
Curly Howard]

PERSPECTIVE: For *Booty and the Beast* Jules and Jack White chose to refurbish not another 1930s Curly film, as they had for the previous *Up in Daisy's Penthouse* and 1952's *A Missed Fortune*, but the more recent and very popular Shemp film *Hold That Lion*. Unlike *Up in Daisy's Penthouse*, this film uses extensive footage from the original, which was possible because *Hold That Lion* starred Shemp as the third Stooge and not Curly. This marks an important turning point in the Stooge corpus. The Columbia short-subject unit had a tight budget and was pressed for experienced personnel after the departure of Hugh McCollum and Edward Bernds. Jules and Jack White had reworked old scripts for *A Missed Fortune* and *Up in Daisy's Penthouse* and reused actual footage from two different Curly films in *Pest Man Wins*, the final release of 1951. Starting with *Booty and the Beast*, using footage from earlier Shemp films now becomes the normal method for filling out the year's contractual number of Stooge productions, with new scenes written specifically to introduce or follow the reedited footage. This is the first of four more such remakes in 1953, and by year's end the White brothers will have become so adept at making refurbished versions of Shemp films that the new versions will be improving on the originals.

The second half of the film replays the train footage from *Hold That Lion* with nary a cut or addition. The only changes come where the name 'Ichabod Slipp' appeared in the original; Moe or Larry voice-over Slipp's name by dubbing in "the crook" or simply "him." That Slipp's name has been utterly deleted reveals that the goal was to create an entirely different story and a new motive for the train footage. The crook is no longer a lawyer cheating the Stooges out of their inheritance but a thief who dupes the incredibly gullible but well-meaning Stooges into cracking a safe for him. The Stooges have not been this gullible since their service station was held up in *Slaphappy Sleuths*, but making the Stooges gullible is a reliable, believable way of immersing them innocently and quickly into a crime. (They were hired to serve as delegates in *Three Dark Horses* just as quickly.) Gullibility is not a property of the Stooges alone, though. In the beginning of the film the crook throws up his hands and surrenders at what he thinks is a gunshot - the sound of the Stooges' jalopy backfiring. In the Stooge world every one can at some point act like a Stooge.

Scriptwriter Jack White blends the new story and the *Hold That Lion* footage by having the Stooges argue about how to spell 'garage,' which makes Moe slap Shemp, backing him into the crook's bag filled with "silver dollars." The crook explains that he had lost his money in Las Vegas, was coming back for more, and was taking the train back to Las Vegas at ten o'clock. This makes the new plot particularly timely since Las Vegas, which in 1952 had only five Strip hotel-casinos, was just becoming popular with Los Angelenos and had begun to find its way into such films as *Paint the Clouds With Sunshine* (1951), *The Las Vegas Story* (1952), and *Las Vegas Shakedown* (1952). Once again, a Stooge film mirrors and preserves for us mid-century developments in American culture.

VISUAL HUMOR (NEW MATERIAL): New slapstick sequences move the plot along twice: once when Shemp gives Moe a hand-wave and is shoved into the crook's bag; and once when Shemp says, "Money gives me itchy palms," drops the bag (to scratch his palm) onto Moe's foot, and thus sees that it is filled with safecracking tools. The new interior sequence turns the Stooges into safecrackers and generates well-timed, plot-related tool abuse with a chisel, hammer, power drill, and four sticks of dynamite. Sometimes prop simplicity provides the purest Stooge slapstick: here Shemp absentmindedly drops the chisel and picks up a dynamite stick by mistake; Moe stops him from hammering it, gets his own hand hammered, tells Shemp to hold his hat, whacks him over the head with the dynamite stick, jams it into his mouth, holds his jaw and bonks him on the head four times. This sort of extended slapstick is common in these refurbished films. Another example: Larry: "I think we're out-a gas." Moe: "Joy-ridin' again, eh?" [NOSE TWEAK] Shemp: "Why don't you try the choke?" Moe: "Thanks! I will!" He chokes Shemp, bangs his head into Larry's, and walks across their laps.

Edwin Bryant's editing creates comic suspense twice: he cleverly ends the safecracking sequence with a delayed result shot, showing the Stooges lying buried under the couch and other debris but only after the crook has left with the dough; and we ourselves see that the security guard is holding the Stooges at gun point only after Larry begins to say "Europe! He's taking a train to Las—!" and pauses in mid-sentence.

An entirely new onomatopoetic, plot-moving gag involves spitting the word *poof* out into someone's face. First Shemp says: "Well our ol' man used to open safes with 'Nitro-Glycerinee. Remember that first *poof*!" and spits in Moe's eye. Then Moe gets him back when Shemp asks, "What would happen if it exploded?" Moe says, "It would just go *poof*!" and spits in Shemp's eye. The third time Larry gets them out of trouble by saying "Every time he gets excited his heart goes *poof*!" and spits in the guard's eye; Moe yanks the throw rug out from under him, and the pistol goes off, shooting a light fixture onto the guard's head (*Boobs in Arms*). Moe feigns a heart attack by holding the wrong side of his chest, recalling the reversed saxophone hand positions in *The Big Idea*. Other variations: climbing the trellis (*Squareheads of the Round Table*); spitting teeth (*Three Loan Wolves*); pulling the carpet (*Matri-phony*); a Stooge jalopy (*Cash and Carry*); Larry falling face first in the mud (*Three Little Beers*); and Shemp 'missing' a leg (*Dizzy Doctors*).

VERBAL HUMOR (NEW MATERIAL): Jack White complements the slapstick with a sequence dependent on Stooge ignorance (Larry: "Hey how do you spell 'jarage' - with a 'g' or a 'j'?" Shemp: "With a 'g, you idiot: 'ga-r-a-j!" Moe: "Fine speller you turned out to be...Don't you know there's an 'e' on the end of it?" Shemp: "You just made that up!"), a set-gag (Larry: "We'll get you a new leg." Moe: "You'll be dancin' in six months." Shemp: "That's good - I never could dance before!"), and a three-pattern variation derived from *Three Troubledoers* (Shemp: "Why don't you drill where you're lookin'?" Larry: "Why don't you look where I'm drillin'?"), now with Moe's tag: "Why don't you two shut up?". Shemp has three particularly interesting lines: "I got a soft head," which is ironic for a Stooge who took the beating he did in *Fright Night*; his diminutive malapropism "Nitro-Glycerinee"; and his kindly tag as he puts the throw rug on top of the unconscious guard: "I don't want this guy to catch a cold".

Playing the nameless crook, Kenneth MacDonald combines his very convincing expository lies with humorous hints ("Why, uh, I must have picked up the wrong satchel at the depot, and the combination of my safe was written on a piece of paper that was in my own satchel...By a strange coincidence, there happens to be some explosives in that satchel....I'll go outside and keep a lookout, I mean get a breath of fresh air"). Other variations: Larry: "Clumsy ox!" (*He Cooked His Goose*); Crook: "So long, suckers!"(*So Long, Mr. Chumps*); Moe: "Here ya' are, chiseler; chisel the knob off that combination!" (*Cash and Carry*).

OTHER NOTES: The film was shot in May, 1952. The working title was *Fun for the Money*. The release title parodies that of the eighteenth-century French fairy tale 'Beauty and the Beast'; in 1932 Warner Brothers released a *Beauty and the Boss*. The uncredited assistant director was Carter DeHaven. In some films the Stooges play friends, in others they play brothers. Here in referring to "our ol' man" (Shemp: "Well our ol' man used to open safes with 'Nitro-Glycerinee") the Stooges suggest they had one father. In the previous film we saw their parents, hence the familial relationship here.

#146 - LOOSE LOOT

Studio: Columbia

Released: April 2, 1953

Running Time: 15"54'"

Credited Production Crew:

Produced & Directed by:	Jules White
Screen Play by :	Jack White
Story by:	Felix Adler
Director of Photography:	Fayte Brown
Art Director:	Walter Holscher
Film Editor:	Edwin Bryant

Credited Cast:

Shemp Howard	
Larry Fine	
Moe Howard	
Kenneth MacDonald	Icabod Slipp
Tom Kennedy	Joe

Uncredited Cast:

Nanette Bordeaux	showgirl
Suzanne Ridgeway	first showgirl
[in stock footage:	
Emil Sitka	[Attorney Poole]

PERSPECTIVE: Insofar as gag motifs are concerned, the entire corpus of 190 Columbia Stooge short-films could be summarized as a collection of original, borrowed, and developed gags fitted and refitted into two-reel segments in endless assortments and variations. This film corroborates this description. The previous *Booty and the Beast* used the entire train scene from the second half of *Hold That Lion*. Now *Loose Loot* revisits the two office scenes from the first half of *Hold That Lion* to send the Stooges in search of their inheritance, deletes from the first scene the battle with the file cabinet sequence, and appends to it a multi-door corridor interwoven chase scene (developed in *Squareheads of the Round Table* and *Dunked in the Deep*), a Stooges-hide-inside-the-container scene (like those recently in *Fiddler's Three* and *Hugs and Mugs*), both a bad guy's head locked-in-a-bentwood-chair sequence and a Stooge caught-between-the-mattress-and-door sequence (*Nutty but Nice*), and a man-in-the-painting gag (*I'll Never Heil Again*).

Sid Caesar, the great television comedian of the 1950s, once remarked: "In comedy it is not what you do but how you do it," and this truism is most valid for a Stooge comedy like *Loose Loot*. The gags the Stooges perform are not predictable until you see the props necessary for the gag (e.g. the mattress) but even then there are new lines written ("Boy, we really flattened him!"), different characters performing different functions (Moe substitutes for Curly, so there are recriminations to be dispensed to Larry and Shemp), and different blends with the next scene (throwing things at Slipp instead of heading for the dumbwaiter). Stooge viewers should never dismiss or devalue a gag just because they have seen it before. The Stooges rarely perform a gag exactly the same way twice, or, if they do, the gag is usually good enough to be repeated and varied still again. The 'old comedy rule' is that three times is the limit, but that says legions about how successful or even more successful the second and third time can be.

Every Columbia Stooge short has unique qualities and gags, and in *Loose Loot* it is the two extended Stooge celebrations that stand out. The first occurs after the mattress scene: with Joe knocked out and Slipp immobilized because his head is locked in the Bentwood chair, the Stooges take two minutes of uninhibited pot shots at Slipp as Moe and Larry pound him with apples, tomatoes, and a beer bottle, and Shemp acts like a carnival barker, makes "applesauce" on his head, and then ("Watch the old master: he'll throw faster, the faster the master!") throws two pieces of "hen-fruit" at Slipp's face. The second is at the end of the film, when they recover their money. Although Moe Hailstone lost his turkey to the painted Napoleon in *I'll Never Heil Again*, he was unable to conquer, let alone enter, that elusive fourth dimension. We saw that dimension again in *The Hot Scots*, but now for the first time the Stooges climb into it. Holding their inheritance in their hand, they have perhaps the most joyous, uncorrupted, uninterrupted celebration in all of Stoogedom – and they do it in a different dimension.

VISUAL HUMOR (NEW MATERIAL): The climax of the multi-door chase is enhanced with well-timed fast motion. The two showgirls are more or less plot-related props for the new footage. The first showgirl [Suzanne Ridgeway] Shemp sees (Moe: "If we find—" Shemp: "I found!") leads to the multi-door chase. The second encounter leads to the fight in the dressing room: one showgirl is wrapping a sash around the other, and Shemp comes between them and makes them bonk heads. One tweaks his nose, so Shemp slaps her on the hip with a sword ("I'll slice you to pieces! Ruff! Ruff!") and chases them both into a closet. They remain there until the two crooks are disposed of. Larry bonking the huge cigar over Shemp's head is another Stooge role reversal.

We saw bearded disguises in (*Sing A Song of Six Pants*); a different beard gag was used in *Hold That Lion*. Joe's swollen hand derives from *Punch Drunks*; the gag is particular delightful when Joe uses his revived hand to punch Larry's face. A shield was used to knock people silly in *The Ghost Talks* and *Who Done It?*. A Bentwood chair was also used in *Hokus Pokus*. Other variations: Slipp slapping Moe's hand with the cold cream (Chopper

Kane smashing the cream puff in Shemp's face in *Fright Night*]; Shemp making "applesauce" on Slipp's head [*Love at First Bite*]; playing keep away [*A Ducking They Did Go*]; Slipp banging into the wall and knocking himself out [recently in *Gents in a Jam*]; a sword blade completely bent into a zig-zag [*Fiddlers Three*]; using spurs as a weapon [*Phony Express*]; and a Stooge giving away his hiding place by sneezing [*Booby Dupes*].

VERBAL HUMOR [NEW MATERIAL]: Jack White wrote several lines to accompany the revived gags. Examples include, when Shemp bends his sword by stabbing Slipp: "That guy must have iron in his blood!"; when Shemp gets hit instead of Slipp: "A bull's-eye in reverse!"; and Shemp's carnival barking: "Watch the old master - he'll throw faster, the faster the master...and the gentleman wins himself a small size panatela!". Shemp's "You hit me with a whatsis - a Vana-Bana" is a play on a 'Havana' cigar, which were still legally imported into the U.S. at that time. Larry's "How could it be you behind there when you're out here? You're crazy!" derives from the kind of confusion begun in *Three Missing Links*. Shemp used "They went that-a-way!" in *Sing a Song of Six Pants*.

OTHER NOTES: The film was shot in May, 1952. The working title was *Filthy Lucre*, the phrase used in the song they sing in Slipp's office [*Hold That Lion*]. The assistant director was Carter DeHaven. A wipe is used to take us from the *Hold That Lion* to the new footage at the 'Circle Follies Theatre.'

In the latter years of Columbia Stooge short film production, the publicity stills were generally of a different nature. Not only were advertizing budgets cut, but the audience was changing - now predominantly children in Saturday morning matinees. Nonetheless, there was still a pre-feature market, and Columbia was still a viable studio, so new and old stars alike posed for photographs before and after shooting. Here the cast includes Tom Kennedy [rear center], who appeared, as did the Stooges, in MGM's *Hollywood Party* (1934). He made a number of two-reelers at Columbia, eleven in a co-starring role with Monte Collins. Of course another reason for the different look of the publicity stills in the mid-1950s was the use of stock footage, which eliminated two days of filming.

#147 - TRICKY DICKS

Studio: Columbia

Released: May 7, 1953

Running Time: 15"50'"

Credited Production Crew:

Produced & Directed by:	Jules White
Story & Screen Play by:	Felix Adler
Director of Photography:	William E. Whitley
Art Director:	George Brooks
Film Editor:	Edwin Bryant

Credited Cast:

Shemp Howard	
Larry Fine	
Moe Howard	
Benny Rubin	Antonio Zucchini Salami Gorgonzola de Pizza
Connie Cezan	Slick Chick
Ferris Taylor	B. A. Copper
Phil Arnold	Chopper (Gilbrave Q. Tiddlywadder)
Murray Alper	Magurk

Uncredited Cast:

Suzanne Ridgeway	police woman

PERSPECTIVE: For almost two full decades now Felix Adler has been creating a wide range of clever scenarios for Stooge comedy. The same writer who invented such disparate comic arrangements as *Hoi Polloi* (the trio confronting a society party), *The Ghost Talks* (the trio confronting spooks in a castle), *Cuckoo on a Choo Choo* (parodying two contemporary feature films), and *Self-Made Maids* (the trio playing their own fiancées and prospective father-in-law), now comes up with another unique method of presenting Stoogeness in *Tricky Dicks*: the Stooges tackle a mystery without leaving their office. The basic centrifugal format - keeping the Stooges stationary and bringing the plot in to them - Adler developed first in *Three Loan Wolves* and then *Sing a Song of Six Pants*, where the Stooges stayed in their tailor shop and assisted the police by capturing a crook who comes in to their shop. But in *Tricky Dicks*, they play the role of police detectives working in a police station, and they spend their day engaging in four different silly phone conversations, battling file cabinet drawers, grilling three different witnesses in four interviews, and ultimately solving the mystery of who killed Slug Magurk, capturing the criminal with the assistance of a hurdy-gurdy monkey.

The specific requirements for the box comedy of narrative format is that the characters who enter the Stooges' space be amusing and/or move the plot along, and that the dialogue maintains an upbeat momentum. 'Slick Chick' [Connie Cezan] beautifully brings out the witlessness of Shemp as a detective; she picks his pocket, takes his matches, and reveals to us plenty more contraband strapped to her legs. Chopper (Gilbrave Q. Tiddlywadder [Phil Arnold]) amuses us while baffling the Stooges with his sophisticated level of vocabulary and compounds the mystery by leading us astray from the actual criminal. The Italian Antonio Zucchini Salamii Gorgonzola de Pizza (whose name reflects the growing popularity of local pizzerias in the early 1950s) surprises us with his British accent and leaves behind the monkey to capture the real crook. Chief B. A. Copper adds intensity to the plot by imposing a 24-hour time limit. And interspersed throughout are the many puns and phone gags as well as a number of slapstick exchanges.

Many of Felix Adler's Stooge films had an underlying theme - not a moral, but a subtext that appears over and over. In this film it is the consistent lack of intelligence and perceptiveness of the Stooges who are not janitors or prisoners but police detectives. Shemp does not see the evidence that Slick Chick is a pick pocket, the Stooges cannot understand Chopper's big words, they throw the real killer out (according to Moe, "a thousand times"), Shemp has to bang his head on the desk to think, and then in the last few minutes they are outsmarted by Chopper who is lying, the crook himself who is not lying, and the monkey. We saw this gullibility emphasized previously in *Booty and the Beast*, but here their ignorance is brilliant.

VISUAL HUMOR: The filing cabinet sequence was the only footage from *Hold That Lion* not used in *Booty and the Beast* or *Loose Loot*, the two previous films. The file cabinet footage here is new, and the monkey shooting the file cabinet drawer is a new gag. The visitor format makes the inter-Stooge slapstick episodic, and most is accompanied by a full complement of verbal gags, for example when Moe orders Larry to "Take this down in short hand!" and Larry pulls his arms closer to his body; when Larry with a dozen pens in his vest pockets answers Moe's "Did you put it down?" with "No, I couldn't find a pencil!"; in the file cabinet sequence; and particularly when Shemp tries to think: (Shemp asks Moe to loosen his scalp, so Moe bonks his head. Shemp has a thought in the back of his head, so Moe clangs him. Shemp: "You knocked it out entirely!" Shemp tries again to think; Moe: "Quiet everybody! Genius at work!" Shemp falls asleep on his outstretched arm. Moe: "Think louder, kid." Shemp snores loudly and quivers his lip. [NOSE TWEAK]). The sequence in which Slick Chick says, "How dare you look like somebody I hate!" and slaps Larry, is of the same type, but it derives from a repeated Judy Malcolm gag in the Columbia Schilling & Lane series (1946-1949). Shemp stealing an ace from the deck and later winning a poker hand with four aces is entirely visual. This was Shemp's best death scene since the near fatal drink in *Who Done It?*. Other variations: the 'BANG' gun [*Studio Stoops*]; making an 'N-B-C' sound [*Hokus Pokus*]; Shemp shooting out water [*Fiddlers Three*]; the three bowling balls [*Grips, Grunts and Groans*] a marksman monkey [*Goofs and Saddles*], Slick Chick being scared by a mouse [*Ants in the Pantry*]; Moe raising Shemp's knee and setting his elbow on it [*I Can Hardly Wait*]; Shemp spitting all over Moe [*Sing a Song of Six Pants*; earlier *Hoi Polloi*]; the Italian stereotype [*Beer and Pretzels*; *Three Little Beers*]; Moe slapping Shemp and Larry for protesting "Did *you*?" [*Three Little Pigskins*]; Copper pounding the table, raining poker chips all over himself [*Listen, Judge*]; Shemp 'using his head' to think [*3 Dumb Clucks*] and getting "a terrific headache" [*In the Sweet Pie and Pie*]; Moe's "Well here's a lump for your cocoa!" [*Meet the Baron*]; a bullet breaking an ink jar all over Larry [*Phony Express*]; shooting B. A. Copper's toupee [*Disorder in the Court*]; the paper spindle, and Larry and Moe putting on bathing caps and taking a shower [[Larry: "Saturday night!"] recently in *Studio Stoops*].

VERBAL HUMOR: Adler's script offers the most compendious collection of phone gags in all of Stoogedom [Moe: "You say you don't know what to do about a woman bein' annoyed by a man with a wooden leg by the name of Smith? Well find out the name of his other leg!". Larry: "You know my sister was engaged to a guy with a wooden leg." Moe: "What happened?" Larry: "She broke it off." Moe: "The engagement?" Larry: "Nah, the leg."]; Moe: "Oh hello, dear... Good-bye, sweetheart....That was the mayor"; Moe: "You say there's a dead horse on Ticonderoga street?...How do you spell 'Ticonderoga'?...Oh you don't know either? Well, drag him over to First Street"; and Shemp: "Release that guy that stole the eleven bottles of whisky...I know he's guilty, but the DA says we can't make a case out of eleven bottles!"). Of similar style is Shemp's monologue ("The body of your friend, Slug Magurk, was found wrapped up in newspapers. Now I know you can't believe everything you see in the newspapers, but the fact remains he's dead!"). Because of their aural nature, none of these allow for accompanying slapstick. The exchanges with Slick Chick depend on the absurdities of dialogue [Slick: "You are handsome, you know." Shemp: "Aw, you just said that." Slick: "No I didn't." Shemp: "Well somebody just said it!"].

All the names are comical, including 'Slick Chick' [Shemp: "Oh, one of those wise dames, eh?"], 'B. A. Copper,' 'Ronald Shrinker, Chief of Police,' 'Gilbrave Q. Tiddlywadder,' and 'Antonio Zucchini Salami Gorgonzola de Pizza' [Larry: "Sounds like a bad meal!"]. Chopper's "Indubitably" resembles Moe's "Indrubitably!" from *Up in Daisy's Penthouse*. "I must have iron in my blood" was used in the previous film, as was the name Ambrose Rose again from *Hold That Lion*. Also used in *Hold That Lion* is Shemp's "I'm loosin' my mind!". Other variations: Shemp: "Where were you born?" Slick: "In bed. I wanted to be near my mother" [*Rhythm and Weep*]; Shemp: "I meant to hit the other monkey" [*What's the Matador?*]; and 'Old Panther Whiskey' [*Love at First Bite*]. Epithets: "nitwit" and "pickle-brains."

OTHER NOTES: The film was shot in July, 1952. The working title was *Cop and Bull Story*. This marks the first Stooge appearance by Benny Rubin [Antonio Zucchini Salami Gorgonzola de Pizza]; he will play mostly ethnics in five more. His career spanned over 50 years, one of his first films being *Hollywood on Parade* in which the Stooges also appeared. Ferris Taylor [B. A. Copper] performed in W. C. Fields' *You Can't Cheat an Honest Man*. There are over seventy shots from that pistol without one reload.

The Stooges manhandle Phil Arnold, who has already played the little man in *Sing a Song of Six Pants* and the voice of 'Tom' in *The Ghost Talks*. He plays Gilbrave Q. Tiddlywadder in this little box comedy called *Tricky Dicks* (1953). He is just one of several suspects, witnesses, and criminals who enter into the Stooges' police precinct for comic justice.

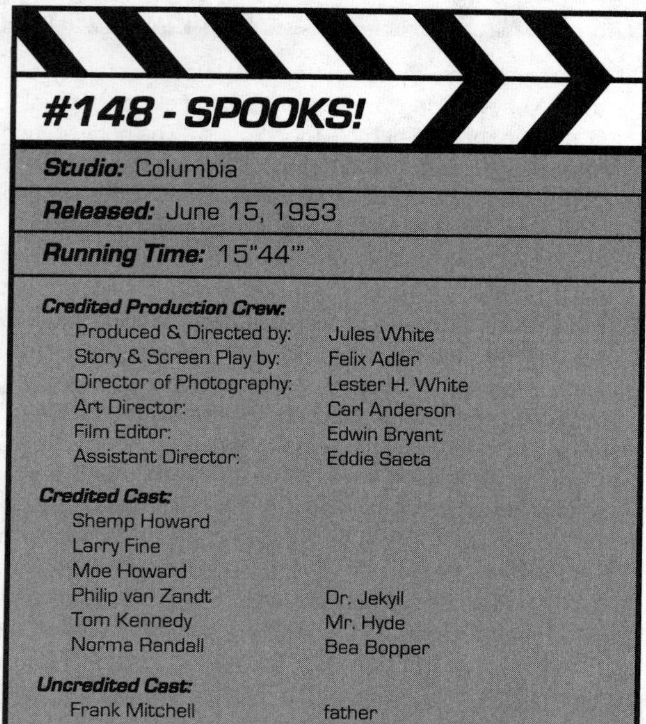

#148 - SPOOKS!

Studio: Columbia

Released: June 15, 1953

Running Time: 15"44'"

Credited Production Crew:

Produced & Directed by:	Jules White
Story & Screen Play by:	Felix Adler
Director of Photography:	Lester H. White
Art Director:	Carl Anderson
Film Editor:	Edwin Bryant
Assistant Director:	Eddie Saeta

Credited Cast:

Shemp Howard	
Larry Fine	
Moe Howard	
Philip van Zandt	Dr. Jekyll
Tom Kennedy	Mr. Hyde
Norma Randall	Bea Bopper

Uncredited Cast:

Frank Mitchell	father

PERSPECTIVE: A fine example of another Stooge production reflecting contemporary changes in Hollywood, *Spooks!* was shot in '3-D.' Its timely release came just months after United Artists released the first 3-D feature, *Bwana Devil*, Arch Obeler's 1952 African adventure film advertised with the exaggerated catch phrase "A Lion in Your Lap!" 3-D, an anaglyphic color process employing polarized light, was invented decades earlier in the 1920s and exhibited already as 'Natural Vision' in *Danger Lights* in 1930. But the process was expensive and difficult to exhibit, requiring two simultaneous projections, so it never caught on. Now in 1952 the film industry was desperately searching for a method to lure the public back to movie theaters and away from the convenience of watching television at home. One of the struggling major studios, 20th-Century Fox, found the ultimate solution to the problem, and that was to shoot films in Henri Chrétien's 'CinemaScope,' the wide-screen system that was to become a permanent feature of film making and theatrical projection. But while Fox was preparing *The Robe*, its first CinemaScope release, the rage for most of 1953 was 3-D. Movie theater audiences donned red and green tinted glasses and watched a number of action films that featured objects thrown, shoved, or projected right at them. It was in this era that Columbia made *Spooks!* and the Stooges' next film, *Pardon My Backfire*, in 3-D.

Even viewed today, the opening credits of *Spooks!* leap right at us. Modern television/video viewers should remember that forty-some years ago they would have been sitting in a theater wearing bi-color glasses looking at these scenes in full-fledged 3-D, and these vivid 3-D effects would have enhanced the pen thrown at Shemp's nose, Moe's eye gouge, Dr. Jekyll's hypodermic, Moe's kicking Shemp, the bat attack, Jekyll's jabbing and throwing the knife at Shemp and the cleaver at Larry, the skeleton emerging from the closet, Hyde swinging the sickle at Moe and shooting fire from the flame thrower, Moe responding with the fire extinguisher, the Roman candle, Hyde advancing with the pitchfork, and the gorilla growling, threatening, and throwing pies to bring the film to a close, totaling over two dozen 3-D effects in under 16 minutes.

Adapting the 3-D environment to the Stooge world creates curious visual effects. 3-D often works best when the object on screen moves slowly towards the audience - like the menacing gorilla - but Stooge slapstick more often relies on Moe's quick hands for its best effect. In *Spooks!* we see one of Moe's gouges shooting forth not at Shemp or Larry but coming slowly and steadily right at us. Similarly, in *Gents in a Jam* and *Three Dark Horses* we saw the Stooges open the door to let the person charging at them go through and run into the next wall. Now the pitchfork-wielding Mr. Hyde comes right at us. In both cases the camera perspective has shifted 90° from side view to front view. In Stooge films we have always watched physical slapstick performed on other victims; now, visually speaking, the physical slapstick is performed on us.

The 3-D effects do not tell the story. To do that Felix Adler wrote a simple 'scare comedy' plot of the sort used recently in *Shivering Sherlocks* and *The Hot Scots*. The Stooges play detectives who encounter a doctor planning to do a brain transplant [*A Bird in the Head*] on a damsel-in-distress. The scare-comedy setting sets up several non 3-D animal gags (the bat with a face like a whiskered Shemp; Shemp scared by a moving stuffed-animal head mounted on the wall), but interestingly the gorilla itself may have been inspired by the 3-D feature *Bwana Devil* with its ferocious lions or the 3-D gorilla film, *Gorilla at Large*, to be released in 1954. Then again, we just saw a monkey conclude the action of the previous Stooge film, *Tricky Dicks*.

Spooks! most appropriately ends with pie throwing in glorious 3-D. Even if it is the gorilla who throws those pies, the film concludes with everyone laughing just as the recent *Loose Loot* ended with the Stooges celebrating inside the fourth dimension. Here instead the Stooges celebrate in the third dimension of 3-D cinema.

VISUAL HUMOR: 3-D effects tend to create a stop-and-go pace, as do some of the extended chase gags. For instance, Jekyll and Shemp stop by the chemical beakers, Shemp says, "What a silly way to make tea," the chase resumes, Shemp stops again, picks up the phone, and says, "Hello?...It's for you," and Jekyll takes the receiver ("Oh! Thank you!") from Shemp ("You're welcome!") but gets conked on the head, which then knocks Jekyll backwards onto the hypodermic needle. An interesting variation of the 3-D concept: the match cut from the beautiful pair of Mary's eyes to her frightened eyes. Some of the extended slapstick involves Larry more than usual: in succession Larry makes a fist, Moe hits it, it circles around and hits Moe but hurts Larry's hand; Moe goes to gouge Larry but Shemp grabs his arm so Moe turns and gouges Shemp; Larry gives Moe a hand-wave with a downward thrust; Moe slaps Larry and gives Shemp a nose bonk. Elsewhere Larry nervously offers cigarettes, scatters them, puts the pack in his mouth, strikes a match on Moe's cheek, realizes what he is doing, and tosses the lit match over to where that Roman candle sits, causing another 3-D effect. Shemp turns to the gorilla and talks before doing a take, as we saw in *Three Missing Links*, just as does Moe to Hyde (Moe to Shemp: "Did you say that?" Hyde: "I said it!" Moe: "Well why don't you stop buttin' in?! How do you like that ugly lookin'— NYAGGH!"). As in the previous film, the verbal and physical humor are particularly well matched, e.g. Shemp: "See, there's somethin's fishy here." Moe: "Yeah, you two suckers!" (DOUBLE SLAP); Shemp: "What's a cranny?" Larry: "This!" [He offers Shemp a fist, which Shemp hits and spins around to hit Shemp's head]; Moe: "What's in your mouth?" Shemp: "Nothin'," Moe sticks his finger in and pulls Shemp by the cheek (*Baby Sitters Jitters*). Other variations: Moe and Shemp standing nose-to-nose, and Miss Bopper opening the door into Shemp's nose (*Love at First Bite*); Moe gouging Larry, Shemp grabbing his arm, and Moe gouging Shemp (*Corny Casanovas*); the stretching doorknob (*A Gem of a Jam*); picking up a phone and handing it to the pursuer (*Slaphappy Sleuths*); the Stooges sleeping and snoring to open the film (*Movie Maniacs*); the Stooges wearing clothes underneath pajamas (*Rockin' Thru the Rockies*); Shemp leaping into Larry's arms (*Oily to Bed, Oily to Rise*); Sherlock Holmes-type hats (*Horses' Collars*); putting a mouse trap on Shemp's tongue (a clothes pin in *Dizzy Detectives*); and Shemp hitting Larry who is under a cloth (*Merry Mavericks*).

VERBAL HUMOR: Felix Adler's script, as often, includes internal rhyme (Larry's "A cleaver tried to cleave me in half!"), three-patterns (Moe: "What did you do?" Larry: "Who'd you kill?" Shemp: "Who do you want us to cover up for?"; Moe: "It came from inside the house." Larry: "Let's investigate!" Shemp: "Let's go home and investigate tomorrow!"), and ironic Stooge ignorance (Shemp about the elk: "A dead cow!"; the sign ('SUPER SLUETH DETECTIVE AGENCY...Dont Knock' with a backward 's'). Role reversal: for the first time Shemp uses the "I can't see...I've got my eyes closed" gag, and he adds a variation after Moe gouges him: "They're open! They're open!". References: Shemp's "George B. Bopper...Oh, a Bebopper! Dig that crazy bopper name...Cool, man! Real George. Give me some skin!" is jive (bebop) slang derived from the jazz movement of the 1940s; the name 'Bea Bopper' is a jive gag as well. 'Congo the gorilla' uses the colonial name for Zaire. The names given to the mad doctor and his assistant, 'Jekyll' and 'Hyde,' derive from the 1886 Robert Louis Stevenson tale (filmed in 1921, 1931, and 1941); Shemp makes one pun on the names (Shemp: "Dr. Jekyll?! We must hide!"). Shemp's throw-away line when he gets a pen stuck on his nose ("Give me a blotter!") refers to an ink blotter. Moe's "Tote that board! Rip those nails!" is a play on "Tote that barge! Lift that Bale!" used first in *Rockin' Thru the Rockies*. And Larry's "Don't worry, mister, we'll bring her back alive!" is another reference to Frank Buck, last heard in *Up in Daisy's Penthouse*. Shemp's mother-in-law joke ("I found a great big chimanee-panzee. He looked just like my mother-in-law!") is the second in the Stooge corpus (*All Gummed Up*); mother-in-law jokes were particularly popular in the late 1940s-1950s. The 'Ticonderoga' joke in the previous film was different from this one (Moe: "We'll be with you before you can say 'Fort Ticonderoga." Larry: "If you can say 'Fort Ticonderoga.'" Moe: "If you can say anything.") and the version in *Back to the Woods*. Other variations: Shemp: "We're trapped like rats!" Moe: "Speak for yourself! (*Nutty but Nice*); "I'm losing my mind!" (*A Gem of a Jam*); "chimanee-panzee (*Dizzy Detectives*); "You can say that again!" (*Micro-Phonies*); and "Gentlemen!" Larry: "Where?" (*Horses' Collars*). Epithets: "mush-head" and "you stubborn mule."

OTHER NOTES: The *Scrapbook* says a 'flat' [2-D] version of this film was released on April 15, 1953, but it also says the film was shot in May. This is the second time an assistant director is credited. The opening credits begin the 3-D effects: the Stooges in black cloaks move towards us and back to under their names; a shivering font emerges from an unfocused white blob on not the comedy mask backdrop, but a spooky room with a bat, all with ominous music until the Stooge theme begins. It lasts 45 seconds. The final screen uses the same spooky room photo. Frank Mitchell [Bea Bopper's father] was part of the vaudevillian team, Mitchell & Durant. He later (1974) teamed with Mousie Garner and Joe DeRita to form a short-lived trio known as 'The New Three Stooges'. Jules White initially had high hopes for 3-D comedy: "I made the first 3-D comedies to hit the screen - and thought we had a whole new life ahead of us. Boy, did I goof!" The only other Stooge 3-D film, *Pardon My Backfire*, was never even released in 3-D. But when *Spooks!* was shown to a preview audience, it was a huge success. White [*Bruskin* 95]: "I've never heard greater screams of laughter nor seen a more riotous reaction in all my life."

#149 - PARDON MY BACKFIRE

Studio: Columbia

Released: August 15, 1953

Running Time: 15"52'"

Credited Production Crew:

Produced & Directed by:	Jules White
Story & Screen Play by:	Felix Adler
Director of Photography:	Henry Freulich
Art Director:	Walter Holscher
Film Editor:	Edwin Bryant
Assistant Director:	Milton Feldman

Credited Cast:

Shemp Howard	
Larry Fine	
Moe Howard	
Benny Rubin	gang leader
Frank Sully	gang member
Phil Arnold	knife thrower

Uncredited Cast:

Ruth Godfrey	Nettie
Angela Stevens	Hettie
Theila Darin	Betty
Fred Kelsey	father
Barbara Bartay	gang moll

PERSPECTIVE: The only other 3-D Stooge film, *Pardon My Backfire* probes stereoscopic depths even further than did the previous *Spooks!*. Director Jules White enhances the 3-D effects by having his actors move the solid props - the fork, cake, screwdriver, knives, and a ricocheting bottle - slowly forth into, and back from, the camera for the setup shot; then for additional and continuous movement he attaches the props to wires and slides them into the camera. But then, because solid props necessarily have to stop short of the lens, White shoots forth in addition a number of liquids - water, lacquer, oil, and grease - to cover the camera lens, making a more immediate impact upon the bi-spectacled audiences. And he even shoots a flame at the camera - three times! Some of these scenes may look cumbersome, especially when contrasted with the rapid timing of Stooge slapstick, but it should be remembered that the intent of these 3-D films in 1953 was not to show just the 'normal' Stooge slapstick but to thrust an object at the camera and let the 3-D effects create an additional thrill for the audience. Compared to the virtual reality glasses of the twenty-first century, 3-D looks sub-standard, but modern viewers should remember that in the 1950s they would be wearing cardboard, polarizing cellophane glasses to see this film on a large screen in a theater crowded with like-minded people. Each era believes in its own cinematic illusions.

Typical of many mid-1950s Stooge narratives, the story is eclectic: courting three like-named girls and quarreling with their father is *The Sitter Downers*, having a limited amount of time to complete a task we just saw in *Tricky Dicks*, working as destructive auto mechanics dates back to *Higher Than a Kite*, and catching crooks has always been a staple of the Shemp films. But Felix Adler unifies all this in a ring composition by inserting Nettie, Hettie, and Betty fore and aft, and Jules White advances the narrative relentlessly with a constant barrage of slapstick, verbal gags, and 3-D effects. Shemp and Larry, for instance, hit Moe in the head, which causes Moe to demonstrate his expertise with a hammer, with which he breaks the windshield, which makes Larry come over and ignite Moe's rear, which causes Shemp to joke "That's a hot one," which causes Moe to squirt grease in Shemp's face [3-D effect], which causes Shemp to wipe his face and toss his greasy glove onto the stool, which the gang moll sits on, causing the gang leader to get jealous and start the 3-D extravaganza fight.

Concentrating on 3-D effects may have inspired making other drastic changes as well, for *Pardon My Backfire* increases the number of Stooge role reversals: Moe struggles with a tire and in his frustration goes "Hhmm!" à la Curly; Larry slaps Shemp; Shemp retaliates by hand-waving Larry, leaving Larry's head wavering in the air before coming back and giving him the final downthrust; Shemp now owns the "poor, sweet, dear, cute, beautiful, little head"; and Curly's "Oh! Oh! Oh! Ohhh-look!" becomes Larry's "Oh-Oh-Oh-h-hhhh!" directed not at a bent saw but at a woman. No Stooge film offers so many transformations of visual gags and Stooge characterizations.

VISUAL HUMOR: New gags: passing serving bowls in time to 'Oh Susanna'; the pneumatic hammer with its contagious vibrations (Larry: "Hey buster!" Gang Leader: "M-my n-name is-s n-not-t b-bus-s-s-t-ter!"); and Moe feeding a wire up into Larry's nose and out his ear, the latter taking us into an internal, anatomical sort of 3-D. Variations on slapstick staples: besides Shemp hand-waving Larry, the coat-pulling struggle at the door, last seen in *Three Dark Horses*, is well choreographed with Moe pulling Larry, Shemp pulling Moe, Larry pulling Shemp, Larry and Moe pulling each other's hair, Shemp crawling between their legs, and Larry and Moe holding each other's hair. A fist game has Shemp slapping at Larry's arm, the hammer he holds circling around and hitting Shemp on the head. A gouge is accompanied by a new verbal exchange (Moe: "Do you like asparagus?" Larry: "Love em'!" Moe: "Well here's a couple of tips for ya'!"). Both Larry and Shemp work on the fender and sock Moe with their elbows. The girls' father gives the Stooges their twentieth filmed triple slap. And that leg of

lamb evokes animalistic eating even by Stooge standards. In scare comedies, one Stooge sees something strange only to have it disappear when another Stooge comes to verify it. Here that happens with the engine wire (Larry and Shemp) and the spraying tire (Moe and Shemp). Other variations: Shemp pulling out the bent fork (*Fiddlers Three*); a gouging in 3-D (*Spooks!*); the car backfiring soot all over Shemp, and shattering a windshield (*Higher Than a Kite*); cutting Shemp's tie with a weapon (*Tricky Dicks*); Larry pulling the wire, knocking Moe's head against the chassis, and Moe tugging Larry back into the engine (*Three Sappy People*); Moe rasping Larry's forehead (*No Census, No Feeling*); kissing a Stooge instead of a woman (*Calling All Curs*); Shemp throwing the bottle, missing, but bouncing it off a tire on the wall and knocking the crook out (*Dizzy Detectives*); and the horn falling to the floor and dying ("They got me!" in *Men in Black*).

VERBAL HUMOR: Adler's script offers literal responses (Moe: "Sit down and eat like a gentleman." Shemp: "I'll eat but I promise nothin'!"; Shemp: "I want cake in the worst way!" Moe: "That's exactly how you're going to get it!"), Stooge logic (Shemp [about the damaged fender]: "You know, I think they hit somethin'"; Shemp: "The light must be off because it ain't on"), mispronunciations intentional (Moe: "Ree-treat!") and unintentional (Larry: "You nincompip!" Shemp: " The word is nincompoop!"), and a gag with the blasting car horn (Larry: "What are ya' yellin' about?"). The romantic Moe: "Anything for a beautiful chick like you!"; "Some sweet music for a sweet thing!"; and "I'm always happy to give a lady a helping hand.".

In the first scene, both the Stooges ("Oh no, not that!") and their fiancées ("Papa! You've spoiled our cake!") make exclamations in unison. Later the Stooges howl in unison, and at the end Nettie, Hettie, and Betty say in unison: "You're heroes! You're wonderful!" (like Hope, Faith, and Charity in *Back to the Woods*). Larry apologizes with the "Pardon my backfire!" of the film title echoed in "Pardon my monkey wrench!".

As in the previous film, Phil Arnold ("I believe it might be advisable to forestall such an eventuality") speaks in big words, and Benny Rubin [Gang Leader] in a subdued Italian accent: "Talk to me couple syllables"; "I am going to kill you to death!" . Moe, skilled in recognition sequences when beasts loom behind him, does a frontal recognition scene ("Take it easy, mister. We were just listenin' to the radio. They were tellin' about three escaped convicts wearin' nice business suits like you. And one of 'em had a scar on his face like you...Hey! It *is* you!") and another about his own rear (Moe: "The guy 'll be burnt up, won't he?" Larry: "I smell rubbish burnin'." Moe: "It's me!"). Twice he boasts of expertise ("Spread out! Let an expert show you how to disconnect it."; "Listen, lame-brain! Let an expert show you how to do this!"). He also wishes he had an odd condiment ("If it only had ketchup!") on a cake; Larry wanted ketchup for hot cakes in *A Missed Fortune*.

Larry says: "Yeah, that's a slick chick!"; we met 'Slick Chick' in *Tricky Dicks*. Other variations: Shemp: "Oh my poor, sweet, dear, cute, beautiful, little head" (*"I Can Hardly Wait"*); Shemp: "Call your shots, will ya'!" (*A Plumbing We Will Go*); Shemp: "Remember: your mother and my mother are both mothers"; and Moe: "Every time you think you weaken the nation" (*Half Shot Shooters*); Moe: "I'm losin' my mind!" (*A Gem of a Jam*); Moe: "I'm gonna get myself a cheap lawyer!" (*Monkey Businessmen*); Larry: "I wonder how much?" Radio: "$1500." Shemp: "Thanks!" Radio: "You're welcome." (*Healthy, Wealthy and Dumb*); Moe: "Are you going to eat that lamb alone?" Larry: "No, I'll wait. Maybe I'll get somethin' else." (*In the Sweet Pie and Pie*). Epithets: "lame-brain" and "lunk-head."

OTHER NOTES: The opening credits show the Stooges, dressed in black to blend into the background, jabbing towards us for an initial 3-D effect. The music accompanying the credits over a shot of the garage lasts 31 seconds. We see the same shot for the final screen also. The film was released in a 'flat' version [2-D], not 3-D. This film marks the first of six Stooge appearances by Frank Sully, who played in hundreds of films spanning his 50-year career. The horn of the car Larry is tuning sounds continuously, as did a whole factory of horns for Laurel & Hardy in *Saps at Sea* (1940).

#150 - RIP, SEW AND STITCH

Studio: Columbia

Released: September 3, 1953

Running Time: 16"32"'

Credited Production Crew:

Produced & Directed by:	Jules White
Screen Play by:	Jack White
Story by:	Felix Adler
Director of Photography:	Ray Cory
Art Director:	Cary Odell
Film Editor:	Edwin Bryant
Assistant Director:	James Nicholson

Credited Cast:

Shemp Howard
Larry Fine
Moe Howard

Uncredited Cast:

[in stock footage:

Vernon Dent	Officer Sharp
Harold Brauer	Terry Hargen
Phil Arnold	little man
Cy Schindell	[torpedo]

PERSPECTIVE: Unlike the earlier reworkings of 1953, *Rip, Sew and Stitch* reuses almost all the footage from a previous Shemp film, *Sing a Song of Six Pants. Up in Daisy's Penthouse*, the first release of 1953, merely reworked an old Curly script, and then the ground-breaking *Booty and the Beast* and *Loose Loot* each used half of a Shemp film [*Hold That Lion*]. But in putting *Rip, Sew and Stitch* together, Jules White makes a notable change in policy by initiating a series of refurbished films that reuse the majority of footage from the prototype. Part of the reason for this, of course, was to save time and therefore money: the less new footage that had to be shot, the less shooting time was required and the less money had to be spent. [The Stooges' salary, established in 1934 on a per-film/per-year basis, did not vary with the change in shooting schedules.] But Jules White was not Harry Cohn, the Columbia boss often accused of sacrificing art for frugality. White had now spent 20 years at the helm of the Columbia short-subjects unit and had always managed to find methods of producing comic innovation despite continually decreasing budgets. With *Rip, Sew and Stitch* he begins not just reusing old footage but fully refurbishing and ultimately improving upon a number of films.

Felix Adler's *Sing a Song of Six Pants* was a very important film in the corpus. With *Three Loan Wolves* it became the model for the Stooge box comedy set in one location into which external characters import narrative developments; we saw just this year the influence of box comedy in *Tricky Dicks*. When White revisited *Sing a Song of Six Pants* in 1953 he decided to enclose the narrative entirely within the confines of the 'Pip Boys' tailor shop. In the original film the policeman, Terry Hargen, his moll Flossie, and the short fellow with the shredded suit jacket [Phil Arnold] visited the tailor shop, but we saw two scenes back at Hargen's hideout. In this newer version those external scenes are eliminated, the policeman has a smaller role in the final scene, and the moll is eliminated completely. This means that the Stooges are even more isolated in this newer version.

The replacement scenes leave more to the Stooges' own comic devices: Moe razors Shemp's hair - providing a different means of getting the razor into the whisk broom to shred Phil Arnold's jacket - and Larry and Shemp then shred a matching pair of pants for him; the Stooges themselves find money in the lapel since the moll is no longer present to do so; Larry salutes and slaps Moe; Shemp argues with him; and in the back room scenes, Shemp strangles Moe, Moe bangs Shemp's knuckles, and Moe hammers Larry's shoes to the floor. There is also one brief scene in which Hargen [not the original actor] sneaks in to get his clothes. He is inserted because Hargen has to be wearing his coat in the finale,

but it was his moll who retrieved it in *Six Pants*. Except for this brief continuity insert, none of the new sequences advance the plot but simply focus on the Stooges stooging. Larry gets so much of it that he calls Moe: "You stupid stooge!"

VISUAL HUMOR [NEW FOOTAGE]: Pulling out Larry's hair has been a Stooge staple for years. Here, Moe razors Shemp's hair and bonks it back onto his head. As in recent films, two slapstick bits are set up verbally [Moe: "Do your knuckles hurt?" Shemp: "No." Moe: "They will!" [CLANG]; Shemp: "I once had a granny who searched every nook and cranny." Moe: "I did, too. You know what she found?" [GOUGE]). We heard a "nook and cranny" joke in *Spooks!*. In the back room, we see Larry coming in but Moe and Shemp do not, so Shemp strangles Moe by mistake - a 'scare comedy' technique. Moe punches Shemp in the stomach and pulls him by his open mouth, just as Moe grabbed Curly by the tongue in *An Ache in Every Stake* and *Sock-A-Bye Baby*, but this derives directly from Moe's two-mouth grab in *Baby Sitters Jitters*. Other variations: Larry's shoesnailed to the ground (*Rhythm and Weep*); saluting and slapping (*Uncivil Warriors*); Moe swinging, missing, and bonking instead (*Hoi Polloi*); and Moe spitting out teeth (*Three Loan Wolves*).

VERBAL HUMOR (NEW FOOTAGE): Script writer Jack White has Moe turn a noun into a verb: "I ought-a razor-blade you!". Shemp offers throw-away lines after he gets his hair bonked back on ("Now my hat won't fit me!"), after Phil Arnold asks for shredded pants ("That guy's mother must have raised him on shredded wheat!"), and after Moe pries Shemp's nose ("What does that look like, a nail?!"). Moe and Shemp kiss each other and say "Viva!" as in *Dutiful but Dumb*. Epithets: "mongoose" and "wart hog."

OTHER NOTES: The working title was *A Pressing Affair*. Shot in regular 2-D, the comic mask screens and the old theme song are returned as well.

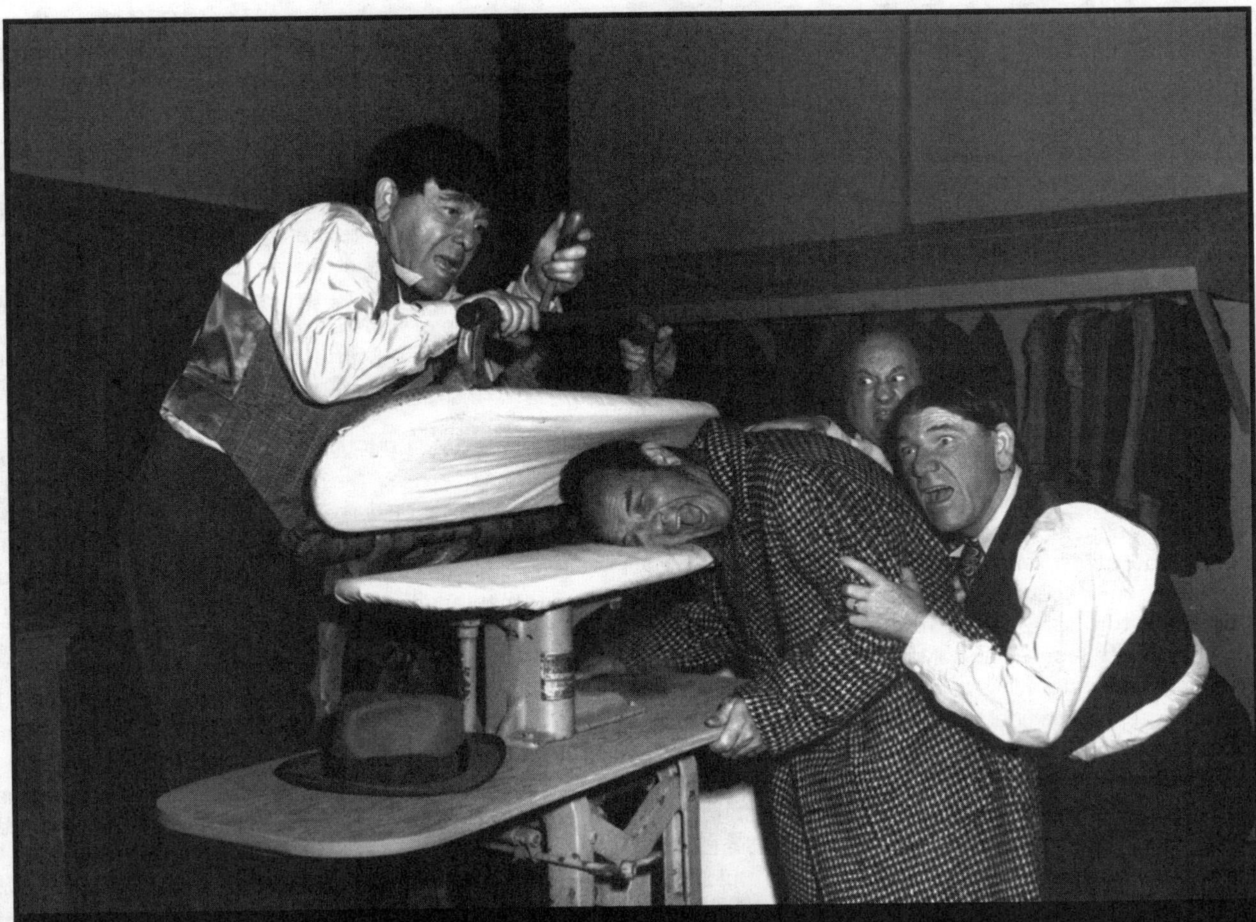

By 1953, Jules White had taken over the duties of both producing and directing all the Stooge short-film productions. To meet the demands of his contracts, he still produced eight Stooge films per year, but now he began 'refurbishing' a number of older Shemp films. This entailed re-editing the old film by inserting new segments, deleting others, and frequently transforming the story. In many instances he, with the help of brother Jack, improved upon the original, usually by tightening its narrative structure. Here in *Rip, Sew and Stitch* he refurbishes 1947's *Sing a Song of Six Pants* by making its box-comedy structure complete and allowing for more isolated Stooging.

#151 - BUBBLE TROUBLE

Studio: Columbia

Released: October 8, 1953

Running Time: 16"30'"

Credited Production Crew:

Produced & Directed by:	Jules White
Screen Play by:	Jack White
Story by:	Felix Adler
Director of Photography:	Ray Cory
Art Director:	Cary Odell
Film Editor:	Edwin Bryant
Assistant Director:	James Nicholson

Credited Cast:

Shemp Howard	
Larry Fine	
Moe Howard	
Emil Sitka	Amos Flint
Christine Mcintyre	Cerina Flint

PERSPECTIVE: *Bubble Trouble* refurbishes *All Gummed Up*. Whether intentional or not, the order of the original 1947 films, #102-*Sing a Song of Six Pants* and #103-*All Gummed Up*, is identical with the order of their respective 1953 refurbishings, #150-*Rip, Sew and Stitch* and #151-*Bubble Trouble*. And as with *Rip, Sew and Stitch*, *Bubble Trouble* is particularly interesting in that Jules White managed not just to save time and money by reworking an older story and reusing older footage but to improve upon an older film that was not ultimately satisfactory. The ending of *All Gummed Up* is one of the oddest, least relevant in any Stooge film. After inventing their youth-inducing formula and rejuvenating Mrs. Flint, the Stooges save their drug store by promising to rejuvenate Amos Flint; but they turn him into an infant and bring the story line to a close four minutes before the films ends; the final quarter consists merely of their victory celebration and its a bubble-gummed cake. In 1950's *Three Hams on Rye* the Stooges spent some three minutes coughing up a feathery cake, but there they were entertaining the film's internal audience and creating success for their play and the film's plot. This ending has no such effect.

To improve *Bubble Trouble* Jules and Jack White switched the two final scenes of *All Gummed Up*, moving Amos's drinking of the Stooges' fountain-of-youth concoction from before the final bubble-blowing scene to after. By doing this they transfer the plot-negative bubble-blowing scene from the more important final position to a harmless transitional scene where it is much more palatable, like the feather-coughing sequence in *Uncivil Warriors*. To enhance the new finale, they transform Amos' metamorphosis. Instead of shrinking into an innocuous infant he theriomorphically becomes a gorilla, allowing the film to conclude with a brief, head-knocking chase sequence, a 3-man vs. gorilla-man struggle, and an ultimate Stooge triumph. And then, as so often, the Stooges screw up anyway and finish with a delightful gag which turns Moe himself into a gorilla. *Bubble Trouble* is therefore a 'director's cut' that improves upon the original release. To make room for this grand finale the Whites drop several brief sequences, most noticeably the three opening retail gags and the jumping beans and the "cotton!" exchange during the concoction sequences. But none of these gags is sorely missed since the more unified version comes to a more logical and exciting conclusion.

Bubble Trouble is the fifth of 1953's nine releases to rework an earlier film, and the improvement in technique over the course of the year is considerable. While the Whites were improving plot flow and logic, the rest of the Columbia production staff was becoming skilled at making seamless edits and making sure the costumes, sets, and props looked virtually identical with the original film. Stooge scenes, whether fresh or six years old, become interchangeable in the hands of such experienced directors, writers, editors, and art directors, just as Stooge slapstick gags have been recast, rejoined, and refurbished time and time again for over two decades.

VISUAL HUMOR (NEW FOOTAGE): The Stooges just finished dealing with a gorilla in *Spooks!*. A new gag used twice here is for both Moe and Amos to do great takes when they see a gorilla in the mirror. Result shots [besides the gorilla and youthful metamorphoses]: Moe's flattened head, and the flattened hammer. Hammering Moe's flattened head out may derive from loosening Shemp's scalp in *Tricky Dicks*; Moe's "The bells!" recalls Charles Laughton's famous bell-ringing sequence in *The Hunchback of Notre Dame* (1939). Moe making Simian faces and walking towards the camera may be an unconscious echo of the in-to-the-camera technique used for this same year's 3-D films. Other variations: twisting and untwisting Moe's foot (*Idle Roomers*); being held by the ankles and banged on the head (*Hold That Lion*); having the serum shoved into Moe's open mouth when he says "Say 'Ah!'" (*Cactus Makes Perfect*); the flower pot falling onto Shemp's head (*Heavenly Daze*); Flint punching through the door, hitting Moe's head, which hits Shemp's, which hits Larry's (*Nutty but Nice*); and using chloroform (*Three Dark Horses*). Amos' transformation into a gorilla, accomplished mostly off camera and then with a dissolve, was a technique common in contemporary horror movies, particularly Wolfman films of the 1940/1950s.

VERBAL HUMOR (NEW FOOTAGE): Since there is a gorilla, there must be a recognition sequence à la *Movie Maniacs* and *Three Missing Links*: the gorilla/Flint kicks Moe from behind; Moe blames Shemp, but the terrified Shemp can manage to say only "Honest, M-m-m-moe. I d-d-d-didn't-t d-d-do it." Moe [pointing to the gorilla]: "I suppose he did it— Nyaggh!!" Shemp's stuttering resembles the pneumatic drill-inspired stuttering in *Pardon My Backfire*. Shemp almost has a recognition sequence at the end of the film (Moe: "It would be better with two talking gorillas!" Shemp: "Yeah, but where we gonna get— No! Moe! That look in your eye! I ain't no gorilla!"). Larry then adds a throw-away line: "It's great being a gorilla - you don't have to pay any income tax!" This presages the film after next, *Income Tax Sappy*. Amos' "So you made a monkey out of me, eh?" we heard in *A Bird in the Head*. Both Amos and Cerina Flint give versions of Shemp's signature: "ee-bee-bee."

OTHER NOTES: The new footage was shot on October 13, 1952, almost exactly one year before its release. The working title was *Drugstore Dubs*. All five cast members are credited. Editing the new and old scenes together is often accomplished with fades, dissolves, and wipes, but edits within scenes are seamless. Laurel & Hardy's *Dirty Work* (1933) also involves a youth serum and a simian, though the story is quite different from that of *Bubble Trouble*. Continuity: Shemp says he wants to get rich exhibiting "the only talking gorilla in captivity," but they were supposed to get rich from the youth serum.

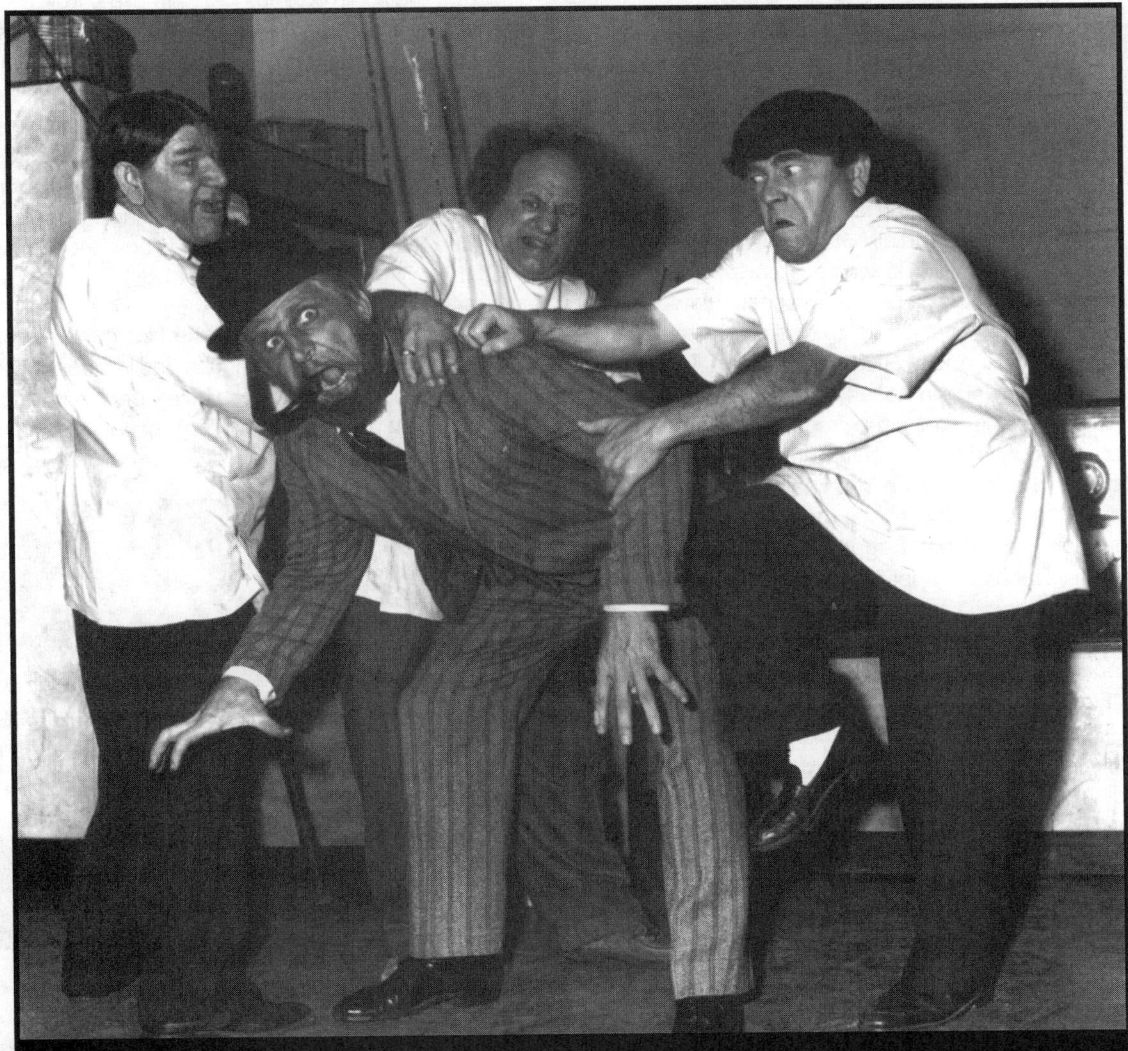

Bubble Trouble (1953) was one of Jules White's most successful refurbishing projects. The original *All Gummed Up* (1947) finished its narrative motivation a few minutes before the end of the film and then filled those minutes with chewing gum gags. Stooge physical humor sequences only rarely do not at some point advance the plot, so White transferred the gum-chewing scene to the middle of the story and added a new ending.

#152 - GOOF ON THE ROOF

Studio: Columbia

Released: December 3, 1953

Running Time: 16"23'"

Credited Production Crew:

Produced & Directed by:	Jules White
Story & Screenplay by:	Clyde Bruckman
Director of Photography:	Sam Leavitt
Art Director:	George Brooks
Film Editor:	Edwin Bryant
Assistant Director:	James Nicholson

Credited Cast:

Shemp Howard	
Larry Fine	
Moe Howard	
Frank Mitchell	Bill
Maxine Gates	Bill's wife

PERSPECTIVE: Clyde Bruckman had not written a script for the Stooges in three years, and for this final release of 1953 - in contrast to the remakes, refurbishings, and 3-D films that comprised all but one (*Tricky Dicks*) of this year's Stooge output - he wrote a script about a very contemporary subject: television, in particular, television sets, and more in particular, television set installation. Between 1952 and 1954 more than five million television sets were installed in U.S. homes in a mad dash to gain access to the top-rated *I Love Lucy, Dragnet*, and other popular shows that were being talked about at work and school, from the malt shop to the pizza parlor, and publicized in all the magazines. This was the period when a TV set began to be thought of as a necessary electronic appliance for the American home, eventually bringing the total of television sets in the US from less than 20 million in 1953 to double that number just four years later.

For most American households, the installation of their first television and its antenna was the cause of at most a little frustration or a minor additional expense. But dismantling the TV set itself, throwing vital parts away, almost smashing a helper over the head with the picture tube, bending the control knob, hammering holes in the wall, starting a fire, electrocuting yourself, knocking down the chimney, and falling through the roof into the living room, not to mention breaking up a young marriage, were complications and damages only the likes of Stooges could create while doing a TV installation. Previously in *Love at First Bite* and *Corny Casanovas* we saw the influence of television sitcoms on Stooge short-films of the early 1950s, and now just like Riley and Lucy the Stooges themselves live in a home - albeit not their own - in which to install a television. Typically, they screw the whole thing up, but how ironic it is that the Stooges who were to have a whole second career of popularity from the late 1950s to the present thanks to television broadcasts of their films could not even install a TV set without ruining it and the house in which their own situation comedy takes place.

Plotwise [a *bona fide* 1950s adverb], the Stooges are house-sitting for Bill who will return with his bride this same day - a comic time constraint - and out of genuine sincerity they volunteer to install his television and clean his house. The latter causes the first six minutes of mayhem with Dutch doors, a bucket of water, and a bar of soap providing just about all the Stooges need to booby-trap the entrance to the kitchen; in fact, the water-bucket-on-the-head result shot is used so many times that Shemp sees Larry in the same predicament and asks ironically: "Is that me?" Once the TV installation disaster begins - brought on by Shemp losing the ring his girl friend found in a Cracker Jack box - we notice similarities with *A Plumbing We Will Go*: isolated Stooges wreaking separate havocs to destroy a house, confusing electricity and water, and falling through a ceiling. But this is no society party; Bill and his new bride come home to find this a nightmarish television situation comedy for them.

VISUAL HUMOR: Because the film consists of two gag scenarios - cleaning the house and installing the TV - most of the physical gags have to rely on the physicality itself and not on driving the plot. This creates some awkward, unmotivated moments, for instance, when Shemp or

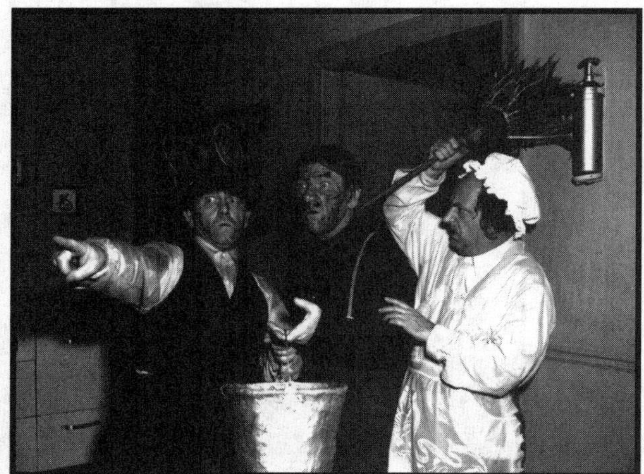

Larry sit on the floor with a bucket on their head; the gag is over, it effects nothing else, and we have to wait for the next gag. The resulting choppiness puts pressure on each individual gag to stand on its own comic merits, which does not always work. The gag scenarios frequently require the Stooges to be separated, so Shemp by himself loses his ring, Larry by himself catches his finger in the phone, and Moe by himself eats the soap sandwich.

The use of the Dutch doors is a welcome addition to Stoogedom. We saw sliding doors featured in *A Snitch in Time* and a swinging door in *Listen, Judge* and *Gents in a Jam*. Other new gags: Shemp trying to "fan the fire out"; Moe shoving the hose down Shemp's pants; and Larry lighting his own nose. New slapstick: Moe giving Shemp three nose bonks and shaking his chin while still holding his nose. Bill's overweight fiancée is a character type we saw already in *Hoi Polloi*. But having her pick Bill up is a new gag; it is set up nicely with Rosebud's "But Bill, darling, a bride never crosses her threshold by herself." Bill: "You're right, little dumplin'". Another result shot: the handle of the brush through Shemp's ears. Moe squirting the fire-extinguisher liquid into his mouth and spitting it onto the fire is a variation on the old gag of not being able to squeeze something out (*3 Dumb Clucks*). Since *Soup to Nuts* the Stooges have eaten odd com-binations of food. Here Moe enjoys his soap sandwich ("Heavenly!") and a drink of vinegar. Larry strikes his match on Shemp's neck as he did in *Spooks!*. Other variations: catching the bucket handle on Moe's throat (*Fright Night*); zipping out of pajamas, being fully dressed underneath (*Rockin' Thru the Rockies*); Larry tripping and dumping the water all over Moe and Shemp (*Back to the Woods*); scooting along the floor on smoking rears (*Heavenly Daze*); Moe putting Larry's chin on his fist and his elbow on his knee (*I Can Hardly Wait*); Larry running towards the fire with the hose and doing a flip when the hose gets stuck (*Out West*); pulling back the covers to reveal Stooge heads at the foot of the bed (*Pardon My Clutch*); and sleeping to open a film (*Movie Maniacs*).

VERBAL HUMOR: Because the Stooges are alone and fight against one another, most of Bruckman's verbal gags are epithets ("mutton-head"; "nitwit"; "ya' snoring hyenas"), curses (Shemp: "I hope you choke!"), insults (Shemp: "He always had a swelled head!"), accusations (Moe: "Stop doin' it *for* me! You're doin' it *to* me!"; Larry: "Get out of my way when I'm fightin' fire and quit blockin' the water!"), and threats (Shemp: "Why?" Moe: "Get another bucketful of water and finish up the mopping or you'll find out 'why' and how!"; Moe: "Say, did you say you were hungry?" Shemp: "I'm starved...Oh I'd love it!" Moe: "You got it!"). Bruckman also penned self-contained Stooges ironies (Shemp: "I nearly ruined the ring my girl won for me in a Cracker Jack box"; Larry: "I need a longer arm or a shorter wall"; Larry: "I smell smoke. You chewin' tobacco?").... Other bits of Stooge irony come when Moe asks Larry about the holes in the wall (Moe: "How you going to explain this to Bill?" Larry: "Woodpeckers!"); when Shemp sees the fire ("Hey Moe, what's cookin'?...If we only had some marshmallows!"); and at the conclusion (Larry: "Let her go, Bill." Moe: "Sure, Bill, then the four of us can live in peace and harmony."). Shemp's "I fall down" we last heard in *Crash Goes the Hash*. Moe comparing the holy wall to "Swiss cheese" we first heard in *Cookoo Cavaliers*.

OTHER NOTES: This film was a reworking of Vernon & Quillan's *Let Down Your Aerial* (1949), though in 1949 there were less than 2 million TV sets in the United States. All five cast members are credited. Frank Mitchell [Bill] had decades earlier formed the Mitchell & Durant vaudeville team, filmed in Fox's anti-Depression revue *Stand Up and Cheer* (1934). Maxine Gates [Bill's wife] will appear in several subsequent Stooge films. This is Clyde Bruckman's final script for the Stooges; he had written or worked on twenty-nine of them. In two years he would commit suicide. At the end of his endurance, Bruckman had come to White for work just the day before he shot himself (using a gun borrowed from friend Buster Keaton); White had nothing for him, but was not aware of Bruckman's extreme desperation [*Bruskin* 77]. White's usual pecking order for writing assignments was Felix Adler, Jack White, then Bruckman. In 1952 Shemp had suffered a mild stroke, but its effects are barely visible in subsequent films.

Between 1952 and 1954, more than five million television sets were installed in American homes. The Stooges do their worst at installing theirs in 1953's *Goof on the Roof*, once again proving just how industrious, up-to-date, and incompetent they can be.

1954

Income Tax Sappy • Musty Musketeers

Pals and Gals • Knutzy Knights

Shot in the Frontier • Scotched in Scotland

#153 - INCOME TAX SAPPY

Studio: Columbia

Released: February 4, 1954

Running Time: 16"28'"

Credited Production Crew:

Produced & Directed by:	Jules White
Story & Screenplay by:	Felix Adler
Director of Photography:	Ray Cory
Art Director:	George Brooks
Film Editor:	Edwin Bryant
Assistant Director:	Abner Singer

Credited Cast:

Shemp Howard	
Larry Fine	
Moe Howard	
Marjorie Liszt	Sis
Benny Rubin	Mr. Cash
Nanette Bordeaux	Mrs. Cash

Uncredited Cast:

Vernon Dent	tax agent
Joe Palma	tax agent

PERSPECTIVE: Like its predecessor *Goof on the Roof*, this first of only six 1954 releases depicts the Stooges in a contemporary setting reflective of life in the early mid-1950s. Contemplating whether to buy a house (the post-war housing boom and 'suburban sprawl' was still in progress) and living together with 'Sis,' they discuss tax deductions and spend the first half of the film filling out their tax forms while making jokes about not paying taxes,

deducting charitable, medical, automobile, and bartender expenses as well as bad debts, while also fighting with a bowling ball, instant glue, a hot dog sandwich, and each other. Nothing is mentioned about their means of employment or source of income, and nothing is mentioned about going to work; what is important is only the scenario inside and about their domicile.

Just as the subject matter of the previous film was inspired by the television installation boom occurring at the time, so the comedic style of both these films is clearly influenced by the television content that was being broadcast every evening. Television situation comedies like *I Love Lucy, I Married Joan*, and *The Adventures of Ozzie and Harriett* were filmed on sound stages made to look like American homes, and even *The Jack Benny Show*, starring a Stooge contemporary, included a domestic format. These shows were reforming short-subject film comedy because each of them took place in an American home, and each week's episode told a different story. This is why these two Stooge films are so house bound, and this is why these two films put the Stooges in the sort of domestic situation they only occasionally found themselves in the past. Such confinement inside the house explains why a "Sis" is written into the script, and it accounts for why so much of the slapstick in these two films consists of revenge-oriented paybacks. The Stooges who have traveled back to the Middle Ages and visited Egypt and Anemia in their films, have often brought their comedy out into the world to express its truest genius. But the comic perspective in 1953-1954 was domesticated, and if you lock up Stooges together, they will end up hitting each other.

The second half of the film puts the Stooges in the wealthy fiscal situation they enjoyed in *Healthy, Wealthy and Dumb*, *A Missed Fortune,* and *Heavenly Daze*. Having made a fortune by anticipating H. & R. Block and today's omnipresent tax accountants and lawyers, they are lavish with their money - throwing away a fifty dollar bill and burning a thousand dollar bill - and entertain one of their best customers. A fine meal always provides the Stooges with an ideal comedy situation and inspirational props, and thanks to some clever writing, Moe's mixology and Larry's turkey carving - two Stooge staples - lead directly to cutting off and hiding Mr. Cash's beard, and with Shemp's food throwing they in turn force Cash to reveal himself as a federal agent. The subsequent chase scene is limited in scope. It is not at all an extended multi-room chase, and one of the reasons for this is that for the first time in many years the Stooges are caught willfully committing a serious crime. Yes, in this film the Stooges are the crooks, so how much chasing could there be before they *really* got into trouble? They were by their own confessions guilty, and this trend will continue in subsequent films of 1954.

VISUAL HUMOR: As in *Love at First Bite*, being confined at home makes the Stooges break into extended slapstick sequences. In the first of three Moe gives a backwards bonk and a gouge, Shemp hand-waves Moe up and down, Moe pounds Shemp and bonks him, turning him sideways so he can kick him in the rear into the breakfront from which a bowling ball crashes over Shemp's head; then

Moe puts a pen in Larry's nose and tells him to hold it while he goes over to Shemp only to get a piece of the ball ("Here's a nice big piece." Moe: "Let me have it!") broken over his own head. In the second, Moe zips Larry's scar up and down half a dozen times, so Larry threatens with his fist, which Moe slaps, circling it around and hitting Larry on the head; then Moe pulls Shemp's ear and slaps him over to get him a cup of coffee, but Shemp picks up the handle from a broken cup and pours the coffee into his pants. The third has Moe going to slug Shemp but hitting Larry instead; Larry protests, so Moe grabs his nose with a large pair of scissors (Shemp: "Looks like a V-8!"), bonking Shemp with the scissors; Larry gets even by squirting instant glue on Moe's hand, which Larry slaps, making it circle and stick to Larry's hair, so Moe rips out a wad of hair and with a nose tweak ("Remind me to kill you later!") sends Larry to make him a sandwich.

New slapstick: Moe giving a backwards bonk and a gouge combo. Shemp's tuxedo front rolling up is an old gag but a Stooge first. Result shot: Mr. Cash with lettuce covering his head, eyebrows and chin. Larry's missing with the kitchen sheers and sheering off half of Mr. Cash's beard off is an expansion of Curly's scissors slipping into Moe's rear in *Slippery Silks*. Shemp squirting a fountain pen into his own face resembles Moe's struggle with the fire extinguisher in the previous film. Other variations: a bowling ball rolling onto Shemp's head (*Three Loan Wolves*); Moe putting the pen in Larry's nose and telling him to hold it (*Squareheads of the Round Table*); Shemp imitating a calculator (*No Census, No Feeling*); a sandwich biting the eater's nose (*Pardon My Scotch*); a living hot dog (*Malice in the Palace*); instant glue (*Healthy, Wealthy and Dumb*; the hair gag also recalls the gum in *Love at First Bite*); drinking ink (*Three Missing Links*); throwing away a fifty-dollar bill (*Hold That Lion*); hot pepper making smoke come out of Moe's mouth (*Playing the Ponies*); and the live crustacean in Larry's soup (*Dutiful but Dumb*).

VERBAL HUMOR: Felix Adler wrote many plot-related tax jokes (Larry: "Makin' out the income tax is nothing...When I get through, the income tax collector will get nothin'!"; Moe: "You know it's funny how people love to gyp on their income tax." Shemp: "That's because it's such a cinch. They never can catch smart guys like us!"; Larry: "How much can I deduct for charity?" Moe: "$3000...but you gotta put down who got the money." Larry: "*I* got it!" Moe: "Oh you'll never get away with that!" Larry: "Why not? Charity begins at home!"; Shemp: "Have you any bad debts?" Moe: "I owe Uncle Jake $1500." Shemp: "Then deduct it from your income tax." Moe: "How can I? I owe *him*." Shemp: "Do you expect to pay it?" Moe: "No." Shemp: "Then it's a bad debt!"; Moe: "How much are you gonna deduct for dependents?" Shemp: "$4400." Larry: "That's eleven dependents! Who are they?" Shemp: "My ex-wife and ten bartenders!")... Related to the tax jokes is Larry's "zipper and hem-stitch" scar ("the zipper is in case I need another operation") which he shows in response to Moe asking about the $2500 he is deducting for his three operations. It leads to one of the extended slapstick sequences.

Benny Rubin's presence means language gags, including Moe's pig Latin ("Arry-lay, ix-nay the eard-bay) as well as Rubin's German accent ("He made a boo-boo...I don't like viniminees [vitamins] anyvay....zalt, mustache, A-number-six-seven-sideways, and condimentees"; cf. Larry's "Oh I'm sorry mine Herring, I mean, Mein Heir!") To make his revelation convincing, Rubin's accent changes very abruptly: "Vat have you done vith my beautiful beard?!...Look what you've done! You've ruined a perfectly good fifty-dollar beard!". Epithets: Moe has used "imbecile" in many paradoxical ways when another Stooge thinks of something clever, but his "You're a smart imbecile" here is a new turn of phrase. Moe calls Shemp and Larry "laughing hyenas"; Mr. Cash he calls "a dirty double-crossing rat". Other insults: Sis: "Don't be chumps"; Cash: "What is wrong with you idiots?!"; more ironic is Cash's "You are a very loose eater!".

References: Mr. Cash's 'A-number six, seven sideways' is a Stooge way of saying 'A-1 Sauce'; Larry's "Charity begins at home" comes from the *New Testament* and the ancient Roman comedian Terence (*Andria* 651). Moe's betting instructions for the third race at Santa Anita ("Five across...that's five, five, and five...fifteen cents altogether") recall his betting instructions in *Love at First Bite*. Larry's "Why don't you call your shots?" was used recently in *Pardon My Backfire*. Other variations: Shemp: "Looks like a V-8!" (*Slippery Silks*); and Moe [before double slapping Larry and Shemp]: "Why didn't you think of that?!" (*Dizzy Doctors*.) A weakness in the script is Moe's reaction to the animated hot dog: "Now I've seen everything!"

OTHER NOTES: The release title is a homonym for 'Income Tax Happy'; The working title was *Tax Saps*. It is unclear what relation Margie Liszt plays to the Stooges. The *Scrapbook* calls her Moe's wife; Larry calls her "Sis." It is difficult to tell if she is wearing a wedding ring. For the second film in a row Moe gives a Curly-esque "Hhmm!". Moe's "wonderful dressing" recipe: oil, vinegar, salt, lots of cayenne pepper, and crumpanella. The punchline to the calculating scene in *Cactus Makes Perfect* refers to deducting taxes from income; in *Income Tax Sappy* it is to deduct income from paying taxes. As always, Stooges do not calculate very well: 100,000 X 7.5¢ = $7500, not "39 dollars, 57 and a half cents."

#154 - MUSTY MUSKETEERS

Studio: Columbia

Released: May 13, 1954

Running Time: 15"55'"

Credited Production Crew:

Produced & Directed by:	Jules White
Screenplay by :	Jack White
Story by:	Felix Adler
Director of Photography:	Gert Anderson
Art Director:	Ross Bellah
Film Editor:	Edwin Bryant
Assistant Director:	Irving Moore

Credited Cast:

Shemp Howard	
Larry Fine	
Moe Howard	
Vernon Dent	King Cole
Phil Van Zandt	Mergatroyd the Magician

Uncredited Cast:

Ruth Godfrey	Lilly
Theila Darin	Tillie
Norma Randall	Millie
Charles 'Heine' Conklin	guard
Virginia Hunter	Princess Alicia [stock footage]
Sherry O'Neill	magician's assistant [stock footage]
Joe Palma	guard [stock footage]

PERSPECTIVE: *Musty Musketeers*, the first of four refurbished films released in 1954, revisits *Fiddlers Three*, originally released in 1948. Jules White was now advancing into the second full year of refurbishing Shemp films, and although this is but a minor step beyond 1953's *Rip, Sew and Stitch* and *Bubble Trouble* which derived from 1947 films, it illustrates to us forty-plus years later how thoroughly White was committed at the time to this new means of Stooge film production. We have seen how adept White had become at producing refurbished films that were, at least insofar as the narrative was concerned, superior to their originals [e.g. *Bubble Trouble*], so now in 1954 the whole Columbia Shemp corpus - over four dozen film to date - becomes his library of raw materials.

To refurbish *Fiddlers Three* producer/director White decided to add both a Stooge romance and a final sword fight. *Fiddlers Three* was one of the longer Shemp films at over seventeen minutes, so White made room for the new sequences by eliminating the original introductory sequence which established the Stooges in their roles as court jesters singing nursery rhymes to 'Old King Cole of Coleslaw-vania. Although these music 'videos' were quite enjoyable in the original film, they put the plot in suspension, and White's goal in this and in most of the subsequent refurbished films was to fit the new version with a more coherent plot. At the beginning of *Fiddlers Three* the Stooges had asked the king permission to get married, but it was never made clear whom the Stooges wished to marry, nor did we ever hear about their marriage again. But at the beginning of *Musty Musketeers* we now see the Stooges go a-calling, a-courting, and a-proposing, which provides a specific reason for them to visit the king, ask his permission to marry the beloved Tillie, Lilly, and Millie, toast their engagement, and only then find themselves involved in helping the king recover his daughter. By establishing this romance at the beginning of the film White can substitute a new and delightfully silly conclusion to replace the 'Pied Piper' ending of the original. The old ending, without the earlier nursery rhyme 'videos' and with the era of 'Million Dollar Legs' six years in the past, would no longer be comprehensible to viewers, particularly since the Stooge audience in the 1950s was mostly children who flocked to 'Kiddie Matinees' on Saturday mornings. Now to bring the whole package to a logical conclusion, 'Tillie-eth,' 'Lilly-eth,' and 'Millie-eth' rush in to hug their beloveds, unfortunately bonking heads and knocking all six of them CUCKOO.

The final sword fight contains plenty of densely packed gags which add to the classic box interior scenes of the original. Old King Cole 'calls for' his sword but gets it in the rear, punches himself 'in the labonza,' and knocks out his courtier in the excitement. Larry wipes out all the bad guys with the vessel he finds stuck on his left hand. And Shemp, in one of the great Stoogizations of all time, locks swords with the evil magician, comes face to face with him, and - instead of issuing a verbal challenge as Errol Flynn, Zorro, or countless movie heroes would do - bites his nose with a loud CRUNCH.

VISUAL HUMOR (NEW FOOTAGE): The Stooges have been knocking on foreheads instead of doors since *Calling All Curs*, but here they knock on all three maidens' foreheads. Other variations: biting the magician's nose [*Uncivil Warriors*]; using a metal vase to conk heads [*Spooks!*]; tossing fruit from the end of a sword [*Malice in the Palace*]; tossing an anchor off ahorse [*Uncivil Warriors*]; and toasting and breaking their mugs [*Woman Haters*].

VERBAL HUMOR (NEW MATERIAL): In picking up where Felix Adler left off in the original film, Jack White applied the '-eth' suffix and other linguistic archaisms to the fist game [Shemp: "See-eth this?...Ouch-eth! Ouch-eth!"] and other slapstick variations [Larry: "Moe-eth! Art thou okay? [SLAP] He is okay."], to the maidens ["Moe-eth! Shempeth! Larry-eth!" Moe: "Tillie-eth!" Shemp: "Lilly-eth!" Larry: "Millie-eth!"), to typical Stooge Brooklynese (Moe: "What a swell joint-eth!"), and to Moe's epithets ("Thou art a matzah-head!"). Shemp also offers an archaic neologism (Moe: "We pray permission to marry our sweethearts forthwith—" Shemp: "If not forthwither—"). In contrast is the contemporary bebop slang (Girls [unison]: "Zoot! That's real George!" Larry: "Dig that crazy talk, man!"; Moe: "Truckin' on down, man!"; and the horse named 'Zoot') first heard in *Spooks!*, and contemporary boxing ring slang (King: "Hit him in the labonza!"). As in many Stooge romances and in another castle-comedy (*Squareheads of the Round Table*), the Stooges sing a song prefaced by a major triad ("Ohhh— A-calling we do come/To woo our maidens fair/We bring them flowers and while away hours/[Shemp:] But get ye not in their hair!).

OTHER NOTES: Background music from the credits continues into the first scene until the Stooges toss anchor. The joins between the old and new footage here are particularly seamless. This is the first of the three 1948 'castle' films to be refurbished; the other two, *Squareheads of the Round Table* and *The Hot Scots*, will be refurbished as *Knutzy Knights* and *Scotched in Scotland* later this same year. Of the three original 1948 films, *Fiddlers Three* was the only one produced and directed by Jules White. This seems to have been the last of Vernon Dent's five dozen Stooge roles. A diabetic, he went blind shortly after this film (he was fully blind by the time of Shemp's funeral in 1955) and died of a heart attack in 1963. The tradition that reports he was a Christian Scientist is incorrect. For a brief biography, see *The 3 Stooges Journal* 76 (1995) 6, 14. The nursery rhyme theme of the original was more appropriate for an earlier era; 1933, for example, produced both W. C. Fields as Humpty Dumpty in *Alice in Wonderland* and the Stooges' own *Nertsery Rhymes*.

Musty Musketeers was one of four refurbished films released in 1954. Deriving from 1948's *Fiddlers Three*, it further develops the Stooge romance with Tillie, Lilly, and Millie ('Tillie-eth,' 'Lilly-eth,' and 'Millie-eth') while scaling down the nursery rhyme elements of the original.

#155 - PALS AND GALS

Studio: Columbia

Released: June 3, 1954

Running Time: 16"41'"

Credited Production Crew:

Produced & Directed by:	Jules White
Screen Play by:	Jack White
Story by:	Clyde Bruckman
Director of Photography:	Gert Anderson
Art Director:	Ross Bellah
Film Editor:	Edwin Bryant
Assistant Director:	Irving Moore

Credited Cast:

Shemp Howard	
Larry Fine	
Moe Howard	
Christine McIntyre	Nell
George Chesebro	Quirt
Norman Willes	Doc Barker [stock footage]

Uncredited Cast:

Norma Randall	Zelle
Ruth Godfrey	Belle
Stanley Blystone	colonel [new and stock footage]
Frank Ellis	Jake [stock footage]
Vernon Dent	doctor [stock footage]
Charles 'Heine' Conklin	bartender [stock footage]
Joe Palma	gang member
Blackie Whiteford	cowboy

PERSPECTIVE: *Pals and Gals* is a refurbishing project, but unlike most of them, this one revisits two different films. Jules White had done something similar in 1946 when Curly was ill, splicing in footage from both *In the Sweet Pie and Pie* and *Hoi Polloi* to fill out several gag scenarios for *Half-Wits Holiday*. But White did not use two different films for *Pals and Gals* because of Stooge illness; he used two different films because he was now availing himself of the entire Stooge corpus for his refurbished productions, as we saw in the previous film, *Three Musketeers*. Refurbishing was now the most common method of Stooge film production: in 1953 five of the nine releases were refurbished films; in 1954 four of the six were refurbished, and in 1955 six of eight. And since White's goal was not merely to save time and money by editing old footage into new films but actually to improve upon the original film, combining footage from two different films would now become a viable means of piecing a new Stooge release together if it meant producing a better product.

Primarily comprising footage from 1947's *Out West*, *Pals and Gals* concludes with footage and a concept from 1937's *Goofs and Saddles*. This is particularly interesting since the previous 1950s refurbishings either borrowed footage from previous Shemp films or reshot an older Curly script. *Pals and Gals* is the first refurbishing project to use both a Shemp film - *Out West* was the second Shemp film - as well as footage from a Curly film. This is a new blend. For *Up in Daisy's Penthouse* White took a Curly film [*3 Dumb Clucks*] and completely reshot it with Shemp taking Curly's role. Here, though, White reuses Shemp footage from *Out West*, edits in non-Curly footage from *Goofs and Saddles*, and reshoots some sequences from *Goofs and Saddles* with Shemp playing Curly's role.

The joined footage looks very smooth to the unknowing eye, and the film proceeds in an orderly narrative. White excises the scenes with the cavalry and the Arizona Kid - Jacques O'Mahoney was involved with such TV Westerns as *The Range Rider* at the time of the re-shooting - and instead places Nell's two sisters, Zelle and Belle, in the downstairs jail cell, bringing in a romantic element like the one added into *Musty Musketeers*. With the US Cavalry scenes excised, White had to replace the dynamite/Cavalry footage which brought *Out West* to a close, so he edited in the wacky finale of *Goofs and Saddles*, reshot the wagon interior scenes with Shemp, and made new footage of the monkey Gattling-gunning the Stooges into their beloved's arms: "Oh! Oh! Oooohhhhh!" Interestingly, in reworking the plot of *Out West* White replaces Doc Barker with Quirt [Jack Chesebro, who played the same role in *Out West*]. Doc dies of a heart attack brought on either by Moe's 'Ickey-may' or an instant pneumonia caused by Shemp soaking him with the fire hose; [Larry mentions pneumonia here but not in *Out West*]. In either case, a criminal charge would be murder or manslaughter, so in two of the last three films the writers felt comfortable inventing Stooge pranks that were actually serious crimes!

VISUAL HUMOR (NEW FOOTAGE): In *Goofs and Saddles*, we saw the US Cavalry riding backwards; here we see the gang members riding backwards. Curly's pistol was stuck in his holster in *Horses' Collars*, and in *Three Troubledoers* Curly drew his pistol only to have the whole holster come with it. Here Shemp tries to withdraw his pistol from his holster but shoots his foot. The Stooges disguising themselves as 'gentlemen' (Larry: "I'm from the South!") with long coats, hats, mustaches, and cigars derives from their several southern films (e.g. *Uncivil Warriors*, *Uncivil War Birds*) and their old 'Southern Gentlemen' characterization with Ted Healy (*Plane Nuts*). As often, the Stooges' first step in escaping is for Moe to gouge the main crook, here Quirt; previously Moe gouged Wick in *Three Dark Horses*, the idol in *Hula-la-la*, and Ghinna Rumma in *Malice in the Palace*. When he is

For *Pals and Gals* (1954) Jules White varied the refurbishing formula by using two previous films, Shemp's *Out West* (1947) and Curly's *Goofs and Saddles* (1937). To do so he had to reshoot this wagon scene originally shot with Curly.

captured, Larry ("I was only kiddin'!") is carried right into the camera, similar to a Curly gimmick in *Calling All Curs*.

VERBAL HUMOR (NEW FOOTAGE): The only new verbal gags here are Shemp's throw-away reaction to the monkey ("A gorilla! Where are we - Africa?"), and the rhyming introduction of the girls (Nell: "Zelle! Belle!" Stooges [unison]: "Well! Well!")... Shemp picks up the Arizona Kid's lingo with: "I'll dry gulch that Doc Barker! That's what I'll do, gal!". When Larry is in jail and worries about being shot at sundown, Moe tells him "Relax, kid. You're practically free!"; in *Out West* he had said "Not if you ain't still in there they won't!".

In the previous film (*Musty Musketeers*) the old knocking-on-the-forehead routine was extended from one victim to all three maidens. Here Curly's painful "Oh! Oh! Oh! Ohhhh-llook!" which Larry transformed into a romantic "Oh! Oh! Oh! Ooooohhhhh!" in *Pardon My Backfire* is now used by all three Stooges to bring the film to its romantic close. There were several unison lines in the previous film, and now they say Shemp's "He and subsequently in *Mummy's Dummies*, *Self-Made Maids*, and *Loose Loot*) in unison. Other variations: Larry offering to the gang members politely "After you, gentlemen" (*All Gummed Up*), Larry's (usually Moe's) "I'm gonna get a cheap lawyer!" (*Monkey Businessmen*).

OTHER NOTES: The working title was *Cuckoo Westerners*. The footage of Doc Barker is credited on screen to Norman Willes, a.k.a. Norman Willis, although his stage name, which was used in *Out West*, was Jack Norman. So that the pre-chase scenes would match up with the chase scenes from *Goofs and Saddles*, Stanley Blystone, who had played the protagonist Longhorn Pete in *Goofs and Saddles*, was asked to don a costume and play a non-speaking role as one of the gang members here in *Pals and Gals*. That way there would not be a blatant mismatch when Blystone is seen [in the old footage] yelling from the window after the Stooges jump onto the wagon and flee. Jules White often took care in making such matches; he used a moviola on the set to make sure new footage matched the old, and he once reportedly ordered Emil Sitka to lose 10 pounds in one week so he would match some earlier footage.

#156 - KNUTZY KNIGHTS

Studio: Columbia

Released: September 2, 1954

Running Time: 15"22'"

Credited Production Crew:

Produced & Directed by:	Jules White
[Story:	Edward Bernds]
Screenplay by:	Felix Adler
Director of Photography:	Ray Cory
Art Director:	Carl Anderson
Film Editor:	Edwin Bryant
Assistant Director:	Irving Moore

Credited Cast:

Shemp Howard	
Larry Fine	
Moe Howard	
Jacques O'Mahoney	Cedric
Christine McIntyre	Elaine
Philip Van Zandt	Black Prince

Uncredited Cast:

Vernon Dent	King Arthur
Harold Brauer	Sir Satchel [stock footage]
Joe Garcia	soldier [stock footage]
Douglas Coppin	soldier
Joe Palma	soldier [in stock footage]; Sir Satchell
Ruth Godfrey	handmaiden

PERSPECTIVE: *Knutzy Knights* incorporates mostly footage from 1948's *Squareheads of the Round Table* but differs from the previous two refurbished films in not adding a Stooge love interest. The original film already featured a non-Stooge love interest between Cedric and Elaine, but so did the original (*Out West*) of the previous film (*Pals and Gals*). The difference is that the romance between the Arizona Kid and Nell could be replaced by the romance between the Stooges and Nell, Zelle, and Belle, whereas the romance between Cedric and Elaine could not be replaced. It lies at the core of the damsel-in-distress plot that drives *Squareheads of the Round Table*, and to replace it would mean eliminating perhaps the most memorable musical sequence in all of Stoogedom - the serenade 'Oh Elaine, Come Out Tonight' sung to the music of Donizetti's *Lucia di Lammermoor* ("the sextet from 'Lucy'" in *Micro-Phonies*) outside Elaine's balcony. Maintaining the essential Cedric-Elaine romance and the Stooges-save-the-damsel plot, Jules White and Felix Adler simply shored up several holes in Edward Bernds' original script which left us unsure whether the king or Cedric or both were to be killed when the trumpets sounded. The final scene of the film is therefore entirely rewritten not so much to change the plot or to make it more amusing but to clarify it.

In *Squareheads of the Round Table* Moe tells Larry and Shemp in a Stooge "yes" pattern what he has overheard the Black Prince telling Sir Satchell: "You know that Black Prince character, the guy that tried to kill our pal Cedric?" Larry & Shemp: "Yes!" Moe: "Well he's gonna kill the king." Larry & Shemp: "No!" Moe: "Yes!" But in the finale there was no mention of any assassination of the king. Now in Adler's revised *Knutzy Knights* the Stooges, dressed in armor, hide with Elaine and overhear Sir Satchell tell the Black Prince: "When the guards hear the fanfare of the trumpets, Cedric's head will fall." Black Prince: "Good! Good! And when the trumpets sound the second time, you shall strike the king down." Jules White thought that including this correction was so critical that he inserted it into the original armament-room scenes where Harold Brauer played Sir Satchell and Joe Palma played a guard - just a few minutes before the new footage in which Joe Palma plays Sir Satchell.

The exposition contains the most innovative rewriting. In *Squareheads of the Round Table* it was left mostly to the Stooges and Cedric to reveal the plot. But Adler now has the Stooges perform a dramatic prologue, a play-within-a-play that parallels the queen's own predicament, a literary device that worked well enough for Shakespeare's *Hamlet*, so why not for *Knutzy Knights*? While explaining the plot it allows Larry to convey Shakespearean emotional extremes from laughter ("tee-hee-hee-hee-hee") to pathos ("boo-hoo-hoo-hoo"), and like *Hamlet*'s play-within-a-play which reenacted an assassination carried out by pouring liquid poison into the sleeping king's ear, this one features an innocuous liquid comically sprayed from Larry's anachronistic eye glasses onto Moe's windshield wiper helmet.

VISUAL HUMOR (NEW FOOTAGE): The play-within-a-play has Moe wearing a fake mustache and a Van-Dyke goatee, Larry in a woman's gown, blonde wig, and glasses, and Shemp with a large oriental mustache. As tears spray out from Larry's glasses all over Moe's windshield wiper helmet, Shemp does the breast-stroke. The blacksmith scene of *Squareheads of the Round Table* established the Stooges as troubadours. Because they are no longer troubadours, different gags had to be used. Instead of Cedric crunching all three Stooges' hands in a "One for all!...every man for himself!" oath which accompanied troubadour dialogue, now Cedric crunches only Shemp's hand; and instead of Shemp joking about a helmet protecting him from a tomato and rock throwing audience he now has a barking helmet (a counterpart to the windshield wiper helmet). Shemp's swollen hand derives from *Loose Loot*, the other two Stooges shying away from a crushing handshake derives from *Gents in a Jam*. Cedric slapping Moe and Larry on the back causing them to bonk their heads together resembles Doc Barker slapping Shemp real hard in *Out West/Pals and Gals;* later Cedric bonks the Black Prince's and Sir Satchell's heads together five times... Other variations: the Stooges helping a weeping woman (*Oily to Bed, Oily to Rise*; *So Long, Mr. Chumps*); and Shemp waving his hand under the handmaiden's chin (*A Pain in the Pullman*). Result shot: Shemp in the helmet and chest pieces.

VERBAL HUMOR (NEW FOOTAGE): The opening subtitles of *Squareheads of the Roundtable* ('In Days of Old'/ 'When Knights were Bold' / 'and Suits were made of Iron') is changed to: "In Days of Old / when Knights were Bold / The Guys were hot / But the Gals were cold'; the 'Three Blind Mice' theme song continues over this script. Before the Stooges perform their play-within-a-play they offer a unison, ungrammatical chant ("We are troubadours one-two-three/Why did my lady send for we?") in the same rhythm as the moron chant of *Half-Wits Holiday*, and an introductory verse: "Good morn to thee, fair princess/Weep not or you'll get bags/ [Moe:] We hope to bring thee laughter/With buffoonery and gags." When the handmaiden says: "You must cheer her up," the Stooges respond with a pun (Larry: "We'll have her splittin' her sides." Shemp: "East side, West side, front side and back again!"), a Shakespearean gag [*Romeo and Juliet* II.ii.33 ("O Romeo, Romeo! wherefore art thou Romeo?")] (Moe: "Wherefore art thou, fair princess?" Larry: "Here I art, Art!"), an extension of an old Stooge-ism (Moe: "Recede!...and proceed!"), an insult (Moe: "I wilt, my beautiful flower - Boy! Are you ugly!..."), and epithet/name calling (Shemp: "Unhand my lass, you brazen ass!" Moe: "Be gone, you scrabble-head!") as well as Larry's melodramatic laughter and weeping.

Throughout the first scene the language is archaic (e.g. Moe: "Thou art a wet weeper!...You will be in his arms ere morning!"), later put into contrast with Larry's anachronistic "I don't understand. This routine killed 'em in Cucamonga!" A similar mixture of archaism and California geographical anachronism is the exchange between Moe and the princess (Moe: "Where can we find Cedric this village blacksmith?" Princess: "Under the spreading chestnut tree, around the corner, by the pawn shop at Pittsfield and Tonsilvania." The reference to Longfellow's spreading chestnut tree ("the village blacksmith... under the spreading chestnut tree") was recently reused in *Musty Musketeers*; the same film also reused 'Coleslaw-vania,' a parallel to the princess's 'Tonsilvania'. Another Stooge epithet: "iron-head". Prop-related armor gags: Shemp: "Get me outta this tin can. I feel like a sardine!...If I only had a can opener!" Moe: "If I had a can opener I'd open your head!". Role reversal: with his hand crunched and swollen, Shemp says Larry's line: "I'll never be able to write under water!"

OTHER NOTES: Ed Bernds wrote the original film, but credit is given only for Felix Adler's screenplay; as usual, credits are given for only the new footage. To replace the prison sequences Cedric now simply bends one of the bars to slip out of his jail cell.

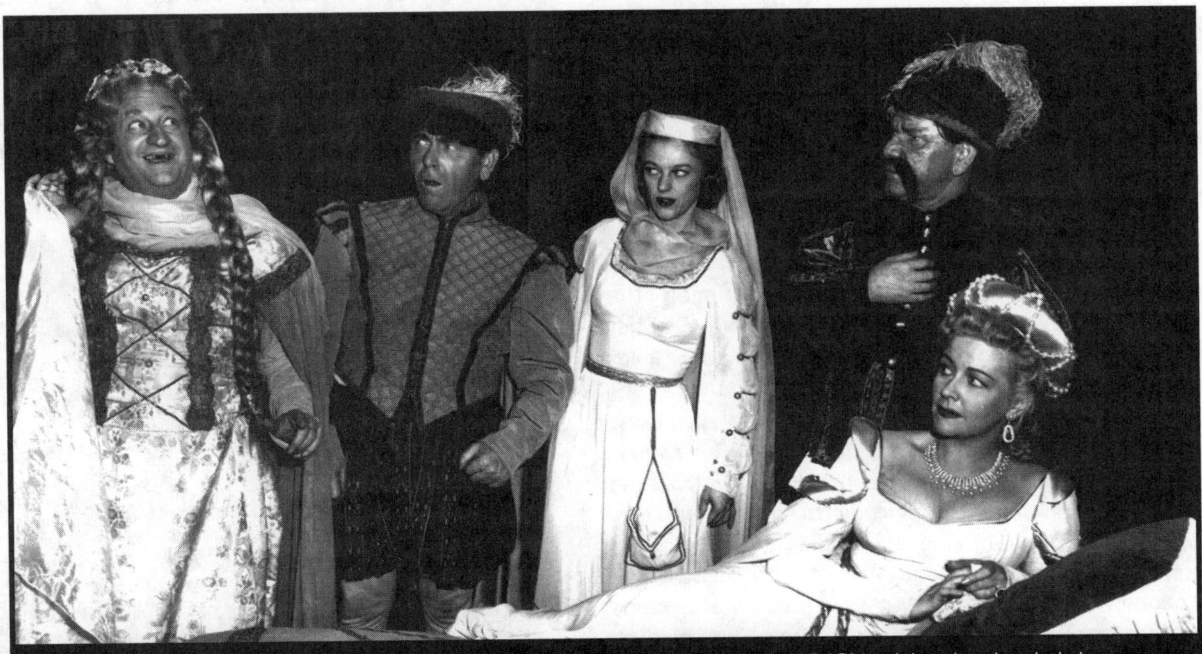

Knutzy Knights (1954) refurbishes the classic *Squareheads of the Round Table* (1948) by tightening the plot's loose ends and adding a play within a play. This theatrical motif worked in *Hamlet*, and it works here...with comic effect.

#157 - SHOT IN THE FRONTIER

Studio: Columbia

Released: October 7, 1954

Running Time: 15"52'"

Credited Production Crew:

Produced & Directed by:	Jules White
Story & Screenplay by:	Felix Adler
Director of Photography:	Ray Cory
Art Director:	George Brooks
Film Editor:	Edwin Bryant
Assistant Director:	Abner Singer

Credited Cast:

Shemp Howard
Larry Fine
Moe Howard

Uncredited Cast:

Emil Sitka	Sheriff
Vivian Mason	Ella
Theila Darin	Bella
Ruth Godfrey [White]	Stella
Joe Palma	a Noonan brother
Kenneth MacDonald	a Noonan brother
Emmett Lynn	Lem, the balladeer
Babe London	Mandy

PERSPECTIVE: In the period between 1952 and 1954 television was consuming Hollywood. *Lux Video Theater* reduced feature films to sixty-minute tele-plays, films inspired such TV series as *Topper* and *Lassie*, and Sid Caesar and Imogene Coca's *Your Show of Shows* offered parodies of films. The writers for *Your Show of Shows* included Mel Brooks and Woody Allen, both of whom would make film parodies in the 1970s, and as sketch comedy proliferated in 1954's comedy-variety shows a number of television writers regularly parodied recent Hollywood releases. This tendency spilled over to the Columbia short-subject unit which was always open to a fresh concept for its two-reeler comedies; besides, the running length of the typical two-reeler was nearly the same as that of a television sketch. *Shot in the Frontier* is such a creation, a sixteen-minute parody of Stanley Kramer's classic 1952 Western, *High Noon*.

This is not the first Stooge parody of a recent, stylish film. Their only Oscar nomination was for *Men in Black*, a parody of *Men in White*, and *Heavenly Daze*, an early Shemp film, loosely parodied the popular *Here Comes Mr. Jordan*. But the mid-1950s becomes especially an era of parody for them: in 1955 the Stooges will parody *Dragnet*, a top-rated TV show, and in the previous year *Cuckoo on a Choo Choo* was an experimental parody of the intensely dramatic *A Streetcar Named Desire* and the batty comedy *Harvey*. And just as *Cuckoo on a Choo Choo* was more aptly called *A Train Named Schmow* during production, so *Shot in the Frontier* might have been better served retaining the working title *Low Afternoon* for clarity's sake. Nonetheless, Jules White did decide to name the villains the '*Noon*-an' brothers.

High Noon follows a newly married but soon abandoned sheriff [Gary Cooper] as he prepares for the arrival of a villainous gang on the noon train and then wins the long-awaited gun battle. Distinguishing *High Noon* is the hero's isolation reinforced by repeated images of the ticking grandfather clock ominously stroking its way towards noon, and the muted beat and haunting tones of the Academy-Award winning 'Do Not Forsake Me, Oh My Darling' by Dmitri Tiomkin and Ned Washington, sung by Tex Ritter. Both *High Noon* and *Shot in the Frontier* begin with the wedding of the protagonists and the wives leaving their husbands. But in *High Noon* Grace Kelly leaves because her husband insists on fighting the Frank Miller gang, while in the Stooge parody Ella, Bella, and Stella leave because the Stooges are too cowardly to fight. This comically perverts the heroism inherent in *High Noon*, as does the iconoclastic gun battle in which Gary Cooper's cleverness and bravery is rolled with Moe and his adversary back and forth and back and forth and back and forth along the dusty street. The Stooge version of the ominous clock ticking is the grandfather clock Larry attempts to turn back, only to have it chime: 'No Use - You're Doomed'! And as for the song, the sonorous tones of Tex Ritter become meek, toothless utterances from the fuzzy Columbia Western stalwart Emmett Lynn, the quietly insistent strains of *High Noon* now reduced to a nerve-jarring TWANG-TWANG.

VISUAL HUMOR: As in *High Noon* much of the parody is shot in exteriors, a rarity in Stooge films of the 1950s. To carry out the parody and concentrate on the duel

Columbia staff writer Felix Adler had been creating Stooge parodies since he wrote the Stooges' only Oscar-nominated film, *Men in Black* [1934], which parodied MGM's *Men in White*. *Shot in the Frontier*, one of two new films in the 1954 releases, parodies Stanley Kramer's now-classic western *High Noon* [1952] with its 'Noonan' Brothers, Emmett Lynn singing a horrible ballad, a ticking clock, and the wedding scene shown here. Television parodies of Hollywood films had come of age in 1954, but the Stooge films, thanks to Adler, had been doing this for decades.

against the Noonans, there is not much inter-Stooge slapstick, although taking their coats off while punching each other, a timing gag structurally similar to saluting and socking each other and getting through a door three abreast, is nicely choreographed, as are the Stooges and Noonans backing around each other on the street, the ring-passing at the wedding ceremony, and Moe's final battle with the last Noonan [Joe Palma]. The latter duel is cleverly constructed. Shemp tries to box [his final boxing routine on film], Larry tries to butt, and then Moe rolls and rolls. A prelude to the duel is when Lem [the guitarist] throws a bag of rice into Shemp's mouth and two boots at Moe's head.

Minor Larryisms: walking bow-legged; kissing the wedding bouquet instead of Stella.The parody requires the Stooges to act with cowardice à la spooky 'scare comedies,' so Shemp backs up with his pistol drawn and steps on a cat's tail [*Dizzy Detectives*], and Moe [à la Ted Healy] talks tough but pushes the others ahead of him. Mandy's missing tooth is a commonplace for Stooge women [*Mummy's Dummies, Scrambled Brains*, more recently Larry in *Knutzy Knights*]. Lem pulling out the smaller ukulele is the opposite of Curly pulling out larger and larger pencils [*Movie Maniacs*]. Larry shooting down a heavy bag onto one Noonan's head recalls the heavy bag dropped in *Soup to Nuts*. A Noonan being shot in the rear but holding his heart is pure Stoogeness, but saying "They got me!" is an old Western cliché the Stooges applied to radios and such in *Men in Black* and *Gents in a Jam*. Shemp using his suspenders as a slingshot but hitting Moe is a variation of the old tree branch sling shot in *Back to the Woods*.

Other variations: Larry scooting his rear along the ground [*I Can Hardly Wait*]; Shemp pouring drinks into his hand without a glass (Curly's pipe in *No Dough Boys*); Larry shooting balloon-like hot dogs (the 'BANG' guns in *Studio Stoops*); the Stooges dusting each other off [*Horses' Collars*]; Larry ramming the iron plate in Noonan's shirt, and bumping into Moe and spilling his beer [*3 Dumb Clucks*]; Larry kicking Noonan in the rear with his spur, and Larry taking a shot of liquor with fireworks sound effects [*Phony Express*]; drinking, then breathing out smoke [*Grips, Grunts and Groans*]; Larry throwing the shotgun, bouncing it off a hanging mattress spring, and hitting the Noonan in the head [*Dizzy Detectives*]; Moe shooting a barrel of gun powder which blows a Noonan clear out of his clothes (shoes in *Half-Shot Shooters*]; the girls hugging their heroes to close the film (recently *Musty Musketeers*); Shemp's Curly-ism "Rruff! Rruff!" [*Sing a Song of Six Pants*]; and Larry running into the wall and spitting out teeth [*Three Loan Wolves*].

VERBAL HUMOR: The lyrics to Lem's song - despite the intermittent twanging - parallel the sentiment of the original 'Do Not Forsake Me, Oh My Darling: "I will never let you go my pretty sweet one/For you're my love to hold, my joy and pride [TWANG, TWANG]/And I hope and trust I'll never meet one/ Who will try to take you from my lovin' side [TWANG, TWANG]." The lyrics are not intended to be humorous, only the twanging. Instead, verbal humor is found in the tombstone epitaphs at 'DIGGS, GRAVES, & BERRY UNDERTAKERS - M. BALMER, MGR...Sorry, no vacancies.' ['Beneath this/monumental stone/lies 80 lbs of/skin and bone'; 'Mama loved papa/ Papa loved women/Mama caught papa /With two girls in swimmin''; and 'Here lies a father of 28/He might have had more/But now it's too late'].

Stooge fear is conveyed in part by a three-pattern [Larry: "I don't see 'em anyplace." Moe: "They must-a got scared and run away." Shemp: "If you think they're scared, I wish you'd tell my knees to quit shakin'" [*Punch Drunks*]], and, as in scare comedies, by Moe's "If you're gonna be a coward, okay. As for me, I'm a-stayin' and I'm a-fightin'...till your last breath!"; also, Larry: "They're comin'!" Shemp: "I'm goin'!"... The Stooges do a fine group-take when Lem says: "The sheriff'll be leavin' town in a half hour; and the Noonan boys'll be gunnin' for ya'. Say, I'll go over and order ya' some coffins." Stooges: "Thanks!".

Variations: Moe: "Here's how!" Shemp: "I know how!" [*Goofs and Saddles*]; Larry: "I gotta have a drink!" Moe: "Me too!" Shemp: "Me three!" [*If a Body Meets a Body*]; 'OLD PANTHER - DISTILLED YESTERDAY - Rotgut, Kentucky' [*Love at First Bite*]; and Moe: "Range: across the street; Elevation: six feet; Weight: 180 pounds; Weather clear! Track fast! They're off!" [*Back to the Woods*]

OTHER NOTES: Initially we see the bow-legged, dusty Stooges as most unlikely heroes. They have always worked well as heroes thrust unwillingly into confrontation, and often it is Moe who fears the most but pushes Shemp/Curly into a higher plane of performance. Here, however, Moe has the toughest battle. The film is filled with sound images: the [false] sound of galloping horses, the guitarist's twang, the periodic orchestral musical accompaniment, and the muffled taunts Moe and Noonan hurl at each other as they roll away from the camera and back. As in *Pals and Gals*, the Stooges are now capable of causing death, and here one Noonan brother is shot dead, after being blown out of his clothes.

Emmett Lynn [Lem, the guitarist] played in many B-westerns, worked as an extra at Columbia [he had a bit part in *The Yoke's on Me*], and co-starred in one two-reeler comedy at Columbia when teamed with Slim Summerville for *Bachelor Daze* in 1944. At about the time *Shot in the Frontier* was being made he had just completed playing the role of 'Nathan' in Fox's first CinemaScope film, *The Robe*. Joe Palma [the last Noonan brother] had two different roles in the previous film, and will substitute for Shemp in 1956. The outdoor Western setting presages the Stooges' last two feature films of the 1960s, *4 for Texas* and *The Outlaws is Coming*.

#158 - SCOTCHED IN SCOTLAND

Studio: Columbia

Released: November 4, 1954

Running Time: 15"31'"

Credited Production Crew:

Produced & Directedby:	Jules White
[Story:	Elwood Ullman]
Screen Play by:	Jack White
Director of Photography:	Ray Cory
Art Director:	Carl Anderson
Film Editor:	Robert B. Hoover
Assistant Director:	Irving Moore

Credited Cast:

Shemp Howard	
Larry Fine	
Moe Howard	
Phil Van Zandt	O. U. Gonga, Dean
Christine McIntyre	Lorna Doone
Charles Knight	Angus [stock footage]

Uncredited Cast:

George Pembroke	McPherson
Ted Lorch	McPherson [stock footage]
Herbert Evans	Earl [stock footage]

PERSPECTIVE: *Scotched in Scotland* is the fourth and last 1954 release that refurbishes a 1947-1948 Shemp film. Not surprisingly, it revisits *The Hot Scots*, the third of the three 1948 'castle' films shot at the *The Bandit of Sherwood Forest* set and the only one Jules White had not yet reworked. As with the others, White chose not to revamp the film entirely but only, since the castle sequences were mostly irreplaceable, to clarify the plot. The Scotland Yard scenario of *The Hot Scots*, although good comedy, fails to account convincingly for the Stooges' presence at Scotland Yard - we hear merely that they answered a 'Wanted: Experienced Yard Men' newspaper ad - and sets up their appearance at Glenheather Castle as a mere accident: a letter asking for three Scotch operatives blows off the Scotland Yard inspector's desk down to the Stooges in the garden below. It used to be that such tenuous plot devices were not only common but ideal for Stooge shorts. Felix Adler developed this common plot-type already in 1934's *Three Little Pigskins* and 1935's *Pop Goes the Easel*, where the Stooges began in one situation which they bungled terribly and then ran to/found themselves in another situation for which they were neither properly trained nor legitimately assigned. But that was in the 1930s and 1940s. Now Jules White is looking not for tangential accident but narrative coherence. Short-film comedy, like any art, and Jules White, like any artist, developed over the years, and with the Columbia Stooge shorts now entering their third decade the Scotland Yard scenario was scrapped.

In *Scotched in Scotland* we see the Stooges in an American office, one of their most familiar and effective expository haunts, where we hear from Dean Gonga that they are being sent overseas for performing so miserably in detective school. The school promised job placement; even Dean Gonga's desk sign says 'We Furnish Jobs.' This gives more detail than the original which never accounted for why the Stooges were in the British Isles in the first place. And just to put the unmistakable mark of Stoogedom on the scene they spill and rub ink all over the dean and go out the door with noses and hair in hand. This will become a typical exiting strategy in the refurbished films.

Once the Stooges get to the castle, the story remains the same but five new scenes are added to help explain 1) what is happening: the servants explain their plan to steal valuable objects, 2) why the servants are wearing disguises in their own castle: to scare those "comic book detectives" away, and 3) why an Arab is hanging around a Scottish castle: we see McPherson (played by a different actor) putting on his Arab disguise. Moe and Lorna's 'cookie' sequence is replaced with a mouse trap, and Moe's dancing sequence and the Arab-in-the-painting sequence are replaced with the parrot-in-the-skull gag in part to create an additional spooky, scare-comedy atmosphere, but also in part to update the film: as McPherson puts on his Arab disguise and searches in the drawer for a knife, he removes a skull, a shaving mug, and a razor, the latter giving the parrot the opportunity to squawk out the contemporary Gillette Razor Company slogan: "How are you fixed for blades? You better look!"

VISUAL HUMOR (NEW FOOTAGE): A new slapstick move: Moe mesmerizing Shemp and Larry by drawing his fists down and up in front of their faces and then giving them each a bonk. A new Stooge office weapon: a stapler. Moe staples Larry's finger and Shemp's nose. Moe used a pen in Larry's nose just recently in *Income Tax Sappy*. Other variations: the flying parrot (*If a Body Meets a Body*, [the owl] in *The Ghost Talks*); the Arab trying to jab Moe with his knife but jabbing Lorna in the rear (*Loose Loot*); Moe and Larry saluting and slapping Shemp (*Uncivil Warriors*); Lorna catching her fingers in a mouse trap (*Goofs and Saddles*); Moe's hair standing on end (*Spook Louder*); and Moe wiping ink on the dean's cheek (*Slaphappy Sleuths*).

VERBAL HUMOR (NEW FOOTAGE): Jack White piggy-backs onto Ellwood Ullman's Scottish diction by having Moe call Larry "McNothing". Reference: 'Dean Gonga' is a play on the Rudyard Kipling character Gunga Din, the subject of the 1939 Gary Cooper film. Of the two other new gags, Larry's pun on Scotch ("You take a tall thin glass, you put the ice in—") substitutes for Moe's line in *The Hot Scots* ("Through these veins flow some of the finest Scotch in the world"), and Moe's 'bicarbonate' quip (Shemp [seeing the skull walking]: "Gho-gho-gho-gho-!" Moe: "You need bicarbonate!") is the most recent in a string of bicarbonate gags dating back to *Soup to Nuts*. The Stooges "graduated with the lowest honors in our school's history," similar to their 'dystinction' of graduating with the lowest temperatures in their class in *Men in Black*; in dentistry school (*The Tooth Will Out)* they were just "lazy, clumsy, and stupid." Another borrowing from *Men in Black* is the phone-answering sequence, here with the Stooges saying a few "Hellos," singing a major triad "Hello," and then saying "Hello" to each other. We last heard "Viva!" in *Rip, Sew and Stitch*.

OTHER NOTES: The working title was *Hassle in the Castle*. Elwood Ullman, who wrote the original story, is not given screen credit, as often. In most of the remakes, the original actors were asked back to shoot new footage (Christine McIntyre here in *Scotched in Scotland*); if not available to shoot new footage, they were written out of the film (the Arizona Kid in *Pals and Gals*). Here McPherson could not be written out since he was so essential to the bedroom scenes, yet Ted Lorch had passed away shortly after shooting the original film. In the new footage, McPherson, now played by George Pembroke, appears without his Arab disguise only once, and there (the fourth scene) he has his back to us and the parrot stands on his shoulder to block his face from view. The Scotland Yard intro to *The Hot Scots* will be reused in *Hot Ice*. In 1954 the Stooges earned the Motion Picture Exhibitors' Laurel Award for making the top two-reel moneymakers, as they had in 1948/1949, 1951, and 1953.

1955

Fling in the Ring • *Of Cash and Hash* • *Gypped in the Penthouse*

Bedlam in Paradise • *Stone Age Romeos* • *Wham-Bam-Slam!*

Hot Ice • *Blunder Boys*

#159 - FLING IN THE RING

Studio: Columbia

Released: January 6, 1955

Running Time: 16"15'"

Credited Production Crew:

Produced & Directed by:	Jules White
[Story:	Clyde Bruckman]
Screenplay by:	Jack White
Director of Photography:	Ray Cory
Art Director:	Edward Ilou
Film Editor:	Robert B. Hoover
Assistant Director:	Eddie Saeta

Credited Cast:

Shemp Howard	
Larry Fine	
Moe Howard	
Richard Wessel	Chopper Kane [stock footage]
Claire Carleton	Kitty Davis [stock footage]
Frank Sully	Big Mike

Uncredited Cast:

Joe Palma	Chuck
Tommy Kingston	Chuck [stock footage]
Harold Brauer	Big Mike [stock footage]
Cy Schindell	Moose [stock footage]
Charles 'Heine' Conklin	Gorilla's trainer [stock footage]

PERSPECTIVE: The four 1954 films that refurbished earlier Shemp efforts shored up narrative holes or added a romantic element. This first 1955 release refurbishes the very first Shemp film, *Fright Night* (1947), changing it just enough to introduce several elements of narrative and visual confusion that the original managed to avoid. The plot of the original was very simple: the Stooges are training a fighter, Chopper Kane, but are pressured by 'Big Mike' [played by Harold Brauer] to have Chopper throw the fight. Blamed unjustifiably for the fight's cancellation, the Stooges fight for their lives against Big Mike's gang in a warehouse, defeat them, and see him carted off by the police.

In this new version, the gangster [played by Frank Sully] is unable to get good odds on Chopper, bets $10,000 that he will throw the fight, but then for some reason lies to the Stooges and mentions nothing about the fix. Just as inexplicably, in the very next scene he does tell them there is a fix. When the fight is canceled, he blames the Stooges for losing his "chance to make ten grand," which means he got odds of 2 to 1 on the challenger, and yet Larry was earlier able to get 5 to 1 odds on Chopper. In the finale of the original, Big Mike warned the Stooges, "When I stand a chance to lose a hundred grand, I like to do something about it - like takin' my pals for a ride, a one way ride," thus setting up the fight at the warehouse. But in the finale of *Fling in the Ring* the warehouse setting is unexplained. And once the fight begins, the Stooges eliminate any dramatic tension by defeating Big Mike [Frank Sully] first; then they proceed to fight...the original Big Mike [Harold Brauer]! We are never told who this other thug is, and we never see what happens to the new Big Mike [Frank Sully]. The script is a mess.

Fling in the Ring is still fun to watch. The training scenes are still well choreographed, Chopper [Dick Wessel] is a delightful concoction of emotional extremes, and the crate-and-barrel chase in the finale has plenty of energy and visual ironies. But it is mostly the old material that is delightful. The new material simply gives Larry a few good new lines but adds the narrative confusion and contradiction. The new prologue leaves

us with the impression that Big Mike is a mean-spirited but inept prankster, slamming the Stooges' fingers in his cigar box and giving them exploding cigars, one of which backfires and blows up in his own face. This makes it seem as if Big Mike is vulnerable, but in the next scene he utterly intimidates the Stooges into trying to fatten and soften up Chopper. The precedent for the initial office scene is clear enough: the previous film (*Scotched in Scotland*) was refurbished by being given an initial office scene in which the Stooges are also first insulted by and then get back at their boss, and we see that here. As for the finale, though, the police cannot come to arrest *two* Big Mikes, so Shemp simply throws his ax in the air (*Slaphappy Sleuths*) and knocks himself out (*Who Done It?*), while Moe spills water and revives the gang (*Back to the Woods*). In one fresh, final moment Moe and Larry try to pull Shemp but merely yank off his outer clothes. Moe exclaims: "He's losin' weight!"

VISUAL HUMOR (NEW FOOTAGE): A new gag is inserted into the gym sequence. In the original Moe takes off Shemp's boxing gloves before the gangsters arrived; here Shemp struggles to pull his gloves off in several different shots, finally doing so and knocking Larry's head into Moe's [*Grips, Grunts and Groans*] to end the scene. This is the first time we have seen anyone smoke an exploding cigar, although in *Gold Raiders* the Stooges threw exploding cigars. Often in these refurbished films physical gags are extended to more than one person, e.g. all three Stooges and all three of their beloveds bonking heads at the end of *Musty Musketeers*. Here the lead-in to the warehouse scene has not just two gangsters punch each other instead of the ducking Stooges [as do the Colonel and Quirt in *Pals and Gals*], but all of them. Painting Big Mike's face in the sliding door derives from the hole-in-the-door sequences in *Loose Loot* and *Nutty but Nice* and the sliding door sequence in *A Snitch in Time*. Other variations: A 'Shave and a Haircut' knock on the door [*Whoops, I'm an Indian*]; and Moe pretending he has broken his gouge fingers [*Dizzy Pilots*].

VERBAL HUMOR (NEW FOOTAGE): Because this is no longer the first Stooge short without Curly, no longer does the gym sign have to emphasize the name 'The Three Stooges' [MUSCLE MANOR - WE TRAIN THE FIGHTERS - The THREE STOOGES Props.']; it now reads 'SLAP-HAPPY GYM - Training Quarters for CHOPPER KANE'. The only significant new dialogue is in the gym scene with the new set of gangsters. Jack White gives gangster vernacular to Mike ("Do as you're told or you'll end up in cement kimonos!") and some Yiddish to Larry ("He'll verbludger him!"). Larry gets the two other punch lines as well (Moe: "We bet every cent we got." Larry: "Yeah, and every dollar, too!"; and Larry: "Better we lose our dough than our lives!").

OTHER NOTES: Dick Wessel [Chopper] is credited as Richard Wessel. The *Scrapbook* reports that Jack White's script ended with Moe and Larry heading towards China on a motorcycle with a sidecar occupied by Shemp. Edward Bernds, the director of the original, complained to the Director's Guild that his work was uncredited; he received small compensation ($2500), and thereafter many of the refurbishings would credit at least the original writer [*Okuda* 17].

#160 - OF CASH AND HASH

Studio: Columbia

Released: February 3, 1955

Running Time: 15"46'"

Credited Production Crew:

Produced & Directed by:	Jules White
[Story:	Del Lord & Elwood Ullman]
Screen Play by:	Jack White
Director of Photography:	Ray Cory
Art Director:	Edward Ilou
Film Editor:	Robert B. Hoover
Assistant Director:	Eddie Saeta

Credited Cast:

Shemp Howard	
Larry Fine	
Moe Howard	
Christine McIntyre	Gladys
Vernon Dent	Captain Mullins [stock footage]
Frank Lackteen	Red Watkins
Kenneth MacDonald	Lefty Loomis

Uncredited Cast:

Duke York	Angel [stock footage]
Stanley Blystone	customer
Cy Schindell	policeman [stock footage]

PERSPECTIVE: Of the sixteen films made during Shemp's final two years (1955-56), fourteen of them are refurbishings, and this is one of the most comprehensively rethought and meticulously reedited. It improves upon the original *Shivering Sherlocks* (1948) by clarifying the plot, simplifying the narrative development, eliminating extraneous material, introducing the film with an attention-getting prologue, inserting a brief car chase and several exterior shots midstream, and then adding a brief denouement that ties up loose ends and brings the film to a more satisfying conclusion. The gun battle at the outset is particularly effective. It adds an exciting touch of crime-drama realism, provides bits of humor for each Stooge, immediately establishes the viability of an exterior setting, and helps us, the viewers, identify the crooks at the same time the Stooges do. The latter is very much an important addition to the film: by making both the Stooges and the viewers eye-witnesses to the gun battle in the street, now both we and the Stooges know who the crooks are while the police do not, and this changes the original who-done-it mystery of *Shivering Sherlocks* to a film of *anagnorisis* ('recognition'). More importantly it makes the search for justice the underlying motivation for everything else that happens in the film. Forty-plus years later we can see the White brothers at work, illustrating their technical expertise at revising an old film, reshooting scenes, and recutting extensively. Stooge viewers rarely have such an opportunity to see the importance of the editing process in producing a fine comedy.

The cafe sequences received the most extensive rewriting and reediting. Jules and Jack White made room for additional material by eliminating the relatively uncomical discussion of Gladys' property as well as the 'clam' soup routine (from *Dutiful but Dumb*) which had just been revised and reused in *Income Tax Sappy* and was irrelevant to the plot of *Shivering Sherlocks* anyway. Then they reedited the chicken soup and fried egg routines to separate them, and at the end of the scene they added the detail that Gladys had a car, which sets up the brief car chase. There is a little confusion as to why Larry orders the chicken soup after telling the customer all they had was roast beef and mashed potatoes - shades of *Fling in the Ring* - but at least the soup gag was used to get Moe and Shemp out of the kitchen and the mashed potatoes on Moe's face. As for the car chase, a limited budget keeps it modest, but at least there is one. Remarkably, in over 160 films the Stooges have only rarely been given a chance to participate in car chases, a commonly employed element of most physical comedy films. But Stooge films were different in their conception and execution, and car chases for them detract from their unique triadic dynamic.

The new denouement shows us how Gladys frees herself from her bonds - in the original we see her left tied and gagged in a chair and then later inexplicably unbound - and it allows the Stooges to discover the stolen money. Fittingly, the money pours out of one of the barrels Shemp drops onto the crooks, meriting Shemp a number of 'ee-bee-bees' and kisses - a unique romantic combination.

VISUAL HUMOR (NEW FOOTAGE): Of the four shooting gags in the prologue, two are new (shooting Larry's bottle of milk and Shemp's pipe bowl) and two are variations (Larry scooting on his rear [*Shot in the Frontier*] and Moe's creased scalp [*Disorder in the Court*]). Complex traditional slapstick is used to spice up new inserts. When the Stooges dress for work, Shemp socks Moe while fluffing out his chef's cap [SLAP, SLAP, POUND, BONK]; emerging from the kitchen Moe and Shemp exchange six slaps and a hand-wave; and Moe slaps Larry just before he points out the customer who happens to be one of the armored car robbers.

In the most recent refurbishings [*Scotched in Scotland*; *Fling in the Ring*] the new introductions often conclude with Moe grabbing the other two Stooges and leading them out (into the old footage). Here just before they enter the crooks' house Moe grabs Shemp's hair,

Of Cash and Hash (1955) is probably the most carefully and meticulously reedited Stooge film the White brothers produced in the mid-1950s. Completely rethinking the narrative development of 1948's *Shivering Sherlocks*, they clarified and streamlined the plot. Above all, they began the film with the attention-getting prologue pictured here, and added a brief denouement to make the conclusion of the film more satisfying. This gun battle, while adding the sort of crime-drama realism seen in 1948's *Crime on Their Hands*, establishes the viability of an exterior setting and helps the viewer and the Stooges identify the crooks, thereby changing the original who-done-it mystery of *Shivering Sherlocks* to a film of *anagnorisis*. Consequently, it makes the search for justice the underlying motivation for the film.

looks at Larry, and says, "You!" Larry grabs his own nose, so Moe grabs his wrist and pulls him and Shemp towards the house.

VERBAL HUMOR (NEW FOOTAGE): Jack White adds a bit of gangster talk to exploit the talents of Frank Lackteen (Larry: "Say, haven't I seen you somewhere before?" Customer: "I was never there!"). He also adds in a pun (Shemp: "I don't like deserted houses." Larry: "Why not? Maybe we'll get dessert!") and a verbal play on directional adverbs (Moe: "We're goin' up there." Shemp: "Not me! I'm goin' down there!").

The extended exchange (Shemp: "You got nothin' to worry about, pal. It's a cinch. Believe me, it's a cinch." Moe: "Oh boy! That's wonderful! That's terrific! Oh boy,we practically got 'em! Where are they?" Shemp: "I don't know.") is a delayed-disappointment timing gag like the old "I've got it!"..."What?"..."A terrific headache!" used most recently in *Musty Musketeers*. In recent refurbished films (*Musty Musketeers*; *Fling in the Ring*), old Stooge standards have been embellished by augmenting the cast. Here both Larry and Shemp each point in a different direction and say, "He went that-a-way!" (*Sing a Song of Six Pants*). The first customer orders "creamed chipped beef on toast" instead of the "short ribs" of the original.

OTHER NOTES: The working title, *Crook Crackers*, plays on the barrel sequence. Only rarely do the Stooges refer to their own slapstick. Here in the cafe Larry calls the slapstick between Moe and Shemp "horsin' around."

#161 - GYPPED IN THE PENTHOUSE

Studio: Columbia

Released: March 10, 1955

Running Time: 16"07"

Credited Production Crew:

Produced & Directed by:	Jules White
Story & Screen Play by:	Felix Adler
Director of Photography:	Ray Cory
Art Director:	Carl Anderson
Film Editor:	Henry Batista
Assistant Director:	Abner E. Singer

Credited Cast:

Shemp Howard	
Larry Fine	
Moe Howard	
Jean Willes	Jane
Emil Sitka	Charlie

Uncredited Cast:

Al Thompson	seated club member

PERSPECTIVE: The first of two fresh scripts for the 1955 releases, *Gypped in the Penthouse* offers two apparently independent stories of two disastrous romantic triangles told in flashback but concluded in real time when all four principles rediscover each other in two interdependent surprise encounters and give expression to emotional frustration. That is to say, it is two stories of twisted romance, jealousy, and revenge, Stooge-style. In the first flashback Larry and Moe vie for the same woman and end up fighting over her; Larry wins the fight and saves his dignity but loses the woman. In the second Shemp and Moe are involved in a marital mix up over the same woman, and Shemp loses both the fight and his dignity, not to mention $50 for masquerading as a woman. Then in the penultimate scene Larry and Shemp both happen upon the man who turns out to be their mutual rival - Moe - and defeat him in a brief struggle, and leaving from that fight they immediately happen upon the woman who turns out to be their mutual romantic interest - Jane - and in a second and brief final battle exact revenge from her, too, only this time with eggs, sugar and milk rather than punches and an inverted fishbowl.

This ultimate victory as well as the setting for the flashbacks depend on the same basic concept: hating women. Misogyny (with its counterpart, male-bashing) has been a common element in slapstick comedy since antiquity, and for the Stooges we find it already in their first Columbia short, *Woman Haters*, in which all three Stooges vied for - and ended up hating - the same woman. In the intervening two decades the Stooges have abused, made fun of, and impersonated women, gotten bossed around, tackled, and triple-slapped by women, and rescued, flirted with, courted, and even married women. Usually when the Stooges are a-wooing they act as a unified trio working on three rhymingly-named women, but on rare occasions since *Woman Haters* they have again been divided and jealous of each other, most notably in *Corny Casanovas* and *He Cooked His Goose*, back-to-back 1952 releases.

By dividing them as jealous rivals, White and Adler create some interesting characterizations and interpersonal relationships for the Stooges functioning as three separate and independent individuals. Shemp plays his usual buffoon role, and Moe is reduced almost entirely to his bad-guy persona. But Larry's characterization is unique: usually confidently flirtatious, here his appearance is so horrid he stops a clock and shatters a mirror; not even curlers or a hair-dryer help. (Ugliness of this scope is usually reserved for Curly, Shemp, or women.) Uniting these three separate Stooges is the desirable 'Jane' [Jean Willes], who helps create the comic mayhem and absorbs a few hits herself. She is a gold digger who keeps a jeweler's glass handy, rejects Larry but keeps his ring, marries Moe only for his (larger) ring, and puts Shemp into jeopardy by lying about her "separated" husband. All of this is encased in the two flashbacks but then emerges with a fine slapstick finale much enhanced by a fifth and romantically unrelated person, the comedic king of innocent bystanders, Emil Sitka [Charlie].

VISUAL HUMOR: The slapstick sequences of this new film resemble contemporary slapstick footage inserted into refurbished films, particularly in fight sequences. Adler and White introduce slapstick sequences with complementary dialogue whether in an exchange (Larry: "What can I do for you?" Moe: "This!" [Moe punches him in the left eye] Larry: "Ow! Didn't you make a mistake?" Moe: "Yeah, I hit the wrong eye!" [Moe punches him in the right eye]) or from an isolated Stooge (Moe: "I'll catch up with you one of these days, wise guy, and when I do - POW!" [He bonks himself]). Fights are filled with extended

Gypped in the Penthouse (1955) features two romantic triangles, Stooge-style.

slapstick [Larry hand-waves Moe, Moe bonks and pounds Larry, Larry clubs Moe, Moe bites Larry's leg and bonks him, Larry tosses a vase, Moe ducks, it hits Jane, Larry taps Moe's shoulder, gouges him, rips his jacket, ties it over his head, then mule kicks him [à la Curly in *Back to the Woods*] into Jane and the couch]. The final fight begins with a variation of the 'missed-punch' gag used recently outside the fight arena in *Fling in the Ring* and the continuous beating Emil Sitka takes in *Gents in a Jam*: Moe and Larry throw punches at each other, miss, and hit Emil Sitka, then Shemp throws a punch at Moe, misses, and hits Sitka, then later Sitka gets hit with a bottle from a backswing. Some of the slapstick humor is understated, e.g. Larry sitting under a hair dryer, and playing with his bubble gum. This is particularly true of Jane's gags: smoking a cigar, having a jeweler's glass handy, and draping her lingerie over the room divider... Slapstick updates: Shemp hand-waved Moe recently in *Income Tax Sappy*, but here Larry mesmerizes Moe with hand-waves before bonking him; and nose bites have become common.

Stooge firsts: Shemp throwing the phone only to have it bounce back at his head; and blowing beer foam on each other. References: The piano sequence [Shemp: "I was tryin' to impersonate that guy with the candelabra!"] was inspired by Liberace, who premiered on NBC television in 1952 and was known for his flashy clothes and signature candelabra; Shemp dresses in a robe, plays a white piano decorated with a candelabra, and finishes with an arpeggio flourish. 'Ugly enough to stop a clock' was a common 1950s expression. Result shot: Shemp on the floor, wrapped in wires and piano keys. This is the first time Larry's hair has blown upwards; previously it has been Moe's.

When Jane puts the ring down her dress, Shemp says into the camera: "There must be a way to get that ring back without getting into trouble with the censor." The Stooges have recently played directly into the camera to end scenes in *Brideless Groom* [Shemp], *Pals and Gals* [Larry], and Moe [*Bubble Trouble*]. The Stooges have been abusing new appliances since *3 Dumb Clucks*; here Shemp struggles with a dishwasher. Changing wet clothes in a woman's apartment we saw in *Three Little Pigskins;* even the style of robe is similar. Shemp had played piano in *Scrambled Brains* and wrecked one in *Brideless Groom*. Throwing up the piano lid only to have it smash back down on him is a variation, although it resembles the phone-throwing bounce-back of the penultimate scene. Accidentally finding Jane on the sidewalk resembles the Stooges finding their father at the conclusion of *3 Dumb Clucks*.

Other variations: the fishbowl on Moe's head [*Hold That Lion*]; shaving at the table [*Hoi Polloi*]; Shemp testing the razor blade on his tongue [*Slaphappy Sleuths*]; the cat and mouse running up Shemp's pants [the crocodile in *Hula-la-la*]; Moe'shooting a light fixture which falls onto his head [*Boobs in Arms*]; and Larry with lipstick all over his face [*G.I. Wanna Home*; *Love at First Bite*].

VERBAL HUMOR: As is customary in Stooge romances, Moe offers an absurdly sweet romantic line [with internal rhyme] ["Ah, my beautiful Jane, while it's in my brain may I dain again to ask you not refrain the chance to make us twain"], Larry acts tough ["Hey! What the hey?"; Jane: "That's the wrong ring!" Larry: "So sue me!"], and there is a song [Shemp: "Home, home on the farm/In Geo-o-rgia, our farm had such charm/And mama's so sweet/ Cooks good things to eat /In Ge-o-rgia, down on the farm"]. Shemp gets in a throw-away line [[caught in the piano wires] "I feel like a pretzel!"], as does Emil Sitka [[smashing the bowl with his cane] "Can I get you a glass of water?"]. Felix Adler includes an old joke for Shemp ["I played that in four sharps. I used to play in five flats but I got kicked out of the last one!"[*Rhythm and Weep*]] and one for Moe ["I flew, and are my arms tired!"]. Both Jane and Moe have something to hide from each other [Jane: "Why are you looking under the bed?" Moe: "Because that's where I hide when I— What am I sayin'?!"; Moe: "How tall was he?!" Jane: "Oh he was about five foot— I tell you there's nobody here!"].

References: Larry's "Mirror, mirror on the wall, who's the fairest of them all?" derives from Disney's *Snow White and the Seven Dwarfs* [1937]; the Stooges will make a feature film about Snow White six years hence. The reference to diamonds [Charlie: "All the dame wants is diamonds: 2 carat, 4 carat, 12 carat"] is roughly contemporary with the song 'Diamonds Are a Girl's Best Friend' [1953]. Epithets: "spotted raccoon" and "caterpillar". As in *Ants in the Pantry* [Curley: "You can depend on us, *toots*!" Moe: "Whadya mean gettin' familiar with the *dame*?"], Moe corrects one chauvinist insult with another: "How dare you call my tomato a 'gold digger'!".

Other variations: Shemp calling the cat a tiger [*Disorder in the Court*]; Larry: "Here's how!" Shemp: "I know how!" [*Goofs and Saddles*]; Shemp: "Too much seltzer!" [*Up in Daisy's Penthouse*]; and 'OLD PANTHER...DISTILLED YESTERDAY... Panther Brewing Co....Rotgut, Kentucky' [*Shot in the Frontier*].

OTHER NOTES: The film was shot in July, 1954. The working title was *Blundering Bachelors*. We hear an odd voice-over while Shemp cleans up the piano.

#162 - BEDLAM IN PARADISE

Studio: Columbia

Released: April 15, 1955

Running Time: 15"51'"

Credited Production Crew:

Produced & Directed by:	Jules White
Screen Play by:	Felix Adler
Story by:	Zion Myers
Director of Photography:	Ray Cory
Art Director:	Carl Anderson
Film Editor:	Paul Borofsky
Assistant Director:	Jerrold Bernstein

Credited Cast:

Shemp Howard	
Larry Fine	
Moe Howard	Moe; Uncle Mortimer
Vernon Dent	lawyer
Philip Van Zandt	the Devil - Mr. Heller
Sylvia Lewis	female Devil - Hellen Blazes

Uncredited Cast:

Vic Travers	Mr. De Peyster [stock footage]
Symona Boniface	Mrs. De Peyster [stock footage]
Marti Shelton	Miss Jones, the angel [stock footage]

PERSPECTIVE: *Bedlam in Paradise* is the most profound of all the mid-1950s refurbishings, for in addition to Shemp's celestial dream from 1948's *Heavenly Daze* this version also conjures up the Devil himself. In doing so Felix Adler turns *Heavenly Daze*'s Stoogification of *Here Comes Mr. Jordan* into a Faustian struggle between the forces of Good and Evil. The Devil's appearance from amidst a sudden flash of light, flame, and smoke immediately presents Shemp with a vivid alternative he did not have to face in the original film's celestial scene: either reform Moe and Larry so he can stay in heaven forever, or go to the Devil. At first the decision seems easy ("I'll reform that Moe and Larry if it kills me. What am I sayin'?...I'm already dead!"), but the Devil brags that he already has "Moe and Larry under my evil influence, and I will thwart you!" He then creates more fire and smoke, from which emerges the horned, aptly named 'Hellen Blazes' dancing in black leotards to jazzy trumpet music and asking: "Why don't you come down and see us some time." Although Shemp does his best to reject the seductive dance of the Devil's temptress, he does succumb to a kiss. Stooges do not take kisses lightly, but when Shemp realizes that he may be facing an eternity of "hot dances," he swears allegiance to the side of Good. In the Stooge world, this means two things: 1) reforming Moe and Larry, and 2) showing the Devil your fist ("See this?!") and bonking him on the head.

To establish the Good-Evil confrontation, Jules White adds Shemp's death scene. As in most of the refurbishings, White wanted to clarify the plot, so he has Shemp say: "I'm gonna kick the bucket...Now you behave. If you don't, I'll come back and haunt ya'!" Moe and Larry try to doctor and comfort him with a hot water bottle, but, Stooges that they are, they quarrel instead. Moe knocks Larry into Shemp and causes Shemp to swallow the glass room-thermometer. Technically, they kill him just as they technically killed Doc Barker in *Pals and Gals*. And killed by Stooges - something unique to this era except for the infamous *The Yoke's On Me* - Shemp ee-bee-bees, barks, shakes, and dies like a Stooge, a fine if more subtle variation on his comic death throes in *Who Done It?*.

Bedlam in Paradise is literally a world apart from *Heavenly Daze*; it has a theological essence that expands Stoogedom to include a choice between eternal reward and punishment. In the original film Moe and Larry hoped to make it rich by investing Shemp's $140 inheritance in the bogus pen that writes under whipped cream. In the new version, which regrettably had to replace the butler (Spiffingham) sequences, Moe and Larry are unknowingly in cahoots with the Devil (Moe: "We've made a small fortune thanks to you"), whom they know only as Mr. 'Heller' and whose horns they do not even notice when he tips his hat. Now their phony pen scam is Satan's idea, so when Shemp turns up the mix-master he is not just being a Stooge but fighting for the side of Good. With a clump of whipped cream slammed into his face, the Devil at that point can only admit defeat: "Well that beats the Devil!"

VISUAL HUMOR (NEW FOOTAGE): As often in refurbished films, there is extended slapstick. Larry heats the hot water bottle by holding it (empty) over the stove, Moe slams him with it in the back of the head, kicking him over to the bed, making him land on Shemp, who swallows the thermometer. We saw Moe bite a thermometer in *Idiots Deluxe* and Curly eat one in *Monkey Businessmen*; a room thermometer burst in *Self-Made Maids*. Larry has to jab a pin into Shemp to get him to open his mouth for the thermometer. In the original footage later in the film Shemp jabs a pin into both Larry and Moe to prove his ghostly presence. A Stooge first: Moe and Larry collapsing the bed. Moe and Larry shake Shemp's belly and hear broken bits of glass, reminding us of the abdominal surgical tools in *Men in Black*. We saw flying Stooges at the conclusion of *Idle Roomers*, but here Shemp's angel rises out of his body and floats towards heaven, a common element in cartoons since the 1940s, as was the struggle between an angel and the Devil.

As do many of the refurbishings of the 1950s, *Bedlam in Paradise* (1955) makes a marvelous parody/fantasy like 1948's *Heavenly Daze* into an even better film. *Bedlam in Paradise* becomes not just a get-rich quick scheme through gadgetry but a theological struggle between the forces of Good and Evil - the latter represented by Hellen Blazes and the Devil himself. But the Devil, like the Nazis during the war years, was no match for Stooges.

Cinematographically, this sequence requires the same kind of double exposure technique used to make Shemp walk through walls. The musical number is the only 'beat-jazz' dance we see in a Stooge film. The number is enhanced visually by contrasting black and white tones, representing Evil and Good; dark tights were popular at the time, e.g. on Judy Garland in *A Star is Born* (1954). The she-devil herself may derive from the one in Bob Hope's *Son of Paleface* (1952). Hellen Blazes advances right towards the camera, as did Larry in *Pals and Gals* and Shemp (verbally) in the previous film (*Gypped in the Penthouse*). After kissing Hellen Blazes, Shemp breathes smoke out of his mouth, a Stooge reaction usually caused by a stiff alcoholic drink or hot food.

VERBAL HUMOR (NEW FOOTAGE): For the opening scene, Felix Adler penned prop-related gags about sickness (Moe: "Galloping hoofs of the heart...Hoof and heart disease!"; Moe [reading the thermometer]: "Ten degrees below zero!") and death (Moe: "He's gone to the dogs"). Larry's race track call ('They're goin' around the first turn. Shemp is in the lead!") derives from *Back to the Woods* and, more recently, *Shot in the Frontier*. To the celestial footage Adler added the joke about reincarnation ("I'll reform that Moe and Larry if it kills me. What am I sayin'?...I'm already dead!"). Throughout the film he inserts jokes about the devil (the names 'Hellen Blazes' and 'Mr. Heller'; Shemp's "Beat it, you devils! Go to blazes!"; and the Devil's "I did give you some devilish good ideas, eh?" and "Well that beats the devil!"). Harkening back to his *Income Tax Sappy*, Adler has Moe reveal to us that he does not understand why 'Mr. Heller' requires no payment for his kindness: "This guy must be in too high an income tax bracket". Reference: Hellen Blazes' "Why don't you come down and see us some time" derives from Mae West's famous "Why don't you come *up* and see me some time" (*Diamond Lil* [1932]). The toast (Larry: "Tootle-oo." Moe: "Skip the gutter." Larry: Break a leg.") varies the toast we heard first in *Pardon My Scotch*.

OTHER NOTES: The new footage was shot on July 9, 1954. The working title was *Gruesome Threesome*. The Devil appeared often in contemporary films. *The Devil and Daniel Webster* was filmed the same year (1941) as *Here Comes Mr. Jordan*, the prototype for *Heavenly Daze*. Roughly contemporary with and perhaps inspirational for *Bedlam in Paradise* were *Meet Mr. Lucifer* (1953) and *Bait* (1954). Sylvia Lewis [Hellen Blazes] had just completed a two-year stint as choreographer and dancer for 'The Ray Bolger Show' on ABC television from October, 1953 to June, 1955; she dances here to music by Jerry Feldman ("Blues") and Mischa Bakaleinikoff ("New End of Blues"). During the voiced-over final line "Dear Uncle Mortimer" we can see Shemp's lips saying "Dear Ma."

#163 - STONE AGE ROMEOS

Studio: Columbia

Released: June 2, 1955

Running Time: 15"48'"

Credited Production Crew:

Produced & Directed by:	Jules White
Screen Play by:	Felix Adler
Story by:	Zion Myers
Director of Photography:	Ira Morgan
Art Director:	Carl Anderson
Film Editor:	Paul Borofsky
Assistant Director:	Jerrold Bernstein

Credited Cast:

Shemp Howard	
Larry Fine	
Moe Howard	
Emil Sitka	B. Bopper, Curator
Virginia Hunter	Aggie [stock footage]
Nancy Saunders	Maggie [stock footage]
Dee Green	Baggie [stock footage]

Uncredited Cast:

Barbara Bartay	secretary
Cy Schindell	caveman [stock footage]
Joe Palma	caveman [stock footage]
Bill Wallace	caveman [stock footage]

PERSPECTIVE: Inventing still another clever method for refurbishing an early Shemp film, Jules White and Felix Adler create a film-within-a-film to give the extensive caveman footage from *I'm a Monkey's Uncle* (1948) a fresh perspective. The newly written introduction lasts nearly six minutes, two or three times longer than most, and this one consists of both a genuine prologue in B. Bopper's office, which gives the footage a modern and scientific perspective, and then a secondary prologue, which takes the Stooges on an anthropological expedition out into the field somewhere between Drinka Gin and

Stone Age Romeos is a brilliant recasting of 1948's *I'm a Monkey's Uncle.* First Felix Adler and Jules White added a prologue which took place in museum curator B. Bopper's office...

...and then added a second prologue out in the wild. At the end of *Stone Age Romeos* we find out that the Stooge's prehistoric film-within-a-film is nothing more than a modern scientific scam.

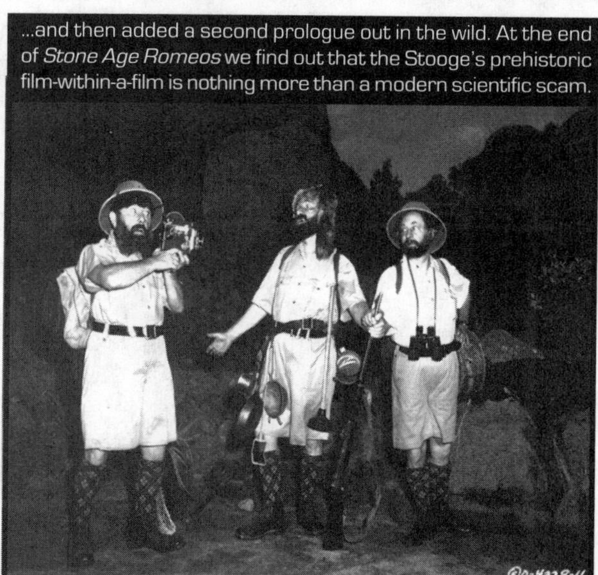

Rigor Mortis along the shores of the Drop Dead Sea. The stock caveman footage itself has several bits edited out, but nothing new is added to it. Then to consolidate the narrative White and Adler conclude the film by returning to the setting and characters of the first new prologue, a technique with which the White brothers had experimented in *Musty Musketeers*.

Both new introductory scenes advance the plot while exploiting a generous portion of pertinent gags. The prologue aims at establishing an atmosphere fit for explorers and knowledgeable men, so the gags develop the idea of an explorer's intrepidness (Shemp: "That's us: we're decrepit"), geographical knowledge ("Moe: "We've explored the South Pole-" Shemp: "and the North Pole-" Larry: "and even the telegraph pole!"), and intelligence (Moe: "That's the dust off your brain!") as well as a knowledge of obscure regions of the earth (squaring the map into sections and then playing checkers on it) and prehistoric life species (Larry: "She's on television. I always watch Dinah Shore!"). Then it comes to a close with the sort of 'exit gag' used frequently in refurbished office prologues: as the Stooges attempt to sign their contract, Shemp squirts ink in Moe's face, so Moe grabs Shemp's tongue with the scissors, Larry's hair with his fist, and leads them out for the exit. This typical, albeit always varied, mid-1950s Stooge exit works like a musical cadence, only it is a lot more painful. Normally, it leads directly into the old footage, but exiting from this office prologue takes them into the next prologue out in the field where Moe discovers "a big bat in the forest climbing monster trees," that is, a fly in Larry's hair. The conclusion to this second prologue uses a different but old and reliable means of changing the direction of a Stooge narrative, a slapstick-motivated change of direction: Moe hits Larry on the head with the rifle, so Larry bends over in pain, which leads him to discover the prehistoric footprint, and off they go.

The brief denouement takes the film into a deeper perspective and a shorter history. It makes us aware that we have been watching a film-within-a-film, but it also utterly transforms the prehistoric time frame of the original film into a modern scam. Just as Moe with his binoculars thinks he is looking at a forest and a giant bat but is really seeing a fly on the back of Larry's head, we think we are looking at footage of prehistoric humans but are really seeing a Stooge film made by the Stooges.

VISUAL HUMOR (NEW FOOTAGE): In the first prologue, the Stooges plan travel by pogo stick, unique in the Stooge corpus. Shemp aiming the camera the wrong way is another example of Stooge ignorance; it is basic Stoogeness to hold objects in the wrong direction, be they nails, guns, or cameras. Shemp's umbrella is presumably not for the sun but in case that "flying bat as big as an elephant" flies over. This is relatively off color for the Stooges. Recently, though, Shemp had made an adult gag about retrieving his ring from Jane's dress in *Gypped in the Penthouse* ("There must be a way to get that ring back without getting into trouble with the censor.").

It is because he is an explorer that Larry keeps string in his ear "so the wind won't blow the dust in my ear." Shemp blowing air into one ear and dust out from the other derives from the mud-sequence in *Goofs and Saddles*. Larry's suggestion that Moe get a windshield wiper recalls the wiper-equipped helmet in *Knutzy Knights*, although here Moe turns Larry's suggestion into a gouge setup. Moe and Larry bonking because of the binoculars strap is a variation of the collision caused by the suitcase in *Ants in the Pantry*. Moe mistaking Larry's scalp for a different eco-system derives from *Who Done It?*. Other variations: Larry playing checkers and getting "crowned" (*Tassels in the Air, Higher Than a Kite*); Shemp squirting ink in Moe's face (*Healthy, Wealthy and Dumb*); Shemp removing his rifle and hitting Moe in the head, and then Larry removing a bag and hitting Moe in the head (*G.I. Wanna Home*); Moe hitting Shemp with the backswing of the rifle and Larry with the foreswing (*3 Dumb Clucks*); the Stooges shot in the rear at a film's conclusion (recently in *Goof on the Roof*); and Bopper shooting himself in the foot (recently Shemp in *Pals and Gals*).

VERBAL HUMOR (NEW FOOTAGE): For the two prologues, Felix Adler created many plot-related gags. Shemp confuses "intrepid" with "decrepit"; Moe calls Shemp a "chipmunk" presumably because he looks like one with that beard; "tadpole," on the other hand, fits in with the other "poles" of the geographical four-pattern (Moe: "We've explored the South Pole-" Shemp: "and the North Pole-" Larry: "and even the telegraph pole!" Moe: "Shut up, tadpole!"). Moe's "Great Scott!" is appropriate since Robert Scott explored the South Pole; (this was also a favorite expression of Basil Rathbone's contemporary cinematic Sherlock Holmes). Also appropriate to the world of exploration is Moe's reference to the Tsetse fly. The Map of Jerkola ("a portion of the earth that is almost unknown") includes Hang Gover, Looks Sea [Look Sea], and Bay of Rum from *You Nazty Spy!*, Jerkola, Straights of Rye, Hot Sea...Tot Sea, and Eye-Land...We-Land [like I-Ran...He-Ran...She-Ran] from *You'll Never Heil Again*, Giva-Dam and Shmow [Lake] from *Malice in the Palace*, and new territories based on mispellings (Pecific Ocean), drinking gags (Bourbon River, Kegoboozia, Isle-Liquor, Yule-Liquor, Wing Ding, Drinka Gin, Canabeer [*Dizzy Pilots*], and Gunga Gin), doublets (Mish Mosh, Pish Posh [*Back to the Woods*]), and geographical puns (Drop Dead Sea, Rigor Mortis).

Larry telling Shemp to mind his own business before Moe hits Shemp with the rifle (Shemp: "You wanna kill him?" Larry: "Mind your own business. Go ahead, Moe.") derives from Curly's classic sweater sequence in *How High is Up?*. Larry's "I can't see! I can't see!...I got my eyes closed!" we most recently heard from Shemp in *Spooks!*. The Stooges sing a major triad of "It's a deal"; their most recent triad was in *Scotched in Scotland*. Reference: Dinah Shore [Larry's pun on "dinosaur"] had a live, twice-weekly, 15-minute musical show on NBC television (1951-1957) that followed the evening network news broadcast; Liberace, whom Shemp imitated in *Gypped in the Penthouse*, debuted as her summer replacement in 1952. A similar Dinah Shore gag appears in 1949's *On the Town*. 'B. Bopper,' whose name is jive (*Spooks!*), has a German accent characteristic for a professor (*Violent is the Word for Curly*).

OTHER NOTES: The new footage was shot on August 26, 1954. The working title was *Caved in Caveman*. The use of the 16mm camera is a Stooge first; presumably this is the camera the Stooges used to film their scam prehistoric footage. There is a certain irony in portraying modern professors *with* beards, cavemen without beards. this is the second consective refurbishing of a Zion Myers script. The film-within-a-film recalls the play-within-a-play in *Knutzy Knights*. We see the map for 35 seconds.

#164 - WHAM-BAM-SLAM!

Studio: Columbia

Released: September 1, 1955

Running Time: 15"54'"

Credited Production Crew:

Produced & Directed by:	Jules White
Screen Play by :	Felix Adler
Story by:	Clyde Bruckman
Director of Photography:	Fred Jackman, Jr.
Art Director:	Cary Odell
Film Editor:	Paul Borofsky
Assistant Director:	Willard Sheldon

Credited Cast:

Shemp Howard	
Larry Fine	
Moe Howard	
Matt McHugh	Claude A. Quacker[stock footage]
Alyn Lockwood	Petunia
Doria Revier	Marigold[stock footage]
Wanda Perry	Narcissus[stock footage]

PERSPECTIVE: *Wham-Bam-Slam!* refurbishes *Pardon My Clutch*, the 1948 film which promised a Stooge camping trip that never got off the ground because the Stooges bought a lemon of a car and their tent collapsed to the ground as did all their baggage. Nonetheless, they did make it down the street to a gas station, and they did encounter the crazy man from the bushes. Both these scenes have been omitted in this newer version, which makes it even more spatially confined than the original. Writer Felix Adler takes advantage of this confinement by clarifying the origins, expanding upon the symptoms, and then curing Shemp's ill health by adding a prologue and reconstructing the finale, both of which build to fine climaxes. Once again a refurbished film improves upon the original by clarifying the plot and tying up loose ends, insofar as the limited range of the original Clyde Bruckman story would allow.

The new prologue incorporates one Stooge wife, Petunia [Alyn Lockwood], from the original film and excludes the other two who are "out shopping." The narrative purpose of the prologue is to establish the previously undiagnosed nature of Shemp's illness and Larry's confidence in his friend Claude's medical ability, while its humor stems primarily from what the Stooges can do with hotcakes: Moe can flip one onto the ceiling and back down onto his face, Larry can eat his with ketchup, mustard, whipped cream, and, preferably, beer, and Shemp can mistake his for a powder puff. Each of these gags is a variation: Moe's pan-to-ceiling-to-face pancake is a variation from *Movie Maniacs* and the classic 'Sword of Damocles' pie in *Half-Wits Holiday*, Larry's odd assortment of condiments is a Stooge comic staple used in *Soup to Nuts*, *Idiots Deluxe*, and more recently in *Goof on the Roof*, and Shemp's eating a powder puff derives from *Three Sappy People*. As always, though, Stooge gags derive their humor not so much from innovation as from execution and timing. Surprise is an important element of comedy, be it in the surprise of what we do not expect or the correct timing of what we do expect. We know Shemp is going to do something after eating that powder puff, but not exactly what nor exactly when. The sudden, powdery explosion from his mouth is quite spectacular.

The new middle scene that replaces the gas station scene is bright and energized, climaxing when Shemp is bitten by a lobster and Moe and Larry do a Cossack dance around him, a rather joyous Stooge moment. For the end of the film Adler wanted to bring Shemp's illness to closure, which the original film failed to do, and so he

makes the double-whammy excitement of Moe getting his foot caught under the car and then Larry and the baggage falling off the car the magical impetus that cures Shemp. It turns out that Larry's friend Claude was right, sort of, so Larry gets to finish the film doing something he has never done in two decades: bonk Moe's head against someone else's - four times!

VISUAL HUMOR (NEW FOOTAGE): New food abuse: Larry sandwiching a stick of butter between two hotcakes and smashing them with his hand. The lobster in the foot bath comes from a lineage of Stooge crustaceans, the feistiest of which was the crab in *Matri-Phony*. In the Cossack dance Larry does not do his deep knee-bend kicks, but he does trip some nice fantastic, especially for someone just hit on the head with a sledgehammer. The most recent Cossack dance we saw was in *Pest Man Wins* (1951). When Shemp passes out at the end of the tooth-extraction sequence, Moe unbuttons his pajama top to find a bullet proof vest. This is unaccounted for. In *Pardon My Clutch* the scene ends with Shemp's cheek quivering; Moe ("We must-a left the root in there!") opens his mouth and looks in.

VERBAL HUMOR (NEW FOOTAGE): Adler wrote two new set gags for the prologue (Larry: "Let me go get him; he'll cure Shemp like *that*!" Moe: "Are you sure?" Larry: "I'm positive." Moe: "Only fools are positive!" Larry: "Are you sure?" Moe: "I'm positive!"; and Larry: "When we were in school, he cured all the pupils there." Moe: "What school?" Larry: "The reform school!").

Claude's business card, which serves to corroborate Larry's confidence in his friend, gives us his full name ('CLAUDE A. QUACKER') and professional abbreviations of the sort we saw in *"I Can Hardly Wait"* (one of the models for *Pardon My Clutch*), including 'F.O.B.' 'N.U.T.Z.' is new, and notice his stinky phone number: 'P.U. 3411'. Other variations: Shemp: "Light as a feather" (*Uncivil Warriors*); Larry: "My favorite fruit" *Fright Night*, Shemp: "Somethin's got me! An octopus!" (*The Sitter Downers*); and Shemp:"poor, dear, sweet lovable toe" (*I Can Hardly Wait*).

OTHER NOTES: The new footage was shot in one day - January 18, 1955. The release title *Wham-Bam-Slam!* has hyphens between the onomatopoetic triad of words and an exclamation point at the end. The working title was *Enjoying Poor Health*.

There were many sub-genres and plotlines in Stooge short-film comedies. *Wham-Bam-Slam!* (1955) was an enhanced box comedy which began with a Stooge vacation that never left home even when they tried it in Clyde Bruckman's *Pardon My Clutch* (1948). This story line was originally developed in Laurel & Hardy's *Perfect Day* (1929), but Stooge trio comedy differs greatly from that of comedy duos. Short-film comedies, like medieval romances, found themselves revived repeatedly, each time varied, each time stylized according to the special abilities of the artists and the requirements of the target audience.

#165 - HOT ICE

Studio: Columbia

Released: October 6, 1955

Running Time: 16"08'"

Credited Production Crew:

Produced & Directed by:	Jules White
Screen Play by:	Jack White
Story by:	Elwood Ullman
Director of Photography:	Fred Jackman
Art Director:	Cary Odell
Film Editor:	Tony DiMarco
Assistant Director:	Willard Sheldon

Credited Cast:

Shemp Howard	
Larry Fine	
Moe Howard	
Kenneth MacDonald	Dapper Malone
Christine McIntyre	Bee [stock footage]
Barbara Bartay	woman in the cafe

Uncredited Cast:

Cy Schindell	Muscles [stock footage]
Bud Fine	thug [stock footage]
Blackie Whiteford	thug [stock footage]

PERSPECTIVE: Unlike any of the recent refurbishings except *Pals and Gals*, *Hot Ice* joins footage from two 1948 films, *Crime on Their Hands* and *The Hot Scots*. Also unlike any of the recent refurbishings, *Hot Ice* includes not even one whole new scene, it adds only a few brief sequences, and none of what little new footage has been added changes the plot significantly. There is a good reason for this. The purpose of these mid-1950s refurbishings was largely to clarify plots and tie up any loose narrative ends, but the plot of *Crime on Their Hands* was already clear and had no loose ends to tie up: the Stooges as eager reporters assigned themselves to finding the Punjab Diamond thieves, and in their search they found not only the thieves and the diamond but also a wild gorilla, and then Shemp accidentally swallows the diamond; in the end the gorilla extracts the diamond, Shemp befriends the gorilla, and the Stooges capture the thieves. There was nothing to clarify or tie up here, so Jules White made the decision to vary the original film by conjoining it with the introduction to *The Hot Scots*.

The Hot Scots and *Crime on Their Hands* both followed a similar narrative formula in portraying the Stooges as wanna-be reporters/detectives who get a case to investigate, so putting the plots of these two films together was a simple matter of grafting the Scotland Yard introduction of one [*The Hot Scots*] onto the Punjab Diamond case of the other. In the previous year Jules & Jack White had already taken the Scottish location of the second half of *The Hot Scots* and joined to it a new prologue that sent the Stooges overseas from America to Scotland, so changing continents here was not a difficult task, and that first half of *The Hot Scots* was begging to be reused in a refurbishing project. The only new writing required for the join was a sentence changing the Stooges from reporters to detectives, and another moving the Dapper Gang from an American to an English location more appropriate for Scotland Yard and *The Hot Scots*. This sentence explains Dapper's plan to "kidnap a girl from the circus to earn the ransom money to pay for passage back to America," presumably to unload the diamond, one of the more convoluted plans in Stoogedom.

White shot three other new sequences. One put Barbara Bartay into her cockney role at 'McGuffey's Cafe' [an English sounding name]. Bartay's accent sounds forced, but the visual gag accompanying it works nicely at demonstrating what stooges the Stooges are at sleuthing, not noticing Nitro, dynamite, and a variety of weapons as they pull them out of her bag. This is the most inspired of the new material, although it unfolds slowly. Like the exploration gags written to introduce the stock footage in *Stone Age Romeos*, the other two new sequences - the drawer and the three beds - are designed as sleuthing gags. Feeling compelled to change the final gag of the film, White has Shemp swallow the diamond a second time so Moe and Larry can ad-lib a tool-fest conclusion. Unfortunately the gorilla is left out of the operation despite his being the best surgeon of the four of them.

VISUAL HUMOR (NEW FOOTAGE): The sleuthing sequence contains a visual three-pattern (Shemp and Larry flip down the covers of a bed. Moe: "Nobody there." Shemp and Larry flip down the covers of a second bed. Moe: "Nobody there." Shemp and Larry flip down the covers of a third bed. A man sits up. Moe: "Nobody there.") and revives two Stooge prop-gag staples: a stethoscope and a file cabinet, the former used in *Men in Black* and nine subsequent films to this point; Moe snaps the stethoscope into his face as in *Three Sappy People*. The file cabinet gag was used first in *Hold That Lion*. The woman bonks their heads together as did Larry at the end of previous *Wham-Bam-Slam!*. Other variations: Moe pounding Shemp so he spits out the drink into Moe's face (*Hoi Polloi*); Larry getting his nose bitten (*Uncivil Warriors*); Shemp speaking half a sentence before the 'anesthetic' takes effect (*A Snitch in Time*); and Larry delivering the 'anesthetic' (*Men in Black*). The ad-libbing at the end of the film includes Moe drilling Shemp's stomach, and Larry trying first a saw on his neck and then a plunger on his face.

VERBAL HUMOR (NEW FOOTAGE): The entire sleuthing sequence is established with a pun (Moe to Larry: "Examine this room carefully. We gotta get to the heart of this case." Larry: "Right, doctor!"). Jack White also introduces a rhyming three-pattern (Larry: "It's liquor!" Moe [taking the glass]: "She's gettin' shickered!" Shemp [taking the glass]: "I'll do it quicker!"), and a prose one ([after they pull out a knife, a bottle of Nitro, two sticks of dynamite, an ax, and a crow bar] Larry: "No diamond." Moe: "Nope, she's as clean as a hound's tooth." Shemp: "Sorry, lady."). 'Shickered' is Yiddish for "drunk," but the little ditty may derive ultimately from the 1931 Ogden Nash poem: "Candy/Is dandy/But liquor/Is quicker". Moe shows some characteristic false bravado: "Step aside! I'll find a clue...I hope". The drawer sequence gets some fresh dialogue (Moe: "Why didn't you tell me I left it open." Shemp: "Sorry, Moe: you left the drawer open." Moe [bowing]: "Ohh, very observant!").

Reference: Moe's "Sorry, ma'am, we gotta get the facts, ma'am" parodies *Dragnet*, the subject of parody in the next film (*Blunder Boys*). Variations: Moe: "What does your watch say?" Larry: "Tick-tick-tick-tick" (*Fright Night*); Moe: "Whadya hear?" Larry: "Termites!" (*3 Dumb Clucks*); and Moe: "Watch your 'p's and 'q's'!" (*Three Missing Links*).

OTHER NOTES: Barbara Bartay uses a German accent in *Stone Age Romeos*, a French one in *Blunder Boys*.

One of Larry Fine's many fine moments, and well worth preserving from the original *Crime on Their Hands*, was the gorilla-cage sequence in *Hot Ice* (1955), where he gets abuse at the hands of the gorilla and a disbelieving Moe.

#166 - BLUNDER BOYS

Studio: Columbia

Released: November 3, 1955

Running Time: 15"54'"

Credited Production Crew:

Produced & Directed by:	Jules White
Story & Screen Play by:	Felix Adler
Director of Photography:	Ray Cory
Art Director:	Cary Odell
Film Editor:	Tony DiMarco
Assistant Director:	Willard Sheldon

Credited Cast:

Shemp Howard	
Larry Fine	
Moe Howard	
Benny Rubin	the Eel
Angela Stevens	Alma Matter, School Registrar
Kenneth MacDonald	F. B. Eye

Uncredited Cast:

Barbara Bartay	beautician
Bonnie Menjum	turkish bather
Marjorie Jackson	turkish bather
Barbara Donaldson	turkish bather
June Lebow	turkish bather
Frank Sully	Watts D. Matter, Dean

PERSPECTIVE: The last completely original film starring Shemp, *Blunder Boys* is Hollywood's first cinematic parody of a TV program - *Dragnet*. By the spring of 1955, when *Blunder Boys* was filmed, the television and film industries were already making mutual invasions into each other's territories: Columbia had formed its television subsidiary Screen Gems, NBC had broadcast a feature film [Laurence Olivier's *Richard III*] before its theatrical release, Paddy Chayevsky's teleplay *Marty* was being turned into a Hollywood film, an episode of *Dragnet* had been written for theatrical release, a number of theatrically released films had included televisions or the world of television broadcasting as a setting or plot device [*A Star is Born, Meet Mr. Lucifer*], and sketch comedy on television now regularly included parodies of major films, much as the Stooges had done in *Cuckoo in a Choo Choo* and *Shot in the Frontier*. Until now no one had parodied a TV program on film, but again the Stooges are on the cutting edge of parody.

Dragnet, sometimes recognized as the most successful police series in television history, premiered on NBC in 1952 and was second in the Nielson ratings in 1953, third in 1954, and third again when this film was made in 1955. The show featured a kind of realism hitherto unknown on television dominated by situation comedies [cf. *Don't Throw That Knife*] and variety shows [cf. Larry's 'Dinah Shore' in *Stone Age Romeos*]. *Dragnet* was different. From Walter Schumann's most memorable four notes [dum-de-dum-dum] ever written for television to the hammered 'MARK VII' conclusion, millions of Thursday night NBC viewers followed 'Joe Friday' in crime dramas narrated in Jack Webb's monotone voice. All these signatures - the musical motto, the stark realism, the nomenclature, and the monotone narrative, are parodied here in *Blunder Boys* with its four-note recurring theme [F-D-G-D], a bare wall, three cops named '-day,' a fist-hammered engraving at the conclusion, and Moe's recurrent narration, including the phrase "These are the facts; nothin' but the facts" which had also made its way into the previous film, *Hot Ice*.

Joe Friday worked with a sidekick who was not as deadpan as he, and the two of them often encountered relatively quirky witnesses. This sets the tone for Shemp's role as a downright silly third member of the team, the 'hang nail of the law.' The Felix Adler story reviews the history of the Stooge detective team from WWII, their criminological education, and their first case, but since the film is a parody the Stooges do not capture the cross-dressing crook. Instead, they fail as detectives, so Shemp's evolving holiday names conclude appropriately on 'Labor Day,' which gives the Stooges a chance to hit each other with tools and, more appropriately, it gives Moe a chance to pound 'VII 1/2 - THE END' into Larry's forehead. Ironically, the Stooges' own 'COLUMBIA - SCREEN GEMS' logo would in just a few years become just as recognizable to millions of television viewers thanks to the proliferation of Stooge films on TV.

VISUAL HUMOR: *Dragnet*'s characteristic location interviews of Los Angeles residents inspired the beauty salon setting and its appropriate gags. [The cross-dresser may be an exaggeration of a typical *Dragnet* crook or from some other inspiration.] The Stooges have often misused modern appliances as props, like the dishwater in *Gypped in the Penthouse*, and here it is both the reducing machine and exercise horse... Many other gags are plot specific, including the recurring badge skits and the handcuff sequence. The slapstick is particularly lively with a double slap, a backwards double bonk, and Moe's "81-C" in which Shemp and Larry intentionally run into Moe's extended fingers to gouge their own eyes. Other well orchestrated movements: circling and twisting around/under/over the handcuffs; two pickax gags in which Shemp pokes himself in the rear with his own backswing and then flings the "cock-eyed ax" into the wall and gets stuck in the rear again; the final gag in which Moe sticks Larry in the rear with his pickax, Larry shovels dirt in Moe's face, Moe takes Shemp's shovel and throws a load of dirt in Larry's face and conks him; and a dazzling, intertwining fist game in which Moe offers Larry the fist,

Shemp slaps it and it hits Larry, Larry offers Moe the fist, Moe slaps it and it hits Shemp, Shemp offers the first, and Moe knocks it back into Shemp's face. In the hotel room the camera circles around the Eel and the Stooges, uncommon cinematography for a Stooge film; they usually play into a stationary camera since it takes much less time (and costs much less) to set up the shot. A physical three-pattern: Larry pulls his money out of his stocking, Shemp collects coins from his belt coin changer, and Moe carefully removes money from a mouse trap he keeps on a chain in his coat pocket.

Larry bites into a "hard apple" grenade much as Curly bit into a "pineapple" in *Saved By the Belle*. Shemp ending up head first in the ceiling is a Stooge first, although it recalls the ceiling fan incident in *Punch Drunks*. Other variations: rolling [in fast motion] across the room (*Shot in the Frontier*); the slow-flying shell (*Three Little Sew and Sews*); Larry knocked silly and accidentally doing something good (Shemp in *Fuelin' Around*); Moe playing with his gum (Larry in *Gypped in the Penthouse*); Larry biting his own leg (*Brideless Groom*); knocking over a waiter with a tray (*He Cooked His Goose*); hitting a table from which a vase falls on Moe's head (*Heavenly Daze*); Moe splitting the table in half and bringing them all to the floor (*Pardon My Scotch*); Shemp saluting and hitting Moe (*Uncivil Warriors*); hiding and reemerging dressed as women (*Pop Goes the Easel*); a Stooge out on a window ledge (*3 Dumb Clucks*); the mud pack and scalding hot towel (*Cookoo Cavaliers*); entering a bath filled with women (*Meet the Baron*); and the Stooges isolated in separate gags near the end of a film (*Three Little Beers*).

VERBAL HUMOR: No Stooge films offers more three-patterns (*Squareheads of the Round Table* had seven) with six separate examples (1) Moe: "When we first started out I never thought we'd be the three fingers on the arm of the law. I'm the first finger." Larry: "I'm the second finger." Shemp: "I'm the hang nail!"; 2) Larry: "In the lexicon of crime, it is theoretically propounded that passion, inhibition, and delinquency are the major contributing factors." Moe: "Not to mention corruption of mind, detestation, and schizophrenia, if I may be so sesquipedalian." Shemp: "A jerk with a quirk may do the work, or, a Turk with a dirk may stick a clerk!"; 3) Moe: "Come out!" Larry: "Come out!" Shemp: "Wherever you are!"; 4) Moe: "We finished our courses in criminology." Larry: "And we graduated." Shemp: "With the lowest possible honors!"; 5) Moe: "And now were ready for our first case, yep, our first case." Larry: "Make mine gin." Shemp: "Make mine cham-pay-nee!"; and 6) Larry: "Moella, shall we take a sun bath?" Moe: "No, no, Larrietta. Let us take a scramola." Shemp: "Not me. I wanna linger with the rest of the girls!") as well as six three-pattern variations on the *Dragnet* "-day" names (in this formula: Moe: "I'm Halliday." Larry: "I'm Tarriday." Shemp: "I'm xx Day!"). Adler also added an extended 'Yes! Yes!' pattern (Captain: "Boys, I want you to pay strict attention." Stooges: "Yes! Yes!" Captain: "There's a robber by the name of 'the Eel,' a slippery cuss." Stooges: "Yes! Yes!" Captain: "He masquerades as a woman but he smokes cigars." Stooges: "Yes! Yes!" Captain: "We have a tip he's going to hold up the Biltless Hotel tonight at 8 o'clock. Stake out and get him." Stooges: "Yes! Yes!" Captain: "Now if you fail, you're through." Stooges: "Yes! Yes!...No! No! We'll get 'im!"), a pun (Moe: "Well that Eel was slippery!"), a fear joke (Moe: "Somebody's rattlin' dice." Shemp: "That's my knees!"), and a deliciously ironic line from the beautician to Moe ("I love your bangs!").

Because the Stooges attend school, there is a sharp contrast between Moe's and Larry's 'sesquipedalian' talk and Shemp's terse rhymes. Shemp's "transfer" joke is specific to college enrollment, as is their usual graduating with the 'lowest possible honors' (*Men in Black, Scotched in Scotland*). The 'La Stinkadora' gag is based on Stooge ignorance, as is Moe's "Very periphrastic!"; cf. Moe: "Don't you two imbeciles know a gentleman when you see one?".

Plot-related gag names: 'F. B. Eye,' 'Biltless [i.e. Biltmore] Hotel', 'Alma Matter,' and her dad 'Dean, Watts D. Matter.' The names Moella and Larrietta derive from *Self-Made Maids*. Epithets: "mongoose," "titmouse," "nitwit," and "Stooge!" Another leads to a unique response from Shemp (Moe: "Hey imbecile!" Shemp: "Oh, that's me!"). Shemp's throw-away lines: "A dog bit me!"; "Now I'll have to eat standin' up!"; [seeing a woman in a bathing suit] "I found somethin'!"; and after Larry hits him with the stocking] "I'll tell Santa Claus on you!" (à la Curly's "You just hit Santa Claus! For that - no toys!" in *Wee Wee Monsieur*). Other variations: "Our first case." Larry: "Make mine gin!" (*Tricky Dicks*); Moe: "We didn't get him, but we got the gate!" (*Fiddlers Three*); and "Viva!" (*Dutiful but Dumb*).

References: Shemp's "Gut gesacht?" is Yiddish for "Well said." Larry's "When in Rome, do as the Romans do" is a proverb attributed to St Ambrose (4th century A. D.).

OTHER NOTES: The working title was *Cuckoo Cops*. Larry's 'second finger of the law' is his middle finger. Times and mores have changed. The Stooges used the flashback technique recently in *Gypped in the Penthouse*. We hear flutes play the Stooge theme thrice. Milton Berle, with Jackie Cooper and Vic Damone, offered a Dragnet parody in his 1954 season. In 1955 the Stooges earned their fifth Motion Picture Exhibitors' Laurel Award.

1956

Husbands Beware • Creeps • Flagpole Jitters

For Crimin' Out Loud • Rumpus in the Harem • Hot Stuff

Scheming Schemers • Commotion on the Ocean

#167 - HUSBANDS BEWARE

Studio: Columbia

Released: January 5, 1956

Running Time: 16"00'"

Credited Production Crew:

Produced & directed by:	Jules White
Screen Play by:	Felix Adler
Story by:	Clyde Bruckman
Director of Photography:	Henry Freulich
Art Director:	Ross Bellah
Film Editor:	Tony DiMarco
Assistant Director:	Eddie Saeta

Credited Cast:

Shemp Howard	
Larry Fine	
Moe Howard	
Maxine Gates	Flora (Moe's wife)
Lou Leonard	Dora (Larry's wife)
Dee Green	Fanny Dinklemeier [stock footage]
Christine McIntyre	Lulu Hopkins [stock footage]

Uncredited Cast:

Emil Sitka	Justice Benton
Doris Colleen	former girl friend [stock footage]
Nancy Saunders	former girl friend [stock footage]
Johnny Kascier	bellhop [stock footage]

PERSPECTIVE: *Husbands Beware* is the first release of 1956, the only year in which all the releases were refurbishings. The first four films maintained the usual balance between stock and new material, but after Shemp's fatal heart attack midway through the production schedule, the remaining four necessarily contained little new footage. Most of the refurbishings were of the 1949 releases since all the 1947-1948 films had already been reworked except *Mummy's Dummies* and *Brideless Groom*. *Mummy's Dummies*, with its exotic sets, was never refurbished. But *Husbands Beware* refurbishes *Brideless Groom*, the delightful 1947 film in which Shemp has to get married to inherit $500,000. Jules White now turns it into a slightly different but equally dynamic tale of three romantically (and gustatorially) disastrous marriages and supreme revenge. The mayhem of the original, highlighted first in the mid-stream beating Shemp takes from Christine McIntyre and then in the final Bassarid riot, is maintained intact, but to it is added a complementary battle between two absolutely titanic wives and their defenseless Stooge husbands.

The film opens with Moe and Larry marrying Shemp's "lovely sisters," a new addition to the uncles and cousins of Shemp's extended family. These brides are nearly twice the size of Moe and Larry, and no sooner do the grooms say "I do" and prepare for their nuptial kisses than the wives deck them with right crosses, shouting, "That's just to show you who's gonna be boss around here!" Belly bumping and kicking them into the kitchen, they reverse gender roles completely by putting the men into the kitchen to cook for them, a comic cultural paradox in the 1950s. Little do the wives know what kind of cooks the Stooges are, though. Earnest as ever, the trio does genuinely try to produce a fine turkey dinner, but of all the Stooge-prepared meals this one turns out the most undelicious with more than a hint of such flavorings as soap, aftershave, powder, turpentine, and fire extinguisher. The Stooges have served many bad meals to many people, but usually their victims cough feathers, smile politely, or pucker their lips. This time is different: the wives throw all three of them out of the house.

The addition of the two bossy, physically dominant wives was a stroke of genius. To make room for the new footage White dropped the dressing scene and the Shemp-in-the-piano sequence; the latter was recently reprised in *Gypped in the Penthouse*, and both would have interfered with the woman-beats-Stooge theme of the new version. Now the film begins, continues, and ends with women that beat the Stooges. The Stooges who regularly hammer each other, gangsters, and beast-men now find themselves socked, manhandled, thrown, belly bumped, and kicked by their wives, shoved, slapped, and shaken by the woman across the hall, and beaten, rifle butted, and bear trapped by the gold diggers in the finale. What this film demonstrates is how Stooge physical humor can depend not only on the Stooges hitting each other but on their being hit by other people, especially 'poor, weak, helpless' women and "lovely" new brides. If there was ever a time for the Stooges to join the Woman Haters Club, this was it.

VISUAL HUMOR (NEW FOOTAGE): Overweight women have been part of Stooge humor since *Hoi Polloi*, but usually as side characters. And physical abuse from a woman has been used as a passing or closing gag (the flying tackle in *Slippery Silks*; the final gag in *Healthy Wealthy and Dumb*). But here the initial punches from Flora and Dora get the film off to a rollicking start and establish the message loud and clear; Flora's belly bump rounds the sequence off with punctuation. We have not seen a belly bump since *Rhythm and Weep* (1946).

Stooge firsts: Flora slamming a muffin against the table, breaking a piece of the table off; and Shemp drying his hands on the kitchen curtains. Turkey preparations: Larry pulling out the turkey's feathers and socking Moe in the jaw with the same motion uses the same kind of elbow movement seen first in *Pardon My Scotch* (drawing the six-inch line into Curly's belly) and *A Pain in the Pullman* (carving the crab shell into Larry's eye); picking up the whole turkey we saw as a feature gag in *I'll Never Heil Again*; shaving the turkey derives from Curly's shaving the ice in *An Ache in Every Stake*; spraying it with the fire extinguisher derives from *Listen, Judge*; putting turpentine on it is a first. Other variations: Moe sharpening the razor on his tongue (*Slaphappy Sleuths*; recently in *Gypped in the Penthouse*); Moe tossing the excess shaving cream into Larry's face (*Cactus Makes Perfect*); and being shot in the rear at a film's conclusion, and scooting their rears along the floor (recently in *Goof on the Roof*).

VERBAL HUMOR (NEW FOOTAGE): Most of Felix Adler's additional dialogue is gagless but establishes motivation (Shemp: "Boy if that's married life I don't want any part of it. I'll never get married." Moe: "But you hooked us, you rat, and we'll get even with you!") and moves the plot from one scenario to the next: at the end of the disastrous turkey dinner Larry notices it is time for them to give a music lesson, leading into the old footage. At the end of the film a twist is added (Moe to Shemp: "Well wise guy, your Uncle Caleb is not dead, you don't have 500,000 dollars, but you ARE married!" Larry: "And now we're even!") to tie these two bits of dialogue together. Shemp's: "Gee, fellas, I didn't know my sisters were so mean. To prove it I'll help ya'," serves to get him into the kitchen scene. Adler adds one pun (Larry: "I'll get a styptic pencil." Moe: "Well watch your styptic!"), two throwaway lines (Shemp's "Oh that's that cheap modern furniture!"; and the Justice of the Peace leaving "to testify at a divorce") and Moe's Curly-esque shaving banter ("Once over lightly? Right sir...Make like this"). References: Larry standing with the feathery turkey on his head and saying, "Do I look like Davy Crockett?" refers to the popular Disney trio of films aired on television in 1954/1955, the first television miniseries, the first major venture by a film studio into television production, and the broadcasts that turned "Disneyland" into ABC's first major hit series and, in several reincarnations, the longest running prime-time series in television network history. Its popularity inspired zillions of children to purchase coonskin caps that looked like, but were more sanitary than, Larry's turkey. Shemp's "So I'm a Cupid!" refers to the ancient Roman god of love and matchmaking. Shemp's "Anyway, better you should support 'em than I" is a common 1950s concept; a man was expected to support his unmarried sisters.

OTHER NOTES: The new footage was shot in one day - May 17, 1955. The working title was *Eat, Drink, and Be Married.* Shemp's recipe for muffins: three ladles of flour, one whole egg (with shell), a pint of milk and lots and lots of baking powder "to make it rich". At the end of the film as Moe and Larry prepare to tell Shemp his uncle is not really dead, a double can be seen in the background substituting for Dee Green.

Husbands Beware was the first release of 1956, a year in which every film was a refurbishing. Beginning with the footage of Clyde Bruckman's *Brideless Groom*, Felix Adler wrote a new opening scene in which Moe and Larry marry two large bossy women (Maxine Gates, Lou Leonard). The cooking and dinner scenes turn into Stooge fiascoes, leading smoothly into the Cousin Basil slugfest and the Bassarid riot of the original. Shot in just one day, this new material both complements and enhances the best of the original stock.

#168 - CREEPS

Studio: Columbia

Released: February 2, 1956

Running Time: 15"40'"

Credited Production Crew:

Produced & directed by:	Jules White
Screen Play by:	Jack White
Story by:	Felix Adler
Director of Photography:	Henry Freulich
Art Director:	Ross Bellah
Film Editor:	Harold White
Assistant Director:	Eddie Saeta

Credited Cast:

Shemp Howard
Larry Fine
Moe Howard

Uncredited Cast:

Phil Arnold	voice of Tom

PERSPECTIVE: With fourteen of the fifteen 1947-1948 Shemp films now refurbished - *Mummy's Dummies* already had a coherent, self-contained story, and its ancient Egyptian sets would have made it relatively expensive to reshoot - *Creeps* is the first refurbishing of a 1949 film. This sets the trend for the six remaining 1956 releases which will refurbish the other six 1949 films and bring the Shemp era to a close. The film which *Creeps* refurbishes, *The Ghost Talks*, began abruptly with the Stooges walking into a castle on a stormy night, and ended just as abruptly with Lady Godiva's appearance and several pies thrown into the Stooges' faces from an unknown assailant. In between were several spooky encounters with animals and skeletons and an extended heart-to-heart conversation with the talking suit of armor who referred to himself as 'Peeping Tom.' The film

somewhat mimicked the fairy-tale quality that *Fiddlers Three* had used successfully a few months earlier, but the story of Peeping Tom and Lady Godiva, as it was told in *The Ghost Talks*, lacked both exposition and a thematic thread as well as a satisfactory conclusion. It was therefore a candidate for one of those effective White brothers' mid-1950s overhauls.

To establish the exposition the Whites add an introductory scene that borrows a page from *Self-Made Maids*. We see a split screen that introduces the Stooges playing both themselves and Stooge babies in a crib. Genetically similar to their parents, the baby Stooges cry and hit each other, demanding that their dads tell them a scary bedtime story. This sets the stage for the spooky castle tale to be told as a flashback, gives Larry a chance to tell the babies that their dads were movers under orders to collect the castle's antiques, and allows Shemp to describe the howling wind.

The castle scenes are simplified to include just the talking armor and 'Red Skeleton,' who was kept in

because the original reference to Red Skelton the radio/motion picture comedian applied now to the star of the *The Red Skelton Show*, a highly rated TV show in the 1955-56 season. The talking armor no longer makes fairy tale references to Lady Godiva, so 'Peeping Tom' is changed to 'Sir Tom' (easily accomplished in a voice-over since Tom did not talk with human lips). No longer a victim in a medieval legend, Tom now becomes a dangerous spook who warns and threatens and then attacks the Stooges during a new guillotine scene [à la *Dizzy Detectives*, a previous scare comedy] that concludes when Tom uses his sword to sheer off Moe's pants and Moe walks towards the camera to end the flashback.

This takes us to the final nursery scene, in which baby Stooge tantrums lead to what would normally be labeled as child abuse: Larry provides a club and a couple of hammers so that the baby Stooges get conked on their heads. If modern behavioral psychologists and sociologists are correct in believing that an abused child has a tendency, by learned behavior, to become an abusive parent, here we get a glimpse of how Moe, Larry, and Shemp must have been put to bed at night when they were children.

VISUAL HUMOR (NEW FOOTAGE): Because they are infants, the baby Stooges are limited in their slapstick movements: baby Larry slaps baby Shemp, and baby Moe double pounds and bonks them both; baby Larry and baby Moe each bonk baby Shemp. Later in the guillotine room we get adult Stooge, plot-related, extended slapstick: Larry attacks Tom ("Why you tin can!") with a large sheers, but misses and gets Moe by the neck; Moe swings a punch at Larry but misses and hits Tom in the visor; Moe bends over to hold his hand, so Tom raises his sword and slices off the rear of Moe's pants, exposing his diamond print boxers; howling in pain, Moe edges closer and closer to the camera as the flashback dissolves. The guillotine blade almost hits Shemp twice, and the 'N-B-C' triple bonking at the end of the film echoes the 'N-B-C' gag in the original footage of *The Ghost Talks*. The flying skull was eliminated in part because a variation had just been used in *Scotched in Scotland*. The barking dog/bat mounted on the wall is the same used in *Spooks!*. Jules White often reused props to save money [*Bruskin* 93].Tom swinging at Shemp but cutting off the head of a statue/bust derives from *Shivering Sherlocks*.

VERBAL HUMOR (NEW FOOTAGE): A remnant of the fairy tale subject matter of *The Ghost Talks* is the impromptu nursery rhyme pun (Moe: "Once upon a time there was a lion." Larry: "It was fifty feet from tail to head/ Fifty feet from head to tail/Hundred feet all together./It was a dandelion!"). This is somewhat reminiscent of the opening rhymes in *Knutzy Knights*. A baby Stooge three-pattern (Baby Shemp: "Tell us about brave knights." Baby Larry: "No knights! Tell us a scary one about ghosts!" Baby Moe: "No knights and no ghosts. Tell us one with a lot of killings and a lot of murders in it so we can sleep reeeaaal good!"). Ironically at one point in the guillotine scene the adult Moe says: "Quit acting like babies!".

OTHER NOTES: The working title was *Three Brave Cowards*. In the opening credits the title is written in wavering letters. Film Editor Harold White was producer/director Jules White's elder son. He worked on a number of Stooge films after this. Ending a film with Stooge children was first attempted in the original ending of *Three Little Pigskins*. In the opening scene we hear one of the babies saying, "Oh no! Fui!", but none of the mouths move.

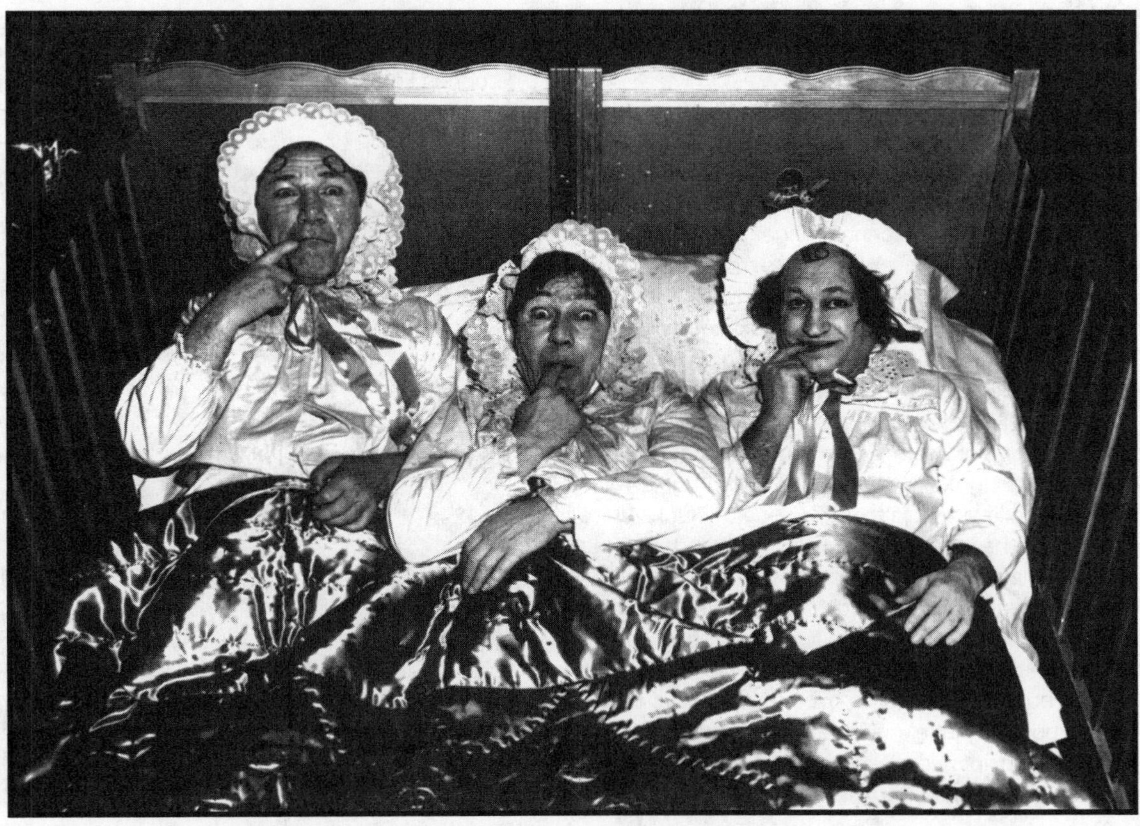

#169 - FLAGPOLE JITTERS

Studio: Columbia

Released: April 5, 1956

Running Time: 15"15'"

Credited Production Crew:

Produced & directed by:	Jules White
Screen Play by:	Jack White
Story by:	Felix Adler
Director of Photography:	Irving Lippman
Art Director:	Cary Odell
Film Editor:	Harold White
Assistant Director:	Willard Sheldon

Credited Cast:

Shemp Howard	
Larry Fine	
Moe Howard	
David Bond	Svengarlic
Vernon Dent	insurance adjustor [stock footage]
Mary Ainslee	Mary [stock footage]

Uncredited Cast:

Frank Sully	Jim
Don Harvey	Jack
Barbara Bartay	chorus girl with ice cream
Beverly Thomas	chorus girl
Bonnie Menjum	chorus girl
Dick Alexander	cop
Ned Glass	agent [stock footage]
Johnny Kascier	delivery boy [stock footage]

PERSPECTIVE: *Flagpole Jitters* refurbishes *Hokus Pokus*, the 1949 film which began and ended with the story of an insurance scam run by the Stooges' upstairs neighbor (Mary), and in between featured the Stooges hypnotic encounter with the magnificent Svengarlic, the magician "who steals your breath away." In terms of plot and characterization the refurbishing is perhaps the most drastic of any. Most of the 1954-1955 refurbishings added prologues and/or conclusions to clarify the plot and fill in narrative holes, but in the previous film (*Creeps*) the story as well as the atmosphere was changed from a spooky fairy tale about a well-meaning armored spirit to an active struggle against a threatening, sword-wielding one. Following this trend, Jules and Jack White utterly reverse the story of *Hokus Pokus*, decriminalizing Mary and transforming Svengarlic into the criminal. As the leader of a gang of safe-crackers, the pointy-goateed Svengarlic gives the film visually a more convincing sinister element than did the white-collar crime of the original, so bowling Svengarlic over on the bicycle now becomes a positive plot element as well as a silly mistake. Such changes do not necessarily make the newer version better than the original, but they certainly offer a fresh variant.

To flesh out the new crime drama, the Whites allow the new plot to develop in the theatrical setting which was barely explained and minimally (ab)used in the original film. It was just outside the theater that Svengarlic hypnotized the Stooges in the original, so now the theater sets the stage for the Stooges' encounter with Svengarlic's torpedoes in the hallway and Svengarlic's planning session in his office. This tightens the story by incorporating the poster-hanging sequence into the crime drama and makes the hypnotism/Bentwood chair gag (Shemp: "You are now in Sing Sing." Moe [through the bars of the chair]: "I am now in Sing Sing." Shemp: "You are now in Boston." Moe: "I am now in Sing Sing." Larry: "You can't get this guy outta Sing Sing!") ironically appropriate since the criminals overhear it. To balance the handle-poking poster-hanging sequence (which revived the prototype, crowded-pit sequence from *Cash and Carry*) the Whites cast the Stooges as the theater's custodians and crowd them into a tiny closet where Moe (as in the *Cash and Carry* pit sequence) takes an incredible beating with buckets, fists, sleeves, and the closet door.

With Mary's white collar crime eliminated, the new version concludes with the Stooges capturing the crooks and making good for their disabled neighbor, an old-fashioned Stooge triumph that builds to a double climax. Not only do we see the original footage of the Stooges standing on and hanging from the flagpole high above the city streets, now we also get the new footage of the Stooges knocking out the crooks with their fall from the

Flagpole Jitters (1956) offers one of the most thoroughly re-edited films from the later period at Columbia's short film unit. The initial footage from 1949's *Hokus Pokus* was reused fairly intact but completely reversed in terms of its plot function. Writer Jack White turned the disabled Mary from a scamming con-artist into a victim, and the hypnotist Svengarlic from a showman into the criminal mastermind - utterly transforming the story while reusing much of the original film.

breaking flagpole, a grand explosion, Shemp pulling down debris, and Moe 'calling' down even more. Now even Svengarlic may not be able to get out of Sing-Sing.

VISUAL HUMOR (NEW FOOTAGE): In the 1950s refurbishings, new footage sometimes echoes a gag from the old footage. Here when Moe closes the janitorial closet door on Larry's head and asks "Was it [the cyclone] like that?" he reprises the gag from the original opening scene wherein Moe hits Shemp with the hammer and says, "All I did was hit you like this." This is not a surprise; the Whites looked at the originals carefully and even ran segments on a moviola they used on the set. Refurbishings also often include old gags expanded to more than one person. Here all three Stooges in the closet have buckets on their heads, a Shemp gag we saw as early as *Fright Night* and then several times in *Goof on the Roof*. The rest of the closet sequence includes Larry taking off his coat and socking Moe with his fist, Moe grabbing Larry's hair and shaking it, and Larry and Shemp slugging Moe in the jaw each time they slide their arm into a sleeve, adapted from the dressing scene in *Up in Daisy's Penthouse*. When Svengarlic's torpedoes slam the door on Moe, we hear wreckage from inside the closet, as in *Studio Stoops* and *Dizzy Doctors*. After hypnotizing the Stooges, Svengarlic winks at two of his gang members, who nod and head for the safe. In *Hokus Pokus* Larry at this point became a cat and meowed at Shemp, who became a monkey and picked through Larry's hair for lice. Prototypes for the chorus girl getting an ice cream cone knocked into her face include *No Census, No Feeling* and *Beer Barrel Polecats*.

VERBAL HUMOR (NEW MATERIAL): After the insurance adjuster stomps on Shemp's foot there is some new footage added to explain the plot (Moe: "Never mind that insurance crook, Mary. We gotta job. We'll earn enough money for your operation and you'll walk again." Larry: "Yeah, we're workin' for the Garden Theatre pastin' up posters, and [to Moe] we better get to work before we get fired!"). As often in these refurbishings, Moe then grabs both Shemp and Larry by the hair and ushers them out. "Oh fui!" was added as a voice-over in the previous film; here we hear Moe say "Now I'll scramble 'em" in a voiceover as he is cooking. The name of the 'Gottrox Wholesale Jewelry Co.' is a variation of 'Mrs. Gotrocks' in *Half-Wits Holiday*. The closet-bound exchange between Moe and Shemp regarding 'Jingle Bells' (Moe: "Jingle bells?" Shemp: "Cow bells." Moe: "Let's try for jingle bells!" [BONK]. Shemp: "Still cow bells." Moe rattles Shemp's head. Shemp: "I hear 'em! Jingle bells!") recalls Shemp's 'Jingle Bells' gag as detective "Christmas Day" in *Blunder Boys*. In the later Shemp years 'yielding gags' are often punctuated with a variation of "heh, heh, heh"; here it occurs in the closet sequence (Moe: "Did you guys slam that door?" Men: "Yeah! What about it?" Moe: "Nothing, you can slam it any time you like, heh-heh-heh-heh-heh-heh!").

OTHER NOTES: The new footage took two days (June 30, July 1) to shoot. Refurbishings were often shot in one day, but this one includes the explosion and debris sequences. This is the first Stooge film of photographer Irving Lippman, a childhood friend of Jules White's in Edendale.

#170 - FOR CRIMIN' OUT LOUD

Studio: Columbia

Released: May 3, 1956

Running Time: 15"28'"

Credited Production Crew:

Produced & directed by:	Jules White
Screen Play by:	Felix Adler
Story by:	Edward Bernds
Director of Photography:	Irving Lippman
Art Director:	Cary Odell
Film Editor:	Harold White
Assistant Director:	Willard Sheldon

Credited Cast:

Shemp Howard	
Larry Fine	
Moe Howard	
Christine McIntyre	Goodrich's niece [stock footage]
Ralph Dunn	niece's husband [stock footage]
Emil Sitka	Councilman Goodrich

Uncredited Cast:

Barbara Bartay	newsgirl
Charles Knight	butler [stock footage]
Duke York	Nikko [stock footage]

PERSPECTIVE: To create *For Crimin' Out Loud*, Jules White and Felix Adler made some small but significant adjustments to the script of 1949's *Who Done It?*. They refurbished and improved upon the original by clarifying the motive for the crime, accounting for an association between the Stooges and the victim (Councilman Goodrich [Emil Sitka]), offering an identification for the third thug [Ralph Dunn], and appending a new introduction with some fine slapstick. The original film had the trappings of a radio play: it opened with Goodrich listening to his radio and hearing about the 'Phantom Gang,' and it closed with a dark-screen battle between the Stooges and the criminals. By 1956 radio serial dramas had fallen out of favor and had been replaced by such television crime dramas as *Dragnet* (cf. *Blunder Boys*), so the radio aspect of the exposition is omitted. Moe instead reads in the newspaper that 'Councilman Goodrich Threatened With Death - Promise to Clean up Vice and Corruption Brings Threat from Racketeers,' and this not only gives a more cogent explanation for why Goodrich is being kidnapped and by whom, it also gives cause for Barbara Bartay to play her oddest 'accent-role' of all as the froggy-voiced "newsboy girl" ("*GOSH, FELLAS. THANKS A LOT!* "). Other narrative holes are filled in when we learn from the now extended telephone conversation that the Stooges "did some investigatin'" previously for Goodrich and that his "niece and her husband are mixed up in rackets," which accounts for Ralph Dunn's role as the husband; this was not made clear in the original.

For Crimin' Out Loud may look like most mid-1950s Stooge refurbishings, but what the film does not show is that when in the new scene Moe offers Shemp his fist ("See that?") and Larry slaps it, circling it around to bonk Larry and Shemp and gouge Moe, this was the final slapstick gag performed on film by a Howard-Fine-Howard combination. On November 22, 1955, before shooting the next film, Shemp was taking a taxi home from, ironically, a boxing match in Hollywood when he slumped over, dead of heart failure. This was the second time this script brought tragedy to the Stooges: shortly after Ed Bernds wrote the original script of *Who Done It?* for the Stooges in 1945, Curly suffered the debilitating stroke that ended his Stooge career.

Born March 17, 1895, Samuel 'Shemp' Horwitz died at age sixty. The fearless boxer with great steps but a glass jaw would dance no more. His legacy to us - in addition to several dozen non-Stooge films - is 73 Stooge films from the last decade (1946-1955) of his earthly existence, minus time for talking to Uncle Mortimer at the Pearly Gates in *Heavenly Daze*, plus four additional refurbishings in 1956, for a total of 77 Shemp Columbia Stooge films. Some twenty-five years after *Soup to Nuts*, this final bit of Howard-Fine-Howard fist-game/gouge footage offers a fitting close to the remarkable continuity of their physical compatibility: 170 Columbia two-reelers later, two Howards and one Fine were still capable of creating a wonderful new slapstick routine with their best props - their hands and their heads.

VISUAL HUMOR (NEW FOOTAGE): Besides the fist game variation, Larry's innovative hand-wave ends by pointing/propelling Moe towards the door. Shemp handing a boiling test tube to Moe, who tosses it into the back of Larry's pants, revisits the hot rivet handlings in *How High Is Up?*. The toupee moving along on top of the running mouse is a variation of the bird-in-the-skull (recently in *Scotched in Scotland*). As often in the new introductory footage appended to refurbished films, Moe grabs Larry and Shemp by the hair and leads them out into the old footage. Other variations: Larry waving the pistol in the other Stooges' faces (*You Nazty Spy!*); and Larry shooting the light fixture which falls on both Larry's and Moe's heads (*Boobs in Arms*).

VERBAL HUMOR (NEW FOOTAGE): Felix Adler creates a kind of three-pattern for two Stooges (Larry: "This report's all wrong." Moe: "This report's all right 'cause I made it out." Larry: "Oh that's what's wrong with it.") and a three-pattern leading to a punchline from a non-Stooge

(Moe: "The new newsboy girl, eh?" Shemp: "Baby, you can peddle your papers here any day." Larry: "And how! She's beautiful!" Newsgirl [in a deep, gravelly voice]: GOSH, FELLAS. THANKS A LOT!"). In refurbished films sometimes individual lines are edited out, others added in via voiceover. This new version omits "The Phantom Gang...tied me up and made me listen to singing commercials" because of the radio references. Added is Larry's pointing out fingerprints on the desk: "they must be Moe's; he was just touching that spot" in a voice-over. Goodrich's gruesome directions to '1313 Hysteria Terrace' ("You drive up Murder Gulch Highway along Bloody Creek till you come to Deadman's Curve, and then you turn right on Poison Bend Road 'til you come to the cemetery. You pass the cemetery to Skeleton Flats and up Hysteria Terrace") expand upon Christine McIntyre's '275 Mortuary Road' address in *Dopey Dicks*.

Adler penned several clever variations on familiar old gags, e.g. singing in major triads (They sing "Hello," then "Yes" a little off key; Larry: "The harmony's bad. We didn't have time to rehearse."), jokes about dandruff (Shemp [after filing the toupee under 'D' for dandruff]: "I told you that thing had dandruff... leaping dandruff!") and time (Moe: "Look at your watch." Larry: "Okay but you have to wait till we go to the pawn shop!"; Moe: "What does your watch say?" Shemp: "It don't say anything. You gotta look at it."- from the original film) as well as a variation of the classic "Remind me to kill you later!" from *Cash and Carry* (Larry: "We got work to do. Kill him later." Moe: "Remind me to kill you later!" Shemp: "I won't have time later." Moe: "Then I'll kill you now!"). The door sign 'MIRACLE DETECTIVE AGENCY - IF WE SOLVE YOUR CRIME IT'S A MIRACLE' derives from *Even As IOU*. Moe's irony: "Don't let' em kill ya' till we get there!". Reference: Moe's "You don't say!" Larry: "He did say!" reflects a common exchange of the period, used even in a television commercial.

OTHER NOTES: The release title parodies the expression 'for cryin' out loud'; the working title was *Nutty Newshounds*. Shemp's fatal outing to the boxing card at the Hollywood Legion Field was in part to celebrate the signing of a contract renewal with Columbia, this now being the Stooges' twenty-second year with the same studio. On hiatus at the time, the trio was scheduled to spend Thanksgiving at a nightclub engagement in Miami, Florida. In the taxi with Shemp at the time of his death was his personal friend Al Winston. [*Besser* 172]. Moe recalled the date of Shemp's death as November 23, 1955, and most accounts repeats that date. But Shemp's death certificate on file with the County of Los Angeles is dated November 22, 1955.

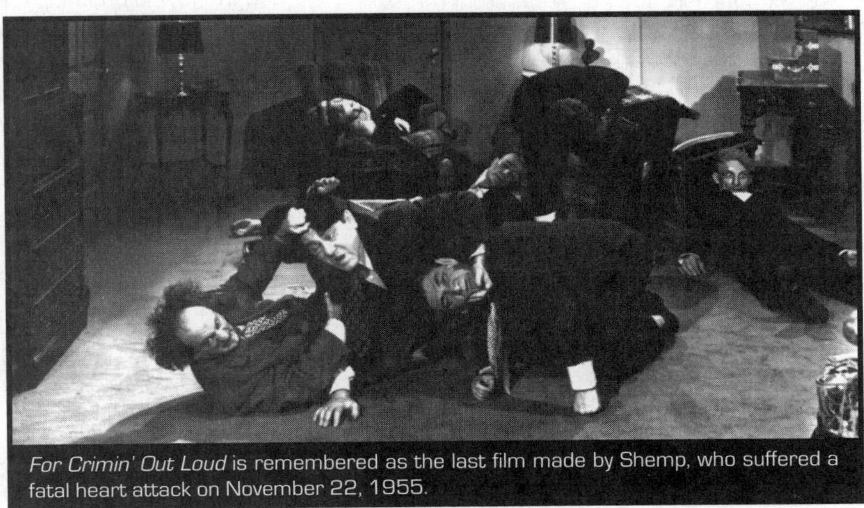

For Crimin' Out Loud is remembered as the last film made by Shemp, who suffered a fatal heart attack on November 22, 1955.

#171 - RUMPUS IN THE HAREM

Studio: Columbia

Released: June 21, 1956

Running Time: 15"56'"

Credited Production Crew:

Produced & directed by:	Jules White
Screen Play by:	Jack White
Story by:	Felix Adler
Director of Photography:	Ray Cory
Art Director:	Ross Bellah
Film Editor:	Harold White
Assistant Director:	Willard Sheldon

Credited Cast:

Shemp Howard	
Larry Fine	
Moe Howard	
Vernon Dent	Hassan Ben Sober [stock footage]
George Lewis	Ghinna Rumma [stock footage]

Uncredited Cast:

Frank Lackteen	Half Adollar [stock footage]
Diana Darrin	Sheba, Reba, or Heba
Ruth Godfrey White	Sheba, Reba, or Heba
Helen Jay	Sheba, Reba, or Heba
Harriette Tarler	harem girl
Suzanne Ridgeway	harem girl

PERSPECTIVE: Despite the unexpected and sudden loss of Shemp, Moe and Larry were required by contract to complete four more films in 1956, so the Columbia short film unit created mechanisms that allowed them to carry on with production of Stooge films until the end of the year. Most of the films were scheduled to be refurbished versions of Shemp films anyway, so it was largely a matter of covering for Shemp's absence in the newly written material by using a double. This was a technique they had used often enough already. For years stunt men like Johnny Kascier, Harold Breen, and Joe Murphy had doubled almost unnoticeably for the various Stooges, and recently in *Scotched in Scotland* George Pembroke doubled for the deceased Ted Lorch's original McPherson role in *The Hot Scots*: Pembroke had a parrot on his shoulder to block his face from the camera in one scene, and in other scenes he wore the Arab disguise. These were minor, non-speaking roles, though. Now they needed to double for a Stooge, and not just any Stooge but the 'third' Stooge.

Rumpus in the Harem refurbishes *Malice in the Palace* (1949). In the opening scene Shemp's absence is neatly obscured. Larry blows a feather while snoring, a variation of the usual trio of snoring Stooges, so we focus on one Stooge and temporarily forget the other two. Moe cannot wake Larry at first; then he has trouble with Shemp. That seems normal, especially when he pounds what appears to be a sleeping Shemp in the belly. Then he discovers a note explaining Shemp's whereabouts. It seems as if there is indeed a trio in that room, although a Stooge fan cannot help but feel a twinge of sorrow when Moe fails to wake Shemp up. Once the story moves to the restaurant and palace footage from *Malice in the Palace*, there would have been no need to double for Shemp if only stock footage were to be used, but because these refurbished films always clarify or develop the plot, some new footage was inserted. For these moments Joe Palma, long an extra and bit actor in Stooge films, impersonated Shemp by wearing a wig and keeping his back to the camera (much as for the double of Curly *fils* in *3 Dumb Clucks*). In one sequence, when Larry says "I got it!...A terrific headache," the camera moves in right past Shemp to focus on Larry. For the final chase sequence Shemp's voice is edited in from previously recorded footage; voicing over was a technique that had already been used earlier in the year in *Creeps* and *For Crimin' Out Loud*.

The redeveloped plot gives the Stooges a genuine reason for going after the Emir of Shmow's diamond - to pay the 1000 Chilblainer virgin tax their sweethearts Sheba, Reba, and Heba have to pay the Sultan of Pish Posh. In *Malice in the Palace* they had gone after the diamond only because they had heard about it from the doorman at the Oasis Hotel (a.k.a. Hassan Ben Sober) and decide to collect a reward. The clarified plot is established in the cutely tearful introductory scene and reinforced in two brief exchanges inserted into the restaurant scenes. The remaining three 1956 releases will have somewhat different solutions to the problem of being Shempless.

VISUAL HUMOR (NEW FOOTAGE): Larry's snoring a feather in and out of his mouth recalls Curly's snoring in the bee in *How High is Up?*. Moe pours hookah water into Larry's gaping mouth, a plot-specific gag; Curly had trouble with a hookah in *I'll Never Heil Again*. When Moe and Larry pull their pajamas off they bonk heads, a consequence often reserved for bowing. The beating in the harem derives from the beating Lulu Hopkins gives Shemp in *Brideless Groom*, later celebrated in *Husbands Beware*. Other variations: wearing clothes underneath their pajamas (*Rockin' Thru the Rockies*); the girls wringing out their hankies and spraying Moe and Larry (the plant in *Heavenly Daze*); Shemp running in circles (*From Nurse to Worse*); and Larry mistakenly trying to leap through the window's shadow on the wall (*Self-Made Maids*). As in the previous film, a gag edited out from the original footage (knocking a guard out with a metal vase) is redone.

The publicity stills for *Rumpus in the Harem* (1956) starkly emphasize the absence of a third Stooge.

VERBAL HUMOR (NEW FOOTAGE): The title is accompanied again by Middle Eastern style music but now reads 'THE ORIENT - "Where Men are Men and Women are Glad of It"' (instead of 'CAFE CASBAHBAH - Meeting place of Black Sheep - Bah-Bah-Bah'); the new title is a variation from *Cactus Makes Perfect*. Shemp's letter contains an ironic 'P.S.' almost worthy of the real Shemp: 'You guys snore so loud I couldn't sleep so I went down to open the restaurant. P.S. If you don't get this note let me know and I'll write you another!"... Jack White's new gags are relatively weak (Larry: "Worse comes to worst we can rob a bank." Moe: "He's been workin' around thieves so much he's beginnin' to think like one!"; Moe to the weeping girls: "Boy, you're really weepy!"; Larry: "But the Emir of Shmow is a cutthroat. Suppose he cuts my throat?" Moe: "So you'll look like you have two mouths!").

White does supply some fine dialogue, however, for the 'helpless' harem women: "Take that you beast... frightening a defenseless woman!...You should be ashamed of yourself scaring us helpless girls!...How dare you invade the privacy of us frail women! And you caught me with my veil down!"... As often in refurbishings, gagless lines of exposition are added in (Moe: "Gee, girls, we don't have the money either...We're only poor owners of a small restaurant"; Larry: "Hey Moe, the Emir of Shmow stole that Rootentooten diamond." Moe: "Yeah, and we're gonna get it back from him, return it to its rightful owner, get a big reward and then pay the taxes for our sweethearts").The girls weep in sequence and in unison: "Our guardian is going to sell us to the Sultan of Pish Posh...unless we each pay a 1000 Chilblainer virgin tax within three days! [unison] And we don't have the money!..."Oh woe is us!" The latter unison lamentation as well as 'Pish Posh' derive from *Back to the Woods*. Other variations: Larry: "Man the lifeboats! Me and the women first" (*Grips, Grunts and Groans*); Moe shouting "Breakfast!" to wake Larry up (*Up in Daisy's Penthouse*); and Larry: "I got it! I got it!" Moe: "What?" Larry: "A terrific headache!" (*In the Sweet Pie and Pie*).

OTHER NOTES: The working title was *Diamond Daffy*. The map from the original film is not used because we just saw one in the introduction to *Stone Age Romeos*. Joe Palma had appeared in nine Shemp films, most notably as the third Noonan brother in *Shot in the Frontier*. In his memoirs (*Once a Stooge, Always a Stooge* [176]), Joe Besser says the rumors at Columbia were that a despondent Moe was contemplating utterly disbanding the Stooges. Harry Cohn nixed Moe's suggestion that he and Larry form 'The Two Stooges,' and the matter was dropped until after Moe and Larry completed these last four films required by their contract. After Christmas, Cohn authorized Jules White to make an offer to Joe Besser to become the third Stooge.

#172 - HOT STUFF

Studio: Columbia

Released: September 6, 1956

Running Time: 15"55'"

Credited Production Crew:

Produced & directed by:	Jules White
Screen Play by:	Felix Adler
Story by:	Elwood Ullman
Director of Photography:	Irving Lippman
Art Director:	Ross Bellah
Film Editor:	Harold White
Assistant Director:	Willard Sheldon

Credited Cast:

Shemp Howard	
Larry Fine	
Moe Howard	
Christine McIntyre	Hazel [stock footage]
Emil Sitka	Professor Snead
Philip Van Zandt	Captain Rork

Uncredited Cast:

Joe Palma	Shemp's double
Gene Roth	His Excellency of Anemia
Connie Cezan	Uranian officer
Evelyn Lovequist	Uranian secretary
Andre Pola	Colonel Clutz
Harold Brauer	Leon [stock footage]
Vernon Dent	general [stock footage]
Jacques O'Mahoney	guard [stock footage]

PERSPECTIVE: *Hot Stuff*, the second Shempless Shemp film, refurbishes the 1949 Cold War satire *Fuelin' Around*. And its new footage demonstrates how Jules White updated not only the target of political satire but also methods of presenting Shemp's double on film. For the previous *Rumpus in the Harem* he determined that the most expedient method of replacing Shemp was to recreate him, so he put Shemp's suit and a wig on Joe Palma, and to perpetrate the masquerade White filmed this 'Shemp' character only from the back. In *Hot Stuff* we can now be given a quick glimpse of 'Shemp's' face because Palma, like the others, is disguised with a beard and buried under a hat. Complimenting the visual presentation is the aural, for instead of supplying voice-overs here Palma is allowed to say "Right!" à la Shemp before he walks out of the hallway scene and later make the sound "ee-bee-bee" as he walks out of the camera frame in the laboratory scene. Although Palma does not look exactly like Shemp nor sound like him, abundant stock footage of the real Shemp from the original *Fuelin' Around* prevents the unaware viewer from noticing the difference. A good long look would reveal the deception, but as with the use of a stunt double, a quick glimpse is all we get. So 'Shemp' is promptly sent to follow the suspicious-looking woman in the hallway scene and told to stand behind the door in the laboratory scene, put out of the way until the real Shemp could be reedited back into the film.

To *Fuelin' Around* are added an introductory plot clarification scene and an introductory plot development scene. The first shows us the Anemian chief, who now in the midst of the 1950s Cold War looks much more like Stalin than Hitler, ordering Rork to visit Professor Snead with the purpose of obtaining the rocket fuel that will allow Anemia to conquer Urania. The comedy here derives from the silly pomposity of Anemian protocol and the 'rotten egg flavor' snort His Excellency takes. The second shows us the Stooges in the Uranian Department of the Inferior, and the gags here come from using a variety of office props [paper spindle, stapler, ink] and flirting with the female staff.

In one sense this flirting is no different from the flirting Curly did in *Punch Drunks* back in 1934 - acting cute, polished, or aggressive. But in the 1950s Stooge flirting, thanks largely to the classic Lulu Hopkins scene in *Brideless Groom*, regularly results in paybacks. In the previous film it was punching and slapping in the harem; in this one it is a verbal put-down ("She said make yourself 'at home,' not 'obnoxious!'"), a nose bite, and a paper spindle in the rear. The Stooges have been criticized for being misogynists, but every time they encounter women recently, the women put them in their place. Their approach to women is certainly no more chauvinistic than typical Rock Hudson/Doris Day romances of the 1950s era, but their aggression is deterred because Stooge women fight back!

VISUAL HUMOR [NEW FOOTAGE]: The Anemian rounded handshake [à la *Malice in the Palace*], salutes, and heel clicks recall the physical political satire in *You Nazty Spy!*

After Shemp's death, stock footage with Shemp was carefully re-edited with new footage that necessarily omitted him.

and *I'll Never Heil Again*. The latter also made use of the globe; here His Excellency keeps his liquor inside one. Two gags are numbered, as was '81-C' in *Blunder Boys*: "number 7" (hand to ear) and "routine number 6" (blowing pepper and hitting with the bottle from behind). Larry gets Rork with the pepper in the same way Moe got him with the ink - during an unguarded laugh. Moe gives Larry multiple (4) nose bonks just as he gave him multiple (11) tack hammer hits in the original film footage.

Newspaper headlines introduced an international, news-oriented plot in *Dutiful but Dumb*. After His Excellency takes a slug of booze, he hears sirens, gongs, and drums (*Gypped in the Penthouse*), and then smoke comes out his mouth (*Shot in the Frontier*). Other variations: the 'Shave and a Haircut' knock (*Back to the Woods*); the Stooges disguised at the outset (*Horses Collars*); 'Operators 5 and 6 7/8' (*You Nazty Spy!*); the Moe slapping salute (*Uncivil Warriors*); using a paper spindle as a weapon (*Studio Stoops*); and using a stapler as a weapon (*Scotched in Scotland*).

VERBAL HUMOR (NEW MATERIAL): Felix Adler adds verbal banter to most of the new slapstick. The officer [Connie Cezan] acts like Moe when she says "Let me see your hand" and then rapidly pounds five staples into it. When Moe wants a kiss she offers: "Sure... You poot, and I'll pucker." When she sits on Moe's lap after she placed the paper spindle on the chair we hear an exchange (Officer: "Is that fun?" Moe: "You're breaking my heart!"). And as Larry pulls the spindle out we hear (Moe: "Oh! Oh! Oh! OH! OH!!" Larry: "It's out." Moe: "Oh"), the latter recalling a similar pattern in *Rockin' Thru the Rockies*. Two new puns: Officer: "You will work under cover." Moe: "Yes, we will work under covers!"; and Officer: "You will go to his new house and pretend you are carpet layers." Larry: "I can't lay carpet!...I'm not that rugged! Get it? 'Carpets'? 'Rugged'? ". Gag newspaper name: *Urania Daily Bladder*.

New Stooge recipes: "pig's feet smothered in lubricating oil, raw potatoes boiled [!] in pure varnish, and head cheese garnished with nails...rusty nails!". The 'Department of Inferior' we heard first in *Three Dark Horses*.

OTHER NOTES: The working title was *They Gassed Wrong*. A SWALLOW sound effect was added to Shemp swallowing the tacks. Another new sequence is added to the laboratory scene: the camera focuses on the key to the cell below and pulls back to show Moe and Larry. Moe: "We gotta get down there somehow." Without the Morse Code scene, however, it is no longer clear how Moe and Larry learn Professor Snead is in the cell beneath them.

#173 - SCHEMING SCHEMERS

Studio: Columbia

Released: October 4, 1956

Running Time: 15"54'"

Credited Production Crew:

Produced & directed:	Jules White
Screen Play by:	Jack White
Story by:	Elwood Ullman
Director of Photography:	Ray Cory
Art Director:	Ross Bellah
Film Editor:	Harold White
Assistant Director:	Willard Sheldon

Credited Cast:

Shemp Howard	
Larry Fine	
Moe Howard	
Christine McIntyre	Mrs. Allen [stock footage]
Emil Sitka	Walter Norfleet
Kenneth MacDonald	Mr. Allen
Dudley Dickerson	Henry, the chef [stock footage]

Uncredited Cast:

Symona Boniface	Clarabell Norfleet [stock footage]
Herbert Evans	Wilks, the butler [stock footage]
Joe Palma	Shemp's double
Al Thompson	party guest [stock footage]
Victor Travers	party guest [stock footage]
Helen Dickson	party guest [stock footage]

PERSPECTIVE: *Scheming Schemers* is delightful chaos, the most outrageous of the four Shempless films with crazy plumbing from 1949's *Vagabond Loafers*, the no-holds-barred pie-fight footage from *Half-Wits Holiday*, and the most elaborate reediting job in Stoogedom. While the previous refurbishings had only several additions and excisions, there are well more than a dozen here with sequences from both films not only spliced into tasty morsels and rearranged but also supplied with voice-overs for 'Shemp' as well as for Larry and Moe. In addition, there were doubles used for both Shemp and Mrs. Allen [originally Christine McIntyre], and, as if the visual and audio editing is not complex enough, the writing takes us in search of that ring upstairs and downstairs in a watery maze of locations as confusing as Shemp's pipe work up in the bathroom. If Jack and Jules White were trying to match madcap confusion in form and content, this film is an utter success.

The rewriting works around Shemp's absence by leaving Shemp [Joe Palma] outside - we see him unloading the truck, his face covered by tools and a work bag - while Moe and Larry find, lose, and refind Norfleet's ring. The Whites then had to rewrite the finale since *Vagabond Loafers* had nothing to do with a lost ring. Their new version ends simply and effectively with Moe and Larry solving the crime via the pie-fight footage and then thinking about Shemp. In the most ironic moment in any Stooge film, Moe asks "Hey, where is that puddin'-head?" and then he and Larry look up. We might think sadly of Shemp's real 'heavenly daze,' but they are thinking only of Shemp the plumber. The film closes with a sequence excised from the middle of the original film and placed now at the conclusion of the new version: Shemp crying from his own pipe labyrinth, "Moe! Larry!"

How appropriate that *Vagabond Loafers* should be the subject of such energetic refurbishing. It was the first Stooge film made from a previously filmed Stooge script [*A Plumbing We Will Go* was itself derived from an earlier film] that combined two classic Stooge characterizations - tradesmen in a wealthy home and crook catchers - and now we have the tradesmen in a wealthy home and the pie fight we saw again in *Pest Man Wins*. The resulting film has the viewer following Mr. Norfleet's ring from hand to sink to pipe to basement to Larry's hair, figuring out how Shemp gets back to the basement, why Larry returns to the washroom, how the party guests and the Stooges get into the pie room, and keeping track of the chef and the painting thieves. The whole experience is a wild ride for the viewer and apparently so emotionally stressful for the frantic Mr. Norfleet that when he gets his valuable ring back he cannot think of anything else except the stolen painting; he does not even notice his washbasin on the floor and heedlessly drinks from his gushing pipes. Desperate to get the painting back, he gets a pie in the face and then offers to reward the Stooges. But ponder what he will find when he goes upstairs to shower the pie bits from his hair.

VISUAL HUMOR (NEW FOOTAGE): More editing occurs where Larry drills several holes in the first-floor bathroom's floor, soaking Moe in the basement below; in the original that water came from Shemp, but now Shemp is in the second-floor bathroom. Film Editor Harold White does a fine job when Moe knocks Larry's pie in the air, making it seem as if it is landing on Symona Boniface's face even though her pie originally fell from the ceiling ['the Sword of Damocles'] in *Half-Wits Holiday*... The sound editing is effectively muted when we hear Larry speaking in a muffled tone ("I'm down here....") from 'inside' the sink. Although the slapstick is reduced to only two active Stooges, Moe and Larry have fine moments in the bathroom when they twice bonk their heads together reaching into the sink and when Larry pries the sink off the wall onto Moe's foot, which in the best Stooge tradition advances the plot: Moe hollers and hops and clanks Larry on the head with his hammer, but when he grabs him by the hair, he finds the ring. For the pie fight they again lack Shemp, but have both Kenneth MacDonald and the footage from *Half-Wits Holiday* to help them; highlights include Larry's second shot hitting Moe in the back of the head, Larry covering his face and squatting ("Are you here, Moe?" Moe [squatting]: "No, I just left." [BLAM]) à la *Pop Goes the Easel*, and Moe gouging MacDonald, grabbing the pipe, and hitting him twice with the pipe (and Larry with the backswing)... Moe becomes a bossy hypocrite for the gag in which Larry drops the tool bag on the floor (CRASH), Moe yells "QUIET!" and throws his own equipment on the floor (CRASH), and yells: "I said 'Quiet!'" (SLAP)... Moe tries to pull a wrench from the tool bag, but it is stuck; he yanks it out and hits himself in the forehead, much as did Larry in the previous film (*Hot Stuff*) when he pulled the paper spindle out of Moe's rear. Other variations: Larry being under the sink while seeming to be *in* the sink (*False Alarms*); Moe sticking the plunger onto Larry's forehead (*Dizzy Pilots*); and Larry getting gouged when he asks Moe: "Is your hand all right? (GOUGE) It's all right...Ow!" (*Musty Musketeers*).

VERBAL HUMOR (NEW FOOTAGE): Jack White's new plumbing lines include anatomical absurdities (Larry: "I won't fit in here [the sink]!" Moe: "By golly, he's right. His ears are in the way!"; Moe: "I got part of him [Larry's hair]. I'll have to take him out in pieces!"), internal rhyme (Larry: "I couldn't find that water shutoff." Moe: "Shutoff, shut-up!"), and a popular, contemporary verbal play (Larry: "What do you think I am, any how?" Moe: "Come on, 'any how'!"). One way of making Shemp seem present is to talk about him (Mr. Norfleet: "Someone stole our new $50,000 painting." Larry to Moe: "Where's Shemp? He loves pictures."). Examples of lines dubbed in are Shemp's "Hold your horses, will ya'?" and Larry's "We can't find the ring while it's leakin'". The line "It's the very latest set" has been edited out because that TV is no longer the 'very latest' model. Variations: Larry: "What idiot left this water running? Oh, *I* did!" (*Hokus Pokus*); Moe: "Don't worry boss. We'll have your ring back before you can say 'Cucamonga'" (*Back to the Woods*); and Moe saying "Hhmm!" (*I'm a Monkey's Uncle*). Epithets: "sap," "knucklehead," and "puddin'-head."

OTHER NOTES: The new footage was shot January 16, 1956. The working title was *Pixilated Plumbers*. A double is used for Christine McIntyre, who had married and retired from Columbia the previous year, when Moe and Larry spy the Allens putting the painting in the pipe; in the original it was Shemp who saw this. Of the three Stooge plumbing films derived ultimately from Sidney & Murray's *Plumbing for Gold*, this is the only one which includes the search for a lost ring.

Scheming Schemers (1956) offers the last footage of the skillful comedienne Christine McIntyre (1911-1984). Born in Nogales, Arizona, Christine studied voice at Chicago Musical College and, after several stage and B Western gigs, was discovered by Hugh McCollum, who was apparently inspired in part by Christine's newly dyed blonde hair. Though she appeared in more than a dozen Stooge short films and many other non-Stooge Columbia comedies, she is best remembered for her delightful singing in *Micro-Phonies* (1945) and *Squareheads of the Round Table* (1948), and the fabulous punch she threw at Shemp in *Brideless Groom* (1947).

#174 - COMMOTION ON THE OCEAN

Studio: Columbia

Released: November 8, 1956

Running Time: 16"34'"

Credited Production Crew:

Produced & directed by:	Jules White
Story & screen Play by:	Felix Adler
Director of Photography:	Ray Cory
Art Director:	Ross Bellah
Film Editor:	Harold White
Assistant Director:	Willard Sheldon

Credited Cast:

Shemp Howard	
Larry Fine	
Moe Howard	
Gene Roth	Bortch [stock footage]
Emil Sitka	Smitty
Harriette Tarler	Emma Blake
Charles Wilson	J. L. Cameron [stock footage]

Uncredited Cast:

Joe Palma	Shemp's double

PERSPECTIVE: This fourth and last of the Shempless Shemp films refurbishes *Dunked in the Deep*, the 1949 film that so effectively isolated the Stooges with a Cold War spy as stowaways aboard a freighter crossing the Atlantic. This is the only refurbished Shemp film of the 1950s directed and written by the original directing and writing team - Jules White and Felix Adler. They accomplished this final refurbishing in two steps, first by incorporating the newspaper office introduction from another 1949 film, *Crime on Their Hands*, and then by updating the spy's microfilmed contraband from the vaguely described "secret files" to more specific "secret atomic documents." The Punjab Diamond theft portion of *Crime on Their Hands* had recently been used in *Hot Ice*, where the introduction of *The Hot Scots* was attached to it, and now the reverse occurs here: the newspaper office introduction of *Crime on Their Hands* is attached to the espionage tale of *Dunked in the Deep*. [We saw a similar division with *Hold That Lion*, the first half reused in *Loose Loot*, the second half in *Booty and the Beast*.] Because Shemp plays such an important role in the chase sequence and ship-board antics of *Dunked in the Deep*, *Commotion on the Ocean* relies very heavily on stock footage, but White joined the two footages neatly, not editing and splicing so frequently as in the previous *Scheming Schemers*.

White and Adler updated the original espionage story by simply changing the newspaper headline from the 'Punjab Diamond' caper to read 'ATOMIC DOCUMENTS MISSING - SUSPECTS BEING SCREENED,' which takes the film out of its original post-war Cold War milieu and puts it into the 'Atomic Period' of the mid-1950s. The high profile arrest, trial, and execution of Ethel and Julius Rosenberg for stealing secret atomic documents just a few years earlier [1951-53] had become a fixture in the American psyche, and feature films like *The Atomic City* [1952] and *The Atomic Man* [1956] had already brought contemporary anti-Soviet spy films into the higher-tech plane. Now it was the Stooges' turn to go atomic. By next year they will be in outer space.

The new footage consists of simple plot exposition inserts [Moe to Bortch: "We've disguised ourselves so we won't be recognized." Larry: "We're lookin' for a foreign spy who stole atomic secret documents." Moe: "We're undercover reporters, so to speak." Larry: "Yeah, and since you speak so many foreign languages, how about helping us tonight?") and an extended sequence which culminates with the hungry Stooges eating a wooden fish and spitting out sawdust à la *Uncivil Warriors*. This fits in neatly with the salami eating sequence of the original, not requiring the presence of Shemp who is "on deck to scout for food" (and who originally found the salami in the first place). As Moe spits out sawdust, he says, "I hope Shemp got somethin' decent to eat," to tie the old and new footages together.

And with this film the era of Howard-Fine-Howard Columbia two-reelers comes to a close after 22 years and 174 films.

VISUAL HUMOR (NEW FOOTAGE): The comedic ancestry of the wooden fish includes the still-mounted wooden fish Curly cooks in *Even As IOU*... Both the porthole and post-salami sea-sickness gags are plot specific; the new inedible fish sequence and the undrinkable booze sequence of the original complement each other like a [not so] fine meal and a [lousy] bottle of wine. When Moe and Larry remove their shoes to sneak around the ship quietly, Larry pulls his off and socks Moe in the face, a variation on gags in the previous two films (Moe pulling a wrench from the bag and hitting himself [*Scheming Schemers*]; and Larry pulling the paper spindle out of Moe's rear [*Hot Stuff*]). Moe smashing the plate over Larry's head brings the eating sequence to a close.

VERBAL HUMOR (NEW FOOTAGE): Shemp's absence requires Adler to write two-patterns, whether the aforementioned expository ones or as a prelude to slapstick (Larry: "You're broad minded." Moe : "You're narrow headed!"[WHAM]). Adler also offers food-related expressions (Moe: "Speaking of food, my stomach thinks my throat is cut!"), internal rhymes (Moe: "Hey, skipper, how would you like to have that kipper?"), and puns (Larry's "Nervous beer!"; and Larry: "That's a dish of fish and it's perfect. You can take my word on it. On fish I'm a 'common-sewer' [connoisseur]"). The latter is used twice, the second time evoking a hit from Moe. Epithet: "flat-head". Larry's joke about Smitty's name ("Smitty. Oh, I know him: 'Under the spreading chestnut tree, the village Smitty stands') is derived from Longfellow's poem, and was used in *Fiddlers Three* and elsewhere.

OTHER NOTES: The new footage was shot in one day, January 17, 1956 - the day after *Scheming Schemers* - as may be apparent from the way Larry swallows and reverses the phrase 'secret atomic documents' to "atomic secret documents".The working title was *Salt Water Daffy*. Stooge address: 'Emma Blake, 1420 Beech St., Rialto, California.'

1957

Hoofs and Goofs • Muscle Up a Little Closer • A Merry Mix-Up

Space Ship Sappy • Guns A Poppin! • Horsing Around

Rusty Romeos • Outer Space Jitters

#175 - HOOFS AND GOOFS

Studio: Columbia

Released: January 31, 1957

Running Time: 15"27"

Credited Production Crew:

Produced & Directed by:	Jules White
Story & Screen Play by:	Jack White
Director of Photography:	Gert Anderson
Art Director:	Paul Palmentola
Film Editor:	Harold White
Assistant Director:	Willard Sheldon

Credited Cast:

Joe Besser	
Larry Fine	
Moe Howard	
Benny Rubin	Mr. Dinkelspiel, the landlord
Harriette Tarler	his daughter
Tony, the Wonder Horse	

PERSPECTIVE: The final four films of 1956 worked well enough as refurbished Shemp films with Joe Palma doubling as Shemp in brief sequences, but this technique would not work for a whole year's worth of films, let alone for the personal appearances the Stooges made during their annual hiatus. Moe seems to have fixed on the idea that Shemp's replacement, the next 'third Stooge,' should resemble Curly, so he first asked burlesque comic Joe DeRita. [*Moe Howard* (152)]: "He was fat and chubby with a round, jovial face, and, with his hair clipped close, he would look a great deal like my brother Curly."] But DeRita was bound by contract to burlesque producer Harold Minsky, so Harry Cohn and Jules White, with Moe's guidance, turned to another chubby burlesque comic, Joe Besser. An experienced stage, film, and television comedian born in St. Louis in 1907, he was only five years younger than Larry. Besser had known the Stooges for decades and had worked with the non-Stooge Shemp, first on Broadway in J. J. Shubert's *The Passing Show of 1932* and later in Abbott & Costello's *Africa Screams* (1949) he had also maintained a close personal friendship with Shemp over the years. Besides resembling Curly in his rotund stature, Joe Besser featured a Curly-esque childlike personality and simple-mindedness. Yet this personality type was not all for the stage: Besser refused to take the slaps, gouges, and conks that Curly, Shemp, and Larry regularly suffered, and his contract, which paid him more than Moe and Larry, stipulated that he was not to receive that kind of pounding.

With Besser's contract for sixteen two-reelers inked on January 1, 1956, Moe and Larry launch into a fresh chapter in Stooge history with *Hoofs and Goofs*. The concept of attributing human speech and thought to an equine figure as the result of metamorphosis is as old as Apuleius' *The Golden Ass* and Shakespeare's *A Midsummer Night's Dream*, and it had been recently revived in the 'Francis, the Talking Mule' films produced from 1950 until 1956, the year *Hoofs and Goofs* was produced. [*Mister Ed* was not developed until 1961.] This takes the Stooges down a comedic path they had trodden only briefly with the talking animals in *Crime On Their Hands* and *Rockin' In the Rockies*.

With the substitution of Joe for Shemp, a certain refocusing in inter-Stooge relationships was necessary. Joe's presence in the film is clearly distinct from Moe's and Larry's. Unlike them, he believes in reincarnation and is determined to recover the soul of sister Birdie. He even bosses them around several times, and he utterly takes charge when it comes time to deliver Birdie's colt. This idea of distinguishing the third Stooge had worked well before in *Heavenly Daze* and *Scrambled Brains*, and now with a non-Howard third Stooge there was a more compelling reason for developing the concept. And yet, as in Shemp's first film, there is a special emphasis on establishing the newcomer's Stoogeness: by making the three Stooges brothers and casting Moe as their little sister, there can be no doubt in the audience's mind that these are indeed 'The Three Stooges,' even if one of the faces is different.

VISUAL HUMOR: Because of the stipulations in Besser's contract, Moe never lays a hand on him except to dump water and a casserole over his head. In contrast, Joe gives Moe and Larry several patsy slaps, which work quite well; these were part of Joe's well developed physical style. His rude awakening to Stoogedom seems to come when he bonks Moe's head and hurts his own hand ("Ow! That hur-r-ts!"). The casserole Birdie dumps on his head at the conclusion of the film was originally designed to be a break-away rolling pin; but Besser protested and the prop was changed. In his autobiography Besser says the Stooges were quite accommodating in keeping him from potential harm. Much of the physical humor is reallocated from Joe to Stooge veteran Benny Rubin [Mr. Dinkelspiel] as the foil, recalling the old Vernon Dent/ Bud Jamison days: plaster falls from the ceiling onto his cake, into his soup, and onto his head; he blindly looks into a cabinet instead of the bedroom; Birdie kicks him face first into the fly paper; he walks across a chair; he gets his glasses back on with the fly paper still attached; he falls down the stairs; and he drinks the ether-laden milk and passes out. He also indulges in some buddy humor when he nudges Moe about hiding a lady [the horse in drag] in the apartment. Dinkelspiel's reliance on glasses recalls Curly in *All the World's A Stooge* and Shemp in *Mummy's Dummies*. The horse carries some of the physical humor as well, dressing in drag [as does Moe later], stretching out across two beds, and displaying a wristwatch on her ankle.

As for Moe and Larry, Moe trips over the chair Larry left in his path, spilling the water; Moe refills the basin but gets knocked over by Larry on the other side of a swinging door (*Playing the Ponies*). A new slapstick wrinkle is Larry saying "Ask me nice" before being slapped by Moe ("That's nice enough!"), although it is similar to "I'll...when I'm good and ready!". Other variations: tying the brick onto Birdie's tail (*Busy Buddies*), the misdirected horse pill (*Even as IOU*), giving their horse a bath (*Flat Foot Stooges*); wringing out the tail into Moe's face (*He Cooked His Goose*); the result shot of Moe with the basin on his head (*Goof on the Roof*); a drunk standing nearby (*Matri-Phony*); and ending the film as if it were all a dream (*Heavenly Daze* and *I Can Hardly Wait*). Decor: there is a painting of a horse on the bedroom wall; and the Stooges lead Birdie past a sign in their apartment lobby: 'NO PETS.'

VERBAL HUMOR: The sounds of speech are very different in this film, created by Joe's well-honed child-like patter ("Don't swat that f-l-l-l-y-y-y-y! You may be hurting Birdie!"; "Hur-r-ry!"; and "That hur-rts!"), Birdie's off-screen voice, and Dinkelspiel's thick German accent and malapropisms ([when plaster falls in his soup] "Thank you very much for the cracker!"; "I'm going upstairs to give those guys two pieces of my mind!"; "Tr-r-r-ampling ar-r-r-ound here like a horse!"; "It schmells like a horse!"; "Who made out the lights?"; "It's dark out here...Yoww!"). Rubin used a thick Italian accent in *Tricky Dicks*. Joe's child-like speech also accommodates classic Stooge ignorance, e.g. Larry: "You're the anesthetist." Joe: "Don't call me names!" It presents a simple-minded cuteness, which is used to bring the film to a conclusion: "Birdie...no salt!".

There are several 'horse' references (Moe's "It's my bronchitis...or maybe it's because I'm a little hoarse today"; Larry's "You're stubborn as a mule!"; Joe's "Horse feathers!"). Equine ironies are heard when Larry urges Birdie to "tip-toe"; and when Birdie tells the Stooges: "You guys don't smell like lilies either!". There are other animal jokes, including the name "Birdie"; Birdie's "A horse?! You worm!"; and Larry's set gag about the chicken (Larry: "Yesterday he imagined he was a chicken." Moe: "We better send him to an institution." Larry: "Oh we can't do that!" Moe: "Why not?" Larry: "We need the eggs!") heard previously in *Listen, Judge*. Moe's "like my ex-mother-in-law" is one of the few mother-in-law jokes in Stooge films; cf. *All Gummed Up*. Other variations: Larry: "You startin' that again?" (*False Alarms*); Moe opening his mouth to pretend he is neighing (*I Can Hardly Wait*); and Birdie's burp (the conclusion of *You Nazty Spy!*). Reference: Birdie's reference to Kim Novack (Joe: "Birdie! You're reincarnated...but you're a horse." Birdie: "So who did you expect - Kim Novack?") is particularly ironic since in the next year she would star in Hitchcock's *Vertigo*, which involves a reincarnation, although not an equine one.

OTHER NOTES: The working titles were *Galloping Bride* and *Horsing Around*. The newly made opening screen shows the Stooges (not a drawing or still photograph) standing against a black background (like the 3-D introductions to *Spooks!* and *Pardon My Backfire*) and, after a brief fanfare, singing a major triad of "Hello," then waving and saying "Hello." The music used is the 'driving' version of 'Three Blind Mice,' newly recorded with a harp introduction and a shortened middle section. All the actors are credited. Some of the scenes are divided by fading to black. Moe's double is obvious in the final scene. Reincarnation was featured in several films of 1957 (*The She Creature* and *The Undead*) in addition to *Vertigo* of the following year. When looking for the girl's father in *Dutiful but Dumb*, Curly looks at a horse and explains: "Don't you believe in reincarnation?". Joe Besser gives a detailed account of how Harry Cohn and Jules White hired him as the 'third Stooge' on pp. 171-80 of his autobiography, *Once A Stooge, Always a Stooge*. Not such a Stooge off camera, Besser negotiated a salary of $3500 per week; Moe and Larry were receiving $1000 less than that. Besser was well known to audiences of the day from his regular appearances on early television variety shows and especially his continuing role as the childish 'Stinky' on *The Abbott and Costello Show* in 1951-1953. He had also starred in 10 shorts at Columbia produced between 1949-1956; that series came to an end when he joined the Stooges. Many of the Joe shorts he filmed as a Stooge were collected into a feature release known as *The Three Stooges Fun-O-Rama* (1959).

This photo from *Hoofs and Goofs* (1957), the first release of the year and the first of sixteen Joe Besser Stooge films, includes a different array of characters - the ethnic-accented Benny Rubin [Mr. Dinkelspiel] and a horse. The latter is scripted as a reincarnated Stooge, and the former takes most of the physical abuse.

When Joe Besser was hired to play the 'third stooge,' he insisted his contract stipulate that he not be forced to take the kind of physical punishment characteristic of the third stooge when played by Curly and Shemp. Man-to-man, Stooge-abuse slapstick had been a trademark of the act since the Ted Healy period in the 1920s, so writer and director Jack and Jules White found different ways to create the physical comedy.

#176 - MUSCLE UP A LITTLE CLOSER

Studio: Columbia

Released: February 28, 1957

Running Time: 16"46'"

Credited Production Crew:

Produced & Directed by:	Jules White
Written By:	Felix Adler
Director of Photography:	Irving Lippman
Art Director:	Cary Odell
Film Editor:	Harold White
Set Decorator:	Robert Priestley
Assistant Director:	Mitchell Gamson

Credited Cast:

Joe Besser	
Larry Fine	
Moe Howard	
Maxine Gates	Tiny, Joe's girl
Harriette Tarler	Mary Brown, Moe's girl
Ruth Godfrey	May Trent, Larry's girl
Matt Murphy	Elmo Drake, trucking foreman

PERSPECTIVE: *Muscle Up A Little Closer* has the distinction of being the first film in which Larry does not frizz his hair and Moe combs his bangs back off his forehead. Changing these trademark silhouettes that had identified them for decades was Joe's suggestion, and since Moe and Jules White knew that replacing Shemp would necessitate stylistic changes, they were receptive to some of Joe's ideas. To accommodate him in the previous film they reallocated the physical beatings the 'third Stooge' usually receives, and now in *Muscle Up a Little Closer* Moe and Larry change their hairdos. It was not an unwelcome suggestion - off camera Moe wore his hair combed back, and Larry was losing hair with every frizz - and it does not interfere with the slapstick: Moe still manages to give Larry a hair pull in the locker room, and two films hence Moe's hair will stand on end at the sight of Sunevian Amazons. Nonetheless, the change would soon be reversed since it made matching up old footage impossible.

Like many Stooge films this one takes place in two distinct locations. The initial domestic scene introduces the Stooges' new hairdos by having the girls compliment them on their haircuts. But we barely notice their hair because soon after Moe knocks on the door [and two foreheads], the humongous Maxine Gates ['Tiny'!] dominates the scene. The Stooges had married Maxine into the family recently in *Husbands Beware*, where she used her massive forearm to break a table with one of Shemp's biscuits, and now here she brings the frantic search for the diamond ring to an earth-shaking climax by collapsing onto the bed [and Larry!] in one of the most tremendous falls in all of Stoogedom.

The hunt for the ring takes the Stooges to plant locations reminiscent of settings used for the early TV sitcom *The Life of Riley*. The packaging room scenes have little to do with the search for the ring, but they give Joe his first opportunity to work in some solo physical gags - sewing the package to his shirt, scrambling eggs on the floor with an acetylene torch, and feigning a heart attack. The latter results in a medical examination with fresh, if understated, material, including the first Stooge reference to 'rock-and-roll.' In the locker room dumbbells knock Larry into a daze [à la *Grips, Grunts and Groans*], and he suffers further abuse from Moe in a sequence cleverly hidden behind intervaled lockers. As the working title *Builder Uppers* suggests, the original concept put the Stooges into the company gym to do some comic exercise. They had been in gyms before to train boxers and wrestlers, but here they parody two newly popular sports: weightlifting and wrestling. Finding the ring-snatching Elmo in the gym, the Stooges are each defeated by him. But these defeats are just preliminaries to the titanic bout between Tiny and Elmo, which owes its headlock, body-throwing, and flying-leap choreography to televised wrestling that was popular at the time. For the second consecutive film, much of the physical comedy is reallocated from Joe and the Stooges to a non-Stooge. This is a major change for Stooge dynamics, but little 'Tiny' is definitely up to the task of beating up Elmo, recovering her ring, and literally carrying her beloved Joe off to their honeymoon.

VISUAL HUMOR: Inventive as ever, Jules White and the Stooges find a way to have Joe take a shove from Moe, fall to the floor, get the package ripped off his shirt, follow his nose along Moe's sleeve, and participate in the climactic battle without ever taking a real hit but appearing to be part of the melee. Typically, Joe throws his shirt into Moe's face without payback. Two of his gags are verbal and [mildly] physical, the first when Moe gives him a drink of water and Joe says "pink pills," spraying water all over Moe; the second when Joe wants to fight Elmo, insists four times "Let go of me!" to Tiny, but as he steps forward the fourth time he notices with disappointed surprise: "Oh! She let go of me!".

The camera enhances several sequences: it shifts from face to face in the first scene; pulls back to reveal the burlap wrapping on Joe's package; and hides Larry behind the locker. Stooge-esque uses for barbells: throwing one across the room like a spear; and hitting two Stooges in the face with each side. Dumbbells are used to roll off the locker onto Larry's head à la *Grips, Grunts and Groans*. Blowing through the stethoscope we saw earlier in *Scrambled Brains*, but having the stethoscope tip plug into the light socket is a new use for this often and effectively used Stooge prop. The Stooges washed their hands for sterility in the beginning of *Calling All Curs*; here Moe washes his hands in a bucket of fire water, holds them up to maintain their sterility, then dries them off on a greasy towel. Joe following his nose along Moe's pointing arm was first used in the Maharaja sequences of *Time Out for Rhythm* and *Three Little Pirates*. Tiny's great crash on the bed recalls the bed collapse in *Bedlam in Paradise*. The result shot, with Joe having one eggshell on his brow, one on his nose, and another in his mouth, resembles the one in *Three Smart Saps*. Other variations: Moe knocking on the door, then Joe's head and Tiny's (*Calling All Curs*); the 'N-B-C' clanging (*Back to the Woods*); Joe picking the box up and the bottom falling out (*Cash and Carry*); and Joe discarding his gum and sticking it under the table (*Love At First Bite*).

VERBAL HUMOR: Joe's "Don't yell-l-l!" - a Stooge first - adds noisy chaos to the lost ring situation. Felix Adler gives him several word plays (Larry: "Let's look before we leap!" Joe: "He's a good looker, and I'm a bad leaper!"; Moe: "Quit stallin'!" Joe: "I'm not stallin'; I'm thinkin'!"; [to Larry with the spring on his nose] Joe: "You're all sprung!"). Like a true Stooge, Joe is a coward ("You get him. I'm afraid I'll kill him!"; cf. Moe: "This is a man's job." Larry: "Where will we find one?"), and lazy (Tiny: "Pick it up!" Joe: "Pick it up?! I can't even bend!"), and has to endure jokes about his head (Tiny: "You're too fat - Look at your head!").

References: Moe speaks in an uncharacteristic combination of short phrases followed by a sentence or explanation ("A frustrated short-order cook. This guy must have come from outer space"; "Weak heart. Get a new one right away"; "That's an involved case of high water pressure"; and "A slight case of musical cardiac - rock-and-roll type - a lot of fat around the heart and plenty of it around the head. Strenuous exercise is what I recommend"). This is an imitation, and many of the verbal gags depend on contemporary references: Moe's "medic" (Moe: "I was in the army medical corps, a medic." Larry: "I saw you on TV!") refers to *Medic*, one of the first medical anthology shows on television; it ran on NBC from 1954-'56. Larry's "I'm mortified" (with the bed spring on his nose) is an allusion to entertainer Jimmy Durante; there have been many Stooge references to Durante over the years, but Durante was still well known from 'The Jimmy Durante Show' originally running on NBC (1954-1956), switching to CBS in 1957. The doubly ethnic set-gag (Larry: "That shipment came in from Japan." Moe: "What was in it?" Larry: "Matzah." Moe: "Just in time for Thanksgiving.") makes fun of the old enemy - Japan - and its cheap exports; a popular gag in the mid-1950s was to describe anything cheap as 'Made in Japan.' The sign: 'SEABISCUIT FOOD CORP. - SEABISCUIT GIVES YOU AN APPETITE LIKE A HORSE' refers to the same champion horse as in *You Nazty Spy!* ('Sea of Biscuit') and *Violent Is the Word for Curly*. Moe's reference to rock-and-roll reflects the late spring of 1956 when the pop charts still mixed standard pop hits by Frank Sinatra and Doris Day with the new genre, e.g. Elvis Presley's 'Heartbreak Hotel' (March), 'Blue Suede Shoes' (April), and 'I Want You, I need You, I Love You' (May), and Chuck Berry's 'Roll Over Beethoven' (June). As for Moe's "this guy must have come from outer space," the film after next would involve space travel; the Soviet 'Sputnik' would not be launched until the following year. Epithet: "bubble-brain". Joe's "You're stretchin' my skull!" recalls Shemp's "You're crushin' my eyebrows!" in *Fright Night*. Other variations: Moe: "Nice time to go to sleep!" (*Uncivil War Birds*); Joe: "That string is an octopus!" (*The Sitter Downers*); Moe: "Keep an eye on him." Larry: "I'll keep both eyes on him!" (*Slaphappy Sleuths*); and Larry: "Something knocked me dizzy." Moe: "You were born that way." (*All the World's a Stooge*).

OTHER NOTES: The film was shot in late June, 1956.The title parodies the Otto Harbach/Karl Hoschna song 'Cuddle Up a Little Closer' written for the 1908 Broadway show *The Three Twins* and revived often in later films, e.g. 1939's *The Story of Vernon and Irene Castle*. This is the first Stooge film to credit a 'Set Decorator' [Robert Priestley] as distinct from the 'Art Director'. Televised wrestling had been regularly scheduled on all three major networks since the summer of 1948. There is an odd voice over ("Oo! Larry! Will ya' help me?!") when Joe bends over to clean up the eggs. The *Scrapbook* reports two deleted sequences at the plant, one involving Moe, Joe, and a concealed salami, the other sticking Joe's ear to a wad of gum on a telephone receiver à la *Love At First Bite*... Larry puts out what seems to be an accidental fire on Joe's trouser leg. All the actors are credited.

#177 - A MERRY MIX-UP

Studio: Columbia

Released: March 28, 1957

Running Time: 15"51'"

Credited Production Crew:

Produced & Directed by:	Jules White
Written By:	Felix Adler
Director of Photography:	Irving Lippman
Art Director:	Paul Palmentola
Film Editor:	Harold White
Set Decorator:	Dave Montrose
Assistant Director:	Irving Moore

Credited Cast:

Joe Besser	Joe, Jack, Jeff
Larry Fine	Larry, Louie, Luke
Moe Howard	Moe, Max, Morris

Uncredited Cast:

Frank Sully	waiter
Nanette Bordeaux	May (Jack's wife)
Suzanne Ridgeway	Jill (Louie's wife)
Harriette Tarler	Letty (Max's wife)
Diana Darrin	Jane (Morris's fiancee)
Ruth Godfrey White	Leona (Luke's fiancee)
Jeanne Carmen	Mary (Jeff's fiancee)

PERSPECTIVE: One of the oldest comic plots is one in which twin brothers separated in their youth turn up years later in the same place at the same time without anyone realizing the coincidence. First one twin converses with his wife or friends and exits; then the other twin appears, not recognizing his twin brother's wife and friends even though they recognize 'him'; confusion reigns since no one is aware that there are two different but identical brothers. Even the brothers themselves do not know that their twin brother is alive, let alone in the same place at the same time. Only the audience knows that there are two brothers causing all the confusion, and this is what makes the situation so eternally comical. This comic tradition begins in ancient Greece and Rome with Plautus' *Menaechmi Brothers* and *Amphitryon*, and then Shakespeare wrote the first well-known English variation, *A Comedy of Errors*. In Shakespeare the tradition takes on two sets of twins - a master and his servant each having a twin brother, who are also master and servant. The best-known twentieth-century version is George Abbott's *The Boys From Syracuse*, which was turned into both a Rodgers & Hart Broadway musical and then a Universal film in 1940. *The Boys From Syracuse* was well-known enough to be referred to during the Mata Hari sequence in *You Nazty Spy!*.

Felix Adler helped write a Laurel & Hardy version (*Our Relations*) in 1936, and now Adler Stoogifies the tradition in *A Merry Mix-Up*. As in *Cookoo on a Choo Choo*, which parodied both *A Streetcar Named Desire* and *Harvey*, the Stooges tend to take parody to extremes, so Adler increases not only the twins to triplets to accommodate the Stooge trio; he also increases the number of fraternal sets from two to three and the women involved with them from two to six. *A Merry Mix-Up* is therefore an extravaganza of a time-honored comic scheme, and the nine Stooges pull it off without a hitch by using split screens and doubles. No Stooge film is photographically so complex.

In 1950's *Self-Made Maids* the Stooges had to differentiate their roles as Stooge men and Stooge fiancées, but here in *A Merry Mix-Up* they must seem similar enough to create the confusion and infuriate their fiancées and wives while still letting us identify each set of Stooge triplets. The physicality of *A Merry Mix-Up* makes up for the relative calm of the first two Joe Besser Stooge shorts, and it even brings about Joe's first 'beating,' a backwards BONK to which he offers a fine reaction. Adding physical excitement to the confusion is the fight between women and the Stooges, the fight between the two sets of women, and all the interaction with the waiter. Like the landlord and horse in *Hoofs and Goofs* and 'Tiny' and Elmo in *Muscle Up A Little Closer*, here, too a non-Stooge bears the brunt of the physical beatings and emotional frustration. For the climax the waiter chases all nine Stooges in and out of three kitchen doors in the first multi-door chase since Joe joined the trio, and ultimately the confusion makes the waiter so witless that he willingly bonks himself into merry oblivion.

VISUAL HUMOR: In addition to the numerous split screens and doubles, Irving Lippman's camera helps differentiate the sets of triplets by focusing on the individual photographs and then the individual groupings of triplets. As in *Hugs and Mugs* romance is shown in a three pattern: Leona kisses Larry; Joe ends up with lipstick lips on his forehead and hides his wallet; Moe makes faces and noises. The Stooges and Jules White are finding ways of making the slapstick with Joe less violent while still varied and amusing. When Moe backwards bonks Joe, Joe grabs his head and struts around in pain (Moe: "What's wrong?!" Joe: "Nuth-in! It was a nice piece of acting, though, wasn't it?"); when Joe asks Moe to pinch him to see if he is dreaming, Moe does (Joe: "Not so har-r-d!"), so Joe pinches him back, Moe imitates him ("Not so har-r-d!" Joe: "You copy!"), Joe lightly slaps Moe, and then he and Larry scare each other; and later the waiter bonks Moe's and Larry's heads together, so Moe gouges him, Joe pounds him, Larry turns him, and Moe kicks him into the door. These are the first gouges in a Joe film... Also adding to the physicality are Larry's

The original concept of 1957's *A Merry Mix-Up* goes back to Shakespeare and Plautus: twins separated at birth later turn up at the same place at the same time. But the ever-inventive Felix Adler did the math and expanded the tale to three sets of Stooge triplets. Here the real Stooges and six Stooge doubles line up for a cast shot. Filming the doubles, along with the Stooge women, was not nearly so simple.

Cossack dance which ends with Moe and Joe bonking heads, Ruth Godfrey's double direction triple slaps, Suzanne Ridgeway's handling of the baseball bat, and still several other Stooge variations (Joe and Larry punching Moe in the face as they put their coats on; Moe popping the champagne into Larry's face; and Larry [Louie] trailing the rest out the kitchen door, banging first into the wall). Other variations: Moe handing the waiter the phone and telling him "It's for you" (*Slaphappy Sleuths*); Joe with lipstick on his forehead (*G.I. Wanna Home*); and the waiter clanging himself a half dozen times on the head to end the film (*Who Done It?*).

VERBAL HUMOR: Narration was a common method for beginning 1950s feature film comedies and cartoons. Also common to romantic comedies of the mid/late-1950s are narrator's exclamations (e.g. "Yipe, what a jackpot!") and patterned expressions (e.g. "These fellows are confirmed bachelors and have three weaknesses: striped ties, pretty girls, and more pretty girls.") as well as a mock-flirtatious exchange (Waiter: "Will this table do?" Joe: "It has pretty legs.") and Jane's wifely gold digging "After we're all married we'll need *lots* of money". Adler writes three-patterns to emphasize the triplet groupings (Moe: "Champagne." Joe: "With bubbles!" Larry: "The cheap variety!"). They weep in a three-pattern major triad, but the most elaborate three-pattern in all of Stoogedom is the one in which they pay each other back (Moe: "And speakin' of money, how about the twenty bucks you owe me?" Larry: "I only got ten, so here's ten and I owe you ten." Joe reminds Moe he owes him twenty dollars, so Moe pays Joe the ten and owes him ten; Larry reminds Joe that he owes him twenty dollars, so Joe pays Larry the ten and owes him ten; Larry gives Moe the ten he owes him; Moe gives Joe the ten he owes him; and Joe gives Larry the ten he owes him.) Another extended triple-pattern works like the pattern made famous by Ma and Pa Kettle (Larry to Joe: "Where do you want to go?" Joe to Larry: "I don't know. Where do you want to go?" Larry to Joe: "I don't know. Where do you want to go?" Joe to Larry: "I don't know. Where do you want to go?" Moe: "Quiet, you stoops! Let's go!" Joe and Larry [unison]: "Where do you want to do?" Moe: "I don't know. Where do you— Come on! Get the coats!"). At one point Adler forms a four-pattern ([Larry]: "I'm Louis!" [Joe]: "I'm Jack!" [Moe]: "I'm Max!" Leona: "I'm mortified!"); the word "mortified" may or may not be associated with Jimmy Durante's use of the same word imitated by Larry in the previous film.

A Stooge first: [They knock the waiter against the door] Joe: "That was good! [The waiter turns back towards them] That's bad!". Other variations: Narrator: "Set of triplets #1 served in the infantry and piled up such an enviable record that they were discharged with the lowest possible honors" (*Men in Black*); Narrator: "They were in the air corps - pilots...kitchen pilots, that is. They'd 'pilot' here, they'd 'pilot' there, they'd 'pilot' anywhere" (*Uncivil Warriors*); Moe: "What'll you have - blonde, brunette, or henna color?" Larry: "Oh, henny color at all!" (*Cookoo Cavaliers*); Larry weeping "They all owed me money!" (*Fright Night*); "'a shingled roof'...It's on the house!" (*Horses' Collars*); and Moe: "Here's how!" Joe: "I know how!" (*Goofs and Saddles*). Reference: Joe's "Seek and we shall find" parodies "Seek and ye shall find" from *Matthew* 7:7. Epithet: "porcupine."

OTHER NOTES: The working title was the alliterative *A Merry Marriage Mix-Up*. This marks the last of eight Stooge appearances by Nanette Bordeaux. For a biography, see Bill Cappello, *The 3 Stooges Journal* 72 (1994) 6-7. Naming one of Larry's brothers Louie is ironic: Larry's name at birth was Louis Feinberg. The *Scrapbook* discusses a disagreement between Jules White and Larry in setting up the very expensive final group sequence; Larry was correct in remaining at his marker and saved the unit a considerable sum of money.

#178 - SPACE SHIP SAPPY

Studio: Columbia

Released: April 18, 1957

Running Time: 16"15'"

Credited Production Crew:

Produced & Directed by:	Jules White
Written By:	Jack White
Director of Photography:	Henry Freulich
Art Director:	William Flannery
Film Editor:	Saul A. Goodkind
Set Decorator:	Frank A. Tuttle
Assistant Director:	Donald Gold

Credited Cast:

Joe Besser	
Larry Fine	
Moe Howard	
Doreen Woodbury	Liza Rimple
Benny Rubin	Prof. A. K. Rimple
Marilyn Hanold	Amazon
Lorraine Crawford	Flora
Harriette Tarler	Fauna
Emil Sitka	Liar's Club Emcee

PERSPECTIVE: *Space Ship Sappy* has the grandest scope of any Stooge film to date, taking the Stooges from a humdrum earthly existence via rocket ship to an outer space adventure on the planet Sunev inhabited by alien female vampires and a giant reptile. The scope of previous films ranged from a garbage can interior (*Shivering Sherlocks*) to an expansive terrestrial golf course (*Three Little Beers*), the depths of the sea (*Three Little Sew and Sews*), the upper atmosphere (*Idle Roomers*), and the Pearly Gates (*Heavenly Daze*). None of these can rival inter-planetary travel, and for all the beatings the Stooges have taken from wives and girlfriends, for all the spooking they have received from parrots in skulls and mischievous butlers, and for all the pursuits by gorillas, crocodiles, and beast-men, they have never encountered anything as grotesque as alien vampirellas or as huge as an alien monster.

Space Ship Sappy covers the alpha and omega of Stooge scenarios by beginning with the Stooges portraying unemployed bums much as they did in their earliest Columbia films of the Depression. They have not suffered this kind of poverty since 1945's *If a Body Meets a Body*, and the last time we saw them living outside on a little patch of land was in 1946's *G.I. Wanna Home*. With holes in his shoes and Larry's shoes in the stew, Moe reads about a 'slipping' stock market as his rear slips through the hole in the hammock. 1956 marked the very heart of the great Bull Market which lifted the 'Dow' to above its pre-Depression lows, so this scene is actually an echo of 1930s Stoogedom. In stark contrast, within minutes they are aboard a space ship hurtling towards Sunev. Space travel had become the rage in films since 1950's *Destination Moon* and *Rocketship XM*, and 1956 was the year for finding beautiful women on other planets (*Forbidden Planet, Fire Maidens From Outer Space*). Budget constraints limited *Space Ship Sappy*. to modest control panel instrumentation, cheap rocket model work, and a mere three Sunevian maidens, but it did allow for the first Stooge 1950s-style 'monster' - even if only an enlarged lizard for a few seconds - and a stock shot of the earth's sphere rapidly disappearing.

Still another Stooge film on the cutting edge, *Space Ship Sappy* not only parodies futuristic space travel and 1950s giant monster and B-horror films but has Amazons speaking contemporary be-bop (literally), Larry making a reference to Elvis Presley - whose 'Hound Dog'/ 'Don't Be Cruel' release was number one in the charts in July/August of 1956 when this film was shot, and Moe referring to Joe's calculating head as an "IBM" in the very year in which IBM surpassed UNIVAC as the most successful manufacturer of mainframe computers. The tickling episode may last too long (40 seconds; cf. the laughing gas sequence in *Boobs in Arms*), and the Sunevian events may unfold too rapidly, but the Stooges have made their first venture into outer space and will return there in two of their upcoming feature films, *Have Rocket - Will Travel* and *The Three Stooges in Orbit*, despite denying the whole trip at the Liars Club.

VISUAL HUMOR: The camera expands the visual scope with special effects (the earth below, the enlarged lizard, the exterior [model] rocket, and the upside-down rocket interior) and more traditional movements (the 'fooler opening' showing us Moe smoking a cigar and reading the newspaper, then pulling back to reveal his shoe soles worn through and his rear sagging through the hammock bottom; and pulling back to reveal the 'LIARS CLUB' sign). In these late films, without a second Howard with whom to indulge in new slapstick, many old favorites are trotted out (e.g. the Cossack dance [*Ants in the Pantry*], and Moe hoisting the shovel and clonging Larry on the head [*Cash and Carry*]). New is Moe lighting his nose instead of his cigar; and Joe offering a new gag in his own style: when Moe asks if he is afraid he shakes and shakes his head 'no' but says "Yes".

Moe spreading out his paper and slugging Larry in the jaw resembles Joe and Larry punching Moe in the face as they put their coats on in the previous *A Merry Mix-Up*. Other variations: Moe slapping Joe back into a hypodermic on the table (*Spooks!*); Joe using himself as a calculator (*No Census, No Feeling*); the port hole sequence (*Dunked in the Deep*); cooking a boot as "fillet of sole and heel" [*A Pain in the Pullman*]; exhaling smoke after a kiss [*Love At First Bite*]; banging each other with duffel bags [*G.I. Wanna Home*], knocking out the professor and his daughter with the door [*Uncivil War Birds*]; Moe having holes in his shoes [*Half Shot Shooters*]; and Moe's hair standing on end [*Spook Louder*].

VERBAL HUMOR: Giving Joe the majority of the punchlines, writer Jack White works him into the Stooge frame of mind, exploiting ignorance of the meaning of words and technical terms (Professor: "Could you read a log?" Moe: "Oh, we read logs, signs on fence posts, comic books"; Larry: "What's our remuneration?" Joe: "Never mind that. What's our salary?"; Professor: "Pay strict attention to flora and fauna." Joe: "Oh boy! Dames!"; Joe: "There's Flora, Fauna and another one!"; and Joe [putting shaving cream on his face]: "You told me to 'grease my pan!'), ignorance of dangerous circumstances (Moe: "If it ain't askin' too much, where are we goin'?" Professor: "To the moon." Stooges: "Oh...to the *moon*!!"; Larry: "This joint looks deserted." Moe: "In fact, I think it's uninhabited." Joe "And there's nobody lives here either!" [three-pattern]; Professor: "Those vomen are vild! They are vampires! Be careful, or they will love you to death!" Joe: "What a wonderful way to die!" Moe: "You know my Uncle Peter died that way - took the undertaker two days to wipe the smile off his face." Larry: "That professor's silly. These innocent kids wouldn't hurt a fly. They're sweet as babies"; Moe [the lizard behind him]: "I wonder what made them run?" Larry: "They probably got a good look at your kisser!" Joe: "What a fine time to joke"; Moe [flying the rocket ship]: "Don't worry: whatever goes up must come down...I know how to run this! I used to fly a kite!...[Joe pulls the control lever off]...You got me outta control!"), ignorance of consequences (Moe: "I'll try to find us a job, even if it kills me."), ignorance of alien names and words (Moe: "You like to smooch with nice men?" Amazons: "Aye-aye-aye." Joe: "The 'ayes' have it!"; Professor: "We have landed on Sunev!" Joe: "And the 'sunev' we leave the better we'll like it!"), and ignorance of corporate names (Larry: "How's your American Can?" Moe: "Oh, that's slipping, too, but Pinpoint Pimple is up 6." Larry: "Squeeze it!"). Ignorance is central to the final gag at the Liars Club (Moe: "One fool at a time!" Larry & Joe: "Go ahead!").

Giving Joe the majority of punchlines emphasizes his stupidity, making the IBM gag particularly poignant (Moe [patting Joe's head]: "Good thinkin', kid. The old IBM is still goin' great!"). Benny Rubin [Professor Rimple] uses the silly German accent and English malapropisms he used recently in *Hoofs and Goofs* ("We are traveling at the rate of 10,000 crummy seconds a second!"; "We are going to the planet of Sunev...It's 'Venus' spelled backwards, but don't you tell somebody!"; "Wait until you see Sunev! It is the most beautiful—, in my life I have never—, this is the most gor—...I wonder what it looks like!". Larry uses the slang term 'kisser' twice ("When I walk down the street all the girls say, 'Look at that kisser'"; Moe: "What made them run?" Larry: "They probably got a good look at your kisser!").

References: Besides contemporary references to IBM, Elvis Presley, and Be-bop, Joe refers to *The Eddy Duchin Story* (1956), another Kim Novack vehicle [cf. *Hoofs and Goofs*]; and Moe refers to L.A. smog (Liza: "The air-temp gauge shows the air outside to be the same as on earth!" Moe: "Oh, smog!"). Epithet: "stupe".

Although *Space Ship Sappy* (1957) is the first film to take the Stooges into outer space, it ranges from this Depression-like opening to the planet Sunev. Along with rocket travel, the last years of Stooge films will contain frequent contemporary references to enliven and update traditional Stooge-isms.

'Branacoma Copper' is reminiscent of 'Anaconda' in *Men in Black*. Moe's lazy characterization ("I'm going to relax!") goes back to *A Pain in the Pullman* through *Hocus Pocus*. Other variations: Moe: "Recede!" (*Pardon My Scotch*); Moe: "Keep an eye out for Flora and Fauna." Joe: "Yeah, I'll keep 'em both open!" (*Slaphappy Sleuths*); Professor: "Gentlemen!" Larry: "Who came in?" (*We Want Our Mummy*); Moe: "It's rainin'" (*Blunder Boys*); and the rock painted with the graffito 'KILROY WAS HERE' (*Half-Wits Holiday*).

OTHER NOTES: In another vampire film, *Son of Dracula* (1943), the villain was 'Alucard,' 'Dracula' spelled backwards. Professor A. K. Rimple's address: '60 Bayview Road'. Shortly after filming, Joe suffered a mild heart attack and was inactive for several weeks.

#179 - GUNS A POPPIN!

Studio: Columbia

Released: June 13, 1957

Running Time: 16"27'"

Credited Production Crew:

Produced & Directed by:	Jules White
Screen Play by :	Jack White
Story by :	Jack White & Elwood Ullman
Director of Photography:	Henry Freulich
Art Director:	Cary Odell
Film Editor:	Saul A. Goodkind
Set Decorator:	Fay Babcock
Assistant Director:	Herb Wallerstein

Credited Cast:

Joe Besser	
Larry Fine	
Moe Howard	
Frank Sully	Sheriff
Joe Palma	Mad Bill Hookup
Vernon Dent	judge [stock footage]

PERSPECTIVE: After four new scripts, this fifth 'Joe film' refurbishes the 1945 'Curly film' *Idiots Deluxe*. Most of Shemp's 1954-56 films refurbished earlier 'Shemp films,' which made the reshooting and editing relatively easy since matching clothes, sets, and Shemp were the major requirements. But now there was a new Stooge who did not look like Shemp, and although he may have been short, fat, and bald, he did not look enough like Curly to blend in with old Curly footage except for indirect or long shots. Nevertheless, constant budgetary constraints compelled Jules White to cut corners, and this film illustrates how much money could be saved in refurbishings while still producing a new comedy. The new footage, remarkably, was filmed in just one day (Nov. 28, 1956), even though the film reuses only one or two minutes of stock footage from *Idiots Deluxe* - almost all of it involving the bear, 45 seconds of which are taken up by the honey-licking scene. So now the Stooges commence the first of six refurbishing projects in the Joe era, and like one of the first Shemp refurbishings (*A Missed Fortune*), this first Joe refurbishing uses a Curly script and preserves much of the original dialogue verbatim. Despite Joe's Curly-esque appearance and naiveté, it is Larry who is given many of Curly's lines (Larry says Curly's: "There's a b-b-b-bear in the window!") and physical gags: Larry takes Curly's deep 'healthy,' breath and coughs; and its now even Larry [for the first and only time] who dents the ax with his head, while Joe gets many of Larry's best lines: "This area's fine for hunting......I just saw a sign that said 'Fine For Hunting'!"

To refurbish *Idiots Deluxe* Jules and Jack White clarify the original plot by giving reasons for Moe's nervous breakdown ("Creditors closed up my business...I have to pay $10,000 or they'll put me in bankruptcy") and then add a new finale involving the apprehension of the outlaw Mad Bill Hickup. The Stooges had not made a Western since 1954, and while the original film took the Stooges merely into "the beautiful country, the babbling brook, the murmuring of the breezes through the treezes, the mooses, and the meeces," *Guns A Poppin!* now plunges the Stooges into a sheriff/outlaw gunfight by blending the threefold knock-the-door-onto-Moe sequence (a Stooge first) with the bullets-in-the-oven climax à la *Phony Express*. What does this have to do with the original plot? Well, apprehending Mad Bill earns the Stooges precisely the $10,000 Moe needs to pay off his creditors...for a moment. But the "nitwits" allow Bill to escape, so Moe goes back into his insanity and back to the courtroom as the flashback ends. The new sequence makes this the second 'Joe film' involving the capture of a crook (*Hoofs and Goofs*), and as usual the Stooges capture the crook but louse up their final triumph at the end of the film. When all is said and done,

the sheriff is still chasing the crook, Larry and Joe are still driving Moe crazy, and the bear is driving off into the sunset.

VISUAL HUMOR (NEW FOOTAGE): Other variations of the original include Larry putting the funnel in Moe's mouth, pouring in several dozen pills and a few ounces of tonic, and shaking his head around; in the original the excited Moe called for his pills, but Curly took them himself. Also, Joe [Larry in the original] plays the top hat with his right hand and a clarinet with his left, while Larry [Curly in the original] plays a trombone with his hands, a cymbal with his head, and a drum with a mallet attached to his rear. New gags include Joe hitting Larry with the drum mallet; Moe swinging the ax at Larry and Joe, knocking the chimney pipe onto his own head, and pulling it off, leaving black ash all over his face (à la *Higher Than A Kite*); and Larry moving the carton of eggs around on the shelf after each gun shot. The shot of the bear driving the car away is beautifully set up by reediting the original bear-in-the-car sequence. In the original the bear rode in the car for the whole scene, but now Moe simply hears the car start and stands at the door where he sees the bear waving good-bye at the wheel of their car, making the vision quite a surprise to Moe and the viewer. Joe takes a head bonk and gets bonked on the head by Mad Bill Hookup's pistol. The new knock-the-door-onto-Moe sequence is nonetheless an elaboration of a gag in *Calling All Curs*. Other variations: Mad Bill taking Moe's gun, whacking him over the head, and handing it back to him (*Fuelin' Around*); and Moe walking towards the camera to end the film (*Bubble Trouble*).

VERBAL HUMOR (NEW FOOTAGE): Joe does get Curly's line in one exchange (Moe: "I'd go too but my nerves won't let me." Joe: "I haven't got the nerve either!"), but another (Joe: "Can't you just see it - hunting and fishing...and far away in the distance, you hear the call of the wolf"...[Larry gives the wolf-whistle]...That's the wrong wolf!") is a role reversal. New punchlines are allocated to each Stooge. Joe's are wonderfully in type, mocking Moe ("'Sunny side over, don't turn 'em down'? Boy, this guy's nuts."), repeating a cowardly threat while hiding behind Moe (Moe: "Stick 'em up or I'll blast ya'!" Joe: "Yeah! Stick 'em up or he'll blast ya'!"), and meekly yelling at the outlaw while missing the point after Bill clubs Moe on the head with his own rifle ("Hey what are you tryin' to do - break his gun?"). Larry gets the kind of throwaway, non-answerable lines Shemp used to specialize in ("You ought-a hold him with a habeas corpuscle!"; "He's got political pull!"; Joe: "That ought-a cure him." Larry: "Or kill him!"; and "If that bear kills me I'll never talk to you again!").

Moe's lines include a literal joke (Larry: "Did you seen a trombone slide?" Moe: "No, but I've seen a dream walking." [*Hollywood on Parade*]) and an ethnic joke. Bill: "Saaayy, that's a nice gun you have there." Moe: "Yeah, I got it for my Bar Mitzvah.") reminiscent of the Yiddish/Japanese gag in *Muscle Up A Little Closer*. Other variations: Larry's "habeas corpuscle" ("habus corpus" in *Healthy, Wealthy and Dumb*); Moe: "Yipe!", and Joe: "Not so lou-oud! ["Not so har-r-rd"] (*A Merry Mix-Up*); "Larry: "Just picture the beautiful country - the babbling brook, the murmuring of the breezes through the treezes, the mooses, and the meeces" (*Don't Throw That Knife*); and Larry: "Listen, you!—" Mad Bill: "What?!" Larry [yielding]: "Just, listen-" (recently in *Hoofs and Goofs* [Moe: "Get a towel!" Larry: "Ask me nice! (SLAP) That's nice enough!"]). Epithets: "imbeciles," "stupe," "birdbrain," and "nitwits."

Guns A Poppin! (1957) was shot in just one day even though very little of the released film is stock from the original *Idiots Deluxe* (1945). Joe Besser was short, fat and bald like Curly, but his movements and verbal delivery were very different. Larry speaks many of the lines which had been allotted to Curly in the original film, and Moe keeps his bear skin.

OTHER NOTES: Although this film was shot November 28, 1956, the week after *Horsing Around,* it was released several months prior to it. The title contains an exclamation point and no hyphens: *Guns A Poppin!*; the working title was *Nerveless Wreck*. This is Joe Palma's first Stooge appearance since substituting for Shemp the previous year. The name 'Mad Bill Hookup' parodies 'Wild Bill Hickok,' the nineteenth-century scout and marshal who was in 1956/57 being immortalized on the syndicated *The Adventures of Wild Bill Hickok* shown on both ABC *and* CBS along with a concurrent Mutual radio broadcast. The stars were Guy Madison and Andy Devine.

#180 - HORSING AROUND

Studio: Columbia

Released: September 12, 1957

Running Time: 15"27'"

Credited Production Crew:

Produced & Directed by:	Jules White
Written By:	Felix Adler
Director of Photography:	Ray Cory
Art Director:	Cary Odell
Film Editor:	William Lyon
Set Decorator:	Fay Babcock
Assistant Director:	Herb Wallerstein

Credited Cast:

Joe Besser	
Larry Fine	
Moe Howard	
Tony, the Wonder Horse	
Emil Sitka	Snapp's owner
Harriette Tarler	showgirl

PERSPECTIVE: *Horsing Around* is the only true sequel in the entire Stooge film corpus. It is a sequel to *Hoofs and Goofs*, the first Joe Besser Stooge film, which established the story of the discovery, concealment, and motherhood of the Stooges' equine sister. There have been other Stooge sequels of sorts, but while *I'll Never Heil Again* and *Punchy Cowpunchers* continue characters and settings from *You Nazty Spy!* and *Out West*, respectively, *Horsing Around* takes place just one week after the story of *Hoofs and Goofs*, uses the same equine characters, maintains Joe's quasi-leadership position, and tries to locate the father of the colt born in the original film, thereby continuing the story of reuniting the quadruped branch of the extended Stooge family tree.

In previous films the Stooges have typically treated animals like humans, most notably in the bath-house sequence of *Flat Foot Stooges*. In *Horsing Around* the Stooges continue this tradition, putting a diaper on the colt, keeping it in a crib, feeding it with a bottle, and dining along with Birdie at the table. Birdie also soaks her fallen arches in a basin of water. But this film now takes this kind of gag to the next step, with Birdie almost turning the Stooges into her humanoid minions: they cook for her, find her a baby sitter, and do her bidding. She turns the Stooges into virtual horses when Larry wears blinders, pulls her in their wagon, and shakes the puddle water off himself like a horse. Larry and Moe even dress in horse drag. In fact, to the extent that Birdie runs over a log and knocks the Stooges wagon wheel off center, she is almost a fourth Stooge.

The conclusion of the film may at first seem very un-Stoogelike. Birdie's reunification with Schnapps is perhaps the most romantically sappy ending in the entire corpus, wherein for a full twenty seconds we see Birdie and Schnapps kissing and speaking endearments while the Stooges look on smiling and sighing. But sappiness has always been a dimension of Stoogedom. *Even As IOU* ended with a similarly equine pony-hugging and the pony saying "Da-da," and from *Three Sappy People* to *Three Smart Saps* to *Income Tax Sappy* to *Space Ship Sappy* (and *Sappy Bull Fighters* yet to come), the Stooges have always had soft spots in their sappy hearts for damsels, children, and animals, even more so in the mid-1950s with the majority of the Stooge movie-going audience being children. Sappiness requires a certain degree of gullibility and innocence, and it entails a chivalrous commitment to someone, all qualities which apply to the Stooges. If the conclusion here strikes us as uncharacteristically inoffensive and cute, it represents just one extreme of Stoogedom. It is just as Stooge-esque as being chased out of town or knocking themselves out. They may be Stooges intellectually and physically, but they can also be nice guys, especially to a sister and brother-in-law.

VISUAL HUMOR: Despite its essential sappiness, the film contains more intra-Stooge slapstick than any previous Joe release, including the first fist game since Shemp's demise (Larry offers his fist; Moe hits it, it circles around and hits Larry on the head; Moe offers his fist, Larry slaps it, and it circles around and hits Larry on the head). Joe is integrated into the slapstick, taking a chicken leg to the forehead, two slaps from Larry, and a basin on the head from Moe. He plays a vital role in a head bonking routine in which Larry gets an idea and calls "Hike!"; they huddle briefly, break, and then hear Joe say: "Hey fellas! Come back! I gotta better idea!"; they bend down, bonk heads, and huddle again; Moe and Larry both pat Joe on the head for his better idea.

Joe is adept at non-violent pantomime, so he puts six spoonfuls of sugar into his ice tea, tastes it, makes a sour face, adds just a tad more sugar, and then likes it (Shemp in *Three Dark Horses*); when they leave the cabin he picks up a scrap of sandwich, takes a bite, and then leaves the scene; and when Moe tells him to "Get rid of the dishes," Joe takes it literally and tosses them out the window ("You told me to 'grease my pan!'" in *Space Ship Sappy*). In contrast to Curly's iron skull, Joe's head is considered delicate: "Not in the head. You know it's soft!" But it is put to good use: Joe slaps at Larry lightly, so Larry slaps him on the shoulder; Joe slaps at him even more lightly, so Larry slaps Joe on the head; Larry feels sorry for him and rubs it a little; Joe smiles: "Make *bigger* circles!". Because of the restrained slapstick in the Joe films, the physical humor tends to depend more on the accompanying dialogue. Joe refuses to pick up the heavy box ("It's heavy-y!"), so Larry picks it up, the bottom opens up, and everything falls out below ("It's light as a feather!"); the trainer chases after Moe and Larry, runs into the top half of the stable Dutch doors ("A truck bit me!"), and gets a rake handle in the back of his head when he steps on the head ("Sneak up on me, will you!"); Moe breaks the board over Larry's head ("You nearly wrecked my hat!" [*Gold Raiders*; cf. "Hey what are you tryin' to do - break his gun?" in *Gun A Poppin!*]); and Moe: "Where we gonna find the ax to chop it with?" Larry: "Use your head!" (*3 Dumb Clucks*). To build an exciting climax, Jules White and editor William Lyon intersperse a simultaneous duet of scenarios with the horse trainer [Emil Sitka] looking for his gun/looking for bullets/ shooting himself in the foot, and the Stooges riding to the rescue/getting soaked with laundry water tossed by a camper/the wagon hitting a rock, making Birdie come loose and pulling Moe off the buckboard; the same technique was used in *Punchy Cowpunchers*. Emil Sitka's nearsightedness derives from Benny Rubin's in the original film (*Hoofs and Goofs*); he talks to Schnapp's hind quarter, blindly kicks a trunk, and puts on pinch-nez in front of his other glasses. His poor eyesight allows the horse outfit ruse to work (*What's the Matador?*, *Three Little Twirps*). Other variations: Moe getting Larry to bend over, then using his head to break the board (*A Pain in the Pullman*); Larry (A little water ain't gonna hurt you!") plunging into the water (Curly's "It ain't deep!" in *Uncivil Warriors*); punching Larry through his hat (*Healthy, Wealthy and Dumb*) and Larry shaking water off like a horse (*Rockin' Thru the Rockies*).

For three grown men who regularly slap, bonk, and poke each other, quarrel, antagonize cops, and capture crooks, the Stooges in contrast can be very 'sappy.' They turn sappy in particular when confronted with children, animals and women, and in 1957's *Horsing Around*, a true sequel to *Hoofs and Goofs*, they mid-wife their reincarnated equine sister to give birth to this pony. Being a Stooge requires more than sheer ignorance and physical abuse; it is actually a rather complex personality type (or species of quasi-human) which covers a broad spectrum of human qualities, emotions, and dysfunctions.

VERBAL HUMOR: Felix Adler's script concentrates on the equine essence of the story, so the Stooges joke about horses (Larry: "Why don't we rent a wagon. After all, our sister is a horse." Moe: "That's really horse sense!"; Moe: "Where are you going to get a baby sitter?" Larry: "There's a horse at Santa Anita owes me a five dollar favor!"; Larry: "I'm beat! I was never cut out to be a horse." Moe: "But you eat like one!" à la Curly in *G.I. Wanna Home*); Birdie the horse is treated like a human ("My insteps were killin' me!"; "My feet are killin' me. I gotta have some new shoes. You know I've always had fallen arches!"; Joe: "She's been runnin' around barefooted all day!"); Birdie eats 'horseradish' salad; and Birdie's colt is named 'Piggy'!. Birdie's crib song: [to the tune of 'Yankee Doodle'] 'Rock and roll my baby/Sleep - I don't mean 'maybe,'/You will grow real big, of course,/ And be a great big circus horse'. The connection with *Hoofs and Goofs* is made in a few expository sentences. Moe holds a picture of Birdie [Moe in drag]: "Our sister Birdie refuses to eat and you're worried about Schnapps." Joe: "You're right, but Birdie is unhappy here. After all, this is a tough place for her to bring up her baby...Remember, she's not like us: she died and was reincarnated".

Felix Adler adds non-horse gags to the dining scene (Larry: "I sure love the caraway seeds in this rye bread." Moe: "Those are not caraway seeds; those are ants!"; Moe [Joe smearing mashed potatoes on his bread]: "Why don't you use butter?" Joe: "That's fattening!"; Moe [accidentally hitting Joe with the chicken leg]: "I'm sorry, Joe." Joe: "'I'm sorry, Joe. I'm sorry, Joe'— Can't you ever say anything like 'I'm *glad*,' once?" Moe: "Yeah, so I'm glad I'm sorry once!" Joe: "That's better!"). Other variations: Joe: "You back-biter!" (*Pop Goes the Easel*); Joe: "Not so lou-oud!" (*Guns A Poppin!*, which was actually shot first); Larry & Joe: "Gesundheit!" (*Violent is the Word for Curly*); the Stooges pulling the wagon with Birdie on top: "Mush!" (*Wee Wee Monsieur*); Moe: "A fine time to go swimmin'!" (*Punch Drunks*); and Birdie: "Quit actin' like Stooges!" ("You remind me of The Three Stooges" in *Crash Goes the Hash*).

OTHER NOTES: The film was shot November 19-21, 1956, the week before the previous release, *Guns A Poppin!*. The same cabin is used for *Guns A Poppin!*. The working titles were *Just Horsing Around* and *Just Fooling Around*. Despite the care taken to protect Joe, he got a one-inch splinter in his hand when shooting the wagon scene. He describes the incident in his autobiography (*Once A Stooge, Always a Stooge*, 193-4). This is the first appearance of a portable radio in a Stooge film. The Stooges' hair is combed back again. As often in these later films, all the actors are credited.

#181- RUSTY ROMEOS

Studio: Columbia

Released: October 17, 1957

Running Time: 16"16'"

Credited Production Crew:

Produced & Directed by:	Jules White
Screen Play by:	Felix Adler
Story by:	Jack White
Director of Photography:	Henry Freulich
Art Director:	Cary Odell
Film Editor:	Saul A. Goodkind
Set Director:	Tom Oliphant
Assistant Director:	Sam Nelson

Credited Cast:

Joe Besser	
Larry Fine	
Moe Howard	
Connie Cezan	Mary/Mabel/Sally

PERSPECTIVE: *Rusty Romeos*, the second remake in the Joe era, is not a revised Curly script but a refurbished Shemp film. For the previous Joe remake, *Guns A Poppin!*, the script of 1945's *Idiots Deluxe* was rearranged so that Larry would have many of Curly's lines, the slapstick was softened, very little original footage was reused, and a new five-minute Western scenario was added to help tie together the original beginning and ending. Here in *Rusty Romeos* the script of 1952's *Corny Casanovas* remains essentially the same with Joe playing Shemp's part [Larry: "The tax won't come out!" Shemp/Joe: "They went in; they must be 'income tacks.'"]. Some of the slapstick bits are reshot almost exactly as they were shot four years before, and some of the old footage is reused as well. And instead of inserting a whole new scene leading up to the end of the film, Jules and Jack White replace Felix Adler's original introductory ladder, dust mop, and Murphy bed sequences with a less violent, quintessential Stooge bed sequence and a new kitchen scene.

Larry for once solos in a cooking sequence. He follows a recipe too literally, of course, but he does manage to use a pastry bag without squirting Moe and actually produces something edible: triangular, pretzel-shaped, and circular Flipper's Fluffy Flabungita Flapjacks. Meanwhile Moe and Joe are daydreaming about their fiancées instead of paying attention to their condiments. Putting ketchup on pancakes and drinking from the sugar bowl instead of a coffee cup does not matter to them, though, since as in the previous film [*Horsing Around*] the Stooges are characterized as saps - romantic saps in this particular case. And as sappy as the Stooges were adoring the horse couple in *Horsing Around*, they are equally sappy in *Rusty Romeos* adoring their one and only Mary, er, Mabel, er, Sally.

In every refurbishing project the Whites attempt to improve upon and clarify the original film, so in the new opening bed sequence they introduce the previously nameless Stooge fiancée(s) as Mary [Joe's], Mabel [Larry's], and Sally [Moe's], hoping the viewer will realize later that Mary/Mabel/Sally are/is one and the same three timing gold digger duping the Stooges out of a very, very small diamond, a toe ring, and a cat-bristling portrait of Joe. Jules White shifts Larry's phone call into the Davenport sequence to correlate the film's two halves, and then, as in *Guns A Poppin!*, he adds a new sequence to tie both ends of the film together: instead of having Shemp/Joe grab the fireplace shovel and knock out Larry and Moe, he has Mary/Mabel/Sally do it, setting up more convincingly her line from the original: "So long, suckers!" Meanwhile, Joe goes back to the Stooges' apartment to retrieve Larry's "continuous shooting automatic" tack rifle. His plan, motivated by jealousy, was to shoot his rivals, but when he sees what this 'Jezebel' has done to them, he turns the rifle on her instead and shoots her rear full of tacks. For once the Stooges get to act like saps as well as reclaim their dignity, and maintaining dignity has always been an important part of being a Stooge. A true Stooge is proud of being a Stooge.

VISUAL HUMOR (NEW FOOTAGE): Larry, not Joe, substitutes for Shemp by doing some boxing steps, but Joe does get his most continuous beating to date: Moe gives him a bonk, so Joe ("I'm mad! I'm fighting mad!") belly bumps Larry [Joe's first belly bump] and then Moe;

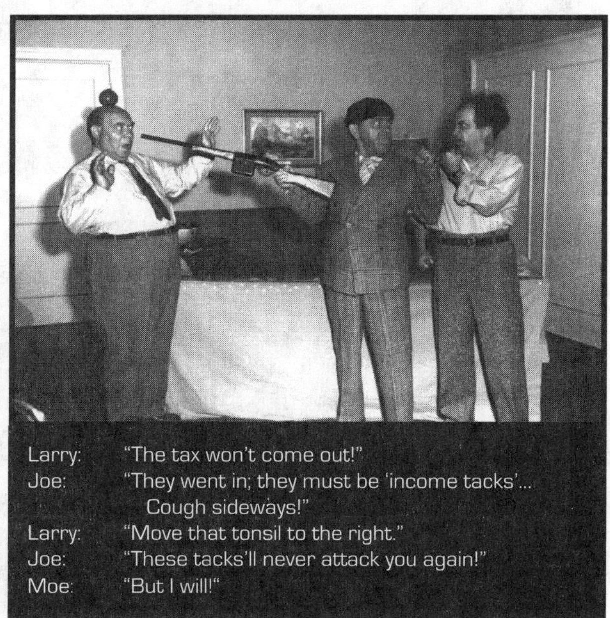

Larry: "The tax won't come out!"
Joe: "They went in; they must be 'income tacks'... Cough sideways!"
Larry: "Move that tonsil to the right."
Joe: "These tacks'll never attack you again!"
Moe: "But I will!"

Moe bonks Joe and Larry pounds him, too, sending him backwards into the wall where a flowerpot slips off a loosened shelf onto his head (*Heavenly Daze*). Later Moe threatens with the hammer but slaps Joe on the head, knocking him back into Larry; in the original Moe clanged Shemp with the hammer who then ("Oh! Oh! Oh! Oh! Look!") pointed to the flattened hammer. Other variations: the Stooges sleeping and snoring to open a film or scene (*Nertsery Rhymes; Hoi Polloi*); Larry wearing curling ribbons in his hair (*Woman Haters*); Larry stroking 'Mabel' (Moe's foot) and plucking 'her eyebrow' (*Calling All Curs: I'm a Monkey's Uncle*); Moe taking a slug of hair tonic (*In the Sweet Pie and Pie*); polishing Joe's bald head with a cloth (*Violent is the Word for Curly*); Joe putting ketchup on his flapjacks (*Idiots Deluxe*); and Moe drinking from the sugar bowl instead of his coffee cup (*Tassels in the Air*).

VERBAL HUMOR (NEW FOOTAGE): The original malapropisms are omitted except "bicyclefocals," "That's a coincidental," and the comment that they have not met each other's "fian-sees". Joe makes two silly replies to Moe's orders (Moe: "You hold your tongue!" Joe: "I can't! It's too slippery!"; Moe: "You watch your Ps and Qs!" Joe:"Okay, L-M-F-F-P-Q."). A Stooge first: Moe: "Do you think you could cook breakfast?" Larry: "I don't think, I know." Moe: "I don't think you know either!". Typical of Stooge romances, the dialogue oscillates from serious threats (Moe: "If I had a machine gun I'd blow you to ribbons!"; Larry: "You send me!" Moe: "I'll send you!") to unpoetic romantic endearments (Joe: "My Mary's eyes - they're like two headlights on a dark night!"; Moe: "Those lips, those nose!"). Epithets: Moe's new name for Joe: "Goldilocks"; Larry and Joe both respond to "Hey imbecile!"; Moe also uses "sponge-head".

References: Joe calling Mary/Mabel/Sally "You Jezebel you!" refers to a wicked, two-timing woman, originally in the Bible [I *Kings* 16], and also the title of the Oscar-producing 1938 Bette Davis film. The exchange about the flapjacks ("What is this: Phi Sigma Delta?" Larry: "No, they're Flipper's Fluffy Flabungita Flapjacks." Moe: "Oh, a new sorority.") makes fun of Larry's 'delta'-shaped flapjack. Larry's recipe (two cups of flour - measuring cups included, two eggs - shells included, and a can of condensed milk - can included) derives from *An Ache in Every Stake*; taking off the can label ("You can't eat paper!") was introduced in *Listen, Judge*. Other variations: Moe: I've gotta get over to my girl's house." Joe: "Me, too!" Larry: "Me three!" (*If a Body Meets a Body*); and Joe: "Nothing to worry about - no blood!" ("Any blood - ignore it!" in *Fright Night*).

OTHER NOTES: The new footage was shot in two days on February 12-13, 1957. The working title was *Sappy Lovers*. All four actors are credited.

Moe, clowning on the set during a cigarette break, cracks Joe and Connie Cezan up while cracking Larry on the head.

#182 - OUTER SPACE JITTERS

Studio: Columbia

Released: December 5, 1957

Running Time: 16"17'"

Credited Production Crew:

Produced & Directed by:	Jules White
Written by:	Jack White
Director of Photography:	William Bradford
Art Director:	Walter Holscher
Film Editor:	Harold White
Set Decorator:	Sidney Clifford
Assistant Director:	Max Stein

Credited Cast:

Joe Besser	
Larry Fine	
Moe Howard	
Emil Sitka	Professor Jones
Gene Roth	Grand Zilch of Suvev
Philip Van Zandt	High Mucky Muck
Don Blocker	zombie

Uncredited Cast:

Joe Palma	Captain Tsimmes
Harriette Tarler	space woman #1
Diana Darrin	space woman #2
Arline Hunter	space woman #3

PERSPECTIVE: The final release of 1957 is the year's second outer-space film, and taking place almost entirely on another planet, *Outer Space Jitters* is the most far-ranging Stooge short film. Stooge comedy often takes place in exotic settings (ancient Egypt, European castles, Western deserts, tropical Pacific isles) with odd peoples and customs for the Stooges to satirize, and now that outer space had become a cinematic exotica of the 1950s, this last release of 1957 finds them again on the planet of Sunev. Despite the similarity of the name 'Sunev,' *Outer Space Jitters* is not a genuine sequel to *Space Ship Sappy*. The latter is an adventure film in which the Stooges unknowingly boarded a rocket ship and briefly encountered Sunevian cannibalistic amazons and a giant reptile. *Outer Space Jitters* eliminates the space travel from/to earth and places the Stooges from the outset on a very different Sunev for a very different set of experiences.

This new Sunev is a celestial Shangri-La with all the modern conveniences, even air-conditioning (which was not common in 1957 even in southern California). To make Sunev seem ultra-modern, Jules White had set decorator Sidney Clifford design plenty of gadgetry enhanced by hydraulic and electrical sound effects. The Stooges then parody this brave new world by wearing derbies on and hot water bottles under their 'space suits,' making fun of the Sunevian diet of clam shells (no problem for a Stooge) and battery acid, and kissing/cooking with the electrically charged, non-cannibal Sunevian women. All this gives *Outer Space Jitters* as much energy as many of the 1950s sci-fi flicks it parodies.

The Stooges' long-standing anti-totalitarian philosophy takes the film to a higher political orbit. Demeaning titles like 'Grand Zilch' and 'High Mucky Muck' recall the Stooges' World War II satires, and a plot in which evil, ambitious men constructing a zombie army for world/universal domination recalls the premise of 1950's *Dopey Dicks*. By the mid-1950s Cold War fears and contemporary sci-fi films like *Forbidden Planet* (1956) and *The Day the Earth Stood Still* (1952) had already assumed that aliens would be smarter than earthlings and hostile by nature, but boasting that "we are way ahead of you earth people," the air-conditioned, button-pushing Grand Zilch of Sunev miscalculates badly when he assumes that futuristic devices and a massive army of immortal zombies are all he needs to defeat Stooge heroes. They may use only a hot water bottle to short circuit the High Mucky Muck, a pant-load of stolen gold to clonk the Grand Zilch, and an on/off switch to deactivate the zombie (the pre-*Bonanza* Dan Blocker), but the Stooges save mankind and continue their string of recent democratic triumphs which had them intercept atomic secrets in microfilm-plugged watermelons (*Commotion On the Ocean*) and keep a secret rocket fuel away from Anemia (*Fuelin' Around*). Forget those Stooge saps we saw in the previous two films. When humankind is at risk, the Stooges become heroes even if their natural instinct is to escape and their emotional motivation is unadulterated fear. The crisis averted, they revert to natural instincts and jump out the window at the film's conclusion.

VISUAL HUMOR: The surprise appearance and make-up of the baby sitter presages a classic 1960 *Twilight Zone* episode, 'Eye of the Beholder,' in which a beautiful woman (Donna Douglas) is considered hideous in a world inhabited by ugly people. As often in scare comedies and beast films since *Idle Roomers* and *Hold That Lion*, the zombie menaces while the Stooges create the humor by not noticing his presence and doing belated takes. First the zombie stands behind Moe while Larry and Joe find themselves unable to utter a single comprehensible syllable; Moe thinks they are playing charades and guesses "a tall word," looks to his right and left, says "Good evening" to the zombie, and finally does a take. Then while Moe tries to open the door, the zombie breathes down his neck ("What are you guys pantin' about? I'm doin' all the work!...Stop snortin' down my neck, Larry...Maybe you ought to take a little bicarbonate of

The Stooges established their anti-totalitarian philosophy in World War II and the Cold War, and now they convey it in *Outer Space Jitters*, the second outer-space Stooge film of 1957, to a higher political orbit. Pioneering sci-fi films like *Forbidden Planet* (1956) had already assumed that aliens would be smarter than earthlings and hostile by nature, but boasting that "we are way ahead of you earth people," the air-conditioned, button-pushing Grand Zilch of Sunev miscalculates badly when he assumes that futuristic devices and a massive army of immortal zombies are all he needs to defeat Stooge heroes. They may use only a hot water bottle to short circuit the High Mucky Muck, a pant-load of stolen gold to clonk the Grand Zilch, and an on/off switch to deactivate the zombie, but simple tools for simple people.

soda, Joe"), Moe leads the zombie by the hand to the opposite door, and only then turns and does his take. Finally, Moe runs into Joe and Larry, and they all scare each other. The Stooges tossing their hats around and onto the [Easter Island-like] statuette dates back to gags commonly used by W. C. Fields. The Stooges have breathed smoke and heard fireworks after kissing women, but this atomic-electric race of Sunevians pops popcorn and cooks a chicken.

Hot water bottles have been used most notably in *False Alarms, All the World's a Stooge*, and *Bedlam in Paradise*. The space harem is the logical extension of Stooge harem scenes in *Malice in the Palace* and *Blunder Boys*. Joe's inadvertently knocking out the Grand Zilch behind him with the gold pants/sack has a long pedigree, esp. *G.I. Wanna Home* and *Three Little Sew and Sews*. The original ending of *Three Little Pigskins* had the Stooges explaining their adventures to their young children. Other variations: Moe's hair standing on end (*Spook Louder*); the Stooges assisting their chewing with head banging, hand coercion, and throat manipulation (*Uncivil Warriors*); Moe strapping Larry to the wall by putting a chord around his throat (*Three Little Twirps*); Moe planing Larry's head (*A Snitch in Time*); Joe's pants falling from the weight of the gold (*Cash and Carry*); the professor's mouth-gag turning out to be a strip of material twenty feet in length (*Malice in the Palace*); and the Stooges standing [split screen] as they talk to their infant Stooge offspring sitting in a triple-wide crib (*Self-Made Maids*).

VERBAL HUMOR: Twice, the Stooges are made fun of as unlikely earth specimens (Grand Zilch: "So these are earth men?"; Sunevian woman #1: "So you're an earth man? What a terrible specimen!"). The script has two three-patterns (Moe: "We'd like to know what's cookin'!" Larry: "Such as dames!" Joe: "You don't happen to have any spare telephone numbers, do ya'?"; and Larry: "Just before we came up here I had some nuts and bolts under glass." Moe: "Could I have a nice salami sandwich smothered in sour cream with cherry jelly?" Joe: "Pickle in the middle and the mustard on top?"), the latter a characteristically odd Stooge food combination. Moe's romantic talk: "Eenie, meenie, minie, moe. I'm Moe - you're for me, Hiya, toots!... Wow! Boy I've heard of hot lips but you're a sizzle!... A two cylindered dynamo!". A polite intra-slapstick exchange: Moe: "Think nothing of it." Larry: "Stout fellow!".

References: "Bewitched, bothered, and bewildered" are lyrics from the song in *Pal Joey*, a 1940 Rodgers & Hart musical made into a film (with Kim Novak) in 1957; Larry looks directly at the camera and adds "And don't forget to see *Pal Joey*, folks!"; needless to say, it was a Columbia production. Larry's "our favorite theater nuisance – popcorn!" refers to kids throwing popcorn in movie theaters during Saturday morning matinees. Stocks: "General Motorcycle" [General Motors], "Anacana-panna Steel" [Anaconda Copper, à la *Men in Black*], and "Tsimmes Incorporated" ['Tsimmes' is a Yiddish word used for the name of Captain Tsimmes (*Wee Wee Monsieur*)]. Other variations: the title 'SUNEV IS VENUS SPELLED BACKWARDS' (*Space Ship Sappy*); Space woman #3 to Joe: "You're a fat one!" (*Three Missing Links*); "Bewitched... Bothered... Bewildered" ("Delighted... Devastated... Dilapidated...Embalmed!" in *Half-Wits Holiday*); Larry reading the ticker tape (*I'll Never Heil Again*); Professor: "Mmbmmbbmm." Moe: "What'd he say?" Larry: "Mmbmmbbmm" (*Hold That Lion*); and Joe: "That hu-u-urts!" (*Hoofs and Goofs*).

OTHER NOTES: The working title was *Outer Space Daze*. The screen credits have 'Don' Blocker. When the Grand Zilch brags about their weather, Moe dubs in "Whadya know! How about that!" for no apparent reason and to no one's moving lips.

1958

Quiz Whizz • Fifi Blows Her Top • Pies and Guys

Sweet and Hot • Flying Saucer Daffy • Oil's Well That Ends Well

#183 - QUIZ WHIZZ

Studio: Columbia

Released: February 13, 1958

Running Time: 15"25'"

Credited Production Crew:

Produced & Directed by:	Jules White
Written by:	Searle Kramer
Director of Photography:	Irving Lippman
Art Director:	John McCormack
Film Editor:	William Lyon
Set Decorator:	Sidney Clifford
Assistant Director:	Jerrold Bernstein

Credited Cast:

Joe Besser	
Larry Fine	
Moe Howard	
Greta Thyssen	Lisa, secretary to
Gene Roth	Montgomery M. Montgomery
Milton Frome	G. Y. Prince
Emil Sitka	J. J. Figby, tax collector
Bill Brauer	R. O. Broad

PERSPECTIVE: Columbia president Harry Cohn terminated the Stooges' contract in December, 1957. So while these six films were being released in 1958, the Stooges were no longer making short films. Nonetheless, to viewers the Stooge world is what they see on film, and the six 1958 releases offer another interesting spectrum of refurbished films and satires of mid-1950s contemporary culture. Here in *Quiz Whizz*, for instance, the Stooges once again almost make it into the big money. In *If a Body Meets a Body* they almost inherit Uncle Bob O. Link's fortune, in *Heavenly Daze* they almost sell a hypo-whipped-cream fountain pen, in *Income Tax Sappy* they cheat the IRS but are arrested, and in *Healthy, Wealthy and Dumb* Curly actually wins a radio quiz only to lose his winnings to New Deal taxation. *Quiz Whizz* adds a new entry into the ledger of Stooge economics. The story was written by Searle Kramer, the same writer who penned *Healthy, Wealthy and Dumb* years ago and who had not written a Stooge script since 1939 (*Calling All Curs*). In this updated version he has Joe winning $15,000 on a TV quiz show, and, like the sci-fi film which preceded this one, nothing could be more contemporary. The 1956/1957 television season was the season of the network quiz show: *The $64,000 Question* with its sweat-producing isolation booth premiered and zoomed to the top of the ratings charts ahead of *I Love Lucy*, Groucho Marx's *You Bet Your Life* was the 7th rated show, *I've Got a Secret* 10th, and the same season saw the debuts of *To Tell the Truth*, *Treasure Hunt*, and the infamous, scandal-ridden *Twenty-One*, which Congress investigated and ultimately forced, along with most of the big money prime-time quiz shows, off the air by the fall of 1958.

We don't know which "five questions about food" Joe answered correctly because the narrative does not include the quiz show itself. We come in one day later after Joe has already lost the prize money. This time it is that Joe has been cheated out of his winnings by con artists, one of whom is an eccentric millionaire named 'Montgomery M. Montgomery' modeled after another popular contemporary television show, CBS' *The Millionaire*, in which each week an eccentric millionaire ordered 'Michael Anthony' (whence 'Montgomery') to give an average person a $1,000,000 check.

Being scammed has been a part of Stoogedom since 1937's *Cash and Carry* and *Playing the Ponies*. It is that naive, gullible part of the Stooge character, along with ignorant imbecility, which allows Joe to invest his winnings with 'John Smith' and not recognize either Smith's disguise or that being "Montgomery's wards" could lead to the Stooges' death. Emphasizing feeble-mindedness, the Stooges don costumes - not commonly done in the Joe era - and play children, reprising a concept that worked well for the Stooges in *All the World's a Stooge* and for Joe Besser as 'Stinky,' the brat in the Little Lord Fauntleroy outfit he had played weekly in *The Abbott and Costello Show*. When the Stooges finally realize what has happened, they have their second elaborate chase of the Joe era. Moe and Larry take the bulk of abuse, but this ninth 'Joe film' demonstrates how well Besser's and the Stooges' comedic styles have blended in one year of working together. From not taking a single hit in *Hoofs and Goofs* and being mimicked by Moe in *A Merry Mix-Up*, Joe now regularly takes head bonks, nose crunches, and even slaps to his head and face while still maintaining his uniquely passive character, jabbing out with his silly little slaps, and speaking in his inimitable vocal patterns ("Not so lou-oud!").

VISUAL HUMOR: The softer slapstick (e.g. Moe kicking Joe in the rear so that he sprays Larry with water, Larry pouring water into Moe's mouth and onto his shirt, Moe spitting out his coffee, Moe biting off a piece of his coffee cup, and jamming the large hat onto the IRS agent's head instead of gouging him for their getaway move) is due to concern for the Stooges' younger audiences as well as for Joe, but Joe is assimilating nicely; he sits on Montgomery's knee (*All the World's a Stooge*), takes a bite of the cigar while chewing, smiling, and grimacing (*Uncivil Warriors*). A visual three-pattern: one knife takes Joe's blond wig off, the next narrowly misses Larry's nose, the last makes Moe's hair stand on end. A Stooge first: Joe telling Montgomery to "Look!" in the other direction so he can spit out the cigar. Prince's secretary sits almost motionless holding cards in her hand...

When the Stooges try to break the door down, Broad opens it, so they fly across the room into the opposite wall; this is the first time the Stooges themselves have been victims of this gag first seen in *Self-Made Maids*. From *Ants in the Panty* come Moe and Larry kissing each other (Moe: "I'm poisoned!"), Montgomery and the secretary preparing a drink with rat poison, and Moe trying to lead Larry and Joe off by the hair but not being able to grab Joe's bald head; Joe's entering while Moe reports him missing is reminiscent of Moe not recognizing either Curly or Larry as he tries to interview them in *No Census, No Feeling*; blindfolded Stooges playing Blind Man's Bluff we first saw in *Three Little Pigskins*; and the secretary clubbing Moe with her foreswing and Larry with her backswing dates back to *Three Little Sew and Sews*. Moe accidentally rips Joe's pants off; Joe lost his pants in *Outer Space Jitters*. Other variations: Moe shooting Joe's tie off (*Tricky Dicks*); the 'BANG' pistol, and running into Venetian blinds (*Studio Stoops*); being backed up against a wall and having knives thrown at them (*Three Little Twirps*); Moe's hair standing on end (*Spook Louder*); Moe slamming the cake into the secretary's face (*Three Sappy People*; recently in *Rusty Romeos*); and the Stooges pointing to one another and saying "He did!" (*Pest Man Wins*).

VERBAL HUMOR: Most distinctive is the self-contradictory, childlike talk masking adult desires for money (Larry: "I don't like toys; I like *money*!" Moe: "Yeah, folding money." [They grab the wad of bills] Larry: "This I like!" Moe: "This I don't blame you!") and women (Secretary: "What nice boys." Larry: "You're not so bad yourself!" Moe to Larry: "You're supposed to be a kid." Larry: "So, I'm a juvenile delinquent!"; and Larry: "How about Post Office?" Secretary: "That's a kid's game." Larry: "Not the way I play it!"). Linguistically they depend on diminutives and mispronunciations (Larry: "He hit me on my wittle cheek"; Moe: "Go on, eat the nice cigar Joey-woey."). Some of this, of course, is not much different from Joe's regular speech pattern ("Go away, you crazy *you*!")... Other gags depend on Joe's naiveté (Larry: "Don't tell me you cashed it!" Joe: "Whada-you think I'm an idiot or somethin'? Of course I didn't cash it...I invested it!"; Moe: "Don't tell me: you bought the Brooklyn Bridge." Joe: "Certainly not...That was sold last week!"; Joe: "His name is John Smith." Larry: "Don't tell me he introduced you to Pocahontas." Joe: "Somebody told ya'!"), Joe's fatness and baldness (Moe: "Joe Besser...height... about 5'5 by 5'5', color of hair: skin"; Larry: "You can't shoot him here! We could never dispose of that body!"), ironic word plays (Moe: "Why didn't you tell us you were here?!" Joe: "I'm no snitch"; Joe [holding a lit cigar]: "I ought-a give you the hot face!"; and the misspelled film title *Quiz Whizz*), and genuine Stooge ignorance (Moe: "Where is this John Smith?" Joe: "In his office, next door to a bar-b-que pit." Larry: "Does bar-b-cues have pits?" Joe: "Whadya hittin' me for? I didn't say it...Incidentally, do bar-b-que have pits?").

References: "Consolidated Fujiyama California Smog Bags...filled with smog" is the second Stooge reference to LA smog (*Space Ship Sappy*) which had been forming since the late 1940s, and the second hint at 'Made in Japan' (*Muscle Up a Little Closer*). Pocahontas and John Smith were the famous Indian/English couple in colonial Virginia. Joe's joke about "Montgomery's wards" (Broad: "His name is Montgomery M. Montgomery." Joe: "Oh boy! We'll be Montgomery's wards!") refers to the name of the long-established department store Montgomery Ward. Larry's reference to "juvenile delinquency" reflects a widely recognized problem in the mid-to-late 1950s evidenced cinematically in *Blackboard Jungle* (1955), *Rock, Rock, Rock!* (1956), and Jerry Lewis's first solo film *The Delicate Delinquent* (1957).

Role-reversal: Larry offers a Curly-esque "Rruff! Rruff!" Also, Larry figures out the words "gyp" and "rob" from the door sign, the first time a sign has been explained to us in the dialogue. The Stooges' chant- "At last we're in the dough. Hi-lee Hi-lo" - is the first since *Knutzy Knights*. The "bar-b-que pit" gag recalls Shemp's question about marshmallows having pits in *All Gummed Up*. Other variations: "Montgomery's Wards" (*I'll Never Heil Again*); Larry: "How about Post Office?" Secretary: "That's a kid's game." Larry: "Not the way I play it!" (*A Pain in the Pullman*); Larry: "Well how about fifty cents on account?" Joe: "On account of that's all we've got." (*So Long, Mr. Chumps*); "Call your shots!" (*A Plumbing We Will Go*); and Joe: "Not so lou-oud!" (*Guns A Poppin!*).

OTHER NOTES: All the actors are credited... Greta Thyssen will play in two more Stooge shorts. She played a part in Fox's *Bus Stop* (1956) but was best known at the time as Jan Murray's assistant 'Pirate Girl' on NBC's *Treasure Hunt*. Milton Frome [G. Y. Prince] had a lengthy career; recently he had been a regular on *The Milton Berle Show* (1953-1955). There is another awkward voice-over from Moe ("Crown 'em, Joe!") when he hits the two crooks with a baseball bat. Joe eating the Havana cigar (*Loose Loot*) is the descendant of everything else the Stooges have eaten over the years, including the clam shells from the previous film; but it also reminds us that during May of 1957, when this film was being made, the exiled Fidel Castro had recently returned to Cuba and was in the early stages of his revolution. In a year or so, a 'Havana' would be contraband in the US and remain so for decades.

#184 - FIFI BLOWS HER TOP

Studio: Columbia

Released: April 10, 1958

Running Time: 16"22"'

Credited Production Crew:

Produced & Directed by:	Jules White
Written by:	Felix Adler
Director of Photography:	Henry Freulich
Art Director:	Cary Odell
Film Editor:	Saul A. Goodkind
Set Decorator:	Tom Oliphant
Assistant Director:	Sam Nelson

Credited Cast:

Joe Besser	
Larry Fine	
Moe Howard	
Vanda Dupre	Fifi
Phil Van Zandt	her husband
Harriette Tarler	Parisian waitress
Christine McIntyre	Katrina [stock footage]

Uncredited Cast:

Yvette Reynard	Maria [stock footage]
Al Thompson	Maria's father [stock footage]
Joe Palma	M.P.
Charles 'Heine' Conklin	bartender
Suzanne Ridgeway	girl in restaurant
Wanda D'Ottoni	girl in restaurant

PERSPECTIVE: *Fifi Blows Her Top* begins as if it is to be merely a 'Joe' remake of 1950's *Love at First Bite*. But after repeating the flashback footage of Larry's and Moe's wartime European romances, the film heads off in a different direction altogether. As with almost every refurbished Stooge film, Jules White (with Felix Adler) succeeds in improving the original which confined the Stooges to their apartment and saw them indulge in some of the heaviest drinking in the entire corpus. The youthful audience which adored the Stooges in the late 1950's would not relate well to a new version of the drunken bout, so White and Adler reduced that entire sequence to a delightful enterprise in which Larry makes a fruity cocktail, shakes it against Joe's head, and dumps it with multiple pineapple rings all over Fifi. The chewing gum sequence and nose-to-nose standoff also had to be reshot because the original footage involved Shemp, but both are varied, refreshed, and brightened in tone.

Joe opens the film in a depressed mood, something extraordinary for a Stooge. Stooges are usually too mindless, gullible, angry, fearful, joyous, or sappy to be depressed. But the late 1950s were an era in which brooding individual psyches come to the fore in the cinema in the likes of Marlon Brando and Anthony Perkins, so Joe is entitled to mope a bit as well. It does not last long, of course, but it justifies the Stooges' reminiscing about their war romances. (In the original it was meeting their fiancées that afternoon that inspired the flashbacks.) After the flashbacks the second half of the film features the reunification of Joe and Fifi in a situation similar to the visit of Rocky Dugan's wife in *Gents in a Jam* (1952): both women make innocent visits, remove their dresses because of Stooge ineptitude, and then have to hide from their husbands. The two films part company there, though, since this one needs to preserve the romance between Joe and the hidden Fifi. Larry is a standout in the cover-up and subterfuge - telling the husband "the line's busy" before he picks up the phone, recognizing the dress on the table, warning Moe in pig Latin, lying about his shirt tail, pretending Fifi was a tiny dog ("squeak, squeak, squeak"), and then creating a diversion out of the husband's saying his wife is also named 'Fifi.' This all ends in an active slapstick conclusion with a baseball bat, bowling ball, and telephone used as weapons.

Jules Whites' limited annual budget forced him to save money on several films per year, so here he reuses old footage in the first part of the film and then sets the finale in a single-room, quite a contrast to the relatively elaborate outer space (*Space Ship Sappy; Outer Space Jitters*), camera-effects filled (*A Merry Mix-Up*), and talking-horse (*Hoofs and Goofs*; *Horsing Around*) films of the previous year's releases. But one-room, television-like, domestic situation comedies had entered into the Stooge corpus as long ago as 1951's *Baby Sitters Jitters* and *"Don't Throw That Knife"* - both involving rocky marriages - and inter-Stooge physical and verbal humor often flourishes in confined spaces, especially now with Joe thoroughly incorporated into the trio and Larry filling in the gaps.

VISUAL HUMOR (NEW FOOTAGE): To convey the humor physically confined in a one-room sitcom, timing gags between the players become critical, e.g. Joe rehearsing a knock while at the same time Fifi makes a real knocking sound at the door; Larry and Joe ("With you a cocktail shaker's a weapon. Let me have that!") struggling with the cocktail shaker and spilling it; and the confused Fifi hearing Joe calling for 'Fifi' (the dog) and opening the trunk by mistake. The alcohol-induced nose-to-nose confrontation of the original is shifted to a sober argument about ironing the dress (Larry: "I smell somethin' awful." Moe: "Well don't brag about it!" Larry: "No, I mean I smell something burning!" Moe: "It's me sizzling!"). The chewing gum sequences are essentially unchanged except for the addition of Joe's appropriate quip: "You're all stuck up!". The degree of Joe's integration into the trio can be seen in this standard Stooge three-pattern now jazzed up with Joe-type gags [Moe to Larry: "Hey! Go heat an iron!" Joe to Larry: "Hey! Go heat an iron!" Moe to Joe: "Shut up!" Joe: "Not so lou-oud!" Moe to Larry: "Go heat an iron!" Larry: "Don't press me! Ha-ha! [Looking at the camera] I guess I told him!" Moe slaps Larry. Joe: "That's good for him! [Moe bonks Joe] That's bad for me!"]. There is also the Stooge first where Joe rests on Moe's shoulder and sobs: "I can't take it," turns back to Fifi ["I'll never let you go!"], turns back to lean again on Moe's shoulder, but, with Moe having moved, falls to the floor. Result shot: Fifi covered in orange and pineapple slices.

When at the conclusion of the film Fifi, still worked up, accidentally slaps Joe when he comes over to congratulate her, she reminds us of the still fitful Curly knocking out Moe and Larry at the conclusion of *Punch Drunks*. The trunk with a false bottom derives from *Don't Throw That Knife*. A similar gag was used in Laurel & Hardy's *Unaccustomed as We Are* [1929]; that duo often hid from jealous husbands. Other variations: Fifi ducking when her husband ducks [*Pop Goes the Easel*]; sweeping dirt under the carpet [*So Long, Mr. Chumps*]; Fifi swinging a baseball bat [*Quiz Whizz*]; Joe taking the bat from Fifi's hand and handing her a bowling ball ("Use this!") instead [*Dizzy Pilots*]; Joe: "That's good for him! [BONK] That's bad for me!" [*A Merry Mix-Up*]; and Moe burning Larry's rear with the iron [*Movie Maniacs*]

VERBAL HUMOR (NEW FOOTAGE): The new wrap-around dialogue for Larry's flashback offers the gag name, "Leilani Baggicaluppi; I called her 'Maria' for short"; she was just 'Maria' in the original. Moe's new dialogue adds Germanic food gags: "Wieners-chnitzel Strasse...I fell for Katrina like a load of Wienerwurst." Joe's flashback maintains Shemp's original French references [Rue de la Schlemiel, Rue de la Pew, "Paris sites," and the name 'Fifi'] and keeps the dog-under-the-table gag but adds jokes about Joe's appetite ["two orders of vichyssoise, two orders of frog legs, and two glasses of Bordeaux wine"; Joe: "I'm expecting—"] and an exchange dependent on Joe's ignorance [M.P.: "Two weeks A.W.O.L., eh?" Joe: "I wrote the admiral for a 10-day extension." M.P.: "10 days? I'll see that you get 10 years!" Joe: "Don't try to make up. I'll have you demoted to an M.P.!...Oh, he is an M.P.!"]. The name of the cafe ['CAFE LA-MER-ESSEN'] is French [*La Mer*] with a German suffix [*Essen*]. While Fifi hides in the trunk, there are various combinations of verbal humor. Twice the Stooges divert the husband's attention by engaging him in group laughter [Husband: "That's a funny shirt you're wearing - white in front and flowered in back." Larry: "It's a new style." Moe: "Ivy League!" They all laugh; Husband: "My wife's name is Fifi." Larry: "What a coincidence! His wife's name is Fifi! What a coincidence!" They all laugh], twice Joe almost gives away the secret [Joe: "Where's Fifi?" Moe: "That's our dog." Joe: "Don't you call her a dog!"; Moe to the husband: "Why don't you see the landlady about a key?" Joe: "Hey I got a— [He has the key in his hand; Moe bonks him] a head-a-a-ache."], and Larry offers a solo, meandering lie ["She's a Fifi, I mean she's French, a French poodle - Australian, German, Swiss - on the other side, and they don't grow very large just like a little mouse, tiny like that - 'squeak, squeak, squeak.' She can hide anywhere"].

References: Joe's "I come from Brooklyn where them 'Bums' are." [Fifi: "'Bums? They explode!"] Joe: "I'll say! They fall apart!" refers to the Brooklyn Dodgers and needs the nickname "Bums" pronounced with a French accent to make the pun work; but when this film was shot in February, 1957 the team had just recently become the Los Angeles Dodgers, and the suitability of the old nickname "Bums" had lessened in the previous two years. The perennially losing Dodgers appeared in both the 1955 and 1956 World Series against the Yankees, winning in 1955. Larry's "To be or not to be" is the same Shakespearean line used in *Three Hams on Rye*. Moe's "Ivy League" style was new in 1957. Larry's "She went to see a dog about a man" is a chiasmus for "He went to see a man about a dog," which was a common euphemism for going to the lavatory. The label on the Stooge trunk ['STAGE SCREEN & RADAR'] parodies the relatively new phrase 'stage, screen, & television'. Larry's "The ess-dray on the able-tay!" is the first pig Latin since *Income Tax Sappy*. Epithet: "stupes". Joe's final "She still loves me!" recalls Larry's [phone-on-the-head] similar proclamation in *Corny Casanovas*. Other variations: Larry's "a French poodle - Australian, German, Swiss - on the other side" ["His mother and my mother were both mothers...on his father's side!" in *Wee Wee Monsieur*]; Fifi: "Thank you too much!" [*Cookoo Cavaliers*]; Joe: "Not so ha-a-ard!" [*A Merry Mix-Up*]; Joe: "Not so lou-oud!" [*Guns A Poppin!*]; Joe: "You're a snitch!" [*Quiz Whizz*]; and Larry: "Skip the gutter!" Moe: "Break a leg!" [*Pardon My Scotch*]

OTHER NOTES: The working title was *Rancid Romance*. For the first time Joe wears a hairpiece [in the flashback]. The film opens with a trunk labeled 'HOWARD, FINE & BESSER,' the first written reference to the new Stooge configuration. *Besser* [195] reports that before filming *Fifi Blows Her Top* Harry Cohn was entertaining the idea of putting the Stooges into a weekly television show, but then scrapped the project at the last minute.

#185 - PIES AND GUYS

Studio: Columbia

Released: June 12, 1958

Running Time: 16"09"'

Credited Production Crew:

Produced & Directed by:	Jules White
Written by:	Jack White
Director of Photography:	Irving Lippman
Art Director:	John McCormack
Film Editor:	Harold White
Set Decorator:	Sidney Clifford
Assistant Director:	Jerrold Bernstein

Credited Cast:

Joe Besser	
Larry Fine	
Moe Howard	
Greta Thyssen	Lulu, secretary to
Milton Frome	Prof. Quackenbush
Gene Roth	Prof. Sedlitz
Emil Sitka	Sappington, the butler
Harriette Tarler	Countess Spritzwasser
Helen Dickson	Mrs. Gotrocks

Uncredited Cast:

Symona Boniface[stock footage]
Barbara Slater [stock footage]
Al Thompson[stock footage]

PERSPECTIVE: Of all the refurbished Stooge films made during the 1950s, *Pies and Guys* strays least from the original script. It recreates 1947's *Half-Wits Holiday*, which turned out to be a significant film: it was during the filming of *Half-Wits Holiday* that Curly suffered a severe stroke and was unable to continue, and the pie fight footage from *Half-Wits Holiday* was reused in *Pest Man Wins* which itself marked a significant turning point as the first Shemp film to reuse extensive material from previous films. Since the pie fight of the original did not contain any footage of Curly or Shemp, this more than any film merited being remade from start to finish with Joe as the third Stooge, as if Joe was serving as a stand-in for an ailing Curly.

For every other Stooge remake to date, including the previous film, Jules White and his staff added scenes and clarified the plot, but this particular refurbishing merely adds some new gag lines (Quackenbush: "Take your serviette." Joe: "I never ate one of those!"; Joe: "Pag-pag-paganinni—" Quackenbush: "Paganini? That's page nine!"), expands older ones ([Moe: "Oh Curlington." Curly: "Yesington?"] becomes Moe: "Oh Joe-ington." Joe: "Yesington? Did you callington me?" Moe: "Indeedington!"), omits others (Sedlitz: "Tutt-tutt and poof-poof, to say nothing of piffle!" Quackenbush: "Poo-poo and hubba-hubba!"), varies the wording (Larry: "There hasn't been a gentleman in our family for five [fifty] generations!") or placement (Larry says "This joint's prettier than the reform school!" when they enter the house; in the original Larry says, "So different from our first party at the reform school!" when they are introduced to Mrs. Smythe Smythe), or assignment of verbal gags (Quackenbush: "There is definite evidence of Vacancy of the Cranium." Curly/Larry: "Oh, thank you, professor!"), reedits the fireplace slapstick and the pie fight to accommodate Joe, adds a brief Cossack dance, and omits the final gag with the professors (Quackenbush: "Here's your check back." Sedlitz: "Yes, professor, and I've learned something, too." Quackenbush: "What's that?" Sedlitz [hitting him with a pie]: "This!"). One particularly welcome improvement is in quickening the pace of the table-manners lesson. The main course of the original is no longer served, and the long, awkward silences are gone as well. Each individual change listed here (and there are several more) is relatively minor, but their sheer number and variety demonstrate the care that Jules and Jack White took in revising Zion Myer's original script.

Pies and Guys should be regarded as a variant of *Half-Wits Holiday*, which itself was a variation of *Hoi Polloi*, itself a parody of George Bernard Shaw's *Pygmalion*. As a whole this remake stands up well because Joe was in his prime for *Pies and Guys*, whereas Curly was already impaired and ultimately incapacitated for *Half-Wits Holiday*. Few Stooge aficionados would rank Joe Besser and Curly Howard on an equal stratum of Stoogitude, but in this particular remake Joe Besser as the third Stooge makes a thoroughly convincing, innately imbecilic, wonderful ignoramus.

VISUAL HUMOR (NEW MATERIAL): Joe now regularly gets double pounded/bonked/slapped in combination slapstick movements, beginning in earnest with *Rusty Romeos*. The introduction to Mrs. Smythe Smythe [Moe: "Very very happy happy!...You know this is our first entrée into society and we find it very delightful." Larry: "So different from our first party at the reform school."] could not be reshot because of Symona Boniface's death in 1950, so the reform school gag was placed elsewhere and in its place the Stooges perform the cigarette lighting sequence, in which Moe uses a lighter to ignite Larry's whole match book so he can light the Countess Spritzwasser's cigarette. Moe's Cossack dance (*Ants in the Pantry*) is very brief, but viewers should recall that Moe was now over 60 years old.

VERBAL HUMOR (NEW MATERIAL): Other changes and substitutions include Joe (instead of Moe) exclaiming "What a Lulu!" and howling (instead of Curly) like a wolf,

Lulu being described as a secretary instead of the professor's daughter, Moe calling Joe the epithet "skin-head...stupe" instead of "flat-top," Moe calling Larry the epithet "feather-brained imbecile" instead of "feather-brain," Moe reading the upside-down book as "Ingenzomen emdelah aysed bubis enangh" instead of the palindrome "Tar ytrid eht sey glub snap snorgatz ramatz, ranaance kiberze," and, of course, the absence of "Nyuk, nyuk, nyuk, nyuk" in the alcove sequence. Other new verbal gags include Moe: "Soup too hot?" Larry: "No, too salty!"; Moe's "It must be your tapeworm...Delicious! Just like the cans my mother used to make!"; and Moe: "You kleptomaniac!" Joe: "If that means what I think it does...I'm guilty!"... Moe 's "ingenzomen" was an ingredient in the youth serum in *Bubble Trouble*... The Page Nine/Paganini gag (Joe: "Pag-pag-paga-ninni—" Quackenbush: "Paganini? That's page nine!") was used earlier in the 1951 feature film *Gold Raiders*. Moe's "Now you watch your P's and Q's" we heard first in *Beer and Pretzels* and *Three Missing Links*.

OTHER NOTES: The film was shot in two days in early May, 1957. The working title was *Easy Come, Easy Go*. Zion Myers is not given screen credit for the story.

The last batch of Columbia Stooge short films was released after the Stooge contract and film production was already terminated. But the essence of Stoogedom is the film corpus they left behind; that was true in the late 1950s (when the Stooge films were first released for television broadcast), and it is true in the early years of the third millennium when everything is available for home viewing. This particular film, *Pies and Guys* (1958) is of special interest because the script is only slightly changed from the original version filmed a decade earlier as *Half-Wits Holiday*, during the filming of which Curly suffered his stroke, and because the pie fight footage was reused in *Pest Man Wins*, the first Shemp film to reuse extensive material from previous films.

#186 - SWEET AND HOT

Studio: Columbia

Released: September 4, 1958

Running Time: 16"17'"

Credited Production Crew:

Produced & Directed by:	Jules White
Screen Play by:	Jerome S. Gottler & Jack White
Story by:	Jerome S. Gottler
Director of Photography:	Irving Lippman
Art Director:	Adam Gosse
Film Editor:	Edwin Bryant
Set Decorator:	Sidney Clifford
Assistant Director:	Mitchell Gamson

Credited Cast:

Joe Besser	Joe, Uncle Joe
Larry Fine	Larry, Uncle Louie
Moe Howard	Dr. Hugo Gansamacher; Tiny's father
Muriel Landers	Tiny Landers

PERSPECTIVE: Music has always been an integral part of Stooge entertainment, beginning in their Ted Healy days on stage, their early film work at MGM [*Dancing Lady*] and their very first Columbia short, the 'Musical Novelty' *Woman Haters*, written by Archie & Jerome Gottler, the latter returning here to co-write this film and bring 24 years of Columbia short films full circle. Over the years the Stooges have danced, sung, and played instruments in dozens of these films, featured the talented Columbia contract comic actress/songstress Christine McIntyre [*Micro-Phonies*], and even displayed new talent, for instance, the Andrews Sisters-like act of 'Lindsay, Laverne, and Betty' in 1944's *Gents Without Cents*. In addition, the Stooges have occasionally played in backstage musicals [*Rhythm and Weep*], backstage dramas [*Three Hams on Rye*], and backlot films [*Movie Maniacs*]. Flexibility and experimentation frequently lead the Stooges into new directions, and now *Sweet and Hot* takes them into the unique and highly improbable genre of the Freudian-psychiatrist-barnyard-musical. From the initial bovine love song with a barnyard chorus to the final mouse terror, this extraordinarily variegated musical takes us from rural charm to a New York nightclub via a psychiatrist's couch and a sodium pententatentaten—, er, Truth Serum-induced flashback to an Andy Hardy-like farm setting, isolating each Stooge as an individual character in two different roles in two different time periods.

The vehicle around which all this happens is Muriel Landers, whom Columbia had signed on for the single featurette *Tricky Chicks* just months earlier; in fact, Landers had sung 'The Heat Is On' for *Tricky Chicks*, and some of that footage is reused here. The plumpness she brings to the film is a quintessential Stooge quality, providing not only a feminine counterpart to the portly Curly and Joe but also an updated musical version of the equally huge June Gittelson [*False Alarms*] and Maxine Gates [*Husbands Beware*]. Like Joe in *Quiz Whizz*, she loves food and allows the promise of lobster and spaghetti tetrazine to lure her to New York. But then we find out she has a problem— stage fright.

To overcome this stage fright she undergoes an examination by Dr. Hugo Gansamacher, a Freudian psychiatrist played by Moe with his hair slicked back and a heavy German accent à la Benny Rubin [*Income Tax Sappy* and *Space Ship Sappy*]. The extensive interview between him and Tiny uses several old and new doctor jokes, and then Tiny and the good doctor reverse roles: *he* lies on the couch. Regaining control, the doctor uses hypnotism and sodium pentathol to help Tiny reexperience a childhood trauma involving her father [Moe] and Uncles Joe and Louie [Larry]. The treatment works, so the freshly emboldened Tiny is ready for the New York club and the musical finale. Now the initial barnyard musical number yields to a 'hot' metropolitan club number, and Tiny's misplaced love for the cow finds new inspiration in Larry's kiss. Musicals regularly end with the 'boy' getting the 'girl,' so the rotund, sweet, and ultimately successful Tiny, whom Larry had told earlier "I think you're prettier than a spotted heifer," ends up with her true love, as is proper for a 'sweet' Stooge musical like this.

VISUAL HUMOR: At the outset, the camera emphasizes the bizarre juxtaposition of romantic music in a barnyard setting by focusing on Tiny singing 'Let's Fall in Love' and then pulling back to show her hugging a cow in the barn. From there editor Edwin Bryant shows us the cow, chicken, dog, horse, bull, mule, nursing piglets, and duck making their calls and noises. The duck footage is from *I'm a Monkey's Uncle*, the hound dog raising his huge ears from Joe Besser's *G. I. Dood It* [1955].The musical genre tones down the slapstick, which comprises new [Moe dropping his looking glass into Tiny's mouth [Tiny: "It's a good thing you don't use binoculars!"]] and varied gags [Moe conking his head against Joe's, bouncing off and conking it against Larry's; Larry pulling Joe out of the way by the ear; and a fist game]. Repetitions: Joe spreads his arms and knocks the bucket onto Larry's head as they prepare to leave for New York, and later in the night club act Tiny spreads her arms and knocks Joe and Larry down; in the psychiatry sequence, Moe bangs his head on the bed tray twice; and Moe's 'Rock and Roll' shuffle is not too different from Larry's soft shoe just outside the barn door.

Result shot: Larry covered with eggs, as in *G.I. Wanna Home*. Tiny sits on the hypodermic needle as did Joe recently in *Space Ship Sappy*. Joe's method of churning butter, which squirts up in his face, is different from the method used in *I'm a Monkey's Uncle*. Other variations: smashed cigars (*Uncivil Warriors*); the reaction to a mouse (*Horses' Collars*); and Joe reaching up to a shelf and having a jar fall on his head (*Fuelin' Around*).

VERBAL HUMOR: The verbal humor in the barn scenes focuses on food. Muriel Landers and Joe are perfectly matched as Larry says, "Think of the money, New York, the theatre, the lights, the food!" To most suggestions they say "Eh" or "Nah," but the mention of food gets their attention (Larry: "Steaks, lobsters, chicken cacciatore, spaghetti tetrazini..." Landers: "I couldn't eat another bite!...When do we eat, I mean, when do we leave?!") In the flashback Landers sings the last lines of 'Yankee Doodle' as "eating big fudge sandwiches/stuffed with lice baloney".

The psychiatric examination has its predecessors in the medical examinations in *Men in Black*, *From Nurse to Worse*, and recently in *Muscle Up a Little Closer;* we saw the Stooges portraying Germanic psychiatrists in *Three Sappy People*. Although Moe's accent is of the extreme sort used recently by Benny Rubin (featured in *Tricky Chicks*), Moe himself used a German accent earlier in the anti-Nazi films, as did Vernon Dent as Dr. Panzer in *A Bird in the Head*; the prototype is Jack Pearl as Baron Munchausen in *Meet the Baron*. Like Pearl and Rubin, Moe combines his thick accent with malapropisms ("Please, my time is lineament!...I mean, limited"; "Open your mouth and push your tongue inside out"; "This is an open and shut case, inside out and upside down"; and "Sodium Pententatentaten—Truth Serum!"), and like Dr. Panzer, Dr. Gansamacher is a bit crazed (Moe: "Ah-hah! Ah-ha-ha-ha! Ha-ha-ha-ha-ha-hah!" Joe: "What is it, doc?" Moe: "Nothing. I just thought of zomething funny!") and a little mean ([Tiny opens her mouth very wide] "I don't want to valk in; I just want to look!"). Most of the other medical gags are in classic question-and-answer format (Moe: "Where you vaz born?" Tiny: "In bed." [cf. *Men in Black; Tricky Dicks*]; Moe: "No, no: I mean, what state?" Tiny: "Kansas." Moe: "What part?" Tiny: "All of me." Moe: "It's a good thing it's a big state!"; Moe: "When you vaz a little girl, you ever did somezing naughty?" Tiny: "Once I drank a bottle of ink." Moe: "Incredible." Tiny: "Uh-uh, indelible!"; and Moe: "What'd you want to be when you were six?" Tiny: "Seven." Moe: "What'd you want to be when you were four?" Tiny: "Seven"). Their word associations bring up the third 'smog' and 'rock-and-roll' references in the Stooge films but the first to Great Neck, New York. Another (Moe: "Nein." Tiny: "Ten." Moe: "Eleven.") is reminiscent of "Hey, you, fore!...Five...Six" in *Three Little Beers*.

Larry and Joe are included by taking things literally (Moe: "Gentlemen, take a chair." Joe and Larry lift up chairs; Moe: "I give him artificial respiration!" Larry: "Artificial?! For what you charge, you give him the real thing!") or being ignorant (Moe: "You are an ochlophobe!" Joe: "Watch your language!" ["You kleptomaniac!" Joe: "If that means what I think it does...I'm guilty!" in the previous film]). Throw-away lines: Moe: "You got those beautiful blue eyes!" Joe: "They just came with her head!"; Tiny: "I can't sing for people!" Joe: "We ain't people! We're your uncles!").

References: Moe uses the German "grossartig" meaning "grand, splendid"; the exclamation "Ach du lieber!" means "Oh dear me!"; and the psychological term "ochlophobe" refers to a person who is 'afraid' of 'crowds.' Moe's name, "Gansamacher" is a Yiddish term referring to a person who can do everything. Other variations: Joe: "Not so lou-oud!" (*Guns A Poppin!*); Joe: "Give it to him, Larry!...He gave it to you!" ("Good for you...Bad for me!" in *A Merry Mix-Up*); and Joe: "Indian giver!" (*Back to the Woods*).

OTHER NOTES: The film was shot in 2 days, in August, 1957. All the actors are credited. Muriel Landers is credited as "Also Starring." She had a brief but regular TV role as Rosa in *Life With Luigi* (1953) and will appear in *Pillow Talk* (1959). Tiny pantomimes playing 'Three Blind Mice' on an imaginary piano, but her fingers move in the wrong direction. This was Joe Besser's least favorite Stooge short. Jules White [*Bruskin* 97-99] commented later that "It was too good; the people were too human and too nice". Not only does Jerome Gottler (*Woman Haters*) bring the Columbia shorts full circle; so does Harold Arlen's song 'Let's Fall in Love,' which Larry played in the second Columbia short, *Punch Drunks*. Jules White [Bruskin 97] "used that song in fifty pictures. I loved it." Ned Washington and Lester Lee's "The Heat is On" originated in Columbia's *Miss Sadie Thompson* (1953).

"Mars Men" attack the Stooges out on a camping trip in the next film, *Flying Saucer Daffy* - one of the most complex and contemporary films the Stooges ever made, and the last short-film they made for Jules White's unit and Harry Cohn's Columbia.

#187 - FLYING SAUCER DAFFY

Studio: Columbia

Released: October 9, 1958

Running Time: 16"07'"

Credited Production Crew:

Produced & Directed by:	Jules White
Written by:	Jack White
Director of Photography:	Frank Jackman
Art Director:	Cary Odell
Film Editor:	Saul A. Goodkind
Set Decorator:	Milton Stumph
Assistant Director:	Jerrold Bernstein

Credited Cast:

Joe Besser	
Larry Fine	
Moe Howard	
Gail Bonney	aunt/mother
Emil Sitka	President of *Facts and Figures Magazine*
Bek Nelson	Tyrin from Planet Zircon
Diana Darrin	Elektra from Planet Zircon

Uncredited Cast:

Harriette Tarler	party girl
Joe Palma	government officer

PERSPECTIVE: The final three Columbia shorts (*Oil's Well That Ends Well*, *Triple Crossed*, *Sappy Bull Fighters*) were filmed before *Flying Saucer Daffy* but released afterwards. Shot December 19-20, 1957, this was the last Stooge Columbia short ever filmed. Since 1934 the Stooges' Columbia contract obligated them to making eight films per year, and they had now completed all sixteen films for 1957-1958. Harry Cohn had the right to pick up the option for 1959, and Moe was saying on the way back to the dressing rooms on the final day of shooting, "Well, fellas, let's keep our fingers crossed that Harry Cohn thinks we're worth another year." [Besser, 197] The trio sat silently removing their makeup, and then in walked Jules White: "Boys, I have bad news. Columbia Pictures is letting you go." It was that abruptly that the Stooges' unparalleled twenty-four consecutive years (and Joe Besser's fourteen years) at Columbia came to an end. Moe and Larry said little, but Joe went up to the office of 'King Cohn' only to hear: "I'll miss you and the boys. You've always come through for me. But what can I say? Television is the rage. Even though your films have made money, short subjects are dead."

This film is a fascinating final offering. Like the previous release *Sweet and Hot*, the story separates the Stooges and joins two otherwise incompatible movie themes - Cinderella and flying saucers. The story of Cinderella, which Disney had animated in 1950, was revived twice metaphorically in 1954's *Sabrina* and *The Barefoot Contessa*, and was turned into a musical with Leslie Caron in 1955's *The Glass Slipper*. Calling himself a "he-Cinderella," Joe wishes for his 'fairy godmother' ("All you need is a glass slipper instead of a bone head!") and suffers repeated abuse from his cousins and brash aunt, the latter a wicked step-mother type playing another tough woman who yells at and beats up Stooges.

Flying saucers were already a part of contemporary cinema. In 1956, Columbia released Ray Harryhausen's now classic *Earth Versus the Flying Saucers*. But when the Soviets launched Sputnik 1 in October, 1957, the US was in 'Sputnik Hysteria.' *Flying Saucer Daffy* was shot just two months later, putting the Stooges once again at the film world's vanguard. Capturing 'SPUTNIK-G.i-8' on a *Polaroid* made *Flying Saucer Daffy* even more avant-garde [as did the use of paper plates!], and four bits of exterior stock, shots of five different newspaper headlines and magazine covers, and flying saucer footage from *Earth Versus the Flying Saucers* make this film one of the most visually elaborate in Stoogedom. Of course, Columbia owned all this material already so it was inexpensive to use.

Sci-fi films usually include a final moral, and here it is that Cinderella Good triumphs over step-Stooge Evil. After Moe and Larry steal Joe's prize-winning photo,

spend their ill-gotten riches like prodigals, and fail to believe in Joe's genuine flying saucer photo, the Zirconian fairy godmothers ultimately reward Joe's big-hearted purity by giving him wealth, a limousine, a big cigar, a ticker tape parade, and their beautiful selves. In contrast, the final scene, the last in a Stooge short, shows us a quasi-Biblical comeuppance with Moe's and Larry's straight-jacketed, head-banging self-punishment.

Flying Saucer Daffy was the last Columbia Stooge short film ever made, though it was not the last one released. It took Curly several years before he found his true persona as a Stooge, and now at the end of his second year Joe Besser was finding his as well. Of course, any actor depends on the story and script provided him, but Jack White - now in his fifth decade of comedy-film writing - developed this story which feature Joe's naive qualities. Here in this limited exterior shot he takes a picture of some 'real' aliens with his Polaroid-type camera, evidence for not only the existence of extraterrestrial beings but the contemporary gadgetry necessary to this comedy.

Joe, calling himself a 'he-Cinderella,' does not enjoy this champagne celebration in 1958's *Flying Saucer Daffy*. The Cinderella motif was recently re-popularized in Disney's animated version of 1950, 1954's *Sabrina* and *The Barefoot Contessa*, and 1955's *The Glass Slipper*. In 1952 the Stooges parodied both *A Streetcar Named Desire* and *Harvey* in the same film (*Cuckoo on a Choo Choo*), and here they combine both science fiction and fairy tale motifs.

VISUAL HUMOR: For all of the initial concern about Joe not taking any hits when he joined the trio, the slapstick is an integral part of this particular, and final, film. Because Joe triumphs in the end, an essential part of the story has to be the physical abuse that Joe suffers before the final reversal. First Moe grabs him by the throat, slaps him on each cheek twice, gouges him, pounds him, and gives him a nose tweak; then the mother slaps him twice with each hand, gouges him, pounds him and kicks him into the punch bowl; and finally Moe and Larry rough him up with two pounds, a slap, a bonk, and two punches to the jaw. When Joe has finally had enough ("That's it!"), the ultimate retribution comes appropriately and surprisingly as a new variation on the fist game, one that Moe and Larry have not seen before, and certainly not from Joe: he holds up two fists: "See this?" Moe & Larry: "Yeah." Joe slugs them each in the face, wields a champagne bottle, conks his aunt with the backswing, and then conks Moe and Larry. An earlier foreshadowing of the final retribution comes when Moe and Larry are about to be arrested: Moe tries to punch Joe but hits Larry instead. Curly used his hand wave and "Hhmm!" sound to ease the frustration of being beaten; Joe uses dialogue: [NOSE TWEAK] Joe: "Do that again! [NOSE TWEAK] Again! [NOSE TWEAK] You do everything I tell ya' to!". Besides the Polaroid camera, flying saucer, and paper plate, another very contemporary item is the frozen 'TV Dinner'; TV dinners became popular in the late 1950s. Joe kneeling and hiding in the tent, then being exposed when Moe and Larry speed off in the car is an elaborate version of the hiding-in-the-box gag used recently in *Fifi Blows Her Top*. Moe and Larry are busted by the Feds, as they were in *Income Tax Sappy* and *Cash and Carry*. Other variations: Moe lighting his nose (*Space Ship Sappy*); Joe "dropping what he is doing" (recently in *Horsing Around*); Larry pulling down cans onto his and Moe's head (recently in *Sweet and Hot*); Moe letting a branch swing into Larry's face, and Larry letting it swing into Joe's [*Uncivil Warriors*]; smoke coming out Joe's mouth and ears after a kiss [*Love at First Bite*]; Joe tripping, shooting his shotgun, and killing a duck [*Back to the Woods*]; the swinging kitchen door [*Crash Goes the Hash*]; and Joe living outdoors [*Space Ship Sappy*].

VERBAL HUMOR: Jack White's opening scene establishes the familial relationships, so we learn quickly that the wicked aunt [Gail Bonney], one of the great Stooge characters, drinks heavily ("Water! Don't you never do that to me again!"), favors Moe and Larry [Aunt: "Darling Larry, you're so considerate of your mother. [She pounds Joe] Why didn't *you* think of that?!"], expects Joe to earn all the money [Aunt "How was the track today." Larry: "Sloppy." Aunt: "Sloppy?! We ain't had rain in weeks." Larry: "Some sow slopped beer in my hat!" Aunt: "Oh, I'll get Joe to get you a new one."], and criticizes Joe despite his efforts [[Joe carrying two grocery bags, two cake boxes, and a smaller brown bag]: "Did you wipe your feet?"; Joe: "You're a doll." Aunt: "Go wash the dishes and then clean out the hearth!"]. The abuse makes Joe co-dependent, buying her two cakes and calling himself an "ingrate." In our first view of her she tosses booze bottle into the fireplace; later she tosses champagne bottles. In contrast, Joe is nice to everyone, his step-family, the aliens, and even, like the Disney Cinderella, to little wild animals: he apologizes to the squirrel for not having any nuts, so he tosses him some chewing gum. Similarly, unlike most aliens in 1950's films, the Zirconians are peaceful ("Do not be afraid...We want to make friends with you earth people"). White writes two literal gags for Moe and Larry [[Larry reading *Facts and Figures*] Moe: "Give me the facts about it." Larry: "Wait till I look over the figures!" [Larry looking at a photo of a woman in a bathing suit.] Moe: "What are you - an accountant?"; and Moe: "What are you lookin' for?!" Larry: "With all that space up there, there might be a space ship!". Epithets: "weasel, " "overstuffed baloney," and "double crossin' rat." Moe uses the diminutive 'Joey'. To illustrate Stooge ignorance, the phrase "Mars Men" is perfect. Lying is an important element in Stooge space films. In the end of *Space Ship Sappy* they won a prize from the Liars Club, in *Outer Space Jitters* it turns out that they were telling their kids a bedtime story, and here there is much about truth, lying, belief, and disbelief. The gag in which Moe hits Joe, making him swear not to tell the truth but then Joe doing 'as he was told' and lying to the government agents, was popular in the late 1950s, early 1960s (e.g. in *A Funny Thing Happened on the Way to the Forum*). Variations: Joe: "Not so lou-ou-ou-ou-oud! [the longest ever] [*Guns A Poppin!*]; Joe: "That's good for you!...That's bad for me!, and "Not so har-ard!" [*A Merry Mix-Up*]; and Moe: "Get us a lawyer! A cheap one!" [*Monkey Businessmen*].

OTHER NOTES: The working title was *Pardon My Flying Saucer*. Edwin Land patented his Polaroid camera in 1947; it became popular in the 1950s. The stock shot of dirty dishes is from Vernon and Quillan's *He Flew the Shrew* (1951). Bek Nelson [Tyrin] played in *Tricky Chicks* with Murial Landers; the following year she had a steady role as Dru Lemp on ABC's *The Lawman*. Gail Bonney [Aunt], who made her career as a character actress, is remembered for her role in *Cat Ballou* (1965). Zirconian business card: 'A. B. CLOUD & CO. - DISTRIBUTORS - SPUTNIK-G.i-8 - NEW AND USED SPACE SHIPS - 200 VAPOR BLVD. - ZIRCON - PHONE: BEEP-BLUEP-BLOP'. The Stooges had made two short films associated with fairy tales previously [*Nertsery Rhymes*; *Fiddlers Three*] and would make a feature in 1961 [*Snow White and the Three Stooges*]. This was not the first Stooge short released before an earlier production; *Movie Maniacs*, for instance, was filmed before *Ants in the Pantry*, but was released later, as was the case with *A Bird in the Head* and *Micro-Phonies*.

The final release of 1958 was *Oil's Well That Ends Well*, a film that gave the Stooges another chance to abuse a pickax. This may not seem extraordinary, but there was much ado about Joe's original Stooge-film contract and how it stipulated that he would not tolerate the usual Stooge abuse. But as his two years proceeded this restriction was apparently relaxed. More importantly, Joe developed some fine comic responses to the abuse, and was capable of dishing it out in return.

#188 - OIL'S WELL THAT ENDS WELL

Studio: Columbia

Released: December 4, 1958

Running Time: 16"09'"

Credited Cast:
Joe Besser
Larry Fine
Moe Howard

Credited Production Crew:

Produced & Directed by:	Jules White
Written by:	Felix Adler
Dirctor of Photography:	Irving Lippman
Art Director:	Adam Gosse
Film Editor:	Edwin Bryant
Set Decorator:	Sidney Clifford
Assistant Director:	Mitchell Gamson

PERSPECTIVE: *Oil's Well That Ends Well* refurbishes *Oily to Bed, Oily to Rise*, the memorable 1939 film that gave us our first "Oh! Oh! Oh! Ohhh-llook!" from Curly and took the Stooges from jobless to employed to fired to heroic crime solvers who by strike oil and rescue three sisters in emotional and financial distress. One of the most memorable images from this or any Stooge film is of Curly sitting atop the oil 'geezer,' but it is actually only one highlight of a film shot in many exterior settings, a specialty of writer Andrew Bennison [*Back to the Woods*]. To revise *Oily to Bed, Oily to Rise* Jules White and Felix Adler jettisoned the original criminal and romantic elements which took the Stooges out to many of those exterior scenes, but they added a new exterior scene - the Stooge's atomic-age attempt at mining for their dad's uranium, a fair exchange for the original's inimitable tool-abuse sequence. Not exterior, but still rural, are the scenes in the cabin - a cow milking scene [*Busy Buddies*] substituting for the cooking sequence in *Guns A Poppin!/ Idiots Deluxe*, and a fine bunk bed sequence, the only one of the Joe era and the first since *G.I. Wanna Home*. As in the original, the 'wishing' theme is predominant, although we still do not learn why Joe has his wishing ability. Joe makes six wishes early on, and now the wishing theme brings the film to a climax when Joe uses his seventh, eighth, and ninth wishes to activate, deactivate, and reactivate the oil gusher. Atop all that black gold, Joe just has to conclude with his titular, Shakespearean pun: "Oil's Well That Ends Well!"

Cast as separate characters in the previous release, the Stooges take advantage of being cast as a trio again, especially with the absence of any other actors, by moving physically in an orchestrated variety that smacks of the old days. The first two scenes send Larry flying: in the first Joe belly bumps Larry so hard he backs into a chair and spills over a table [with a $100 bill attached, thereby advancing the plot], and in the second the cow knocks him against the wall. The third scene broadens out spatially in the exterior with Joe walking back and forth and almost sitting on the dynamite plunger twice before actually blowing up his brethren. The bunk bed scene expands vertically, forwards, and backwards in a dozen triadic permutations, and the fifth scene takes Joe even higher in the classic 'geezer' scene which requires him again to sit twice before the explosive action can occur.

Being cast together again also increases the amount of inter-Stooge slapstick. For the first time since Joe joined the trio every scene contains a complex slapstick exchange. In the first scene Joe repays Larry's nose tweak with a belly bump; in the second Moe gives Larry an eye-gouging lesson; in the third Moe and Larry battle with a shovel and a hammer and Joe engages in a gouging routine; by the fourth Joe seems more of a Stooge than ever as he engages in the tightly choreographed bunk bed routine; and in the fifth scene he rises even higher on his oil gusher in what at least looks like the most physically extensive gag in his stint as the third stooge.

VISUAL HUMOR (NEW MATERIAL): The abundant slapstick includes lively variations. Larry misses Moe with his shovel on his first turn, then clangs him on the second [*Back to the Woods*; *Cash and Carry*]; Larry hits Moe with his hammer, Moe breaks a rock over his head, Larry points to the ground [*A Pain in the Pullman*], saying a simplified version of the original film's new Curlyism "Oh look!", and slugs Moe; Larry "pumps" the cow's tail and gets kicked back into the wall, flour falling on his head [*Busy Buddies*, *Vagabond Loafers*]; and Joe tosses a piece of "broken" dynamite, tossing other dynamite sticks to Larry [*Yes, We Have No Bonanza*], and then almost sits on the dynamite plunger twice before actually blowing Moe and Larry up. There are two gouging variations: a broken finger routine [Joe blocks Moe's gouge, they both laugh, Moe gouges him in the back of the head, Joe says: "He broke his fingers," and Moe gouges him the right way [*Three Dark Horses*]], and the gouging lesson [Larry goes to gouge Moe, but Moe blocks it: "You don't know how to do that. Look." He puts Larry's hand in the blocking position and gouges him with two hands]. Joe's sliding inside Moe's pajama leg is a Stooge first. Felix Adler films often compliment slapstick with dialogue. Best here perhaps is when Larry claims the lower berth [HAIR PULL, SEVEN SLAPS] Moe: "Who's sleeping in the lower?" Larry: "You are!" Joe slaps Moe rapidly seventeen times from the rear. Moe: "Who is sleeping in the lower?..." "Well who is?!" Joe: "You are!" [SLAP] Larry: "On second thought we better take the upper." Joe: "That was better than the first thought." Other examples: Moe squeezing milk into Joe's face [Joe: "Try another faucet. Maybe it gives chocolate flavor. [Moe squeezes a different teat] Tastes the same!"]; Larry tapping at the rock and clanging Moe with a backswing [Moe: "It was only the head!"], slamming a rock over Larry's head [Larry: "Oww! Ohh! Oh, look!" Moe: "How do you like that?!"], Larry pointing to the ground, Moe bending over, Larry clanging him on the head with the hammer [Larry: "How do you like that?!"]; and with Joe's leg slipped into Moe's pajama leg [Joe: "You're following me!"]. Another Curlyism: Joe waves his finger in Moe's face and mesmerizes him. Twice the viewer sees what Moe does not: Larry about to throw a can hard at Moe's back but tossing it lightly when Moe turns toward him; and Joe mouthing 'I hate him!' into the camera. The latter was an ad-lib which Joe had used in his 1944 feature film *Hey, Rookie!* [*Besser* 185]. Result shots: Larry, a blackened face, with an exploded cigar in his mouth [*Fling in the Ring*]; and Moe and Larry half buried in the rock debris. Several of the bunk-bed gags [boosting Larry in the wrong direction; banging their heads on the wall and passing out] are from *A Pain in the Pullman*.

VERBAL HUMOR [NEW MATERIAL]: Many gags depend on Stooge ignorance, particularly about cows [Moe: "What comes from cows?" Larry: "Steak!"; Larry: "What good's a cow? You know milk comes in bottles...all sizes!"; Larry: "What good's that milk bottle gonna do him? How's he gonna get a cow to sit on a little thing like that?" Moe: "How do you think?" Larry: "Oh, the same way they get them to sit on the little cans!"; Larry: "All you have to do is turn on the faucet....You have to pump it!"; and Joe's "Try another faucet. Maybe it gives chocolate flavor!" and "How now, brown cow!"] and uranium mining ["What does the Geiger Counter say?" "Click-click, click-click"; and Moe: "Eureka!" Larry: "We're looking for uranium, not 'eureka'"]. Joe's relatively gentile character now often fends off Moe's insults verbally [Moe: "You're a nitwit imbecile." Joe: "Flattery will get you no place!"; Moe: "You clumsy ox!" Joe: "Don't you call me 'clumsy'!"; and Joe: "You're such a weakling, you can't lift a little me." Moe: "It would take a derrick to lift a ton of blubber like you!" Joe: "You're just saying that!"]. At one point the dialogue turns a bit eerie: Joe: "I got my wish again!...Hey, I'm scared." Moe [backing away]: "So am I". References: The Stooges tell us their dad is "in the hospital in Colfax," a small mining town north of Sacramento; Joe's last line, "Well, oil's well that ends well," is borrowed from the title of Shakespeare's 1601/1603 comedy of the same name, although before him John Heywood [fl. 1550-80] had translated the Latin proverb [*Si finis bonus est, totum bonum erit*] from which it derives; Joe's "How now, brown cow" was a popular rhyming expression in the 1950s. Epithets: "You double-crosser!" and "imbeciles!" [twice]. Variations: Moe: "Every time you think you weaken the nation" [*Half-Shot Shooters*]; Moe: "What does the Geiger counter say?" Larry: "Click-click, click-click" [*Fright Night*]; Joe: "Cut that out, you crazy you!" [*Quiz Whizz*]; Larry: "Good night, mother. Wind up the cat and put out the clock" ["Oh Nellie, you're here at last!" in *A Pain in the Pullman*]; Moe: "I'm beginnin' to think you're haunted" [*Men in Black*].

Oil's Well That Ends Well resembles its classic 1939 predecessor *Oily to Bed, Oily to Rise* in specific borrowings. But now in the Atomic Age, the Stooges search for uranium. Along the way there is much verticality, first with this bunk bed which the Stooges attempt to mount in a variety of permutations, and ultimately with the oil 'geezer.'

OTHER NOTES: The film was shot on August 26-27, 1957, using the same cabin as for *Guns A Poppin!* and *Horsing Around*. Filmed before *Flying Saucer Daffy*, *Oil's Well That Ends Well* was issued as the final release of 1958. The final three Columbia Stooge releases are refurbishings; of the sixteen 'Joe films,' seven were refurbishings. The only reused footage is that of Curly atop the oil gusher and being yanked off with a rope. This is only film other than *Self-Made Maids* to use only the Stooges as actors.

Triple Crossed • Sappy Bullfighters

#189 - TRIPLE CROSSED

Studio: Columbia

Released: February 2, 1959

Running Time: 15"48"'

Credited Production Crew:

Produced & Directed by:	Jules White
Written by:	Warren Wilson
Director of Photography:	Fred Jackman
Art Director:	Cary Odell
Film Editor:	Saul A. Goodkind
Set Decorator:	Milton Stumph
Assistant Director:	Jerrold Bernstein

Credited Cast:

Joe Besser
Larry Fine
Moe Howard

Uncredited Cast:

Angela Stevens	Millie
Mary Ainslee	Belle [stock footage]
Diana Darrin	Miss Lapdale [stock footage]
Connie Cezan	Belle
Johnny Kascier	waiter [stock footage]

PERSPECTIVE: As with 1958's *Pies and Guys, Triple Crossed* takes an older script - 1952's *He Cooked His Goose* - and reshoots it with Joe substituting for Shemp as the third Stooge. Reshooting older scripts instead of fully refurbishing their introductions and conclusions, as had been the norm in 1953-1956, was more common in the final two years of Stooge production, and the causes for this included increased pressures on studio profits and the public's changing preferences for entertainment. The separation of theater chains from film studios had now deprived the studios of most of their booking leverage, and the newly independent theater operators found that by showing double features (rather than a single feature preceded by cartoons, short films, or newsreels) they could attract a broader assortment of audiences. Also, the now established dominance of television kept many former theater-goers, particularly children who were now the primary audience for cartoons and shorts, at home; the most popular comedic vehicle was the half-hour television situation comedy, direct competition to the two-reeler short. With such major changes taking place in the entertainment industry throughout America, the old and relatively expensive short-subject film genre found itself unable to thrive. By December 1957, Columbia's short film unit was facing permanent shutdown .

The pressure to produce the eight new Stooge films per year as cheaply as possible was greater than ever. For the previous *Oil's Well That Ends Well*, not a single non-Stooge actor was employed despite the use of seven in the original film. And the shooting for *Triple Crossed* was limited to a single day, the time previously allotted to shoot merely introductions and conclusions, to refurbishing projects. (White used to take four days to shoot an entire film.) To maximize the amount of old footage that could be reused, Jules White chose a film which featured neither Curly nor Shemp but Larry, in this case a Felix Adler creation which had Larry, "the two-timin' porcupine," victimizing Moe and Shemp. To replace the Shemp scenes they had only to substitute the kitchen scene for the scene with Shemp in Millie's living room and reshoot the scenes in Belle's apartment with Joe now dressed in street clothes, custom underwear, and a Santa Claus suit. Angela Stevens was available to voice over every "Shemp" with "Joe" in the opening scene, but Mary Ainslee was not available to reprise Belle. Jules White called upon Connie Cezan to stand in and, like Joe Palma in the last four 'Shemp films,' be shot only from behind. Shemp is not so easily gotten rid of, though: as if he is still hiding in the chimney, it is his hand we see pointing and his yell we hear when Moe shoots at him.

New sequences offer us Joe almost taking a bite out of a frog sandwich - the frog replacing the clam of the original - and Joe shooting up Millie's kitchen instead of a turkey. One incident in the new kitchen scene subtly represents how modern both the times and the Stooges have become: Joe slams his fist into the cake Millie is making from a box mix, à la the contemporary Betty

Crocker, instead of one of the patented Stooge scratch-cake recipes.

VISUAL HUMOR (NEW MATERIAL): The freshest gag is Joe's taking aim at the turkey but shooting down a kitchen shelf and some plates instead ("The barrel must have been bent!"). Joe ripping off Larry's collar, Larry ripping off Joe's lapel, and Joe ripping off Larry's lapel is an old Laurel & Hardy gag. The concluding slapstick combines two old reliable routines. First Joe throws a punch at the ducking Larry and hits Moe, and Moe throws another and hits Joe. Then Millie stops them: "Stop! Don't hit him!" Larry [smiling]: "Thanks!" Millie: "Let *me* do it!" She socks Larry in the jaw (*Pardon My Clutch*). Joe winks at the camera to close the film, as did Curly in *Oily to Bed, Oily to Rise*; Joe had talked directly into the camera in the previous film ("I hate him!"), which also happens to derive from *Oily to Bed, Oily to Rise*. Other variations: the frog sandwich (the frog jumping into Shemp's hat in *The Ghost Talks*); and Joe pulling out a towel-sized hanky from his lapel pocket (the mouth gag in *Outer Space Jitters*).

VERBAL HUMOR (NEW MATERIAL): This is writer Warren Wilson's only Stooge script. He uses the new kitchen scene to establish Joe's characterization as a falsely accused Stooge who will tell white lies despite an innate honesty (Millie: "Now no fibs, Joey: How many shots?" Joe: "None. I hit it with my car!"; Joe: "The barrel must have been bent!"; Millie: "You say Larry's a chiseler, but he says you're just a playboy, are you?" Joe: "No! That fuzzy-topped porcupine!"). This ambiguity is repeated in the final line of the film: "You see I'm no playboy...I think." In between Joe is self-effacing ("I'm an ingrate...I hate myself!") as he was in *Flying Saucer Daffy*.

Wilson adds a pun to the underwear scene ("Any man would like this. You could wear it for a sun suit, underwear, or 'any wear'!"), and he works a few extra gags around the Christmas theme: (Joe [shoving Larry into Moe]: "Look what Santa Claus brought you!"; Joe [emerging as Santa]: "Merry Christmas, everyone! Merry, merry, merry, merry Christmas!... Merry, m-m-m-m-merry—" This replaces Shemp's "Helloooo, children!" Wilson also tries to clarify the association between Christmas and lingerie ("Larry: "I just got you a job with Plotnick...men's custom-made underwear and novelties, and Santa Claus suits") which the original film failed to do. Epithets: the rivalry between the Stooges generates much name calling (Larry: "You big hunk-a blubber!"; Joe: "That fuzzy-topped porcupine!"; Joe: "That double-crossin' skunk Larry!"; Joe: "Why that two-timing chiseler!"). This generates the semi-final gags (Moe: "You snake in the grass! You skunk! You—" Larry: "Philanderer?" Moe: "I can't say philander! You mixed me up. Where was I?" Larry: "Skunk!" Moe: "Oh, yeah! You dirty baboon!"). Moe needing Larry to fill in the noun was used with "imbecile" in *Listen, Judge* and "scrutiny" in *Hold That Lion*. Moe's "I can't say philander" parallels " I can't say Worcestershire" (*Half-Wits Holiday*).

OTHER NOTES: The shooting date, December 18, 1957, was the day before shooting commenced for *Flying Saucer Daffy* (December 19-20), the last Stooge short to be filmed. The working title was *Chiseling Chisler*.

Triple Crossed (1959) refurbished a unique film from the Shemp era which featured Larry as a two-timing, romantic scam artist. The script of *He Cooked His Goose* (1952) provided the romantic quintet, so Joe simply replaced Shemp in the film. Nonetheless, it is still Shemp's Santa-Claus arm that comes down and out from the chimney.

#190 - SAPPY BULL FIGHTERS

Studio: Columbia

Released: June 4, 1959

Running Time: 15"12'"

Credited Production Crew:

Produced & Directed by:	Jules White
Written by:	Jack White
Director of Photography:	Irving Lippman
Art Director:	Walter Holscher
Film Editor:	Harold White
Set Decorater:	Sidney Clifford
Assistant Director:	Max Stein

Credited Cast:

Joe Besser	
Larry Fine	
Moe Howard	
Greta Thyssen	Greta
George Lewis	Jose

Uncredited Cast:

Joe Palma	bull ring attendant
Eddie Laughton	bull ring attendant[stock footage]
Cy Schindell	bull ring attendant [stock footage]

PERSPECTIVE: *Sappy Bull Fighters* is a refurbished version of *What's the Matador?*, the 1942 film that casts the Stooges as unemployed showmen getting a gig in a Mexican bull ring via a beautiful woman's bedroom thanks to a mistaken suitcase. Beginning in a US booking agency, *What's the Matador?* expanded to a number of exterior scenes, added minor characters in Mexico and plenty of other Hispanic flavorings, and also included the Stooges' first bedroom 'comedy of manners.' *Sappy Bull Fighters* maintains each of these elements but simplifies them considerably, as required now by the limited budget of a Columbia short-subject unit facing its demise.

A limited budget for a Stooge film meant less elaborate sets and costumes (the exposition of the original is replaced simply with an opening sign; the pre-bull ring scenes in the new version take place in just two rooms backstage at the Teatro Internacional, with the Stooges wearing street clothes), a limited use of extras (other than the wife [Greta Thyssen] and husband [Gorge Lewis] the plot requires for the 'comedy of manners' sequence, the only non-Stooge actor is a dog; a frog was added in the previous film), and effective use of stock footage (like the oil geyser footage in *Oil's Well to End Well*, the old bull-fight footage here is visually exciting and works well as the film's action climax). A limited budget also meant a brief shooting schedule, and of all the 190 films to date, this one more than any other could have used a few more takes during shooting and a little more care in post-production. There are a few brief dead-air moments that interrupt the comic flow, the limited back and forth movement in the shots of Joe riding the bull fail to match the violent movements of the original footage, and even the sound effects for the suitcase hits are muted or absent. In a sad way, this film offers a fitting conclusion to the Columbia Stooge corpus, the product of an entertainment world that had lost interest in short films and a studio that was losing money in the process of making them. Then again, a number of the recent releases have been of much higher technical quality.

Sappy Bull Fighters was released in June, 1959, and although it was the last Stooge short-film to be released and is always listed as Columbia Stooge short #190, it was actually shot almost two years earlier, in July, 1957. At the time of its release, Columbia had already terminated their contract with the Stooges eighteen months earlier (December 20, 1957) just after the shooting of *Flying Saucer Daffy* had been completed. At the beginning of *Sappy Bull Fighters* the Stooges are unemployed showmen, and Joe comments: "He wanted us to do ten extra shows for free." Nothing could be more ironic: in January, 1958, one month after the Stooges' contract had been terminated, Screen Gems, Columbia's television subsidiary, released 78 Stooge shorts to television, and before *Sappy Bull Fighters* was shown theatrically Screen Gems released another 40 films to television. By 1959 those Stooge films were being shown on 156 of 534 television stations nationwide, earning Columbia $12 million, of which the Stooges received not one cent in residuals. As it turned out, the Stooges did a lot more than "ten extra shows for free."

VISUAL HUMOR (NEW MATERIAL): The slapstick in the first scene would normally flow from Greta kissing Joe to the "Bull ring here we come, gosh!" rumba to Joe hitting Moe with the suitcase to Moe hitting Joe to the suitcase opening to finding that it was Greta's suitcase, but there are interruptions and dead air. The new gags are quite simple: Joe putting his head down into a pile of eggs (a simplified version of the egg sequence in *G.I. Wanna Home*); and Joe getting 'kissed' by the dog instead of Greta. Joe scares the bull away by making a face and barking à la Curly. Similarly, after Moe gouges him, Joe gives Moe a hand-wave, his first (and last); in *Oil's Well That Ends Well* Joe mesmerized Moe by waving his finger in front of this face. Other variations: the dog 'weeping' with the Stooges (*So Long, Mr. Chumps*); the chanted "Bull ring here we come, gosh!" (recently "At last we're in the dough...Hi-lee Hi-lo" in *Quiz Whiz*); Joe belly bumping Larry and Moe (*Rusty Romeos*); drinking hot sauce and breathing smoke (*Playing the Ponies*); using the suitcase as a weapon [*Myrt and Marge*; *A Pain in the Pullman*]; Moe bonking Joe and Larry repeatedly [ten times] on their foreheads [*They Stooge to Conga*]; and Larry getting the suitcase thrown at him after saying, "We forgot our suitcase. Let me have it!" [*Three Sappy People*]

VERBAL HUMOR (NEW MATERIAL): There are two new verbal exchanges depending on literal interpretations (Greta: "Join me in a cocktail?" Joe: "There isn't room in there for the both of us!"; Joe: "You know babe, I sure could go for you." Greta: "You don't have to go anywhere for me!"). Both were common gags of the period, as was Moe's response when Greta offers them a snack: "You twisted our arms." Also new is Joe's comment to the real bull in the ring: "Hey you guys even smell like a bull!". As in the original, Jose [now played by George Lewis instead of Harry Burns] speaks in comical Spanish-English malapropisms: "Your nose has grown real long, I think...What has happened to your hair; it is bald-headed on the top!...I will kill them to pieces!" However, Jose now bribes the two bull ring attendants in English: "Let the bull out". The misplaced insult gag (Joe: "Who is that idiot?" Greta: "That idiot is my husband, I mean—") was used in the original at the booking agency. For the first and only time Joe does the "I can't see! I can't see!...My eyes are closed" gag. Other variations: Moe: "What are you - a man or a mouse?" [*Three Troubledoers*]; and Joe: "Squeak-squeak" [*Fifi Blows Her Top*]; weeping in a major triad (*A Merry Mix-Up*). Epithets: Moe: "You stupid Stooge!"; and Joe to his hat: "You double-crosser you!"

OTHER NOTES: The title screen contains three words, *Sappy Bull Fighters*. The working title was *That's Bully*. Born Jorge Lewis in Guadalajara, Mexico, George Lewis [Jose] had a long film career. He would play 'Don Alejandro' in ABC's *Zorro*, which premiered in October, 1957, just a few months after this film was shot. In the introductory Mexican music ('La Cucaracha'), the exaggerated sliding trombones lead into the 'Three Blind Mice' theme and the brief exposition; the Stooges' name is ironically crossed out on the sign.

Jules White [*Bruskin* 76]: "Toward the end, I was shooting a picture a day with lots of stock footage, and nobody knew or cared." Shortly before his death Jules White recollected that before being ordered to do so by Harry Cohn he had himself determined to shut down the unit and "leave them laughing" [*Bruskin* 104]. He offered a private laugh of his own: on the introductory poster shot, under 'GRETA - CANCIONES Y BAILES' ["songs and dances"], it reads 'Julio Blanco,' Spanish for 'Jules White'; see Richard Finegan, 'Notes on Stooge Film Music and Other Oddities,' *The 3 Stooges Journal* 79 (1996) 4].

Although the first batch of 78 Stooge shorts were not sold to television until 1958, ABC television had apparently purchased exclusive rights to broadcast thirty shorts as early as October 1949. The sale of Stooge films to television was part of a tacit, industry-wide agreement that no films made after 1948 would be released to television. A regular schedule of recent Hollywood films did not appear on television until NBC's *Saturday Night at the Movies* premiered in 1961.

It was Jules White who urged Harry Cohn's son, Ralph and other Screen Gems executives to distribute six Stooge comedies. This experiment (in New England) was a success, whence the larger release for television distribution. Harry Cohn, tyrant that he was, never let the Stooges abandon their two-reeler career, as they wanted, to make feature films, thus keeping their unparalleled short-film output intact and paving the way for their unparalleled wave of popularity on television. He is reported [*Scripts* 26] to have said something like: "The Stooges were the only stars at Columbia who made me laugh... They were not only funny; they never made a picture that lost money". Cohn died on February 27, 1958 at age 67, after the first release of Stooge films to television, but before their popular resurgence. During Joe's bull ride you can still hear a brief "woob-woob-woob" from Curly.

After shooting *Flying Saucer Daffy* on December 20, 1957, Jules White informed the Stooges that the twenty-four year association between Columbia and the Three Stooges had come to an end. However, the last of the Stooge short films [*Sappy Bull Fighters*] was not released in theaters until June, 1959, and in the meanwhile Columbia had found a new medium for distribution - television. Before the year was out, the Three Stooges were more popular and in greater demand than ever.

1959 - 1970
LATE FEATURE FILMS

Have Rocket - Will Travel • *Stop! Look! and Laugh!*

Snow White and the Three Stooges • *The Three Stooges Meet Hercules*

The Three Stooges in Orbit • *The Three Stooges Go Around the World in a Daze*

It's a Mad, Mad, Mad, Mad World • *4 for Texas* • *The Outlaws Is Coming* • *Kook's Tour*

HAVE ROCKET - WILL TRAVEL

Studio: Columbia

Released: August 1, 1959

Running Time: 1'16'14"'

Credited Cast:

The Three Stooges	
Jerome Cowan	J. P. Morse
Anna Lisa	Dr. Ingred Naarveg
Bob Colbert	Dr. Ted Benson

Uncredited Cast:

Marjorie Bennett	Mrs. Huntingford
Don Lamond	newspaperman
Nadine Ducas	French dancer
Robert J. Stevenson	robot's voice
Dal McKennon	unicorn's voice

Credited Production Crew:

Director:	David Lowell Rich
Producer:	Harry Romm
Written by:	Raphael Hayes
Music:	Mischa Bakaleinikoff
Title Song:	George Duning & Stanley Styne
Photography:	Ray Cory
Editor:	Danny B. Landres
Assistant Director:	Floyd Joyer
Art Director:	John T. McCormack
Set Decorator:	Darrell Silvera
Narration:	Don Lamond
Sound:	Harold Lewis

PERSPECTIVE: Columbia mogul Harry Cohn terminated the Stooges' contract the very day the Stooges completed shooting *Flying Saucer Daffy*, December 20, 1957. The market for short films had evaporated in the era of television sitcoms and theatrical double features, so after 24 years the Stooges were suddenly without studio employment. Several times they had flirted with television: in 1949 they produced a pilot ('*Jerks of All Trades*') for a television series on ABC, and in 1957 Harry Cohn briefly considered producing a different television project for the trio, but destiny had in store a very different sort of television presence and greater success for the Stooges.

Now 60 years of age, Moe first considered retirement, and then when he was planning a tour for their live act he found that Joe Besser, unwilling to leave his ailing wife in LA., had already signed a Fox contract for the Bing Crosby feature *Say One For Me*. So just to put on a live act he and Larry had to search for a "new Curly." They auditioned and rejected old comrade Mousie Garner, then Larry recommended Joe DeRita, who had starred in four Columbia shorts in 1946-1948 and whom he had seen in 'Minsky's Follies of 1958' in Las Vegas. In October, 1958, after what Moe described as a miserable debut in Bakersfield, the act was again on the verge of retirement. But when performing in Pittsburgh just weeks later, with DeRita now called 'Curly-Joe' and sporting a Curly-esque shaved head, the Stooges began to ride the wave of a most unexpected, television-induced nationwide Stooge hysteria. Just one month after their film contract was terminated, Columbia's television subsidiary, Screen Gems, had released 78 old Stooge shorts for television distribution, and although Harry Cohn did not live to see it, within months their old films were appearing on 25% of all the television stations in the US with huge ratings in major cities. Wildly popular again, the Stooges earned as much as $25,000 for one-day personal appearances. Columbia, who still owned the copyright to their films, immediately cashed in by releasing *Three Stooges Fun-O-Rama*, a grouping of Joe Besser Stooge shorts. But then the new bosses at Columbia inked the new Stooge configuration to make a feature film, and for the first time ever the Stooges were to enjoy sole top-billing in a decently budgeted feature film tailor made for their humor.

Writer Raphael Hayes and director David Lowell Rich had not worked on Stooge short films, but *Have Rocket - Will Travel* reuses plot motifs from *Space Ship Sappy* and *Outer Space Jitters* (launching into space accidently; landing on Venus [no longer 'Sunev']; encountering a monster and mad robot; a ticker tape parade; newspaper headlines; and a triumphant party). Fleshing out the plot are the Stooge robots, romance, and a monkey and talking unicorn as well as plenty of traditional Stooge routines (hammer and pick-and-shovel abuse, an explosive recipe, a multi-door chase, a classic Stooge party, and two pies in Moe's face). Curly-Joe participates fully in the physical humor, taking gouges, slaps, and bonks, ruining a pickax with his skull ("Oo! Oo! Oo! Look!"), and bouncing off a spring in his pants. Unlike any of the previous fourteen Stooge feature films, this one is real Stooge stuff for 75 minutes.

VISUAL HUMOR: Good Stooge slapstick tends to propel the plot: Moe hits Larry with a shovel and knocks him down, which allows Larry to see that the space ship's door is clear; Larry sicks Curly-Joe on Moe, which makes the ship fall down the cliff; the plumbing disaster leads to their blasting off from earth; and the fire-breathing tarantula ignites the rocket so they can leave Venus. New gags: the robot Stooges (even if the film technique is the same used in *Self-Made Maids* and *A Merry Mix-Up*); floating in zero gravity; and standing on the hatch while trying to lift it. For the first time we see a Stooge, here Curly-Joe, watching television. Larry's reaction to drinking the fuel is the best since Shemp's in *Who Done It?* The concept of shrinking the Stooges derives from Columbia's

Joe Besser spent only two years with the Stooge act. After a brief search, Moe and Larry next hired Joe DeRita as the third Stooge. He was an experienced stage and film comedian, but Stooging, as both Curly and Joe Besser found out, is a skill that takes time to acquire. At first their act failed on the road, but within months the new Stooge craze fostered by the recent success of their films on television put them in high demand. Joe shaved his head, took the name 'Curly-Joe,' and they were offered contracts to make feature films.

The Seventh Voyage of Sinbad (1958) and *The Incredible Shrinking Man* (1957), the driverless car from *Forbidden Planet* (1956), and the monster tarantula from *Tarantula* (1955); their own *Space Ship Sappy* had a 'giant' iguana. The robot triple slapping the Stooges is the first triple slap since *A Merry Mix-Up*.

Larry's requiring "anesthetic" and an operation has a long pedigree, beginning with their Oscar-nominated *Men in Black*. Other variations: sleeping at the opening of the film (*Movie Maniacs*); Larry keeping his shoes in the refrigerator (Shemp's hot towel in *Hokus Pokus*); Moe hit by a pick and shovel (*Cash and Carry*); knocking in the 'Shave and a Haircut' rhythm (*Back to the Woods*); Larry hitting Moe ("That was me!") by mistake during a multi-door chase (*Spook Louder*); Curly-Joe trapped in the maze of pipes (*A Plumbing We Will Go*); the talking radio tube (*Men in Black*); confusing coffee for fuel (*Tassels in the Air*); pouring popcorn into something hot (*Slaphappy Sleuths*); pushing and pulling each other out of the way (*Rockin' Thru the Rockies*); stuffing Larry down the sink (*False Alarms*); J.P. falling into the flooded basement (*Meet the Baron*; *Swing Parade of 1946*); Larry blowing soap bubbles (*Calling All Curs*); J.P. tripping and getting his foot caught in a bucket (*Punchy Cowpunchers*); Moe's side stroke (*Uncivil Warriors*); befriending a talking horse (recently in *Hoofs and Goofs*); Curly-Joe's mattress spring, Curly-Joe lifting his pinkies to eat, and Larry losing his shoe on the dance floor (*Hoi Polloi*); crawling out of a riotous party (*Three Sappy People*); Curly-Joe trying to sneak away with a piece of cake (*Ants in the Pantry*, *Three Little Sew and Sews*); and Curly-Joe looking at Moe who looks at Larry who looks to the woods and then back at Moe who looks at Curly-Joe when they see the car (*Uncivil Warriors*). The background music interferes with a slapstick sound effect when Moe pounds Curly-Joe (Larry: "Where are we?" Curly-Joe: "Looks like Death Valley."): we hear musical sounds from stringed instruments and not POUND.

VERBAL HUMOR: Raphael Hayes' script appropriately juxtaposes rocket science with Stooge ignorance, be it ignorance about the crashed rocket (Curly-Joe: "Maybe it's lost." Larry: "Maybe they sent it over to be cleaned and polished."); fuel (Moe: "Hydrogen, Boron, Kerosene, Beryllium." Larry: "No wonder Dr. Ingrid's got a problem." Curly-Joe: "She couldn't make up her mind which one to use!"); ultra-sonics ("color television set"), meteors (Curly-Joe: "They're throwin' things at us!"); control panels ("Push buttons!" [thrice]), the inter-space communicator ("Hi-Fi set"); or Venus' surface (Curly-Joe: "A watermelon!"). Even the monkey knows more than they do (Moe: "If I was in there as long as he was I'd have known where *all* the buttons were!"). Moe knows a little chemistry ("Caffeine and H2O...[Larry: "Wha'?]...Coffee, jug-head."), and they all know a little Latin (Ingrid: "Ab uno disce omnes." Larry: "She talks Latin!" Stooges [unison]: "E pluribus unum!"; later Larry says, ironically: "Why didn't I learn French instead of Latin?...[seeing a brunette on the couch]...Oh! A Latin!"), but they do not know what real intelligence is (Ingrid: "I respect men who show an interest in the sciences; it's a mark of intelligence." Curly-Joe: "For a lady scientist, she's not only pretty, she's also got brains."). J.P. agrees ("These idiots!...I do not believe that there are three more stupid, incompetent, stumble-footed men on this earth!"). Ironically, because of his romantic frustration Ted concludes: "You know who are the happiest and best adjusted people in this institution? Those maintenance men - Moe. Larry and Curly-Joe. They're not married to any kind of science at all!"

The script plays with language and delivery patterns. Besides the scientific jargon and Latin, the unicorn speaks archaic English ("Thy language is most odd and thou hast a strange look."], Curly-Joe shakes the hammer and says "Hammer-hammer-hammer," and the car and robot voices inspire several traditional Stooge patterns [Car: "Do not delay! I am waiting!" Larry: "I am Larry!" Moe: "I am Moe!" Curly-Joe: "And I am Curly-Joe!" [three-pattern]; Curly-Joe: "That's a fine way to treat the first space travelers!" Larry: "Yeah, who does he think he is?" [a bolt of energy strikes them] Voice: "That is who I am!" Moe: "I'm gettin' out-a here!" Larry: "Me, too!" Curly-Joe: "Me, three!" [*If a Body Meets a Body*]; and Curly-Joe: "Hey car!" Moe: "Speak respectfully!" Curly-Joe: "Hey automobile!" [*Disorder in the Court* Attorney: "Address the judge as 'Your Honor.'" Curly: "Well, it was like this, My Honor—"]]. Fear of the unknown inspires other Stooge patterns [Moe: "Don't you wanna go down in history?" Larry & Curly-Joe: "No!" Moe: "Don't you wanna astound the world?" Larry & Curly-Joe: "No!" Moe: "Don't you wanna become celebrated and famous?" Larry & Curly-Joe: "No!" Moe: "Don't you wanna help Dr. Ingrid?" Larry & Curly-Joe: "Oh, yeah!"; and Moe: "All right! We're goin' that way...[pushing Curly-Joe ahead]...Go ahead!"]. The Stooge robots do the same [Robot Moe: "Operation Big Switch." Robot Larry: "Check!" Robot Moe: "We'll change them into electrical energy. Robot Curly-Joe: "Check, check!"]. Some of the threats are space-related [Curly-Joe: "You got space madness." Moe: "I'll make a satellite out of ya'!"; Moe: "You're on another world! Act like human beings!"], as are other gags [Larry: "Your outside head [helmet] is broken!"; Moe: "Now look here, my good m-, my good ma-, whatever you are!"; Moe: "There's life here." Curly-Joe [rubbing his burnt rear]: "Yeah, I can still feel it!"] and puns [Robot: "I destroyed them all and turned them into electrical energy. Moe: "Shocking!"].

Epithets: the name calling is prolific ["jug-head" five times, "imbeciles" twice, "nitwit" twice]; one is turned into an exchange [Moe: "Now plug it in right, you nitwit!" Curly-Joe: "Yeah, ya' nitwit!" Moe: "I'll do the name callin' around here!"]; others are "you mental midget," "lame-brain," and "dimwits," the latter of the Stooge robots. There are two gags about the Stooges' looks [Curly-Joe: "Who is in the mirror. Moe: "It's me." Curly-Joe: "Oh good. I thought it was me!"; Curly-Joe: "They made [Robot] Moe real ugly, didn't they, Larry?" Larry: "I dunno. I think he's uglier in person!" Moe mixes the fuel with popcorn and an old favorite, sodium bicarbonate, but without the usual nonsense ingredients; later in the ship Moe asks for the 'grammapatiola'.

References: the 'Hi-Fi set' and 'color television' were high tech in 1959. Moe's "One of these days, one of these days—" derives from the Jackie Gleason [*Honeymooners* [1955-1956]] tag, but it is given an appropriate Stooge variation [Curly-Joe: "Yeah, one of these days [GOUGE] you're gonna poke my eyes out!"]. Ingrid's Latin "*Ab uno disce omnis*" is a proverb meaning "From this one thing learn everything"; it derives from Vergil [*Aeneid* 2.66], as does "*E pluribus unum*." Curly-Joe's "Looks like Death Valley" is virtually correct and breaks the cinematic illusion briefly. Larry's internal rhyme "Isn't he quisn't" was used in the 1949 television pilot '*Jerks of all Trades*'. The "Right! Right!" gag [Larry & Curly-Joe: "Right! Right!" Moe: "Boys... Everything all right?" Larry & Curly-Joe: "Right! Right!"] goes back to Ted Healy and *Dancing Lady* [1934]. Other variations: Moe: "Get off of me you baby hippopotamus!" ["Hippopotamus no good for this trick!" in *No Dough Boys*]; and Moe: "What did it say?" Curly-Joe: "Beep-beep-beep-beep" [*Fright Night*]

OTHER NOTES: The title is spelled 'Have Rocket — Will Travel'. The title is derived from *'Have Gun, Will Travel,'* the third highest rated television show from 1958 to 1960 [after 'Gunsmoke' and 'Wagon Train'] in the era of TV westerns. Though there were two years between filmings, this feature film appeared in theaters just two months after the final short [*Sappy Bull Fighters*], so audiences barely noticed a hiccup in Stooge film releases. The overture begins with a variation of the Stooges' 'Three Blind Mice' theme. Background music is heard throughout the opening Stooge scenes; some of it, with a bassoon emphasis, sets a mood too unsophisticated even for Stoogedom. Moe accurately claims that they are the first space travelers: Yuri Gargarin was not launched in his Vostok craft until April 12, 1961. Moe's hair blows up at lift off, which is an aerodynamic and gravitational impossibility.

Joe DeRita was born in Philadelphia in 1909; he was two years younger than Joe Besser, seven years younger than Larry [who was also born in Philadelphia] and twelve years younger than Moe. Besides his four Columbia shorts, he appeared in five feature films for various studios, most recently as 'the hangman' in Fox' *The Bravados* [1958]. *Larry* [223-225] recollects that after seeing Lou Costello [recently separated from Bud Abbott] in a Las Vegas show at the Dunes, Minsky in his office afterwards asked Larry if the Stooges would replace Costello after he left to fulfill a prior film commitment. Larry agreed, but added that there were only two Stooges now since Joe Besser was unable to leave his ailing wife. It was Minsky who then put Moe and Larry in contact with Joe DeRita. Jerome Cowan [J. P.] had a long film career that included the role of Miles Archer in *The Maltese Falcon*; in 1960 he had a regular role on *The Tab Hunter Show.* Don Lamond [narrator] was married to Larry's daughter, Phyllis. Bob Colbert [Ted] went on to play Brent Maverick in *Maverick's* semi-final year and more science fiction in ABC's *The Time Tunnel* [1966-1967]. Director David Lowell Rich worked in television [eventually earning an Emmy Award in 1978 for 'The Defection of Simas Kudirka'] and directed a wide range of feature films - odd comedies [*Chu Chu and the Philly Flash* [1981]], heavy-handed soap operas [*Madame X* [1965]], and off-beat psycho dramas [*Eye of the Cat* [1969]]. The film recouped a third of its $380,000 cost in just five days.

STOP! LOOK! AND LAUGH!

Studio: Columbia

Released: February 8, 1961

Running Time: 1'17"50'"

Credited Cast:

The Original Three Stooges - Moe, Larry, Curly
Paul Winchell with Jerry Mahoney & Knucklehead Smiff
The Marquis Chimps
Officer Joe Bolton

Credited Production Crew:

Director:	Jules White
Director [Cinderella]:	Lou Brandt
Director [Winchell]:	Don Appell
Producer:	Harry Romm
Written by:	Sid Kuller [Cinderella]
Music:	Mischa Bakaleinikoff
Title Song:	George Duning & Stanley Styne
Photography:	William Steiner [Winchell]
Editor:	Jerome Thoms
Art Director:	Robert Bryer [Cinderella]
Assistant Director:	Milton Feldman

PERSPECTIVE: This seemingly harmless concoction caused one of the largest legal disputes in Stoogedom to date. About the time *Have Rocket — Will Travel* was released, Moe was in the process of replacing long-term manager and producer Harry Romm with his son-in-law Norman Maurer. After arguing over percentages for the next feature film - Romm wanted 50%, the Stooges 75% - Romm cut the Stooges out completely and made his own deal with Columbia. The result was *Stop! Look! and Laugh*!, but the Stooges took the matter to court, succeeded in getting an injunction to delay the theatrical release of the film, won a cash settlement, and signed a lucrative contract ($50,000 plus 50% of the profits) for their next Columbia feature, *The Three Stooges Meet Hercules*.

To make *Stop! Look! and Laugh!* Romm interwove segments of eleven 'Curly' shorts and a chimpanzee version of Cinderella into a film narrating a day at home with Paul Winchell and his two dummy children, Jerry Mahoney and Knucklehead Smiff. The sneaky, recalcitrant Jerry keeps trying to outwit Winchell so he can sleep late and stay home from school, while Knucklehead is being, well, a knucklehead. Their almost Stooge-like quips (Winchell: "You're completely exasperating, frustrating, and incorrigible!" Knucklehead: "I wish you'd tell that to my mother; she thinks I'm a jerk!") lead into the Stooge segments: mention of Mexico leads to the bullfight in *What's the Matador?*, a call to the auto mechanic puts *Higher Than a Kite* on the other end of the line, and a call to the plumbers evokes segments from *A Plumbing We Will Go*. One particularly interesting lead-in gets Winchell, Jerry, and even us to watch the Western *Goofs and Saddles* within the TV frame. The whole day-in-the-life story ends rather interactively when Winchell literally 'steps into' *Half-Wits Holiday* and gets a pie in the face.

The presentation of the Stooge segments is not at all unadulterated. Smooth edits divorce gags from their original stories and remove them from context. Despite what critics maintain, Stooge comedy is plot oriented; individual gags often need the developing tensions of an unfolding narrative to blossom fully. In addition, a persistent musical soundtrack hinders the impact of the original Stooge sound effects by creating a second layer of sound between us and the film, as if some annoying person has the radio on in the next room. Nonetheless, in 1960, before the era of VCRs but after the era of theatrically released short films, only *Stop! Look! and Laugh!* offered Stooge shorts on the big screen. For the first TV generation of kids, this was a chance to go to the local movie theater to see their beloved Stooges in a Saturday matinee featuring a very popular television ventriloquist, his silly dummies, and a slew of cutely dressed chimpanzees. Thirty-seven years later Stooge watchers viewing this as a 'film' will find it a very different experience, but the 2000s viewer needs to change channels to the late 1950s/early 1960s, the golden age of children's television, when personable show hosts reached through the TV screen to young minds confident of getting innocent humor, a sense of calm, and genuine familial bonding.

VISUAL HUMOR: The eleven films used here are *Oily to Bed, Oily to Rise, How High is Up?, Violent is the Word for Curly, Sock-A-Bye Baby, Higher Than a Kite, What's the Matador?, Calling All Curs, Goofs and Saddles, Micro-Phonies, A Plumbing We Will Go*, and *Half-Wits Holiday*. Watching the Western *Goofs and Saddles* within the TV frame recalls Curly-Joe watching a TV Western while soaring through space in *Have Rocket — Will Travel*.

VERBAL HUMOR: Knucklehead's stupidity is similar to Stooge ignorance of grammar (Knucklehead: "They can't teach me nothin'" Winchell: "'They can't teach me *anything*.'" Knucklehead: "Oh, you must be stupid, too?"), math (Winchell: "How much is 1+1?" Knucklehead: "11."), and vocabulary (Winchell: "You're completing exasperating, frustrating, and incorrigible!" Knucklehead: "I wish you'd tell that to my mother; she thinks I'm a jerk!"). Title Song: 'When the Stooges start to clown, /Stop! Look! and Laugh! / When the dummies snoop around, / Stop! Look! and Laugh! /When those crazy chimpanzees/ Do the things that people do, /

Call it monkey business if you please, / but if it pleases you, / Then get in and join the fun, / Stop! Look! and Laugh! / And we do mean every one, / Stop! Look! and Laugh! / It's the show you can fret, / It's the show you won't forget, / So on your marks! Get set! / and Stop! Look! and Laugh!'

OTHER NOTES: The film was released in New York along with *The Three Worlds of Gulliver*. The opening credits include 'Writers of various segments': Adler, Bernds, Bruckman, Collins, Giebler, Goodman, Kramer, Myers, Ullman, Ward, White (Jack); 'Producers of various segments': Chase, Lord, McCollum, White (Jules); 'Directors of Photography - various segments': Cano, Kelley, Kline, O'Connell, Siegler; 'Film Editors - various segments': Batista, Borofsky, Bryant, Nelson, Seid; 'Directors of various segments': Bernds, Chase, Lord. Jules White, long-time Columbia short subject unit boss and Stooge film director is credited with most of the direction. The founder/president of Screen Gems, Ralph Cohn (Harry's son), wanted White to join him at Screen Gems in 1958, but White declined, saying later, "I could have been a millionaire, but with all the pressure I would not have lived to enjoy it." White actually had relatively little contact with the Stooges after the short subject unit closed; he and Moe had had somewhat of a falling out. Although not credited, most of the voice-overs for the Marquis Chimps in the Cinderella sequence were done by June Foray, who the same year was providing the voice for Rocket J. Squirrel in 'Rocky and His Friends'. The title has a model in 1939's light comedy *Stop, Look, and Love*.

Paul Winchell was a very popular television personality, particularly with children, during the 1957-1960 seasons. Appearing in various game and variety shows between 1948 and 1960, Winchell's own *The Paul Winchell - Jerry Mahoney Show* ran on NBC during prime time for four seasons, from 1950-1954. It shifted over to CBS' Saturday morning children's lineup until 1956 before moving to ABC's Sunday lineup through 1961.

In *Stop! Look! and Laugh!* (1961), Winchell and his chimps were written around segments from eleven Columbia Stooge films, but producer Harry Romm was sued by the Stooges. Found to be entirely in the wrong, Romm was issued an injunction, and he had to delay his planned theatrical release - for which this pressbook ad was printed - and pay damages to The Three Stooges.

SNOW WHITE AND THE THREE STOOGES

Studio: Twentieth-Century Fox

Released: June 21, 1961

Running Time: 1'47"21'"

Credited Cast:

Carol Heiss	Snow White
The Three Stooges	[Moe, Larry, Curly-Joe]
Edson Stroll	Quatro [Prince Charming]
Patricia Medina	Queen
Guy Rolfe	Oga
Michael David	Rolf
Buddy Baer	Hordred
Edgar Barrier	King Augustus
Peter Coe	Captain

Uncredited Cast:

Lisa Mitchell	Linda
Chuck Lacey	Frederick
Owen McGivney	Physician
Gloria Doggett	skater
Leon McNabb	skater
Blossom Rock	servant
Leslie Farrell	young snow white
Craig Cooke	young prince
Burt Mustin	farmer
Richard Collier	turnkey
Herbie Faye	cook
Edward Innes	second cook

Credited Production Crew:

Director:	Walter Lang
Producer:	Charles Wick
Story:	Charles Wick
Screenplay:	Noel Langley and Elwood Ullman
Songs:	'A Place Called Happiness,' 'I Said it Then; I Say It Now,' and 'Because I'm in Love' by Harry Harris; 'Once in A Million Years' by Earl Brent
Music:	Lyn Murray
Ice Choreographer:	Ron Fletcher
Photography:	Leon Shamroy
Art Director:	Jack Martin Smith and Maurice Ransford
Set Decorations:	Walter M. Scott and Paul S. Fox
Assistant Director:	Eli Dunn
Editor:	Jack W. Holmes
Sound:	Arthur Kirbach and Frank W Moran

PERSPECTIVE: Between Columbia feature films, the Stooges signed with Twentieth-Century Fox to co-star in their first and only feature-length, Technicolor, CinemaScope film, *Snow White and the Three Stooges.* This was the second feature the Stooges made for Fox, the first being *Soup to Nuts* some thirty-one years earlier. Although Fox was hoping to cash in, then as now, on the Stooges' surging popularity, the Stooges are billed only as 'Also Starring.' The new star ("Introducing") around whom the film was really designed was Carol Heiss, World Champion Women's Figure Skater 1956-1960 and the Olympic gold-medalist at the 1960 Squaw Valley winter games. As it turned out, this was Carol Heiss' only Hollywood film, but to have the Stooges share the billing and serve merely as comic relief and emotional support was not at all unique: these types of support roles had been common for them in their feature films of the 1930s, 1940s, and 1950s.

The studio planned to employ either Frank Tashlin or Walter Lang as director. Tashlin had begun his career writing several successful comedies starring Red Skelton and Jack Carson [*The Fuller Brush Man* [1948], *The Good Humor Man* [1950]], but then turned to writing/directing many Jerry Lewis films; just the previous year he had written and directed Lewis' fairy tale adaptation, *Cinderfella*, no doubt part of the inspiration for this Stooge film. Walter Lang, the director of the Stooges' *Meet the Baron* in 1933, had more recently established his fame directing family-oriented, lavish Technicolor musicals like his Oscar-nominated *The King and I* [1956]. Fox decided on Lang, and the resulting film, Lang's last, is indeed full of rich colors, lavish costumes and sets, romantic musical numbers, two ice-skating extravaganzas, soldiers and horses galloping through broad exteriors, in-castle sword play, frequent special effects, and much else thanks to a $3 million budget.

The opening credits show some fine comic promise as the Stooges parody the storybook format with yelling, hair pulling, and Moe's great slap of Curly-Joe, but then they disappear for nearly twenty minutes. When they reappear, they are cast as peddlers, as they were in the 1951 feature film *Gold Raiders*, with Curly-Joe playing the 'Shemp' role as the plant in the audience. The comedic moments dwindle in number from that point, most often limited to such malapropisms as Joe's "To whom is your first duty? To youm, that's whom!" and "If she likes you, all the crowned feet of Europe will be at your head." Then after Quarto [i.e. the 'fourth' Stooge] and then Snow White are presumed dead, the Stooges play sympathetic, gentle, non-comic heroes. The Stooges have played unlikely heroes many times in their careers, and for a number of years now they have been reducing their slapstick and taking on a kindly disposition on behalf of the many children in their new audience, but even Moe later recognized the relative lack of humor in this film as a "Technicolor mistake."

VISUAL HUMOR: In the opening credits, at the mention of a lovely child we see Larry blinking his eyes innocently inside the story book frame (Moe: "Not you! Come out-a there!") and then grabbed by the hair; at the mention of "her hair as black as ebony" we see Curly-Joe stroking his bald head (Moe: "Who let you in?" Curly-Joe: "My hair used to be black." Moe: "Out! Before you get a pair of eyes to match!" [SLAP]); and at the mention of the 'handsome' Prince Charming of Bravuria we see Moe (Larry: "He said 'handsome!'" Curly-Joe: "Come on! Get out-a there!") being tugged at from both sides (Moe: "I'm a citizen!"). Finally we see the miniaturized Stooges running across the bottom of the screen as the narrator adds, "If by now you're wondering what on earth the Three Stooges have to do with the fairy tale of Snow White, it's very simple: in this version we are telling the tale of 'Snow White and the Three Stooges'. Action scenes use the Stooges as support: hiding Snow White in the bushes; disguising themselves as vegetable merchants, entering the palace, and overcoming the kitchen help with two mallets, a half-dozen pies and a frying pan; smuggling

food to Quatro and conking the jailer with a mallet and the tray; freeing Quatro; diving for safety into a hanging curtain, falling, and then clubbing Oga on the shin and grabbing his magic sword; fleeing for their lives in a wagon (*Goofs and Saddles*); and Curly-Joe giving Snow White a flower, getting a kiss, and stepping off sprightly singing, "Hi Ho! The Merry-O! A hunting we will go!"

Other than the plot-related beatings, slapstick is reduced to several forehead slaps, hair pulls, one trio collision, and one belly bump. The sound effects are often muted or non-existent. For the sound effect to the bonk Moe gives Curly-Joe (after wishing Oga 'Happy Birthday') we hear a skin slap only; there is also no sound effect when they bump into each other in the hall. Stooge musicianship: Curly-Joe's concertina socks Moe in the face, and Larry's bow gets thrust into Moe's mouth, then Curly-Joe prepares to play but catches his concertina on Larry's violin, recalling the musical sequence in *Disorder in the Court*. The flashback technique (recounting how the Stooges adopted Quatro) was used in several Stooge shorts and in two previous Stooge features, *Turn Back the Clock* and *Stop! Look! and Laugh!*. The latter also had a ventriloquist and his dummies; Quinto here fills the former role. Other variations: Larry reaching up (recently in *Flying Saucer Daffy*) and dumping flour onto Joe (recently in *Oils' Well That Ends Well*); and eggs dropping onto Moe's head (recently in *Sweet and Hot*).

VERBAL HUMOR: The screenplay by Noel Langley turns Moe early on into a bombastic 'YUK' huckster ("Hair in such abundance that the chipmunks nest there in the mating season"; "It was imparted to my illustrious partner and myself by an incumbent judo expert in gratitude for saving his life when threatened by an emotionally unstable cobra on the far-flung mud banks of the flooded Hooglie. Now, as a river, the Hooglie is only 'ooglie.'"); similarly, Curly-Joe later: "He was too young for it to register on his cogitative faculties." Towards the end of the film the Stooges become genteel (Curly-Joe: "I wish we were more of us, and prettier." Snow White: "I wouldn't want you to be any different. I love you just as you are - all three of you." Larry: "Gee, only our mother ever said that without laughing in our faces"; Moe: "We stole a couple of—, that is, we're minding some eggs for an absent-minded duck we ran into.").

Long-time Stooge writer Elwood Ullman wrote in a pun (Moe: "The reason it's a 'standing invitation' is because the beds are too short to lie down in!"), gags involving Stooge ignorance (Moe: "You're better than we ever were." Curly-Joe: "Yeah, but he cheats: he's got brains!"; Joe: "We've been incarcerated." Larry: "Not to mention being thrown in the clink!"), ironies (Curly-Joe: "Are we still alive?" Moe: "Of course we're still alive: otherwise we wouldn't be freezing to death!"; Guard: "This man is to be executed." Moe: "Not on an empty stomach!"; Guard: "How come a whole loaf of bread for just one man?" Curly-Joe: "Because it's his last meal. Now if it was me, I'd start off with oysters in white wine—"), a Spoonerism for Curly-Joe ("Hark! Hooses' horfs, I mean, horses' hoofs!"), and for Moe several epithets ("soft-boiled egg-head," "mangy floor mop," "ignoramus"), threats ("I'll touch your nose with my fist if you don't wish us off this mountain!"; Moe: "Out! Before you get a pair of eyes to match!"), and insults (Curly-Joe: "I sleep curled up in a ball." Moe: "That's why you keep rollin' out of bed!" Larry: "I can sleep on my head." Moe: "Why not? It's full of feathers!"). The Stooges swear fealty to Snow White in a three-pattern (Moe: "You can count on us!" Larry: "Come what may!" Curly-Joe: "Ad infinitum!" - recalling *Restless Knights*) and offer another three-pattern to Oga as they bow obsequiously (Moe: "Thank you, your worship." Larry: "You're very kind, your worship." Curly-Joe: "Happy Birthday, your worship!"). Other variations: Moe: "I'll get a cheap lawyer!" (*Monkey Businessmen*); and Moe: "I'm a citizen!" (*Punch Drunks*). The Stooge hunting song: 'A hunting we have went,/We followed every scent,/We even scared a polar bear/A hunting we have went'. References: Curly-Joe's "I wish the queen would go to Hades!" is a pagan euphemism for 'go to Hell.' Curly-Joe's 'Ad infinitum' is a Latin motto meaning "Forever!"

OTHER NOTES: The film premiered in Philadelphia on May 26. Billed as only 'Also Starring' in the opening credits, the Stooges are only fourth on the list of closing credits . The Stooges had been placed in fairy-tale settings earlier in *Nertsery Rhymes* and *Fiddlers Three*, and in an updated Cinderella story in *Flying Saucer Daffy*. Screenwriter Noel Langley had co-written *The Wizard of Oz* (1939). Edson Stroll [Quarto] went on to do more comedy as 'Virgil Edwards' in ABC's *McHale's Navy* (1962-1966). The British Patricia Medina [Queen], wife of actor Joseph Cotten, had played in swashbuckler costumers since the late 1940s, including the comedy *Abbott and Costello in the Foreign Legion* (1950). Buddy Baer [Hordred], brother of former heavyweight boxing champion Max Baer [father of Max Baer, Jr, who played 'Jethro' on the *Beverly Hillbillies*], had himself been a prizefighter. He played in Abbott and Costello's *Africa Screams* (1949) along with both Shemp and Joe Besser. Larry talked about the 'Baer' family in *Three Loan Wolves*. Almost lost is Herbie Faye [cook], best known as 'Private Sam Fender' in *The Phil Silvers Show* (1955-1959), who went on to play in 1960s comic films (*The Fortune Cookie*) and 1970s sitcoms.

When the Stooges moved to Hollywood in the 1930s, Moe hoped to make feature films. It took almost 30 years, but he got less than he hoped for in the amply budgeted, Technicolor, CinemaScope extravaganza *Snow White and the Three Stooges* (1961).

THE THREE STOOGES MEET HERCULES

Studio: Columbia

Released: January 26, 1962

Running Time: 1'28"43'"

Credited Cast:

The Three Stooges	[Moe, Larry, Curly-Joe]
Vicky Trickett	Diane Quigley
Quinn Redeker	Schuyler Davis
George N. Neise	Ralph Dimsal/King Odius
Samson Burke	Hercules
The McKeever Twins	
Mike Mckeever	Ajax, the Cyclops
Marlin McKeever	Argo, the Cyclops
Emil Sitka	Shepherd/Greek Humor man
Hal Smith	Thesus, King of Rhodes
John Cliff	Ulysses
Lewis Charles	Achilles the Heel
Barbara Hines	Anita
Terry Huntingdon	Hecuba
Diana Piper	Helen
Gregg Martell	Simon

Uncredited Cast:

Gene Roth	harbor captain
Edward Foster	Freddie the Fence
Cecil Elliott	matron
Rusty Wescoatt	Philo, the hortator

Credited Production Crew:

Director:	Edward Bernds
Producer:	Norman Maurer
Screenplay:	Elwood Ullman
Story:	Norman Maurer
Music:	Paul Dunlap
Photography:	Charles S. Welborn
Art Director:	Don Ament
Editor:	Edwin Bryant
Set Decorations:	William Calvert
Narration:	Don Lamond
Assistant Director:	Herb Wallerstein
Sound:	James Flaster

PERSPECTIVE: The two sci-fi shorts of 1957 [*Space Ship Sappy, Outer Space Jitters*] and the 1959 feature *Have Rocket — Will Travel* established the travel/adventure plot-type to be used in most of the Stooges' 1960s feature films. But in these earlier films the Stooges visited the future; now they travel back through time to ancient Greece. In the 1940s the Stooges parodied ancient Egypt in *Mummy's Dummies* and ancient Rome in *Matriphony*, but in those films the Stooges lived in ancient times. Now, because the concept of time travel had been popularized recently in George Pal's *The Time Machine* [1960], they travel back to antiquity to encounter the great mythological hero Hercules.

The ancient world was very popular in the cinema in 1961. Cecil B. DeMille's *Samson and Delilah* had reaped a fortune for Paramount in 1949, so all the other studios brought out the togas throughout the 1950s. In 1953 Columbia offered *Salome*, *Serpent of the Nile*, and *Slaves of Babylon*, stock footage from which enhances this Stooge production, and the most highly regarded of all the 'ancient' films, MGM's *Ben-Hur* [1959], inspired *The Three Stooges Meet Hercules* to parody its galley scene and chariot race. Greco-Roman-type films were particularly abundant in Italy, so in 1959 Joseph E. Levine used saturation booking to make the cheaply produced Italian *Hercules* highly profitable in the U.S., consequently making the character of Hercules all the rage. The next decade saw over two dozen Hercules films starring either championship body-builders like Steve Reeves or appropriately named strongmen like Alan Steel and the Stooges' own Samson Burke.

The first 'Meet' feature film was actually the Stooges' co-feature *Meet the Baron*, but only after *Enemy Agents Meet Ellery Queen* [1942] did it become common to include the names of both stars and adversaries in film titles. Abbott and Costello starred in seven '*Abbott and Costello Meet—*' films [1948-1955], and that series inspired Norman Maurer to develop the concept of '*The Three Stooges Meet Hercules*,' the crowning glory of Stooge feature films and their finest effort of the 1960s. In its initial theatrical release the film grossed over $2,000,000, four times its cost, which encouraged Columbia to sign the Stooges to make three more features. The dual popularity of the Stooges and Hercules brought in the crowds, but what made the film so enjoyable was the veteran team of director Edward Bernds and writer Elwood Ullman returning to Stooge films for the first time since 1952. Paying little attention to extraneous romance or subplots, they focused instead on what the Stooges did best - working with tools, throwing pies, confronting, defeating, or escaping tough guys, brutes, monsters, and a room full of women, uttering appropriately ignorant anachronisms ["I haven't eaten in 3000 years!"], and indulging in such delicious ironies as knocking the mighty Hercules silly, threatening to poke out the eyes of a Siamese Cyclops, rowing a *Ben-Hur*-like galley around the Mediterranean to a rumba beat, and doing a classic tool-abuse prison break while the cleverest man in history, Ulysses, watches in bewilderment.

VISUAL HUMOR: Hercules sometimes served as a comic butt in ancient Greece and Rome, and he fares the same here. Besides the Stooges knocking him silly with doors, making him run through the open door in fast motion [*Gents in a Jam*], pushing a pipe through the floor into his chin [*Out West*], smashing a fruit bowl into his face and knocking him back into the wall so a vase falls on his head [*Malice in the Palace*], there is the wonderful moment when Odius yells at the strongman and makes him drop his head and sulk for making so much noise crushing walnuts with his biceps. Moments later, Curly-Joe toasts wine all over him. One of the better visual anachronisms is the warm up jacket with 'HERCULES' on it. Parody often requires exaggeration and compounding, thus making an ancient one-eyed Cyclops into a two-eyed, two-headed Siamese Cyclops, whose finest moment involves shushing each other/itself. There is more irony when Moe threatens: "Let go, you, or I'll poke your eyes out!" Odius takes a fine fall when he lands head first on the earth and steps into the pond. Cutting trees down with a picked chariot continues the parody of *Ben-Hur*.

The slapstick is sporadic but effective. In the opening drug store scene we patiently wait for Moe to club Larry and Curly-Joe with the mortar, and later Moe gives Curly-Joe a great wallop with the one cup he does not drop; the splattered mess enhances the next scene, although the accompanying music and relative absence of accompanying dialogue is unfortunate. By this time the Stooges had come under some criticism for their violence and its potential influence on children, so the film lacks the gouge and other patently hurtful slapstick excesses. Curly-Joe's physical skills do not include the quickness of Curly and Shemp, but he does yeoman's work when bailing the leak, punching the huge hole in the hull, and grimacing as Hercules cracks the walnuts. Other variations: mixing a strange concoction, covering a room in suds (*Pardon My Scotch*); Curly-Joe picking up a waste basket and dropping papers out the bottom (recently in *Muscle Up A Little Closer*); entering the women's bath (*Meet the Baron, Blunder Boys*); Hercules punching through the door (*Nutty but Nice*); and the trap door in the floor (*We Want Our Mummy*).

VERBAL HUMOR: Elwood Ullman wrote many verbal gags, including linguistic (Moe: "Thou better escapest whilst thou cannest"), mythological (Curly-Joe: "You can't tell one [Hydra] head from another without a program...Cerberus - that pooch could be a tough one!"), political (Curly-Joe: "Self-confidence, initiative, and referendum"), electrical (Moe: "I'm positive the negative won't fit"), malapropisms and neologisms(Moe: "continmumum"; Larry: "He's got his cathawhatsis where his anawhosis ought to be"; Curly-Joe's "Old Nebuch-kibitzer"; the silly dialect the Siamese Cyclops speaks to itself/each other), anachronisms (Curly-Joe's "I haven't eaten in 3000 years," "Guess we made the crew," and "Just like a floatin' Vic Tanny."; Moe's "If we want a singer we'll call for Perry Como," "I'll report you to the Masseurs' Union," and "Hey conductor!"; Larry's "You mean I haven't been born yet?"; and 'The Greek Humor Man' cart), puns (Curly-Joe: "Galleys? We're gonna do some cookin'?"), internal rhymes (Moe: "Thesus has gone to pieces"; Moe: "I wish I had a bald-headed screwdriver" [for a bald-headed screw]), sarcasm (Moe: "Nooo! We always take a bath with our clothes on. That's how we do our laundry!"; and Schuyler: "I do have to pick up a deflection attenuator." Moe: "I know, we can't do without one of those!") and insults (Odius: "Immortals?... Impossible!";

The publicity campaign for *The Three Stooges Meet Hercules* was considerable, particularly compared to the limited publicity allotted to the comedy shorts the Stooges had produced at Columbia. The film grossed over $2 million.

Moe: "Even though you got two heads you only got half a brain!"; Curly-Joe: "We're outnumbered!" Moe: "You're out-brained, too!"; Moe: "Any idiot can see that." Larry: "Well you ought to know!"; and Curly-Joe: "If he turns out to be a heel as well as a wolf, this could be the start of the Dimsal family"). Moe is ignorant here (Schuyler: "If I could just shorten the wave length." Moe [handing him sheers]: "Here why don't you snip a piece off the end"). Three-pattern (Moe: "I'll take the right flank." Larry: "I'll take the left flank." Curly-Joe: I'll take a tranquilizer!")

Emil Sitka, as usual, does a great job as the confused shepherd; Stooge reaction is similar to the (Spanish) directions gag in *What's the Matador?*. The Ithaca New York/Greece pun is similar to the Syracuse pun in *You Nazty Spy!*. Other variations: "I'll hire a cheap lawyer," and "Find yourself a cheap blacksmith" (*Monkey Businessmen*); Moe: "Head for the time machine, and don't spare the horse power!" (*Three Dark Horses*); Moe: "He's a victim of circumstantial circumstances" (*Beer and Pretzels*); and "Backbiter!" (*Pop Goes the Easel*). References: Nebuch-kibitzer: a pseudo-Yiddish hybrid of 'kibitz' and Nebuchad-nezzar [Nebechadrezzar] II, King of Babylon around 575 BC, the Babylonian king in the *Book of Daniel* and in Columbia's *Slaves of Babylon*; Vic Tanny: a 1960s exercise guru; Perry Como: a singer who had a variety show on NBC from 1955-1963; Atlas Missile: our first ICBM, still being tested in 1961; the sign 'Have Muscles Will Travel': television's *Have Gun, Will Travel* was still on the air in 1962; Cerberus, the Wild Horses of Diomede, and the Iron [Stymphalian] Birds of Arcadia: three of Hercules' twelve labors; and Larry's "It's all Greek to him": parodies "It was Greek to me" from Shakespeare (*Julius Caesar* I.ii.288).

OTHER NOTES: The shooting dates were June 6-22, 1961. The film is copyrighted in 1961, but the first date we see when they go back in time is 1962. The working title was *Hercules and the Three Stooges*. Stock is also taken from *Half-Shot Shooters* [chimney exploding] and *You Can't Take It With You* (1938) [fireworks]. Larry was reportedly knocked unconscious while filming the chariot sequence. The Greek sign transliterates English sounds into Greek letters: ΗΑΡΒΩΡ ΩΦ ΡΗΩΔΕΣ (HARBOR OF RHODES); ΣΕΩΕΝ ΨΑΛΜΣ (SEVEN PSALMS (PALMS?)); ΡΗΟΔΕΣ INN (RHODES INN). But ΘΛΩΠΞ ΡΛΣΕ (ULOPX RLSE) is nonsense. Don Lamond, the narrator, had a bit role in *Have Rocket — Will Travel.* Vicki Trickett [Diane] played in a number of light comedies in the early 1960s, e.g. *Gidget Goes Hawaiian;* 'Diane' was essentially the same name used in the 'ancient' *Matri-Phony* ['Diana']. Of the McKeever twins Mike and Marlin [the Siamese Cyclops], the latter was a linebacker for the Los Angeles Rams at the time. Hal Smith [King Thesus] was at this time playing the role of Otis Campbell in *The Andy Griffith Show.* Rusty Wescoatt [hortator] earlier in his career had used his given name, William Norton Bailey, when he acted in serials in the later 1940s, early 1950s. Historical adjustments: Schuyler guesses the date of Ulysses' battle as 900 BC, but he is several centuries too late; the shepherd says the distance from Ithaca to Rhodes is 1200 miles, but it is less than 500; the correct plural of 'Cyclops' is 'Cyclopes'; and the ancient Greek name is 'Theseus,' not 'Thesus'. A derivative mythological Stooges film was the Italian/Chinese feature *The Three Stooges vs. The Wonder Women* (1975), where a different group faces Amazon warriors.

THE THREE STOOGES IN ORBIT

Studio: Columbia

Released: July 4, 1962

Running Time: 1'27"28'"

Credited Cast:

The Three Stooges	[Moe, Larry, Curly-Joe]
Carol Christensen	Carol Danforth
Edson Stroll	Captain Tom Andrews
Emil Sitka	Professor Danforth
George N. Neise	Ogg
Rayford Barnes	Zogg
Norman Leavitt	Williams, the butler
Nestor Paiva	Martian leader
Don Lamond	Col. Smithers
Peter Brocco	Dr. Appleby
Thomas Glynn	George Galveston
Jean Charney	WAF Sergeant
Peter Dawson	General Bixby
Maurice Manson	Mr. Lansing, TV producer
Duane Ament	clerk

Uncredited Cast:

Bill Dyer	Colonel Lane
Roy Engel	Welby, F.B.I. agent
Jane Wald	bathing girl
Cheerio Meredith	woman in tooth paste ad
Rusty Wescoatt	pie baker

Credited Production Crew:

Director:	Edward Bernds
Producer:	Norman Maurer
Screenplay:	Elwood Ullman
Story:	Norman Maurer
Music:	Paul Dunlap
Photography:	William F. Whitley
Art Director:	Don Ament
Editor:	Edwin Bryant
Set Decorations:	Richard Mansfield
Assistant Director:	Eddie Saeta
Sound:	William Bernds

PERSPECTIVE: Producer Norman Maurer introduced Columbia executives to his plan for the next 'The Three Stooges Meet' film, *The Three Stooges Meet the Martians*, by showing them the unsold 1960 TV pilot, *The Three Stooges Scrapbook*. The premise was this: evicted from their rooms, the Stooges end up in a mansion owned by a wealthy man who happens to have a Martian spy in his employ, from whom they flee in their pajamas and hitch a ride to the television studio where they are employed as cartoon show hosts. We see much of this pilot footage here in the first twenty minutes of the feature, but Maurer sold them on an expanded version by adding the "sea-going helitank, or a land-going helisub, or an airborn what-in-hell," a brief trip to space, and a battle against the Martians.

The Stooges had already made two shorts and one feature (*Have Rocket — Will Travel*) involving space travel, and wacky submarines (*Three Little Sew and Sews*), eccentric scientists (*Fuelin' Around*), and crazy inventions (*Dopey Dicks*) had been part of Stoogedom since the World War II era. But their previous space missions had been to Venus/Sunev, so this is the first time the Stooges participate in the modern obsession with a Martian invasion that began with H. G. Wells' 1898 novel *War of the Worlds*, intensified with Orson Wells' infamous 1938 radio broadcast, and culminated cinematically in George Pal's 1953 film version of the same. 'Martian films' proliferated in the 1950s - recently there had been *The Angry Red Planet* (1959) - but perhaps even more influential, at least insofar as the word 'Orbit' in the revised title is concerned, was John Glenn's heroic US orbital mission on February, 1962, two months before the film was shot. This great moment boosted the prestige of the American space program vis à vis the Soviets, and once *The Three Stooges in Orbit* is put into this perspective, we understand why the Martian leader yells quasi-Russian phonemes and pounds his shoe on the desk as did USSR Premier Nikita Khrushchev at the United Nations General Assembly in 1960.

The subject matter for the film is again a large-scale adventure, although in this case the Stooges travel from earth to the extra-terrestrial, not back or forth in time. As in the previous film, narration and animated credits start things off, and then Edward Bernds and Elwood Ullman have the Stooges appear on screen almost non-stop, again minimizing the romantic subplot. With gadgetry, a bathing woman, stock military and aerial footage, and sequences from Columbia's *Earth's Flying Saucers* (1956) they create a visually exciting, aurally complex canvas on which the Stooges paint their characteristic acts of unlikely but determined heroism. Amidst the political satire and the struggle against aliens is an ample offering of contemporary references, most notably the exploitation of "the thing they're all going daffy about" - the 'Twist,' which Chubby Checker introduced in the summer of 1960 and which had already found its way into such 1961-1962 films as *Twist Around the Clock*, *Hey, Let's Twist*, and *Don't Knock the Twist*.

Contemporary and successful as ever, this newest Stooge feature grossed $1.5 million.

VISUAL HUMOR: Plotwise, the most important contemporary reference is the sequence the Martians see on television – a silly toothpaste commercial, L.A. freeway traffic, sirens, explosions, twisting and Keystone Cops footage - that causes them to cancel their invasion of earth. Two slapstick sequences also propel the plot, the first when Curly-Joe pokes a hole in the wall with his chisel and engages in a fight with the Martian who then blasts a hole in the other wall wide enough for the machine to get out; the second where Larry squirts oil in Curly-Joe's face, causing him to fall onto the controls, start up the machine, and spin Moe around on the rotor and then off, ruining the Martian telescreen. Curly-Joe gets clanked twice by the thrown hot plate with a fine sound effect, but elsewhere there is an uncharacteristically dull sound for head banging. The ricochet gag is used twice, once with Moe outside Curly-Joe's door in the mansion, once in the machine during the meteor shower; the first belonged to the original TV pilot. Other highlights of the original pilot include hiding the food in the TV, turning the table over to hide the food (and then turning the table over by mistake), and creating an echo with multiple slaps, not to mention hitching a ride on a (normal) helicopter. Some of the dialogue enhances slapstick gags, e.g. Curly-Joe: "It was an accident." Moe: "This is on purpose!" (SLAM). Moe's reacts to the professor's claims much as he did to Schuyler's talk about the time machine in the previous film. The submarine depositing bras is a gag used recently in *Operation Petticoat* (1959). The gadgetry invented by the professor recalls the Rube Goldberg contraptions used in the first Stooge film, *Soup to Nuts*. Other variations: subtitles for comic effect (*Punchy Cowpunchers*); Moe pulling Curly-Joe by the back of the coat before boarding the helicopter (*Rockin' Thru the Rockies*); a mysterious mansion with secret passageways (*Spook Louder*); fighting over bed covers with an unrecognized fiend (*The Hot Scots*); Larry's nose following Moe's pointing arm (*Time Out for Rhythm*); Moe saluting and hitting Larry in the nose with his elbow (*Uncivil Warriors*); Moe riding on the propeller, and Curly-Joe pulling out the emergency brake (*Dizzy Pilots*); Lansing getting his foot caught in the wash bucket (*Have Rocket — Will Travel*); leading Curly-Joe to the opposite wall so the "pointy part" faces in the right direction (*Loco Boy Makes Good*); and the soot on the Martian (*Higher Than a Kite*).

VERBAL HUMOR: Ullman wrote several notable gags depending on internal rhyme (Larry: "It'll even revolutionize revolutions!"; Larry: "Mr. Galveston of Galveston"), repetition (using the "I don't think I know" gag [Curly-Joe: "What do you think- I'm dumb?" Moe: "I don't think; I know!" Curly-Joe: "Well I don't think you know either."] twice and adding "Didn't we just do that?" the second time) and a malapropism (Curly-Joe: "It gives me great pleasure on this monotonous occasion—" Moe: "Hey! It's 'momentous'— 'mo-mentous.'" Curly-Joe: "Now what are you givin' me two words for when I'm havin' so much trouble with one?") nicely varied later (Moe: "It is a great pleasure on this momentous occasion—" Curly-Joe: "Hey, you're stealin' my line... On this monotonous occasion—" Larry: "Hey this is gettin' monotonous." Moe: "It's 'momentous!'"). Ullman has the Stooges indulge in self-deprecation and ignorance (Larry: "What a team! He's got the brains, and we've got—" Moe: "What?" Larry:

The Stooges hold on for life above deck on their flying submarine ("all purpose military vehicle") in *The Three Stooges in Orbit* (1963), one of three feature films they made in 1962-63 at the height of their post-television-release stardom. Rube Goldberg's gadgetry was part of their first film, 1930's *Soup to Nuts*, and it is instrumental here.

"—the enthusiasm"; Larry: "How stupid can you get?" Curly-Joe: "I dunno. I guess you can get pretty stupid"; Moe: "What do you usually do when somebody mails you a bomb?" Curly-Joe: "I mail it back!" Moe: "You bird brain! You dunk it in water and put it out of commission! Sometimes I think you're dumb." Curly-Joe: "Dumb?! Well!"; Moe: "Visibility zero!" Curly-Joe: "You can't see either!"; and Larry, seeing the 'MAGAZINE' sign: "Look out for that bookstore!").

The Martian language is not the bebop of earlier space films or the electronically enhanced Siamese Cyclops lingo in *Hercules*. It includes a few syllables of the Stooges' pseudo-Russian Maharaja lingo, apt for the Russian references. (Larry reverses syllables in "Azaconey-capanna-allawattah!"). Curly-Joe's physical move- ment is relaxed and subtle; so is his verbal delivery, e.g. "Mrs. McGinnis! You're looking the same as ever!" and "I'm not afraid of that pop gun; it probably shoots corks. 'Caz-aconey' yourself!"). Epithets: "mental midget!" (*Have Rocket — Will Travel*), "bird-brained idiot," "lame-brain," "apple-brain," "bubble-brain," "bird-brain," "abominable snowman," "jug-heads," and "lug-heads." Three-pattern à la *Uncivil Warriors* (Professor: "Prepare for the water test!" Moe: "Prepare for the water test!" Larry: "Prepare for the water test!"). The other type of pattern gag (Moe: "Do you jug-heads mean to tell me you're gonna let fear stand in the way of our careers?" Larry & Curly-Joe: "Yes!" Moe: "Do you mean to tell me that you're too chicken to face up to that kooky butler?" Larry & Curly-Joe: "Yes!" Moe: "With three against one?" Larry & Curly-Joe: "Absolutely!") was used recently in *Have Rocket — Will Travel.* Moe calling Larry a "chicken," saying "Follow me!" and pushing both ahead of him became a classic pattern in *Dizzy Detectives*.

Other variations: 'Hotel Costa Much' (*Healthy, Wealthy and Dumb*); "Doesn't look a day over 98" (*No Census, No Feeling*); Curly-Joe: "Maybe we'll get a ticket." Larry: "Can you get one for my friend?" (*Men in Black*); "Half empty or half full" (*Soup to Nuts*); Moe: "Remind me to wallop you later." Curly-Joe: "I'll make a note of it," and Danforth: "Look out for that first step!" (*Cash and Carry*); "Skip the gutter" (*Pardon My Scotch*); Moe: "Looks like a country club for zombies!" Larry: "You ought-a know!" (*The Three Stooges Meet Hercules*); Larry: "What's that for?!" Moe: "That's for not thinkin' of it before!" (*Hoi Polloi*); Curly-Joe: "Termites?" (*3 Dumb Clucks*); Curly-Joe: "One of those crazy desert cloudbursts!" (*Heavenly Daze*); Curly-Joe: "I'll clean it up when I'm ready! Moe: "So?" Curly-Joe: "So, I'm ready!" (*Plane Nuts; Men in Black*); Owl: "Whoo!" Curly-Joe: "Me, that's who!" (*The Ghost Talks*); Moe: "You're all right. It was only a blow on the head." (Moe: "Did you get hurt?" Dinkelspiel: "No, I fell on my head" in *Hoofs and Goofs*); and Moe: "I don't think; I know!" Curly-Joe: "Well I don't think you know either" (*Rusty Romeos*). References: Curly-Joe's "And leave the driving to us!" was a well-known phrase from Greyhound Bus commercials of the period; later we hear a variation (General: "And leave the court martial to us!"). Aerial footage of Disneyland, built in the previous decade, causes the Martian to say: "Hit them where it hurts most!" Also fairly new in 1962 were credit cards, hence Curly-Joe/Moe: "A tourist from Mars...with a card from the Diner's Club." Moe knows that 'AEC' (Curly-Joe: "Automobile Exchange Company!") stands for the 'Atomic Energy Commission,' [established in 1946 but replaced by the Nuclear Regulatory Commission in 1975]. The Nike missiles Andrews mentions were some of the first American surface-to-air missiles developed after World War II. 'Caruso' was the great Neapolitan tenor, the first to make recordings. 'Magic lantern' was the seventeenth-century device that was the forerunner of the movie camera. And 'Land of Sky Blue Waters' belonged to a television commercial for Hamm's Beer.

OTHER NOTES: Part of the humor relies on the rivalry between the Army, Navy, and Air Force, a common motif in post-war military comedies. The original pilot for *The Three Stooges Scrapbook* was in color; in this feature we see that footage in black and white. The Stooges would introduce Stooge cartoons - 156 of them - for real beginning in October 1965. This particular one from the original pilot was 'The Spain Mutiny.' The concept of "electronic cartoons" was actually what Norman Maurer's Artiscope, developed in 1954, was designed to do - recreate human-like motions in animated form. The exchange about Social Security (Larry: "They're going to blow up the whole world!" Curly-Joe: "They can't do that: we'll never get our Social Security!") is quite different in concept from when the Stooges were young men; back then the 'Social Security Tax' was one of their deductions in *Healthy, Wealth and Dumb.* The Stooges have been fired from show business jobs in a number of previous films, first in *Beer and Pretzels.* Nestor Paiva [Martian leader], bald and dark complexioned, normally played [earthly] ethnic roles. A comparison can be made between the Stooges' facial reactions to the G-forces in this film and those during the lift off in *Space Ship Sappy*, which was made before manned space travel.

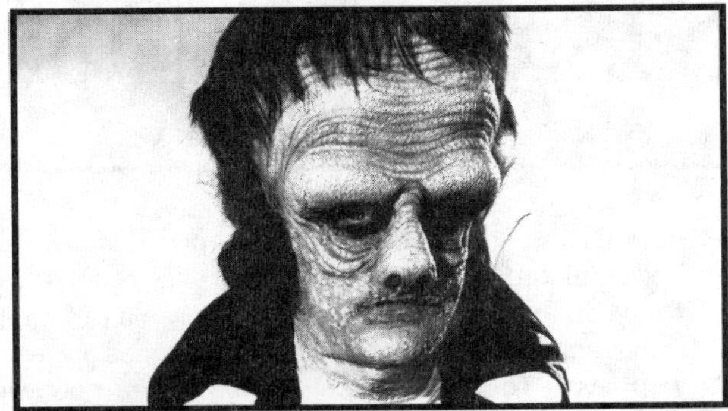

THE THREE STOOGES GO AROUND THE WORLD IN A DAZE

Studio: Columbia

Released: August 21, 1963

Running Time: 1'33"01'"

Credited Cast:

The Three Stooges	[Moe, Larry, Curly-Joe]
Jay Sheffield	Phileas Fogg III
Joan Freeman	Amelia Carter
Walter Burke	Lory Filch
Peter Forster	Vickers Cavendish
Maurice Dallimore	Crotchet
Richard Devon	Maharaja
Anthony Eustrel	Kandu
Iau Kea	Itchy Kitchy
Bob Kino	Charlie Okuma, Itchy's manager
Phil Arnold	Sumo refereee
Murray Alper	Gus
Don Lamond	Bill
Jack Greening	McPherson

Uncredited Cast:

Emil Sitka	butler
Jeffrey Maurer	Timmy, the flute boy
Audrey Betz	flute boy's mother
Ramsey Hill	Gatesby
Colin Campbell	Willoughby
Michael St. Clair	first mate
Ron Whelan	Harry
Kei Chung	Chinese guard
John Sheffield	Peters
Mark Harris	Tremble
Aki Aelong	Chinese Non Com
Tom Symonds	Bowers
Gerald Jann	Chinese general
Laurie Main	Carruthers
Magda Harout	hand maiden
Joe Wong	Chinese Joe
Harold Fong	Chinese Larry
Guy Lee	Chinese Moe

Credited Production Crew:

Director:	Norman Maurer
Producer:	Norman Maurer
Screenplay:	Elwood Ullman
Story:	Norman Maurer
Music:	Paul Dunlap
Photography:	Irving Lippman
Art Director:	Don Ament
Editor:	Edwin Bryant
Set Decorations:	James M. Grove
Assistant Director:	Eddie Saeta
Sound:	William Bernds
Special Effects:	Richard Albain

PERSPECTIVE: In 1956, Broadway producer Michael Todd adapted Jules Verne's 1873 French novel *Around the World in Eighty Days* into a memorable film of epic length and scope. Its 178 minutes surrounded audiences with lavish Technicolor shots taken with a new wide-screen system, Todd-AO. The narrative was little more than a glorified travelogue with forty-four movie-star cameos sprinkled liberally throughout numerous episodic sequences. Seven years later, producer/director/writer Norman Maurer adapted Stooge comedy to *Around the World in Eighty Days* by writing the trio into the various episodes, a narrative format in which the Stooges had been thriving for decades in their two-reelers and travel-adventure features of the 1960s as they ran from authorities, disguised themselves, took on odd jobs, and helped various people in distress. And so in Turkey they hide themselves and get banged around inside steamer trunks (à la *Fiddlers Three*); in India they rescue a damsel-in-distress (*So Long, Mr. Chumps*), break out of prison (*3 Dumb Clucks*) when Larry plays 'Pop Goes the Weasel' (*Punch Drunks*), and perform an updated version of their Maharaja routine (*Time Out For Rhythm; Three Little Pirates*); in China they brainwash Communist psychiatrists into anti-authoritarian Sino-Stooges; and in Japan and San Francisco Curly-Joe wrestles against champion Sumo wrestler Itchy Kitchy (*Grips, Grunts and Groans*).

Part of the uniqueness of this film is in casting the Stooges as man-servants. Throughout their careers the Stooges have portrayed tradesmen, bums, criminals, husbands, courtiers, and actors, and they have been rich, poor, and middle class, but while they have often been someone else's employees, they have not really played someone else's servants, especially servants who have to serve with such precision. Phileas Fogg III expects his breakfast at 7:49, leaves his club at 5:18, and has to return to the Reformers' Club within exactly 80 days. In part the humor comes from maintaining this precision (putting a thermometer in orange juice), and in part it

comes in spite of it [swallowing the thermometer]. Made all the more poignant by the British setting, the emphasis on temporal precision provides a structure ripe for that inimitable Stooge bending, wrenching, and breaking.

Because Verne's novel takes its heroes around the world, the Stooges get ample opportunity to employ and confront various accents and ethnic stereotypes, a significant part of their humor ever since they demolished the French artist's painting in *Pop Goes the Easel.* Always ready for political satire as well, the Stooges make fun of the British class system, Indian colonialism, Chinese communism, and Japanese commercialism, not to mention President Kennedy's fitness program ("Kennedy-style hikin': at least we're keepin' fit") and Vietnam policy ("*We not soldiers. We technicians!*"). The international setting also allows Maurer to include ample stock footage, which, as in *The Three Stooges in Orbit*, adds visual authenticity and scope.

VISUAL HUMOR: When Joe Besser joined the Stooges in 1956, it took several films before the three comedians fully blended their physical humor, and in the 1930s it took several years before Curly developed his full repertoire of physical movements. In his fifth feature film Joe DeRita hits full stride in his physical interplay. He takes a great shot in the head with a frying pan, bounces all over the place in the Sumo match, and covers a lot of arm waving territory when the belly dancer bumps him through the curtains. He is an active participant in the slapstick free-for-alls at the end of the trunk-dropping and Maharaja sequences as well as at the very end of the film, where Moe bonks him ten times, bonks and pounds both Curly-Joe and Larry and gives them nose

crunches, and they crush Moe's face with their forearms. Curly-Joe also has a unique characteristic: he is able to smell "Ham and eggs, sunny side up."

Quite extraordinary, in terms of Stooge history, is the Chinese episode in which Moe reprimands his Chinese counterpart that they no longer gouge eyes ("Uh-uh. That's number 21. We don't do that anymore. We do the number 47, like this—" [SLAP]). We have not seen an eye gouge since *Have Rocket – Will Travel.* Result shots: the trunks fallen on Moe; Larry dropping the trunks; and the truck stowaways climbing out of the toppled furniture and boxes.

Visual references: the Chinese Stooges paint glasses and a mustache on a poster of Chairman Mao Tse-tung, Chairman of the Chinese Communist Party and China's Premier from 1949-1976; Itchy Kitchy breaks a board and a tree branch with his bare hand, popular images of karate in the early 1960s. A new weapon: a wet newspaper. Itchy Kitchy's fantastic collapse into the Sumo ring recalls Tiny's huge bed flop in *Muscle Up a Little Closer*; it is foreshadowed when Curly-Joe throws Kandu and the Maharaja face down onto the collapsing table piled with food. Other variations: interior shots inside the trunks [*Boobs in Arms*]; driving through a wall [*Punch Drunks*]; breaking through the door and [in fast motion] running into the wall [recently in *The Three Stooges Meet Hercules*]; fighting with lights out [*Nutty but Nice*]; Larry pouring hot coffee on Moe's foot [*Listen, Judge*]; Moe swallowing the thermometer [*Monkey Businessmen*]; Moe banging Larry on the head with a silver tray [*3 Dumb Clucks*]; Curly-Joe knocking Moe over with the swinging door, breaking the dishes [*Crash Goes the Hash*]; Larry giving Moe "a hand" [*A Plumbing We Will Go*]; grabbing food through the ship's window

(*Idle Roomers*); Moe knocking guards out with a vase (*Malice in the Palace*); using a periscope (recently in *The Three Stooges in Orbit*); Itchy Kitchy wringing Curly-Joe's foot (and his shoe without the foot, but Curly-Joe says "Ooo!" anyway), and Fogg punching Filch, whose head snaps back into Cavendish's (*Grips, Grunts and Groans*); Curly-Joe doing a double flip as the hose unrolls (*Out West*); Curly-Joe firing a shot in the air that ricochets four times and then hits Larry's head (*So Long, Mr. Chumps*); Moe squirting cream from a goat's udder (*Busy Buddies*); and chickens laying eggs on Curly-Joe's head (*Sweet and Hot*).

VERBAL HUMOR: As in all the Columbia feature scripts penned by Elwood Ullman, verbal gags are plentiful and varied, beginning with written gags (initial apologies to Jules Verne in the credit titles; the Tokyo sign for 'FLIED LICEBERGERS'; the subtitle: 'CENSORED (in Chinese-type script) AND DON'T COME BACK'). Besides the political verbal gags already mentioned, ethnic gags exploit British stuffiness (Moe: "I was so embarrassed I felt like turning in my sideburns!"; Larry: "Who will lay out your day tods for day wear?" Moe: "And your night tods for nightmares?"; Moe: "There was a strong will: died two months after the doctors gave him up." Curly-Joe: "The only time he was ever late in his life!"), foreign names (Itchy Kitchy, Kandu, Musselbini, and Ginga Din (Gunga Din's sister)), other speech patterns and accents ("And now everyone welcome to watch training exercise, but prease to remember buying tickets to the next match at the Tokyo Sports Palace - this not being on television" (*No Dough Boys*)), mixed stereotypes (Japanese Sumo manager: "Oy Vay!"), costumes (Curly-Joe: "Hello, Rahah!...My Uncle Gus had a Lodge uniform that looked exactly like yours - the Royal Order of the Timberwolves"), foods (Larry (drifting in the China sea with only fortune cookies to eat): "It says you're goin' on a long trip!"), and prisons (Moe: "We prefer the penthouse"; of the straw beds: "We need a change of linens").

There are also literal interpretations ([Fogg discusses a river bridge.] Curly-Joe: "Don't worry. We'll cross that bridge when we come to it!"; Curly-Joe spills champagne on Moe and Larry: "Don't worry about it. It's on them." Moe: "No, it's on the both of us!"), and two license gags (Curly-Joe: "What kind of phony rap did you pin on him." Kandu: "Charming cobras without a license"; Moe: "Let me see your license!" Curly-Joe: "Who's got a license?"). As in the previous film, there are self-deprecating jokes about Stooge ignorance (Larry: "I had enough brains to steal this from the duke's palace next door. You thought I was stupid, didn't you?" Moe: "Now I'm sure of it!"; Curly-Joe: "Kippers take 11 minutes to broil, sausage take four minutes more, 4 goes into 12 twenty...It can't be done!"; Larry: "We're goin' around the world on our wits!" Moe: "With your wits you won't get past the front door!"; Curly-Joe: "Sorry, Moe. Low bridge." Moe: "Pardon me, low mentality!"; Moe: "Sorry, general: with these boys, no brainee to washee!"; Moe: "This is a crazy, mixed up car." Curly-Joe: "Well I'm a crazy mixed up driver!"; Moe: "Hit it, maestro!" Larry: "Who's 'maestro'?" Moe: "You, you fool!"; and Fogg: "Turn at the next corner." Curly-Joe: "Left?" Fogg: "Right." [Curly-Joe turns left.] Moe: "Right, you knucklehead!" Fogg: "I said 'left!'" Curly-Joe: "See, right *was* left!" Moe: "Wha'?" Curly-Joe: "I dunno."). Yet, it was Curly-Joe's idea to ship themselves C.O.D.

The Maharaja sequence contains variations of set gags (Larry: "Shoot *what* raisin from *which* gentleman's head?" Moe: "Oh pardon me for calling you a 'gentleman'"; Moe: "The Rajah says that this time he will throw the razor's edge daggers at random." Larry: "Random? Get him up here. Hey Randy!"; Moe: "a *mblpblbplbl* shots out of a possible 300!" Curly-Joe: "That's without bullets!"; Moe "You gonna hit a man with glasses?...Go ahead!"). Moe offers slapstick setup lines ("Here's one [plate] you missed!"; "You know, a sharp crack deserves a sharp answer!"; "How would you like a coffee break in the head?"; to Larry: "Why didn't you play in a higher key?"). Curly-Joe is adapting to post-slapstick throw-away lines à la Shemp ("Oh, Moe. That hurt me more than it did you!"; "You crazy? You wanna give her a bad impression?"; "You wanna get me wet?!"; Moe: "Easy now!" Curly-Joe: "Easy for who?!"; and Moe: "Did you hurt yourself?" Curly-Joe: "Well I didn't do myself any good!").

He and Larry both offer lines after dropping the trunks (Curly-Joe: "Somethin's missing!" Larry: "They didn't build the house right!"). Also like Shemp is Curly-Joe's fear when Itchy Kitchy demonstrates what he will do to his opponent: "His opponent ain't stayin'!" He adapts an old Stooge-ism when his karate chop fails: "I hurt my wittle hand." Moe and Larry both appeal in Borscht-belt patterns (Moe: "That's a young man?"; Larry: "Galley shmalley!"; and Larry: "I'm goin' back for gas." Moe: "The only gas you're gonna get is on your stomach!" Larry [hit on the head]: "That's my stomach?!").

Moe's "Surprise me some time: do something right!" recalls his surprise that Curly-Joe and Larry did do something right in *The Three Stooges In Orbit* when the Martian blasted the hole in the wall. Other variations: Moe: "Get the number of that truck!" (*Three Missing Links*); Moe: "Man the life boats! Women and children first!" (*Grips, Grunts and Groans*); Moe: "Watch your Ps and Qs" (*Beer and Pretzels*); Moe: "Don't you know me? Don't I belong with ya'?" ("Don't you know? You been around me many years! Don't you know what I look like?" in *Who Done It?*); Moe: "Remind me to kill you later!" (*Cash and Carry*). Epithets: "nitwits," "frizzle-top," "mongoose," "imbecile," "porcupine," "button-head," "Beetle-brain," and "zombie!" References: Moe: "His man Friday—" Larry: "and Saturday!" parody the *Robinson Crusoe* character (and Columbia's hit 1940 film *His Girl Friday*). The Stooges play 'Odds and Evens,' a British game. Two television references: Curly-Joe thinking of 'Folgers' Coffee [a contemporary commercial]; and Moe holding up the wine: "Route 66...A very wonderful year!" [CBS' *Route 66* aired 1960-1964].

The Stooges relax with fellow cast and crew members on the set of *The Three Stooges Go Around the World in a Daze* (1963), their parody of Michael Todd's *Around the World in Eighty Days* (1956). The episodic travelogue of the original story easily accommodated Stooge episodic comedy.

OTHER NOTES: The multiple working titles (*The Three Stooges Go Around the World on Eighty Cents, The Three Stooges Go 'Round the Globe on Eighty Cents, The Three Stooges Circle the Globe on Eighty Cents, Around the World on Eighty Cents, The Three Stooges Circle the World on Ninety-Nine Cents, The Three Stooges Go Around the World on Seventy-Nine Cents, The Three Stooges Go Around the World on $1.98, The Three Stooges Meet Phileas Fogg and Merry Go Round the World*) were the result of negotiations with United Artists who claimed the right to Verne's original title [which, actually, was *Le Tour du monde en quatre-vingts jours*!]. The film was shot in May, 1963; John Kennedy had sent "military advisers" to Vietnam late in 1961. This was Joe DeRita's favorite Stooge film. It earned $1 million, a fair return on the investment, but not enough to make the brass at Columbia enthusiastic about another multiple-film contract. As fodder for the Stooge parody, the introductory scenes of the original film contained a white-collar bank robbery, a meeting at the 'Reform Club,' a fastidious Fogg who keeps to a time table precise to the minute and requires "toast heated to 93-degrees," the bet with Stuart [Finlay Currie], and, not coincidentally, a comedian [Cantinflas] for a butler. There is no restriction that Fogg cannot spend his own money; there are also different stops during the journey except for India, Japan, and San Francisco. Hong Kong is necessarily exchanged for Communist China.

Jay Sheffield [Phileas Fogg III] had no other major film roles; he had a supporting role in the film *Tammy and the Millionaire* (1967) as well as in the TV series *Tammy* (1965). The previous year Joan Freeman [Amelia] played a continuing role in the notorious TV series *Bus Stop* criticized for sadism and violence; the Stooges, having eliminated the old #21, were no longer under such criticism. Peter Forster [Vickers Cavendish] had a lengthy film career, he was the father of Brian Forster, who played Christopher Partridge on *The Partridge Family* (1971-1974). Norman Maurer's son, Jeffrey, plays the boy who takes Larry's flute at the Sumo match.

IT'S A MAD, MAD, MAD, MAD WORLD

Studio: United Artists

Released: November 7, 1963

Running Time: 2'52"53'"

Credited Cast:

Spencer Tracy	Captain T. G. Culpeper
Milton Berle	J. Russell Finch
Sid Caesar	Melville Crump
Buddy Hackett	Benjy Benjamin
Ethel Merman	Mrs. Marcus
Mickey Rooney	Ding Bell
Dick Shawn	Sylvester Marcus
Phil Silvers	Otto Meyer
Terry Thomas	Lt. Col. J. Algernon Hawthorne
Jonathan Winters	Lonnie Pike
Edie Adams	Monica Crump
Dorothy Provine	Emmeline Finch
Eddie 'Rochester' Anderson	taxi driver #1
Jim Backus	Tyler Fitzgerald
Ben Blue	airplane pilot
Joe E. Brown	union official
Alan Carney	police sergeant
Chick Chandler	
Barrie Chase	Mrs. Haliburton
Lloyd Corrigan	mayor
William Demerest	Aloysius, Chief of Police
Selma Diamond	voice of Culpepper's wife
Andy Devine	Sheriff Mason
Peter Falk	taxi driver #2
Norman Fell	police detective
Paul Ford	Colonel Wilberforce
Stan Freberg	deputy sheriff
Louise Glenn	voice of Billie Sue
Leo Gorcey	taxi driver #3
Sterling Holloway	fireman on ladder
Edward Everett Horton	Dinckler, man on street
Marvyn Kaplan	Irwin, gas station attendant
Buster Keaton	Jimmy the crook
Tom Kennedy	traffic cop
Don Knotts	Ford driver
Charles Lane	airport manager
Ben Lessy	George, the steward
Mike Mazurki	hitchhiker
Charles McGraw	lieutenant
Cliff Morton	
ZaSu Pitts	Gertie
Carl Reiner	tower director
Madlyn Rhue	police secretary
Arnold Stang	gas station attendant
Nick Stuart	truck driver
The Three Stooges	firemen
Sammee Tong	Chinese laundryman
Jesse White	radio tower operator
Jimmy Durante	Smiler Grogan

Uncredited Cast: ["A Few Surprises"]

Jerry Lewis	crazy driver
Howard Da Silva	airport officer
Jack Benny	man in car in the desert

Credited Production Crew:

Director:	Stanley Kramer
Producer:	Stanley Kramer
Screenplay:	William and Tania Rose
Story:	William and Tania Rose
Music:	Ernest Gold
Photography:	Ernest Laszlo
Art Director:	Gordon Gurnee
Editor:	Fred Knutson
Set Decorations:	Joseph Kish
Sound:	John Kean
Special Effects:	Danny Lee

PERSPECTIVE: At the height of their resurgent popularity in the 1960s, the Stooges took time out from their Columbia feature-film productions to appear in two features made by other studios. Both offered merely cameo roles. But apparently the Stooges' own feature-films of the early 1960s had not just entertained young fans whose first Stooges exposure was locally hosted television showings of their old classics; they also captured the attention of Hollywood film makers and moved the Stooges up a notch in the estimation of their peers. No longer considered just another old comedy team who survived beyond Laurel & Hardy, the Marx Brothers, Abbott & Costello, and Dean Martin & Jerry Lewis, the Stooges were now successful, money-generating film stars, albeit past their prime. In 1961 Fox had used them in their Carol Heiss *Snow White* vehicle, and now there were two more opportunities.

Stanley Kramer, the Oscar-nominated producer and director of such important recent films as *The Defiant Ones* (1958) and *Judgment at Nuremberg* (1961), had in 1952 produced *High Noon*, which the Stooges parodied in 1954's *Shot in the Frontier*. In fact, in the wake of the artistic success of *High Noon*, Columbia mogul Harry Cohn signed Kramer to a multi-film, $25 million contract, meaning that Columbia employed both Kramer and the Stooges at the same time, although in 1953 alone Kramer earned about what all six Stooges combined earned from their entire tenure at Columbia. Kramer left Columbia in 1954, and now nine years later he creates Hollywood's first and only epic comedy: Nothing is like it in scope. *It's a Mad, Mad, Mad, Mad World* was shot in widescreen Cinerama, runs almost three hours in length, and employs four dozen comedians, some as principals, others - Jerry Lewis, Buster Keaton, and the Three Stooges - in cameos.

The film begins with Jimmy Durante driving over a cliff, but living long enough for Milton Berle, Ethel Merman, Sid Caesar, Buddy Hackett, Mickey Rooney, Phil Silvers, Terry Thomas, and Jonathan Winters to find out about $350,000 buried under "a big 'W'" in a Santa Rosita park. Thereafter the story follows the non-stop, madcap race for the loot, and the Stooges' five-second cameo comes at one of the most intense moments of the film: a maddened Sid Caesar is destroying a hardware store, Phil Silvers has ruined his car by driving into a river, and Mickey Rooney/Buddy Hackett find themselves trying to land an airplane after their drunken pilot gets knocked out. Amidst all this maddening destruction, we see emergency equipment and a crowd gathering for the crash landing, and as the camera pans left we hear 'Three Blind Mice' and see Larry, Moe, and Curly-Joe dressed as firemen holding fire extinguishers and an ax. They do not say anything, move a muscle, or make a face. With so much destruction in the film already, it would be anticlimactic to have the Stooges offer their own demolition scene. They just stand there, the Gods of Destructive Ineptitude, giving viewers a glorious vision: the sheer contemplation of what additional destruction these paragons might inflict.

OTHER NOTES: The 'Three Blind Mice' theme song was familiar to contemporary audiences from television reruns of the Stooges' Columbia two-reelers. The Stooges had worked previously with Jimmy Durante in such early features as *Meet the Baron*, *Hollywood Party*, and *Start Cheering*, and they mimicked Durante nearly a half dozen times in their two-reelers. ZaSu Pitts [telephone operator] played opposite the Stooges as well in MGM's *Meet the Baron* [1930]. The film was nominated for six Academy Awards. Versions of the video available for purchase/rental have different running times. The original 70mm print included 8 minutes of music and a 16-minute intermission; the 35mm version ran 154 minutes.

The Three Stooges had long ago developed an international following. In 1939, the summer before they made *You Nazty Spy!*, they made a tour of the United Kingdom, and they were always popular south of the border where clown-style humor thrived. Here is a Mexican lobby card from Stanley Kramer's epic comedy, *It's a Mad, Mad, Mad, Mad World*, released in the US in 1963, and elsewhere in 1964. Interestingly, this lobby card features the Stooges in a photo of their very brief, silent cameo despite that the cast of the film was filled with more than a dozen well-known screen and television celebrities. And yet the Stooges are not even listed in the cast. Then again, who did not know who these three fellows were?

4 FOR TEXAS

Studio: Warner Brothers

Released: December 18, 1963

Running Time: 1'54"42'"

Credited Cast:

Frank Sinatra	Zackariah Thomas
Dean Martin	Joe Jarrett
Anita Ekberg	Elya Carlson
Ursula Andress	Maxine Richter
Charles Bronson	Matson
Victor Buono	Harvey Burden
Edric Connor	Prince George
Virginia Christine	
Ellen Corby	
Nick Dennis	Angel
Richard Jaeckel	Mancini
Mike Mazurki	Chad
Wesley Addy	Trowbridge
Marjorie Bennett	Miss Ermaline
Jack Elam	Dobie
Jesslyn Fak	widow
Fritz Feld	maître d'
Percy Helton	Ansel
Jonathan Hole	Renèe
Jack Lambert	Monk
Paul Langton	Beauregard
Keith McConnell	
Teddy Buckner and his All-Stars	
Michele Montau	
Maidie Norman	
Bob Steele	
Mario Siletti	
Eva Six	
Abraham Sofaer	
Michael St. Angel	
Grady Sutton - bank messenger	
Ralph Volkie	
Max Wagner	
William Washington	
Dave Willock	
The Three Stooges [Moe, Larry, Curly-Joe]	

Credited Production Crew:

Director:	Robert Aldrich
Producer:	Robert Aldrich
Screenplay:	Teddi Sherman and Robert Aldrich
Music:	Nelson Riddle
Photography:	Ernest Laszlo
Art Director:	William Glasgow
Editor:	Michael Luciano
Set Decorations:	Raphael Bretton
Assistant Directors:	Tom Connors and Dave Salven

PERSPECTIVE: The second 1963 feature film in which the Stooges made a guest appearance was Warner Brothers' *4 for Texas*, a Technicolor curiosity starring two members of the 'Rat Pack' - Frank Sinatra and Dean Martin. The Hollywood 'Rat Pack' originally described Humphrey Bogart's circle of friends ('The Holmby Hills Rat Pack'), but the same term was applied later to Frank Sinatra's circle of friends who became the darling bad boys of the Hollywood press and the Las Vegas showroom scene while shooting the infamous Vegas caper film, *Ocean's Eleven* in 1960. The Rat Pack membership included a half-dozen revolving celebrities, but the core always consisted of Frank Sinatra and Dean Martin, who made four major films together in this period. *4 for Texas* was the third of these films. Produced, directed, and co-written by Robert Aldrich for Warner Brothers, the film matches the two handsome Rat Packers with the two most glamorous and chesty Swedish beauties of the time - Anita Ekberg and Ursula Andress. Other cast members include Aldrich regular Victor Buono (later of television *Batman* fame), Charles Bronson (who would become a superstar in the 1970s), and listed after thirty-five other actors, 'Special Guest Stars: THE THREE STOOGES.'

This would be the last time the Stooges would ever appear in a feature-film in which they did not star, making a total of fourteen such features. This particular appearance is longer than the five-second cameo in United Artists' *It's a Mad, Mad, Mad, Mad World*, but their role as three delivery men who disappear from the film as soon as their scene is finished has no bearing on the plot. Nonetheless, on camera for three minutes, they are featured in three consecutive sequences. They appear ninety minutes into the film to provide an odd sort of comic interlude. The film to this point and afterwards contains mostly brawls, threatening banter, and unfulfilled romances and teasing, so the Stooges' arrival causes an abrupt pause in the flow of the film: the men building the riverboat gambling casino take time off to gather round and watch, and even Dean Martin and Ursula Andress interact with and laugh at the Stooges' antics.

Typically the Stooges in non-starring roles are compelled to do their routines quickly and suddenly, out of narrative context. This tends to hollow their routines by stripping them of any comic momentum; it is much like asking Olivier to walk in front of the camera and "do some Shakespeare." The Stooges' comic routines run smoothly enough here, but it is no coincidence that both had been inserted into previous feature films. The 'point-to-the-right' routine (*Rockin' In the Rockies*; *Start Cheering*) and the 'Tell him, Tex' routine (*Gold Raiders*), both of which originated in two-reelers, were apparently routines which the Stooges thought worked well enough out of context, true also for the triple slap. In fact, here they get triple slapped twice - once by one of the widows, and once by Dean Martin - the only time they are triple slapped by two different people in a single film and the final triple slaps of their lengthy film career.

VISUAL HUMOR: The 'point-to-the-right' routine first appeared in *Pardon My Scotch* twenty-eight years earlier. The 'Tell him, Tex' routine is actually a combination of that phrase, introduced in *Pardon My Clutch* and *Punchy Cowpunchers*, and the 'the state [CLAP-CLAP-CLAP-CLAP] of Texas' routine they first filmed for their 1949 TV pilot *'Jerks of All Trades.'* The old widow hitting Moe on the head with a parasol and giving the Stooges a triple slap stems from a long line of women who have beaten on the Stooges, particularly in *Brideless Groom*, and *Husbands Beware*. In the previous film the 'flute boy's' mother hit Larry incessantly with her purse. Moe barking and the widow roaring back is also a two-reeler routine [e.g. *3 Dumb Clucks*] already inserted into a feature - *Start Cheering*.

VERBAL HUMOR: Curly-Joe's easy delivery creates a breezy comic effect in one exchange (Moe: "This guy's a nitwit." Curly-Joe: "Yeah, he's stupid!"). Several verbal gags were used previously in feature-films: "Recede!" [*Myrt and Marge*; *Swing Parade of 1946*], and "I'm dealing with two mental midgets here!" [*Have Rocket — Will Travel*; *The Three Stooges in Orbit*]. In the three-pattern (Larry: "She reminds me of my mother!" Moe: "You never had a mother!" Curly-Joe: "Shame on you!"), Moe's response comes from a long-line of mother jokes, e.g. "My mother and your mother are both mothers" [*Half-Shot Shooters*] and "My mother knows my name!" [*Movie Maniacs*].

Other variations: Moe's "Remind me to have you stuffed!" [*So Long, Mr. Chumps*]; and Moe's "Give her an adjective!" [*Hold That Lion*]. When Joe [Dean Martin] ends up in the river, he says, "If I had to take a bath, you could have waited till Saturday!" This is a gag used in several variations, e.g. *Rockin' Thru the Rockies*, though it is not unique to the Stooges.

Reference: Moe's "Get your mother out-a here, Whistler!" refers to James Whistler's (1834-1903) famous painting, 'The Artist's Mother,' commonly 'Whistler's Mother.' Cf. their 1949 TV pilot ("You've heard of Whistler?" Moe: "I listen to his radio program all the time.").

OTHER NOTES: The correct title of this film uses the numeral: *4 for Texas*. Director Robert Aldrich was successful immediately before and after this film with dark comedies/horror films like *Whatever Happened to Baby Jane?* (1962) and *Hush Hush Sweet Charlotte* (1964), starring such major Hollywood titans as Bette Davis, Joan Crawford, and Olivia de Havilland. The crowd laughter at Stooge pranks recalls the party crowd reaction in *Ants in the Pantry*.

Proof of how 'hip' Stoogedom had become in the mid-1960s is the Stooge 3-minute shtick in *4 For Texas* (1963), a film featuring Ursula Andress and the Rat Pack's Frank Sinatra and Dean Martin - who triple-slaps the Stooges.

THE OUTLAWS IS COMING

Studio: Columbia

Released: January 14, 1965

Running Time: 1'28"12'"

Credited Cast:

The Three Stooges [Moe, Larry, Curly-Joe]

Nancy Kovack	Annie Oakley
Adam West	Kenneth Cabot
Mort Mills	Trigger Mortis
Don Lamond	Rance Roden
Rex Holman	Sunstroke Kid
Emil Sitka	Mr. Abernathy/witch doctor/ colonel
Henry Gibson	Charlie Horse
Murray Alper	Chief Crazy Horse
Tiny Brauer	bartender
Marilyn Fox	first girl
Sidney Marion	Hammond
Audrey Betz	fat squaw
Jeffrey Alan [Maurer]	kid
Lloyd Kino	Japanese 'Beatle'
Paul Frees	narrator

Special Guests:

Curly-Joe Bolton	Rob Dalton
Bill Camfield	Wyatt Earp
Hal Fryar	Johnny Ringo
Johnny Ginger	Billy the Kid
Wayne Mack	Jesse James
Ed T. McDonnell	Bat Masterson
Bruce Sedley	Cole Younger
Paul Shannon	Wild Bill Hickok
Sally Starr	Belle Starr

Credited Production Crew:

Produced & Directed by:	Norman Maurer
Screenplay:	Elwood Ullman
Story:	Norman Maurer
Music:	Paul Dunlap
Photography:	Irving Lippman
Art Director:	Robert Peterson
Editor:	Aaron Nibley
Set Decorations:	James M. Crowe
Sound:	James Z. Flaster
Special Effects:	Richard Albain
Assistant Director:	Donald Gold

PERSPECTIVE: Norman Maurer was riding in an elevator in Columbia's New York offices with a script of this film, then known as *The Three Stooges Meet the Gunslingers*. Veteran Columbia executive Leo Jaffe looked at the cover artwork and said, "That's funny! Let's make the picture." The result was *The Outlaws Is Coming*, which was then promoted with an innovative marketing plan: the gunslinger roles were all played by hosts of local daytime Stooge programs. Because these personable, high profile celebrities from the major television markets kept chatting to Stooge fans daily about making the film and were occasionally even visited by the Stooges themselves, their audiences anxiously awaited the film which ultimately grossed $1 million. It was the favorite feature-film of both Moe and Norman Maurer, and three decades later *The Outlaws Is Coming*, the last major Stooge Hollywood film, remains a treasure which captures the older Stooges at their best. Bungling and quarreling their way through another wild adventure, the Stooges encounter outlaws, Indians, women, and bullies, abuse machinery and gadgetry, work with glue, tools, explosives, drink hard liquor, beat the bad guys in a climactic chase sequence, and save the buffalo, penultimately triumphing only to have Mother Nature rain on their ride into the sunset.

This is not to say that the Stooges of 1965 are the same as the Stooges of 1939. Moe, the catalyst of Stooge slapstick, is now 68, and he is working with his fourth 'third Stooge' and a new generation of technical crew. All this and angry PTA groups have brought a halt to extensive gouging, wrenching, and slapping, which necessarily limits interactivity between the Stooges. When Moe cannot consistently hit the third Stooge it puts distance between not only Moe and Curly-Joe, but also Moe and Larry, since genuine Stooge slapstick requires Larry's reactions. You cannot blame Curly-Joe, who wriggles his rotund shape, exudes a profound ignorance, and employs a full repertoire of facial expressions, nor Moe who does give Larry a backwards bonk/hair pull while pounding/bonking Curly-Joe, engages in the recently popular one-on-two pattern [Moe: "Do you mean to say that you would let Mr. Cabot face all these dangers alone?" Larry & Curly-Joe: "Yes!" [DOUBLE SLAP]], and initiates a brief round of inter-Stooge hitting in the final sequence. Their comedy style has simply softened, so a potentially classic scene like the one with spilled glue [as in *A Snitch in Time*] ends with Moe yelling in the shrillest of tones instead of the traditional repercussive wallops, leaving us yearning for closure.

The humor depends more than ever, luckily, on writer Ellwood Ullman, a Stooge veteran of nearly thirty years, and director Norman Maurer, who compensates physically with the glued-gun battle, the pie-throwing wagon chase, the most imaginative Stooge Indian sequences since *Back to the Woods*, and a host of camera techniques detailed below. Ullman complements all this verbally by inserting an extraordinary number of contemporary references easily recognized by the TV-oriented Stooge audience, making this film quite a memorable document of American popular culture in 1964.

VISUAL HUMOR: Maurer, who was so fond of animation, experiments visually by varying typical film parameters

(speakers turn to the camera to 'break the proscenium' when Moe says " A Japanese Beatle?", when Curly-Joe mouths "I'll get the flash powder ready," and when the chief says proudly "My son, the doctor!") and toying with images of the printed word (Trigger Mortis shoots up the opening credits written on glasses, bottles, mugs, mirrors, the piano, and a woman's belly; a Gattling gun fires black spots into the picture and forms the words 'THE END'; smoke signals read like modern electronic communiqué along the bottom of screen (like a television crawl), or are sent by a strange contraption, or in a unique kind of Indian syllabary, or via a peace pipe Morse Code; Abernathy reads the 'Buffalo Census Chart' down the wall and onto the floor; and Larry and Curly-Joe read the printer's ink on Moe's face and 'turn pages' by moving

his head). There are several effective fast motion sequences, and having Curly-Joe dance as an Indian flapper in two-piece lingerie does not fall under the category of 'normal' visual parameter either.

Maurer helps energize scenes by combining gags. Moe orders Curly-Joe to "drop everything" (recently in *Flying Saucer Daffy*), so Curly-Joe does so, vaulting the can of glue onto a shelf from where it spills onto Moe's chair (*A Snitch in Time*); then the glue scene itself is divided into two, surrounding some gun play with Annie and Cabot. Another example: interweaving Joe's cigar with the 'meter maid' sequence by having a half-dozen cowboys run to wipe the paint off their horses, swinging open the saloon door and smashing Curly's Joe's cigar. After the first flash powder explosion we get the most elaborate result shot in all the feature films, with five people buried in/under animal trophies and tattered paraphernalia. That explosion is used to set up the second explosion during the Indian sequences, Curly-Joe increasing the anticipation with "This is gonna be dynamite!" Twice we hear an anemic xylophone sound effect for the 'Buffalo Census Chart' and for Moe rolling ink down Curly-Joe's face and tongue.

Anachronistic references: the Roaring Twenties type Gattling-gun drive-by shooting; developing the exposed photographic plate like a Polaroid (cf. *Flying Saucer Daffy*); smoke signal contraptions; a meter maid; and the parking sign. Maurer nicely varies several old gags originating in *Horses' Collars*: Annie shoots a bullet up Trigger's pistol barrel, and the Stooges take their drinks, breathe smoke and flames and then boast, "They watered it!"; one of Annie's shots ricochets four times (*The Three Stooges Go Around the World in a Daze*) before spinning the roulette wheel to a winning number. Other variations: clothes pin gas masks (*Cookoo Cavaliers*); the swinging door (*Playing the Ponies*); smashed cigars (*Uncivil Warriors*); the Sunstroke Kid throwing the Stooges into the water trough and getting splashed (*We Want Our Mummy*); Larry toasting all over the Sunstroke Kid (*The Three Stooges Meet Hercules*); the top of the 'tank' (*The Three Stooges in Orbit*) getting knocked off by the tree branch, the meat grinder gun, and throwing the pots and pans (*Goofs and Saddles*) and pies (*The Three Stooges Meet Hercules*); the [fast motion] cavalry riding to the rescue (*Out West*), Oakley shooting off Bill's mustache and setting the gun belt off (*Phony Express*); the Stooges passing security at the powwow (*Three Little Beers*); and a melee giving the Stooges a chance to crawl to safety (*Three Sappy People*).

VERBAL HUMOR: There are more verbal gags in this film than in any other feature of the 1960s. Many are topical and referential: 1) Hollywood and film: the title is modeled after the grammatically arresting ad slogan 'THE BIRDS IS COMING' for Hitchcock's *The Birds* (1963); Moe's "Boys, you got a rat right here in Casper city with a capital 'R' and that stands for 'Rotten' and that rhymes with 'Roden'" is a parody of Robert Preston's memorable pattern song in *The Music Man* (1962); Wild Bill Hickok asks the "Mirror, mirror on the wall" à la *Snow White and the Seven Dwarfs* (1937); the fat squaw is named 'Zsa-Zsa' à la Zsa-Zsa Gabor; Moe's "That's a good way to lose the West" recalls the 1962 MGM film *How The West Was Won*; and two self-referential gags demonstrate a film consciousness (Colonel: "Never in the history of motion pictures has the United States Cavalry ever been late!"; Curly-Joe: "Just like the big-budget Westerns: we're gonna get to ride off into the sunset."). 2) Television programs: the opening narration and 'William Tell Overture' are from *The Lone Ranger* (1949-57); the kid [Jeffrey Maurer] says, "He's even faster than Mr. Dillon!" like Festus Haggen in *Gunsmoke* (1955-75); Moe calls the medicine man "Kildare" after NBC's *Dr. Kildare* (1961-66); and Curly-Joe's "Me squaw hootenanny!" refers to ABC's folksy *Hootenanny* (1963-1964). The contemporary expression, "My X, the Y," (Chief: "My son, the doctor") would the same year be used for NBC's *My Mother The Car*. Moe promising the reformed outlaws "You may even get into TV!" is self-referential since these actors were already Stooge TV show hosts, and gunslingers *Bat Masterson* (1958-61), [*The Life and Legend of*] *Wyatt Earp* (1955-61); Billy the Kid [*The Tall Man*] (1960-62), and *Wild Bill Hickok* (1951-58) already had television shows; so did *Annie Oakley* (1953-56). 3) Television commercials: Curly-Joe's "Greasy kids' stuff" was a phrase used in Vitalis ads; Rhoden and Trigger's "12,000 soldiers or 12,000 miles...whichever comes first" parodies a typical automobile ad stipulation; and beeping out the competitive brands and the bartender's description of the Stooges ("You know these guys are BEEP-BEEP-BEEP-BEEP") originated with beeping out a competitor's name, a replacement for the 'Brand X' boxes of the 1950s. 4) Rock-and-Roll: The Beatles entered the mainstream when they played on Ed Sullivan on February 9, 1964, so Moe compares hairdos and asks the viewers, "A Japanese Beatle?"; screaming fans holler "Ringo!" as if outlaw Johnny Ringo is Beatle drummer Ringo Starr; Larry and Curly-Joe make fun of Wild Bill Hickok's long hair; the skunk's name is 'Elvis'; and Moe says the cocktail cactus "is doing the Twist!" 5) Classical music: "too much pizza in my 'pizzicata'"; "a reverse cadenza"; Curly-Joe refers to Mozart [1756-91], and Larry to Paderewski [the Polish pianist/composer who died in 1941]. 6) Business: Charlie Horse's "A fleet deal"; Curly-Joe's "ATT is splittin' two for one!" and Moe's "Escrow Indians." (*Rockin' Thru the Rockies*). 7) History: Moe calls Curly-Joe 'Gutenberg,' the inventor of the printing press in 1455; and Larry calls the tank a 'Monitor,' the Civil War iron-clad battle ship, familiar then because the US was celebrating the 100th anniversary of the end of its Civil War.

Set gags include puns (Larry: "What are they, Blackfeet?" Curly-Joe: "I can't see their feet, but the rest of 'em don't look too clean!"; Larry: "You got a Colt?" Curly-Joe: "I got a horse pistol. I raised it from a colt!"; Larry: "You find anything?" Curly-Joe: "Just a pair of mules." Larry: "How'd they get them past the room clerk?" Curly-Joe: "Not that kind!"; and Larry: "[This lingerie] must belong to Wild Bill Hickok. He wears his hair down to there!" Curly-Joe: "That's probably why he's 'wild.'") and gags based on Stooge ignorance (Cabot: "Boys! Please! I'm working." Moe: "That's all right. You're not bothering us!"; Cabot: "We are here for the express purpose of saving them from extinction." Curly-Joe: "What he say?") and fear (Curly-Joe: "Well, if you're gonna stay here and you two guys are gonna stay here, there's only one thing I can say...Good luck!"; Curly-Joe: "There's only one thing I'd ask for if I had to tangle with that guy." Larry: "You mean a fair fight?" Curly-Joe: "No, I mean a head start!"; Sunstroke Kid: "Whisky! And leave the bottle!" Curly-Joe: "I'll have a coke...and leave the bottle...[The Kid orders them a Tarantula Fizz]... What's holdin' up my Tarantula Fizz?" Moe: "Put two tarantulas in mine!"; Larry: "Wyoming! It's full of gunslingers, gila monsters, rattlesnakes, and Indians!" Curly-Joe: "And besides it's against our religion. We're devout cowards!"; and Curly-Joe: "In a few days we'll be laughing at this whole thing...[They all laugh, but then Moe yells at Curly-Joe for laughing]...All right, all right. Shut up: I'm worrying!").

Throwaway and gag-ending lines abound and are given mostly to Curly-Joe, who now chuckles after saying them (the skunk raises his tail: "He's aimin'! Put that down, you!"; Moe has hair glued to his hand: "You didn't shave your hand today, did you?"; he accuses the women of having nightmares: "Whenever you have sauerkraut and lobster - happens every time!"; and he looks at the war paint: "I see stripes are in style this season...Greasy kids' stuff!"), and Moe (about Curly-Joe's horn: "That looks like an unborn piccolo!"; he adds explosive powder: "It's

better to be half safe than half sure!"; and their wheels are shot off: "How do ya' like that? A flat tire!"); cf. Trigger's "Lucky for you I gotta reload!" Charlie Horse, the educated Indian with a degree in poetry, speaks in modern slang: "You know, if you cut out that broken English and that cornball pantomime, this transaction would proceed a lot faster!"; "Cool it, pale daddy. We dig the set up. We don't want to go through that Indian jazz again!"; "He wants to sell us that souped up hot rod!"; "With that swingin' tooter we'll have two buffalo in every teepee!"

Other mixed-ethnic jokes include names ("Japanese Beatle"; "Cleveland Indians") and phrases ("GERONIMO, AND ALL THAT JAZZ"). Gag names: 'Trigger Mortis,' 'The Sunstroke Kid,' and 'Buffalo (Chip) McAdams.' Epithets include "chowder-head," "clumsy idiot," "idiots," "imbecile," and "mongoose." "Idiots" is used to introduce the Stooges into the film; "Mongoose" leads into an echo of the *The Music Man* gag combined with scene-ending slapstick. (Larry: "Is that with a capital 'M'?" Moe: "No, that's with a capital gun!" [Moe bonks Larry with the pistol butt]. "Give me an 'A'"..."'A!'" is a standard musician's gag, used thrice here - twice by the Stooges, once by the Indians. Gag signs: '3 UNDERTAKERS - NO WAITING'; 'SHORT HORN [i.e. Long Horn] SALOON'; and 'SHERIFF WANTED - NO EXPERIENCE NECESSARY.'

Variations: "Do you mean to say you would let Mr. Cabot face all these dangers alone?" Larry & Curly-Joe: "Yes!" (*Have Rocket — Will Travel*); Moe: "You talk like an idiot." Curly-Joe: "Then you understand me," and "I'm a success!" (*The Three Stooges Meet Hercules*); Moe: "We'd rather you hang us from that tree." Charlie Horse: "Why, that tree won't be ready for sixty years!" Curly-Joe: "We'll wait." (*In the Sweet Pie and Pie*); "How are you fixed for blades? (*Scotched in Scotland*); "Never in the history of motion pictures has the United States Cavalry ever been late!" and "one day old" Bourbon (*Out West*); Moe: "Watch your Ps and Qs" (*Three Missing Links*); Moe: "I'm gonna get myself a cheap lawyer" (*Monkey Businessmen*); Curly-Joe: "Jealousy will get you nowhere!" (*Hula-la-la*); Moe: "Sounds like an internal hot foot" (*No Census, No Feeling*); the Stooges confirming their Indian disguises by saying "Ug" (*Whoops, I'm an Indian*); Moe: "Every time you got it, I get it!" (*"I Can Hardly Wait"*); and Larry's "1-2-3-4...what comes after four?" (*Back From the Front*).

OTHER NOTES: The film was shot in May 1964 at both the Columbia Ranch and at the B-BAR-B Buffalo Ranch outside Gillette, Wyoming. The copyright date of the film is 1964; it premiered January 1 in San Antonio. The 1995 video release of this film from Columbia incorrectly credits 'THE THREE STOOGES - Starring: Moe Howard, Larry Fine and Curly-Joe Howard.' Jeffrey Alan [Maurer] is Norman's son, Moe's grandson. The writing on the woman's belly in the opening credits precedes *Laugh In* by three years. Henry Gibson [Charlie Horse] was a regular on that show, and also played 'Wrongo Starr' on *F Troop*. After this film Adam West starred in *Batman* (1966-68). Nancy Kovack [Annie Oakley] often played in action/adventure films (*Jason and the Argonauts*, *Tarzan and the Valley of Gold*). Photographer Irving Lippman began working on Stooge films in 1955 (*Flagpole Jitters*). In the closing credits the Indian chief is named 'Chief Crazy Horse,' but the only time we hear his name in the film Roden calls him 'Chief Battle Horse.' For the second time we see Moe shirtless (*The Three Stooges in Orbit*). The Stooges' concern for the buffalo in 1871 is fairly accurate: conservation becomes a concern at the close of the Civil War, and Yosemite was made our first national park in 1872.

Curly-Joe's "Hey fellas, just like the big-budget Westerns: we're gonna get to ride off into the sunset" turns out to be ironic: this was their last Hollywood feature film.

Columbia and producer Norman Maurer created tremendous anticipation for the release of *The Outlaws Is Coming* by casting the hosts of daytime Stooge programs as such famous Western characters as Billy the Kid and Wild Bill Hickok. During post-production the Stooges themselves made personal appearances on their local programs to advertize the film, which ultimately grossed $1 million. Those from the Philadelphia area, like the author, will easily spot Sally Starr [as Belle Starr] in the center of this publicity photo.

KOOK'S TOUR

Studio: A Normandy Production

Released: February 5, 1970

Running Time: 51"22'"

Credited Cast:
Joe DeRita
Larry Fine
Moe Howard
Moose the dog

Credited Production Crew:

Created & Produced by:	Norman Maurer
Written & Directed by:	Norman Maurer
Director of Photography:	James T. Flocker
Film Editor:	Pat Somerset
Sound:	Audio Effects
Special Effects:	Jeffrey Allen
Wardrobe:	Joan Howard

Uncredited Cast:
Norman Maurer
Jeffrey Maurer

PERSPECTIVE: *Kook's Tour* is intended to document a five-week Stooge vacation in the wilderness of Idaho and Wyoming. Moe narrates the film in a serious tone while the "ex-Stooges" ("We quit!") fish, camp, tour, and fish some more. At times we know we are watching a scripted romp, but at others we forget the crew behind the camera and watch the semi-retired Stooges at play as if in a lighthearted home movie. When Moe cracks the old joke, "The arrow points half way: I don't know if it's half empty or half full," the other two groan and tell him, "Forget the jokes!"; and when Moe combs his hair down over his forehead, he laughs at himself and combs it back the 'normal' way. But this ex-Stooge mask of denial cannot hide their comic characterizations: Curly-Joe plays a tough guy with a litter fetish, Larry plays a virtually invisible Stooge so inept that even Moose the dog proves superior, and Moe as often plays the kind-hearted boss who rarely shows his kind-heartedness.

Kook's Tour is a different kind of Stooge film. It follows an itinerary instead of a plot, and its non-studio exteriors give it an extraordinary look. And it is in color! Yet it is clearly a Stooge film filled with physical and verbal silliness, bickering, gadgetry, and variegated inter-Stooge activity. Even the film's concept, Stooge R & R, has its roots in 1945's *Idiots Deluxe*, and Larry's isolation as the 'third Stooge' goes back to 1946's *Three Loan Wolves* and even 1934's *Woman Haters*. If this is the only Stooge film without their trademark slapstick and verbal gags, it is because at ages 71 and 67 Moe and Larry consciously avoid and even ridicule them. The recent Columbia features may have already diminished inter-Stooge slapstick, but Norman Maurer and the "ex-Stooges" were clearly looking for something different here. Maurer even edited out a pie-fight sequence honoring Moe's birthday.

The Stooges filmed this comic travelogue in the fall of 1969 as a TV pilot designed originally for 39 half-hour shows. But tragedy struck during the editing process early in 1970. Larry's speech may seem slightly slurred throughout *Kook's Tour*, but on January 9 he suffered a debilitating stroke. Paralyzed on his left side and permanently confined to a wheel-chair, he had to retire to the Motion Picture and Television Home and Hospital in Woodland Hills where he lived happily for five years, making a number of inspirational personal appearances. Larry genuinely felt as if the stroke had improved his luck, so he called his dictated autobiography *'Stroke of Luck.'* Moe later acted in one feature film (*Doctor Death: Seeker of Souls* [1973]) and made several memorable television appearances, but attempts at making a Stooge feature with Emil Sitka and Curly-Joe proved unsuccessful, and five years later he succumbed to lung cancer. When Moe, the unflappable professional, concludes *Kook's Tour*, "Poor Larry. Maybe his luck will improve after we...head our rig for the inland waters of Japan," he must know this will never happen. His " Sayonara" is the Stooges' filmed farewell, and with *Kook's Tour* the film corpus of the Three Stooges comes to a close.

VISUAL HUMOR: Despite the absence of traditional inter-Stooge slapstick, there is plenty of physical activity and interactivity. Larry's physical condition seems well enough for him to pull off the camouflage gag and be unseen by the others (*Heavenly Daze*), get hit in the face with a branch (*Uncivil Warriors*), give Curly-Joe a half-hearted chin wave, and catch Moe's hand in the winch. Curly-Joe gets smashed in the face by the littering woman's bag (recently in *The Three Stooges Go Around the World in a Daze* and *The Outlaws Is Coming*), bangs his head on the boat windshield, as does Larry later, and walks absent-mindedly into the water and falls in. Moe accidently throws salt into Larry's face. And as a trio they lose their boat, rent paddle boats and crash into each other (with traffic noise sound effects), get chased (in fast motion) by park rangers and an angry loving couple, and get rained on as soon as they sit down for an elegant dinner. In addition to the liberal use of fast motion (used six times), the camouflage scene ends with a freeze frame, as did many television episodes of the 1970s. The toned black and white segments we see at the opening of the film are from three recent features - *The Three Stooges Meet Hercules, The Three Stooges Go Around the World in a Daze*, and *The Outlaws Is Coming*. The Stooges have

used contraptions like the fake geyser pump, the motorcycle vacuum cleaner, and the camera trap [designed by Jeff Maurer] in their films since *Termites of 1938*, and (non-Stooge) gadgetry goes all the way back to *Soup to Nuts*. Other variations: Curly-Joe shaking off with/like the dog (*We Want Our Mummy*); Curly-Joe unsuccessfully trying to climb into the upper berth (recently in *Oil's Well That Ends Well*).

VERBAL HUMOR: Gags are derived from the fact that Moe, Larry, and Curly-Joe used to be Stooges, for instance the interrupted three-pattern (Curly-Joe: "I used to get paid a lot of money for takin' your insults, but no more, buddy boy! No more!" Larry: "He's right! We're ex-Stooges, and we're ought-a start acting like ex-Stooges." Moe: "Well, sometimes I-I-I! ...Ya' turned the boat loose!"). Moe as the boss muses about the others ("Curly-Joe was used to getting clobbered with those kind of instruments, not using them"; "Poor Larry. For fifty years the scripts never let him do anything right. I guess it's become a habit"), gets angry at them ("Imbecile! For fifty years I've been surrounded by imbeciles, and I'm still surrounded by imbeciles!"), or holds back ([tempted to gouge the phone, as in *False Alarms*]: "I gotta be careful with those old habits!"). Yet Moe is the one who says the "The arrow points half way: I don't know if it's half empty or half full!" gag, first used in *Soup to Nuts* (1930), making it the longest-running Stooge verbal gag and the only one used in their first and last films.

Because they are three old friends out on a camping trip, not to mention ex-Stooges, teases and insults abound (Moe: "You look like a dirty lawn in the fall!"; Curly-Joe: "Watch out for the bears: they're liable to think you're a berry bush and chew your arm off!"; Curly-Joe: "Sounds like my stomach." Moe: "Your stomach never sounded so good"; Moe: "In a place like this even Larry could catch a fish." Curly-Joe: "You wanna bet?!"; and Moe: "I wouldn't be surprised if he's out there now with a stick of dynamite trying to catch a fish!"). Moe teases Curly-Joe about his weight ("Admiral Blimp"; "With all that blubber he'll float!"; Curly-Joe: "This doesn't fit my personality." Moe: "It doesn't fit your belly either!"). But Curly-Joe shows no respect for Moe when he calls him "Captain Moe" and "Chef Moe." Epithets: "imbeciles," "dummy," and "fatso." Instead of bossing his companions, Moe asks nicely, "Curly-Joe: please take care of the wood. Larry: please take care of the fire." But when Larry asks, "What are you going to do?" and Moe says, "Nothing." Moe is reverting to an old joke from *Violent is the Word*

The Stooges are loaded into the hull of a TWA CargoJet as they leave for their vacation film, *Kook's Tour* (1970). Designed as a television pilot, the film was never broadcast, and Larry's debilitating stroke during post-production terminated the project. Video copies have just recently been made available.

for Curly. As the 'third Stooge' Larry gets extra punchlines (Moe: "Just relax...and we'll all go to lunch before the man with the white coat comes." Larry: "Is he comin' to lunch, too?"; Moe: "It's beautiful down there!" Larry: "If it's so beautiful down there, what are we doin' up here?") and most of the throw-away lines ("That's my fish! Mine! My fish! Mine!"; [about the geyser]: "That's a crazy way to make coffee, ain't it?"; Curly-Joe: "The only place in the world's what got something like that, you know that? You don't know that; I know that." Larry: "You must-a read it somewhere"; [after Moe tosses the salt in Larry's face] Curly-Joe: "Let's you and I set the table." Larry: "Yeah, it's safer there"; and Larry: "I wish I was a dog!").

Other variations: Larry: "I snored so loud I kept myself awake!" (*Three Missing Links*; *Rumpus in the Harem*); Moe: "That's a 'geezer.'" Curly-Joe: "'Geezer,' 'geyser'— it's fantastic!" (*Oily to Bed, Oily to Rise*). References: the "Twenty-One Club of the wilderness" refers to the famous New York restaurant of the 1960s; "immaculate contraption" parodies 'immaculate conception.' With "Hi! Remember us? That's how we made our living for fifty consecutive years," Moe dates himself back to 1919-20, before 'The Three Stooges' had actually formed, but when he himself was already in show business. The self-conscious off-color joke (Curly-Joe: "Look at the size of those mountains. It's like the Swiss Alps." Moe: "You don't know your Alps from your Tetons." Curly-Joe: "Now don't get nasty: this might get on television.") is one of the very few in the entire Stooge corpus (cf. Shemp's umbrella for the "bat...as big as an elephant...in case it rains" in *Stone Age Romeos*, and Shemp thinking about offending the censor in *Gypped in the Penthouse*).

OTHER NOTES: When Larry suffered his stroke, plans for the 39-show series were cancelled. What we see here Norman Maurer edited to a television hour (51 minutes), but it was never broadcast. The film had limited video cassette distribution to the public in 1973 at Sears outlets, and then in 1975 Niles Film released a Super-8 version. In 2000 it was released again on video.

After Larry's stroke, Maurer reshot the close up in the corn flake sequence using his own hands. In his personal appearances at Los Angeles schools, Larry was accompanied by Babe London ('Nora' in *Scrambled Brains*). Maurer and son also appear as the litterers; the woman is played by Maurer's secretary. Moose was Norman Maurer's Labrador retriever. The *Scrapbook* lists the following locations in Idaho and Wyoming: 'Snake River, Jackson Lake and Lodge, Old Faithful Geyser and Inn, Castle and Sawmill Geysers, Yellowstone National Park and Lake, Bridge Bay Marina, Grand Canyon [of the Yellowstone], Jack Lott's Ranch, Henry's Lake, Staley Springs Lodge, Fishing Bridge at Big Springs, Massacre Rocks at Snake River outside American Falls, Redfish Lake and Marina, Lowman Highway on Idaho State 21 before Lowman, Idaho, Lucky Peak near Boise, Lake Pend Oreille and Priest Lake,' as well as 'Angeles National Forest, Charlton Flats Picnic Area on Angeles Crest Highway, Lake Piru, Moe Howard's home, and Los Angeles International Airport.' We see the Stooges signing a few autographs at the airport and greeting fans at Yellowstone.

Kook's Tour has a very understated mood. Many parts seem unscripted, but Norman Maurer was developing a relaxed style, reinventing Stooge comedy for actors that were pushing seventy. Moe made one feature film and a half-dozen TV appearances over the next few years, but *Kook's Tour* brings the Stooge film corpus to an end.

INDEX

SELECT BIBLIOGRAPHY

Alleman, Richard. *The Movie Lover's Guide to Hollywood.* New York: Harper & Row, Publishers, 1985.

The American Film Institute catalog of motion pictures produced in the United States. 7 Vols. New York : Bowker, 1971-.

Baxter, John. *Sixty Years of Hollywood.* South Brunswick, NJ and New York: A. S. Barnes and Company, 1973.

Besser, Joe, with Jeff and Greg Lenburg. *Once a Stooge, Always a Stooge* [revised ed. of *Not Just a Stooge]*. Santa Monica, CA: Roundtable Publishing, Inc., 1990.

Brooks, Tim, and Earle Marsh. *The Complete Directory to Prime Time Network and Cable TV Shows, 1946-Present*[6]. New York: Ballantine Books, 1995.

Bruskin, David N., ed. *Behind the Three Stooges: The White Brothers.* Los Angeles: Directors Guild of America, 1993. [*Bruskin*]

Buxton, Frank, and Bill Owen. *Radio's Golden Age.* NC: Easton Valley Press, 1966.

Carone, James, as told by Larry Fine. *Stroke of Luck.*. Hollywood: Siena Publishing Company, 1973. [*Larry*]

Dick, Bernard F., ed. *Columbia Pictures: Portrait of a Studio.* Lexington, KY: The University of Kentucky Press, 1992.

The Star-Spangled Screen: The American World War II Film. Lexington, KY: The University of Kentucky Press, 1985.

Durbano, Art. *TV Guide's Television Almanac.* NC: News America Publications, Inc., 1995.

Eames, John Douglas. *The MGM Story: The Complete History of FIfty Roaring Years.* New York: Crown Publishers, Inc., 1975.

Everson, William K., *The Complete Films of Laurel & Hardy.* Secaucus, NJ: Citadel Press, 1967.

Feinberg, Morris. *Larry: The Stooge in the Middle.* San Francisco: Last Gasp of San Francisco, 1984.

Forrester, Jeffrey. *The Stooge Chronicles.* Chicago: Contemporary Books, Inc., 1981.

The Stoogephile Trivia Book. Chicago: Contemporary Books, Inc., 1982.

Forrester, Tom, with Jeffrey Forrester. *The Stooges' Lost Episodes.* Chicago: Contemporary Books, Inc., 1988.

Hansen, Tom, with Jeffrey Forrester. *Stoogemania.* Chicago: Contemporary Books, 1984.

Howard, Moe. *Moe Howard and The Three Stooges.* Secaucus, NJ: Citadel Press, 1977. [*Moe*]

Lenburg, Jeff, Joan Howard Maurer, and Greg Lenburg. *The Three Stooges Scrapbook.* Secaucus, NJ: Citadel Press, 1982.

MacDonald, J. Fred. *Don't Touch That Dial!: Radio Programming in American Life, 1920-1960.* Chicago: Nelson-Hall Inc., Pub, 1979.

Maltin, Leonard. *Movie Comedy Teams*[2]. New York: New American Library, 1985.

Maurer, Joan Howard. *Curly: An Illustrated Biography of the Superstooge.* Secaucus, NJ: Citadel Press, 1985. [*Curly*]

Maurer, Joan Howard. *The Three Stooges Book of Scripts.* Two volumes. Secaucus, NJ: Citadel Press, 1984. [*Scripts*]

McNeil, Alex. *Total Television: A Comprehensive Guide to Programming From 1948 to the Present*[3]. New York: Penguin Books, 1991.

Okuda, Ted, with Edward Watz. *The Columbia Comedy Shorts: Two-Reel Hollywod Film Comedies, 1933-1958.* Jefferson, NC: McFarland & Company, Inc., Publishers, 1986. [*Okuda*]

Ragan, David. *Who's Who in Hollywood.* Two volumes. New York: Facts on File, Inc., 1992.

Rosten, Leo, *The Joys of Yiddish.* NewYork: McGraw Hill, 1966.

Scordato, Mark and Ellen. *The Three Stooges.* New York: Chelsea House Publishers. 1995.

Slide, Anthony. *Great Radio Personalities - In Historic Photographs.* New York: Dover Publications, Inc., 1982.

Smith, Ronald L. *The Stooge Fans' I.Q. Test.* New York: S.P.I. Books, 1993.

St. John, Robert. *Encyclopedia of Radio and Television Broadcasting.* Milwaukee, WI: Cathedral Square Publishing Company, 1967.

Taylor, A. Marjorie. *The Languages of World War II.* New York: The H. W. Wilson Company, 1944.

The Three Stooges Journal. Issues 1-84.

Thomas, Bob. *King Cohn: The Life and Times of Harry Cohn.* New York: G. P. Putnam's Sons, 1967.

Volk, Daniel. *The Films of the Stooges: Larry, Curly, & Moe...The Columbia Shorts.* Daniel Volk, 1988.

Walker, John, ed. *Halliwell's Filmgoer's Companion*[12]. New York: Harper Collins Publishers, 1997.

Walker, John. *Halliwell's Film Guide*[8]. New York: Harper Collins Publishers, 1991.